Applied Choice Analysis

The second edition of this popular book brings students fully up to date with the latest methods and techniques in choice analysis. Comprehensive yet accessible, it offers a unique introduction to anyone interested in understanding how to model and forecast the range of choices made by individuals and groups. In addition to a complete rewrite of several chapters, new topics covered include ordered choice, scaled MNL, generalized mixed logit, latent class models, group decision making, heuristics and attribute processing strategies, expected utility theory, and prospect theoretic applications. Many additional case studies are used to illustrate the applications of choice analysis with extensive command syntax provided for all Nlogit applications and datasets available online. With its unique blend of theory, estimation, and application, this book has broad appeal to all those interested in choice modeling methods and will be a valuable resource for students as well as researchers, professionals, and consultants.

David A. Hensher is Professor of Management, and Founding Director of the Institute of Transport and Logistics Studies (ITLS) at The University of Sydney Business School.

John M. Rose was previously Professor of Transport and Logistics Modelling at the Institute of Transport and Logistics Studies (ITLS) at The University of Sydney Business School and moved to The University of South Australia as co-director of the Institute for Choice in early March 2014.

William H. Greene is the Robert Stansky Professor of Economics at the Stern School of Business, New York University.

T0382647

Applied Choice Analysis

Second Edition

David A. Hensher

The University of Sydney Business School

John M. Rose

The University of Sydney Business School*

William H. Greene

Stern School of Business, New York University

* John Rose completed his contribution to the second edition while at The University of Sydney. He has since relocated to The University of South Australia

CAMBRIDGE
UNIVERSITY PRESS

CAMBRIDGE
UNIVERSITY PRESS

University Printing House, Cambridge CB2 8BS, United Kingdom

Cambridge University Press is part of the University of Cambridge.

It furthers the University's mission by disseminating knowledge in the pursuit of education, learning and research at the highest international levels of excellence.

www.cambridge.org
Information on this title: www.cambridge.org/9781107465923

© David A. Hensher, John M. Rose and William H. Greene 2015

First published 2005
Second edition 2015
4th printing 2021

Printed in the United Kingdom by TJ Books Limited, Padstow Cornwall

A catalogue record for this publication is available from the British Library

Library of Congress Cataloguing in Publication data
Hensher, David A., 1947–
Applied choice analysis / David A. Hensher, The University of Sydney Business School, John M. Rose,
The University of Sydney Business School, William H. Greene, Stern School of Business, New York University. – 2nd edition.
   pages   cm
John M. Rose now at University of South Australia.
Includes bibliographical references and index.
ISBN 978-1-107-09264-8
1. Decision making – Mathematical models.   2. Probabilities – Mathematical models.   3. Choice.   I. Rose,
John M.   II. Greene, William H., 1951–   III. Title.
QA279.4.H46   2015
519.5′42–dc23

2014043411

ISBN 978-1-107-09264-8 Hardback
ISBN 978-1-107-46592-3 Paperback

Additional resources for this publication at www.cambridge.org/9781107465923

Contents

Part IV   Advanced topics

Figures

Tables

Preface

I'm all in favor of keeping dangerous weapons out of the hands of fools. Let's start with typewriters.

(Frank Lloyd Wright 1868–1959)

Almost without exception, everything human beings undertake involves a choice (consciously or subconsciously), including the choice not to choose. Some choices are the result of habit while others are fresh decisions made with great care, based on whatever information is available at the time from past experiences and/or current inquiry.

Over the last forty years, there has been a steadily growing interest in the development and application of quantitative statistical methods to study choices made by individuals (and, to a lesser extent, groups of individuals or organizations). With an emphasis on both understanding how choices are made and on forecasting future choice responses, a healthy literature has evolved. Reference works by Louviere *et al.* (2000) and Train (2003, 2009) synthesize the contributions. However while these sources represent the state of the art (and practice), they are technically advanced and often a challenge for both the beginner and practitioners.

Discussions with colleagues have revealed a gap in the choice analysis literature – a book that assumes very little background and offers an entry point for individuals interested in the study of choice regardless of their starting position. Writing such a book increasingly became a challenge for us. It is often more difficult to explain complex ideas in very simple language than to protect one's knowledge base with complicated deliberations. The first edition published in 2005 was written in response to this gap in the literature in order to serve the needs of practitioners, seasoned researchers, and students.

There are many discussion topics that are ignored in most books on choice analysis, yet are issues which students have pointed out in class, and been noted by researchers in general, as important in giving them a better understanding of what is happening in choice modeling. The lament that too many books on discrete choice analysis are written for the well informed is common, and was sufficient incentive to write the first edition of this book and a subsequent need to revise it to include the many new developments since 2004 (when the first edition was completed), as well as to clarify points presented in the first edition on which many readers sought further advice. The new topics, in addition to a complete rewrite of most previous chapters, include ordered choice, generalized mixed logit, latent class models, statistical tests (including partial effects and model output comparisons), group decision making, heuristics, and attribute processing strategies, expected utility theory, prospect theoretic applications, and extensions to allow for non-linearity in parameters. The single case study has been replaced by a number of case studies, each chosen as an example of data that best illustrate the application of one or more choice models.

This book for beginners in particular, but also of value to seasoned researchers, is our attempt to meet the challenge. We agreed to try and write the first draft of the first edition without referring to any of the existing material as a means (hopefully) of encouraging a flow of explanation. Pausing to consult can often lead to terseness in the code (as writers of novels can attest). Further draft versions leading to the final product did, however, cross-reference to the literature to ensure that we had acknowledged appropriate material. This book in both its first and second edition guises, however, is not about ensuring that all contributors to the literature on choice are acknowledged, but rather ensuring that the novice choice analyst is given a fair go in their first journey through this intriguing topic.

We dedicate this book to the beginners, but we also acknowledge our research colleagues who have influenced our thinking as well as co-authored papers over many years. We thank Michiel Bliemer for his substantial input to Chapter 6 as well as Andrew Collins and Chinh Ho for their case studies using NGene. We also thank Waiyan Leong and Andrew Collins for their substantial contribution to Chapter 21. We especially recognize Dan McFadden (2000 Nobel Laureate in Economics), Ken Train, Chandra Bhat, Jordan Louviere, Andrew Daly, Moshe Ben-Akiva, David Brownstone, Michiel Bliemer, Juan de Dios Ortúzar, Joffre Swait, and Stephane Hess. Colleagues and doctoral students at the University of Sydney read earlier versions. In particular, we thank Andrew Collins, Riccardo Scarpa, Sean Puckett, David Layton, Danny Campbell, Matthew Beck, Zheng Li, Waiyan Leong, Chinh Ho, Kwang Kim and Louise Knowles, and the 2004–2013 graduate classes in Choice Analysis as well as participants in the annual short courses on choice analysis and choice experiments at The University of Sydney and various other locations in Europe, Asia, and the United States, who were guinea pigs for the first full use of the book in a teaching environment.

Part I

Getting started

1 In the beginning

Education is a progressive discovery of our own ignorance.

(Will Durant, 1885–1991)

1.1 Choosing as a common event

Why did we *choose* to write the first edition of this primer and then a second edition? Can it be explained by some inherent desire to seek personal gain or was it some other less self-centered interest? In determining the reason, we are revealing an underlying objective. It might be one of maximizing our personal **satisfaction** level or that of satisfying some community-based objective (or social obligation). Whatever the objective, it is likely that there are a number of reasons why we made such a *choice* (between writing and not writing this primer) accompanied by a set of constraints that had to be taken into account. An example of a reason might be to "promote the field of research and practice of choice analysis"; examples of constraints might be the time commitment and the financial outlay.

Readers should be able to think of choices that they have made in the last seven days. Some of these might be repetitive and even habitual (such as taking the bus to work instead of the train or car), buying the same daily newspaper (instead of other ones on sale); other choices might be a once-off decision (such as going to the movies to watch a latest release or purchasing this book). Many choice situations involve *more than one choice* (such as choosing a destination and means of transport to get there, choosing where to live and the type of dwelling, or choosing which class of grapes and winery in sourcing a nice bottle of red or white).

The storyline above is rich in information about what we need to include in a study of the choice behavior of individuals or groups of individuals (such as households, lobby groups, and organisations). To arrive at a choice, an

3

individual must have considered a set of **alternatives**. These alternatives are usually called the **choice set**. Logically, one must evaluate at least two alternatives to be able to make a choice (one of these alternatives may be "not to make a choice" or "not participate at all"). At least one actual (or potential) **choice setting** must exist (e.g. choosing where to live, choosing who to vote for, or choosing among alternative future green sources of vehicle fuels) but there may be more than one choice (e.g. what type of dwelling to live in, whether to buy or rent, and how much to pay per week if rented). The idea that an individual may have to consider a number of choices leads to a set of inter-related choices. Some choice situations might also involve subjective responses on a psychological scale (such as the rating of a health scheme, the amenity of a suburb, or a bottle of wine); or on a best–worst scale in which they choose the most preferred (or best) alternative or attribute and the least preferred (or worst) alternative or attribute.

Determining the set of alternatives to be evaluated in a choice set is a crucial task in choice analysis. Getting this wrong will mean that subsequent tasks in the development of a choice model will be missing relevant information. We often advise analysts to devote considerable time to the identification of the choices that are applicable in the study of a specific problem. This is known as **choice set generation**. In identifying the relevant choices, one must also consider the range of alternatives, and start thinking about what influences the decision to choose one alternative over another. These influences are called **attributes** if they relate to the description of an alternative (e.g., travel time of the bus alternative, vintage of a bottle of wine), but an individual's prejudices (or tastes) will also be relevant and are often linked to **socio-economic characteristics** (SECs) such as personal income, age, gender, and occupation.

To take a concrete example, a common problem for transportation planners is to study the transport-related choices made by a sample of individuals living in an urban area. Individuals make many decisions related to their transportation needs. Some of these decisions are taken occasionally (e.g., where to live and work) while others are taken more often (e.g., departure time for a specific trip). These examples highlight a very important feature of choice analysis – the temporal perspective. Over what time period are we interested in studying choices? As the period becomes longer, the number of possible choices that can be made (i.e., are not fixed or pre-determined) are likely to increase. Thus if we are interested in studying travel behavior over a five-year period, then it is reasonable to assume that an individual can make choices related to the locations of both living and working, as well as the means of transport and departure time. That is, a specific choice of means of transport may indeed be changed as a consequence of the person changing where they reside or work. In a shorter period such as one year, choosing among modes of transport may be conditional on where one lives or works, but the latter is not able to be changed given the time that it takes to relocate one's employment.

The message in the previous paragraphs is that careful thought is required to define the choice setting so as to ensure that all possible behavioral responses (as expressed by a set of choice situations) can be accommodated when a change in the decision environment occurs. For example, if we increase fuel prices, then the cost of driving a car increases. If one has only studied the choice of mode of transport then the decision maker will be "forced" to modify the choice among a given set of modal alternatives (e.g., bus, car, train). However it may be that the individual would prefer to stay with the car but to change the time of day they travel so as to avoid traffic congestion and conserve fuel. If the departure time choice model is not included in the analysis, then experience shows that the modal choice model tends to force a substitution between modes, which in reality is a substitution between travel at different times of the day by car.

Armed with a specific problem or a series of associated questions, the analyst now recognizes that to study choices we need a set of choice situations (or outcomes), a set of alternatives and a set of attributes that belong to each alternative. But how do we take this information and convert it to a useful framework within which we can study the choice behavior of individuals? To do this, we need to set up a number of behavioral rules under which we believe it is reasonable to represent the process by which an individual considers a set of alternatives and makes a choice. This framework needs to be sufficiently realistic to explain past choices and to give confidence in likely behavioral responses in the future that result in staying with an existing choice or making a new choice. The framework should also be capable of assessing the likely support for alternatives that are not currently available, be they new alternatives in the market or existing ones that are physically unavailable to some market segments. These are some of the important issues that choice modelers will need to address and which are central to the journey throughout this book.

Before we overview the structure of the book, we thought it useful to go back in time and get an appreciation of the evolution of choice modeling, which began at least ninety years ago.

1.2 A brief history of choice modeling

It is eighty-seven years since Thurstone's classic 1927 paper on the *law of comparative judgment*, in which he assumes that the response of an individual to a pair of alternatives, i, j, is determined by the discriminal processes $v_i = f(\alpha_i) + \varepsilon_i$ and $v_j = f(\alpha_j) + \varepsilon_j$. The terms $f(\alpha_i)$ and $f(\alpha_j)$ represent a single-valued function of unknown parameters α_i and α_j, characteristics of the "objects participating in the i, j pair." These parameters are referred to by Thurstone as "affective values" of the corresponding objects (or alternatives); ε_i and ε_j are elements of the discriminal processes specific to the randomly selected individual and are assumed by Thurstone to obey a normal bivariate **distribution** function. The difference process $(v_i - v_j)$ is distributed normally with mean $f(\alpha_i) - f(\alpha_j)$ and **variance** $\sigma^2_{ij} = \sigma^2_i + \sigma^2_j + 2\rho_{ij}\sigma_i\sigma_j$ where ρ_{ij} is the correlation between the alternatives. The individual is assumed to judge $X_i > X_j$ when $(v_j - v_i) > 0$. Thus the probability that a randomly sampled individual will be observed to judge $X_i > X_j$ is $Prob_{ij} = \Phi\{f(\alpha_i) - f(\alpha_j) / \sigma_{ij}\}$. This response function is referred to as a statement of the law of comparative judgment. McFadden (2001) described the Thurstone contribution as a model of imperfect discrimination in which alternative i with true stimulus level V_i is perceived with a normal error as $V_i + \varepsilon_i$ and Thurstone showed that the probability $P_{\{i,j\}}(i)$ that alternative i is chosen over alternative j has a form that we now call binomial probit. The emphasis on probabilistic choice theory can be credited to both Thurstone (1945) and a lesser-known author, Hull (1943).

An alternative to the normal response function proposed by Bradley and Terry (1952) and Luce (1959) is of special interest because of its psychological interpretation (Restle 1961, Bock and Jones 1968). The authors proposed a model for the probability that X_i is ranked above X_j in the pair X_i, X_j, as $Prob_{ij} = \{\pi_i/(\pi_i + \pi_j)\}$, $i = 1,2,\ldots,n$; $j = 1,2,\ldots,n$. π_i and π_j are positive parameters characteristic of alternatives X_i and X_j. Bradley and Terry (1952) introduce $\pi_i + \pi_j$ in the denominator to **normalize** π_i so that $Prob_{ij} + Prob_{ji} = 1$. Luce (1959) developed the theoretical foundations in a precise form, in which π_i can be interpreted as the probability that X_i will be ranked first among all n alternatives. The probability that X_i will be ranked first in any subset of alternatives, and in particular in the subset $\{X_i, X_j\}$ in any subset of alternatives follows from Luce's *principle of independence from irrelevant alternatives*, which states that the ratio π_i/π_j is constant regardless of what other alternatives are in the subset. This became known as the IIA rule or constant shares assumption. Importantly, this model was transformed into the logistics response function by setting $\pi_i/\pi_j = \exp(\alpha_i - \alpha_j)$. Bradley and Terry (1952) were the first (in the psychological literature) to estimate the logit response function by using a maximum likelihood estimator, although the logistic form goes back many years in Bioassay (see Ashton 1972 for a review and summary of the contribution of Berkson). Estimates of the natural log of π_i/π_j were obtained by employing logistic deviates $y_{ij} = \ln\{prob_{ij}/(1-prob_{ij})\}$. After exponential transformation of parameters (what later became the representative or observed component of *utility*), the Bradley–Terry–Luce (BTL) model becomes equivalent to Thurstone's Case V model, except that the logistic's density replaces the Gaussian density of Thurstone's response function. The principle of IIA has the exact same effect as constant correlation of discriminal processes for all pairs of alternatives (stimuli). This implies that the conditional probability of an individual's choice between any two alternatives, given their choice between any other two alternatives, is equal to the unconditional probability. The famous *red bus/blue bus* example introduced by Mayberry in Quandt (1970) and due to Debreu (1960), has been used extensively to highlight the risk of empirical **validity** of IIA, which became the springboard for many of the developments in discrete choice models to circumvent the rigidity of IIA.

Marschak (1959) generalized the BTL model to **stochastic utility maximization** over multiple alternatives, and introduced it to economics, referring for the first time to Random Utility Maximization (RUM) (also see Georgescu-Roegen 1954). Marschak explored the testable implications of maximization of random preferences, and proved for a finite set of alternatives that choice probabilities satisfying Luce's IIA axiom were consistent with RUM. An extension of this result established that a necessary and sufficient condition for RUM with independent errors to satisfy the IIA axiom was that the ε_i be identically distributed with a Type I Extreme Value distribution, $\text{Prob}(\varepsilon_i \le c) = \exp(-e^{-c/\sigma})$, where σ is a scale factor and c is a location parameter. The sufficiency was proved by Anthony Marley and reported by Luce and Suppes (1965).

In the 1960s a number of researchers realized that the study of choices among mutually exclusive (discrete) alternatives was not appropriate through the application of ordinary least squares (OLS) regression. Given that the dependent variable of interest was discrete, typically binary (1, 0), the use of OLS would result in predicted outcomes violating the boundary limits of probability. Although under a binary choice setting, probabilities in the range 0.3 to 0.7 tended to satisfy a common range of a linear OLS (or linear probability model form), any probabilities at the extremities were likely to be greater than 1.0 and less than 0. To avoid this, a transformation is required, the most popular being the logistic (log of the odds) transformation. Software to estimate a binary logit (or probit) model started to appear in the 1960s, replacing the popular discriminant analysis method. The early programs included PROLO (PRObit-LOgit) written by Cragg at the University of British Columbia and which was used in many PhD theses in the late 1960s and early 1970s (including Charles Lave 1970, Thomas Lisco 1967, and David Hensher 1974). Peter Stopher (at Northwestern University, and now at Sydney) in the late 1960s had written a program to allow for more than two alternatives, but as far as we are aware it was rarely used. During the period of the late 1960s and early 1970s there were a number of researchers developing logit software for multinomial logit, including McFadden's code that became the basis of QUAIL (programmed in particular by David Brownstone), Charles Manski's program (XLogit) used by MIT students such as Ben-Akiva, Andrew Daly's ALogit, Hensher and Johnson's BLogit, and Daganzo and Sheffi's TROMP. Bill Greene had a version of Limdep in the 1970s that began with Tobit and then Logit.

Despite the developments in software (mainly binary choice and some limited multiple choice capability), it was not until the link was made between McFadden's contribution at Berkeley (McFadden 1968) and a project undertaken by Charles River Associates to develop a joint mode and destination choice model (Domencich and McFadden 1975), that we saw a significant growth in research designed to deliver practical tools for modeling interdependent discrete choices involving more than two alternatives. By the late 1960s, McFadden had developed an empirical model from Luce's choice axiom (centered on IIA as described above). Letting $P_C(i)$ denote the probability that a subject confronted with a set of mutually exclusive and exhaustive alternatives C will choose alternative i, given the IIA property, Luce showed that if his axiom holds, then one can associate with each alternative a positive "strict utility" w_i such that $P_C(i) = w_i / \sum_{k \in C} w_k$. Taking the strict utility for alternative i to be a parametric exponential function of its attributes x_i, $w_i = \exp(x_i\beta)$, gave a practical statistical model for individual choice data. McFadden called this the *conditional logit model* because it reduced to a logistic in the two-alternative case, and had a ratio form analogous to the form for conditional probabilities (McFadden 1968, 1974). McFadden (1968, 1974) proved necessity (given sufficiency had already been shown), starting from the implication of the Luce axiom that multinomial choice between an object with strict utility w_1 and m objects with strict utilities w_2 matched binomial choice between an object with strict utility w_1 and an object with strict utility mw_2.

In McFadden (2001), the author explains that he "initially interpreted the conditional logit model as a model of a decision making bureaucracy, with random elements coming from **heterogeneity** of tastes of various bureaucrats. It was then transparent that in an empirical model with data across decision-makers, the randomness in utility could come from both inter-personal and intra-personal variation in preferences, and from variations in the attributes of alternatives known to the decision-maker but not to the observer." This led in his classic 1974 paper on the conditional logit model to introduce the idea of an *extensive* margin for discrete decisions in contrast to the *intensive* margin that operates for a representative consumer making continuous decisions. This was a defining distinction between the economist's and the psychologist's interpretation of randomness.

The 1970s saw much activity in finessing the multinomial logit model based on the form developed by Dan McFadden. In addition to the Charles River Associates project (published as the book by Domencich and McFadden 1975), which introduced inclusive value to connect levels calculated as probability weighted averages of systematic utility components at the next level down in the tree (with Ben Akiva separately developing the log sum formula for exact calculation of inclusive values – see Ben Akiva and Lerman 1979) McFadden directed the Travel Demand Forecasting Project (TDFP), which set out to develop a comprehensive framework for transportation policy analysis using disaggregate behavioral tools. TDFP used the introduction of BART to test the ability of disaggregate travel demand models to forecast a new transportation mode. On the methodological front, TDFP developed methods for choice-based sampling and for simulation, and statistical methods for estimating and testing **nested** logit models, that laid the foundation for later results. Some of the ideas that led to the eventual discovery of the nested logit had been laid down by Marvin Manheim (1973), and Alan Wilson barely missed it when proposing the combined distribution-mode split function for the famous SELNEC transport model (Wilson *et al.* 1969).

The concern with the limitation of the IIA condition led to the development of the nested logit model (referred to as tree logit by Andrew Daly) in which the idea of dissimilarity noted over forty-five years before in psychology finally was treated explicitly in the RUM framework through the recognition that the variance associated with the unobserved influences in the random component is likely to be different across the finite set of alternatives in a choice set, but possibly similar for subsets of alternatives. This had appeal to those interested in decision trees, although it must be pointed out that the nesting structure is a mechanism to accommodate differential variance in the unobserved effects that may not align with intuition in the construction of decision trees. With the knowledge that the distribution of the variance associated with the unobserved effects can be defined by a location and a **scale parameter**, the nested logit model had found a way of explicitly identifying and parameterizing this scale, which became known alternatively as composite cost, inclusive value, logsum and expected maximum utility. The contributions to this literature, in particular the theoretical justification under RUM, are attributable to Williams (1977) and Daly and Zachary (1978), with a later generalization by McFadden (2001). In particular, the Williams–Daly–Zachary analysis provides the foundation for derivation of RUM-consistent choice models from social surplus functions, and connects RUM-based models to **willingness to pay** (WTP) for projects.

The period from the mid 1970s to 2010 saw an explosion of contributions to theory, computation and empirical applications of **closed-form** discrete-choice models of the multinomial logit (MNL) and nested logit (NL) variety. The most notable development of closed-form models occurred when it was recognized that the nested logit model reveals crucial information to accommodate the pooling of multiple data sets, especially revealed and stated preference data. Although Louviere and Hensher (1982, 1983) and Louviere and Woodworth (1983) had recognized the role of stated choice data in the study of discrete choices in situations where new alternatives and/or existing alternatives with stretched attribute levels outside of these observed in real markets exist, it was the contribution of Morikawa (see Ben Akiva and Morikawa 1991) that developed a way to combine data sets while accounting for differences in scale (or variance) that was the essential feature of the choice model that had to be satisfied if the resulting model was able to satisfy the theoretical properties of RUM. Bradley and Daly (1997, but written in 1992) and Hensher and Bradley (1993) had shown how the nested logit method could be used as a "nested logit trick," to identify the scale parameter(s) associated with pooled data sets and to adjust the parameter estimates so that all absolute parameters can be compared across data sets.

Despite great progress in linking multiple choices and multiple data sets, some critical challenges remained. These centered initially on open-form models such as multinomial probit, which in the 1980s was difficult to estimate beyond a few alternatives, given the need to accommodate multiple integrals through analytical solutions. The need for numerical integration was required, but it was not until a number of breakthroughs associated with the notion of simulated **moments** (McFadden 1989) that the door opened to ways of accommodating more complex choice models, including models that could account for the fuller range of sources of unobserved heterogeneity in preferences.

The era of open-form models such as random parameter logit (also referred to as mixed logit) and error components logit, enabled researchers to account for random and systematic sources of taste (or preference) heterogeneity, to allow for the correlated structure of data common to each sampled individual (especially the case for stated choice data), and to obtain richer insights into preference and scale heterogeneity (and heteroskedasticity) associated with structural and latent influences on choices.

1.3 The journey ahead

The following sections of this primer will introduce the main rules that are needed to start understanding the richness of methods available to study. We will start right from the beginning and learn to "walk before we run." We will be pedantic in the interest of clarity, since what is taken for granted by the long-established choice analyst is often gobbledy-gook to the beginner. Intolerance on the part of such "experts" has no place in this book.

We have found in our graduate teaching and short courses that the best way to understand the underlying constructs that are the armory of choice analysis is to select one or, at most, a limited number of specific choice problems and follow them through from the beginning to the end. However, the main feedback on the 1st edition is the request to use a number of data sets that show the diversity of relevance of choice analysis, including the popular choose 1 (or first preference) labeled choice data, unlabeled choices, best–worst attribute and alternative designs, **ordered choices**, and choices involving more than one agent, in the context of mixtures of (or stand alone) settings of revealed and stated preference data. While readers will come from different disciplinary backgrounds such as economics, geography, environmental science, marketing, health science, statistics, engineering, transportation, logistics, and so forth, and will be practising in these and other fields, the tools introduced through a limited number of case studies should be sufficient to demonstrate that they are universally relevant.

A reader who insists that this is not so is at a disadvantage; they are committing the sin of assuming uniqueness in behavioral decision making and choice response. Indeed the great virtue of the methods developed under the rubric of choice analysis is their universal relevance. Their portability is amazing. Disciplinary boundaries and biases are a threat to this strength. While it is true that specific disciplines have a lot to offer to the literature on choice analysis, we see these offerings as contributions to the bigger multi-disciplinary effort.

The selected data sets used throughout the book have all of the properties we need to be able to illustrate the following features of choice analysis:

1. There are more than two alternatives. This is important because a choice situation involving more than two alternatives introduces a number of important behavioral conditions that do not exist when studying a binary choice.

2. It is possible to view the set of alternatives as more than one choice (e.g., choosing between public and private modes, choosing among the private modes, and choosing among the public modes). This will be important in order to show later how to set up a choice problem with more than one (inter-related) choice decision.

3. Two types of choice data have emerged as the primary sources of choice response. These are known as **revealed preference** (RP) and **stated preference** (SP) or stated choice (SC) data. RP data refer to situations where the choice is made in real market situations; in contrast SP data refer to situations where a choice is made by considering hypothetical situations (which are typically the same alternatives in the RP data set, but they are described by different levels of the same attributes to those observed in actual markets, as well as additional attributes not in the data collected from actual markets). SP data are especially useful when considering the choice among existing and new alternatives since the latter are not observed in RP data.

4. Often in choice modeling we over- and under-sample individuals observed to choose specific alternatives. This is common where particular alternatives are dominant or popular. For example, it is common to over-sample existing choosers of bus and train and under-sample car users in cities where the car dominates. In establishing the relative importance of the attributes influencing the choice among the alternatives we would want to correct for this over- and under-sampling strategy by weighting the data to ensure reproduction of the population **choice shares**. These weighted choice shares are more useful than the sample choice shares, and are essential when obtaining **elasticity** estimates.

5. The data have a large number of attributes describing each alternative and characteristics describing the socio-economic profile of each sampled trip maker (e.g., personal income, age, car ownership status, occupation). This gives the analyst plenty of scope to explore the contributions of

attributes of alternatives and characteristics of individuals to explaining choice behavior.

6. The alternatives are well defined and are described by labels such as bus, train, car drive alone, and car ride share. A data set with labeled alternatives is preferred over one where the alternatives are not well defined in terms of a label (called unlabeled alternatives) such as abstract alternatives that are only defined by combinations of attributes. Labeled alternatives enable us to study the important role of alternative-specific constants.

7. Finally, the case studies are associated with activities that most analysts have had personal experience with. Thus the applications should be very familiar.

The following chapters set out the process of choice analysis in a logical sequence consistent with what researchers and practitioners tend to do as they design their study and collect all the necessary inputs to undertake data collection, analysis, and reporting. We begin with a discussion on what we are seeking to understand in a study of choice (Chapter 2); namely, the role of an individual's preferences and the constraints that limit the ability to choose alternatives that are the most preferred in an unconstrained setting. Having established the central role of preferences and constraints, we are ready to formalize a framework within which a set of behavioral rules can be introduced to assist the analyst in accommodating these individual preferences, recognizing that the analyst does not have as much information about these individual preferences as the individual decision maker being studied (Chapter 3). The behavioral rules linking utility and choice are used to develop a formal model of choice in which we introduce the sources of individual preferences (i.e., attributes), constraints on such preferences (i.e., characteristics of individuals, peer influences, and other contextual influences), and the available set of alternatives to choose from. Once we have clarity on the crucial link between utility (sources of preference) and choice, we are ready (in Chapter 4) to introduce the family of choice models such as multinomial logit, nested logit, probit, mixed logit (and its growing number of variants), **latent class**, and ordered logit and probit. We focus on explaining the meaning of likelihood (and log-likelihood (LL)) functions, and how these are written out as a representation of the relationship between the functional form of the utility expressions and the choice probabilities. Chapter 5 is devoted to the estimation strategies that are available to obtain parameter (or marginal utility) estimates. These include the standard range of algorithms as well as simulated maximum likelihood that is used in more complex models such as mixed logit. We spend time on explaining important features of estimation such as the variance-covariance matrix (which is increasingly required in the design of choice experiments – see Chapter 6), the hessian, and what to do with a singular matrix.

With a choice modeling framework set out, and the range of models available, we are ready to introduce a very specific data paradigm that has become a very popular way of studying choice. Known as choice experiments, the literature has moved forward in leaps and bounds since the 1st edition of the book. We have totally rewritten the material on design of stated preference or stated choice experiments (as Chapter 6), introducing new software (NGene) that can accommodate most of the efficient designs that are used in the state of practice choice modeling applications.

We are now at the stage in the book where we have introduced the main features of choice models, some data issues, and the estimation of models using a simple MNL model to gain an understanding of the essential empirical features of a choice model. In Chapter 7 we introduce the main tools that are used to assist in determining "how good" the model is. Known as statistical inference, there are many tests but the most relevant ones are the likelihood ratio test, AIC, BIC, the **Wald test**, the **Delta method**, the **Lagrange multiplier test**, and the **Krinsky–Robb** (KR) test. We also introduce **bootstrapping** and show how to use variance functions to obtain standard errors for the WTP distributions. To complete the journey through the fundamental elements of the choice modeling process (referred to as Part I of the book), Chapter 8 introduces a number of themes that are often overlooked as well as the main behavioral outputs of choice models. These include endogeneity, random regret, partial or **marginal effects**, elasticities (point and arc), and WTP.

With a choice modeling framework set out, we are ready to introduce the choice modeling software. The two chapters in Part II focus on Nlogit, the software used throughout the book to illustrate how choice models can be estimated using various data sets. Although there are a number of software options available for model estimation, we have selected Nlogit5 for two reasons – it is the most popular software package for choice model estimation, and it is the package that the authors have greatest expertise in using (William Greene and David Hensher are the developers of Nlogit). Chapters 9 and 10 set out the basis procedures in Nlogit5 with which analysts must be familiar that are precursors to running choice models. These include installing the software, reading in data, creating project files, editing data, and transforming data.

Part III of the book is a journey beginning with the multinomial logit model (Chapter 11), including Chapter 13 on getting more from your model, through to the nested logit model (Chapter 14), the mixed logit model

(Chapter 15), latent class (Chapter 16), binary choices (Chapter 17), ordered logit (Chapter 18), and data fusion (especially SP–RP), including the topic of **hypothetical bias** (Chapter 19). Chapter 12 is a diversion to the important topic of how to handle unlabeled data. The mixed logit chapter includes all of the variants such as **scaled multinomial logit**, generalized mixed logit, in preference and WTP space, and error components, as well as latent class models (separated into Chapter 16), the latter being a discrete distribution interpretation of a fixed or random parameter mixed logit model.

The final three chapters (Part IV) are new developments that were not included in the 1st edition. As model functional form becomes more complex, the need for nonlinear (in parameters) estimation becomes increasingly relevant. The old grid search methods need to be replaced with a joint estimation capability. Chapter 20 introduces the nonlinear random para-meters model form as a frontier in choice analysis; illustrated after setting out the new model form with a number of nonlinear models associated with expected utility theory and variants of prospect theory (such as rank depen-dent utility theory and cumulative prospect theory). Chapter 21 brings together the growing literature on attribute processing, more broadly referred to as process heuristics, which recognizes that respondents typically make choices in the context of a set of rules that condition how each attribute or alternative is processed. This is a lengthy new chapter given the growing importance of this literature in choice modeling. The final chapter, Chapter 22, moves beyond the single decision maker (or chooser) to a recognition that many choices are made by groups of individuals. We show how standard choice modeling methods can be used with data appropriate to a multiple agent setting, in establishing the influence (or power) of each decision maker in arriving at a group choice (be it cooperative or non-cooperative).

Throughout the book we add numerous hints under the boxed heading of "as an aside." This format was chosen as a way of preserving the flow of the argument while placing useful tips where they can best be appreciated. Finally, the data sets used to illustrate the application of specific choice modeling methods are not provided with the book; however a few of the data sets will be made available on a service site for analysts to access (http://sydney.edu.au/itls/ACA-2015).

2 Choosing

As soon as questions of will or decision or reason or choice of action arise, human science is at a loss.

(Noam Chomsky, 1928 –)

2.1 Introduction

Individuals are born traders. They consciously or subconsciously make decisions by comparing alternatives and selecting an action that we call a choice outcome. As simple as the observed outcome may be to the decision maker (i.e., the chooser), the analyst who is trying to explain this choice outcome through some captured data will never have available all the information required to be able to explain the choice outcome fully. This challenge becomes even more demanding as we study the population of individuals, since differences between individuals abound.

If the world of individuals could be represented by one person, then life for the analyst would be greatly simplified, because whatever choice response we elicit from that one person could be expanded to the population as a whole to get the overall number of individuals choosing a specific alternative. Unfortunately there is a huge amount of variability in the reasoning underlying decisions made by a population of individuals. This variability, often referred to as heterogeneity, is in the main not observed by the analyst. The challenge is to find ways of observing and hence measuring this variability, maximizing the amount of measured variability (or observed heterogeneity) and minimizing the amount of unmeasured variability (or unobserved heterogeneity). The main task of the choice analyst is to capture such information through data collection, and to recognize that any information not captured in the data (be it known but not measured, or simply unknown) is still relevant to an individual's choice, and must somehow be included in the effort to explain choice behavior.

2.2 Individuals have preferences and they count

What we need is a conceptual framework that focuses on identifying the underlying influences on an individual's choice behavior. A useful way of revealing the necessary information is to start with a search for what these influences are. We will draw on ideas (in the main) from economics and (to a lesser extent) psychology and decisions sciences, starting with the notion that it is an individual's **preferences** for specific alternatives (be they goods or services) that best determine what alternative is chosen. The word "preference" is used in common parlance – we often state that "we prefer to drive a car to work than catch public transport" or "we prefer scary movies to romantic movies." If we delve deeper and try and understand the transport statement a little better, we would find that the reasons for preferring the car over public transport are related to travel time, comfort, convenience, security, and even status (depending on what type of car is driven!). We might also be told, however, that not all reasoning is grounded in positive issues – parking is a problem at the destination (in terms of availability and price), and one might even include good-citizen considerations such as air pollution, global warming, and car crashes leading to huge costs to society in terms of lost productivity, not to mention trauma.

Even taking into account these underlying reasons that drive preferences, there will always be a number of constraints that deny the full achievement of the most preferred alternative. For example, an individual may not be able to afford to purchase a car (a personal and/or household income constraint). Assuming that the income constraint is not binding (for the time being), it makes very good sense to try and find out more about the preferences so that, regardless of the current budget constraint, if in the future this constraint is modified (i.e., tightened or relaxed) we can usefully establish what set of alternatives would be most preferred. To progress along this line of reasoning, we need to take a closer look at how preferences are formed.

Where to start? Let us assume that we are discussing whether an individual will choose the car as a driver or the train for the journey to work. We will keep it simple, limiting the discussion to two alternatives, although we can easily generalize the situation to many alternatives once we have a basic understanding on how preferences are revealed. Let us also assume that we have had extensive discussions with a sample of travelers and have identified the many reasons for choosing car or train. This list is likely to be quite long, but we will take the top two attributes – travel time and out-of-pocket cost. Later you will see that the selection of these two attributes is a gross simplification of what are the underlying influences on preferences for car or train travel; in a serious data collection we have to measure a greater number of the potentially relevant attributes. Indeed, even travel time itself is a complex attribute because it includes all types of travel time – walking to a train station, waiting for a train, time in the train, the proportion of in-train time that the person is seated, time in the car, time parking a car, time walking to workplace after parking the car or alighting from the train and travel time variability (or reliability) over repeated trips.

To be able to progress, we have to decide on how we might measure the underlying influences that define an individual's preferences for car over train or vice versa. Putting aside a concern about the image of a particular form of transport (which may ultimately be an important influence on preference formation, especially for new means of transport), we have assumed that the choice between car and train is determined by a comparison of the travel times and costs of the trip. But how relevant or important is time compared to cost, and does it differ within each alternative? Throughout the development of choice analysis, we have sought to find a way of measuring an individual's preferences through what we call the "sources of preferences." Once the sources are identified, they have to be measured in units that enable us to compare various combinations of the attributes across the alternatives, and hopefully be confident that the alternative with the highest (positive) value or index is the most preferred. Whether we can say that an alternative is preferred by an exact number (i.e., a *cardinal measure*) or simply state that it is more preferred (i.e., an *ordinal measure*) is a more challenging question, but for this book we can safely put that issue aside.

The best way to progress the measurement of preferences is to recognize that if the only influencing attribute were travel time, then it would be a simple exercise to compare the travel times, and conclude that the alternative that has the shorter travel time to the given destination would be preferred. However, here we have two attributes (and usually many more). So how do we measure an individual's preferences in a multi-attribute environment?

We will begin by looking at each mode of transport separately. Take the car with its travel time and cost. To reveal an individual's preferences, we will invite them to evaluate different combinations of travel time and cost associated with a particular trip (whose distance travelled is known). We need to ensure that all combinations are realistic, although at the same time noting that some combinations may be outside of the individual's existing experiences (in the sense that there is no current technology available that can deliver a particular combination, e.g., an automatic pilot operating the vehicle using a global positioning system (GPS technology) to steer – which is not far off; or institutional constraints such as 100 kph that legally limits a particular travel time over the fixed distance). To be able to convert the combinations of time and cost into a unit (or metric) that enables a comparison, it is common practice to define a response space in either satisfaction or utility space. We need to explain this since it is crucial that the reader understands the meaning.

The build up of knowledge of an individual's preferences begins by taking one commodity or good (which we call an alternative). Let us begin with the bus alternative and seek out an individual's preference for different combinations of travel time and cost (i.e., bus fare). We might start by selecting a range over which we will select a number of travel times and fares. Let this be 10–60 minutes and $0.20–$5.00. Preferences are revealed by asking an individual to evaluate combinations of travel time and cost, and to provide either a numerical score or a ranking. A numerical score implies an ability to quantify with some precision a preference order and is referred to as *cardinal measurement*. A ranking score implies relativity (including equivalence) but admits that precision by cardinal measurement is not possible. Such a ranking is known as *ordinal measurement*. Despite the ongoing debate about the relative merits of cardinal and ordinal measurement, we will be adventurous and assume a capability to assign a numerical measure to each combination of travel time and cost. But what might this numerical measure be? In psychology, it is referred to as "level of satisfaction"; in economics it is called "level of utility." These are essentially the same (although economists typically reserve the nomenclature "utility" for ordinal measurement). Typically this measure is a relative one.

Using the notion of satisfaction, we need to give it some numerical dimension (i.e., a scale) that is easy to understand, and is capable of being used to compare combinations of travel time and cost. We will use a scale over the range 0–100, where 100 is the highest level of satisfaction. We will further assume that the scale has a meaningful zero, and hence we can compare pairs of levels on the scale. A pair is a ratio and hence it is known as a **ratio scale**. If we were to assume that zero was not meaningful, then we cannot infer whether or not a fixed difference between two combinations (e.g., 20 versus 30 on the satisfaction scale with 30 versus 40) is exactly the same on satisfaction. Another way of saying this is that over a fixed interval, the preference is not linear.

Continuing with a ratio scale satisfaction response, we would elicit a response from an individual for each offered combination of travel time and

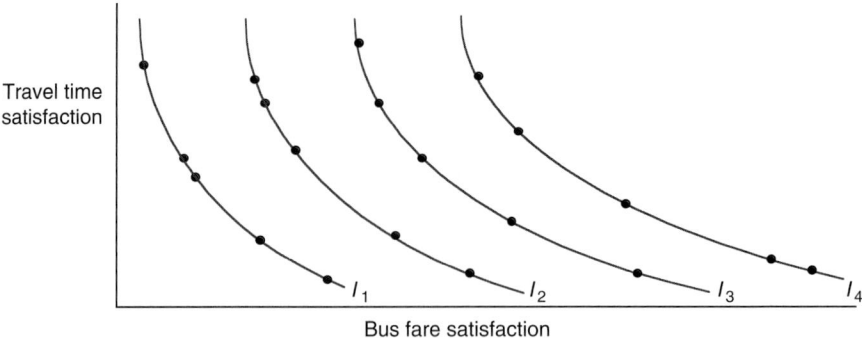

Bus fare satisfaction

Figure 2.1   Identification of an individual's preferences for bus use

cost. Although in theory one can offer an infinite number of combinations subject to the range of travel time and cost, in practice we tend to select a sufficient number to be able to trace out the levels of satisfaction that are likely to arise from the "consumption" of any one of the total (but finite) set of possible combinations. What we are doing here is plotting the combinations of travel time and cost in satisfaction space as a way of revealing preferences.

To illustrate what such a plot might look like, for one alternative (the bus mode) we define in Figure 2.1 the vertical axis as levels of satisfaction associated with travel time, and the horizontal axis as levels of satisfaction associated with bus fares. Assume that we invited an individual to evaluate the 20 combinations, by indicating on a satisfaction rating scale what rating they would assign to each combination of time and fare, and then we plotted the responses in satisfaction space. They do because of the IC line but it is not clear that the two points I have circled here have some satisfaction without the line. We have specifically plotted a number of combinations with the same levels of satisfaction to be able to introduce another way of representing preferences. If we join together all points with the same level of satisfaction we can conclude that an individual is *indifferent* as to which of these combinations is chosen. This indifference in level of satisfaction has led to the definition of a set of **indifference curves** as a way of depicting individual preferences.

In the satisfaction space in Figure 2.1, there are literally thousands of possible points of difference and equality in satisfaction. The indifference curves enable us to make some meaningful sense out of all the potentially useful information on what we might call the *shape of the preferences of individuals*. This exercise can be repeated for each alternative since it is likely that the same combinations of levels of attributes might produce different levels of satisfaction across the alternative modes of transport. For example, holding cost fixed, 20 minutes in a bus might be associated with a different level of satisfaction than 20 minutes in a car as a driver. What we are starting to recognize is that the preferences (as revealed through levels of satisfaction) of an individual across alternatives will vary and indeed this is likely to be the case even across individuals.

This heterogeneity in preferences is what choice analysis is all about – to try and explain these preferences across a sample of individuals, given the choice set. In taking stock of what information we now have about preferences, it should be recognized that we have made a number of (implicit) assumptions to assist in measuring the levels of satisfaction (which we might also start to refer to as levels of utility):

1. We have assumed that any other influences on preference formation except levels of travel time and cost of a specific alternative are held fixed at whatever levels they might be at the time of the evaluation.
2. These other influences include the state of technology, an individual's ability to pay (i.e., their personal income), the levels of attributes associated with that alternative that are additional to travel time and cost, the levels of all attributes associated with other (competing and/or complementary) alternatives, and preferences for other alternatives.

The state of technology refers to the levels of attributes offered in the market by existing modes of transport. By referring to these other potential influences on choice behavior as fixed influences, we commonly use the nomenclature that an individual chooses levels of the two attributes (travel time and cost) and assigns a level of satisfaction, holding "all other influences constant" (also referred to as **ceteris paribus**). This statement hints at a preference for the combination of travel time and cost that provides the highest level of satisfaction (or utility). To be able to say that an individual prefers this combination implies that an individual acts *as if* they are maximizing the level of satisfaction. This is commonly referred to as a behavioral rule expressed as *utility-maximizing behavior.*

As desirable as the selection of the combination of attributes is, all other things being equal, that gives the highest level of utility, this solution may not be achievable. This is because a person's income (or budget) cannot afford the cost, and/or the state of technology does not permit that combination. The next task is to recognize these constraints and establish the utility-maximizing combination within the financial budget.

We need to make a modification to the presentation now. Instead of working with two attributes of a single alternative (i.e., time and cost for bus), we will instead introduce an additional alternative (i.e., car) and look at

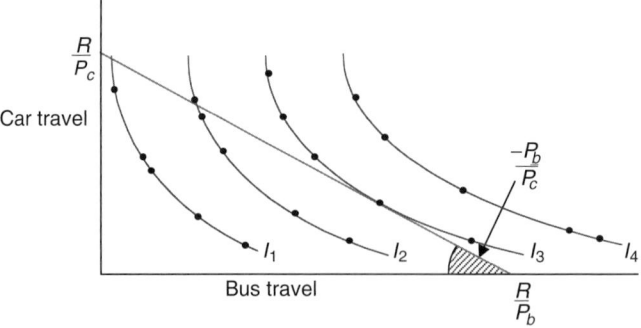

Figure 2.2   The budget or resource constraint

the preferences for bus versus car travel (either in terms of a single attribute such as cost, or in terms of combinations of attributes such as time and cost). Note that if we evaluate more than one attribute associated with each alternative, then to be able to stay with a simple two-dimensional diagram, we will need to add up each attribute. In the current context we would have to convert travel time to dollars, and add it to fares for bus and operating costs for car to get what is referred to as the generalized cost or generalized price of a trip. We discuss issues of converting attributes into dollar units in a later chapter on WTP, but for the time being we will assume that we have a single attribute associated with bus and car, called cost. Within this revised setting of two modes, we will define the budget constraint as an individual's personal income. In Figure 2.2 we overlay this budget constraint on a set of preference (or indifference) curves to identify the domain within which preferences can be realized. How do we present the budget constraint? There are three main elements in the definition of the budget constraint:

1. The total resources (R) available (e.g., personal income) over a relevant time period (which we refer to as resources available per unit of time);
2. The unit price associated with car (P_c) and bus (P_b) travel; and
3. Whether these unit prices are influenced by the individual (as a price maker) or the individual has no influence, and simply takes prices as given (i.e., a price taker).

Let us define the price of a unit of car travel as P_c and the price of a bus trip as P_b. We will also assume that the individual is a price taker and so has no influence over these unit prices. The slope of the budget constraint is the ratio of the prices of the two modal trips. To explain why this is so, if we assume that all of the budget is spent on car travel, then the maximum amount of car travel that one can "consume" is the total resources (R) divided by P_c. Likewise the

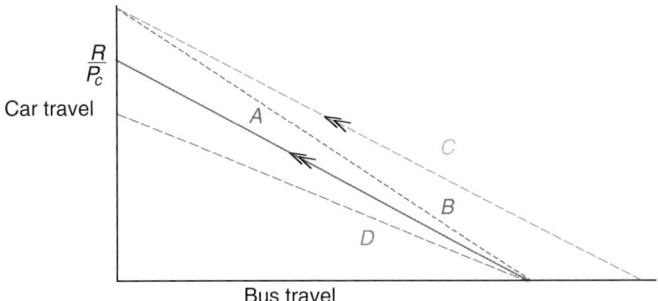

Figure 2.3   Changes to the budget or resource constraint

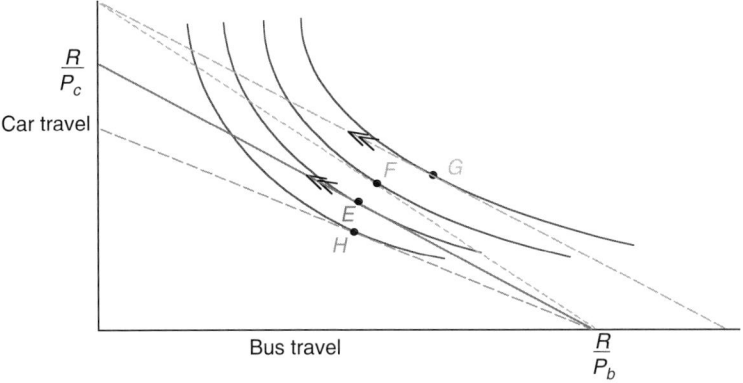

Figure 2.4   Individual preferences subject to a budget constraint

total amount of bus travel that can be undertaken is R/P_b. As a price taker, the unit price is constant at all levels of car and bus travel cost, and so is a straight line. To illustrate what happens to the budget line when we vary price and resources, in Figure 2.3, starting with the original budget constraint (denoted as line A) we present line B for a reduction in the price of car travel, line D for an increase in the price of car travel, and line C for an increase in total resources (holding prices fixed at P_c and P_b).

In Figure 2.4, when we overlay the budget constraint with the preference curves, we can see the possible combinations of the two modal trips that an individual can choose in order to maximize utility subject to the resource constraint. This will be at point E where an indifference curve is tangential to the budget constraint for the prices P_c and P_b, and resources R. The individual cannot improve their level of utility without varying the total amount of resources and/or the unit prices of the two modal trips. In Figure 2.4 we show other utility-maximizing solutions under a reduction in the unit price of car travel (point F), an increase in total personal income (point G), and an increase in the unit price of bus travel (point H).

In the discussion above we have used a car trip being traded against a bus trip. It is common, however, in developing an understanding of the role of preferences and constraints, to select one attribute of an alternative (or good or service) and evaluate its role *vis-à-vis* not spending money on that alternative, given the total available resources. This single attribute is typically the unit price of the alternative (e.g., the bus fare). However we can see from Figure 2.1 that alternatives have many attributes as descriptors of sources of satisfaction (or utility), and hence we would want to preserve this detail in a real application. This would be achieved by converting each attribute's levels into a dollar value, and adding them up to produce what is called a *generalized price*. In presenting the material in a two-dimensional diagram, the best way to continue the discussion is to treat the horizontal axis as the amount of the travel mode (i.e., bus) consumed as defined by the number of trips per unit of time (say, over a month), and the vertical axis as another use of resources that are available after allocating funds to bus use (call it savings or expenditure on commodity Y).

Figure 2.5 has three budget constraints and three indifference curves that serve to illustrate how utility-maximizing levels of bus travel and expenditure on other activities are determined. You will see that the amount of bus travel varies as we vary the price of bus travel, increasing as bus fares decrease, and decreasing as bus fares increase. Figure 2.5 is especially useful

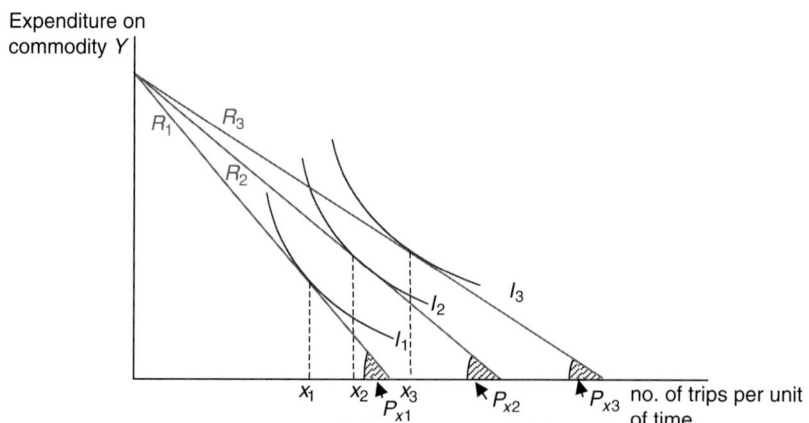

Figure 2.5   Indifference curves with budget constraints

in establishing a relationship between the frequency of choice and an attribute influencing such a choice, all other things being equal (or constant). We can now make a very important statement: "Given an individual's preferences (as represented by the shapes of the indifferent curves), available budget and unit prices of alternatives (in this example bus travel and all other activities), and holding all other considerations constant, under the rule of utility maximisation we can trace out the relationship between the unit price of bus travel and the amount of bus travel." What we have here is the *individual's demand function*.

We have avoided using the word "demand" up to now since our focus is on "choice." These two constructs are related and need to be clarified. When we observe an individual doing something such as undertaking a bus trip, we have observed the outcome of a choice and also information that represents the demand for the activity (i.e., bus travel). The observed choice outcome observed over a period of time enables us to measure the number of times a specific choice is made (whether it is made under habitual choice or a fresh re-evaluation each time, the latter known as variety seeking). Importantly, to be able to interpret the sum of all choice outcomes as a measure of an individual's demand for a specific activity (be it a purchase of a durable good (e.g., a car), consumption of a good (e.g., a chocolate bar), or use of an alternative such as bus), we must record situations where such an activity is not undertaken at all. This has led to a useful distinction between **conditional choice** and **unconditional choice**. The former tells us that a specific choice is conditional on something else. For example, the choice of mode of transport for the journey to work is conditional on a prior choice to work or not to work. It may also be conditional on the prior choice to work away from home versus work at home (conditional on the decision to work). An unconditional choice is one that is not conditioned on any prior choice. It is only when we have taken into account all of these prior (or in some cases joint) conditions that we can refer to individual (unconditional) demand. An important point to recognize for later is that the alternative "not to choose any of the alternatives offered" is a very important alternative, where it is a valid response, if we are to convert an individual **choice outcome** into a measure of individual demand.

With this distinction clarified, we can now use the information in Figure 2.5 to derive the individual's *demand function* for a specific alternative. We do this by simply reading off from Figure 2.6a the combinations of unit price and number of bus trips and plotting them in Figure 2.6b against a vertical axis for price and a horizontal axis for the *quantity* demanded.

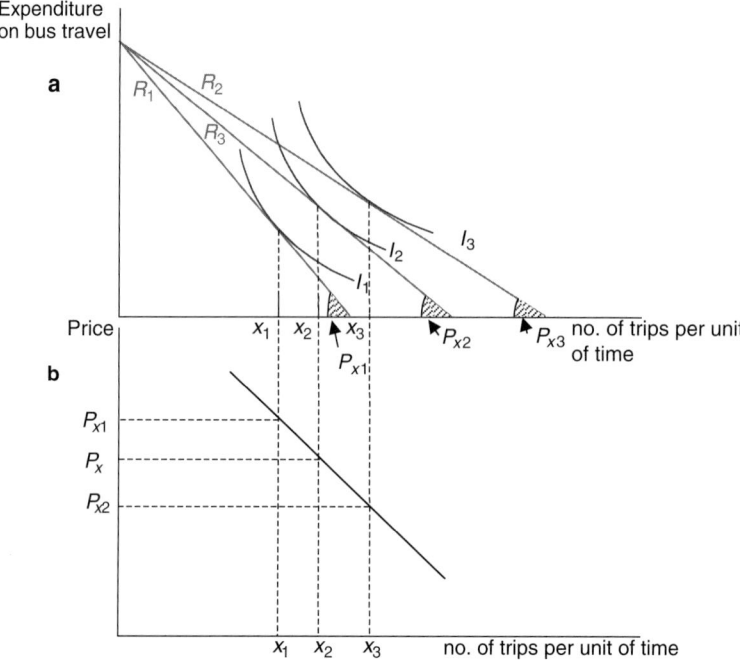

Figure 2.6   Demand curve construction

Figure 2.6 has provided the necessary information to derive one demand curve for an individual. Movements along this demand curve are attributed to changes in the price of bus travel, all other considerations held constant. However other influences may change from time to time for many reasons, and then we have a problem in interpreting movements along a given demand curve. Simply put, we cannot observe movements along a given demand curve (called change in the *quantity* demanded) when something other than what is on the vertical axis changes. If an individual's personal income increases, we might expect a change in the quantity of bus travel because the additional income might enable the individual to buy a car and switch from bus to car travel for some of the trips per unit of time. What we now have is more than a change in the quantity of bus travel; we also have a change in the *level* of demand.

That is, the demand curve itself will change, resulting in an additional demand curve that accounts for both the reduction in bus travel and the increase in car travel. Since Figure 2.6 is focused on bus travel, we will only be able to observe the change in bus travel in this diagram. We will also need an additional diagram (Figure 2.7) to show the amount of travel that has

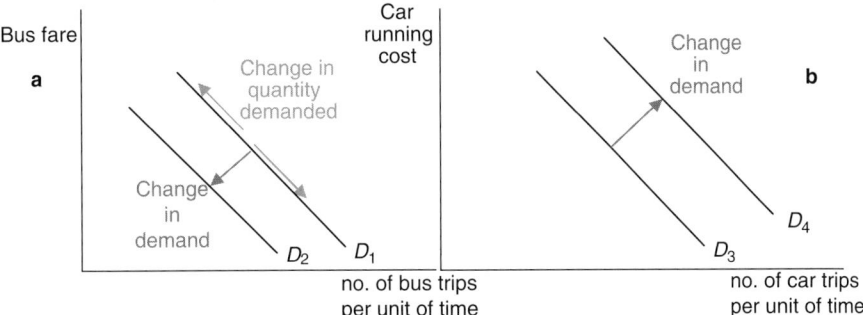

Figure 2.7   Changes in demand and changes in quantity demanded

substituted car for bus. A movement between demand curves is referred to as *a change in demand* (in contrast to a change in the quantity demanded when an individual moves along a given demand curve). We now have a **substitution effect** and an **income effect**; the latter due to a change in income and the former due to a change in the unit price. These concepts are developed in more detail in Hensher and Brewer (2001, 197–201).

2.3 Using knowledge of preferences and constraints in choice analysis

We are now able to focus again on choice analysis, armed with some very important constructs. The most important is an awareness of how we can identify an individual's preferences for specific alternatives, and the types of constraints that might limit the alternatives that can be chosen. The shapes of the preference curves will vary from individual to individual, alternative to alternative, and even at different points in time. Identifying the influences molding a specific set of preferences is central to choice analysis. Together with the constraints that limit the region within which preferences can be honored, and the behavioral decision rule used to process all inputs, we establish a choice outcome.

The challenge for the analyst is to find a way of identifying, capturing, and using as much of the information that an individual takes on board when they process a situation leading to a choice. There is a lot of information, much of which the analyst is unlikely to observe. Although knowledge of an individual's choice, and the factors influencing it, is central to choice analysis, the real game is in being able to explain choices made by a *population* of individuals. When we go beyond an individual to a group of individuals (as a sample or a full population census) we reveal an even greater challenge for the analyst – how best to take into account the huge amount of variation in reasoning underlying the same choice outcome, and indeed the rejection of the non-chosen alternatives.

Choice analysis is about explaining variability in behavioral response in a sampled population of individuals (or other units of choice making such as households, firms, community groups, etc.). An early reminder of the importance of this is in order. There are some relatively simple ways of attacking this very important matter. One might limit the compilation of data to a few easy to measure attributes of alternatives and descriptors of individuals. Furthermore one might use relatively aggregate measures of these. For example, it is not uncommon in transport studies to use the average income of individuals living in a specific suburb instead of an individual's actual income. It is also not uncommon to use the average travel time between specific locations based on a sample of individuals travelling between those locations, instead of an individual's actual (or most likely perceived) travel time. It is also not uncommon to then take the proportion of travelers choosing an alternative as the dependent variable, effectively moving away from a study on individual choice to a study of spatially aggregated individuals. What we will observe is that much of the variability in sources of potential influence on choice behavior associated with individuals is eliminated by aggregation (or averaging). When this occurs, we have indeed less variability to explain and indeed statistical methods will handle this in a way that produces a higher explanation of behavioral response. This is a fallacy – when there is less variability to explain, it is easier to explain and you tend to get a better fitting statistical model (e.g., a very high overall goodness of fit measure such as R^2 in a linear model). You feel good but you should not. There is a very high chance that you have explained a high amount of only a small amount of the true behavioral variance in the data on individuals. What we still have left is a huge amount of unobserved variability that is central to explaining the choice made. Its relevance increases when the analyst adopts so-called simple ways of trying to explain choice behavior. One is not eliminating the problem, but rather simply ignoring (or avoiding) it.

The next step is to set out a framework within which we can capture the sources of behavioral variability at the individual decision making level. We must recognize that the sources of variability are initially unobserved by the analyst (but known with certainty by the decision maker, at least for the time being); and that the analyst's challenge is to try and capture as much of the variability through a set of observed influences, while finding ways of accommodating the remaining unobserved (to analyst) influences. We cannot ignore the latter because they are very much relevant sources of variability. How we account for these unobserved influences is at the center of choice analysis. This task, known as linking choice and utility, is the focus of Chapter 3.

3 Choice and utility

To call in the statistician after the experiment is done may be no more than asking him to perform a post-mortem examination: he may be able to say what the experiment died of.

(Ronald Fisher)

3.1 Introduction

As seen in Chapter 2, individual preferences, subject to any **constraints** faced by those operating in a market, will give rise to choices. These choices in the aggregate sum to represent the total demand for various goods and services within that market. Rather than attempt to model demand based on aggregate level data, **discrete choice** models seek to model demand using disaggregate level data. Note that this does not necessarily mean that different discrete choice models are estimated for each individual, although some researchers do attempt such feats (e.g., Louviere *et al.* 2008). Rather, models dealing with aggregate level demand data typically work with variables where each data point represents the amount of some good or service sold at a specific point in time, whereas discrete choice models are typically applied to data where each data point represents an individual choice situation, where the sum of the choices combine to produce information about overall demand.

Importantly, to be able to refer to "demand" we have to allow for the presence of a "no choice," since some goods and services are not consumed by an individual. Throughout this chapter and the rest of the book, we will refer to both choice and demand, and treat them as interchangeable words. In doing so, we also recognize the broader context within which discrete choice models can be used, that often distinguishes between discrete choice models and a complete system of demand models, the latter at a more aggregate economy wide level, in contrast to discrete choice models that are most commonly applied at a sectoral level (e.g., transport or health). Truong and Hensher (2012), among others, develop the theoretical linkages between *discrete choice models* and *continuous choice models*, where discrete choice models focus on the structure of tastes or preferences at the individual level, while continuous demand models can be used to describe the interactions between these preferences at the industry or sectoral level, extendable to an entire economy.

Working with disaggregate level data poses many challenges that those working with more aggregate level data might not have to worry about. In particular, disaggregate level data requires that data be captured pertaining to the specific context within which each observed decision was made (for aggregate level data, it is usually sufficient to know that X number of widgets were sold last month, Y the month before. The circumstance under which each and every widget was purchased is of little to no relevance, although the average price per widget, etc. might also come in handy). As such, the analyst may need to capture data related to the *decision context* related to each observed choice (e.g., was a trip made for work or non-work, purposes), the alternatives that were available to the decision maker at the time the choice was made (e.g., a bus, train, and car, or just a bus and train), relevant variables that describe those same alternatives which may have influenced the choice (e.g., the times and costs of the various modes), as well as the characteristics of the individual decision makers themselves (e.g., their age, gender, income, etc.).

The decision context will *typically* be used as a segmentation instrument, with different choice models estimated for different decision contexts. In some instances, however, data collected over multiple decision contexts may be pooled and the decision context used as an explanatory variable used to help explain differences in choice patterns. The alternatives (which are also referred to as **profiles** or **treatment combinations**, depending on what literature one reads), and the variables that describe them (when a variable relates to an alternative, we use the term attribute) group together to form what is known as either a choice situation (which we will adopt throughout), choice set, choice task, choice **observation**, profile combination, or even a run. Any information about the characteristics of the decision makers may also be used as explanatory variables to help explain differences in observed choices over the sampled population.

Of particular importance to the modeling process are the choice situations consisting of information related to the various alternatives that were available at the time a choice was observed to have been made (one can still estimate a choice model without knowing anything about the specific choice context or the decision makers, although having such information may result in better modeling outcomes). Discrete choice models require that each choice situation consists of an *exhaustive* and *finite* set of *mutually exclusive* alternatives. This implies that data on all relevant alternatives (including any null alternative, such as an alternative representing the status quo) is captured and that there exists some natural limit to the number of alternatives present, which is hopefully not too large. The fact that the alternatives are mutually exclusive suggests that decision makers are able to choose only one alternative per choice situation. These requirements combined point to the fact that discrete choice models are more concerned with questions about *what* is chosen rather than *how much* is chosen.

Given data about the choice situations and what alternatives were chosen, discrete choice models involve the estimation of a series of regression like equations, one per alternative. These equations predict the amount of (relative) utility each decision maker assigns to each of the alternatives. The utilities for the alternatives are then linked to predict, up to a probability, which of the alternatives will be chosen. In this way, discrete choice models involve the simultaneous estimation of a number of equations, up to the number of alternatives present within the data. Unlike linear regression models, however, these equations do not directly predict the observed outcome, which in this case would be the observed choices. Rather, the "regression like" equations predict the latent utility for each of the alternatives, which are then subsequently used to predict the choice outcomes.

This chapter sets out to describe in a general sense the above story. We begin with a discussion about modeling in general, with the aim of showing what discrete choice models are by beginning with the familiar regression model framework. We then extend the discussion to a treatise on utility, using the remainder of the chapter to explain the alternatives available to researchers in terms of modeling.

3.2 Some background before getting started

The objective of fitting a statistical model to data is typically to determine what, if any, relationship exists between two or more variables and, where a relationship is present, what the strength of that relationship is. Most undergraduate and postgraduate students will be familiar with the concept of linear regression models which are often used to identify the relationship between one or more independent variables with a single dependent variable. Assuming there to be k independent variables, x, and denoting the dependent variable Y, the *linear regression model* may be represented as shown in Equation (3.1):

$$Y_n = \beta_0 + \beta_1 x_{1n} + \beta_2 x_{2n} + \ldots + \beta_k x_{kn} + \varepsilon_n, \tag{3.1}$$

where β_0 and $\beta_k = \beta_1, \beta_2, \ldots, \beta_k$ are parameters to be estimated, the former representing a constant term, the latter the relationship between variable $x_k = x_1, x_2, \ldots, x_K$ and Y. The subscript n in Equation (3.1) is used to denote that there are n observations or data points. ε in Equation (3.1) reflects a degree of impreciseness in the relationship, often referred to as *error* or *white noise* and represents, in part, factors other than the k independent variables that might influence Y.

As the very name of the model implies, linear regression models require *linear relationships* between the dependent variable, Y_n, and the k independent variables, x_{kn}. Often, to ensure such a relationship, it is necessary to add to or transform one or more of the variables in some manner. Common transformations of either one or both of the dependent and independent variables include taking the logs of the variables, squaring the variables, or adding interaction terms. The specific transformation employed is designed to ensure that the linear relationship between the independent and dependent variables is maintained. For example, in Figure 3.1, using simulated data (the data is provided in Appendix 3A), we plot as a dotted line the relationship between X and Y. As can be seen, the line of best fit for this data is non-linear. In the same figure, we now plot X against the log of Y, which we show as a dashed

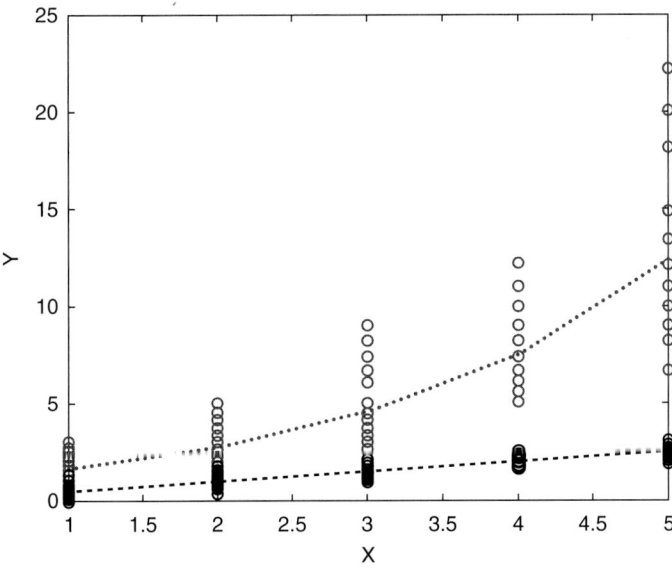

Figure 3.1   Example: log versus linear relationship

line. The relationship between X and $\log(Y)$ is a much better linear approximation than the relationship between X and Y, suggesting that the $\log(Y)$ and not Y should be used in any linear regression model estimated on this data.

While it may be possible to transform the data to ensure that the linearity assumption is maintained, one assumption of the linear regression model that cannot be so easily overcome is that the dependent variable must be continuous in nature, such that $Y_n \in (-\infty, \infty)$. No such assumptions are necessary with regards to the independent variables, however. In many cases, the dependent variable of interest will not be continuous, but rather take a finite number of **discrete** values. In Chapter 2, we suggested just such a dependent variable; that being some form of discrete choice, where one alternative out of a set is observed to be chosen. Assuming that Y_n takes the value one if alternative n is chosen, or zero otherwise, the dependent variable is represented as a *categorical* or *dichotomous* variable and hence definitely cannot be treated as if it is truly **continuous** (i.e., $Y_n \in (0, 1)$). It is important to note, however, that despite our use of the term "discrete choice," as in discrete choice models, the underlying econometric models which represent the focus of this book can be applied to any data where the dependent variable is categorical, and not just choice data. In this sense, the models we present are far more flexible in terms of the data to which they may be applied than otherwise might seem the case, and in some literature they are referred to as *categorical dependent variable* models.

To understand the concern with using linear regression models for data involving categorical dependent variables, and to further demonstrate that the methods discussed within this book can be extended beyond disaggregate level choice data, consider as an example the party make-up of The United States Congress. Each State is divided into voting districts representing approximately 700,000 people who elect a Congress person to act as their representative, typically belonging to either the Republican or Democratic Party. Suppose a researcher was interested in determining whether districts with a larger proportion of minority groups (i.e., persons who identify as being non-Caucasian) are more likely to be represented by a Democratic Party member in Congress. Plotted in Figure 3.2 is data on congressional party affiliation against the proportion of the population considered to be from minority groups for each of the 168 congressional voting districts.[1] As shown in Figure 3.2, the Y values take only the value zero (Republican Party) or one

---

[1] The data was obtained from http://ballotpedia.org/Portal:Congress accessed on 17 October 2013. Data on 430 voting districts was used for the analysis due to missing data related to five voting districts.

Table 3.1 Linear regression results

	Par.	(t-ratio)
Constant	0.091	(2.39)
% Minority	1.438	(11.74)
Model fit		
R^2	0.244	

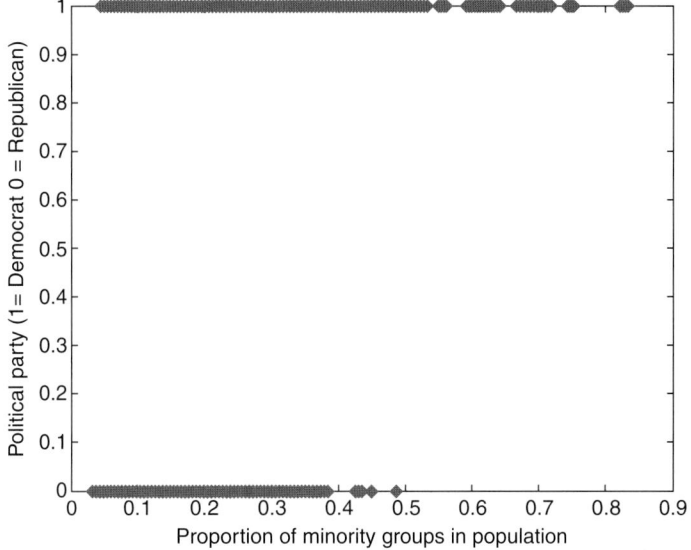

Figure 3.2   Plot of Congressional party affiliation against proportion of minority groups in voting districts

(Democratic Party). Note that the assignment of zero or one to a party is arbitrary and does not reflect any particular order or preference for one party or another.

Despite our earlier discussion regarding the need for a continuous dependent variable, it is still possible to estimate a linear regression model based on this data using party affiliation as the dependent variable and the proportion of the population that identify with a minority group as the independent variable. Table 3.1 shows the results of this analysis. The resulting model produces an R^2 of 0.244, and statistically significant parameter estimates. The positive parameter associated with the proportion of the population that identifies as being part of a minority group suggest that as the proportion of non-white residents increases in a district, the higher the likelihood that that district will be represented by a Democratic Party representative. The model

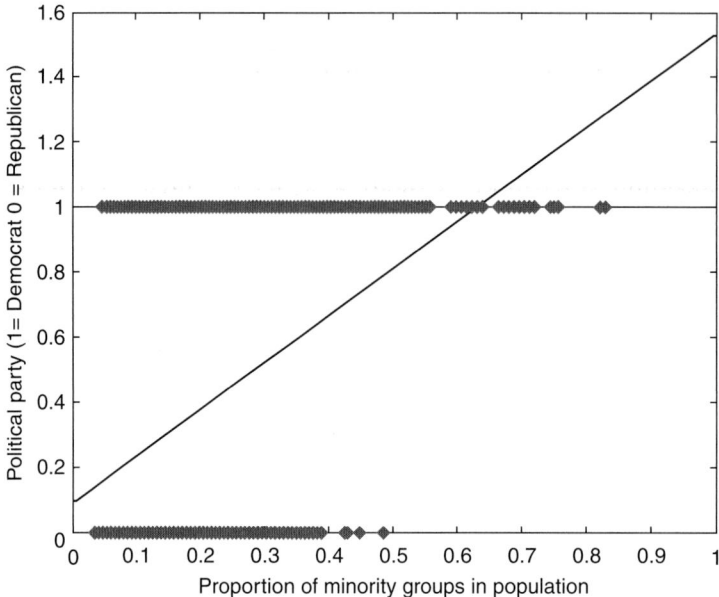

Figure 3.3   Linear regression model of Congressional party affiliation against proportion of minority groups in voting districts

was estimated using Nlogit 5.0. The syntax for this and other models are provided in Appendix 3B. The syntax for estimating models in Nlogit will be explained further in later chapters.

Figure 3.3 plots the linear regression line based on this model. A number of issues becomes readily apparent. Firstly, given the fact that the results of a linear regression model should be interpreted as if the dependent variable is continuous, the model will predict non-zero-one outcomes. Thus for example, the model will predict for a district with a 50 percent non-white population to have a congressional representative belonging to a party equivalent to 0.810. While it might be tempting to treat this outcome as a probability, and suggest that as the result is closer to one, the district is more likely to have a Democratic Party member as their congressional representative than a Republican, the linear regression model should not be interpreted this way, given that the regression line is continuous and hence the model is in fact predicting a congressional member belonging to a party coded as 0.810. The second concern with using linear regression models on data with a categorical dependent variable can also be seen clearly from Figure 3.3: the model may potentially predict outcomes outside of the zero and one range (whether it does will depend on the parameter estimates, and the values of the X variable). For the present example, a district with only 70 percent of the population identifying as being from a minority group will be predicted as having a party affiliated Congress person of 1.097 (noting that 70 percent falls within the data range). This further substantiates the fact that the previous prediction of 0.810 should not be treated as if it is a probability of party representation, as probabilities by definition are constrained to be between zero and one. It is worth noting that there are models such as tobit regression that ensure compliance with lower and upper limit constraints; however this does not change the issue of interpretation of the predictions as probabilities.

To resolve the above issues, it is necessary to transform the dichotomous dependent variable into a continuous variable. As noted above, transformations of the dependent variable are possible when using linear regression models, provided that the dependent variable remains (or becomes) continuous. Indeed, numerous studies have employed transformed dependent variables in the past. For example, as discussed above, a common transformation involves taking the log of the dependent variable and using this in the regression model, as shown in Equation (3.2):

$$\log(Y_n) = \beta_0 + \beta_1' x_{1n} + \beta_2' x_{2n} + \ldots + \beta_k' x_{kn} + \varepsilon_n, \tag{3.2}$$

where $'$ is used to indicate that the estimates obtained in Equation (3.2) would be expected to differ from those obtained from a model estimated as per Equation (3.1).

Where a transformation of the dependent variable is used, it is not possible to directly calculate the impact of the independent variables upon the dependent variable Y due to the transformative process used. It is therefore necessary to retrieve the relationship mathematically. For example, given the above, consider the impact upon Y given a one unit change in x_k. In this case, a Δx_{kn} will result in a $\exp(\beta_k' x_{kn})$ change in Y, whereas previously a change in x_k is predicted to result in a β_k change in Y.

The transformation of a dependent variable results in what is sometimes referred to as a *link function*. Consider Equation (3.3):

$$f(Y_n) = Y_n^* = \beta_0 + \beta_1 x_{1n} + \beta_2 x_{2n} + \ldots + \beta_k x_{kn} + \varepsilon_n, \tag{3.3}$$

where $f(Y_n)$ is any transformative function of Y producing Y_n^*. Here, Y_n^* is used in model estimation and not Y_n where the $f(Y_n)$ is the transformative link between the two values. In the previous example, the $f(Y_n) = \log(Y_n)$.

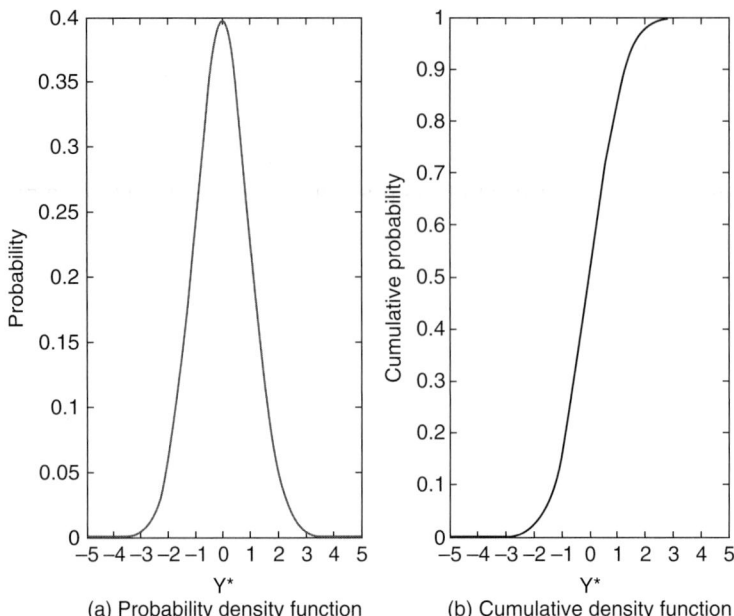

(a) Probability density function   (b) Cumulative density function

Figure 3.4   PDF and CDFs for Normal distribution: 1

In the case of a categorical dependent variable, it is necessary to locate a link function that will transform Y into a continuous variable such that $Y_n \in (0, 1)$ while $Y_n^* \in (-\infty, \infty)$. Unfortunately, the most common link functions used within the linear regression framework are not workable when the dependent variable is dichotomous (e.g., the log of zero is undefined).

Fortunately, under certain distributional assumptions, it is possible to convert any real number drawn from a random variable into a probability. The reverse is also true, allowing one to move from a probability back to the real number. For example, assuming a normal distribution, it is possible to calculate the Z-score for a random variable such that the cumulative normal distribution Φ of the Z-score will be $\Phi(Z) \in (0, 1)$.

Figure 3.4 plots the **probability density function** (PDF) and **cumulative density function** (CDF) for a (discrete) random variable Y^* which is assumed to be normally distributed. The PDF of a random variable represents the relative likelihood that the random variable will take a particular value while the probability that the variable will lie within some range is calculated as the integral over that range (i.e., the area under the PDF curve). The CDF represents the probability that a random variable, Y^*, with some density (represented by its PDF) will be located at some value less than or equal to Y_n.

For example, assume that Y^* is a random variable drawn from a standard normal distribution and that the analyst is interested in calculating the probability that Y^* is observed to take on a value less than or equal to some known value, say $Y_n^* = -1.0$. This is graphically represented in Figure 3.5(a) sub-panel (a) as the area under the PDF to the left of $Y_n^* = -1.0$. The precise probability of this occurring assuming that Y^* is drawn from a standard normal distribution is 0.1587, which is calculated from the CDF shown in sub-panel (b). Likewise, the probability that Y^* is observed to take on a value less than or equal to some known value, $Y_n^* = 1.0$ is 0.8413, as shown in Figure 3.5(b).

Relating this back to the problem at hand, assuming the right hand side of our regression equation is normally distributed, then:

$$Y_n = \Phi(\beta_0 + \beta_1 x_{1n} + \beta_2 x_{2n} + \ldots + \beta_k x_{kn} + \varepsilon_n)$$
$$\Phi^{-1}(Y_n) = Y_n^* = \beta_0 + \beta_1 x_{1n} + \beta_2 x_{2n} + \ldots + \beta_k x_{kn} + \varepsilon_n$$
(3.4)

where Φ is the Greek symbol (upper case) Phi, representing the CDF of the Normal distribution.

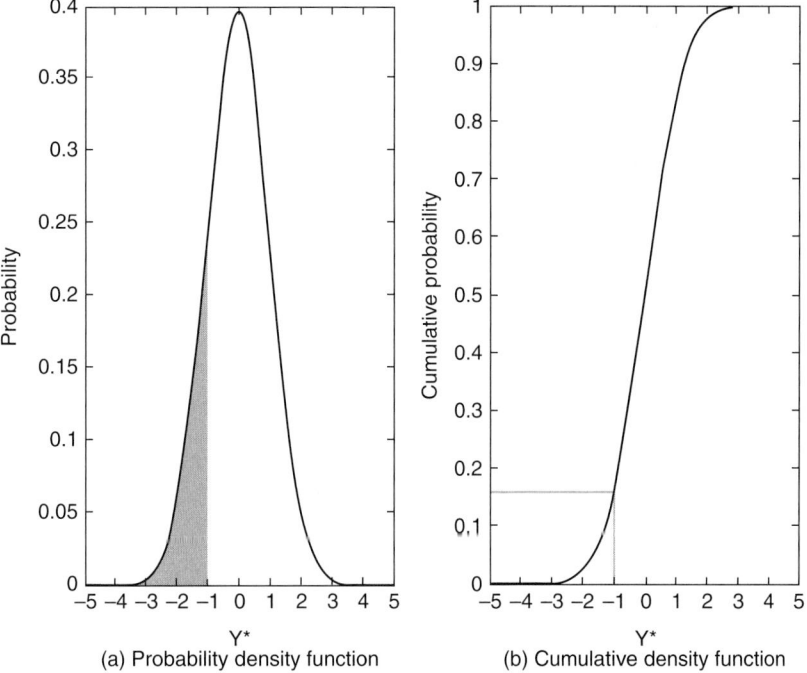

(a) Probability density function   (b) Cumulative density function

Figure 3.5   PDF and CDFs for Normal distribution: 2

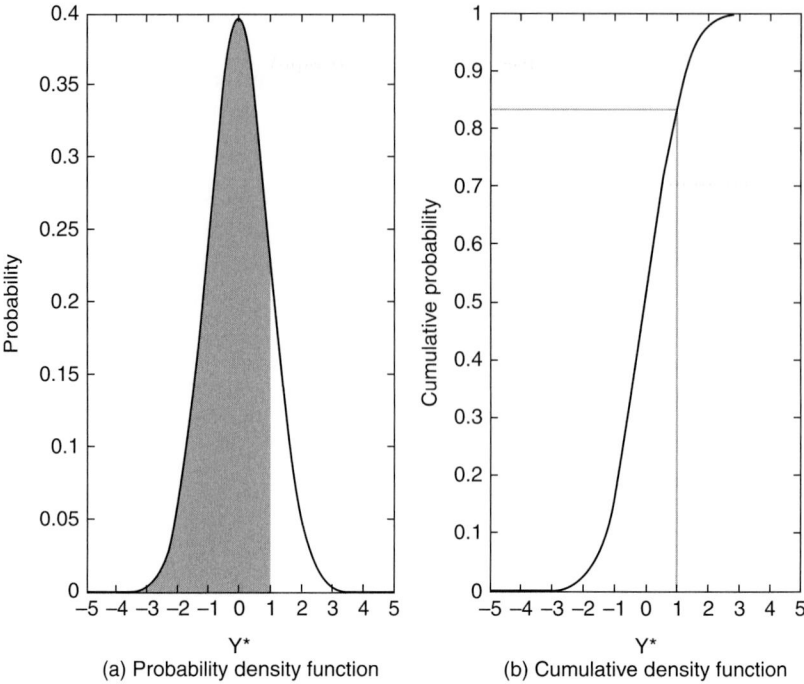

(a) Probability density function   (b) Cumulative density function

Figure 3.5   (cont.)

In Equation (3.4), the link function is $f(Y_n) = \Phi^{-1}(Y_n)$, which has been termed the probability unit link function, subsequently shortened to **probit**, and the resulting model is termed the probit model. Y^* represents a latent variable which is assumed to be Normally distributed.

In the case of a binary outcome, the probit model is known as a bivariate probit model, and Equation (3.4) relates to the outcome coded as outcome 1. To demonstrate, Table 3.2 presents the results of a probit estimated on the previously described data. We discuss the probit model in more detail in Chapter 4; however, it is sufficient to state at this time that it is possible to substitute values for the independent variables, much like with a linear regression model, to calculate the value of the latent variable Y^*.

For example, assuming that a voting district had 50 percent of its residents identify as belonging to a minority group, then Y^* in the above example would be equal to 1.899. Given that Y^* is assumed to be distributed standard normal, this value can be treated as if it were a Z-score. Hence, in this instance, the model predicts that a voting district made up of 50 percent minority groups has a probability of 0.88 of having a representative belonging to the party coded as 1, the Democratic Party. Given that probabilities sum to one, it is easy to calculate

Table 3.2 Probit model results

	Par.	(t-ratio)
Constant	−1.309	(−9.39)
% Minority	4.926	(9.25)
Model fit		
LL	−235.326	
ρ^2	0.207	

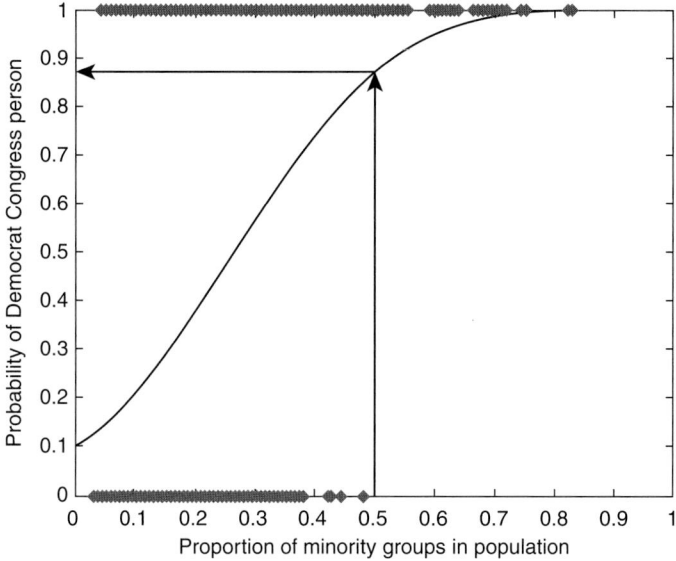

Figure 3.6   Probit model of Congressional party affiliation against proportion of minority groups in voting districts

that the same district will have a 0.12 probability of having a Republican Party member as its elective representative. Likewise, the reader can confirm that a district with a 70 percent minority group make-up will have a 0.98 probability of having a Democratic Party member as its elective representative.

Unlike the linear regression model, the probit model predictions derived from the latent variable Y^* are probabilities and therefore bounded between zero and one. Plotting the probit probabilities over the range of the x variable results in an S-shaped curve known as a *sigmoidal curve*. The sigmoidal curve for the model estimated above is shown in Figure 3.6. As shown in Figure 3.6, a district with 50 percent of its population identifying as belonging to a minority group will have a 0.88 probability of having a Congress person belonging to the party coded as 1, in this case the Democrat Party.

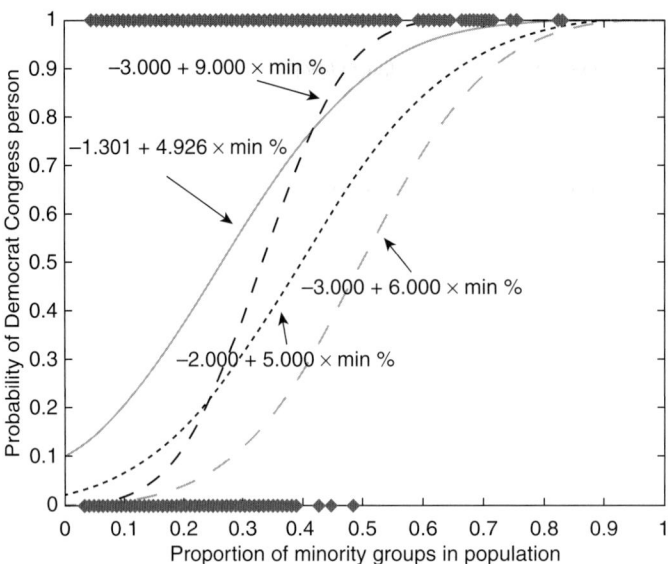

Figure 3.7 Sigmoid curve examples of alternative probit models

The shape of the sigmoidal curve will depend on the parameter estimates. Figure 3.7 plots the sigmoidal curve of the bivariate probit under various assumptions of the parameter estimates. As can be seen in the plot, the slope, and where the curve connects with the upper and lower x-axis, will depend on both the constant terms and parameter estimates associated with the independent variable.

An alternative model to the probit is the logit model. As with the probit model, we discuss the logit model in more detail in Chapter 4; however, it is sufficient to state at this time that the logit model is related to what are known as *odds ratios*. The odds ratio represents the odds of an outcome occurring based on some known probability. The odds of an outcome occurring may be calculated as per Equation (3.5):

$$Odds(Y) = \frac{p}{1-p}, \tag{3.5}$$

where p is the probability of outcome $Y = 1$ occurring. The odds as derived by Equation (3.5) are constrained to be within the positive domain such that $Odds(Y) \in (0, \infty)$. As such, rather than use the odds ratio, it is customary to use the log of the odds ratio instead which extends to both sides of the real line. That is $\log|Odds(Y)| \in (-\infty, \infty)$. Table 3.3 presents the odds and log odds for probabilities ranging between zero and one.

Table 3.3 Odds ratios and log-odds

p	$Odds(Y)$	$log(Odds(Y))$
0	0	$-\infty$
0.1	1/9	−2.197
0.2	1/4	−1.386
0.3	3/7	−0.847
0.4	2/3	−0.405
0.5	1	0.000
0.6	1 and 1/2	0.405
0.7	2 and 1/3	0.847
0.8	4	1.386
0.9	9	2.197
1	∞	∞

For the logit model, the link function used is the log of the odds ratio. Algebraically the logit probabilities for the binary outcome case can be derived as per Equation (3.6). As stated above, we discuss the logit model in more detail in Chapter 4, where we extend it to the multinomial case. We also discuss the multinomial case in Section 3.3:

$$
\begin{aligned}
\log\left(\frac{p_n}{1-p_n}\right) &= Y_n^* = \beta_0 + \beta_1 x_{1n} + \beta_2 x_{2n} + \ldots + \beta_k x_{kn} + \varepsilon_n \\
\frac{p_n}{1-p_n} &= \exp(Y_n^*) \\
p_n &= (1-p_n)\exp(Y_n^*) \\
p_n &= \exp(Y_n^*) - \exp(Y_n^*)p_n \\
p_n\left(1 + \exp(Y_n^*)\right) &= \exp(Y_n^*) \\
p_n &= \frac{\exp(Y_n^*)}{1 + \exp(Y_n^*)}
\end{aligned}
\tag{3.6}
$$

Table 3.4 presents the results of a logit model based on the same data described above. The logit formula (for the binary case) is given in Equation (3.6). Assuming a voting district with a 50 percent non-white population, the latent variable Y^* will be equal to 1.899 based on the reported model results. As with the probit model, the logit model predicts the probability of an outcome occurring. Substituting 1.899 into Equation (3.6) leads to a prediction of 0.87 that the district will have a Democrat as its elected Congressional member.

Table 3.4 Logit model results

	Par.	(*t*-ratio)
Constant	−2.165	(−8.65)
% Minority	8.130	(8.69)
Model fit		
LL	−235.868	
ρ^2	0.205	

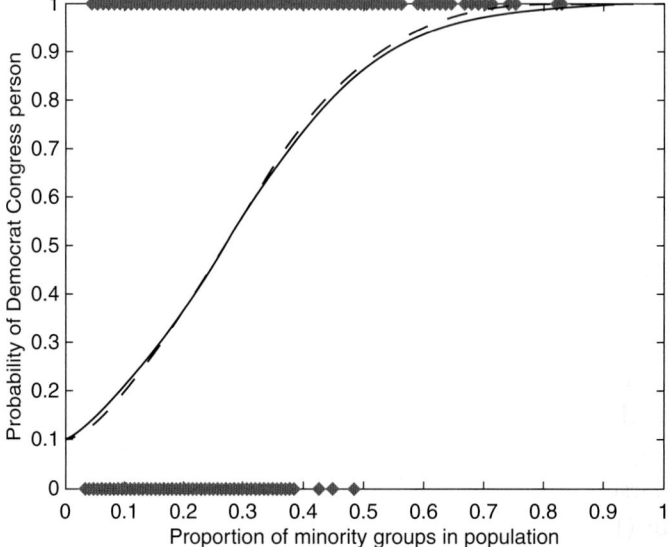

Figure 3.8   Logit and probit models of Congressional party affiliation against proportion of minority groups in voting districts

Similar to the probit model, the logit model probabilities produce a sigmoidal curve over the range of the independent variables. The sigmoidal probabilities for the above model are shown in Figure 3.8 as a continuous line. Also shown in the figure is the sigmoidal curve for the probit model reported in Table 3.2 (shown as a dashed line). As can be seen in the figure, the two models tend to predict very similar results, with the main differences being close to the zero and one probabilities.

We return to discuss both the probit and logit models in Chapter 4. In Section 3.3, with the preceding background, we return to a discussion of utility and choice.

3.3 Introduction to utility

In Section 3.2, we introduced the concept of link functions, which provide a mechanism to relate dichotomous dependent variables to a latent variable in an econometric model of interest. When the categorical dependent variable relates to choices, the latent variable, previously designated as Y^*, is termed utility. Let U_{nsj} denote the utility that decision maker n in choice situation s will derive from consuming or possessing alternative j. Typically, U_{nsj} may be partitioned into two separate components, an observed or modeled component, V_{nsj}, and a residual unobserved and un-modeled component, ε_{nsj}, such that:

$$U_{nsj} = V_{nsj} + \varepsilon_{nsj}. \tag{3.7}$$

In the sections that follow, we discuss both components of utility in detail, starting with the observed or modeled component of utility. Before we do so however, although briefly mentioned in Chapter 2, it is worth reiterating that in general, economics recognizes two different types of utilities: **cardinal** and **ordinal** *utility* (in economics, other types of utility also exist, such as expected utility, which deals specifically with risky choices; however, we will ignore these other forms of utility here and discuss them in Chapter 20). Cardinal utility is a theory of utility under which the utility obtained from an alternative is not only measurable but the magnitude of the measurement is also meaningful. First envisaged by Bernoulli (1738) and later expanded upon by Bentham (1789), under cardinal utility theory, utility is measured in units known as "*utils*," which is based on a ratio scale such that a direct comparison between the utilities gained from two alternatives is behaviorally interpretable. For example, assuming a person would gain 10 utils from consuming an apple but only 5 for consuming an orange, cardinal utility would conclude that the person would receive precisely half the pleasure of eating the orange than they would from eating an apple. Ordinal utility (Pareto 1906), on the other hand, suggests that the utilities obtained from two alternatives are indicative of the order of preference between the two goods, but the values themselves are meaningless (i.e., utility is measured on an ordinal scale). Hence, in our apple and orange example, all the analyst would be able to conclude is that the person concerned prefers apples to oranges; however, we are unable to say precisely by how much. That is, in ordinal utility theory, zero utility does not represent an absence of preference. Taking the apple and orange example, it would be possible to subtract 10 from each of the utilities so that the utility for apples is now measured as zero while the utility for oranges is –5. Once again, all we are able to conclude under ordinal utility theory is that the person prefers apples to oranges, and not that they are indifferent to apples but have a dislike (what is referred to as a *disutility*) for oranges. For this reason, when dealing with ordinal utility theory, it is common to refer to *relative utility*, as the absolute value of utility is meaningless. The distinction between cardinal and ordinal utility is important here as the utilities derived from discrete choice models are interpreted as being ordinal.

The fact that utilities obtained from discrete choice models are measured on an ordinal scale is important in that it implies that only differences in utility matter, not the absolute value of utility. In making this statement, however, it is necessary to make a distinction between the *level* and *scale* of utility. The level of utility represents the absolute value of utility. Adding or subtracting a constant to/from the utilities of all J alternatives, while changing the level of utility, will maintain the relative differences of utility between each of the alternatives. For example, subtracting 10 from the utilities of both the apple and orange alternatives above did not change the differences in utility between either. The scale of utility refers to the relative magnitude of utility. Consider an example where the utilities of all J alternatives are multiplied by the same value. The resulting utilities will not change in terms of their relative preference rankings; however, the utility differences will change. For example, multiplying the utility for both apples and oranges by 2 will produce a utility of 20 for apples and 10 for oranges such that apples are still preferred to oranges, but the relative difference in the utilities for the two alternatives is now 10. Table 3.5 demonstrates the difference between utility level and utility scale for the apple and orange example.

Table 3.5 Utility level versus utility scale

	Level				Scale		
	U(Apple)	*U(Orange)*	*Difference*		*U(Apple)*	*U(Orange)*	*Difference*
Uj*	*10*	*5*	*5*	*Uj**	*10*	*5*	*5*
−0.25	9.75	4.75	5	×0.25	2.5	1.25	1.25
−0.50	9.5	4.5	5	×0.50	5	2.5	2.5
−0.75	9.25	4.25	5	×0.75	7.5	3.75	3.75
+1.25	11.25	6.25	5	×1.25	12.5	6.25	6.25
+1.50	11.5	6.5	5	×1.50	15	7.5	7.5
+1.75	11.75	6.75	5	×1.75	17.5	8.75	8.75
+2.00	12	7	5	×2.00	20	10	10

The fact that only differences in utility matter has a number of important implications in terms of the identification of discrete choice models. Firstly, it is only possible to estimate parameters when there exist differences across the alternatives. This has important ramifications for the estimation of model constants and covariates, which we discuss later. Secondly, while the scale of utility does not matter, in that multiplying the utilities of all of the alternatives by the same amount will not change the relative preference rankings, it does play an important role econometrically. Consider Equation (3.8), in which we multiply utility by some positive amount (i.e., $\lambda > 0$):

$$\lambda U_{nsj} = \lambda (V_{nsj} + \varepsilon_{nsj}). \tag{3.8}$$

What becomes apparent from Equation (3.8) is that the scale of the observed component of utility is intrinsically linked to that of the unobserved component, in that both components are affected. We will discuss the unobserved effects in detail in Section 3.4; however, for the present it is sufficient to state that the unobserved effects are assumed to be randomly distributed with some density. Given this fact, it is easy to show that the scale of the observed component of utility will necessarily affect both the mean and variance of the unobserved component of utility. In the latter case, by precisely λ^2, given that $\mathrm{var}(\lambda \varepsilon_{nsj}) = \lambda^2 \mathrm{var}(\varepsilon_{nsj})$.

Note that Equations (3.7) and (3.8) make use of subscript j. This implies that each alternative, j, present within a person's choice set, will have its own utility function. To relate this back to our discussion in Section 3.2, we note that each of the models was represented by a single equation even though there existed two possible outcomes; a Democratic or Republican Party representative. As should be clear now from the discussion above, the latent variable for the outcome coded as zero in Section 3.2 was simply normalized to zero and it was for this reason that the Equations related to the outcome coded as one. In the case of binary outcomes, it is necessary to normalize the utility of one alternative to zero. This is because there will exist an infinite number of utility functions that may reproduce the same relative utility differences.

In many instances, however, there will exist more than one possible mutually exclusive non-continuous outcome. For example, there might exist a third political party that could be voted in, or a person may potentially have three or more possible modes of transport to choose from when travelling to work. In such cases, each alternative will have its own unique utility function, one of which may or may not be normalized to zero. How and when to normalize utility will form a large basis of the remainder of this chapter, where we concentrate on the observed component of utility, leaving discussion of the unobserved component of utility to Chapter 4. We are now ready to delve in some detail into the sources of observed and unobserved utility.

3.4 The observed component of utility

The observed component of utility associated with alternative j, V_{nsj}, is typically defined as a function of k variables, x_{nsjk}, with associated preference weights, β, such that:

$$V_{nsj} = f(x_{nsjk}, \beta, \lambda), \tag{3.9}$$

where x_{nsjk} is a **vector** of k attributes describing alternative j and/or covariates describing either the decision maker (e.g., age, income) or some aspect related to the decision context (e.g., whether the purchase is for personal use of the individual making the choice or a gift), and β is a vector of parameters to be estimated. λ is a scalar representing a scale parameter that links V_{nsj} to ε_{nsj}. For the purposes of the current discussion, we will assume that λ equals one, and hence will ignore it for the present, noting only that the parameter serves to scale the utility of each of the alternatives, J. We return to a discussion of λ in Chapter 4.

The parameters represent unknowns to be estimated and reflect the weights that decision makers attach to each of the attributes of an alternative, or that reflect the influence a covariate has upon the utility of that alternative (see Section 3.4.1 for a further discussion of the precise interpretation of the parameter estimates). Once estimated, the parameters will take on numerical values, such that the combination of the parameters and the variables will in turn produce a numerical value representing the overall utility a decision maker holds for that alternative.

The specific functional form that the observed utility function takes is defined by the analyst, with the only restriction being limitations imposed by the software used to estimate the models as well as the imagination of the analyst themselves. For whatever reason, the most common utility function reported within the discrete choice literature involves a simple linear combination of the attributes and parameter estimates, as shown in Equation (3.10). Note that this is similar to the specifications used in Section 3.2:

$$V_{nsj} = \sum_{k=1}^{K} \beta_k x_{nsjk}. \tag{3.10}$$

When a linear utility function such as that described in Equation (3.10) is used, different names for the parameters have been used within the literature, including **parameters**, parameter estimates, **coefficients**, **marginal utilities**, preference weights, taste weights, **tastes**, sensitivities, etc. The terms parameters, parameter estimates, and coefficients reflect the outcomes of some form of estimation procedure, while preference weights and taste weights suggest a more behavioral interpretation of these outcome estimates. Marginal utility, on the other hand, reflects an economic interpretation of the model, where the term *marginal* refers to a small change, in this case to the associated attribute. Independent of the name used, the interpretation remains the same assuming a linear in the attributes, linear in the parameters utility function, We discuss the issue of non-linear utility functions in Section 3.4.5. Given a unit change in attribute k, utility will change by an amount equivalent to β_k.

3.4.1 Generic versus alternative-specific parameter estimates

At this stage, it is worth noting that in order for there to be a choice to be made, the decision maker must face a situation in which there exists $j \geq 2$ alternatives (if there is only one alternative, then there is no choice), even if one of the choices is to not choose, or remain with the current status quo. Depending on what the alternatives being described are, there may exist a set of attributes that are common across all, or at least a subset of the alternatives (e.g., if the alternatives are bus and car, then an attribute that might be common to both alternatives is, say, travel time, even though the value of travel time might differ between the two modes). In such cases, the analyst may choose to constrain the parameters across two or more of the alternatives to be the same and estimate what are known as generic parameters. In some cases, the analyst may do this after finding that the parameters are not statistically different across alternatives (i.e., for empirical reasons – "the data told me so"). In other cases, the analyst may estimate generic parameters for theoretical reasons (e.g., the analyst may argue that a dollar is a dollar and that it should not matter what the dollar is spent on – "theory told me so"). In yet other cases, the way the alternatives are described may also require that the estimates be treated as generic (e.g., for unlabeled choice experiments more on this in Chapter 6). In Equation (3.11), the generic parameter estimates are given the same subscript β_k, suggesting that they are the same estimates across the two utility functions:

$$V_{ns,car} = \sum_{k=1}^{K} \beta_k x_{ns,car,k,}$$

$$V_{ns,bus} = \sum_{k=1}^{K} \beta_k x_{ns,bus,k}. \tag{3.11}$$

Utility functions may also be specified to contain what are termed *alternative-specific parameter* (ASP) estimates. An alternative-specific parameter is one which is allowed to differ across alternatives (and hence is not constrained to be the same, as with generic parameter estimates; i.e., β_{kj} is not constrained to equal β_{ki}). An example of this is given in Equation (3.12), where the parameter estimates associated with the two different utility functions are represented by different subscripts:

$$V_{ns,car} = \sum_{k=1}^{K} \beta_{k,car} x_{ns,car,k},$$

$$V_{ns,bus} = \sum_{k=1}^{K} \beta_{k,bus} x_{ns,bus,k}. \tag{3.12}$$

As with generic parameter estimates, the analyst may wish to specify alternative-specific parameter estimates for a number of reasons. Firstly, the data may suggest that the amount of (dis)-utility a decision maker will obtain for a specific attribute is not uniform across alternatives (e.g., a minute spent in an air-conditioned car with a functioning radio may be worth more to a person travelling to work on a hot summer day than a minute spent on an overcrowded non-air-conditioned bus full of commuters who forgot to bathe in the past week). Note, however, that the specification of alternative-specific parameter estimates does not preclude the resulting estimates being statistically equal to one another. Second, an attribute may belong to one, or a subset of alternatives, and hence cannot by definition belong to all J alternatives (e.g., for a specific trip, a decision maker may be faced with a decision to use their car and pay for petrol, possible tolls and parking, or take the bus and pay the bus fare (it is unlikely they will have to pay for tolls or parking the bus, however)). In such cases, the parameter associated with a specific attribute may be non-zero for some alternatives (although it could be statistically equal to zero also), but zero for other alternatives simply due to the non-presence of that attribute.

In some instances, it is possible that a subset of the parameters will be generic, while others will be alternative-specific. In Equation (3.13), for example, time is assumed to be associated with a generic parameter, while toll, parking costs, and fare are assumed to have alternative-specific parameter estimates:

$$V_{ns,car} = \beta_1 time_{ns,car} + \beta_{2,car} toll_{ns,car} + \beta_{3,car} parking\ cost_{ns,car},$$
$$V_{ns,bus} = \beta_1 time_{ns,bus} + \beta_{2,bus} fare_{ns,bus}. \tag{3.13}$$

Of course, different combinations of alternative-specific and generic parameter estimates are possible across multiple utility functions, as shown in Equation (3.14):

$$V_{ns,car} = \beta_{1,car} time_{ns,car} + \beta_{2,car} toll_{ns,car} + \beta_{3,car} parking\ cost_{ns,car},$$
$$V_{ns,bus} = \beta_{1,pt} time_{ns,bus} + \beta_{2,bus} fare_{ns,bus} + \beta_{3,bus} waiting\ time_{ns,bus},$$
$$V_{ns,train} = \beta_{1,pt} time_{ns,train} + \beta_{2,rail} fare_{ns,train},$$
$$V_{ns,tram} = \beta_{1,pt} time_{ns,tram} + \beta_{2,rail} fare_{ns,tram}. \tag{3.14}$$

3.4.2 Alternative-specific constants

Another form of alternative-specific parameter estimate, known as an *alternative-specific constant* (ASC), reflects something about the utility of an alternative not related to an attribute specified in the utility function. Rather, ASCs say something about the alternative that is not measured elsewhere in V_{nsj}. For example, the variables in the utility functions of a bus alternative may relate to the times and costs of the bus trip; however, if variables related to convenience and comfort are important to the decision process of choosing between the various transport modes, but have not been measured by the analyst, or not included in the utility specification, then these variables end up in the unobserved effects. The ASCs of the model reflect the average of the variables that have not been measured (as well as other effects such as experimental design or survey biases (see Chapter 6)), that is they represent the average of the unobserved effects.

We will return to the ASCs in Sections 3.4.5.2 and Chapter 4; however, for the present it is sufficient to note that for any choice model, one can estimate up to $J-1$ ASCs only. This is because only differences in utility matter, not the absolute values. Once again, given J alternatives, there will exist an infinite number of combinations for the ASCs that will reproduce the same levels of utility differences. For example, assume the utility for car, bus and train are 15,

10, and 8, respectively. Firstly, this implies that individuals prefer cars to buses and buses to trains. Second, the difference between the utility for car and bus is 5, car and train 7, and bus and train 2. If we were to change the utility levels by subtracting 8 from the utility of each alternative, the utilities now become 7, 2 and zero. Note that the relative preference rankings between the alternatives remain the same as, too, the differences between the utilities. Likewise, changing the utility levels to be −85, −90, and −92 by subtracting 100 from each of the original values reproduces the exact same result in terms of the relative utility differences. For this reason, in estimating the model, the analyst will need to set the level of utility by normalizing at least one of the ASCs to some arbitrary value, with the most common value selected being zero. Once more, this does not imply preference indifference for the selected alternative as one can only consider relative utility values for two or more alternatives. Further, the fact that utility is measured on an ordinal scale implies that the choice of which alternative to normalize the ASC to zero does not matter, as the utility levels implied by the ASCs will simply adjust by adding or subtracting the same value to the utility of each of the alternatives to reproduce the same utility differences. For example, assuming the ASCs for car, bus and train are 2, 1, and 0, respectively (where the train ASC has been set to zero), then the same differences in utility will be maintained if we set the ASC for the bus alternative to be zero, such that the ASCs would now be 1, 0 and −1, hence preserving the relative differences.

Taking our earlier example, Equation (3.15) allows for ASCs for the car, bus, and train alternatives that will be relative to the tram alternative. Note that, as with any other parameter, constants may be also made to be generic across two or more alternatives. Treating constants as generic parameters, however, should only be done if, empirically, the ASCs for two or more alternatives are found to be statistically equivalent:

$$
\begin{aligned}
V_{ns,car} &= \beta_{0,car} + \beta_{1,car} time_{ns,car} + \beta_{2,car} toll_{ns,car} + \beta_{3,car} parking\ cost_{ns,car}, \\
V_{ns,bus} &= \beta_{0,bus} + \beta_{1,pt} time_{ns,bus} + \beta_{2,bus} fare_{ns,bus} + \beta_{3,bus} waiting\ time_{ns,bus}, \\
V_{ns,train} &= \beta_{0,train} + \beta_{1,pt} time_{ns,train} + \beta_{2,rail} fare_{ns,train}, \\
V_{ns,tram} &= \qquad\quad \beta_{1,pt} time_{ns,tram} + \beta_{2,rail} fare_{ns,tram}.
\end{aligned}
\tag{3.15}
$$

Although in Equation (3.15) we have represented the ASCs as parameters that are not associated with any variables, an alternative representation would be to write $\beta_{0j} x_{nsjk}$, where $x_{nsjk} = 1, \forall n, s, j$ (mathematically, the symbol $\forall$ means "for all"). In this representation, the x_{nsjk} is constant for the J alternatives, while the ASCs vary (with at least one ASC normalized to zero).

3.4.3 Status quo and no choice alternatives

At this point, it is worthwhile considering choice situations in which there exists the possibility to choose "not to choose," or to remain with some status quo alternative. Many choice situations present decision makers with examples of both types of alternatives. For example, a person can elect to stay at home and not see a movie if three potential movie alternatives showing at a local cinema at some preferred time do not appeal to them. Likewise, a decision maker facing the expiration of their rental agreement may elect to simply renew their current rental contract or move apartments, hence signing a new lease. In the case of a **no choice** alternative, the alternative labelled "*none*" will be devoid of any attribute levels (e.g., there is no movie ticket price, no time spent at the cinema, etc., associated with not going to the movies). The absence of attributes, however, does not mean that the decision maker is indifferent to that alternative. In the movie example, if the three movies on offer are romantic comedies, then staying at home and not attending any of them might be the most preferred option.

Despite the name, a *no choice* alternative remains an alternative with some level of utility, and as such the analyst may elect to have neither attributes or ASCs enter into the utility function associated with the alternative, as per Equation (3.16a):

$$
\begin{aligned}
V_{ns,movieA} &= \beta_{0A} + \beta_1 genre_{nsA} + \beta_2 ticket\ price_{nsA} + \beta_3 movie\ length_{nsA}, \\
V_{ns,movieB} &= \beta_{0B} + \beta_1 genre_{nsB} + \beta_2 ticket\ price_{nsB} + \beta_3 movie\ length_{nsB}, \\
V_{ns,movieC} &= \beta_{0C} + \beta_1 genre_{nsC} + \beta_2 ticket\ price_{nsC} + \beta_3 movie\ length_{nsC}, \\
V_{ns,no\ choice} &= 0
\end{aligned}
\tag{3.16a}
$$

or allow the alternative to have an ASC, as in Equation (3.16b):

$$
\begin{aligned}
V_{ns,movieA} &= \beta_{0A} + \beta_1 genre_{nsA} + \beta_2 ticket\ price_{nsA} + \beta_3 movie\ length_{nsA}, \\
V_{ns,movieB} &= \beta_{0B} + \beta_1 genre_{nsB} + \beta_2 ticket\ price_{nsB} + \beta_3 movie\ length_{nsB}, \\
V_{ns,movieC} &= \phantom{\beta_{0C} +} \beta_1 genre_{nsC} + \beta_2 ticket\ price_{nsC} + \beta_3 movie\ length_{nsC}, \\
V_{ns,no\ choice} &= \beta_{0,no\ choice}.
\end{aligned}
\tag{3.16b}
$$

Given that utility is ordinal, which alternative the ASCs are associated with does not matter. As such, results obtained from models based on Equations (3.16a) and (3.16b) will functionally be equivalent to one another.

Where a status quo alternative is present, the alternative will typically have attributes that will take specific levels (e.g., the current apartment where a person lives will have some level of rental, number of bedrooms, etc.). As such, unlike a "no choice" alternative, status quo alternatives will typically be described by a set of attributes. Similar to situations involving a "no choice" alternative, the analyst is free to select which alternatives to specify ASCs for, provided they belong to no more than $J-1$ of the alternatives. Hence, the status quo alternative may either not include an ASC (as in Equation 3.17a) or may include an ASC (as in Equation 3.17b), with the choice of where the ASCs are placed being once again completely arbitrary:

$$V_{ns,ApartmentA} = \beta_{0A} + \beta_1 rent_{nsA} + \beta_2 number\ of\ bedrooms_{nsA} + \beta_3 number\ of\ bathrooms_{nsA},$$
$$V_{ns,ApartmentB} = \beta_{0B} + \beta_1 rent_{nsB} + \beta_2 number\ of\ bedrooms_{nsB} + \beta_3 number\ of\ bathrooms_{nsB},$$
$$V_{ns,ApartmentC} = \beta_{0C} + \beta_1 rent_{nsC} + \beta_2 number\ of\ bedrooms_{nsC} + \beta_3 number\ of\ bathrooms_{nsC},$$
$$V_{ns,status\ quo} = \qquad \beta_1 rent_{nsSQ} + \beta_2 number\ of\ bedrooms_{nsSQ} + \beta_3 number\ of\ bathrooms_{nsSQ}.$$

$$(3.17a)$$

$$V_{ns,ApartmentA} = \beta_{0A} + \beta_1 rent_{nsA} + \beta_2 number\ of\ bedrooms_{nsA} + \beta_3 number\ of\ bedrooms_{nsA},$$
$$V_{ns,ApartmentB} = \beta_{0B} + \beta_1 rent_{nsB} + \beta_2 number\ of\ bedrooms_{nsB} + \beta_3 number\ of\ bedrooms_{nsB},$$
$$V_{ns,ApartmentC} = \qquad \beta_1 rent_{nsC} + \beta_2 number\ of\ bedrooms_{nsC} + \beta_3 number\ of\ bedrooms_{nsC},$$
$$V_{ns,status\ quo} = \beta_{0SQ} + \beta_1 rent_{nsSQ} + \beta_2 number\ of\ bedrooms_{nsSQ} + \beta_3 number\ of\ bedrooms_{nsSQ}.$$

$$(3.17b)$$

3.4.4 Characteristics of respondents and contextual effects in discrete choice models

As with ASCs, the fact that only differences in utility matter has another important implication for the specification of discrete choice models. The only parameters that can be estimated are those that capture differences across alternatives. For attributes that describe something specific about each alternative, such differences exist. For variables associated with descriptions of respondents and other contextual influences that are not attribute descriptions of alternatives also have a role in choice models, and are often referred to as *characteristics* or *covariates*. They are constants across the alternatives and hence no differences will exist between the alternatives. For example, a decision maker's gender does not change because they are considering a car as opposed to a bus. To demonstrate the issue, let v_n represent a covariate related to decision maker n in choice context s. Considering a two alternative case, it is possible to write out the utility functions for a discrete choice model as follows:

$$V_{ns1} = \sum_{k=1}^{K} \beta_k x_{ns1k} + \delta_1 v_n,$$

$$V_{ns2} = \sum_{k=1}^{K} \beta_k x_{ns\,2k} + \delta_2 v_n. \tag{3.18}$$

where δ_j represents an alternative-specific parameter associated with the covariate v_n. Unfortunately, v_n does not differ between the two alternatives, and given that only differences in utility matter, it is not possible to estimate the absolute values for δ_1 and δ_2, assuming that $\delta_1 \neq \delta_2$, as there will exist an infinite number of possible values that either parameter could take that will reproduce the same relative utility differences. For this reason, it is necessary to normalize the parameter associated with one of the alternatives to some value in order to be able to estimate the rest. Although any value could be chosen, it is most common to normalize the parameter associated with a particular covariate to zero for at least one of the alternatives.

Equation (3.19) includes age and gender of the decision maker in the system of utility functions associated with the model. Note that age enters into the car, bus, and tram alternatives and have alternative-specific parameter estimates, while a covariate representing the season of the year enters solely into the utility function for the train alternative. The variable relating whether the decision maker is female or not is associated with both train and tram, and is generic for these two alternatives in this example:

$$
\begin{aligned}
V_{ns,car} &= \beta_{0,car} + \beta_{1,car} time_{ns,car} + \beta_{2,car} toll_{ns,car} + \beta_{3,car} parking\ cost_{ns,car} + \beta_{4,car} age_n, \\
V_{ns,bus} &= \beta_{0,bus} + \beta_{1,pt} time_{ns,bus} + \beta_{2,bus} fare_{ns,bus} + \beta_{3,bus} waiting\ time_{ns,bus} + \beta_{4,bus} age_n \\
V_{ns,train} &= \beta_{0,train} + \beta_{1,pt} time_{ns,train} + \beta_{2,rail} fare_{ns,train} + \beta_{3,train} season + \beta_{4,rail} female_n, \\
V_{ns,tram} &= \qquad\qquad \beta_{1,pt} time_{ns,tram} + \beta_{2,rail} fare_{ns,tram} + \beta_{3,tram} age_n + \beta_{4,rail} female_n.
\end{aligned}
$$

$$\tag{3.19}$$

Given that utility is measured on an ordinal scale, the parameters related to covariates are interpreted in a relative sense, both within and between alternatives. That is, assuming the age parameter to be positive and statistically significant for the car alternative, one interpretation for the age parameter would be that, *holding all else equal*, older decision makers have a higher utility for the car alternative relative to younger decision makers. Alternatively, comparing across the utility functions, one can interpret the parameter as suggesting that relative to the train alternative (where the parameter has been constrained to be equal to zero), older decision makers have a higher utility for the car alternative, *all else being equal*. Generic covariate parameters may similarly be interpreted.

The presence of a no choice or status quo alternative offers a number of options to the analyst where covariates are concerned. As with ASCs, the analyst may allow a covariate to enter into all utility functions excluding the no choice (or status quo) alternative and estimate either generic or alternative-specific parameter estimates for it. For example, in Equation (3.20a), age now enters into the utility functions of non-no choice alternatives with a generic parameter. In this case, β_4 will be interpreted relative to the no choice alternative with a positive parameter, suggesting that older decision makers are more likely to choose one of the travel modes relative to not travelling, all else being equal, while a negative parameter suggests the opposite to be true. Of course, age could be allowed to have alternative-specific parameter estimates, in which case the degree to which age influences the preferences of the various travel modes is assumed to be different relative to the no choice alternative:

$$
\begin{aligned}
V_{ns,car} &= \beta_{0,car} + \beta_{1,car}time_{ns,car} + \beta_{2,car}toll_{ns,car} + \beta_{3,car}parking\ cost_{ns,car} + \beta_4 age_n, \\
V_{ns,bus} &= \beta_{0,bus} + \beta_{1,pt}time_{ns,bus} + \beta_{2,bus}fare_{ns,bus} + \beta_{3,bus}waiting\ time_{ns,bus} + \beta_4 age_n \\
V_{ns,train} &= \beta_{0,train} + \beta_{1,pt}time_{ns,train} + \beta_{2,rail}fare_{ns,train} + \beta_4 age_n, \\
V_{ns,tram} &= \qquad\quad \beta_{1,pt}time_{ns,tram} + \beta_{2,rail}fare_{ns,tram} + \beta_4 age_n, \\
V_{ns,no\ choice} &= \beta_{0,no\ choice}.
\end{aligned}
$$

$$(3.20a)$$

In Equation (3.20b), age enters into the no choice alternative only. Here, the parameter estimate will be interpreted relative to the non-no choice alternatives such that a positive age parameter is indicative of older decision makers having a preference not to travel via one of the travel modes, while a negative parameter suggests that older decision makers prefer to select one of the travel modes. Note that Equations (3.20a) and (3.20b) effectively tell the same story and indeed, β_4 from Equation (3.20a) would be the same as $\beta_{4,no\ choice}$ from Equation (3.20b); however, the sign will be reversed. That is, we would expect that $\beta_4 = -\beta_{4,no\ choice}$. This relationship will only hold, however, if the parameter for age in Equation (3.20a) is generic across all of the non-no choice alternatives:

$$V_{ns,car} = \beta_{0,car} + \beta_{1,car} time_{ns,car} + \beta_{2,car} toll_{ns,car} + \beta_{3,car} parking\ cost_{ns,car},$$
$$V_{ns,bus} = \beta_{0,bus} + \beta_{1,pt} time_{ns,bus} + \beta_{2,bus} fare_{ns,bus} + \beta_{3,bus} waiting\ time_{ns,bus},$$
$$V_{ns,train} = \beta_{0,train} + \beta_{1,pt} time_{ns,train} + \beta_{2,rail} fare_{ns,train},$$
$$V_{ns,tram} = \beta_{1,pt} time_{ns,tram} + \beta_{2,rail} fare_{ns,tram},$$
$$V_{ns,no\ choice} = \beta_{0,no\ choice} + \beta_{4,no\ choice} age. \tag{3.20b}$$

Independent of how one interprets the parameters of covariates, it is important to note that the covariates themselves should not be interpreted as direct sources of utility. The utility of an alternative is related to the characteristics or attributes of that alternative (Lancaster 1966). Belonging to a particular covariate grouping does not in and of itself provide more or less utility for a particular alternative; however, something about the alternative may appeal more or less to particular covariate groupings. Covariates in discrete choice models therefore act as proxies for unmeasured attributes. Thus, for example, if the parameter for gender is found to be statistically significant for the train alternative, then it is likely that gender is acting as a proxy for some latent or unobserved characteristic related to train as a mode, such as safety, which is more important (either positively or negatively) for one gender relative to the other.

We now turn to a discussion of the options available to researchers in terms of variable and parameter transformations.

3.4.5 Attribute transformations and non-linear attributes

How an analyst codes data may be viewed as somewhat arbitrary and hence so too how variables enter into the utility functions of discrete choice models. Firstly, the analyst may select to represent numerical variables using different units of measure. For example, income may be coded in 10s, 100s, or 1,000s of units. Such arbitrary **coding** will not change the relative utilities for the alternatives; it will simply scale the magnitude of the resulting parameter estimates to maintain the same utility values. For example, a parameter for income may be equal to −0.5 if the variable is measured in 10s of units, or −0.05 if measured in 100s of units.

Secondly, the analyst may transform the variables to reflect some complex underlying decision rule that the analyst believes decision makers are using when evaluating the alternatives. For example, rather than assume that the variables enter into utility in the same fashion as the data was collected, the analyst may choose to apply some form of transformation to one or more of the variables, such as taking the log of a variable (i.e., $\log(x_{nsjk})$) or squaring it (i.e., x^2_{nsjk}) prior to it entering into the utility functions of one or more of the alternatives. For example, consider Equation (3.21), representing the utility functions for two alternatives, car and bus. For the car alternative, toll is entered into the utility function both as x_{nsjk} and x^2_{nsjk} while time enters into both the car and bus alternatives as the square of the original attribute. Similar to Train (1978), the fare attribute associated with the bus alternative is divided by income to reflect the fact that decision makers with different incomes may have a different marginal utility associated with the fare attribute. Further, the age variable is assumed to enter into the bus alternative as the natural log of age:

$$V_{ns,car} = \beta_{0,car} + \beta_{1,car}time^2_{ns,car} + \beta_{2,car}toll_{ns,car} + \beta_{3,car}toll^2_{ns,car} + \beta_{4,car}parking\ cost_{ns,car},$$

$$V_{ns,bus} = \beta_{1,pt}time^2_{ns,bus} + \beta_{2,bus}\frac{fare_{ns,bus}}{income_n} + \beta_{3,bus}waiting\ time_{ns,bus} + \beta_{4,bus}\log(age_n).$$

$$(3.21)$$

Another commonly applied transformation is what is known as the Box–Cox transformation. Building on the earlier work of Tukey (1957), Box and Cox (1964) proposed the following power transformation:

$$x'_{nsjk} = \begin{cases} \dfrac{x^{\lambda}_{nsjk} - 1}{\gamma}, & \gamma \neq 0 \\ \log(x_{nsjk}), & \gamma = 0 \end{cases}. \qquad (3.22)$$

where γ is a parameter to be estimated.

Given that the transformation requires that the log of x_{nsjk} be taken if $\gamma=0$, this type of transformation can be applied to variables that take positive values only. Note that other power transformations have been proposed within the literature (e.g., Manly 1976; John and Draper 1980; Bickel and Doksum 1981); however, the Box–Cox transformation remains the most commonly used transformation of its type to date.

When a variable enters into utility in a non-linear transformed state, one needs to account for the transformation when interpreting its contribution to overall utility. For example, consider the toll attribute in Equation (3.21). The marginal contribution to utility for the toll attribute is now a function of *toll* and *toll²*, and as such, both effects need to be considered jointly and not separately. For example, a one unit change in toll will change the utility for the car alternative by $\beta_{2,car} + \beta_{3,car}$ toll (noting that $toll^2 = 1^2 = 1$). Similarly, in the above example, one cannot consider the impact of fare upon the utility of bus, without jointly considering the decision maker's income. One common trick, which we already introduced in our discussion surrounding Equation (3.19) without comment, is to invoke the *ceteris paribus* assumption. *Ceteris paribus* is a Latin phrase adopted by economists, which translates to "all else being equal" or "all else being held constant." For example, one could state that holding income constant, as fare changes, utility for bus will change by $\beta_{2,bus}$. Likewise, one could interpret the impact of income upon utility holding fare constant. For variables transformed using the Box–Cox transformation, one cannot interpret the results without considering the value of the λ parameter. This is because the value of each data point will depend on the value of γ. We return to discussing how to correctly interpret the parameters for non-linear transformed variables in Section 3.4.5.2.

3.4.5.1 Interaction effects

A common transformation often used within the literature is the inclusion of interaction terms within the utility functions of discrete choice models. An interaction term involves the multiplication of two or more variables, such as $x_{nsjk}x_{nsjl}$, where the variables may represent attributes, covariates, or combinations of both. When two variables are multiplied together, the resulting interaction term is known as a two-way interaction. Where three variables are multiplied together, a three-way interaction term is created, with a similar naming convention used for the multiplication of four, five, or more variables. To demonstrate, consider the car alternative in Equation (3.23), which includes a two-way interaction between travel time and toll cost, and a three-way interaction between travel time, toll cost, and parking costs, while the utility function for the bus alternative allows for a two-way interaction term between travel time and age:

$$
\begin{aligned}
V_{ns,car} &= \beta_{0,car} + \beta_1 time_{ns,car} + \beta_{2,car} toll_{ns,car} + \beta_{3,car} parking\ cost_{ns,car} \\
&\quad + \beta_{4,car}(time_{ns,car} \times toll_{ns,car}) \\
&\quad + \beta_{5,car}(time_{ns,car} \times toll_{ns,car} \times parking\ cost_{ns,car}), \\
V_{ns,bus} &= \qquad \beta_1 time_{ns,bus} + \beta_{2,bus} fare_{ns,bus} + \beta_{3,bus}(time_{ns,bus} \times age_n).
\end{aligned}
$$

$$(3.23)$$

Sometimes within the literature, in addition to the other names given to the parameter estimates of discrete choice models, the parameters are referred to as some type of "**effect**." For example, a parameter associated with a single variable will often be referred to as a **main effect**, while the parameters associated with an interaction term will be termed as an **interaction effect**, or more specifically as a two-way or three way interaction effect, etc. Hence, β_1 in the above example represents the main effect associated with travel time, whereas $\beta_{3,bus}$ represents the two-way interaction effect between the bus travel time and age interaction term.

As with other non-linear transformations, the inclusion of interaction terms requires that particular care be taken when interpreting the model outputs. For example, the travel time attribute now enters into the utility function of the car alternative three times, and hence the impact upon the utility for car given a one unit change in travel time is now a function of all three appearances. As such, it is common to invoke the *ceteris paribus* rule when interpreting models involving interaction terms. For example, in the Equation (3.23), the impact on the utility for the car alternative, given a one unit change in travel time, given a toll and parking cost, will be: $\beta_1 + \beta_{4,car}toll_{ns,car} + \beta_{5,car}(toll_{ns,car} \times parking\ cost_{ns,car})$, *ceteris paribus*.

3.4.5.2 Dummy, effects, and orthogonal polynomial coding

Another common data transformation is to use what are known as non-linear coding schemes. Consider the season attribute associated with the train alternative in Equation (3.19). Assuming that one lives in a country that experiences four seasons – summer, autumn (or fall depending on where you live), winter and spring – then the four seasons might be coded as 1, 2, 3, and 4 (known as a linear coding scheme), respectively. Given how the utility function has been specified, every time we change season by one unit, *ceteris paribus*, the utility level for train changes by an amount equal to $\beta_{3,train}$. That is, the utility for the difference between summer and autumn (fall) is the same as the utility for the difference between autumn (fall) and winter. To be more explicit, the model implies that as one moves from summer to autumn (fall), utility will change by $\beta_{3,train}$, just as moving from autumn (fall) to winter will result in a change in utility by an amount equal to $\beta_{3,train}$. Assuming $\beta_{3,train}$ to be positive, Figure 3.9 demonstrates this effect. The parameter represents the slope of the curve, such that moving from one (coded) season to another will reproduce an equal (linear) increase in utility for the train alternative.

Realistically, however, such an outcome is unlikely. Summer may be particularly hot and the air-conditioning on the trains ineffective, whereas in winter, the air-conditioning may induce hypothermia amongst those brave enough to use the system. As such, commuters may prefer to use the train in the more temperate seasons; however, due to the way the variable has been coded, this pattern of preferences cannot be detected by the model. Further,

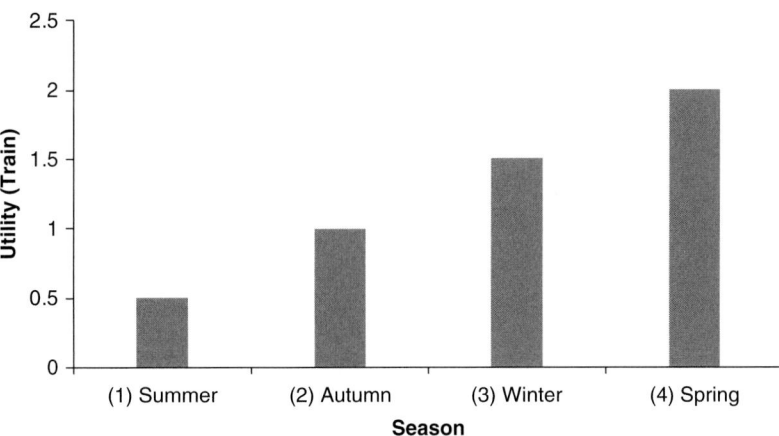

Figure 3.9   Marginal utility for season (linear coding)

the resulting parameter estimate may become a function of how the variable is coded. If, for example, the season variable was coded 1 = autumn (fall), 2 = summer, 3 = winter and 4 = spring, then the slope of the line, that is the parameter estimate, may be very different, leading the analyst to a completely different interpretation of the relationship between season and the utility obtained for the train alternative.

Several non-linear coding schemes exist; however for the sake of brevity we limit ourselves to a discussion of only three such schemes, these being **dummy coding**, **effects coding** and *orthogonal polynomial coding schemes*. All three schemes allow for a non-linear relationship between the levels of attributes and utility, and in each case involve the analyst constructing a number of new variables being recoded. For each non-linear coding scheme, the number of new variables created will be equivalent to the number of levels associated with that attribute, l_k, minus one. Thus, taking our previous season example, the variable for season has four levels (i.e., $l_k = 4$), hence, the recoding of the season variable into any of the non-linear coding schemes will require the creation of three new variables (i.e., $l_k - 1 = 3$). When using *dummy* coding, each newly constructed variable will be associated with one of the original levels, taking the value 1 if that level appears in the data, or zero otherwise. For example, let x_{nsjk1}, x_{nsjk2}, and x_{nsjk3} represent the newly constructed variables for our season example. Although any mapping is possible, let us assume that summer is associated with x_{nsjk1}, autumn (fall) with x_{nsjk2}, and winter with x_{nsjk3}. If in the data, a choice observation was recorded in the summer, then x_{nsjk1} will take the value one while x_{nsjk2} and x_{nsjk3} will both take the values zero. If, on the other hand, a choice situation occurred in winter, then x_{nsjk3} will take the value one while x_{nsjk1} and x_{nsjk2} will both take the values zero.

Dummy or *effects* coding differ only in how the last level, referred to as the base level, is coded. In *dummy* coding, the base level receives a value of zero for each of the newly constructed dummy coded variables. Thus, if the mode choice was made in spring, then x_{nsjk1}, x_{nsjk2}, and x_{nsjk3} will simultaneously be coded as zero. In *effects* coding, however, the base level receives a value of minus one (-1) for each of the newly constructed effects coded variables, such that x_{nsjk1}, x_{nsjk2}, and x_{nsjk3} will simultaneously be coded as minus one if the choice situation were recorded in spring. The *dummy* or *effects* coding schemes for up to seven levels are given in Table 3.6, panels (a) and (b), respectively.

The reason we only require $l_k - 1$ dummy or effects codes is due to colinearity between the resulting data if all l_k variables are constructed and used. Typically, most people think of **correlation** as being bivariate, that is between two random variables (e.g., $\rho(x_{nsjk}, x_{nsjl})$). Mathematically, however, correlation can exist between linear combinations of multiple variables (e.g., $\rho(x_{nsjk}, x_{nsjl} + x_{nsjm})$). Unfortunately, dummy and effects coding produce perfect correlations between the resulting variables. Consider by way of example a three level variable where the analyst constructs three dummy or effects coded variables. To demonstrate the issue, if we were to observe that for the first two dummy or effects coded variables, one of them took the value one, we would know immediately that the third column would have to take the value zero. On the other hand, if we observed that neither of the first two variables took the value one, then by deduction, the last variable must be equal to one. As such, for both the dummy and effects coding schemes, if we know the values of $l_k - 1$ variables, we know the value of the last L_k dummy or effects coded variable. Indeed, one of the variables will always be redundant in terms of the information provided.

Equation (3.24) represents the utility function for the train alternative based on Equation (3.19) assuming that the season variable has now been either dummy or effects coded. Note that in writing out the new utility function, we have dropped the train subscript for the sake of expediency:

$$V_{ns} = \beta_0 + \beta_1 time_{ns} + \beta_2 fare_{ns} + \beta_{31} x_{summer} + \beta_{32} x_{n,autumn} + \beta_{33} x_{n,winter} + \beta_4 female_n.$$

$$(3.24)$$

The interpretation of dummy or effects coded variables requires a substitution of relevant values into the utility expression. Assuming that a choice observation is associated with a summer month, for example, the variable x_{summer} will

Table 3.6 Non-linear coding schemes

(a) Dummy coding

l_k	2	3		4			5				6					7					
	X_{nsjk1}	X_{nsjk1}	X_{nsjk2}	X_{nsjk1}	X_{nsjk2}	X_{nsjk3}	X_{nsjk1}	X_{nsjk2}	X_{nsjk3}	X_{nsjk4}	X_{nsjk1}	X_{nsjk2}	X_{nsjk3}	X_{nsjk4}	X_{nsjk5}	X_{nsjk1}	X_{nsjk2}	X_{nsjk3}	X_{nsjk4}	X_{nsjk5}	X_{nsjk6}
1	1	1	0	1	0	0	1	0	0	0	1	0	0	0	0	1	0	0	0	0	0
2	0	0	1	0	1	0	0	1	0	0	0	1	0	0	0	0	1	0	0	0	0
3		0	0	0	0	1	0	0	1	0	0	0	1	0	0	0	0	1	0	0	0
4				0	0	0	0	0	0	1	0	0	0	1	0	0	0	0	1	0	0
5							0	0	0	0	0	0	0	0	1	0	0	0	0	1	0
6											0	0	0	0	0	0	0	0	0	0	1
7																0	0	0	0	0	0

(b) Effects coding

l_k	2	3		4			5				6					7					
	X_{nsjk1}	X_{nsjk1}	X_{nsjk2}	X_{nsjk1}	X_{nsjk2}	X_{nsjk3}	X_{nsjk1}	X_{nsjk2}	X_{nsjk3}	X_{nsjk4}	X_{nsjk1}	X_{nsjk2}	X_{nsjk3}	X_{nsjk4}	X_{nsjk5}	X_{nsjk1}	X_{nsjk2}	X_{nsjk3}	X_{nsjk4}	X_{nsjk5}	X_{nsjk6}
1	1	1	0	1	0	0	1	0	0	0	1	0	0	0	0	1	0	0	0	0	0
2	-1	0	1	0	1	0	0	1	0	0	0	1	0	0	0	0	1	0	0	0	0
3		-1	-1	0	0	1	0	0	1	0	0	0	1	0	0	0	0	1	0	0	0
4				-1	-1	-1	0	0	0	1	0	0	0	1	0	0	0	0	1	0	0
5							-1	-1	-1	-1	0	0	0	0	1	0	0	0	0	1	0
6											-1	-1	-1	-1	-1	0	0	0	0	0	1
7																-1	-1	-1	-1	-1	-1

(c) Orthogonal polynomial coding

l_k	2	3		4			5				6					7					
Effect:	Linear	Linear	Quadratic	Linear	Quadratic	Cubic	Linear	Quadratic	Cubic	Quartic	Linear	Quadratic	Cubic	Quartic	Quintic	Linear	Quadratic	Cubic	Quartic	Quintic	Sextic
	X_{nsjk1}	X_{nsjk1}	X_{nsjk2}	X_{nsjk1}	X_{nsjk2}	X_{nsjk3}	X_{nsjk1}	X_{nsjk2}	X_{nsjk3}	X_{nsjk4}	X_{nsjk1}	X_{nsjk2}	X_{nsjk3}	X_{nsjk4}	X_{nsjk5}	X_{nsjk1}	X_{nsjk2}	X_{nsjk3}	X_{nsjk4}	X_{nsjk5}	X_{nsjk6}
1	-1	-1	1	-3	1	-1	-2	2	-1	1	-5	5	-5	1	-1	-3	5	-1	3	-1	1
2	1	0	-2	-1	-1	3	-1	-1	2	-4	-3	-1	7	-3	5	-2	0	1	-7	4	-6
3		1	1	1	-1	-3	0	-2	0	6	-1	-4	4	2	-10	-1	-3	1	1	-5	15
4				3	1	1	1	-1	-2	-4	1	-4	-4	2	10	0	-4	0	6	0	-20
5							2	2	1	1	3	-1	-7	-3	-5	1	-3	-1	1	5	15
6											5	5	5	1	1	2	0	-1	-7	-4	-6
7																3	5	1	3	1	1

take the value one, while x_{autumn} and x_{winter} will both take the value zero, and *ceteris paribus*, the seasonal impact on the utility for the train alternative will be equivalent to β_{31}. Assuming that a choice observation was recorded to have occurred in winter, however, the variable x_{winter} will now take the value one while x_{summer} and x_{autumn} will both simultaneously be equal to zero. Under this scenario, the seasonal impact on the utility for the train alternative will now be equal to β_{33}, *ceteris paribus*. The substitution of values differs only for the base level for dummy and effects coded variables. Assuming that the data has been dummy coded, the base level associated with spring will requires that x_{summer}, x_{autumn}, and x_{winter} be simultaneously equal to zero, and hence the utility will be equal to zero, *all else being equal*.

It is important to note that, given that utility is measured on an ordinal scale, a utility of zero does not mean that the decision maker is indifferent to or has no preference for spring. Rather, the other parameters will be estimated relative to this base dummy coded level. Given that the ASC of an alternative represents the average of the unobserved or un-modeled effects for that alternative, the fact that the base level is forced to have a marginal utility of zero has led some researchers to suggest that the marginal utility for the base level of a dummy coded variable, not being independently measured, is perfectly confounded with the ASC for that alternative. As such, some researchers add the ASC to the resulting marginal utilities when dealing with dummy coded variables.

Unlike dummy coded variables, effects coded variables do not take a zero value for the base level, but rather minus one. Taking our season example, the variables x_{summer}, x_{autumn}, and x_{winter} will simultaneously be assigned values of minus one such that the seasonal impact on the utility for the train alternative will now be equal to $-\beta_{31} - \beta_{32} - \beta_{33}$, all else being equal. As such, the base level of an effects coded variable will produce a unique utility value which is no longer perfectly confounded with the alternatives ASC. This is one of the reasons why many researchers prefer to use effects coding rather than dummy coding. Table 3.7 summarizes this discussion.

A second reason that effects coding is generally preferred to dummy coding lies in what happens when two variables are non-linearly coded. Assume now that both the season and female variables in Equation (3.24) are dummy coded (hence male is coded as 0 for the later variable). As seen above, the marginal utility for spring has been normalized to be equal to zero within the season dummy coding scheme; however, so too has male for the gender-related variable. Both base levels have been normalized to the same value, and both are perfectly confounded with the model's ASCs. As such, one cannot say whether being male or making a choice in spring will have a greater impact on

Table 3.7 Dummy and effects coding marginal utilities

Season	Dummy coding				Effects coding			
	x_{summer}	x_{autumn}	x_{winter}	Effect	x_{summer}	x_{autumn}	x_{winter}	Effect
Summer	1	0	0	β_{31}	1	0	0	β_{31}
Autumn (fall)	0	1	0	β_{32}	0	1	0	β_{32}
Winter	0	0	1	β_{33}	0	0	1	β_{33}
Spring	0	0	0	0	−1	−1	−1	$-\beta_{31} - \beta_{32} - \beta_{33}$

Table 3.8 Relationship between effects coding and ASC

Level	Average utility	Effects code
Summer	−0.225	−0.800
Winter	0.875	0.300
Autumn	1.175	0.600
Spring	0.475	−0.100
Average	0.575	0.575

the utility for train, as both effects have been forced to be equal. If both season and gender are effects coded, however, then the base level for season will be equal to $-\beta_{31} - \beta_{32} - \beta_{33}$, while the marginal utility associated with being male will be $-\beta_4$. As such, the base levels for both variables now take on unique values, and one can compare $-\beta_{31} - \beta_{32} - \beta_{33}$ to $-\beta_4$ to determine which has the greater overall impact on utility (Table 3.8).

As an aside, in models where all variables are effects coded, the ASC of an alternative and the effects coded variables will have a very specific interpretation. To demonstrate, we show how the effects codes and ASCs of just such a model are estimated. Consider the example in Table 3.8. In the table, we compute the hypothetical average utilities over a sample of respondents for each level of an effects coded variable with four levels. Note that while in the model, we would have three effects codes, it is still possible to compute the average utility over the sample for all three levels. Thus, for example, over all N respondents, the average utility for summer might be calculated as −0.225 while the average utility over the same respondents for the winter level is 0.875. Once computed, the average of these averages is calculated, which we call the grand mean. The effects coded parameters are then calculated as the difference in the average utility for that level from the grand mean. The grand mean itself will be the ASC for the model. As such, the effects code may be interpreted as reflecting the average difference in utility for that level relative to the average utility for all of the effects coded variables. Note that this interpretation only works when all variables in the model are effects coded, however.

Table 3.9 Dummy and effects coding rescaling

	Dummy parameter	*Effects parameter*
Summer	−0.7	−0.8
Autumn (Fall)	0.4	0.3
Winter	0.7	0.6
Spring	0	−0.1

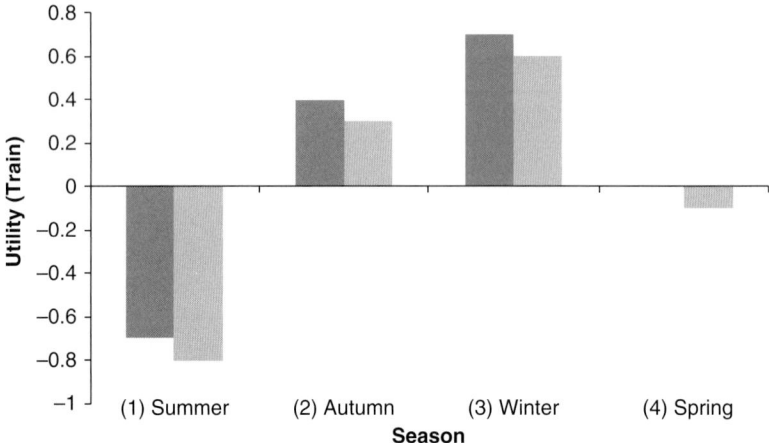

Figure 3.10   Marginal utility for season (dummy and effects coding)

For both the dummy and effects coding schemes, the choice of which level to set as the base is completely arbitrary. This is because utility is measured on an ordinal scale, and the parameters will be estimated relative to whatever level is set as the base. Further, *all else being equal*, the choice of coding scheme should not matter in terms of the final model results, only in how the results are interpreted. This is because moving from dummy coding to effects coding (or vice versa) will, if done correctly, lead simply to a rescaling of the parameter estimates by precisely $-\sum_{l}^{L-1} \beta_{kl}$, such that the predicted utilities for the alternatives will remain exactly the same. To demonstrate, consider an example where the season variable is effects coded and produces parameter estimates for summer, autumn (fall) and winter of −0.8, 0.3, and 0.6, respectively. The base level associated with spring will be −0.1 (i.e., −(−0.8 + 0.3 + 0.6)). If we were to use dummy codes as opposed to effects codes, the parameters for summer, autumn, and winter would rescale by −0.1, to become −0.7, 0.4, and 0.7, respectively. Table 3.9 and Figure 3.10 show this rescaling.

Table 3.10 Dummy and effects coding with a status quo alternative: 1

Situation (s)	Policy (j)	Fish saved	Constant	Dummy coding x_{10}	x_{20}	x_{30}	Effects coding x_{10}	x_{20}	x_{30}
1	A	10	1	1	0	0	1	0	0
1	B	20	1	0	1	0	0	1	0
1	C	10	1	1	0	0	1	0	0
1	Do nothing	0	0	0	0	0	−1	−1	−1
2	A	30	1	0	0	1	0	0	1
2	B	10	1	1	0	0	1	0	0
2	C	20	1	0	1	0	0	1	0
2	Do nothing	0	0	0	0	0	−1	−1	−1

> *As an aside*, one instance when the parameter estimates for dummy and effects coding will not rescale to reproduce the same result is when the base level of a variable is associated with only one particular alternative, typically a status quo alternative. To demonstrate, taking an environmental economics example, assume that a researcher is investigating potential policies related to improving the quality of water for a particular river. One attribute is the number of fish each policy will save, where for the status quo alternative representing "*doing nothing*," the value for this attribute will be zero. Assuming that each policy will save at least some fish, the attribute associated with each policy will never take the value zero. In such cases, many researchers in setting up the data will assign as the base level the attribute level with the lowest value, which in this case would be saving zero fish. To demonstrate how the data might look, consider Table 3.10.

In Table 3.10, we have used a data format whereby each row of data represents an alternative, and each column a variable. Groups of rows represent a choice observation. For example, assuming a decision maker is faced with the choice between three policy alternatives, A, B, or C, and the choice not to do anything, then each block of four rows will represent one choice observation. This particular data format convention is used by software such as Nlogit and is further discussed in Chapter 10. Within the table, choice situations consisting of four alternatives are shown. Assuming that the number of fish saved attribute takes four levels (0, 10, 20, and 30), both dummy and effects coding will require the creation of three additional variables. Note that in Table 3.10, we have also included a column for model constants (ASCs) following the discussion presented after Equation (3.15).

Coding the data as shown causes a number of problems when attempting to estimate the model. Firstly, x_{10}, x_{20}, and x_{30} will induce near perfect correlations within the data. To see why, consider any two of the three dummy or effects coded variables. If either of these two columns takes the value one, then we know that the last column must be zero (i.e., if either x_{10} or $x_{20} = 1$, then x_{30} must equal 0). If, on the other hand, neither of the two columns takes the value one, then the last column must be equal to one. As such, we know the value of the last column by knowing the value of the other columns (this is the same reason we only need l_k-1 columns when we use dummy or effects coding). Hence, the information for any one dummy or effects coded variable is contained within the other variables, and in this way at least one variable is mathematically redundant. Second, the base level for both the dummy and effects coded variables are perfectly confounded with an alternative, in this case the no choice alternative. In the previous example used to describe dummy and effects coding, the season in which a choice observation was recorded was not specific to any particular alternative, and over the data set will hopefully be associated with each alternative at some point in time (the fact that we used the season dummy for only the train alternative is beside the point; in some observations, the choice observation will be for summer, in others winter, etc.). Whereas the correlation resulting in the need for only l_k-1 columns results from correlations caused by linear combination of the columns, now we have correlation in both the columns and rows of the data. This latter point means that the base level of the dummy or effects code will act like a model ASC as it is a constant for that alternative for all choice observations within the data. As such, one can no longer estimate $J-1$ ASCs, as the base level of the dummy or effects coded variable will not only represent the base level of the variable but also a constant for that alternative. Hence, whereas before one could have estimated an ASC for policies A, B, and C after normalizing the ASC for the no choice alternative to zero, now we would be able to estimate ASCs for only two of the policies as the third ASC *is the base level of the dummy or effects coded variable* associated with the no choice alternative. Further, as an ASC represents the mean of the unobserved effects for that alternative, the difference in the coding of the base level between the dummy and effects coding schemes applies not only with that variable as before, but now to the entire alternative. For this reason, the two coding schemes will produce different model results!

Cooper *et al.* (2012) propose using a hybrid coding scheme for such data, combining both dummy and effects codes. This coding scheme involves effects coding the values not perfectly correlated with an alternative (using our example, this would be for levels 10, 20, and 30) while setting the values for the correlated level to be zero. Note that it is necessary to use only l_k-1 of the

Table 3.11 Dummy and effects coding with a status quo alternative: 2

				Hybrid dummy and effects coding	
Situation (s)	Policy (j)	Fish saved (00)	Constant	x_{10}	x_{20}
1	A	10	1	1	0
1	B	20	1	0	1
1	C	10	1	1	0
1	Do nothing	0	0	0	0
2	A	30	1	−1	−1
2	B	10	1	1	0
2	C	20	1	0	1
2	Do nothing	0	0	0	0

non-alternative correlated levels in setting up this hybrid scheme, as shown in Table 3.11.

Orthogonal polynomial coding differs substantially from both dummy and effects coding in terms of how the variables are recoded within the data, and how the results should be interpreted. Similar to dummy or effects coding, the analyst creates $l_k - 1$ variables when using orthogonal polynomial coding; however, each of the newly constructed variables, while being associated with a particular level, represents a particular polynomial effect. The first variable represents a linear transformation of the original variable (x_{nsjk}), the second a quadratic transformation (x_{nsjk}^2), the third a cubic transformation, (x_{nsjk}^3), etc. Taking an example of a variable described by four attribute levels, the marginal utility associated with orthogonal polynomial coding for that variable is equivalent to:

$$V_{nsj} = \beta_{11} x_{nsjk} + \beta_{12} x_{nsjk}^2 + \beta_{13} x_{nsjk}^3. \tag{3.25}$$

Here, however, the levels the variable can take are discrete, and the polynomial transformation is achieved via how the variable is recoded. Hence, the interpretation of the results obtained from models estimated on data using an orthogonal polynomial coding scheme do not require that one apply a power transformation to each of the variables, as this is already accounted for in the coding. Hence, the effect that a particular level will have on the utility of an alternative is given as:

$$V_{nsj} = \beta_{11} x_{nsjk1} + \beta_{12} x_{nsjk2} + \beta_{13} x_{nsjk3}. \tag{3.26}$$

Table 3.12 Dummy, effects, and orthogonal polynomial coding correlation comparisons

	(a) Dummy codes			(b) Effects codes			(c) Orthogonal codes		
Original code	X_{nsjk1}	X_{nsjk2}	X_{nsjk3}	X_{nsjk1}	X_{nsjk2}	X_{nsjk3}	X_{nsjk1}	X_{nsjk2}	X_{nsjk3}
1 (Summer)	1	0	0	1	0	0	−3	1	−1
2 (Autumn)	0	1	0	0	1	0	−1	−1	3
3 (Winter)	0	0	1	0	0	1	1	−1	−3
4 (Spring)	0	0	0	−1	−1	−1	3	1	1
Correlation structure	X_{nsjk1}	X_{nsjk2}	X_{nsjk3}	X_{nsjk1}	X_{nsjk2}	X_{nsjk3}	X_{nsjk1}	X_{nsjk2}	X_{nsjk3}
x_{nsjk1}	1			1			1		
x_{nsjk2}	−0.33	1		0.5	1		0	1	
x_{nsjk3}	−0.33	−0.33	1	0.5	0.5	1	0	0	1

Continuing with the season example, in setting up the orthogonal polynomial coding scheme, the analyst will generate $l_k - 1$ or three variables. Table 3.11 provides the values that each of these variables will take, which for the season example are replicated in the first part of Table 3.12. If, for example, the season variable indicates that the observation was recorded in summer, the first orthogonal polynomial coded variable will take the value −3, the second 1, and the third −1. If however the season was autumn, then the values −1, −1, and 3 are used. Note that unlike dummy or effects codes, each of the $l_k - 1$ variables will take non-zero values for all levels and hence, the impact on overall utility will require using all of the parameter estimates. To demonstrate this and what precisely the coding scheme is doing, let us assume four different example sets of parameters. In the first example, the parameters are assumed to be −0.9, 0, and 0 for β_{31}, β_{32} and β_{33}, respectively. In the second example, assume now that the parameters are now 0, 0.5, and −0.4, while in the third example they become −0.6, 0.8, and −0.4. In the last example, assume that the parameters take the values −0.8, 0.3, and 0.6. Table 3.13 shows the utility for each of the seasons applying the orthogonal polynomial coding scheme for all for sets of parameter estimates.

Plotting the resulting utilities demonstrates what the coding scheme is doing (see Figure 3.11). In the first example, β_{32} and β_{33} are not statistically significant and the results imply a linear relationship between each of the seasons and utility for the train alternative. In the second example, only the second parameter is statistically significantly different from zero and a quadratic relationship between the seasons and utility is inferred. For the last two examples, complex relationships are inferred.

Table 3.13 Orthogonal polynomial coding example results

	β_{31}	β_{32}	β_{33}				
Example (1)	−0.9	0	0				
Example (2)	0	0.5	0				
Example (3)	−0.6	0.8	−0.4				
Example (4)	−0.8	0.3	0.6				
Original code	X_{nsjk1}	X_{nsjk2}	X_{nsjk3}	$V_{nsj}(1)$	$V_{nsj}(2)$	$V_{nsj}(3)$	$V_{nsj}(4)$
1 (Summer)	−3	1	−1	2.7	0.5	3	2.1
2 (Autumn)	−1	−1	3	0.9	−0.5	−1.4	2.3
3 (Winter)	1	−1	−3	−0.9	−0.5	−0.2	−2.9
4 (Spring)	3	1	1	−2.7	0.5	−1.4	−1.5

At the base of Table 3.12, we present the correlation structures inferred for each of the three different non-linear coding schemes. As can be seen, dummy and effects codes induce correlations between each of the constructed variables, while orthogonal polynomial coding does not. It is for this reason that orthogonal polynomial coding is generally preferred (see, e.g., Louviere *et al.* 2000, 269, who recommend that orthogonal polynomial coding be used wherever possible); however the interpretation of orthogonal polynomial coding may be somewhat more difficult to describe to those less familiar with such a coding scheme.

To finish our discussion, we present an example of how the data might appear under all three coding schemes. In doing so, we use −999 to represent missing data (the value used in Nlogit5). In our example (Table 3.14), the season variable only applies to the train alternative, and hence we have used the missing value code to represent this (although in reality, we would not do this, as we may wish to apply the season variable to another alternative in another model).

3.4.6 Non-linear parameter utility specifications

Although much less common in practice, it is also possible to estimate discrete choice models allowing for non-linear parameter estimates (e.g., Fader *et al* 1992). The parameter estimates in such models may be a function of other parameters, other variables, or a combination of both. Chapter 20 provides details of how to do this using Nlogit5:

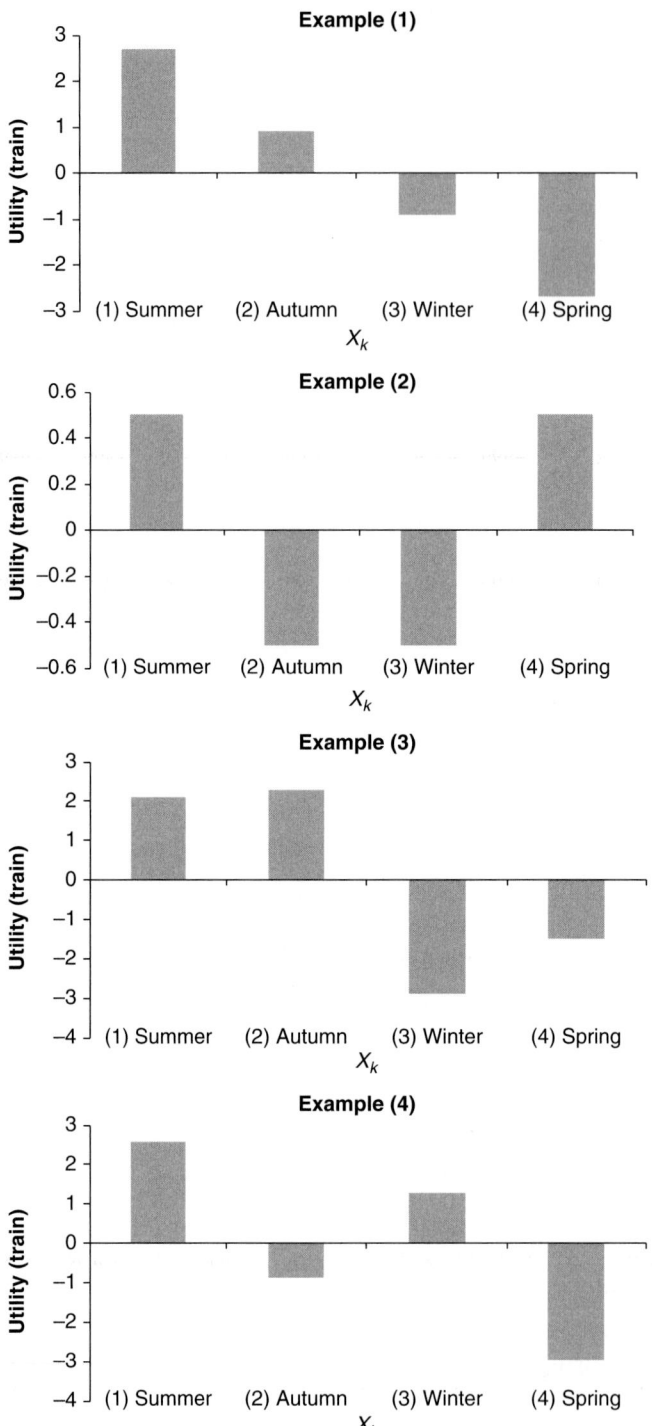

Figure 3.11   Plots of orthogonal polynomial coding example results

Table 3.14 Example data set up for dummy, effects, and orthogonal polynomial coding

				Dummy coding			Effects coding			Orthogonal polynomial coding		
n	s	Mode (j)	Season	X_{nsjk1}	X_{nsjk2}	X_{nsjk3}	X_{nsjk1}	X_{nsjk2}	X_{nsjk3}	X_{nsjk1}	X_{nsjk2}	X_{nsjk3}
1	1	car	1	−999	−999	−999	−999	−999	−999	−999	−999	−999
1	1	bus	1	−999	−999	−999	−999	−999	−999	−999	−999	−999
1	1	train	1	1	0	0	1	0	0	−3	1	−1
1	1	tram	1	−999	−999	−999	−999	−999	−999	−999	−999	−999
1	2	car	3	−999	−999	−999	−999	−999	−999	−999	−999	−999
1	2	bus	3	−999	−999	−999	−999	−999	−999	−999	−999	−999
1	2	train	3	0	0	1	0	0	1	1	−1	−3
1	2	tram	3	−999	−999	−999	−999	−999	−999	−999	−999	−999
2	1	car	2	−999	−999	−999	−999	−999	−999	−999	−999	−999
2	1	bus	2	−999	−999	−999	−999	−999	−999	−999	−999	−999
2	1	train	2	0	1	0	0	1	0	−1	−1	3
2	1	tram	2	−999	−999	−999	−999	−999	−999	−999	−999	−999
2	2	car	4	−999	−999	−999	−999	−999	−999	−999	−999	−999
2	2	bus	4	−999	−999	−999	−999	−999	−999	−999	−999	−999
2	2	train	4	0	0	0	−1	−1	−1	3	1	1
2	2	tram	4	−999	−999	−999	−999	−999	−999	−999	−999	−999

$$\beta_k = G(x_{nsjl}, \beta_l). \tag{3.27}$$

One example where non-linear parameter utility specifications are becoming increasingly used involves models in which either an entire utility function or all utility functions within the model are multiplied by a single parameter (e.g., Fiebig *et al.* 2010, Greene and Hensher 2010b). For example, in Equation (3.28), the utility functions for all J alternatives are multiplied by a common parameter β_l.

$$V_{nsj} = \beta_l \sum_{k=1}^{K} \beta_{jk} \, x_{nsjk} = \sum_{k=1}^{K} \beta_l \beta_{jk} \, x_{nsjk}. \tag{3.28}$$

The marginal impact on utility for a change in x_{nsjk} will be $\beta_l \beta_{jk} = \theta_{jk}$, however, as β_l is common to all θ_{jk}, the resulting estimates are likely to be correlated, not only within each alternative but also between alternatives (Hess and Rose 2012).

Models allowing for non-linearity in the parameters utility specifications have also been applied to data dealing with risky choices (e.g., Anderson *et al.*

2012; Hensher *et al.* 2011; and Chapter 20). "Risk" in such studies has typically been defined in terms of uncertainty in observing what outcome is likely to occur prior to the choice being made. In defining risk, each potential outcome is defined as occurring up to some probability, and decision makers are assumed to know both the potential outcome and the probability that an outcome will actually occur (in reality, it is a little more complicated than this, as research has shown that decision makers are likely to use what are known as subjective as opposed to objective probabilities when making decisions, where the latter is the actual probability associated with an outcome, while the former is the decision maker's interpretation of the probability; this recognizes that for some outcome, the decision maker's perception (i.e., the subjective probability) of an objective probability (i.e., the real life mathematical probability) will typically be either an over- or under-weighting of the objective probability). For example, prior to driving to work, a commuter will not know precisely how long the trip will take due to unknowns such as the degree of traffic congestion, how many traffic lights (or robots for our South African readers) they will be stopped by, the weather, etc. Nevertheless, based on previous experience, the same car commuter will likely have an expectation as to the minimum and maximum amount of time the trip might take, as well as an expectation as to the most likely amount of time (probably an average of the travel times over repeated similar trips). The car commuter is also likely to have some idea about the likelihood of each outcome actually occurring (e.g., the shortest and longest travel times are more likely to occur with much less frequency than the average travel time). Based on this same scenario, Hensher *et al.* (2011) modeled choice data in which car commuters were presented with competing routes described by a range of travel times, each with an associated probability of occurring. Let p_{nsoj} be the probability that decision maker n in choice situation s will experience for route j a travel time of x_{nsoj}. Hensher *et al.* (2011) parameterized their model such that:

$$\kappa_{nsoj} = \beta_l \left[\left(\sum_{o=1}^{O} \omega(p_{nsoj}) x_{nsoj}^{1-\alpha} \right) / (1-\alpha) \right], \tag{3.29}$$

where $\omega(p_{nso}) = \exp(-\tau(-\ln(p_{nso}))^{\gamma})$ and β_l, α, τ, γ are parameters to be estimated. Note that $\omega(p_{nso})$ is a non-linear weighting function, representing the assumed relationship between the objective probability, p_{nso}, and the subjective probability actually used in making the choice. The specific functional form reported here for the weighting function represents one of four non-linear weighting functions estimated in the original Hensher *et al.* (2011) paper.

Non-linear in the parameter utility specifications remain to date relatively uncommon. This is because such specifications will usually require very rich data capable of supporting such decision processes, as well as the need to impose complex restrictions or normalizations in order to allow for the parameters of interest to be estimated. Further, until recently, very few if any commercial software allowed for the estimation of non-linear in the parameters models, meaning that only those with sophisticated programing abilities were in a position to estimate such models. Nevertheless, it is envisaged that such specifications will become increasingly more common as an increasing amount of commercial software becomes available in the future. Chapter 20 introduces this literature and how to estimate such models using Nlogit5.

3.4.7 Taste heterogeneity

The discussion to date has assumed, for a given variable, that the parameters are fixed over respondents, implying that all decision makers (or groups of decision makers) share the same marginal utility as one another. For example, in our discussion on orthogonal polynomial coding, all decision makers, n, were assumed to have a marginal utility of $\beta_{31} = -0.9$ under the first example discussed. The inclusion of an interaction term relaxes this assumption, allowing different covariate segments to have different marginal utilities for a particular variable. For example, a utility function containing the following term, $\beta_1 x_{nsj1} + \beta_2 x_{nsj1} gender_n$, would imply a marginal utility of β_1 for gender = 0, and $\beta_1 + \beta_2$ for gender = 1. Here, however, all decision makers within gender class 0 share the same marginal utility, as do all decision makers within gender class 1. While it is possible to add additional interaction terms, for example, to $\beta_1 x_{nsj1} + \beta_2 x_{nsj1} gender_n + \beta_3 x_{nsj1} gender_n age_n$, to uncover further taste variations, it is unlikely that the analyst will be able to discover all possible sources of taste differences.

Several types of discrete choice models allow for heterogeneity in the tastes exhibited by different decision makers within some sampled population without having to rely on interaction terms. These models involve allowing the parameter estimates to be drawn from some underlying distribution, which can be either continuous or discrete in nature. As such, these models allow the parameters to be distributed over respondents such that β_k is now represented as β_{kn}. We discuss three such models within this text; the probit model (Chapters 4 and 17), the mixed multinomial logit model (Chapters 4 and 15) and the latent class model (Chapters 4 and 16).

3.5 Concluding comments

Despite the name, discrete choice modeling need not be about choices, at least in the sense that most people think about them. The econometric models and underlying economic or psychological theories may be adapted to fit any discrete outcome. For example, Jones and Hensher (2004) apply discrete choice models to model corporate bankruptcies, insolvencies, and takeovers. Likewise, the substantive example used in Section 3.2 dealt with election outcomes (i.e., voting), which at the aggregate level represent disaggregate choices that, however, should be thought of differently. Although the majority of this chapter has dealt with the issue of utility, as discussed in Section 3.2, discrete choice models relate, via a link function, some latent variable to the observed outcomes, and it just so happens that the latent variable is called utility when the outcomes are disaggregate choices.

Whether dealing with choices or otherwise, this chapter set out the basis for modeling the observed component of discrete choice models. The chapter sought to explain the alternatives available to the analyst when writing out the utility functions of discrete choice models, as well as the various interpretations that each approach has. The chapter has made reference to material to follow. Although we have introduced probit and logit models, link functions, choice probabilities, etc., the next few chapters will go into far more detail about the different econometric models and how they are estimated. In particular, in outlining the various econometric models over the next few chapters, a significant amount of time will be devoted to the unobserved effects of discrete choice models and the impact that different assumptions about them have on discrete choice models.

Appendix 3A: Simulated data

X	X contd	X contd	X contd	Y	Y contd	Y contd	Y contd
4	1	5	5	8.2	1.8	18.2	10
1	5	5	2	1.8	6.7	18.2	1.8
4	4	1	5	6.7	10	1	13.5
5	2	4	4	13.5	2.7	6	6
4	4	1	4	5	8.2	3	5.5
4	1	1	1	7.4	3	1.6	1.3

X	X contd	X contd	X contd	Y	Y contd	Y contd	Y contd
5	4	1	3	12.2	9	2.7	3.3
3	2	5	1	4.1	2.5	9	1.6
5	1	1	3	20.1	2.5	1.3	4.1
3	5	3	1	5	13.5	4.5	1.1
3	5	5	3	5	12.2	10	3.7
3	5	1	3	5	8.2	2	4.5
3	1	3	2	3.7	1.8	4.5	2.5
2	4	1	4	4.5	6.7	1.6	8.2
1	3	3	5	1.2	4.1	4.1	14.9
3	4	2	3	3.7	9	1.5	4.1
3	5	2	3	5	11	2	8.2
3	2	3	5	5	3.7	4.5	13.5
3	4	2	2	5	5.5	3.7	2.2
5	4	3	1	14.9	9	5	2
2	5	5	2	1.5	11	10	2
2	1	1	–	2.5	1.5	1.2	–
3	3	1	–	5	4.1	1.6	–
1	1	3	–	2.2	1.6	3	–
4	1	5	–	9	1.8	9	–
4	4	2	–	7.4	5.5	3.3	–
2	5	2	–	2	9	4.1	–
2	3	5	–	2.2	4.1	14.9	–
5	2	1	–	22.2	2.5	2	–
4	2	2	–	11	4.1	4.1	–
5	4	5	–	11	8.2	13.5	–
1	3	1	–	1.8	9	1.8	–
2	3	5	–	5	2.7	12.2	–
4	3	5	–	12.2	6	8.2	–
5	2	2	–	13.5	2	2.2	–
1	3	4	–	1.5	4.1	11	–
1	3	1	–	1.6	7.4	1.5	–
2	3	1	–	3.7	3.3	1.1	–
4	5	2	–	5	10	3.7	–
3	5	5	–	6.7	13.5	12.2	–
2	2	5	–	5	3	14.9	–
4	1	1	–	9	1.6	1.8	–
2	4	3	–	2.5	6	5	–

Appendix 3B: Nlogit syntax

Model 1: Linear regression model

```
REGRESS;Lhs=Party;Rhs=ONE,min$
```
```
-----------------------------------------------------------------------------------
Ordinary     least squares regression ...........
LHS=PARTY    Mean                   =       .46279
             Standard deviation     =       .49919
----------   No. of observations    =          430  DegFreedom   Mean square
Regression   Sum of Squares         =      26.0374            1     26.03737
Residual     Sum of Squares         =      80.8673          428       .18894
Total        Sum of Squares         =     106.905           429       .24919
----------   Standard error of e    =       .43467  Root MSE        .43366
Fit          R-squared              =       .24356  R-bar squared   .24179
Model test   F[  1,    428]         =   137.80596  Prob F > F*      .00000
Model was estimated on Dec 02, 2013 at 05:13:26 PM
-----------+-----------------------------------------------------------------------
           |                   Standard               Prob.         95% Confidence
    PARTY| Coefficient        Error        t       |t|>T*           Interval
-----------+-----------------------------------------------------------------------
Constant|     .09081**       .03799     2.39       .0173      .01634       .16528
     MIN|    1.43778***      .12248    11.74       .0000     1.19772     1.67783
-----------+-----------------------------------------------------------------------
Note: ***, **, * ==>  Significance at 1%, 5%, 10% level.
-----------------------------------------------------------------------------------
```

Model 2: Probit model

```
PROBIT;Lhs=Party;Rhs=ONE,min$
Normal exit:   5 iterations. Status=0, F=     235.3260
--------------------------------------------------------------------------
Binomial Probit Model
Dependent variable                   PARTY
Log likelihood function        -235.32597
Restricted log likelihood      -296.86149
Chi squared [   1 d.f.]         123.07103
Significance level                .00000
McFadden Pseudo R-squared        .2072870
Estimation based on N =     430, K =    2
Inf.Cr.AIC   =     474.7 AIC/N =     1.104
Model estimated: Dec 02, 2013, 17:13:26
Hosmer-Lemeshow chi-squared =   17.71639
P-value=  .02346 with deg.fr. =         8
```

```
-----------+--------------------------------------------------------------------------
           |                  Standard              Prob.         95% Confidence
    PARTY|  Coefficient      Error       z       |z|>Z*            Interval
-----------+--------------------------------------------------------------------------
           |Index function for probability
Constant|    -1.30938***     .13944     -9.39     .0000      -1.58267    -1.03608
     MIN|     4.92644***     .53252      9.25     .0000       3.88272     5.97017
-----------+--------------------------------------------------------------------------
Note: ***, **, * ==>  Significance at 1%, 5%, 10% level.
-----------------------------------------------------------------------------------------
```

Model 3: Logit model

```
LOGIT;Lhs=Party;Rhs=ONE,min$
Normal exit:   6 iterations. Status=0, F=      235.8677
-----------------------------------------------------------------------------------------
Binary Logit Model for Binary Choice
Dependent variable                     PARTY
Log likelihood function        -235.86766
Restricted log likelihood      -296.86149
Chi squared [   1 d.f.]         121.98766
Significance level                .00000
McFadden Pseudo R-squared        .2054623
Estimation based on N =     430, K =    2
Inf.Cr.AIC   =     475.7 AIC/N =     1.106
Model estimated: Dec 02, 2013, 17:13:26
Hosmer-Lemeshow chi-squared =    17.54945
P-value=  .02487 with deg.fr. =         8
-----------+--------------------------------------------------------------------------
           |                  Standard              Prob.         95% Confidence
    PARTY|  Coefficient      Error       z       |z|>Z*            Interval
-----------+--------------------------------------------------------------------------
Constant|    -2.16536***     .24463     -8.85     .0000      -2.64482    -1.68591
     MIN|     8.12953***     .93524      8.69     .0000       6.29649     9.96256
-----------+--------------------------------------------------------------------------
Note: ***, **, * ==>  Significance at 1%, 5%, 10% level.
```

4   Families of discrete choice models

4.1 Introduction

The purpose of Chapter 3 was to provide an introduction to models estimated on data with categorical dependent variables. In doing so, we demonstrated how more commonly known model frameworks, such as the linear regression model, are inappropriate for this type of data. The model estimated on discrete choice data must accommodate the nature of the process that generates the data. The observed data on choices reveal, in discrete categorical form, the preferences of the individual over a discrete set of alternatives. The preferences, in turn, are embodied in latent continuous variables, termed utilities, that express the intensity of those preferences. The observed outcomes reveal only the relative preferences for the set of alternatives being modeled. If the latent preferences were observable we could, in principle, analyze them with regression methods. When only relative preferences, expressed in discrete outcomes, are revealed, different methods are called for.

As shown in Chapter 3, the analyst can specify a set of utility functions associated with the alternatives being modeled. Each utility function was shown to consist of two components, an observed component and an unobserved component. Chapter 3 focused on the observable components of the model of utility. Through their informed specification, the analyst has control over this part, being able to determine which variables enter into it, and how. Chapter 3 discussed the various choices analysts have available in specifying the observed component of utility for discrete choice models, including specifying generic and alternative specific parameters, using non-linear coding, and using linear and non-linear functions of data and parameters. Chapter 3 also mentioned two types of econometric models, *probit* and *logit*, which are based on two different specifications of the random parts of the utility functions in the random utility models of interest in this chapter.

In this chapter, we examine the unobserved component of utility in more detail and demonstrate how assumptions about unobserved effects dictate the specific econometric model being estimated. Given that the unobservable component of utility is, well, unobserved, at least by the analyst, it is necessary to make a number of assumptions about how this component of utility is distributed over the sampled population. It is these assumptions that lead to different econometric models, including the probit and logit models. The different assumptions about the unobserved component of utility also lead to different methods for calculating the probabilities for the observed outcomes. The purpose of this chapter is to discuss the assumptions typically made about the unobserved component of utility and demonstrate how these assumptions lead to different econometric models. We will also set out the theoretical differences between the various econometric models available to the analyst, within the framework of the unobserved effects, which will be explored in later chapters. Some of the econometric detail is provided in later chapters where we show how to estimate specific model forms and interpret the range of behavioral outputs using Nlogit. We will cross-reference to the specific chapters.

4.2 Modeling utility

Let U_{nsj} denote the utility of alternative j perceived by respondent n in choice situation s. We assume that U_{nsj} may be partitioned into two separate components, an observable component of utility, V_{nsj}, and a residual, unobservable component, ε_{nsj}, such that:

$$U_{nsj} = V_{nsj} + \varepsilon_{nsj}. \tag{4.1}$$

The observable component of utility is typically assumed to be a linear relationship of observed attribute levels, x, of each alternative j and their corresponding weights (parameters), β, with a positive scale factor, σ_n such that:

$$U_{nsj} = \sigma_n \sum_{k=1}^{K} \beta_{nk} x_{nsjk} + \varepsilon_{nsj}, \tag{4.2}$$

where β_{nk} represents the marginal utility or parameter weight associated with attribute k for respondent n. The unobserved component, ε_{nsj}, is often assumed to be an independently and identically (**IID**) distributed EV1 distribution or more flexibly with a normal distribution. We will develop the implications of the distributional assumption in detail below. The individual scale factor in Equation (4.2) is normalized to one in most applications. (We refer to such models as *constant variance models*.) An alternative representation that preserves the preference order in Equation (4.2), as long as σ_n does not vary across alternatives, is:

$$U^*_{nsj} = \sum_{k=1}^{K} \beta_{nk}x_{nsjk} + (\varepsilon_{nsj}/\sigma_n).$$

(4.3)

It can be seen that the variance of ε_{nsj} is inversely related to the magnitude of $\sigma_n \sum_{k=1}^{K} \beta_{nk}x_{nsjk}$ via σ_n. If ε_{nsj} has an EV1 distribution with this scale parameter, then $\mathrm{Var}(\varepsilon_{nsj}/\sigma_n) = \pi^2/6$; if, instead, ε_{nsj} is normally distributed, then $\mathrm{Var}(\varepsilon_{nsj}/\sigma_n) = 1$. In addition to the information on the levels of the attributes, x in Equation (4.2) may also contain up to $J-1$ alternative-specific constants (ASCs) that capture the residual mean influences of the unobserved effects on choice associated with their respective alternatives. This x takes the value 1 for the alternative under consideration or zero otherwise. The utility specification in Equation (4.2) is flexible in that it allows for the possibility that different respondents may have different marginal utilities for each attribute being modeled. In practice, it is not generally feasible to estimate individual specific parameter weights. As such, it is common to estimate parameter weights for the population that vary randomly around a mean, such that:

$$\beta_{nk} = \bar{\beta}_k + \eta_k z_{nk},$$

(4.4)

where $\bar{\beta}_k$ represents the mean of the distribution of marginal utilities held by the sampled population, η_k represents a deviation or spread of preferences among sampled respondents around the mean marginal utility, and z_{nk} represents random draws taken from a pre-specified distribution for each respondent n and attribute k. Rather than assuming that the marginal utility has some distribution over both n and s, as would be dictated by z_{nsk}, this alternative model specification allows for a distribution over only n such that z_{nsk} becomes z_{nk}. In this version of the model, preferences are assumed to vary between individuals (n) but not within an individual, given a sequence of observed choices made by individual n (s). The assumption that preferences vary between and not within respondents accounts for the panel nature of **stated choice** (SC) data (see Ortúzar and Willumsen 2011; Revelt and Train 1998; Train 2009) – these act like "random effects." Within the literature, when z_{ns} is employed, the resulting model is known as a *cross-sectional discrete choice model*, while z_n produces what is referred to as a *panel discrete choice model*, as it takes into account the panel nature of repeated choice observations.

We now discuss a number of models that account for various levels of generality. The main features of the utility model that analysts are interested in generalizing are heterogeneity in the marginal utilities and scale variation, which implies different kinds of heteroskedasticity. The models we discuss are not an exhaustive list of models capable of addressing scale heterogeneity and other features. For example, two models not developed in detail here are the *heteroskedastic Extreme value* (HEV) model, mainly as a result of its lack of popularity within the wider literature and the *cross-nested logit* (CNL) model due its lack of suitability for typical data collected by researchers (although the latter is included in Section 14.9 of Chapter 14). Our discussion is provided as an overview of some of the main methods currently employed in well-known applications.

4.3 The unobserved component of utility

For a given choice situation, the analyst will rely on data on the attributes describing the alternatives faced by a decision maker, covariates representing the characteristics of the decision maker, and the context in which the decision is being made. Also required are the observed choice outcomes. These data are then used to form utility specifications that explain the observed choice outcomes. The analyst, however, will never observe the actual utility that the decision maker holds towards each of the alternatives. Utility is a latent construct known only (even if subconsciously) to the decision maker. To further complicate matters, the analyst will rarely, if ever, observe all of the variables that lead to each decision maker's level of utility for each of the alternatives, labeled j. In part, this might be the result of failing to ask for all relevant information from each decision maker, or that the decision makers themselves cannot relate fully the relevant information to the analyst. As such, the utility, U_{nsj} will never actually equal the model specified by the analyst, V_{nsj}. To reconcile these two utility constructs, an additional term is required. This additional term, first introduced in Equation (3.7), is given as Equation (4.5), where U_{nsj} equals $V_{nsj} + \varepsilon_{nsj}$, such that ε_{nsj} captures the factors that affect utility but are not measured within V_{nsj} and not directly observable by the analyst:

$$U_{nsj} = V_{nsj} + \varepsilon_{nsj}. \tag{4.5}$$

Assuming that each decision maker acts as a utility maximiser, they will choose the alternative for which they will derive the largest amount of utility. Given that the specific value ε_{nsj} is unknown for all n, s, and j, the total utility, U_{nsj}, for each decision maker will also be unknown. As such, while the analyst may be able to calculate the amount of utility for each alternative associated with the observed component of the model, it remains impossible to calculate precisely the overall utility that each decision maker will hold for any given alternative. (That is, even assuming that V_{nsj} is observable. Typically, in the context of a model, V_{nsj} will also involve unknown parameters that must be estimated using the observed data.) To demonstrate, consider a scenario in which decision maker n is faced with a choice between four possible alternatives, car, bus, train, and tram. Assume further that based only on their relative times and costs, the decision maker would value the four choices, in relative terms, at 2, 3, –2 and 0 for V_{nj}, for car, bus, train, and tram, respectively. The utility functions for this example are given as Equation (4.6):

$$\begin{aligned}
U_{n,car} &= \ \ 2 + \varepsilon_{n,car}, \\
U_{n,bus} &= \ \ 3 + \varepsilon_{n,bus}, \\
U_{n,train} &= -2 + \varepsilon_{n,train}, \\
U_{n,tram} &= \ \ 0 + \varepsilon_{n,tram}.
\end{aligned} \tag{4.6}$$

Given this scenario, it is tempting to state that the decision maker would select the bus alternative; however, whether they actually choose the bus will depend on the values they hold for $\varepsilon_{n,car}$, $\varepsilon_{n,bus}$, $\varepsilon_{n,train}$, and $\varepsilon_{n,tram}$. For example, suppose for our hypothetical decision maker, $\varepsilon_{n,car} = -1$, $\varepsilon_{n,bus} = -3$, $\varepsilon_{n,train} = 5$, and $\varepsilon_{n,tram} = 0$. Then, the alternative with the highest total utility will be train. Despite all other modes of transport offering greater amounts of utility in terms of what was modeled, the train alternative will be chosen. The chooser has a strong preference for rail travel. Perhaps they are a train buff, a variable not included in the observed component of the model.

In order to make any progress at modeling choices, it is necessary to make a number of assumptions about the unobserved components of utility. The most common assumption is that for each alternative, j, ε_{nsj}, will be randomly distributed with some density, $f(\varepsilon_{nsj})$, over decision makers, n, and choice situations, s. Further assumptions about the specific density specification adopted for the unobserved effects, ε_{nsj} (e.g., the unobserved effects are drawn from a **multivariate** normal distribution) lead to alternate econometric models.

Assuming that there exists some joint density such that $\varepsilon_{ns} = \langle \varepsilon_{ns1}, \ldots, \varepsilon_{nsJ} \rangle$ represents a vector of the J unobserved effects for the full choice set, it becomes possible to make probabilistic statements about the choices made by the decision makers. Specifically, the probability that respondent n in choice situation s will select alternative j is given as the probability that outcome j will have the maximum utility:

$$
\begin{aligned}
P_{nsj} &= \text{Prob}(U_{nsj} > U_{nsi}, \forall i \neq j) \\
&= \text{Prob}(V_{nsj} + \varepsilon_{nsj} > V_{nsi} + \varepsilon_{nsi}, \forall i \neq j)
\end{aligned}
\tag{4.7}
$$

which can also be written as:

$$
P_{nsj} = \text{Prob}(\varepsilon_{nsj} - \varepsilon_{nsi} > V_{nsi} - V_{nsj}, \forall i \neq j).
\tag{4.8}
$$

Equation (4.8) reflects the probability that the differences in the random terms, $\varepsilon_{nsi} - \varepsilon_{nsj}$ will be less than the differences in the observed components of utility, $V_{nsi} - V_{nsj}$.

The fact that discrete choice models are probabilistic in nature is important for a number of reasons. The probabilities described in Equations (4.7) and (4.8) represent the translation between the categorical dependent variable and the latent utility. The properties of probabilities provide a natural link between the utility functions of the j alternatives. While it might appear that the utility specifications are independent of each other (indeed, one could think of them as separate regression equations), the fact that for a mutually exclusive and exhaustive set of alternatives, the probability of any one alternative being selected is constrained to be between zero and one, and the sum of the probabilities for all alternatives must sum to one, means that the utilities are related via their associated probabilities. Thus, if the utility for one alternative increases, *ceteris paribus*, the probability that that alternative will be selected increases and, correspondingly, the probabilities that other alternatives will be selected will fall, even though the utilities for the remaining alternatives do not change. It is the choice probabilities that link the separate utility functions together in one single model.

The relationship between the modeled utility and the choice probabilities is non-linear. In Chapter 3, we demonstrated that choice probabilities are not linear in shape over changes in x. A unit change in an attribute x, will result in a different change in the predicted choice probabilities given different initial values of x. To illustrate, consider the change in probability that a voting district will have elected a Democratic Party member given an increase from

0.5 to 0.6 in the proportion of people identifying as belonging to a minority group in that district. Based on the model results reported in Chapter 3, such an increase will result in an increase in the latent variable Y^* of 0.493 for the probit model and 0.813 for the logit model, with associated increases of 0.074 and 0.068 in the probabilities that the district will have elected a Democrat in the 2012 election (i.e., from 0.876 to 0.950 for the probit model and from 0.870 to 0.938 for the logit model). Now consider instead an increase in the proportion of people in that district identifying as belonging to a minority group from 0.6 to 0.7, still an overall increase of 0.1. The change in the latent variables Y^* for both the probit and logit models remain unchanged; Y^* is predicted to increase by 0.493 and 0.813 for the probit and logit models, respectively. But, now the probability that a Democrat would have been elected within that district increases from 0.950 to 0.984 for the probit model and from 0.938 to 0.971 for the logit model, representing absolute changes of only 0.034 for both models compared to 0.074 and 0.068 before. The same change in the independent variable produces only half the change in the predicted probabilities.

The non-linear relationship between changes in the independent variables and the choice probabilities, even if the utility functions are linear in the parameters and the attributes, has significant implications for how discrete choice models are estimated and interpreted. Linear regression models may be estimated using ordinary least squares (OLS). It is not possible to estimate non-linear discrete choice models using the same method. (We hinted at this in Chapter 3 when we presented the results for the probit and logit models.) While there exist several possible approaches to estimating discrete choice models, the most common is to use **maximum likelihood estimation** (MLE). We discuss MLE in Chapter 5. This method is used, and not OLS, due to the non-linear relationship between the utility functions and the estimated choice probabilities.

4.4 Random utility models

Choice models are built around two families of distributions for the random component of the utility function. Most recent studies rely on the Gumbel, or Type 1 Extreme value distribution (EV1) discussed above. This model was used in the earliest developments and remains the basic framework of choice. Contemporary studies generally build outward from this essential model. The alternative is the multivariate normal. The normal distribution is more natural in terms of modeling individual behavior; however, it is less practical in terms of actual estimation and analysis, for the reasons noted below.

4.4.1 Probit models based on the multivariate normal distribution

Discrete choice models in which the unobserved effects are assumed to be drawn from a multivariate normal distribution are known as *probit models*. Let $\varepsilon_{ns} = \langle \varepsilon_{ns1}, \ldots, \varepsilon_{nsJ} \rangle$ be a vector representing the J unobserved effects for individual n and choice situation s. Assuming that $\boldsymbol{\varepsilon}_{ns}$ follows a multivariate normal distribution with a mean vector of zero and **covariance** matrix $\boldsymbol{\Omega}_\varepsilon$ denoted as:

$$\boldsymbol{\varepsilon}_{ns} \sim \mathrm{N}[\mathbf{0}, \boldsymbol{\Omega}_\varepsilon], \tag{4.9}$$

the density of $\boldsymbol{\varepsilon}_{ns}$ is:

$$\phi(\boldsymbol{\varepsilon}_{ns}) = \frac{1}{(2\pi)^{J/2} |\boldsymbol{\Omega}|^{1/2}} \exp\left(-\frac{1}{2} \boldsymbol{\varepsilon}'_{ns} \boldsymbol{\Omega}_e^{-1} \boldsymbol{\varepsilon}_{ns}\right), \tag{4.10}$$

where $|\boldsymbol{\Omega}|$ is the determinant of $\boldsymbol{\Omega}_e$. Figure 4.1 shows a plot for a multivariate normal distribution assuming two alternatives.

The symmetric covariance matrix $\boldsymbol{\Omega}_e$ will have J variance terms (i.e., $\sigma_{ii} \, \forall i$) and $((J-1)J)/2$ unique covariance terms (i.e., $\sigma_{ij} \, \forall i \neq j$), with a total of $((J+1)J)/2$ distinct elements. For example, if J equals 5, $\boldsymbol{\Omega}_e$ will have 5 variance terms and

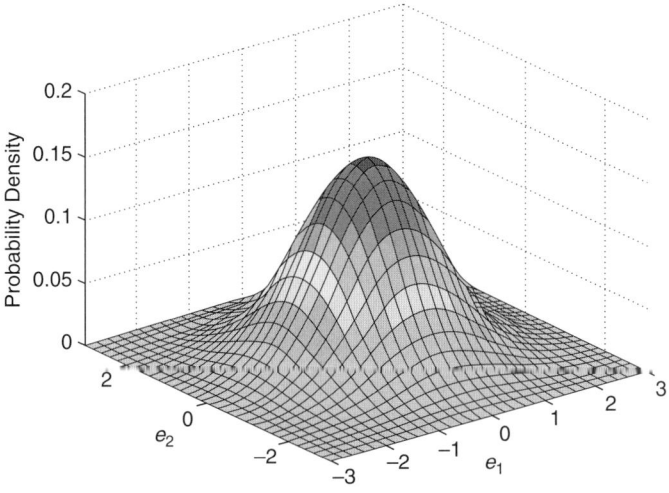

Figure 4.1   Multivariate Normal distribution for two alternatives

10 unique covariance terms (i.e., $((5-1)5)/2 = 10$), making a total of 15 independent terms (i.e., $((5+1)5)/2 = 15$). For the five alternative case, assuming that the specification is fully identified (which is it is unlikely to be – see below), we may therefore rewrite Equation (4.9) as:

$$
\varepsilon_{ns} \sim N \left(\begin{pmatrix} 0 \\ 0 \\ 0 \\ 0 \\ 0 \end{pmatrix}, \begin{pmatrix} \sigma_{11} & \sigma_{12} & \sigma_{13} & \sigma_{14} & \sigma_{15} \\ \sigma_{12} & \sigma_{22} & \sigma_{23} & \sigma_{24} & \sigma_{25} \\ \sigma_{13} & \sigma_{23} & \sigma_{33} & \sigma_{34} & \sigma_{35} \\ \sigma_{14} & \sigma_{24} & \sigma_{34} & \sigma_{44} & \sigma_{45} \\ \sigma_{15} & \sigma_{25} & \sigma_{35} & \sigma_{45} & \sigma_{55} \end{pmatrix} \right). \tag{4.11}
$$

4.4.1.1 Normalization of the unobserved effect and the impact upon the observed component of utility

Based on Equation (4.8), only differences in utility matter for the choices made. Selecting one of the alternatives as the base, the utility for this alternative is differenced from the utilities of the remaining alternatives. In order to establish that U_j is the maximum among J utilities, we will make $J-1$ comparisons, and thus be concerned with only $J-1$ random terms, each in the difference of $J-1$ utilities and U_j. The implication for the choice model is that we cannot actually learn about a $J \times J$ covariance matrix Ω from observed outcomes. Some normalization is necessary. There are numerous possible ways that the covariance matrix can be normalized to accommodate this idea. One that works well is simply to normalize "on one of the utility functions"; we make one of the utilities a "base" alternative. The resulting normalized matrix, if this is the last alternative, in our $J = 5$ example, would be:

$$
\varepsilon_{ns} \sim N \left(\begin{pmatrix} 0 \\ 0 \\ 0 \\ 0 \\ 0 \end{pmatrix}, \begin{pmatrix} \theta_{11} & \theta_{12} & \theta_{13} & \theta_{14} & 0 \\ \theta_{12} & \theta_{22} & \theta_{23} & \theta_{24} & 0 \\ \theta_{13} & \theta_{23} & \theta_{33} & \theta_{34} & 0 \\ \theta_{14} & \theta_{24} & \theta_{34} & \theta_{44} & 0 \\ 0 & 0 & 0 & 0 & 1 \end{pmatrix} \right). \tag{4.12}
$$

Even after accommodating the need to think in terms of utilities relative to each other, there remains a loose end in the specification of the covariance matrix. Consider the statement of the random utility model in Equation (4.1), now with our normalization:

$$U_{nsj} - U_{nsi} = (V_{nsj} - V_{nsi}) + (\varepsilon_{nsj} - \varepsilon_{nsi}), \tag{4.13}$$

where $\mathrm{Var}(\varepsilon_{nsj} - \varepsilon_{nsi}) = \theta_{jj}$. Alternative j is most preferred if these differences are all positive. Now, suppose that every utility function is divided by the same positive scale, τ. Our comparison would be:

$$(U_{nsj} - U_{nsi})/\tau = (V_{nsj} - V_{nsi})/\tau + (\varepsilon_{nsj} - \varepsilon_{nsi})/\tau. \tag{4.14}$$

But, the scaling does not affect the comparison. If j were the most preferred alternative without the scaling of the utilities, it is still the preferred alternative after the scaling. The empirical implication is that even after accommodating the idea that, for modeling purposes, utilities are considered only relative to each other, we must also accommodate this scaling ambiguity. Once again, there are many ways to do this by modifying the covariance matrix so that in terms of observable information, the matrix is "observable" (that is, estimable). Again, a straightforward way to proceed is to normalize one more of the remaining variances to one, and implicitly scale the entire remaining matrix. This would appear as follows:

$$\varepsilon_{ns} \sim N\left(\begin{pmatrix} 0 \\ 0 \\ 0 \\ 0 \\ 0 \end{pmatrix}, \begin{pmatrix} \lambda_{11} & \lambda_{12} & \lambda_{13} & \lambda_{14} & 0 \\ \lambda_{12} & \lambda_{22} & \lambda_{23} & \lambda_{24} & 0 \\ \lambda_{13} & \lambda_{23} & \lambda_{33} & \lambda_{34} & 0 \\ \lambda_{14} & \lambda_{24} & \lambda_{34} & 1 & 0 \\ 0 & 0 & 0 & 0 & 1 \end{pmatrix} \right), \tag{4.15}$$

so that throughout the matrix, $\lambda_{ii} = \theta_{ii}/\theta_{44}$ and $\lambda_{ij} = \theta_{ij}/\sqrt{\theta_{44}}$. That is, the normalization process impacts upon the unobserved effects, both variance and covariances related to the J alternatives. We emphasize there are an infinite number of possible ways to normalize and scale the covariance matrix to satisfy the requirements. (See the work of Moshe Ben-Akiva and Joan Walker for studies on different ways that the covariance matrix may be normalized in models based on the normal distribution.) The empirical implication is that the normalization is necessary for "identification." We hope to learn about Ω from observed data. But the observed data on choices only contain a certain amount of information, and no more, without further assumptions by the analyst. Choice data on $J = (5)$ outcomes only provide sufficient information to analyze a matrix such as that in Equation (4.13), or a transformation of such a matrix. Second, we must note that normalization and scaling have implications for the deterministic parts of utility, V_{nsi}, as well as the unobserved part. To see this at work, reconsider the original unnormalized, unscaled model:

$$U_{nsj} = \boldsymbol{\beta}' \mathbf{x}_{nsj} + \varepsilon_{nsj}.$$

We now know based on this discussion that given the observed choice data, we cannot actually learn about $\boldsymbol{\beta}$. Because of the need for a scale normalization – in terms of our 5 choice example, all we can learn about is a scaled vector, $\boldsymbol{\beta}/\sqrt{\theta_{44}}$.

4.4.1.2 An empirical example

In Chapter 3, we provided an empirical example of a data set exploring the relationship between the proportion of people identifying as belonging to a minority group in a voting district and the likelihood that that district elected a Republican or Democrat as their congressional representative during the 2012 United States federal election. In doing so, we reported the results of a binary probit model. Let us now consider a similar study in which we expand the previously used data to consider the multinomial outcome of whether a voting district voted for either a male or female Republican Party member or a male or female Democrat Party member during the 2012 congressional elections. Equation (4.16) sets out the utility functions used in this demonstration. The model has four utility functions with three ASCs, where we set the last ASC associated with voting for male Democratic Party members to zero. For the two utility functions associated with voting for male or female Republican Party members, alternative-specific parameter estimates are used, related to the proportion of people identifying as belonging to a minority group in a voting district. For the two utility functions related to voting for Democrat Party members, we use a dummy variable related to whether the vote took place in one of the 17 Southern States in the United States (i.e., Alabama, Arkansas, Delaware, Florida, Georgia, Kentucky, Louisiana, Maryland, Mississippi, Missouri, North Carolina, Oklahoma, South Carolina, Tennessee, Texas, Virginia, and West Virginia) or not (1 = yes, 0 = no). Alternative-specific parameter estimates are used for these dummy variables. For the last utility function, we also include a variable representing the proportion of the voting district that are female:

$$
\begin{aligned}
U_{rep,fem} &= \beta_{01} + \beta_{min1} minority_n + \varepsilon_{rep,fem}, \\
U_{rep,mal} &= \beta_{02} + \beta_{min2} minority_n + \varepsilon_{rep,mal}, \\
U_{dem,fem} &= \beta_{03} \qquad\qquad\quad + \beta_{sou3} South_n + \varepsilon_{dem,fem}, \\
U_{dem,mal} &= \qquad\qquad\qquad\quad \beta_{sou4} South_n + \beta_{fem4} female + \varepsilon_{dem,mal}.
\end{aligned}
\tag{4.16}
$$

As well as specifying the observed component of utility, it is necessary to also stipulate the covariance matrix of the unobserved terms for the model. We do so in Equation (4.17). In this instance, we normalize the **standard deviations** of all four unobserved error terms to be equal to 1, while estimating a single covariance that is between the first two utility specifications related to districts voting for either a female or male Republican Party member:

$$
\Omega_e =
\begin{pmatrix}
1 & \rho_{12} & 0 & 0 \\
\rho_{12} & 1 & 0 & 0 \\
0 & 0 & 1 & 0 \\
0 & 0 & 0 & 1
\end{pmatrix}.
\tag{4.17}
$$

Referring to Equation (4.13), it is clear that the matrix in Equation (4.17) contains more restrictions than we need for identification. Our choice data would actually allow us to estimate two variances and three covariances in Ω_e. This specification is said to be **overidentified**. Estimation results for the model appear in Table 4.1.

4.4.1.3 Calculating probit choice probabilities

The main obstacle to actual use of the multinomial probit model detailed above until the mid 1990s was the complication of actually computing the multivariate normal probabilities. This section will sketch the problem and the modern solution. Return to the original choice model – the four-outcome case will suffice to demonstrate the computation:

$$
U_{nj} = V_{nj} + \varepsilon_{nj}, j = 1, \ldots, 4 \text{ where }
\begin{pmatrix}
\varepsilon_{n1} \\
\varepsilon_{n2} \\
\varepsilon_{n3} \\
\varepsilon_{n4}
\end{pmatrix}
\sim N
\left[
\begin{pmatrix}
0 \\
0 \\
0 \\
0
\end{pmatrix},
\begin{pmatrix}
\lambda_{11} & \lambda_{21} & \lambda_{31} & 0 \\
\lambda_{21} & \lambda_{22} & \lambda_{32} & 0 \\
\lambda_{31} & \lambda_{32} & 1 & 0 \\
0 & 0 & 0 & 1
\end{pmatrix}
\right].
\tag{4.18}
$$

Table 4.1 Estimated probit model for voting choices

	Republican female		Republican male		Democrat female		Democrat male	
	Par.	(*t*-rat.)	Par.	(*t*-rat.)	Par.	(*t*-rat.)	Par.	(*t*-rat.)
Observed component of utility								
Constant	9.390	(1.96)	9.473	(2.24)	7.129	1.69)	–	–
% Minority	−7.787	(−4.20)	−7.688	(−7.87)	–	–	–	–
Southern State (1 = yes)	–	–	–	–	−1.894	(−6.09)	−1.299	(−5.88)
% Females	–	–	–	–	–	–	15.221	(1.83)
Unobserved component of utility								
Standard dev.	1.000	–	1.000	–	1.000	–	1.000	–
Correlation matrix of unobserved effects								
	Republican female		Republican male		Democrat female		Democrat male	
Republican female	1.000	–	0.997	(8.54)	0.000	–	0.000	–
Republican male	0.997	(8.54)	1.000	–	0.000	–	0.000	–
Democrat female	0.000	–	0.000	–	1.000	–	0.000	–
Democrat male	0.000	–	0.000	–	0.000	–	1.000	–
Model fit								
LL	−383.967							
ρ^2	0.356							

Consider the probability that the individual chooses alternative 1. For convenience at this point, we will drop the observation subscript. This means that:

$$U_1 - U_2 > 0 \text{ or } (V_1 + \varepsilon_1) - (V_2 + \varepsilon_2) > 0 \text{ or } \varepsilon_1 - \varepsilon_2 > V_2 - V_1 \text{ or } w_{12} > A_{12},$$
$$U_1 - U_3 > 0 \text{ or } (V_1 + \varepsilon_1) - (V_3 + \varepsilon_3) > 0 \text{ or } \varepsilon_1 - \varepsilon_3 > V_3 - V_1 \text{ or } w_{13} > A_{13},.$$
$$U_1 - U_4 > 0 \text{ or } (V_1 + \varepsilon_1) - (V_4 + \varepsilon_4) > 0 \text{ or } \varepsilon_1 - \varepsilon_4 > V_4 - V_1 \text{ or } w_{14} > A_{14}.$$

The three random terms, (w_{12}, w_{13}, w_{14}), are linear combinations of joint normally distributed variables, so they are joint normally distributed. The means are obviously (0,0,0). The 3×3 covariance matrix is:

$$\Sigma_{[1]} = \begin{pmatrix} 1 & -1 & 0 & 0 \\ 1 & 0 & -1 & 0 \\ 1 & 0 & 0 & -1 \end{pmatrix} \begin{pmatrix} \lambda_{11} & \lambda_{21} & \lambda_{31} & 0 \\ \lambda_{21} & \lambda_{22} & \lambda_{32} & 0 \\ \lambda_{31} & \lambda_{32} & 1 & 0 \\ 0 & 0 & 0 & 1 \end{pmatrix} \begin{pmatrix} 1 & 1 & 1 \\ -1 & 0 & 0 \\ 0 & -1 & 0 \\ 0 & 0 & -1 \end{pmatrix}$$

$$= \begin{pmatrix} \lambda_{11} + \lambda_{22} - 2\lambda_{12} & \cdots \\ \cdots & \ddots \end{pmatrix}.$$

$$(4.19)$$

We require the trivariate normal probability:

$$\text{Prob(Alt 1 is chosen)} = \int_{V_2-V_1}^{\infty} \int_{V_3-V_1}^{\infty} \int_{V_4-V_1}^{\infty} \phi_3(w_1, w_2, w_3 | \Sigma_{[1]}) dw_3 dw_2 dw_1,$$

$$(4.20)$$

where $\phi_3(\ldots)$ denotes the trivariate normal density in Equation (4.20) with means zero and covariance matrix $\Sigma_{[1]}$. The practical complication is in computing the three variate normal integral. There is no function that can be used. The GHK simulator, invented in the early 1990s, is a method (an algorithm) that is used to approximate these integrals using Monte Carlo simulation. The calculation is approximate, and extremely computer intensive (time consuming) even with modern technology. Simulation-based computations and the GHK simulator are developed in further detail in Chapter 5.

4.4.2 Logit models based on the multivariate Extreme value distribution

The logit model is the most common type of discrete choice model. Logit models are derived under the assumption that the unobserved effects are drawn from a multivariate *generalized Extreme value* (GEV) distribution. GEV distribution on which the model is based is a complex and extremely flexible distribution requiring three parameters to describe its shape and underlying properties. Depending on the values of these parameters, the GEV distribution will collapse to several other types of distributions, for example the Gumbel, Fréchet, and Weibull distributions, otherwise referred to as the Type 1 GEV, Type 2 GEV, and Type 3 GEV distributions, respectively. Logit models are derived under the specific assumption that the unobserved effects are drawn from a Type 1 GEV or Gumbel distribution, which is often referred to simply as an EV1 distribution. Since the model is constructed from a set of EV1 variables, the MEV model applies.

Although the probability density function of the Type 1 GEV model is very different from that of a multivariate normal distribution, visually the two distributions look somewhat similar. The main difference between the two distributions lies in the tail, related to extreme values. Unlike a normal distribution, the Type 1 GEV distribution is skewed. The standardized distribution has a skewness coefficient of +1.13956 compared to zero for the symmetric normal distribution. The tails of the GEV1 distribution are actually thinner than those of the normal – the kurtosis value for the GEV1 is 2.4 compared to 3.0 for the normal.

Before discussing the Type 1 GEV distribution in detail, it is easier to discuss normalization of the logit model first. This is because the properties of the Type 1 GEV distribution will be a function of the model normalization process. The logit model requires the same sorts of identification restrictions as the probit model, with the need to set both the level and scale of utility in order to be able to estimate the parameters of interest. The approach to ensuring identification of the logit model, however, is different from how it is handled within the probit model framework.

The utility functions are:

$$U^*_{nsj} = V^*_{nsj} + \varepsilon^*_{nsj}. \tag{4.21}$$

Let the variance of the unobserved effect for alternative j be $\mathrm{Var}(\varepsilon^*_{nsj}) = \sigma^2_j$. This value equals $\frac{\pi^2}{6\lambda^2_j}$ for the unstandardized Type 1 GEV distribution, where λ_j is the scale parameter mentioned in Section 4.2. As before, because only rankings of alternatives, and not actual utilities, can be observed, it is necessary to normalize the scale of the utility function – we do not have information for estimation of an unknown scale parameter. We do this by scaling the utility by λ_j as:

$$U_{nsj} = \lambda_j V_{nsj} + \varepsilon_{nsj}. \tag{4.22}$$

The standardized GEV1 random variable in (4.22) that does not have a separate scale parameter – i.e., when the scale equals one – has variance $\pi^2/6$. Thus, $\mathrm{Var}(\lambda_j\varepsilon^*_{nsj}) = \frac{\pi^2}{6}$. This is in contrast to the normalized probit model in which the standardized random effect has $\mathrm{Var}[\varepsilon_{nsj}] = 1$. The standardized GEV1 variable also has a non-zero mean, $E[\varepsilon_{nsj}] = 0.57721$ (the constant 0.57721 is the *Euler–Mascheroni constant*, $\gamma = -\Gamma'(1)$).

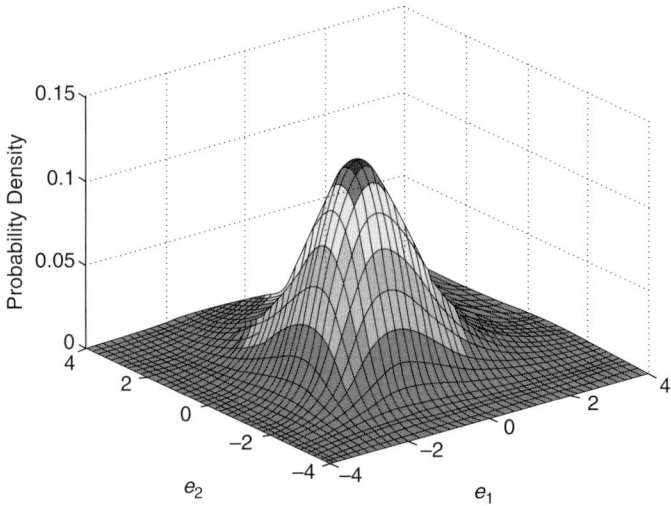

Figure 4.2   GEV distribution for two alternatives

Logit models are usually specified under the general assumption that the variances of the unobserved effects are the same for all alternatives j. Consistent with the notation used earlier, where $\boldsymbol{\varepsilon}^*_{ns} = \langle \varepsilon^*_{ns1}, \ldots, \varepsilon^*_{nsJ} \rangle$ represents the vector of unobserved effects, assuming $J = 5$, we can express Equation (4.22) as Equation (4.23):

$$\varepsilon_{nsj} \sim GEV1 \left(\begin{pmatrix} 0.57721/\lambda_1 \\ 0.57721/\lambda_2 \\ 0.57721/\lambda_3 \\ 0.57721/\lambda_4 \\ 0.57721/\lambda_5 \end{pmatrix}, \begin{pmatrix} \sigma_{11} & \sigma_{12} & \sigma_{13} & \sigma_{14} & \sigma_{15} \\ \sigma_{12} & \sigma_{22} & \sigma_{23} & \sigma_{24} & \sigma_{25} \\ \sigma_{13} & \sigma_{23} & \sigma_{33} & \sigma_{34} & \sigma_{35} \\ \sigma_{14} & \sigma_{24} & \sigma_{34} & \sigma_{44} & \sigma_{45} \\ \sigma_{15} & \sigma_{25} & \sigma_{35} & \sigma_{45} & \sigma_{55} \end{pmatrix} \right). \quad (4.23)$$

Figure 4.2 shows a plot for a Type 1 GEV distribution assuming two alternatives, setting $\lambda_j = 1, \forall j$. Note that we now recognize that different alternatives may have different scale parameters via the inclusion of the subscript j.

The logit model requires the same level and scale normalizations as the probit model in order to be able to estimate the parameters of interest. The approach to ensuring identification of the logit model, however, is different from how it is handled within the probit model framework. Although there exist different types of logit models (e.g., multinomial logit, nested logit, mixed multinomial logit), logit models are generally derived under the assumption

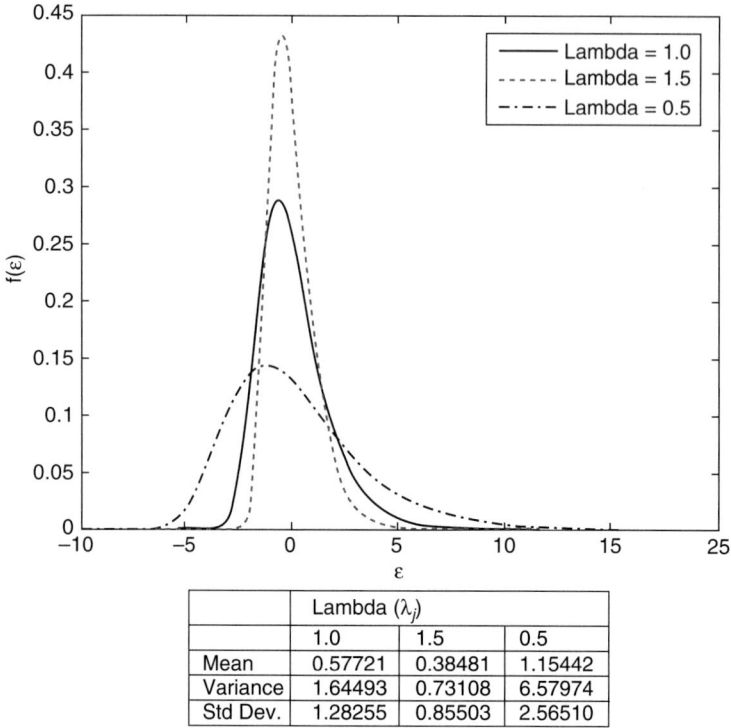

Figure 4.3   EV1 distributions under different scale assumptions

that the variances of the unobserved effects are the same for all alternatives j. The assumption that the variances of the unobserved effects are constant across alternatives j requires some form of normalization of σ_j^2.

> *As an aside*, given that only differences in utility matter, the fact that the mean of the Type 1 GEV distribution is not zero is of no consequence. The difference will be zero for any pair of alternatives, i and j, assuming $\lambda_j = \lambda_i$. Nevertheless, the distribution is clearly dependent on the scale parameter as demonstrated in Figure 4.3, where the probability density function of a **univariate** Type 1 EV distribution is plotted for three different values of σ_j^2.

A further normalization is required in order for the variances of the unobserved effects to be constant across the alternatives. Given that $\mathrm{var}(\varepsilon_{nsj}^*) = \frac{\pi^2}{6\lambda_j^2}$, for the variances of the unobserved effects to be constant across all alternatives, it is also necessary to make λ_j equal for all alternatives. While it is possible to select any value for λ_j, it is most common to set $\lambda_j = 1$ such that

$\mathrm{Var}(\varepsilon_{nsj}) = \frac{\pi^2}{6} = 1.6449$, which is equivalent to saying that $\sigma_{11} = \sigma_{22} = \ldots = \sigma_{55}$ in Equation (4.23). Note that this suggests that normalizing the variance of the unobserved effects is therefore equivalent to normalizing the scale of utility.

Further restrictions or normalizations are imposed, depending on the specific logit model being estimated. The simplest logit model, the *multinomial logit (MNL) model*, restricts all covariances to be zero such that Equation (4.23) becomes:

$$\varepsilon^*_{nsj} \sim IID\ EV1 \left(\begin{pmatrix} 0.57721 \\ 0.57721 \\ 0.57721 \\ 0.57721 \\ 0.57721 \end{pmatrix}, \begin{pmatrix} \pi^2/6 & 0 & 0 & 0 & 0 \\ 0 & \pi^2/6 & 0 & 0 & 0 \\ 0 & 0 & \pi^2/6 & 0 & 0 \\ 0 & 0 & 0 & \pi^2/6 & 0 \\ 0 & 0 & 0 & 0 & \pi^2/6 \end{pmatrix} \right). \tag{4.24}$$

IID is used to indicate that the random variables are independently and identically distributed. Here, "independent" implies zero covariances or correlations between the j unobserved effects, while "identical" implies that the distributions of the unobserved effects are all the same. Note that we have also used the term EV1 in Equation (4.24) as opposed to GEV, as this is more consistent with the language used in the literature.

The computation of the multinomial probit probabilities in Equation (4.20) is complex, and requires an involved approximation that uses Monte Carlo simulation. The expression in Equation (4.10) that involves integrals that need to be approximated is denoted an "open-form" computation. In contrast, the probabilities for a MLN model are considerably simpler, and can be computed in closed form. It has been shown in many sources, such as Train (2009), that for a MLN model:

$$\mathrm{Prob}\ (\mathrm{Alt}\ j\ \text{is chosen}) = \frac{\exp(V_{nsj})}{\sum_{j=1}^{J} \exp(V_{nsj})}, j = 1, \ldots, J. \tag{4.25}$$

Assuming that the utility functions themselves are straightforward, the probabilities in Equation (4.25) can be computed simply by plugging relevant quantities into the formula, with no approximations required. This is one of the appealing features of the logit form of choice model. We do note that, with advances in software and continuous improvements in computing speed, this advantage has become a bit less compelling.

4.4.3 Probit versus logit

In estimating any discrete choice model, because only comparisons of utilities are possible and because there is never any observable information that reveals the scale of the utility functions, it is necessary to normalize both the scale and utility levels in order for the model to be identified. (By "identified" we mean that the feature of the model is estimable with observed data.) As we have seen, the process of normalization of both scale and the utility level differs for logit and probit models, with these differences impacting upon how one should interpret the two models. The variance of the unobserved effects for the logit model are normalized to be equal to 1.0, such that the scale parameter is equal to $\lambda = \sqrt{\frac{\pi^2}{6}} = \sqrt{1.6449}$. This implies that the observed component of the logit model will be precisely $\sqrt{\frac{\pi^2}{6}}$ greater in magnitude than an equivalent probit model in which the scale of the model was normalized to be 1.0. The obvious place that this becomes visible is in the estimated "coefficients" in the utility functions. In general, the probit and logit models do not represent fundamentally different utility structures. Since marginal utilities are estimated only up to scale, the general finding is that in most applications, when otherwise similar models are estimated as probit versus logit specifications, the coefficients in the logit model are usually roughly 1.3–1.5 times larger than those in an otherwise similar probit model.

4.5 Extensions of the basic logit model

The logit (MNL) model with constant variances and zero covariances is a fairly restrictive form. In this regard, the probit model is somewhat more attractive. However, the probit form is rather cumbersome and, as we have seen, still quite complicated to estimate. The logit form is a convenient starting point for a large number of interesting extensions.

Choice analysis has often been described as a way of explaining variations in the behavior of a sample of individuals. The consequence of this view is that a key focus of model development has been the search for increasing sources of variance, or heterogeneity, in the candidate observed and unobserved influences on choice making.

Recent emphasis has been given to the treatment of scale, in particular recognition of variance in utility over different choice situations. This is referred to as **scale heterogeneity**. Scale heterogeneity is a relatively old problem (see Hensher *et al.* 1999 and Louviere 2000, for the historical context), but it is only in recent years that we have seen a concerted effort to develop estimation capability within the family of logit models to account for it at the respondent level. For example, Fiebig *et al.* (2010), formalizing the campaign led by Louviere and his colleagues (1999, 2002, 2006, 2008) to recognize this claimed important source of variability that has been neglected by a focus on revealing preference heterogeneity (now aligned with the mixed logit model). Papers by Breffle and Morey (2000) and Hess *et al.* (2010) are other contributions.

It is early days to be definitive about the empirical implications of the role of scale and the extent to which preference and scale heterogeneity are independent or proportional. What is clear, however, is that the specification of a model that allows for both sources of heterogeneity induces correlation among the observed attributes, and this should be accounted for (see Train and Weeks 2005).

In investigating the potential role of scale heterogeneity, we need to estimate a number of models that accommodate mixtures of **preference heterogeneity** and scale heterogeneity. The sets of interest include, in addition to the basic MNL model, the standard mixed logit model (with random parameters), the MNL model extended to allow for scale heterogeneity, and a **generalized mixed logit** model in which both random parameters (to account for preference heterogeneity) and variation in the variance condition associated with the random component (known as scale heterogeneity) are included.

We have decided not to introduce the mixed logit model with non-linear utility functions until Chapter 20. This general form departs from a standard linear-in-parameters random utility model, with utility functions defined over J_{ns} choices available to individual n in choice situation s, $W(n,s,m) = U(n,s,m) + \varepsilon_{nsm}$, $m = 1,\ldots,J_{ns}$; $s = 1,\ldots,S_i$; $n = 1,\ldots,N$, with the IID, Type I EV1 distribution assumed for the random terms ε_{nsm}. The utility functions that accommodate non-linearity in the unknown parameters, even where the parameters are non-random, are built up from an extension of the mixed multinomial logit (MMNL) structure, outlined in this chapter and Chapter 15.

4.5.1 Heteroskedasticity

As we examined earlier, it is not possible to learn the scales of the utility functions from observed choice data. We did observe, however, that relative scales can be determined. See, for example, Equation (4.15). With the normalization of one of the scale factors to one, we could specify the logit model as:

$$\varepsilon_{nsj}^* \sim EV1 \left(\begin{pmatrix} 0.57721 \\ 0.57721 \\ 0.57721 \\ 0.57721 \\ 0.57721 \end{pmatrix}, \begin{pmatrix} \theta_1^2 \pi^2/6 & 0 & 0 & 0 & 0 \\ 0 & \theta_2^2 \pi^2/6 & 0 & 0 & 0 \\ 0 & 0 & \theta_3^2 \pi^2/6 & 0 & 0 \\ 0 & 0 & 0 & \theta_5^2 \pi^2/6 & 0 \\ 0 & 0 & 0 & 0 & \pi^2/6 \end{pmatrix} \right).$$

$$(4.26)$$

Note that we no longer state that the random terms are IID – they remain independent, but they are not identically distributed. The normalization is $\theta_5 = 1$. The heteroskedasticity specified in Equation (4.26) is with respect to the set of utility functions. All individuals are still characterized by the same scale factor. Later in the book (see Chapter 15) we will examine models in which characteristics of the individuals (such as age, education, income, and gender) also influence the scaling of the utilities. For present purposes, the extension might appear as shown in Equation (4.27):

$$\text{Var}[\varepsilon_{nsj}] = (\theta_j^2 \, \pi^2/6) \exp(\gamma' \mathbf{w}_n). \tag{4.27}$$

θ_j is as in Equation (4.26), $\mathbf{w}_n$ is the set of characteristics indicated, and γ is a set of coefficients to be estimated. With Equation (4.27), we have two types of heterogeneity in the scaling: across the utility functions and across individuals in the population.

A number of authors have used what is known as the Heteroskedastic MNL (HMNL) model to explore issues related to scale heterogeneity (e.g., Dellaert et al. 1998; Hensher et al. 1999, 2013; Louviere et al. 2000; Swait and Adamowicz 2001a, 2001b; Swait and Louviere 1993). The utility specification of the HMNL is given as:

$$U_{nsj} = \left(1 + \sum_q^Q \delta_q w_{nq}\right) \sum_{k=1}^{K} \beta_k x_{nsjk} + \varepsilon_{nsj}, \tag{4.28}$$

where δ_q is a parameter associated with covariate w_q (there being up to Q covariates). The 1 in Equation (4.28) is required if $\sum_q^Q \delta_q w_q$ enters the equation linearly as shown above so that if δ_q equals zero, we revert back to the unscaled model, not to zero (no model). (See e.g., Dellaert *et al.* 1998.) Swait and Adamowicz (2001a, 2001b) assume an exponential formulation like Equation (4.27) for the multiplicative scale and hence can drop the 1. Note that in Equation (4.28), scale is constrained to be positive by taking the exponential of $\sum_q^Q \delta_q w_q$, in which case the 1 is no longer required.

In this model, the parameter estimates associated with each attribute x are fixed parameters while scale is estimated as a function of observables. Dellaert *et al.* (1999) make scale a function of the attribute level differences as well as the attribute levels contained within the data; Swait and Adamowicz (2001) make scale a function of entropy in order to model the influence of task complexity and respondent effort. Hensher *et al.* (2013) make scale a function of the perceived acceptability of an alternative and reported threshold level of attribute acceptance.

Swait and Adamowicz (2001a, 2001b) note that the HMNL model, like the MNL and multinomial probit models, is characterized "by translational and rotational invariance, but unlike the simple MNL model, it does not have the Independence of Irrelevant Alternatives (**IIA**) property" as a result of scale being a function of objectively observable characteristics. DeShazo and Fermo (2002) and Hensher *et al.* (2005) make scale a function of various measures of choice complexity and other factors affecting cognitive effort using a covariance heterogeneity model (see below and Section 14.8 in Chapter 14). Other approaches are based on modeling the variance by using socio-economic characteristics that proxy the ability to deal with cognitive effort, such as familiarity with similar choice tasks in the market place or education attainment (for example, Scarpa *et al.* 2008).

4.5.2 A multiplicative errors model

Fosgerau and Bierlaire (2009) operationalized an alternative discrete choice model that also allows for differences in error variance or scale. Rather than assume a linear additive relationship between the observed and unobserved component of utility, Fosgerau and Bierlaire propose a model in which the two terms are multiplicative such that the utility for alternative j in choice set s held by respondent n may be represented as:

$$U_{nsj} = V_{nsj}\varepsilon_{nsj}. \qquad (4.29)$$

Assuming that both V_{nsj} and ε_{nsj} are positive, Fosgerau and Bierlaire (2009) note that it is possible to take logs of V_{nsj} and ε_{nsj} without affecting choice probabilities, and in doing so the model is equivalent to an additive model, where V_{nsj} is replaced by $\ln(V_{nsj})$. Assuming, for example, that $V_{nsj} < 0$ and $\varepsilon_{nsj} > 0$, Equation (4.29) may be equivalently rewritten as:

$$U_{nsj}^* = -\ln(-V_{nsj}) - \ln \varepsilon_{nsj}. \qquad (4.30)$$

Adopting the assumption that $-\ln(\varepsilon_{nsj}) = {\xi_{nsj}}/{\sigma_n}$, Equation (4.30) then becomes:

$$U_{nsj}^* = -\ln(-V_{nsj}) + {\xi_{nsj}}/{\sigma_n} \quad = -\sigma_n \ln(-V_{nsj}) + \xi_{nsj}. \qquad (4.31)$$

The CDF of the error term for this new model, assuming ε_{nsj} is Extreme value distributed, is:

$$F(\varepsilon) = \exp(-\sigma\varepsilon), \qquad (4.32)$$

that is a generalization of an exponential distribution. This is different to the CDF assumed for logit models and, as such, the multiplicative errors (ME) model might be considered to fall outside of the logit family of discrete choice models. Nevertheless, in estimating Equation (4.29), the authors assumed ε_{nsj} is EV1 distributed. This form can be estimated using Nlogit with the non-linear model form presented in Chapter 20.

4.6 The nested logit model

The most common model used to date in the literature to account for scale heterogeneity is the nested logit (NL) model. The NL model is typically set up with a hierarchical tree-like structure linking alternatives that share common scale or error variances. Each **branch** or nest of the model, which sits above the **(elemental) alternatives** in the tree, also will have its own utility as well as scale. The NL model allows for a (partial) parameterization of scale at each level of the model (after some normalization). The scale parameters within the model are inversely related to the error (co)variances of the common set of alternatives linked to that branch or nest and are multiplicative with the utility of those same alternatives. The NL model is estimated in Chapter 14.

> *As an aside*, The NL tree structure is designed to accommodate the differences in error variances (including correlated alternatives) between alternatives (including the degenerate branch for one alternative), and as such should not be interpreted as a decision tree.

Let λ_b represent the scale parameter at the top branch level or nest and $\mu_{(j|b)}$ represent the scale at the elemental alternative level of the tree. The utility of an alternative located at the lower level of the tree-like structure nested within branch or nest b is given as Equation (4.33):

$$U_{nsj} = \mu_{(j|b)} \sum_{k=1}^{K} \beta_k x_{nsjk} + \varepsilon_{nsj}, \tag{4.33}$$

where $\mu_{(j|b)} = \frac{\pi^2}{6var(\varepsilon_{nsj|b})}$.

From Equation (4.33), the influence of scale and error variance upon utility can clearly be seen. As the error variance increases, the magnitude of $\mu_{(j|b)}$ decreases and hence the observed component of utility decreases. Likewise, a decrease in error variance will result in an increase in $\mu_{(j|b)}$ and an increase in the magnitude of the observed component of utility.

The utility at the upper level of the tree structure is linked to the utility of the alternatives contained within the "nest" below such that:

$$\lambda_b \left(\frac{1}{\mu_{(j|b)}} \log \left(\sum_{b \in j} \exp \left(\mu_{(j|b)} V_{nsj|b} \right) \right) \right), \tag{4.34}$$

where $\mu_{(j|b)} = \frac{\pi^2}{6var(\varepsilon_b)}$ represents the scale at the upper branch level.

The NL model remains over-parameterized, requiring the normalization of one or more parameters for model identification. It is typical to normalize either $\mu_{(j|b)}$, or λ_b to 1.0 for one or more of the branches or nests. Normalizing $\mu_{(j|b)} = 1.0$ results in models that are said to be normalized to random utility 1 (RU1) while normalizing $\lambda_b = 1.0$ produces random utility 2 (RU2) models (see, e.g., Carrasco and Ortúzar 2002 and Hensher and Greene 2002). In either case, what is actually being estimated in the model is λ_b or $\frac{1}{\mu_{(j|b)}}$, rather than both $\mu_{(j|b)}$ and λ_b separately. The estimated parameters are often referred to as **inclusive value**, or IV parameters within the literature. In Chapter 14 we use the RU2 specification, given the controversy over whether an upper or lower normalization is appropriate (see Ortúzar and Willumsen (2011), 241–8 for an overview of the debate).

In addition to allowing for different scales across subsets of alternatives, the NL model also induces correlations between the utilities for alternatives contained within a common branch (Ben-Akiva and Lerman 1985). The correlation structure for alternatives i and j in branch b is given as Equation (4.35):

$$corr(U_{j|b}, U_{i|b}) = 1 - \frac{\lambda_b}{\mu_{(j|b)}}.$$

(4.35)

The link between the scales contained at each level of the tree structure can best be seen when examining the choice probabilities produced from the NL model. These are calculated using Equation (4.36):

$$P_{nsj} = P_{njs|b}.P_{nbs}$$

$$= \frac{\exp\left(\mu_{(j|b)} V_{nsj|b}\right)}{\sum_{i\in J_b} \exp\left(\mu_{(i|b)} V_{nsi|b}\right)} \cdot \frac{\exp\left(\frac{\lambda_b}{\mu_{(j|b)}}\log\left(\sum_{b\in J_b}\exp\left(\mu_{(j|b)} V_{nsj|b}\right)\right)\right)}{\sum_{b=1}^{B}\exp\left(\frac{\lambda_b}{\mu_{(i|b)}}\log\left(\sum_{i\in J_b}\exp\left(\mu_{(i|b)} V_{nsi|b}\right)\right)\right)},$$

(4.36)

where $P_{njs|b}$ is the conditional probability that respondent n will select alternative j in choice task s given that alternative j belongs to branch b and P_{nbs} is the probability of respondent n choosing branch b.

In estimating the model, $E(P_{nsj})$ is substituted for the probability given in Equation (4.36). As such, the model does not have a panel specification equivalent.

4.6.1 Correlation and the nested logit model

The model with a full unrestricted covariance matrix is not estimable. But we have just seen that various restrictions allow the estimation of some extensions of the basic model. Thus, in Equation (4.26), the assumption of zero covariances and normalization of θ_5 to one allows the estimation of four relative variances. The model in (4.26) is, in fact, "overidentified." There are actually more restrictions than necessary. We were able to estimate a probit model with some covariances across the utilities. The same is true of the logit model.

For example, Equation (4.37) shows a configuration in which there are two covariance parameters that allow correlation across two sets of alternatives:

$$\varepsilon_{nsj}^* \sim EV1 \left(\begin{pmatrix} 0.57721 \\ 0.57721 \\ 0.57721 \\ 0.57721 \\ 0.57721 \end{pmatrix}, \begin{pmatrix} \sigma^2 & \sigma_a & \sigma_a & 0 & 0 \\ \sigma_a & \sigma^2 & \sigma_a & 0 & 0 \\ \sigma_a & \sigma_a & \sigma^2 & 0 & 0 \\ 0 & 0 & 0 & \sigma^2 & \sigma_b \\ 0 & 0 & 0 & \sigma_b & \sigma^2 \end{pmatrix} \right). \tag{4.37}$$

The configuration in Equation (4.37) gives rise to a "nested logit model." Consider, for example, a choice setting in transport with five alternatives, (bus, train, light rail) and (car as passenger, car as driver). The five alternatives are arranged in two blocks of "similar" alternatives. We can imagine a choice process suggested by a tree such as:

	————— Public —————	Bus
		Train
Commute		Light rail
	————— Private —————	Car/Passenger
		Car/Driver

A choice model such as the one in Equation (4.37) might be suggested by this arrangement.

4.6.2 The covariance heterogeneity logit model

The covariance heterogeneity logit (CHL) model extends the NL model by allowing a decomposition of the inclusive value parameters (see Section 14.8 in Chapter 14). This is accomplished by making the scale parameters a function of covariates, as shown in Equation (4.38) where δ_q and w_q are as previously defined (in Equation 4.28):

$$\mu_{(j|b)}^* = \mu_{(j|b)} \times e^{\sum_{q=1}^{Q} \delta_q w_q}. \tag{4.38}$$

The scale parameters in Equation (4.36), for example, are replaced by Equation (4.38) in the CHL model, while the exponentiation of $\sum_{q}^{Q} \delta_q w_q$ ensures that scale remains positive.

4.7 Mixed (random parameters) logit model

The mixed logit model differs from the MNL model in that it assumes that at least some of the parameters are random, following a certain probability distribution, as suggested earlier in Equation (4.4). These random parameter distributions are assumed to be continuous over the sampled population. This model form takes on many names including mixed logit, random parameters logit, kernel logit, and mixed multinomial logit (MMNL). The choice probabilities of the MMNL model, P_n^*, therefore now depends on the random parameters with distributions defined by the analyst. The MMNL model is summarized in Equation (4.39):

$$\text{Prob}(choice_{ns} = j | \mathbf{x}_{nsj}, \mathbf{z}_n, \mathbf{v}_n) = \frac{\exp(V_{nsj})}{\sum_{j=1}^{J_{ns}} \exp(V_{nsj})} \tag{4.39}$$

where

$$V_{nsj} = \boldsymbol{\beta}_n' \mathbf{x}_{nsj}$$

$$\boldsymbol{\beta}_n = \boldsymbol{\beta} + \boldsymbol{\Delta} \mathbf{z}_n + \boldsymbol{\Gamma} \mathbf{v}_n.$$

$\mathbf{x}_{nsj}$ = the K attributes of alternative j in choice situation c faced by individual n;

$\mathbf{z}_n$ = a set of M characteristics of individual n that influence the mean of the taste parameters; and

$\mathbf{v}_n$ = a vector of K random variables with zero means and known (usually unit) variances and zero covariances.

The multinomial choice model embodies both observed and unobserved heterogeneity in the preference parameters of individual n. Observed heterogeneity is reflected in the term $\boldsymbol{\Delta} \mathbf{z}_n$ while the unobserved heterogeneity is embodied in $\boldsymbol{\Gamma} \mathbf{v}_n$. The structural parameters to be estimated are the constant vector, $\boldsymbol{\beta}$, the $K \times M$ matrix of parameters $\boldsymbol{\Delta}$, and the non-zero elements of the lower triangular **Cholesky matrix, $\boldsymbol{\Gamma}$**.

A number of interesting special cases are straightforward modifications of the model. Specific non-random parameters are specified by rows of zeros in $\boldsymbol{\Gamma}$. A pure random parameters MNL model results if $\boldsymbol{\Delta} = \mathbf{0}$ and $\boldsymbol{\Gamma}$ is diagonal. The basic multinomial logit model results[1] if $\boldsymbol{\Delta} = \mathbf{0}$ and $\boldsymbol{\Gamma} = \mathbf{0}$.

---

[1] One can, however, allow for deterministic taste heterogeneity via interaction terms with respondent-specific characteristics.

The expected probability over the random parameter distribution can be written as:

$$E(P_n^*) = \int_{\beta} P_n^*(\beta) f(\beta)|\Omega) d\beta, \tag{4.40}$$

where $f(\beta|\Omega)$ is the multivariate probability density function of β given the distributional parameters θ. By using a transformation of β such that the multivariate distribution becomes semi-parametrical, we can write Equation (4.40) as:

$$E(P_n^*) = \int_{z} P_n^*\Big(\beta(z|\Omega)\Big) \phi(z) dz, \tag{4.41}$$

where $\beta(z|\Omega)$ is a function of z with parameters Ω, and where $\phi(z)$ is the multivariate non-parametrical distribution of z. It is common to use several (independent) univariate distributions[2] instead of using a single multivariate distribution, such that Equation (4.41) can be written as:

$$E(P_n^*) = \int_{z_1} \cdots \int_{z_K} P_n^*\Big(\beta_1(z_1|\theta_1), \ldots, \beta_K(z_K|\theta_K)\Big) \phi_1(z_1) \cdots \phi_K(z_K) dz_1 \cdots dz_K. \tag{4.42}$$

Having separate univariate distributions for each parameter has the benefit that different distributions can be easily mixed. For example, if $\beta_1 \sim N(\mu, \sigma)$, and $\beta_2 \sim U(a, b)$, then $E(P_n^*)$ is written as:

$$E(P_n^*) = \int_{z_1} \int_{z_2} P_n^*\Big(\beta_1(z_1|\mu, \sigma), \beta_2(z_2|a, b)\Big) \phi_1(z_1) \phi_2(z_2) dz_1 dz_2, \tag{4.43}$$

where $\beta_1(z_1|\mu, \sigma) = \mu + \sigma z_1$ with $z_1 \sim N(0, 1)$ following a standard normal distribution, and $\beta_2(z_2|a, b) = a + (b - a)z_2$ with $z_2 \sim U(0, 1)$ following a standard uniform distribution. Other distributions can be used as well, such as the log-normal distribution in which the transformation $\beta(z|\mu, \sigma) = e^{\mu} e^{\sigma z}$ is used, with $z \sim N(0, 1)$. Note that a fixed parameter is a special case of a random parameter, such that all equations also hold in the case that only some

---

[2] Note that if one would not like to assume independent random variables, then one can sample directly from the multivariate distribution. In the case of a multivariate normal distribution, this is possible through a Cholesky decomposition (see, e.g., Greene 2002).

of the parameters are considered random. For a fixed parameter β_k we simply take $\beta_k(z_k|\mu_k) = \mu_k$, and $\phi_k(z) = 1$.

In Chapter 15, we discuss the range of distributional assumptions and set up a MMNL model to allow for heterogeneity in the mean of a random parameter, as well as heteroskedasticity and heterogeneity in the variance of a random parameter, recognizing the possibility of correlated random parameters.

4.7.1 Cross-sectional and panel mixed multinomial logit models

MMNL models can be estimated using a single **cross-section** data set or a **panel data** set. An example of the latter is *stated choice data* (see Chapter 6), in which a respondent is offered a sequence of choice sets and asked to make a choice of an alternative from each choice set. This data, often called an "instantaneous panel," engenders (potential) correlation between observations common to a respondent.

The log-likelihood (LL) functions of the cross-sectional MMNL are derived under the same assumptions of choice observation independence as made with the MNL model. The difference between these two models and the MNL model, however, is that the choice probabilities used for the MNL are replaced with the expected choice probabilities given in Equation (4.40). Using the same mathematical rules used to derive the MNL model LL function, and noting additionally that because of independence $E(P_1 P_{n2}) = E(P_1)E(P_{n2})$, the LL function of the cross-sectional MMNL model may be represented as:

$$\log E(L_N) = \sum_{n=1}^{N} \sum_{s \in S_n} \sum_{j \in J_{ns}} y_{nsj} \log E(P_{nsj}). \tag{4.44}$$

The derivation of the LL functions of the panel formulations of the MMNL model differs from those of their equivalent cross-sectional forms, as well as from that of the MNL model, in that the choice observations are no longer assumed to be independent within each respondent (although the independence across respondents' assumption is maintained). Mathematically, this means that $E(P_1 P_2) \neq E(P_1)E(P_2)$, hence the LL functions of the panel MMNL may be represented as:

$$\log E(L_N) = \sum_{n=1}^{N} \log E \left(\prod_{s \in S_n} \prod_{j \in J_{ns}} (P_{nsj})^{y_{nsj}} \right), \tag{4.45}$$

or:

$$\log(L_N) = \sum_{n=1}^{N} \log E(P_n^*). \tag{4.46}$$

4.7.2 Error components model

It is possible to estimate an alternative specification to Equation (4.4), leading to a utility heteroskedastic interpretation. This approach is commonly referred to as the error components (EC) model (details in Section 15.8 of Chapter 15), a model which has been proposed as an elegant way to account for flexible **substitution patterns** across alternatives which goes beyond the patterns typically achievable by means of generalized Extreme value models, such as the nested and cross-nested logit models presented above and in Chapter 14 (see Brownstone and Train 1999).

Alternatives whose utility have some form of covariance share error components, which are typically distributed zero-mean random normal with a standard deviation to be estimated. As such, the estimation of error components requires that x takes the value 1 for the subset of alternatives under consideration or zero otherwise. That is, rather than associating different attributes or other such variables, EC models use a series of dummy variables to place subsets of alternatives into different "branches" or "nests." In this way, the model may approximate a covariance structure more complex than the typical NL model by forming complex covariance structures between alternatives. Dropping subscript s, the EC model becomes:

$$U_{nsj} = \sum_{k=1}^{K} \beta_k x_{nsjk} \pm \sum_{l=1}^{L} \eta_l z_{lns} d_{lb}, +\varepsilon_{nsj}, \tag{4.47}$$

where $d_{lb} = \begin{cases} 1 & \text{if } j \text{ is in nest } b \\ 0 & \text{otherwise.} \end{cases}$

The interpretation of the ECs therefore relates to their associations with specific alternatives and not with attributes as with more traditional random taste models. Each estimated EC represents the residual random error variances linking those alternatives, and by estimating different ECs for different subsets of alternatives it is possible to estimate complex correlation structures among the error variances of the various alternatives being modeled. Indeed, the use of ECs in a model induces particular covariance structures among the modeled alternatives, and hence represents a relaxation of the IID assumption typically associated with most logit type models.

The covariance structure is shown in Equation (4.48):

$$Cov(U_{nsi}, U_{nsj}) = E(\eta_i z_{nsi} d_{bi} + \varepsilon_{nsi})'(\eta_j z_{nsj} d_{bj} + \varepsilon_{nsj})$$
$$= \begin{cases} \vartheta_b & \text{if alts } i \text{ are in nest } b \\ 0 & \text{otherwise.} \end{cases} \tag{4.48}$$

With variance for each alternative in nest b equal to:

$$Var(U_{nsj}) = E(\eta_j z_{nsj} d_{bj} + \varepsilon_{nsj})^2 = \vartheta_b + \pi^2/6\sigma_n^2. \tag{4.49}$$

An EC model form can be included in a random parameters logit model or can be applied with fixed parameters. In addition, systematic sources of influence on the mean estimates of the variance parameters associated with each error component can also be explored (see Section 15.8 of Chapter 15). See Greene and Hensher (2007) for further details.

4.8 Generalized mixed logit

The generalized mixed logit model builds on the specifications of the mixed logit model developed in Train (2003, 2009), Hensher and Greene (2003), and Greene (2007), among others, and the "generalized multinomial logit model" proposed in Fiebig et al. (2010) – see also Greene and Hensher (2010b).

A growing number of authors has stated that the mixed logit model and multinomial choice models, more generally, do not adequately account for scale heterogeneity (e.g., Feibig et al. 2010 and Keane 2006). Scale heterogeneity across choices is easily accommodated in the model already considered by random alternative-specific constants. As in the earlier implementation, we accommodate both observed and unobserved heterogeneity in the model.

The starting position is the standard mixed multinomial logit model, Equation (4.39), modified accordingly as Equation (4.50) (see also Section 15.10 of Chapter 15):

$$\beta_n = \sigma_n[\beta + \Delta z_n] + [\gamma + \sigma_n(1 - \gamma)] \Gamma v_n, \tag{4.50}$$

where

$\sigma_n = \exp[\ \bar{\sigma} + \boldsymbol{\delta}'\mathbf{h}_n + \tau w_n]$, the individual specific standard deviation of the idiosyncratic error term;

$\mathbf{h}_n$ = a set of L characteristics of individual n that may overlap with $\mathbf{z}_n$;

$\boldsymbol{\delta}$ = the parameters in the observed heterogeneity in the scale term;

w_n = the unobserved heterogeneity, standard normally distributed;

$\bar{\sigma}$ = a mean parameter in the variance;

τ = the coefficient on the unobserved scale heterogeneity;

γ = a weighting parameter that indicates how variance in residual preference heterogeneity varies with scale, with $0 \leq \gamma \leq 1$.

The weighting parameter, γ, is central to the generalized model. It controls the relative importance of the overall scaling of the utility function, σ_n, versus the scaling of the individual preference weights contained in the diagonal elements of $\boldsymbol{\Gamma}$. Note that if σ_n equals one (i.e., $\tau = 0$), then γ falls out of the model and Equation (4.50) reverts back to the base case random parameters model in Equation (4.39). A non-zero γ cannot be estimated apart from $\boldsymbol{\Gamma}$ when σ_n equals one. When σ_n is not equal to one, then γ will spread the influence of the random components between overall scaling and the scaling of the preference weights. In addition to the useful special cases of the original mixed model, some useful special cases arise in this model. If $\gamma = 0$, then a scaled mixed logit model emerges, given in Equation (4.51):

$$\boldsymbol{\beta}_n = \sigma_n[\boldsymbol{\beta} + \Delta \mathbf{z}_n + \boldsymbol{\Gamma} \mathbf{v}_n]. \tag{4.51}$$

If, further, $\boldsymbol{\Gamma} = \mathbf{0}$ and $\boldsymbol{\Delta} = \mathbf{0}$, a "scaled multinomial logit" (SMNL) model is implied (Equation (4.52)). This is a MNL model (i.e., no random parameters) with scale allowed to vary across the sample:

$$\boldsymbol{\beta}_n = \sigma_n \boldsymbol{\beta}. \tag{4.52}$$

The full model, in the unrestricted form or in any of the modifications, is estimated by maximum simulated likelihood (see see Chapter 5). Fiebig *et al.* (2010) note two minor complications in estimation. Firstly, the parameter $\bar{\sigma}$ in σ_n is not separately identified from the other parameters of the model. We will assume that the variance heterogeneity is normally distributed. Neglecting the observed heterogeneity (i.e., $\boldsymbol{\delta}'\mathbf{h}_n$) for the moment, it will follow from the general result for the **expected value** of a log-normal variable that $E[\sigma_n] = \exp (\bar{\sigma} + \tau^2/2)$. That is, $\sigma_n = \exp(\bar{\sigma})\exp(\tau w_n)$ where $w_n \sim N(0,1)$, so $E[\sigma_n] = \exp(\bar{\sigma})E[\exp(\tau w_n)] = \exp(\bar{\sigma})\exp\big(E[\tau w_n] + \frac{1}{2}\mathrm{Var}[\tau w_n]\big) = \exp(\bar{\sigma} + \tau^2/2)$.

It follows that $\bar{\sigma}$ is not identified separately from τ, which appears nowhere else in the model. Some normalization is required. A natural normalization would be to set $\bar{\sigma} = 0$. However, it is more convenient to normalize σ_n so that $E[\sigma_n^2] = 1$, by setting $\bar{\sigma} = -\tau^2/2$ instead of zero.

A second complication concerns the variation in σ_n during the simulations. The log-normal distribution implied by $\exp(-\tau^2/2 + \tau w_n)$ can produce extremely large draws and lead to overflows and instability of the estimator. To accommodate this concern, in Nlogit we have truncated the standard normal distribution of w_n at -1.96 and $+1.96$. In contrast to Fiebig *et al.* who propose an acceptance/rejection method for the random draws, we have used a one draw method, $w_{nr} = \Phi^{-1}[.025 + .95U_{nr}]$, where $\Phi^{-1}(t)$ is the inverse of the standard normal CDF and U_{nr} is a random draw from the standard uniform population. This will maintain the smoothness of the estimator in the random draws. The acceptance/rejection approach requires, on average, $1/.95$ draws to obtain an acceptable draw, while the inverse probability approach always requires exactly one.

Finally, in order to impose the limits on γ, γ is reparameterized in terms of α, where $\gamma = \exp(\alpha)/[1 + \exp(\alpha)]$ and α is unrestricted. Likewise, to ensure $\tau \geq 0$, the model is fit in terms of λ, where $\tau = \exp(\lambda)$ and λ is unrestricted. **Restricted** versions in which it is desired to restrict $\gamma = 1$ or 0 and/or $\tau = 0$ are imposed directly during the estimation, rather than using Extreme values of the underlying parameters, as in previous studies. Thus, in estimation, the restriction $\gamma = 0$ is imposed directly, rather than using, for example, $\alpha = -10.0$ or some other large value. See Section 15.9 of Chapter 15, where we estimate a number of generalized mixed logit models.

4.8.1 Models estimated in willingness to pay space

This generalized mixed model also provides a straightforward method of reparameterizing the model to estimate the taste parameters in willingness to pay (WTP) space, which has recently become a behaviorally appealing alternative way of directly obtaining an estimate of WTP. It is possible to re-specify the utility function so as to estimate the WTP estimates directly when these are of primary empirical interest (see Train and Weeks 2005; Fosgerau 2007, 2007; Scarpa *et al.* 2008; Sonnier *et al.* 2007; Hensher and Greene 2011). Given Equation (4.50), if $\gamma = 0$, $\Delta = 0$ and the element of $\boldsymbol{\beta}$ corresponding to the cost variable β_c is normalized to 1.0 while a non-zero constant is moved outside the brackets, the following reparameterized model emerges:

$$\boldsymbol{\beta}_n = \sigma_n \boldsymbol{\beta}_c \left[\left(\tfrac{1}{\tfrac{1}{\beta_c}} \right) (\boldsymbol{\beta} + \boldsymbol{\Gamma} \mathbf{v}_n) \right] = \sigma_n \boldsymbol{\beta}_c \left[\boldsymbol{\theta}_c + \boldsymbol{\Gamma}_c \mathbf{v}_n \right]. \tag{4.53}$$

In the simple multinomial logit case ($\sigma_n = 1$, $\boldsymbol{\Gamma} = \mathbf{0}$), this is a one to one transformation of the parameters of the original model. Where the parameters are random, however, the transformation is no longer that simple. We, as well as Train and Week (2005), have found, in application, that this form of the transformed model produces generally much more reasonable estimates of WTP for individuals in the sample than the model in the original form in which WTP is computed using ratios of parameters (Hensher and Greene 2011).[3]

Assuming utility is separable in price, c_{nsj}, and other non-price attributes x_{nsjk} it is possible write out Equation (4.54) in WTP space:

$$\begin{aligned} U_{nsj} &= \sigma_n \left[c_{nsj} + \frac{1}{\beta_{nc}} \sum_{k=1}^{K} \beta_{nk} x_{nsjk} \right] + \varepsilon_{nsj}, \\ &= \sigma_n c_{nsj} + \sigma_n \sum_{k=1}^{K} \theta_{nk} x_{nsjk} + \varepsilon_{nsj} \end{aligned} \tag{4.54}$$

where the price parameter has been normalized to 1.0 and where θ_{nk} represents a direct parameterization of WTP for the remaining non-price attributes x_{nsjk}. As can be seen from Equation (4.54), scale also plays a dominant role in the model. Indeed, this is noted by Scarpa *et al.* (2008), who discuss the confound between scale and preference heterogeneity, stating that

If the scale parameter varies and [the taste parameters] are fixed, then the utility coefficients vary with perfect correlation. If the utility coefficients have correlation less than unity, then [the taste parameters] are necessarily varying in addition to, or instead of, the scale parameter. Finally, even if [the scale parameter] does not vary over [respondents] . . ., utility coefficients can be correlated simply due to correlations among tastes for various attributes.

Applications to date indicate that it remains an empirical matter whether specific data sets support utility specifications in the conventional preference space or in the specialized WTP space (Balcombe *et al.* 2009). However, it is clear that WTP space specifications afford the researcher much more control

---

[3] The paper by Hensher and Greene (2011), like Train and Weeks (2005) supports the WTP space framework for estimating WTP distributions given that the evidence on the range is behaviorally more plausible, despite the overall goodness-of-fit being inferior to the utility space specifications.

on the distributional features of marginal WTP in the underlying population (Thiene and Scarpa 2009).

4.9 The latent class model

A popular alternative to the MMNL model, in which we have a continuous distribution on the random parameters, is a latent class (LC) model in which discrete distributions are used to define the underlying latent structure of preferences as represented by parameters assigned to explanatory variables through a class assignment that is an alternative way of representing preferences. Intuitively, what we have in a LC model is a number of classes that each describes the role of specific attributes up to a probability of class membership of the sample of respondents. If one had a very large number of classes (say, 200) then one would start to see what looks like a continuous distribution for a parameter estimate associated with an attribute, each level being relevant according to the probability of class membership. It is this interpretation that places the LC model within the broad setting of mixed logit models. In addition, for **fixed parameters** within a class, it is also possible to allow random parameterization within a class, as we show in Section 16.3. Chapter 16 develops and applies in some detail the LC model in its fixed and random parameter form; in this chapter we set out the fixed parameter version only to highlight the main elements of this model form.

The choice probabilities for the LC model differ somewhat from those given by the previous models. Beginning with the MNL model (the framework in which most LC models are developed), there now exist three sets of probabilities calculated by the LC model. Firstly, consider the probability that a sampled respondent belongs to a particular LC, c. Within the LC model, this probability is derived via the class assignment model, and is given in Equation (4.55):

$$P_{nc} = \frac{\exp(V_{nc})}{\sum_{c \in C} \exp(V_{nC})}, \tag{4.55}$$

where $V_{nc} = \delta_c h_n$, represents the observed component of utility from the class assignment model and h_n are respondent-specific covariates that condition class membership.

In addition to the class assignment probability, there also exists a probability of respondent n selecting alternative j in choice situation s given membership of class c. This we represent in Equation (4.56):

$$P_{nsj|c} = \frac{\exp(V_{nsj|c})}{\sum_i \exp(V_{nsi|c})},$$ (4.56)

where $V_{nsj|c}$ represents the observed component of utility.

The LC model can be estimated on either a single cross-section or a panel data set, just like the MMNL model. This distinction between the cross-sectional and panel formulations has implications for the specification of the estimable model. Moving from an assumption of independence of choice observations (a cross-section) to one where the marginal utilities within respondent are correlated impacts (a panel) on Equation (4.55) will influence the parameter estimates. Equation (4.56) may also be calculated in both versions of the LC model; however, what is directly being modeled in the panel formulation of the model is not the within choice task choice probabilities as given by Equation (4.56), but the probability of observing the particular sequences of choices made. Mathematically, this is represented as the product of the probabilities calculated in Equation (4.56). We represent this now as Equation (4.57):

$$P_{nj|c} = \prod_s \frac{\exp(V_{nsj|c})}{\sum_i \exp(V_{nsi|c})}.$$ (4.57)

Both versions of the LC model calculate a set of probabilities conditioned on the observed choices (which we term alternative conditioned class probabilities). This final set of probabilities are calculated based on both the class assignment probabilities (Equation (4.55)) and the within choice situation choice probabilities (Equation (4.56)) in the cross-sectional formulation of the model and Equation (4.57) in the panel version, all conditioned on the observed choices. We represent these probabilities for the cross-sectional and panel formulations of the model as Equations (4.58) and (4.59), respectively:

$$P_{ns|c} = \frac{y_{nsi}P_{nsj|c}.P_{nc}}{\sum_{c \in C} y_{nsi}P_{nsi|c}.P_{nc}}, \forall c \in C.$$ (4.58)

$$P_{ns|c} = \frac{\prod_s y_{nsi} P_{nsj|c} \cdot P_{nc}}{\sum_{c \in C} \prod_s y_{nsi} P_{nsj|c} \cdot P_{nc}}, \forall c \in C. \tag{4.59}$$

If the number of choice tasks observed per respondent equals one, then Equation (4.59) will collapse to Equation (4.58). Analysts wanting to use the LC model in its various forms can now go to Chapter 16.

4.10 Concluding remarks

This chapter has taken the reader on a journey through the (historical) development of discrete choice models, mainly logit (and some limited discussion of probit), to show the growth in behavioral richness that is now available in the progression of choice models from the very basic multinomial logit to the advanced versions of mixed multinomial logit. The latter can allow for scale and preference heterogeneity in various guises including decomposition to recognize sources of the systematic explanation of variation in the distribution of preferences and scale in a sample.

A challenge for the analyst is to compare the model forms, noting the progression in behavioral richness in closed-form models (MNL and nested logit) where a partial relaxation of IID occurs, and the migration to open-form models associated with the growing family of mixed multinomial logit models that allow for continuous preference distributions for observed attributes describing alternatives as well as variance heterogeneity (through scale and error components) in the unobserved influences on utility. The LC model form is linked to the open-form mixed multinomial logit model through a discrete (in contrast to a continuous) distribution of attribute parameterization through class assignment, as well as allowing for continuous distributions on parameters within a class.

In several of the following chapters (especially Chapters 11–16), we show the user how to estimate the full range of models presented in this chapter, including applying the statistical tests presented in Chapter 7.

5   Estimating discrete choice models

An approximate answer to the right problem is worth a good deal more than an exact answer to an approximate problem.

(Tukey 1962)

5.1 Introduction

Chapters 3 and 4 introduced a number of new concepts and models to the reader, including the probit and logit models. As seen in Chapter 4, probit and logit models are derived under different assumptions about the error term. For probit models, the error terms are assumed to be multivariate Normally distributed, while logit models assume a multivariate extreme value Type 1 distribution, or some restriction thereof. In Chapter 4, we briefly discussed the fact that discrete choice models are estimated using a method known as maximum likelihood estimation. The current chapter seeks to explain maximum likelihood estimation in the context of discrete choice models. In doing so, we also briefly discuss several of the more common algorithms used in estimating discrete choice models.

In addition to discussing maximum likelihood estimation, we also introduce the related concept of simulated maximum likelihood. A number of the models introduced in Chapter 4 do not have analytically tractable solutions when one attempts to compute their choice probabilities. Such models are said to be of open form, requiring simulation of the choice probabilities. We therefore discuss the several common simulation approaches used in estimating discrete choice models.

5.2 Maximum likelihood estimation

Given data, the objective of the analyst is to estimate the unknown parameters, β. While there exist several methods to do so, the most common approach when dealing with discrete choice data is to use a method known as maximum likelihood estimation. Maximum likelihood estimation involves the analyst specifying some objective function, known as a likelihood function, where the only unknowns are the parameters which are related to the data via the analyst's defined utility specifications, and then maximizing the function. Given that the parameters are the only unknowns, the data being fixed, they remain the only component of the equation that can change in maximizing the likelihood function. The difficulty therefore is in deriving a likelihood function that is appropriate for the problem, identifying the parameters that best fit the data.

The likelihood function of discrete choice models is designed to maximize the choice probabilities associated with the alternatives that are observed to be chosen in the data. That is, the likelihood function is defined in such a way as to maximize the predictions obtained by the model. To demonstrate, let y_{nsj} equal one if j is the chosen alternative in choice situation s faced by decision maker n, and zero otherwise. In other words, y represents the observed choice outcomes within some data. Then the parameters can be estimated by maximizing the likelihood function L:

$$L_{NS} = \prod_{n=1}^{N} \prod_{s \in S_n} \prod_{j \in J_{ns}} (P_{nsj})^{y_{nsj}}. \tag{5.1}$$

where N denotes the total number of decision makers, S_n is the set of choice situations faced by decision maker n, and P_{nsj} is a function of the data and unknown parameters β.

To appreciate how Equation (5.1) works, consider an example data set involving two decision makers who were observed to have each made choices in two separate choice situations. Let us assume that the first decision maker had three alternatives to choose from in the first situation, coded 1, 2, and 3, but only the first two alternatives in the second situation. Further, let us assume that the second decision maker observed alternatives 2 and 3 in the first choice situation but had four alternatives in the second choice situation they faced, coded 1, 2, 3, and 4. Let each alternative be represented by three attributes, x_1, x_2, and x_3 and that the model has generic parameters, with no constants. The data as described are presented in Table 5.1 alongside an indicator variable, y_{nsj}, representing which of the j alternatives were observed to have been chosen in each choice situation s.

Let us assume that the analyst has estimated the parameters related to x_1, x_2, and x_3 to be −0.2, 0.2, and 0.2, respectively. Based on these parameters, the

Table 5.1 Example of likelihood estimation: 1

N	S	J	y_{nsj}	x_1	x_2	x_3	V_{nsj}	P_{nsj}	$P_{nsj}^{y_{nsj}}$
1	1	1	0	15	4	6	−1.000	0.115	1.000
1	1	2	1	5	2	6	0.600	0.571	0.571
1	1	3	0	10	6	4	0.000	0.313	1.000
1	2	1	1	10	4	4	−0.400	0.354	0.354
1	2	2	0	5	2	4	0.200	0.646	1.000
2	1	2	1	15	6	2	−1.400	0.731	0.731
2	1	3	0	20	4	4	−2.400	0.269	1.000
2	2	1	0	20	6	6	−1.600	0.221	1.000
2	2	2	0	15	4	2	−1.800	0.181	1.000
2	2	3	1	10	2	2	−1.200	0.329	0.329
2	2	4	0	15	4	4	−1.400	0.270	1.000
								$L_{NS} =$	**0.049**

utilities associated with each of the alternatives are calculated, as are the choice probabilities, assuming an MNL model. The utilities and choice probabilities are also given in Table 5.1. Given the choice probabilities, we are able to apply Equation (5.1) to calculate the likelihood function. Noting that for $y_{nsj} = 0$, $(P_{nsj})^0 = 1$, while for $y_{nsj} = 1$, $(P_{nsj})^1 = P_{nsj}$, the likelihood function for the model is 0.049.

Now consider that for the same data a new model is estimated, and the parameters are now found to be −0.301, 0.056, and −0.189 for x_1, x_2, and x_3, respectively (actually these are the parameter estimates which maximize the likelihood function). Given the new parameter estimates, the utilities are re-calculated as are the choice probabilities, both of which are presented in Table 5.2. Note now that the model likelihood is much larger than for the previous estimates. Also, note that for three of the four choice situations, the choice probabilities for the chosen alternatives are larger, suggesting that, for these choice situations, the model is a better predictor of these outcomes. This is precisely what Equation (5.1) seeks to do. By maximizing Equation (5.1), the analyst is attempting to maximize the choice probabilities for the chosen alternatives within the data. Nevertheless, as demonstrated in the example below, it may not be possible to maximize the choice probabilities for all choice situations. In other words, the objective is to locate the parameters that will produce the best choice probabilities over the entire sample, not just at the individual choice situation level.

The fact that one or more choice probabilities may be worse off despite the overall model likelihood improving may be indicative of a number of issues.

Table 5.2 Example of likelihood estimation: 2

N	S	J	y_{nsj}	x_1	x_2	x_3	V_{nsj}	P_{nsj}	$P_{nsj}^{y_{nsj}}$
1	1	1	0	15	4	6	−5.427	0.038	1.000
1	1	2	1	5	2	6	−2.527	0.685	0.685
1	1	3	0	10	6	4	−3.432	0.277	1.000
1	2	1	1	10	4	4	−3.544	0.199	0.199
1	2	2	0	5	2	4	−2.150	0.801	1.000
2	1	2	1	15	6	2	−4.560	0.880	0.880
2	1	3	0	20	4	4	−6.555	0.120	1.000
2	2	1	0	20	6	6	−6.821	0.020	1.000
2	2	2	0	15	4	2	−4.672	0.171	1.000
2	2	3	1	10	2	2	−3.277	0.691	0.691
2	2	4	0	15	4	4	−5.049	0.117	1.000
								$L_{NS} =$	**0.083**

Firstly, the analyst may have mis-specified the utility expressions. For example, perhaps the correct utility specification should have involved some form of transformation of one or more of the independent variables. Or perhaps there exists one or more interaction terms that have not been accounted for in the model specification. Secondly, there may exist either scale or preference heterogeneity that has not been allowed for in the model specified. Or perhaps different decision makers make use of different mental algebra in making their choices (i.e., attribute processing – see Chapter 21), which the estimated model ignores. Thirdly, there may be omitted variables that if included would ensure a solution whereby all the choice probabilities for the chosen alternatives would improve as the model likelihood improves. Only when all the choice probabilities for the chosen alternatives are equal to one can any of the above be ruled out; however, in such a case the choices would be completely deterministic, in the sense that if one can predict perfectly the choices made in all choice situations by all decision makers, then there exists no error and the analyst will have perfect knowledge of the decision processes of all decision makers. In such a scenario, the choice models described herein may fail, given that the choice probabilities are derived under the assumption that there does exist error within the data, which represents somewhat of a paradox.

Putting aside the above, it is more common to maximize the log of the likelihood function rather than the likelihood function itself. This is because taking the product of a series of probabilities will typically produce values that are extremely small, particularly as n, s, and j increase. Unfortunately, most software will be unable to adequately handle such small numbers, having to resort to rounding, which in turn will affect the estimation results. By taking the logs of the probabilities first, large negative values will result which, when multiplied, produce even larger negative values. As such, the log-likelihood (LL) function of the model, shown below, is typically preferred:

$$LL_{NS} = \ln\left[\prod_{n=1}^{N}\prod_{s\in S_n}\prod_{j\in J_{ns}}(P_{nsj})^{y_{nsj}}\right].\tag{5.2}$$

Further assumptions are often made about the LL function, resulting in different econometric models. For example, the MNL model assumes that the choice observations are independent over both decision makers and choice situations. As such, and using the mathematical properties $\ln(P_{1sj}P_{2sj}) = \ln(P_{1sj}) + \ln(P_{2sj})$ and $\ln(P_{nsj})^{y_{njs}} = y_{nsj}\ln(P_{nsj})$, and applying the same mathematical rules to choice situations, s, Equation (5.2) may be rewritten as Equation (5.3):

$$LL_{NS} = \sum_{n=1}^{N}\sum_{s\in S_n}\sum_{j\in J_{ns}} y_{nsj}\ln(P_{nsj}).\tag{5.3}$$

This is the LL function of the MNL model. For any choice situation, s, as the probability of P_{nsj} increases, $\ln(P_{nsj})\rightarrow 0$ and hence for $y_{nsj}=1$, $y_{nsj}\ln(P_{nsj})\rightarrow 0$. Thus, as the probability approaches one for a chosen alternative within choice situation, s, the choice situation-specific LL approaches zero. The objective is therefore to locate (sample) population parameter estimates that maximize (noting that the log of any value between zero and one will be negative, hence we wish to maximize, not minimize) as many within choice situation LLs as possible. In doing so, it is important to note that in estimating the parameters, as with the likelihood function, the choice situation-specific LL may increase for some choice situations; however, it is hoped that over all choice situations the majority of within choice situation LLs gets smaller.

Table 5.3 shows for the same sample data used to demonstrate the likelihood function, the calculations for the LL function. Note that the parameters found by maximizing the LL function are precisely the same as those obtained by maximizing the likelihood function. That is, the parameters are found to be −0.301, 0.056, and −0.189 for x_1, x_2, and x_3, respectively. Note, however, that the object function being optimized, the LL, is now negative (as is expected).

Table 5.3 Example of log-likelihood estimation

N	S	J	y_{nsj}	x_1	x_2	x_3	V_{nsj}	P_{nsj}	$\ln(P_{nsj})$	$y_{nsj}\ln(P_{nsj})$
1	1	1	0	15	4	6	−5.427	0.038	−3.278	0.000
1	1	2	1	5	2	6	−2.527	0.685	−0.378	−0.378
1	1	3	0	10	6	4	−3.432	0.277	−1.283	0.000
1	2	1	1	10	4	4	−3.544	0.199	−1.616	−1.616
1	2	2	0	5	2	4	−2.150	0.801	−0.222	0.000
2	1	2	1	15	6	2	−4.560	0.880	−0.128	−0.128
2	1	3	0	20	4	4	−6.555	0.120	−2.122	0.000
2	2	1	0	20	6	6	−6.821	0.020	−3.913	0.000
2	2	2	0	15	4	2	−4.672	0.171	−1.764	0.000
2	2	3	1	10	2	2	−3.277	0.691	−0.369	−0.369
2	2	4	0	15	4	4	−5.049	0.117	−2.141	0.000
									$LL_{NS} =$	**−2.491**

Table 5.4 Example of log-likelihood estimation using count data

N	S	J	c_{nsj}	x_1	x_2	x_3	V_{nsj}	P_{nsj}	$\ln(P_{nsj})$	$c_{nsj}\ln(P_{nsj})$
1	1	1	2	15	4	6	0.127	0.302	−1.199	−2.398
1	1	2	3	5	2	6	0.736	0.554	−0.591	−1.772
1	1	3	1	10	6	4	−0.609	0.144	−1.935	−1.935
1	2	1	0	10	4	4	−0.193	0.375	−0.982	0.000
1	2	2	2	5	2	4	0.320	0.625	−0.469	−0.939
2	1	2	1	15	6	2	−1.121	0.324	−1.128	−1.128
2	1	3	2	20	4	4	−0.385	0.676	−0.391	−0.783
2	2	1	0	20	6	6	−0.385	0.248	−1.396	0.000
2	2	2	1	15	4	2	−0.705	0.180	−1.716	−1.716
2	2	3	0	10	2	2	−0.192	0.300	−1.204	0.000
2	2	4	4	15	4	4	−0.289	0.273	−1.300	−5.200
									$LL_{NS} =$	**−15.869**

> *As an aside*, in the examples above we assumed discrete choice data; however, the same technique can be used to estimate the parameters for other related types of data – for example, count or proportions data. For count data, decision makers are observed to select each alternative, j, more than once, or not at all. That is, rather than making a discrete choice, decision makers may select how many times each alternative will be chosen. When dealing with count data, the choice indicator, y_{nsj}, is replaced by the count variable, c_{nsj}, in the LL function. An example of this is given in Table 5.4, assuming now that the parameters for x_1, x_2, and x_3 are now estimated to be −0.019, −0.208, and 0.208, respectively.

Table 5.5 Example of log-likelihood estimation using proportion data

n_s	S	J	π_{sj}	x_1	x_2	x_3	V_{nsj}	P_{nsj}	$\ln(P_{nsj})$	$\pi_{sj}n_s\ln(P_{nsj})$
10	1	1	0.300	15	4	6	1.833	0.319	−1.144	−3.432
10	1	2	0.600	5	2	6	2.446	0.588	−0.531	−3.185
10	1	3	0.100	10	6	4	0.605	0.093	−2.372	−2.372
3	2	1	0.666	10	4	4	0.975	0.380	−0.969	−1.936
3	2	2	0.333	5	2	4	1.467	0.620	−0.477	−0.477
1	3	2	0.100	15	6	2	−0.496	0.227	−1.485	−0.148
1	3	3	0.900	20	4	4	0.733	0.773	−0.257	−0.231
8	4	1	0.250	20	6	6	1.342	0.450	−0.798	−1.597
8	4	2	0.000	15	4	2	−0.125	0.104	−2.265	0.000
8	4	3	0.125	10	2	2	0.366	0.170	−1.774	−1.774
8	4	4	0.375	15	4	4	0.854	0.276	−1.286	−3.858
									$LL_{NS}=$	**−19.009**

Likewise, the use of proportions data as opposed to discrete choice outcomes requires an adjustment of the LL function of the model. In this case, the choice indicator, y_{nsj}, is replaced by the observed proportion of times an alternative is observed to be selected, π_{sj}, times the number of times that 10 decision makers were observed to make choices for the first choice situation, with three selecting the first alternative, six the second, and one the last alternative. This information may be converted to 0.3, 0.6, and 0.1 for alternatives one, two, and three, respectively. Alternatively, the researcher may ask decision makers to indicate the probability with which they are likely to select each alternative. For example, assume a single decision maker, when presented with the third choice situation, indicated that they would likely select alternative two with a probability of 0.1 and alternative three with a probability of 0.9. The calculations for the LL, assuming now that the parameters are equal to −0.024, −0.185, and 0.490 x_1, x_2, and x_3 respectively, are given in Table 5.5.

Putting aside the specific type of dependent variable for the present, we note that there exist an infinite number of parameter estimate combinations for which one could calculate the LL function. By calculating the LL function for each combination of parameter estimates, or a relatively large subset thereof, and plotting the LL for each parameter combination, the resulting plot represents the surface of the LL function. Understanding the LL surface is important as it provides insights into potential algorithms that may be used to locate the parameter estimates for the data, the topic of discussion in Section 5.6, as well as potential issues that one must consider when estimating discrete choice models.

Table 5.6 Binary choice data example

s	x_{11}	x_{12}	x_{21}	x_{22}
1	8	4	6	0
2	9	5	5	0
3	10	5	4	1
4	5	2	9	2
5	8	2	6	4
6	7	4	7	1
7	4	0	10	5
8	8	1	6	3
9	10	4	4	0
10	5	3	9	3

To demonstrate, consider discrete choice data consisting of two alternatives each described by 2 variables and 10 choice situations. The data for all 10 choice situations is presented in Table 5.6. Further assume that 100 decision makers were observed to have all 10 choice situations and selected which of the alternatives they most preferred in each situation, thus providing the analyst with a total of 1,000 choice observations.

Assume now that the analyst was to estimate an MNL model on the data. For simplicity, assume that the model has generic parameters and no constants. The utility specification for this model is given as Equation (5.4):

$$V_{nsj} = \beta_1 x_{nsj1} + \beta_2 x_{nsj2}. \tag{5.4}$$

Given the above information, we simulate the utilities for all 1,000 choice observations by assuming that $\beta_1 = -0.5$ and $\beta_2 = 0.7$, and taking random draws from an EV1 IID distribution to replicate the error structure of the assumed sample population (we discuss methods for drawing from distributions in Section 5.5). Given knowledge of the utilities, and assuming that decision makers will select the alternative that maximizes their utility, it is then possible to simulate the choice index, y_{nsj}, for each observation. Given data simulated as described above, one would expect to retrieve the input parameter estimates assuming the same utility specification by maximizing the LL function given in Equation (5.3). Rather than do this, however, we jointly vary the parameter estimates systematically in increments of 0.1 between the ranges of -1.0 and 1.0 (i.e., $(\beta_1,\beta_2)=(-1,-1),(-1,-0.9),\ldots,$ $(0,0),\ldots,(1,0.9),(1,1))$ and calculate the log-likelihood for each parameter

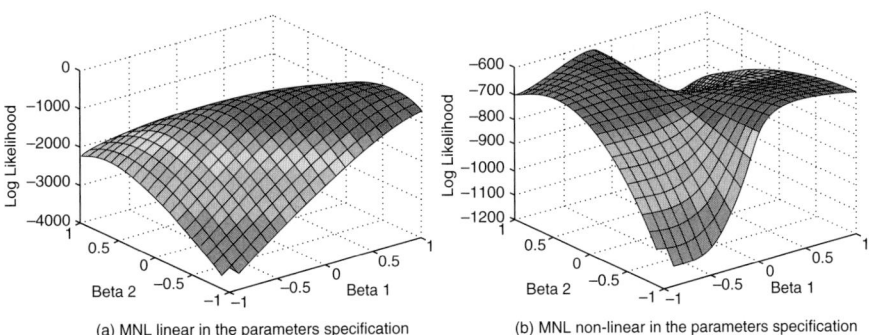

(a) MNL linear in the parameters specification   (b) MNL non-linear in the parameters specification

Figure 5.1   Log-likelihood function surfaces

pair. Figure 5.1a plots the results of this exercise. As can be seen from the plot, the LL function is always negative and approaches its maximum value when $\beta_1 = -0.5$ and $\beta_2 = 0.7$, suggesting that these are the estimates most likely to have come from this data.

For MNL models with linear in the parameters' utility specifications, the surface of the LL function will be globally concave, meaning that there will exist one maxima which should be relatively straightforward to locate. For all other models, including MNL models with non-linear in the parameters' specifications, there may exist multiple (local) maxima. In such instances, location of the global maxima may not always be so straightforward. To demonstrate, consider now that the analyst was to specify an MNL model using the following non-linear in the parameters specification (which can be estimated in Nlogit5 – see Chapter 20) based on the same simulated discrete choice data:

$$V_{nsj} = \beta_1 x_{jns1}^{(1-\exp(\beta_2 x_{jns2}))^{0.5}}. \tag{5.5}$$

Figure 5.1b plots the LL surface over the same range of parameter combinations based on this new utility specification. Note now that the LL surface is no longer globally concave and has two maxima, one local (i.e., when $\beta_1 = 0.9$ and $\beta_2 = -0.3$ the LL function equals -619.500) and one global (i.e., when $\beta_1 = -1.0$ and $\beta_2 = 0.3$ the LL function equals -604.008). Although the two LLs appear to be quite different in value, depending on a number of factors it is possible when estimating the model that they end up with the estimated parameters associated with the local optima, being unaware that there exists a different global optima. This is because most algorithms do not plot the entire surface of the LL function in the manner described above, as doing so would be highly inefficient and time consuming. As such, the algorithms employed will typically be dependent on the start parameters used when estimating the model, and hence it is advised that one make use of multiple start values when estimating any discrete choice model other than a linear in the parameters MNL model (e.g., Liu and Mahmassani 2000). In later chapters you will see how we can select start values from more advanced models such as mixed logit for even more advanced models such as generalized mixed logit. One should avoid start values set to zero except for simple MNL models, and fortunately most software now use MNL start values as the default set.

5.3 Simulated maximum likelihood

Several discrete choice models assume that (some of) the parameters are randomly distributed over the population, where typically the random parameters are assumed to follow certain parametric probability distributions (there also exist several models that allow for non- or semi-parametric representations of the probability distributions (e.g., Briesch *et al.* 2010; Fosgerau 2006; Klein and Spady 1993); however, these models remain outside of the scope of the current text). The probit model is an example of one such model, where (subject to restrictions) the error terms are parameters to be estimated under the assumption that they are Normally distributed over the sample population. Further, as discussed in Chapter 4, the probit model can be extended to allow for tastes to be Normally (and log-Normally) distributed over the sampled population. Likewise, the MMNL model allows tastes to vary over the population according to some analyst defined continuous distribution (see Chapter 15). Of importance is the fact that, for these models, the estimated parameters describe the moments of the assumed distributions for the sampled population. Where a particular individual resides within the distribution is not known (i.e., their assignment is random without an interaction with the source of a potential systematic influence which could place a respondent at a particular location on a distribution). Thus, for each individual, it is necessary to evaluate the choice probabilities over the entire real line represented by the population level distributions. Hence, the probability that respondent n in choice situation s will choose alternative j can be written as:

$$L_{nsj} = \int_{\beta} P_{nsj}(\beta) f(\beta|\theta) d\beta, \tag{5.6}$$

where $f(\beta|\theta)$ is the multivariate probability density function of β, given the distributional parameters θ. The P_{nsj} may be either a logit or probit choice probability, depending on the model assumed. Equation (5.6) can be generalized by adopting a transformation of β such that the multivariate distribution may be represented in a form that is parameter-free. Thus:

$$L_{nsj} = \int_{z} P_{nsj}\left(\beta(z|\theta)\right)\phi(z)dz, \tag{5.7}$$

where $\beta(z|\theta)$ is a function of z with parameters θ, and where $\phi(z)$ is a multivariate standard distribution of z. Models involving multivariate distributions are generally limited to situations in which all random parameters are assumed to be normally distributed, and involve correlating the random parameters via a process known as Cholesky decomposition (see Section 5.5). Where one or more parameters are not normally distributed, or even when all random parameters are normally distributed, it is far more common to assume (independent) univariate distributions such that Equation (5.7) can be written as:

$$L_{nsj} = \int_{z_1} \cdots \int_{z_K} P_{nsj}\left(\beta_1(z_1|\theta_1), \ldots, \beta_K(z_K|\theta_K)\right)\phi_1(z_1)\cdots\phi_K(z_K)dz_1\cdots dz_K. \tag{5.8}$$

The assumption of separate univariate distributions for each parameter allows for the mixing of different distributions within the same model for different random parameters. For example, if we have one normal, $\beta_1 \sim N(\mu,\sigma)$, and one uniform, $\beta_2 \sim U(a,b)$, distribution, then L_{nsj} may be written as:

$$L_{nsj} = \int_{z_1}\int_{z_2} P_{nsj}\left(\beta_1(z_1|\mu, \sigma), \beta_2(z_2|a, b)\right)\phi_1(z_1)\phi_2(z_2)dz_1 dz_2, \tag{5.9}$$

where $\beta_1(z_1|\mu, \sigma) = \mu + \sigma z_1$ with $z_1 \sim N(0, 1)$ and $\beta_2(z_2|a, b) = a + (b - a)z_2$ with $z_2 \sim U(0, 1)$.

The integrals in Equation (5.6)–(5.9) do not have a closed analytical form, meaning that they must be evaluated using either Pseudo-Monte Carlo (PMC) or Quasi-Monte Carlo methods. These methods involve simulating the parameters and choice probabilities, and involve taking R draws for each of the

K random terms or parameters, calculating the choice probabilities for each of the draws, and averaging the probabilities over the draws. That is, let $\beta^{(r)}$ denote a $K \times 1$ vector of parameters associated with draw r, $r=1,\ldots,R$, such that $\beta^{(r)} = [\beta_1^{(r)}, \ldots, \beta_K^{(r)}]$, with corresponding random distributions described by probability density functions $\phi_k(\beta_k|z_k)$. Given data, X, the approximation of the choice probability can be formalized as:

$$L_{nsj} = E(P_{nsj}) \approx \frac{1}{R}\sum_{r=1}^{R} f(\beta^{(r)}|X). \tag{5.10}$$

The simulated LL function is then computed using the expected probability computed from Equation (5.10). That is, the expected likelihood function (or, typically, the logarithm) is maximized based on the simulated draws, where the maximization process is referred to as simulated maximum likelihood. That is, the LL function of the model becomes:

$$L\Big(E(L_{NS})\Big) = \ln E\left(\left[\prod_{n=1}^{N}\prod_{s\in S_n}\prod_{j\in J_{ns}} (P_{nsj})^{y_{nsj}}\right]\right). \tag{5.11}$$

Assuming independence between the responses of the individual decision makers, n and choice situations s, the simulated maximum likelihood becomes:

$$\begin{aligned} L\Big(E(L_{NS})\Big) &= \log E\left(\prod_{n=1}^{N}\prod_{s\in S_n}\prod_{j\in J_{ns}} (P_{nsj})^{y_{nsj}}\right) \\ &= \sum_{n=1}^{N}\sum_{s\in S_n}\sum_{j\in J_{ns}} y_{nsj}\log E(P_{nsj}), \end{aligned} \tag{5.12}$$

which represents the simulated LL function for the cross-sectional version of the model.

Assuming independence between the responses of the individual decision makers, the simulated maximum likelihood becomes:

$$\begin{aligned} L\Big(E(L_{NS})\Big) &= \log E\left(\prod_{n=1}^{N}\prod_{s\in S_n}\prod_{j\in J_{ns}} (P_{nsj})^{y_{nsj}}\right) \\ &= \sum_{n=1}^{N}\log E\left(\prod_{s\in S_n}\prod_{j\in J_{ns}} (P_{nsj})^{y_{nsj}}\right). \end{aligned} \tag{5.13}$$

To demonstrate how simulated maximum likelihood works in practice, consider the same data described in Table 5.1. Let the first two parameters associated with x_1 and x_2 be randomly distributed such that $\beta_1 \sim N(-0.301, 0.100)$ and $\beta_2 \sim N(0.056, 0.020)$ while the third parameter is a fixed parameter equal to -0.189. Table 5.7 demonstrates the calculations of the choice probabilities and the model LL function, assuming the cross-sectional MMNL model specification for $R = 5$ random draws (we discuss in Section 5.4 how these specific draws were selected). For each choice situation s, different draws are taken for each of the random parameters, such that the total number of draws over the sample is $N.S.R = 2 \times 2 \times 5 = 20$. As shown in the table, for each draw, $\tilde{\beta}^{(r)}$, the utility is calculated as per normal, as are the choice probabilities, based on the logit choice formula (we discuss the specific calculation of probit choice probabilities in Section 5.6). That is:

$$P^r_{nsi} = \frac{e^{V^r_{nsi}}}{\sum\limits_{j=1}^{J} e^{V^r_{nsj}}}. \tag{5.14}$$

At the base of each choice situation, the average choice probability is shown with the expected choice probability for the chosen alternative placed in **bold**. The last column of the table calculates the choice situation-specific contribution to the model simulated LL, as well as the model simulated log-likelihood based on the parameter values provided.

Note that at the base of each choice situation, we have also calculated and shown the average simulated utility for each alternative. This has been done for purely cosmetic purposes. Indeed, it is worthwhile stressing that the average probability is used to calculate the simulated LL and not the average simulated utilities. This is because $E\left(\dfrac{e^{V^r_{ni}}}{\sum\limits_{j=1}^{J} e^{V^r_{nsj}}}\right) \neq \dfrac{e^{E(V^r_{nsi})}}{\sum\limits_{i=1}^{J} e^{E(V^r_{nsj})}}$. We leave it to the

reader to confirm that the choice probabilities for the chosen alternatives would be 0.707, 0.181, 0.859, and 0.745 for the four choice situations, respectively, if the average utilities were (incorrectly) used, leading to simulated LL of -2.503, as opposed to the correct value of -2.249. Although there is only a small discrepancy in this instance, as the number of choice observations increase so too will the differences, resulting in very different model outcomes.

Table 5.7 Example of simulated log-likelihood estimation (cross-sectional model)

n	s	r	y_{nsj}	x_{i1}	x_{i2}	x_{i3}	x_{21}	x_{22}	x_{23}	x_{31}	x_{32}	x_{33}	x_{41}	x_{42}	x_{43}	$\tilde{\beta}_1^r$	$\tilde{\beta}_2^r$	β_3	V_{ns1}^r	V_{ns2}^r	V_{ns3}^r	V_{ns4}^r	P_{ns1}^r	P_{ns2}^r	P_{ns3}^r	P_{ns4}^r	$y_{nsj}\ln E(P_{nsj})$
1	1	1	2	15	4	6	5	2	6	10	6	4	–	–	–	−0.301	0.047	−0.189	−5.461	−2.545	−3.484	–	0.037	0.692	0.271	–	
1	1	2	2	15	4	6	5	2	6	10	6	4	–	–	–	−0.369	0.064	−0.189	−6.404	−2.847	−4.055	–	0.021	0.753	0.225	–	
1	1	3	2	15	4	6	5	2	6	10	6	4	–	–	–	−0.234	0.031	−0.189	−4.513	−2.239	−2.904	–	0.064	0.618	0.318	–	
1	1	4	2	15	4	6	5	2	6	10	6	4	–	–	–	−0.416	0.053	−0.189	−7.164	−3.108	−4.599	–	0.014	0.805	0.181	–	
1	1	5	2	15	4	6	5	2	6	10	6	4	–	–	–	−0.269	0.071	−0.189	−4.888	−2.337	−3.022	–	0.049	0.632	0.319	–	
																		Average:	−5.686	−2.615	−3.613	–	0.037	**0.700**	0.263	–	−0.357
1	2	1	1	10	4	4	5	2	4	–	–	–	–	–	–	−0.333	0.040	−0.189	−3.924	−2.340	–	–	0.170	0.830	–	–	
1	2	2	1	10	4	4	5	2	4	–	–	–	–	–	–	−0.186	0.059	−0.189	−2.382	−1.569	–	–	0.307	0.693	–	–	
1	2	3	1	10	4	4	5	2	4	–	–	–	–	–	–	−0.455	0.080	−0.189	−4.980	−2.868	–	–	0.108	0.892	–	–	
1	2	4	1	10	4	4	5	2	4	–	–	–	–	–	–	−0.285	0.020	−0.189	−3.529	−2.142	–	–	0.200	0.800	–	–	
1	2	5	1	10	4	4	5	2	4	–	–	–	–	–	–	−0.350	0.049	−0.189	−4.059	−2.407	–	–	0.161	0.839	–	–	
																		Average:	−3.775	−2.265	–	–	**0.189**	0.811	–	–	−1.665
2	1	1	2	–	–	–	15	6	2	20	4	4	–	–	–	−0.212	0.066	−0.189	–	−3.165	−4.738	–	–	0.828	0.172	–	
2	1	2	2	–	–	–	15	6	2	20	4	4	–	–	–	−0.390	0.035	−0.189	–	−6.016	−8.413	–	–	0.917	0.083	–	
2	1	3	2	–	–	–	15	6	2	20	4	4	–	–	–	−0.252	0.055	−0.189	–	−3.832	−5.581	–	–	0.852	0.148	–	
2	1	4	2	–	–	–	15	6	2	20	4	4	–	–	–	−0.317	0.074	−0.189	–	−4.688	−6.798	–	–	0.892	0.108	–	
2	1	5	2	–	–	–	15	6	2	20	4	4	–	–	–	−0.148	0.043	−0.189	–	−2.336	−3.538	–	–	0.769	0.231	–	
																		Average:	–	−4.008	−5.814	–	–	**0.851**	0.149	–	−0.161
2	2	1	3	20	6	6	15	4	2	10	2	2	15	4	4	−0.487	0.060	−0.189	−10.518	−7.447	−5.131	−7.825	0.004	0.084	0.854	0.058	
2	2	2	3	20	6	6	15	4	2	10	2	2	15	4	4	−0.293	0.085	−0.189	−6.491	−4.438	−3.141	−4.816	0.023	0.183	0.669	0.125	
2	2	3	3	20	6	6	15	4	2	10	2	2	15	4	4	−0.359	0.027	−0.189	−8.153	−5.656	−3.914	−6.034	0.011	0.134	0.763	0.092	
2	2	4	3	20	6	6	15	4	2	10	2	2	15	4	4	−0.223	0.051	−0.189	−5.296	−3.526	−2.510	−3.903	0.037	0.217	0.598	0.148	
2	2	5	3	20	6	6	15	4	2	10	2	2	15	4	4	−0.402	0.069	−0.189	−8.764	−6.135	−4.262	−6.513	0.009	0.121	0.787	0.083	
																		Average:	−7.844	−5.440	−3.792	−5.818	0.017	0.148	**0.734**	0.101	−0.309

$$L(E(L_{NS})) = -2.491$$

To demonstrate how the simulated LL calculation differs for the panel version of the model, we show the calculations for the same data in Table 5.8. The first thing to note is that, in taking the draws, the same draws are used for each decision maker across choice situations. For example, for $n = 1$, $r = 1$, the draw for the first random parameter is -0.301 for choice situations one and two. Likewise, the second draw for the same decision maker is -0.369 for the same parameter and choice situation. As such, unlike the cross-sectional version of the model, although the number of draws is kept the same, that being $R = 5$ in this example, the actual number of simulated draws generated is less, being equal to $N.R$ as opposed to $N.R.S$, or $2 \times 5 = 10$ in this case. The second thing to note is that the choice probabilities are calculated for each choice situation; however, the simulated LL function is calculated based on the within decision maker expected value of the product of choice probabilities, suggesting that what is actually being modeled is the probability of observing the sequence of choices made by the decision maker s, as opposed to the within choice probabilities. Thus for example, the simulated LL for decision maker one is computed as:

$$\ln\left[\left(\begin{array}{l} 0.692 \times 0.804 + 0.753 \times 0.847 + 0.618 \times 0.751 \\ +0.805 \times 0.878 + 0.632 \times 0.769 \end{array}\right)\Big/5\right] = \ln(0.130)$$
$$= -0.2043.$$

(5.15)

Note that even though we have assumed the same parameter estimates for the cross-sectional and panel versions of the MMNL model in our examples, in practice the two models will tend to produce very different estimates and simulated LL functions. Further, in practice the log-likelihood function of the panel version of the model will typically be better than that of the cross-sectional version of the same model, all else being equal. Unfortunately, the two models are not necessarily nested in that they are maximizing different log-likelihood functions (Equation (5.12) versus Equation (5.13)), and hence a direct comparison may not be possible between the two. Nevertheless, theory would suggest that in short run panels such as with stated preference data, tastes are likely to be consistent within decision maker n across choice observations, and hence the panel model may be the more appropriate model to estimate on such data. Finally, we note that in the case of each decision maker observing a single choice situation, the two models will be necessarily the same, as the product of s in the panel model will disappear.

Table 5.8 Example of simulated log-likelihood estimation (panel model)

n	s	r	y_{nsj}	x_{11}	x_{12}	x_{13}	x_{21}	x_{22}	x_{23}	x_{31}	x_{32}	x_{33}	x_{41}	x_{42}	x_{43}	$\tilde{\beta}_1^{\,r}$	$\tilde{\beta}_2^{\,r}$	β_3	V_{ns1}^r	V_{ns2}^r	V_{ns3}^r	V_{ns4}^r	P_{ns1}^r	P_{ns2}^r	P_{ns3}^r	P_{ns4}^r	$\ln\left(E\left(P_{n1j}^{y_{n1j}}\cdot P_{n2i}^{y_{n2i}}\right)\right)$
1	1	1	2	15	4	6	5	2	6	10	6	4	–	–	–	−0.301	0.047	−0.189	−5.461	−2.545	−3.484	–	0.037	0.692	0.271	–	
1	1	2	2	15	4	6	5	2	6	10	6	4	–	–	–	−0.369	0.064	−0.189	−6.404	−2.847	−4.055	–	0.021	0.753	0.225	–	
1	1	3	2	15	4	6	5	2	6	10	6	4	–	–	–	−0.234	0.031	−0.189	−4.513	−2.239	−2.904	–	0.064	0.618	0.318	–	
1	1	4	2	15	4	6	5	2	6	10	6	4	–	–	–	−0.416	0.053	−0.189	−7.164	−3.108	−4.599	–	0.014	0.805	0.181	–	
1	1	5	2	15	4	6	5	2	6	10	6	4	–	–	–	−0.269	0.071	−0.189	−4.888	−2.337	−3.022	–	0.049	0.632	0.319	–	
																		Average:	−5.686	−2.615	−3.613	–	0.037	**0.700**	0.263	–	
1	2	1	1	10	4	4	5	2	4	–	–	–	–	–	–	−0.301	0.047	−0.189	−3.578	−2.167	–	–	0.196	0.804	–	–	**−2.043**
1	2	2	1	10	4	4	5	2	4	–	–	–	–	–	–	−0.369	0.064	−0.189	−4.184	−2.470	–	–	0.153	0.847	–	–	
1	2	3	1	10	4	4	5	2	4	–	–	–	–	–	–	−0.234	0.031	−0.189	−2.967	−1.861	–	–	0.249	0.751	–	–	
1	2	4	1	10	4	4	5	2	4	–	–	–	–	–	–	−0.416	0.053	−0.189	−4.705	−2.730	–	–	0.122	0.878	–	–	
1	2	5	1	10	4	5	5	2	4	–	–	–	–	–	–	−0.269	0.071	−0.189	−3.164	−1.960	–	–	0.231	0.769	–	–	
																		Average:	−3.720	−2.238	–	–	**0.190**	0.810	–	–	
2	1	1	2	–	–	–	15	6	2	20	4	4	–	–	–	−0.333	0.040	−0.189	–	−5.130	−7.253	–	–	0.893	0.107	–	
2	1	2	2	–	–	–	15	6	2	20	4	4	–	–	–	−0.186	0.059	−0.189	–	−2.818	−4.243	–	–	0.806	0.194	–	
2	1	3	2	–	–	–	15	6	2	20	4	4	–	–	–	−0.455	0.080	−0.189	–	−6.715	−9.525	–	–	0.943	0.057	–	
2	1	4	2	–	–	–	15	6	2	20	4	4	–	–	–	−0.285	0.020	−0.189	–	−4.538	−6.383	–	–	0.864	0.136	–	
2	1	5	2	–	–	–	15	6	2	20	4	4	–	–	–	−0.350	0.049	−0.189	–	−5.333	−7.559	–	–	0.903	0.097	–	
																		Average:	–	−4.907	−6.993	–	–	**0.882**	0.118	–	
2	2	1	3	20	6	6	15	4	2	10	2	2	15	4	4	−0.333	0.040	−0.189	−7.550	−5.211	−3.627	−5.588	0.014	0.150	0.732	0.103	
2	2	2	3	20	6	6	15	4	2	10	2	2	15	4	4	−0.186	0.059	−0.189	−4.504	−2.935	−2.121	−3.313	0.050	0.241	0.544	0.165	
2	2	3	3	20	6	6	15	4	2	10	2	2	15	4	4	−0.455	0.080	−0.189	−9.743	−6.875	−4.763	−7.253	0.006	0.100	0.826	0.068	
2	2	4	3	20	6	6	15	4	2	10	2	2	15	4	4	−0.285	0.020	−0.189	−6.721	−4.578	−3.192	−4.956	0.020	0.172	0.689	0.118	
2	2	5	3	20	6	6	15	4	2	10	2	2	15	4	4	−0.350	0.049	−0.189	−7.838	−5.431	−3.779	−5.809	0.013	0.143	0.746	0.098	
																		Average:	−7.271	−5.006	−3.496	−5.384	0.021	0.161	**0.707**	0.111	**−0.465**

$$L\left(E\left(L_{NS}\right)\right) = -2.508$$

With the above discussion in mind, we now turn to a consideration of methods related to how to draw from densities. In doing so, we discuss a number of methods that have been employed in the past.

5.4 Drawing from densities

Several discrete choice models rely on simulation in order to calculate the choice probabilities and hence the LL functions necessary to estimate the parameters of the model specified. As shown in Section 5.3, simulation involves repeatedly drawing from a density, calculating some statistic of interest, and averaging over the draws. For discrete choice models, the statistics of interest are the choice probabilities. In Section 5.3, we demonstrated the simulation process used to calculate the choice probabilities for two versions of the MMNL model, noting that similar simulation procedures were used in calculating the choice probabilities of probit models, although the specific calculations of probit choice probabilities differ to those used for logit models (Section 5.6 deals specifically with the simulation of probit choice probabilities). This section deals specifically with how the draws are taken from a density, independent of the model being estimated.

Typically, a density may be described in one of two related ways; either in terms of its probability density function (PDF) or cumulative density function (CDF). As noted in Section 3.2, the PDF of a random variable represents the relative likelihood that the random variable will take a particular value while the probability that the variable will lie within some range is calculated as the integral over that range (i.e., the area under the PDF curve). The CDF represents the probability that a random variable with some density (represented by its PDF) will be located *at some value less than or equal to some other value*, defined as Y_n^* in Section 3.2.

Most simulation methods begin by taking draws from the CDF of the density, which are then converted or translated to the PDF of the same related density. As before, let $\beta^{(r)}$ represent a $K \times 1$ vector of parameters associated with draw r, $r = 1, \ldots, R$. Using methods described in detail below, R uniformly distributed random numbers on the interval $[0,1]$ are drawn, which for the kth random parameter we denote $u_k^{(r)}$. Given $u_k^{(r)}$, the draws for the kth random parameter are computed by:

$$\beta_k^{(r)} = \Phi_k^{-1}\left(u_k^{(r)}\right), \tag{5.16}$$

where $\Phi_k(\beta_k|z_k)$ denotes the cumulative distribution function corresponding to the probability density function $\phi_k(\beta_k|z_k)$.

To understand why draws from the CDF are first taken and later transformed into draws from the PDF, recall that the objective of drawing from a density is to estimate the population moments of the random parameter distributions. As we will describe in Section 5.6, estimation of discrete choice models involves an iterative process in which the parameter estimates are systematically changed in a manner that is designed to locate improvements of the (simulated) LL. Rather than draw directly from the PDF of the multivariate parameter distribution at any one iteration, it is typical to draw from the associated CDF when estimating the parameter estimates of the model. By fixing the probabilities of the CDF for each of the simulated draws, equivalence in terms of the coverage of the multivariate parameter distribution space is ensured, as the parameter moments update during the estimation procedure. The simulated maximum likelihood procedure therefore involves first the generation of multidimensional finite sequences that fill the 0–1 interval (and hence approximate probabilities) which are then translated to draws taken from the density functions of the random parameters.

To demonstrate, consider two different PDFs (as will be the case over different iterations of the search process). It might not be possible to simply draw the same values for $\beta_k^{(r)}$ or, even where it is possible, changes in the density of the distribution imply different mass probabilities of observing the draws. To demonstrate, consider for example the probability mass of drawing a value equal to 2.0 for $\beta_k^{(r)}$. Now consider two PDFs representing different potential densities for $\beta_k^{(r)}$; the first being a standard Normal distribution and the second a Normal distribution with a mean of -1.0 and a standard deviation of 0.75. Figure 5.2 plots the PDFs of these two distributions. For the first PDF based on a standard Normal distribution, the probability mass for $\beta_k^{(r)} = 1.0$ is 0.054, while for the second the mass probability is equal to 0.0002, representing a much less likely outcome (represented by the fixed line arrow). Fixing the mass probability to 0.054, the draw for $\beta_k^{(r)}$ based on the second PDF would be 0.198, which is very different to 2.000.

Rather than fix the values of the draws for $\beta_k^{(r)}$ directly, it is far easier to hold constant the probabilities of taking a particular set of draws. This is where working with the CDF is easier as the CDF directly describes the probability that a random variable with some density (represented by its PDF) will be located at some value less than or equal to some value. For example, consider the CDFs associated with the PDFs described above. These are shown in Figure 5.3, where we fix the draw for $u_k^{(r)}$ to 0.6, resulting in different draws for the two different densities described.

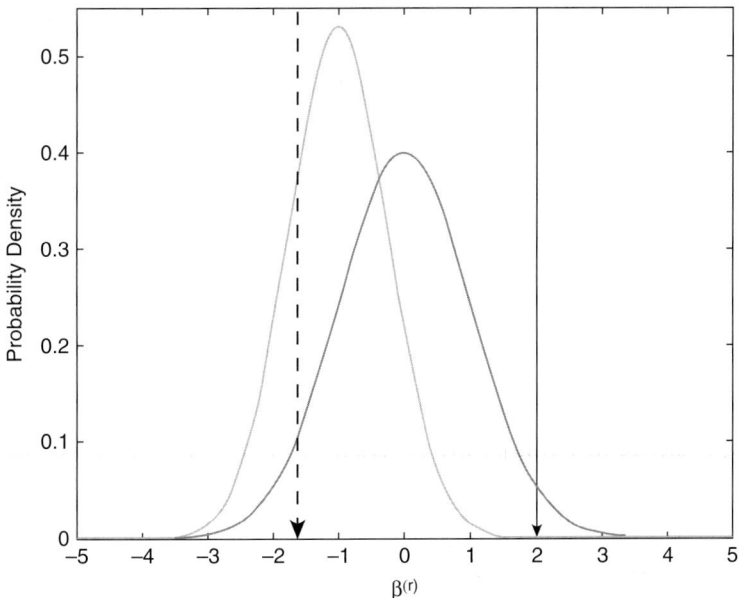

Figure 5.2   Example for drawing from two different PDFs

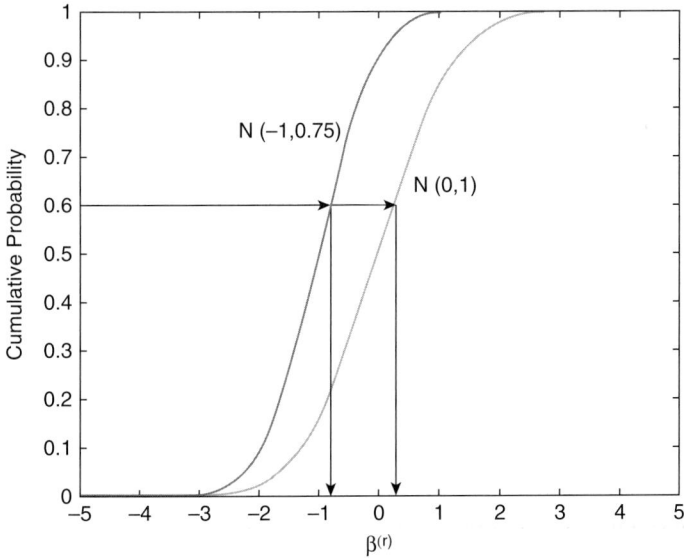

Figure 5.3   Example for drawing from two different CDFs

To generate the sequences of probabilities used in model estimation, there exist a number of different simulation procedures available to the analyst. The simplest method involves the use of pseudo-random draws (often referred to as Pseudo-Monte Carlo (PMC) draws), where parameters are randomly selected from a distribution. While simple to implement, different sets of random draws are likely to produce different coverage over the distribution space, possibly leading to different model results, particularly when a low number of draws is used in estimation. By using a more systematic approach in selecting points when sampling from a distribution, a number of authors have shown how precision of the simulation process may potentially be improved (see, e.g., Bhat 2001, 2003; Hess *et al.* 2006; Sándor and Train 2004). Such techniques are commonly referred to within the literature as Quasi-Monte Carlo (QMC) draws (also often referred to as **intelligent draws**), with the most common QMC methods being the use of Halton sequences (see Bhat 2001, 2003; Halton 1960; Sándor and Train 2004) or modified Latin Hypercube sampling (MLHS) draws (see Hess *et al.* 2006).

Given this background, we now describe different approaches commonly used to draw from densities, within the discrete choice literature. We begin with a brief discussion of PMC draws before moving on to QMC draws.

5.4.1 Pseudo-random Monte Carlo simulation

PMC simulation involves the analyst having the computer generate the random draws. Unfortunately, computers are not able to generate truly random numbers, as any number generated will be a function of the specific program code used to generate the number, which is fixed. Most computers therefore rely on some constantly changing variable, such as time, to generate random numbers and as such any random number generated by a computer is therefore strictly not random. That is, computer generated random draws are actually pseudo-random draws.

As per the discussion surrounding Equation (5.16), and the discussion in Section 5.3, the computer first generates either $N.S.R$ pseudo-random numbers for cross-sectional models, or $N.R$ pseudo-random numbers for panel models, the values of which are constrained to be between 0 and 1. In generating these values, the analyst may either fix the seed of the program, so that in estimating the same model repeatedly, the model will be guaranteed to converge to the same result, or not, in which different results may be obtained over repeated model estimations. Note, however that, as the number of draws, R, increases to infinity, the same results should be observed over

▲	A	B	C	D	E	F	G
1		Step 1				Step 2	
2	r	u®1	u®2		r	u®1	u®2
3	1	=RAND()	=RAND()		1	=NORMINV(B3,-2.5,0.4)	=NORMINV(C3,1.4,0.25)
4	2	0.388206	0.288864		2	-2.613598873	1.26082374
5	3	0.338382	0.904622		3	-2.666753205	1.727086627
6	4	0.628155	0.102044		4	-2.369212032	1.082502358
7	5	0.338441	0.638461		5	-2.666688217	1.48858722
8	6	0.170891	0.43212		6	-2.880259337	1.35725522
9	7	0.675593	0.266131		7	-2.317835672	1.243861146
10	8	0.769221	0.455223		8	-2.205486748	1.371880796
11	9	0.963127	0.804354		9	-1.784725656	1.614319567
12	10	0.777247	0.462837		10	-2.194828568	1.376677488

Figure 5.4   Example of PMC draws

different estimation runs even when the different seeds are used. Independent of whether the seed is set or not, the pseudo-random draws are retained and re-used over different iterations (see Section 5.6). These draws are then converted to draws taken from the density functions of the random parameters.

Figure 5.4 demonstrates this process using Microsoft Excel. In step 1, we generate two sequences of pseudo-random numbers for $R=10$ draws using the rand() function. Although not shown in the figure, these values should then be fixed, by first copying the values and then using paste special to convert the formulas to values. Next, assuming normal distributions, the Excel equation Norminv(<prob>, <mean>, <std dev>) function is used to convert the 0–1 draws to the density functions of the random parameters. Here, the first reference of the equation is to the probability, which is represented by the 0–1 sequences. Next, the equation requires the analyst to specify the mean and standard deviation of the random parameter.

Randomness of the draws is not a prerequisite in the approximation of the integral in Equation (5.6). Rather, Winiarski (2003) has posited that correlation between draws for different dimensions can have a positive effect on the approximation, and draws which are distributed as uniformly as possible over the area of integration as being more desirable. Hence, selecting draws deterministically so that they possess these properties represents a potential way to minimize the integration error (for further discussion, see Niederreiter 1992 or Fang and Wang 1994). QMC simulation methods are almost identical to the PMC simulation method, except that they use deterministic sequences in generating the population of values in $u_k^{(r)} \sim U(0, 1)$. In QMC methods, the numbers in $u_k^{(r)}$ are taken from different intelligent quasi-random sequences, also termed low discrepancy sequences. One argument for the use of QMC approaches is that QMC sequences result in faster convergence to the true value of the numerical integration than PMC simulation. We discuss this further in Section 5.4.7.

Given this discussion, we now consider several QMC approaches commonly used in estimating discrete choice models. In particular, we focus on Halton, random Halton, shuffled Halton, Sobol, and MLHS methods. We also discuss antithetic draws. We begin with a discussion of Halton sequences.

5.4.2 Halton sequences

Halton sequences (Halton 1960) are constructed according to a deterministic method based on the use of Prime numbers. Formally, the rth element in the Halton sequence based on Prime p_k (where p_k represents the Prime number used as the base for the kth parameter) is obtained by taking the radical inverse of integer r in base p_k by reflection through the radical point, such that:

$$r = \sum_{\ell=0}^{L} b_\ell^{(r)} p_k^\ell, \tag{5.17}$$

where $0 \leq b_\ell^{(r)} \leq p_k - 1$ determines the L digits used in base p_k in order to represent r (i.e., solving Equation (5.17)), and where the range for L is determined by $p_k^L \leq r < p_k^{L+1}$. The draw is then obtained as:

$$u_k^{(r)} = \sum_{\ell=0}^{L} b_\ell^{(r)} p_k^{-\ell-1}. \tag{5.18}$$

In words, the process of construction begins by listing integers in base 10 beginning with 0 up to R and converting each value to integers with base p_k. For example, assuming Prime 2, the values 0, 1, 2, 3, 4 are converted to 0, 1, 10, 11, 100. Next, the newly constructed values are decimalized after the order of values is reversed. For example, 0, 1, 10, 11, 100 now become 0.0, 0.1, 0.01, 0.11, and 0.001, respectively. Finally, the values are converted back to base 10, which in the example above returns the values 0, 0.5, 0.25, 0.75, and 0.125.

To demonstrate the process more comprehensively, we present for $R = 20$, the conversions of integer values for Primes 2 to 37 numbers, representing 12 dimensions (each sequence based on a different Prime is referred to as a dimension, hence there are 12 prime numbers leading to 12 sequences in this example). The following steps are involved.

Table 5.9 Conversion of Base numbers for Primes 2 to 37

Base 10 integer	Prime 2	Prime 3	Prime 5	Prime 7	Prime 11	Prime 13	Prime 17	Prime 19	Prime 23	Prime 29	Prime 31	Prime 37
0	0	0	0	0	0	0	0	0	0	0	0	0
1	1	1	1	1	1	1	1	1	1	1	1	1
2	10	2	2	2	2	2	2	2	2	2	2	2
3	11	10	3	3	3	3	3	3	3	3	3	3
4	100	11	4	4	4	4	4	4	4	4	4	4
5	101	12	10	5	5	5	5	5	5	5	5	5
6	110	20	11	6	6	6	6	6	6	6	6	6
7	111	21	12	10	7	7	7	7	7	7	7	7
8	1000	22	13	11	8	8	8	8	8	8	8	8
9	1001	100	14	12	9	9	9	9	9	9	9	9
10	1010	101	20	13	A	A	A	A	A	A	A	A
11	1011	102	21	14	10	B	B	B	B	B	B	B
12	1100	110	22	15	11	C	C	C	C	C	C	C
13	1101	111	23	16	12	10	D	D	D	D	D	D
14	1110	112	24	20	13	11	E	E	E	E	E	E
15	1111	120	30	21	14	12	F	F	F	F	F	F
16	10000	121	31	22	15	13	G	G	G	G	G	G
17	10001	122	32	23	16	14	10	H	H	H	H	H
18	10010	200	33	24	17	15	11	I	I	I	I	I
19	10011	201	34	25	18	16	12	10	J	J	J	J
20	10100	202	40	26	19	17	13	11	K	K	K	K

Step 1. List the integers zero to R in Base 10. Most readers will be familiar with Arabic numerals that consist of 10 digits, zero to nine. Arabic numerals presented in this way are said to be in decimal, or base 10 units. Working in base 10, all digits are used to count from zero up to nine, after which two digits are required to represent numbers between 10 and 99, three digits for values in the hundreds, etc. In Binary or base 2, there are only two digits available, zero and one, while when working in base 3, there are three digits available, zero, one, and two. For numbers presented in base 10 or greater, more than ten digits will be required. Unfortunately, the counting system adopted by Western societies is such that we have only nine digits available (perhaps the Babylonians who developed a mathematical system equivalent to base 60 had it right!). Hence, for base 11, we require 11 digits, however we only have ten numerals available. As such, it is common to use capital letters, A, B, C, D, E, etc. to represent the decimal numbers 10, 11, 12, 13, and 14, etc. The base values for Prime numbers two to 37 (dimensions two and 12) are shown in Table 5.9.

Step 2. For each integer in Table 5.9, reverse the order of the digits and convert the resulting value into a decimal number by placing the reversed value after the decimal point. We treat the letters as a special case, substituting the value that the letter represents and keeping that value unchanged. The result of this process is shown in Table 5.10.

Step 3. For each decimalized number, convert the number back to Prime 10 using Equation (5.19):

$$u_k^{(r)} = \sum_{\ell=1}^{L} b_l^{(r)}/p_k^l, \tag{5.19}$$

where p_k represents the Prime number used as the base for the kth parameter, and $b_l^{(r)}$ represents the lth digit after the decimal place for draw r. For example, consider the 13th value for Prime 2, 0.1011. Based on Equation (5.19), this translates to $\frac{1}{2^1} + \frac{0}{2^2} + \frac{1}{2^3} + \frac{1}{2^4} = 0.6875$. Likewise, consider the 20th draw based on Prime 3, that being 0.202. The conversion back to base 10 would be $\frac{2}{3^1} + \frac{0}{3^2} + \frac{2}{3^3} = 0.7407407$. For the non-decimal values (i.e., the ones that we used letters to represent previously), the process is somewhat simplified in that the conversion back to base 10 is:

$$u_k^{(r)} = b_l^{(r)}/p_k. \tag{5.20}$$

Thus, for example, consider the 12th draw for the sequence generated using Prime 13. The $\frac{12}{13} = 0.9230769$.

Step 4. Remove the first row, related to $r = 0$.

Using the process as described above, the Halton sequence for the $R = 20$ is given in Table 5.11. Note that in addition to deleting the first row of the sequence related to $r = 0$, it is commonly advised to also delete the rows associated with $r = 1$ to 10 (see Bratley *et al.* 1992 or Morokoff and Caflisch 1995). Although not necessary, this is done as the generated sequences may be sensitive to the starting point chosen. Note that where the first r (not including the $r = 0$) rows are discarded, it is necessary to construct longer sequences to derive the necessary number of draws. For example, if the analyst wishes to make use of 500 Halton draws, but at the same time delete the first 10, then 510 draws must be constructed.

Halton sequences generated in the above fashion will exhibit a certain degree of correlation, particularly among sequences generated from higher Prime numbers. Indeed, when two large Prime-based sequences associated with two high dimensions are paired, the sampled points increasingly lie on

Table 5.10 Converting the Base values to decimals

r	Prime 2	Prime 3	Prime 5	Prime 7	Prime 11	Prime 13	Prime 17	Prime 19	Prime 23	Prime 29	Prime 31	Prime 37
0	0	0	0	0	0	0	0	0	0	0	0	0
1	0.1	0.1	0.1	0.1	0.1	0.1	0.1	0.1	0.1	0.1	0.1	0.1
2	0.01	0.2	0.2	0.2	0.2	0.2	0.2	0.2	0.2	0.2	0.2	0.2
3	0.11	0.01	0.3	0.3	0.3	0.3	0.3	0.3	0.3	0.3	0.3	0.3
4	0.001	0.11	0.4	0.4	0.4	0.4	0.4	0.4	0.4	0.4	0.4	0.4
5	0.101	0.21	0.01	0.5	0.5	0.5	0.5	0.5	0.5	0.5	0.5	0.5
6	0.011	0.02	0.11	0.6	0.6	0.6	0.6	0.6	0.6	0.6	0.6	0.6
7	0.111	0.12	0.21	0.01	0.7	0.7	0.7	0.7	0.7	0.7	0.7	0.7
8	0.0001	0.22	0.31	0.11	0.8	0.8	0.8	0.8	0.8	0.8	0.8	0.8
9	0.1001	0.001	0.41	0.21	0.9	0.9	0.9	0.9	0.9	0.9	0.9	0.9
10	0.0101	0.101	0.02	0.31	10	10	10	10	10	10	10	10
11	0.1101	0.201	0.12	0.41	0.01	11	11	11	11	11	11	11
12	0.0011	0.011	0.22	0.51	0.11	12	12	12	12	12	12	12
13	0.1011	0.111	0.32	0.61	0.21	0.01	13	13	13	13	13	13
14	0.0111	0.211	0.42	0.02	0.31	0.11	14	14	14	14	14	14
15	0.1111	0.021	0.03	0.12	0.41	0.21	15	15	15	15	15	15
16	0.00001	0.121	0.13	0.22	0.51	0.31	16	16	16	16	16	16
17	0.10001	0.221	0.23	0.32	0.61	0.41	0.01	17	17	17	17	17
18	0.01001	0.002	0.33	0.42	0.71	0.50	0.11	18	18	18	18	18
19	0.11001	0.102	0.43	0.52	0.81	0.61	0.21	0.01	19	19	19	19
20	0.00101	0.202	0.04	0.62	0.91	0.71	0.31	0.11	20	20	20	20

Table 5.11 Halton sequences for Primes 2 to 37

R	Prime 2	Prime 3	Prime 5	Prime 7	Prime 11	Prime 13	Prime 17	Prime 19	Prime 23	Prime 29	Prime 31	Prime 37
1	0.5	0.3333333	0.2	0.1428571	0.090909	0.0769231	0.0588235	0.0526316	0.0434783	0.0344828	0.0322581	0.027027
2	0.25	0.6666667	0.4	0.2857143	0.181818	0.1538462	0.1176471	0.1052632	0.0869565	0.0689655	0.0645161	0.0540541
3	0.75	0.1111111	0.6	0.4285714	0.272727	0.2307692	0.1764706	0.157894	0.1304348	0.1034483	0.0967742	0.0810811
4	0.125	0.4444444	0.8	0.5714286	0.363636	0.3076923	0.2352941	0.2105263	0.173913	0.137931	0.1290323	0.1081081
5	0.625	0.7777778	0.04	0.7142857	0.454545	0.3846154	0.2941176	0.2631579	0.2173913	0.1724138	0.1612903	0.1351351
6	0.375	0.2222222	0.24	0.8571429	0.545455	0.4615385	0.3529412	0.3157895	0.2608696	0.2068966	0.1935484	0.1621622
7	0.875	0.5555556	0.44	0.0204082	0.636364	0.5384615	0.4117647	0.368421	0.3043478	0.2413793	0.2258065	0.1891892
8	0.0625	0.8888889	0.64	0.1632653	0.727273	0.6153846	0.4705882	0.4210526	0.3478261	0.2758621	0.2580645	0.2162162
9	0.5625	0.037037	0.84	0.3061224	0.818182	0.6923077	0.5294118	0.4736842	0.3913043	0.3103448	0.2903226	0.2432432
10	0.3125	0.3703704	0.08	0.4489796	0.909091	0.7692308	0.5882353	0.5263158	0.4347826	0.3448276	0.3225806	0.2702703
11	0.8125	0.7037037	0.28	0.5918367	0.008264	0.8461538	0.6470588	0.5789474	0.4782609	0.3793103	0.3548387	0.2972973
12	0.1875	0.1481481	0.48	0.7346939	0.099174	0.9230769	0.7058824	0.6315789	0.5217391	0.4137931	0.3870968	0.3243243
13	0.6875	0.4814815	0.68	0.877551	0.190083	0.0059172	0.7647059	0.6842105	0.5652174	0.4482759	0.4193548	0.3513514
14	0.4375	0.8148148	0.88	0.0408163	0.280992	0.0828402	0.8235294	0.7368421	0.6086957	0.4827586	0.4516129	0.3783784
15	0.9375	0.2592593	0.12	0.1836735	0.371901	0.1597633	0.8823529	0.7894737	0.6521739	0.5172414	0.483871	0.4054054
16	0.03125	0.5925926	0.32	0.3265306	0.46281	0.2366864	0.9411765	0.8421053	0.6956522	0.5517241	0.516129	0.4324324
17	0.53125	0.9259259	0.52	0.4693878	0.553719	0.3136095	0.0034602	0.8947368	0.7391304	0.5862069	0.5483871	0.4594595
18	0.28125	0.0740741	0.72	0.6122449	0.644628	0.3905325	0.0622837	0.9473684	0.7826087	0.6206897	0.5806452	0.4864865
19	0.78125	0.4074074	0.92	0.755102	0.735537	0.4674556	0.1211073	0.0027701	0.826087	0.6551724	0.6129032	0.5135135
20	0.15625	0.7407407	0.16	0.8979592	0.826446	0.5443787	0.1799308	0.054017	0.8695652	0.6896552	0.6451613	0.5405405

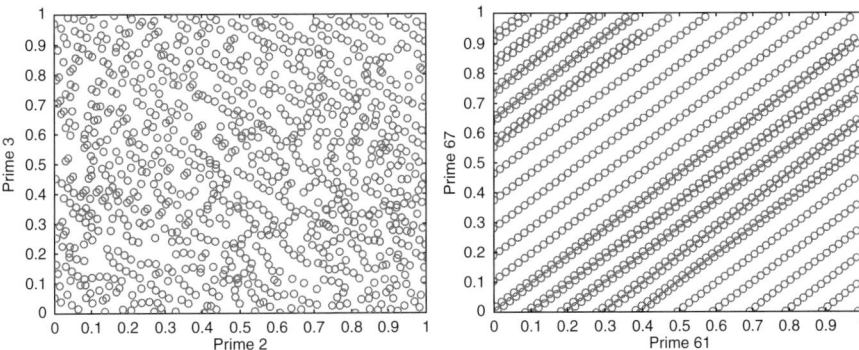

Figure 5.5   Coverage of Halton sequences using different Primes ($R = 1,000$)

parallel lines. This is illustrated in Figure 5.5. The panel on the left of Figure 5.5 plots the space covered or evaluated for $R = 1,000$ draws based on Halton sequences generated from Primes 2 and 3. The panel on the right of Figure 5.5 plots for the same number of draws the coverage based on Halton sequences generated from Primes 61 and 67 (dimensions 18 and 19). As shown in the figure, the use of higher dimensions leads to a rapid deterioration in the uniformity of the coverage of Halton sequences, with a noticeable deterioration after only five dimensions (i.e., Prime 13 onwards) (e.g., Bhat 2001, 2003).

To break this correlation, researchers have suggested several ways in which the Halton sequences can be randomized. We discuss two of these approaches in Sections 5.2.2 and 5.2.3. Nevertheless, in addition to increasingly worsening correlation structures, the use of higher dimensions leads to a need to use more draws. This can clearly be seen in Table 5.11 by comparing the sequences generated from Primes 2 to 19 (dimensions one to eight) to sequences generated from Prime 23 onwards.

For the first set of sequences, the Halton sequences cover the zero-one space at least once before starting again. For example, examining the sequence generated from Prime 19, the sequence begins with a value close to zero, before increasing to close to one (draw 18), before starting the cycle once more with a value close to zero. As such, within 20 draws, sequences generated using Primes 2 to 19 will have completed at least one cycle between zero and one. Note that for sequences generated from Prime numbers greater than 19, this is not the case. Indeed, for Prime 37, the sequence requires 36 draws before it begins the cycle anew. As a consequence, higher dimensional Halton sequences based on larger Prime numbers will require many more draws in

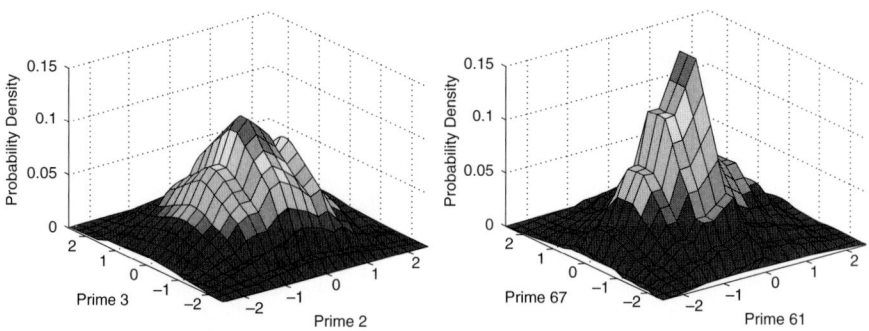

Figure 5.6   Multivariate Normal distributions for 100 Halton sequences based on different Primes

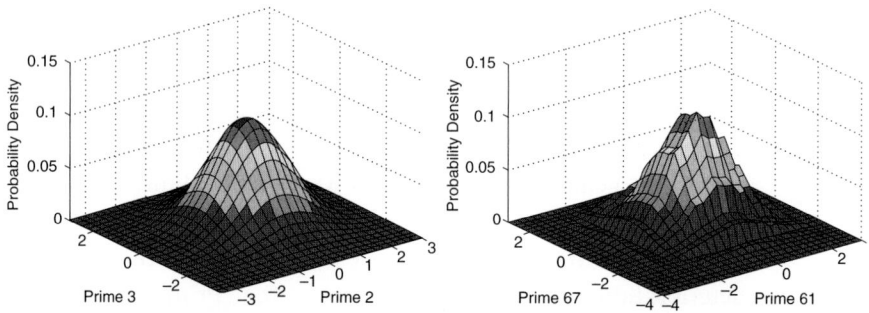

Figure 5.7   Multivariate Normal distributions for 1,000 Halton sequences based on different Primes

order to properly simulate distributions of interest. To demonstrate, consider Figure 5.6, in which we use 100 Halton draws based on Primes 2 and 3, and 61, and 67, to simulate two multivariate Normal distributions. As can be seen, while neither plot provides a decent representation of a multivariate Normal distribution, the multivariate Normal distribution constructed from the Halton sequences generated using Primes 2 and 3 performs significantly better than that generated using Primes 61 and 67.

Based on the same Prime numbers, Figure 5.7 shows the two multivariate Normal distributions generating using 1,000 draws from each sequence. As can be seen, after 1,000 draws, the multivariate normal distribution based on the Halton sequences generated from lower Prime numbers approximate the distribution quite well whereas the multivariate normal distribution based on the higher dimensional Halton sequences is less well represented.

To further demonstrate the need to use larger numbers of draws when using larger dimensions of Halton sequences, Figure 5.8 plots the multivariate

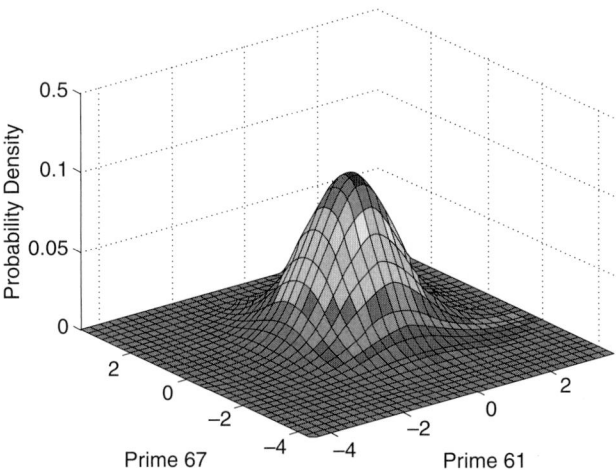

Figure 5.8   Multivariate Normal distribution for 5,000 Halton draws based on Primes 61 and 67

normal distribution based on Halton sequences generated from Primes 61 and 67, assuming 5,000 draws. As can be seen from the figure, the use of 5,000 draws provides an adequate approximation for the multivariate normal distribution, much better than 1,000 draws.

5.4.3 Random Halton sequences

Wang and Hickernell (2000) describe a procedure to randomize Halton sequences. They propose for each of the k dimensions, generating a random number, Z_k, which can take any integer value between zero and some large number. For each dimension, Halton sequences are then constructed for $R + Z_k$ draws, such that the length of each sequence will differ by some random amount. For each dimension, the final sequence is constructed by deleting the first Z_k draws. For example, assume the analyst wishes to simulate two different dimensions. Using Primes 2 and 3, the analyst draws two random integers, five and eight. The **randomization** process would then involve constructing 25 draws based on Prime 2 and 28 draws based on Prime 3. This is shown in the left hand side of Table 5.12. Next, the first five Halton sequences are deleted for the first sequence, while the first eight draws are deleted from the second sequence, thus resulting in precisely 20 draws for both sequences.

Note that randomizing the generation process using the procedure as described will lead to different sequences being generated in different time intervals, unless the seed of the randomization process is fixed. Further, note

Table 5.12 Example of randomized Halton draws process

r	Prime 2	Prime 3	r	Prime 2	Prime 3
1	**0.5**	**0.333333**	1	0.375	0.037037
2	**0.25**	**0.666667**	2	0.875	0.37037
3	**0.75**	**0.111111**	3	0.0625	0.703704
4	**0.125**	**0.444444**	4	0.5625	0.148148
5	**0.625**	**0.777778**	5	0.3125	0.481481
6	0.375	**0.222222**	6	0.8125	0.814815
7	0.875	**0.555556**	7	0.1875	0.259259
8	0.0625	**0.888889**	8	0.6875	0.592593
9	0.5625	0.037037	9	0.4375	0.925926
10	0.3125	0.37037	10	0.9375	0.074074
11	0.8125	0.703704	11	0.03125	0.407407
12	0.1875	0.148148	12	0.53125	0.740741
13	0.6875	0.481481	13	0.28125	0.185185
14	0.4375	0.814815	14	0.78125	0.518519
15	0.9375	0.259259	15	0.15625	0.851852
16	0.03125	0.592593	16	0.65625	0.296296
17	0.53125	0.925926	17	0.40625	0.62963
18	0.28125	0.074074	18	0.90625	0.962963
19	0.78125	0.407407	19	0.09375	0.012346
20	0.15625	0.740741	20	0.59375	0.345679
21	0.65625	0.185185			
22	0.40625	0.518519			
23	0.90625	0.851852			
24	0.09375	0.296296			
25	0.59375	0.62963			
26	–	0.962963			
27	–	0.012346			
28	–	0.345679			

that the process need not break the correlation structure as advertised, particularly when larger Prime numbers are used to construct the Halton sequences. For example, panel (a) of Figure 5.9 plots the unit space covered or evaluated for $R = 1,000$ draws based on randomized Halton sequences generated from Primes 61 and 67, where $Z_{61} = 663$ and $Z_{67} = 931$. As can be seen in the plot, a similar correlation pattern as existed before remains. Further still, as can be seen in panel (b) of Figure 5.9, which plots the multivariate normal distribution simulated using the same randomized Halton draws, even with 1,000 draws the approximation to the assumed density remains less than desirable.

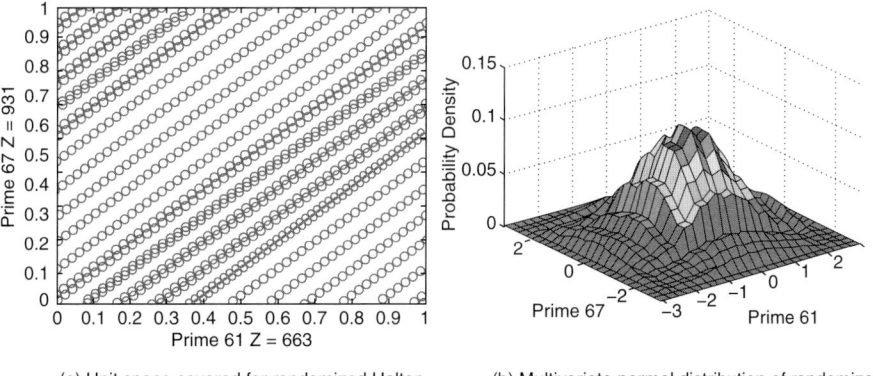

(a) Unit space covered for randomized Halton

(b) Multivariate normal distribution of randomized sequence Halton sequence

Figure 5.9   Example of randomized Halton draws based on Primes 61 and 67

5.4.4 Shuffled Halton sequences

In the current section, we introduce the approach discussed by among others Tuffin (1996), where the modified draws are obtained by adding a random draw ξ_k to the individual draws in dimension k, and by subtracting one from any draws that now fall outside the 0–1 interval. That is:

$$u_k^{(r)'} = \begin{cases} u_k^{(r)} + \xi_k, & \text{if } u_k^{(r)} + \xi_k \le 1, else \\ u_k^{(r)} + \xi_k - 1. \end{cases} \tag{5.21}$$

In generating randomized Halton sequences in this fashion, different random draws are used for each dimension. As with randomized Halton sequences, it is necessary to fix the random values by setting the random seed so as to allow for comparisons across simulation runs. Further, similar to randomized Halton draws, shuffled Halton sequences will not necessarily solve all of the issues related with the use of higher dimensions of Halton sequences. For example, let $\xi_{61} = 0.47328$ and $\xi_{67} = 0.33709$. Figures 5.10 and 5.11 plot the coverage over unit space for 1,000 and 5,000 shuffled Halton sequences as well as the associated multivariate Normal distributions, based on Primes 61 and 67 (dimensions 18 and 19). As shown in the plots, the shuffling process does not appear to compensate for the requirement that a greater number of draws is required when constructing Halton sequences using higher level prime numbers.

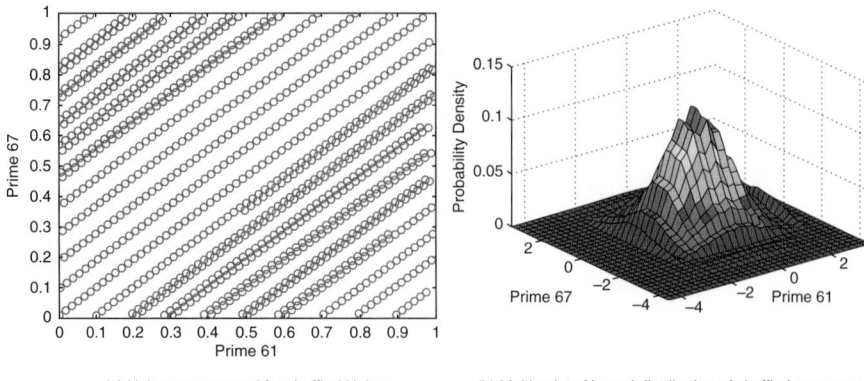

(a) Unit space covered for shuffled Halton

(b) Multivariate Normal distribution of shuffled sequence Halton sequence

Figure 5.10 Example of 1,000 shuffled Halton draws based on Primes 61 and 67

5.4.5 Modified Latin Hypercube sampling

The Modified Latin Hypercube sampling (MLHS) procedure described by Hess *et al.* (2006) generates multi-dimensional sequences by combining randomly shuffled versions of one-dimensional sequences made up of uniformly spaced points. Formally, the individual one-dimensional sequences of length R are constructed as:

$$u_k^{(r)} = \frac{r-1}{R} + \xi_k, \quad r = 1, \ldots, R, \tag{5.22}$$

where ξ_k is a random number drawn between 0 and $1/R$, and where a different random draw is used in each of the K different dimensions. In the resulting sequence, the distances between adjacent draws are all equal to $1/R$, satisfying the condition of equal spacing. Multi-dimensional sequences are constructed by a simple combination of randomly shuffled one-dimensional sequences, where the shuffling disrupts the correlation between individual dimensions.

In words, the process begins by listing integers from 1 to R and subtracting 1 from this number. For example, assuming $R = 5$, we obtain the values 0, 1, 2, 3, 4. Each value of the sequence is then divided by R, thus giving values of 0, 0.2, 0.4, 0.6, and 0.8 in the current example. These values then form the basis for each MLHS sequence to be generated. Next a different random number between 0 and $1/R$ is generated for each sequence that is then added to each value in the sequence. For example, assuming that a random value of 0.096 is drawn, then the sequence now becomes 0.096, 0.296, 0.496, 0.696, and 0.896.

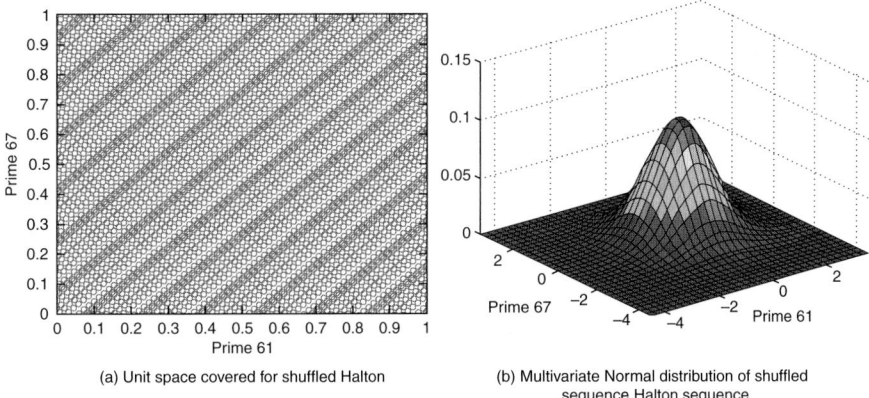

(a) Unit space covered for shuffled Halton

(b) Multivariate Normal distribution of shuffled sequence Halton sequence

Figure 5.11   Example of 5,000 shuffled Halton draws based on Primes 61 and 67

	A	B	C	D	E	F
1						
2	ς_k	=1/MAX($A$5:$A$14)*RAND()	0.0955	0.0379	0.0256	0.0902
3						
4	R	u^r_1	u^r_2	u^r_3	u^r_4	u^r_5
5	1	=($A5-1)/$A$14+B$2	0.0955	0.0379	0.0256	0.0902
6	2	0.1187	0.1955	0.1379	0.1256	0.1902
7	3	0.2187	0.2955	0.2379	0.2256	0.2902
8	4	0.3187	0.3955	0.3379	0.3256	0.3902
9	5	0.4187	0.4955	0.4379	0.4256	0.4902
10	6	0.5187	0.5955	0.5379	0.5256	0.5902
11	7	0.6187	0.6955	0.6379	0.6256	0.6902
12	8	0.7187	0.7955	0.7379	0.7256	0.7902
13	9	0.8187	0.8955	0.8379	0.8256	0.8902
14	10	0.9187	0.9955	0.9379	0.9256	0.9902

Figure 5.12   Example of generating MLHS draws in Microsoft Excel

Finally, the order of values within each sequence is randomized. Thus, the final sequence might therefore be 0.296, 0.896, 0.696, 0.496, and 0.096.

Figure 5.12 demonstrates the construction of 10 MLHS random draws for five different sequences using Microsoft Excel rand functions. In row 2 we compute the rand draws for ξ_k by first calculating $1/R$ and multiplying this value by different random draws for each of the five sequences. The random draws are taken from a random uniform distribution based on the Microsoft Excel rand() function. The MLHS draws are then calculated as per Equation (5.22).

Once the random draws have been computed, the analyst should fix the values ξ_k or else the draws will continually change every time an operation is

	A	B	C	D	E	F
1						
2	ζ_k	0.0187	0.0955	0.0379	0.0256	0.0902
3						
4	R	u^r_1	u^r_2	u^r_3	u^r_4	u^r_5
5	1	0.1187	0.7955	0.6379	0.5256	0.1902
6	2	0.7187	0.9955	0.7379	0.8256	0.5902
7	3	0.2187	0.6955	0.4379	0.2256	0.4902
8	4	0.6187	0.0955	0.2379	0.4256	0.9902
9	5	0.4187	0.1955	0.9379	0.9256	0.3902
10	6	0.3187	0.8955	0.5379	0.6256	0.0902
11	7	0.5187	0.5955	0.0379	0.3256	0.7902
12	8	0.7187	0.3955	0.3379	0.1256	0.8902
13	9	0.9187	0.2955	0.1379	0.7256	0.2902
14	10	0.8187	0.4955	0.8379	0.0256	0.6902

Figure 5.13 Randomization of MLHS draws in Microsoft Excel

performed in Excel. Further, the analyst should take the draws as calculated and randomize each column, as shown in Figure 5.13.

5.4.6 Sobol sequences

Like Halton sequences, Sobol sequences (Sobol 1967) represent deterministic sequences of probabilities. Unlike Halton sequences, however, all dimensions of Sobol sequences are based on Prime 2 but with different permutations. The use of a low base therefore ensures a small cycle length which is not necessarily present in Halton sequences generated using higher order Prime numbers. The generation of multi-dimensional Sobol sequences involves undertaking the same steps independent of the dimension. We provide a brief description of the generation process here; however, the interested reader is referred to Galanti and Jung (1997) for a more detailed exposition. The process begins by generating a set of r odd integer values, m_r, such that $0 < m_r < 2^r$. To generate the integers, the coefficients of a primitive polynomial of modulo 2 are first derived. The coefficients, c_q, which will take the values 0 or 1 are the values of interest. A primitive polynomial of degree d is given as Equation (5.23):

$$P = x^d + c_1 x^{d-1} + c_2 x^{d-2} + \dots + c_{d-1} x + 1. \tag{5.23}$$

Table 5.13 shows the first five primitive polynomials where the first dimension will use the first primitive polynomial, the second dimension the second, etc.

Table 5.13 Example primitive polynomials

Degree	Primitive polynomial	
0	1	–
1	$x+1$	–
2	x^2+x+1	–
3	x^3+x+1	x^3+x^2+1

For higher dimensions, several primitive polynomials will exist from which the analyst may randomly select one.

Next, the set of values, m_r are located for each draw r using the coefficients of the primitive polynomial and a recursive relationship for $r > d$ such that:

$$m_r = 2c_1 m_{r-1} \oplus 2^2 c_2 m_{r-2} \oplus ... \oplus 2^{d-1} c_{d-1} m_{r-d+1} \oplus 2^d c_{r-d} m_{r-d}, \qquad (5.24)$$

where $c_1, c_2, . . ., c_{d-1}$ are the coefficients of the primitive polynomial of degree d and $\oplus$ is the bit-by-bit exclusive-or (EOR) operator. For example, $14 \oplus 8$ expanded to base 2 is represented as:

$01110 \oplus 11000 = 10110.$

As Equation (5.24) generates values for m_r for $r > d$ only, the first "d" odd integers must be supplied rather than constructed. Any odd values can be chosen provided the condition $0 < m_r < 2^r$ is satisfied. A set of direction numbers are next generated by converting each m_r value into a binary fraction in the base 2 number system such that:

$$v(r) = \frac{m_r}{2^r} \text{ in base 2.} \qquad (5.25)$$

Once the direction numbers have been calculated, a sequence of non-negative integers ($n = 0, 1, 2, . . ., R-1$) is converted into their representation in the base 2 number system. Finally, the rth sobol number $\phi(r)$ for $n = 0, 1, 2, . . ., R-1$ is calculated using the Antonov and Saleev (1979) recursive algorithm:

$$\phi(n+1) = \phi(n) \oplus v(q), \qquad (5.26)$$

where $\phi^k(0) = 0$, $v(q)$ is the qth direction number and q is the rightmost zero bit in the base two expansion. For example, the rightmost zero value for $n = 9$ represented in the base 2 number system (1001) corresponds to $q = 2$.

To demonstrate, consider the construction of the first six Sobol draws using the third-degree primitive polynomial:

$$P = x^3 + c_1 x^2 + 1 = 1.x^3 + 1.x^2 + 0.x + 1.$$

which implies $c_1 = 1$ and $c_2 = 0$. The recurrence relationship (Equation (5.24)) then becomes:

$$m_r = 2m_{r-1} \oplus 2^3 m_{r-3} \oplus m_{r-3}.$$

Arbitrarily choosing m_1, m_2, and m_3 to equal 1, 3, and 7, respectively, then for $r = 4$ to 6 we obtain the values in Table 5.14 for m_r and $v(r)$.

The last step involves calculation of the actual generation of the draws themselves. For the first draw, we consider $n = 0$ for which the binary expansion of 0 is 0.0, hence insinuating $q = 1$, meaning that we apply $v(1)$ to Equation (5.25). Hence for the first draw, we obtain, $\phi(1) = \phi(0) \oplus v(1) = 0.1 \oplus 0.1 = 0.1$, which in base 10 gives the value 0.5. For the second draw, assuming $n = 1$, the binary expansion is 0.01, and hence the rightmost zero value is for $q = 2$. As such, for the second draw, we obtain $\phi(2) = \phi(1) \oplus v(2) = 0.10 \oplus 0.11 = 0.01$ which in base 10 returns the value 0.25. The generation of the remaining values continues in this manner. The entire process is shown in Table 5.14.

Table 5.15 presents the first 10 Sobol draws for the first 10 dimensions of Sobol sequences.

Figure 5.14 plots the coverage in unit space for 250 Sobol draws based on dimensions one and two, and 19 and 20. Although in higher dimensions, patterns become increasingly discernible, coverage of the space tends to remain superior to Halton sequences with the same number of draws. Nevertheless, as shown in Figure 5.15, the number of draws required to adequately simulate

Table 5.14 Example calculations for constructing Sobol draws

			Base 2 conversion					Base 10	Base 2	
r	$2m_{i-1}$	$2^3 m_{i-3}$	$2m_{i-3}$	$2m_{i-1}$	$2^3 m_{i-3}$	$2m_{i-3}$	m_r	$v(r)$	$v(r)$	$\Phi(r)$
1	–	–	–	–	–	–	1	1/2	0.1	0.5
2	–	–	–	–	–	–	3	3/4	0.11	0.25
3	–	–	–	–	–	–	7	7/8	0.111	0.75
4	14	8	1	1110	1000	1	7	7/16	0.0111	0.125
5	14	24	3	1110	11000	11	23	23/32	0.10111	0.625
6	46	56	7	101110	111000	111	17	17/64	0.010001	0.375

Table 5.15 Sobol draws

R	Sobol 1	Sobol 2	Sobol 3	Sobol 4	Sobol 5	Sobol 6	Sobol 7	Sobol 8	Sobol 9	Sobol 10
1	0.5000	0.5000	0.5000	0.5000	0.5000	0.5000	0.5000	0.5000	0.5000	0.5000
2	0.7500	0.2500	0.7500	0.2500	0.7500	0.2500	0.7500	0.2500	0.2500	0.7500
3	0.2500	0.7500	0.2500	0.7500	0.2500	0.7500	0.2500	0.7500	0.7500	0.2500
4	0.3750	0.3750	0.6250	0.1250	0.8750	0.8750	0.1250	0.6250	0.1250	0.8750
5	0.8750	0.8750	0.1250	0.6250	0.3750	0.3750	0.6250	0.1250	0.6250	0.3750
6	0.6250	0.1250	0.3750	0.3750	0.1250	0.6250	0.8750	0.8750	0.3750	0.1250
7	0.1250	0.6250	0.8750	0.8750	0.6250	0.1250	0.3750	0.3750	0.8750	0.6250
8	0.1875	0.3125	0.3125	0.6875	0.5625	0.1875	0.0625	0.9375	0.1875	0.0625
9	0.6875	0.8125	0.8125	0.1875	0.0625	0.6875	0.5625	0.4375	0.6875	0.5625
10	0.9375	0.0625	0.5625	0.9375	0.3125	0.4375	0.8125	0.6875	0.4375	0.8125

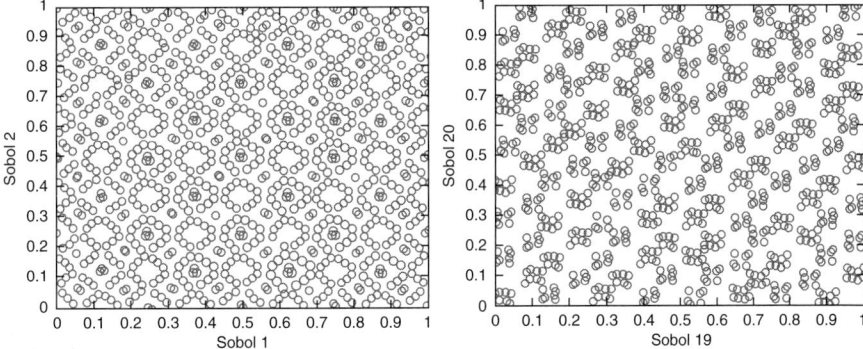

Figure 5.14   Coverage of Sobol sequences

multivariate distributions, in this case, multivariate Normal distributions, may be many more than are used in most published research to date.

Although we do not do so here, it is also possible to randomize or shuffle Sobol sequences. This can be done using the same methods used to randomize or shuffle Halton sequences (see Sections 5.4.2 and 5.4.3).

5.4.7 Antithetic sequences

As a method, antithetic sequences (Hammersley and Morton 1956) simply represents a systematic modification of any other type of sequence, and as such can be applied to PMC or any QMC method. Therefore, unlike the other methods described here, the generation of antithetic sequences first requires

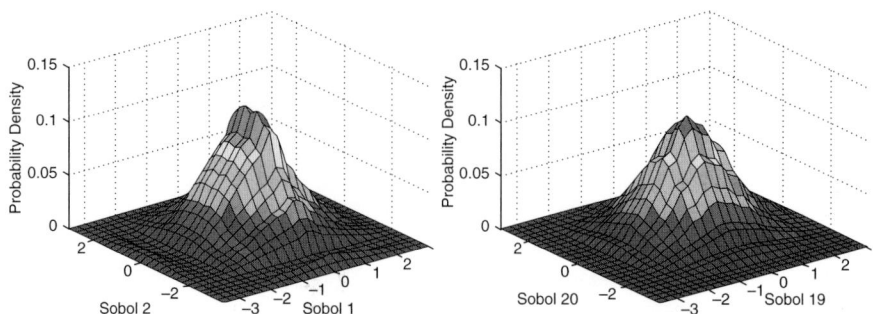

Figure 5.15 Multivariate Normal distributions for 250 Sobol draws based on different dimensions

the generation of another form of sequences. The process of generating antithetic draws involves taking each value drawn from an existing density and using these to construct new draws by inflecting the original values around the midpoint of the original density. For example, given that the standard uniform density is bounded at 0 and 1 and centered at 0.5, the antithetic variate of a draw d_1 can be constructed as $d_2 = 1 - d_1$.

In the case of a k-dimensional problem, the typical approach to generating antithetic draws involves constructing the full factorial of original and antithetic variates. Thus, each draw from the original sequence will result in 2^k draws. For example, consider a case involving three random parameters using Halton sequences. Specifically, consider the draw associated with $r = 11$, such that $d_{11} = [d_{11}^1, d_{11}^2, d_{11}^2] = [0.8125, 0.7037, 2800]$. The resulting antithetic draws are given in Equation (5.27):

$$
\begin{bmatrix} d_{11,1} \\ d_{11,2} \\ d_{11,3} \\ d_{11,4} \\ d_{11,5} \\ d_{11,6} \\ d_{11,7} \\ d_{11,8} \end{bmatrix}
=
\begin{bmatrix}
d_{11}^1 & d_{11}^2 & d_{11}^3 \\
1 - d_{11}^1 & d_{11}^2 & d_{11}^3 \\
d_{11}^1 & 1 - d_{11}^2 & d_{11}^3 \\
d_{11}^1 & d_{11}^2 & 1 - d_{11}^3 \\
1 - d_{11}^1 & 1 - d_{11}^2 & d_{11}^3 \\
1 - d_{11}^1 & d_{11}^2 & 1 - d_{11}^3 \\
d_{11}^1 & 1 - d_{11}^2 & 1 - d_{11}^3 \\
1 - d_{11}^1 & 1 - d_{11}^2 & 1 - d_{11}^3
\end{bmatrix}
=
\begin{bmatrix}
0.8125 & 0.7037 & 0.2800 \\
0.1875 & 0.7037 & 0.2800 \\
0.8125 & 0.2963 & 0.2800 \\
0.8125 & 0.7037 & 0.7200 \\
0.1875 & 0.2963 & 0.2800 \\
0.1875 & 0.7037 & 0.7200 \\
0.8125 & 0.2963 & 0.7200 \\
0.1875 & 0.2963 & 0.7200
\end{bmatrix}.
$$

$$(5.27)$$

An issue with the use of antithetic draws lies in the fact that the number of draws will have to be a multiple of 2^k. That is, unlike Halton, Sobol, and MLHS draws, where the analyst can specify any value for R, the use of antithetic draws requires specific values of R to be chosen. The restriction that the number of draws must be a multiple of 2^k implies a lower bound on the minimum number of draws that are possible. Thus, the use of antithetic draws may involve greater estimation time requirements than other draw types that do not have this restriction.

5.4.8 PMC and QMC rates of convergence

A practical concern is the reduction of the computational time needed for the simulation as well as the numerical error of the simulation itself. Both issues are related to the rate at which the simulation converges to the true value. There are several approaches to reduce the simulation error; however, the easiest approach is to simply increase the number of draws, R. Doing so will result in increased computation time. The alternative approach is to make use of more intelligent draws. For PMC, the convergence rate is $O(1/\sqrt{R})$ (see Niederreiter 1992), which compares to $O(1/R)$ in optimal circumstances or $O\left((\ln(R))^K/R\right)$, where K is the number of dimensions, in the upper limit (e.g., see Caflisch 1998 or Asmussen and Glynn 2007). The values derived from these equations represent the state that the probabilistic error bound that the Monte Carlo method, either PMC or QMC, for numerical integration will yield. Note that convergence for PMC simulations is independent of the number of dimensions being evaluated, as is the best case for QMC methods. Nevertheless, in theory, under less than optimal conditions, the convergence rate of QMC methods is dependent on the number of dimensions, and hence can be slower to reach convergence than PMC. Table 5.16 shows the convergence rates of PMC and QMC simulation methods based on the above discussion.

Note that the lower bound of the probabilistic error for QMC will always be smaller than that of PMC. Typically, for dimensions higher than 5, the upper bound for QMC methods will be inferior to the bound of PMC; however, in practice, the convergence rates of QMC methods are usually observed to be much smaller than suggested by the theoretical upper bound. As such, the accuracy of QMC approaches is generally thought to increase faster as R increases than PMC methods (for further discussion of this, see Asmussen and Glynn 2007).

The above discussion summarizes the literature on Monte Carlo simulations in general; however, when the object being simulated involves a non-linear transformation, the above might not hold. Problems arise when dealing with discrete choice models, as the simulation of the maximum

Table 5.16 Convergence rates of PMC and QMC simulation methods

			QMC	
R	K	PMC	$O(1/R)$	$O((ln(R))^K/R)$
50	1	0.14142	0.02000	0.07824
100	2	0.10000	0.01000	0.21208
100	5	0.10000	0.01000	20.71230
1000	1	0.03162	0.00100	0.00691
1000	2	0.03162	0.00100	0.04772
1000	5	0.03162	0.00100	15.72841
5000	1	0.01414	0.00020	0.00170
5000	2	0.01414	0.00020	0.01451
5000	5	0.01414	0.00020	8.96422
5000	10	0.01414	0.00020	401,786.16490
10000	5	0.01000	0.00010	6.62794
10000	10	0.01000	0.00010	439,295.54628
10000	15	0.01000	0.00010	29,116,233,957.87300
10000	20	0.01000	0.00010	1,929,805,769,851,870.00000

likelihood function requires the estimation of the log of the simulated choice probabilities. As such, even though the simulated probabilities themselves may be unbiased for the true probabilities for a given number of draws, R, the logs of the probabilities may not be. If this is the case, then the simulated maximum likelihood function will also be biased. While this bias will decrease as R increases, one must also consider the impact of the number of choice observations. Train (2009) provides a discussion of these issues and hence we omit a detailed treatise here, providing only a brief summary of the arguments.

Firstly, as argued by Train (2009), if R is fixed, then the simulated maximum likelihood function will fail to converge to the true parameter estimates as the number of choice observations in the sample, S, increases. If R increases at the same rate as S, the simulated maximum likelihood function will be consistent; however, the estimator will not be asymptotically normal, meaning that it will not be possible to estimate the standard errors (see Section 5.7). Indeed, R must increase at a rate greater than $\sqrt{s}$ for the simulated maximum likelihood function to be consistent, asymptotically normal, and efficient, in which case it will be equivalent to the maximum likelihood estimator. The corollary of this is that the number of draws used in practice should increase as the number of choice observations increases in a sample.

5.5 Correlation and drawing from densities

The discussion to date has implicitly assumed that the random parameters are drawn from univariate distributions. This is because in the simulation process as described, each individual random estimate, whether it be a random taste parameter or random error term, is assigned to a unique PMC or QMC generated sequence. In theory, although not in practice, each sequence is unrelated to each other. Earlier we noted that correlation between draws for different dimensions can have a positive effect on the approximation of whatever integral is being evaluated. In describing the various QMC methods, we plotted the coverage of the draws in the 0–1 space and related the resulting patterns to correlation. To demonstrate the issue further, in Table 5.17, we show the correlation structures for the first 12 dimensions of Halton sequences assuming 50, 100, 500, and 1,000 draws. As shown in the table, several of the sequences are non-trivially correlated when a low number of draws is taken. Nevertheless, we note that the correlations tend to shrink as the number of draws increases. While correlation between the draws may aid in evaluating the integral of interest, it also has implications for interpreting the results. For example, let:

$$
\begin{aligned}
\beta_{n1} &= \bar{\beta}_1 \pm \eta_1 z_{n1} \text{ and} \\
&= \bar{\beta}_1 \pm \omega_1, \\
\beta_{n2} &= \bar{\beta}_2 \pm \eta_2 z_{n2} \\
&= \bar{\beta}_2 \pm \omega_2,
\end{aligned}
\tag{5.28}
$$

represent two random parameters where z_{n1} and z_{n2} are random draws from two univariate distributions – say, two standard Normals – and $\bar{\beta}_k$ and η_k are the mean and deviation parameters of the two distributions, $k = 1, 2$. Let ω_1 and ω_2 represent the simulated standard deviations of the two distributions. Given the above, we note that if z_{n1} and z_{n2} are correlated, then by definition so too must ω_1 and ω_2 and hence β_{n1} and β_{n2}. As such, while the analyst has assumed that β_{n1} and β_{n2} are independent and interpreted the model as if this were the case, the simulation process has induced correlations (or covariances) between the two random parameters.

The assumption that correlation exists between random terms need not be a concern. Indeed, in reality, some or all of the tastes that decision makers have towards different attributes may be correlated. For example, there might exist a time–cost trade-off such that decision makers who are more time sensitive are less cost sensitive, while those who are more cost sensitive are less time sensitive. In this case, one would expect there to exist a negative correlation between the tastes for time and cost. Likewise, the flexibility of the probit model allows for correlation between the random error terms. In both of these cases, the assumption that the random estimates should be drawn from uncorrelated univariate distributions no longer holds. The problem is that in drawing from univariate densities as we have described above, the degree of correlation is an input into the model that, aside from using different numbers and types of draws, the analyst has no control over or, without performing post-estimation simulations, any way of retrieving.

Rather than draw from separate univariate distributions, the solution is to draw directly from the multivariate distribution. In doing so, it should be possible to estimate the covariances of the random terms and hence recover the degree of correlation between the estimates. Unfortunately, this is not so straightforward and to date is only truly feasible if one is working with a multivariate Normal distribution. The process involves making use of a process known as Cholesky factorization or, alternatively, a Cholesky transformation. Let β_n be a vector of K normally distributed elements such that:

$$\beta_n \sim N(\bar{\beta}, \Omega_r), \tag{5.29}$$

where Ω_r represents the covariance matrix of β_n. Note that Ω_r differs from the covariance matrix Ω_e described in Chapter 4. Ω_e was the covariance matrix of the error terms, while Ω_r represents the covariances of the random parameter estimates.

In the multivariate case, the aim is to estimate all the elements of Ω_r. This includes the off-diagonal elements which describe the covariances (and hence correlations) between the random parameter estimates. Cholesky factorization involves constructing a lower triangular matrix, C, such that $\Omega_r = CC'$, as shown in Equation (5.30):

$$\begin{pmatrix} \eta_{11} & \eta_{21} & \eta_{31} & \eta_{41} \\ \eta_{21} & \eta_{22} & \eta_{32} & \eta_{42} \\ \eta_{31} & \eta_{32} & \eta_{33} & \eta_{43} \\ \eta_{41} & \eta_{42} & \eta_{43} & \eta_{44} \end{pmatrix} = \begin{pmatrix} s_{11} & 0 & 0 & 0 \\ s_{21} & s_{22} & 0 & 0 \\ s_{31} & s_{32} & s_{33} & 0 \\ s_{41} & s_{42} & s_{43} & s_{44} \end{pmatrix} \begin{pmatrix} s_{11} & s_{21} & s_{31} & s_{41} \\ 0 & s_{22} & s_{32} & s_{42} \\ 0 & 0 & s_{33} & s_{43} \\ 0 & 0 & 0 & s_{44} \end{pmatrix}.$$

$$\tag{5.30}$$

The Cholesky decomposition matrix is that matrix given immediately to the right of the equal sign in Equation (5.30), in which the upper off-diagonal elements are all equal to zero. To calculate the elements of this matrix given Ω_r the following equations are utilized:

$$s_{11} = \sqrt{\eta_{11}}, \forall k = l = 1 \text{ (the first diagonal element) else} \tag{5.31a}$$

$$s_{kl} = \sqrt{\eta_{kl} - \sum_{k}^{k-1} s_{kl}^2}, \forall k = l \neq 1 \text{(all other diagonal elements) else} \tag{5.31b}$$

$$s_{kl} = (\eta_{kl})/s_{kl}, \forall k = 1, i \neq l \text{(lower off-diagonal elements in the first column)} \tag{5.31c}$$

$$s_{kl} = (\eta_{kl} - \sum_{k}^{k-1} s_{km}s_{ml})/s_{kk}, \forall k \neq 1, k \neq l \text{ (lower off-diagonal}$$

elements not in the first column). $\tag{5.31d}$

Once computed, the values for ω_k may then be determined such that:

$$\begin{pmatrix} \omega_1 \\ \omega_2 \\ \omega_3 \\ \omega_4 \end{pmatrix} = \left(\begin{pmatrix} s_{11} & 0 & 0 & 0 \\ s_{21} & s_{22} & 0 & 0 \\ s_{31} & s_{32} & s_{33} & 0 \\ s_{41} & s_{42} & s_{43} & s_{44} \end{pmatrix} \begin{pmatrix} z_1 \\ z_2 \\ z_3 \\ z_4 \end{pmatrix} \right), \tag{5.32}$$

which may be rewritten as:

$$\begin{aligned} \omega_1 &= s_{11}z_1, \\ \omega_2 &= s_{21}z_1 + s_{22}z_2, \\ \omega_3 &= s_{31}z_1 + s_{32}z_2 + s_{33}z_3, \\ \omega_4 &= s_{41}z_1 + s_{42}z_2 + s_{43}z_3 + s_{44}z_4, \end{aligned} \tag{5.33}$$

where s_{kl} are parameters to be estimated and z_k are draws from univariate standard Normal distributions.

As an aside, Equations (5.31a–d) are not used in practice. As stated above, it is the elements in *C* that are estimated and not those in Ω_r. That is, in practice the matrix *C* is computed, from which Ω_r is later determined. Equations (5.31a–d) assume that Ω_r is known, and from this are used to calculate the elements of *C*. As such, we show these equations simply to demonstrate the relationship between the two matrices (see Appendix 5A).

From Equation (5.33), it can be seen that the Cholesky factorization process correlates the K terms based on K independent components, z_k. For example, in the above, $\hat{\omega}_2$ and $\hat{\omega}_1$ are correlated due to the common influence of z_1. Note that the two terms are not perfectly correlated given that z_2 affects only $\hat{\omega}_2$ and not $\hat{\omega}_1$. Similar patterns of correlation are derived for the other paired combinations of $\hat{\omega}_k$ values.

To demonstrate the above, assume that the following Cholesky matrix was obtained from a hypothetical model:

$$C = \begin{pmatrix} 1.361 & 0 & 0 & 0 \\ 0.613 & 0.094 & 0 & 0 \\ -0.072 & -0.037 & 0.219 & 0 \\ 0.106 & 0.109 & -0.095 & 0.039 \end{pmatrix}, \tag{5.34}$$

such that:

$$\begin{aligned} \hat{\omega}_1 &= 1.361z_1, \\ \hat{\omega}_2 &= 0.613z_1 + 0.094z_2, \\ \hat{\omega}_3 &= -0.072z_1 - 0.037z_2 + 0.219z_3, \\ \hat{\omega}_4 &= 0.106z_1 + 0.109z_2 - 0.095z_3 + 0.039z_4. \end{aligned} \tag{5.35}$$

Given the above estimates, the covariance matrix of random terms, Ω_r, is thus computed as:

$$\begin{aligned} \Omega_r &= \begin{pmatrix} 1.361 & 0 & 0 & 0 \\ 0.613 & 0.094 & 0 & 0 \\ -0.072 & -0.037 & 0.219 & 0 \\ 0.106 & 0.109 & -0.095 & 0.039 \end{pmatrix} \begin{pmatrix} 1.361 & 0.613 & -0.072 & 0.106 \\ 0 & 0.094 & -0.037 & 0.109 \\ 0 & 0 & 0.219 & -0.095 \\ 0 & 0 & 0 & 0.039 \end{pmatrix} \\[2mm] &= \begin{pmatrix} 1.853 & 0.835 & -0.098 & 0.144 \\ 0.835 & 0.385 & -0.048 & 0.075 \\ -0.098 & -0.048 & 0.055 & -0.033 \\ 0.144 & 0.075 & -0.033 & 0.034 \end{pmatrix}. \end{aligned}$$

$$\tag{5.36}$$

Note that the multivariate case will collapse to the univariate case when $s_{kl} = 0, \forall k \neq l$. That is:

$$\begin{pmatrix} \eta_{11} & 0 & 0 & 0 \\ 0 & \eta_{22} & 0 & 0 \\ 0 & 0 & \eta_{33} & 0 \\ 0 & 0 & 0 & \eta_{44} \end{pmatrix} = \begin{pmatrix} s_{11} & 0 & 0 & 0 \\ 0 & s_{22} & 0 & 0 \\ 0 & 0 & s_{33} & 0 \\ 0 & 0 & 0 & s_{44} \end{pmatrix} \begin{pmatrix} s_{11} & 0 & 0 & 0 \\ 0 & s_{22} & 0 & 0 \\ 0 & 0 & s_{33} & 0 \\ 0 & 0 & 0 & s_{44} \end{pmatrix}.$$

(5.37)

Given the covariance matrix, Ω_r it is a simple process to calculate the correlation structure between the random terms, using Equation (5.38):

$$\rho(\eta_k, \eta_l) = \frac{\text{cov}(\eta_k, \eta_l)}{\sigma_{\eta_k} \times \sigma_{\eta_l}}.$$

(5.38)

We leave it to the reader to confirm that the correlation structure of the hypothetical random parameters given the covariance matrix in Equation (5.36) is:

$$\rho(\eta_k, \eta_l) = \begin{pmatrix} 1.000 & 0.988 & -0.310 & 0.576 \\ 0.988 & 1.000 & -0.330 & 0.660 \\ -0.310 & -0.330 & 1.000 & -0.759 \\ 0.576 & 0.660 & -0.759 & 1.000 \end{pmatrix}.$$

(5.39)

To demonstrate how the process works in practice, assume now that the four random parameters have the following moments: $\beta_1 \sim N(-0.5, 0.1)$, $\beta_2 \sim N(0.25, 0.05)$, $\beta_3 \sim N(-1.00, 0.60)$, and $\beta_4 \sim N(0.80, 0.20)$. Further assume that the random parameters are correlated, with C equal to Equation (5.34). Given this information, four steps are followed.

Step 1: For each random parameter, k, draw R independent uniformly distributed random numbers on the interval [0,1]. For example, Figure 5.16 shows the first 15 out of 100 draws generated from Halton sequences for $K=4$ random parameters.

Step 2: Transform the R independent uniformly distributed random numbers into standard Normal distributions. Figure 5.17 demonstrates this transformation using the Microsoft Excel formula normsinv() (see cell I22). As shown in the figure, the univariate standard Normal distributions have correlations close to zero (Table 5.17).

◢	A	B	C	D	E
1		Parameter moments			
2		R_1	R_2	R_3	R_4
3	mu	-0.5	0.25	-1	0.8
4	std dev.	0.1	0.05	0.6	0.2
5					
6		Cholesky matrix			
7		R_1	R_2	R_3	R_4
8	R_1	1.361	0.000	0.000	0.000
9	R_2	0.613	0.094	0.000	0.000
10	R_3	-0.072	-0.037	0.219	0.000
11	R_4	0.106	0.109	-0.095	0.039
12					
13		Correlation matrix of draws			
14		P_2	P_3	P_5	P_7
15	P_2	1.000	-0.030	-0.007	-0.031
16	P_3	-0.030	1.000	-0.020	-0.031
17	P_5	-0.007	-0.020	1.000	-0.043
18	P_7	-0.031	-0.031	-0.043	1.000
19					
20		Halton draws			
21	r	P_2	P_3	P_5	P_7
22	1	0.500	0.333	0.200	0.143
23	2	0.250	0.667	0.400	0.286
24	3	0.750	0.111	0.600	0.429
25	4	0.125	0.444	0.800	0.571
26	5	0.625	0.778	0.040	0.714
27	6	0.375	0.222	0.240	0.857
28	7	0.875	0.556	0.440	0.020
29	8	0.063	0.889	0.640	0.163
30	9	0.563	0.037	0.840	0.306
31	10	0.313	0.370	0.080	0.449
32	11	0.813	0.704	0.280	0.592
33	12	0.188	0.148	0.480	0.735
34	13	0.688	0.481	0.680	0.878
35	14	0.438	0.815	0.880	0.041
36	15	0.938	0.259	0.120	0.184

Figure 5.16   Draw R uniformly distributed random numbers on the interval [0,1]

	A	B	C	D	E	F	G	H	I	J	K
1			**Parameter moments**								
2		R_1	R_2	R_3	R_4						
3	mu	-0.5	0.25	-1	0.8						
4	std dev.	0.1	0.05	0.6	0.2						
5											
6			**Cholesky matrix**								
7		R_1	R_2	R_3	R_4						
8	R_1	1.361	0.000	0.000	0.000						
9	R_2	0.613	0.094	0.000	0.000						
10	R_3	-0.072	-0.037	0.219	0.000						
11	R_4	0.106	0.109	-0.095	0.039						
12											
13			**Correlation matrix of draws**						**Correlation matrix of standard Normals**		
14		P_2	P_3	P_5	P_7			Z_1	Z_2	Z_3	Z_4
15	P_2	1.000	-0.030	-0.007	-0.031		Z_1	1.000	-0.053	-0.021	-0.046
16	P_3	-0.030	1.000	-0.020	-0.031		Z_2	-0.053	1.000	-0.041	-0.068
17	P_5	-0.007	-0.020	1.000	-0.043		Z_3	-0.021	-0.041	1.000	-0.071
18	P_7	-0.031	-0.031	-0.043	1.000		Z_4	-0.046	-0.068	-0.071	1.000
19											
20			**Halton draws**						**Standard Normal draws**		
21	r	P_2	P_3	P_5	P_7		r	Z_1	Z_2	Z_3	Z_4
22	1	0.500	0.333	0.200	0.143		1		=NORMSINV(C22)	2	-1.068
23	2	0.250	0.667	0.400	0.286		2	-0.674	0.431	-0.253	-0.566
24	3	0.750	0.111	0.600	0.429		3	0.674	-1.221	0.253	-0.180
25	4	0.125	0.444	0.800	0.571		4	-1.150	-0.140	0.842	0.180
26	5	0.625	0.778	0.040	0.714		5	0.319	0.765	-1.751	0.566
27	6	0.375	0.222	0.240	0.857		6	-0.319	-0.765	-0.706	1.068
28	7	0.875	0.556	0.440	0.020		7	1.150	0.140	-0.151	-2.045
29	8	0.063	0.889	0.640	0.163		8	-1.534	1.221	0.358	-0.981
30	9	0.563	0.037	0.840	0.306		9	0.157	-1.786	0.994	-0.507
31	10	0.313	0.370	0.080	0.449		10	-0.489	-0.331	-1.405	-0.128

Figure 5.17   Transforming random draws to standard normal draws

Step 3: Matrix multiply the univariate standard Normal distributions with the Cholesky matrix, C. In Microsoft Excel, we do this using the sumproduct formula, multiplying the standard Normal draws by the relevant elements from the Cholesky matrix. An example of this is given in cell P22 of the screen capture shown in Figure 5.18. As shown in the correlation matrix given in cells N15:Q18, the new simulated draws display the predicted correlation structure given in Equation (5.39).

Step 4: Calculate the draws for β_n, such that $\beta_{nk} = \bar{\beta}_k + \varpi_k$. This is shown in columns T to W in Figure 5.19.

The correlated draws derived in Step 4 are then used in the simulation process.

While it is possible to apply the Cholesky factorization process to other multivariate distributions, we note that this should not be done in practice. That is, the process as outlined above should only ever be applied to multivariate Normal distributions. To demonstrate why, we apply the Cholesky transformation assuming a multivariate uniform distribution. Assume now that:

Table 5.17 Correlation structure of Halton sequences for dimensions 1 to 12 for 50 to 1,000 draws

(a) 50 draws

	p_2	p_3	p_5	p_7	p_{11}	p_{13}	p_{17}	p_{19}	p_{23}	p_{29}	p_{31}
p_2	1.000	-0.047	-0.035	-0.075	-0.026	-0.100	0.016	-0.059	-0.011	-0.022	0.036
p_3	-0.047	1.000	-0.049	-0.069	-0.047	0.029	0.006	-0.026	-0.035	0.057	0.001
p_5	-0.035	-0.049	1.000	-0.033	-0.102	0.001	-0.038	-0.058	0.041	0.083	0.043
p_7	-0.075	-0.069	-0.033	1.000	-0.093	-0.067	-0.021	-0.095	-0.034	0.061	-0.051
p_{11}	-0.026	-0.047	-0.102	-0.093	1.000	-0.143	0.038	-0.116	0.222	-0.054	0.074
p_{13}	-0.100	0.029	0.001	-0.067	-0.143	1.000	-0.014	0.149	-0.101	0.123	-0.003
p_{17}	0.016	0.006	-0.038	-0.021	0.038	-0.014	1.000	0.305	-0.185	0.140	0.240
p_{19}	-0.059	-0.026	-0.058	-0.095	-0.116	0.149	0.305	1.000	0.006	-0.092	-0.043
p_{23}	-0.011	-0.035	0.041	-0.034	0.222	-0.101	-0.185	0.006	1.000	0.053	-0.051
p_{29}	-0.022	0.057	0.083	0.061	-0.054	0.123	0.140	-0.092	0.053	1.000	0.721
p_{31}	0.036	0.001	0.043	-0.051	0.074	-0.003	0.240	-0.043	-0.051	0.721	1.000

(b) 100 draws

	p_2	p_3	p_5	p_7	p_{11}	p_{13}	p_{17}	p_{19}	p_{23}	p_{29}	p_{31}
p_2	1.000	-0.030	-0.007	-0.031	-0.016	-0.048	-0.029	-0.017	-0.014	-0.029	0.034
p_3	-0.030	1.000	-0.020	-0.031	0.003	-0.014	-0.054	-0.051	-0.037	0.014	-0.010
p_5	-0.007	-0.020	1.000	-0.043	-0.038	0.001	0.010	0.012	-0.015	-0.058	-0.072
p_7	-0.031	-0.031	-0.043	1.000	0.010	-0.002	-0.030	-0.030	0.017	-0.030	-0.011
p_{11}	-0.016	0.003	-0.038	0.010	1.000	0.009	-0.017	-0.030	0.025	0.016	-0.058
p_{13}	-0.048	-0.014	0.001	-0.002	0.009	1.000	-0.043	-0.005	0.010	-0.070	0.011
p_{17}	-0.029	-0.054	0.010	-0.030	-0.017	-0.043	1.000	-0.131	-0.017	0.006	-0.090
p_{19}	-0.017	-0.051	0.012	-0.030	-0.030	-0.005	-0.131	1.000	-0.068	0.003	0.042
p_{23}	-0.014	-0.037	-0.015	0.017	0.025	0.010	-0.017	-0.068	1.000	-0.086	0.121
p_{29}	-0.029	0.014	-0.058	-0.030	0.016	-0.070	0.006	0.003	-0.086	1.000	0.404
p_{31}	0.034	-0.010	-0.072	-0.011	-0.058	0.011	-0.090	0.042	0.121	0.404	1.000

(c) 500 Draws

	p_2	p_3	p_5	p_7	p_{11}	p_{13}	p_{17}	p_{19}	p_{23}	p_{29}	p_{31}
p_2	1.000	-0.009	0.000	-0.010	-0.004	-0.004	-0.014	-0.008	-0.009	-0.005	0.002
p_3	-0.009	1.000	-0.006	-0.011	0.001	-0.004	-0.003	-0.013	-0.003	-0.003	-0.004
p_5	0.000	-0.006	1.000	-0.006	-0.005	-0.007	-0.007	0.002	-0.014	-0.013	0.000
p_7	-0.010	-0.011	-0.006	1.000	-0.005	-0.004	0.000	-0.006	0.004	-0.002	0.001
p_{11}	-0.004	0.001	-0.005	-0.005	1.000	-0.005	-0.007	0.006	-0.016	-0.003	0.000
p_{13}	-0.004	-0.004	-0.007	-0.004	-0.005	1.000	0.008	0.012	-0.014	0.004	0.007
p_{17}	-0.014	-0.003	-0.007	0.000	-0.007	0.008	1.000	0.020	-0.007	0.019	-0.016
p_{19}	-0.008	-0.013	0.002	-0.006	0.006	0.012	0.020	1.000	-0.010	-0.004	0.001
p_{23}	-0.009	-0.003	-0.014	0.004	-0.016	-0.014	-0.007	-0.010	1.000	-0.014	-0.025
p_{29}	-0.005	-0.003	-0.013	-0.002	-0.003	0.004	0.019	-0.004	-0.014	1.000	0.066
p_{31}	0.002	-0.004	0.000	0.001	0.000	0.007	-0.016	0.001	-0.025	0.066	1.000

(d) 1,000 draws

	p_2	p_3	p_5	p_7	p_{11}	p_{13}	p_{17}	p_{19}	p_{23}	p_{29}	p_{31}
p_2	1.000	-0.004	0.000	-0.004	-0.004	-0.002	-0.004	-0.003	-0.003	-0.001	0.001
p_3	-0.004	1.000	-0.003	-0.005	-0.001	-0.006	-0.002	-0.006	-0.003	-0.005	-0.006
p_5	0.000	-0.003	1.000	-0.005	-0.001	-0.001	-0.002	-0.002	-0.002	-0.005	-0.002
p_7	-0.004	-0.005	-0.005	1.000	-0.003	-0.003	0.003	0.000	-0.002	-0.005	-0.005
p_{11}	-0.004	-0.001	-0.001	-0.003	1.000	0.002	0.002	0.003	-0.006	0.000	-0.013
p_{13}	-0.002	-0.006	-0.001	-0.003	0.002	1.000	0.004	0.006	0.001	-0.006	-0.006
p_{17}	-0.004	-0.004	-0.002	0.003	0.002	0.004	1.000	0.013	0.001	0.011	-0.013
p_{19}	-0.003	-0.006	-0.002	0.000	0.003	0.006	0.013	1.000	0.008	-0.006	-0.002
p_{23}	-0.003	-0.003	-0.002	-0.002	-0.006	0.001	0.001	0.008	1.000	-0.003	0.010
p_{29}	-0.001	-0.005	-0.005	-0.005	0.000	-0.006	0.011	-0.006	-0.003	1.000	0.043
p_{31}	0.001	-0.006	-0.002	-0.005	-0.013	-0.006	-0.013	-0.002	0.010	0.043	1.000

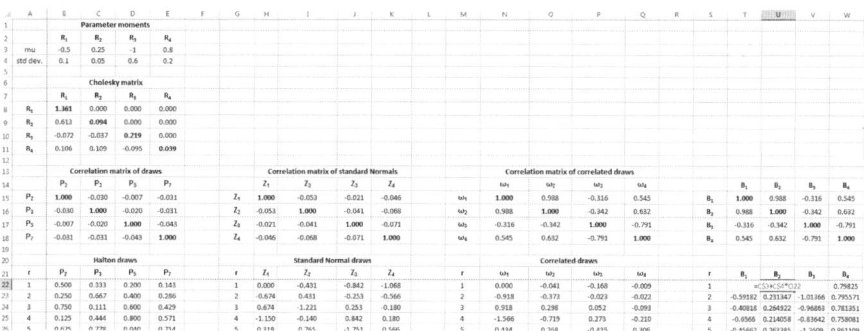

Figure 5.18 Correlating the random draws

Figure 5.19 Correlated random draws

$\beta_1 \sim U(-0.8, -0.1)$, $\beta_2 \sim U(0.1, 0.5)$, $\beta_3 \sim U(-1.00, -0.20)$,   and $\beta_4 \sim U(1.0, 2.0)$. Keeping the same Cholesky matrix, C, we apply the Cholesky transformation using the same process described above.

Figure 5.20 shows the results of this process. As can be seen, the resulting simulated draws are correlated in the manner predicted. The issue, however, is that while the final draws are correlated correctly, the upper and lower moments of the resulting uniform distributions are no longer related to the bounds of the input parameters. Thus, for example, the interval for β_4 was [1,2]; however, the application of the Cholesky transformation results in an interval between [0.952,1.202]. Similar issues arise when Cholesky factorization is applied to other distributions based on the Normal, such as log-Normals. As such, most applications allowing for correlated parameters are restricted to drawing from a multivariate Normal distribution.

▲	A	B	C	D	E	F	G	H	I	J	K	L	M	N	O	P	Q
1			Parameter moments														
2			R_1	R_2	R_3	R_4											
3		Lower	-0.8	0.1	-1	1											
4		Upper	-0.1	0.5	-0.2	2											
5																	
6			Cholesky matrix														
7			R_1	R_2	R_3	R_4											
8		R_1	1.361	0.000	0.000	0.000											
9		R_2	0.613	0.094	0.000	0.000											
10		R_3	-0.072	-0.037	0.219	0.000									B_1	B_2	B_3	B_4
11		R_4	0.106	0.109	-0.095	0.039							Min	-0.793	0.116	-1.056	0.952
12													Max	0.138	0.371	-0.846	1.202
13			Correlation matrix of draws					Correlation matrix of correlated draws									
14			P_2	P_3	P_5	P_7		ω_1	ω_2	ω_3	ω_4			B_1	B_2	B_3	B_4
15		P_2	1.000	-0.030	-0.007	-0.031	ω_1	1.000	0.988	-0.309	0.557	B_1	1.000	0.988	-0.309	0.557
16		P_3	-0.030	1.000	-0.020	-0.031	ω_2	0.988	1.000	-0.333	0.642	B_2	0.988	1.000	-0.333	0.642
17		P_5	-0.007	-0.020	1.000	-0.043	ω_3	-0.309	-0.333	1.000	-0.776	B_3	-0.309	-0.333	1.000	-0.776
18		P_7	-0.031	-0.031	-0.043	1.000	ω_4	0.557	0.642	-0.776	1.000	B_4	0.557	0.642	-0.776	1.000
19																	
20			Halton draws					Correlated draws									
21		r	P_2	P_3	P_5	P_7	r	ω_1	ω_2	ω_3	ω_4	r	B_1	B_2	B_3	B_4
22		1	0.500	0.333	0.200	0.143	1	=SUMPRODUCT($B$9:$C$9,B22:C22)		0.076		1	-0.32355	0.235278	-1.00387	1.075755
23		2	0.250	0.667	0.400	0.286	2	0.340	0.216	0.045	0.072	2	-0.56177	0.18653	-0.96434	1.072357
24		3	0.750	0.111	0.600	0.429	3	1.021	0.471	0.073	0.051	3	-0.08532	0.288223	-0.94164	1.051013
25		4	0.125	0.444	0.800	0.571	4	0.170	0.119	0.149	0.008	4	-0.68089	0.147463	-0.88042	1.008038

Figure 5.20   Correlated uniform draws

To conclude our discussion regarding correlated draws, we note that although we have couched the discussion in terms of random parameters, the same processes hold for calculating the error structure of probit models, a topic to which we now return.

5.6 Calculating choice probabilities for models without a closed analytical form

Given the knowledge of how to draw from different densities, we are now able to describe how the choice probabilities may be calculated for models in which the choice probabilities do not have a closed analytical form. This includes the probit model and any logit model where there are random parameter estimates, including the MMNL and GMNL models. Such models require that the choice probabilities be simulated using either PMC or QMC methods.

We begin first with a discussion of how to calculate the choice probabilities of the probit model.

5.6.1 Probit choice probabilities

In Section 3.2, we briefly touched on how to calculate the choice probabilities for the binary probit model. In this section, we extend the discussion to the more general multinomial probit model.

The choice probabilities of the multinomial probit model may be expressed as:

$$P_{nsj} = \int I(V_{nsj} + \varepsilon_{nsj} > V_{nsi} + \varepsilon_{nsi}, \forall j \neq i)\phi(\varepsilon_n)d\varepsilon_n, \tag{5.40}$$

where $I(.)$ is an indicator variable of whether the statement is holds, and $\phi(\varepsilon_n)$ is the joint Normal density with a mean of zero and covariance matrix Ω_e.

The multivariate probit model with fixed parameter estimates requires simulation of the error terms in Ω_e in order to calculate the choice probabilities. For probit models with random taste parameters, simulation of the random parameters will also be necessary. There exist several methods to simulate the multivariate probit choice probabilities. We now discuss the three main methods applied within the literature.

5.6.1.1 Accept–reject simulator

The simplest method used to simulate the choice probabilities for probit models is known as the accept–reject (AR) simulator. First proposed for probit models by Manski and Lerman (1981), the AR simulator involves simulating the choice index for the sampled data R times and then averaging over the R simulation runs. The process begins by taking a draw from Ω_e (and Ω_r if the model assumes random taste parameters) and, given the draws, calculating the utilities of all J alternatives, including error terms. Given that the density of Ω_e is multivariate Normal and assuming that any random parameters are multivariate Normal, then the draws may be correlated as per Section 5.5. Next, assuming that for each choice situation a decision maker will choose the alternative with the highest utility, the choice index is constructed such that the alternative with the highest utility is assigned a value 1, while all other alternatives are assigned a value of 0. Label the simulated choice index for each alternative I_j^1. The process is then repeated R times using different simulated draws. The choice probability for alternative j is then simply computed as $\dfrac{1}{R}\sum\limits_{r-1}^{R} I_j^r$.

To demonstrate, consider the multinomial probit model results reported in Table 4.1 of Chapter 4. The modeled components of utility are reproduced as Equation (5.41):

$$V_{d1} = 9.390 - 7.787\%min_d,$$
$$V_{d2} = 9.473 - 7.688\%min_d,$$
$$V_{d3} = 7.129 - 1.894south_d,$$
$$V_{d4} = \quad - 1.299south_d + 15.221\%fem_d,$$

(5.41)

where index d represents voting district $d = 1$ to 430, %min represents the proportion of individuals residing in voting district d who describe themselves as belonging to a minority group, *south* is a dummy variable equal to one if the voting district belongs to a Southern state, or zero otherwise, and %*fem* is a variable representing the proportion of females living in the district.

We demonstrate how the AR simulator works assuming that district $d = 1$ from the constructed data set. For district $d = 1$, %*min* = 0.337, *south* = 1, and %*fem* = 0.485. Let V_j represent the vector of modeled utilities. Based on the values of the variables for $d = 1$, and the parameter estimates as given in Equation (5.41), $V_j = (6.766, 6.882, 5.235, 6.083)$.

To proceed, now let ε_n^r represent a J-dimensional vector of errors drawn from a multivariate Normal distribution with mean zero and covariance Ω_e. Given:

$$\rho(e_i, e_j) = \begin{pmatrix} 1.000 & 0.997 & 0 & 0 \\ 0.997 & 1.000 & 0 & 0 \\ 0 & 0 & 1.000 & 0 \\ 0 & 0 & 0 & 1.000 \end{pmatrix},$$

(5.42)

the Cholesky transformation for Ω_e is computed:

$$C = \begin{pmatrix} 1.000 & 0 & 0 & 0 \\ 0.997 & 0.072 & 0 & 0 \\ 0 & 0 & 1.000 & 0 \\ 0 & 0 & 0 & 1.000 \end{pmatrix},$$

(5.43)

which we use to correlate the elements contained within ε_n^r as described in Section 5.5.

Assuming that Halton sequences are used, for $r = 1$, we obtain $\varepsilon_n^1 = (0.000, -0.031, -0.842, -1.068)$. The utilities for each of the j alternatives may now be constructed such that $U_{nsj}^1 = V_{nsj} + \varepsilon_{nsj}^1$. Note that if random taste parameters are assumed, V_{nsj} will require that one or more of the parameters be drawn from a simulated distribution and hence also require a superscript leading to $U_{nsj}^1 = V_{nsj}^1 + \varepsilon_{nsj}^1$. Let U_n^1 represent the vector of utilities. Given the above information, we obtain $U_n^1 = (6.766, 6.851, 4.393, 5.015)$. In this case, $j = 2$ is observed to have the highest utility of the four alternatives, and hence the choice index becomes $I_n^1 = (0, 1, 0, 0)$. Repeating the process for $r = 2$, we obtain $\varepsilon_n^2 = (-0.674, -0.642, -0.253, -0.566)$ such that $U_n^2 = (6.092, 6.240, 4.982, 5.517)$. Once again, the second alternative is observed to have the highest utility $I_n^2 = (0, 1, 0, 0)$. We repeat this process $R = 1,000$ times. The simulated probability for alternative j is then computed as the average number of times that alternative is accepted over the R draws. We leave it to the reader to confirm that the simulated choice probabilities are 0.041, 0.620, 0.077 and 0.262 for $j = 1$ to 4, respectively.

The AR simulator represents the simplest approach to calculating the choice probabilities for probit models (indeed, the approach is general in the sense that it can be applied to any model, and hence is not limited to just probit models). Nevertheless, the approach is rather crude and can cause problems in estimation. The primary concern is that, depending on the draws taken, it is not uncommon for an alternative to have a zero probability of being chosen. This is an issue in simulated maximum likelihood estimation which requires that the log of the probability be taken. Unfortunately, the log of zero is undefined and hence the simulated maximum likelihood cannot be computed. The likelihood that an alternative will be zero will increase when (a) the true choice probability over the sample is low, (b) when a small number of draws is taken, and (c) if there are a large number of alternatives present.

Also of concern is the fact that the simulated probabilities are not smooth in the parameters. This is a problem, as most estimation procedures require that the simulated maximum likelihood be twice differentiable (see Section 5.7). Unfortunately, this requires that the simulated probabilities be smooth in the parameters that is not the case and, as such, the estimation procedures commonly used may not perform as required. To overcome this problem, larger step sizes are sometimes used than would ordinarily be the case.

5.6.1.2 Smoothed AR simulator

Proposed by McFadden (1989), this process involves simulating the choice probabilities in precisely the same way as the AR simulator; however, rather than simulate the choice index, the smoothed AR simulator makes use of the logit probability equation. The smoothed AR simulator begins by taking a draw from Ω_e (and Ω_r if the model assumes random taste parameters) and, given the draws, calculating the utilities of all J alternatives. That is $U_{nsj}^r = V_{nsj}^r + \varepsilon_{nsj}^r$. Given the simulated utilities, the logit probabilities are next calculated such that:

$$P^r_{nsi} = \frac{e^{\lambda U^r_{nsi}}}{\sum_{j=1}^{J} e^{\lambda U^r_{nsj}}}, \tag{5.44}$$

where $\lambda > 0$ is a scale factor specified by the analyst.

The value of λ determines the degree of smoothing. As $\lambda \to 0$, $\lambda U^r_{nsj} \to 0$, $\forall j$, and $P^r_{nsj} \to \frac{1}{J}$, $\forall j$. Conversely, as $\lambda \to \infty$, $\lambda U^r_{nsj} \to \infty$, $\forall j$, and $P^r_{nsj} \to (0, 1)$, $\forall j$. In the latter case, the smooth AR simulator will approximate the AR simulator, along with the difficulties associated with it in estimating the model. Further, as $\lambda U^r_{nsj} \to \infty$, $\forall j$, the exponentiation required to calculate the logit probabilities becomes increasingly difficult for software to handle. The aim of the analyst is, therefore, to select a value of λ that is not too low as to force the choice probabilities to be $\frac{1}{J}$, $\forall j$, or too large that the method replicates almost perfectly the AR simulator or creates problems in calculating the choice probabilities.

The above process is repeated for a large number of draws, R, over which the value of λ is fixed. The simulated choice probabilities are then averaged over the draws, such that $E[P^r_{nsi}] = \frac{1}{R} \sum_{r=1}^{R} P^r_{nsi}$.

Based on the same example used previously to describe the operation of the AR simulator, for the first observation we draw $\varepsilon^1_n = (0.000, -0.031, -0.842, -1.068)$ and obtain $U^1_n = (6.766, 6.851, 4.393, 5.015)$. Assuming that $\lambda = 60$ and substituting the simulated utilities into Equation (5.44), in vector notation we obtain $P^1_n = (0.006, 0.994, 0.000, 0.000)$. In this instance, $\lambda = 60$ was selected as values greater than 60 created difficulties in exponentiating the utilities while values less than 60 tended to produce choice probabilities that differed substantially from those derived using the other approaches. For the second set of draws, we obtain choice probabilities $P^2_n = (0.000, 1.000, 0.000, 0.000)$, while for the third set of draws, $P^3_n = (0.170, 0.830, 0.000, 0.000)$. Repeating the process for 1,000 draws, we obtain simulated choice probabilities of 0.048, 0.615, 0.077, and 0.260 for $j = 1$ to 4, respectively.

5.6.1.3 GHK simulator

The final probit simulator we discuss is the GHK simulator, named after three authors who independently developed the method – Geweke (1989, 1991), Hajivassiliou (Hajivassiliou and McFadden 1998), and Keane (1990, 1994). In comparison to the AR and smoothed AR simulator approaches, the GHK simulator is much more complex to implement; however, several researchers have reported that it is far more accurate in simulating the desired choice probabilities (e.g., Borsh-Supan and Hajivassiliou 1993).

The GHK simulator works with utility differences and assumes that the model is normalized for both scale and level. In working with utility differences, the approach iteratively sets each of the J alternatives as the base utility, each time calculating the choice probability for the base alternative. As such, the GHK simulator can be quite slow in practice; however, as stated above, compared to other methods, it is generally far more accurate.

The process begins by selecting one of the alternatives as the base alternative. For the moment, assume that alternative i is chosen as the base (and hence we will calculate the choice probability for this alternative). Adopting the notation used in Chapter 4, the utility differences are:

$$U_{nsj} - U_{nsi} = (V_{nsj} - V_{nsi}) - (\varepsilon_{nsj} - \varepsilon_{nsi})$$
$$\tilde{U}_{nsji} = \tilde{V}_{nsji} + \tilde{\varepsilon}_{nsji}. \tag{5.45}$$

The choice probabilities are then computed as:

$$P_{nsi} = P(\tilde{U}_{nsji} < 0, \forall j \neq i). \tag{5.46}$$

In practice, the calculations involved in deriving Equations (5.45) and (5.46) are complex, being further complicated by the fact that one or more of the error terms, and hence differences in the error terms, are likely to be correlated in the probit model. We therefore describe the GHK procedure using the same example as was used to demonstrate the workings of the AR and smoothed AR simulators.

The first step of the GHK simulator involves selecting an alternative for which the choice probabilities are to be derived and using this as the base in calculating the utility differences, as suggested by Equation (5.45). Before doing so, however, it is important that the model be normalized for both scale and level effects. As noted in Section 4.4.4.1, any normalization of one component of utility must also impact upon the other. Hence, normalization of the unobserved effects must also carry through to the observed component of utility. For this reason, we begin with determining $\tilde{\varepsilon}_{nsji}$, so as to understand how the observed component of utility is affected. In the current example:

$$\Omega_e = \begin{pmatrix} 1 & \rho_{12} & 0 & 0 \\ \rho_{12} & 1 & 0 & 0 \\ 0 & 0 & 1 & 0 \\ 0 & 0 & 0 & 1 \end{pmatrix} = \begin{pmatrix} 1.000 & 0.997 & 0 & 0 \\ 0.997 & 1.000 & 0 & 0 \\ 0 & 0 & 1.000 & 0 \\ 0 & 0 & 0 & 1.000 \end{pmatrix}, \tag{5.47}$$

which is expressed in terms of a correlation matrix. Re-arranging Equation (5.38), we are able to express this in terms of a covariance matrix, which in this instance remains unchanged from Equation (5.47).

The next step involves framing Equation (5.47) in terms of error differences. Setting alternative 1 as the base, the matrix of the vector of error differences is:

$$\tilde{\Omega}_{e1} = \begin{pmatrix} 0.00516 & 0.00258 & 0.00258 \\ 0.00258 & 2.00000 & 1.00000 \\ 0.00258 & 1.00000 & 2.00000 \end{pmatrix}, \tag{5.48}$$

and the normalized covariance for the matrix of the error differences is:

$$\tilde{\Omega}_{e1}^{*} = \begin{pmatrix} 1.0000 & 0.5000 & 0.5000 \\ 0.5000 & 387.5969 & 193.7984 \\ 0.5000 & 193.7984 & 387.5969 \end{pmatrix}. \tag{5.49}$$

Equation (5.49) is obtained by dividing all elements in Equation (5.48) by the first element in the $\tilde{\Omega}_{e1}$ As noted above, this same operation must also be performed on the vector of differences in the observed components of utility. As before, the modeled or observed utilities for each of the J alternatives were observed to be $V_j = (6.766, 6.882, 5.235, 6.083)$. Setting $j = 1$ as the base alternative, we obtain:

$$\tilde{V}_{nsj1} = \begin{pmatrix} 0.1158 & -1.5314 & -0.6834 \end{pmatrix}. \tag{5.50}$$

Dividing each element of Equation (5.50) by $\sqrt{0.00516}$ (see Section 4.4.1) we now get:

$$\tilde{V}_{nsj1}^{*} = \begin{pmatrix} 1.6119 & -21.3184 & -9.5139 \end{pmatrix}, \tag{5.51}$$

which is the vector of differences in the observed utilities normalized for both scale and level.

The next step in the process requires the estimation of the Cholesky factor for $\tilde{\Omega}_{e1}^{*}$. We first convert $\tilde{\Omega}_{e1}$ into a correlation matrix which can be done via Equation (5.38). Let ρ_{e1}^{*} be the converted correlation matrix, such that:

$$\rho_{e1}^{*} = \begin{pmatrix} 1.0000 & 9.8437 & 9.8437 \\ 9.8437 & 1.0000 & 75115.6781 \\ 9.8437 & 75115.6781 & 1.0000 \end{pmatrix}, \tag{5.52}$$

resulting in a Cholesky matrix:

$$
C_1 = \begin{pmatrix} 1.0000 & 0.0000 & 0.0000 \\ 0.5000 & 19.6811 & 0.0000 \\ 0.5000 & 9.8342 & 17.0480 \end{pmatrix},
\tag{5.53}
$$

that notationally corresponds to:

$$
C_1 = \begin{pmatrix} s_{11} & 0 & 0 \\ s_{21} & s_{22} & 0 \\ s_{31} & s_{32} & s_{33} \end{pmatrix}.
\tag{5.54}
$$

Given the above, we are now able to express the differences in the observed utilities accounting for the correct degree of correlation expressed in Equation (5.52). That is, the model may be written as:

$$
\begin{aligned}
\tilde{U}_{ns21} &= \tilde{V}_{ns21} + s_{11}z_1 = 1.6119 + z_1, \\
\tilde{U}_{ns31} &= \tilde{V}_{ns31} + s_{21}z_1 + s_{22}z_2 = -21.3184 + 0.5z_1 + 19.6811z_2, \\
\tilde{U}_{ns41} &= \tilde{V}_{ns41} + s_{31}z_1 + s_{32}z_2 + s_{33}z_3 = -9.5139 + 0.5z_1 + 9.8342z_2 + 17.0480z_3,
\end{aligned}
\tag{5.55}
$$

where $z_j \sim N(0,1), \forall j$.

With the utility functions thus derived, it is then possible to calculate the choice probability for the base alternative, i. The choice probabilities are calculated using a recursive process, as shown in Equation (5.56):

$$
\begin{aligned}
P_{nsi} &= P(\tilde{U}_{nsji} < 0, \forall j \neq i) \\
&= P\left(z_1 < \frac{-\tilde{V}_{ns1i}}{s_{11}}\right) \times P\left(z_2 < \frac{-(\tilde{V}_{ns2i} + s_{21}z_1)}{s_{22}} \middle| z_1 < \frac{-\tilde{V}_{ns1i}}{s_{11}}\right) \\
&\times \cdots \\
&\times P\left(z_J < \frac{-(\tilde{V}_{nsJi} + \sum_{j=1}^{J-1} s_{Jj}z_j)}{s_{JJ}} \middle| \begin{matrix} z_1 < \frac{-\tilde{V}_{ns1i}}{s_{11}} \\ \cdots \text{ and } z_{J-1} < \frac{-(\tilde{V}_{nsJ-1i} + \sum_{j=1}^{J-2} s_{J-1j}z_j)}{s_{J-1J-1}} \end{matrix}\right), \forall j \neq i
\end{aligned}
\tag{5.56}
$$

where J is the total number of alternatives.

For the current example, where there exist $J = 4$ alternatives, this translates to:

$$P_{nsi} = P(\tilde{U}_{nsji} < 0, \forall j \neq i)$$

$$= P\left(z_1 < \frac{-\tilde{V}_{ns1i}}{s_{11}}\right) \times P\left(z_2 < \frac{-(\tilde{V}_{ns2i} + s_{21}z_1)}{s_{22}} \middle| z_1 < \frac{-\tilde{V}_{ns1i}}{s_{11}}\right)$$

$$\times P\left(z_3 < \frac{-(\tilde{V}_{ns3i} + s_{31}z_1 + s_{32}z_2)}{s_{33}} \middle| z_1 < \frac{-\tilde{V}_{ns1i}}{s_{11}} \text{ and } z_2 < \frac{-(\tilde{V}_{ns2i} + s_{21}z_1)}{s_{22}}\right).$$

$$(5.57)$$

To operationalize Equation (5.56), the GHK procedure involves first calculating:

$$\tilde{P}^1_{nsi} = P\left(z_1 < \frac{-\tilde{V}_{ns1i}}{s_{11}}\right) = \Phi\left(\frac{-\tilde{V}_{ns1i}}{s_{11}}\right) \qquad (5.58)$$

which will be a fixed value. Next, a draw is taken from a truncated standard Normal distribution. This is achieved by first drawing a standard uniform distribution, $u^r_1 \sim U(0,1)$. Given u^r_1, the truncated standard Normal distribution is calculated as $z^r_1 = \left(u^r_1 \Phi(-\tilde{V}_{ns1i}/s_{11})\right)$. Next, compute:

$$\tilde{P}^2_{nsi} = P\left(z_2 < \frac{-(\tilde{V}_{ns2i} + s_{21}z_1)}{s_{22}} \middle| z_1 = z^r_1\right) = \Phi\left(\frac{-(\tilde{V}_{ns2i} + s_{21}z^r_1)}{s_{22}}\right). \qquad (5.59)$$

A second draw is taken from a truncated standard Normal distribution by first taking a draw from a standard uniform distribution, u^r_2 such that $z^r_2 = \Phi^{-1}\left(u^r_2 \Phi\left(-(\tilde{V}_{ns2i} + s_{21}z_1)/s_{22}\right)\right)$. Given z^r_2 we next calculate:

$$\tilde{P}^3_{nsi} = P\left(\frac{-(\tilde{V}_{ns3i} + s_{31}z_1 + s_{32}z_2)}{s_{33}} \middle| z_1 = z^r_1, z_2 = z^r_2\right)$$

$$= \Phi\left(\frac{-(\tilde{V}_{ns3i} + s_{31}z^r_1 + s_{32}z^r_2)}{s_{33}}\right). \qquad (5.60)$$

This process is repeated for all alternatives j not equal to i, such that the final calculation in the series is:

$$\tilde{P}^J_{nsi} = P\left(z_J < \frac{-(\tilde{V}_{nsJi} + \sum_{j=1}^{J-1} s_{Jj}z_j)}{s_{JJ}} \,\middle|\, z_1 = z_1^r, \ldots, z_{J-1} = z_{J-1}^r \right)$$

$$= \Phi\left(\frac{-(\tilde{V}_{nsJi} + \sum_{j=1}^{J-1} s_{Jj}z_j^r)}{s_{JJ}} \right), \tag{5.61}$$

where $z_j^r = \Phi^{-1}\left(u_j^r \Phi\left(-(\tilde{V}_{nsJi} + \sum_{j=1}^{J-1} s_{Jj}z_j^r)/s_{2JJ} \right) \right)$, and u_j^r is a draw from a standard uniform distribution.

The simulated choice probability for the rth draw is then:

$$P^r_{nsi} = \tilde{P}^{1r}_{nsi} \times \tilde{P}^{2r}_{nsi} \times \ldots \times \tilde{P}^{Jr}_{nsi}. \tag{5.62}$$

The process is repeated for $r = 1,\ldots, R$ draws and the simulated probability calculated as:

$$E(P_{nsi}) = \frac{1}{R} \sum_{r=1}^{R} P^r_{nsi}. \tag{5.63}$$

Equation (5.63) provides the simulated probability for alternative i. To obtain the choice probabilities for the remaining j alternatives, $j \neq i$, a new base alternative is selected and the entire process repeated.

To carry through with our example, we begin by calculating Equation (5.58). In this case, $\tilde{P}^1_{ns1} = \Phi\left(\frac{1.6119}{1}\right) = 0.053$ (in Microsoft Excel, this can be calculated using the normdist() formula). Next, we draw from a standard uniform distribution u_1^r, making use of Sobol sequences (see Section 5.4.5). We label this u_1^1, that takes the value 0.5. Given u_1^1, we now compute $z_1^1 = \Phi^{-1}\left(u_1^1 \Phi(-\tilde{V}_{ns11}/s_{11}) \right) = \Phi^{-1}\left(0.5\Phi(0.053) \right) = -1.931$ (calculated using the norminv() formula in Microsoft Excel). $\tilde{P}^2_{nsi}$ is calculated next such that $\tilde{P}^{2r}_{ns1} = 1 = \Phi\left(\frac{-(\tilde{V}_{ns21} + s_{21}z_1^1)}{s_{22}}\right) = \Phi\left(\frac{-(-21.3184 + 0.5 \times -1.931)}{19.6811}\right) = 0.871$. Next, drawing from a standard uniform from the second dimension of the Sobol sequence, $u_2^1 = 0.5$, $z_2^1 = \Phi^{-1}\left(u_2^1 \Phi\left(-(\tilde{V}_{ns21} + s_{21}z_1^1)/s_{22} \right) \right) = \Phi^{-1}\left(0.5\Phi\left(-(-21.3184 + 0.5 \times 0.5)/19.6811 \right) \right) = 1.132$, which allows us to calculate $\tilde{P}^{3r}_{ns1} = 1 = \Phi\left(\frac{-(-9.5139 + 0.5 \times -1.931 + 9.8342 \times -0.162)}{17.0480}\right) = 0.761$. The probability may then be calculated for $r = 1$ as $P^1_{ns1} = 0.053 \times 0.871 \times 0.761 = 0.0354$. Taking 1,000

Sobol draws, $E(P_{ns1}) = 0.035$. The choice probabilities for the remaining alternatives were calculated as 0.632, 0.073, and 0.259, respectively.

5.7 Estimation algorithms

There exists within the literature a number of algorithms for locating the parameters of discrete choice models. In this section, we briefly discuss the most widely used algorithms, noting that those discussed do not represent anywhere near a definitive list of those used within the discrete choice literature. The algorithms discussed make use of the principles of calculus, in particular, the derivatives of the LL function with respect to the parameter estimates. We therefore start with a discussion from this perspective, before going into the details of the various algorithms themselves.

5.7.1 Gradient, Hessian, and Information matrices

In calculus, a derivative represents the fundamental tool for studying the behavior of functions, and in particular locating maxima or minima points of the function being evaluated. Given that the goal is to find the maximum of some pre-specified LL function defined in terms of unknown parameter estimates, the most commonly used algorithms make use of the derivatives of the LL function with respect to the parameter estimates in order to locate the parameters that best fit the data. The first derivative of the LL function with respect to the parameter estimates represents the slope of the tangent line to the LL function at the point being evaluated, that is for a given set of parameter estimates, and provides information as to whether the function is increasing or decreasing at that point, and by how much it is increasing or decreasing. The second derivatives indicate whether the first derivatives are increasing or decreasing.

The process for locating the parameter estimates is iterative. Adopting the notation of Train (2009), let β^t be a $K \times 1$ vector of parameters attained after t iterations from the starting value. The gradient at β^t is then of first derivatives of the LL function, $LL_{NS}^t(\beta)$, evaluated at β^t. For each choice situation, s, faced by decision maker n, the gradient can be calculated as:

$$g_{ns}^t = \left(\frac{\partial LL_{ns}(\beta)}{\partial \beta} \right)_{\beta^t} = \left(\frac{\partial \ln P_{ns}(\beta)}{\partial \beta} \right)_{\beta^t}, \tag{5.64}$$

where g_{ns} is referred to as the *score* of the observation.

The gradient of the model, g_{NS}^t, is calculated as the average score over all observations, such that:

$$g_{NS}^t = \sum_{n=1}^{N}\sum_{s=1}^{S}\frac{g_{ns}(\beta_t)}{NS} = E\left(\frac{\partial LL_{ns}(\beta)}{\partial\beta}\right)_{\beta^t},$$ (5.65)

where we use LL_{ns} to denote the observation-specific contribution to the model LL LL_{NS}, where n denotes the decision maker and s the choice situation.

The gradient will be model-specific given that each model will have its own unique LL function. For example, consider the MNL model. Re-arranging the LL of the MNL model, we obtain:

$$LL_{NS}^t = \sum_{n=1}^{N}\sum_{s\in S_n}\sum_{i\in J_{ns}} y_{nsj}\ln(P_{nsj})$$

$$= \sum_{n=1}^{N}\sum_{s\in S_n}\sum_{i\in J_{ns}} y_{nsj}\ln\left(\frac{e^{V_{nsj}}}{\sum_{i=1}^{J}e^{V_{nsi}}}\right)$$ (5.66)

$$= \sum_{n=1}^{N}\sum_{s\in S_n}\sum_{i\in J_{ns}} y_{nsj}\left(V_{nsj} - \ln\sum_{i=1}^{J}e^{V_{nsi}}\right).$$

The first derivative of the LL function is thus calculated as:

$$\frac{\partial LL_{NS}^t}{\partial\beta_k^t} = \frac{\partial}{\partial\beta_k}\left(\sum_{n=1}^{N}\sum_{s\in S_n}\sum_{i\in J_{ns}} y_{nsj}(V_{nsj} - \ln\sum_{i=1}^{J}e^{V_{nsi}})\right)$$

$$= \sum_{n=1}^{N}\sum_{s\in S_n}\sum_{i\in J_{ns}} y_{nsj}\left(\frac{\partial V_{nsj}}{\partial\beta_k} - \frac{\partial}{\partial\beta_k}\ln\sum_{i=1}^{J}e^{V_{nsi}}\right)$$ (5.67)

$$= \sum_{n=1}^{N}\sum_{s\in S_n}\sum_{i\in J_{ns}} y_{nsj}\left(\frac{\partial V_{nsj}}{\partial\beta_k^t} - \frac{1}{\sum_{i=1}^{J}e^{V_{nsi}}}\sum_{i=1}^{J}e^{V_{nsi}}\frac{\partial V_{nsi}}{\partial\beta_k^t}\right).$$

Assuming a linear in the parameters, linear in the variables utility specification, then $\frac{\partial V_{nsj}}{\partial\beta_k^t} = x_{nsjk}$ and hence:

$$\frac{\partial LL_{NS}^t}{\partial \beta_k^t} = \sum_{n=1}^{N}\sum_{s\in S_n}\sum_{i\in J_{ns}} y_{nsj}\left(\frac{\partial V_{nsj}}{\partial \beta_k^t} - \frac{\sum_{i=1}^{J} e^{V_{nsi}}\frac{\partial V_{nsi}}{\partial \beta_k^t}}{\sum_{j=1}^{J} e^{V_{nsi}}}\right)$$

$$= \sum_{n=1}^{N}\sum_{s\in S_n}\sum_{i\in J_{ns}} y_{nsj}\left(x_{nsjk} - \sum_{i=1}^{J}\frac{e^{V_{nsi}}}{\sum_{i=1}^{J} e^{V_{nsi}}}x_{nsik}\right)$$

$$= \sum_{n=1}^{N}\sum_{s\in S_n}\sum_{i\in J_{ns}} y_{nsj}\left(x_{nsjk} - \sum_{i=1}^{J} P_{nsi}x_{nsik}\right).$$

(5.68)

The gradients for other models, while different, may be similarly computed. Daly (1987) provides the gradients for the nested logit model, while Bliemer and Rose (2010) provide the gradients for both the panel and cross-sectional versions of the MMNL models.

When the gradients of a model are unknown or too complex to compute analytically, numerical approximation may be used instead. This involves first calculating the LL for a given set of parameter estimates, and then subsequently either adding or subtracting a small value, δ_k, to each parameter one at a time, re-calculating the LL value for each parameter change (e.g., $\beta_k^t + 0.000001$). The gradient for each parameter estimate is then computed as the average over the sample of the difference between the LL calculated using the original parameter values and the newly calculated LL, divided by the amount added or subtracted from the parameter estimate. Let $(g_{NS}^k)^t$ represent the gradient for the kth parameter, then the procedure as described is simply:

1. Calculate the LL for the model assuming β^t. Designate the LL function as $LL_{ns}^t(\beta^t)$.
2. Recalculate the LL assuming that $\beta_1^t + \delta_1$, fixing the remaining $k-1$ parameters at the values given in β_t. Designate this new LL as $LL_{NS}^t(\beta_1)$.
3. The gradient for the first parameter is then calculated as:

$$(g_{NS}^1)^t = E\left[\frac{\left(LL_{ns}^t(\beta^t) - LL_{ns}^t(\beta_1)\right)}{\delta_1}\right].$$

4. Recalculate the LL assuming that $\beta_2^t + \delta_2$, fixing the remaining $k-1$ parameters at the values given in β^t. Designate this new LL as $LL_{NS}^t(\beta_2)$.

5. The gradient for the first parameter is then calculated as:

$$\left(g_{NS}^2\right)^t = E\left[\frac{\left(LL_{ns}^t(\beta^t) - LL_{ns}^t(\beta_2)\right)}{\delta_2}\right].$$

6. Repeat for the remaining k parameter estimates.

The use of numerically computed gradients as opposed to those derived analytically, while allowing greater flexibility in terms of the complexity of the models one can estimate, will result in significantly increased computational burden. This is because the LL will need to be calculated $k + 1$ times, compared to just once if the analytical derivatives are used, alongside the need to perform additional calculations to compute the change in LLs.

Occasionally, for greater accuracy, the above process is performed for values of $\pm\delta_k$, such that the gradient for each parameter is calculated twice, once for the addition and once for the subtraction of δ_k, and $(g_{NS}^k)^t$ computed as the average of the two. While doing so improves the accuracy of the calculated gradient, it comes at the cost of having to perform many more calculations.

In addition to the gradients, the algorithms described herein also make use of the second derivatives to locate the parameter estimates that maximize the LL functions of discrete choice models. Taking the second derivatives of the LL function with respect to the parameter estimates results in a $K \times K$ matrix which is commonly referred to as the Hessian matrix, given as:

$$H_{NS}^t = E\left(\frac{\partial^2 LL_{ns}(\beta)}{\partial\beta\partial\beta'}\right)_{\beta^t}. \tag{5.69}$$

The negative of this matrix, called the Fisher Information matrix, or simply Information matrix, is therefore computed as:

$$I_{NS}^t = -E\left(\frac{\partial^2 LL_{ns}(\beta)}{\partial\beta\partial\beta'}\right)_{\beta^t}. \tag{5.70}$$

In econometrics, the Information matrix is considered important, as the higher the information, represented as larger values contained within I_{NS}, the better the ability to estimate the parameter estimates.

As with the gradients, the Hessian and Information matrices will be model-specific, given that different discrete choice models are defined by different LL functions. Similar to the calculation of the model gradients, it may be possible to compute the Hessian and Information matrices analytically, although for more advanced models the mathematics becomes somewhat tedious. As such, it is far more common for more complex models to compute the Hessian and Information matrices by other means. Indeed, it is the calculation of the Hessian matrix that distinguishes the various algorithms we discuss below.

Before discussing a number of algorithms commonly used to compute the Hessian matrices of discrete choice models, we first discuss the concepts of direction and step-length, which dictate how to determine what the best values for the parameters are in each subsequent iteration t, as well as model convergence.

5.7.2 Direction, step-length, and model convergence

Taking a second-order Taylor's series expansion of the LL at iteration $t+1$ around the LL at iteration t, we obtain:

$$LL_{NS}(\beta^{t+1}) = LL_{NS}(\beta^t) + (\beta^{t+1} - \beta^t)' g_{NS}^t$$
$$+ \frac{1}{2}(\beta^{t+1} - \beta^t)' g_{NS}^t H_{NS}^t (\beta^{t+1} - \beta^t). \tag{5.71}$$

Taking the derivative of Equation (5.71) with respect to the estimates in iteration $t+1$, and setting this to zero, we obtain:

$$\frac{\delta LL_{NS}(\beta^{t+1})}{\beta^{t+1}} = g_{NS}^t + H_{NS}^t(\beta^{t+1} - \beta^t) = 0,$$
$$H_{NS}^t(\beta^{t+1} - \beta^t) = -g_{NS}^t, \tag{5.72}$$
$$\beta^{t+1} - \beta^t = -(H_{NS}^t)^{-1} g_{NS}^t,$$
$$\beta^{t+1} = \beta^t - (H_{NS}^t)^{-1} g_{NS}^t.$$

Let $\Omega_p = -(H_{NS})^{-1}$, such that:

$$\beta^{t+1} = \beta^t + \Omega_p^t g_{NS}^t. \tag{5.73}$$

In theory, Ω_p should also be represented with a subscript N; however, we drop this in order to remain consistent with the notation adopted in later chapters. Equation (5.73) states that the parameters at iteration $t+1$ are equal to the current parameter values plus $\Omega_p^t g_{NS}^t$.

As with the Information matrix, Ω_p contains information as to the ability to estimate the parameter estimates. Indeed, given that Ω_p is the inverse of the Information matrix, the smaller the elements contained within Ω_p, the better the ability to estimate the model parameter estimates. In addition to its role in assisting in the location of the parameter estimates, the matrix Ω_p plays another important role from an econometrics perspective. This matrix, which is often referred to within the literature as the variance-covariance matrix, or simply covariance matrix, contains information as to the robustness of the parameter estimates as well as any relationships that exist between them, and plays an important role in experimental design (see Chapter 6) as well as in conducting tests of statistical inference about the parameter estimates themselves (see Chapter 7).

Despite being referred to as the covariance matrix, note that Ω_p differs from the covariance matrix of error terms, Ω_e, as defined in Chapter 4. As shown in Chapter 4, the elements contained within the covariance matrix of error terms relate to the unobserved effects of the model and, depending on which model is estimated and what normalizations are used, may be thought of as parameters to be estimated. For example, in Section 4.3.2, we estimated, using a probit model, a correlation term (which maps to a covariance term) from Ω_e. As we show in Chapters 6 and 7, the elements in Ω_p are not parameters *per se*, but rather provide information about the parameters themselves. Hence, all estimates, whether they be parameter estimates, scale terms, or modeled error terms, will be represented within Ω_p. This is important to note, as despite presenting our discussion in terms of parameter estimates, the discussion chapter extends to all estimates. That is, the vector of parameter estimates, β, may be considered to contain not just parameters associated with specific variables (i.e., β_k), but also any other parameters associated with a model being estimated, such as those related to scale, λ_j, and even the error terms, σ_{ij}, contained within Ω_e.

As we show in the following sections, the computation of Ω_p can be somewhat difficult and definitely more than a little time consuming, all of which is exacerbated by the fact that Ω_p needs to be computed over multiple iterations, t. To save both computational effort and time, some software will multiply $\Omega_p^t g_{NS}^t$ by a scalar, α, as shown in Equation (5.74):

$$\beta^{t+1} = \beta^t + \alpha \Omega_p^t g_{NS}^t, \tag{5.74}$$

where $\Omega_p^t g_{NS}^t$ is commonly referred to within the literature as the direction, while α is called the step-length.

For each iteration t, α is systemically varied and the LL calculated given the resulting vector of estimates β^{t+1}, without resorting to having to recalculate either Ω_p^t or g_{NS}^t. Typically, the process begins by calculating the LL and $\Omega_p^t g_{NS}^t$ as previously described, assuming that $\alpha = 1.0$. Next, α is halved (i.e., α is set to 0.5) and β^{t+1} recalculated fixing $\Omega_p^t g_{NS}^t$ to the original values obtained when $\alpha=1.0$. If the LL function is greater than when $\alpha = 1.0$, then α is halved again (i.e., α now equals 0.25) and the values of β^{t+1} recalculated, again keeping $\Omega_p^t g_{NS}^t$ fixed to the original values obtained when $\alpha = 1.0$. The new parameter values are then used to recompute the LL function, and if the LL function thus obtained represents an improvement from when $\alpha = 0.5$, then α is once more halved (i.e., α is set to 0.125) and the process repeated. This continues until no further improvement in the LL is observed to occur. If no improvement in the LL was achieved after the first halving of α, then α is set to 2.0 and the LL calculated as described above. If this produces an improvement in the LL value, then α is doubled and the process repeated. The doubling of α continues until no further improvements in the LL function are achieved. When no further improvement in the LL function is observed given either a further halving or doubling of α, the procedure will move to the next iteration, and the process repeated.

In theory, the LL will be at its maximum when the gradient vector is zero. In practice, this is unlikely to ever occur due to the impreciseness of the calculations generated using computers, for example due to rounding, etc. As such, the gradient vector is likely to get close to zero, but never actually arrive at zero. For this reason, a number of criteria have been developed to determine when to the stop the iterative search process, a point known as model convergence. The most common criterion employed makes use of the following statistic:

$$h_t = g_{NS}^{t'} \Omega_p^t g_{NS}^t. \tag{5.75}$$

h_t in Equation (5.75) will be a scalar distributed χ^2 with K degrees of freedom. It is therefore possible to use h_t to set up a hypothesis test where, in this instance, the test is whether the elements of the gradient vector are simultaneously equal to zero or not. Typically, however, to ensure true convergence, very small values of h are specified by the analyst (e.g., $h = 0.0000001$) and the iterative process terminated only once $h_t \geq h$. Other convergence criteria have been proposed and used, primarily related to the gradient vector. Nevertheless, the criterion above remains the most commonly applied one within the literature. We refer the interested reader to Train (2009) for further information on other criteria.

Given the above background, we are now able to move onto the specific algorithms used to estimate discrete choice models. We begin with a discussion of the Newton–Raphson algorithm.

5.7.3 Newton–Raphson algorithm

The Newton–Raphson (NR) procedure involves analytically calculating the Hessian matrix, and using this to obtain the parameter estimates of the model via Equation (5.72). That is, the NR algorithm makes use of the analytical second derivatives of the LL function with respect to the parameter estimates, as opposed to some form of approximation of the matrix. For example, continuing with the MNL model, then:

$$
\begin{aligned}
\frac{\partial^2 LL^t_{NS}}{\partial \beta^t_k \partial \beta^t_l} &= \frac{\partial}{\partial \beta^t_l} \left(\sum_{n=1}^{N} \sum_{s \in S_n} \sum_{i \in J_{ns}} \left(y_{nsj} \frac{\partial V_{nsj}}{\partial \beta^t_k} - \sum_{i=1}^{J} P_{nsi} \frac{\partial V_{nsi}}{\partial \beta^t_k} \right) \right) \\
&= -\sum_{n=1}^{N} \sum_{s \in S_n} \sum_{i \in J_{ns}} \left(\sum_{i=1}^{J} \frac{\partial P_{nsi}}{\partial \beta^t_l} \frac{\partial V_{nsi}}{\partial \beta^t_k} + \sum_{i=1}^{J} \left(P_{nsi} \frac{\partial^2 V_{nsi}}{\partial \beta^t_k \partial \beta^t_l} \right) \right), \\
&= -\sum_{n=1}^{N} \sum_{s \in S_n} \sum_{i \in J_{ns}} P_{nsj} \frac{\partial V_{nsi}}{\partial \beta^t_k} \left(\frac{\partial V_{nsj}}{\partial \beta^t_l} - \sum_{i=1}^{J} P_{nsi} \frac{\partial V_{nsi}}{\partial \beta^t_l} \right)
\end{aligned} \tag{5.76}
$$

where

$$
\frac{\partial^2 V_{nsj}}{\partial \beta^t_k \partial \beta^t_l} = 0, \tag{5.77}
$$

and

$$
\begin{aligned}
\frac{\partial P_{nsj}}{\partial \beta^t_l} &= \frac{\partial}{\partial \beta^t_l} \left(\frac{e^{V_{nsj}}}{\sum_{i=1}^{J} e^{V_{nsi}}} \right) \\
&= \left(\frac{1}{\sum_{i=1}^{J} e^{V_{nsi}}} \right)^2 \left(\frac{\partial}{\partial \beta^t_l} (e^{V_{nsj}}) \sum_{i=1}^{J} e^{V_{nsi}} - e^{V_{nsj}} \frac{\partial}{\partial \beta^t_l} \left(\sum_{i=1}^{J} e^{V_{nsi}} \right) \right) \\
&= \left(\frac{e^{V_{nsj}} \frac{\partial V_{nsj}}{\partial \beta^t_l} \sum_{i=1}^{J} e^{V_{nsi}}}{\sum_{i=1}^{J} e^{V_{nsi}} \sum_{i=1}^{J} e^{V_{nsi}}} - \frac{e^{V_{nsj}}}{\sum_{i=1}^{J} e^{V_{nsi}}} \frac{\sum_{i=1}^{J} e^{V_{nsi}} \frac{\partial V_{nsi}}{\partial \beta^t_l}}{\sum_{i=1}^{J} e^{V_{nsi}}} \right) \\
&= P_{nsj} \left(\frac{\partial V_{nsj}}{\partial \beta^t_l} - \sum_{i=1}^{J} P_{nsi} \frac{\partial V_{nsi}}{\partial \beta^t_l} \right).
\end{aligned} \tag{5.78}
$$

As with the gradients, if a linear in the parameters, linear in the variables utility specification is assumed, then $\frac{\partial V_{nsj}}{\partial \beta_k^t} = x_{nsjk}$ such that:

$$\frac{\partial^2 LL_{NS}^t}{\partial \beta_k^t \partial \beta_l^t} = -\sum_{n=1}^{N} \sum_{s \in S_n} \sum_{i \in J_{ns}} P_{nsj} x_{nsik} \left(\frac{\partial V_{nsj}}{\partial \beta_l^t} - \sum_{i=1}^{J} P_{nsi} \frac{\partial V_{nsi}}{\partial \beta_l^t} \right). \tag{5.79}$$

Substituting the relevant values into Equation (5.78) will produce the Hessian matrix for the MNL model, the negative inverse of which will be the covariance matrix of the model. Like the gradients, the equations necessary for deriving the Hessian matrix of different choice models will differ given the divergent LL functions of the various possible models. Daly (1987) and Bliemer et al. (2009) provide the equations required to compute the Hessian for the nested logit model, while Bliemer and Rose (2010) provide those for both the panel and cross-sectional versions of the MMNL models.

For models where the analytical derivatives are unknown, or too difficult to compute, alternative approaches that approximate the Hessian will need to be adopted. The specific approximation adopted represents the defining differences of the algorithms that we now discuss.

5.7.4 BHHH algorithm

For many discrete choice models, it might not be possible to analytically calculate the Information matrix, or even where it is possible, the mathematics might be so difficult that making use of some form of approximation is preferable. One algorithm that makes use of an approximation of the Information matrix is the BHHH algorithm (pronounced as B triple H), named after the authors Berndt, Hall, Hall, and Hausman, who proposed the algorithm in 1974. The algorithm makes use of the observation-specific scores that, as we saw previously, are simply the derivatives of the LL function with respect to the parameters calculated at the level of each observation. For choice situation s, the observation specific $K \times K$ Information matrix, is calculated as the outer product of that observations score, such that:

$$I_{ns}^t = g_{ns}(\beta_t) g_{ns}(\beta_t)' = \begin{pmatrix} g_{ns}^1 g_{ns}^1 & g_{ns}^1 g_{ns}^2 & \cdots & g_{ns}^1 g_{ns}^K \\ g_{ns}^1 g_{ns}^2 & g_{ns}^2 g_{ns}^2 & \cdots & g_{ns}^2 g_{ns}^K \\ \vdots & \vdots & \ddots & \vdots \\ g_{ns}^1 g_{ns}^K & g_{ns}^2 g_{ns}^K & \cdots & g_{ns}^K g_{ns}^K \end{pmatrix}, \tag{5.80}$$

where g_{ns}^k is the kth element of $g_{ns}(\beta_t)$, where β_t has been omitted purely for the purposes of convenience. The elements of the Information matrix for the model are then computed by simply summing the corresponding elements of the choice specific Information matrices, such that $I_{NS}^t = \sum_{n=1}^{N} \sum_{s=1}^{S} I_{ns}^t$.

Use of the BHHH algorithm offers both advantages and disadvantages over the NR algorithm. With regards to advantages, the BHHH algorithm will generally require less time to estimate, as the algorithm requires only the estimation of the model gradients, which are then used to compute the Information matrix given as Equation (5.79). The NR algorithm, on the other hand, requires additional calculations be made to compute the second derivatives of the model's LL function with respect to the parameter estimates, leading to longer estimation times. Nevertheless, experience suggests that the BHHH algorithm can be somewhat slower and require substantially more iterations than the NR algorithm to reach model convergence, particularly when the algorithm is far from the maximum of the LL function. This is because the BHHH algorithm will tend to produce small step changes when far from the maximum, and hence require more iterations than the NR algorithm to reach model convergence. Second, the BHHH algorithm, as an approximation of the Information matrix, does not require the analyst to first calculate, then program, the second derivatives of the LL function. This means that the algorithm can be easily applied to any model, no matter how complex, and hence is extremely portable. Third, unlike the NR algorithm, the Information matrix obtained from the BHHH algorithm is guaranteed to be positive definite at each iteration, meaning that it will always be possible to invert the matrix (which is necessary to obtain the estimates of Ω_p required in Equation 5.72) and that improvements in LL function will be observed at each iteration.

Nevertheless, the BHHH algorithm does suffer from a number of shortcomings. Aside from tending to provide a poor approximation to the Information matrix when far from the maximum of the LL function, the major disadvantage of the BHHH algorithm is that the Information matrix produced by the algorithm will converge to the true Information matrix, assuming that the model is correctly specified, only as $NS \rightarrow \infty$. That is, the BHHH can yield values that are very different to the true values in small samples.

5.7.5 DFP and BFGS algorithms

The most commonly used algorithms for econometric problems such as choice models are the "variable metric" methods. The variable metric methods use an approximation to the inverse of the Hessian that evolves as the iterations proceed. In this class of methods, two common approaches are a "rank 2 update," by Davidon, Fletcher, and Powell (DFP) and a "rank 3 update" by Broyden, Fletcher, Goldfarb, and Shanno (BFGS). The update aspect refers to how the approximation to the (inverse) of the Hessian is obtained. For DFP, the recursion begins at a positive definite matrix, typically the identity matrix:

$$\mathbf{W}^{*(0)} = \mathbf{I}.$$

Then,

$$\mathbf{W}^{*(t+1)} = \mathbf{W}^{*(t)} + \mathbf{a}^{(t+1)}\mathbf{a}^{(t+1)'} + \mathbf{b}^{(t+1)}\mathbf{b}^{(t+1)'} = \mathbf{W}^{*(t+1)} + \mathbf{E}^{(t+1)}, \quad (5.81)$$

where $\mathbf{a}^{(t+1)}$ and $\mathbf{b}^{(t+1)}$ are two vectors that are computed using the gradients at the current and previous iterations, $g^{(t+1)}$ and $g^{(t)}$. Notice that the update matrix, $\mathbf{E}^{(t+1)}$ is the sum of two outer products and thus has rank 2 – hence the name. The BFGS algorithm adds a third term, $\mathbf{c}^{(t+1)}\mathbf{c}^{(t+1)'}$ which produces a rank 3 update. Precise details on the computation of $\mathbf{E}^{(t+1)}$ appear in Appendix E of Greene (2012, 1099). After a sufficient number of iterations, $\mathbf{W}^{*(t)}$ will provide an approximation to the negative inverse of the second derivatives matrix of the LL. In some applications, this approximation has been used as the estimator of the asymptotic covariance matrix of the coefficient estimators. As a general outcome, while the approximation is sufficiently accurate for optimization purposes, it is not sufficiently accurate to be used directly for computing standard errors. After optimization (or during, on the side), it is necessary to compute the estimator of the asymptotic covariance matrix for the **maximum likelihood estimation** (MLE) separately.

5.8 Concluding comment

This chapter has provided a detailed presentation of the methods used to obtain parameter estimates for choice models that have both fixed and random parameters. It concludes the set of chapters that provides the theoretical and econometric setting within which discrete choice models are developed.

In the remaining chapters we focus on model implementation and interpretation, using Nlogit5.

Before introducing Nlogit5 and the various choice models, we make a diversion to introduce three important themes. The first (Chapter 6) is an important data paradigm, namely choice experiments, since such data is increasingly being used in discrete choice modeling. The second theme (Chapter 7) is the statistical tests that are used in hypothesis tests and variance estimation, which are essential in comparing the overall performance of models as well as contrasts of parameter estimates and WTP distributions across different models. The third set of themes (Chapter 8) are ones that are often not given sufficient attention, and include the issue of endogeneity, the relationship between conditional and unconditional parameter estimates in models with random parameters in particular, and the asymmetry of WTP.

Appendix 5A Cholesky factorization example

The calculations used to compute the Cholesky matrix in Equation (5.37) are:

$$s_{11} = \sqrt{\eta_{11}} = \sqrt{1.853} = 1.361 \qquad\qquad \text{from (5.33a)}$$

$$s_{21} = (\eta_{21})/s_{11} = (0.835)/(1.361) = 0.613 \qquad\qquad \text{from (5.33c)}$$

$$s_{22} = \sqrt{\eta_{22} - s_{21}^2} = \sqrt{0.3852 - (0.613)^2} = 0.094 \qquad\qquad \text{from (5.33b)}$$

$$s_{31} = (\eta_{31})/s_{11} = (-0.098)/(1.361) = -0.072 \qquad\qquad \text{from (5.33c)}$$

$$s_{32} = [\eta_{32} - s_{31} \times s_{21}]/s_{22} = [-0.048 - (-0.072 \times 0.613)]/0.094$$
$$= -0.037 \qquad\qquad \text{from (5.33d)}$$

$$s_{33} = \sqrt{\eta_{33} - s_{32}^2 \times s_{31}^2} = \sqrt{-0.098 - [(-0.037)^2 \times (-0.072)^2]}$$
$$= 0.219 \qquad\qquad \text{from (5.33b)}$$

$$s_{41} = (\eta_{41})/s_{11} = (0.144)/(1.361) = 0.106 \qquad\qquad \text{from (5.33c)}$$

$$s_{42} = [\eta_{42} - s_{41} \times s_{21}]/s_{22} = [0.075 - (0.106 \times 0.6136)]/0.094$$
$$= 0.109 \qquad\qquad \text{from (5.33d)}$$

$$s_{43} = [\eta_{43} - s_{42} \times s_{32} - s_{41} \times s_{31}]/s_{33} = \begin{bmatrix} 0.075 - (0.109 \times - 0.037) \\ -(0.106 \times - 0.072) \end{bmatrix}/0.219$$
$$= -0.095$$

from (5.33d)

$$s_{44} = \sqrt{\eta_{44} - s_{43}^2 \times s_{42}^2 \times s_{41}^2} = \sqrt{0.034 - [(-0.095)^2 \times (0.109)^2 \times (0.106)^2]}$$
$$= 0.039$$

from (5.33b)

6 Experimental design and choice experiments

As far as the laws of mathematics refer to reality, they are not certain; and as far as they are certain, they do not refer to reality.

(Einstein 1921)

This chapter was co-authored with Michiel Bliemer and Andrew Collins.

6.1 Introduction

This chapter might be regarded as a diversion from the main theme of discrete choice models and estimation; however, the popularity of stated choice (SC) data developed within a formal framework known as the "design of choice experiments" is sufficient reason to include one chapter on the topic,[1] a topic growing in such interest that it justifies an entire book-length treatment. In considering the focus of this chapter (in contrast to the chapter in the first edition), we have decided to focus on three themes. The first is a broad synthesis of what is essentially experimental design in the context of data needs for choice analysis (essentially material edited from the first edition). The second is an overview in reasonable chronological order of the main developments in the literature on experimental design, drawing on the contribution of Rose and Bliemer (2014), providing an informative journey on the evolution of approaches that are used to varying degrees in the design and implementation of choice experiments. With the historical record in place, we then focus on a number of topics which we believe need to be given a more

---

[1] This chapter draws on the first edition and a number of papers which were written primarily by John Rose and Michiel Bliemer, with some inputs from papers by David Hensher and Andrew Collins. Andrew Collins provided some examples on how to use Ngene; Chinh Ho contributed the case study Ngene design on BRT versus LRT.

189

detailed treatment, which includes sample size issues, best–worst designs, and pivot designs. We draw on the key contributions in Rose and Bliemer (2012, 2013); Rose (2014); and Rose *et al.* (2008). We use Ngene (Choice Metrics 2012), a comprehensive tool that complements Nlogit5 and which has the capability to design the wide range of choice experiments discussed in this chapter, and to provide syntax for use in a few of the designs. We refer the reader to the Ngene manual for more details (www.choice-metrics.com/doc umentation.html).

Unlike most survey data, where information on both the dependent and explanatory variables is captured directly from respondents, SC data is unique in that typically only the *choice response variable* is provided by the respondent. With the exception of covariate information, which is often ignored in most analysis, the primary variables of interest, consisting of **attributes** and their associated levels, are designed in advance and presented to the respondent in the form of competing alternatives in SC studies. However, increasing evidence of both an empirical (e.g., Bliemer and Rose 2011; Louviere, Street *et al.* 2008) and a theoretical nature (e.g., Burgess and Street 2005; Sándor and Wedel 2001, 2002, 2005) suggests that the specific allocation of the attribute levels to the alternatives presented to respondents may impact to a greater or lesser extent on the reliability of the model outputs, particularly when small samples are involved. As such, rather than simply randomly assign the attribute levels shown to respondents over the course of an experiment, experimental design theory has been applied to allocate the attribute levels to the alternatives in some systematic manner.

The objective of this chapter is twofold. Firstly, it is argued that, despite the disparate nature of the existent literature, there does indeed exist a unified experimental design theory for the construction of SC experiments. Furthermore, this theory is capable of accommodating each of the design paradigms that have appeared within the literature at one time or another. Second, in presenting this theory it is discussed how the various researchers in this field have actually been reliant on this theory, many without knowing it, but under very different sets of assumptions. It is these *assumptions* that define the different approaches, and not differences in the underlying experimental design theory.

The remainder of this chapter is set out as follows. Section 6.2 discusses what exactly an experimental design is, and why it is important. Section 6.3 outlines a number of decisions that are required prior to generating the experimental design. Section 6.4 then provides a discussion of the theory of experimental design as it relates to SC studies. Section 6.5 provides a selective historical overview of key research groups working in the area of experimental design theory for SC studies. Section 6.6 gives brief comments on the main points covered in the previous sections. The remaining sections focus on some specific topics that are of growing interest, such as pivot designs and best–worst designs. The chapter concludes with some example applications using Ngene (Choice Metrics 2012) syntax to design the choice experiment. We refer those readers interested in more advanced theoretical aspects of experimental design to other texts such as Louviere *et al.* (2000), which provide a more detailed treatment of the topic (but only up to the late 1990s), the manual accompanying Ngene (Choice Metrics 2012), and recent papers by Bliemer and Rose (2014) and Rose and Bliemer (2009, 2011, 2014).

> *As an aside*, This chapter draws on the many papers by Rose and Bliemer and Bliemer and Rose to highlight some of the main developments in the literature on choice experiments since the first edition. In addition we provide a number of examples of how the Ngene software, which complements Nlogit, can be used to design choice experiments.

6.2 What is an experimental design?

The foundation for any SC experiment is an **experimental design**. An **experiment** defined in scientific terms involves the observation of the effect upon one variable, a response variable, given the manipulation of the levels of one or more other variables. The manipulation of the levels of the variables does not occur in a haphazard manner. Rather, we turn to a specialized form of statistics to determine what manipulations to make, and when to make them. Thus we can say that the manipulations occur by design. Hence the name experimental design!

Many different fields have developed a rich literature related to the concept of experimental design. Unfortunately, they have done so with little broad consultation. The result has been a diverse use of terminology that has only aided in the mystique of this topic. For example, the manipulated variables mentioned in the previous paragraph have alternatively been termed *factors*, independent variables, explanatory variables and attributes (when they are related to the characteristics of a good or service), depending upon which literature one reads. The levels have been called **factor levels**, **attribute levels**, or simply just levels. Given our earlier distinction in Chapter 3 between attributes and socio-demographic characteristics, we have chosen to continue with the terms *attribute* and *attribute levels*. We do so noting that the experimental designs we discuss throughout this book involve the manipulation of the levels of goods and services only.

We also note that much of the literature refers to each individual attribute level as a **treatment**. A combination of attributes, each with unique levels, is called a **treatment combination**. Treatment combinations thus describe the profile of the alternatives within the choice set. Again, different literatures have developed their own terminology – for example, marketing, which refers to treatment combinations as **profiles**. We will use the terms *treatment* and *treatment combination* throughout. The language associated with the field of experimental design can become quite complicated, quickly.

Figure 6.1 summarizes the process used to generate stated preference experiments. This process begins with a refinement of the problem, to ensure

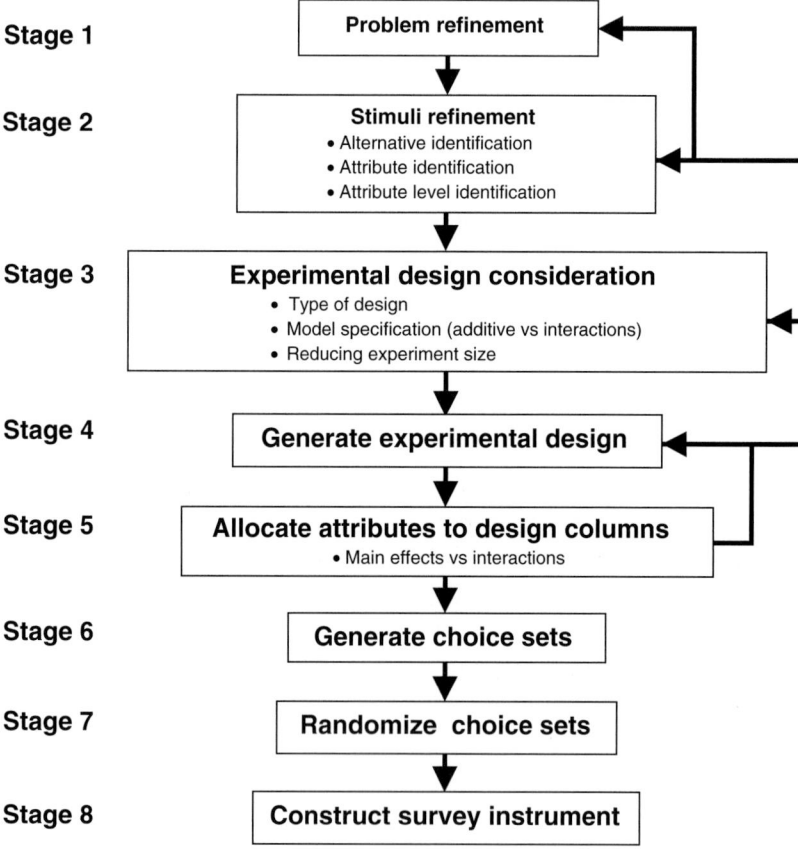

Figure 6.1   Experimental design process

that the analyst has an understanding of what the research project hopes to achieve by the time of completion.

Once the problem is well understood, the analyst is required in stage two to *identify* and *refine* the stimuli to be used within the experiment. It is at this stage of the research that the analyst decides on the list of alternatives, attributes, and attribute levels to be used. This refinement may result in further scrutiny of the problem definition and as a result a return to the problem refinement stage of the process. Moving from **stimuli refinement**, the analyst must now make several decisions as to the statistical properties that will be allied with the final design.

As an aside, the first two stages of the process consist of refining the analyst's understanding of behavioral aspects of the problem as they relate to decision makers. It is hoped that this understanding of the behavioral impacts will regulate the analyst's decision process at the time of considering the statistical properties of the design. Often, however, statistical considerations must take precedence. Statistically inefficient designs, designs that are unwieldy in size, or possibly even the non-availability of a design that fits the behavioral requirements established in the earlier stages, may trigger a return to the first two stages of the design process.

Provided that the analyst is sufficiently happy to continue at this point, the *experimental design* may be generated in stage three. While it is preferable to generate such designs from first principles, such a derivation requires expert knowledge. For the beginner, we note that several statistical packages are capable of generating simple experimental designs that may be of use (e.g., SPSS®, SAS®, and Ngene®). Following the generation of the experimental design, the analyst must allocate in stage four the attributes selected in stage two to specific columns of the design. Again, a return to previous stages of the design process may be necessary if the design properties do not meet the criteria established at earlier stages of the process.

Once the attributes have been allocated to columns within the design, the analyst manipulates the design to produce the response stimuli in stage five. While several forms of response stimuli are available to the analyst, we concentrate in this book on only one type, that of choice. Thus, the sixth stage of the design process sees the analyst construct choice sets that will be used in the survey instrument (e.g., a questionnaire). To overcome possible biases from order effects, the order of appearance of these choice sets is randomized across the survey instrument shown to each respondent. As such, several versions are created for each single choice experiment undertaken. The final stage of the experimental design process is to construct the survey, by inserting the choice sets as appropriate into the different versions and inserting any other questions that the analyst may deem necessary to answer the original research problem (such as questions on revealed preference (RP) data or socio-demographic characteristics (SECs)).

The remainder of this section provides a more in depth examination of stages one through five as described above.

6.2.1 Stage 1: problem definition refinement

Let us continue our discussion on experimental design through the use of an example, a simple hypothetical example that will demonstrate how the specialist (or at least the authors) go about deriving experimental designs for choice experiments. Consider an example whereby an analyst has been approached by an organization to study inter-city transport demand between two cities. The first stage in an analyst's journey towards deriving an SP choice experiment is to *refine their understanding of the problem being studied*. The analyst begins by asking the question "Why is this research being undertaken?" By defining the problem clearly from the outset, the questions that "need" to be asked may be determined, as well as irrelevant questions that can be avoided.

Let us assume that the organization that approached our analyst wishes to estimate mode share changes given the introduction of a new alternative means of travel between the two cities. With such a brief, the analyst may ask several questions. What are the existing modal alternatives available? What are their attributes? What determinants drive demand for travel between the two cities? Who are travelers? Are travel patterns consistent over time or are they seasonal? Many more **research questions** exist that the analyst may wish to ask. Through asking questions such as those mentioned above, the analyst can begin to refine their understanding of the problem.

> *As an aside*, we note that at this stage of the research the analyst should not be wed to any particular methodological approach to answer the research questions. Rather the questions the analyst arrives at from the problem refinement process should decide the approach to be taken. Hence the approach does not decide which questions should be asked. *As a further aside*, we note that given the possibility of deriving several possible research questions from a single research problem, the analyst may be required to employ several research approaches to satisfactorily resolve the problem.

One benefit of establishing research questions is that they aid in **hypothesis** generation. The generation of hypotheses hones even further the questions that the analyst may be required to ask of the population under study. For example, the analyst may hypothesize that one of the determining factors affecting modal choice in traveling between the two cities of interest is the conditions of the roads between the two cities. For example, poorly maintained roads may result in higher patronage of modes that do not rely on the road system (i.e., trains or aircraft). In setting up such hypotheses, the analyst begins to build upon the types of questions that need to be asked of the population of travelers. For the above example, without asking questions related to the road conditions experienced and without attempting to obtain information as to the impacts of such conditions upon mode choice, this hypothesis will remain just that, a hypothesis.

Only once the research problem has been properly refined should the analyst proceed. We will assume that the analyst has garnered a sufficient understanding of the problem to meaningfully proceed. We will further assume that given the necessity to estimate modal market shares in the presence of a new modal alternative, the analyst has decided upon the use of a **stated preference experiment**. The next stage of the design process is the refinement of the stimuli to be used in the experimental design.

6.2.2 Stage 2: stimuli refinement

6.2.2.1 Refining the list of alternatives

The next stage of the experimental design process is *stimuli refinement*. Beginning with alternative identification and refinement, we now have a two-stage process. The first stage involves defining the universal but finite list of alternatives available to decision makers within the context being studied. In defining such a list, one must identify each and every possible alternative (even if a number of alternatives are available to only a small subset of the total number of decision makers) in order to meet the global utility-maximizing rule first introduced in Chapter 3. We recall that this rule states that failure to identify all the alternatives produces, as a constraint, a threshold on the utility-maximizing outcome.

In deriving the universal but finite list of alternatives, it is suggested that the analyst expend a considerable level of effort. Secondary data searches, in depth interviews, and focus groups may aid in alternative identification. Often attending the location at which the decision takes place can also prove insightful.

Whether the analyst proceeds to the second stage of alternative identification and refinement is dependent on the number of alternatives identified in the first stage of the process. The second stage involves the culling of alternatives from the list. While this breaks with the global utility-maximizing rule, for studies that have identified large numbers of alternatives the analyst may be left with little choice but to cull alternatives in order to reach a manageable number to study. We note several ways to reduce the number of alternatives to be used within a study. Firstly, the analyst may assign a randomly sampled number of alternatives taken from the universal but finite list of alternatives to each decision maker (plus the chosen). Hence, each decision maker is presented with a different sub-set of alternatives. Thus, while in the aggregate (provided enough decision makers are surveyed) the entire population of alternatives may be studied, each individual decision maker views a reduced set of alternatives within their given choice set (essentially they adopt a **process heuristics** such as ignoring certain alternatives – see Chapter 21). While such an approach appears more appealing than simply removing alternatives from all decision makers' choice sets, the experimental designs for such studies tend to be quite large and complex. This process, however, under the strict condition of IID (see Chapter 4), does not violate the global utility maximization assumption. When we deviate from IID, the global utility maximization assumption is violated.

The second approach to reducing the alternatives is to exclude "**insignificant**" alternatives. The problem here is that the analyst is required to make the somewhat subjective decision as to what alternatives are to be considered insignificant and therefore removed from the study. However in making such a decision, the analyst is placing more weight on practical, as opposed to theoretical, considerations. A third approach is to use experiments that do not name the alternatives (i.e., the analyst defines generic or unlabeled alternatives).

If the universal, but finite, list of alternatives is relatively small (typically up to 10 alternatives although we have often studied the choice among 20 alternatives), the analyst may decide not to reject alternatives from the choice analysis at all. We end this discussion by stating that the analyst should be guided in their decision by the research problem in determining how best to proceed.

6.2.2.2 Refining the list of attributes and attribute levels

Having identified the list of alternatives to be studied, the analyst must now determine the *attributes* and *attribute levels* for these alternatives. This is not an easy task. Firstly, we note that each alternative may incorporate a mix of common as well as different attributes and even if two alternatives have similar attributes the levels of those attributes may differ from alternative to alternative. For example, in selecting between two modes of transport for a trip to work, consider the attributes which result in preference formation if those two transport modes are train and automobile. In looking at the train alternative, decision makers are likely to examine such attributes as frequency of service, waiting times (which may incorporate time spent waiting at the station and time taken walking to the station) and fares. None of these attributes is associated with driving a car to work. Instead, decision makers are likely to consider such car-related attributes as fuel, toll, and parking costs. Both modes do share some attributes that decision makers are likely to consider. For example, departure time from home, arrival time at work, and comfort. Yet, despite these attributes being shared by both alternatives, the levels decision makers cognitively associate with each alternative are likely to be different. There is no need for the decision maker to travel to the station if they choose to travel by car, and hence they are likely to be able to leave home later if this mode of transport is selected (assuming favorable traffic conditions). The levels one attaches to comfort may differ across the alternatives. Indeed, we invite the reader to consider what the attribute *comfort* means in the context of traveling to work either by train or by car. A discussion of the meaning of comfort is an excellent group discussion theme. It reveals the ambiguities in meaning and measurement of many attributes one may wish to use as part of a choice study.

Continuing with the example of *comfort*, interesting questions are raised as to how the analyst is to communicate attributes and attribute levels to decision makers (recalling that in SP tasks the analyst relates the attributes and attribute levels to respondents). What does the word "comfort" really mean, and does it mean the same thing to all decision makers? In the context of a train trip, does comfort refer to the softness of the seats aboard the train? Or could comfort relate to the number of other patrons aboard which affects the personal space available for all on board? Alternatively, could comfort refer to the temperature or ambience aboard the train? Or is it possible that decision makers perceive comfort to be some combination of all of the above, or perhaps even none of the above but rather some other aspect that we have missed, such as getting a seat? And what does comfort refer to in the context of a car trip?

> *As an aside*, the consequences of attribute ambiguity may not be apparent at first. We note that what the analyst has done by inclusion of an ambiguous attribute is more than likely add to the unobserved variance in choice between the alternatives without adding to their ability to explain any of the new increase in variation observed. Further, looking ahead, consider how the analyst may use such attributes after model estimation. Assuming that the attribute is statistically significant for the train alternative, what recommendations can the analyst make? The analyst may recommend improving comfort aboard trains; however questions remain as to how the organization responsible for the running of the trains may proceed. What aspects of comfort should be improved? Will the specific improvements result in persuading all decision makers to switch modes, or just those who perceive comfort as relating to those areas in which improvements were made? Failure to correctly express attribute descriptors results in lost time and money for all parties.

Earlier, we hinted at the solution to attribute ambiguity, although we did not mention it at the time. Returning to waiting time, we noted different components of travel time that may be important to how preferences are formed. Decision makers may attach a different **importance weight** (or marginal utility) to time spent walking to a station than they do to time spent waiting at the station itself. Walking to the station, it is unlikely that they will be able to drink a coffee and read the newspaper (unless they walk slowly). Waiting at the station, these actions become relatively easy, although waiting may be monotonous compared to walking. Or consider how decision makers perceive time spent while in (1) heavily congested (but still moving) traffic versus (2) heavily congested traffic that frequently requires stopping versus (3) free-flowing traffic conditions. Can the analyst attach a single meaning to travel time that captures the importance of travel time under all three conditions, or are separate weights required? If one believes the answer is that separate weights are required, then the analyst is required to break the attribute into unambiguous components that are well understood by decision makers.

When identifying the attributes to be used in an experiment, the analyst must consider the concept of **inter-attribute correlation**. Despite the use of the word **correlation**, inter-attribute correlation is not a statistical concept. Rather, inter-attribute correlation refers to the cognitive perceptions decision makers bind to the attribute descriptions provided. As we will show later, an experimental design may be statistically uncorrelated (i.e., **orthogonal**) in terms of the design used but correlated perceptually in terms of the attributes employed. For example, consider the frequently noted price–quality heuristic often employed by decision makers. This heuristic suggests that decision makers act as if higher priced alternatives display higher levels of quality (however quality is defined). That is, price acts as a *proxy* for quality. Thus, while we may generate an experimental design that allows for the independent estimation of importance weights for price and quality, decision makers may not necessarily treat these attributes as being independent. While we may test for this at the time of estimation, dependent upon the characteristics of the design used, the problem remains that inter-attribute correlation may result in cognitively unacceptable combinations of attributes within the design. Assuming a price–quality heuristic, how will decision makers react to a high price, low quality alternative? One possible result of such combinations is that they will stop taking the experiment seriously, thus biasing the results. Design strategies exist to overcome the problem of inter-attribute correlations, such as nested designs; however, implementing such designs may prove beyond the beginner (nevertheless, we discuss the nesting of attributes in Appendix 6A).

In such cases, we suggest that the beginner identifies attributes that may act as proxies for other attributes and select and use the most appropriate attribute for the study.

Having identified the attributes to be used in the experiment, the analyst must now derive attribute labels and **attribute level labels**. We define *attribute levels* as the levels assigned to an attribute as part of the experimental design process. These are represented by numbers that will have meaning for the analyst but not for the decision maker being surveyed. Attribute level labels, on the other hand, are assigned by the analyst and are related to the experimental design only insofar as the number of attribute level labels must equal the number of attribute levels for a given attribute. Attribute level labels are the narrative assigned to each attribute level that will (if the experiment is designed correctly) provide meaning to the decision maker. Attribute level labels may be represented as numbers (i.e., **quantitative** attributes such as travel time may have attribute level labels of 10 minutes, 20 minutes, etc.) or as words (i.e., **qualitative** attributes such as color may have attribute level labels of green and black).

The identification and refinement of the attribute levels and attribute level labels to be used in an experiment is not an easy task, requiring several important decisions to be made by the analyst. The first decision is how many attribute levels to assign to each attribute, noting that the number of levels does not have to be the same for each attribute. Let us consider the attribute *travel time* for a single alternative. For any given decision maker, there will exist for this attribute different quantities of utility associated with the various levels that may be taken. That is, the utility for 5 minutes of travel time is likely to be different to the utility attached to 10 minutes of travel time. Is the utility attached to 5 minutes of travel time likely to be different to the utility attached to 5 minutes and 10 seconds of travel time? Each "possible" attribute level may be mapped to a point in utility space. The more levels we measure of an attribute, the more information (and hopefully accuracy) we capture in utility space.

Figure 6.2 illustrates this point. Figure 6.2 shows in utility space the level of utility derived from a single attribute at varying levels. The utility brought about by the levels of a single attribute has been referred to as **part-worth** utility in some literatures such as marketing, or **marginal utility** in others. As we move from Figure 6.2(a) to 6.2(d) we note the analyst's ability to detect more complex utility relationships as more levels (and hence more observations) are added. Indeed, starting with Figure 6.2(a), the analyst would be forced to conclude that the utility relationship for the attribute is linear given a change in the attribute level from level one to level two. Examination of

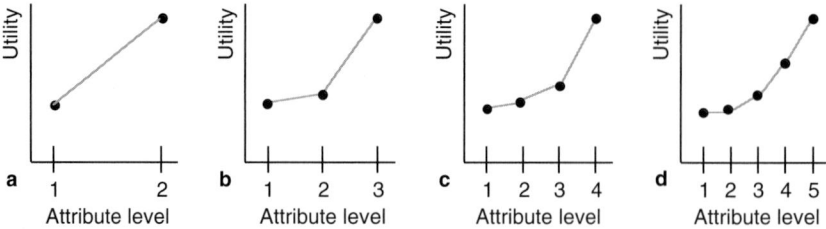

Figure 6.2   Mapping part-worth utility

Figure 6.2(b), in which a third attribute level is added, suggests a non-linear relationship in terms of utility over the range of the attributes' levels. This relationship would go undetected if only two attribute levels had been used. Figures 6.2(c) and 6.2(d) suggest that had only three levels been used, the analyst still would not have a true understanding of the real relationship that exists (although three attribute levels would suffice to provide knowledge of a good approximation of the true underlying utility function).

Ultimately, we would like to observe the level of satisfaction at each point in utility space by taking observations for each level of an attribute. As we will see later, this is not always possible. Thus, the analyst may be forced to compromise in terms of the number of attribute levels to use. Deciding on the number of attribute levels to assign is a complex issue, relating to the number of observations in utility space one wishes to obtain. A separate, but no less important, issue is how to identify the extreme ranges (sometimes referred to as the *end-points*) of the attribute levels to use.

The analyst can best identify the attribute level label extremes by examining the experiences related to that attribute of the decision makers being studied. Returning to the example of travel time for a single alternative, a process consisting of a secondary data search combined with focus groups may have identified that decision makers experience travel times varying from 11 hours to 15 hours for travel between two cities. The analyst may use these experiences to derive the extremes of the attribute level labels to be used in their experiment. However, rather than use these (observed) levels, the analyst should consider using values outside of the identified range. We suggest this for modeling purposes. It is well known that statistical models generally predict poorly outside of the range of data used for model estimation. Assume that 11 hours and 15 hours represent the extremes of the travel times used to estimate a model. If conditions change such that journeys now take much less than 11 hours or longer than 15 hours, any predictions from the model for the new conditions should be treated with caution.

Selecting attribute level labels outside of the conditions experienced, however, must be done with care. This is because the selected levels must be such that decision makers may reasonably believe them to be feasible and the analyst has confidence in the shape of the utility expression outside of the empirically identified domain. Taking the car alternative, for example, if trip lengths are currently on average around 11–15 hours, presenting decision makers with a hypothetical car trip of 8 hours is likely to have a detrimental effect on how seriously the decision maker takes the SP task.

> *As an aside*, while we have concentrated on a quantitative example we note that the above holds for qualitative attributes as well. We make a distinction between nominal and ordinal scale qualitative attributes. A **nominal qualitative attribute** may be one such as the color used for the bus alternative, where no natural order exists between the levels assumed. Selecting attribute levels to use for such attributes involves an in depth study as to what levels are likely to result in changes to preference (e.g., should the analyst use as levels the colors blue or red or green?). Ordinal qualitative attributes assume that some natural order exists among the levels. Taking the bus alternative as an example once more, the demeanor of the bus driver may be a significant attribute in preference formation for this alternative. Demeanor may be measured on some non-quantitative continuum ranging from "grumpy" to "gregarious," where gregarious is naturally rated higher than grumpy. Assigning attribute level labels to points between these extremes is a tedious task, requiring much work for the number of descriptive labels that may exist between these two extremes.

To conclude, we note the existence of the axiom "garbage in, garbage out." The meaning of this axiom is quite simple. If a computer programer enters invalid data into a system, the resulting output produced will also be invalid. Although originating in computer programing, the axiom applies equally well to other systems, including systems dealing with decision making. The point to take away from this is that the analyst is best to spend as much time identifying and refining the lists of alternatives, attributes, attribute levels, and attribute level labels to be used before proceeding to the formal design of the experiment.

6.2.3 Stage 3: experimental design considerations

Having identified the alternatives, attributes, the number of attribute levels, and the attribute level labels, the analyst must now make decisions as to the design to be used. Let us reiterate from the outset that it is best if the analyst's understanding of the behavioral impacts regulate the decision process at the time of considering the statistical characteristics of the design. While this represents the best outcome, you will find that often the designs available will constrain the behavior(s) that the analyst is able to explore.

Table 6.1 Full factorial design

Treatment combination	Comfort	Travel time
1	Low	10 hours
2	Low	12 hours
3	Low	14 hours
4	Medium	10 hours
5	Medium	12 hours
6	Medium	14 hours
7	High	10 hours
8	High	12 hours
9	High	14 hours

That said, a number of different classes of designs are available to the analyst. We discuss the most common designs that the reader may wish to use. We begin with the most general class of design available, the **full factorial design**. We also introduce orthogonal designs initially and then move to the **efficient designs** that are growing in popularity. All of the designs presented can be implemented in Ngene.

We define a *full factorial design* as a design in which all possible treatment combinations are enumerated. To demonstrate, we return to our earlier example. Assume that through a process of secondary data search and focus groups, the analyst identifies two salient attributes, comfort and travel time. For the time being, we will assume the existence of only one alternative. During the preliminary research phase, relevant ranges of the attributes are also obtained. Those interviewed suggest three relevant levels for the comfort attribute. For convenience we designate these as low, medium, and high. Typical ranges for the attribute travel time lead our analyst to propose the use of three levels, 10 hours, 12 hours, and 14 hours. A full factorial design is a design in which all possible combinations of the attribute alternatives are used. We show these combinations in Table 6.1.

Rather than write out the combinations as in Table 6.1, the experimental design literature has created a coding format that may be used to represent the possible combinations. This coding format assigns a unique number to each attribute level, beginning with 0, then 1, and proceeding to L−1, where L is the number of levels for that attribute. Thus given 3 levels the coding would be 0, 1, and 2. For attributes with 4 levels the coding used would be 0, 1, 2, and 3. Using this coding scheme, Table 6.1 becomes Table 6.2.

We could use any coding that allows for a unique mapping between the level and the assigned value. A useful alternative to the coding structure

Table 6.2 Full factorial design coding

Treatment combination	Comfort	Travel time
1	0	0
2	0	1
3	0	2
4	1	0
5	1	1
6	1	2
7	2	0
8	2	1
9	2	2

demonstrated in Table 6.2 is known as **orthogonal coding**. Orthogonal coding uses values for codes which, when summed over any given *column* (not row), equal 0. To achieve this effect, we code an attribute such that when we assign one level a positive value, we assign a second level the same value, only negative. This works in the case where we have an even number of levels. In the case of odd numbers of levels, the median level is assigned the value 0. For example, in the case of a two level attribute, we assign the values of 1 and -1 for the two levels. For a three level attribute we assign the values -1, 0, and 1.

As an aside, convention suggests that we use only odd numbers in such coding i.e. -3, -1, 0, 1, 3, etc. Table 6.3 shows the orthogonal codes for the equivalent design codes used in Table 6.2 above for attributes up to six levels. Note that by convention, -5 and 5 are not used in orthogonal coding.

The analyst may choose to stop at this point of the design process and use the design as it is. By having decision makers rate or rank each of the treatment combinations, the analyst has elected to perform **conjoint analysis**. We focus on choice analysis and not conjoint analysis and as such require some mechanism that requires decision makers to make some type of choice. To proceed, we note that the treatment combinations above represent possible product forms that our single alternative may take. For a choice to take place we require treatment combinations that describe some other alternative (recalling that choice requires at least two alternatives).

Assuming that the second alternative also has two attributes that are deemed important in preference formation, we now have a total of four attributes: two attributes for each alternative. As discussed earlier, these attributes do not have to be the same across alternatives, and even if they are the attribute levels each

Table 6.3 Comparison of design codes and orthogonal codes

Number of levels	Design code	Orthogonal code
2	0	−1
	1	1
3	0	−1
	1	0
	2	1
4	0	−3
	1	−1
	2	1
	3	3
5	0	−3
	1	−1
	2	0
	3	1
	4	−3
6	0	−7
	1	−3
	2	−1
	3	1
	4	3
	5	7

assumes do not have to be the same. For ease, we will assume that the attributes for the two alternatives are the same. Let us assume that the attribute levels for the comfort attribute are the same for both alternatives, but that for alternative 2 we observe attribute levels of 1 hour, 1.5 hours, and 2 hours for the travel time attribute (as opposed to 10, 12, and 14 hours for alternative 1). Taking the full factorial design for two alternatives, each with two attributes with three levels, 81 different treatment combinations exist. How did we arrive at this number?

The full enumeration of possible choice sets is equal to L^{JH} for labeled choice experiments (defined in Section 6.2.3.1) and L^H for unlabeled experiments. Thus, the above example yields 81 (i.e., $3^{(2 \times 2)} = 3^4$) possible treatment combinations (assuming a labeled choice experiment; for an unlabeled choice experiment, we could reduce this to nine treatment combinations (i.e., 3^2)).

Table 6.4 Choice treatment combination

	Alternative 1		Alternative 2	
Treatment combination	Comfort	Travel time	Comfort	Travel time
1	Low	10 hours	Low	1 hour

Table 6.5 Labeled choice experiment

	Car		Plane	
Treatment combination	Comfort	Travel time	Comfort	Travel time
1	Low	10 hours	Low	1 hour

6.2.3.1 Labeled versus unlabeled experiments

Rather than have decision makers rate or rank a treatment combination, we may now have them choose which of the alternatives they would select given the levels each alternative assumes. Table 6.4 shows the first treatment combination for the example described above. As we will show later, the treatment combinations for designs such as that represented in Table 6.4 become the choice sets we use in the experiment. In Table 6.4, the analyst elected to use generic titles for each of the alternatives. The title *Alternative 1* does not convey any information to the decision maker other than that this is the first of the alternatives. Experiments that use generic titles for the alternatives are called **unlabeled experiments**. Instead, the analyst may have elected to label each of the alternatives in the experiment (e.g., car). We have done this in Table 6.5. We term such experiments **labeled experiments**.

The decision as to whether to use labeled or unlabeled experiments is an important one. One of the main benefits of using unlabeled experiments is that they do not require the identification and use of all alternatives within the universal set of alternatives. Indeed, alternative 1 above may be used to describe alternatives as diverse as cars, buses, and trains. That is, the attribute levels are sufficiently broad enough as to relate to various modes of travel.

We acknowledge a further benefit in the use of unlabeled experiments. Recall the IID assumption introduced in Chapter 4 that imposed the restriction that the alternatives used in the modeling process be uncorrelated. This assumption is less likely to be met under labeled experiments than under unlabeled experiments. To explain, we note that a label attached to an alternative acts somewhat like an attribute for that alternative (albeit an attribute whose level is constant across treatment combinations). This has several consequences. Firstly, if we acknowledge that an alternative's name becomes an attribute in labeled experiments (the different alternatives being the attribute levels), the perceptions decision makers hold with regard to the alternatives may be correlated with the attributes used within the experiment. That is, the alternative, *plane*, may be correlated with both the comfort and travel time attributes. This represents a failure in terms of meeting the IID model assumption.

As an aside, a further problem arising from the use of labeled experiments develops from the perceptual assumptions decision makers hold for each labeled alternative. To date, we have kept our example simple for pedagogical purposes. Clearly, however, in reality, mode choice depends on more than the two attributes we have identified. Decision makers may use assumptions surrounding the labels attached to alternatives as proxies for these omitted attributes. We invite the reader to return to our earlier discussion on the IID assumption in Chapter 4 to see how omitted attributes are treated. The message here is that one should spend as much time as is feasible in identifying which attributes, attribute levels, and attribute level labels to use in an experiment.

In using labeled experiments, if the analyst identifies the relevant attributes for the experiment then problems brought about by decision makers making inferences about the levels of omitted attributes from the labels will also be minimized. Further, violations of the IID assumption are testable, and if observed may be dealt with through the use of more advanced modeling techniques such as nested logit modeling (Chapters 14 and 15), which will require the design of a choice experiment that accounts for the underlying assumptions of the more advanced model (see Bliemer and Rose 2010a, Bliemer *et al.* 2009).

The above does not suggest that one should avoid labeled experiments. Indeed, the decision to use a labeled as opposed to an unlabeled experiment should be made in the context of the research problem. Indeed, if one wishes to estimate alternative-specific parameter estimates, it is best to use labeled experiments. Also, one may elect to use labeled experiments for the purpose of realism. When decision makers venture to a point of physical distribution (e.g., a supermarket), they do not select among generic alternatives, but rather from a number of branded goods and services. Having decision makers select from breakfast cereal A or B may not represent a realistic task. Further, the branded name for a good or service may be an important contributor to choice among segments of decision makers. For example, some decision makers may elect to fly with Qantas, without consideration of the attribute levels associated with Qantas or their competitors, simply because of the brand name Qantas. The same logic has engendered an emotional attachment to light rail compared to bus rapid transit (Hensher *et al.* 2014, in press). The brand name connotes an historical accumulation of utility associated with attribute levels experienced in the past, and as such is a very powerful influence on choice, often downgrading the role of currently observed (actual or perceived) attribute levels.

> *As an aside*, in general, where the focus is on prediction and forecasting in contrast to establishing willingness-to-pay (WTP) for specific attributes, a labeled experiment is preferred. However, one can take a set of parameters estimated from an unlabeled experiment and, provided one is happy to stay with generic parameters for all attributes, then introduce alternative-specific constants as **calibration constants** to fit the model to a set of actual labeled alternatives to reproduce actual market shares. These calibrated constants are not part of the SP estimation process but are introduced in the application stage (see Chapter 13).

Whether the analyst decides on a labeled or unlabeled experiment, several more considerations are required to be made by the analyst in selecting a design. We note in our example that the analyst requires decision makers to make 81 choices, one for each treatment combination. The analyst may believe that presenting decision makers with 81 choice sets may place a significant level of **cognitive burden** on respondents, with the likely result of a decrease in response rates and/or a decrease in response reliability. There are a number of different strategies that may be adopted to reduce the number of choice sets given to decision makers. These are (1) reducing the number of levels used within the design, (2) using fractional factorial designs, (3) blocking the design, and (4) using a fractional factorial design combined with a blocking strategy.

Before we discuss each of these strategies, let us expand upon the example. Rather than two alternatives, let us now assume the existence of four alternative modes of transport – car, bus, train, and plane. Retaining the initial two attributes, the attribute levels associated with each alternative are shown in Table 6.6. Using this as the basis for a design, there are now 6,561 possible treatment combinations (recall L^{JH}).

6.2.3.2 Reducing the number of levels

Reducing the number of levels within the design will dramatically reduce the design size; however, such a reduction comes at a cost in terms of the amount of information the design obtains in terms of observations gained. One such strategy often employed is to utilize the attribute levels at the extremes only.

Table 6.6 Attribute levels for expanded number of alternatives

Attribute \ Alternative	Car	Bus	Train	Plane
Comfort	Low	Low	Low	Low
	Medium	Medium	Medium	Medium
	High	High	High	High
Travel time	10 hours	10 hours	10 hours	1 hour
	12 hours	12 hours	12 hours	1½ hours
	14 hours	14 hours	14 hours	2 hours

That is, each attribute will have only two attribute levels, both at the two extremes of the attribute level range. Such designs are known as end-point designs (as promoted in Louviere *et al.*, 2000, Chapter 5). For the example above, using an end-point design reduces the number of treatment combinations to 256. End-point designs are particularly useful if the analyst believes that linear relationships exist among the part-worth utilities, or if the analyst is using the experiment as an exploratory tool.

6.2.3.3 Reducing the size of experimental designs

Rather than use all 6,561 possible treatment combinations, it is possible for the analyst to use only a fraction of the treatment combinations. Designs in which we use only a fraction of the total number of treatment combinations are called *fractional factorial* designs. To choose which treatment combinations to use, the analyst may randomly select a number of treatment combinations from the total number of treatment combinations without replacement. However, random selection is likely to produce statistically inefficient or sub-optimal designs. What is required is a scientific method that may be used to select the optimal treatment combinations to use. Figure 6.3 shows the steps used to derive a statistically efficient fractional factorial design.

In order to proceed, the analyst must have an understanding of a number of statistical concepts. We begin with the concept of **orthogonality**. Orthogonality is a mathematical constraint requiring that all attributes be statistically independent of one another. Strictly speaking, orthogonality requires that each possible pair of attribute levels appears an equal number of times over the design. In practice, orthogonality has been interpreted as implying zero correlations between attributes. An orthogonal design is therefore often assumed to be a design in which the columns of the design display zero correlations (note that the attributes themselves may be perceptually correlated but statistically independent).

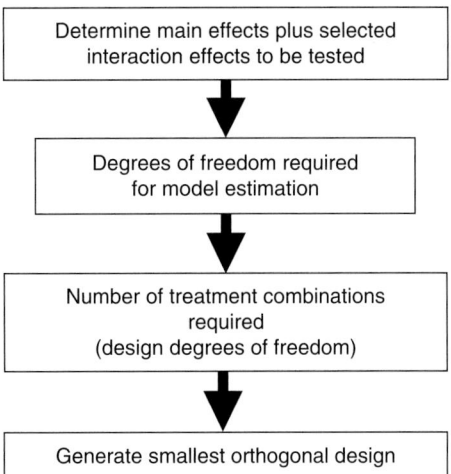

Figure 6.3   Stages in deriving fractional factorial designs

> *As an aside*, the number of rows which represent the number of alternative combinations of attribute levels are critical to the determination of column orthogonality; but once the orthogonality is established for a given number of rows, we can easily remove columns without affecting the orthogonality. Removing rows, however, will affect the orthogonality. In studies we often give individuals sub-sets of rows, which is fine assuming that when we pool the data for analysis, we retain an equal number of responses for each row. The importance of sampling becomes paramount in preserving the orthogonality.

Under very strict assumptions, as with **multicollinearity** in linear multiple regression, non-orthogonal designs render determination of the contribution of each independent attribute difficult, as the attributes are confounded with one another. Statistically, non-orthogonality tends to produce higher amounts of shared variation with lower unique variation from which individual attribute estimates are derived. Parameters estimated from non-orthogonal designs are often assumed to be incorrectly estimated and, in some instances, have the incorrect sign although, as we argue later, this is not correct, unless very large correlations are present within the design.

> *As an aside*, full factorial designs mathematically display orthogonality, that is why we have ignored this important concept to date.

A second concept that requires exploration is that of **main effects** and **interaction effects**. We define an *effect* as the impact a particular treatment has on some response variable. In choice analysis, the response variable is choice. Thus, an effect is the impact that a particular attribute level has on choice. For experimental designs we define an effect as the difference in treatment means. A *main effect* (ME) is defined as the direct independent effect of each attribute upon the response variable, choice. The main effect, therefore, is the difference in the means of each level of an attribute and the overall or grand mean. An *interaction effect* is an effect upon a response variable, choice, obtained by combining two or more attributes which would not have been observed had each of the attributes been estimated separately.

The following illustrates the differences. Equation (6.1) is the linear representative component of utility first presented in Chapter 3:

$$V_i = \beta_{0i} + \beta_{1i}f(X_{1i}) + \beta_{2i}f(X_{2i}) + \beta_{3i}f(X_{3i}) + \ldots + \beta_{Ki}f(X_{Ki}), \qquad (6.1)$$

where

β_{1i} is the weight (or parameter) associated with attribute X_1 and alternative i;

β_{0i} is a parameter not associated with any of the observed and measured attributes, called the alternative-specific constant (ASC), which represents on average the role of all the unobserved sources of utility.

Using Equation (6.1), an ME is the effect each attribute has on the response variable (V_i in Equation 6.1) independent of all other attribute effects. Examination of Equation (6.1) suggests that the impact of any attribute, for example X_{1i}, on V_i, is equivalent to its associated parameter weight, in this instance β_{1i}. Thus the β_{ki}s represent our estimates of MEs. For any given design, the total number of MEs that we can estimate is equivalent to the number of attribute levels present in the design.

What we have not shown in Equation (6.1) are the *interaction terms*. An interaction occurs when the preference for the level of one attribute is dependent upon the level of a second attribute. A good example of this is nitro-glycerine. Kept separately, nitro and glycerine are relatively inert; however, when combined an explosive compound is created. This is not a chemistry text, however, and a useful example for students of choice is warranted. The part-worth utility functions might thus look like Equation (6.2):

$$\begin{aligned} V_i = \beta_{0i} &+ \beta_{1i}f(X_{1i}) + \beta_{2i}f(X_{2i}) + \beta_{3i}f(X_{3i}) + \ldots + \beta_{Ki}f(X_{Ki}) + \beta_{Li}f(X_{1i}X_{2i}) \\ &+ \beta_{Mi}f(X_{1i}X_{3i}) + \ldots + \beta_{Oi}f(X_{1i}X_{ki}) + \beta_{Pi}f(X_{2i}X_{3i}) + \ldots + \beta_{Zi}f(X_{1i}X_{2i}X_{3i}\ldots X_{Ki}), \end{aligned}$$
$$(6.2)$$

where

$f(X_{1i}X_{2i})$ is the two-way interaction between the attributes X_{1i} and X_{2i} and β_{Ki} is the interaction effect. $f(X_{1i}X_{2i}X_{3i}\ldots X_{Ki})$ is the kth-way interaction and β_{Zi} is the related interaction effect.

Returning to our example, assume that the analyst identified color as being an important attribute for the bus alternative. Research showed that for trips of 10 hours or less, decision makers had no preference for the color of the bus. However, for trips over 10 hours, bus patrons prefer light colored buses to dark colored buses (the analyst suspects that dark color buses become hotter and therefore more uncomfortable over longer distances). As such, the preference decision makers have for the bus alternative is not formed by the effect of color independent of the effect of travel time but rather is formed due to some combination of both.

Because the level of one attribute when acting in concert with a second attribute's level affects utility for that alternative, the analyst should not examine the two variables separately, but rather in combination with one another. That is, the bus company should not look at the decision of which color bus to use as separate to the decision of what route to take (affecting travel times). Rather, the two decisions should be considered together in order to arrive at an optimal solution. In terms of our model, if an interaction effect is found to be significant, then we need to consider the variables collectively (though the model itself does not tell us what the optimal combination is). If the interaction effect is found not to be significant, then we examine the main effects by themselves in order to arrive at the optimal solution.

As an aside, one might confuse the concept of interaction with the concept of correlation. *Correlation* between variables is said to occur when we see movement in one variable similar to the movement in a second variable. For example, a positive correlation may be said to exist if, as price increases, we also observe quality increasing. While this looks remarkably like the concept of interactions discussed above, it is not. The concept of an interaction between two attributes is about the *impact* two attributes are having when acting in concert. Thus, in the example described earlier, we are not interested in whether, as the level of color changes from light to dark, travel time increases. Rather we are interested in the impact certain combinations of color and travel time may have on bus patronage (i.e., increasing utility for the bus alternative relative to the other alternatives). That is, which combinations of color and travel time will sell more bus tickets? Put simply, a correlation is said to be a relationship between two variables, whereas an interaction may be thought of as the impact two (or more) variables have on a third (response) variable.

Interaction and main effects are important concepts and must be fully understood by the analyst. One benefit of using full factorial designs is that all the main effects and all the interaction effects may be estimated independent of one another. That is, the analyst may estimate parameters for all main effects and interaction effects such that there is no **confoundment** present. As we argue later, however, the above arguments relate to linear models. Due to the exponentiation in the choice probabilities, discrete choice models are non-linear models, and the same arguments about the desirability of orthogonality as a statistical property will hold only under very strict conditions. Unfortunately, in reducing the number of treatment combinations, fractional factorial designs force confoundment upon these effects. Strategies exist to minimize these confoundments such that those effects of interest may be estimated independent of all other effects. We address these strategies later.

Let J equal the number of alternatives, S the number of choice situations, and H the number of parameters to be estimated. Finally we define **degrees of freedom**. The degrees of freedom required for an experiment. In layman's terms, a degree of freedom represents a single piece of information available to the analyst. Consider a single choice task S. In the choice task there will be J probabilities calculated. Given that the sum of all J probabilities must by definition be equal to one, we can calculate the Jth alternative, given information about the remaining J–1 probabilities. As such, each choice situation will have J–1 pieces of unique information, from which the last can be calculated. As the analyst requires a certain amount of information (degrees of freedom) in order to estimate a model, the analyst requires knowledge of how much information is present within a design and how much information is required to estimate a model.

To determine the minimum number of treatment combinations necessary for a fractional factorial, the analyst is obligated to establish how many degrees of freedom are required for estimation purposes. This determination is dependent on the number of parameters to be estimated at the time of modeling, which in turn is dependent on how the analyst is likely to specify the model. To demonstrate, recall that the representative component of utility (ignoring interactions) for any alternative may be written as a linear function such that:

$$V_i = \beta_{0i} + \beta_{1i} f(X_{1i}) + \beta_{2i} f(X_{2i}) + \beta_{3i} f(X_{3i}) + \ldots + \beta_{Ki} f(X_{Ki}). \tag{6.3}$$

If, for argument's sake, the attribute *comfort* for the car alternative is the first attribute associated with alternative i, then using our notation this attribute enters the utility function of Equation (6.3) through X_{1i}. At the time of modeling, we will derive a weight, β_{1i} associated with this attribute.

Using the coding suggested in Table 6.6, the imposition of a linear effect on utility can easily be shown. Our estimate of the level of utility associated with a low level of comfort is obtained by substituting 0 (the non-orthogonal code used in the design for a low level of comfort; this value would be −1 if using the orthogonal coding method) into $f(X_{1i})$ to obtain:

$$V_i = \beta_{0i} + \beta_{1i} \times 0 = \alpha_i + 0 \tag{6.4}$$

ceteris paribus (all other things being equal). The utility we estimate for the medium level of comfort, *ceteris paribus*, is given as:

$$V_i = \beta_{0i} + \beta_{1i} \times 1 = \alpha_i + \beta_{1i} \tag{6.5}$$

and for a high level of comfort:

$$V_i = \beta_{0i} + \beta_{1i} \times 2 = \alpha_i + 2\beta_{1i}. \tag{6.6}$$

Note that every time we increase the amount of comfort by one unit, *ceteris paribus*, our utility level increases by the amount β_{1i}. That is, the utility for the difference between a low level of comfort and a medium level of comfort is the same as the utility for the difference between a medium level of comfort and high level of comfort. This is unlikely to be true. Consider the case of air travel. The three levels of comfort may translate to comfort levels experienced in coach, business, and first class. Those who are lucky enough to have traveled first class will acknowledge a significant difference between first class and business class, much more so than between business and coach. The answer to this problem lies in two alternative coding approaches.

6.2.3.4 Dummy and effects coding

Dummy coding allows for non-linear effects in the levels of attributes. We have introduced this topic in Chapter 3, but it is useful to revisit it here. This is accomplished through the creation of a number of variables for each attribute being coded. The number of new variables created is equivalent to the number of levels of the attribute being coded, minus one. Thus in the example above, where we have three comfort levels, we need to create two variables. For simplicity's sake, let us call these new variables *Comfort1* and *Comfort2*. We associate *Comfort1* with the high level of comfort such that every time the attribute comfort is at the high level, we will place a 1 in the column *Comfort1* of our data set. If the attribute was other than high then we will place a 0 in the *Comfort1* column. Similarly *Comfort2* will equal 1 if a medium level of comfort was experienced and 0 otherwise. As we have only two variables but three levels, the third level, a low comfort level, is represented as a 0 in both *Comfort1* and *Comfort2*. This coding is shown in Table 6.7.

Table 6.7 Dummy coding

Attribute level	Variable	
	Comfort1	Comfort2
High	1	0
Medium	0	1
Low	0	0

Such coding allows for non-linear effects to be tested in the levels of the attributes. Returning to Equation (6.3), *Comfort1* would now be associated with $f(X_{1i})$ and *Comfort2* with $f(X_{2i})$. Consequently we now have two β parameters associated with our single comfort attribute, β_{1i} and β_{2i}. The utility associated with a high level of comfort, *ceteris paribus*, now becomes:

$$V_i = \beta_{0i} + \beta_{1i} \times 1 + \beta_{2i} \times 0 = \alpha_i + \beta_{1i} \tag{6.7}$$

and for medium comfort:

$$V_i = \beta_{0i} + \beta_{1i} \times 0 + \beta_{2i} \times 1 = \alpha_i + \beta_{2i}. \tag{6.8}$$

The utility associated with a low comfort level becomes:

$$V_i = \beta_{0i} + \beta_{1i} \times 0 + \beta_{2i} \times 0 = \alpha_i. \tag{6.9}$$

What we now have is a different value of utility associated with each level of the attribute coded. We have therefore overcome the problem noted with the more traditional coding method of linear changes in the response variable given one unit changes in the explanatory variable.

We have left β_{0i} in Equations (6.4) through (6.9) quite deliberately. Examination of Equation (6.9) shows that the utility associated with the base level will always, by default, equal β_{0i}. That is, we are not measuring the utility associated with low comfort at all, but rather the average overall utility level when we look at the utility for the base level. This suggests that by dummy coding the data we have perfectly confounded the base level of an attribute with the overall or *grand mean*. Each attribute we dummy code will also be perfectly confounded with the grand mean. The question is then: What have we measured? Have we measured the utility for the base level or the overall or grand mean?

It is for the above reason that we prefer effects coding as opposed to dummy coding. Effects coding has the same advantage of dummy coding in that non-linear effects in the attribute levels may be measured, but it dispenses with the disadvantage of perfectly confounding the base attribute level with the grand mean of the utility function.

To effects code, we follow the procedure set out above for dummy coding; however, instead of coding the base level 0 across our newly created variables, we now code the base level as −1 across each of these new variables. Thus for our example we now have the coding structure in Table 6.8.

Design and choice experiments

Table 6.8 Effects coding structure

Attribute Level	Variable	Comfort1	Comfort2
High		1	0
Medium		0	1
Low		−1	−1

Table 6.9 Effects coding formats

	Variable 1	Variable 2	Variable 3	Variable 4
Level 1	1			
Level 2	−1			
Level 1	1	0		
Level 2	0	1		
Level 3	−1	−1		
Level 1	1	0	0	
Level 2	0	1	0	
Level 3	0	0	1	
Level 4	−1	−1	−1	
Level 1	1	0	0	0
Level 2	0	1	0	0
Level 3	0	0	1	0
Level 4	0	0	0	1
Level 5	−1	−1	−1	−1

As we have not changed the coding for the high and medium comfort levels, Equations (6.7) and (6.8) still hold. However the estimate of utility associated with the change of the coding for the low level of comfort, now becomes:

$$V_i = \beta_{0i} + \beta_{1i} \times (-1) + \beta_{2i} \times (-1) = \beta_{0i} - (\beta_{1i} + \beta_{2i}). \tag{6.10}$$

We note that the utility for the base level is now no longer perfectly confounded with alternative i's grand mean, but rather may be estimated as $\beta_{0i} - \beta_{1i} - \beta_{2i}$. As such, the effect of the base level is therefore equivalent to $- \beta_{1i} - \beta_{2i}$ around β_{0i}.

In Table 6.9, we show the coding structure for attributes up to five levels. For attributes with more than five levels, the analyst is simply required to add more variables.

To demonstrate the importance of the coding choice (i.e., the use of a single (linear) attribute or several dummy or effects coded variables representing a single attribute), consider Figure 6.4.

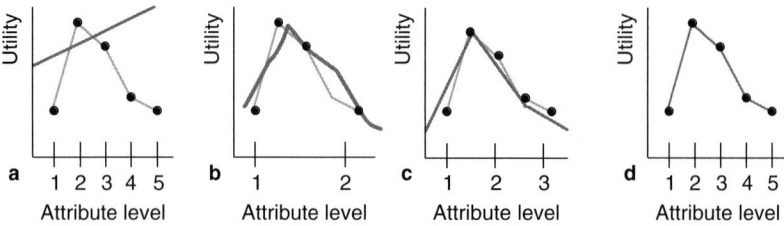

Figure 6.4   Estimation of linear versus quadratic effects

Figure 6.4 assumes the existence of some complex part-worth (marginal) utility function (taken from Figure 6.2(d)). Assuming the estimation of a single parameter (i.e., slope coefficient) for this attribute, we arrive at the case represented by 6.4(a). In such a case, the analyst will not be able to establish the true utility function to any degree of accuracy. As we estimate more parameters (i.e., more slope coefficients) for the attribute through the use of dummy or effects codes, the analyst may obtain a better understanding of the true utility function as shown in Figures 6.4(b) through 6.4(d).

> *As an aside*, because the estimation of a single parameter for an attribute will produce a linear estimate (i.e., slope), we refer to such estimates as *linear estimates*. An attribute estimated with two dummy (or effects) parameters is known as a quadratic estimate and subsequent dummy (or effects) parameters are known as polynomials of degree L−1 estimates (where L is the number of dummy or effects parameters).

What the above discussion suggests is that the more complex the part-worth utility function, the better off one is to move to a more complex coding structure capable of estimating more complex non-linear relationships. Of course, prior to model estimation, beyond experience and information gleaned from other studies, the analyst will have no information as to the complexity of a part-worth utility function. This would suggest that the analyst is best to assume the worst and produce models capable of estimating complex non-linear relationships. However, as we shall see, this comes at a considerable cost, and may be far from the best strategy to employ.

6.2.3.5   Calculating the degrees of freedom required

Recall the earlier definition provided for degrees of freedom:

The degrees of freedom for an experiment is $S \times (J-1)$, where S is the number of the choice situations and J is the number of alternatives in each choice situation. This number must be greater than or equal to the number of independent (linear) constraints placed upon it during the modeling process. The independent (linear) constraints are the β parameters we estimate, including any constants.

The above definition suggests that the more parameters an analyst desires to estimate, the greater the number of degrees of freedom required for estimation purposes. That is, the more complex non-linear relationships we wish to detect, the more parameters we are required to estimate, and in turn the more degrees of freedom we require for model estimation. As we shall show, *more degrees of freedom mean larger designs.*

Assuming the estimation of a main effects only model (ignoring interactions between attributes), the degrees of freedom required of a design depend on the types of effects to be estimated and whether the design is labeled or unlabeled. For our example, each (labeled) alternative (i.e., car, bus, train, and plane, i.e., $J = 4$) has two attributes defined on three levels. Assuming estimation of linear effects only, the degrees of freedom required for the design is equal to eight (i.e., $4 \times 2 + 1$). As noted above, the degrees of freedom required of a design corresponds to the number of parameters to be estimated over all alternatives. Consider the utility functions for each of the four alternatives given that the marginal utilities (or part-worths) are assumed to be linear. The utility functions will be estimated as shown below (ignoring constant terms):

$$V_{car} = \beta_{1car} \times comfort + \beta_{2car} \times TT$$

$$V_{bus} = \beta_{1bus} \times comfort + \beta_{2bus} \times TT$$

$$V_{train} = \beta_{1train} \times comfort + \beta_{2train} \times TT$$

$$V_{plane} = \beta_{1plane} \times comfort + \beta_{2plane} \times TT$$

Over the four alternatives, the number of parameters to be estimated is 8. Thus, a minimum of 8 degrees of freedom would be required for the design used to estimate all of the parameters within the above system of utility functions. The design requires $S \times (J - 1) \geq 8$. Given that $J = 4$, $S \times (3) \geq 8$, hence $S \geq 3$ (rounding up to the nearest integer). As such, the design would need a minimum of 3 choice situations.

Assuming the estimation of non-linear effects, the degrees of freedom required increases to 16 (i.e., $((3-1) \times 4 \times 2)$. Under the assumption that the marginal utilities for each attribute are non-linear, the utility functions become:

$$V_{car} = \beta_{1car} \times comfort(low) + \beta_{2car} \times comfort(medium) + \beta_{3car} \times TT(10\ hours)$$
$$+ \beta_{4car} \times TT(12\ hours)$$

$$V_{bus} = \beta_{1bus} \times comfort(low) + \beta_{2bus} \times comfort(medium) + \beta_{3bus} \times TT(10\ hours)$$
$$+ \beta_{4bus} \times TT(12\ hours)$$

$$V_{train} = \beta_{1train} \times comfort(low) + \beta_{2train} \times comfort(medium) + \beta_{3train} \times TT(10\ hours)$$
$$+ \beta_{4train} \times TT(12\ hours)$$

$$V_{plane} = \beta_{1plane} \times comfort(low) + \beta_{2plane} \times comfort(medium) + \beta_{3plane} \times TT(1\ hour)$$
$$+ \beta_{4pane} \times TT(1\tfrac{1}{2}\ hours)$$

A total of 16 parameters is required to be estimated (ignoring constant terms). Given the requirement of an additional degree of freedom, the above model specification would require a minimum of 16 degrees of freedom. Give $S \times (J - 1) \geq 16$, the minimum number of choice situations (rounded up to the nearest integer) would be 6.

For unlabeled choice experiments, the degrees of freedom required are somewhat reduced. The minimum degrees of freedom required of a design may be calculated using the formulas given in Table 6.10.

As with main effects, the degrees of freedom required for an interaction effect depends on how the interaction effect is to be specified in the model. To demonstrate, consider the three utility specifications below:

$$V_i = \beta_{0i} + \beta_{1i} \times comfort + \beta_{2i} \times TT + \beta_{3i} \times \mathbf{comfort \times TT}$$

$$V_i = \beta_{0i} + \beta_{1i} \times comfort(low) + \beta_{2i} \times comfort(medium) + \beta_{3i} \times TT(10\ hours)$$
$$+ \beta_{4i} \times TT(12\ hours) + \beta_{5i} \times \mathbf{comfort(low) \times TT(10\ hours)} + \beta_{6i} \times \mathbf{comfort(low)}$$
$$\times \mathbf{TT(12\ hours)} + \beta_{7i} \times \mathbf{comfort(medium) \times TT(10\ hours)}$$
$$+ \beta_{8i} \times \mathbf{comfort(medium) \times TT(12\ hours)}$$

$$V_i = \beta_{0i} + \beta_1 i \times comfort(low) + \beta_{2i} \times comfort(medium) + \beta_{3i} \times TT(10\ hours)$$
$$+ \beta_{4i} \times TT(12\ hours) + \beta_{5i} \times \mathbf{comfort \times TT}.$$

Table 6.10 Minimum treatment combination requirements for main effects only fractional factorial designs

Effects \ Experiment	Unlabeled	Labeled
Linear	$S(J - 1) \geq H$	$S(J - 1) \geq H$
Non-linear (dummy or effects coded variables)	$S(J - 1) \geq (L - 1)H$	$S(J - 1) \geq (L - 1)JH$

In the first utility specification, the main effects are estimated as linear effects and the interaction effect as the multiplication of the two linear main effects. Thus, the interaction effect requires the estimation of only a single parameter and hence necessitates only a single degree of freedom. In the second utility specification, the main effects have been estimated as non-linear effects (i.e., they have been either dummy or effects coded). Interaction effects may thus be estimated for each combination of the non-linear main effects. Under this specification, 4 interactions are generated requiring 4 parameter estimates and an additional 4 degrees of freedom. The last utility specification shows an example whereby the main effects are estimated as non-linear effects; however, the interaction effect is estimated as if the main effects were linear in effect. As such, only a single parameter will be estimated for the interaction effect requiring only a single degree of freedom for estimation. The total number of degrees of freedom required for this specification is 6.

The degrees of freedom required for the estimation of interaction terms therefore depend on how the utility functions are likely to be estimated. The degrees of freedom from an interaction term estimated from linear main effects (two or more) will be one. Two-way interaction terms estimated from non-linear main effects will be equal to $(L_1 - 1) \times (L_2 - 1)$, where L_1 is the number of levels associated with attribute 1 and L_2 is the number of levels associated with attribute 2. The degrees of freedom associated with the addition of attributes to an interaction (e.g., three-way interactions) require the addition of multiplication terms to Equation (6.12) (e.g., $(L_1 - 1) \times (L_2 - 1) \times (L_3 - 1)$).

Given knowledge of all of the above, we are now ready to proceed with the design of an experiment. Firstly, the analyst is required to determine which effects of interest are to be modeled. It is usual to model all main effects (treated as either linear or non-linear) and ignore any possible interaction effects; hence, the smallest number of effects to be estimated is equivalent to the number of main effects (i.e., parameters). This will produce a model equivalent to Equation (6.1). Such designs are called **orthogonal main effects only designs** assuming orthogonality is retained as a statistical property. We noted earlier that reducing the number of treatment combinations through the use of fractional factorial designs results in confoundment of effects. Main effects only designs are designs in which the main effects are independently estimable of all other effects but the interaction effects will be confounded with one another.

For our example, we have 8 attributes each with 3 levels (2 attributes for each of the 4 alternatives). Assuming that non-linear estimates are required, each attribute requires 2 degrees of freedom for main effects to be estimated, suggesting that the design generated requires at minimum 16 degrees of freedom (each attribute requires 2 degrees of freedom (i.e., 3 − 1) to estimate each of the dummy or effects coded parameters. Estimating all 8 attributes therefore requires a total of 16 degrees of freedom (i.e., 8 × 2)). Hence, the minimum degrees of freedom required is actually 16. With $J = 4$, noting $S \times (J − 1) \geq 16$, the minimum number of treatment combinations (rows) is 6 (rounding up to the nearest integer). Unfortunately, if the analyst wishes to maintain orthogonality, the search for an orthogonal array with 8 columns, each with 3 levels will reveal that a greater number of treatment combinations is required. That is, while we can generate a 16-row design, such a design will not be orthogonal. Indeed, the minimum number of rows for 8 attributes each with 3 levels and maintaining orthogonality is 18; 18 treatment combinations may be far more manageable for a decision maker to handle than the full 6,561 treatment combinations generated by the full factorial design. The point to note is that orthogonality is often found by selecting designs that satisfy the number of degrees of freedom but often have more rows than the number of degrees of freedom.

The use of a main effects only design significantly reduces the number of treatment combinations required. However, this reduction comes at a cost. Recall that $J − 1$ alternatives within each treatment combination represents a separate piece of information. By using only a fraction of the total number of possible treatment combinations, the analyst has in effect thrown away a significant proportion of information. The effect of this lost information will never be known. To emphasis the point, consider what information has been lost through the use of a main effects only design. The analyst is only capable of estimating the main effects. No interaction terms are estimable (a degree of freedom problem), and even if they were they are likely to be confounded with one another (again, we later show that this is strictly not true for non-linear discrete choice models). Thus the analyst has assumed that all the interaction effects are not significant, an assumption that cannot be tested. For our example, there exist 28 two-way interaction terms. Assuming 8 attributes (we will call them attributes A, B, C, D, E, F, G, and H) the 28 treatment combinations are as shown in Table 6.11.

There also exist a number of three-, four-, five-, six-, seven-, and eight-way interactions. All these *are assumed* to be statistically insignificant (i.e., their parameters in Equation (6.2) are equal to 0). Recalling our earlier discussion on interaction terms, if any one of these interaction terms is in reality not statistically insignificant, then ignoring the non-significant interactions will produce sub-optimal results in terms of our model estimated and the predictions derived from that model.

Table 6.11 Enumeration of all two-way interactions

A	B	C	D	E	F	G	H
AB	BC	CD	DE	EF	FG	GH	
AC	BD	CE	DF	EG	FH		
AD	BE	CF	DG	EH			
AE	BF	CG	DH				
AF	BG	CH					
AG	BH						
AH							

Fortunately, the analyst is able to generate designs that allow for the estimation of selected interaction effects. Such designs require advance knowledge as to which interactions are likely to be statistically significant. The ability to estimate interaction effects comes at the cost of design size, however. The more interaction effects the analyst wishes to estimate the more treatment combinations are required. Let us assume that our analyst believes that the interaction between comfort and travel time will be significant for the car alternative and similarly for the bus alternative. Therefore, the analyst wishes to estimate two two-way interaction effects. Taking the two-way interaction effect for the car alternative and assuming non-linear effects, the degrees of freedom for the interaction effect is 4 (i.e., $(3 - 1) \times (3 - 1)$) (one if linear effects are used). Similarly, the two-way interaction for the bus alternative is also 4. Thus the analyst now requires a design with 24 degrees of freedom (16 main effects degrees of freedom plus 8 two-way interaction degrees of freedom). Again, a search for an orthogonal array shows that the smallest number of treatment combinations is 27 and not 24. Thus the analyst must generate a design with 27 treatment combinations. So how do we determine which 27 treatment combinations to select (recall that there exist 6,561 such combinations)?

6.2.3.6 Blocking the design

Before answering the above question, let us finish this section by discussing another method used to reduce the number of treatment combinations shown to any particular respondent. This technique is known as blocking. **Blocking** involves the analyst introducing another orthogonal column to the design, the attribute levels of which are used to segment the design. That is, if this new attribute has 3 levels, then the design will be broken down into 3 different segments (blocks). Each block is then given to a different respondent, the result of which is that 3 different decision makers are required to complete the full design. Assuming that the analyst has done as described above, then for the design with 27 treatment combinations, each decision maker would receive 9 of the 27 treatment combinations. If a 9-level column was used, then 9 respondents would each receive 3 treatment combinations. Note that we could have blocked the full factorial design (although the block would not be orthogonal; full factorial designs allocate all possible orthogonal columns to the attributes); however, as can be seen from the above, the sample size required for a blocked design increases exponentially as the number of treatment combinations within a block decreases for a fixed number of treatment combinations.

As an aside, a design is only orthogonal if the complete (fractional factorial or full factorial) design is used. Thus, if blocks of block size nine are used and only two of the three decision makers complete the experiment, the (pooled) design used at the time of estimation will not be orthogonal. Acknowledgement of this fact has largely been ignored by both academics and practitioners. One wonders how many carefully crafted orthogonal designs in reality have maintained their statistical properties after the data have been collected and used in model estimation!

As a further aside, note that we suggested a blocking strategy that involves the use of an extra column that is orthogonal to the other design columns. By using an orthogonal column for the block, the attribute parameter estimates will be independent of the assigned blocks. This is important statistically; however, it may not always be possible to add an extra design column for the purpose of blocking without increasing the number of treatment combinations, as for every design there exists a finite number of orthogonal columns available that the analyst may choose from. It is therefore not uncommon to move to a larger design in order to locate an additional design column that may be allocated as a blocking variable. Note, however, that unless it is the desire of the analyst to test the effect of a blocking variable, assuming that there exists an additional design column that may be allocated as the blocking variable, we do not have to increase the number of treatment combinations as a result of an increase in the degrees of freedom required.

Increasing the number of treatment combinations within a design is but one alternative in accommodating an additional blocking column. Nevertheless more complex designs may make this strategy unworkable. In such cases, the analyst may elect to randomly allocate treatment combinations to different decision makers. While this strategy may result in a confoundment between the treatment combinations given to decision makers and the parameter estimates, this approach may be the only strategy available to the analyst.

6.2.4 Stage 4: generating experimental designs

In this rather long section we work through the main issues with which an analyst needs to have some familiarity when deciding on what design strategy to adopt. We will begin with the earliest forms of designs – namely, orthogonal designs, and move to designs that are less concerned with orthogonality and more concerned with parameter estimate precision. The latter places less concern on avoiding correlation among attributes within and between alternatives, focusing instead on ensuring that the chosen design satisfies a number of **statistical efficiency** criteria. These latter designs are called efficient or optimal designs. The manual accompanying Ngene (Choice Metrics 2012) details many of the designs and can be downloaded (for free) from the Choice Metrics site.

Independent of the specific application area, experimental design theory has at its core two common objectives: (i) the ability to detect independently the effects of multiple variables on some observable outcome, and (ii) the improvement of the statistical efficiency of the experiment. In many cases, these two objectives are not in themselves independent, with designs that allow for an independent assessment of various variables on some dependent variable being the same as those that are considered to be statistically efficient. SC experimental design theory, as we shall see, appears to be one of these cases.

6.2.4.1 Generating orthogonal designs

Generating the actual experimental design is not a straightforward task. Indeed, conversations with colleagues and students have led us to believe that this is the least understood concept related to the choice modeling process. In this section, we will lay bare how the reader may generate simple experimental designs using computer software. Using software to generate experimental designs is not the preferred method; however, to describe exactly how the expert generates experimental designs would require an entire book. We have therefore chosen to demonstrate, using SPSS as an example (but we could have easily used Ngene), how to obtain workable designs. The reader who wishes to become a serious choice analyst is advised to research beyond this book to learn exactly how experts generate designs (for example, see Kuehl 2000).

To proceed from this point, the analyst must consider whether a main effects only design is to be generated or whether a main effects plus selected interactions design is required. Given a main effects only design, the analyst may name the attributes such that each design column that will be generated will be assigned to a specific attribute (e.g., SPSS will generate a column in the design called *comfort*). Examination of the design process outlined in Figure 6.1 suggests that for main effects only designs, the generation of the design (stage four) and the allocation of attributes to design columns (stage five) occur simultaneously. If the analyst wishes to test for specific interaction effects (e.g., the two-way interaction between the *comfort* and *travel time* attributes for the car alternative) then stages four and five of the design process occur sequentially such that the analyst provides SPSS with generic attribute names and assigns the generated design columns at a later stage of the design process. We see why this is so as our discussion progresses.

> *As an aside*, the orthogonal design developed in SPSS can also be developed in Ngene. Later in the chapter we show how you can use Ngene to design most choice experiments.

Returning to our earlier example, we note that the analyst requires a main effects plus selected (two-way) interaction design (i.e., the two way interaction between the attributes comfort and travel time for the car alternative, and the two-way interaction between comfort and travel time for the bus alternative). Note that the analyst must pre-specify which interactions are to be tested before a design can be generated, as well as whether linear or non-linear effects (or some combination of the two) are to be estimated.

To generate an experimental design in SPSS, the following actions are required. Go to the *Data* option in the toolbar menu. In the pop down menu select *Orthogonal Design* and then *Generate...* This will open the *Generate Orthogonal Design* dialog box. We show these dialog boxes in Figure 6.5.

To progress, the analyst uses the *Generate Orthogonal Design* dialog box to name the attributes to be generated. We do this by typing the names of the attributes (factors) into the Factor Name box and pressing the *Add* button after each entry. Once the *Add* button has been pressed, the attribute name will appear in the box next to the *Add* button. Note that SPSS allows for designs with up to 10 attributes (we shall discuss later how one may generate larger designs). Continuing with our example, the analyst provides each of the attributes with generic titles. For this example, we will use the names, A, B, C, D, E, F, G, H, and I. Note that we have provided 9 attribute names, and not 8. We will use one of these attributes (we do not know which yet) as a blocking attribute.

Next the analyst must specify the number of *attribute levels*. For main effects only designs, the analyst provides attribute names that are specific to

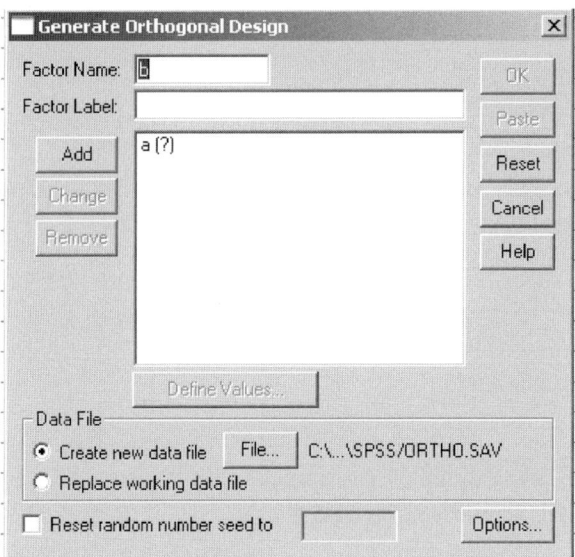

Figure 6.5   Generating designs using SPSS

the attribute. As such, the number of attribute levels to be related to a specific attribute must specifically be applied to that attribute (e.g., we must assign 3 levels to the comfort attribute for the car alternative). If for the case of main effects plus selected interactions designs, generic titles have been used, the analyst must be careful to assign the correct number of attribute levels as required in the experiment (e.g., if 2 attributes are at 2 levels and 4 are at 3 levels, then attributes A and B will be assigned 2 levels and attributes C, D, E, and F will be assigned 3 levels each). To assign the attribute levels, we note that there appears a [?] next to each attribute name. This symbol signifies that there are no attribute levels assigned to this attribute. To assign levels, select the attribute and press the *Define Values...* pushbutton. This will open the *Generate Design: Define Values* dialog box (see Figure 6.6). Note that you may select more than one attribute at a time to assign attribute levels if the numbers of levels for the attributes are the same.

SPSS allows for up to 9 attribute levels for each attribute. For our example, we wish to assign each attribute 3 attribute levels. We will title these 0, 1, and 2 in line with our coding format established earlier. We enter these values as shown in Figure 6.6. Once the attribute levels have been correctly specified we press *Continue*.

Upon returning to the *Generate Orthogonal Design* dialog box, the analyst will notice that the attribute levels are now specified next to the attribute

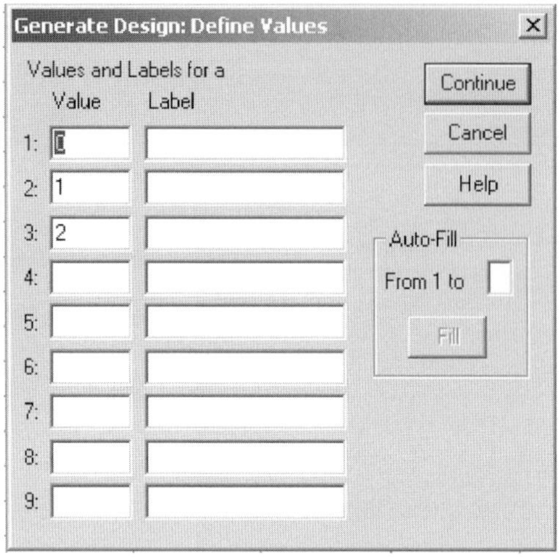

Figure 6.6   Specifying the number of attribute levels per attribute

names. Before we can continue, the analyst must be aware of the number of treatment combinations required due to the degrees of freedom necessary for estimation purposes. In generating a design for any number of attributes and attribute levels, SPSS will generate the smallest design available (although this is not strictly true, as we will see) capable of estimating non-linear effects. As we have seen, the smallest experimental design possible (that we would consider using) is a main effects only design. Thus, if a larger design as a result of a greater number of degrees of freedom is required for estimation purposes (e.g., due to the necessity to estimate interaction effects), we are required to inform SPSS of this. We do this by selecting the options button in the *Generate Orthogonal Design* dialog box. This will open the *Generate Orthogonal Design: Options* dialog box. Following on from our earlier example, we note that the minimum number of treatment combinations required for a design with main effects plus 2 two-way interactions, where each attribute within the design has 3 levels, is 24. We therefore place 25 in the *Minimum number of cases to generate:* box and press *Continue*. (We put 25 instead of 24 purely to demonstrate that *S* has to be greater than the degrees of freedom required of the design. We could put 24 here.)

The analyst is now ready to generate an experimental design. Before doing so, however, the analyst may elect to generate the design in a file saved somewhere on their computer, or to have the design replace the active worksheet in SPSS. This decision is made in the *Generate Orthogonal Design* dialog box in the section titled *Data File* (Figure 6.7). Having selected where the design is outputted to generate the design, press the *OK* button.

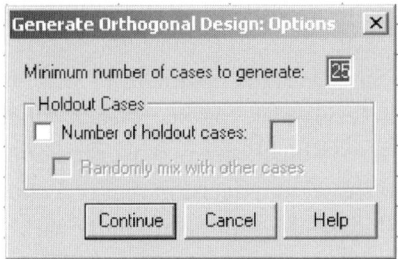

Figure 6.7   Specifying the minimum number of treatment combinations to generate

> *As an aside*, note that the reader is best to generate statistical designs from first principles rather than use statistical packages such as SPSS. To prove why, we invite the reader to generate a design with 8 attributes each with 3 levels without specifying the minimum number of treatment combinations to generate. In doing so, the reader should note that the design generated will have 27 treatment combinations. This is certainly not the smallest design possible. As we noted earlier, we are able to generate a workable design capable of estimating non-linear effects for each attribute from first principles that has only 18 treatment combinations for the attributes and attribute levels as specified. While the 27 treatment combination is useful, this highlights one problem in using computer programs to generate designs.

> *As a further aside*, note that SPSS will generate a different design each time the process described is followed. Thus, if the reader uses SPSS to generate two designs without changing any inputs to the program, two completely different designs will be generated. As such, the reader is advised that should they follow our example and attempt to replicate the design we display in the next section, it is probable that they will obtain a different looking design. No matter what the design generated, SPSS ensures that the design generated will be orthogonal.

6.2.4.2 Assigning an attribute as a blocking variable

We noted earlier that the analyst may choose to create a blocking variable in order to reduce the number of choice sets each decision maker will be given. Optimally, this blocking variable will be orthogonal to the other design attributes. As such, we generate the blocking variable at the time of design generation. For main effects only designs, the analyst is best to name the specific variable in some fashion that will specifically identify the design column generated as being related to the blocking variable. For main effects plus selected interaction designs, the analyst does not pre-specify which design column will be used as the blocking variable, although there exists an exception to this rule.

Consider our example in which 27 treatment combinations are generated using SPSS. If we allocate to each attribute of the design 3 levels (as we have in the example), then the blocking variable (whichever design column it may be) will have to assume 3 levels also. As such, each block will have 9 treatment combinations (i.e., have a block size of 9, worked out by dividing 27 by 3). If, however, we wish to show each decision maker 3 choice sets and not 9, then we would have to allocate at least one attribute with 9 levels and use this attribute as our blocking variable (i.e., we would have 9 blocks of block size 3).

6.2.5 Stage 5: allocating attributes to design columns

We noted in the previous section that if a main effects only design is required, stages four and five of the design process will be conducted simultaneously. As such, the analyst may proceed directly to stage six of the design process. If, however, main effects plus selected interactions are of interest, then the generation of the design is separated from the allocation of the attributes to the design columns generated.

To allocate the attributes to design columns, the analyst is required to code the attribute levels using orthogonal codes, as opposed to the design codes used up until this point. Table 6.12 shows a design generated using SPSS in which we have coded the attribute levels using orthogonal codes.

We prefer to use orthogonal coding due to some desirable properties we observe from such coding. Primarily, orthogonal codes allow the analyst to observe the design columns for the interaction effects. To generate the interaction columns of a design, the analyst simply multiplies the appropriate main effects columns together. For example, columns A and B represent the main effects columns for two attributes (although we are unsure which two attributes at this stage). To obtain the interaction column for the A and B columns (i.e., the AB interaction) the analyst multiplies each of the terms of the A and B columns. Taking the first treatment combination of Table 6.12, the AB interaction term is equal to 1 (i.e., -1×-1). This process is followed for higher order interactions. For example, the ADEF interaction column is obtained by multiplying the A, D, E, and F columns together. For the first treatment, the ADEF interaction is observed to take the level, 0 (i.e., $-1 \times 0 \times 0 \times -1$). For our example, the analyst may generate columns for the two-way interactions, three-way interactions, and four-way interactions, up to the nine-way interaction (e.g., ABCDEFGHI).

Table 6.12 Orthogonal coding of fractional factorial design

Treatment combination	A	B	C	D	E	F	G	H	I
1	−1	−1	1	0	0	−1	0	−1	1
2	1	0	1	−1	−1	0	0	−1	−1
3	0	0	1	0	−1	−1	1	0	0
4	0	0	0	1	0	−1	−1	0	−1
5	1	−1	0	−1	1	1	−1	0	1
6	0	1	0	−1	−1	1	1	−1	−1
7	−1	1	0	0	−1	0	−1	0	0
8	0	−1	0	0	1	0	0	1	−1
9	1	0	0	0	0	0	1	−1	1
10	1	1	1	0	1	−1	−1	1	−1
11	0	−1	−1	1	−1	0	1	1	1
12	−1	0	−1	0	1	1	1	1	−1
13	−1	1	−1	1	0	0	0	0	−1
14	1	1	−1	−1	0	−1	1	1	0
15	−1	−1	0	1	1	−1	1	−1	0
16	0	−1	1	−1	0	0	−1	1	0
17	−1	0	1	1	−1	1	−1	1	1
18	−1	−1	−1	−1	−1	−1	−1	−1	−1
19	1	−1	−1	0	−1	1	0	0	0
20	−1	1	1	−1	1	0	1	0	1
21	1	0	−1	1	1	0	−1	−1	0
22	0	1	−1	0	0	1	−1	−1	1
23	−1	0	0	−1	0	1	0	1	0
24	1	1	0	1	−1	−1	0	1	1
25	0	1	1	1	1	1	0	−1	0
26	1	−1	1	1	0	1	1	0	−1
27	0	0	−1	−1	1	−1	0	0	1

> *As an aside*, it is good practice to test the effect of blocks on the experiment. This may include testing the interaction of the blocking variable with the attribute columns of the design. If we use up to the nine-way interaction, then we have included the blocking variable in the interaction effect. Doing so, however, will require that the blocking variable be included in the model, which in turn requires that the degrees of freedom for that variable be included in the determination of how many treatment combinations are required.

The analyst is not required to generate all of the interaction columns in order to determine which attributes to allocate to which design columns. As a

	A	B	C	D	E	F	G	H	I	J	K	L	M	N	O	P	Q
1	Treatment Combination	A	B	C	D	E	F	G	H	I	AB	AC	AD	AE	AF	AG	AH
2	1	-1	-1	1	0	0	-1	0	-1	1	=$B2*C2	=$B2*D2	=$B2*E2	=$B2*F2	=$B2*G2	=$B2*H2	=$B2*I2
3	2	1	0	1	-1	-1	0	0	-1	-1	0	1	-1	-1	0	0	-1
4	3	0	0	1	0	-1	-1	1	0	0	0	0	0	0	0	0	0
5	4	0	0	0	1	0	-1	-1	0	-1	0	0	0	0	0	0	0
6	5	1	-1	0	-1	1	1	-1	0	1	-1	0	-1	1	1	-1	0
7	6	0	1	0	-1	-1	1	1	-1	-1	0	0	0	0	0	0	0
8	7	-1	1	0	0	-1	0	-1	0	0	-1	0	0	1	0	1	0
9	8	0	-1	0	0	1	0	0	1	-1	0	0	0	0	0	0	0
10	9	1	0	0	0	0	0	1	-1	1	0	0	0	0	0	1	-1
11	10	1	1	1	0	1	-1	-1	1	-1	1	1	0	1	-1	-1	1
12	11	0	-1	-1	1	-1	0	1	1	1	0	0	0	0	0	0	0
13	12	-1	0	-1	0	1	1	1	1	-1	0	1	0	-1	-1	-1	-1
14	13	-1	1	-1	1	0	0	0	0	-1	-1	1	-1	0	0	0	0
15	14	1	1	-1	-1	0	-1	1	1	0	1	-1	-1	0	-1	1	1
16	15	-1	-1	0	1	1	-1	1	-1	0	1	0	-1	-1	1	-1	1
17	16	0	-1	1	-1	0	0	-1	1	0	0	0	0	0	0	0	0
18	17	-1	0	1	1	-1	1	-1	1	1	0	-1	-1	1	-1	1	-1
19	18	-1	-1	-1	-1	-1	-1	-1	-1	-1	1	1	1	1	1	1	1
20	19	1	-1	1	0	-1	1	0	0	0	-1	-1	0	-1	1	0	0
21	20	-1	1	1	-1	1	0	1	0	1	-1	-1	1	-1	0	-1	0
22	21	1	0	-1	1	1	0	-1	-1	0	0	-1	1	1	0	-1	-1
23	22	0	1	-1	0	0	1	-1	-1	1	0	0	0	0	0	0	0
24	23	-1	0	0	-1	0	1	0	1	0	0	0	1	0	-1	0	-1
25	24	1	1	0	1	-1	-1	0	1	1	1	0	1	-1	-1	0	1
26	25	0	1	1	1	1	1	0	-1	0	0	0	0	0	0	0	0
27	26	1	-1	1	1	0	1	1	0	-1	-1	1	1	0	1	1	0
28	27	0	0	-1	-1	1	1	-1	0	0	1	0	0	0	0	0	0

Figure 6.8 Calculating interaction design codes using Microsoft Excel

rule of thumb, the analyst should generate all interactions up to the order of the highest order interaction the analyst wishes to estimate. For our example, the highest order interaction the analyst desires to test is a two-way interaction. Thus, all two-way interaction columns should be produced. Had it been the desire of the analyst to test a four-way interaction (e.g., the interaction between the travel time attributes for each of the alternatives) then all two-way, three-way, and four-way design columns should be examined. Table 6.13 shows the design columns for all main effects and all two-way interactions columns for the design shown in Table 6.12.

> *As an aside*, Table 6.13 was derived using Microsoft Excel as shown in Figure 6.8. In Figure 6.8, cells K2 through P2 show the calculations of the two-way interaction effects, while cells K3 through Q28 show the results of similar calculations for each remaining row of the design.

The next stage of the process is to generate the complete correlation matrix for all main effects and interaction terms. This is shown in Table 6.14. Examining the correlation matrix in Table 6.14 reveals that all of the main effects are uncorrelated with all other main effects. Using the terminology of the experimental design literature, we say that the main effects are un-confounded with each other.

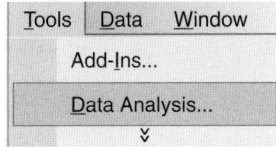

Figure 6.9   Microsoft Excel commands to generate correlations

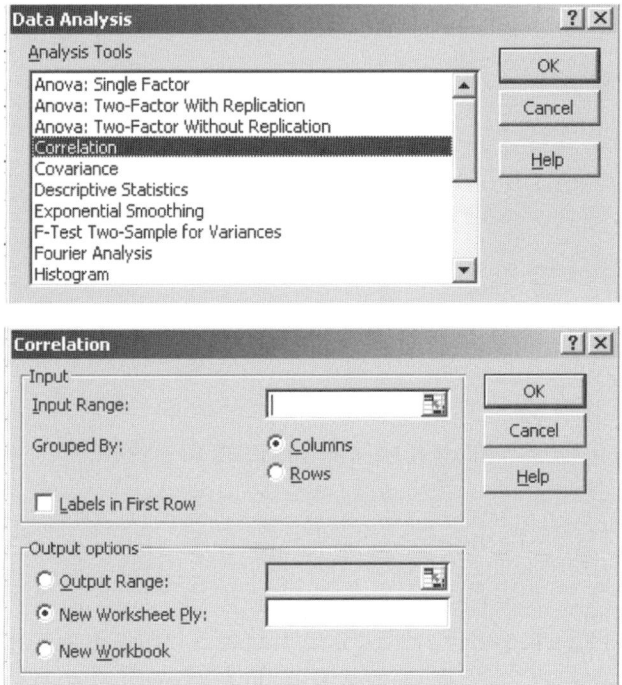

Figure 6.10   Microsoft Excel Data Analysis and Correlation dialog boxes

> *As an aside*, the correlation matrix shown as Table 6.14 was also derived using Microsoft Excel. This can be done by first selecting the *Tools* toolbar option followed by the *Data Analysis...* option as shown in Figure 6.9. Note that the *Data Analysis* option is not automatically installed with Microsoft Excel. If the option is not present in the *Tools* Toolbar dropdown menu, the reader will need to add the option via the *Add-Ins...* option, also shown in Figure 6.9.

Selecting *Data Analysis...* from the *Tools* dropdown menu will open the *Data Analysis* dialog box (see Figure 6.10). From the *Data Analysis* dialog box the analyst next selects the heading *Correlation* before pressing *OK*. This will open the *Correlation* dialog box also shown in Figure 6.10.

Table 6.13 Orthogonal codes for main effects plus all two-way interaction columns

Treatment Number	1	2	3	4	5	6	7	8	9	10	11	12	13	14	15	16	17	18	19	20	21	22	23	24	25	26	27
A	-1	-1	0	0	0	1	0	0	0	1	1	0	-1	-1	-1	0	-1	-1	-1	-1	-1	1	0	-1	1	0	0
B	-1	0	0	0	-1	-1	-1	0	1	1	0	-1	-1	1	-1	0	1	-1	-1	-1	1	0	1	0	0	-1	0
C	1	1	1	0	0	0	-1	0	0	1	-1	-1	-1	-1	0	-1	-1	-1	1	-1	0	-1	0	0	1	1	-1
D	0	-1	0	1	-1	1	0	0	0	0	1	0	-1	0	-1	1	1	-1	-1	-1	-1	0	-1	-1	1	1	1
E	0	-1	-1	0	-1	-1	-1	1	0	1	1	1	0	1	1	0	1	-1	1	0	0	0	0	0	1	0	1
F	-1	0	-1	-1	1	-1	-1	0	0	0	-1	1	-1	-1	-1	0	-1	-1	1	1	0	1	1	1	-1	1	-1
G	0	0	1	-1	-1	1	-1	0	0	-1	0	1	0	-1	1	-1	1	1	0	1	-1	-1	0	0	0	-1	0
H	-1	-1	0	0	0	-1	0	1	-1	1	1	1	0	0	1	-1	1	-1	0	0	-1	-1	-1	1	-1	0	0
I	1	1	0	-1	1	-1	0	0	-1	1	1	0	-1	1	-1	0	0	1	0	-1	0	0	0	0	0	-1	0
AB	1	0	0	0	-1	0	-1	0	1	1	0	1	-1	0	0	0	-1	1	1	1	0	0	0	-1	0	0	0
AC	-1	1	0	0	0	0	1	0	0	0	0	1	1	-1	1	0	1	-1	0	-1	1	0	0	1	0	0	0
AD	0	-1	0	0	-1	0	0	0	0	0	0	0	0	1	0	0	-1	-1	1	0	-1	0	1	1	1	1	0
AE	0	-1	0	0	1	0	0	0	0	-1	0	-1	0	-1	0	0	0	-1	-1	-1	0	0	0	-1	0	0	0
AF	1	0	0	0	1	0	-1	0	0	1	0	1	1	1	1	0	0	1	0	1	0	0	1	1	0	0	0
AG	0	0	0	0	-1	0	-1	0	-1	1	0	0	0	-1	-1	1	0	1	1	0	-1	0	0	0	0	1	0
AH	1	1	0	0	0	0	1	0	0	1	0	1	1	0	1	1	-1	1	0	0	-1	0	-1	1	0	0	0
AI	-1	-1	0	0	1	0	0	0	-1	-1	1	-1	1	0	0	0	0	1	0	-1	0	1	0	-1	-1	-1	0
BC	-1	0	0	0	0	1	-1	0	1	-1	0	0	-1	1	1	-1	0	1	1	0	1	0	0	0	1	-1	0
BD	0	0	0	0	1	-1	0	0	0	-1	0	0	0	1	-1	1	0	1	0	0	-1	-1	0	1	0	-1	0
BE	0	0	0	0	0	-1	0	0	-1	-1	1	0	1	0	1	0	0	1	0	1	0	0	0	0	1	0	0
BF	1	0	0	0	-1	1	0	-1	0	0	1	-1	-1	-1	-1	1	0	1	0	1	0	1	0	-1	0	1	0
BG	0	0	0	0	-1	1	1	0	0	-1	1	-1	0	1	-1	1	0	1	1	0	0	-1	0	0	0	-1	0
BH	1	0	0	0	1	-1	0	-1	0	-1	1	-1	-1	0	1	1	0	1	1	0	-1	-1	0	0	1	0	0
BI	-1	0	0	0	1	-1	0	1	0	1	-1	1	0	-1	1	-1	0	-1	0	1	0	1	0	1	0	1	0
CD	0	-1	0	0	0	0	0	0	0	0	-1	-1	-1	0	0	0	0	1	-1	-1	-1	0	0	0	1	0	0
CE	0	-1	-1	0	0	0	0	0	0	-1	0	-1	0	0	0	1	0	1	1	1	0	0	0	0	1	0	-1
CF	-1	0	-1	0	0	0	0	0	0	1	1	-1	-1	-1	0	-1	0	1	-1	0	-1	-1	0	-1	1	1	1
CG	0	0	1	0	0	0	0	0	0	1	1	1	0	1	0	-1	0	1	0	1	1	1	0	0	0	1	0

CH	0	0	-1	0	-1	1		0	-1	-1	1	-1	1	1	0	0	0	0	0	0	0	0	-1
CI	-1	-1	0	0	1	0		1	0	0	1	1	1	1	0	0	0	0	0	0	0	0	1
DE	-1	0	-1	-1	-1	1		1	0	0	0	0	1	0	0	0	-1	0	0	0	0	0	0
DF	-1	-1	-1	-1	0	0		1	1	-1	0	0	0	0	0	0	-1	0	-1	0	0	0	0
DG	0	-1	0	0	-1	-1		1	1	1	0	0	0	0	0	0	-1	0	0	0	0	0	0
DH	0	0	-1	-1	1	0	-1	1	-1	1	0	0	0	0	0	0	1	0	1	0	0	1	0
DI	-1	-1	0	0	0	0		1	0	0	0	-1	-1	0	0	0	0	0	-1	0	1	0	0
EF	-1	0	-1	0	0	0	-1	1	0	0	0	0	0	0	0	-1	1	1	1	1	0	0	0
EG	0	0	0	0	1	1	-1	1	0	0	-1	-1	-1	0	0	0	0	0	-1	-1	0	-1	0
EH	0	0	-1	0	1	-1	0	1	0	0	0	1	-1	0	0	0	0	0	0	0	0	-1	0
EI	-1	-1	0	0	0	0	-1	1	0	1	0	1	1	0	0	0	1	0	1	0	0	0	0
FG	0	0	1	1	-1	0	0	1	0	0	0	-1	0	0	0	0	1	1	1	-1	0	0	0
FH	-1	-1	-1	1	1	0	0	1	-1	-1	0	-1	0	0	-1	-1	-1	0	0	0	0	0	1
FI	0	-1	0	0	-1	0	0	1	1	0	0	1	0	1	1	1	1	-1	1	1	0	0	-1
GH	0	0	0	0	-1	1	0	1	-1	1	0	-1	-1	1	1	1	1	0	1	0	0	0	0
GI	0	-1	0	0	-1	0	0	1	0	0	0	1	-1	1	1	1	1	0	-1	0	0	0	0
HI	0	0	0	1	1	0	0	1	0	0	0	-1	-1	-1	-1	-1	1	1	1	0	0	0	-1

As an aside, the correlation coefficient used by Microsoft Excel is the Pearson product moment correlation coefficient. This statistic is strictly appropriate only when the variables used in the test are **ratio scaled**. This is clearly not the case here. The full design with interaction columns (Table 6.13) could be exported into SPSS and either the Spearman rho or Kendall's tau-b correlations be calculated; however, neither of these is strictly appropriate for the data either. The appropriate measure to use for the design would be the J-index; however, unless the analyst has access to specialized software, this correlation coefficient will need to be calculated manually. This calculation is beyond the scope of this book, and as such we rely on the Pearson product moment correlation coefficient, assumed to be an approximation for all similarity indices.

In the *Correlation* dialog box, all the cells shown in Figure 6.10 are selected in the *Input Range*: cell. By selecting the first row that includes the column headings, the analyst is also required to check the *Labels in First Row box*. This will show the column headings as part of the Excel correlation output, otherwise Excel will assign generic column headings to the resulting correlation matrix output.

Note, however, the existence of correlations with the main effects columns and several of the interaction effects columns (e.g., design column A is correlated with the BF interaction column), as shown in Table 6.14. This is an unfortunate consequence of using fractional factorial designs. By using only a fraction of the available treatment combinations, fractional factorial designs must confound some of the effects. Unless designs are generated from first principles, the analyst has no control over which effects are confounded (another reason why the serious choice analyst is best to learn how to generate statistical designs from first principles and not rely on computer packages).

As an aside, experience suggests that it is more likely that two-way interactions are statistically significant than three-way or higher interactions. Thus, designs in which all main effects are un-confounded with all two-way interactions are preferable. To demonstrate why this is so, return to our earlier discussion of the effects of confoundment. Confoundment produces model effects similar to the effects of multicollinearity in linear regression models. That is, the parameter estimates we obtain at the time of estimation are likely to be incorrect, as are their standard errors, and as such so are any tests we perform on attribute **significance**. Taking this example, unless the analyst specifically tests the statistical significance of the attributes assigned to the B and F design columns (we have not yet allocated attributes to columns), the analyst can never be sure that the parameter estimates for the main effect for the attribute assigned to column A are correct. We note that design column A is also confounded with the CI, EG, and FH

interaction columns. As with the BF interaction, the significance of any of these interactions also poses problems for model estimation. We draw the reader's attention to the
fact that the other main effects columns are also correlated with other interaction effects.
Does the analyst test for these effects also? To do so will require larger designs due to
the requirement for degrees of freedom. Thus the only way to proceed is to assume that
these interaction effects are insignificant in practice. While this assumption may seem
unwise, the analyst can cut the odds in assuming interaction effects to be insignificant
through selecting specific interaction effects to test. The selection of which effects to test
for occurs prior to design generation. For example, the analyst in our example believed
that the interactions between the comfort attribute and travel time attribute for the car
and bus alternatives were likely to be significant. This determination was made in
advance of the design generation.

To continue, the analyst first assigns the attributes for which interaction
effects are to be tested. The analyst revisits the correlation matrix and identifies the two-way interaction columns for correlations with the main effects
columns. Examination of Table 6.14 reveals that the AD, BC, BE, BI, CD, CE,
CF, DF, and EF two-way interaction columns are all un-confounded with all
main effects design columns (but not with other two-way interaction columns). The analyst requires four design columns (two for the car interaction
and two for the bus interaction). What is required is to determine which of the
columns to use given the correlations among the main effects and two-way
interaction columns. The analyst may assign any of the columns as suggested
by the interaction combinations suggested above. That is, for the interaction
between the comfort and travel time attributes the analyst may assign the
comfort attribute to column A and the travel time attribute to column D (or
comfort to D and travel time to A). Alternatively, the B and C, B and E, B and
I, C and D, C and E, C and F, D and F, or E and F columns could be used. The
analyst must also assign the attributes for the bus alternative to one of these
combinations.

But which combinations should be used? Again, the correlation matrix
provides the answer. Once the analyst has identified which interaction
design columns are un-confounded with the main effects design columns,
the next step is to examine the correlations among the two-way interactions.
Doing so, we note that the AD interaction column is confounded with the
BC, BE, BI, CE, and EF design interaction columns. Hence, if the analyst
were to assign the attributes of the car alternative to the A and D columns
and the bus alternative attributes to any of the combinations of the interaction columns mentioned above, then the estimated interaction effects will be

Table 6.14 Design correlation

	A	B	C	D	E	F	G	H	I	AB	AC	AD	AE	AF	AG	AH	AI	BC	BD	BE	BF	BG	BH
A	1	0	0	0	0	0	0	0	0	0	0	0	0	0	0	0	0	0	0	0	-0.6	0	0
B	0	1	0	0	0	0	0	0	0	0	0	0	0	-0.6	0	0	0	0	0	0	0	0	0
C	0	0	1	0	0	0	0	0	0	0	0	0	0	0	0	0	-0.6	0	0	0	0	0	0
D	0	0	0	1	0	0	0	0	0	0	0	0	0	0	0	0	0	0	0	0	0	-0.6	0
E	0	0	0	0	1	0	0	0	0	0	0	0	0	0	-0.6	0	0	0	0	0	0	0	0
F	0	0	0	0	0	1	0	0	0	-0.6	0	0	0	0	0	-0.6	0	0	0	0	0	0	-0.6
G	0	0	0	0	0	0	1	0	0	0	0	0	-0.6	0	0	0	0	0	-0.6	0	0	0	0
H	0	0	0	0	0	0	0	1	0	0	0	0	0	-0.6	0	0	0	0	0	0	-0.6	0	0
I	0	0	0	0	0	0	0	0	1	0	-0.6	0	0	0	0	0	0	0	0	0	0	0	0
AB	0	0	0	0	0	-0.6	0	0	0	1	0	0	0	-0.3	0	0.5	0	0	0	0	0.25	0	0.5
AC	0	0	0	0	0	0	0	0	-0.6	0	1	0	0	0	0	0	0.25	0	0.25	0	0	-0.3	0
AD	0	0	0	0	0	0	0	0	0	0	0	1	0	0	0	0	0	0.3	0	0.3	0	0	0
AE	0	0	0	0	0	0	-0.6	0	0	0	0	0	1	0	0.25	0	0	0	0.25	0	0	0	0
AF	0	-0.6	0	0	0	0	0	-0.6	0	-0.3	0	0	0	1	0	0.25	0	0	0	0	0.25	0	0
AG	0	0	0	0	-0.6	0	0	0	0	0	0	0	0.25	0	1	0	0	-0.3	0	0	0	0	0
AH	0	0	0	0	0	-0.6	0	0	0	0.5	0	0	0	0.25	0	1	0	0	0	0	0	0	0.5
AI	0	0	-0.6	0	0	0	0	0	0	0	0.25	0	0	0	0	0	1	0	0.5	-0.3	0	0.25	0
BC	0	0	0	0	0	0	0	0	0	0	0	0.25	0	0	-0.3	0	0	1	0	0.5	0	0	0
BD	0	0	0	0	0	0	-0.6	0	0	0	0.25	0	0.25	0	0	0	0.5	0	1	0	0	0.25	0
BE	0	0	0	0	0	0	0	0	0	0	0	0.25	0	0	0	0	-0.3	0.5	0	1	0	0	0
BF	-0.6	0	0	0	0	0	-0.6	0	0	0.25	0	0	0.25	0	0	0	0	0	0	0	1	0	-0.3
BG	0	0	0	-0.6	0	0	0	0	0	0	-0.3	0	0	0	0	0	0.25	0	0.25	0	0	1	0
BH	0	0	0	0	0	-0.6	0	0	0	0.5	0	0	0	0	0	0.5	0	0	0	0	-0.3	0	1
BI	0	0	0	0	0	0	0	0	0	0	0	0.5	-0.3	0	0.25	0	0	0	0	0	0	0	0
CD	0	0	0	0	0	0	0	0	0	0.3	0	0	0.3	0	0.5	0.3	0	0	0	0	0	0	0.3
CE	0	0	0	0	0	0	0	0	0	0	0	0.3	0	0.3	0	0.5	0	0.5	0	0.5	0	0	0
CF	0	0	0	0	0	0	0	0	0	0	0	0	0.3	0	0.3	0	0.5	0	0	0	0	0.3	0
CG	0	0	0	0	0	0	0	-0.6	0	-0.3	0	0.5	0	0.5	0	0	0	0	0	0	0.25	0	0
CH	0	0	0	0	0	0	-0.6	0	0	0	0	0.25	0.5	0	0	0	0	0	0.25	0	0	0	0
CI	-0.6	0	0	0	0	0	0	0	0	0	-0.3	0	0	0	0	0	0.25	0	0.25	0	0.25	0.5	0.25
DE	0	0	0	0	0	0	0	-0.6	-0.6	0.25	0.25	0	0	0.25	0	0	0	0	0	0	0.5	0	0
DF	0	0	0	0	0	0	0	0	0	0	0	0	0.25	0	0.5	0	-0.3	0	0	0.5	0	0	0
DG	0	-0.6	0	0	0	0	0	0	0	0	0	0.5	0	0.5	0	0.25	0.25	0	0.25	0	0	-0.3	0
DH	0	0	0	0	-0.6	0	0	0	0	0	0	0	0	0.25	0	0.25	0	0.25	0	0	0	0	0
DI	0	0	0	0	-0.6	0	0	0	0	0.5	0	0	0	-0.3	0.25	0	0	0.25	0	0	0.25	0	0
EF	0	0	0	0	0	0	0	0	0	0	0.25	0.25	0	0	0	0	0.5	0	0.5	0	0	0.25	0
EG	-0.6	0	0	0	0	0	0	0	0	0	0	0	-0.3	0	0.25	0	0	0	0	0	0.25	0	0.25
EH	0	0	-0.6	0	0	0	0	0	0	-0.6	0	0.5	0	0	0	0	0	0	0	0	0	0.25	0
EI	0	0	0	-0.6	0	0	0	0	-0.6	0	-0.3	0	0	0.5	0	0	0	0	0	0	0.25	0.5	0
FG	0	0	0	0	0	0	0	0	-0.6	0	0.5	0.5	0	0	0	0	0	0.25	0	0.25	0	0	0
FH	-0.6	-0.6	0	0	0	0	0	0	0	0	0	0	0	0.25	0	-0.3	0	0	0	0	0.25	0	0.25
FI	0	0	0	0	0	0	-0.6	0	0	0	0	-0.3	0.5	0	0	0	0	0.25	0.25	0.25	0	0	0
GH	0	0	-0.6	0	0	0	0	0	0	0	0	0.25	0	0	0	0	0.25	0	0	0.25	0	0	0
GI	0	0	0	0	0	-0.6	0	0	0	0.25	0	0.25	0	0	0	0.25	0	0.5	0	0.5	0	0	0.25
HI	0	0	0	0	-0.6	0	0	0	0	0	0	0	0	0	0.25	0	0	0.25	0	0	0	0.25	0

confounded. Thus, should the analyst decide to use the A and D columns for one interaction effect, the other interaction attributes should be assigned to the C and D, C and F, or the D and F columns. Note that we cannot assign two attributes to the D column; therefore, the second two attributes for which an interaction effect is to be tested must be assigned to the C and F

Table 6.14 (cont.)

BI	CD	CE	CF	CG		CH	CI	DE	DF	DG	DH	DI	EF	EG	EH	EI	FG	FH	FI	GH	GI	HI
0	0	0	0	0	A	0	-0.6	0	0	0	0	0	0	-0.6	0	0	0	-0.6	0	0	0	0
0	0	0	0	0	B	0	0	0	0	-0.6	0	0	0	0	0	0	0	-0.6	0	0	0	0
0	0	0	0	0	C	0	0	0	0	0	0	0	0	0	0	0	0	0	0	-0.6	0	0
0	0	0	0	0	D	0	0	0	0	0	0	0	0	0	-0.6	-0.6	0	0	0	0	0	0
0	0	0	0	0	E	0	0	0	0	0	-0.6	-0.6	0	0	0	0	0	0	0	0	0	-0.6
0	0	0	0	0	F	0	0	0	0	0	0	0	0	0	0	0	0	0	0	0	-0.6	0
0	0	0	0	0	G	-0.6	0	0	0	0	0	0	0	0	0	0	0	0	-0.6	0	0	0
0	0	0	0	-0.6	H	0	0	-0.6	0	0	0	0	0	0	0	-0.6	0	0	0	0	0	0
0	0	0	0	0	I	0	0	-0.6	0	0	0	0	0	0	-0.6	0	-0.6	0	0	0	0	0
0	0.25	0	0	-0.3	AB	0	0	0.25	0	0	0	0.5	0	0	0	-0.3	0	0	0	0	0.25	0
0	0	0	0	0	AC	0	-0.3	0.25	0	0.5	0.25	0	0.25	0	0.5	0	0.5	0	0	0	0	0
0.5	0	0.3	0	0.5	AD	0.3	0	0	0	0	0	0	0.3	0	0	0	0.5	0	-0.3	0.3	0.3	0
-0.3	0.25	0	0.25	0	AE	0.5	0	0	0.25	0	0	0	0	-0.3	0	0	0	0.5	0	0	0	0
0	0	0.25	0	0.5	AF	0	0	0.25	0	0.5	0	-0.3	0	0	0	0.5	0	0.25	0	0	0	0
0.25	0.5	0	0.5	0	AG	0	0	0	0.5	0	0.25	0.25	0	0.25	0	0	0	0	0	0	0	0.25
0	0.25	0.5	0	0	AH	0	0	0	0	0.25	0	0	0	0	0	0	0	-0.3	0	0	0.25	0
0	0	0	0	0	AI	0	0.25	0	-0.3	0.25	0	0	0.5	0	0	0	0	0	0	0.25	0	0
0	0	0.5	0	0	BC	0	0	0	0	0	0.25	0.25	0	0	0	0	0.25	0	0.25	0	0.5	0.25
0	0	0	0	0	BD	0.25	0.25	0	0	0.25	0	0	0.5	0	0	0	0	0	0.25	0	0	0
0	0	0.5	0	0	BE	0	0	0	0.5	0	0	0	0	0	0	0	0.25	0	0.25	0.25	0.5	0
0	0	0	0	0.25	BF	0	0.25	0.5	0	0	0	0.25	0	0.25	0	0.25	0	0.25	0	0	0	0
0	0	0	0.25	0	BG	0	0.5	0	0	-0.3	0	0	0.25	0	0.25	0.5	0	0	0	0	0	0.25
0	0.25	0	0	0	BH	0	0.25	0	0	0	0	0	0	0.25	0	0	0	0.25	0	0	0.25	0
1	0.25	0	0.25	0.5	BI	0.25	0	0	0.25	0	0	0	0.25	0.5	0	0	0	0	0	0	0.25	0
0.3	1	0	0.5	0	CD	0	0	0	0.5	0	0	0	0	0.3	0	0	0	0	0	0	-0.3	0
0	0	1	0	0	CE	0	0	0	0	0.3	0	0	0	0	0	0	0.3	-0.3	0.3	0	0.5	0
0.3	0.5	0	1	0	CF	0	0	0	0.5	0	0	0	0	0.3	-0.3	0.3	0	0	0	0	0	0.5
0.5	0	0	0	1	CG	0.25	0	0.25	0	0	0	-0.3	0.25	0	0	0.5	0	0	0	0.25	0	0
0.25	0	0	0	0.25	CH	1	0	0	0	0	0	0	-0.3	0	0	0	0	0	0.5	-0.3	0	0
0	0	0	0	0	CI	0	1	0	0	-0.3	0	0	0.25	0.5	0	0	0	0.5	0	0	0	0
0	0	0	0	0.25	DE	0	0	1	0	0	-0.3	0.25	0	0	0.25	0.25	0.25	0	0	0	0	0
0.25	0.5	0	0.5	0	DF	0	0	0	1	0	0	0	0	0.25	0	0	0	0	0	0.25	0	0
0	0	0.25	0	0	DG	0	-0.3	0	0	1	0	0	0.25	0	0	0	0	0.25	0	0	0	0
0	0	0	0	0	DH	0	0	-0.3	0	0	1	0.5	0	0	0.25	0	0.25	0	0	0	0	0.5
0	0	0	0	-0.3	DI	0	0	0.25	0	0	0.5	1	0	0	0	-0.3	0	0	0	0	0	0.5
0.25	0	0	0	0.25	EF	-0.3	0.25	0	0	0.25	0	0	1	0	0	0	0	0	0	0.5	0	0
0.5	0.25	0	0.25	0	EG	0	0.5	0	0.25	0	0	0	0	1	0	0	0	0.5	0	0	0	0
0	0	0	-0.3	0	EH	0	0	0.25	0	0	0.25	0	0	0	1	0.25	0.5	0	0	0	0	-0.3
0	0	0	0.25	0.5	EI	0	0	0	0	0	0	-0.3	0	0	0.25	1	0	0	0	0	0	0.25
0	0	0.25	0	0	FG	0	0	0	0	0	0.25	0	0	0	0.5	0	1	0	-0.3	0	0.25	0
0	0	-0.3	0	0	FH	0	0.5	0	0	0.25	0	0	0	0.5	0	0	0	1	0	0	0	0
0	0	0.25	0	0	FI	0.5	0	0	0	0	0	0	0	0	0	0	-0.3	0	1	0	0.25	0
0.25	0	0	0	0.25	GH	-0.3	0	0	0	0	0	0	0.5	0	0	0	0	0	0	1	0	0
0	-0.3	0.5	0	0	GI	0	0	0	0	0	0	0	0	0	0	0	0.25	0	0.25	0	1	0
0	0	0	0.5	0	HI	0	0	0	0	0	0.5	0.5	0	0	-0.3	0.25	0	0	0	0	0	1

columns. Had the B and C columns been utilized for the car attributes, the reader is invited to check that either D and F or E and F columns may be used for the second two attributes for which the analyst wishes to obtain interactions.

As an aside, assuming the A and D columns and B and C columns were the ones used, the two two-way interactions may be treated as being independent of all main effects, but not of all other two-way interaction effects. Indeed, as with the main effects, the analyst must assume that the two-way interactions for the BC, BE, BI, CE, and EF interaction terms are insignificant in order to proceed (and that is only for the AD interaction). If, however, it turns out in practice that any other interactions are significant, then the problem of estimating models with correlated data arises once more. That these interactions are insignificant statistically is an assumption of which there exists no way of testing. We have said nothing of the confoundment that exists with higher order interaction terms.

Assuming that the analyst elected to assign the car alternative attributes to the A and D columns and the bus alternative attributes to the C and F design columns, the remainder of the attributes may be distributed to the remaining design columns. No interaction terms are required for these and hence confoundement of the interaction terms for these remaining attributes is not an issue. Note that, for our example, all attributes have three levels each, hence it matters not to which design columns we assign the remaining attributes to. Had the design required one attribute to have four levels, then that attribute would be assigned to the design column with four attribute levels (or a pair of design columns each of two levels). Table 6.15 shows the attributes as they might be allocated to the design columns for the experimental design introduced in Table 6.11. Note that we have allocated column I to be the block variable.

As an aside, the reader should be aware of the issue of **balanced designs** versus **unbalanced designs**. A *balanced design* is a design in which the levels of any given attribute appear the same number of times as all other levels for that particular attribute. For example, for the design described in Table 6.15, for each attribute, the level coded −1 occurs nine times, 0 nine times, and 1 nine times. An *unbalanced design* is a design in which the attribute levels do not appear the same number of times within each attribute for the design. The use of balanced versus unbalanced designs is of interest as early research conducted suggests that the unbalanced attributes of an unbalanced design are often found to be statistically significant, not so much because the attribute itself is statistically significant but because attention is drawn to that attribute at the time of the survey.

Table 6.15 Attributes assigned to design columns

	comf1 (CAR)	ttime1 (CAR)	comf2 (bus)	ttime2 (bus)	comf3 (train)	ttime3 (train)	comf4 (plane)	ttime4 (plane)	block
Design column Treatment combination	A	D	C	F	E	B	G	H	I
1	−1	0	1	−1	0	−1	0	−1	1
2	1	−1	1	0	−1	0	0	−1	−1
3	0	0	1	−1	−1	0	1	0	0
4	0	1	0	−1	0	0	−1	0	−1
5	1	−1	0	1	1	−1	−1	0	1
6	0	−1	0	1	−1	1	1	−1	−1
7	−1	0	0	0	−1	1	−1	0	0
8	0	0	0	0	1	−1	0	1	−1
9	1	0	0	0	0	0	1	−1	1
10	1	0	1	−1	1	1	−1	1	−1
11	0	1	−1	0	−1	−1	1	1	1
12	−1	0	−1	1	1	0	1	1	−1
13	−1	1	−1	0	0	1	0	0	−1
14	1	−1	−1	−1	0	1	1	1	0
15	−1	1	0	−1	1	−1	1	−1	0
16	0	−1	1	0	0	−1	−1	1	0
17	−1	1	1	1	−1	0	−1	1	1
18	−1	−1	−1	−1	−1	−1	−1	−1	−1
19	1	0	−1	1	−1	−1	0	0	0
20	−1	−1	1	0	1	1	1	0	1
21	1	1	−1	0	1	0	−1	−1	0
22	0	0	−1	1	0	1	−1	−1	1
23	−1	−1	0	1	0	0	0	1	0
24	1	1	0	−1	−1	1	0	1	1
25	0	1	1	1	1	1	0	−1	0
26	1	1	1	1	0	−1	1	0	−1
27	0	−1	−1	−1	1	0	0	0	1

> *As a further aside*, the formulas shown in Table 6.10 are used to calculate the minimum degrees of freedom necessary for estimating the desired number of parameters. The numbers derived may, however, not represent the true minimum number of treatment combinations necessary to achieve an orthogonal design, due to the necessity to maintain attribute level balance within each attribute. For example, let M = 2, A = 3, and L = 2. The minimum number of treatment combinations assuming the estimation of non-linear effects in the marginal utilities in a labeled choice experiment is equal to $(2-1) \times 2 \times 3 + 1$ or 7.

However, such a design will not be balanced as each attribute has 2 levels which must appear an equal number of times over 6 choice sets. This represents an additional constraint, such that the smallest possible design will have a number of treatment combinations equal to or greater than that calculated using the relevant formula shown in Table 6.10, but also be a number that produces an integer when divided by all L.

Before proceeding to stage six of the design process, the analyst may wish to sort the experimental design by the blocking variable. Doing so informs the analyst which mixture of treatment combinations will be shown to various decision makers. Looking at Table 6.16, we see that one out of every three decision makers will be given treatment combinations 2, 4, 6, 8, 10, 12, 13, 18, and 26. Other decision makers will be presented with treatment combinations 3, 7, 14, 15, 16, 19, 21, 23, and 25. Yet other decision makers will be given treatment combinations 1, 5, 9, 11, 17, 20, 22, 24, and 27.

We have, in generating a fractional factorial design for the example described, managed to reduce the number of treatment combinations from 6,561 (the full factorial design) to 27. Further, we have managed to reduce the 27 treatment combinations to 9 in terms of how many treatment combinations each decision maker will be presented with (in the guise of choice sets). We have done so by confounding higher order interaction effects that we are required to assume will be statistically insignificant.

The experimental design shown in Table 6.16 represents a workable design capable of estimating all main effects and two two-way interactions. However returning to the method of how the design was derived, we note that the degrees of freedom used to determine the number of treatment combinations for the design was such that non-linear effects could be estimated for each attribute. That is, the analyst may elect to dummy or effects code each attribute and estimate a parameter for each dummy or effect variable thus created. It is therefore worthwhile examining how the design will look should the analyst elect to use effects codes (for dummy codes one simply has to replace all −1s with 0s). Using the orthogonal code of −1 in Table 6.15 to represent the base level (i.e., the level that will take the value −1 in our effects code), the design will be shown as in Table 6.15.

Note that we did not effects code column I of Table 6.16. This is because this column represents the blocking column of the design for which we will not be estimating a parameter when we estimate our choice model (although we could in order to determine whether the block assigned was a significant contributor to the choice outcome). Table 6.18 shows the correlation matrix for the design shown in Table 6.17.

Table 6.16 Using blocking variables to determine allocation of treatment combinations

	comf1 (CAR)	ttime1 (CAR)	comf2 (bus)	ttime2 (bus)	comf3 (train)	ttime3 (train)	comf4 (plane)	ttime4 (plane)	block
Design column Treatment combination	A	D	C	F	E	B	G	H	I
2	1	−1	1	0	−1	0	0	−1	−1
4	0	1	0	−1	0	0	−1	0	−1
6	0	−1	0	1	−1	1	1	−1	−1
8	0	0	0	0	1	−1	0	1	−1
10	1	0	1	−1	1	1	−1	1	−1
12	−1	0	−1	1	1	0	1	1	−1
13	−1	1	−1	0	0	1	0	0	−1
18	−1	−1	−1	−1	−1	−1	−1	−1	−1
26	1	1	1	1	0	−1	1	0	−1
3	0	0	1	−1	−1	0	1	0	0
7	−1	0	0	0	−1	1	−1	0	0
14	1	−1	−1	−1	0	1	1	1	0
15	−1	1	0	−1	1	−1	1	−1	0
16	0	−1	1	0	0	−1	−1	1	0
19	1	0	−1	1	−1	−1	0	0	0
21	1	1	−1	0	1	0	−1	−1	0
23	−1	−1	0	1	0	0	0	1	0
25	0	1	1	1	1	1	0	−1	0
1	−1	0	1	−1	0	−1	0	−1	1
5	1	−1	0	1	1	−1	−1	0	1
9	1	0	0	0	0	0	1	−1	1
11	0	1	−1	0	−1	−1	1	1	1
17	−1	1	1	1	−1	0	−1	1	1
20	−1	−1	1	0	1	1	1	0	1
22	0	0	−1	1	0	1	−1	−1	1
24	1	1	0	−1	−1	1	0	1	1
27	0	−1	−1	−1	1	0	0	0	1

Examination of Table 6.18 shows that there now exist correlations within the design. Design orthogonality has been lost. Indeed, design orthogonality will exist for linear main effects designs only. Once one moves towards designs capable of estimating non-linear effects using such methods as effects or dummy coding, one automatically introduces correlations (we leave it to the reader to show the correlation structure formed when dummy codes are used instead of effects codes for the above example).

Table 6.17 Effects coding design of Table 6.15

Design column / Treatment combination	A1	A2	D1	D2	C1	C2	F1	F2	E1	E2	B1	B2	G1	G2	H1	H2	I
2	1	0	-1	-1	1	0	0	1	-1	-1	0	1	0	1	-1	-1	-1
4	0	1	1	0	0	1	-1	-1	0	1	0	1	-1	-1	0	1	-1
6	0	1	-1	-1	0	1	1	0	-1	-1	1	0	1	0	-1	-1	-1
8	0	1	0	1	0	1	0	1	1	0	-1	-1	0	1	1	0	-1
10	1	0	0	1	1	0	-1	-1	1	0	1	0	-1	-1	1	0	-1
12	-1	-1	0	1	-1	-1	1	0	1	0	0	1	1	0	1	0	-1
13	-1	-1	1	0	-1	-1	0	1	0	1	1	0	0	1	0	1	-1
18	-1	-1	-1	-1	-1	-1	-1	-1	-1	-1	-1	-1	-1	-1	-1	-1	-1
26	1	0	1	0	1	0	1	0	0	1	-1	-1	1	0	0	1	-1
3	0	1	0	1	1	0	-1	-1	-1	-1	0	1	1	0	0	1	0
7	-1	-1	0	1	0	1	0	1	-1	-1	1	0	-1	-1	0	1	0
14	1	0	-1	-1	-1	-1	-1	-1	0	1	1	0	1	0	1	0	0
15	-1	-1	1	0	0	1	-1	-1	1	0	-1	-1	1	0	-1	-1	0
16	0	1	-1	-1	1	0	0	1	0	1	-1	-1	-1	-1	1	0	0
19	1	0	0	1	-1	-1	1	0	-1	-1	-1	-1	0	1	0	1	0
21	1	0	1	0	-1	-1	0	1	1	0	0	1	-1	-1	-1	-1	0
23	-1	-1	-1	-1	0	1	1	0	0	1	0	1	0	1	1	0	0
25	0	1	1	0	1	0	1	0	1	0	1	0	0	1	-1	-1	0
1	-1	-1	0	1	1	0	-1	-1	0	1	-1	-1	0	1	-1	-1	1
5	1	0	-1	-1	0	1	1	0	1	0	-1	-1	-1	-1	0	1	1
9	1	0	0	1	0	1	0	1	0	1	0	1	1	0	-1	-1	1
11	0	1	1	0	-1	-1	0	1	-1	-1	-1	-1	1	0	1	0	1
17	-1	-1	1	0	1	0	1	0	-1	-1	0	1	-1	-1	1	0	1
20	-1	-1	-1	-1	1	0	0	1	1	0	1	0	1	0	0	1	1
22	0	1	0	1	-1	-1	1	0	0	1	1	0	-1	-1	-1	-1	1
24	1	0	1	0	0	1	-1	-1	-1	-1	1	0	0	1	1	0	1
27	0	1	-1	-1	-1	-1	-1	-1	1	0	0	1	0	1	0	1	1

There therefore exists a trade-off in being able to detect non-linear effects and the introduction of correlations. Unfortunately, programs such as SPSS are only able to generate designs based on the number of degrees of freedom necessary to estimate non-linear effects. As such, should one be interested in non-linear effects, one will have to use a much larger design than is necessary if the design one wishes to produce is constructed by programs such as SPSS or Ngene, another reason why one should learn how to generate designs from first principles.

Table 6.18 Correlation matrix for effects coded design

	a1	a2	d1	d2	c1	c2	f1	f2	E1	e2	b1	b2	g1	g2	h1	h2	i
a1	1																
a2	0.5	1															
d1	0	0	1														
d2	0	0	0.5	1													
c1	0	0	0	0	1												
c2	0	0	0	0	0.5	1											
f1	0	0	0	0	0	0	1										
f2	0	0	0	0	0	0	0.5	1									
e1	0	0	0	0	0	0	0	0	1								
e2	0	0	0	0	0	0	0	0	0.5	1							
b1	0	0	0	0	0	0	0	0	0	0	1						
b2	0	0	0	0	0	0	0	0	0	0	0.5	1					
g1	0	0	0	0	0	0	0	0	0	0	0	0	1				
g2	0	0	0	0	0	0	0	0	0	0	0	0	0.5	1			
h1	0	0	0	0	0	0	0	0	0	0	0	0	0	0	1		
h2	0	0	0	0	0	0	0	0	0	0	0	0	0	0	0.5	1	
i	0	0	0	0	0	0	0	0	0	0	0	0	0	0	0	0	1

Independent of whether we wish to detect linear effects or non-linear effects, we have left ourselves open to one major criticism. This criticism does not relate to the processes in generating the design. Rather, we may be criticized for failing to heed our own advice. The astute reader will note that our original research problem was framed such that the analyst wished to estimate mode share changes given the introduction of a new alternative means of travel between the two cities. The design we generated is for currently existing alternatives only. We require additional design columns for the attributes of the new alternative. Taking this into account we are required to generate another (probably larger) design.

Let us assume that this new alternative has two attributes that the analyst believes will be significant in determining whether the alternative will be chosen or not (perhaps focus groups were conducted to determine these). Each attribute will have three attribute levels. The full factorial design will have 59,049 possible treatment combinations (i.e., $3^{(5 \times 2)}$). Given this, it is likely the analyst will wish to generate a fractional factorial design to reduce the number of treatment combinations. Unfortunately this is not possible using SPSS as the total number of attributes that may be handled is 10. The analyst requires 11 (10 attributes and one blocking variable). Fortunately, the analyst may proceed by

Table 6.19 3^4 Fractional factorial design

Treatment combination	A	B	C	D
1	-3	-3	-3	-3
2	1	1	-3	1
3	3	3	-3	3
4	-1	-1	-3	-1
5	-1	3	1	-3
6	3	1	-1	-3
7	1	-1	3	-3
8	-3	3	3	1
9	3	-3	3	-1
10	-3	1	1	-1
11	-1	1	3	3
12	-1	-3	-1	1
13	1	-3	1	3
14	1	3	-1	-1
15	3	-1	1	1
16	-3	-1	-1	3

using SPSS to generate a base design and then use this base design to generate the other attribute columns as required. Let us use a simpler (smaller) design example to demonstrate how. Table 6.19 shows a design generated by SPSS for four attributes each with four levels. Note that we have used orthogonal coding.

The analyst may generate the additional design columns required using a number of different approaches. Firstly, the analyst may use the existing treatment combinations and use these as the additional design columns. To do so, the analyst might randomize the treatment combinations and assign these randomized treatment combinations to the new design columns while retaining the existing design for the original columns. We do this in Table 6.20.

In assigning the randomized treatment combinations, it is important that the analyst check that a randomized treatment combination is not assigned next to its replicate treatment combination (i.e., randomized treatment combination one is not assigned next to the original treatment combination one).

Table 6.21 shows the correlation matrix for the above design. The design produced, as is the case here, is not likely to be orthogonal. As such, the problems associated with modeling with correlated data are likely to be experienced.

An alternative approach is to take the **foldover** of the design and to use it as the new design columns. Taking the foldover involves the reproduction of the

Table 6.20 Randomizing treatment combinations to use for additional design columns

Treatment combination	A	B	C	D	Random treatment combination	E	F	G	H
1	−3	−3	−3	−3	2	1	1	−3	1
2	1	1	−3	1	16	−3	−1	−1	3
3	3	3	−3	3	15	3	−1	1	1
4	−1	−1	−3	−1	6	3	1	−1	−3
5	−1	3	1	−3	4	−1	−1	−3	−1
6	3	1	−1	−3	10	−3	1	1	−1
7	1	−1	3	−3	9	3	−3	3	−1
8	−3	3	3	1	14	1	3	−1	−1
9	3	−3	3	−1	8	−3	3	3	1
10	−3	1	1	−1	1	−3	−3	−3	−3
11	−1	1	3	3	12	−1	−3	−1	1
12	−1	−3	−1	1	5	−1	3	1	−3
13	1	−3	1	3	3	3	3	−3	3
14	1	3	−1	−1	7	1	−1	3	−3
15	3	−1	1	1	11	−1	1	3	3
16	−3	−1	−1	3	13	1	−3	1	3

Table 6.21 Correlation matrix for randomizing treatment combinations

	A	B	C	D	E	F	G	H
A	1							
B	0	1						
C	0	0	1					
D	0	0	0	1				
E	−0.1	−0.05	−0.15	0.2	1			
F	0.2	−0.4	0	0	0	1		
G	0.6	−0.05	0.15	0	0	0	1	
H	0.25	−0.25	0	0.5	0	0	0	1

design such that the factor levels of the design are reversed (e.g., replace 0 with 1 and 1 with 0). If orthogonal codes have been used we may achieve this effect by multiplying each column by −1. Table 6.22 shows the foldover for our simplified example. Columns E through H of Table 6.22 represent the foldover columns.

Unfortunately, the way SPSS generates designs means that using the foldover to generate extra design columns is not a desirable approach to the

Table 6.22 Using the foldover to generate extra design columns

Treatment combination	A	B	C	D	E	F	G	H
1	-3	-3	-3	-3	3	3	3	3
2	1	1	-3	1	-1	-1	3	-1
3	3	3	-3	3	-3	-3	3	-3
4	-1	-1	-3	-1	1	1	3	1
5	-1	3	1	-3	1	-3	-1	3
6	3	1	-1	-3	-3	-1	1	3
7	1	-1	3	-3	-1	1	-3	3
8	-3	3	3	1	3	-3	-3	-1
9	3	-3	3	-1	-3	3	-3	1
10	-3	1	1	-1	3	-1	-1	1
11	-1	1	3	3	1	-1	-3	-3
12	-1	-3	-1	1	1	3	1	-1
13	1	-3	1	3	-1	3	-1	-3
14	1	3	-1	-1	-1	-3	1	1
15	3	-1	1	1	-3	1	-1	-1
16	-3	-1	-1	3	3	1	1	-3

problem. Examination of the correlation matrix for the design presented in Table 6.22 shows that the additional attribute columns are perfectly (negatively) correlated with the existing design columns. As such, using the foldover to generate additional design columns is not an option for those using SPSS to generate a design (Table 6.23).

As an aside, assuming that the analyst wishes to estimate non-linear effects, even had no correlations been observed, the above designs would be unusable as a result of insufficient degrees of freedom. That is, for 4 attributes each with 4 levels, 16 treatment combinations provide a sufficient amount of degrees of freedom for estimation purposes (i.e., we require 3 × 4 = 12 degrees of freedom for main effects only). For 8 attributes each with 4 levels we require 24 degrees of freedom (i.e., 3 × 8) for a main effects only design. As such, 16 treatment combinations will provide an insufficient amount of degrees of freedom. In our defense, the above is used only as an example of procedure. The reader should note that had we done the above correctly, we would specify the minimum number of treatment combinations to be generated as 24 before proceeding to generate the additional columns.

We conclude that the analyst is best to use the first method to generate additional design columns (at least if SPSS is used to generate the design). Unless all decision makers respond to the questionnaire, then the design as entered into the computer will not be orthogonal anyway (i.e., for

Table 6.23 Correlation matrix for designs using foldovers to generate additional columns

	A	B	C	D	E	F	G	H
A	1							
B	0	1						
C	0	0	1					
D	0	0	0	1				
E	−1	0	0	0	1			
F	0	−1	0	0	0	1		
G	0	0	−1	0	0	0	1	
H	0	0	0	−1	0	0	0	1

orthogonality, it is the rows of the design which are important and not the columns). We can remove columns and not lose orthogonality. If we lose rows (treatment combinations) then the design will no longer be orthogonal. Thus if a block of a design is not returned by one decision maker, orthogonality will be lost. In practice, this fact is largely ignored. We continue our discussion on the experimental design process in Chapter 7.

6.2.6 Generating efficient designs

Statistical efficiency in experimental design terms relates to an increased precision of the parameter estimates for a fixed sample size. Statistical efficiency is therefore linked to the standard errors likely to be obtained from the experiment (and to a lesser effect the covariances – see Chapter 5), with designs that can be expected to (i) yield lower standard errors for a given sample size, or (ii) the same standard errors given a smaller sample size, being deemed more statistically efficient. Fortunately, while different criteria have been applied at various times to measure statistical efficiency, the underlying definition of statistical efficiency has changed little, even if it has not been appropriately applied in all cases. Once it is understood that, independent of the specific problem being examined, experimental design theory (as applied in the case of the SC context) is concerned with the standard errors (and covariances) of the parameters obtained from models to be estimated from data collected using a generated design, it is clear that what is of prime consideration is the relationship between the design and the resulting model variance-covariance matrix (from whence the standard errors are derived).

Experimental design theory originated in fields other than SC and discrete choice analysis, and hence developed specifically to address models tailored to particular data types corresponding to the problems that were being addressed at the time. Indeed, the original theories dealt specifically with experimental problems where the dependent variable was continuous in nature. As such, the resulting design theory was developed specifically for models capable of handling such data; hence much of the work on experimental design theory has concentrated on use of analysis of variance (ANOVA) and linear regression type models (see Peirce 1876). From a historical perspective this has had a significant impact on the SC literature. The original SC studies, unsurprisingly, concentrated on introducing and promoting the benefits of the new modeling method and did not concentrate specifically on the issue of experimental design (see Louviere and Hensher 1983 and Louviere and Woodworth 1983). As such, these earlier works understandably borrowed from the early theories on experimental design without considering whether they were appropriate or not for use with models applied to such data. Over time, the designs used in these earlier SC studies became the norm and have largely remained so ever since.

Sporadic research over the years, however, has looked at the specific problem of experimental designs as related to econometric models estimated on discrete choice data. In order to calculate the statistical efficiency of a SC design, Fowkes and Wardman (1988), Bunch et al. (1996), Huber and Zwerina (1996), Sándor and Wedel (2001), and Kanninen (2002), among others, have shown that the common use of logit models to analyze discrete choice data requires *a priori* information about the parameter estimates, as well as the final econometric model form that will be used in estimation. Specifically, information on the expected parameter estimates, in the form of *priors* is required in order to calculate the expected utilities for each of the alternatives present within the design. Once known, these expected utilities can in turn be used to calculate the likely choice probabilities. Hence, given knowledge of the attribute levels (the design), expected parameter estimate values, and the resultant choice probabilities, it becomes a straightforward exercise to calculate the asymptotic variance-covariance (AVC) matrix for the design, from which the expected standard errors can be obtained. The AVC matrix of the design, Ω_N, can be determined as the inverse of the Fisher Information matrix, I_N, which is computed as the negative expected second derivatives of the log-likelihood (LL) function, considering N respondents, of the discrete choice model to be estimated (see Train 2009 and Chapter 5). By manipulating the attribute levels of the alternatives, for known (assumed) parameter values, the analyst is able to minimize the elements within the AVC matrix, which in the case of the diagonals means lower standard errors and hence greater reliability in the estimates at a fixed sample size (or even at a reduced sample size).

In taking this approach, these authors have remained consistent with the underlying theory of experimental design as defined previously. Indeed, the theory for generating SC experimental designs has as its objective the same objective when dealing with linear models; that is, the minimizing of the variances and covariances of the parameter estimates. What is different, however, is the econometric models to which the theory is being applied. As discussed above, other differences have also emerged related to the various assumptions that are required to be made when dealing with data specifically generated for logit type models.

The efficiency of a design can be derived from the AVC matrix. Instead of assessing a whole AVC matrix, it is easier to assess a design based on a single value. Therefore, efficiency measures have been proposed in the literature in order to calculate such an efficiency value, typically expressed as an efficiency "error" (i.e., a measure for the inefficiency). The objective then becomes to minimize this efficiency error.

The most widely used measure is called the *D-error*, which takes the determinant of the AVC matrix Ω_1 assuming only a single respondent.[2] A design with the lowest *D*-error is called *D-optimal*. In practice, it is very difficult to find the design with the lowest *D*-error, therefore we are satisfied if the design has a sufficiently low *D*-error, called a *D-efficient* design. Different types of *D*-error have been proposed in the literature, depending on the available information on the prior parameters $\tilde{\beta}$. We will distinguish three cases (also see Bliemer and Rose 2005b, 2009 and Rose and Bliemer 2004, 2008):

(a) *No information is available*

If no information is available (not even the sign of the parameters), then set $\tilde{\beta} = 0$. This leads to a so-called D_z-error ("z" from "zero").

(b) *Information is available with good approximations of β*

If the information is relatively accurate, $\tilde{\beta}$ is set to the best guesses, assuming that they are correct. This leads to a so-called D_p-error ("p" from "priors").

(c) *Information is available with uncertainty about the approximations of β*

Instead of assuming fixed priors $\tilde{\beta}$, they are assumed to be random following some given probability distribution to express the uncertainty about the true value of β. This Bayesian approach leads to a so-called D_b-error("b" from "Bayesian").

The *D*-errors are a function of the experimental design X and the prior values (or probability distributions) $\tilde{\beta}$, and can be mathematically formulated as:

---

[2] The assumption of a single respondent is just for convenience and comparison reasons and does not have any further implications. Any other sample size could have been used, but it is common in the literature to base it on a single respondent.

$$D_z\text{-error} = \det\left(\Omega_1(X, 0)\right)^{1/H}, \tag{6.11}$$

$$D_p\text{-error} = \det\left(\Omega_1(X, \tilde{\beta})\right)^{1/H}, \tag{6.12}$$

$$D_b\text{-error} = \int \tilde{\beta}\det\left(\Omega_1(X, \tilde{\beta})\right)^{1/H} \phi(\tilde{\beta}|\theta)d\tilde{\beta}. \tag{6.13}$$

where H is the number of parameters to be estimated. Note that the AVC matrix is a matrix. In order to let the D-error be independent of the size of the problem, the D-error is normalized by the power $1/H$. We recommend removing the rows and columns corresponding to the model constants in the AVC matrix, as these parameters in general do not have a clear meaning in a SC experiment (in contrast to revealed choices). As the standard errors of these model constants can become fairly large, they could dominate the D-errors, therefore we advise removing them before taking the determinant (and at the same time also adjusting the value of H).

Besides the D-error, other inefficiency measures have been proposed as well. Another well-known efficiency error is called the **A-error**, and the design with the lowest A-error is called *A-optimal*. Instead of taking the determinant, the A-error takes the trace of the AVC matrix, which is the summation of all the diagonal elements of the matrix. Therefore, the A-error only looks at the variances and not at the covariances. In order to normalize the A-error it is divided by H (the same recommendation about the model constants applies). Similar to the D-error, different A-errors can be determined based on the availability of information on the parameters. The error is mathematically formulated as:

$$A_p\text{-error} = \frac{\text{tr}\left(\Omega_N(X, \tilde{\beta})\right)}{H}. \tag{6.14}$$

The A_z-error and A_b-error can be derived using formulations equivalent to Equations (6.11) and (6.13). The A-error should be used with caution in case not all parameter values are of equal scale. By the simple summation of the variances it is likely that parameters with large values will overshadow the other parameters. Therefore, we suggest using a weighted summation. Using weights, it is also possible to give more importance to certain parameters – that is, enable the estimating of these parameters more accurately than others.

Rose and Bliemer (2013) defined a new efficiency measure, the s-error, which provides the theoretical minimum sample size required for a design. Noting that the AUC matrix is most commonly computed assuming only a single respondent, and that the AUC matrix can be calculated for any sample size such that

$$\Omega_N = \frac{\Omega}{N} \tag{6.15}$$

Rose and Bliemer (2013) showed that re-arranging the t-ratios for the hth parameter

$$t_h = \frac{\dfrac{\beta_h}{\text{s.e.n}}}{\sqrt{n_h}}$$

gives

$$n_h = t_h^2 \frac{\text{s.e}_h^2}{\beta_h} \tag{6.16}$$

The s-error is then given as the $\max(n_h)$ under assumptions about the desired values and non-zero betas. The problem of finding an efficient design can be described as follows:

Given feasible attribute levels Λ_{jk} for all j and k, given the number of choice situations S, and given the prior parameter values $\tilde{\beta}$ (or probability distributions of $\tilde{\beta}$), determine a level balanced design X with $x_{jks} \in \Lambda_{jk}$ that minimizes the efficiency error in Equation (6.11), (6.12), (6.13), or (6.14).

Note that in this formulation attribute level balance is added as a requirement, consistent with current state of practice. It should be stressed that an efficient design does not necessarily require attribute level balance. In fact, a more efficient design may be found by removing the level balance requirement.

In order to solve the problem of determining the most efficient design, one could determine the full factorial design and then evaluate each different combination of S choice situations from this full factorial. The combination with the lowest efficiency error is the optimal design. However, this procedure is not feasible in practice due to an extremely high number of possible designs to evaluate. For example, consider the problem of determining an efficient design for a hypothetical case with three alternatives as shown in Table 6.24. The full factorial design has $2^1 \times 3^8 \times 4^2 = 209,952$ choice situations. Suppose that we would like to find an efficient design with $S = 12$ choice situations. Selecting 12 choice situations from this set of 209,952 different choice situations yields 7.3×10^{63} possible different designs. Clearly, it is not feasible to evaluate all possible designs, hence a smart algorithm is necessary to find a design that is as efficient as possible.

Table 6.24 Example dimensions for generating an efficient design

Attributes	Alternatives		
	Car (route A)	*Car (route B)*	*Train*
Travel time (min.)	{10, 20, 30}	{15, 30, 45}	{15, 25, 35}
Delay/waiting time (min.)	{0, 5, 10}	{5, 10, 15}	{5, 10}
Toll cost/fare ($)	{2, 4, 6, 8}	{0, 1, 2, 3}	{4, 6, 8}

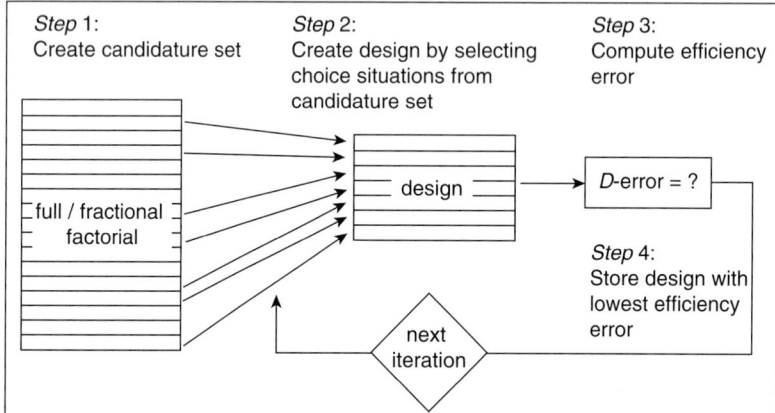

Figure 6.11 Modified Federov algorithm

There are row-based algorithms and column-based algorithms for finding an efficient design. In a *row-based algorithm*, choice situations are selected from a pre-defined candidature set of choice situations (either a full factorial or a fractional factorial) in each iteration. *Column-based algorithms* (such as RSC *(Relabeling, Swapping & Cycling)* algorithms) create a design by selecting attribute levels over all choice situations for each attribute. Row-based algorithms can easily remove bad choice situations from the candidature set at the beginning (e.g., by applying a utility balance criterion), but it is more difficult to satisfy attribute level balance. The opposite holds for column-based algorithms, in which attribute level balance is easy to satisfy, but finding good combinations of attribute levels in each choice situation is more difficult. In general, column-based algorithms offer more flexibility and can deal with larger designs, but in some cases (for unlabeled designs and for specific designs such as constrained designs, see Section 6.3) row-based algorithms are more suitable.

The *Modified Federov algorithm* (Cook and Nachtsheim 1980) is an example of a row-based algorithm and is illustrated in Figure 6.11. First, a candidature set is determined, either the full factorial (for small problems), or a

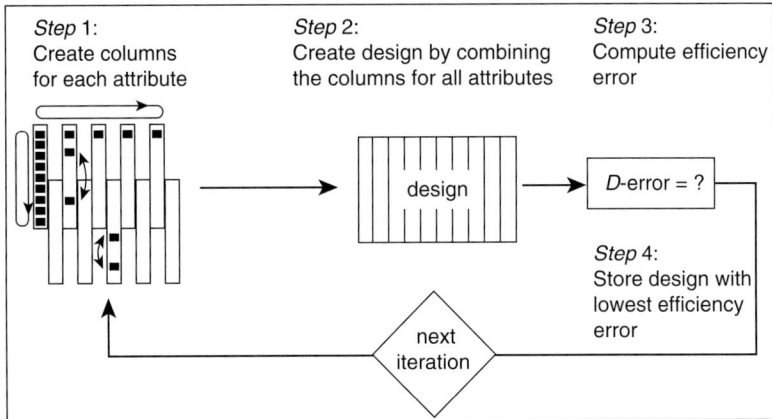

Figure 6.12   RSC algorithm

fractional factorial (for large problems). Then, a (attribute level balanced) design is created by selecting choice situations from the candidature set. After that, the efficiency error (e.g., D-error) is computed for this design. Finally, if this design has a lower efficiency error than the current best design, the design is stored as the most efficient design so far, and one continues with the next iteration, repeating the whole process again. The algorithm terminates if all possible combinations of choice situations have been evaluated (which is in general not feasible), or after a pre-defined number of iterations. Construction of D_z-optimal, as described in Street *et al.* (2005), is also row-based, in which in a smart way combinations of choice situations are made.

RSC algorithms (Huber and Zwerina 1996; Sándor and Wedel 2001) are column-based algorithms, illustrated in Figure 6.12. In each iteration, different columns for each attribute are created, which together form a design. This design is evaluated and if it has a lower efficiency error than the current best design, then it is stored. The columns are not created randomly, but – as the name suggests – are generated in a structured way using relabeling, swapping, and cycling techniques. Starting with an initial design, each column could be altered by relabeling the attribute levels. For example, if the attribute levels 1 and 3 are relabeled, then a column containing the levels (1,2,1,3,2,3) will become (3,2,3,1,2,1). Swapping means that some attribute levels switch place – for example, if the attribute levels in the first and fourth choice situation are swapped, then (1,2,1,3,2,3) would become (3,2,1,1,2,3). Finally, cycling replaces all attribute levels in each choice situation at the time by replacing the first attribute level with the second level, the second level with the third, etc. Since this impacts all columns, cycling can only be performed if all attributes have exactly the same sets of feasible levels (e.g., where all variables are dummy coded). Sometimes only swapping is used, sometimes only relabeling and swapping is used, as special cases of this algorithm type.

A genetic algorithm, also a column-based algorithm, has been proposed by Quan *et al.* (2011). In this algorithm, a population of designs is (randomly) created, and new designs are determined by cross-over of designs in the population (combining columns of two designs, called the parents, creating a new design, called the child). The fittest designs in the population, measured by their efficiency, will most likely survive in the population, while less fit designs with a high efficiency error will be removed from the population (i.e., die). Mutation in the population takes place by randomly swapping attribute levels in the columns. Genetic algorithms seem to be quite powerful in finding efficient designs relatively quickly.

If for some reason orthogonality is required in a D_p design, one could construct a single orthogonal design, from this design easily create a large (but not huge) number of other orthogonal designs, and then evaluate all these orthogonal designs and select the most efficient one. Creating other orthogonal designs from a single orthogonal design is relatively simple.

Evaluating each design for the efficiency error is the most time consuming part of each algorithm; therefore the number of D-error or other efficiency error evaluations should be kept to a minimum by putting more intelligence into the construction of the designs. In determining Bayesian efficient designs this becomes even more important, as the integral in Equation (6.13) cannot be computed analytically, but only by simulation. Mainly pseudo-random Monte Carlo simulations have been performed for determining the Bayesian D-error for each design, which enables the approximation of this D-error by taking the average of all D-errors for the same design using pseudo-random draws for the prior parameter values. This is clearly a computation intensive process, such that finding Bayesian efficient designs is a very time consuming task. Bliemer *et al.* (2008) have proposed using quasi-random draws (such as Halton or Sobol sequences) or preferably Gaussian quadrature methods instead of pseudo-random draws, which require fewer simulations and therefore enable the evaluation of more designs in the same amount of time.

Manually determining efficient designs is only possible for the smallest hypothetical experiments. Computer software such as SAS and Ngene are able to generate efficient designs. SAS, however, is limited to MNL models and does not include Bayesian efficiency measures, while Ngene is able to determine efficient designs for the ML, NL, and ML models, including Bayesian efficient designs.

6.3 Some more details on choice experiments

In this section we introduce a number of themes related to the ongoing development of improved choice experiments. This is designed to illustrate the challenges that still face the development of behaviorally meaningful SC designs. Firstly, constraints on combinations of attribute levels are imposed in order to rule out infeasible combinations in choice situations, leading to *constrained designs* (Section 6.3.1). Second, the assumptions that all respondents face the same choice situations will be relaxed. Instead, the choice situations presented to the respondents will depend on their actual situation – for example, their current revealed preference. Pivoting attribute levels around these personal values creates more realistic choice situations specific for each respondent. This leads to efficient **pivot designs** (Section 6.3.2). Third, we will discuss the inclusion of covariates (i.e., socio-demographic variables), which are different from the attribute variables in the model. If covariates are not considered when creating a design, then the efficiency in the design will be lost in the data when estimating the model with covariates. By determining a *design with covariates* one can optimize the design for each group of respondents, and maybe even select optimal sample sizes within each of these groups (see Section 6.3.3).

6.3.1 Constrained designs

Sometimes certain combinations of attribute levels in a choice situation are not feasible. These infeasible choice situations need to be avoided by adding constraints. Level constrained designs are most apparent in applications in health economics. For example, consider two alternatives, treating and not treating a patient. Then the attribute "age of death" in these alternatives should be such that in each choice situation this age for the treating alternative is never lower than the non-treating alternative, and the attribute "current age" cannot be higher than the "age of death." In transportation, one could think of route alternatives with different departure times, free-flow travel times, and arrival times. Clearly, the arrival times should be later than the departure times, and the different between the arrival and departure time should be greater than or equal to the free-flow travel time.

There are different ways of including above mentioned constraints. A straightforward way, implemented in Ngene, is using an extended version of the modified Federov algorithm (discussed in Section 6.2.6) by adding an extra step. After having determined the candidature set, choice situations that do not satisfy the constraints are removed from this set. This ensures that all designs generated from this candidature set will be feasible.

Note that it may be hard or even impossible to find an attribute level balanced design satisfying the constraints, especially when the constraints impose many restrictions. Also note that in theory RSC algorithms can also be used (see Section 6.2.6), but that after each relabeling, swapping, or cycling all choice situations need to be checked for feasibility. Ensuring that all choice situations are feasible could be difficult, hence RSC algorithms may not be suitable.

6.3.2 Pivot designs

From a cognitive and contextual point of view, the assumption that all respondents face the same choice situation may not be optimal. The use of a respondent's *knowledge base* to derive the attribute levels of the experiment has come about in recognition of a number of supporting theories in behavioral and cognitive psychology and economics, such as **prospect theory**, case-based decisions theory, and minimum-regret theory. This leads to the notion of so-called *reference alternatives*, which may be different for each respondent. As Starmer (2000, 353) remarks: "While some economists might be tempted to think that questions about how reference points are determined sound more like psychological than economic issues, recent research is showing that understanding the role of reference points may be an important step in explaining real economic behavior in the field." Reference alternatives in SC experiments act to frame the decision context of the choice task within some existing memory schema of the individual respondents and hence make preference-revelation more meaningful at the level of the individual.

In a pivot design the attribute levels shown to the respondents are pivoted from the reference alternatives of each respondent. In Table 6.25 an example is shown, where for compactness only the first alternative is presented. The actual underlying design is shown in grey, where the attributes are either a relative pivot (as in the travel time), or an absolute pivot (as in the toll cost). The attribute levels shown in the SC experiment are based on the reference alternative of the respondents. For example, suppose that respondent 1 has answered in an earlier question in the survey that he or she currently has a travel time of 10 minutes and pays a toll of $2, then the attribute levels for the first alternative in the first choice situation will be determined as 10 − 1 = 9 minutes (10 percent less travel time), and a toll cost of 2 + 2 = $4 ($2 extra). Therefore, this choice situation will be different from the choice situation presented to respondent 2 (facing a travel time of 27 minutes and a toll of $5 for the first alternative in the first choice situation).

Table 6.25 Designs pivoted from a reference alternative

	Design		Respondent 1 (travel time = 10, toll = 2)		Respondent 2 (travel time = 30, toll = 3)	
	Travel time (min.)	Toll cost ($)	Travel time (min.)	Toll cost ($)	Travel time (min.)	Toll cost ($)
1.	−10%	+2	9	4	27	5
2.	+10%	+1	11	3	33	4
3.	+30%	+0	12	2	36	3
4.	+10%	+2	11	4	33	5
5.	−10%	+0	9	2	27	3
6.	+30%	+1	12	3	36	4

Hence, instead of creating a design with the actual attribute levels, a pivot design is created with relative or absolute deviations from references. Suppose that a single pivot design is created. The efficiency of this design depends on the references of the respondents, as these determine the actual attribute levels in the choice situations and therefore the AVC matrix. However, the references of the respondents are typically not available in advance. Rose *et al.* (2008) have compared several different approaches for finding efficient pivot designs:

(a) Use the population average as the reference (yields a single design)
(b) Segment the population based on a finite set of different references (yields multiple designs)
(c) Determine an efficient design on the fly (yields a separate design for each respondent)
(d) Use a two-stage process in which the references are captured in the first stage and the design is created in the second stage (yields a single design).

Intuitively, approach (a) should give the lowest efficiency (individual reference alternatives may differ widely from those assumed in generating the design), while approach (d) should yield the highest efficiency (likely to produce truly efficient data). This was also the outcome of the Rose *et al.* study. Approach (a) worked relatively well, and approach (b) only performed marginally better. Approach (c) and (d) performed best. The outcomes were also compared with an orthogonal design, which performed poorly. Pivot designs for approaches (a) and (b) are relatively easy to generate, for approaches (c) and (d) more effort is needed. Approach (c) requires a **Computer-Assisted Personal Interview** **(CAPI)** or an internet survey, and an efficient design is generated while the respondent is answering other questions. Approach (d) is sensitive to drop-outs, as the design will only be optimal if all respondents in the second stage participate again in the survey. An example of the design of a pivot experiment using Ngene is given in Section 6.5.

6.3.3 Designs with covariates

Including covariates (e.g., socio-economic data such as income, gender, car-ownership, etc.) in the model estimation may result in loss of efficiency when the design was determined ignoring these covariates. So far, only attributes have been considered in the model specification, but it is common to include covariates in the estimation process. Analysts should primarily be interested in the efficiency of the SC data collected rather than being concerned about the efficiency of the underlying SC design. Designs should be constructed in a manner that will reflect the final data to be collected, including any possible covariates.

Rose and Bliemer (2006) demonstrate how efficient SC experiments may be constructed to account for covariates, and how minimum quotas may be established in order to retain a fixed level of efficiency. The procedures for doing this are not much different for constructing efficient designs without considering any covariates. Assuming categorical covariates (or continuous covariates coded categorically), it is possible to calculate the AVC matrix for a SC study by constructing a set of segments based on combinations of covariates, and assigning to each segment one or more SC designs. If multiple covariates are to be analyzed, the analyst may wish to construct a full factorial or fractional factorial of the possible combinations formed by the covariates and assign to each the generated design. Next, the analyst may generate segment-specific efficient designs that minimize the AVC matrix for the pooled data. Procedures similar to those discussed in Rose and Bliemer may be used to do this; however, rather than having one design, the analyst now has to deal with multiple "stacked" or pooled designs.

If the covariates are continuous in nature, then the above methods cannot be handled easily. If the above procedure is to be employed, then the number of segments that can be formed may be so large as to not be computationally possible to handle. If this is the case, then the analyst may have to resort to Monte Carlo simulations to simulate the likely data that is expected to be collected. While this will generally take much longer to locate an efficient design than when using the true analytical AVC matrix, given the full factorial of possible covariate combinations that may possibly be formed by combining certain covariates, the use of Monte Carlo simulations may actually require much less time in this instance.

6.4 Best–worst designs

In recent years there has been growing interest within the discrete choice framework on seeking responses to scenarios where stakeholders select both the best option and worst option (or attribute) from a set of alternatives, and this literature recognizes the additional behavioral information in the best and worst response mechanism (e.g., Marley and Louviere 2005; Marley and Pihlens 2012). The best–worst scaling delivers more efficient and richer discrete-choice elicitation than other approaches, and is gaining popularity as a way to narrow down a set of attributes for a traditional choice experiment from a much larger set that are candidate influences on preferences. It is hence an attractive method for the preference assessment of the large number of statements or attributes, which far exceed the number that might be included in a comprehensive and comprehendable SC experiment.

Recent advances in survey design for SC experiments suggest that obtaining a ranking from an iterative set of best–worst choices offers significant advantages in terms of cognitive effort (for example, see Auger *et al.* 2007; Cohen 2009; Flynn *et al.* 2007; Louviere and Islam 2008). In addition to the standard choice response (the most preferred option), best–worst designs include a response mechanism to reveal the respondents' perceived worst alternative. This method can be implemented at the attribute or statement level or at a choice alternative level. As is common practice with best–worst choice data, the observation for the worst choice is assumed to be the negative of the best choice data. Under this assumption, preferences for the least preferred choice are assumed to be the negative inflection of preferences for the most preferred choice (see Marley and Louviere 2005; Marley and Pihlens 2012). Best–worst scaling as a data collection method has been increasingly used in studying consumer preference for goods or services (Collins and Rose 2011; Flynn *et al.* 2007; Louviere and Islam 2008; Marley and Pihlens 2012). Best–worst data are typically analyzed using conditional logit models.

In a recent study (Hensher *et al.* 2014), involving sets of statements (Table 6.26) on the design of bus rapid transport (BRT) and light rail transit (LRT), a Bayesian *D*-efficient design was developed assuming normally distributed priors, with means of zero and standard deviations of one. The design allows for all main effects and was constructed to allow for best–worst choices. In generating the design, it was assumed that the alternative chosen as best was deleted when constructing the pseudo-worst choice task. To generate the design, spherical-radial transformed draws were used (see Gotwalt *et al.* 2009), assuming

Table 6.26 Full list of statements used in construction of a best–worst design

Id	Design statements favoring LRT in a best–worst experiment
1	There are fewer bus stops than light rail (tram) stations so people have to walk further to catch a bus
2	Light rail (tram) systems provide better network coverage than bus systems
3	A new light rail (tram) line can bring more life to the city than a new bus route in a bus lane or dedicated corridor
4	A light rail (tram) service looks faster than a bus service in a bus lane or dedicated corridor
5	Light rail (tram) lines are fixed, so light rail (tram) stops provide more opportunity for new housing than a bus route which can be changed very easily
6	New light rail (tram) stops will improve surrounding properties more than new bus stops or a new bus route in a bus lane or dedicated corridor
7	Light rail (trams) are more environmentally friendly than buses in a bus lane or dedicated corridor
8	More jobs will be created surrounding a light rail (tram) route than a bus route in a bus lane or dedicated corridor
9	A light rail (tram) is more likely than a bus service in a bus lane or dedicated corridor to still be in use in 30 years' time
10	Light rail (tram) services stop nearer to more people than bus services
11	Light rail (tram) services are less polluting than buses
12	Light rail (tram) services are more likely to have level boarding (no steps up or down to get on the vehicle) than buses
13	Light rail (trams) are quieter than buses
14	Light rail (tram) services have been more successful for cities than bus services in a bus lane or dedicated corridor
15	Light rail (trams) are more permanent than buses in a bus lane or dedicated corridor
16	Light rail (trams) provide more opportunities for land redevelopment than buses in a bus lane or dedicated corridor
17	Light rail (trams) provide more focussed development opportunities than buses in a bus lane or dedicated corridor
18	Light rail (trams) are more likely to be funded with private investment than buses in a bus lane or dedicated corridor
19	Light rail (trams) support higher population and employment growth than buses in a bus lane or dedicated corridor
20	Putting down rails and buying light rail (trams) makes a light rail (tram) system cheaper than bus services running in a bus lane or a dedicated corridor
21	Light rail (tram) systems have lower operating costs than bus services provided in a bus lane or dedicated corridor
22	Light rail (tram) systems have lower operating costs per person carried than bus services provided in a bus lane or dedicated corridor
23	Building a new light rail (tram) line will cause less disruption to roads in the area than a new bus route in a bus lane or dedicated corridor
24	Overall, light rail (trams) and light rail (tram) track have lower maintenance costs than buses in a bus lane or dedicated corridor
25	Light rail (tram) stops have greater visibility for passengers than bus stops
26	Light rail (trams) have lower accident rates than buses in a bus lane or dedicated corridor

Table 6.26 (cont.)

Id	Design statements favoring LRT in a best–worst experiment
27	Light rail (trams) provide a more liveable environment than buses in a bus lane or dedicated corridor
28	Light rail (trams) have greater long-term sustainability than buses in a bus lane or dedicated corridor
29	Light rail (trams) provide more comfort for travelers than buses
30	Light rail (tram) systems are quicker to build and put into operation than bus services in a bus lane or dedicated corridor
31	The long-term benefits of a new light rail (tram) line are higher than a new bus route in a bus lane or dedicated corridor
32	House prices will rise faster around new light rail (tram) stops than bus stops associated with a bus lane or dedicated corridor
33	Light rail (trams) provide better value for money to taxpayers than buses in a bus lane or dedicated corridor

three radii and two randomly rotated orthogonal matrices. The final design had 22 choice tasks. An Illustrative preference screen is given in Figure 6.13. The underlying experimental design is given in Appendix 6A. The Nlogit syntax used to estimate a choice model is given in Table 6.27. Each respondent was given four best–worst choice tasks.

To show how the data is set up, we present part of the data set for the first respondent in Table 6.28. The names of each variable in Table 6.27 are column headings in Table 6.28. There are 4 choice sets, each represented by 7 rows. The first 4 rows (*cset*=4) are the unlabeled alternatives for the full choice set, and the last 3 rows (*cset*=3) are the same unlabeled alternatives minus the most preferred alternative in the 4-alternative set. *Altype* is an indicator (1,–1) to identify the two specifications for the best (1) and the worst (–1) preference regime. It is used to construct a sign reversal for the attribute levels under the worst preference form. *Altij* indicates which alternative is associated with each row, noting again that the best alternative has been removed from the worst choice set. The *choice* column indicates which alternative was chosen as the best and as the worst. We have listed the first 10 statements (out of the full set of 66, i.e., 33 BRT preferred and 33 LRT preferred to show the sign reversal in the worst preferred choice set). The full model set up in Nlogit shows the way in which the data are used. There are only 4 alternatives but the relevant set is recognized via *cset* and *altij* for each of the 8 (i.e., 4 and 3 alternative choice sets for each of 4 choice scenarios). Given the dummy variable nature of this specific data, the marginal utility (or parameter estimate) is relative to one of the alternatives, arbitrarily selected as the 33rd statement for both the BRT favoring and LRT favoring statements, where the BRT favoring statement is

Table 6.27 Nlogit syntax for estimating a choice model

nlogit
;lhs=choice,cset,Altij
;choices=A,B,C,D
;smnl;pts=200
;pds=4;halton
;model:
U(A,B,C,D) = <AASC,BASC,CASC,0>+
s1b*stat101+s2b*stat102+s3b*stat103+s4b*stat104+s5b*stat105+s6b*stat106+s7b*stat107+s8b*stat108
    +s9b*stat109+s10b*stat110+s11b*stat111+s12b*stat112+s13b*stat113+s14b*stat114+s15b*stat115
    +s16b*stat116+s17b*stat117+s18b*stat118+s19b*stat119+s20b*stat120+s21b*stat121+s22b*stat122
    +s23b*stat123+s24b*stat124+s25b*stat125+s26b*stat126+s27b*stat127+s28b*stat128+s29b*stat129
    +s30b*stat130+s31b*stat131+s32b*stat132/
s1lr*stat201+s2lr*stat202+s3lr*stat203+s4lr*stat204+s5lr*stat205+s6lr*stat206+s7lr*stat207+s8lr*stat208
    +s9lr*stat209+s10lr*stat210+s11lr*stat211+s12lr*stat212+s13lr*stat213+s14lr*stat214+s15lr*stat215
    +s16lr*stat216+s17lr*stat217+s18lr*stat218+s19lr*stat219+s20lr*stat220+s21lr*stat221+s22lr*stat222
    +s23lr*stat223+s24lr*stat224+s25lr*stat225+s26lr*stat226+s27lr*stat227+s28lr*stat228+s29lr*stat229
    +s30lr*stat230+s31lr*stat231+s32lr*stat232$

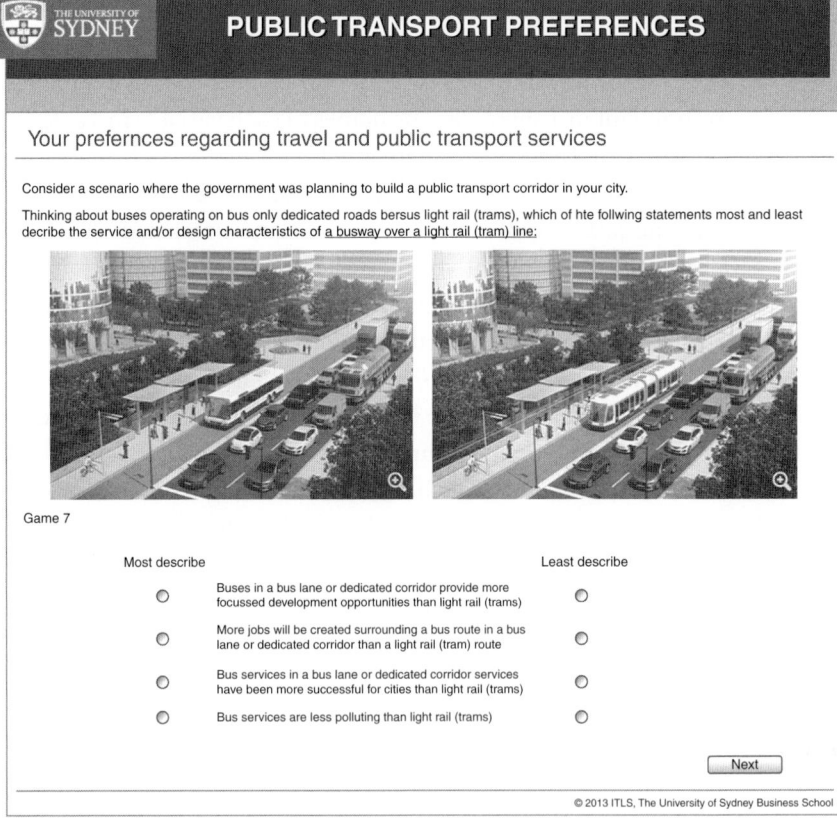

Figure 6.13 Example best–worst scenario for design statements

Table 6.28 The data set up for analysis of best–worst data

RespId	GameNo	BlockId	GameId	BusImg	TramImg	Versus	CSet	AtlType	Altij	Choice	StateId	State01	State02	State03	State04	State05	State06	State07	State08	State09	State10
1	1	15	3	2	2	1	4	1	1	0	27	0	0	0	0	0	0	0	0	0	0
1	1	15	3	2	2	1	4	1	2	0	9	0	0	0	0	0	0	0	0	1	0
1	1	15	3	2	2	1	4	1	3	1	30	0	0	0	0	0	0	0	0	0	0
1	1	15	3	2	2	1	4	-1	4	0	25	0	0	0	0	0	0	0	0	0	0
1	1	15	3	2	2	1	3	-1	1	0	-27	0	0	0	0	0	0	0	0	0	0
1	1	15	3	2	2	1	3	-1	2	0	-9	0	0	0	0	0	0	0	0	-1	0
1	1	15	3	2	2	1	3	-1	4	1	-25	0	0	0	0	0	0	0	0	0	0
1	3	15	1	1	1	2	4	1	1	1	7	0	0	0	0	0	0	1	0	0	0
1	3	15	1	1	1	2	4	1	2	0	20	0	0	0	0	0	0	0	0	0	0
1	3	15	1	1	1	2	4	1	3	0	30	0	0	0	0	0	0	0	0	0	0
1	3	15	1	1	1	2	4	1	4	0	26	0	0	0	0	0	0	0	0	0	0
1	3	15	1	1	1	2	3	-1	2	0	-20	0	0	0	0	0	0	0	0	0	0
1	3	15	1	1	1	2	3	-1	3	0	-30	0	0	0	0	0	0	0	0	0	0
1	3	15	1	1	1	2	3	-1	4	0	-26	0	0	0	0	0	0	0	0	0	0
1	5	15	4	1	2	2	4	1	1	0	30	0	0	0	0	0	0	0	0	0	0
1	5	15	4	1	2	2	4	1	2	0	21	0	0	0	0	0	0	0	0	0	0
1	5	15	4	1	2	2	4	1	3	1	22	0	0	0	0	0	0	0	0	0	0
1	5	15	4	1	2	2	4	1	4	0	10	0	0	0	0	0	0	0	0	0	1
1	5	15	4	1	2	2	3	-1	1	0	-30	0	0	0	0	0	0	0	0	0	0
1	5	15	4	1	2	2	3	-1	2	0	-21	0	0	0	0	0	0	0	0	0	0
1	5	15	4	1	2	2	3	-1	4	1	-10	0	0	0	0	0	0	0	0	0	-1
1	7	15	2	2	1	1	4	1	1	0	20	0	0	0	0	0	0	0	0	0	0
1	7	15	2	2	1	1	4	1	2	0	25	0	0	0	0	0	0	0	0	0	0
1	7	15	2	2	1	1	4	1	3	0	13	0	0	0	0	0	0	0	0	0	0
1	7	15	2	2	1	1	4	1	4	0	6	0	0	0	0	0	1	0	0	0	0
1	7	15	2	2	1	1	3	-1	2	0	-25	0	0	0	0	0	0	0	0	0	0
1	7	15	2	2	1	1	3	-1	3	0	-13	0	0	0	0	0	0	0	0	0	0
1	7	15	2	2	1	1	3	-1	4	1	-6	0	0	0	0	0	-1	0	0	0	0

associated with the s1b to s32b parameters and the LRT favoring statement is associated with the s1lr to s32lr parameters. Given the panel nature of the data, we have used a scaled multinomial logit (SMNL) model (see Chapters 4 and 15) to account for the correlated nature of the 4 choice sets.

The example above is one format for a best–worst experiment. Rose (2014) sets out the range of options in some detail. There are three unique approaches to best–worst survey response mechanisms. In case 1, respondents are asked to choose the most and least preferred object from a set of objects (e.g., Louviere *et al.* 2013). In case 2, the task consists of respondents viewing a set of attributes, each described by a series of attribute levels, and being asked to select the most and least preferred attribute or level out of the set shown (e.g., Beck *et al.* 2013). Case 3 involves the respondents viewing a set of alternatives, each described by a number of attributes and levels, and being asked to select the best and worst alternative from those shown (e.g., Rose and Henser 2014). See Appendix 6B on how Ngene sets up the designs for each of these three cases.

6.5 More on sample size and stated choice designs

Although we have discussed sample size issues in the historical overview, we believe that this topic is of sufficient importance for us to devote a full section to it. In general, little has been known about the sample size requirements for models estimated from SC data. Traditional orthogonal designs and existing sampling theories do not adequately address the issue and hence researchers have had to resort to simple rules of thumb or ignore the issue and collect samples of arbitrary size, hoping that the sample is sufficiently large enough to produce reliable parameter estimates, or are forced to make assumptions about the data that are unlikely to hold in practice. In this section, we demonstrate how a proposed sample size computation by Bliemer and Rose (2005a), and Rose and Bliemer (2005, 2012, 2013) can be used to generate so-called *S*-efficient designs using prior parameter values to estimate panel mixed multinomial logit models. Sample size requirements for such designs in SC studies are investigated. In a numerical case study, it is shown that a *D*-efficient and even more an *S*-efficient design require a (much) smaller sample size than a random orthogonal design in order to estimate all parameters at the level of statistical significance. Furthermore, it is shown that wide level range has a significant positive influence on the efficiency of the design and therefore on the reliability of the parameter estimates.

Identifying methods for reducing the number of respondents required for SC experiments is important for many studies given increases in survey costs. Such reductions, however, must not come at the cost of a lessening in the reliability of the parameter estimates (i.e., in terms of low standard errors) obtained from models of discrete choice. For while SC studies provide a realistic means of capturing decisions made in real markets, reliability in the parameter estimates is attained through the pooling of choices made by different respondents. For example, a typical SC experiment might require the pooling of choices made by 200 respondents, each of whom is observed to make 8 choices, thus producing a total of 1,600 choice observations. Several authors, publishing mainly in the marketing literature, have examined various methods to reduce the number of sampled respondents required to complete choice tasks while maintaining reliability in the results generated (e.g., Bunch *et al.* 1996; Huber and Zwerina 1996; Carlsson and Martinsson 2002).

The usual method of reducing the sample size in SC experiments conducted in health and transport studies appears to be assigning respondents to different choice tasks in a orthogonal fractional factorial experimental design using either a blocking variable (e.g., Hensher and Prioni 2002) or via random assignment (e.g., Garrod *et al.* 2002). Through the use of larger block sizes (i.e., each block has a larger number of choice tasks) or by the use of a greater number of choice tasks being randomly assigned per respondent, analysts may decrease the number of respondents while retaining a fixed number of choice observations collected. It should be noted, however, that while such strategies reduce the number of respondents required for SC experiments, they also reduce the variability observed in other covariates collected over the sample.

Yet despite practical reasons to reduce survey costs, particularly through reductions in the sample sizes employed in SC studies, questions persist as to the minimum number of choice observations required to obtain reliable parameter estimates for discrete choice models estimated from SC data. Although theory exists as to the calculation of sample size requirements for SC data, these traditional theories tend to relate to the precision with which the choice proportions obtained from SC data can be measured. However, these choice proportions in SC experiments may not be the output of most interest. Presently, the traditional sampling theories do not address the issue of minimum sample size requirements in terms of the reliability of the parameter estimates produced, which is far more likely to be of interest to the analyst.

Although the topic of sample size calculations for SC data has already been presented and discussed within the scientific community, this section represents a synthesis of this earlier work, with one major extension. We extend the theory of how to calculate the sample size requirements for SC studies to consider the panel version of a mixed multinomial logit (MMNL) model. In doing so, we highlight several issues related to the topic of interest. We demonstrate how it is possible to determine the likely asymptotic efficiency (i.e., reliability) of the parameter estimates of discrete choice models estimated from SC data at different sample sizes.

6.5.1 *D*-efficient, orthogonal, and *S*-efficient designs

In order to illustrate the theory of efficient designs and discuss issues of sample size, we will consider the following discrete choice problem. This section draws on Rose and Bliemer (2013). Consider a choice experiment involving two alternatives each described by four attributes. For simplicity, we assume that all parameters are generic, although the theory is easily extended to alternative specific parameter estimates. In generating the design, we assume that each respondent will view 12 choice tasks each. We examine the impact of using different numbers of choice tasks. The utility functions for the problem are:

$$V_{js} = \beta_1 x_{sj1} + \beta_2 x_{sj2} + \beta_3 x_{sj3} + \beta_4 x_{sj4}, \; s = 1, \dots, 12. \tag{6.17}$$

Within the SC experiment, the eight attributes (four per each alternative) can take on different levels over the different choice tasks shown to respondents. Let us assume that each attribute can take on one of three levels, more precisely, $L_k = \{1,2,3\}$ for $k = 1,\dots,4$. These values were chosen for demonstration purposes. Following common practice, we constrain ourselves to attribute level balanced designs (although such a constraint may result in the generation of a sub-optimal design).

We will examine three different design types: (a) a *D*-efficient design, (b) an orthogonal design, and (c) an *S*-efficient design. The *D*-efficient design aims to minimize all (co)variances of all parameter estimates, the orthogonal design minimizes the correlations between the attribute values to zero, and the sample size efficient design aims to minimize the sample size needed to obtain statistically significant parameter estimates. In order to generate the *D*- and *S*-efficient designs, it is necessary to assume prior parameter estimates. For the current case study, we have selected for illustrative purposes the following prior parameter estimates in generating the designs:

$$\beta_1 \sim N(0.6, 0.2), \beta_2 \sim N(-0.9, 0.2), \beta_3 = -0.2 \text{ and } \beta_4 = 0.8.$$

As such, we treat the first two parameters as random parameters drawn from a Normal distribution with a certain mean and standard deviation. The last two parameters are treated as fixed parameters. In generating and evaluating each of the designs, we employ Gaussian quadrature with six abscissae associated with each random parameter (see Bliemer *et al.* 2008), which should provide a very accurate approximation of the random parameter distributions and the resulting simulated likelihood, and a simulated sample of 5,000 respondents to obtain the choice vector needed for computing the AVC matrix of the panel MMNL model (see Bliemer and Rose 2010).

The three designs are presented in Table 6.29, where each represents the expected simulated probability that alternative *j* will be chosen in choice task *s*. In line with common practice, the orthogonal design generated was selected at random. Methods of manipulating the attribute levels so as to generate and locate *D*-efficient designs are discussed in detail in Kessels *et al.* (2009) and Quan *et al.* (2011), among other sources. For finding the *D*-efficient designs and *S*-efficient designs presented here, we used several simple randomization and swapping heuristics on the attribute levels using Ngene 1.2 (ChoiceMetrics, 2012).

As expected, the worst performing design in terms of *D*- and *S*-error is the orthogonal design. The orthogonal design is also the only design in which some choice probabilities show some dominant alternatives, namely in choice tasks 3 and 4 the second alternative will be chosen in most cases (94 and 93 percent, respectively). More worrying, the orthogonal design has one choice task with identical alternatives (see choice task 10), and four choice tasks with strict dominating alternatives (choice tasks 1, 3, 4, and 8), in which one alternative is better or equal in all of the attributes. Note that this cannot be observed from the choice probabilities, but has to be identified by inspecting the levels for each attribute in conjunction with the sign of the prior parameter value. In generating the *D*- and *S*-efficient design, we implemented extra checks that ensure that no choice tasks with identical alternatives or strictly dominant alternatives are generated. Strictly dominant alternatives should be avoided at all times and excluded from the data set to avoid biases in parameter estimates.

The *D*-error of the orthogonal design is roughly three times larger than the *D*-error of the *D*-efficient design. This means roughly that on average the standard error of the parameter estimates using the orthogonal design will be $\sqrt{3} \approx 1.73$ times larger than the average standard error of the estimates using the *D*-efficient design (they are in fact on average 1.76 times larger). This in turn means that almost twice as many observations using the orthogonal

Table 6.29 Designs

		D-efficient					Orthogonal					S-efficient				
s	j	x_{sj1}	x_{sj2}	x_{sj3}	x_{sj4}	$E(P_{sj})$	x_{sj1}	x_{sj2}	x_{sj3}	x_{sj4}	$E(P_{sj})$	x_{sj1}	x_{sj2}	x_{sj3}	x_{sj4}	$E(P_{sj})$
1	1	1	1	2	1	0.28	2	1	2	2	0.73	2	1	1	2	0.76
1	2	3	3	2	3	0.72	2	1	3	1	0.27	2	3	2	3	0.24
2	1	2	1	3	2	0.82	3	3	2	3	0.88	2	1	3	1	0.45
2	2	2	3	2	2	0.18	2	3	1	1	0.12	2	3	1	3	0.55
3	1	1	3	2	3	0.21	3	3	3	1	0.06	1	1	3	2	0.45
3	2	3	1	2	1	0.79	3	1	2	2	0.94	3	3	3	3	0.55
4	1	1	1	3	2	0.36	1	2	3	1	0.07	1	3	2	3	0.36
4	2	3	3	1	3	0.64	2	2	1	3	0.93	2	1	3	1	0.64
5	1	2	3	1	3	0.55	3	1	1	1	0.76	3	2	3	1	0.55
5	2	2	1	3	1	0.45	3	3	2	2	0.24	1	2	2	2	0.45
6	1	3	2	3	2	0.68	1	1	3	3	0.75	1	1	2	2	0.59
6	2	1	2	1	2	0.32	3	3	2	2	0.25	3	3	1	2	0.41
7	1	1	2	1	3	0.68	2	3	2	2	0.50	2	3	1	3	0.41
7	2	3	2	3	1	0.32	1	3	3	3	0.50	3	1	3	1	0.59
8	1	3	3	1	2	0.45	2	2	3	2	0.80	2	3	2	3	0.45
8	2	1	1	3	2	0.55	1	2	3	1	0.20	2	1	2	1	0.55
9	1	3	2	1	1	0.50	3	1	2	3	0.72	3	2	2	1	0.55
9	2	1	2	3	3	0.50	1	1	1	3	0.28	1	2	1	2	0.45
10	1	3	2	2	1	0.36	1	2	1	1	0.50	3	3	3	3	0.50
10	2	1	2	1	3	0.64	1	2	1	1	0.50	1	1	2	2	0.50
11	1	2	1	2	1	0.72	1	3	1	3	0.13	1	2	1	2	0.50
11	2	2	3	2	2	0.28	3	1	2	2	0.87	3	2	3	1	0.50
12	1	2	3	3	3	0.36	2	2	1	2	0.40	3	2	1	1	0.40
12	2	2	1	1	1	0.64	2	2	3	3	0.60	1	2	1	3	0.60
D-error	0.326						0.985					0.454				
S-error	57.51						512.43					49.49				

design are required in order to obtain the same values for the standard errors. This demonstrates that information on prior parameter estimates can clearly help significantly in making a more efficient design. In cases where one has no information on the parameter estimates whatsoever, it is common practice to assume that the prior parameter estimates are all equal to zero. As mentioned in Rose and Bliemer (2005), assuming all zero priors (i.e., assuming that no information exists on any of the parameters, not even the sign), an orthogonal design will be the most efficient design.

Therefore, an orthogonal design will be a good design in a worst case scenario (i.e., when no prior information is available to the analyst). Unfortunately, it may be possible to generate a large number of different orthogonal designs for any given choice experiment. As such, the orthogonal design presented in Table 6.29 is but one out of many possible orthogonal designs that could have been generated. It is therefore worth noting that had another orthogonal design been generated, that it may have performed better or worse than the design shown here, given the priors that we have assumed (although, theoretically, an orthogonal design can never outperform a D-optimal design in efficiency, as orthogonality is just another constraint on the design). In our case, the best orthogonal design we were able to locate has a D-error of 0.77, while the worst one has a D-error of 1.10. Regrettably, when no prior information is available, there is no way of telling which orthogonal design will be the best.

Looking at the S-error, we can immediately see the orthogonal design struggles in finding good t-ratios for at least one or more parameters. While the D- and S-efficient designs require around 50 respondents for all t-ratios to be above 1.96, the orthogonal design requires ten times as many. To investigate this further, we will have a closer look at the minimum sample size requirements for each parameter separately, using the equations for computing the t-ratio at any sample size provided in Equation A6.2.7 and A6.2.8.

The asymptotic t-ratios corresponding to the three designs assuming different sample sizes are shown in Figure 6.14. The dashed line indicates a t-ratio of 1.96, and the S-error is indicated. This figure provides an insight into the design and statistical characteristics of the parameter estimates.

In all three designs, it appears difficult to obtain statistically significant parameter estimates for the standard deviation parameters. The asymptotic standard error of the parameter estimates can be positively influenced by making the attribute level range wider, as will be demonstrated in Section 6.5.2. Estimating parameter β_3 also appears relatively difficult, which may be partly explained by the fact that its contribution to the overall utility, accounting also for the relative magnitude of the attribute level for the related attribute relative to the other parameters, is closer to zero. As such, greater statistical power in the form of a larger sample size is required for this parameter. Using the S-efficient design, a sample size of 50 respondents (yielding $50 \times 12 = 600$ choice observations) appears to be sufficient for obtaining significant parameter estimates for all of the attributes, while (by definition) larger sample sizes are necessary when using the other two designs. The orthogonal design performs poorly, requiring a sample size of 513 respondents for all parameters to be statistically significant. Compared to the orthogonal design, the D-efficient design was able to improve on the t-ratios of all parameters, such that both the lowest and highest t-ratios were improved. In contrast, the S-efficient design focuses on the lowest t-ratio and

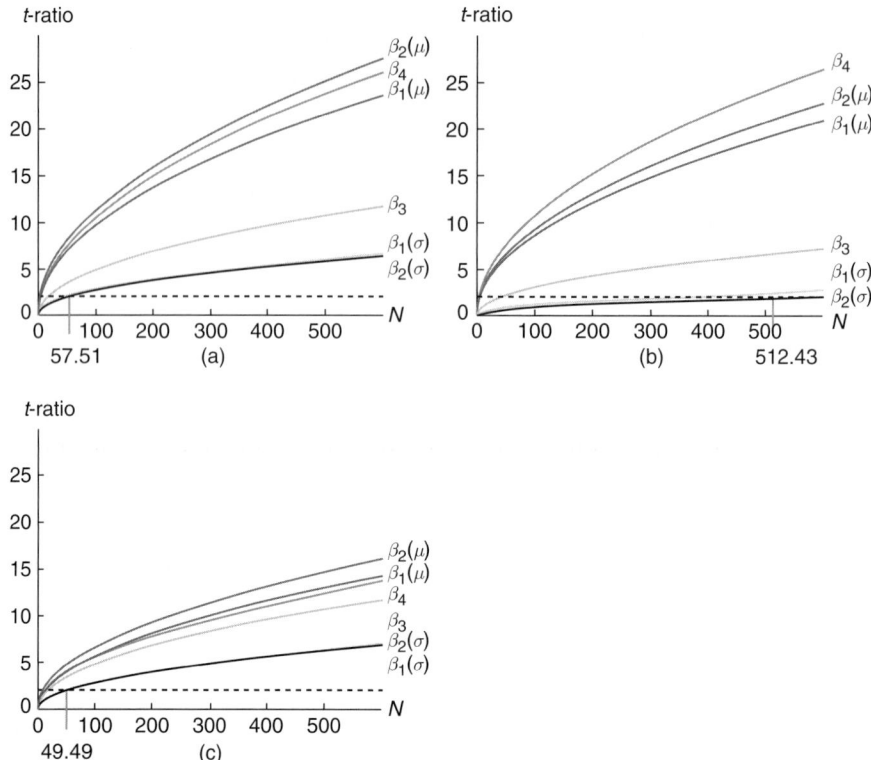

Figure 6.14   Asymptotic *t*-ratios for different sample sizes for the (a) *D*-efficient design, (b) orthogonal design, and (c) *S*-efficient design

improves this at the expense of other parameters. Hence, this results in an improvement in the lower bound, but at the cost of lower *t*-ratios for most other parameters (even compared to the orthogonal design). As a consequence, the difference band between the lowest and highest *t*-ratios for an *S*-efficient design will be much narrower than for other designs.

6.5.2   Effect of number of choice tasks, attribute levels, and attribute level range

In order to analyze the impact of different designs on *D*-efficiency and *S*-efficiency, we analyze the following effects: (i) effect of the number of choice tasks, *S*; (ii) effect of the number of attribute levels; and (iii) the effect of the attribute level range.

Previously, it was assumed that each respondent reviewed twelve choice tasks, which are essentially arbitrarily chosen (although for attribute level balance it should be a multiple of the number of attribute levels). Typically, all choice tasks are shown to each respondent and in order to avoid a too high burden on the respondent, the number of choice tasks is preferably limited. Alternatively, one could give each respondent only a sub-set (block) of the complete design, but it should be noted that such a blocking strategy should be part of the design generation process for a panel MMNL model, as there will only be dependent choice observations within each block, not across blocks. Simultaneous optimization of the design and the blocking scheme is therefore not trivial for the panel MMNL model and is beyond the scope of this chapter.

The minimum number of choice tasks, S, is determined by the number of degrees of freedom, which is essentially the number of parameters to estimate, K. It needs to hold that in our case study, since $K = 6$, the minimum is therefore $S = 6$. A D-efficient design can be found using this minimum number of choice tasks, whereas there does not exist an orthogonal design with this number of choice tasks. As such, in many instances orthogonal designs will be required to be (much) larger than is necessary. Using the same attribute levels as before, we vary the number of choice tasks, from 6 to 27. Finding larger designs with 30 or more choice tasks tends to be problematic, as it is increasingly difficult to find additional choice tasks without any strictly dominant alternative. For each design size, a D- and S-efficient design is constructed. The D-errors and S-errors are shown in Table 6.30. As the D-error and S-error will always decrease with the design size, in order to make a fair comparison we investigate whether the overall efficiency is improved by normalizing for the design size. The D-error is normalized to a single choice task by multiplying the D-error by S. Also, for comparison reasons, the S-error is normalized by multiplying it times S, resulting in the number of observations. If the normalized D-error decreases, it means that the decrease of the D-error is not just because an extra choice task is added, but because it actually increases the overall efficiency. Similarly, if the normalized S-error decreases, it means that we can obtain the same t-ratio of the most difficult to estimate parameter using fewer observations in total.

Clearly, the D-error and S-error will decrease with larger designs; however, once normalized to the number of choice tasks, the increase in efficiency due to a larger design is not that great. Looking at designs optimized for D-error, the drop in the normalized D-error from 18 to 27 choice tasks is small. Very small designs are not very efficient, but there does not seem to be a reason to generate very large designs. A similar conclusion can be drawn for designs that are optimized for S-error, where there is a steep initial decline in the number of observations required when moving from a very small design to a larger design, while this decline becomes smaller for even larger designs. However, the decrease in the normalized S-error is noticeably larger than the decrease in

Table 6.30 Effect of the number of choice tasks on *D*-error and *S*-error

Number of choice tasks	$S = 6$	$S = 9$	$S = 12$	$S = 15$	$S = 18$	$S = 21$	$S = 24$	$S = 27$
			Designs optimized for D-error					
D-error (D)	0.779	0.455	0.326	0.256	0.210	0.179	0.155	0.137
Normalized *D*-error (D.S)	**4.67**	**4.10**	**3.91**	**3.84**	**3.77**	**3.75**	**3.72**	**3.70**
S-error (N)	253.4	91.9	57.5	43.3	32.8	24.3	20.8	17.6
Normalized *S*-error (N.S)	**1520**	**827**	**690**	**650**	**590**	**510**	**498**	**476**
MNL normalized *D*-error	2.47	2.47	2.44	2.47	2.46	2.47	2.48	2.50
			Designs optimized for S-error					
D-error (D)	1.184	0.706	0.454	0.378	0.356	0.263	0.211	0.182
Normalized *D*-error (D.S)	**7.10**	**6.35**	**5.45**	**5.67**	**6.41**	**5.52**	**5.06**	**4.91**
S-error (N)	174.1	89.1	49.5	35.0	28.0	22.7	19.0	15.8
Normalized *S*-error (N.S)	**1045**	**802**	**594**	**524**	**504**	**476**	**456**	**428**
MNL normalized *S*-error	153.3	151.1	150.6	150.7	150.8	150.9	151.0	151.2

the *D*-error. As mentioned before, the standard deviation parameters are the most difficult ones to estimate in our panel MMNL model, and it seems that collecting more data from a single respondent (i.e., using a larger design) contributes to the efficiency of estimating these parameters. This is an interesting result, as it is different from the conclusions that can be drawn for the MNL model. If we would optimize for an MNL model (with parameters $\beta_1 = 0.6$, $\beta_1 = -0.9$, $\beta_3 = -0.2$, and $\beta_4 = 0.8$), we observe from Table 6.30 that there is no need to go beyond 12 choice tasks, as the choice tasks that provide the most information are already in the design, and the normalized *D*-error and *S*-error may even go up. This is consistent with the conclusion in Bliemer and Rose (2011) that, in terms of the normalized *D*- or *S*-error, a relatively small design for an MNL model is just as efficient (and often more efficient) as a large design. For the panel MMNL, it seems that at least the standard deviation parameters benefit from larger designs. Note that this analysis is from a statistical point of view, and it is questionable whether a respondent is actually willing to face 27 choice tasks.

Using 12 choice tasks, we also vary the number of levels for each attribute from two to four levels, and simultaneously make the attribute level range narrower and wider. The attribute levels are shown in Table 6.31. For each combination of number of levels and level range, in total nine combinations, we again find *D*- and *S*-efficient designs.

The lowest *D*-errors and the minimum sample sizes (based on the *S*-error calculation) for all combinations are listed in Table 6.32. There is a consistent

Table 6.31 Different number of attribute levels and level ranges

	Narrow range	Medium range	Wide range
2 levels	(1.5, 2.5)	(1, 3)	(0, 4)
3 levels	(1.5, 2, 2.5)	(1, 2, 3)	(0, 2, 4)
4 levels	(1.5, 1.83, 2.17, 2.5)	(1, 1.67, 2.33, 3)	(0, 1.33, 2.67, 4)

Table 6.32 Effect of number of levels and level range on D-error and sample size

		Optimized for D-error			Optimized for S-error		
		Narrow range	Medium range	Wide range	Narrow range	Medium range	Wide range
2 levels	D-error	**0.933**	**0.278**	**0.106**	1.049	0.347	0.118
	S-error	279.9	47.0	13.5	**211.4**	**38.0**	**11.0**
3 levels	D-error	**1.280**	**0.326**	**0.116**	1.725	0.454	0.139
	S-error	446.9	57.5	14.1	**420.4**	**49.5**	**12.1**
4 levels	D-error	**1.602**	**0.380**	**0.130**	2.049	0.529	0.182
	S-error	647.2	75.6	16.3	**558.7**	**65.7**	**13.8**

pattern that favors two-level designs with a wide level range, in terms both of D-error and of sample size requirements (such designs are sometimes referred to as end-point designs, see Louviere *et al.* 2000). While it appears that the number of levels does make a difference, it is the attribute level range that has a substantial impact upon the overall efficiency of the design (and has been shown by Louviere and Hensher (2001) to have the greatest impact on the WTP estimates). Therefore, it is recommended for linear relationships to choose the attribute level range as wide as realistically makes sense. Table 6.33 lists the D- and S-efficient designs in the case of two levels with wide range. By moving to such an end-point design, the minimum sample size for obtaining statistically significant parameter estimates has decreased from around 50 to 11. For completeness, we also list an orthogonal design in Table 6.33, which performs poorly and is again problematic (it contains identical alternatives in choice tasks 7 and 12, and strictly dominant alternatives in choice tasks 3, 5, and 9). The two efficient designs show similarities, having 7 out of 12 choice tasks in common.

A remark has to be made with respect to the number of levels. Designs with only a few attributes (e.g., two or three) may not always benefit from using two levels and a wide level range. This is due to the fact that the designs are likely to have dominant alternatives (that is, an alternative that will be chosen with a

Table 6.33 End-point designs

		D-efficient					Orthogonal					S-efficient				
s	j	x_{sj1}	x_{sj2}	x_{sj3}	x_{sj4}	$E(P_{sj})$	x_{sj1}	x_{sj2}	x_{sj3}	x_{sj4}	$E(P_{sj})$	x_{sj1}	x_{sj2}	x_{sj3}	x_{sj4}	$E(P_{sj})$
1	1	0	0	4	0	0.58	4	4	0	4	0.91	4	0	4	0	0.84
1	2	4	4	0	0	0.42	0	0	4	0	0.09	0	4	0	4	0.16
2	1	4	4	4	4	0.72	4	0	4	0	0.33	0	0	4	0	0.58
2	2	0	0	0	0	0.28	0	0	4	4	0.67	4	4	0	0	0.42
3	1	0	0	0	4	0.81	0	4	0	4	0.04	4	4	0	4	0.59
3	2	4	0	4	0	0.19	0	0	0	4	0.96	4	0	4	0	0.41
4	1	0	4	0	0	0.19	4	0	4	4	0.92	4	4	0	4	0.42
4	2	4	4	4	0	0.81	4	0	0	0	0.08	0	0	4	4	0.58
5	1	4	4	4	4	0.28	0	0	0	0	0.01	0	4	4	4	0.09
5	2	0	0	4	4	0.72	4	0	4	4	0.99	4	0	4	0	0.91
6	1	4	0	0	0	0.50	0	4	4	0	0.00	0	0	4	4	0.50
6	2	0	0	4	4	0.50	4	0	0	0	1.00	4	0	0	0	0.50
7	1	0	4	0	4	0.59	0	4	4	0	0.50	4	0	0	0	0.91
7	2	0	0	4	0	0.41	0	4	4	0	0.50	0	4	0	4	0.09
8	1	4	0	0	0	0.74	0	0	4	4	0.93	4	4	0	0	0.33
8	2	4	4	4	4	0.26	0	4	0	4	0.07	0	4	0	4	0.67
9	1	0	0	4	4	0.58	4	0	0	0	1.00	0	0	4	0	0.72
9	2	4	4	0	4	0.42	0	4	0	0	0.00	4	4	4	0	0.28
10	1	4	4	4	0	0.19	4	4	0	0	0.04	0	4	0	4	0.41
10	2	0	4	0	4	0.81	4	4	0	4	0.96	0	0	0	0	0.59
11	1	4	0	4	0	0.84	0	0	0	4	0.99	0	0	0	0	0.28
11	2	0	4	0	4	0.16	4	4	4	0	0.01	4	4	4	4	0.72
12	1	0	4	0	4	0.09	4	4	4	4	0.50	4	4	4	4	0.28
12	2	4	0	0	0	0.91	4	4	4	4	0.50	0	0	4	4	0.72
D-error	0.106						0.541					0.118				
S-error	13.5						171.3					11.0				

high probability). Choice tasks with dominant alternatives do not provide much (if any) information and therefore yield high D-errors. Including more attribute levels avoids these dominant alternatives and, therefore, for very small designs using more than two attribute levels seems to be preferred. Furthermore, for small designs not many possible attribute level combinations exist when using only two levels. This means that the number of choice tasks should be small, otherwise choice tasks with strictly dominant alternatives occur. Again, adding more attribute levels solves this problem. In practice, the number of attributes will generally be (much) larger than two or three attributes, such that it does not really cause problems. A negative consequence of using only two levels, however, is that one is restricted to testing linear relationships for that attribute (see Hensher *et al.* 2005) instead of non-linear effects with dummy or effects coding.

6.5.3 Effect of wrong priors on the efficiency of the design

Up to this point, we have assumed that the prior parameter values correspond to the true parameter values held by the population. This represents a strong assumption that is unlikely to hold in practice, but it is necessary for creating efficient designs. Assuming that the true parameter values are different from the priors, given the designs in Table 6.29, we can compute the asymptotic (co)variance matrix based on the "true" parameter values and compare these with the asymptotic (co)variance matrix using the prior parameter values.

Figure 6.15 plots the impact upon **design efficiency** given mis-specification of the prior parameter estimates. Using the S-error as the measure expressing

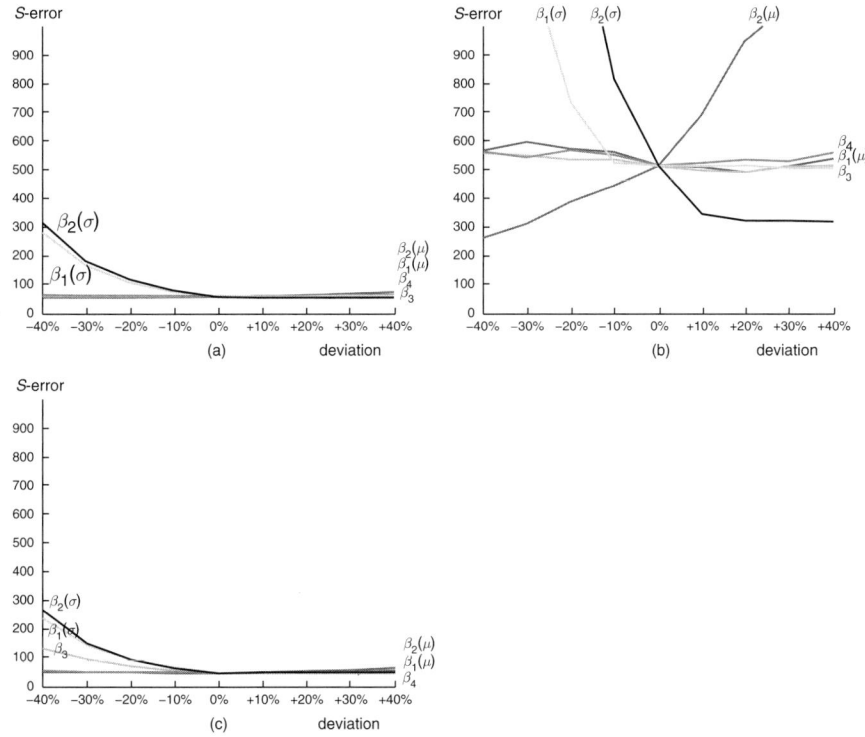

Figure 6.15   Impact of prior misspecification on the sample size for the (a) *D*-efficient design, (b) orthogonal design, and (c) *S*-efficient design

the overall efficiency of the design, we determine the *S*-errors when each true parameter independently deviates between −40 percent and +40 percent of its prior parameter value.

A number of points are worth noting from this exercise. Firstly, the *D*-efficient and *S*-efficient designs are much more robust against prior mis-specification than the orthogonal design, with lower losses of efficiency due to parameter mis-specification. Second, especially mis-specifying the standard deviation priors seems to result in large efficiency losses (although in the orthogonal design also mis-specification of one of the mean priors can lead to significantly larger required sample sizes). It is interesting to note that the smaller the magnitude of the standard deviation parameters relative to what was assumed in the design generation process, the greater the loss of efficiency experienced for all types of designs.

Robustness of a design can be improved by assuming Bayesian priors (i.e., probability distributions) instead of local (fixed) priors, as argued in Sándor and Wedel (2001), and for which efficient algorithms for the MNL model have been proposed in Kessels *et al.* (2009). However, generating Bayesian efficient designs for the panel MMNL model is computationally extremely challenging and at this moment not feasible except for the smallest of designs.

6.6 Ngene syntax for a number of designs

In this section we provide three examples of the generation of SC experimental designs in Ngene. The examples introduce the reader to the syntax, which is similar to Nlogit, and demonstrate a sub-set of the overall feature set. The Ngene manual (ChoiceMetrics, 2012) is freely downloadable from www.choice-metrics.com.

6.6.1 Design 1: standard choice set up

Consider the following syntax:

```
Design
;alts=A,B,C
;rows=18
;block=2
;eff=(rppanel, d)
;rdraws=halton(250)
;rep=250
;cond:
```

```
if(A.att1=2, B.att1=[4,6]),
if(A.att2<3, B.att2=[3,5])
;model:
U(A) = A0[-0.1] +
       G1[n,-0.4,0.1]   * att1[2,4,6] +
       G2[u,-0.4,-0.2]  * att2[1,3,5] +
       A1[0.7]          * att3[2.5,3,3.5] +
       A2[0.6]          * att4[4,6,8] /
U(B) = B0[-0.2] +
       G1               * att1 +
       G2               * att2 +
       B1[-0.4]         * att7[2.5,4,5.5] +
       B2[0.7]          * att8[4,6,8]
$
```

The syntax begins with Design, and is terminated by a $. In between are a series of commands, referred to as properties in Ngene. Several properties are compulsory when generating efficient designs, including ;alts, ;rows, and ;eff. The names of the choice alternatives are specified with ;alts. The number of choice tasks in the experimental design is specified with ;rows. The choice tasks can be blocked, so that each respondent is assigned to a sub-set of the tasks. In this example, ;block=2 generates two blocks, of nine choice tasks each. The efficiency measure on which to optimize the design is controlled by the ;eff property where, in this example, the design is optimized on the D-error, assuming that a panel specification of the mixed logit model is to be estimated. If random parameters are employed, the type and number of draws can be controlled by ;rdraws. Here we use 250 Halton draws. Generating designs using the panel specification of the mixed logit model requires the iteration over a number of simulated respondents, where this number can be specified with ;rep. The higher this number, the more accurate the computations, but the longer the computation time.

In some choice settings, certain combinations of attribute levels should not be shown together within a choice task. This may be due to logical constraints, or to increase the behavioral plausibility of the choice tasks. This is particularly common within the health economics literature, in studies that consider mortality and health outcomes (e.g., Viney *et al.* 2005). Ngene allows constraints to be imposed on the attribute levels generated. Two constraints are specified in the example with ;cond. If the attribute att1 in alternative A assumes the level 2, this same attribute in alternative B is constrained so that it could only assume the levels of 4 and 6. Put another way, the level 2 cannot appear for attribute att1 in both alternatives A and B. The second constraint demonstrates an inequality constraint. A careful reading of this constraint reveals that a similar function to the first constraint is achieved in this particular instance.

Ngene specifies the utility functions through the ;model property, using a structure which is similar but not identical to Nlogit. In the example, the utility structure is specified for the first two alternatives, but not alternative C, which can be treated as a "no-choice" or "opt-out" alternative.

Where the utility structure is specified, the utility of each alternative is the sum of one or more utility components, or "part-worths." Each part-worth will contain, at a minimum, the name of a parameter. The value inside the square bracket represents a parameter prior, which is the analyst's expectation of what the parameter might be post-model estimation. If the parameter is specified only, the part-worth is an alternative-specific constant (A0 and B0 in this example). Alternatively, the parameter may be multiplicatively associated with an attribute of the choice alternative. However, unlike in model estimation, where the attribute will be a variable in the data set used for estimation, we specify for each attribute a set of levels that may be used to generate the experimental design. In the example, att1 is an attribute that may assume levels 2, 4, and 6. The same attribute can be specified across multiple alternatives, and it is not necessary to specify the levels more than once.

The parameters may be specified as generic or alternative-specific. Any parameter that enters more than one alternative may be considered generic. As with the attributes, it is not necessary to specify the parameter priors more than once. It is sufficient to do so where the parameter is first introduced. In the example, parameters G1 and G2 are generic, while A1, A2, B1, and B2 are alternative-specific, as of course are the alternative-specific constants A0 and B0. Unlike in Nlogit, random parameters are specified directly in the utility functions. Where random parameters are introduced, it is necessary to specify prior values for each moment of the distribution. In the example, parameter G1 is normally distributed, with mean −0.4 and standard deviation 0.1. G2 is uniformly distributed, with lower bound −0.4 and upper bound −0.2.

The above syntax was run in Ngene. Many candidate designs were generated, and after three hours, the best design was:

Choice situation	a.att1	a.att2	a.att3	a.att4	b.att1	b.att2	b.att7	b.att8	Block
1	6	5	3	4	2	1	4	4	1
2	6	3	2.5	6	4	3	4	4	2
3	2	3	3.5	6	4	3	4	6	2
4	6	1	3	4	2	5	2.5	6	1
5	6	5	2.5	6	6	3	4	4	2
6	2	5	2.5	4	6	3	2.5	8	1
7	6	5	3	8	2	5	4	8	2
8	4	3	3.5	8	6	5	4	6	1
9	4	5	2.5	6	4	1	2.5	6	2
10	4	3	3.5	8	6	1	5.5	4	1
11	4	5	2.5	6	4	5	2.5	4	1
12	4	1	2.5	4	2	3	5.5	8	1
13	2	1	3	8	6	3	5.5	4	2
14	2	3	3.5	8	4	5	5.5	6	1
15	6	3	3	8	4	1	5.5	8	1
16	6	5	3.5	4	6	1	5.5	8	2
17	2	1	3	6	4	3	2.5	6	2
18	4	1	3.5	4	2	5	2.5	8	2

This design has a *d*-error of 0.329256. While for the same design specification this measure can be compared across designs, it is not in itself particularly informative. That said, a value greater than 1 is generally indicative of a poor experimental design. Another red flag is if the choice probabilities for specific alternatives are very high or very low, where Ngene allows these probabilities to be interrogated.

6.6.2 Design 2: pivot design set up

Now consider a second example, which generates a pivot design. Such designs can accommodate reference alternatives, where the reference alternative is commonly based on a recent experience. The attribute levels of some or all of the attributes of the non-reference alternative pivot around the reference alternative, and when the experiment is being designed, these attribute levels are typically conceptualized in terms of percentage or absolute shifts from the reference alternative level. Crucially, since different respondents are likely to have different reference alternatives, different respondents are likely to experience different experimental designs in terms of the levels they face. Since the efficiency of the design is a function of the actual attribute levels, there are implications in terms of the efficiency of the design, and whether to generate a single underlying design (in terms of shifts from the reference alternative), or multiple designs for different segments. This issue is investigated in Rose *et al.* (2008). One approach to generating a pivot design is demonstrated in the example below:

```
Design
;alts(small)  = alt1, alt2, alt3
;alts(medium) = alt1, alt2, alt3
;alts(large)  = alt1, alt2, alt3
;rows = 12
;eff = fish(mnl,d)
;fisher(fish) = des1(small[0.33]) + des2(medium[0.33]) + des3(large[0.34])
;model(small):
U(alt1) = b1[0.6] * A.ref[2]      + b2[-0.2] * B.ref[5]           /
U(alt2) = b1      * A.piv[-1,0,1] + b2[-0.2] * B.piv[-25%,0%,25%] /
U(alt3) = b1      * A.piv[-1,0,1] + b2[-0.2] * B.piv[-25%,0%,25%]
;model(medium):
U(alt1) = b1[0.6] * A.ref[4]      + b2[-0.2] * B.ref[10]          /
U(alt2) = b1      * A.piv[-1,0,1] + b2[-0.2] * B.piv[-25%,0%,25%] /
U(alt3) = b1      * A.piv[-1,0,1] + b2[-0.2] * B.piv[-25%,0%,25%]
;model(large):
U(alt1) = b1[0.6] * A.ref[6]      + b2[-0.2] * B.ref[15]          /
U(alt2) = b1      * A.piv[-1,0,1] + b2[-0.2] * B.piv[-25%,0%,25%] /
U(alt3) = b1      * A.piv[-1,0,1] + b2[-0.2] * B.piv[-25%,0%,25%]
$
```

Here, three different reference alternative segments are considered, by specifying three different sets of utility functions, each labeled within the ;model property, as small, medium, and large. In the "small" reference alternative, attribute A takes on a level of 2, and B a level of 5. Note how the same attribute can be considered either a reference level, by suffixing the attribute name with .ref, or a pivot level, by suffixing with .piv. For attribute A, the pivoting is expressed in absolute terms, with shifts of −1, 0, and 1, while for attribute B the pivoting is in percentage terms, with shifts of −25%, 0%, and +25%.

The ;fisher property serves two purposes. Firstly, it allows weights to be assigned to each of the reference alternative segments. Here the weights are roughly equal, but if one segment was anticipated to be more common, its weight could be increased accordingly. Second, the ;fisher property dictates how many distinct designs should be generated. Since each segment is associated with a unique identifier, des1, des2, and des3, three designs are generated, one for each segment. This is referred to as a heterogenous design. Note that this approach is different from generating three separate designs independently, as here only a single Fisher Information matrix is calculated, as a weighting of the various segments, and from this combined matrix the overall efficiency is calculated (note how the ;fisher property is linked to the ;eff property by the label "fish" in this example). This is consistent with estimating a single model from all respondents, irrespective of what reference alternative they experience.

Alternatively, a homogenous design could be generated. This results in a single design only, albeit one with an efficiency measure informed by the three reference alternative segments. A homogenous design could be specified by using:

```
;fisher(fish) = des1(small[0.33], medium[0.33], large[0.34])
```

Below is the first of three sub-designs from a candidate heterogenous pivot design generated in Ngene. Note how the pivot levels are represented as either absolute or percentage shifts.

```
Design – des1
```

Choice situation	alt1.a	alt1.b	alt2.a (pivot)	alt2.b (pivot)	alt3.a (pivot)	alt3.b (pivot)
1	2	5	1	0%	−1	0%
2	2	5	0	25%	0	−25%
3	2	5	1	−25%	−1	25%
4	2	5	0	−25%	0	25%
5	2	5	0	25%	0	0%
6	2	5	1	−25%	−1	0%
7	2	5	−1	0%	1	−25%
8	2	5	−1	0%	1	0%
9	2	5	−1	−25%	1	25%
10	2	5	0	0%	0	25%
11	2	5	−1	25%	1	−25%
12	2	5	1	25%	−1	−25%

6.6.3 Design 3: *D*-efficient choice design

This third example of an SC survey aims to understand how the government should spend money on building infrastructure and gain voters' support and what service attributes of public transport infrastructure, be it a Bus Rapid Transit (BRT) system or a Light Rail Transit (LTR) system, are important to voters. The service attributes are classified into four groups shown in

Table 6.34 Pre-defined attributes and attribute levels for survey design

Attributes	Name	Attribute level	# levels
Description of investment			
Construction cost	cost	0.5, 1, 3, 6 b$	4
Construction time	time	1,2,5,10	4
% metropolitan population serviced	pop	5,10,15,20	4
% route dedicated to this system only and no other means of transport	roway	25,50,75,100	4
Operating and maintenance cost per year (million)	opcost	2,5,10,15 m$	4
Service levels:			
Service capacity in one direction (passengers/hour)	capa	5k, 15k, 30k	4
Peak frequency of service, every . . .	pfreq	5,10,15 mins	3
Off-peak frequency of service, every . . .	ofreq	5,10,15,20 mins	4
Travel time (door-to-door) compared to car	tcar	−10, 10, 15, 25 %	4
Fare per trip compared to car-related costs (fuel, tolls, parking)	fare	±20, ±10%	4
Features of the system:			
Off-vehicle prepaid ticket required	prepaid	Yes, No	2
Integrated fare	ticket	Yes, No	2
Waiting time incurred when transferring	wait	1, 5,10,15 mins	4
On-board staff for passenger safety and security	staff	present, absent	2
Ease of boarding public transport vehicle	board	level boarding, steps	2
General characteristics of investment:			
Operation is assured for a minimum of	yearop	10,20,30,40,50,60 years	6
Risk of it being closed down after the assured minimum period	close	0,25,50,100%	4
Attracting business around stations/stops	buss	low, medium, high	3
% car trips switching to this option within first 3 years of opening	shiftcar	0,5,10,20 %	4
Overall environmental friendliness compared to car	env	±25,−10,±5, 0 %	6
The two systems described above are actually	brt	BRT, LRT	2

Table 6.34, alongside the attribute levels and attribute names. The survey is designed with the same route length for BRT and LRT systems, which are referred to as System A (*sysA*) and System B (*sysB*) in the choice experiment. Thus, the survey is designed as unlabeled with an exception being that the differences between BRT and LRT systems are treated as an attribute in the experiment, as voters may have different images about bus-based and rail-based systems.

An example Ngene syntax for generating an efficient design is as follows:

```
Design
;alts = sysA, sysB
;rows = 24
;block =12
;eff = (mnl,d)
;cond:
if(sysA.pfreq =[10],sysA.ofreq =[10,15,20]),
if(sysA.pfreq =[15],sysA.ofreq =[15,20]),
if(sysA.pfreq =[20],sysA.ofreq =[20]),
if(sysB.pfreq =[10],sysB.ofreq =[10,15,20]),
if(sysB.pfreq =[15],sysB.ofreq =[15,20]),
if(sysB.pfreq =[20],sysB.ofreq =[20])
;model:
U(sysA) = cost[0]*cost[0.5,1,3,6] + time*time[1,2,5,10] + pop*pop[5,10,15,20]
+ roway*roway[25,50,75,100] + opcost*opcost[2,5,10,15] + capa*capa[5,15,30] +
pfreq*pfreq[5,10,15] + ofreq*ofreq[5,10,15,20] +  tcar*tcar[-10,10,15,25]  +
fare*fare[-20,-10,10,20]       +        prepaid.dummy*prepaid[0,1]          +
ticket.dummy*tick[0,1] +  wait*wait[1,5,10,15]  +  staff.dummy*staff[0,1]   +
board.dummy*board[0,1]      +        yearop*yearop[10,20,30,40,50,60]       +
close*close[0,25,50,100]      +       buss.dummy[0|0]*buss[0,1,2]           +
shiftcar*shiftcar[0,5,10,20]    +   env*env[-25,-10, -5, 0,5,25]            +
BRT.dummy[0]*BRT[0,1]/
U(sysB) = cost*cost   + time*time + pop*pop + roway*roway  + opcost*opcost  +
capa*capa   +    pfreq*pfreq    +  ofreq*ofreq + tcar*tcar   + fare*fare    +
prepaid.dummy*prepaid + ticket.dummy*tick  +  wait*wait + staff.dummy*staff +
board.dummy*board + yearop*yearop + close*close + buss.dummy*buss +
shiftcar*shiftcar + env*env + BRT.dummy*BRT$
```

Each respondent is asked to answer 2 choice tasks. Given the number of levels for each attribute and the desire to maintain attribute level balance, the survey is designed with 24 rows (i.e., choice tasks) and blocked into 12 blocks so that each respondent will be assigned a block with 2 choice tasks (24 tasks/12 blocks = 2 tasks per block). This design use a D-error measure for finding an efficient design for estimating MNL models, which is specified in the syntax with the ;eff = (mnl,d) command. In addition, a set of conditions is employed to require the peak-hour level of service to be no worse than the off-peak level of service. This is executed in Ngene by a ;cond: command, which in this example limits the off-peak level of service to a set of attribute levels. The first condition states that if the level of peak-hour frequency of System A is 10 (minutes), then the allowed levels of off-peak frequency of System A are 10, 15, and 20 (minutes). When the level of peak frequency is 5 minutes, the off-peak frequency can be any of the pre-defined levels, and thus no condition is required.

This survey is designed for estimating MNL models using a ;model: command to define the utility functions of the alternatives (System A and

System B), set up like Nlogit. When generating an efficient design, each parameter must have a prior value, which can be fixed (e.g., MNL model) or random (e.g., mixed logit model). Prior parameters are specified within square brackets, immediately following the parameter names. For example, the syntax above uses zeros as the prior parameters of all service attributes but only construction cost is explicitly specified with a prior of zero (*cost[0]*), while prior parameters associated with other attributes are left empty to receive the Ngene default value of zero. When priors are not available, as in the case of this study, zero priors may be used to create a pilot survey and distribute to a small proportion of the sample. This pilot survey provides data for model estimation to obtain priors for generating an efficient design for a main survey.

The above syntax also shows how Ngene handles designs with non-linear relationships through the model utility functions with dummy coded attributes. To specify dummy variables, the parameter names need to be followed by the syntax .dummy, such as *prepaid.dummy* in the above example. Prior parameters of dummy variables are required for *l–1* levels and must be specified within square brackets, separated by a | symbol. An example syntax is *buss.dummy[0|0]*buss[0,1,2]*, where the first two levels of attracting business around stations/stops have been assigned a prior value of 0. Effect coded variables are handled in a similar way with .effect being used after parameter name in place of the .dummy syntax.

The pre-defined levels of each attribute are specified within square brackets, following attribute names and being separated by a comma (,). The attribute levels and prior parameters should only be defined the first time the attributes appear in the utility function. For example, in the above syntax all attribute levels and prior parameters are defined in the utility function of System A and are not defined again in the utility function of System B.

A screenshot below shows a design generated by Ngene using the above syntax. The output includes information on the efficiency measures related to the design, which in this case are *D*-error, *A*-error, percentage of utility balance (*B* estimate) and minimum sample size (*S* estimate) for estimating significant parameters, assuming the priors are correct. As zero priors are used, utilities of System A and System B are both zero, which produces a design with 100 percent utility balancing and a minimum sample size of zero (i.e., no need to do the survey if all parameters are not statistically different from zero).

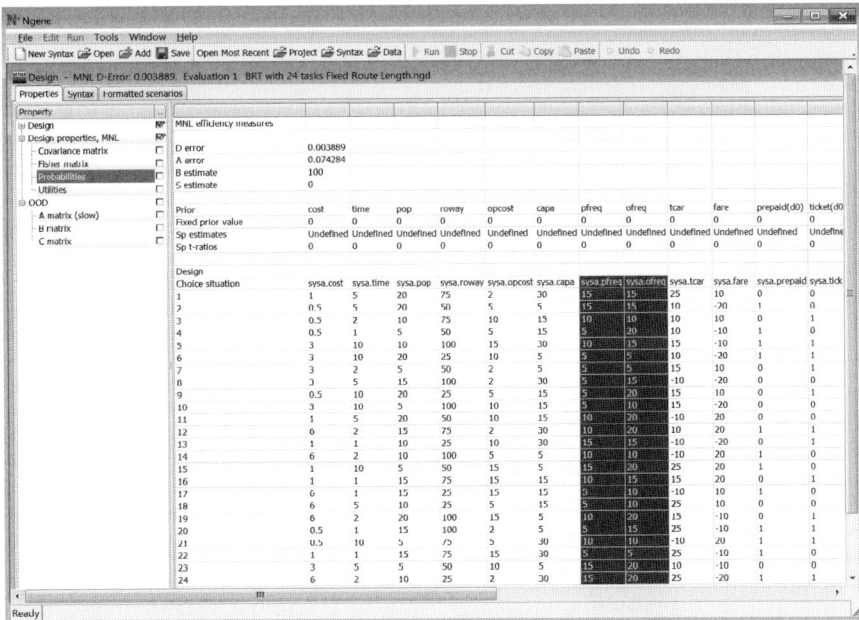

Underneath the efficiency measures is information related to each parameter included in the model, except for constants which by default are excluded by Ngene from optimizing the design based on the user's specified efficiency measure. The *Sp t-ratios* represent the expected *t*-ratio for each of the parameters if one respondent were given the survey, while *Sp estimates* indicate the number of respondents needed to obtain a significant estimate of each parameter. At the 5 percent level of significance, the *Sp estimate* for each parameter is calculated as the square of (1.96/*Sp t ratio*). The minimum sample size (*S estimate*) is the maximum value of all *Sp estimates*.

The survey itself is presented as a matrix of attribute levels, where each row corresponds to one choice task. The survey is designed with a command ;rows = 24 and thus the survey includes 24 rows or choice situations. Each column represents one attribute associated with each alternative and the cells represent attribute levels. Highlighted in the screenshot above are the attribute levels of peak frequency and off-peak frequency of System A. This design has met the conditions of peak service levels, being at least as frequent as off-peak service levels (specified with the ;cond: command). We leave it to the reader to explore what happens to attribute level balance when conditions are included in the survey.

A screenshot of an example choice task faced by respondents is provided below.

 **Delivering better public transport for our cities**

Route Mode Games (2 of 2)

We now want you look at various scenarios that describe differnt ways in which taxpayers money might be spent on building new infrastructure.

The Table below summarises a scenario of two public transport systems (called and) with the same Rute Length.

We ask you to review these systems and then choose an answer for each of the following questions.

Attributes	System A	System B
Route lenght in each direction	30 km	
Description of investement:		
Construction cost	$6000m	$500m
Construction time	10 years	1 years
% metropolitan population serviced	20 %	5 %
% route dedicated to this system only and no other means of transport	75 %	50 %
Operating and maintenance cost per year (millions)	$10m	$5m
Service Levels:		
Service capacity in one direction (passengers/hour)	15,000	15,000
Peak frequency of service, every...	5 mins	5 mins
Off-peak frequency of service, every...	5 mins	20 mins
Travel time (door-to-door) compared to car	15% quicker	10% quicker
Fare per trip compared to car-related costs (fuel, tolls, parking)	15% higher	10% lower
Features of the system:		
Off-vehicle prepaid ticket required	Yes	No
Integrated fare	No	Yes
Waiting time incurred when transferring	1 mins	15 mins
On-board staff for passenger safety and security	absent	present
Ease of boarding public transport vehicle	level boarding	steps
General characteristics of investment:		
Operation is assured for a minimum of	60 years	10 years
Risk of it being closed down after the assured minimum period	100%	0%
Attracting business around stations/stops	High	Medium
% car trips switching to this option within first 3 years of opening	10%	5%
Overall environmental friendliness compard to car	10% worse	5% better

	BRT	LRT
The two systems described above are actually		
Given this additional information		
Which investment would benefit your metropolitan area better?	◎	◎
Which investment would you prefer personally?	◎	◎
Which investment is better value for tax payers money?	◎	◎
If you were voting now, which one would you vote for?	◎	◎
Which investment would improve the liveability of the metroplitan area more?	◎	◎

Next

© 2014 ITLS, The University of Sydney Business School

6.7 Conclusions

One important point that we hope that the reader does take away from this chapter is the inappropriate use of a number of statistical measures which have come to be prevalent within the literature. In particular, we deliberately point out two such measures, one which is designed specifically to optimize designs for linear models and the second which is used to optimize designs assuming an MNL model specification with generic local priors equal to zero under orthonormal codes (i.e., the specific case examined by Street and Burgess 2004). While use of these measures are perfectly valid if one wishes to optimize a design under these express assumptions, applying these measures to determine how optimal a design is generated under other assumptions (including different model specification, prior parameter assumptions, and coding structures) is both incorrect and misleading (we are not implying that those who devised these measures have applied the measures incorrectly; however, we can attest to the fact that a number of reviewers have over time applied them inappropriately to infer that designs are not optimal, even when generated under different sets of assumptions). In this chapter, it has been argued that the use of orthogonal designs for non-linear models, such as the logit model, will be inefficient under most, but not all, assumptions made during the design generation phase (e.g., the specific case examined by Street and Burgess has shown that orthogonal designs are optimal under some assumptions). Nevertheless, orthogonal designs remain to this day the most widely used design type. Such prevalence is the result of the fact that orthogonal designs appear to (and actually do) work well in most cases, and it is important to understand why this is the case.

Designs of all types, whether orthogonal or non-orthogonal, are generated under assumptions about the true population parameter estimates (i.e., the priors that are assumed). These assumptions are either explicitly acknowledged by those generating the design or implicitly made without their knowledge. Perhaps unknown to many, an orthogonal design will be the optimal design under the assumption of locally optimal parameter estimates set at zero (see Bliemer and Rose 2005a). As per Figure 6.3, if the true population parameters differ from those that are assumed in the design generation phase, then the design will generally lose statistical efficiency. The impact of such a loss of efficiency can be seen in Figure 6.16. Figure 6.16 shows the relationship between the standard errors

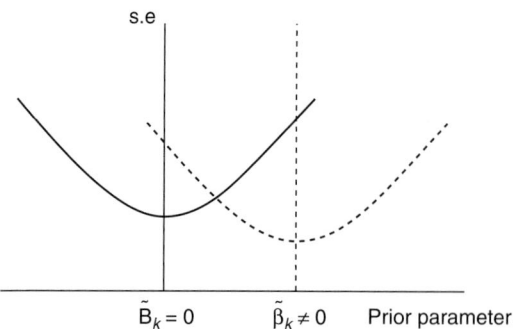

Figure 6.16 Implications of prior parameter misspecification and loss of efficiency

and the parameter priors assumed for two different locally optimal designs generated under zero prior parameters and non-zero prior parameters. As shown in the figure, if the prior parameter is incorrectly specified, this will typically result in an increased standard error at the true parameter value, *all else being equal.* Note that this does not mean that the true parameter cannot be estimated by the design, but simply that a larger sample size would be required to detect the statistical significance of the parameter estimate than otherwise would have been the case had the prior parameter assumed been correct. It is for this precise reason that orthogonal designs have appeared to work well in the past and will likely continue to work well into the future. That is, the sample sizes used in practice have in most cases reported in the literature been such that they have sufficiently outweighed any loss of efficiency in the design as the true parameters diverge from those assumed in generating the design. The point of those advocating non-orthogonal designs generated under non-zero prior parameter estimates, however, is that in undertaking SC experiments, one would assume that the attributes chosen will have some influence in the choices made by the respondents, and hence the true population parameters will be non-zero. In such cases, the argument is that these designs will outperform orthogonal designs given similar sample sizes, or produce the same results as an orthogonal design but with smaller sample sizes.

It is important to note that the above discussion is predicated on the assumption of *all else being equal.* That is, it assumes that there exists no link between the population parameter estimates and the design itself. Several articles have convincingly argued that the design may result in unintended biases of the parameter estimates (e.g., Louviere and Lancsar

2009). In theory however, this should not be the case. McFadden (1974) showed that asymptotically the parameter estimates should converge to the population parameters, independent of the data matrix (i.e., design in this instance). Using Monte Carlo simulations, McFadden further showed that this was the case in quite small finite samples, with as few as 50 choice observations. Numerous studies using simulation have led to the same conclusions (e.g., see Ferrini and Scarpa 2007). However, the arguments put forward by Louviere and Lancsar (2009) remain compelling. They posit that if the design attributes correlate with unobserved omitted covariates or latent contrasts such as personality profiles or other such characteristics, then the resulting parameters obtained from different designs will indeed be influenced by the specific design used. Such biases will not exist in simulated data unless they are assumed in the data generation process, which makes empirical studies far more important in determining if these biases are real or not. This thus represents an important area of research that is urgently required, as the existence of any such biases may require a different line of enquiry in terms of generating designs than has occurred in the past, as outlined in this chapter.

Similarly, the impact of designs upon scale also represents an important research area. Louviere *et al.* (2008) and Bliemer and Rose (2011) found scale differences across various designs relating to how easy or hard the resulting questions are as generated from the design. Both Louviere *et al.* and Bliemer and Rose found, for example, that orthogonal designs tended to lead to lower error variances than efficient designs, possibly as a result of the presence of dominated alternatives. Given that efficient designs are less likely to have dominated alternatives than orthogonal designs, the questions arising from the use of orthogonal designs will be easy to answer, resulting in lower error variance. As such, there exists the very real possibility that any move away from orthogonal designs to other designs represents a trade-off between capturing more information per question versus lowering error variance. Once more, further research is required to address this specific issue.

Appendix 6A: Best–worst experiment

Id	blockId	gameId	descridA	descridB	descridC	descridD	busimg	tramimg
1	1	1	24	28	26	10	1	2
2	1	2	8	36	57	4	2	1
3	1	3	17	14	11	2	2	2
4	1	4	4	46	40	64	1	1
5	2	1	16	18	7	2	2	2
6	2	2	65	39	49	51	2	1
7	2	3	20	7	12	23	1	1
8	2	4	46	34	62	45	1	2
9	3	1	35	8	54	65	2	1
10	3	2	22	32	24	60	2	2
11	3	3	4	38	45	3	1	1
12	3	4	23	27	5	24	1	2
13	4	1	40	36	65	3	1	1
14	4	2	13	20	24	19	1	2
15	4	3	63	24	17	7	2	1
16	4	4	54	6	50	57	2	2
17	5	1	25	13	63	7	1	2
18	5	2	37	6	4	34	2	1
19	5	3	29	20	2	30	2	2
20	5	4	3	8	43	6	1	1
21	6	1	28	56	13	11	1	1
22	6	2	49	48	40	42	2	2
23	6	3	5	28	12	21	1	2
24	6	4	36	62	64	50	2	1
25	7	1	19	63	10	30	1	1
26	7	2	39	43	53	40	1	2
27	7	3	20	11	27	32	2	1
28	7	4	40	59	45	35	2	2
29	8	1	55	45	8	37	2	2
30	8	2	7	2	28	19	1	1
31	8	3	34	65	38	47	2	1
32	8	4	56	10	16	21	1	2
33	9	1	61	42	46	53	2	2
34	9	2	32	18	30	5	1	2
35	9	3	16	25	60	58	1	1
36	9	4	45	50	51	42	2	1
37	10	1	1	58	13	23	1	1
38	10	2	43	52	47	45	1	2
39	10	3	58	30	14	12	2	1
40	10	4	6	52	39	38	2	2
41	11	1	24	11	31	12	2	2
42	11	2	65	61	55	57	1	1
43	11	3	8	50	44	52	1	2
44	11	4	56	27	1	63	2	1
45	12	1	7	66	23	26	2	1
46	12	2	61	64	43	54	1	2
47	12	3	31	2	60	9	1	1
48	12	4	34	49	35	43	2	2
49	13	1	27	30	9	15	2	2
50	13	2	50	38	33	37	2	1
51	13	3	15	56	58	7	1	2
52	13	4	51	44	54	40	1	1
53	14	1	42	8	33	52	2	2
54	14	2	31	23	56	25	2	1
55	14	3	28	32	66	9	1	1
56	14	4	35	41	6	61	1	2
57	15	1	44	62	41	49	1	1
58	15	2	9	17	20	58	2	1
59	15	3	26	1	19	17	2	2
60	15	4	41	43	42	38	1	2
61	16	1	59	41	8	51	2	2
62	16	2	30	1	31	28	1	2
63	16	3	62	54	8	48	2	1
64	16	4	14	13	21	66	1	1
65	17	1	36	45	49	54	1	1
66	17	2	32	29	10	17	2	2
67	17	3	44	61	3	47	2	1
68	17	4	63	21	58	32	1	2

Id	blockId	gameId	descridA	descridB	descridC	descridD	busimg	tramimg
69	18	1	63	21	58	32	2	1
70	18	2	44	61	3	47	1	1
71	18	3	32	29	10	17	2	2
72	18	4	36	45	49	54	1	2
73	19	1	14	13	21	66	1	2
74	19	2	62	54	8	48	1	1
75	19	3	30	1	31	28	2	2
76	19	4	59	41	8	51	2	1
77	20	1	19	15	14	16	1	2
78	20	2	50	3	41	39	2	2
79	20	3	62	39	47	59	2	1
80	20	4	21	9	19	25	1	1
81	21	1	35	41	6	61	1	1
82	21	2	28	32	66	9	1	2
83	21	3	52	46	57	49	2	1
84	21	4	14	7	32	31	2	2
85	22	1	51	44	54	40	2	2
86	22	2	15	56	58	7	1	1
87	22	3	26	16	32	13	2	1
88	22	4	51	55	62	43	1	2
89	23	1	10	25	11	15	2	2
90	23	2	52	4	61	62	2	1
91	23	3	60	63	15	29	1	1
92	23	4	8	65	46	50	1	2
93	24	1	57	51	3	64	2	2
94	24	2	7	26	21	31	2	1
95	24	3	65	60	30	56	1	1
96	24	4	48	35	52	36	1	2
97	25	1	5	31	17	16	1	2
98	25	2	59	55	42	36	2	1
99	25	3	43	52	47	45	2	2
100	25	4	1	58	13	23	1	1
101	26	1	22	26	27	14	1	2
102	26	2	38	49	61	59	2	1
103	26	3	33	40	55	6	1	1
104	26	4	60	14	23	28	2	2
105	27	1	56	10	16	21	2	2
106	27	2	34	65	38	47	2	1
107	27	3	7	2	28	19	1	2
108	27	4	55	45	8	37	1	1
109	28	1	18	58	22	11	1	2
110	28	2	47	35	51	33	2	1
111	28	3	17	15	28	18	1	1
112	28	4	41	64	34	55	2	2
113	29	1	36	62	64	50	2	2
114	29	2	5	28	12	21	1	2
115	29	3	49	48	40	42	2	1
116	29	4	28	56	13	11	1	1
117	30	1	1	7	15	5	2	1
118	30	2	54	47	4	55	1	2
119	30	3	37	6	4	34	2	2
120	30	4	25	13	63	7	1	1
121	31	1	54	6	50	57	1	1
122	31	2	63	24	17	7	2	2
123	31	3	13	20	24	19	2	1
124	31	4	40	36	65	3	1	1
125	32	1	46	51	6	48	1	1
126	32	2	2	16	22	1	1	2
127	32	3	45	33	48	61	2	2
128	32	4	11	7	29	66	2	1
129	33	1	46	34	62	45	2	1
130	33	2	20	7	12	23	2	2
131	33	3	66	17	25	27	1	1
132	33	4	38	40	8	46	1	2
133	34	1	4	46	40	64	2	1
134	34	2	17	14	11	2	2	2
135	34	3	7	12	56	2	1	2
136	34	4	48	53	50	34	1	1

Appendix 6B: Best–worst designs and Ngene syntax

Rose (2014) has developed a number of alternative ways of designing best–worst choice experiments. In this Appendix, we show how the data has to be set up for each of three cases together with the Ngene syntax used to obtain an appropriate design matrix, given the selected optimal design criterion.

Best worst scaling (Case 1)

Best	Attribute	Worst
◯	Singapore	◯
◯	Emirates	◯
◯	Qantas	◯
◯	Virgin	◯

Figure 6B.1   Example best–worst case 1 task

6B.1 Best–worst case 1

Case 1 involves respondents being shown sub-sets of alternatives and being asked which alternative is best and which is worst. Note that unlike discrete choice experiments, the alternatives are not represented as bundles of attributes. Consider an example of four alternatives, selected from 1. Air NZ, 2. Delta, 3. Emirates, 4. Jetstar, 5. Qantas, 6. Singapore, 7. United, and 8. Virgin. An example of a choice question is shown in Figure 6B.1.

As an aside, The Ngene syntax should work for all model types by changing the efficiency measure, independent of case type.

The data is set up as per a normal DCE, where the attributes are dummy codes for the alternatives shown. Each task, however, is repeated, once for best and once for worst. For worst, the coding is the same; however, −1 is used instead of 1. An example is presented in Table 6B.1, where the first task is an example of the above task.

The Ngene syntax for this design would look like:

```
Design
;eff=(mnl,d)
;alts = A, B, C, D ? this is the number of options to show
;rows = 12
;prop = bw1(bw)
;con
;model:
U(A) = Airline.d[0|0|0|0|0|0|0] * Airline[1,2,3,4,5,6,7,8]/
U(B) = Airline.d * Airline[1,2,3,4,5,6,7,0]/
U(C) = Airline.d * Airline[1,2,3,4,5,6,7,8]/
U(D) = Airline.d * Airline[1,2,3,4,5,6,7,8]
$
```

Table 6B.1 Example B/W case 1 task data set up 1

Resp	Set	Altij	Cset	Bestworst	AirNZ	Delta	Emirates	JetStar	Qantas	Singapore	United	Choice
1	1	1	4	1	0	0	0	0	0	1	0	0
1	1	2	4	1	0	0	1	0	0	0	0	1
1	1	3	4	1	0	0	0	0	1	0	0	0
1	1	4	4	1	0	0	0	0	0	0	0	0
1	1	1	4	−1	0	0	0	0	0	−1	0	0
1	1	2	4	−1	0	0	−1	0	0	0	0	0
1	1	3	4	−1	0	0	0	0	−1	0	0	0
1	1	4	4	−1	0	0	0	0	0	0	0	1
1	2	1	4	1	1	0	0	0	0	0	0	0
1	2	2	4	1	0	0	1	0	0	0	0	0
1	2	3	4	1	0	0	0	0	1	0	0	0
1	2	4	4	1	0	0	0	0	0	0	1	1
1	2	1	4	−1	−1	0	0	0	0	0	0	0
1	2	2	4	−1	0	0	−1	0	0	0	0	1
1	2	3	4	−1	0	0	0	0	−1	0	0	0
1	2	4	4	−1	0	0	0	0	0	0	−1	0

Or

```
Design
;eff=(mnl,d)
;alts = A, B, C, D
;rows = 12
;prop = bw1(bw)
;model:
U(A,B,C,D) = Airline.d[0|0|0|0|0|0|0] * Airline[1,2,3,4,5,6,7,8]$
```

To include ordering effects, you can include constants:

```
Design
;eff=(mnl,d)
;alts = A, B, C, D
;rows = 12
;prop = bw1(bw)
;con
;model:
U(A) = A[0]  + Airline.d[0|0|0|0|0|0|0] * Airline[1,2,3,4,5,6,7,8]/
U(B) = B[0]  + Airline.d * Airline[1,2,3,4,5,6,7,8]/
U(C) = C[0]  + Airline.d * Airline[1,2,3,4,5,6,7,8]/
U(D) =         Airline.d * Airline[1,2,3,4,5,6,7,8] $
```

You can have non-zero priors. Some researchers take different approaches to constructing the worst task, where they delete the alternative chosen as best when constructing the worst task. The assumption is that the respondent is comparing the worst from the remaining set of alternatives shown. Below is an example of this. The two approaches represent two different assumptions as to how respondents are answering these questions. The syntax for this type of design becomes:

```
Design
;eff=(mnl,d)
;alts = A, B, C, D
;rows = 12
;prop = bw1(b,w)
;con
;model:
U(A) = A[0] + Airline.d[0|0|0|0|0|0|0] * Airline[1,2,3,4,5,6,7,8]/
U(B) = B[0] + Airline.d * Airline[1,2,3,4,5,6,7,8]/
U(C) = C[0] + Airline.d * Airline[1,2,3,4,5,6,7,8]/
U(D) =        Airline.d * Airline[1,2,3,4,5,6,7,8] $
```

and the assumed data structure being optimized is shown in Table 6B.2. The design also allows for more than one best–worst ranking, for example:

```
Design
;eff=(mnl,d)
;alts = A, B, C, D
;rows = 12
;choices = bw1(bw,b)
;model:
U(A,B,C,D) = Airline.d[0|0|0|0|0|0|0] * Airline[1,2,3,4,5,6,7,8]$
```

Table 6B.2 Example B/W case 1 task data set up 2

Resp	Set	Altij	Cset	Bestworst	AirNZ	Delta	Emirates	JetStar	Qantas	Singapore	United	Choice
1	1	1	4	1	0	0	0	0	0	1	0	0
1	1	2	4	1	0	0	1	0	0	0	0	1
1	1	3	4	1	0	0	0	0	1	0	0	0
1	1	4	4	1	0	0	0	0	0	0	0	0
1	1	1	3	−1	0	0	0	0	0	−1	0	0
1	1	3	3	−1	0	0	0	0	−1	0	0	0
1	1	4	3	−1	0	0	0	0	0	0	0	1
1	2	1	4	1	1	0	0	0	0	0	0	1
1	2	2	4	1	0	0	1	0	0	0	0	0
1	2	3	4	1	0	0	0	0	1	0	0	0
1	2	4	4	1	0	0	0	0	0	0	1	0
1	2	2	3	−1	0	0	−1	0	0	0	0	1
1	2	3	3	−1	0	0	0	0	−1	0	0	0
1	2	4	3	−1	0	0	0	0	0	0	−1	0

Table 6B.3 Example B/W case 2 task attribute levels

Attribute	Level 1	Level 2	Level 3
Seat pitch	28 inches	30 inches	32 inches
Entertainment	Single cabin screen	Limited movies	Full entertainment
Alcohol payment	Pay for alcohol	Free alcohol	
Stop over	No stop over	3 hour stop over	5 hour stop over

Best worst scaling (Case 2)

Best	Attribute	Worst
○	Seat pitch 30'	○
○	Limited movies	○
○	Pay for alcohol	○
○	5 hour stopover	○

Figure 6B.2   Example best–worst case 2 task

6B.2 Best–worst case 2

Case 2 differs from case 1 in that the method concentrates on attributes, not alternatives. Consider an example with four attributes, seat pitch, entertainment, alcohol payment, and stop over. The attribute levels of the four levels are given in Table 6B.3.

An example of a choice question is shown in Figure 6B.2.

The data is set up as per a normal DCE, where the attributes are dummy codes of the attribute levels. Each task, however, is repeated, once for best and once for worst. For worst, the coding is the same, however, −1 is used instead of 1. An example is presented in Table 6B.4, where the first task is an example of the above task.

The Ngene syntax to optimize this is:

```
Design
;eff=(mnl,d)
 ;alts = Seat, Movie, Pay, Stop
;rows = 12
;choices = bw1(bw)
;con
;model:
U(Seat)  = seat.dummy[0|0]  * seat[0,1,2] /
U(Movie) = Movie.dummy[0|0]*Movie[0,1,2] /
U(Pay)   = Pay[0]*Pay[0,1] /
U(Stop)  = Stop.dummy[0|0]*stop[0,1,2] $
```

Table 6B.4 Example B/W case 2 task data set up 1

Resp	Set	Altij	Altn	Cset	Bestworst	Inch28	Inch30	CabScr	LimMov	Pay	Hour1	Hour3	Choice
1	1	1	1	4	1	0	1	0	0	0	0	0	0
1	1	2	2	4	1	0	0	0	1	0	0	0	1
1	1	3	3	4	1	0	0	0	0	0	0	0	0
1	1	4	4	4	1	0	0	0	0	0	0	0	0
1	1	1	5	4	−1	0	−1	0	0	0	0	0	0
1	1	2	6	4	−1	0	0	0	−1	0	0	0	0
1	1	3	7	4	−1	0	0	0	0	0	0	0	1
1	1	4	8	4	−1	0	0	0	0	0	0	0	0
1	2	1	1	4	1	1	0	0	0	0	0	0	0
1	2	2	2	4	1	0	0	1	0	0	0	0	0
1	2	3	3	4	1	0	0	0	0	1	0	0	1
1	2	4	4	4	1	0	0	0	0	0	0	1	0
1	2	1	5	4	−1	−1	0	0	0	0	0	0	1
1	2	2	6	4	−1	0	0	−1	0	0	0	0	0
1	2	3	7	4	−1	0	0	0	0	−1	0	0	0
1	2	4	8	4	−1	0	0	0	0	0	0	−1	0

The command above is still B/W1 (it will be changed soon). You can also have constants in the design, such that the syntax and data structure assumed are:

```
Design
;eff=(mnl,d)
;alts = Seat, Movie, Pay, Stop
;rows = 12
;choices = bw2(bw)
;con
;model:
U(Seat) = ASCseat[0] + seat.dummy[0|0] * seat[0,1,2] /
U(Movie) = ASCMovie[0] + Movie.dummy[0|0]*Movie[0,1,2] /
U(Pay) = ASCPay[0] + Pay[0]*Pay[0,1] /
U(Stop) =            Stop.dummy[0|0]*stop[0,1,2] $
```

As with case 1, some researchers tend to delete the best when constructing the worst task (Table 6B.5). The Ngene syntax to do this is:

```
Design
;eff=(mnl,d)
;alts = Seat, Movie, Pay, Stop
;rows = 12
;choices = bw2(b,w)
;con
;model:
```

Table 6B.5 Example B/W case 2 task data set up 1 with constants

Resp	Set	Altij	Altn	Cset	Bestworst	Seat	Mov	Alc	Inch28	Inch30	CabScr	LimMov	Pay	Hour1	Hour3	Choice
1	1	1	1	4	1	1	0	0	0	1	0	0	0	0	0	0
1	1	2	2	4	1	0	1	0	0	0	0	1	0	0	0	1
1	1	3	3	4	1	0	0	1	0	0	0	0	0	0	0	0
1	1	4	4	4	1	0	0	0	0	0	0	0	0	0	0	0
1	1	1	5	4	-1	1	0	0	0	-1	0	0	0	0	0	0
1	1	2	6	4	-1	0	1	0	0	0	0	-1	0	0	0	0
1	1	3	7	4	-1	0	0	1	0	0	0	0	0	0	0	1
1	1	4	8	4	-1	0	0	0	0	0	0	0	0	0	0	0
1	2	1	1	4	1	1	0	0	1	0	0	0	0	1	0	0
1	2	2	2	4	1	0	1	0	0	0	1	0	0	0	0	0
1	2	3	3	4	1	0	0	1	0	0	0	0	1	0	1	1
1	2	4	4	4	1	0	0	0	0	0	0	0	0	0	0	0
1	2	1	5	4	-1	1	0	0	-1	0	0	0	0	0	0	1
1	2	2	6	4	-1	0	1	0	0	0	-1	0	0	0	0	0
1	2	3	7	4	-1	0	0	1	0	0	0	0	-1	0	0	0
1	2	4	8	4	-1	0	0	0	0	0	0	0	0	0	-1	0

```
U(Seat)  = ASCseat[0] + seat.dummy[0|0] * seat[0,1,2] /
U(Movie) = ASCMovie[0] + Movie.dummy[0|0]*Movie[0,1,2] /
U(Pay)   = ASCPay[0] + Pay[0]*Pay[0,1] /
U(Stop)  =             Stop.dummy[0|0]*stop[0,1,2] $
```

and the data structure would be as given in Table 6B.6.

The design also allows for more than one best–worst ranking, for example:

```
Design
;eff=(mnl,d)
;alts = Seat, Movie, Pay, Stop
;rows = 12
;choices = bw2(bw,b)
;con
;model:
U(Seat)  = ASCseat[0] + seat.dummy[0|0] * seat[0,1,2] /
U(Movie) = ASCMovie[0] + Movie.dummy[0|0]*Movie[0,1,2] /
U(Pay)   = ASCPay[0] + Pay[0]*Pay[0,1] /
U(Stop)  =             Stop.dummy[0|0]*stop[0,1,2] $
```

You can also assume that in the presence of multiple best–worst questions, they choose:

```
Design
;eff=(mnl,d)
;alts = Seat, Movie, Pay, Stop
;rows = 12
;choices = bw2(b,b,b)
;con
;model:
U(Seat)  = ASCseat[0] + seat.dummy[0|0] * seat[0,1,2] /
U(Movie) = ASCMovie[0] + Movie.dummy[0|0]*Movie[0,1,2] /
U(Pay)   = ASCPay[0] + Pay[0]*Pay[0,1] /
U(Stop)  =             Stop.dummy[0|0]*stop[0,1,2] $
```

6B.3 Best–worst case 3

Case 3 differs significantly from cases 1 and 2. Case 3 looks most like a traditional DCE; however, it differs in terms of the response mechanism. Unlike a traditional DCE which involves a pick one task, the best–worst case 3 task involves asking respondents to select the best and worst alternatives

Consider the following example (Figure 6B.3).

The data can be set up in a number of different ways, depending on how the analyst believes that the respondents completed the task. For example, if the analyst did not impose the order that the questions were asked, it is

Table 6B.6 Example B/W case 2 task data set up 2

Resp	Set	Altij	Altn	Cset	Bestworst	Seat	Mov	Alc	Inch28	Inch30	CabScr	LimMov	Pay	Hour1	Hour3	Choice
1	1	1	1	4	1	1	0	0	0	1	0	0	0	0	0	0
1	1	2	2	4	1	0	1	0	0	0	0	1	0	0	0	1
1	1	3	3	4	1	0	0	1	0	0	0	0	0	0	0	0
1	1	4	4	4	1	0	0	0	0	0	0	0	0	0	0	0
1	1	1	5	3	−1	1	0	0	0	−1	0	0	0	0	0	0
1	1	3	7	3	−1	0	0	1	0	0	0	0	0	0	0	1
1	1	4	8	3	−1	0	0	0	0	0	0	0	0	0	0	0
1	2	1	1	4	1	1	0	0	1	0	0	0	0	0	0	0
1	2	2	2	4	1	0	1	0	0	0	1	0	0	0	0	0
1	2	3	3	4	1	0	0	1	0	0	0	0	1	0	0	1
1	2	4	4	4	1	0	0	0	0	0	0	0	0	0	1	0
1	2	1	5	3	−1	1	0	0	0	0	0	0	0	0	0	1
1	2	2	6	3	−1	0	1	0	−1	0	−1	0	0	0	0	0
1	2	4	8	3	−1	0	0	0	0	0	0	0	0	0	−1	0

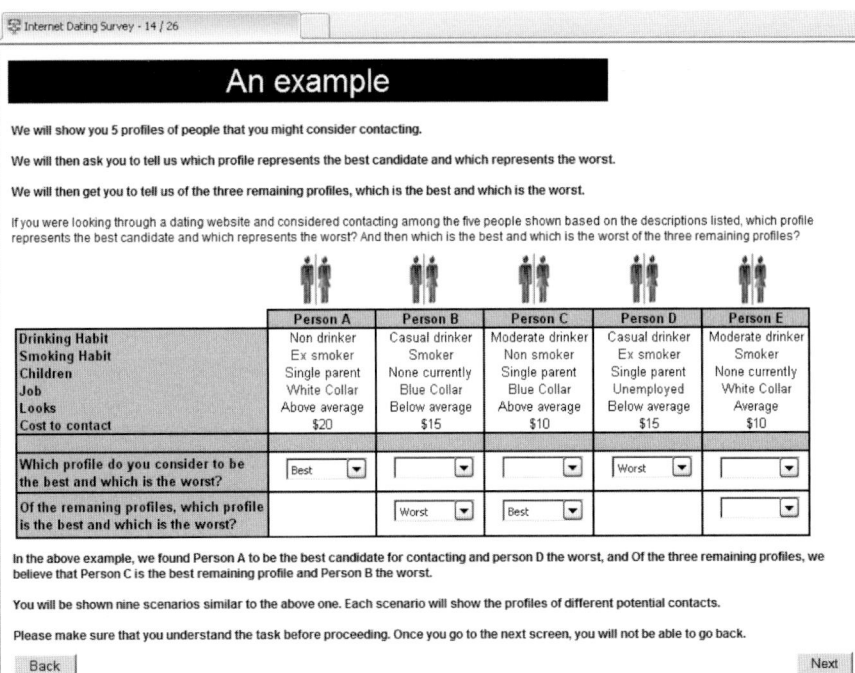

Figure 6B.3 Example best–worst case 3 task

possible that they answered best, next best, next best, and so on. Alternatively, the respondent may have answered best, worst, next best, next worst, and so on.

Assuming best, next best, next best, and so on, the data would be set up as in Table 6B.7 (representing a traditional rank explosion exercise).

The Ngene syntax for the above design would look like:

```
Design
;alts =A,B,C,D,E
;eff= (mnl,d,mean)
;rows=24
;bdraws=halton(100)
;choices = bw3(b,b,b,b)
;model:
U(A) = Dr.dummy[(u,-1,-0.5)|(u,-0.5,0)]*drink[0,1,2] + Sm.dummy[(u,-1,-
0.5)|(u,-0.5,0)]*Smoke[0,1,2]
+ Ch.dummy[(u,-1,-0.5)|(u,-0.5,0)]*Child[0,1,2]+ Jo.dummy[(u,-1,-0.5)|
(u,-0.5,0)]*Job[0,1,2]
+ Lo.dummy[(u,-1,-0.5)|(u,-0.5,0)]*Looks[0,1,2] + Cst[(n,-0.05,0.01)]
*Cost[5,10,15,20] /
```

Table 6B.7 Example B/W case 3 task data set up 1 (best–best–best–best– ...)

Resp	Set	RespSet	Explode	Altij	Altn	Cset	Choice	Drink	Smoke	Child	Job	Looks	Cost
1	1	1	1	1	1	5	1	0	1	1	0	2	20
1	1	1	1	2	2	5	0	1	2	0	1	0	15
1	1	1	1	3	3	5	0	2	0	1	1	2	10
1	1	1	1	4	4	5	0	1	1	1	2	0	15
1	1	1	1	5	5	5	0	2	2	0	0	1	10
1	2	1	2	2	7	4	0	1	2	0	1	0	15
1	2	1	2	3	8	4	1	2	0	1	1	2	10
1	2	1	2	4	9	4	0	1	1	1	2	0	15
1	2	1	2	5	10	4	0	2	2	0	0	1	10
1	3	1	3	2	12	3	0	1	2	0	1	0	15
1	3	1	3	4	14	3	0	1	1	1	2	0	15
1	3	1	3	5	15	3	1	2	2	0	0	1	10
1	4	1	4	2	17	2	1	1	2	0	1	0	15
1	4	1	4	4	19	2	0	1	1	1	2	0	15

```
U(B) = Dr*drink + Sm*Smoke+ Ch*Child+ Jo*Job + Lo*Looks + Cst*Cost /
U(C) = Dr*drink + Sm*Smoke+ Ch*Child+ Jo*Job + Lo*Looks + Cst*Cost /
U(D) = Dr*drink + Sm*Smoke+ Ch*Child+ Jo*Job + Lo*Looks + Cst*Cost /
U(E) = Dr*drink + Sm*Smoke+ Ch*Child+ Jo*Job + Lo*Looks + Cst*Cost $
```

The attributes are dummy coded in the syntax for this example; however, in theory, the method itself does not impose any particular coding structure. Some researchers take a different track for the explosions by deleting the alternative chosen as best or worst in the previous pseudo-observation. In this case, the assumption is that the respondent is comparing the next best or next worst from the remaining set of alternatives. This data set up is shown in Table 6B.8. Note that the two approaches represent two different assumptions as to how respondents are answering these questions.

The Ngene syntax for the above design would look like:

```
Design
;alts =A,B,C,D,E
;eff= (mnl,d,mean)
;rows=24
;bdraws=halton(100)
;choices = bw3(b,w,b,w)
;model:
U(A) = Dr.dummy[(u,-1,-0.5)|(u,-0.5,0)]*drink[0,1,2] + Sm.dummy[(u,-1,-
0.5)|(u,-0.5,0)]*Smoke[0,1,2]
+ Ch.dummy[(u,-1,-0.5)|(u,-0.5,0)]*Child[0,1,2]+ Jo.dummy[(u,-1,-0.5)|
```

Table 6B.8 Example B/W case 3 task data set up 3 (best–worst–best–worst– . . .)

Resp	Bestworst	Explode	Altij	Altn	Cset	Choice	Drink	Smoke	Child	Job	Looks	Cost
1	1	1	1	1	5	1	0	1	1	0	2	20
1	1	1	2	2	5	0	1	2	0	1	0	15
1	1	1	3	3	5	0	2	0	1	1	2	10
1	1	1	4	4	5	0	1	1	1	2	0	15
1	1	1	5	5	5	0	2	2	0	0	1	10
1	−1	2	2	7	4	0	−1	−2	0	−1	0	−15
1	−1	2	3	8	4	0	−2	0	−1	−1	−2	−10
1	−1	2	4	9	4	1	−1	−1	−1	−2	0	−15
1	−1	2	5	10	4	0	−2	−2	0	0	−1	−10
1	1	3	2	12	3	0	1	2	0	1	0	15
1	1	3	3	13	3	1	2	0	1	1	2	10
1	1	3	5	15	3	0	2	2	0	0	1	10
1	−1	4	2	17	2	1	−1	−2	0	−1	0	−15
1	−1	4	5	20	2	0	−2	−2	0	0	−1	−10

```
(u,-0.5,0)]*Job[0,1,2]
+ Lo.dummy[(u,-1,-0.5)|(u,-0.5,0)]*Looks[0,1,2] + Cst[(n,-0.05,0.01)]
*Cost[5,10,15,20] /
U(B) = Dr*drink + Sm*Smoke+ Ch*Child+ Jo*Job + Lo*Looks + Cst*Cost /
U(C) = Dr*drink + Sm*Smoke+ Ch*Child+ Jo*Job + Lo*Looks + Cst*Cost /
U(D) = Dr*drink + Sm*Smoke+ Ch*Child+ Jo*Job + Lo*Looks + Cst*Cost /
U(E) = Dr*drink + Sm*Smoke+ Ch*Child+ Jo*Job + Lo*Looks + Cst*Cost $
```

Appendix 6C An historical overview

In this appendix, we provide an abridged historical overview of research into the experimental design theory as applied to SC type data, drawn from Rose and Bliemer (2014). It is acknowledged that there exists a vast number of papers and researchers who have examined this issue making it impossible to discuss in detail all the developments. As such, we concentrate on what are perceived to be the major contributions.

6C.1 Louviere and Hensher (1983), Louviere and Woodworth (1983), and others

The first SC studies focused on introducing the method and promoting its benefits over the standard stated preference techniques used at the time (such as traditional conjoint methods). These early studies, therefore, did not concern themselves specifically with experimental design issues and simply borrowed design construction methods from elsewhere. As it turned out, the "elsewhere" happened to be from the very methods that SC methods sought to replace; traditional conjoint design methodology.[3] Traditional conjoint studies involve respondents ranking or rating alternatives (rather than picking one) constructed from either a full factorial or fractional factorial design which are not grouped together in choice tasks but presented all at once, and are estimated using linear models such as linear regression (MANOVA was also popular at one stage). As such, the experimental design theory at the time focused largely on linear regression type models used for this sort of data.

The variance-covariance (VC) matrix of a linear regression model is given in Equation (6C.1):

$$VC = \sigma^2 (X'X)^{-1}, \tag{6C.1}$$

where σ^2 is the model variance, and X is the matrix of attribute levels in the design or in the data to be used in estimation.

Fixing the model variance for the present (which simply acts as a scaling factor), the elements of the VC matrix for linear regression models will generally be minimized when the columns of the X matrix are orthogonal. As such, when such models are estimated, the orthogonality of data is considered important as this property ensures that (a) the model will not suffer from multicollinearity, and (b) the variances (and covariances) of the parameter estimates are minimized. As such, orthogonal designs, at least in relation to linear models, meet the two criteria for a good design mentioned earlier; they allow for an independent determination of each attribute's contribution on the dependent variable and they maximize the power of the design to detect statistically significant relationships (i.e., maximize the t-ratios at any given sample size). Of course, the role that sigma plays may be important and as such cannot always be ignored as suggested above. This is because it may be possible to locate a non-orthogonal design which produces non-zero covariances and slightly larger variances, but has smaller elements overall when scaled by sigma. Nevertheless, orthogonal designs will tend to perform well overall for this type of model.

---

[3] This is not to suggest that research into aspects associated with the specific use of orthogonal designs as applied to discrete choice data were not undertaken in the early years of SC studies. For example, Anderson and Wiley (1992) and Lazari and Anderson (1994) looked at orthogonal designs capable of addressing problems of availability of alternatives. See Louviere *et al.* (2000) for a review of orthogonal design theory as applied to SC methods.

Despite the fact that discrete choice data is often applied to non-linear models, the question as to whether designs generated for linear models might be appropriate for such data remained surprisingly uncommented on for a number of years. Where an examination of the problem was made, often an inappropriate analysis was conducted that resulted in the not surprising conclusion that orthogonal designs are preferred to non-orthogonal designs. For example, Kuhfeld et al. (1994) compared balanced and unbalanced orthogonal designs to non-orthogonal designs using the Information matrix associated with linear models (specifically Equation 6C.1 without sigma) despite applying the designs to non-linear logit models. It is little surprising that they concluded that while "preserving orthogonality at all costs can lead to decreased efficiency," particularly when a balanced orthogonal design was not available, "non-orthogonal designs will never be more efficient than balanced orthogonal designs, when they exist."

Such misconceptions continue to this day. To demonstrate, consider the frequent practice of either (i) reporting the following design statistic in SC studies or (ii) the use of the statistic itself as the objective function to be maximized when generating a SC design (e.g., Kuhfeld et al. 1994; Lusk and Norwood 2005):

$$D\text{-efficiency} = \frac{100}{S|(X'X)^{-1}|^{1/K}}, \tag{6C.2}$$

where S is the number of observations (i.e., choice sets), K is the number of attributes or parameters in the design, and X the design matrix. This measure is uninformative with respect to the operating conditions of discrete choice modeling under random utility theory because Equation (6C.2) is derived under the assumption that the model is linear in nature. The relationship between this equation and that of the VC matrix of the homoskedastic linear regression model, clearly demonstrates the relationship between the two. Indeed, Equation (6C.2) will return a value of 100 percent for an orthogonal design and lower values for non-orthogonal designs. However, as is argued later, design orthogonality of this type does not imply efficiency of non-linear discrete choice models.

Nevertheless, it is important to note that the apparent success (or rather lack of failure) of studies applying such designs meant that the use of orthogonal designs remained mostly unchallenged. Even with increasing evidence that non-orthogonal designs might be more appropriate for discrete choice models, orthogonal designs remain largely entrenched within the literature and continue to be the most common design method used.

6C.2 Fowkes, Toner, Wardman *et al.* (Institute of Transport, Leeds, 1988–2000)

In the late 1980s, writing in the transport literature, researchers from Leeds University began to question the appropriateness of using orthogonal designs for discrete choice type data. In a series of research papers spanning over a decade, Fowkes, Toner, and Wardman (among others) questioned the use of fractional factorial designs based on orthogonal arrays and discussed the importance of experiments that were realistic and made sense to the respondents as well as improving the robustness of the parameter estimates. Dealing specifically with the binary choice tasks, the Leeds group designs were generated under the assumptions of *non-zero priors* for both *generic* and alternative-specific parameters. Such designs are referred to as *locally optimal*, as the assumed parameter priors are known with certainty and the designs are optimized precisely for these parameter values. If the true parameter estimates differ from the assumed parameters (i.e., the parameter priors were mis-specified), then the design will lose efficiency; see Figure 6C.1. Rather than concerning themselves directly with minimizing the standard errors of the parameter estimates, the Leeds group designs sought to minimize the variances of ratios of parameters (i.e., they were concerned with *willingness to pay* (WTP) issues) that they were able to calculate from the model AVC matrix using the Delta method (see Chapter 7).

Rather than assume pre-defined fixed attribute levels, this class of designs was generated so as to allow the attribute levels of the design to take any value, including non-integers, and hence be *continuous*. In letting go of specific pre-determined attribute levels and allowing the attributes to take any value, under specific conditions it is possible to locate a design that will optimize the objective function of interest using a number of mathematical techniques such as non-linear programing. The Leeds group were able to utilize such

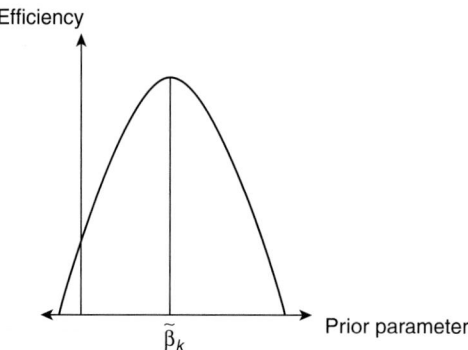

Figure 6C.1 Locally optimal parameter priors and parameter prior misspecification

methods to locate designs that minimized the variances of the ratio of two parameters, and as such generate designs which can be considered to be *optimal* under the assumptions for which they were generated.

Careful examination of the designs that were generated by this group led to the observation that many of the resulting choice tasks were not realistic from the perspective of the respondent. For this reason additional requirements were imposed on the generated designs in which a reasonable coverage of so-called "boundary values" were sought and obtained (see Fowkes and Wardman 1988; Fowkes *et al.* 1993; Toner *et al.* 1998, 1999; Watson *et al.* 2000 for further discussion of these designs). Further examination of these designs by the Leeds group found that they tended to retrieve very specific choice probabilities, which they referred to as "Magic P's." This finding was later independently rediscovered by other researchers working in other discipline areas, in particular by Kanninen in 2002.

6C.3 Bunch, Louviere and Anderson (1996)

In 1996, two similar papers appeared simultaneously in the marketing literature dealing with experimental design theory as related to SC data. The first we discuss here (Bunch *et al.* 1996[4]) appears only in the form of a working paper. This paper dealt specifically with strategies for generating designs for *multinomial logit (MNL)* models assuming either *zero* or *non-zero local priors* for *generic* parameter estimates. Unlike the earlier work coming out of the Leeds group, Bunch *et al.* assumed *fixed attribute levels* using *orthogonal polynomial* coding in estimation (we discuss this coding structure further when we discuss the work of Street and Burgess below). As their objective function, Bunch *et al.* considered designs that minimized the elements of the resulting AVC matrix rather than with the variances of ratios of parameter estimates.

Bunch *et al.* (1996) promoted the use of the *D-error* statistic, applying it to the expected AVC matrix of the design as constructed for the MNL model. The *D-error* statistic, not to be confused with the *D-efficiency* measure suggested by Kuhfeld *et al.* (1994), is calculated by taking the determinant of the AVC matrix assuming a single respondent, Ω_1, and normalizing this value by the number of parameters, K. Minimizing the *D-error* statistic corresponds to minimizing, on average, the elements contained within the expected AVC

---

[4] An earlier version of the paper appeared in 1994; however, we prefer the later date as this version remains freely accessible on the lead authors' own webpage.

matrix. Designs which minimize the *D-error* statistic are therefore called *D-optimal* designs.

Keeping in line with earlier empirical work in SC, Bunch *et al.* (1996) searched only among *orthogonal designs*. In doing so, they considered both simultaneously and sequentially constructed orthogonal designs in the generation process. A simultaneous orthogonal design is one where the attributes of the design are orthogonal not only within alternatives, but also between alternatives. This requires that the design be generated simultaneously for all alternatives. A sequentially constructed orthogonal design is one where the attributes of the design may be orthogonal within an alternative, but not necessarily between alternatives (see Louviere *et al.* 2000). As such, their designs also kept the same properties as orthogonal designs, including attribute level balance constraints.

Unlike the designs generated by the Leeds group, the use of pre-specified fixed attribute levels makes it generally difficult to locate the design matrix which will be optimal. As such, algorithms are required which search over the design space by re-arranging the attribute levels of the design and testing the efficiency measure after each change. Only if all possible designs are tested can one conclude that the design is optimal. For designs with large design dimensions, this is not always possible, and for this reason such designs are more correctly referred to as *efficient designs*. Given that Bunch *et al.* (1996) considered designs which were orthogonal, only a sub-set of all possible designs was examined. For this reason, the class of designs generated by Bunch *et al.* are more correctly referred to as *locally optimal D-efficient* designs, as opposed to *D-optimal* designs. Although algorithms for locating SC designs are important, and formed a central part of the Bunch *et al.* paper, for reasons of space we do not discuss this aspect of the design generation process here (see Kessels *et al.* 2006 for an excellent discussion of design algorithms).

6C.4 Huber and Zwerina (1996)

At the same time as Bunch *et al.* (1996), a paper by Huber and Zwerina (1996) appeared in the marketing literature. This paper covered much of the same material discussed in Bunch *et al.*; however, a number of important and often subtle differences do exist between the two papers. Before discussing these differences, however, it is worth noting the many similarities between the two papers. As with the work of Bunch *et al.*, Huber and Zwerina concerned themselves with optimal designs specifically generated for the *MNL* model assuming *non-zero local priors* for *generic* parameter estimates, although they

Option A			Option B			Option A			Option B		
A1	**A2**	**A3**	**A1**	**A2**	**A3**	**A1**	**A2**	**A3**	**A1**	**A2**	**A3**
10	3	2	10	3	2	10	3	2	10	3	2
20	−5	4	30	−5	6	20	−5	4	20	−5	4
30	3	6	20	−5	4	30	3	6	30	3	4
10	−5	6	20	3	4	30	−5	6	10	3	4
30	−5	2	10	−5	2	30	−5	2	10	−5	2
20	3	4	30	3	6	20	−5	6	20	3	6

(a)   (b)

Figure 6C.2 Different definitions of attribute level balance

assumed *effects coded* variables as opposed to *orthogonal polynomial* coding. Further, as with Bunch *et al.*, they assumed fixed design levels drawn from the underlying experimental design. Finally, they also concluded that minimizing the *D-error* statistic provided the best designs (in terms of generating statistically efficient designs).

It is the differences between the two papers and the reaction of the literature to these differences, however, which is more telling. Unlike Bunch *et al.* (1996), Huber and Zwerina (1996) did not confine the design space to consist only of orthogonal designs. In letting go of orthogonality as a design criterion (or, more precisely, constraint), they also relaxed the concept of attribute level balance somewhat. Whereas previously attribute level balance assumed that each level appeared an equal number of times within every column of the design (a strict definition of attribute level balance; see Figure 6C.2a), a new definition of attribute level balance was adopted that assumed that the level would appear an equal number of times for an attribute, independent of which alternative that attribute appeared in (and hence levels must appear an equal number of times across columns of the design but not necessarily within each column; see Figure 6C.2b). To demonstrate, consider the design in panel (a), in which the levels 10, 20, and 30 each appear twice for attribute A1 for both options A and B. Likewise, the levels of A2 and A3 appear an equal number of times in each column, independent of the alternative to which they belong. In the second design shown in panel (b), the levels do not appear an equal number of times within each column; however, over both options A and B, each level appears exactly four times each within the corresponding attributes.

Two important and far reaching findings were obtained from this paper, however. Firstly, Huber and Zwerina found that under *non-zero local priors*, non-orthogonal designs produced better designs in the form of more statistically efficient outcomes. While important, it is the second finding which has had a somewhat larger, if less desirable impact on the literature. In their paper, Huber and Zwerina concluded that designs that produce roughly equal choice probabilities among the J alternatives were more statistically efficient than designs that resulted in less equal distributions of the choice probability. This finding unfortunately contradicted the earlier findings obtained from the Leeds group, as well as the later work of other researchers in this field, who found that under certain conditions (actually the same conditions assumed by Huber and Zwerina), optimal designs were obtained not under designs that produced alternatives with choice shares equal to $1/J$ but, rather, that optimal designs resulted from constructing alternatives that would produce certain choice probabilities which were not probability (or utility) balanced (the Magic P's discovered by the Leeds group). Unfortunately, it was the message of utility or probability balance which gained wider traction within the literature and not that letting go of orthogonality may result in statistical gains when applied to SC models. Unfortunately, to this day, a number of papers continue to generate probability balanced designs when assuming non-zero priors.

6C.5 Sándor and Wedel (2001, 2002, 2005)

A number of years passed before the next significant breakthrough occurred within the literature, again within marketing. In 2001, Sándor and Wedel introduced Bayesian efficient designs to the SC design field. Assuming an *MNL* model, with *generic parameters* applied to *effects coded* variables and *fixed attribute levels*, Sándor and Wedel relaxed the assumption of perfect *a priori* knowledge of the parameter priors through adopting a Bayesian-like approach to the design generation process. Rather than assuming a single fixed value for each parameter prior, the efficiency of the design is calculated over a number of simulated draws taken from *prior parameter distributions* assumed by the analyst. Different distributions may be associated with different population moments representing different levels of uncertainty with regard to the true parameter values. In this way, by optimizing the efficiency of the design over a range of possible parameter prior values (drawn from the assumed parameter prior distributions), the design is made as robust as possible, at least within the range of the assumed distributions. This is represented in Figure 6C.3, where a Uniform Bayesian prior parameter distribution represented by the dashed rectangle is assumed with lower bound μ_L and upper bound μ_u. As shown in the figure, such designs will generally be less

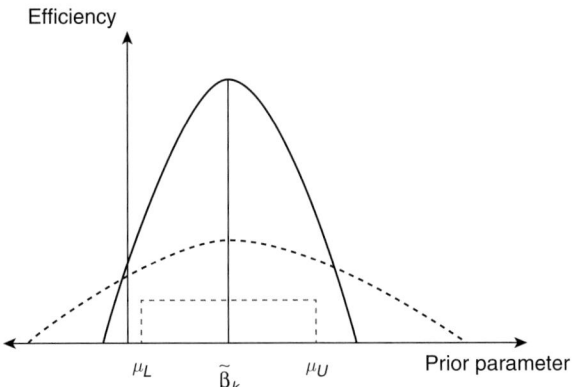

Figure 6C.3 Bayesian versus locally optimal designs

efficient than an equivalent locally optimal design (represented by the non-dashed line) but will be more robust to prior parameter mis-specification. As with Huber and Zwerina (1996), they found that non-orthogonal designs outperformed orthogonal designs based on the Bayesian equivalent of the *D-error* statistic.

In subsequent research Sándor and Wedel (2002, 2005), assuming *generic* parameter estimates for *effects coded* variables and *fixed attribute levels* as well as *locally optimal prior* parameter estimates, derived the AVC matrix for the cross-sectional version of the *mixed MNL (MMNL)* model. As such, they were the first to generate designs for a model other than the MNL model. In doing so, they retained the use of the *D-error* statistic as their design criterion and, as such, despite differences in assumptions made in terms of model type and how the prior parameters are generated, retained as their design objective, the desire to locate a design that results in smaller standard errors (and covariances).

6C.6 Street and Burgess (2001 to current)

An independent stream of research on generating designs for SC studies began to appear in 2001 within the statistics and marketing literatures, and centers around what can be referred to as Street and Burgess type designs (see Burgess and Street 2005; Street and Burgess 2004; Street *et al.* 2001, 2005). Like earlier researchers, Street and Burgess assume an *MNL* model specification in deriving the AVC matrix for their designs; however, the mathematical derivations used to obtain to the AVC matrix are performed in a somewhat different manner. Whereas other researchers derive the second derivatives with respect to the parameter such that:

$$\Omega_N = I_N^{-1}, \text{ with } I_N = -E_N\left(\frac{\partial^2 \log L}{\partial\beta\partial\beta'}\right), \tag{A6.3.3}$$

where $E_N(.)$ is used to express the large sample population mean, Street and Burgess calculate the second derivatives with respect to total utility V, such that:

$$\Omega_N = I_N^{-1}, \text{ with } I_N = -E_N\left(\frac{\partial^2 \log L}{\partial V \partial V'}\right). \tag{A6.3.4}$$

This difference in the mathematical derivations of the AVC matrix has resulted in significant confusion within the literature, with claims that the Street and Burgess approach is unrelated to the more mainstream SC experimental design literature as discussed herein. This view has been further enhanced given the fact that the resulting matrix algebra used to generate the AVC matrices under the two derivations appears to be very different. Recently, however, Bliemer and Rose (2014) were able to show that Street and Burgess designs are simply a special case of the more general methods used by other researchers, as described earlier.

Aside from the assumption of an MNL model specification estimated, Bliemer and Rose (2014) were able to reproduce Street and Burgess type designs using the same methods used by the other researchers discussed above, if they assumed the data were coded using an *orthonomal coding* structure. Beginning with a sequentially generated orthogonal design using the methods first described by Bunch *et al.* (1996), Street and Burgess designs can be constructed after first converting the design (see Table 6C.1a) into orthogonal contrast codes (Table 6C.1b) (see Keppel and Wickens 2004). The orthogonal contrast codes are then converted into the orthonormal coding structure by first computing the sum of the squares of each column (shown at the base of the columns) and then dividing each column of the orthogonal contrast code by this number (see Table 6C.1c).

The AVC matrix of the design is then computed under the assumption of *zero local priors*, assuming that the parameters are *generic* across alternatives. The elements of the resulting AVC matrix are then normalized by dividing each value by the product of the number of levels, L_k, of each attribute k of the original design (i.e., by $\prod_{k=1}^{K} L_k$). The design can then be optimized using the same *D-error* measure promoted by other researchers.

Table 6C.1 Design codes to orthogonal contrast codes

(a) Design codes					(b) Orthogonal contrast codes						
S	A1	A2	B1	B2	S	A1a	A1b	A2a	B1a	B1b	B2a
1	0	0	2	1	1	−1	1	−1	1	1	1
2	1	1	0	0	2	0	−2	1	−1	1	−1
3	2	1	1	0	3	1	1	1	0	−2	−1
4	2	0	1	1	4	1	1	−1	0	−2	1
5	0	0	2	1	5	−1	1	−1	1	1	1
6	1	1	0	0	6	0	−2	1	−1	1	−1
7	1	0	0	1	7	0	−2	−1	−1	1	1
8	2	0	1	1	8	1	1	−1	0	−2	1
9	0	1	2	0	9	−1	1	1	1	1	−1
10	1	0	0	1	10	0	−2	−1	−1	1	1
11	2	1	1	0	11	1	1	1	0	−2	−1
12	0	1	2	0	12	−1	1	1	1	1	−1
						8	24	12	8	24	12

(c) Orthonormal coding

S	A1a	A1b	A2a	B1a	B1b	B2a
1	−0.35	0.20	−0.29	0.35	0.20	0.29
2	0.00	−0.41	0.29	−0.35	0.20	−0.29
3	0.35	0.20	0.29	0.00	−0.41	−0.29
4	0.35	0.20	−0.29	0.00	−0.41	0.29
5	−0.35	0.20	−0.29	0.35	0.20	0.29
6	0.00	−0.41	0.29	−0.35	0.20	−0.29
7	0.00	−0.41	−0.29	−0.35	0.20	0.29
8	0.35	0.20	−0.29	0.00	−0.41	0.29
9	−0.35	0.20	0.29	0.35	0.20	−0.29
10	0.00	−0.41	−0.29	−0.35	0.20	0.29
11	0.35	0.20	0.29	0.00	−0.41	−0.29
12	−0.35	0.20	0.29	0.35	0.20	−0.29

The major contribution of Street and Burgess, however, has been to derive a method that can be used to locate the optimal design under the above set of assumptions without having to resort to complex (iterative) algorithms. This involves first determining the maximum value of the determinant of the AVC matrix. To do this, they first calculate the value M_k, which represents the largest number of pairs of alternatives that can assume different levels for each attribute, k, in a choice situation. This value for each attribute k, can be established using Equation (6C.5). Note that the particular formula to adopt to calculate M_k is a function of the number of alternatives in the design, J, and the number of levels of attribute k, L_k:

$$
M_k = \begin{cases}
(J^2 - 1)/4, & L_k = 2,\ J\ \text{odd}, \\
J^2/4, & L_k = 2,\ J\ \text{even}, \\
\left(J^2 - (L_k x^2 + 2 \times 7 + y)\right)/2, & 2 \leq L_k \leq J, \\
J(J - 1)/2, & L_k \geq J.
\end{cases}
\tag{6C.5}
$$

and x and y are positive integers that satisfy the equation $J = L_k x + y$ for $0 \leq y \leq L_k$. For the case where an attribute has levels $2 \leq L_k \leq J$, the analyst will need to fit integer values for y between zero and L_k to obtain values of x that satisfies this equation. Any value of y that results in an integer value of x represents a possible candidate for the design.

Once the value of M_k has been established for each attribute, the maximum value of the determinant of C is calculated as:

$$
\det(C_{\max}) = \prod_{k=1}^{K} \left(\frac{2M_k}{J^2(L_k - 1)\prod_{i \neq k} L_i} \right)^{L_k - 1} \times 100.
\tag{6C.6}
$$

Equation (6C.6) provides a measure, as a percentage, as to how optimal a design is under the specific assumptions outlined above; that is, the design is constructed assuming an *MNL* model specification, using *orthonormal coding* with *locally optimal priors* for *generic* parameters equal to *zero*. Unfortunately, in a case of selectively choosing criteria to promote one design paradigm over another, the measure has been incorrectly applied by some to infer that designs generated under different sets of assumptions are not optimal. That is, that these equations should only be used to optimize designs under the specific conditions that the equations were derived for, and not to infer anything about designs generated under other sets of assumptions.

6C.7 Kanninen (2002, 2005)

In 2002, Kanninen independently rediscovered the fact that optimal designs generated under the assumption of an *MNL* model specification with *non-zero local priors* for *generic* parameter estimates and restricted to two alternatives tended to retrieve specific non-balanced choice probabilities. As with the work of the Leeds group, Kanninen was able to show analytically that utility or probability balance in choice tasks represented an undesirable property, and in doing so suggested rules that minimized the variance of estimates in an optimal manner, based on desirable choice probabilities or what the Leeds group referred to as "Magic P's." Kanninen (2002) proposed a design approach where $K - 1$ attribute levels are first generated for the *two* alternatives, typically using an orthogonal design or Street and Burgess design. The last Kth attribute for each alternative is then generated as a *continuous variable* (usually a price attribute). The values of these continuous variables are chosen such that the choice probabilities take certain values that minimize the elements of the AVC matrix under the assumption of non-zero prior parameters.

Although the boundary value method of the Leeds group is somewhat different in derivation, the implications remain the same, and similar results are achieved. The main differences between the two methods, however, lie in the fact that the designs generated by the Leeds group were constructed so as to minimize the variances of the ratios of two parameters (i.e., dealing with WTP issues), whereas the approach adopted by Kanninen works directly with the variances of the parameter estimates using the *D-error* measure. Another difference between the two approaches is that the Leeds group promoted the idea of having all the attributes of the design treated as continuous (given transport applications where the attributes often considered are times and costs, this is possible), while Kanninen designs tend to allow only one attribute to be treated as continuous (again, this is in line with the literature where these designs have been applied, marketing and environmental economics in which many of the attributes are qualitative in nature and it makes little to no sense to allow them to be shown to respondents as a continuous attribute level).

Kanninen (2002) and Johnson *et al.* (2006) have determined the desirable probabilities for a limited number of designs (i.e., those involving two alternatives; see Table 6C.2).

One concern with these designs, however, is that they are optimal for the parameter priors assumed. While this is true of other designs, the values that the continuous variables take are particularly sensitive in terms of the priors assumed, and may change markedly given different parameter estimates. Thus, Kanninen (2002) recommends a continual process of updating the design once data is collected and more likely parameter estimates obtained.

6C.8 Bliemer, Rose, and Scarpa (2005 to current)

Writing in the transportation and environmental economics literature, Bliemer, Rose, and Scarpa have sought to extend the theory of experimental

Table 6C.2 Optimal choice probability values for specific designs

Number of attributes (K)	Number of unique choice situations in the design	Optimal choice–percentage split for two-alternative model
2	2	0.82 / 0.18
3	4	0.77 / 0.23
4	4	0.74 / 0.26
5	8	0.72 / 0.28
6	8	0.70 / 0.30
7	8	0.68 / 0.32
8	8	0.67 / 0.33

Source: Adapted from Johnson *et al.* 2006.

design to more advanced discrete choice models, as well as address issues related to the sample size requirements for these types of studies. In 2004, Rose and Bliemer began by examining the impact that relaxing the assumption of orthogonality has on the performance of logit models, in particular *MNL* models assuming *non-zero local priors* (Rose and Bliemer 2004). In line with earlier work, they concluded that orthogonality as a design principle did not appear to be a desirable property for the non-linear logit models. Bliemer and Rose (2005b) next sought to extend the methods advocated by Bunch *et al.* (1996) for MNL model specifications assuming *non-zero local priors* to allow for *alternative specific* and *generic* parameter estimates. Concurrently, Bliemer and Rose (2005a) and Rose and Bliemer (2005) turned their attention towards issues of sample size requirements for SC experiments. Throughout this work, *fixed attribute levels* were assumed in the design generation process.

Bliemer and Rose pointed out that the AVC matrix for discrete choice models is inversely related to the square root of the sample size N. As such, the analyst can calculate the values contained within the AVC matrix for any sample size, simply by determining the AVC for a single respondent and then dividing the resulting matrix by $\sqrt{N}$. Using this relationship, Figure 6C.4 reveals the consequences of investing in larger sample sizes for a given design X^I. While initial gains can be achieved in terms of improvements to the expected asymptotic standard errors achieved from models estimated based on the design from adding more respondents, such improvements occur at a diminishing rate until each additional respondent added will have only a marginal impact on the expected asymptotic standard errors. Hence, increasing the sample size beyond a certain limit will typically have little impact on the statistical significance of the parameter estimates achieved from SC

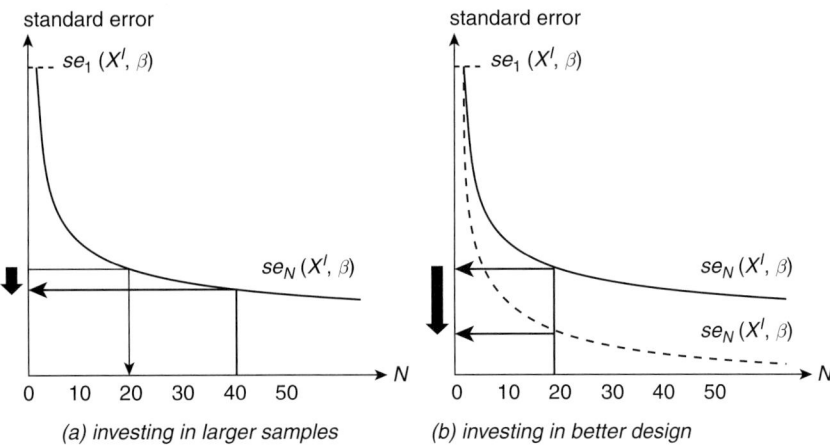

Figure 6C.4 Comparison of investing in larger sample sizes versus more efficient designs

studies. Figure 6C.4b reveals the impact for a given set of population parameters of investing in a better design X^{II} (i.e., more efficient design). Typically,
larger decreases in the standard error can be achieved by investing in finding a
more efficient design than by investing in a larger sample. Note that the
relationships shown in Figure 6C.4 are an inescapable property of the logit
model; however, the rate of decline represented in the curve will be specific to
the design.

Given the above, Bliemer and Rose were able to use this relationship to
provide an insight into the sample size requirements for SC experiments.
Seeing that the square roots of the diagonal elements of the AVC matrix
represent the asymptotic standard errors for the parameter estimates, and the
asymptotic t-ratios are simply the parameter estimates divided by the asymptotic standard errors (Equation (6C.7)), it is possible to determine the likely
asymptotic t-ratios for a design assuming a set of prior parameter estimates:

$$t_k = \frac{\beta_k}{\sqrt{\sigma_k^2/N}}. \tag{6C.7}$$

Rearranging Equation (6C.7):

$$N_k = \frac{t_k^2 \sigma_k^2}{\beta_k}. \tag{6C.8}$$

Equation (6C.8) allows for a determination of the sample size required for
each parameter to achieve a minimum asymptotic t-ratio, assuming a set of

non-zero prior parameter values. To use these equations, the analyst might use the prior parameters used in generating the design, or test the sample size requirements under various prior parameter mis-specifications. Once the sample size is determined for all attributes, the analyst can then select the sample size that will be expected to result in all asymptotic *t*-ratios taking a minimum pre-specified value (e.g., 1.96). Such designs are called *S-efficient* designs. Bliemer and Rose noted, however, that sample sizes calculated using this method should be considered as an absolute theoretical minimum. The method assumes certain asymptotic properties that may not hold in small samples. Further, the method does not consider the stability of the parameter estimates, nor at what sample size parameter stability is likely to be achieved. Comparing samples sizes using Equation (6C.8) for different parameters may also give an indication which parameters will be more difficult to estimate (at a certain level of significance) than other parameters.

Rose and Bliemer (2006) next extended the theory of SC designs to include covariates in the utility functions and hence also in the AVC matrices of the designs. Assuming an *MNL* model with *non-zero local priors* and combinations of *alternative-specific* and *generic parameters*, they were able to demonstrate a method capable of jointly minimizing the elements of the AVC matrix while determining the optimal number of respondents to sample from different segments. This was accomplished by determining optimal weights to apply to different segments of the Fisher Information matrix based on how many respondents belong to each segment.

Rose *et al.* (2008) next looked at SC studies requiring pivot (or customized) designs where the levels of the design alternatives are represented as percentage differences from some pre-specified respondent-specific status quo alternative, rather than as specific pre-defined levels chosen by the analyst. Again, assuming an *MNL* model specification with *non-zero local priors* and combinations of *alternative-specific* and *generic parameters*, they explored a number of design procedures capable of optimizing designs at the individual respondent level.

Meanwhile, Ferrini and Scarpa (2007), writing in the environmental economics literature, extended the optimal design theory to *panel error component* models assuming *non-zero local priors* and *fixed attribute levels*. In considering the panel version of the model, this paper represented a significant leap forward in the theory of SC experimental design, as it was the first to consider the issue of within respondent preference correlations which theoretically exist over repeated choice tasks. Unlike earlier papers, however, Ferrini and Scarpa used simulation to derive the AVC matrix of the model rather than more common analytical derivations.

Scarpa and Rose (2008) looked at various design strategies assuming an *MNL* model specification with *non-zero local priors* and *generic parameters*. Unaware of the earlier work of the Leeds group, they also used the delta method to derive the variance of the ratio of two parameters and advocated optimizing on this measure if WTP was the primary concern of the study.

Bliemer *et al.* (2009) next applied experimental design theories assuming *non-zero local priors* with designs assuming *fixed attribute levels* in order to estimate *nested logit (NL)* models. They were able to show that designs generated assuming an MNL model specification do not necessarily perform well when the "true" scale parameter of the data is assumed to move further from 1.0.

In 2010, Bliemer and Rose were able to analytically derive the AVC matrix for the *panel version of the MMNL* model. Via a number of case studies involving both *non-zero local priors* and *Bayesian priors* together with both *alternative-specific* and *generic parameters*, they were able to compare the design efficiencies for designs generated assuming MNL, cross-sectional MMNL and panel MMNL model specifications. They found that designs generated specifically for MNL model and panel MMNL model specifications performed similarly; however, designs generated for a cross-sectional MMNL specification were very different in terms of the resulting statistical efficiency and sample size requirements (see Bliemer and Rose 2010a).

One criticism often leveled at those advocating the generation of the efficient design approach to SC studies is the need to know in advance the precise econometric model that will be estimated once the data has been collected. There unfortunately exist many forms of possible discrete choice models that analysts may wish to estimate once SC data has been collected (e.g., MNL, NL, GEV, MMNL). Unfortunately, the LL functions of different model types are typically different from each other, and given that the AVC matrix for such models is mathematically given as the inverse of the second derivatives of the model's LL function, the AVC matrix for each type of model will also therefore be different. As such, the construction of efficient designs requires not only an assumption as to the parameter priors assumed, but also what AVC matrix the analyst is attempting to optimize.

Given differences in the AVC matrices of different discrete choice models, attempts at minimizing the elements of the AVC matrix assuming one model may not necessarily minimize the elements of the AVC matrix of another model. Similar to the problem involving knowledge of the parameter estimates with certainty (given by local priors), the analyst is unlikely to know precisely what model is likely to be estimated in advance. The problem then becomes one of having to select the most likely model that will be estimated once data has been collected. To address this specific issue, Rose *et al.* (2009) advocated the use of a model averaging approach, where different weights could be applied to the Fisher Information matrices obtained assuming different model specifications given a common design. Included in the model averaging process were MNL, cross-sectional error components and MMNL, and panel error components and MMNL model specifications.

More recently, Rose *et al.* (2011) sought to extend upon the earlier research originating from both the Leeds group and Kanninen to a wider range of SC problems. Unfortunately, they found that it was only possible to derive the optimal choice probabilities for designs generated under the assumption of a MNL model specification involving two alternatives and *non-zero local priors* parameters and *generic parameter* estimates. To overcome this limitation, they demonstrated how the Nelder–Mead algorithm could be used to locate the optimal choice probabilities for any model type with any number of alternatives and any type of prior parameters, including non-zero Bayesian priors. In contrast to the case with two alternatives and all generic parameters, fixed Magic Ps do not seem to exist for this more general case.

6C.9 Kessels, Goos, Vandebroek, and Yu (2006 to current)

Research groups centered at the Universities of Antwerp and Leuven have also been active in promoting the application of experimental design theory in the generation of SC experiments. A significant proportion of the work originating from this group deals specifically with algorithms for generating these types of designs and are hence beyond the scope of this current chapter (see, e.g., Kessels *et al.* 2006, 2009 and Yu *et al.* 2008). However, this group has also been actively looking at other areas of SC experimental design theory. In particular, they have examined designs for the cross-sectional MMNL model under *non-zero Bayesian priors* and *generic parameters* (see Yu *et al.* 2009) as well as designs generated for *NL* models including *no-choice alternatives* under the assumption of *non-zero Bayesian priors* (see Vermeulen *et al.* 2008). Yu *et al.* (2006) also looked at efficient designs assuming non-zero priors for both main and interaction effects. This group has also addressed issues related to interaction effects assuming an *MNL* model specification and *non-zero Bayesian priors*. Finally, this group has actively examined a wide range of design criteria beyond the *D-error* statistic, including *G-* and *V-*error measures which are designed to minimize the prediction error variance. A closer examination of these measures, however, demonstrates that they still work with the AVC matrix, and while they might not lead to designs that will minimize the standard errors obtained from the design, they do remain consistent with the general theory of experimental design.

One acknowledged limitation of the current chapter lies in the way that we have attempted to present the outputs of the various research groups in chronological order of publication. Unfortunately, such an approach need not reflect the true history of the research efforts of those involved in this field. The issue lies in the variable length of time that it takes for academic research to be published, which admittedly may be longer in some disciplines than others. Further, we have attempted where possible to reference formally published work over working papers, which may distort the true chronology of events. For example, the work by Rose *et al.* (2009) advocating the use of a model averaging process in generating designs when the final model type is unknown also employs designs generated for panel MMNL model specifications, prior to publication of the paper by Bliemer and Rose (2010a) specifically dealing with panel MMNL model designs. This is because the 2010a paper has as its origins a 2008 conference paper originally written in 2007, whereas the 2009 paper remains a conference paper. Likewise, the Bunch *et al.* (1996) paper was originally written in 1994; however, the final working paper that is now available dates from 1996. As such, we ask that care be taken in interpreting the exact timeline of events.

7 Statistical inference

7.1 Introduction

This chapter will discuss some issues in statistical inference in the analysis of choice models. We are concerned with two kinds of computations, hypothesis tests and **variance estimation**. To illustrate the analyses, we will work through an example based on a *revealed preference (RP)* data set. In this chapter, we present syntax and output generated using Nlogit to demonstrate the concepts covered. The syntax and output is, for the more familiar reader, largely self-explanatory; however, for the less familiar reader, we refer you to Chapter 11, which you may wish to read before going further. The multinomial logit model for the study is shown in the following Nlogit set up which gives the utility functions for four travel modes: bus, train, busway and car, respectively:

```
;Model:
u(bs) = bs + actpt*act + invcpt*invc + invtpt*invt2 + egtpt*egt + trpt*trnf /
u(tn) = tn + actpt*act + invcpt*invc + invtpt*invt2 + egtpt*egt + trpt*trnf /
u(bw) = bw + actpt*act + invcpt*invc + invtpt*invt2 + egtpt*egt + trpt*trnf /
u(cr) =             TC*TC + PC*PC        + invtcar*invt + egtcar*egt
```

The attributes are act = access time, invc = in vehicle cost, invt2 = in vehicle time, egt = egress time, trnf = transfer wait time, tc = toll cost, pc = parking cost, and invt = in vehicle time for car. Where a particular example uses a method given in more detail in later chapters, we will provide a cross-reference.

7.2 Hypothesis tests

Hypothesis tests are carried out using a variety of methods appropriate for the situation. The most common tests compare *nested models*. These are cases in which one model is obtained by a restriction on the parameters of a (larger) model. A test of whether a specific parameter in a model equals zero is an example. The test of the MNL model as a restriction on the nested logit model, in which all of the inclusive parameters are restricted to equal one, is another example. Tests of *non-nested models* involve competing models in which neither model encompasses the other. Arguably, neither model is strictly "right" but it might be argued that one or the other is closer to the "truth." Two competing possible specifications of the tree in a nested logit setting might provide an example. Another case would be a competition between a **random utility maximization (RUM)** specification and a *random regret minimization* (RRM) model (see Chapter 8). Finally, *specification tests* involve the competition of a specified null model against a larger universe of alternative models. The **Hausman test** of the IIA assumption in a multinomial logit model against, generally, models that do not impose this assumption is a widely considered example.

7.2.1 Tests of nested models

Nested models are tested generally using one of three methodologies: likelihood ratio, Wald, and Lagrange multiplier (LM) tests. We examine them in turn.

7.2.1.1 Likelihood ratio test

Choice models are usually estimated by optimizing a criterion function such as a log-likelihood (LL), as explained in detail in Chapter 5. Modelers occasionally use the generalized method of moments (GMM) method instead, and there are also Bayesian MCMC applications. However, the method of maximum likelihood overwhelmingly dominates this subject area. Whatever criterion function is used for estimation, the function can be used as a device for testing the hypothesis of a restriction on a model. The general result is that the criterion function degrades when a restriction is imposed – the LL function goes down or the GMM quadratic form goes up. The test statistic is twice the difference in the criterion and has a Chi-squared distribution, with degrees of freedom equal to the number of restrictions (Equation 7.1):

$$LR = 2(\log L \,|\, \text{unrestricted model} - \log L \,|\, \text{restricted model}). \qquad (7.1)$$

Note that the test requires that the restricted model have a smaller number of free parameters. The multinomial logit model, for example, is a special case of the nested logit model where all of the inclusive value parameters are equal to one. To illustrate the likelihood-ratio test (LRT), we will test for a nesting structure in our choice model (see Chapter 14 for nested logit models). Full results and the set up appear below. The LL for the nested logit is −199.25552. The LL for the MNL is −200.40253. Twice the difference is the estimated Chi-squared statistic, which is only 2.294. With two degrees of freedom, the critical value (95 percent) is 5.99. So the hypothesis of the MNL model is not rejected by this test. The LL function for the nested logit model is not significantly larger than that for the MNL model:

```
? LR Test of MNL vs. nested logit
? This first model is a nested logit model.
? Note the tree definition after the list of choices (see Chapter 14 for
details)
NLOGIT
;lhs = choice, cset, altij
;choices = bs,tn,bw,cr
;tree=bwtn(bw,tn),bscar(bs,cr)
;model:
u(bs) = bs + actpt*act + invcpt*invc + invtpt*invt2 + egtpt*egt + trpt*trnf /
u(tn) = tn + actpt*act + invcpt*invc + invtpt*invt2 + egtpt*egt + trpt*trnf /
u(bw) = bw+ actpt*act + invcpt*invc + invtpt*invt2 + egtpt*egt + trpt*trnf /
u(cr) = invtcar*invt + TC*TC + PC*PC + egtcar*egt
? Capture the unrestricted log likelihood
CALC ; llnested = logl $
? This second model is a simple MNL model - note no tree definition.
NLOGIT
;lhs = choice, cset, altij
;choices = bs,tn,bw,cr
;model:
u(bs) = bs + actpt*act + invcpt*invc + invtpt*invt2 + egtpt*egt + trpt*trnf /
u(tn) = tn + actpt*act + invcpt*invc + invtpt*invt2 + egtpt*egt + trpt*trnf /
u(bw) = bw+ actpt*act + invcpt*invc + invtpt*invt2 + egtpt*egt + trpt*trnf /
u(cr)     =     invtcar*invt    +      TC*TC     +    PC*PC  + egtcar*egt $
? Capture the restricted log likelihood, then compute the statistic.
? The Ctb(..) function in CALC reports the 95% critical value for the
? chi squared with two degrees of freedom.
CALC ; loglmnl = logl $
CALC ; List ; LRTest = 2*(llnested-loglmnl) ; Ctb(0.95,2) $
```

The estimation results for this test are shown below. For convenience, some of the computer generated output is omitted:

```
-------------------------------------------------------------------------------
FIML Nested Multinomial Logit Model
Dependent variable                  CHOICE
Log likelihood function      -199.25552   ←
Response data are given as ind. choices
Estimation based on N =    197,   K = 14
Response data are given as ind. choices
Number of obs.=   197, skipped    0 obs
```

CHOICE	Coefficient	Standard Error	z	Prob. $\|z\|>Z*$	95% Confidence Interval	
	Attributes in the Utility Functions (beta)					
BS	-1.66524**	.80355	-2.07	.0382	-3.24017	-.09030
ACTPT	-.07931***	.02623	-3.02	.0025	-.13071	-.02791
INVCPT	-.06125	.05594	-1.09	.2735	-.17089	.04839
INVTPT	-.01362	.00936	-1.45	.1457	-.03197	.00473
EGTPT	-.04509**	.02235	-2.02	.0437	-.08890	-.00128
TRPT	-1.40080***	.46030	-3.04	.0023	-2.30297	-.49863
TN	-3.90899	2.80641	-1.39	.1637	-9.40946	1.59148
BW	-4.26044	2.91116	-1.46	.1433	-9.96621	1.44533
INVTCAR	-.04768***	.01232	-3.87	.0001	-.07183	-.02354
TC	-.11493	.08296	-1.39	.1659	-.27752	.04766
PC	-.01771	.01906	-.93	.3527	-.05507	.01965
EGTCAR	-.05896*	.03316	-1.78	.0754	-.12395	.00603
	IV parameters, tau(b|l,r),sigma(l|r),phi(r)					
BWTN	.55619**	.26662	2.09	.0370	.03363	1.07874
BSCAR	.99522***	.24722	4.03	.0001	.51069	1.47976

Discrete choice (multinomial logit) model
Dependent variable   Choice
Log likelihood function   -200.40253   ←
Estimation based on N =   197,   K = 12

CHOICE	Coefficient	Standard Error	z	Prob. $\|z\|>Z*$	95% Confidence Interval	
BS	-1.87740**	.74583	-2.52	.0118	-3.33920	-.41560
ACTPT	-.06036***	.01844	-3.27	.0011	-.09650	-.02423
INVCPT	-.08571*	.04963	-1.73	.0842	-.18299	.01157
INVTPT	-.01106	.00822	-1.35	.1782	-.02716	.00504
EGTPT	-.04117**	.02042	-2.02	.0438	-.08119	-.00114
TRPT	-1.15503***	.39881	-2.90	.0038	-1.93668	-.37338
TN	-1.67343**	.73700	-2.27	.0232	-3.11791	-.22894
BW	-1.87376**	.73750	-2.54	.0111	-3.31924	-.42828
INVTCAR	-.04963***	.01166	-4.26	.0000	-.07249	-.02677
TC	-.11063	.08471	-1.31	.1916	-.27666	.05540
PC	-.01789	.01796	-1.00	.3192	-.05310	.01731
EGTCAR	-.05806*	.03309	-1.75	.0793	-.12291	.00679

[CALC] LRTEST = 2.2940253
[CALC]   = 5.9914645

7.2.1.2 Wald test

The coefficients of the model are estimated without imposing the restrictions of the **null hypothesis**. The *Wald distance* is a measure of the distance of the estimated parameters from the hypothesized values. A familiar example is the simple *t* test of how far an estimated parameter is from zero (or, in the case of nested logit, how far the inclusive parameter estimate is from 1.0). The **Wald statistic** is computed as a quadratic form in the distance of the parameters from the null hypothesis using the inverse of the appropriate covariance matrix. The statistic has a Chi-squared distribution with degrees of freedom equal to the number of restrictions.

The Wald statistic is computed as follows. The full parameter vector for the model is denoted β. For simplicity, we do not distinguish among the different types of parameters in the model, such as the utility parameters versus the inclusive value parameters in a nested logit model. Let **b** denote the estimator of β, and let **V** denote the estimated asymptotic covariance matrix for **b**. The hypothesis of the restrictions is:

$$H_0 : \mathbf{R}\beta - \mathbf{q} = \mathbf{0}, \tag{7.2}$$

where **R** is a matrix of constants, with each row being the parameters in a constraint, and **q** is a vector of constants. The alternative hypothesis is "not the null." The Wald statistic is:

$$W = (\mathbf{Rb} - \mathbf{q})'[\mathbf{RVR}']^{-1}(\mathbf{Rb} - \mathbf{q}). \tag{7.3}$$

In some cases, the Wald test is built into software such as NLOGIT. In others, you would use matrix algebra to obtain the result. NLOGIT contains a **WALD** command that allows you to specify the constraints (they may be non-linear as well) and that does the matrix algebra for you. In the example below, we use **WALD**, and then show how to use matrix algebra to obtain the same result.

The command below specifies a nested logit model as per Chapter 14. The inclusive value (IV) parameters are the 13th and 14th in the estimated parameter vector. In Section 7.2.1, we used a likelihood ratio to test the null hypothesis that both parameters equal one. We now test the hypothesis using **WALD**, and using matrix algebra:

```
Nlogit
;lhs = choice, cset, altij
;choices = bs,tn,bw,cr
;model:
u(bs) = bs + actpt*act + invcpt*invc + invtpt*invt2 + egtpt*egt + trpt*trnf /
u(tn) = tn + actpt*act + invcpt*invc + invtpt*invt2 + egtpt*egt + trpt*trnf /
u(bw) = bw+ actpt*act + invcpt*invc + invtpt*invt2 + egtpt*egt + trpt*trnf /
u(cr) = invtcar*invt + TC*TC + PC*PC + egtcar*egt
;tree=bwtn(bw,tn),bscar(bs,cr)$
```

```
? Wald Test
WALD ; parameters = b ; labels = 12_c,ivbwtn,ivbscar
? in the above line, there are 12 parameters plus 2 IV parameters
 ; covariance = varb
 ; fn1 = ivbwtn-1 ; fn2 = ivbscar - 1 $
? Same computation using matrix algebra
MATRIX ; R = [0,0,0,0,0,0,0,0,0,0,0,0,1,0 / 0,0,0,0,0,0,0,0,0,0,0,0,0,1] ;
q=[1/1] $
MATRIX ; m = R*b - q ; vm = R*Varb*R' ; list ; w = m'<vm>m $
```

FIML Nested Multinomial Logit Model
Dependent variable   CHOICE
-----------+---

	Standard		Prob.	95% Confidence	
CHOICE	Coefficient	Error	z	|z|>Z*	Interval	
	Attributes in the Utility Functions (beta)					
BS|	-1.66524**	.80355	-2.07	.0382	-3.24017	-.09030
ACTPT|	-.07931***	.02623	-3.02	.0025	-.13071	-.02791
INVCPT|	-.06125	.05594	-1.09	.2735	-.17089	.04839
INVTPT|	-.01362	.00936	-1.45	.1457	-.03197	.00473
EGTPT|	-.04509**	.02235	-2.02	.0437	-.08890	-.00128
TRPT|	-1.40080***	.46030	-3.04	.0023	-2.30297	-.49863
TN|	-3.90899	2.80641	-1.39	.1637	-9.40946	1.59148
BW|	-4.26044	2.91116	-1.46	.1433	-9.96621	1.44533
INVTCAR|	-.04768***	.01232	-3.87	.0001	-.07183	-.02354
TC|	-.11493	.08296	-1.39	.1659	-.27752	.04766
PC|	-.01771	.01906	-.93	.3527	-.05507	.01965
EGTCAR|	-.05896*	.03316	-1.78	.0754	-.12395	.00603
	IV parameters, tau(b|1,r),sigma(1|r),phi(r)					
BWTN|	.55619**	.26662	2.09	.0370	.03363	1.07874
BSCAR|	.99522***	.24722	4.03	.0001	.51069	1.47976

-----------+---
WALD procedure. Estimates and standard errors for nonlinear functions and
joint test of nonlinear restrictions.
Wald Statistic   =   3.01209
Prob. from Chi-squared[2] =   .22179
Functions are computed at means of variables
-----------+---

	Standard		Prob.	95% Confidence	
WaldFcns	Function	Error	z	|z|>Z*	Interval	
Fncn(1)|	-.44381*	.26662	-1.66	.0960	-.96637	.07874
Fncn(2)|	-.00478	.24722	-.02	.9846	-.48931	.47976

===========+---

	W|	1
-----------+--------------
| | 1\| | 3.01209 |

The Wald statistic, 3.01209, appears at the top of the results for the **WALD** command. As before, the critical value with two degrees of freedom is 5.99, so the Wald test does not reject the hypothesis of the MNL model either. The P value given can be used to assess the significance level of the test. Since we are testing at the $\alpha = 5$ percent significance level, the P value of 0.22179, being larger than α, indicates that the null hypothesis should not be rejected. The last result shows that the same value for the Wald statistic can be computed using matrix algebra.

7.2.1.3 Lagrange multiplier test

When the model is estimated without imposing the restrictions of the hypothesis, the derivatives of the criterion function (usually the LL) will equal zero at the optimizer. If the restrictions of the hypothesis are imposed during the estimation, the derivatives of the full model will no longer equal zero at the restricted optimizer. The Lagrange multiplier (LM) test is a test of the hypothesis that these derivatives are actually "close" to zero. It is a Wald statistic based on the derivatives of the criterion function. The LM statistic is a Chi-squared statistic with degrees of freedom equal to the number of restrictions.

In most cases in which one might use the LM test, the LRT can also be computed. The LM statistic requires computation of the full model at the restricted parameter estimates, which means that the full model can be computed. The test is most useful when the full model is difficult to estimate. In all choice models in Chapter 4, we are generally able to employ the LRT.

Nlogit provides a generic device for carrying out LM tests. One provides the restricted estimates as the starting values for the estimator, then instructs the program not to compute any iterations away from the starting values by stating **;Maxit = 0** in the estimation command. In the next example, we will once again test the hypothesis of the MNL model against the alternative of a nested logit model. The results shown below present the estimates of the nested logit model when the two IV parameters are constrained to equal one. Recall, the LR statistic for this hypothesis is 2.294 and the Wald statistic is 3.012. The LM statistic computed below is 2.221. This is also a Chi-squared test with two degrees of freedom, so the hypothesis of the MNL is not rejected, again:

```
Nlogit
;lhs = choice, cset, altij
;choices = bs,tn,bw,cr
;model:
u(bs) = bs + actpt*act + invcpt*invc + invtpt*invt2 + egtpt*egt + trpt*trnf /
```

```
u(tn) = tn + actpt*act + invcpt*invc + invtpt*invt2 + egtpt*egt + trpt*trnf /
u(bw) = bw+ actpt*act + invcpt*invc + invtpt*invt2 + egtpt*egt + trpt*trnf /
u(cr) = invtcar*invt + TC*TC + PC*PC + egtcar*egt $
Nlogit
;lhs = choice, cset, altij
;choices = bs,tn,bw,cr
;tree=bwtn(bw,tn),bscar(bs,cr)
;model:
u(bs) = bs + actpt*act + invcpt*invc + invtpt*invt2 + egtpt*egt + trpt*trnf /
u(tn) = tn + actpt*act + invcpt*invc + invtpt*invt2 + egtpt*egt + trpt*trnf /
u(bw) = bw+ actpt*act + invcpt*invc + invtpt*invt2 + egtpt*egt + trpt*trnf /
u(cr) = invtcar*invt + TC*TC + PC*PC + egtcar*egt
;start= b,1,1 ; maxit=0$
```

```
FIML Nested Multinomial Logit Model
Dependent variable                    CHOICE
LM Stat. at start values              2.22071   ←
LM statistic kept as scalar           LMSTAT
Number of obs.= 197, skipped        0  obs
```
-----------+--

CHOICE	Coefficient	Standard Error	z	Prob. |z|>Z*	95% Confidence Interval	
	Attributes in the Utility Functions (beta)					
BS	−1.87740**	.83515	−2.25	.0246	−3.51426	−.24055
ACTPT	−.06036***	.02329	−2.59	.0095	−.10601	−.01472
INVCPT	−.08571**	.03648	−2.35	.0188	−.15721	−.01420
INVTPT	−.01106	.00951	−1.16	.2447	−.02969	.00757
EGTPT	−.04117**	.01715	−2.40	.0164	−.07478	−.00755
TRPT	−1.15503***	.44365	−2.60	.0092	−2.02456	−.28550
TN	−1.67343	1.21664	−1.38	.1690	−4.05801	.71115
BW	−1.87376	1.27169	−1.47	.1406	−4.36623	.61872
INVTCAR	−.04963***	.01461	−3.40	.0007	−.07827	−.02099
TC	−.11063	.08912	−1.24	.2145	−.28531	.06405
PC	−.01789	.02130	−.84	.4009	−.05964	.02385
EGTCAR	−.05806*	.03207	−1.81	.0703	−.12091	.00480
	IV parameters, tau(b|l,r),sigma(l|r),phi(r)					
BWTN	1.0***	.36193	2.76	.0057	.29063D+00	.17094D+01
BSCAR	1.0***	.25775	3.88	.0001	.49482D+00	.15052D+01

-----------+--

7.2.2 Tests of non-nested models

There is relatively little general methodology for testing non-nested models. A result that is used in some circumstances was developed by Vuong (1989). Consider two competing models to be estimated by maximum likelihood. For the two models, labeled "*A*" and "*B*," the LL functions are the sums of the individual contributions:

$$\log L^j = \sum_{i=1}^{N} \log L_i|j, \; j = A, B. \tag{7.4}$$

We consider the individual differences, $v_i = (\log L_i|A) - (\log L_i|B)$. Note that if model B was nested within model A, then $2\sum_{i=1}^{N} v_i$ would be the LR statistic for testing the null hypothesis of model B against the alternative of model A. However, in this case, the models are not nested. The Vuong statistic is:

$$V = \frac{\bar{v}}{s_v/\sqrt{N}}, \; \bar{v} = \frac{\sum_{i=1}^{N} v_i}{N}, \; s_v = \sqrt{\frac{\sum_{i=1}^{N}(v_i - \bar{v})^2}{N-1}}. \tag{7.5}$$

Thus, V is the standard t statistic that is used to test the null hypothesis that $E[v_i] = 0$. s_v is the sample standard deviation, and $\bar{v}$ is the average of the LR statistics across the sample. Under the assumptions needed to justify use of the statistic, the large sample distribution of V is standard normal. Under the hypothesis of model A, V will be positive. If sufficiently large, i.e., greater than 1.96, the test favors model A. If V is sufficiently negative, i.e., less than −1.96, the test favors model B. The range between −1.96 and +1.96 is inconclusive (at the 5 percent significance level).

Consider two competing nested logit models:

```
?;tree=bwtn(bw,tn),bscar(bs,cr)
?;tree=Bus(bs,bw),trncar(tn,cr)
u(bs) = bs + actpt*act + invcpt*invc + invtpt*invt2 + egtpt*egt + trpt*trnf /
u(tn) = tn + actpt*act + invcpt*invc + invtpt*invt2 + egtpt*egt + trpt*trnf /
u(bw) = bw + actpt*act + invcpt*invc + invtpt*invt2 + egtpt*egt + trpt*trnf /
u(cr) = invtcar*invt + TC*TC + PC*PC + egtcar*egt
```

The two proposed models involve the same parameters, though a different structure for the tree. The results are shown below. The test results superficially favor the second tree structure; V is negative. But the value of the test statistic, −0.391, is squarely in the inconclusive region. We note that the LL for the first model is slightly larger. But this is not definitive when the models are non-nested; nor does it imply the direction of the outcome of the Vuong test. Results are shown only for the test itself. Estimated models are omitted for convenience:

```
NLOGIT
;lhs = choice, cset, altij
;choices = bs,tn,bw,cr
;model:
u(bs) = bs + actpt*act + invcpt*invc + invtpt*invt2 + egtpt*egt + trpt*trnf /
u(tn) = tn + actpt*act + invcpt*invc + invtpt*invt2 + egtpt*egt + trpt*trnf /
u(bw) = bw+ actpt*act + invcpt*invc + invtpt*invt2 + egtpt*egt + trpt*trnf /
u(cr) = invtcar*invt + TC*TC + PC*PC + egtcar*egt
;tree=bwtn(bw,tn),bscar(bs,cr) $
CREATE ; llmdl1 = logl_obs $
NLOGIT
;lhs = choice, cset, altij
;choices = bs,tn,bw,cr
;model:
u(bs) = bs + actpt*act + invcpt*invc + invtpt*invt2 + egtpt*egt + trpt*trnf /
u(tn) = tn + actpt*act + invcpt*invc + invtpt*invt2 + egtpt*egt + trpt*trnf /
u(bw) = bw+ actpt*act + invcpt*invc + invtpt*invt2 + egtpt*egt + trpt*trnf /
u(cr) = invtcar*invt + TC*TC + PC*PC + egtcar*egt
;tree=Bus(bs,bw),trncar(tn,cr) $
CREATE ; LLmdl2 = logl_obs$
CREATE ; dll = llmdl1 - llmdl2 $
CALC ; for[choice=1];list;dbar = xbr(dll)$
CALC ; for[choice=1];list;sd=sdv(dll)$
CALC ; list ; v = sqr(197)*dbar/sd$
```

Results of the test are inconclusive.

[CALC]	DBAR	=	-.0043908
[CALC]	SD	=	.1575719
[CALC]	V	=	-.3911076

In the second example below, we consider the RUM and RRM models as competing models. The Vuong test, however, is inconclusive once again. This is the set up for testing RUM versus RRM. The evidence vaguely favors RUM – the test statistic is positive, which favors the first model – but the test is inconclusive – the value is only 0.155:

```
NLOGIT
;lhs = choice, cset, altij
;choices = bs,tn,bw,cr ?/0.2,0.3,0.1,0.4
;model:
u(bs) = bs + actpt(0)*act + invcpt*invc + invtpt*invt2 + egtpt*egt + trpt*trnf /
u(tn) = tn + actpt*act + invcpt*invc + invtpt*invt2 + egtpt*egt + trpt*trnf /
u(bw) = bw+ actpt*act + invcpt*invc + invtpt*invt2 + egtpt*egt + trpt*trnf /
u(cr) = invtcar*invt + TC*TC + PC*PC + egtcar*egt $
CREATE ; llmnl=logl_obs $
RRLOGIT
... same model specification $
```

```
CREATE ; llrrm = logl_obs $
CREATE ; dll = llmnl - llrrm $
CALC ; for[choice=1];list; tst(dll,0) $
----------------------------------------------------------------------------
One sample t test of mean of DLL      =             .00000
----------------------------------------------------------------------------
Sample            Mean      Std. Dev.  Std. Error  Sample
DLL               .00085     .07740     .00551      197
95% Confidence interval for population mean
                  -.01002 to      .01173
Test statistic =     .155     P value =      .87737
Degrees of freedom   196   Critical value = 1.9721
----------------------------------------------------------------------------
```

7.2.3 Specification tests

Specification tests are typically based on a null hypothesis that is the specification of the model of interest against an alternative that is broadly and ambiguously defined. In choice modeling, the most familiar of these would be the Hausman test against the null hypothesis of the IIA assumptions of the MNL model. In this instance, the alternative hypothesis is the universe of candidate specifications that do not impose this feature. Another common specification test that is tangential to our discussion here is that of the normal distribution of the disturbance in certain models against the alternative of the universe of non-normal distributions.

Specification testing is generally carried out using a strategy designed for the purpose at hand. There is no omnibus procedure such as the Wald statistic in the case of nested models. The test that interests us here, the IIA test (see Chapter 4), is based on the availability of two different estimators of the *same model parameters* that should resemble each other if the null hypothesis is true, but will be statistically different if not. Consider the choice model:

```
NLOGIT
;lhs = choice, cset, altij
;choices = bs,tn,bw,cr
;model:
u(bs) = bs + actpt*act + invcpt*invc + invtpt*invt2 + egtpt*egt + trpt*trnf /
u(tn) = tn + actpt*act + invcpt*invc + invtpt*invt2 + egtpt*egt + trpt*trnf /
u(bw) = bw + actpt*act + invcpt*invc + invtpt*invt2 + egtpt*egt + trpt*trnf /
u(cr) = invtcar*invt + TC*TC + PC*PC + egtcar*egt $
```

Under the assumptions of the multinomial logit model, estimates of the generic parameters in the model, that is *actpt, invcpt, invtpt, egtpt,* and *trpt,* should be estimable in a choice model that does not include, for example, train (*tn*) as an alternative. If this choice were removed from the model, and all individuals who chose that alternative were removed from the sample, the remaining three choices with the associated data should be sufficient to estimate these same parameters. That is an implication of the MNL model. It will generally not be the case in other models, such as the multinomial probit model or any model that relaxes the IIA condition. The strategy, then, will be to estimate the model parameters under these two scenarios and use a Wald statistic to measure the difference. A remaining detail is to define how the covariance matrix for the difference is to be computed. Hausman's (1978) famous result (see Hausman and McFadden 1984), adapted for this application, is:

$$\text{Est.Var}[\mathbf{b}_0 - \mathbf{b}_1] = \begin{array}{l} \text{Variance of the estimator that uses less information} - \\ \text{Variance of the estimator that uses more information.} \end{array} \quad (7.6)$$

The following carries out this test. The model command is modified directly to remove the second alternative. The ;IAS = tn removes the observations from the sample. (These are flagged as the 46 "bad observations.") In computing a Hausman test, it is a good idea to check the definiteness of the covariance matrix. It is not guaranteed to be positive definite. When it is not, the test statistic is not valid. The MATRIX commands below list the characteristic roots of the matrix. As they are all positive, the test can proceed. The test statistic is Chi-squared with five degrees of freedom. The value is 16.11. The 95 percent critical value for the Chi-squared variable with five degrees of freedom is 11.07, so on this basis, the IIA assumption is rejected. This suggests that a nested logit structure might be tested since (as shown in Chapters 4 and 14), it permits relaxation of IIA between branches:

```
NLOGIT
 ;lhs = choice, cset, altij
 ;choices = bs,tn,bw,cr
 ;model:
 u(bs) = bs + actpt*act + invcpt*invc + invtpt*invt2 + egtpt*egt + trpt*trnf /
 u(tn) = tn + actpt*act + invcpt*invc + invtpt*invt2 + egtpt*egt + trpt*trnf /
 u(bw) = bw+ actpt*act + invcpt*invc + invtpt*invt2 + egtpt*egt + trpt*trnf /
 u(cr) = invtcar*invt + TC*TC + PC*PC + egtcar*egt $
MATRIX ; b1 = b(2:6) ; v1 = varb(2:6,2:6) $
?b(2:6) are the 5 generic parameters (noting 1=bs) actpt, invcpt, invtpt, egtpt and
trpt
NLOGIT
 ;lhs = choice, cset, altij
 ;choices = bs,tn,bw,cr
 ;model:
 u(bs) = bs + actpt*act + invcpt*invc + invtpt*invt2 + egtpt*egt + trpt*trnf /
```

```
u(bw) = bw+ actpt*act + invcpt*invc + invtpt*invt2 + egtpt*egt + trpt*trnf /
u(cr) = invtcar*invt + TC*TC + PC*PC + egtcar*egt
;ias=tn $
+---------------------------------------------------------------------------+
|WARNING:    Bad observations were found in the sample. |
|Found  46 bad observations among     197 individuals.  |
|You can use ;CheckData to get a list of these points.  |
+---------------------------------------------------------------------------+
MATRIX ; b0 = b(2:6) ; v0 = varb(2:6,2:6) $
MATRIX ; d = b0 - b1 ; vd = v0 - v1 $
MATRIX ; list ; root(vd)$
? varb(2:6,2:6) are rows 2-6 and columns 2-6 of varb.
?The matrix commands are carrying out a Hausman test. Since the matrix vd
?might not be positive definite - in a finite sample it might not be - it is necessary
?to check. Root(vd) computes the roots. If any are not positive, the Hausman
?test calculation is not valid.
   Result|              1
-------------+-----------------------
        1|         .288220
        2|         .00134785
        3|         .00108021
        4|        .311733E-03
        5|        .465482E-04
|-> matrix ; list ; d'<vd>d $
   Result|              1
-------------+-----------------------
        1|         16.1104
```

When the entire model is generic, Nlogit can carry out the test automatically (i.e., you do not have to include the matrix commands to identify the parameters of interest). The following shows, for example, a model in which only the public transport alternatives are included in the choice set, and the constant terms are removed from the utility functions. The "?" removes the line that defines the utility function for car from the command. In the first model, **;ias=cr** removes the drivers from the sample. In the second, **;ias=tn,cr** removes both drivers and those who choose the train. Since the model is now completely generic across the alternatives, the Hausman statistic can be computed by the program. The program reports a value of 6.8644, and a Chi-squared value with five degrees of freedom. The critical value is 11.07, as before. This implies that if we restrict attention to those who choose the public modes, the IIA assumption appears to be valid. Specifically this suggests that an MNL model is acceptable for the choice among the public transport alternatives *bs* and *bw*:

```
NLOGIT
...
;model:
u(bs) = actpt*act + invcpt*invc + invtpt*invt2 + egtpt*egt + trpt*trnf /
u(tn) = actpt*act + invcpt*invc + invtpt*invt2 + egtpt*egt + trpt*trnf /
u(bw) = actpt*act + invcpt*invc + invtpt*invt2 + egtpt*egt + trpt*trnf
?u(cr) = invtcar*invt + TC*TC + PC*PC + egtcar*egt
;ias=cr $
NLOGIT
...
;model:
u(bs) = actpt*act + invcpt*invc + invtpt*invt2 + egtpt*egt + trpt*trnf /
u(tn) = actpt*act + invcpt*invc + invtpt*invt2 + egtpt*egt + trpt*trnf /
u(bw) = actpt*act + invcpt*invc + invtpt*invt2 + egtpt*egt + trpt*trnf
?u(cr) = invtcar*invt + TC*TC + PC*PC + egtcar*egt
;ias=tn,cr $

------------------------------------------------------------------------------
Discrete choice (multinomial logit) model
Dependent variable            Choice
... results omitted ...
Number of obs.=   197, skipped  117 obs
Hausman test for IIA. Excluded choices are
TN       CR
ChiSqrd[ 5] =   6.8644, Pr(C>c) = .2309
-----------+------------------------------------------------------------------
```

7.3 Variance estimation

Statistical inference, such as some hypothesis tests, confidence intervals, and estimation generally, relies on computation of variances of estimators. There are several ways to proceed. The starting point is the estimator of the asymptotic covariance matrix of the estimator of the model parameters. We will focus on maximum likelihood estimation at this point and, for simplicity, the multinomial logit model. The principles are general, however. This topic is of great relevance to analysts who wish to obtain WTP estimates and need to establish the standard errors and confidence intervals associated with the mean estimates. Central to this activity is the information obtained from a variance-covariance matrix of parameter estimates.

We discuss various appropriate approaches below.

7.3.1 Conventional estimation

The LL for the MNL model (see Chapter 4) is:

$$\log L(\beta) = \sum_{i=1}^{N}\sum_{j=1}^{J} d_{ij}\log P(\beta, x_{ij}), \tag{7.7}$$

where $P(\beta,x_{ij})$ is the multinomial logit probability for outcome j and $d_{ij} = 1$ if individual i chooses alternative j and zero otherwise. The maximum likelihood estimator of β is denoted $\mathbf{b}$. The first derivatives of the LL function with respect to β are:

$$\begin{aligned}\mathbf{g} = \frac{\partial \log L(\beta)}{\partial \beta} &= \sum_{i=1}^{N}\sum_{j=1}^{J} d_{ij}(x_{ij} - \bar{x}_i) \\ &= \sum_{i=1}^{N}\mathbf{g}_i\end{aligned} \tag{7.8}$$

where $\bar{x}_i = \sum_{j=1}^{J} P(\beta, x_{ij})x_{ij}$. The second derivatives are:

$$\begin{aligned}\mathbf{H} = \frac{\partial^2 \log L(\beta)}{\partial \beta \partial \beta'} &= \sum_{i=1}^{N}\sum_{j=1}^{J} -P_{ij}(x_{ij} - \bar{x}_i)(x_{ij} - \bar{x}_i)' \\ &= \sum_{i=1}^{N}\mathbf{H}_i\end{aligned} \tag{7.9}$$

The conventional estimator of the covariance matrix of $\mathbf{b}$ is the negative inverse of the second derivatives matrix:

$$\text{Est.Var}[\mathbf{b}]_{\mathbf{H}} = (-\mathbf{H})^{-1}. \tag{7.10}$$

This matrix forms the basis of the standard errors reported with the estimates in Section 7.2.1. The theory that justifies the usual estimator above also implies an alternative estimator, the BHHH estimator (see Chapter 5):

$$\text{Est.Var}[\mathbf{b}]_{\mathbf{BHHH}} = \mathbf{B}^{-1} \quad \text{where} \quad \mathbf{B} = \left[\sum_{i=1}^{N} \mathbf{g}_i\mathbf{g}'_i\right]. \tag{7.11}$$

In some cases, derivation of and programing of the second derivatives is extremely complicated. The BHHH estimator is a convenient attractive alternative. While some of the estimators in NLOGIT, such as the MNL, are based on the Hessian, several others, such as the HEV model, use the BHHH estimator.

7.3.2 Robust estimation

The objective of *robust covariance matrix* estimation is to devise an estimator that will appropriately estimate the covariance matrix even though the basic assumptions of the model might be violated. The best known application is the *White estimator*, that appropriately estimates the asymptotic covariance matrix of the ordinary (unweighted) least squares estimator, even in the presence of heteroskedasticity. For maximum likelihood estimators, the common such estimator is:

$$\text{Est.Var}[\mathbf{b}]_{\text{Robust}} = (-\mathbf{H})^{-1}\mathbf{B}(-\mathbf{H})^{-1}. \tag{7.12}$$

In order for the estimator above to be appropriate, it must be the case that the parameter estimator, itself, remains consistent even with the failure of the model assumptions. Thus, the ordinary least squares (OLS) estimator of the linear regression model remains consistent (and unbiased) whether or not there is heteroskedasticity. In the settings of the choice models discussed in this book, it is difficult (we are tempted to suggest impossible, but there are exceptions in practice) to devise failures of the model assumptions under which the MLE would still be consistent. As such, use of the so-called robust estimator in this setting seems in the main, unjustified, but it is useful for the analysts to be aware of this since the authors have occasionally found that the inclusion of ;**robust** resolves problems with standard errors. It is worth noting that under the full set of model assumptions, without violations, the robust estimator estimates the same matrix as the conventional estimator. That is, it is generally benign, even if mostly redundant.

A specific exception to this observation might apply to models based on stated choice (SC) experiments, in which individuals answer multiple choice scenarios. In this case, the data for an individual consist of a "cluster" of responses that must be correlated since the same individual is answering the questions. Consider, then, estimating a simple MNL model in an SC experiment in which each individual provides T choice responses. Referring to the earlier definitions, the "cluster corrected" estimator for this case would be constructed as follows:

$$\mathbf{H} = \frac{\partial^2 \log L(\boldsymbol{\beta})}{\partial \boldsymbol{\beta} \partial \boldsymbol{\beta}'} = \sum_{i=1}^{N} \sum_{t=1}^{T} \sum_{j=1}^{J} -P_{ijt}(\mathbf{x}_{ijt} - \bar{\mathbf{x}}_{it})(\mathbf{x}_{ijt} - \bar{\mathbf{x}}_{it})' \tag{7.13}$$

$$\mathbf{C} = \sum_{i=1}^{N} \left(\sum_{t=1}^{T} \mathbf{g}_{it} \right) \left(\sum_{t=1}^{T} \mathbf{g}_{it} \right)' \tag{7.14}$$

$$\text{Est.Var}[\mathbf{b}]_{\text{Cluster}} = (-\mathbf{H})^{-1} \mathbf{C} (-\mathbf{H})^{-1}, \tag{7.15}$$

where $\mathbf{g}_{it} = \sum_{j=1}^{J} d_{ijt}(\mathbf{x}_{ijt} - \bar{\mathbf{x}}_{it})$. This becomes a bit complicated internally when the number of responses, T, varies across individuals. Nlogit provides a way to adjust for this complication.

> *As an aside*, We would encourage analysts to use the **;robust** command to see if the standard errors change in a noticeable way. If they do, then this might suggest some potential problems with the model specification.

7.3.3 Bootstrapping of standard errors and confidence intervals

Bootstrapping is a technique used to deduce the properties (usually mean and variance) of the sampling distributions of estimators by using the variation in the observed sample under an assumption that the pattern of variation in the observed sample mimics reasonably accurately the counterpart in the population. (Limdep Reference Manual R21, R536)

In many cases, it is uncertain what formula should be used to compute the asymptotic covariance matrix of an estimator. The least absolute deviations estimator for a linear regression is a well-known example. In these cases, a more reliable and common strategy is to use a parametric bootstrap procedure instead. This requires drawing from the estimated asymptotic distribution of the parameter estimates, and computing the non-linear function for each independent draw. If this process is repeated many times, any feature of the sampling distribution of the non-linear function can be accurately estimated. Since the moments of these distributions may not exist, confidence regions should be estimated directly using percentiles of the sampling distribution. These calculations can be carried out with minimal programing in most econometric software packages such as Nlogit.

More intuitively, the idea is as follows. We typically have just one data set. When we compute a statistic on the data, we only know that one statistic (e.g., some mean estimate of WTP); we do not see how variable that statistic is. The bootstrap creates a large number of datasets (say, R repetitions) that we might have seen and computes the statistic on each of these data sets. Thus we get a distribution of the statistic. The strategy to create data that "we might have seen" is key.

The bootstrap estimator of the covariance matrix is computed by using the following iteration. For R repetitions, sample N observations randomly from the current sample, *with replacement*. Thus, each of the R random samples will consist of a different set of N observations (each time with some observations being drawn more than once, and others not being drawn at all). The model is then re-estimated with each random sample. Denote by $\mathbf{b}(r)$ the rth replicate. The bootstrap estimator is then:

$$\text{Ext.Var}[\mathbf{b}]_{\text{Bootstrap}} = \frac{1}{R}\sum_{r=1}^{R}[\mathbf{b}(r) - \mathbf{b}][\mathbf{b}(r) - \mathbf{b}]'. \tag{7.16}$$

The following demonstrates the technique for our multinomial logit model used in earlier examples. Note in the *execute* command that generates the bootstraps, we have accounted for the fact that in this sampling setting an "observation" consists of "cset" rows of data. We use the North West transport data set (that is also used in Chapters 11 and 13–15) to illustrate the way in which Nlogit obtains "revised" standard errors for each parameter estimate, together with confidence intervals:

```
LOAD;file="C:\Projects\NWTptStudy_03\NWTModels\ACA Ch 15 ML_RPL models\nw15jul03-
3limdep.SAV.lpj"$
Project file contained 27180 observations.
create
 ;if(employ=1)ftime=1
 ;if(whopay=1)youpay=1$
sample;all$
reject;dremove=1$ Bad data
reject;altij=-999$
reject;ttype#1$ work =1

?Standard MNL Model
Nlogit
    ;lhs=resp1,cset,Altij
    ;choices=NLRail,NHRail,NBway,Bus,Bway,Train,Car
    ;asc
    ;model:
U(NLRail)= NLRAsc + cost*tcost + invt*InvTime + acwt*waitt+
           acwt*acctim + accbusf*accbusf+eggT*egresst
              + ptinc*pinc + ptgend*gender + NLRinsde*inside /
U(NHRail)= TNAsc + cost*Tcost + invt*InvTime + acwt*WaitT + acwt*acctim
          | eggT*egresst | accbusf*accbusf
              + ptinc*pinc + ptgend*gender + NHRinsde*inside /
U(NBway) = NBWAsc + cost*Tcost + invt*InvTime + waitTb*WaitT + accTb*acctim
           + eggT*egresst + accbusf*accbusf+ ptinc*pinc + ptgend*gender /
U(Bus) =   BSAsc + cost*frunCost + invt*InvTime + waitTb*WaitT + accTb*acctim
           + eggT*egresst+ ptinc*pinc + ptgend*gender/
```

```
U(Bway) =   BWAsc + cost*Tcost + invt*InvTime + waitTb*WaitT + accTb*acctim
            + eggT*egresst + accbusf*accbusf+ ptinc*pinc + ptgend*gender /
U(Train) =  TNAsc + cost*tcost + invt*InvTime + acwt*WaitT + acwt*acctim
            + eggT*egresst + accbusf*accbusf+ ptinc*pinc + ptgend*gender /
U(Car) =    CRcost*costs + CRinvt*InvTime + CRpark*parkcost + CReggT*egresst$
Normal exit:   5 iterations. Status=0, F=    3130.826
```

```
Discrete choice (multinomial logit) model
Dependent variable                  Choice
Log likelihood function     -3130.82617
Estimation based on N =   1840, K =   6
Inf.Cr.AIC  =   6273.7 AIC/N =    3.410
R2=1-LogL/LogL* Log-L fncn R-sqrd  R2Adj
Constants only  -3428.8565  .0869 .0863
Response data are given as ind. choices
Number of obs.=  1840, skipped    0 obs
```

RESP1	Coefficient	Standard Error	z	Prob. |z|>Z*	95% Confidence Interval	
A_NLRAIL	.34098***	.08886	3.84	.0001	.16683	.51514
A_NHRAIL	.64197***	.08600	7.46	.0000	.47342	.81053
A_NBWAY	-.95132***	.14913	-6.38	.0000	-1.24362	-.65903
A_BUS	.00090	.08913	.01	.9920	-.17378	.17558
A_BWAY	.02057	.09015	.23	.8195	-.15611	.19726
A_TRAIN	.30541***	.08478	3.60	.0003	.13924	.47158

```
Normal exit:   6 iterations. Status=0, F=    2487.362
```

```
Discrete choice (multinomial logit) model
Dependent variable                  Choice
Log likelihood function     -2487.36242
Estimation based on N =   1840, K =  20
Inf.Cr.AIC  =   5014.7 AIC/N =    2.725
R2=1-LogL/LogL* Log-L fncn R-sqrd  R2Adj
Constants only  -3130.8262  .2055 .2037
Response data are given as ind. choices
Number of obs.=  1840, skipped    0 obs
```

RESP1	Coefficient	Standard Error	z	Prob. |z|>Z*	95% Confidence Interval	
NLRASC	2.69464***	.33959	7.93	.0000	2.02905	3.36022
COST	-.18921***	.01386	-13.66	.0000	-.21637	-.16205
INVT	-.04940***	.00207	-23.87	.0000	-.05346	-.04535
ACWT	-.05489***	.00527	-10.42	.0000	-.06521	-.04456
ACCBUSF	-.09962***	.03220	-3.09	.0020	-.16274	-.03650
EGGT	-.01157**	.00471	-2.46	.0140	-.02080	-.00235
PTINC	-.00757***	.00194	-3.90	.0001	-.01138	-.00377

PTGEND	1.34212***	.17801	7.54	.0000	.99323	1.69101
NLRINSDE	-.94667***	.31857	-2.97	.0030	-1.57106	-.32227
TNASC	2.10793***	.32772	6.43	.0000	1.46562	2.75024
NHRINSDE	-.94474***	.36449	-2.59	.0095	-1.65913	-.23036
NBWASC	1.41575***	.36237	3.91	.0001	.70551	2.12599
WAITTB	-.07612***	.02414	-3.15	.0016	-.12343	-.02880
ACCTB	-.06162***	.00841	-7.33	.0000	-.07810	-.04514
BSASC	1.86891***	.32011	5.84	.0000	1.24151	2.49630
BWASC	1.76517***	.33367	5.29	.0000	1.11120	2.41914
CRCOST	-.11424***	.02840	-4.02	.0001	-.16990	-.05857
CRINVT	-.03298***	.00392	-8.42	.0000	-.04065	-.02531
CRPARK	-.01513**	.00733	-2.07	.0389	-.02950	-.00077
CREGGT	-.05190***	.01379	-3.76	.0002	-.07894	-.02486

-----------+--

?Parametric Bootstrapping of MNL Model

```
proc$
Nlogit
    ;lhs=resp1,cset,Altij
    ;choices=NLRail,NHRail,NBway,Bus,Bway,Train,Car
    ;model:
U(NLRail)= NLRAsc + cost*tcost + invt*InvTime + acwt*waitt+
            acwt*acctim + accbusf*accbusf+eggT*egresst
               + ptinc*pinc + ptgend*gender + NLRinsde*inside /
U(NHRail)= TNAsc + cost*Tcost + invt*InvTime + acwt*WaitT + acwt*acctim
           + eggT*egresst + accbusf*accbusf
               + ptinc*pinc + ptgend*gender + NHRinsde*inside /
U(NBway)= NBWASC + cost*Tcost + invt*InvTime + waitTb*WaitT + accTb*acctim
           + eggT*egresst + accbusf*accbusf+ ptinc*pinc + ptgend*gender /
U(Bus)=   BSAsc + cost*frunCost + invt*InvTime + waitTb*WaitT + accTb*acctim
           + eggT*egresst+ ptinc*pinc + ptgend*gender/
U(Bway)=  BWAsc + cost*Tcost + invt*InvTime + waitTb*WaitT + accTb*acctim
           + eggT*egresst + accbusf*accbusf+ ptinc*pinc + ptgend*gender /
U(Train)= TNAsc + cost*tcost + invt*InvTime + acwt*WaitT + acwt*acctim
           + eggT*egresst + accbusf*accbusf+ ptinc*pinc + ptgend*gender /
U(Car)=   CRcost*costs + CRinvt*InvTime + CRpark*parkcost + CReggT*egresst$
endproc $
|-> execute ; n=100 ; pds = cset ; bootstrap = b $
Completed  100 bootstrap iterations.
```

Results of bootstrap estimation of model.
Model has been reestimated   100 times.
Coefficients shown below are the original
model estimates based on the full sample.
Bootstrap samples have 1840 observations.
Estimated parameter vector is B   .
Estimated variance matrix saved as VARB. See below.

```
-----------+----------------------------------------------------------------------------
           |                 Standard                      Prob.        95% Confidence
BootStrp|  Coefficient      Error        z        |z|>Z*           Interval
-----------+----------------------------------------------------------------------------
     B001|    2.69464***     .34831      7.74       .0000     2.01197     3.37731
     B002|    -.18921***     .01565    -12.09       .0000      -.21989     -.15854
     B003|    -.04940***     .00216    -22.89       .0000      -.05363     -.04517
     B004|    -.05489***     .00580     -9.46       .0000      -.06626     -.04352
     B005|    -.09962***     .03819     -2.61       .0091      -.17447     -.02477
     B006|    -.01157**      .00467     -2.48       .0132      -.02072     -.00242
     B007|    -.00757***     .00164     -4.61       .0000      -.01079     -.00436
     B008|    1.34212***     .19793      6.78       .0000       .95419     1.73005
     B009|    -.94667***     .35724     -2.65       .0081     -1.64685     -.24649
     B010|    2.10793***     .32810      6.42       .0000     1.46486     2.75100
     B011|    -.94474**      .43006     -2.20       .0280     -1.78765     -.10184
     B012|    1.41575***     .36756      3.85       .0001       .69534     2.13617
     B013|    -.07612***     .02150     -3.54       .0004      -.11825     -.03398
     B014|    -.06162***     .00754     -8.17       .0000      -.07641     -.04683
     B015|    1.86891***     .30646      6.10       .0000     1.26825     2.46956
     B016|    1.76517***     .33121      5.33       .0000     1.11601     2.41433
     B017|    -.11424***     .02791     -4.09       .0000      -.16894     -.05954
     B018|    -.03298***     .00401     -8.22       .0000      -.04084     -.02512
     B019|    -.01513*       .00807     -1.88       .0606      -.03094      .00067
     B020|    -.05190***     .01207     -4.30       .0000      -.07555     -.02825

Maximum repetitions of PROC

|-> Completed 100 bootstrap iterations.
```

The mean estimates of each of the 20 parameters for each of 100 repetitions is shown below (which is available as an Nlogit output called Matrix-Bootstrp):

7.4 Variances of functions and willingness to pay

Choice modelers should know that the estimated parameters are not individually useful. Because the scale of the error terms is not identified, the scale of the individual parameters is also not identified (see Chapter 4). Therefore we typically look at ratios of the parameters (usually identifying willingness to pay (WTP) in the model), or use the parameters to carry out demand simulations. Even though these are the quantities of interest for policy analysis, it is very rare that any confidence region is given.

	1	2	3	4	5	6	7	8	9	10	11	12	13	14	15	16	17	18	19	20
1	0.165915	-0.00108075	-0.00031882	-0.00093639	-0.00141862	-0.0002714	-0.00033161	0.014501	-0.0416866	0.156543	-0.052072	0.135927	0.00074836	-0.0005873	0.140558	0.140354	0.00530359	0.00057696	-5.01E-06	0.00266974
2	-0.00108075	0.00025531	5.67E-06	1.64E-05	-8.75E-05	-1.44E-06	-2.48E-06	-8.29E-05	-8.07E-05	-0.00082322	-0.00011817	-0.00090936	4.38E-05	-2.69E-05	-0.00073693	-0.00075016	7.84E-05	6.07E-06	-1.51E-06	4.31E-05
3	-0.00031882	5.67E-06	0.00025531	1.58E-06	3.45E-06	4.49E-07	3.28E-08	-5.99E-05	0.00019033	-0.00030549	0.00018437	0.00030189	2.45E-06	3.66E-06	-0.00029544	-0.00027027	5.31E-06	1.98E-06	-5.15E-06	-2.97E-06
4	-0.00093639	1.64E-05	1.58E-06	2.90E-05	-8.42E-06	3.10E-06	-1.56E-06	-4.75E-05	-1.57E-05	-0.00083698	6.86E-05	-0.00035509	1.83E-05	-1.35E-06	-0.00035213	-0.00039051	-1.43E-05	-2.12E-06	-4.16E-06	-2.38E-06
5	-0.00141862	-8.75E-05	3.45E-06	-8.42E-06	0.00116714	-1.51E-06	2.17E-05	1.66E-06	-4.65E-05	-0.00026013	-0.00034723	-0.00027256	-6.15E-06	-4.88E-06	-0.0001988	-0.00013342	9.05E-06	1.35E-06	-3.43E-06	3.54E-06
6	-0.0002714	-1.44E-06	4.49E-07	3.10E-06	-1.51E-06	1.19E-05	1.66E-06	3.66E-06	-5.16E-06	-0.0003223	6.66E-05	-0.00035772	2.86E-06	2.86E-06	-0.00013342	-6.21E-06	-4.78E-07	2.03E-06	3.66E-06	-8.04E-06
7	-0.00033161	-2.48E-06	3.28E-08	-1.56E-06	2.17E-05	1.66E-06	-0.00010648	0.0287223	-0.00063502	-0.0003223	-0.00047477	-0.00035772	-3.56E-06	2.86E-06	0.0143727	0.0170331	-6.21E-06	-4.78E-07	2.03E-06	2.78E-05
8	0.014501	-8.29E-05	-5.99E-05	-4.75E-05	1.66E-06	3.66E-06	-0.00010648	0.0287223	0.13527	0.0135027	-0.00735094	0.00538133	-3.56E-06	2.86E-06	0.0143727	0.0170331	-6.21E-06	-4.78E-07	2.03E-06	2.78E-05
9	-0.0416866	-8.07E-05	0.00019033	-1.57E-05	-4.65E-05	-5.16E-06	-0.00063502	0.13527	0.13117	0.153527	0.0747337	-0.0317211	-0.0365324	0.0747337	-0.0395635	-0.0377989	-0.00292165	0.0003657	6.94E-05	-0.00109926
10	0.156543	-0.00082322	-0.00030549	-0.00083698	-0.00026013	-0.0003223	-0.0003223	0.0135027	0.153527	0.153527	-0.0516432	0.133401	-0.0516432	0.153527	0.137201	0.137854	0.00541778	0.00058943	-0.00011974	0.00259394
11	-0.052072	-0.00011817	0.00018437	6.86E-05	-0.00034723	6.66E-05	-0.00047477	-0.00735094	0.0747337	-0.0516432	0.171229	0.151222	-0.0422974	-0.0516432	-0.0454265	-0.0435231	-0.00184781	-7.62E-05	0.00011958	-0.00154621
12	0.135927	-0.00090936	0.00030189	-0.00035509	-0.00027256	-0.00035772	-0.00035772	0.00538133	-0.0317211	0.133401	0.151222	0.151222	-0.00059645	-0.00181177	0.137492	0.139309	0.00047328	-0.00037522	0.00037522	0.00226945
13	0.00074836	4.38E-05	2.45E-06	1.83E-05	-6.15E-06	2.86E-06	-3.56E-06	-3.56E-06	-0.0365324	-0.0516432	-0.0422974	-0.00059645	0.00062433	-0.00073468	-0.00060203	-0.00107577	3.01E-06	2.52E-06	3.58E-06	2.38E-05
14	-0.0005873	-2.69E-05	3.66E-06	-1.35E-06	-4.88E-06	2.86E-06	2.86E-06	2.86E-06	0.0747337	0.153527	-0.0516432	-0.00181177	-0.00073468	6.85E-05	-0.00088243	-0.00105089	-1.43E-05	-4.65E-06	-4.00E-06	-7.49E-06
15	0.140558	-0.00073693	-0.00029544	-0.00035213	-0.0001988	-0.00013342	0.0143727	0.0170331	-0.0395635	0.137201	-0.0454265	0.137492	-0.00060203	-0.00088243	0.147924	0.140278	0.00541487	0.00055942	-0.00028294	0.00269406
16	0.140354	-0.00075016	-0.00027027	-0.00039051	-0.00013342	-6.21E-06	0.0170331	-0.0377989	-0.0377989	0.137854	-0.0435231	0.139309	-0.00107577	-0.00105089	0.140278	0.147181	0.00524183	0.00055933	-0.00033699	0.00248947
17	0.00530359	7.84E-05	5.31E-06	-1.43E-05	9.05E-06	-6.21E-06	-6.21E-06	-6.21E-06	-0.00292165	0.00541778	-0.00184781	0.00047328	3.01E-06	-1.43E-05	0.00541487	0.00524183	0.00094587	3.75E-06	-2.68E-06	9.51E-06
18	0.00057696	6.07E-06	1.98E-06	-2.12E-06	1.35E-06	-4.78E-07	-4.78E-07	-4.78E-07	0.0003657	0.00058943	-7.62E-05	-0.00037522	2.52E-06	-4.65E-06	0.00055942	3.75E-06	3.75E-06	1.30E-05	-2.68E-06	9.51E-06
19	-5.01E-06	-1.51E-06	-5.15E-06	-4.16E-06	-3.43E-06	2.03E-06	2.03E-06	2.03E-06	6.94E-05	-0.00011974	0.00011958	0.00037522	3.58E-06	-4.00E-06	-0.00028294	-0.00033699	-2.68E-06	-2.68E-06	6.94E-05	-1.59E-05
20	0.00266974	4.31E-05	-2.97E-06	-2.38E-06	3.54E-06	-8.04E-06	2.78E-05	2.78E-05	-0.00109926	0.00259394	-0.00154621	0.00226945	2.38E-05	-7.49E-06	0.00269406	0.00248947	9.51E-06	9.51E-06	-1.59E-05	0.0002128

Var(B): (note obtained by copying into Excel first to select a nice format)

	1	2	3	4	5	6	7	8	9	10	11	12	13	14	15	16	17	18	19	20
1	2.81132	-0.18297	-0.04719	-0.0587	-0.08487	-0.0129	-0.01025	1.52097	-0.80526	2.23291	-1.24002	1.5981	-0.08306	-0.06737	2.12124	2.00761	-0.08996	-0.03434	-0.02993	-0.02727
2	2.81809	-0.19565	-0.05041	-0.05373	-0.09894	-0.0046	-0.01084	1.05731	-1.48296	2.212	-0.75482	1.30451	-0.05598	-0.05658	1.98883	1.7691	-0.12627	-0.03712	-0.01732	-0.03975
3	2.57788	-0.16473	-0.04799	-0.05383	-0.12556	-0.01483	-0.00855	1.2352	-0.93535	2.02848	-0.95269	1.68349	-0.10294	-0.06565	1.98603	1.82105	-0.08978	-0.03574	-0.01876	-0.05305
4	2.72124	-0.20624	-0.05206	-0.05977	-0.12502	-0.01191	-0.00591	1.00162	-0.35361	2.08802	0.144309	1.69511	-0.12123	-0.06904	1.94814	1.92527	-0.16506	-0.03334	-0.00619	-0.07128
5	3.10422	-0.19186	-0.0529	-0.05186	-0.13337	-0.01026	-0.00917	1.51472	-0.8931	2.51209	-1.19772	1.96268	-0.09026	-0.07051	2.39108	2.28459	-0.11165	-0.0317	-0.01721	-0.05128
6	2.26865	-0.17854	-0.04674	-0.05343	-0.07078	-0.00367	-0.00419	1.11763	-1.02347	1.55317	-0.96239	0.945271	-0.09843	-0.0466	1.40398	1.2679	-0.10378	-0.03228	-0.02315	-0.04116
7	2.64665	-0.19094	-0.04852	-0.05103	-0.10226	-0.0098	-0.00932	1.22533	-0.81653	2.01424	-0.40033	1.67191	-0.04997	-0.06453	1.91512	1.7967	-0.12918	-0.03108	-0.01454	-0.06142
8	2.95462	-0.20911	-0.04987	-0.06669	-0.14387	-0.00292	-0.00796	1.47679	-0.84789	2.22025	-0.86707	1.14534	-0.07631	-0.06957	1.65506	1.84138	-0.15149	-0.0339	-0.01023	-0.05318
9	3.94335	-0.22067	-0.05146	-0.0609	-0.07346	-0.01419	-0.01076	1.75702	-1.04462	3.38164	-1.29255	2.58201	-0.07182	-0.0797	3.12254	3.20887	-0.07018	-0.02479	-0.01899	-0.0371
10	2.3672	-0.17675	-0.04986	-0.05405	-0.09359	-0.01581	-0.00714	1.28591	-0.24646	1.93488	-0.6456	1.07259	-0.04502	-0.05956	1.66166	1.50386	-0.12367	-0.03414	-0.00404	-0.05521
11	2.14678	-0.18001	-0.04616	-0.04792	-0.09858	-0.00342	-0.00821	1.36864	-0.76515	1.5971	-0.50044	1.15732	-0.05448	-0.06056	1.4869	1.41516	-0.0529	-0.03324	-0.03708	-0.06938
12	2.44026	-0.16694	-0.04531	-0.05312	-0.11442	-0.00862	-0.00839	1.16039	-1.17276	1.85154	-0.73539	1.28129	-0.10735	-0.05588	1.64287	1.65119	-0.08345	-0.03322	-0.02959	-0.05177
13	3.3571	-0.21865	-0.04727	-0.05328	-0.09548	-0.01134	-0.01254	1.40929	-1.59061	2.47015	-1.15611	1.82621	-0.05721	-0.06369	2.43317	2.17521	-0.09886	-0.03484	-0.02007	-0.04865
14	2.53811	-0.178	-0.04811	-0.05772	-0.11028	-0.01634	-0.00833	1.26671	-0.43714	1.91162	-0.44643	1.22869	-0.06285	-0.06446	1.4911	1.44315	-0.13651	-0.03213	-0.006	-0.08345
15	1.98343	-0.16758	-0.05016	-0.04312	-0.10192	-0.00794	-0.00854	1.78754	-0.90579	1.4132	-1.18115	0.952768	-0.08152	-0.06762	1.43979	1.36476	-0.13479	-0.03576	-0.01312	-0.05379
16	2.77402	-0.18195	-0.05423	-0.05537	-0.09696	-0.01472	-0.01023	1.00378	-0.9336	2.08753	-1.00619	1.41782	-0.05852	-0.06762	1.88161	1.72324	-0.18225	-0.03737	-0.00612	-0.05093
17	2.91102	-0.18798	-0.04823	-0.0502	-0.06937	-0.00916	-0.00766	1.0609	-1.17684	2.29573	-1.66289	1.50493	-0.02153	-0.0598	2.04183	1.66466	-0.07818	-0.03431	-0.00714	-0.04823
18	3.14602	-0.18882	-0.04862	-0.04952	-0.20991	-0.01007	-0.01011	1.73221	-1.15075	2.5057	-0.97251	1.95995	-0.0833	-0.07368	2.16754	2.40897	-0.1131	-0.03049	-0.0108	-0.04351
19	2.5014	-0.17099	-0.04794	-0.06049	-0.15066	-0.01169	-0.00625	1.54847	-1.13953	1.83937	-1.13264	1.2547	-0.08383	-0.0659	1.37629	1.53763	-0.09286	-0.03412	-0.00749	-0.07202
20	2.39102	-0.18341	-0.05032	-0.05362	-0.18438	-0.00305	-0.00914	1.50861	-0.75403	1.87434	-1.14347	1.01835	-0.07678	-0.06803	1.5235	1.54669	-0.14127	-0.03358	-0.01595	-0.06478
21	3.22899	-0.19643	-0.05095	-0.06732	-0.04383	-0.02249	-0.00901	1.50592	-1.04799	2.62052	-0.8391	1.90627	-0.09959	-0.06952	2.4624	2.22293	-0.13523	-0.02884	-0.00925	-0.05363
22	2.49108	-0.20118	-0.04985	-0.05959	-0.08565	-0.01404	-0.00695	1.352	-0.99131	1.89138	-0.90557	1.13537	-0.08202	-0.06649	1.69282	1.54012	-0.12144	-0.0378	-0.01682	-0.03921
23	3.2374	-0.1882	-0.04949	-0.06673	-0.11753	-0.01456	-0.00807	1.5467	-0.55589	2.51868	-1.43623	1.50086	-0.05532	-0.0636	1.96525	1.87111	-0.09445	-0.03186	-0.01444	-0.05095
24	2.83047	-0.17427	-0.04973	-0.05205	-0.08511	-0.01522	-0.00812	1.46867	-1.16228	2.2206	-0.83146	1.55752	-0.0503	-0.05633	1.94142	1.89116	-0.08498	-0.03183	-0.02514	-0.03981
25	2.77202	-0.1917	-0.04864	-0.06041	-0.12566	-0.01607	-0.00932	1.49141	-0.81905	2.11683	-0.6124	1.38759	-0.07963	-0.06996	1.79877	1.79339	-0.10592	-0.03504	-0.2071	-0.05756
26	2.56711	-0.20678	-0.04618	-0.06222	-0.13406	-0.00878	-0.00519	1.44289	-0.85722	2.0132	-0.69176	1.2517	-0.09212	-0.0569	1.50269	1.61936	-0.13511	-0.03085	-0.019	-0.04761
27	3.23474	-0.16288	-0.05218	-0.05453	-0.08053	-0.01027	-0.00857	1.48734	-1.55624	2.68776	-1.75428	1.7691	-0.05716	-0.08203	2.59825	2.43802	-0.0927	-0.02824	-0.0202	-0.02825
28	2.2625	-0.17636	-0.0464	-0.05338	-0.12389	-0.01	-0.00676	1.56733	-0.28504	1.66127	0.116758	0.718882	-0.04073	-0.0638	1.28315	1.13038	-0.13454	-0.02764	-0.01455	-0.07632
29	2.61633	-0.19692	-0.05114	-0.05401	-0.09596	-0.02175	-0.00927	1.44821	-0.67327	2.17097	-0.74266	1.61842	-0.10641	-0.05408	2.06534	1.94799	-0.11057	-0.03484	-0.02568	-0.05713
30	2.80843	-0.19552	-0.0477	-0.05466	-0.10292	-0.01629	-0.00948	1.25976	-0.94786	2.24202	-1.62568	1.72198	-0.09595	-0.05969	2.07177	1.91855	-0.1182	-0.03194	-0.02503	-0.05645
31	2.71947	-0.18924	-0.0492	-0.05237	-0.06242	-0.01621	-0.00926	1.35839	-1.01852	2.04652	-0.75197	1.28989	-0.06746	-0.04765	1.81893	1.70068	-0.16304	-0.03122	-0.00156	-0.06033
32	2.95597	-0.18995	-0.05056	-0.05252	-0.13936	-0.01862	-0.01262	1.35268	-1.02157	2.34785	-0.88923	1.55905	-0.00878	-0.06968	2.12957	1.88312	-0.0932	-0.04102	-0.02358	-0.04445
33	2.0589	-0.17867	-0.04898	-0.05507	-0.05338	-0.009	-0.00724	1.23153	-0.80042	1.44277	-0.48732	0.705188	-0.06554	-0.06855	1.46379	1.0651	-0.1566	-0.03618	-0.00797	-0.0387
34	2.61638	-0.1827	-0.0477	-0.05621	-0.10418	-0.01065	-0.00863	1.2044	-1.28756	2.4202	-0.85117	1.48749	-0.05863	-0.06795	1.93929	1.81402	-0.11776	-0.03051	-0.01544	-0.05143
35	2.79489	-0.20199	-0.04678	-0.06574	-0.10138	-0.018	-0.00903	1.40822	-0.81104	2.22641	-1.25682	1.42656	-0.0662	-0.05338	1.77326	1.68907	-0.09727	-0.03703	-0.00371	-0.0837
36	2.51444	-0.17489	-0.05021	-0.0531	-0.10651	-0.01867	-0.00748	1.49798	-0.11466	1.82296	-0.18897	1.02318	-0.04938	-0.05784	1.58219	1.47589	-0.15924	-0.03064	-0.0015	-0.03358
37	0.98574	-0.21921	-0.04842	-0.05488	-0.05117	-0.00836	-0.00398	1.37423	-0.62738	0.331399	-0.17352	-0.36942	-0.05966	-0.05683	0.124198	0.100593	-0.12998	-0.04374	0.003924	-0.10913
38	3.06507	-0.20754	-0.04911	-0.05301	-0.10635	-0.00962	-0.01231	1.51725	-0.82811	2.46964	-1.1568	1.81187	-0.05026	-0.06773	2.38122	2.18079	-0.11148	-0.03006	-0.02521	-0.06244
39	3.31969	-0.20555	-0.05173	-0.06063	-0.09401	-0.01751	-0.0065	1.42213	-0.96057	2.55146	-0.96278	2.00537	-0.0765	-0.06887	1.14033	1.04435	-0.12419	-0.02969	-0.00419	-0.04336
40	2.04124	-0.21879	-0.04627	-0.05943	-0.072	-0.01885	-0.00393	1.11167	-0.62812	1.45083	-0.69045	0.767981	-0.08066	-0.0529	2.16103	2.09061	-0.13321	-0.03703	-0.02795	-0.08431
41	2.98034	-0.18286	-0.05328	-0.05877	-0.11699	-0.01133	-0.00722	1.37904	-1.43477	2.46139	-1.38785	1.69772	-0.07746	-0.06499	2.16103	2.09061	-0.0775	-0.03496	-0.02989	-0.05863
42	3.16544	-0.19069	-0.04747	-0.05065	-0.09147	-0.01649	-0.00682	1.47533	-1.37752	2.6037	-1.05634	2.07543	-0.07563	-0.06606	2.33698	2.27288	-0.05107	-0.02658	-0.02588	-0.06464
43	3.10965	-0.19328	-0.04995	-0.06513	-0.13171	-0.01296	-0.00558	1.42002	-1.4035	2.51408	-1.28524	1.46141	-0.04971	-0.06553	1.94017	1.77966	-0.08576	-0.03384	-0.01466	-0.05805
44	2.62787	-0.20805	-0.05138	-0.05435	-0.09166	-0.00683	-0.00527	1.1766	-1.0842	2.17529	-1.3063	1.229	-0.06766	-0.05037	1.83722	1.63284	-0.12416	-0.03202	-0.014	-0.04684
45	2.37621	-0.19193	-0.05089	-0.03864	-0.14647	-0.01113	-0.00623	1.12176	-1.19713	1.86862	-0.78461	1.53052	-0.08386	-0.07385	2.10631	2.07361	-0.11531	-0.03584	-0.01002	-0.06369

46	3.17222	-0.18174	-0.05333	-0.05974	-0.1155	-0.00696	-0.01078	1.4535	-1.67472	2.54421	-1.15203	-0.06158	-0.06722	2.18401	2.10444	-0.1029	-0.03324	-0.00439	-0.04247
47	2.95095	-0.1617	-0.05109	-0.0507	-0.18614	-0.00964	-0.01248	1.19089	-1.32231	2.4869	-0.58043	-0.0507	-0.06013	2.01828	1.94035	-0.11471	-0.02991	-0.02425	-0.03644
48	2.99199	-0.1956	-0.05349	-0.06168	-0.06434	-0.00529	-0.01426	1.23891	-1.31825	2.26075	-0.71209	-0.06428	-0.05956	2.04794	1.63261	-0.05372	-0.03928	-0.02372	-0.05111
49	2.29455	-0.19736	-0.0461	-0.04584	-0.07291	-0.0088	-0.01368	1.51337	-0.33932	1.62878	-0.335	-0.08855	-0.0672	1.75667	1.64039	-0.1607	-0.02905	-0.00769	-0.05697
50	2.98313	-0.18612	-0.04946	-0.05846	-0.1318	-0.01029	-0.01648	1.32688	-0.82229	2.35077	-0.6845	-0.06263	-0.06014	2.04867	1.92991	-0.14129	-0.0327	-0.0059	-0.0699
51	2.5045	-0.19816	-0.04634	-0.05125	-0.13205	-0.00977	-0.01795	1.43752	-0.41064	1.89174	-0.42894	-0.09516	-0.05406	1.58647	1.54188	-0.15657	-0.03152	-0.02179	-0.05347
52	2.43068	-0.17349	-0.04904	-0.06129	-0.10145	-0.00673	-0.01658	1.2732	-0.46946	2.02286	-0.64993	-0.1181	-0.05356	1.79601	1.69256	-0.14662	-0.03057	-0.00349	-0.0564
53	2.75678	-0.15434	-0.05198	-0.05826	-0.06112	-0.00559	-0.01581	1.24625	-0.8529	2.1026	-0.74841	-0.0392	-0.08183	1.88525	1.64962	-0.09423	-0.03449	-0.0067	-0.06674
54	2.77522	-0.16273	-0.05021	-0.05548	-0.08262	-0.0095	-0.01176	1.56674	-1.35775	2.07649	-0.9251	-0.10404	-0.06119	2.07197	1.86698	-0.11333	-0.03232	-0.01322	-0.04813
55	2.80767	-0.1603	-0.04772	-0.05522	-0.14742	-0.00838	-0.00521	1.17797	-1.0311	2.18692	-1.25558	-0.06462	-0.07936	1.90168	1.92702	-0.11263	-0.02995	-0.00821	-0.04171
56	2.79175	-0.17703	-0.05142	-0.05966	-0.17103	-0.0084	-0.00091	1.49696	-1.16735	2.20933	-1.20499	-0.11687	-0.07533	2.06002	2.12009	-0.08374	-0.03759	-0.01749	-0.05251
57	2.9819	-0.17449	-0.04968	-0.05553	-0.06397	-0.00755	-0.01341	1.4479	-0.92529	2.32797	-0.94322	-0.06127	-0.05815	2.10833	1.87698	-0.12032	-0.02859	-0.0053	-0.04822
58	2.77843	-0.18974	-0.05043	-0.05546	-0.1185	-0.0088	-0.01883	1.46535	-0.77753	2.23648	-0.7434	-0.0739	-0.06112	1.94037	1.76184	-0.11675	-0.03292	-0.01324	-0.05457
59	3.02765	-0.17303	-0.05287	-0.06042	-0.09038	-0.00802	-0.01121	1.36309	-1.06731	2.39519	-1.33398	-0.07153	-0.05533	1.93236	1.82162	-0.13308	-0.03208	-0.00897	-0.02596
60	2.025	-0.14003	-0.04104	-0.05174	-0.14117	-0.00559	-0.00998	0.944203	-1.15478	1.44992	-1.33189	-0.07328	-0.05291	1.066	1.09713	-0.12764	-0.02812	-0.02329	-0.04763
61	2.31248	-0.19131	-0.04877	-0.05194	-0.11191	-0.00801	-0.00883	1.17341	-0.75476	1.80224	-0.46079	-0.09509	-0.08021	1.7131	1.64153	-0.10458	-0.0328	-0.03411	-0.08643
62	2.27008	-0.18105	-0.05036	-0.04992	-0.10247	-0.00506	-0.00706	1.07515	-0.97857	1.75761	-0.7434	-0.03431	-0.06306	1.42756	1.35662	-0.0794	-0.04086	-0.01185	-0.06606
63	3.04276	-0.20755	-0.05255	-0.06411	-0.15023	-0.00912	-0.01603	1.53682	-0.61502	2.45696	-1.33398	-0.0557	-0.0516	1.80433	1.71237	-0.14561	-0.03393	-0.00196	-0.06927
64	2.43177	-0.18065	-0.05223	-0.05471	-0.1093	-0.00912	-0.01941	1.54572	-0.67672	1.80062	-0.68812	-0.05519	-0.082	1.64031	1.62111	-0.17906	-0.03743	-0.00152	-0.05657
65	2.38757	-0.18295	-0.0515	-0.05126	-0.05804	-0.00819	-0.0171	1.52026	-1.2963	1.82133	-1.2963	-0.09993	-0.06873	1.91553	1.68603	-0.09618	-0.0336	-0.02981	-0.04833
66	2.83914	-0.21156	-0.05648	-0.05409	-0.06105	-0.00693	-0.0171	1.57635	-1.58025	2.2265	-1.42363	-0.09158	-0.06768	2.06946	1.83772	-0.15771	-0.03357	-0.00436	-0.0519
67	3.41428	-0.22346	-0.04928	-0.06038	-0.12469	-0.00646	-0.00374	1.11737	-0.98978	2.71023	-0.98978	-0.05444	-0.05117	2.29396	2.246	-0.11001	-0.02745	-0.0158	-0.03817
68	3.02309	-0.19251	-0.04946	-0.06104	-0.09613	-0.00792	-0.00792	1.06884	-1.7921	2.29943	-1.7921	-0.08864	-0.06861	2.04873	2.03048	-0.09626	-0.03441	-0.00699	-0.05666
69	2.06503	-0.19379	-0.04922	-0.04105	-0.05705	-0.00728	-0.01287	1.24259	-0.98585	1.52202	-0.66483	-0.07504	-0.06235	1.54577	1.50693	-0.1177	-0.03714	-0.01071	-0.06162
70	2.5089	-0.18348	-0.05208	-0.0547	-0.0844	-0.00797	-0.01045	1.54436	-0.72763	1.99424	-0.67102	-0.06523	-0.06778	1.91189	1.74991	-0.11276	-0.03271	-0.00568	-0.04884
71	2.31269	-0.1964	-0.04787	-0.05397	-0.06141	-0.01151	-0.0078	1.39917	-0.92023	1.6933	-0.74485	-0.05482	-0.07159	1.44782	1.36107	-0.14627	-0.03496	-0.00813	-0.04053
72	3.18683	-0.19111	-0.05014	-0.05286	-0.12052	-0.00657	-0.01007	1.50497	-0.59918	2.58377	-1.12222	-0.10131	-0.06615	2.35493	2.20985	-0.11105	-0.03074	-0.01639	-0.03552
73	2.32795	-0.21771	-0.04971	-0.05763	-0.08125	0.002855	-0.01377	1.21188	-0.9629	1.73549	-2.05236	-0.09158	-0.05665	1.65563	1.42218	-0.19034	-0.03176	-0.011	-0.0787
74	2.74255	-0.2134	-0.04927	-0.0547	-0.08259	-0.00646	-0.00374	1.55652	-1.42871	2.14646	-0.99659	-0.08501	-0.06235	1.65162	1.8296	-0.11061	-0.02827	-0.01145	-0.05084
75	2.32231	-0.19572	-0.04686	-0.05851	-0.13564	-0.00845	-0.00792	1.40853	-0.80771	1.78096	-0.41756	-0.05726	-0.0635	1.39931	1.27066	-0.14147	-0.03322	-0.01451	-0.05987
76	2.17538	-0.15281	-0.04638	-0.05665	-0.10705	-0.00563	-0.01449	1.34533	-0.34237	1.68484	-0.57325	-0.08859	-0.06523	1.40836	1.41189	-0.12695	-0.03311	-0.02154	-0.04748
77	2.72412	-0.18967	-0.04675	-0.05486	-0.08014	-0.00521	-0.01155	1.20552	-0.47215	2.16914	-1.28922	-0.02048	-0.05727	1.68026	1.43029	-0.11599	-0.03031	-0.01114	-0.05632
78	1.91814	-0.20056	-0.04787	-0.04981	-0.07038	-0.0051	-0.01095	1.35744	-0.69987	1.35364	-0.58791	-0.06613	-0.05868	1.12906	0.994532	-0.13906	-0.03598	-0.02282	-0.04005
79	2.20662	-0.19111	-0.05014	-0.0591	-0.19346	-0.0078	-0.01007	1.22383	-0.78591	1.7236	-1.40426	-0.1051	-0.05209	1.47565	1.46771	-0.17259	-0.0361	-0.01918	-0.07653
80	3.00024	-0.20155	-0.04971	-0.0447	-0.07123	-0.01056	-0.02152	1.3618	0.008392	2.41963	-0.10384	-0.11646	-0.04384	2.21873	2.00268	-0.08718	-0.03597	-0.02102	-0.05196
81	2.20187	-0.2134	-0.05136	-0.06568	-0.11397	-0.00652	-0.00711	1.44177	-1.43173	1.66829	-0.89508	-0.08945	-0.06371	1.54451	1.46267	-0.15077	-0.03238	-0.01829	-0.08065
82	2.53619	-0.19302	-0.05227	-0.05507	-0.10307	-0.00749	-0.00749	1.40546	-0.74195	2.02886	-1.0698	-0.14272	-0.05792	1.77499	1.67692	-0.12723	-0.03339	-0.01941	-0.05259
83	3.07634	-0.18124	-0.04843	-0.05315	-0.04816	-0.00829	-0.01513	1.36687	-0.65342	2.45959	-0.92009	-0.0704	-0.06133	2.41075	2.08162	-0.12378	-0.02955	-0.00477	-0.04278
84	2.62186	-0.18269	-0.05022	-0.05243	-0.09648	-0.00508	-0.01195	1.25873	-1.15127	2.07582	-1.2258	-0.01773	-0.06556	1.65728	1.56637	-0.1088	-0.03532	-0.0042	-0.05806
85	2.36809	-0.19074	-0.04722	-0.06074	-0.08951	-0.00741	-0.01415	1.42243	-0.46385	1.89498	-0.63004	-0.0644	-0.0578	1.56259	1.39717	-0.09157	-0.03669	-0.02342	-0.04998
86	3.03783	-0.18852	-0.04997	-0.04965	-0.16869	-0.00721	-0.0133	1.35547	-0.86968	2.54437	-0.82365	-0.09182	-0.06534	1.97871	2.03655	-0.13738	-0.03159	-0.00819	-0.05135
87	2.39716	-0.20259	-0.04947	-0.05404	-0.09892	-0.00953	-0.0132	1.26216	-0.59307	1.81611	-1.04873	-0.11095	-0.04688	1.77885	1.50949	-0.1551	-0.04477	-0.01328	-0.03575
88	2.81868	-0.17311	-0.04979	-0.06111	-0.11221	-0.01095	-0.01013	1.49612	-1.14932	2.19736	-2.43795	-0.2896	-0.06482	1.7804	1.71047	-0.15689	-0.03217	-0.01479	-0.03366
89	2.47773	-0.18815	-0.05315	-0.06111	-0.12201	-0.01025	-0.00337	1.42279	-1.30915	1.73941	-1.28193	-0.12024	-0.05135	1.37722	1.2405	-0.13661	-0.035	-0.00701	-0.09087
90	2.73949	-0.20917	-0.05012	-0.05907	-0.08778	-0.00909	-0.01025	1.25704	-1.65573	2.08618	-0.85935	-0.04961	-0.06128	1.74798	1.63899	-0.1383	-0.02646	-0.02607	-0.05491
91	2.49617	-0.17754	-0.04636	-0.05771	-0.04394	-0.01006	-0.0058	1.29957	-1.18184	1.89537	-0.59179	-0.0654	-0.07338	1.91722	1.4971	-0.12395	-0.02655	-0.01569	-0.06601
92	2.97021	-0.18326	-0.04997	-0.06133	-0.06877	-0.0093	-0.00863	1.36207	-0.88372	2.36211	-0.54977	-0.1002	-0.06614	2.05749	2.10231	-0.04135	-0.03335	-0.0259	-0.05501
93	3.06323	-0.20994	-0.0478	-0.05702	-0.07107	-0.00915	-0.00754	1.52055	-1.05284	2.35792	-0.89739	-0.11499	-0.05139	2.30026	2.05679	-0.09196	-0.03088	-0.01414	-0.04017

	1	2	3	4	5	6	7	8	9	10	11	12	13	14	15	16	17	18	19	20
94	2.72454	-0.18678	-0.05211	-0.05204	-0.14971	-0.01677	-0.00832	1.51471	-0.79036	2.11146	-1.24719	1.61151	-0.07906	-0.04786	1.75335	1.6258	-0.09117	-0.03622	-0.01129	-0.0631
95	2.97069	-0.19496	-0.0478	-0.05339	-0.13895	-0.01569	-0.00773	1.26759	-1.17626	2.42418	-1.2627	1.7293	-0.07298	-0.06396	2.05353	2.18491	-0.12313	-0.03155	-0.01629	-0.04242
96	3.09314	-0.20704	-0.04933	-0.06206	-0.05454	-0.01123	-0.00886	1.15129	-0.79159	2.50301	-0.65512	1.48748	-0.04611	-0.07176	2.15281	2.09623	-0.13545	-0.03061	-0.01253	-0.04733
97	2.33055	-0.17391	-0.04829	-0.05447	-0.08478	-0.00941	-0.00731	1.32992	-0.57779	1.7923	-0.40595	0.911452	-0.05697	-0.07259	1.65931	1.40245	-0.14603	-0.02682	-0.01474	-0.06252
98	2.7949	-0.20094	-0.05231	-0.05729	-0.13112	-0.01601	-0.00546	1.08688	-1.18668	2.04567	-0.83092	1.30328	-0.05069	-0.06604	1.55092	1.56347	-0.15077	-0.03867	-0.00622	-0.04771
99	2.48321	-0.2049	-0.05136	-0.06118	-0.0833	-0.00932	-0.00439	1.21036	-1.53589	1.87442	-0.9157	1.17197	-0.09312	-0.0538	1.53231	1.40838	-0.11112	-0.03792	-0.02194	-0.05207
100	2.64511	-0.19791	-0.04907	-0.05448	-0.08583	-0.01236	-0.00722	1.38516	-0.41325	2.06043	-0.44269	1.17563	-0.05055	-0.07039	1.7151	1.76961	-0.10696	-0.03234	-0.02115	-0.0764

> *As an aside*, David Brownstone in 2000 made the important comment: "Judging from reading many applied papers, the implied assertion is that if the individual coefficients have high *t*-statistics, then any nonlinear combination of them must also have high *t*-statistics."
>
> This is obviously incorrect. Even if the asymptotic normal approximation to the joint distribution of the parameter estimates is accurate, there is no reason why the ratios of any two of these parameters would even have a mean or a variance. If the parameter estimates are uncorrelated, then the ratios will typically have a Cauchy distribution (which has no finite moments). This fact suggests that standard delta-method approximations (see above and also Greene 1997, 127 and 916) will not yield reliable inferences, although the resulting standard error estimates are certainly better than nothing!

Computation of aggregate WTP measures, involves computing functions of estimated parameters. Using the same RP data:

```
nlogit
;lhs = choice, cset, altij
;choices = bs,tn,bw,cr
;model:
u(bs) = bs + actpt*act + invcpt*invc + invtpt*invt2 + egtpt*egt + trpt*trnf /
u(tn) = tn + actpt*act + invcpt*invc + invtpt*invt2 + egtpt*egt + trpt*trnf /
u(bw) = bw + actpt*act + invcpt*invc + invtpt*invt2 + egtpt*egt + trpt*trnf /
u(cr) = invtcar*invt + TC*TC + PC*PC + egtcar*egt $
```

Car drivers' willingness to pay higher tolls for a shorter trip would be measured by:

$$wtp = invtcar/tc.$$

Since *invtcar* and *tc* are estimated parameters with sampling variances, *wtp* is also an estimated parameter. A more involved example is provided by partial effects (see Chapters 8 and 13 for more details) calculations. Consider a binary choice model based on our example for whether an individual chooses to drive or take some other mode. A logit model would appear as:

$$\text{Choose car} = 1[\alpha + \beta_1 invt + \beta_2 tc + \beta_3 pc + \beta_4 egt + \varepsilon > 0]$$
$$= 1[\boldsymbol{\beta}'\mathbf{x} + \varepsilon > 0].$$

where ε has a standardized logistic distribution (mean zero, variance one). The econometric model that follows is:

$$\text{Prob(choose car)} = \frac{\exp(\boldsymbol{\beta}'\mathbf{x})}{1 + \exp(\boldsymbol{\beta}'\mathbf{x})} = \Lambda(\boldsymbol{\beta}'\mathbf{x}). \tag{7.17}$$

The partial effects (see Chapter 8) in this model are:

$$\frac{\partial \Lambda(\beta'\mathbf{x})}{\partial \mathbf{x}} = \Lambda(\beta'\mathbf{x})[1 - \Lambda(\beta'\mathbf{x})]\,\beta = \delta(\beta'\mathbf{x}). \tag{7.18}$$

Once again, the computed function is a function of the estimated parameters, and will inherit a sampling variance that must be estimated.

This section is concerned with methods of obtaining asymptotic covariance matrices for estimators such as these. Two equally effective and widely used methods are the delta method and the Krinsky–Robb (KR) method. The standard errors for a WTP ratio are defined as in Equation (7.19):

$$s.e._{\left(\frac{\beta_k}{\beta_c}\right)} \cong \sqrt{\frac{1}{\beta_c^2}\left[Var(\beta_k) - \frac{2\beta_k}{\beta_c}.Cov(\beta_k, \beta_c) + \left(\frac{\beta_k}{\beta_c}\right)^2 Var(\beta_c)\right]}. \tag{7.19}$$

7.4.1 Delta method

Let $\mathbf{f}(\mathbf{b})$ be a set of one or more functions of an estimator, $\mathbf{b}$ that estimate the vector $\mathbf{f}(\beta)$. The Jacobian of the functions is $\Gamma(\beta) = \frac{\partial \mathbf{f}(\beta)}{\partial \beta'}$. We estimate this matrix using our estimates of β with $\mathbf{G}(\mathbf{b})$. Let $\mathbf{V}$ be the estimator of the variance matrix of $\mathbf{b}$, discussed in Section 7.3. The delta method estimates the sampling variance of $\mathbf{f}(\mathbf{b})$ with the matrix:

$$\mathbf{W} = \mathbf{G}\mathbf{V}\mathbf{G}'. \tag{7.20}$$

For the *wtp* example, $\mathbf{V}$ would be the 2×2 matrix of sampling variances and covariance for (*invtcar,tc*) and $\mathbf{G}$ would be the 1×2 (one function × two parameters) matrix:

$$\mathbf{G} = [\partial wtp/\partial invtcar, \partial wtp/\partial tc] = [1/tc, -invtcar/tc^2]. \tag{7.21}$$

For the vector of partial effects:

$$\mathbf{G} = (1 - 2\hat{\Lambda})\hat{\Lambda}(1 - \hat{\Lambda})\mathbf{b}\mathbf{x}', \ \hat{\Lambda} = \Lambda(\mathbf{b}'\mathbf{x}). \tag{7.22}$$

For functions such as these partial effects, which are functions of the data as well as the parameters, there is a question as to how to handle the data part. It is common to do the computation at the means of the data – this produces the "partial effects at the means." Many applications have suggested instead computing "average partial effects." To compute the average partial effects, the effects are computed at each observation, and the effects themselves, rather than the data, are averaged. The delta method must be modified in this case – the change requires only that the average Jacobian, rather than the Jacobian at the means, be used to compute **W**. (See Greene 2012 for details.)

Nlogit provides two devices for computing variances of functions. The **WALD** command used in Section 7.2.1.2 can be used for basic functions of variables. For functions such as partial effects that involve the data, two commands, **SIMULATE** and **PARTIALS**, are used to do the relevant averaging or summing over the observations and deriving the appropriate variances (both discussed in detail in Chapter 13). Both procedures can be used for the delta method or the KR method described in Section 7.4.2.

This first example uses the delta method to compute a WTP measure based on the MNL model. We use two data sets (the RP component as above and the SC data from the same survey). The model is estimated first. The estimated WTP is reported as the function value by the **WALD** command. The evidence below suggests that the mean estimate of WTP (i.e., value of travel time savings in \$/min.) is not statistically significantly different from 0 ($z = 1.23$), at the 95 percent level of confidence for the RP data set but is statistically significant ($z = 3.44$) for the SC data:

```
?RP Data set
nlogit
;lhs = choice, cset, altij
;choices = bs,tn,bw,cr
;model:
u(bs) = bs + actpt*act + invcpt*invc + invtpt*invt2 + egtpt*egt + trpt*trnf /
u(tn) = tn + actpt*act + invcpt*invc + invtpt*invt2 + egtpt*egt + trpt*trnf /
u(bw) = bw+ actpt*act + invcpt*invc + invtpt*invt2 + egtpt*egt + trpt*trnf /
u(cr) = invtcar*invt + TC*TC + PC*PC + egtcar*egt $
Wald ; Parameters = b ; Covariance = Varb
     ; Labels = 8_c,binvt,btc,c11,c12
? Note that 8_c means c1,c2,c3,c4,c5,c6,c7,c8, which are first 8 parameters in
output
     ; fn1 = wtp = binvt/btc $
-----------------------------------------------------------------------------
Discrete choice (multinomial logit) model
Dependent variable              Choice
Log likelihood function      -200.40133
Estimation based on N =     197, K =   12
Inf.Cr.AIC  =     424.8 AIC/N =    2.156
R2=1-LogL/LogL* Log-L fncn R-sqrd R2Adj
Constants only must be computed directly
            Use NLOGIT ;...;RHS=ONE$
```

```
Chi-squared[ 9]             =      132.82086
Prob [ chi squared > value ] =    .00000
Response data are given as ind. choices
Number of obs.=   197, skipped    0 obs
```

CHOICE	Coefficient	Standard Error	z	Prob. |z|>Z*	95% Confidence Interval	
BS	-1.87740**	.74583	-2.52	.0118	-3.33920	-.41560
ACTPT	-.06036***	.01844	-3.27	.0011	-.09650	-.02423
INVCPT	-.08571*	.04963	-1.73	.0842	-.18299	.01157
INVTPT	-.01106	.00822	-1.35	.1782	-.02716	.00504
EGTPT	-.04117**	.02042	-2.02	.0438	-.08119	-.00114
TRPT	-1.15503***	.39881	-2.90	.0038	-1.93668	-.37338
TN	-1.67343**	.73700	-2.27	.0232	-3.11791	-.22894
BW	-1.87376**	.73750	-2.54	.0111	-3.31924	-.42828
INVTCAR	-.04963***	.01166	-4.26	.0000	-.07249	-.02677
TC	-.11063	.08471	-1.31	.1916	-.27666	.05540
PC	-.01789	.01796	-1.00	.3192	-.05310	.01731
EGTCAR	-.05806*	.03309	-1.75	.0793	-.12291	.00679

```
***, **, * ==> Significance at 1%, 5%, 10% level.
```

WALD procedure. Estimates and standard errors for nonlinear functions and joint test of nonlinear restrictions.

```
Wald Statistic            =      1.52061
Prob. from Chi-squared[ 1] =     .21753
Functions are computed at means of variables
```

WaldFcns	Function	Standard Error	z	Prob. |z|>Z*	95% Confidence Interval	
WTP	.44859	.36378	1.23	.2175	-.26441	1.16158

```
***, **, * ==> Significance at 1%, 5%, 10% level.
```

?SC Data Set
```
|-> Nlogit
   ;lhs=resp1,cset,Altij
   ;choices=NLRail,NHRail,NBway,Bus,Bway,Train,Car
   ;model:
   U(NLRail)= NLRAsc + cost*tcost + invt*InvTime + acwt*waitt+
   acwt*acctim + accbusf*accbusf+eggT*egresst
           + ptinc*pinc + ptgend*gender + NLRinsde*inside /
   U(NHRail)= TNAsc + cost*Tcost + invt*InvTime + acwt*WaitT + acwt*acctim
   + eggT*egresst + accbusf*accbusf
           + ptinc*pinc + ptgend*gender + NHRinsde*inside /
```

```
    U(NBway)=  NBWAsc + cost*Tcost + invt*InvTime + waitTb*WaitT + accTb*acctim
    + eggT*egresst + accbusf*accbusf+ ptinc*pinc + ptgend*gender /
    U(Bus)=  BSAsc + cost*frunCost + invt*InvTime + waitTb*WaitT + accTb*acctim
    + eggT*egresst+ ptinc*pinc + ptgend*gender/
    U(Bway)=  BWAsc + cost*Tcost + invt*InvTime + waitTb*WaitT + accTb*acctim
    + eggT*egresst + accbusf*accbusf+ ptinc*pinc + ptgend*gender /
    U(Train)=  TNAsc + cost*tcost + invt*InvTime + acwt*WaitT + acwt*acctim
    + eggT*egresst + accbusf*accbusf+ ptinc*pinc + ptgend*gender /
    U(Car)=  CRcost*costs + CRinvt*InvTime + CRpark*parkcost + CReggT*egresst$
Normal exit:   6 iterations. Status=0, F=    2487.362

Discrete choice (multinomial logit) model
Dependent variable                Choice
Log likelihood function     -2487.36242
Estimation based on N =    1840, K =  20
Inf.Cr.AIC  =   5014.7 AIC/N =    2.725
R2=1-LogL/LogL* Log-L fncn R-sqrd R2Adj
Constants only must be computed directly
               Use NLOGIT ;...;RHS=ONE$
Response data are given as ind. choices
Number of obs.= 1840, skipped     0 obs
```

RESP1	Coefficient	Standard Error	z	Prob. |z|>Z*	95% Confidence Interval	
NLRASC	2.69464***	.33959	7.93	.0000	2.02905	3.36022
COST	-.18921***	.01386	-13.66	.0000	-.21637	-.16205
INVT	-.04940***	.00207	-23.87	.0000	-.05346	-.04535
ACWT	-.05489***	.00527	-10.42	.0000	-.06521	-.04456
ACCBUSF	-.09962***	.03220	-3.09	.0020	-.16274	-.03650
EGGT	-.01157**	.00471	-2.46	.0140	-.02080	-.00235
PTINC	-.00757***	.00194	-3.90	.0001	-.01138	-.00377
PTGEND	1.34212***	.17801	7.54	.0000	.99323	1.69101
NLRINSDE	-.94667***	.31857	-2.97	.0030	-1.57106	-.32227
TNASC	2.10793***	.32772	6.43	.0000	1.46562	2.75024
NHRINSDE	-.94474***	.36449	-2.59	.0095	-1.65913	-.23036
NBWASC	1.41575***	.36237	3.91	.0001	.70551	2.12599
WAITTB	-.07612***	.02414	-3.15	.0016	-.12343	-.02880
ACCTB	-.06162***	.00841	-7.33	.0000	-.07810	-.04514
BSASC	1.86891***	.32011	5.84	.0000	1.24151	2.49630
BWASC	1.76517***	.33367	5.29	.0000	1.11120	2.41914
CRCOST	-.11424***	.02840	-4.02	.0001	-.16990	-.05857
CRINVT	-.03298***	.00392	-8.42	.0000	-.04065	-.02531
CRPARK	-.01513**	.00733	-2.07	.0389	-.02950	-.00077
CREGGT	-.05190***	.01379	-3.76	.0002	-.07894	-.02486

```
|-> Wald ; Parameters = b ; Covariance = Varb
    ; Labels = 16_c,bcrcst,bcrinvt,c19,c20
    ; fn1 = wtp = bcrinvt/bcrcst $
```

```
WALD procedure. Estimates and standard errors for nonlinear functions and
joint test of nonlinear restrictions.
Wald Statistic            =      11.82781
Prob. from Chi-squared[ 1] =        .00058
Functions are computed at means of variables
-----------+----------------------------------------------------------------------
           |                  Standard              Prob.      95% Confidence
WaldFcns|    Function        Error       z      |z|>Z*          Interval
-----------+----------------------------------------------------------------------
     WTP|    .28870***       .08395     3.44    .0006        .12417     .45323
```

This second example fits a binary logit model to the choice of whether to drive or not for the SC data set. In the three commands, the "if[altij = 4];" restricts the analysis to the sub-set of the sample in which the variable altij equals 4 – that is the outcome row for (cr) in the choice model. The **LOGIT** command then fits a binary logit model to the outcome. The two **PARTIALS** commands compute partial effects for the four indicated variables. The first computes the average partial effects. The second computes the partial effects at the means of the variables in the model. The results are broadly similar, though perhaps less so than we might expect based on only sampling variability. In fact, average partial effects and partial effects at the means are slightly different functions:

```
LOGIT     ; if[altij = 4] ; lhs = choice ; rhs = one,tc,pc,egt,invt $
PARTIALS ; if[altij = 4] ; effects : tc / pc / egt / invt ; summary $
PARTIALS ; if[altij = 4] ; effects : tc / pc / egt / invt ; summary ;
means $
----------------------------------------------------------------------------------
Binary Logit Model for Binary Choice
Dependent variable                    CHOICE
Estimation based on N =     175, K =     5
Inf.Cr.AIC   =      187.2 AIC/N =     1.070
-----------+----------------------------------------------------------------------
           |                  Standard              Prob.      95% Confidence
 CHOICE|    Coefficient     Error       z      |z|>Z*          Interval
-----------+----------------------------------------------------------------------
Constant|    3.01108***     .61209     4.92    .0000      1.81141    4.21075
     TC|     -.14627*       .07817    -1.87    .0613      -.29948     .00694
     PC|     -.02721        .01721    -1.58    .1139      -.06093     .00652
    EGT|     -.07195**      .03287    -2.19    .0286      -.13638    -.00753
   INVT|     -.04110***     .01042    -3.94    .0001      -.06152    -.02068
-----------+----------------------------------------------------------------------
***, **, * ==>  Significance at 1%, 5%, 10% level.
----------------------------------------------------------------------------------
```

```
--------------------------------------------------------------------------
Partial Effects for Logit Probability Function
Partial Effects Averaged Over Observations
--------------------------------------------------------------------------

                 Partial    Standard
(Delta method)   Effect     Error      |t|   95% Confidence Interval
--------------------------------------------------------------------------
      TC         -.02461     .01265    1.95     -.04940        .00019
      PC         -.00458     .00282    1.63     -.01010        .00094
      EGT        -.01210     .00527    2.30     -.02243       -.00178
      INVT       -.00691     .00148    4.68     -.00981       -.00402

--------------------------------------------------------------------------
Partial Effects Computed at data Means
--------------------------------------------------------------------------

                 Partial    Standard
(Delta method)   Effect     Error      |t|   95% Confidence Interval
--------------------------------------------------------------------------
      TC         -.03348     .01805    1.85     -.06887        .00190
      PC         -.00623     .00393    1.59     -.01392        .00147
      EGT        -.01647     .00739    2.23     -.03096       -.00198
      INVT       -.00941     .00232    4.06     -.01395       -.00487
--------------------------------------------------------------------------
```

7.4.2 Krinsky–Robb method

A popular application of choice models is to obtain estimates of WTP as mentioned above; however, where such measures are non-linear functions of estimated parameters (such as double bounded contingent valuation[1] or asymmetric WTP estimates around reference points), it is suggested that procedures such as the delta method are inappropriate as they yield symmetric confidence intervals. Specifically, the delta method is consistent with the derivation of a discrete choice model, but it assumes the standard errors are normally distributed, and the utility specification is linear in parameters and linear in attributes (LPLA). Take the example of the functional form for WTP where the cost variable is a quadratic form:

$$WTP = \frac{\frac{d}{dx_k}\beta_k x_k}{\frac{d}{dx_c}\beta_c x_c^2} = \frac{\beta_k}{2\beta_c x_c}.$$

Obtaining the variance (in Equation (7.19)) involves some complex calculations, see Table 7.1.

---

[1] For example: "Would you be willing to pay \$X? Yes/No. If Yes, would you be willing to pay \$Z (where Z>X)? Yes/No. If No, would you be willing to pay \$Y (where Y<X)? Yes/No."

Table 7.1 Non-linearity implications in defining the covariance structure

First note that, $\frac{\beta_k}{-2\beta_c x_c} = -\beta_k(2\beta_c x_c)^{-1}$, this makes the use of the product rule to derive the gradient easier:

$$\nabla g\left(-\beta_k(2\beta_c x_c)^{-1}\right) = \begin{bmatrix} f' \\ h' \end{bmatrix} = \begin{bmatrix} \dfrac{\partial\left(-\beta_k(2\beta_c x_c)^{-1}\right)}{\partial \beta_k} \\ \dfrac{\partial\left(-\beta_k(2\beta_c x_c)^{-1}\right)}{\partial(\beta_c)} \end{bmatrix} = \begin{bmatrix} -(2\beta_c x_c)^{-1} \\ \beta_c(2\beta_c x_c)^{-2} \end{bmatrix}. \tag{1}$$

So that:

$$Var[g(\beta_{ML})] \approx \nabla g(\beta)' Var(\beta_{ML}) \nabla g(\beta)$$
$$= [-(2\beta_c x_c)^{-1}] \begin{bmatrix} Var(\beta_k) & Cov(\beta_k, \beta_c) \\ Cov(\beta_k, \beta_c) & Var(\beta_c) \end{bmatrix} \begin{bmatrix} -(2\beta_c x_c)^{-1} \\ \beta_k(2\beta_c x_c)^{-2} \end{bmatrix} \tag{2}$$

Multiplying the first row vector by the matrix gives:

$$[-(2\beta_c x_c)^{-1} Var(\beta_k) + \left(\beta_k(2\beta_c x_c)^{-2}\right) Cov(\beta_k, \beta_c)$$

$$-(2\beta_c x_c)^{-1} Cov(\beta_k, \beta_c) + (\beta_k) + \left(\beta_k(2\beta_c x_c)^{-2}\right) Var(\beta_c)] \tag{3}$$

Then, multiplying the resulting row vector by the final **column vector** gives:

$$\left(-(2\beta_c x_c)^{-1}\right)[-(2\beta_c x_c)^{-1} Var(\beta_k) + \left(\beta_k(2\beta_c x_c)^{-2}\right) Cov(\beta_k, \beta_c)]$$

$$-\left(\beta_k(2\beta_c x_c)^{-2}\right)[(2\beta_c x_c)^{-1} Cov(\beta_k, \beta_c) + \left(\beta_k(2\beta_c x_c)^{-2}\right) Var(\beta_c)] \tag{4}$$

Collecting terms

$$\rightarrow Var\left(\frac{\beta_k}{-2\beta_c x_{itc}}\right) = \left((2\beta_c x_c)^{-2}\right)[Var(\beta_k) - \left(\beta_k(2\beta_c x_c)^{-1}\right) Cov(\beta_k, \beta_c)]$$

$$-\left(\beta_k(2\beta_c x_c)^{-3}\right)[Cov(\beta_k, \beta_c) + \left(\beta_k(2\beta_c x_c)^{-1}\right) Var(\beta_c)] \tag{5}$$

Non-symmetric confidence intervals obtained using KR simulations are recommended (see Haab and McConnell 2002; Creel and Loomis 1991). The KR method of Krinsky and Robb (1986) is based on Monte Carlo simulation (i.e., the method requires simulation of the standard errors). The procedure involves the following steps (automated in Nlogit):

1. Estimate the WTP model with any functional form.
2. Obtain the vector of parameter estimates and the variance-covariance (VCV) matrix V(est β).
3. Calculate the Cholesky decomposition, C, of the VCV matrix such that CC'=V(estβ).

4. Randomly draw from standard normal distribution a vector x with k independent elements.

5. Calculate a new vector of parameter estimates Z such that $Z = \beta + C' x$.

6. Use the new vector Z to calculate the WTP measures.

7. Repeat steps 4, 5, and 6 N (e.g., $>=5,000$) times to obtain an empirical distribution of WTP.

8. Sort the N values of the WTP function in ascending order.

9. Obtain a 95 percent confidence interval around the mean/median by dropping the top and bottom 2.5 percent of the observations.

In matrix notation, **b** is the estimator of β and **V** is the variance matrix that is estimated for **b**. To apply the K&R method, we draw a large sample of random draws from the asymptotic normal distribution of **b**, that is from the normal distribution with mean **b** and variance matrix **V**; call these replicates $\mathbf{b}_r$, $r = 1, \ldots, R$. Using $\mathbf{b}_r$, we compute R repetitions of $\mathbf{f}_r = \mathbf{f}(\mathbf{b}_r)$ and compute the sample variances of the sample of estimated functions. (The mechanics of the sampling method are discussed in, e.g., Greene 2012.)

This first example repeats the test carried out in Section 7.2.1.2 that uses the delta method. We have estimated a nested logit model, and are interested in testing the null hypothesis of the MNL model. The two functions of the parameter vector are $f^1(\mathbf{b}) = b_{ivbwtn} - 1$ and $f^2(\mathbf{b}) = b_{ivbscar} - 1$. (Admittedly, these are trivial functions.) The K&R method is used by drawing a large number of draws (e.g., 500) from the 14 variate normal distribution and using the 500 draws on $f^1(b_r)$ and $f^2(b_r)$ to compute the necessary 2×2 covariance matrix. This matrix is then used to carry out the Wald test. The results of the test based on the K&R method and the delta method are shown below. The results are identical in this example, as expected, because the expressions are LPLA:

```
Nlogit
   ;lhs=resp1,cset,Altij
   ;choices=NLRail,NHRail,NBway,Bus,Bway,Train,Car
   ;tree=ptnew(NLRail,NHRail,NBWay),Allold(bus,train,bway,car)
   ;RU2
   ;model:
   U(NLRail)= NLRAsc + cost*tcost + invt*InvTime + acwt*waitt+
   acwt*acctim + accbusf*accbusf+eggT*egresst
   + ptinc*pinc + ptgend*gender + NLRinsde*inside /
   U(NHRail)= TNAsc + cost*Tcost + invt*InvTime + acwt*WaitT + acwt*acctim
   + eggT*egresst + accbusf*accbusf
      + ptinc*pinc + ptgend*gender + NHRinsde*inside /
```

```
    U(NBway)=  NBWAsc + cost*Tcost + invt*InvTime + waitTb*WaitT + accTb*acctim
    + eggT*egresst + accbusf*accbusf+ ptinc*pinc + ptgend*gender /
    U(Bus)=   BSAsc + cost*frunCost + invt*InvTime + waitTb*WaitT + accTb*acctim
    + eggT*egresst+ ptinc*pinc + ptgend*gender/
    U(Bway)=   BWAsc + cost*Tcost + invt*InvTime + waitTb*WaitT + accTb*acctim
    + eggT*egresst + accbusf*accbusf+ ptinc*pinc + ptgend*gender /
    U(Train)=  TNAsc + cost*tcost + invt*InvTime + acwt*WaitT + acwt*acctim
    + eggT*egresst + accbusf*accbusf+ ptinc*pinc + ptgend*gender /
    U(Car)=   CRcost*costs + CRinvt*InvTime + CRpark*parkcost + CReggT*egresst$
Normal exit:  6 iterations. Status=0, F=     2487.362
```

```
Discrete choice (multinomial logit) model
Dependent variable                    Choice
Log likelihood function     -2487.36242
Estimation based on N =    1840, K =   20
Inf.Cr.AIC  =    5014.7 AIC/N =    2.725
R2=1-LogL/LogL* Log-L fncn R-sqrd R2Adj
Constants only must be computed directly
           Use NLOGIT ;...;RHS=ONE$
Response data are given as ind. choices
Number of obs.= 1840, skipped    0 obs
```

RESP1	Coefficient	Standard Error	z	Prob. |z|>Z*	95% Confidence Interval	
NLRASC	2.69464***	.33959	7.93	.0000	2.02905	3.36022
COST	-.18921***	.01386	-13.66	.0000	-.21637	-.16205
INVT	-.04940***	.00207	-23.87	.0000	-.05346	-.04535
ACWT	-.05489***	.00527	-10.42	.0000	-.06521	-.04456
ACCBUSF	-.09962***	.03220	-3.09	.0020	-.16274	-.03650
EGGT	-.01157**	.00471	-2.46	.0140	-.02080	-.00235
PTINC	-.00757***	.00194	-3.90	.0001	-.01138	-.00377
PTGEND	1.34212***	.17801	7.54	.0000	.99323	1.69101
NLRINSDE	-.94667***	.31857	-2.97	.0030	-1.57106	-.32227
TNASC	2.10793***	.32772	6.43	.0000	1.46562	2.75024
NHRINSDE	-.94474***	.36449	-2.59	.0095	-1.65913	-.23036
NBWASC	1.41575***	.36237	3.91	.0001	.70551	2.12599
WAITTB	-.07612***	.02414	-3.15	.0016	-.12343	-.02880
ACCTB	-.06162***	.00841	-7.33	.0000	-.07810	-.04514
BSASC	1.86891***	.32011	5.84	.0000	1.24151	2.49630
BWASC	1.76517***	.33367	5.29	.0000	1.11120	2.41914
CRCOST	-.11424***	.02840	-4.02	.0001	-.16990	-.05857
CRINVT	-.03298***	.00392	-8.42	.0000	-.04065	-.02531
CRPARK	-.01513**	.00733	-2.07	.0389	-.02950	-.00077
CREGGT	-.05190***	.01379	-3.76	.0002	-.07894	-.02486

```
Normal exit:  28 iterations. Status=0, F=      2486.231
```

```
-----------------------------------------------------------------------------------
FIML Nested Multinomial Logit Model
Dependent variable                 RESP1
Log likelihood function       -2486.23068
Restricted log likelihood     -3621.05512
Chi squared [ 22](P= .000)   2269.64888
Significance level                 .00000
McFadden Pseudo R-squared        .3133961
Estimation based on N =    1840, K =  22
Inf.Cr.AIC   =    5016.5 AIC/N =     2.726
R2=1-LogL/LogL* Log-L fncn R-sqrd R2Adj
No coefficients -3621.0551   .3134 .3117
Constants only can be computed directly
            Use NLOGIT ;...;RHS=ONE$
At start values -2487.3624   .0005-.0020
Response data are given as ind. choices
BHHH estimator used for asymp. variance
The model has 2 levels.
Random Utility Form 2:IVparms = Mb|l,Gl
Number of obs.= 1840, skipped    0 obs
-----------+-----------------------------------------------------------------------
           |                  Standard              Prob.      95% Confidence
     RESP1| Coefficient       Error       z       |z|>Z*         Interval
-----------+-----------------------------------------------------------------------
           |Attributes in the Utility Functions (beta)
    NLRASC|   2.50852***      .35399     7.09      .0000     1.81472   3.20232
      COST|   -.17977***      .01550   -11.60      .0000     -.21014   -.14940
      INVT|   -.04607***      .00314   -14.69      .0000     -.05221   -.03992
      ACWT|   -.05176***      .00627    -8.25      .0000     -.06406   -.03947
   ACCBUSF|   -.09067***      .03143    -2.89      .0039     -.15226   -.02907
      EGGT|   -.01076**       .00434    -2.48      .0132     -.01927   -.00225
     PTINC|   -.00717***      .00193    -3.72      .0002     -.01095   -.00339
     PTGEND|  1.27200***      .17781     7.15      .0000      .92349   1.62051
  NLRINSDE|   -.79922***      .30048    -2.66      .0078    -1.38814   -.21029
      TNASC|  1.96138***      .31850     6.16      .0000     1.33713   2.58562
  NHRINSDE|   -.76401**       .34238    -2.23      .0256    -1.43506   -.09297
    NBWASC|   1.37009***      .34763     3.94      .0001      .68874   2.05144
    WAITTB|   -.07264***      .02386    -3.04      .0023     -.11941   -.02586
     ACCTB|   -.05855***      .00916    -6.39      .0000     -.07650   -.04059
     BSASC|   1.74362***      .30317     5.75      .0000     1.14941   2.33782
     BWASC|   1.64330***      .31035     5.30      .0000     1.03504   2.25157
    CRCOST|   -.10797***      .02752    -3.92      .0001     -.16190   -.05403
    CRINVT|   -.03105***      .00424    -7.33      .0000     -.03935   -.02274
    CRPARK|   -.01429**       .00685    -2.09      .0370     -.02773   -.00086
    CREGGT|   -.04953***      .01592    -3.11      .0019     -.08073   -.01832
           |IV parameters, RU2 form = mu(b|l),gamma(1)
     PTNEW|   1.21849***      .13886     8.77      .0000      .94632   1.49066
    ALLOLD|   1.05917***      .07644    13.86      .0000      .90935   1.20900
```

K and R:

```
wald ; parameters = b ; labels  = 20_c,ivpt,ivcar
     ; covariance = varb
     ; fn1 = ivpt-1 ; fn2 = ivcar - 1 ; k&r ; pts=500 $
```

```
-----------------------------------------------------------------------------
WALD procedure. Estimates and standard errors for nonlinear functions and
joint test of nonlinear restrictions.
Wald Statistic                =      2.46781
Prob. from Chi-squared[ 2] =        .29115
Krinsky-Robb method used with    500 draws
Functions are computed at means of variables
```

WaldFcns	Function	Standard Error	z	Prob. |z|>Z*	95% Confidence Interval	
Fncn(1)	.21849	.14012	1.56	.1189	-.05614	.49312
Fncn(2)	.05917	.07731	.77	.4441	-.09236	.21070

Wald:

```
wald ; parameters = b ; labels  = 20_c,ivptn,ivold
     ; covariance = varb
     ; fn1 = ivptn-1 ; fn2 = ivold - 1 ; pts=500 $
```

```
-----------------------------------------------------------------------------
WALD procedure. Estimates and standard errors for nonlinear functions and
joint test of nonlinear restrictions.
Wald Statistic                =      2.51379
Prob. from Chi-squared[ 2] =        .28454
Functions are computed at means of variables
```

WaldFcns	Function	Standard Error	z	Prob. |z|>Z*	95% Confidence Interval	
Fncn(1)	.21849	.13886	1.57	.1156	-.05368	.49066
Fncn(2)	.05917	.07644	.77	.4389	-.09065	.20900

A second example computes the WTP (as the value of travel time savings in $/min.) for the car alternative as the ratio *binvtcr/binvccr*. The result of interest is reproduced here from the nested logit model directly above. The mean estimate is $0.288/min. with a standard error obtained using the K&R method of $0.101/min. and a 95 percent confidence interval of $0.089/min. to $0.486/min. With a z value of 2.84 we can conclude that the mean estimate is statistically significantly different from zero:

WaldFcns	Function	Standard Error	z	Prob. |z|>Z*	95% Confidence Interval	
WTP	0.28755***	0.10122	2.84	.0045	.08917	.48594

The confidence interval is reasonably wide but, encouragingly, it includes a range of values that are all positive, a behavioral condition one would like to have when a negative value makes little behavioral sense:

```
wald ; parameters = b ; labels  = 16_c,binvccr,binvtcr,c19,c20,ivptn,ivold
     ; covariance = varb
     ; fn1 = ivptn-1 ; fn2 = ivold - 1
     ;fn3 = wtp = binvtcr/binvccr ; k&r ; pts=500 $
```

```
-----------------------------------------------------------------------------------
WALD procedure. Estimates and standard errors for nonlinear functions and
joint test of nonlinear restrictions.
Wald Statistic           =      10.68424
Prob. from Chi-squared[ 3] =       .01356
Krinsky-Robb method used with   500 draws
Functions are computed at means of variables
-----------+-----------------------------------------------------------------------
```

WaldFcns	Function	Standard Error	z	Prob. |z|>Z*	95% Confidence Interval	
Fncn(1)	.21849*	.12854	1.70	.0892	-.03344	.47041
Fncn(2)	.05917	.07147	.83	.4078	-.08092	.19926
WTP	.28755***	.10122	2.84	.0045	.08917	.48594

```
     ? Mean and standard error from a nested logit model
     |-> create ; wtpd=rnn(0.28755,0.10122)$ Mean and standard error from
     a nested logit model
     |-> kernel;rhs=wtpd $
     -----------------------------------------------
     Kernel Density Estimator for WTPD
     Kernel Function      =      Logistic
     Observations         =         10680
     Points plotted       =           500
     Bandwidth            =       .014237
     Statistics for abscissa values-------
     Mean                 =       .287357
     Standard Deviation =         .101135
     Skewness             =      -.015106
     Kurtosis-3 (excess) =       -.035446
     Chi2 normality test=         .010422
     Minimum              =      -.136909
     Maximum              =       .686246
     Results matrix       =        KERNEL
```

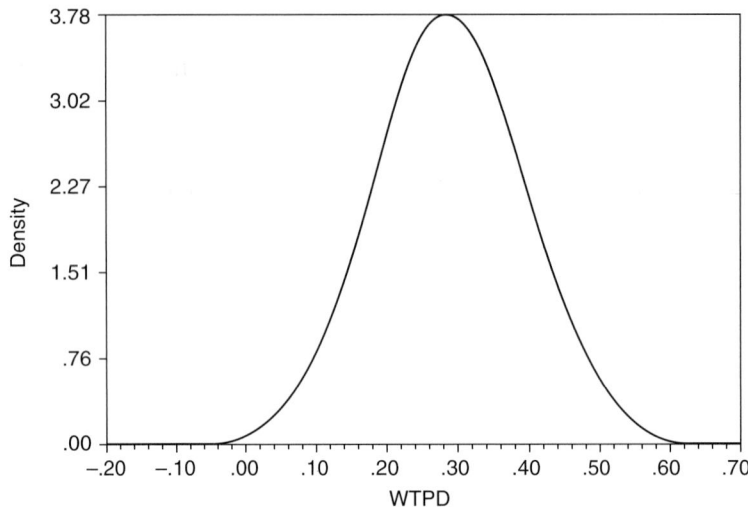

Kernel density estimate for   WTPD

Figure 7.1   Kernel plot of the WTP distribution using Krinsky–Robb derived standard errors

In this example, the Krinsky–Robb method produces a good result (Figure 7.1), but this is not always the case. An often observed empirical situation is one with a very large confidence interval (including a sign change over the range), due typically to the reciprocal variable, 1/*binvccr*. The sample of draws on *binvccr* can include values that are quite close to zero, and it only takes a few reciprocals of these values to produce essentially infinite values of *wtp* that can not be averaged away. Taking a larger number of draws does not help because the near zero values grow in number proportionally with the sample size.

The kernel estimator for the sample of draws on 1/*btc* shown below (Figure 7.2) for another model demonstrates the problem. The more general issue is that certain functions, such as ratios of coefficients, are inherently unstable. For computation of *wtp*, the ratio of two asymptotically normally distributed estimators has an infinite variance – precisely because of the substantive mass near zero.

> *As an aside*, one way to try and minimize this unpalatable result is to identify systematic sources of influence on the parameters associated with the numerator and the denominator, so that the connection between the attribute parameters for each respondent has some behavioral sense as proxied by a "third party" influence such as a socio-economic characteristic.

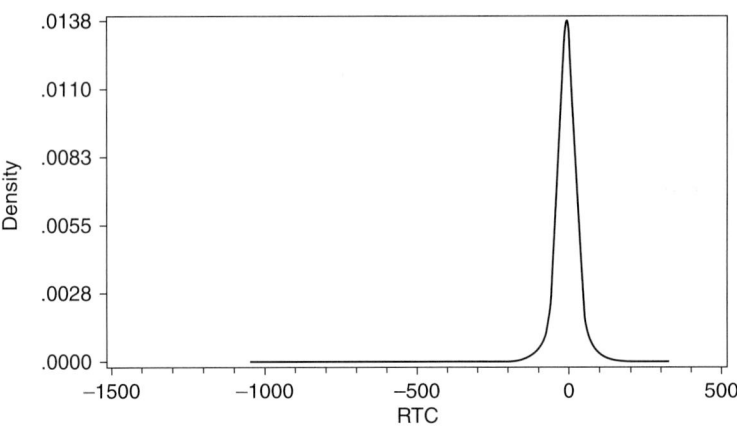

Figure 7.2   Kernel plot of the inverse of a cost parameter

```
Wald ; Parameters = b ; Covariance = Varb
     ; Labels = 8_c,binvt,btc,c11,c12
     ; fn1 = wtp = binvt/btc ; k&r ; pts = 500 $

create ; xtc=rnn(-.110632,.0847106)$
create ; rtc = 1/xtc $
kernel;rhs=Rtc $
```

WALD procedure. Estimates and standard errors for nonlinear functions and
joint test of nonlinear restrictions.
Wald Statistic   =   .00168
Prob. from Chi-squared[1] =   .96729
Krinsky-Robb method used with   500 draws
Functions are computed at means of variables

WaldFcns	Function	Standard Error	z	Prob. $|z|>Z*$	95% Confidence Interval	
WTP	.44859	10.93804	.04	.9673	-20.98958	21.88676

Based on delta method

WaldFcns	Function	Standard Error	z	Prob. $|z|>Z*$	95% Confidence Interval	
WTP	.44859	.36378	1.23	.2175	-.26441	1.16158

8 Other matters that analysts often inquire about

No matter how much one tries to cover the major themes in which choice analysts are interested, we find that there are topics left out that are often listed as future inclusions. In this chapter we identify topics that often arise out of conference debates, referees' suggestions to improve a paper, and question emails to the Limdep/logit list or directly to the authors.

8.1 Demonstrating that the average of the conditional distributions aggregate to the unconditional distribution

This section is the outcome of a discussion between David Hensher, Bill Greene, and Ken Train in July 2012. It is an important discussion, given that it is not often understood that the density f(b) is the "average" of the densities f(b|i), obtained when you integrate one of the variables out of a joint density. When Ken Train in his 2003 book discusses the topic of conditional distributions, this is what he means when he refers to aggregating up the conditional densities to get the population (marginal) density. Specifically he says (2003, 272): "For a correctly specified model at the true population parameters, the conditional distribution of tastes, aggregated over all customers, equals the population distribution of tastes." However, crucially, that does not mean that the moments of the marginal density are the averages of the moments of the conditional densities. They are not, since Var(b) = E[Var[b|i]] + Var[E[b|i]]. Neither term is zero, and if you just average the conditional variances you get the first term which, by itself, is meaningless. In the remaining sections of this chapter, we focus on the mean of a distribution and not the variance.

8.1.1 Observationally equivalent respondents with different unobserved influences

A population of people has the same observed attributes. Each person faces several choice situations and chooses one alternative in each situation. The number of choice situations and the characteristics of each alternative in each situation are the same for all people in the population. The people differ in their unobserved utility coefficients, β, and in the additive term that enters utility for each alternative in each choice situation (which is the IID extreme value term in a mixed logit). The density of β in the population is denoted $f(\beta)$.

Let i be a vector that identifies one alternative for each of the choice situations, and let C be the set of all possible distinct vectors of this form. We refer to "choosing i" as choosing, in each choice situation, the alternative identified in i for that choice situation. Here are the well-known terms: conditional on β, the probability of choosing i is $L(i \mid \beta)$, which for a mixed logit model is a product of standard logit probabilities. The (unconditional) probability of choosing i is then:

$$P(i) = \int L(i|\beta)f(\beta)d\beta. \tag{8.1}$$

The density of β conditional on i is:

$$g(\beta|i) = L(i|\beta)f(\beta)/P(i). \tag{8.2}$$

This is the distribution of β in the sub-population of people who choose i. Now for aggregation: the average of the conditional densities (aka, the expected conditional density, or the aggregate conditional density) is:

$$a(\beta) \equiv \sum_{i \in C} g(\beta|i)S(i), \tag{8.3}$$

where $S(i)$ is the share of people who choose i. If the model is correctly specified, then $P(i) = S(i)$, such that:

$$a(\beta) \equiv \sum_{i \in C} g(\beta|i)P(i). \tag{8.4}$$

Substituting Equation (8.2) into Equation (8.4) gives:

$$\begin{aligned}
a(\beta) &= \sum_{i \in C} [L(i|\beta)f(\beta)/P(i)]P(i) \\
&= \sum_{i \in C} [L(i|\beta)f(\beta) \\
&= f(\beta) \sum_{i \in C} [L(i|\beta)] \\
&= f(\beta)
\end{aligned}$$

since $\sum_{i \in C} L(i \mid \beta) = 1$. That is, the average of the conditional distributions is the unconditional distribution. Stated more directly, if you calculated the conditional distribution for each person based on that person's choices, and then averaged the conditional distributions over all people in the population, then you would get the unconditional distribution – provided only that the model is correctly specified such that $P(i) = S(i)$. If you do this exercise, and the average of the conditionals is not the same as the unconditional, then it means that the model is mis-specified.

Here is the intuition: $f(\beta)$ is the density of β over all people in the population. The population consists of sub-populations of people, where each sub-population contains people who make the same choices. $g(\beta \mid i)$ is the density of β in the sub-population of people who choose i. When you take the density in each sub-population, and aggregate it over all the sub-populations, you get back the density in the population.

8.1.2 Observationally different respondents with different unobserved influences

Let s be the observed attributes of people, with density $m(s)$ in the population. Let x be the observed attributes of all the alternatives in all the choice situations, which varies over people with density $q(x)$ in the population. The density of β is allowed to vary with the attributes of people: $f(\beta \mid s)$ is the density of β among people with attributes s, such that the density of β in the population is $f(\beta) \equiv \int_s f(\beta \mid s)m(s)ds$. The probability of choosing i conditional on s, x and β is $L(i \mid \beta, s, x)$. The probability of choosing i conditional on s and x but not β is:

$$P(i|s, x) = \int L(i|\beta, s, x)f(\beta|s)d\beta. \tag{8.5}$$

The density of β conditional on i, x, s is:

$$g(\beta|i, s, x) = [L(i|\beta, s, x)f(\beta|s)]/P(i|s, x). \tag{8.6}$$

This is the conditional distribution that you would calculate for a person, given their attributes, the characteristics of the choices they faced, and their observed choices. The average of the conditional densities within the sub-population with the same s and x is:

$$a(\beta|s, x) \equiv \sum\nolimits_{i \in C} g(\beta|i, s, x)S(i|s, x). \tag{8.7}$$

where $S(i \mid s, x)$ is the share of people with s and x who choose i. In a correctly specified model, $P(i \mid s, x) = S(i \mid s, x)$, such that, using the same steps as above:

$$a(\beta|s, x) = f(\beta|s).\tag{8.8}$$

Other averages can also be calculated. The average of the conditional densities within the sub-population of people with the same attributes s but different x is:

$$a(\beta|s) \equiv \int x \sum_{i \in C} g(\beta|i, s, x) S(i|s, x) q(x) dx = f(\beta|s).\tag{8.9}$$

That is, the average of the conditional distributions within each demographic group (i.e., attributes s) is the unconditional distribution within that group. The average of the conditional densities over the entire population is:

$$a(\beta|s) \equiv \int s \int x \sum_{i \in C} g(\beta|i, s, x) S(i|s, x) q(x) m(s) dx \, ds\tag{8.10}$$

$$= \int s f(\beta|s) m(s) \, ds\tag{8.11}$$

$$= f(\beta),\tag{8.12}$$

where $f(\beta)$ is the density of β in the entire population, aggregated over the attributes of people.

Essentially, the conditional distributions provide no new information about the population. The conditioning just breaks the population into sub-groups and finds the distribution in each sub-group. But the sub-groups necessarily aggregate back to the population.

When the aggregation is done over a sample (as opposed to the population, as in the above derivations), then the sample average of conditionals might not match the unconditional, because the sample does not capture the full integration over the density of s and x, and the sample share choosing i need not be exactly the population share. However, the difference just represents sampling noise (and/or mis-specification, as discussed above). It does not provide additional or alternative information about the distribution of β in the population.

8.2 Random regret instead of random utility maximization

Interest in alternative behavioral paradigms to random utility maximization (RUM) has existed ever since the dominance of the RUM formulation. One alternative is known as *random regret minimization* (RRM), which suggests that, when choosing between alternatives, decision makers aim to minimize anticipated regret. Although the idea of regret is not new, its incorporation into the same discrete choice framework of RUM is very recent, driven in large measure by the contributions of Caspar Chorus (Chorus 2010; Chorus *et al.* 2008a, 2008b), in which the chosen alternative depends on the anticipated performance of non-chosen alternatives. Specifically, RRM assumes that an individual's choice among a finite set of alternatives is influenced by the wish to avoid the situation where one or more non-chosen alternatives performs better than the chosen one, on one or more attributes – which would cause regret. This behavioral choice rule translates into one in which an individual is assumed to act as if they are minimizing anticipated regret in contrast to maximizing utility. This rule is applicable when the alternatives have attributes that matter in common, which is typically the case in many choice applications.

The notion that anticipated regret influences behavior is not new. Rather, as some have argued, regret is "the emotion that has received the most attention from decision theorists" (Connolly and Zeelenberg 2002). There is an extensive and growing literature in experimental psychology and neurobiology that shows that anticipated regret influences decision making (e.g., Kahneman and Tversky 1979; Zeelenberg 1999; Corricelli *et al.* 2005). Although generally the notion of regret is associated with risky choices in particular, it is also readily applicable to riskless choices, as long as alternatives are defined in terms of multiple attributes. This follows from the idea that the process of making trade-offs between different attributes of different alternatives implies that – in most situations – one has to decide to live with a sub-optimal performance on one or more attributes in order to achieve a satisfactory outcome on other attributes. It is this situation which can be postulated to cause regret at the level of specific attributes. The extension of the earlier binary choice framework to multiple choice alternatives was based on Quiggin's (1982) principle of Irrelevance of Statewise Dominated Alternatives (ISDA), which states that a choice from any given choice set is not affected by adding or removing an alternative that is inferior for every state of the world. It implies that regret only depends on the best available choice alternative. In what follows, we set out the RRM under a condition that all alternatives compete. This is not the same as a model in which regret is specified as a (non-)linear function of the difference between the *best forgone* choice alternative and the chosen alternative (as set out in Chorus *et al.* 2008a, 2008b).

The various versions of the RRM model are summarized (from Rasouli and Timmermans 2014) in Equations (8.13a–c), with $n \in Nn \in N$ representing the set of choice alternatives. RRmax denotes the original model specification in which regret is judged against the best alternative for each attribute separately. RRsum denotes the specification that defines regret as the maximum utility differences between the chosen alternative and *all* forgone alternatives that result in a higher utility on the attribute of interest. RRexp represent the most recent "new regret specification", based on the logarithm function and all pairwise comparisons.

The RRexp form came about as a result of applications in a multiple choice setting (see Chorus 2010) when it was found that the the the max operators imply a non-smooth likelihood function, which may create problems in deriving marginal effects and elasticities. Consequently the original regret specification (RRMax) was replaced by the RRexp new regret model specification (set out in the following paragraphs and the empirical application in Nlogit in Chapter 13):

$$RRmax = \sum_{k=1}^{K} max\left[0, \beta_k \left\{x_k^{n'} - x_k^{n}\right\}\right] \tag{8.13a}$$

$$RRsum = \sum_{n' \neq n \in C} \sum_{k=1}^{K} max\left[0, \beta_k \left\{x_k^{n'} - x_k^{n}\right\}\right] \tag{8.13b}$$

$$RR_{exp} = \sum_{n' \neq n \in C} \sum_{k=1}^{K} \ln\left[1 + \exp\left(\beta_k \left\{x_k^{n'} - x_k^{n}\right\}\right)\right]. \tag{8.13c}$$

It should be noted, however, that Rasouli and Timmermans (2014) raise concerns about developments such as RRexp and show in one empirical study that the RRmax form offers a much better statistical fit and has close links with the original theoretical form.

In a later paper, Quiggin (1995) indicated that the absence of a fully developed model of choice over general (or multiple) sets of alternatives has precluded significant use of regret theory in economic applications, and raised doubts about the general validity of the theory. He then states that "the general version of regret theory offered in this paper however may allay these concerns." *While remaining consistent with the intuition behind the original version, it removes the restriction to pairwise (or even finite) choice sets.* This permits a comparison of regret theory with alternative approaches, not merely in laboratory settings, but in application to real world economic problems. Quiggin says that "On the other hand, the generalization offered here is the only extension of regret theory which satisfies the very weak ISDA **rationality** criterion. If this extension is found to be unsatisfactory, regret theory must be abandoned or radically modified, at least as a normative model. The failure to meet the stronger IRDA (Irrelevance of Regret Dominated Alternatives) criterion provides some grounds for normative objections to the general model proposed here, but these objections do not appear fatal." In a nutshell Quiggin shows that "a simple non-manipulability requirement is sufficient to characterize the functional form for regret theory with general choice sets."

Let us take an example that questions the ISDA property. In order to keep the ISDA property, it seems reasonable that regret should be measured only by the best possible value under each criterion. However, this may not make much sense, as is illustrated in the following hypothetical situation. Suppose that the following are the utilities associated with four alternatives: Alt1 = 30, Alt2 = 32, Alt3 = 31, Alt4 =100. In this example there is just one alternative with a high utility (i.e., 100 utils). Therefore, it is reasonable to expect that someone choosing Alt 1 (30 utils) feels some but limited regret for not having chosen Alt4. This reaction may be rationalized because his/her choice is not as bad when it is compared to that of most of the other alternatives. However, the same person may feel much stronger regret for choosing the alternative with only 30 utils if the utilities were as follows: Alt1 = 30, Alt2 = 98, Alt3 = 97, Alt4 =100. This is understandable because in the new hypothetical example the chosen alternative has a relatively low utility compared to all of the other alternatives. Therefore, intuitively in the previous example, it makes more sense to compute regret in terms of the entire set of alternatives. Thus, the concepts of regret and rejoicing may be more realistically expressed in terms of the criteria values of the entire set of alternatives than in terms of only the best criteria values. However, on the other hand, if regret is computed by considering all the alternatives, then adding or deleting a dominated alternative may alter the initial rankings and thus leaves the ranking of the alternatives open to manipulations like the "Money Pump" idea of Quiggin (1994).

We will now set out the model of interest based on the RRexp form. A decision maker faces a set of J alternatives, each being described in terms of M attributes, x_m, that are comparable across alternatives. The RRM model postulates that when choosing between alternatives, decision makers aim to minimize anticipated random regret, and that the level of anticipated random regret that is associated with a considered alternative i is composed out of a systematic regret R_i and an i.i.d. random error ε_i which represents unobserved heterogeneity in regret and whose negative is Extreme value Type I distributed with variance $\pi^2/6$.

Systematic regret is in turn conceived to be the sum of all so-called binary regrets that are associated with bilaterally comparing the considered alternative with each of the other alternatives in the choice set.[1] The level of binary regret associated with comparing the considered alternative i with another alternative j equals the sum of the regrets that are associated with comparing the two alternatives in terms of each of their M attributes. This attribute level regret in turn is formulated as follows:

$$R_{i \leftrightarrow j}^m = \ln[1 + \exp(\beta_m.\{x_{jm} - x_{im}\})]. \tag{8.14}$$

This formulation implies that regret is close to zero when alternative j performs (much) worse than i in terms of attribute m, and that it grows as an approximately linear function of the difference in attribute values where i performs worse than j in terms of attribute m. In that case, the estimable parameter β_m (for which also the sign is also estimated) gives the approximation of the slope of the regret-function for attribute m. See Figure 8.1 for a visualization.

In combination, this implies the following formulation for systematic regret: $R_i = \sum_{j \neq i} \sum_{m=1..M} \ln\left(1 + \exp[\beta_m \cdot (x_{jm} - x_{im})]\right)$. Acknowledging that minimization of random regret is mathematically equivalent to maximizing the negative of random regret, choice probabilities may be derived using a variant of the multinomial logit-formulation[2]: the choice probability associated with alternative i equals $P_i = \exp(-R_i)/\sum_{j=1..J} \exp(-R_j)$.

The parameters estimated within a RRM framework, have a different meaning than those estimated within a RUM framework. The RUM parameters represent the contribution of an attribute to an alternative's utility, whereas the RRM parameters represent the *potential* contribution of an attribute to the regret associated with an alternative. An attribute's actual contribution to regret depends on whether an alternative performs better or worse on the attribute than the alternative it is compared with. As a result, in contrast with linear additive utilitarian choice models, the RRM model implies semi-compensatory behavior. This follows from the convexity of the regret

---

[1] This heuristic across alternatives has similar behavioral properties to the parameter-transfer rule advocated by Hensher and Layton (2010) within an alternative. Furthermore, the symmetrical form devised initially by Quiggin with regret and rejoice has similar properties to the best–worse (BW) processing rule that focuses on contrasts between alternatives (see Marley and Louviere 2005).

[2] Note that, as has been formally shown in Chorus (2010), the two models (RRM and RUM) give identical results when choice sets are binary. A referee asked whether the findings would be sensitive to six alternatives in contrast to the three alternatives used herein. We are unable to provide a definitive response since it will depend on a number of considerations, including whether the differences in attribute levels between pairs of alternatives are likely to vary significantly or not. This is an area of relevance in future research.

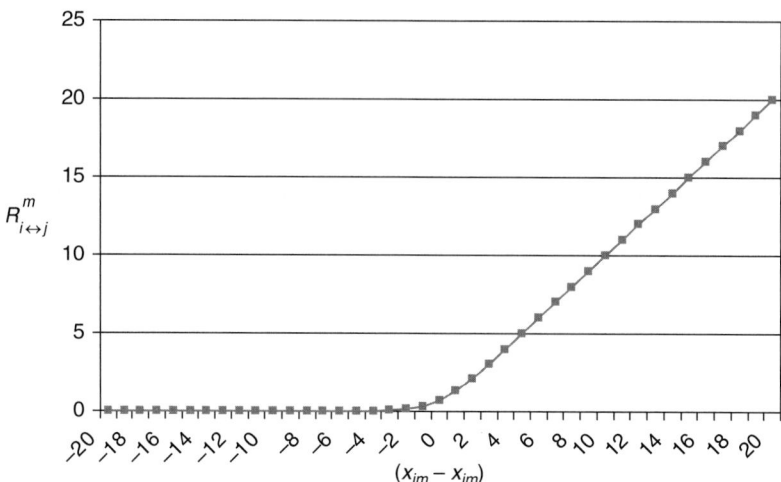

Figure 8.1   Visualization of attribute level regret (for $\beta_m = 1$)

function depicted in Figure 8.1: improving an alternative in terms of an attribute on which it already performs well relative to other alternatives generates only small decreases in regret, whereas deteriorating to a similar extent the performance on another equally important attribute on which the alternative has a poor performance relative to other alternatives may generate substantial increases in regret. Therefore, the extent to which a strong performance on one attribute can compensate a poor performance on another depends on the relative position of each alternative in the set.

As a result of the conceptual difference between RUM- and RRM-based parameter estimates, the best way to establish the behavioral implications of RUM versus RRM is not through interpretation of the parameter estimates but through the direct choice elasticities. Direct choice elasticities derived in the RUM as well as in the RRM context provide a measure of the relationship between a 1 percentage change in the level of the attribute and the percentage change in the probability of choosing the alternative characterized by that specific attribute. Importantly, RRM-based direct elasticities associated with a change in an alternative's attribute depend on the relative performance of *all* the alternatives in the choice tasks, rather than depending only on the performance (choice probability) of the specific alternative. This follows directly from the behavioral premise, underlying the RRM approach, that the regret associated with an alternative's attributes depends on its performance on these attributes relative to the performance of other alternatives on these attributes.

We formally derive the formulae for direct elasticity that has not been derived or implemented in previous papers on RRM. The definition of R_i is:

$$R_i = \sum\nolimits_{j \neq i} \sum\nolimits_{m=1}^{M} \ln\{1 + \exp[\beta_m(x_{jm} - x_{im})]\}. \tag{8.15}$$

To simplify Equation (8.15) for ease of manipulation, we add back and then subtract the i term in the outer sum. This gives us Equation (8.16):

$$R_i = \left\{ \sum\nolimits_{j=1}^{J} \sum\nolimits_{m=1}^{M} \ln\{1 + \exp[\beta_m(x_{jm} - x_{im})]\} \right\} - M \ln 2. \tag{8.16}$$

By definition:

$$P_i = \frac{\exp[-R_i]}{\sum\nolimits_{j=1}^{J} \exp[-R_j]}. \tag{8.17}$$

To differentiate the probability, we use the result $\partial P_i/\partial x_{lm} = P_i \partial \ln P_i/x_{lm}$. Then:

$$\ln P_i = -R_i - \ln \Sigma_{j=1}^{J} \exp(-R_j), \text{ so,}$$

$$\frac{\partial \ln P_i}{\partial x_{lm}} = \frac{-\partial R_i}{\partial x_{lm}} - \frac{\partial \ln \Sigma_{j=1}^{J} \exp(-R_j)}{\partial x_{lm}}$$

$$= \frac{-\partial R_i}{\partial x_{lm}} - \frac{\Sigma_{j=1}^{J} \partial \exp(-R_j)/\partial x_{lm}}{\Sigma_{j=1}^{J} \exp(-R_j)}$$

$$= \frac{-\partial R_i}{\partial x_{lm}} - \frac{\Sigma_{j=1}^{J} \exp(-R_j)\partial(-R_j)/\partial x_{lm}}{\Sigma_{j=1}^{J} \exp(-R_j)} \tag{8.18}$$

$$= \frac{-\partial R_i}{\partial x_{lm}} - \sum\nolimits_{j=1}^{J} P_j \frac{\partial(-R_j)}{\partial x_{lm}}$$

$$= \left(\sum\nolimits_{j=1}^{J} P_j \frac{\partial R_j}{\partial x_{lm}} \right) - \frac{\partial R_i}{\partial x_{lm}}$$

We still require $\partial R_i/\partial x_{lm}$, which is given in Equation (8.19):

$$\frac{\partial R_i}{\partial x_{lm}} (\text{where } l \neq i) = \beta_m \frac{\exp[\beta_m(x_{lm} - x_{im})]}{1 + \exp[\beta_m(x_{lm} - x_{im})]} = \beta_m q(l, i, m),$$

$$\frac{\partial R_i}{\partial x_{im}} (\text{i.e., where } l = i) = -\beta_m \sum\nolimits_{j \neq i}^{J} \frac{\exp[\beta_m(x_{jm} - x_{im})]}{1 + \exp[\beta_m(x_{jm} - x_{im})]}$$

$$= -\beta_m \sum\nolimits_{j=1}^{J} q(j, i, m),$$

where $q(j, j, m) = 0$.   (8.19)

$$\frac{\partial \ln P_i}{\partial x_{lm}} = \beta_m \left[\left(\sum\nolimits_{j=1}^{J} P_j q(j, i, m) \right) - q(l, i, m) \right].$$ (8.20)

Combining terms, the first part of Equation (8.17) is common to both $l = i$ (own elasticities) and $l \neq i$ (cross-elasticities), while the second term in Equation (8.17) involves either the second or the first term in Equation (8.18), respectively. The elasticity, $\partial \ln P_i / \partial \ln x_{lm}$, is then a simple multiplication of Equation (8.17) or Equation (8.19) by x_{lm}. One oddity, unfortunately, is that the sign results that hold for the MNL are not ensured here. The elasticities appear to be reasonably well behaved; however, some peculiar sign reversals can occur.

8.3 Endogeneity

It is not uncommon for analysts to be warned about the possible presence of *endogeneity bias*. Many analysts and others often criticize a model in terms of the presence of endogeneity bias without explaining exactly what this bias is, and what can be done to test for its presence or absence.

In simple terms, endogeneity bias can arise from a number of sources such as measurement error, missing attributes, and simultaneity, and is observed when a specific variable included in the observed effects is correlated with the error term associated with the utility expression containing the explanatory variable of interest. To ensure that the observed component of a model is purged of its endogeneity bias (that is, the part that is correlated with the random error component), one would undertake the following tasks: firstly, test the extent to which the attribute(s) of interest have a systematic influence on the standard deviation of the error component and, second, identify other exogenous variables that are correlated with the attribute of interest, but not with the error component, that could be used as instrumental variables, or simply as evidence of no endogeneity bias. An important finding is one in which we observe that the attribute of interest purges the correlation, effectively eliminating the possibility of endogeneity bias.

In general, the choice model assumes $V + \varepsilon$, which implies that ε is independent of V. If there are some interaction effects that are not accounted for, then one or more variables may end up in both V and ε and hence both terms are no longer orthogonal. For example, if there is a price/quality trade-off, and only price appears in V, then the interaction between price and quality resides in the ε. Then price is in both V and ε and the two are no longer independent. A useful paper on this topic is Petrin and Train, http://elsa. berkeley.edu/~train/petrintrain.pdf. This issue can occur for any variable.

Some analysts (and journal referees) often have a broader definition of endogeneity. Take the example of mode choice and crowding on public transport. Some analysts interpret endogeneity as relating to choices – that is, the issue of crowding occurs because people choose to travel, and one is modeling mode choice (the dependent variable) as a function of choice (leading to crowding), so that choices are on both the LHS and RHS of the equation. In our opinion, this is an invalid inference. Yes, crowding occurs due to people's choices; however, you are modeling respondent preferences in response to other people's choices, not their own. So while the system may have an inherent endogeneity concern, a *particular individual's* preferences are formed on the basis of crowding being exogenous.

8.4 Useful behavioral outputs

Choice modelers typically focus on the derived behavioral outputs from an estimated model, such as how sensitive a sampled respondent's choice (up to a probability) is to a change in the level of an attribute, and how much they are willing to pay to save a unit of a specific attribute. In this section, we set out the underlying theory for the measurement of elasticities and willingness to pay (WTP) associated with specific attributes.

8.4.1 Elasticities of choice

Formally, an **elasticity** may be defined as a unitless measure that describes the relationship between the percentage change for some variable (i.e., an attribute of an alternative or the SEC of a decision maker) and the percentage change in the quantity demanded, *ceteris paribus*. The percentage change in quantity demanded need not be confined to the alternative to which the attribute observed to change belongs, but may also be observed to occur in other competing alternatives. It is for this reason that economists have defined two types of elasticities: *direct elasticities* and *cross-elasticities*. From Louviere *et al.* (2000, 58), direct and cross-elasticities may be defined as:

A direct elasticity measures the percentage change in the probability of choosing a particular alternative in the choice set with respect to a given percentage change in an attribute of that same alternative. A cross-elasticity measures the percentage change in the probability of choosing a particular alternative in the choice set with respect to a given percentage change in an attribute of a competing alternative.

Not only is there a distinction between the form that elasticities may take, there exists also a distinction between how one may calculate the elasticity for an attribute or SEC. The two main methods of calculation are the **arc elasticity** method and the **point elasticity** method. We will ignore the differences between the two estimation methods for the present and note that the default Nlogit output (see Chapter 13) is a point elasticity (except where a dummy variable is used, in which case an arc elasticity is provided, based on the average of the before and after probabilities and attribute levels). We discuss arc elasticities in Chapter 13 and how they can be derived for any measurement unit (e.g., ratio or ordinal) using Nlogit's simulation capability.

The direct point elasticity for the MNL model is given as Equation (8.22), given the definition of the partial effect (or derivative of probability with respect to derivative of X):

$$
\frac{\partial P_i}{\partial X_{ik}} = \frac{\partial}{\partial X_{ik}} \left(\frac{\exp(V_{iq})}{\sum_m \exp(V_{mq})} \right)
$$

$$
= \frac{\exp(V_{iq}) \frac{dV_{iq}}{dX_{ik}} \sum_m \exp(V_{mq}) - \exp(V_{iq})\exp(V_{iq})\frac{\partial V_{iq}}{\partial X_{ik}}}{\left(\sum_m \exp(V_{mq}) \right)^2}
$$

$$
= \frac{\partial V_{iq}}{\partial X_{ik}} P_{iq}(1 - P_{iq}) \tag{8.21}
$$

$$
E_{X_{ikq}}^{P_{iq}} = \frac{\partial P_{iq}}{\partial X_{ikq}} \cdot \frac{X_{ikq}}{P_{iq}} = \frac{\partial V_{iq}}{\partial X_{ikq}} X_{ikq}(1 - P_{iq}). \tag{8.22}
$$

Equation (8.22) is interpreted as the elasticity of the probability of alternative i for decision maker q with respect to a marginal change in the kth attribute of the ith alternative (i.e., X_{ikq}), as observed by decision maker q. Louviere *et al.* (2000) show that, through simplification, the direct *point* elasticity Equation (8.21) for the MNL model for each observation becomes:

$$E_{X_{ikq}}^{P_{iq}} = -\beta_{ik} X_{ikq}(1 - P_{iq}) \tag{8.23}$$

and the cross-point elasticity is given in Equation (8.24):

$$\frac{\partial P_{iq}}{\partial X_{jkq}} = \frac{\partial}{\partial X_{jk}}\left(\frac{\exp(V_{iq})}{\sum_m \exp(V_{mq})}\right) = \frac{-\exp(V_{iq})\exp(V_{jq})\frac{\partial V_{jq}}{\partial X_{jkq}}}{\left(\sum_m \exp(V_{mq})\right)} = -\frac{\partial V_{jq}}{\partial X_{jkq}} P_{iq} P_{jq}$$

$$E_{X_{jkq}}^{P_{iq}} = \frac{\partial P_{iq}}{\partial X_{jkq}} \cdot \frac{X_{jkq}}{P_{iq}} = -\frac{\partial V_{jq}}{\partial X_{jqk}} X_{jqk} P_{jq}.$$

$$\tag{8.24}$$

Examination of the subscripts used within Equation (8.24) will reveal that the cross-point elasticity is calculated for alternative j independent of alternative i. As such, the cross-point elasticities with respect to a variable associated with alternative j will be the same for all $j, j \neq i$ and, as a consequence, a choice model estimated using MNL will display uniform cross-elasticities across all $j, j \neq i$. This property relates to the IID assumption underlying the MNL model. More advanced models (such as those described in later chapters) which relax the IID assumption use different formulae to establish elasticities, and as such allow for non-uniform cross-elasticities to be estimated. Equations (8.22) and (8.24) yield elasticities for each individual decision maker.

To calculate sample elasticities (noting that the MNL choice model is estimated on sample data), the analyst may either (1) utilize the sample average X_{ik} and average estimated P_i for the direct point elasticity, and X_{jk} and average estimated P_j for the direct cross-elasticities, or (2) calculate the elasticity for each individual decision maker and weight each individual elasticity by the decision maker's choice probability associated with a specific alternative (this last method is known as **probability weighted sample enumeration** (PWSE), and uses **;pwt** in Nlogit). Alternative aggregation method (3), known as **naive pooling**, is to calculate the elasticity for each individual decision maker but not weight each individual elasticity by the decision maker's associated choice probability.

Louviere *et al.* (2000) warn against using aggregation (1) and (3). They reject method (1) when using logit choice models due to the non-linear nature of such models, which means that the estimated logit function need not pass through the point defined by the sample averages. Indeed, they report that this method of obtaining aggregate elasticities may result in errors of up to

20 percent (usually over-estimates) in elasticities. Approach (3) to aggregating elasticities is rejected on the grounds that it fails to recognize the contribution of the choice outcome of each alternative.

Heeding this warning, and using the PWSE technique, the aggregate elasticities are calculated using Equation (8.25), where $\hat{P}_{iq}$ is an estimated choice probability and $\bar{P}_i$ refers to the aggregate probability of choice of alternative i:

$$E_{X_{jkq}}^{\bar{P}_i} = \left(\sum_{q=1}^{Q} \hat{P}_{iq} E_{X_{jkq}}^{P_{iq}} \right) / \sum_{q=1}^{Q} \hat{P}_{iq}. \tag{8.25}$$

The use of PWSE has important ramifications for the direct cross-elasticities estimated. Because uniform cross-elasticities are observed as a result of the IID assumption when calculated for individual decision makers, the use of sample enumeration, which weights each individual decision maker differently, will produce non-uniform cross-elasticities. Naive pooling, which does not weight each individual elasticity by the decision maker's associated choice probability, will however, display uniform cross-elasticities. Analysts should not be concerned that the sample cross-elasticities for an attribute differ between pairs of alternatives; the individual-level cross-elasticities are strictly identical for the IID model.

Independent of how the elasticities are calculated, the resulting values are interpreted in exactly the same manner. For direct elasticities, we interpret the calculated elasticity as the percentage change of the choice probability for alternative i given a 1 percent change in X_{ik}. For cross-elasticities, we interpret the calculated elasticity as the percentage change of the choice probability for alternative j given a 1 percent change in X_{ik}. If the percentage change in the probability for either the direct or cross-elasticity is observed to be greater than 1, that elasticity is said to be *relatively elastic*. If the percentage change in the probability for either the direct or cross-elasticity is observed to be less than 1, that elasticity is said to be *relatively inelastic*. If a 1 percent change in a choice probability is observed given a 1 percent change in X_{ik}, then the elasticity is described as being *unit elastic*. Table 8.1 summarizes each scenario, including the impact on revenue (or cost) given that X_{ik} is the price of alternative i, noting that $\varepsilon = E_{X_{jkq}}^{\bar{P}_i}$.

8.4.2 Partial or marginal effects

A partial or marginal effect reflects the rate of change in one variable relative to the rate of change in a second variable. However, unlike elasticities,

Table 8.1 Relationship between elasticity of demand, change in price and revenue

	Absolute value of elasticity observed	Direct elasticity	Cross-elasticity	Price increase	Price decrease	Diagram
Perfectly inelastic	$\varepsilon = 0$	1 percent increase in X_i results in a 0 percent decrease in P_i	1 percent increase in X_i results in a 0 percent increase in P_j	Revenue increases	Revenue decreases	
Relatively inelastic	$0 < \varepsilon < 1$	1 percent increase in X_i results in a less than 1 percent decrease in P_i	1 percent increase in X_i results in a less than 1 percent increase in P_j	Revenue increases	Revenue decreases	
Unit elastic	$\varepsilon = 1$	1 percent increase in X_i results in a 1 percent change in P_i	1 percent increase in X_i results in no percent change in P_j	Revenue unchanged	Revenue unchanged	
Relatively elastic	$1 < \varepsilon < \infty$	1 percent increase in X_i results in a greater than 1 percent decrease in P_i	1 percent increase in X_i results in a greater than 1 percent increase in P_j	Revenue decreases	Revenue increases	
Perfectly elastic	$\varepsilon = \infty$	1 percent increase in X_i results in an ∞ percent decrease in P_i	1 percent increase in X_i results in an ∞ percent increase in P_j	Revenue decreases	Revenue increases	

marginal effects are not expressed as percentage changes. Rather, marginal effects are expressed as unit changes. More specifically, we interpret the marginal effect for a choice model as the change in probability given a unit change in a variable, *ceteris paribus*.

A further similarity exists between marginal effects and elasticities in that, as with elasticities, marginal effects may be represented as both direct and cross-effects. Direct marginal effects represent the change in the choice probability for an alternative given a 1 unit change in a variable of interest, that variable belonging to that same alternative, *ceteris paribus* (see Equation 8.21). Cross-marginal effects represent the impact a 1 unit change in a variable has upon the choice probabilities of competing alternatives to which that attribute does not belong, *ceteris paribus*.

However unlike elasticities (unless treated as a 100 percent change), marginal effects assigned to categorically coded data do make sense. Using gender as an example, a 1 unit change in the gender variable represents the change in choice probabilities (i.e., both direct and cross) given a change from male to female (or vice versa). As we discuss later (below and in Chapter 13), however, the method of calculating marginal effects for categorical data is different from the calculation performed for continuous level data.

A further difference concerns the notion that a marginal effect represents an absolute change in the choice probabilities, while an elasticity represents a proportional change. To show why, consider a marginal effect of 0.1 and an elasticity of 0.1. For the marginal effect, we interpret this as a change in the choice probability for all decision makers of 0.1 given a 1 unit change in the variable for which the marginal effect was calculated, *ceteris paribus*. For the elasticity, we would say that a 1 percent change in the variable of interest will result in a 0.1 percent change in the choice probabilities, *ceteris paribus*. Assuming that the observed choice probabilities for two alternatives are 0.5 and 0.4, a 0.1 percent change (i.e., an elasticity) represents changes of 0.005 and 0.004, respectively, not 0.1 (i.e., a marginal effect).

The direct marginal effect for the MNL model is given as Equation (8.26). The astute reader will note the relationship between the marginal effect and elasticity formula of Equation (8.22). It is the second component of Equation (8.22) that translates a marginal effect to an elasticity. That is, it is the second component of Equation (8.22) that converts Equation (8.26) to a percentage rather than unit change in the dependent choice variable:

$$M_{X_{ikq}}^{P_{iq}} = \frac{\partial P_{iq}}{\partial X_{ikq}}. \tag{8.26}$$

It can be shown that at the level of the individual decision maker, Equation (8.26) is equivalent to Equation (8.27) when calculating a direct marginal effect:

$$M_{X_{ikq}}^{P_{iq}} = \frac{\partial P_{iq}}{\partial X_{ikq}} = [1 - P_{iq}]\beta_k. \tag{8.27}$$

It can also be shown that for cross-marginal effects, Equation (8.26) becomes Equation (8.28) at the level of the individual decision maker:

$$M_{X_{jkq}}^{P_{iq}} = -\beta_{jk}P_{jq}. \tag{8.28}$$

As with elasticities, since the choice model is estimated on a sample of choice data, and not choice data for a single individual, the marginal effect for a variable should be calculated for the aggregate sample and not at the level of the individual decision maker.

To calculate an aggregate marginal effect, the analyst may, as with the calculation of the aggregate elasticities, either (1) utilize the average estimated P_i for the direct marginal effect and average estimated P_j for the cross-marginal effect (i.e., equivalent to using the sample means in estimated aggregate elasticities) or (2) calculate the marginal effect for each individual decision maker and weight each individual marginal effect by the decision maker's associated choice probability (i.e., probability weighted sample enumeration), or (3) calculate the marginal effect for each individual decision maker but not weight each individual marginal effect by the decision maker's associated choice probability (i.e., employ naive pooling). As with the calculation of aggregate elasticities, the authors advise against the use of the probability means and naive pooling and advocate the use of PWSE to calculate marginal effects for discrete choice models.

As an aside, to demonstrate why the marginal effect for a categorical variable is calculated differently from that of a continuous variable, marginal effects are mathematically equivalent to the slopes of lines tangent to the cumulative probability curve for the variable for which the marginal effect is being calculated, as taken at each distinct value of that variable (Powers and Xie 2000). We show this in Figure 8.2 for an individual decision maker. Given that the tangent can be taken at any point along the cumulative distribution for the variable, x_i, our earlier discussion with regard to the use of the sample means, sample enumeration or naive pooling is of particular importance, as it is these approaches which dictate where on the cumulative distribution curve that the tangent (i.e., the marginal effect) is calculated.

For categorical variables, a cumulative distribution function curve may be drawn for each level that the variable of concern may take. We show this for a dummy coded (0, 1) variable in Figure 8.3, in which two curves are present. As with continuous level data, the marginal effects as given by the tangents to the cumulative distribution functions are not constant over the range of the variable x_i. However as suggested by Figure 8.3, the maximum difference between the cumulative distribution function for the two levels occurs at Prob(Y=1) = 0.5. It is at this point that many researchers calculate the marginal effects (i.e., the tangents to the curves).

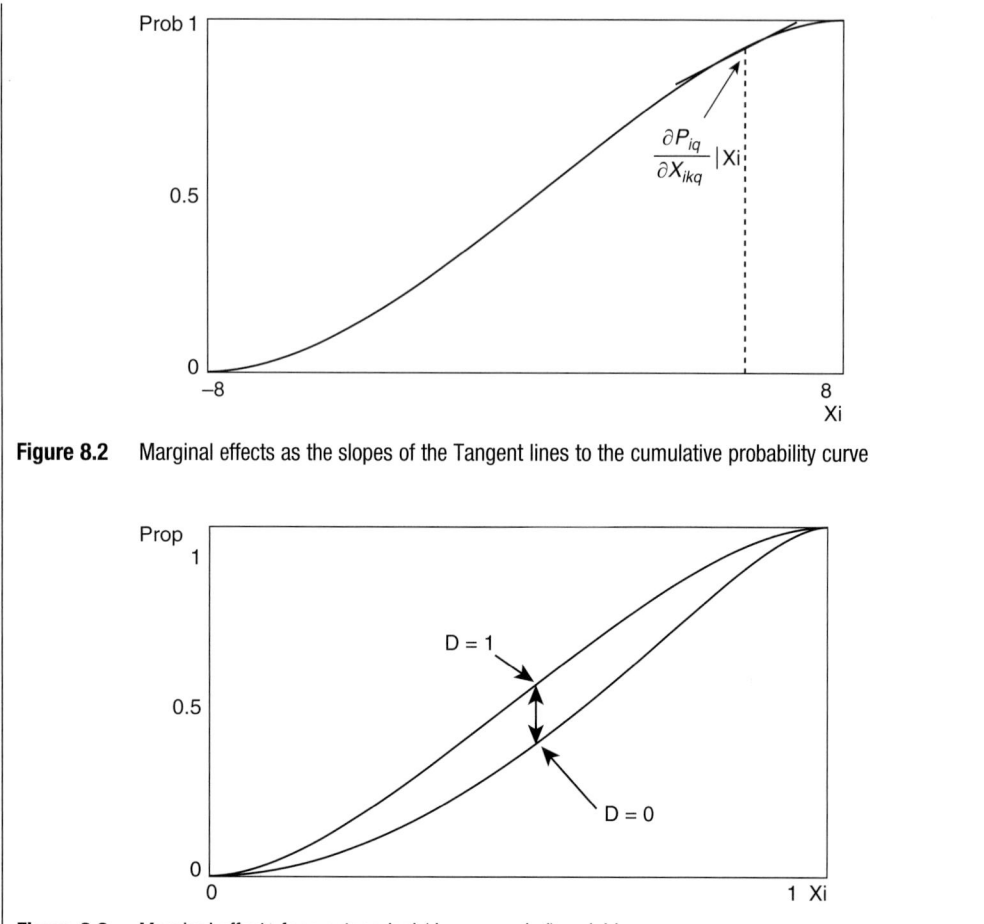

Figure 8.2   Marginal effects as the slopes of the Tangent lines to the cumulative probability curve

Figure 8.3   Marginal effects for a categorical (dummy coded) variable

For categorical variables, a cumulative distribution function curve may be drawn for each level that the variable of concern may take. Looking ahead (see Chapter 13), Nlogit treats the cumulative distribution function as a continuous variable when calculating a marginal effect, independent of whether the variable for which the marginal effect is sought is continuous or not.

8.4.3 Willingness to pay

An important output from choice models is the **marginal rate of substitution** (MRS) between specific attributes of interest, with a financial variable typically being in the trade-off so that the MRS can be expressed in dollar terms. The MRS is more commonly referred to as a WTP estimate.

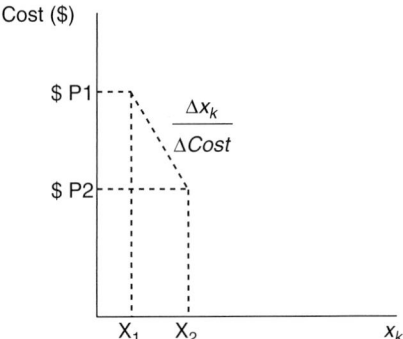

Figure 8.4   WTP as a trade-off between attributes

Using the trade-off between travel time and travel cost as an example (see Figure 8.4), the marginal WTP as the measure of value of time savings (VTTS) describes how much the cost attribute, x_c, would be required to change given a 1 unit change in an attribute, x_k, such that the change in total utility will be zero. The marginal WTP is calculated by taking the ratio of the derivatives of both the attribute of interest and cost, which in the case of a linear in the attributes indirect utility specification is given by Equation (8.29):

$$WTP_k = \frac{\Delta x_k}{\Delta x_c} = \frac{\frac{\partial V_{nsj}}{\partial x_k}}{\frac{\partial V_{nsj}}{\partial x_c}} = \frac{\beta_k}{\beta_c}. \tag{8.29}$$

where V_{nsj} is the utility for respondent n in choice task s for alternative j, and β_k and β_c are the marginal (dis)utilities for the attribute of interest and cost, respectively.

Sometimes an attribute is expressed in natural logarithmic form. When this occurs this is an "additional non-linearity" that requires a different treatment when taking derivatives. For example, if x_k is defined as $\ln(x_k)$, then Equation (8.29) becomes Equation (8.30):

$$WTP = \frac{\frac{\partial}{\partial x_k}\beta_k \ln(x_k)}{\frac{\partial}{\partial x_c}\beta_c x_c} = \frac{\beta_k \frac{1}{x_k}}{\beta_c} = \frac{\beta_k}{\beta_c x_k}. \tag{8.30}$$

Another popular transformation is to include an interaction between two attributes, such as between x_k and x_l, where the latter could be a socio-economic characteristic or another attribute of an alternative. The WTP becomes Equation (8.31):

$$WTP = \frac{\frac{\partial}{\partial x_k}\beta_k x_k x_l}{\frac{\partial}{\partial x_c}\beta_c x_c} = \frac{\beta_k x_l}{\beta_c}. \tag{8.31}$$

8.4.3.1 Computing confidence intervals for WTP

It is often the case that analysts wish to use a more complex non-linear functional form in which the WTP is itself a function of the levels of specific attributes. We would not only want to obtain the mean estimate of WTP but also obtain the variance, and use both outputs to obtain the asymptotic standard error and confidence intervals. This fuller set of output is essential if one is to know the extent of relevance of the mean as a robust estimate. It is also necessary information when one wishes to compare mean estimates based on different functional forms using the same data or comparing evidence from different data sets.

As an example, take the utility function given in Rose *et al.* (2012):

$$V = \ldots + \beta_1 x_k + \beta_2 x_k x_c + \beta_3 x_c^2 + \ldots.$$

The mean WTP is given by $-(\hat{\beta}_1 + \hat{\beta}_2 \bar{x}_c)/(\hat{\beta}_2 \bar{x}_k + 2\hat{\beta}_3 \bar{x}_c)$, while the variance can be computed as:

$$\mathrm{var}(WTP_k) = \left(\begin{array}{c} \dfrac{\partial V}{\partial \beta_1} \\[2mm] \dfrac{\partial V}{\partial \beta_2} \\[2mm] \dfrac{\partial V}{\partial \beta_3} \end{array} \right)^T_{\beta=\hat{\beta}} \cdot \Omega \cdot \left(\begin{array}{c} \dfrac{\partial V}{\partial \beta_1} \\[2mm] \dfrac{\partial V}{\partial \beta_2} \\[2mm] \dfrac{\partial V}{\partial \beta_3} \end{array} \right)_{\beta=\hat{\beta}}$$

$$= \frac{1}{(\hat{\beta}_2 \bar{x}_k + 2\hat{\beta}_3 \bar{x}_c)^2} \left(\begin{array}{c} -1 \\[2mm] \dfrac{(\hat{\beta}_1 + \hat{\beta}_2 \bar{x}_c)\bar{x}_k}{\hat{\beta}_2 \bar{x}_k + 2\hat{\beta}_3 \bar{x}_c} - \bar{x}_c \\[4mm] \dfrac{2\bar{x}_c(\hat{\beta}_1 + \hat{\beta}_2 \bar{x}_c)}{\hat{\beta}_2 \bar{x}_k + 2\hat{\beta}_3 \bar{x}_c} \end{array} \right)^T \left(\begin{array}{ccc} \mathrm{var}(\hat{\beta}_1) & \mathrm{cov}(\hat{\beta}_1,\hat{\beta}_2) & \mathrm{cov}(\hat{\beta}_1,\hat{\beta}_3) \\[2mm] \mathrm{cov}(\hat{\beta}_2,\hat{\beta}_1) & \mathrm{var}(\hat{\beta}_2) & \mathrm{cov}(\hat{\beta}_2,\hat{\beta}_3) \\[2mm] \mathrm{cov}(\hat{\beta}_3,\hat{\beta}_1) & \mathrm{cov}(\hat{\beta}_3,\hat{\beta}_2) & \mathrm{var}(\hat{\beta}_3) \end{array} \right)$$

$$\left(\begin{array}{c} -1 \\[2mm] \dfrac{(\hat{\beta}_1 + \hat{\beta}_2 \bar{x}_c)\bar{x}_k}{\hat{\beta}_2 \bar{x}_k + 2\hat{\beta}_3 \bar{x}_c} - \bar{x}_c \\[4mm] \dfrac{2\bar{x}_c(\hat{\beta}_1 + \hat{\beta}_2 \bar{x}_c)}{\hat{\beta}_2 \bar{x}_k + 2\hat{\beta}_3 \bar{x}_c} \end{array} \right). \tag{8.32}$$

In Chapter 13, we use the Wald procedures (from Chapter 7) to illustrate how the analyst can obtain the empirical estimates of the mean, the standard error, and the confidence intervals.

8.4.3.2 Symmetry versus asymmetry in WTP

This section draws on material in Hess *et al.* (2008), which is a good example of how one can account for the asymmetric nature of WTP (or, in this example, VTTS). In a linear model, the observed utility of alternative *i* is given by an equation like Equation (8.33), using various time and cost variables in an unlabeled choice experiment in which the inclusion/exclusion of the toll indicates the type of road that is used (i.e., of tolled versus free route). The unlabeled stated choice alternatives were pivoted around a reference (or revealed preference) alternative:

$$V_i = \delta_i + \delta_{Toll(i)} + \delta_{FC(i)} + \beta_{FF}FF_i + \beta_{SDT}SDT_i + \beta_C C_i + \beta_T Toll_i , \qquad (8.33)$$

where δ_i is a constant associated with alternative *i* (normalized to zero for the third alternative[3]), and β_{FF}, β_{SDT}, β_C, and β_T are the parameters associated with free flow travel time (FFT), slowed-down travel time (SDT), running cost (C), and road tolls (Toll), respectively. Travel time attributes are expressed in minutes, while travel cost attributes are expressed in Australian dollars ($AU). The two additional parameters, $\delta_{Toll(i)}$ and $\delta_{FC(i)}$, are only estimated in the case where a toll is charged for alternative *i* and in the case where alternative *i* includes no free flow time (i.e., FC = fully congested).

The above specification can be adapted to work with differences in relation to a reference or revealed preference (RP) alternative, as opposed to using the absolute values presented to respondents in the SC experiments. The use of a referencing approach relates to prospect theory (Kahneman and Tversky 1979), according to which, due to limitations on their ability to cognitively solve difficult problems, decision makers simplify the choice process by evaluating the gains or losses to be made by choosing a specific alternative, relative to a neutral or status quo point. For the reference alternative *r*, the utility function is rewritten to include only the three dummy variables δr (ASC), $\delta_{Toll(r)}$ (toll road dummy), and $\delta_{FC(r)}$ (fully congested dummy).

---

[3] The significance of an ASC related to an unlabeled alternative simply implies that after controlling for the effects of the modeled attributes, this alternative has been chosen more or less frequently than the base alternative. It is possible that this might be the case because the alternative is close to the reference alternative, or that culturally, those undertaking the experiment tend to read left to right. Failure to estimate an ASC would in this case correlate the alternative order effect into the other estimated parameters, possibly distorting the model results.

For SC alternative j (where $j \neq r$), the observed utility function is given by:

$$V_{j,\text{new}} = \delta_j + \delta_{\text{Toll}(j)} + \delta_{\text{FC}(j)} + \beta_{\text{FF(inc)}}\max(FF_j - FF_r, 0) + \beta_{\text{FF(dec)}}\max(FF_r - FF_j, 0)$$

$$+ \beta_{\text{SDT(inc)}}\max(SDT_j - SDT_r, 0) + \beta_{\text{SDT(dec)}}\max(SDT_r - SDT_j, 0)$$
$$+ \beta_{\text{C(inc)}}\max(C_j - C_r, 0) + \beta_{\text{C(dec)}}\max(C_r - C_j, 0)$$
$$+ \beta_{\text{Toll(inc)}}\max(Toll_j - Toll_r, 0) + \beta_{\text{Toll(dec)}}\max(Toll_r - Toll_j, 0). \qquad (8.34)$$

This specification is obtained through taking differences for the four attributes relative to the reference alternative, where separate coefficients are estimated for increases (inc) and decreases (dec), hence allowing for asymmetrical responses. The resulting model structure is still very easy to estimate and also apply, which is crucial for practical large-scale modeling analyses.

A point that deserves some attention before describing the results of the modeling analysis is the way in which the models deal with the repeated choice nature of the data. Not accounting for the possible correlation between the behavior of a given respondent across the individual choice situations can potentially have a significant effect on model results, especially in terms of biased standard errors. In an analysis looking at differences between the responses to gains and losses, issues with over- or under-estimated standard errors can clearly lead to misleading conclusions.

Rather than relying on the use of a lagged response formulation (cf., Train 2003) or a jackknife correction approach (cf., Cirillo *et al.* 2000), we can make use of an error components specification of the mixed logit (MMNL) model (see Section 15.8 of Chapter 15)[4] to account for individual-specific correlation. With $V_{n,t,\text{RP,base}}$, $V_{n,t,\text{SP1,base}}$, and $V_{n,t,\text{SP2,base}}$ giving the base utilities for the three alternatives[5] for respondent n and choice situation t, the final utility function (for respondent n and choice situation t) is given by Equation (8.35) for the reference alternative and two stated preference alternatives:

$$U_{n,t,RP} = V_{n,t,\text{RP,base}} + \theta\xi_{n,RP} + \varepsilon_{n,k,RP}$$
$$U_{n,t,SP,1} = V_{n,t,\text{SP1,base}} + \theta\xi_{n,SP1} + \varepsilon_{n,k,SP1}$$
$$U_{n,t,SP,2} = V_{n,t,\text{SP2,base}} + \theta\xi_{n,SP2} + \varepsilon_{n,k,SP2} \qquad (8.35)$$

---

[4] Our method differs from the commonly used approach of capturing serial correlation with a random coefficients formulation, where tastes are assumed to vary across respondents but remain constant across observations for the same respondent. This approach not only makes the considerable assumption of an absence of inter-observational variation (cf. Hess and Rose 2007), but the results are potentially also affected by confounding between serial correlation and random taste heterogeneity.

[5] Independently of which specification is used, i.e. models based on Equation (8.33).

where $\varepsilon_{n,k,RP}$, $\varepsilon_{n,k,SP1}$, and $\varepsilon_{n,k,SP2}$ are the IID draws from a Type I Extreme value distribution, and $\xi_{n,RP}$, $\xi_{n,SP1}$ and $\xi_{n,SP2}$ are draws from three independent Normal variates with a zero mean and a standard deviation of 1. To allow for correlation across replications for the same individual, the integration over these latter three variates is carried out at the respondent level rather than the individual observation level. However, the fact that independent N(0,1) draws are used for different alternatives (i.e., $\xi_{n,RP}$, $\xi_{n,SP1}$ and $\xi_{n,SP2}$) means that the correlation does not extend to correlation across alternatives but is restricted to correlation across replications for the same individual and a given alternative. Finally, the fact that the separate error components are distributed identically means that the model remains homoskedastic.

Letting $j_{n,t}$ refer to the alternative chosen by respondent n in choice situation t (with $t = 1,\ldots,T$), the contribution of respondent n to the log-likelihood (LL) function is then given by:

$$LL_n = \ln \left(\int_{\xi n} \left(\prod_{t=1}^{T} P(j_{n,t} | V_{n,t,RP,base}, V_{n,t,SP1,base}, V_{n,t,SP2,base}, \right.\right.$$

$$\left.\left. \xi_{n,RP}, \xi_{n,SP1}, \xi_{n,SP2}, \theta) \right) f(\xi_n) d\xi_n \right), \tag{8.36}$$

where ξ groups together $\xi_{n,RP}$, $\xi_{n,SP1}$, and $\xi_{n,SP2}$, and where $f(\xi_n)$ refers to the joint distribution of the elements in ξ, with a diagonal covariance matrix.

Using the example for VTTS, in Table 8.2 we summarize the trade-offs between the various estimated parameters, giving the monetary values of changes in travel time, as well as the WTP a bonus in return for avoiding congestion and road tolls. These trade-offs were calculated separately for the

Table 8.2 WTP indicators for base models ($AUD2005)

	versus β_C		versus β_{Toll}	
	Non-commuters	Commuters	Non-commuters	Commuters
β_{FF} ($/hour)	13.39	13.30	12.62	15.95
β_{SDT} ($/hour)	14.95	16.60	14.09	19.90
δ_{FC} ($)	4.89	−0.95*	4.61	−1.14[1]
δ_{Toll} ($)	0.74	1.14	0.70	1.37

Note: 1 Numerator of trade-off not significant beyond 25 percent level of confidence.

Table 8.3 WTP indicators for asymmetrical models $ (AUD2005)

	versus β_C		versus β_{Toll}	
	Non-commuters	Commuters	Non-commuters	Commuters
β_{FF} ($/hour)	9.99	7.27	6.72	6.40
β_{SDT} ($/hour)	15.51	13.70	10.44	12.07
δ_{FC} ($)	-0.18^1	-2.01^2	-0.12^1	-1.77^2
δ_{Toll} ($)	1.82	1.45	1.22	1.28

Notes:
[1] Numerator of trade-off not significant beyond 4 percent level of confidence.
[2] Numerator of trade-off not significant beyond 93 percent level of confidence.

travel cost and road toll coefficient, where the low level of differences needs to be recognized when comparing the results. The main differences between the two sets of trade-offs and across the two population segments arise in the greater willingness by commuters to accept increases in road tolls, and the higher sensitivity to slowed-down time for commuters.

In an asymmetrical model, the calculation is slightly different, as we now have separate parameters for increases and decreases, suggesting different possible combinations of VTTS calculations. As an example, the willingness to accept increases in travel cost in return for reductions in free flow time would be given by $-\beta_{FF}(dec)/\beta_C(inc)$. This approach was used to calculate WTP indicators for the two components of travel time with the two separate cost components, where trade-offs were also calculated for δ_{FC} and δ_T. The results of these calculations are summarized in Table 8.3.

In comparison with the results for the base model, there are some significant differences. The willingness to accept (WTA) increases in travel cost in return for reductions in free flow time decreases by 25 percent and 45 percent for non-commuters and commuters, respectively. Even more significant decreases (47 percent and 60 percent) are observed when looking at the WTA increases in road tolls. While the WTA increases in travel cost in return for reductions in slowed-down time stays almost constant for non-commuters, it decreases by 17 percent for commuters (when compared to the base model). When using road tolls instead of travel cost, there are decreases in both population segments, by 26 percent and 39 percent, respectively. These differences are yet another indication of the effects of allowing for asymmetrical response rates.

Part II

Software and data

9   Nlogit for applied choice analysis

Programming today is a race between software engineers striving to build bigger and better idiot-proof programs, and the Universe trying to produce bigger and better idiots. So far, the Universe is winning.

(Cook, The Wizardry Compiled 1989)

9.1   Introduction

This book uses the computer program, Nlogit, which will enable you to explore the models that are discussed in the book using your own computer. Nlogit is a a major commercial package published by Econometric Software, Inc. (ESI), which is used worldwide by discrete choice modelers in many disciplines such as Transport, Economics, Agriculture, Health, Marketing, Statistics, and all the social sciences (you might want to visit the website, www.NLOGIT.com). This chapter will describe how to install and use this program on your computer.

9.2   About the software

9.2.1   About Nlogit

Nlogit is an extension of another very large, integrated econometrics package, Limdep, that is used worldwide by analysts of models for regression, discrete choice, sample selection, censored data, count data, models for panel data, etc. Nlogit includes all of the capabilities of Limdep plus the package of estimators for models of multinomial choice, such as the multinomial logit (MNL), multinomial probit (MNP), nested logit, mixed logit, generalized mixed logit, ordered logit, latent class, and several others including a very general non-linear random parameters capability in which users write out their own non-linear in parameter and variables functional forms for estimation as a logit model (see Chapter 19), and, in addition, some tools for analyzing discrete choice models such as the model simulator described elsewhere in this book.

9.2.2 Installing Nlogit

Nlogit is a Windows-based program. It will self-install on most machines. Just double click the installation program in any Windows explorer. Windows will find the program and invoke the installation package. This in turn will install the program and place startup icons in your *Start* menu, in the programs menu, and on your desktop. You can start Nlogit from any of these icons just by double clicking it. (You can install Nlogit on a Macintosh computer with a suitable Windows emulator such as *Parallels*.)

9.3 Starting Nlogit and exiting after a session

9.3.1 Starting the program

You can start Nlogit from any of the program icons or menu entries. The main desktop will appear, as shown in Figure 9.1.

9.3.2 Reading the data

In order to do any analysis, you must now input the data to the program. As an example, we take our data that is placed in an Nlogit data file named <*AppliedChoice.lpj*> (the .lpj suffix is a Windows recognized file type which stands for "limdep project file"). Note that this data is not available to readers but is used by the authors as a way of illustrating the NLOGIT set up. You can use your own data to work through the process explained below. To read the data into NLOGIT, use *File, Open Project. . .*, then make your way to this file. We can select the file by by double clicking the file name, and then you are ready to begin. The process is shown in Figure 9.2. Figure 9.3 shows how your desktop will appear after you load your project into the program.

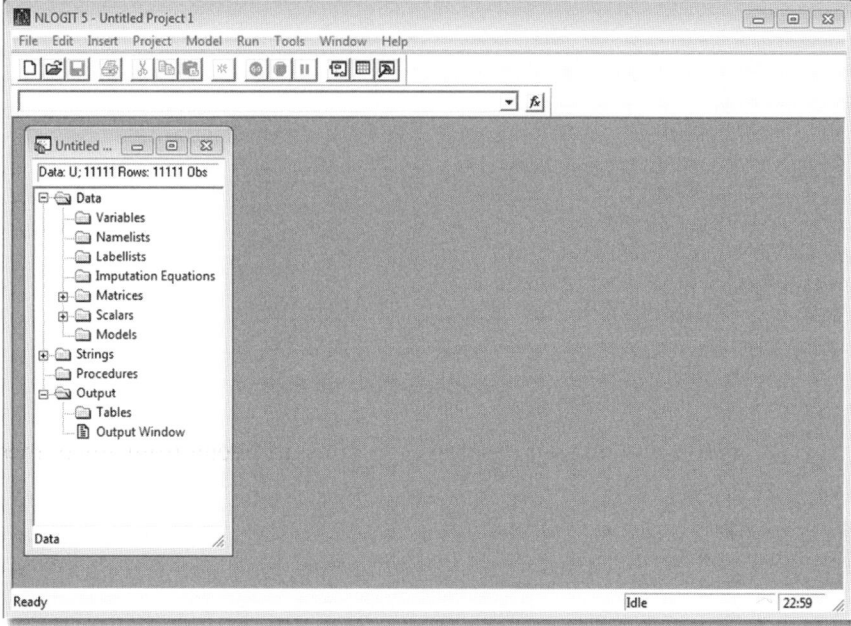

Figure 9.1   Initial Nlogit desktop

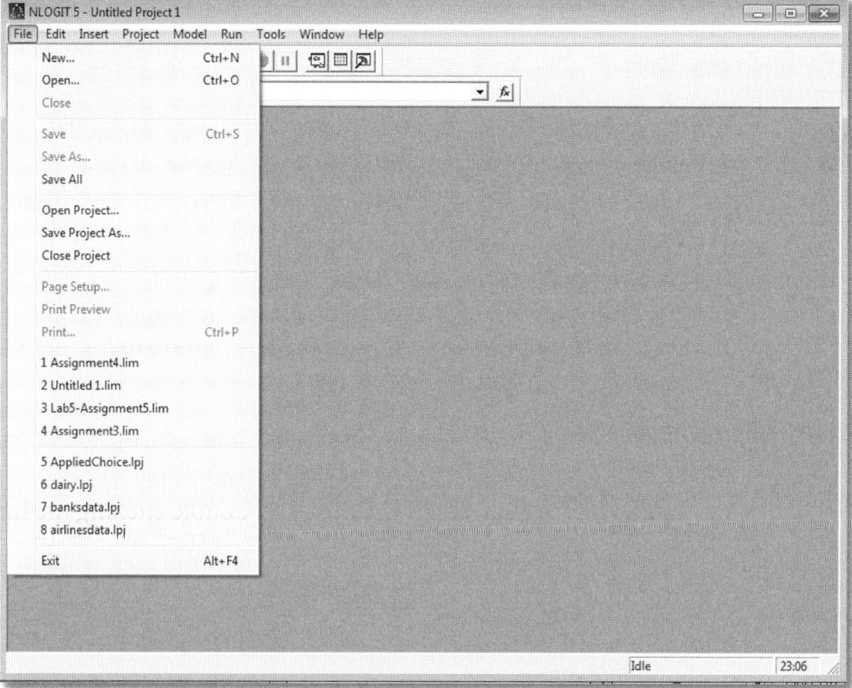

Figure 9.2   File Menu on Main Desktop and Open Project. . .Explorer

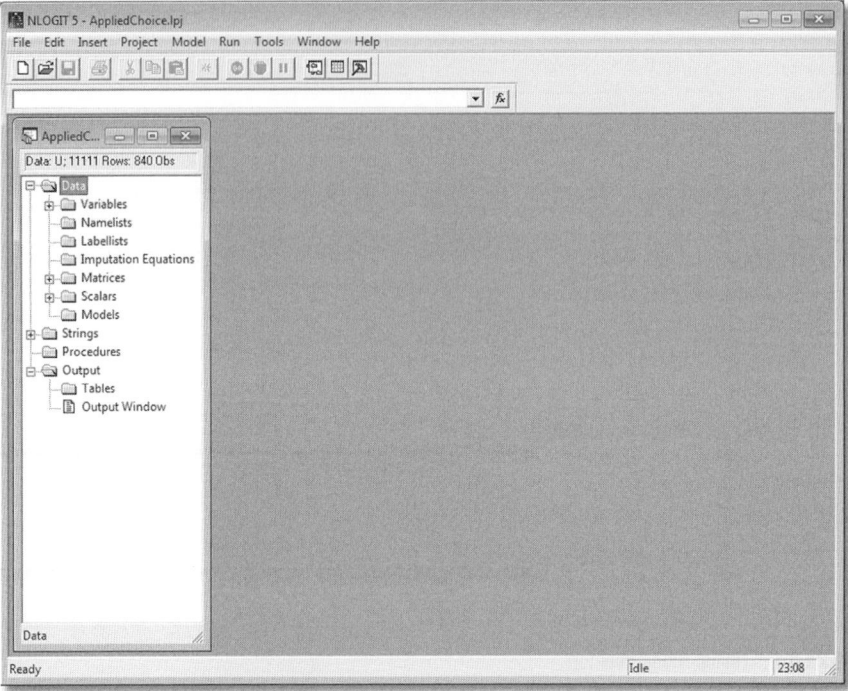

Figure 9.3   Nlogit desktop after Project File Input

9.3.3 Input the data

Nlogit can read many kinds of data files, including rectangular ASCII files and spreadsheet files from programs such as Microsoft Excel®. The program operation to do so is an **IMPORT** or a **READ** command. Importing data is discussed in detail in this chapter (note, once again, that this version of the program will only be able to import its own data set). The data set specific to this text is discussed below. We find that converting XLS or XLSX files to CSV files is the best way to ensure the data is fully compatible with Nlogit.

9.3.4 The project file

All data are stored in the project file. You will be able to create new variables and add them to your project file. When you leave Nlogit, you will be offered a chance to save the project file. You should do this. Later, when you restart the program, you will find *AppliedChoice.lpj* in the bottom part of the file menu in the recent files, and you can load the data into the program by selecting this file from the *File* menu.

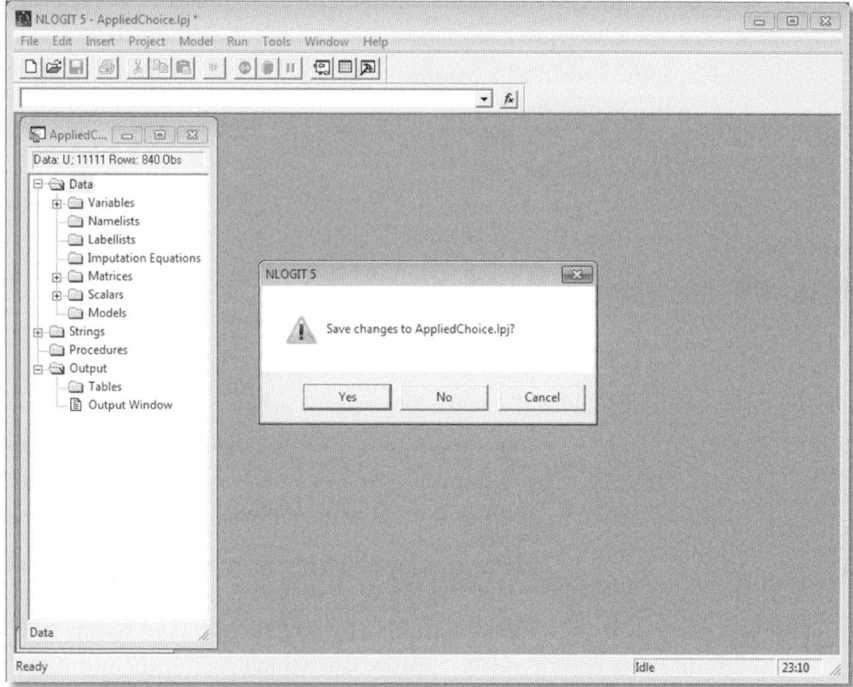

Figure 9.4   Dialog for Exiting Nlogit and Saving the Project File

9.3.5 Leaving your session

When you are ready to leave your session, you should use *File*, *Exit* to close the program (double clicking the Nlogit icon at the extreme upper left of the desktop, or single clicking the red ×button at the extreme upper right will also close the program). When you leave Nlogit, you are given an opportunity to save your work, as shown in Figure 9.4. You should save your project file if you have made any changes that you wish to keep.

9.4 Using Nlogit

Once you have started the program and input your data, you are ready to analyze them. The functions you will perform with Nlogit will include many options such as the following:

a. Compute new variables or transform existing variables.
b. Set the sample to use particular sets of observations in your analyses.

c. Use program tools such as the scientific calculator to compute statistics.

d. Use the descriptive statistics package to learn about your data set.

e. Compute linear regressions.

f. Use the Nlogit features to estimate and analyze discrete choice models.

g. Present all outputs as graphs and tables.

9.5 How to Get Nlogit to do what you want

There are two methods of giving "commands" or instructions to Nlogit. Both will produce identical results. The row of desktop commands at the top of your screen, *File, Edit, Insert, Project*, etc., all invoke dialog boxes that will query you about the information needed to carry out your instructions. There are also dialog boxes for specifying models invoked by the *Model* command. These are standard, Windows style, dialogs that generally require minimal information from you, sometimes nothing more than clicking boxes or buttons to indicate a decision. The alternative method is for you to type commands to Nlogit and to submit these commands to a processor which carries them out for you.

The two methods have their advantages and disadvantages. The dialog boxes are convenient, but have three shortcomings: (1) It is usually necessary to redo all steps completely if you want to repeat an operation; dialog boxes do not remember anything. (2) The dialog boxes do not always provide all the different variations for an instruction you want carried out. (3) Ultimately, command entry by the dialog boxes will become tedious and slow. The command entry is self-documenting – once you enter a command by the method discussed below, the command itself is retained and you can reuse it. Also, commands look like what they are trying to do. For example, the command **CREATE; LOGX = Log(x)$** carries out a function similar to what it looks like (i.e., creates a variable called *logx* which is the natural log of a variable called *x*). The discussion below will describe how to use the Text Editor to enter instructions. You may want to experiment with the menus and dialogs as well.

9.5.1 Using the Text Editor

In order to submit commands to Nlogit's command processor, you will first type them in the "Text Editor." The command (Text) Editor is a basic, standard text processor in which you enter lines of text that are commands to Nlogit. The editor also uses standard features such as Cut/Copy/Paste, highlight, drag and

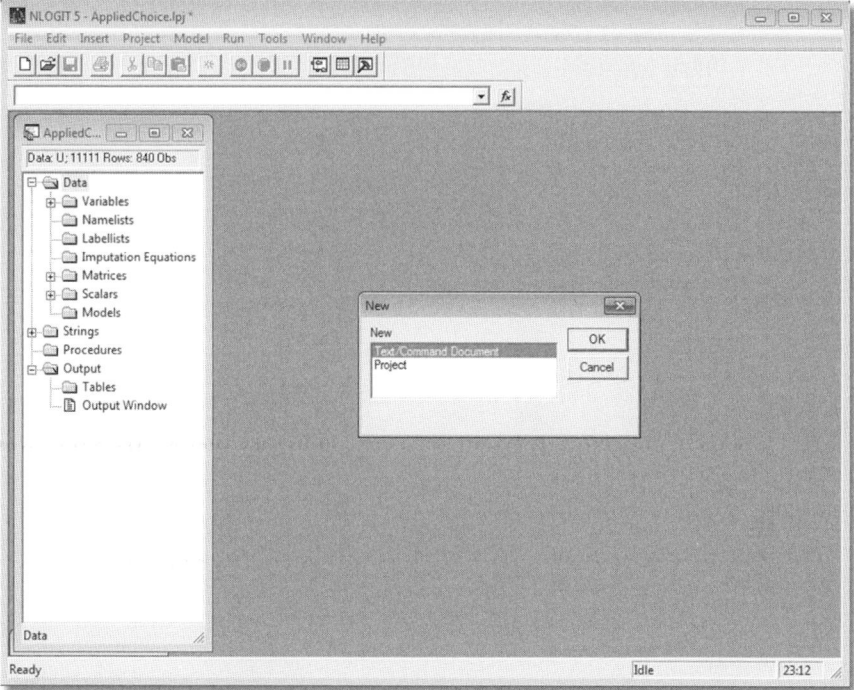

Figure 9.5   Dialog for Opening the Text Editor

drop, etc. Use *File*, *New* then *OK* (assuming Text/Command Document is high-lighted as in Figure 9.5) to open the text editing screen. This will appear as in Figure 9.6. You are now ready to type your instructions. Figure 9.7 shows some examples (the format of the instructions is discussed below and elsewhere in the book). Typing an instruction in the editor is the first step in getting your command carried out. You must then "submit" the instruction to the program. This is done in two ways, both using the "Go" button that is marked in Figure 9.7. To submit a single line of text to the program for execution, put the blinking text cursor on that line, then with your mouse, press the Go button. The instruction will then be executed (assuming it has no errors in it). To submit more than one line at the same time (or one line), highlight the lines as you would in any word processor, then, again, press "Go."

9.5.2 Command format

Nlogit instructions all have the same format. Each new instruction must begin on a new line (see Figure 9.7). Within any instruction, you may use lower case

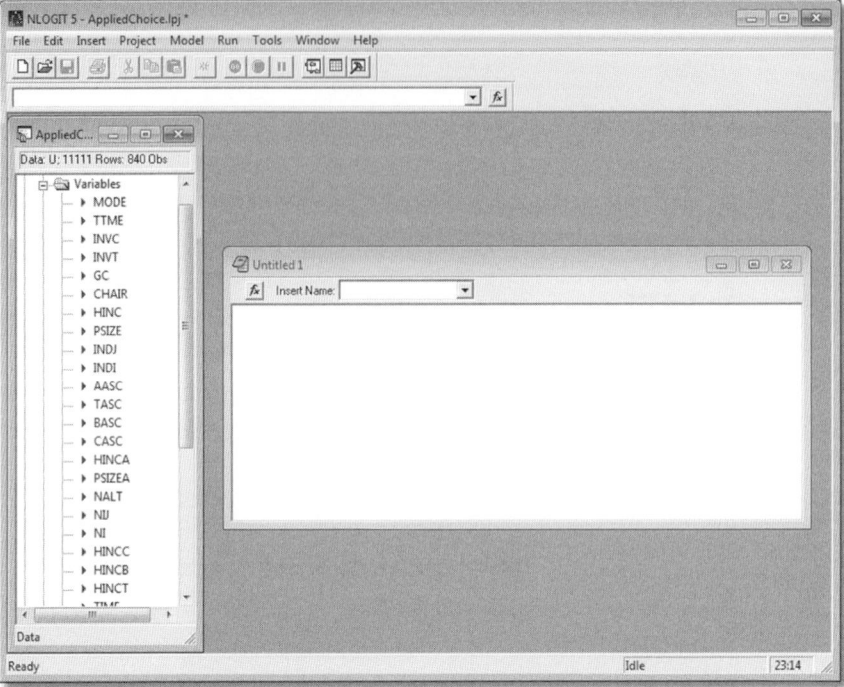

Figure 9.6   Text Editor Ready for Command Entry

or capital letters, and you may place spaces anywhere you wish. An instruction may use as many lines as desired. The general format of a command is:

```
VERB; other information ...$
```

The command always begins with a verb followed by a semicolon and always ends with a dollar sign ($). Commands often give several pieces of information. These are separated by semicolons. For example, when you wish to compute a regression, you must tell Nlogit what the dependent (LHS) and independent (RHS) variables are. You might do this as follows:

```
REGRESS ; LHS = y ; Rhs = One,X $
```

The order of command parts generally does not matter either – the RHS variables could appear first. The other element of commands that you need at this point is the naming convention. Nlogit operates on variables in your data set. Variables all have names, of course. In Nlogit, variable names must have one to eight characters, must begin with a letter, and may use only letters, digits, and the underscore character.

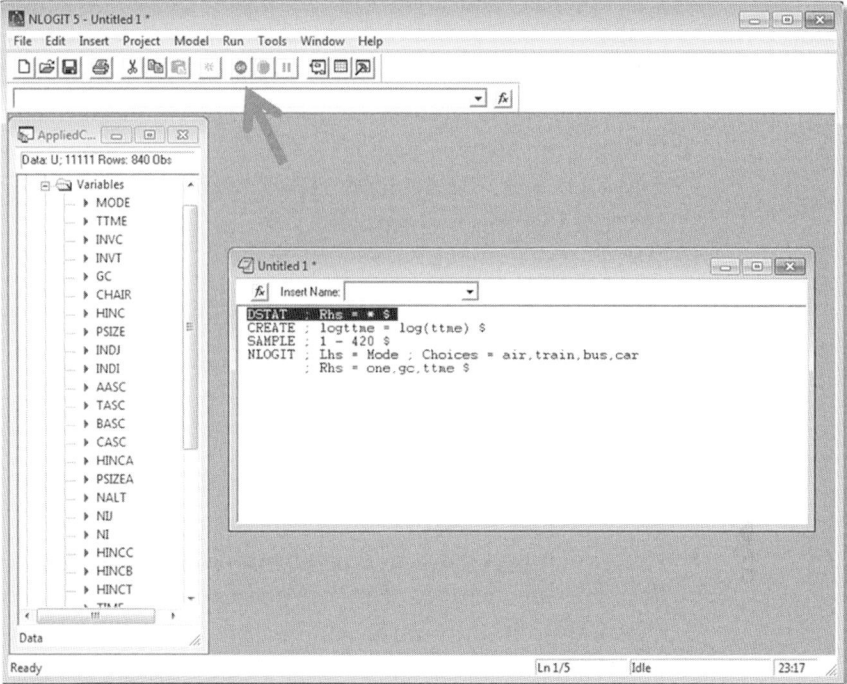

Figure 9.7   Commands in the Text Editor

9.5.3 Commands

Nlogit recognizes hundreds of different commands, but for your purposes, you will only need a small number of them – they are differentiated by the verbs. The functions of the program that you will use (once your data are read in and ready to analyze) are as follows. Note that the actual command is written in **boldface** below. Comments appear after the $ character. If you actually include these in your commands, the comments that follow the $ are ignored by the program.

(1) Data analysis

DSTATS; RHS = the list of variables $ For descriptive statistics:

REGRESS; Lhs = dependent variable; Rhs = independent variable $

Note: ONE is the term used for the constant term in a regression. Nlogit does not put one in automatically; you must request that a constant be estimated.

LOGIT; Lhs = variable; Rhs = variables$ For a binomial logit model.

PROBIT; Lhs = variable; Rhs = variables$ For the binomial probit model.

NLOGIT; various different forms$ The Nlogit command is the command most used throughout this text. The various forms are discussed at length in Chapters 10, 11, 14, and 16

CROSSTAB; Lhs = variable; RHS = Variable$

HISTOGRAM; Rhs = a variable$

KERNEL; Rhs = one or more variables$

Each of these includes many optional features. For example, **HISTOGRAM** and **KERNEL** allow different display formats by modifying the command. There are many different kinds of regressions as well.

(2) Sample setting

SAMPLE; first observation – last observation$

SAMPLE; ALL$ To use the entire data set.

REJECT; decision rule$ For removing observations from the sample. They are not "deleted." They are just marked and bypassed until you restore them in the sample.

(3) New variables

CREATE; name = expression; name = expression . . .$

(4) Scientific calculations

CALCULATE; expression$ Examples appear below.

MATRIX; expression$ Examples appear below.

As an aside, any text after a question mark (**?**) is not read by Nlogit. This allows the analyst to make comments in the command editor that may be useful in future sessions. Also note that spacing of characters in the commands typed is not essential (i.e., the words may run into each other); however, the use of spacing often makes it easier to follow what the command is, and will help in locating errors.

9.5.4 Using the project file box

The variables in the data set, once loaded, may be accessed using the Project File Box. The Project File Box is the box shown to the LHS of the Nlogit desktop. Before loading the data set, the Project File Box is titled "Untitled Project 1" (see Figure 9.1). Once a project file (i.e., a lpj file) has been read into Nlogit, the name of the Project File Box will take on the name of the file read (see Figure 9.3). If data are read into Nlogit using a file extension other than .lpj (e.g., .txt, .xls, .SAV) then the Project File Box will retain the "Untitled Project 1" title.

> *As an aside*, the .SAV file extension, the file extension name used by SPSS, was also historically used by Nlogit. Nlogit no longer uses this file extension. The two program files are not compatible; hence those attempting to read data from SPSS must first save the data into another format (such as .txt, .xls, etc.) before reading it into Nlogit. We do note an extremely useful and not very expense utility program, StatTransfer, that can be used to convert native "save" files from dozens of programs into the format of the others. You can use StatTransfer to convert an SPSS .SAV file to an Nlogit .LPJ file – the operation takes a few seconds.

The Project File Box contains several folders that will allow the analyst to access various useful screens. Double clicking on the Data folder, for example, will open up several other sub-folders, one of which is a Folder titled Variables (Figure 9.7). Double clicking on the Variables folder will allow the analyst to view the names of all the variables in the data set (including any that have been created since reading in the data). By double clicking on any one of the variable names, the Data Editor will be opened displaying up to 5,000 rows of the data for all of the variables, in a spreadsheet format. (Nlogit makes no claims to be a spreadsheet program. If spreadsheet capabilities are required, the authors tend to use other programs such as Microsoft Excel or SPSS and import the data into Nlogit.) Other useful Nlogit functions may be accessed via the Project File Box, such as the scientific calculator.

9.6 Useful hints and tips

Nlogit is an extremely powerful program that allows the analyst to perform many statistical functions and estimate a wide variety of models. Yet despite its wide range of capabilities, those new to Nlogit often have difficulties with the program. While in the chapters that follow, we use the Text/command editor to write out the full set of commands for the models we estimate, the slightest error in spelling or omission of a necessary character will result in the program being unable to carry out the desired function. This is not the fault of the program, but of the analyst. Thus, extreme care must be made in writing out the commands correctly. As mentioned above, the analyst may use the command toolbars rather than the Text/command editor; however, this usually comes at the cost of flexibility. Whilst the authors prefer to use the Text/command editor to write out the commands, it is sometimes useful to use the command toolbars if the source of an error cannot be located. When using the command toolbars Nlogit will show the command syntax for the initiated command in the output file, thus allowing the analyst to see what the command should look like and perhaps help in locating the original error. Nevertheless, as noted earlier, the command toolbars do not always offer the full range of outputs that may be generated using the Text/command editor and, as such, this error locating strategy may not always be possible.

> *A tip*, You can "copy" commands that are echoed by the dialog boxes in the output window, and then paste them into your Text Editor. This is useful if you want to estimate a basic model using the dialog box; then add features to it, which will be easier in the Text Editor format.

9.6.1 Limitations in Nlogit

There are a few limitations on the commands used and models that may be estimated in Nlogit. The two most specific limitations worth noting are:

1. 10,000 character limit to commands (not including comments made after question marks). This is extremely unlikely to be a constraint.
2. 150 parameter limit in the estimation of most models, but 300 parameters in the models that are estimated with the Nlogit command. Panel data models that involve fixed effects may have hundreds of thousands of groups – there are essentially no limits.

Only in extreme cases will these limitations be a barrier for the analyst. Indeed, it is highly unlikely that one would ever need a command that has greater than 10,000 characters or estimate a model that has more than 300 parameters. Even if the 10,000 character limit is reached, often creative renaming of variables and parameters or using program shortcuts such as "namelists" that can represent up to 100 variable names, may overcome the problem. The issue of estimating 300 parameters is less easily solved; however, very few studies will ever require the estimation of a choice model with that number of parameters.

9.7 Nlogit software

The full Nlogit package includes many features not listed above. These include nearly 200 varieties of regression models, models for count data, discrete choice models such as probit and logit, ordered discrete data models, limited dependent variable models, panel data models, and so on. There are also a large variety of other features for describing and manipulating data, writing programs, computing functions and partial effects, graphics, etc. You can learn more about these on the website for the program, www.NLOGIT.com.

As noted earlier, Nlogit is an expanded version of Limdep. There are signatures in the program that will indicate this to you, if you have any doubt. You will be able to see the name Nlogit on the program icons, and find some additional data in the Help About box after you start the program.

10 Data set up for Nlogit

10.1 Reading in and setting up data

In teaching courses on discrete choice modeling, we have increasingly observed that many participants struggle with *the look of choice data*. Courses and texts on econometrics often provide the reader with an already formatted data set (as does this book) yet fail to mention how (and why) the data were formatted in the manner they were. This leaves the user to work out the whys and the hows of data formatting by themselves (albeit with the help of lists such as the Limdep List: see http://limdep.itls.usyd.edu.au). The alternative is for the non-expert to turn to user manuals; however, such manuals are often written by experts for experts. We have found that even specialists in experimental design or econometrics have problems in setting up their data for choice modeling.

We now focus on how to format choice data for estimation purposes. We concentrate on data formatting for the program Nlogit from Econometric Software. While other programs capable of modeling choice data exist in the market, we choose to concentrate on Nlogit because this is the program that the authors are most familiar with (indeed Greene and Hensher are the developers of Nlogit). Nlogit also offers all of the discrete choice models that are used by practitioners and researchers. The release of Nlogit5.0 in August 2012 came with a comprehensive set of (four) online manuals (and no hard copy manuals). The discussion here complements the manuals. All the features of Nlogit that are used here are available in version 5.0 (dated September 2012).

Nlogit is particular in terms of how data must be formatted. We readily admit to spending many hours frustrated by the many and varied errors that Nlogit is capable of generating only to learn that the difficulty arose solely due to incorrect data formatting (always as a result of our own doing). Our objective in writing this chapter is to help the novice avoid this frustration.

10.1.1 The basic data set up

The data set up for choice analysis using Nlogit is now cenventional. Those familiar with panel data formats will see some similarity, but those accustomed to other choice modeling techniques using older statistical packages may be unfamiliar with the data requirements for choice modeling with Nlogit. Unlike some other statistical packages, where each specific row of data represents all of an independent observation, usually that of a separate subject, in the main Nlogit expects the use of several rows of data to represent a single subject. In other treatments of panel data, this is sometimes called the "long" format as opposed to the single line, "wide" format. (Nlogit is also equipped to handle the wide data format, as we will later see, though it is less convenient for choice modeling.)

We consider an example to illustrate the most general data format set up. Let us assume that choice data were collected on travel mode choice for three individuals (a rather small sample, but sufficient to illustrate the data formatting required). Assume that each individual was shown a total of two choice sets, each choice set with four alternatives – say, car, bus, train, and plane. Keeping our example simple, we assume that each alternative has only two attributes, say comfort (clearly defined in some manner) and travel time. We divide the data format into a number of blocks, each block representing an individual choice set as given to each subject. Each row within a block corresponds to an alternative within that choice set. Taking the example as described above, each individual subject will be represented by two blocks (the two choice sets), and within each separate block there will exist four rows of data (the four alternatives). As such, each individual will be represented by eight rows of data (number of blocks multiplied by the number of alternatives within each block). The data as described will look as shown in Table 10.1.

> (*As a quick aside*, the reader does not have to use the attribute names we have use below. In Nlogit names are limited to eight characters and must begin with an alpha code, but are otherwise unrestricted.)

Each decision maker in this example will be represented by eight rows of data. The *alti* variable is an accounting index that informs Nlogit which alternative is assigned to a line of data. In the example above, we have assumed a fixed choice set size with each alternative appearing in each and every choice set. Some designs allow for alternatives to appear in one choice set but not in others. For example, let us add a fifth alternative to our example, say, a high

Table 10.1 Most general choice data format in Nlogit

	id	alti	cset	choice	Comfort1	Comfort2	TTime
Car	01	1	4	1	1	0	14
Bus	01	2	4	0	1	0	12
Train	01	3	4	0	−1	−1	12
Plane	01	4	4	0	0	1	2
Car	01	1	4	0	0	1	10
Bus	01	2	4	1	0	1	14
Train	01	3	4	0	0	1	12
Plane	01	4	4	0	−1	−1	1.5
Car	02	1	4	0	0	1	12
Bus	02	2	4	0	1	0	14
Train	02	3	4	0	−1	−1	12
Plane	02	4	4	1	1	0	1.5
Car	02	1	4	0	−1	−1	12
Bus	02	2	4	0	0	1	12
Train	02	3	4	1	−1	−1	10
Plane	02	4	4	0	−1	−1	1.5
Car	03	1	4	0	−1	−1	12
Bus	03	2	4	1	1	0	14
Train	03	3	4	0	0	1	14
Plane	03	4	4	0	0	1	2
Car	03	1	4	1	1	0	14
Bus	03	2	4	0	0	1	10
Train	03	3	4	0	1	0	14
Plane	03	4	4	0	−1	−1	1.5

speed rail proposal, called the "Very Fast Train" (VFT) between Sydney and Melbourne. If we retain the fixed choice set size of four alternatives then within each choice set, one alternative will have to fall out. In Table 10.2 the first decision maker was presented with a choice set which consisted of a choice between travel using a car, a bus, a plane, or a VFT. The second choice set for this decision maker consisted of the alternatives, car, bus, train, and plane.

The choice set size does not have to be a fixed size. The variable *cset* is designed to inform Nlogit of the number of alternatives within a particular choice set. In both Tables 10.1 and 10.2 the choice set sizes were fixed at four alternatives. With revealed preference (RP) data, some alternatives may not be present at a particular physical distribution point at the time of purchase (choice). The stated preference (SP) equivalent is to use availability designs (see Louviere *et al.* 2000, Chapter 5). In either case, the number of alternatives present varies across choice sets. In Table 10.3 the first choice set has only

Table 10.2 Varying the alternatives within choice sets

	id	alti	cset	choice	Comfort1	Comfort2	TTime
Car	01	1	4	1	1	0	14
Bus	01	2	4	0	1	0	12
Plane	01	4	4	0	0	1	2
VFT	01	5	4	0	1	0	8
Car	01	1	4	0	0	1	10
Bus	01	2	4	1	0	1	14
Train	01	3	4	0	0	1	12
Plane	01	4	4	0	−1	−1	1.5

Table 10.3 Varying the number of alternatives within choice sets: 1

	person	alti	cset	choice	Comfort1	Comfort2	TTime
Car	01	1	3	1	1	0	14
Bus	01	2	3	0	1	0	12
VFT	01	5	3	0	1	0	8
Car	01	1	5	0	0	1	10
Bus	01	2	5	1	0	1	14
Train	01	3	5	0	0	1	12
Plane	01	4	5	0	−1	−1	1.5
VFT	01	5	5	0	−1	−1	6

three of the five alternatives present, while the second choice set has all five alternatives present. The variable *cset*, which is repeated in each row of data in the choice set, gives the number of choices in the choice set. (In general, a variable such as *cset* is needed only when choice sets have differing numbers of choices. If the choice set always has the same number of choices, this will be indicated to the program in a different way.)

The *choice* variable indicates which alternative within a choice set was chosen. A "1" indicates that an alternative was selected, while a "0" indicates that it was not. As such, the sum of the choice variable should equal 1 within each choice set and within an individual sum to the number of choice sets given to that individual. Across individuals, this variable should sum to the total number of choice sets. Returning to Table 10.1, decision maker one chooses alternative one, car, in the first choice set and alternative two, bus, in the second. Decision maker two chose plane and train, respectively.

> *As an aside*, for situations where every observation has the exact same alternatives (and listed in the same order), it is not necessary to define *alti* and *cset*. Nlogit will count the number of alternatives based on the names assigned to the choice alternatives in the Nlogit input command syntax and assume that each observation has these alternatives and, most importantly, that the alternatives are in the same order in each decision maker's choice sets.

The last three variables in our mock data set require some explanation. Taking the case of comfort, we began with only one comfort attribute, but in our data set we have two comfort variables. Comfort, being a qualitative attribute, requires that words rather than numbers be attached as descriptors at the time of survey. For analytical purposes, we are required to numerically code these word descriptors. One possible way of coding qualitative data is to attach a unique numeric value for each level of the attribute within one variable. Thus, assuming three levels of comfort (low, medium, and high), we could create a single variable (call it comfort) such that low = 0, medium = 1 and high = 2 (note that any unique values could have been used). Taking this coding structure, for decision maker one, Table 10.1 becomes Table 10.4.

The reason we do not code qualitative (or any classification) data in the manner suggested by Table 10.4 is simple. The use of such a coding structure unnecessarily ascribes a linear relationship to the effects of the levels of the attribute. That is, at the time of modeling, we will derive a single parameter associated with the attribute comfort. Note that each alternative will have its own β parameter if we allow for an alternative-specific model specification (as discussed in Chapter 3). This is a problem that led us to effects and dummy coding in Chapter 3.

Table 10.4 Varying the number of alternatives within choice sets: 2

	id	Alti	cset	choice	Comfort	TTime
Car	01	1	4	1	0	14
Bus	01	2	4	0	0	12
Train	01	3	4	0	2	12
Plane	01	4	4	0	1	2
Car	01	1	4	0	1	10
Bus	01	2	4	0	1	14
Train	01	3	4	0	1	12
Plane	01	4	4	1	2	1.5

We did not effects code the travel time attribute. This is not to suggest that we could not have effects or dummy coded the variable (by partitioning it into a series of ranges). Indeed, to test for non-linear effects over the range of the attribute, it is sometimes necessary to do so. Nevertheless doing so at this stage will not add to our general discussion, and hence we will assume linearity over the ranges of the travel time attributes.

Thus far we have said little about socio-demographic characteristics (SECs). The SECs of a decision maker are invariant across decisions provided that there is not a significant time lapse involved in the decision making process. As such, when we enter socio-demographic data, the levels of the data are constant for an individual (but vary across individuals). For our example, let us assume that we have collected data on the age of each decision maker. We show how this age variable is entered into Nlogit in Table 10.5. Other socio-demographic characteristics would be entered in a similar fashion.

10.1.2 Entering multiple data sets: stacking and melding

The analyst may have occasion to combine multiple choice data sets, the most common amalgamation being a combination of SP and RP data (a topic discussed in detail in Chapter 19). When combining different data sources, whether the data are SP and RP, or some other combination, the data sources will be stacked, one upon the other. If, however, the two data sources are collected from the same decision makers, we may meld the two data sets such that the data for each decision maker is kept intact independent of which data source it originated from.

10.1.3 Handling data on the non-chosen alternative in RP data

Handling RP data poses significant challenges. As noted in previous chapters, the analyst is often only able to capture information on the chosen alternative. Further, we often only collect RP data for a single decision context. As such, if we enter RP data as suggested above, for each individual we would have only one line of data. The choice variable would therefore take on the constant value of one given that the single line of data represents the chosen alternative for each individual. Given that there is no information on the non-chosen alternatives it would appear that at no stage was a choice made (recalling that we need at least two alternatives for a choice). This represents a modeling problem.

Table 10.5 Entering socio-demographic characteristics

	id	Alti	cset	choice	Comfort1	Comfort2	TTime	Age
Car	01	1	4	1	1	0	14	40
Bus	01	2	4	0	1	0	12	40
Train	01	3	4	0	−1	−1	12	40
Plane	01	4	4	0	0	1	2	40
Car	01	1	4	0	0	1	10	40
Bus	01	2	4	1	0	1	14	40
Train	01	3	4	0	0	1	12	40
Plane	01	4	4	0	−1	−1	1.5	40
Car	02	1	4	0	0	1	12	32
Bus	02	2	4	0	1	0	14	32
Train	02	3	4	0	−1	−1	12	32
Plane	02	4	4	1	1	0	1.5	32
Car	02	1	4	0	−1	−1	12	32
Bus	02	2	4	0	0	1	12	32
Train	02	3	4	1	−1	−1	10	32
Plane	02	4	4	0	−1	−1	1.5	32
Car	03	1	4	0	−1	−1	12	35
Bus	03	2	4	1	1	0	14	35
Train	03	3	4	0	0	1	14	35
Plane	03	4	4	0	0	1	2	35
Car	03	1	4	1	1	0	14	35
Bus	03	2	4	0	0	1	10	35
Train	03	3	4	0	1	0	14	35
Plane	03	4	4	0	−1	−1	1.5	35

What is required is information on (at least one) non-chosen alternative(s). The best solution is to gather the information from those making the decision; however, this is not always possible. In practice, four solutions have been employed. We will assume that in the aggregate, information on the attribute levels for all alternatives within the choice set are available, although at an individual observation level they are available only for the chosen alternative.

The first approach involves taking the averages of the attribute levels (or medians for qualitative attributes) for each alternative for those who chose each of them. For any given individual, the chosen alternatives attribute levels as observed are retained. The calculated averages (or median) attribute levels are then substituted as the attribute levels for the non-chosen alternatives. This first method involves taking the average for the attribute levels of each observed alternative and substituting these averages (or medians) as the values for the attribute levels of the non-chosen alternatives for those who did not choose them. Thus for each individual, while we retain the information on the individual's chosen alternative, we generate data on the non-chosen alternatives by using the averages of the non-chosen alternative's attribute levels as chosen by the other decision makers. It is worth noting that there is a risk that these averages promote a better set of attribute levels than what would be the levels if we knew the actual levels available to the person who has the alternative as the non-chosen. Indeed we note that such a strategy certainly reduces the variance of the attribute level distribution in the sampled population.

The second method employs a similar approach. We sample across a distribution of decision makers such that we have a proportion of decision makers observed to have chosen each of the alternatives. Rather than taking the average of the observed attribute levels for each alternative and substituting these as the attribute levels for the non-chosen alternatives, as in method one, we take the observed levels unamended and distribute these as the attribute levels for those who did not choose those alternatives. This distribution can be done randomly, or alternatively we may attempt to match the non-chosen alternatives attribute levels to specific decision makers through a matching of socio-demographic characteristics. For transport studies, a matching of trip origin and destination is also very useful. The benefit of this approach is the preservation of variability in the attribute level distribution.

> *As an aside*, both methods are far from desirable. We would prefer to capture information on the attribute levels of non-chosen alternatives as they actually exist for the decision maker. While the above represent strategies to estimate what these levels might actually be, it is likely that the actual attribute levels for the non-chosen alternatives are somewhat different. A better strategy may be to gain information from the decision maker based on their perception of the attribute levels for the non-chosen alternative. This approach is likely to produce data that will require much data cleansing. However, it is more likely that decision makers base their choices on their perceptions of what attribute levels an alternative takes rather than the actual levels (or some view from others) that that alternative takes. Thus it may be argued that the capturing of perceptual data will produce more realistic behavioral models. This is the third "solution" to the problem of capturing information on the non-chosen alternative.

The fourth solution, similar to the first two, is to synthesize the data. This requires expert knowledge as to how the data are synthesized. The norm is to use known information such as travel distances or other socio-demographic characteristics and to condition the synthesized data on these. But, like the first two approaches, synthesizing the data leaves one open to the criticism that the created data may not represent the alternatives actually faced by decision makers and as such the estimation process will be tainted. If such synthesized data can be developed from perceptual maps associated with non-chosen alternatives, this may be an appealing solution.

10.2 Combining sources of data

Returning to the example, we no longer have enough decision makers to obtain information on the non-chosen alternatives. We therefore will increase our data set size to 200 (i.e., four alternatives each with 50 respondents), and assume that among those 50 decision makers each alternative was observed to have been chosen at least once. We may now use the observed attribute levels for those who choose car as the attribute levels for the car alternative associated with individuals who choose the bus, train, and plane alternatives.

In combining data sources into a single data set, such as SP and RP data, we need to create a dummy variable that specifies which data set the data originated from. In Table 10.6 we call this variable SPRP. This variable takes the value 1 if the observation is RP or 0 if SP. The SPRP variable will allow the analyst to estimated SP and RP models separately, but will not be used in models combining both data sources. For combined models, this is done through the *alti* variable. The *alti* variable is adjusted to reflect the fact that some alternatives belong to one data source (e.g., RP) while others belong to a second data source (e.g., SP). In Table 10.6, we use values of one through four for the *alti* variable to denote the alternatives belonging to the RP sub-data set, and five through eight to represent alternatives from the SP sub-data set. Thus, the car alternative is represented as one in the *alti* variable when dealing with the RP data and five when dealing with the SP data set (we discuss the combining of data sources further in Chapter 19).

Table 10.6 presents the data set for the first two of our 50 decision makers. We observe that individual one in reality selected to travel by car, a trip which took ten and a half hours and which they described as being of medium comfort. As this person did not take a bus, train, or plane, we have inserted the average (medium for qualitative attributes) attribute levels from those who did select those modes. Thus the average travel time from those decision makers observed to have chosen the bus mode was eleven and a half hours. Similarly, the average travel time for those selecting the train was twelve hours, and one

Table 10.6 Combining SP–RP data

	id	alti	cset	Choice	SPRP	Comfort1	Comfort2	TTime	Age
Car	01	1	4	1	1	0	1	10.5	40
Bus	01	2	4	0	1	−1	−1	11.5	40
Train	01	3	4	0	1	−1	−1	12	40
Plane	01	4	4	0	1	1	0	1.33	40
Car	01	5	4	1	0	1	0	14	40
Bus	01	6	4	0	0	1	0	12	40
Train	01	7	4	0	0	−1	−1	12	40
Plane	01	8	4	0	0	0	1	2	40
Car	01	5	4	0	0	0	1	10	40
Bus	01	6	4	1	0	0	1	14	40
Train	01	7	4	0	0	0	1	12	40
Plane	01	8	4	0	0	−1	−1	1.5	40
Car	02	1	4	0	1	0	1	10	32
Bus	02	2	4	0	1	−1	−1	11.5	32
Train	02	3	4	0	1	−1	−1	12	32
Plane	02	4	4	1	1	1	0	1.25	32
Car	02	5	4	0	0	0	1	12	32
Bus	02	6	4	0	0	1	0	14	32
Train	02	7	4	0	0	−1	−1	12	32
Plane	02	8	4	1	0	1	0	1.5	32
Car	02	5	4	0	0	−1	−1	12	32
Bus	02	6	4	0	0	0	1	12	32
Train	02	7	4	1	0	−1	−1	10	32
Plane	02	8	4	0	0	−1	−1	1.5	32

hour and twenty minutes for those choosing the plane. Individual two was observed to have chosen to travel by plane.

The observant reader will note that if we combine the data sources as suggested above, we have only one RP data choice set but multiple SP data choice sets per individual traveller. Some researchers have suggested that, when combined, RP data should be weighted so as to have equal representation as the SP data set. Weighting each observation is really something that should be decided by the analyst according to what behavioral strengths each data source has. We call this *Bayesian determination*. If we believe that the RP data are equally as useful as the SP data, then we may wish to equally weight them. With, say, one RP observation and eight SP observations, one would either weight the RP data by 8.0 or the SP data by 0.125. We are of the opinion that such weighting should not take place. We reason that RP data is, by its very nature, ill conditioned (i.e., it may be invariant and is likely to suffer from multicollinearity; see Chapter 4), while SP data arguably provides better quality inputs to estimation, especially on the attributes of alternatives. As such, while we use the RP data to provide information on market shares and to capture information on real choices, we believe that we are best to obtain our parameters or taste weights associated with each attribute from SP data sources (except for the alternative-specific constant in labeled choice sets) and export the SP attribute parameters to the RP environment where the model is calibrated to reproduce the actual market shares of observed alternatives.

> *As an aside*, calibration cannot and should not be undertaken on new alternatives, for obvious reasons. What does the analyst **calibrate** against? In addition, choice-based sampling is only valid for RP alternatives.

Thus, we remain unconcerned that SP data may *swamp* RP data at the time of estimation. We do remind the analyst, however, that if the interest is in prediction and deriving elasticities, that the RP model should be used but with the transferred attribute parameters from the SP model. We discuss this in Chapter 19. SP models as stand alone models are only useful for measuring the willingness to pay (WTP) for attributes (i.e., in valuation) and not for prediction and behavioral response (i.e., in deriving elasticities) *unless* the SP model is calibrated through alternative-specific constants, in order to reproduce the base RP shares for the sub-set of alternatives observed in real markets.

10.3 Weighting on an exogenous variable

The choice variable in an RP data set represents an endogenous variable within our system of equations. When we wish to correct for over- and under-sampling on the choice response we refer to choice-based weights (which will be discussed in Chapter 13). However, it is often the situation that the sample is drawn using some non-choice (or exogenous) criteria such as income and gender, drawing observations in a way that over-samples in cells (e.g., high income by gender) with a small population incidence and under-samples in cells with a large population incidence. To correct for such sampling we can re-weight the data using exogenous weights based on the criteria used to design the sample. The analyst may establish an exogenous

Table 10.7 Exogenous weights entered

	id	alti	cset	choice	agent	sprp	comfort1	comfort2	ttime	Age
Car	01	1	4	1	0.6	1	0	1	10.5	40
Bus	01	2	4	0	0.6	1	−1	−1	11.5	40
Train	01	3	4	0	0.6	1	−1	−1	12	40
Plane	01	4	4	0	0.6	1	1	0	1.3	40
Car	01	5	4	1	0.6	0	1	0	14	40
Bus	01	6	4	0	0.6	0	1	0	12	40
Train	01	7	4	0	0.6	0	−1	−1	12	40
Plane	01	8	4	0	0.6	0	0	1	2	40
Car	01	5	4	0	0.6	0	0	1	10	40
Bus	01	6	4	1	0.6	0	0	1	14	40
Train	01	7	4	0	0.6	0	0	1	12	40
Plane	01	8	4	0	0.6	0	−1	−1	1.5	40
Car	02	1	4	0	0.3	1	0	1	10	32
Bus	02	2	4	0	0.3	1	−1	−1	11.5	32
Train	02	3	4	0	0.3	1	−1	−1	12	32
Plane	02	4	4	1	0.3	1	1	0	1.25	32
Car	02	5	4	0	0.3	0	0	1	12	32
Bus	02	6	4	0	0.3	0	1	0	14	32
Train	02	7	4	0	0.3	0	−1	−1	12	32
Plane	02	8	4	1	0.3	0	1	0	1.5	32
Car	02	5	4	0	0.3	0	−1	−1	12	32
Bus	02	6	4	0	0.3	0	0	1	12	32
Train	02	7	4	1	0.3	0	−1	−1	10	32
Plane	02	8	4	0	0.3	0	−1	−1	1.5	32

weighting variable within the data set to be used to weight the data during estimation. For example, we may wish to weight the data differently for the different sexes. For our example, we do not have a gender variable, so let us assume that the analyst wishes to weight the data on the age variable. For example, assume that the analyst wishes to weight the data such that data for those 40 years and older are weighted by 1.5 and those under the age of 40 by 0.5. The weighting variable is shown in Table 10.7.

10.4 Handling rejection: the no option

A significant number of choice contexts allow the chooser *not to choose* (although not choosing is technically a choice), or to delay their choice. In

Mode Description	Car	Bus	Train	Plane	I would not travel
Comfort Level	Medium	High	Low	Low	
Travel Time	12 hours	12 hours	10 hours	1.5 hours	
Given these options I would choose	☐	☐	☐	☐	☐

Figure 10.1   Choice set with the no travel alternative

our example we have ignored the *no choice* alternative and constrained the decision maker into making a choice from the listed alternatives. We call this a *conditional choice*. However, what if the decision maker may elect not to travel? Table 10.8 presents an example of a choice set for our travel example with the *elect not to travel* alternative.

> *As an aside*, it is useful to think of any choice analysis in which the no-choice alternative is excluded, as a conditional choice. Given the definition of demand in Chapter 2, another way of expressing this is that any choice analysis that ignores no choice is effectively a conditional demand model. That is, conditional on choosing an alternative, we can identify a probability of choosing it. The only circumstance in which the conditional demand is equivalent to unconditional demand is where the probability of making no choice is zero.

If one elects not to travel, then we have no observable attribute levels for this alternative. We see this in the choice set shown in Figure 10.1. Given that the attribute levels are not observed, we treat them as missing values. As each row of data represents an alternative we are required to insert a row of data for the not-travel alternative in which the attribute levels are coded as missing. The (default) missing value code for Nlogit is −999.

> *As an aside*, when collecting data for use in Nlogit we strongly recommend that any missing data be either imputed in the data set or assigned a −999 code (the default in Nlogit for missing data). Nlogit will also accept other non-numeric data, such as the word "*missing*" to indicate missing values. In any event, it is a good idea to have something in place to signify a missing value. Some ambiguities as to how to interpret the data can arise if "blank" is used to indicate missing values.

In adding the no choice or **delay choice alternative**, we add to the number of existing alternatives within our data set. As such, we need to adjust our *alti*

Table 10.8 Adding the no choice or delay choice alternative

	Id	Alti	cset	choice	Comfort1	Comfort2	TTime	Age
Car	01	1	5	1	1	0	14	40
Bus	01	2	5	0	1	0	12	40
Train	01	3	5	0	−1	−1	12	40
Plane	01	4	5	0	0	1	2	40
None	01	5	5	0	−999	−999	−999	40
Car	01	1	5	0	0	1	10	40
Bus	01	2	5	0	0	1	14	40
Train	01	3	5	0	0	1	12	40
Plane	01	4	5	0	−1	−1	1.5	40
None	01	5	5	1	−999	−999	−999	40
Car	02	1	5	0	0	1	12	32
Bus	02	2	5	0	1	0	14	32
Train	02	3	5	0	−1	−1	12	32
Plane	02	4	5	1	1	0	1.5	32
None	02	5	5	0	−999	−999	−999	32
Car	02	1	5	0	−1	−1	12	32
Bus	02	2	5	0	0	1	12	32
Train	02	3	5	1	−1	−1	10	32
Plane	02	4	5	0	−1	−1	1.5	32
None	02	5	5	0	−999	−999	−999	32
Car	03	1	5	0	−1	−1	12	35
Bus	03	2	5	1	1	0	14	35
Train	03	3	5	0	0	1	14	35
Plane	03	4	5	0	0	1	2	35
None	03	5	5	0	−999	−999	−999	35
Car	03	1	5	1	1	0	14	35
Bus	03	2	5	0	0	1	10	35
Train	03	3	5	0	1	0	14	35
Plane	03	4	5	0	−1	−1	1.5	35
None	03	5	5	0	−999	−999	−999	35

and *cset* variables. In the example, we now have five alternatives (ignoring VFT as a possible alternative) and hence the *cset* variable will take on the value 5. The *alti* variable will now take on the values 1 to 5, 5 equating to the choice not to travel alternative. We show this in Table 10.8. In Table 10.8 the attribute levels for the *choose not to travel* alternative are set to the missing value code of −999. Socio-demographic characteristics remain unchanged over the new alternative, hence we are not required to treat such data as missing. Again, the reader can see this in Table 10.8. In Table 10.8 individual one elected not to travel in the second choice set.

As an aside, in Nlogit the *alti* indexing must begin at 1 and include all values up to the maximum number of alternatives. This does permit each individual to have a different number of alternatives in their choice set. For example, individual one may have alternatives 1, 2, 4, 5 and individual two may have alternatives 1, 2, 3, 4, 5. The only situation in which we do not need to have an *alti* variable (and a *cset* variable) is where all individuals have choice sets with identical alternatives which are presented in the data in the same order for each individual. We call the latter a fixed choice set and the case of varying *alti* and *cset* a variable choice set. Analysts who use RP and SP data in a combined data set must take this into account when using the sub-data set (e.g., SP), as the *alti* values for the second data set will begin at the value immediately following the last value of the first data set (e.g., in Table 10.6). It will need to be transformed back to 1, 2, etc. This is very easy. One simply creates a new *alti* index (say *altz*) equal to *alti*-z where z is the highest RP *alti* value. The variable *altz* then replaces *alti* in the SP stand alone analysis after you have rejected the RP data lines.

As a further aside, it is interesting to consider the *no choice* or *delay choice* alternatives in terms of RP data studies. Although we have placed the *no choice* alternative in the context of an SP experiment in Table 10.8, the analyst should be prepared to collect RP data on individuals who have elected not to choose or to delay choice. In doing so, one not only captures information on market shares (the aggregates of those who chose among the alternatives) but also on potential demand (those who chose plus those who operate within the market but have elected not to purchase in the current period). Gathering data on non-choosers also allows the analyst to test hypotheses as to differences between decision makers who elected to choose and those that did not.

10.5 Entering data into Nlogit

There are several methods of entering data into Nlogit. By far the most common will be to import a data file prepared by some other program or gathered from an external source, such as a website. A second method, which you will very rarely use, is to enter the data directly into Nlogit's spreadsheet style Data Editor. Finally, Nlogit, like other familiar programs, has its own type of "save" file that can be used to transport data from one user to another and one computer to another. We will refer to this as a *project file* as we proceed. The advantage of the project file is that it enables you to transport work from one session to another and easily from one computer to another. In principle, you need only import a data set once. Thereafter, you will use the project file to hold and move data. We consider each of these in turn.

For most functions in Nlogit, two mechanisms are available to the analyst to initiate actions. These are the command menus and the Text/Document Editor. The commands as described in this and the following chapters are instructions that are to be entered into the Text/Document Editor. While the menus are perhaps more comfortable for the beginner, we have elected not to discuss them in any further detail unless certain commands contained in the command menus are absolutely necessary to access some other Nlogit function. We made this decision because the choice modelers will quickly learn how to use Nlogit using the more convenient and efficient Text/Document Editor and leave the menus and dialog boxes behind.

10.6 Importing data from a file

You will usually analyze data that have been prepared by another program such as Microsoft Excel, SAS, etc., or have been obtained from an external source, such as a website. These files may come in a variety of formats. The most common will be an ASCII character data set with a row of variable names in the first line of the file and the data values in rows to follow, with values separated by commas. The data, for example, might appear thus:

```
MODE,CHSET,COMFORT,TTIME,BLOCK,COMFORT1,COMFORT2
1,2,1,14,-1,1,0
2 ,2,1,12,-1,1,0
3,2,-1,12,-1,-1,-1
4,2,0,2,-1,0,1
1,4,0,10,-1,0,1
2,4,0,14,-1,0,1
3,4,0,12,-1,0,1
4,4,-1,1.5000000,-1,-1,-1
```

(We have changed it slightly by adding the variable CHSET and dropping the repetition of TTIME.) This is a "comma separated values," or CSV file, and it is the most common interchange format used to transport data files. An alternative format that was very common until about 2010 was the .XLS format used by Microsoft Excel. Current versions of Excel use yet another format, the .XLSX format. Still other data formats include "Fortran formatted" data sets, binary, DIF, and space or tab separated ASCII files. NLOGIT can

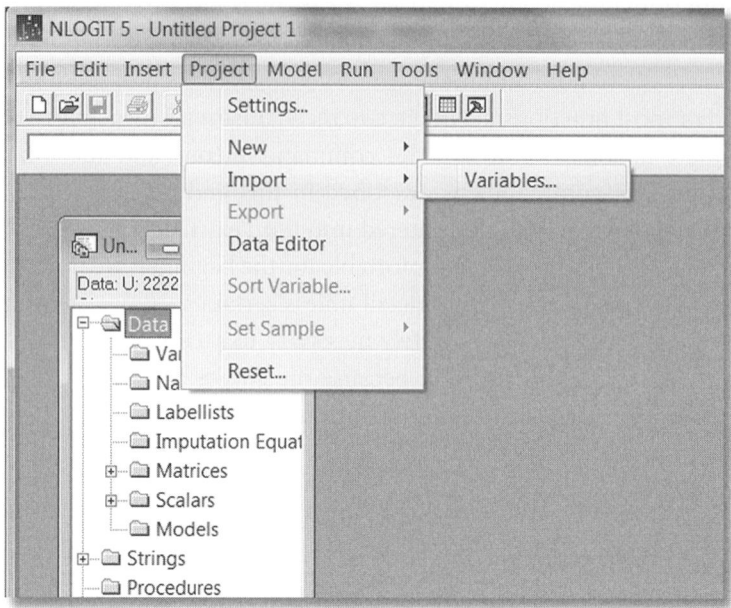

Figure 10.2 Importing variables

read all of these and some others using a specialized command, **READ**, that is documented in the manual for the program. For current purposes, we will focus on the CSV format that is most common.

We created a file, which we call **10A.csv** (using Microsoft Excel). For this example, we select Project:Import/Variables . . . in the desktop menu shown in Figure 10.2 to open the Windows Explorer in Figure 10.3. The default format is the .csv file. We select the file, then click Open (Figure 10.4), and the data file will be read. The Project window will be updated to show the variables you have read.

You can read an .XLS data set the same way. Notice in Figure 10.4 that at the bottom of the window, the file type *.csv is selected. You can select *.xls instead by opening the menu in this small window. (The third type is *.* all files.)

A tip, Stat Transfer, published by Circle Systems, Inc. (stattransfer.com) is a delightful utility program that can be used to convert files written by about thirty different programs, including Limdep and Nlogit as well as SAS, SPSS, Minitab, RATS, Stata, and so on. You can convert a file written by almost any contemporary program directly into a project file readable by Nlogit, and skip the importation step altogether.

The preceding should be useable for most situations. But there is an unlimited variety of ways to write data files, and you may need some additional flexibility.

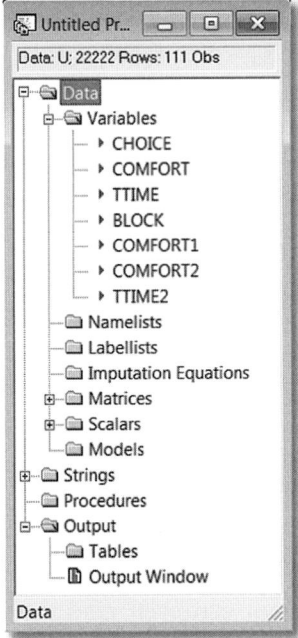

Figure 10.3 Variables in untitled project

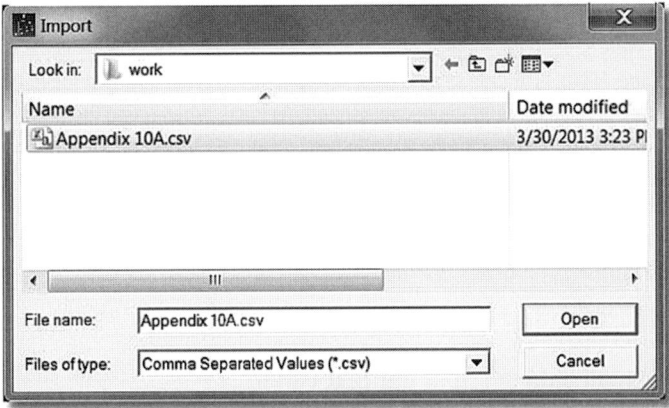

Figure 10.4 Importing CSV data

Nlogit provides a command, **READ**, that can be used to read a file (including the files shown above). The **READ** command is used in the command editor discussed above. It takes two forms, depending on whether the names for the variables are in the data file (as shown above) or not (in which case, the data file contains only the numeric data). For a data file that contains the names in one or more lines at the top of the file, the command is:

READ ; **Nvar = number of variables**
　　　 ; **Nobs = number of observations**
　　　 ; **Names = the number of lines of names are at the top of the file (usually 1)**
　　　 ; **File=the full path to the file. $**

You could read a CSV file with this command, for example, with NVAR = 6, Names = 1 and Nobs = whatever is appropriate. (Some special consideration would be needed to make sure that the program recognizes the observation labels. This is documented in detail in the manual.) The second type of file might have no names in it. For this, you provide names in the **READ** command with:

READ ; **Nvar = number of variables**
　　　 ; **Nobs = number of observations**
　　　 ; **Names = a list of Nvar names, separated by commas.**
　　　 ; **File=the full path to the file. $**

There are many types of data files. Nlogit can even read the internal file formats for a few programs, such as Stata 10 and 11. (We make no guarantee about future versions here. The people at Stata change their native format from time to time.) For the many possibilities, we strongly recommend having a copy of Stat Transfer at close reach.

> *As an aside*, Nlogit is unable to read data saved in the .XLS file format if the data is saved as a workbook (i.e., has more than one worksheet). As such, when using the .XLS file format, the analyst is best to save the file as a worksheet. Also note that Nlogit will not be able to read Excel formulas (this is one of the most common problems in reading in data). The XLSX file is also unreadable. For transporting from recent versions of Excel, just use Save As. . . and save the data file in the .csv format. The CSV format has been proven to be the most portable and reliable.

10.6.1 Importing a small data set from the Text Editor

This is an operation that the authors of this text use often to do a quick on the fly import of a data set. You can lift up data in a document file, an open spreadsheet program, or even (depending on the way it was written) a .pdf file, drop them into Nlogit's text/command editor, and read them directly from there. I am looking at a data set in Excel in Figure 10.5.

I would like to compute some statistics using the first 10 observations on the three variables G, PG, and Y. I can do the following:

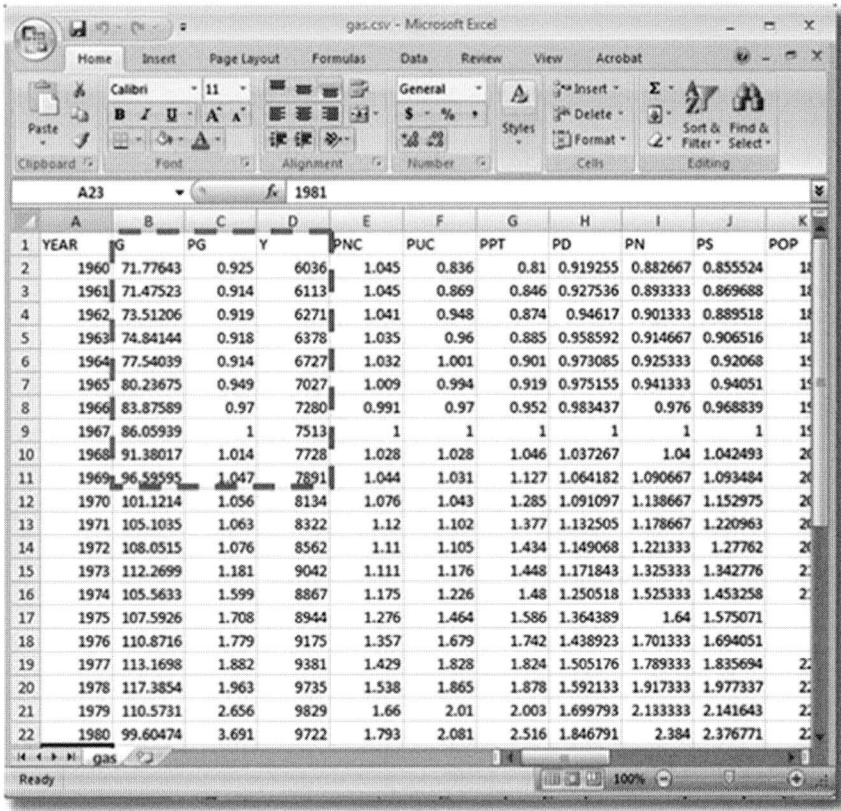

Figure 10.5 Excel data set

1. Launch Nlogit while Excel is open. Open a new Text/Command editing window in Nlogit. Put the one line, short command IMPORT $ at the top of the window, as shown in Figure 10.6.

2. Copy the data in Excel by highlighting the values, including the names, then use Edit/Copy.

3. Paste the data into your Edit window in Nlogit, which will appear as in Figure 10.7.

   Notice that the Text Editor inherits the cell borders. Ignore that.

4. Highlight everything that is now in the window, the IMPORT$ command, the names line, and all ten rows of data, and press GO.

You are done. The data will be in the project, and ready to analyze. You can use this style of importing data for anything that you can drop into the editing window. This includes data from Excel, as you see above, tables that are picked up from a .doc file, or a .txt file. In some cases, this will even work with extracts from .pdf files. (There is some variety there.)

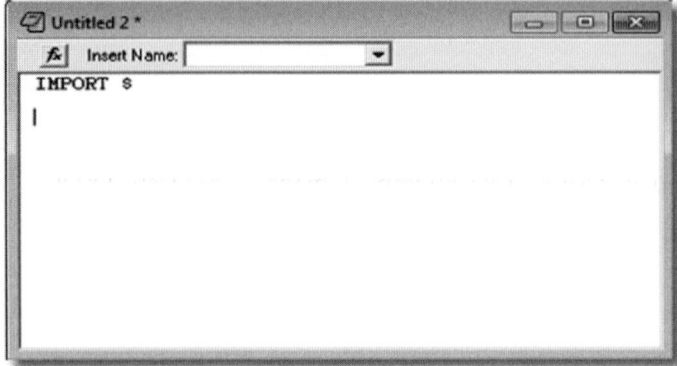

Figure 10.6   Import command

IMPORT $		
G	PG	Y
71.77643	0.925	6036
71.47523	0.914	6113
73.51206	0.919	6271
74.84144	0.918	6378
77.54039	0.914	6727
80.23675	0.949	7027
83.87589	0.97	7280
86.05939	1	7513
91.38017	1.014	7728
96.59595	1.047	7891

Figure 10.7   Imported data

As an aside, Nlogit uses the value −999 as the default missing value. When you import data from another source, it is a good idea to mark empty cells with something distinctive that indicate missing values. Blanks will work in a csv file – ",1, ,2" will be correctly read as 1, −999,2. But, if the file is not comma delimited, blanks might be misread. Alphanumeric or non-numeric data will be treated as missing values by Nlogit, so ",1,missing,2" would be more reliable. The convention of an isolated "." is also respected, so ",1,.,2" will also be read correctly. Again, if you are not using a comma separated values file, it is (always) necessary to be careful how missing values are indicated.

10.7 Entering data in the Data Editor

Nlogit provides a spreadsheet style Data Editor. The editor is minimally functional – it is used only to enter and view data and to make corrections by hand if desired. (No attempt is made to replicate Excel – presumably, the user has Excel or some equivalent program.) In order to enter data in the program "directly," it is necessary first to create the empty columns in the Data Editor. The command to create new variables, for example, x, y and z is:

CREATE ; x, y, z $

I.e., just **CREATE** the variables, with the names separated by commas. There is also a dialog box that can be used, Use Project:New/Variable. . . to open the window, enter the names of the variables to be created in the window, separated by commas, and press *OK* (Figure 10.8).

Either approach opens up the empty columns in the data set. You can see the data set (whether read, imported, loaded, or typed in directly) by viewing the Data Editor (Figure 10.9).

Once all the variables have been named, the analyst next enters the data into the *Data Editor* in a manner similar to most other statistics and spreadsheet programs. To gain access to the Data Editor, the analyst double clicks on the variable name in the *Project* dialogue box (Figure 10.10). This will open up

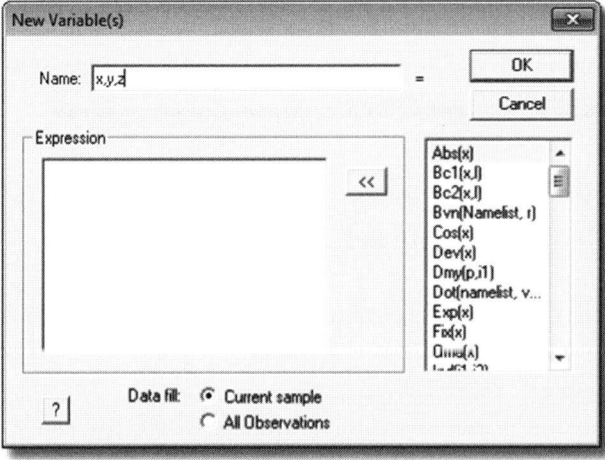

Figure 10.8   Names of variables to be created

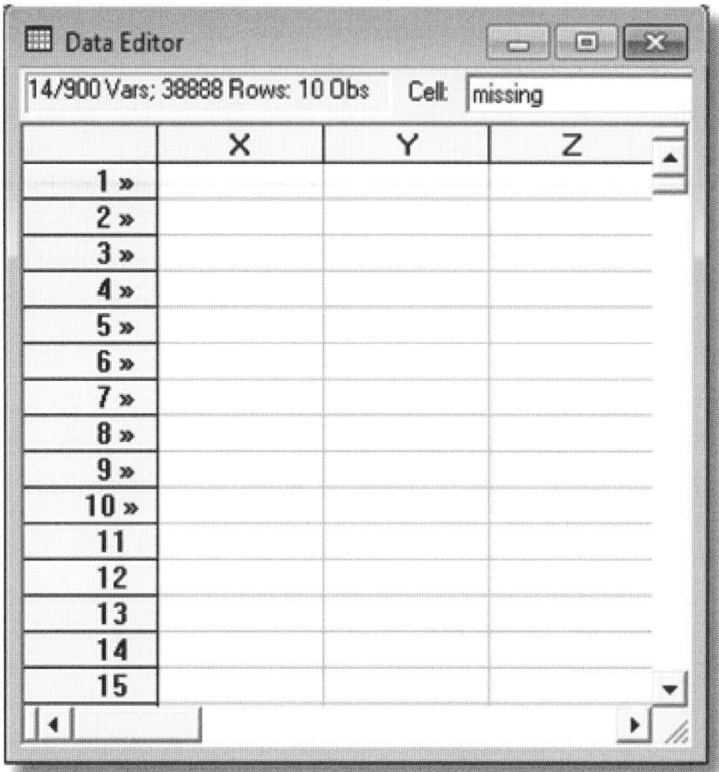

Figure 10.9 View data in Editor

the Data Editor in which the data may be entered. An alternative way to open the Data Editor is to press the Activate Data Editor button (second from right) in the desktop menu, indicated below.

10.8 Saving and reloading the data set

The project file, .lpj format, is used to save your work from session to session, and to exchange data sets from one Nlogit program to another (e.g., on a different computer). Use File:Save Project As. . . (Figure 10.11).

This will open a Windows explorer window where you can specify where you want the project to be saved.

Figure 10.10 Data Editor button

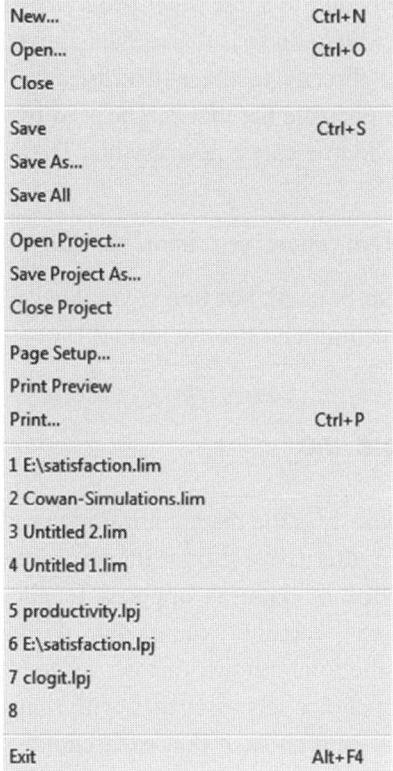

Figure 10.11 Saving data

There are several ways to reload a project that you have saved:

- In Windows explorer, when you double click a file name that has the suffix .lpj, Windows will automatically launch Nlogit and then Nlogit will reload the project file. The .lpj format is "registered" with Windows, so it is a recognized file format.
- After you launch Nlogit, you can use File "Open Project" to open a Windows explorer and navigate to the file then open it.

- The recently used project files will be listed at the end of the File menu. If the project you wish to load was one of the four most recently used projects, it will appear in the File menu, and you can select it from the list.

10.9 Writing a data file to export

If you wish to export data from Nlogit to some other program, there are two ways to proceed. A very reliable way to do so is to use Stat Transfer to convert the Nlogit project file (.lpj file) directly to the native format of the target program. If you want to write a portable file that can be read by many other programs, your best choice will be to create a new .csv file. The command is:

EXPORT ; list of variable names …
     ; File=<the file name and location where you want the file written> $

(There are other formats that can be used, but unless you have a compelling reason to use one of them, we recommend the csv format.)

10.10 Choice data entered on a single line

The data format described previously is the most commonly used format for choice analysis using Nlogit. An alternative formatting approach is to enter each choice set into a single line of data, as opposed to allocating each alternative within a choice set to a separate row of data. Using the single row per choice set data format, the total number of rows related to any given individual is the total number of choice sets associated with that individual.

Table 10.9 shows how data is entered such that each choice set is represented by a single row of data (for space reasons, Table 10.9 shows only the first three individuals). In this data context the choice variable no longer consists of 0s and 1s but rather assumes a unique number corresponding to the alternative chosen. In our example, the first alternative is car. Hence if this is the alternative chosen the choice variable is coded 1. Similarly the choice variable is coded 2 for bus, 3 for train. We have created an index variable, *ind*, which specifies to which individual the choice set belongs. (This is the format that is used by some other programs. Note that *id* is the same as *ind*.)

Although Nlogit can estimate models using data in this format, we prefer the data format as set out earlier in the chapter. The single line format severely

Table 10.9 Data entered into a single line

id	choice	Ind	Comfort1 (Car)	Comfort2 (Car)	Ttime1 (Car)	Comfort3 (Bus)	Comfort4 (Bus)	Ttime2 (Bus)	Comfort5 (Train)	Comfort6 (Train)	Ttime3 (Train)	age
1	1	1	1	0	14	1	0	12	−1	−1	12	40
1	2	1	0	1	10	0	1	14	0	1	12	40
2	3	2	0	1	12	1	0	14	−1	−1	12	32
2	3	2	−1	−1	12	0	1	12	−1	−1	10	32
3	2	3	−1	−1	12	1	0	14	0	1	14	35
3	1	3	1	0	14	0	1	10	1	0	14	35

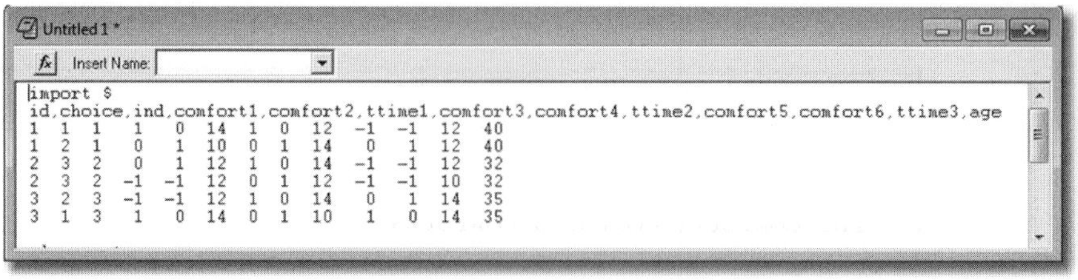

Figure 10.12 Editing data

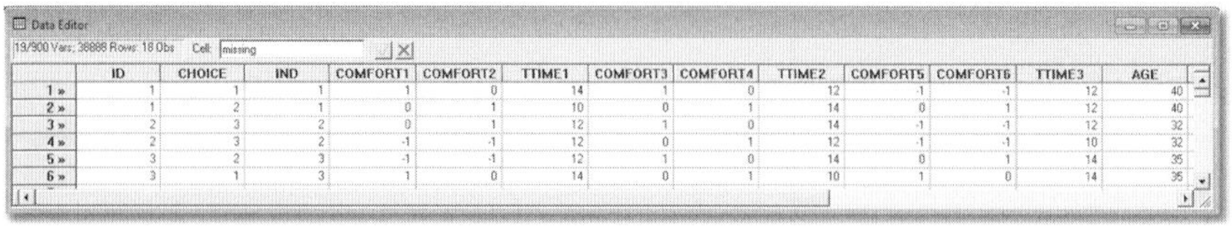

	ID	CHOICE	IND	COMFORT1	COMFORT2	TTIME1	COMFORT3	COMFORT4	TTIME2	COMFORT5	COMFORT6	TTIME3	AGE
1 »	1	1	1	1	0	14	1	0	12	-1	-1	12	40
2 »	1	2	1	0	1	10	0	1	14	0	1	12	40
3 »	2	3	2	0	1	12	1	0	14	-1	-1	12	32
4 »	2	3	2	-1	-1	12	0	1	12	-1	-1	10	32
5 »	3	2	3	-1	-1	12	1	0	14	0	1	14	35
6 »	3	1	3	1	0	14	0	1	10	1	0	14	35

Figure 10.13 Data shown in Data Editor

restricts the range of computations that can be done with the data in Nlogit. In the interests of brevity we do not discuss the modeling procedures associated with single line data analysis. Rather we refer those interested in modeling with such data to the Nlogit user manual.

Nlogit provides an internal device to convert one line data sets to the multiple line format. It is a command built to look like a model command, but converts data instead. To illustrate, we will convert the data in Table 10.9. Since it is a very small data set, we first import it using the procedure described in Section 10.6.1. The editing window is shown in Figure 10.12.

The result in the Data Editor is shown in Figure 10.13.

The command to convert the data is **NLCONVERT**, as shown in Figure 10.14.

The LHS list is the choice variable. The command indicates that there are three choices in the choice set. (This feature requires that the number of choices in the choice set be fixed. This is one of the disadvantages of this "wide" data format.) The sets of RHS variables are the attributes. Since there are three choices, each attribute set provides a set of three variables, one for each alternative. There are three sets of attribute variables, hence three attributes in the final data set. The RH2 variables are variables that will be replicated in each choice within the choice set. Notice that with 6 choice situations and 3 choices in the choice set, the new data set will have 18 rows. The result of the conversion is shown in Figure 10.15. (If instructed with ; **CLEAR**, the command will erase the original variables.) The response of the program in Figure 10.16 shows the computations that were done.

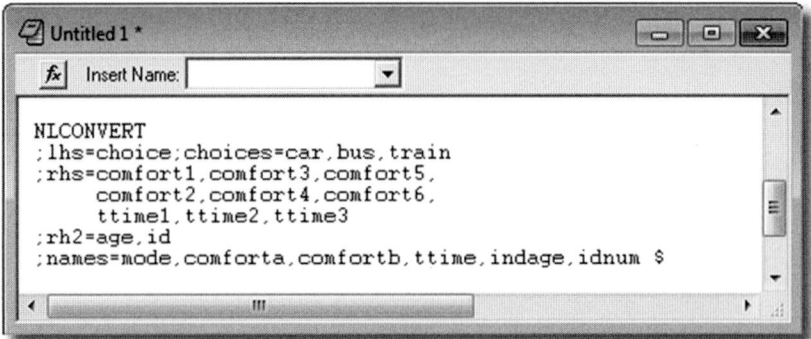

Figure 10.14 Data converter

	TTIME3	AGE	MODE	COMFORTA	COMFORTB	TTIME	INDAGE	IDNUM
1 »	12	40	1	1	0	14	40	1
2 »	12	40	0	1	0	12	40	1
3 »	12	32	0	-1	-1	12	40	1
4 »	10	32	0	0	1	10	40	1
5 »	14	35	1	0	1	14	40	1
6 »	14	35	0	0	1	12	40	1
7 »			0	0	1	12	32	2
8 »			0	1	0	14	32	2
9 »			1	-1	-1	12	32	2
10 »			0	-1	-1	12	32	2
11 »			0	0	1	12	32	2
12 »			1	-1	-1	10	32	2
13 »			0	-1	-1	12	35	3
14 »			1	1	0	14	35	3
15 »			0	0	1	14	35	3
16 »			1	1	0	14	35	3
17 »			0	0	1	10	35	3
18 »			0	1	0	14	35	3
19								
20								

Data Editor — 19/900 Vars; 38888 Rows: 18 Obs   Cell: missing

Figure 10.15 Finalized data

10.11 Data cleaning

The final task for the analyst in entering data should, as always, be the cleaning of the data. Data should always be checked for inaccuracies before analysis. The simplest and quickest check of data is to perform an analysis of descriptive statistics. The command to generate descriptive statistics is

Dstats ;rhs=*$

```
================================================================
Data Conversion from One Line Format for NLOGIT
The new sample contains      18 observations.
================================================================
Choice set in new data set has 3 choices.
CAR      BUS        TRAIN
----------------------------------------------------------------
There were 1 choice variables coded 1,..., 3 converted to binary
Old variable = CHOICE, New variable = MODE
----------------------------------------------------------------
There were 3 sets of variables on attributes converted. Each
set of 3 variables is converted to one new variable
New Attribute variable COMFORTA is constructed from
COMFORT1 COMFORT3 COMFORT5
New Attribute variable COMFORTB is constructed from
COMFORT2 COMFORT4 COMFORT6
New Attribute variable TTIME    is constructed from
TTIME1    TTIME2    TTIME3
----------------------------------------------------------------
There were 2 characteristics that are the same for all choices.
Old variable = AGE    , New variable = INDAGE
Old variable = ID     , New variable = IDNUM
================================================================
```

Figure 10.16 Summary of converted data

The results for the data in Table 10.1 are:

```
Descriptive Statistics for 7 variables
```

Variable	Mean	Std.Dev.	Minimum	Maximum	Cases	Missing
ID	2.0	.834058	1.0	3.0	24	0
ALTI	2.500000	1.142080	1.0	4.0	24	0
CSET	4.0	0.0	4.0	4.0	24	0
CHOICE	.250000	.442326	0.0	1.0	24	0
COMFORT1	-.041667	.806450	-1.000000	1.0	24	0
COMFORT2	.041667	.858673	-1.000000	1.0	24	0
TTIME	9.750000	4.932148	1.500000	14.0	24	0

The * signifies in Nlogit, "all variables." Thus the command will generate descriptive statistics for all variables within the data set. Inserting specific names (separated by commas) instead of * will generate descriptive statistics only for those variables named. The descriptive statistics for the *all variable* case are shown above. What the analyst should look for is unusual looking data. Examination of the output reveals that all variables are within their expected ranges (for example, we would expect the *choice* variable to have a minimum value of 0 and a maximum value of 1). A quick examination of such output can save the analyst a significant amount of time and avoid problems at the time of model estimation.

Examination of the descriptive statistics table is useful for locating possible data entry errors, as well as possibly suspect data observations. The analyst, however, needs to be aware that the output table generated above is inclusive of observations for *all* alternatives. Examining the descriptive statistics for alternatives independently may yield further interesting information. A command we could use for the example above is:

Dstats ; For [alti] ; rhs=comfort1,comfort2,ttime $

The addition of the **;For[alti]** to the **Dstats** command has Nlogit produce descriptive statistics for the observations that are specific to each value present within the *alti* variable.

```
----------------------------------------------------------------------
Setting up an iteration over the values of ALTI
The model command will be executed for     4 values
of this variable. In the current sample of          24
observations, the following counts were found:
Subsample    Observations   Subsample    Observations
ALTI    =   1          6   ALTI    =   2          6
ALTI    =   3          6   ALTI    =   4          6
----------------------------------------------------------------------
Actual subsamples may be smaller if missing values are
being bypassed. Subsamples with 0 observations will
be bypassed.
----------------------------------------------------------------------
```

```
--------------------------------------------------------------------------
Subsample analyzed for this command is ALTI    =    1
-----------+--------------------------------------------------------------
Variable|  Mean       Std.Dev.   Minimum   Maximum  Cases Missing
-----------+--------------------------------------------------------------
COMFORT1|     0.0    .894427  -1.000000      1.0      6        0
COMFORT2|     0.0    .894427  -1.000000      1.0      6        0
   TTIME|  12.33333  1.505545     10.0      14.0      6        0
-----------+--------------------------------------------------------------
Subsample analyzed for this command is ALTI    =    2
-----------+--------------------------------------------------------------
COMFORT1|  .500000    .547723      0.0       1.0      6        0
COMFORT2|  .500000    .547723      0.0       1.0      6        0
   TTIME|  12.66667  1.632993     10.0      14.0      6        0
-----------+--------------------------------------------------------------
```

```
Subsample analyzed for this command is ALTI    =    3
----------- +------------------------------------------------------------------
COMFORT1 |   -.333333    .816497   -1.000000   1.0       6         0
COMFORT2 |   -.166667    .983192   -1.000000   1.0       6         0
TTIME |      12.33333   1.505545      10.0     14.0      6         0
----------- +------------------------------------------------------------------
Subsample analyzed for this command is ALTI    =    4
----------- +------------------------------------------------------------------
COMFORT1 |   -.333333    .816497   -1.000000   1.0       6         0
COMFORT2 |   -.166667    .983192   -1.000000   1.0       6         0
TTIME |       1.666667    .258199    1.500000   2.0       6         0
----------- +------------------------------------------------------------------
```

It may be worthwhile to examine the correlation structure of the data. The command to do so is:

Dstats ;rhs=*; Output=2$

```
----------- +------------------------------------------------------------------
Cor.Mat. |      ID      ALTI     CSET    CHOICE  COMFORT1  COMFORT2    TTIME
----------- +------------------------------------------------------------------
       ID | 1.00000   .00000   .00000    .00000   .06464   -.06071    .04228
     ALTI |  .00000  1.00000   .00000   -.17213  -.25963   -.15517   -74871
     CSET |  .00000   .00000   .00000    .00000   .00000    .00000    .00000
   CHOICE |  .00000  -.17213   .00000   1.00000   .39613   -.02862    .17936
 COMFORT1 |  .06464  -.25963   .00000    .39613  1.00000    .50491    .33613
 COMFORT2 | -.06071  -.15517   .00000   -.02862   .50491   1.00000    .16169
    TTIME |  .04228  -.74871   .00000    .17936   .33613    .16169   1.00000
```

> *As an aside*, the analyst may wish to examine the covariance matrix. The command for this is **output=1$**. Using the command **output=3$** will generate both the covariance and correlation matrices. The correlation matrix for our example is shown above. As with descriptive statistics, it may be worthwhile examining the correlation matrix for each alternative independently. In Nlogit, the correlation matrix is based on a Pearson product moment specification between two variables. Strictly, this is valid when contrasting ratio scaled variables (and is usually acceptable for interval scaled variables); however for classificatory variables (e.g., **ordinal scaled**) other indicators of similarity are preferred. The Prelis pre-processor in LISREL is useful for this task.

To premise the importance of this, consider an SP choice experiment with three blocks. As previously mentioned, one can remove columns (i.e., attributes) from the design without loss of orthogonality; however, the same is not true for the removal of rows (i.e., treatment combinations or choice sets). As such, design orthogonality requires the return of all data for all blocks of the design. There can be no missing data. For small sample sizes (e.g., the total sample size is three respondents, each assigned to one of three blocks of a design), maintaining orthogonality is relatively straightforward. For larger sample sizes (e.g., when the sample size is in the hundreds), maintaining orthogonality is a non-trivial task.

For example, consider a design blocked into three. If 100 decision makers complete the first block and 100 complete the second but only 99 complete the third block, design orthogonality will be lost over the entire sample. The degree of the loss of orthogonality is a question of correlation and hence multicollinearity.

> *As an aside*, for an experimental design to remain orthogonal, either the entire design must be given to each decision maker (and any missing data result in the entire data related to that individual being removed from the data set) or some sampling strategy put in place to ensure that complete designs are returned across all decision makers. Unfortunately, any such strategy is likely to result in questions being raised regarding sampling bias. Computer Assisted Personal Interviews (CAPI) or Internet Aided surveys (IASs) may help alleviate this problem somewhat by detecting portions of a design (blocks) that have been under-utilized in sampling and assign new individuals to these. Alternatively, the randomization process might involve randomly assigning the first decision maker to a block and subsequent decision makers to other unused blocks without replacement. Once the entire design is complete, the process repeats itself, starting with the next decision maker sampled. In either case, the analyst must consider whether such strategies are strictly random. At the end of the day, it is likely that the analyst will have to live with some design non-orthogonality, which with efficient or optimal designs is less of a concern compared with the more traditional orthogonal designs.

Appendix 10A: Converting single line data commands

The commands to convert the data in Table 10.6 into multiple line choice data are recreated below. We have also included the commands to generate the additional descriptive tables for each alternative as well as the correlation matrix, as described in the main text:

```
CREATE
;car=(choice=1);bus=(choice=2);train=(choice=3);plane=(choice=4)
;cset=4
;alt1=1
;alt2=2
```

```
;alt3=3
;alt4=4$
WRITE
;id, alt1, cset, car, comfort1, comfort2, ttime1, age,
id, alt2, cset, bus, comfort3, comfort4, ttime2, age,
id, alt3, cset, train, comfort5, comfort6, ttime3, age,
id, alt4, cset, plane, comfort7, comfort8, ttime4, age
;file= <wherever the analyst specifies.dat>
;format=((8(F5.2,1X)))$


reset
read; file = <specified file location .dat>; nvar = 8 ;nobs = 24
;names = id, alt, cset, choice, comfort1, comfort2, ttime, age$
dstats;rhs=*$

Dstats ;rhs=*; Str=alti$

dstats;rhs=*
output=two$
```

Appendix 10B: Diagnostic and error messages

Altogether, there are well over 1,000 specific conditions that are picked up
by the command translation and computation programs in Limdep and
Nlogit. Most diagnostics are self-explanatory and will be obvious. For
example:

```
82 ;Lhs - variable in list is not in the variable names table.
```

states that your Lhs variable in a model command does not exist. No doubt
this is due to a typographical error – the name must be mis-spelled. Other
diagnostics are more complicated and in many cases it is not quite possible to
be precise about the error. Thus, in many cases, a diagnostic will say something like "the following string contains an unidentified name" and a part of
your command will be listed – the implication is that the error is somewhere
in the listed string. Finally, some diagnostics are based on information that is
specific to a variable or an observation at the point at which it occurs. In that
case, the diagnostic may identify a particular observation or value. In the
listing below, we use the conventions:

<AAAAAAAA>	indicates a variable name that will appear in the diagnostic
<nnnnnnnnnnnn>	indicates an integer value, often an observation number, that is given
<xxxxxxxxxxxx>	indicates a specific value that may be invalid, such as a "time" that is negative.

We note that it should be extremely rare, but occasionally, an error message will occur for reasons that are not really related to the computation in progress (we can't give an example – if we knew where it was, we'd remove the source before it occurred). This is on the same level as the ubiquitous "page fault" that Windows often throws up when something entirely different has occurred. You will always know exactly what command produces a diagnostic – an echo of that command will appear directly above the error message in the output window. So, if an absolutely unfathomable error message shows up, try simplifying the command that precedes it to its bare essentials and, by building it up, reveal the source of the problem.

Finally, there are the "program crashes." Obviously, we intend for these never to occur, but they do. The usual ones are division by zero and "page fault." Once again, we cannot give specific warning about these, since if we could, we'd prevent the problem. If you do get one of these, please let us know at Econometric Software. Also, please keep in mind that it is essential for us to reproduce the error in order to fix it. That means that if you write to Econometrics Software with one of these cases, we ask that you include sufficient resources (data and commands) for us to reproduce the error.

Part III

The suite of choice models

11 Getting started modeling: the workhorse – multinomial logit

An economist is an expert who will know tomorrow why the things he predicted yesterday didn't happen today.

(Laurance J. Peter 1919–90)

11.1 Introduction

In this chapter we demonstrate, through the use of a labeled mode choice data set (summarized in Appendix 11A to this chapter), how to model choice data by means of Nlogit. In writing this chapter we have been very specific. We demonstrate line by line the commands necessary to estimate a model in Nlogit. We do likewise with the output, describing in detail what each line of output means in practical terms. Knowing that "one must learn to walk before one runs," we begin with estimation of the most basic of choice models, the multinomial logit (MNL). We devote Chapter 12 to additional output that may be obtained for the basic MNL model and later chapters (especially Chapters 21–22) to more advanced models.

11.2 Modeling choice in Nlogit: the MNL command

The basic commands necessary for the estimation of choice models in Nlogit are as follows:

```
NLOGIT
;lhs = choice, cset, altij
;choices =<names of alternatives>
;Model:
U(alternative 1 name) = <utility function 1>/
U(alternative 2 name) = <utility function 2>/
...
U(alternative i name) = <utility function i>$
```

We will use this command syntax with the labeled mode choice data described in Chapter 10, shown here as:

```
Nlogit
;lhs = choice, cset, altij
;choices = bs,tn,bw,cr
;model:
u(bs) = bs + actpt*act + invcpt*invc + invtpt*invt2 + egtpt*egt
+ trpt*trnf /
u(tn) = tn + actpt*act + invcpt*invc + invtpt*invt2 + egtpt*egt
+ trpt*trnf /
u(bw) = bw + actpt*act + invcpt*invc + invtpt*invt2 + egtpt*egt
+ trpt*trnf /
u(cr) =                  invccr*invc + invtcar*invt + TC*TC +
PC*PC + egtcar*egt $
```

While other command structures are possible (e.g., using RHS and RH2 instead of specifying the utility functions – we do not describe these here and refer the interested reader to Nlogit's help references), the above format provides the analyst with the greatest flexibility in specifying choice models. It is for this reason that we use this command format over the other formats available.

The first line of the above command, as with all commands in Nlogit, informs the program as to the specific function being undertaken by the analyst. This is similar to the **create** and **dstats** commands discussed previously. The command **NLOGIT** informs the program that the analyst intends to estimate a discrete choice model.

The next command line specifies the components of the LHS of the choice model (**lhs**). The semi-colon is obligatory. The order of the command is always the choice variable (*choice* in this instance) followed by the variable representing the number of alternatives within each choice set (i.e., *cset*) followed by the variable indicating the alternative represented within each row of data (i.e., *altij*). If these names are placed in an order other than that shown, Nlogit is likely to produce an error message such as:

```
Error: 1099: Obs.  1 responses should sum to 1.0. Sum is 2.0000.
```

indicating that there exists more than one choice per choice set somewhere within the data set. Such an error is likely if (1) the data have been incorrectly inputted or (2) the order of the command line has not been correctly entered as suggested above.

The next command:

```
;choices = <names of alternatives>
```

requires the analyst to name each of the alternatives. It is important that the names appear in the exact order as the coding of the *altij* variable otherwise the analyst is likely to misinterpret the resulting output. This is the only place in the command syntax where order matters. For example, in the *altij* variable for the case study, the bus alternative is coded 1 while the train alternative is coded 2. As such, whatever names the analyst gives these two alternatives should appear in the order of the bus followed by the train. The remaining alternatives should also appear in the same order indicated by the *altij* variable.

The remaining commands specify the utility functions (in any order) for each of the alternatives:

```
;model:
U(<alternative 1 name>) = <utility function 1>/
U(<alternative 2 name>) = <utility function 2>/
...
U(<alternative i name>) = <utility function i>$
```

The utility specification begins with the command **;model:** and each new utility function is separated by a slash (/). The last utility function ends with a dollar sign ($) informing Nlogit that the entire command sequence is complete. Note the use of a colon (:) after the word **model** rather than a semi-colon (;).

The utility function for an alternative represents a linear equation corresponding to the functional relationship of attributes (and socio-demographic characteristics, or SDCs) upon the utility level derived for that alternative. Each utility function is equivalent to the utility function shown in Equation (11.1):

$$V_i = \beta_{0i} + \beta_{1i} f(X_{1i}) + \beta_{2i} f(X_{2i}) + \beta_{3i} f(X_{3i}) + \dots + \beta_{Ki} f(X_{Ki}), \qquad (11.1)$$

where

β_{1i} is the weight (or parameter) associated with attribute X_1 and alternative i

β_{0i} is a parameter not associated with any of the observed and measured attributes, called the *alternative-specific constant* (ASC), which represents on average the role of all the unobserved sources of utility.

As an aside, the constant β_{0i} need not be made specific to each alternative (i.e., an alternative-specific constant in the literature); however, it is debatable as to why an analyst would ever wish to constrain a constant to be equal across two or more alternatives (known as a generic parameter) when the alternatives are labeled. Given that the constant term is representative of the average role of all the unobserved sources of utility, constraining the constant terms of two or more labeled alternatives to be equal forces the average role of all the unobserved sources of utility for those alternatives to be equal. In most cases, this represents a questionable proposition for labeled alternatives.

The utility functions specified by the analyst need not be the same for each alternative. Different attributes and SDCs may enter into one or more utility functions or may enter into all or several utility functions but be constrained in different ways or transformed differently across the utility functions (e.g., with log transformations). Indeed, some utility functions may have no attributes or SDCs enter into them at all. We have discussed all the many ways of entering attributes into the utility expressions for each alternative in Chapter 3, and will not repeat this here. We will focus on how to use Nlogit in defining the functional form of the elements in a utility expression.

In specifying a utility function, the analyst must define both the parameters and the variables of the linear utility equation. This is done in a systematic manner with the parameter specified first and the variable specified second. Both are separated with an asterisk (*). We show this below:

```
;Model:
U(<alternative 1 name>) = <parameter>*<variable> /
```

The variable name must be consistent with a variable present within the data set. A parameter may be given any name so long as the name is no more than eight characters long and begins with an alpha code. In naming the parameter, the analyst is best to choose names that represent some meaning to the variable related to that parameter although, as mentioned, any name will suffice.

If the same parameter name is used more than once across (and within) alternatives, the parameter estimated will be the same for however many utility functions that name was used. That is to say that the parameter will be generic across those alternatives. For example:

```
;Model:
U(<alternative 1 name>) = <parameter 1>*<variable 1>/
U(<alternative 2 name>) = <parameter 1>*<variable 1>/....
```

will produce a single parameter estimate which is generic to both utility functions for variable 1. If different parameter names are used for similar variables, then parameter estimates specific to each alternative will be generated. Thus:

```
;Model:
U(<alternative 1 name>) = <parameter 1>*<variable 1>/
U(<alternative 2 name>) = <parameter 2>*<variable 1> /....
```

will estimate a specific parameter for alternative 1 which may be different to the parameter estimated for alternative 2.

To specify that the analyst wishes to estimate a constant term for an alternative, a parameter name for that constant term must also be specified (although no variable name is required). For example:

```
;Model:
U(<alternative 1 name>) = <constant> +<parameter>*<variable>/
```

will produce an estimate of the constant term for alternative 1. Note that only one constant can be specified per utility function. Thus:

```
;Model:
U(<alternative 1 name>) = <constant> + <mistake> + <parame-
ter>*<variable> /
```

will produce an error in the output stating that Nlogit was unable to estimate standard errors or reliable parameter estimates for the model specified. We show this below:

```
+-------------+------------------+---------------------+-----------+----------+
|Variable | Coefficient   |  Standard Error |b/St.Er.|P[|Z|>z]|
+-------------+------------------+---------------------+-----------+----------+
  CONSTANT       .09448145       .70978218        .133    .8941
  MISTAKE        .09448145    ......(Fixed Parameter).......
  PARAMETE      -.08663454    ......(Fixed Parameter).......
```

Using a specific example, the utility function for an alternative named *bs* (i.e., bus) might look thus:

```
;Model:
u(bs) = bs + actpt*act + invcpt*invc + invtpt*invt2 + egtpt*egt
+ trpt*trnf /
```

If a second utility function were specified as shown below, the model output will have a single generic parameter associated with all five attributes for both alternatives *bs* and *tn* but will estimate constant terms specific to each alternative (known as ASCs):

```
u(tn) = tn + actpt*act + invcpt*invc + invtpt*invt2 + egtpt*egt
+ trpt*trnf /
```

We show this in the following Nlogit output table. For this example, a single generic parameter named *actpt* is estimated for all three public transport alternatives while separate ASC terms are estimated:

```
|-> reject;SPRP=0$
|-> Nlogit
   ;lhs = choice, cset, altij
   ;choices = bs,tn,bw,cr?/ 0.2,0.3,0.1,0.4
   ;show
   ;descriptives;crosstabs
   ;model:
   u(bs) = bs + actpt*act + invcpt*invc + invtpt*invt2 + egtpt*egt +
trpt*trnf /
   u(tn) = tn + actpt*act + invcpt*invc + invtpt*invt2 + egtpt*egt +
trpt*trnf /
   u(bw) = bw + actpt*act + invcpt*invc + invtpt*invt2 + egtpt*egt +
trpt*trnf /
   u(cr) =                  invccr*invc + invtcar*invt + TC*TC + PC*PC +
egtcar*egt $
```

```
Normal exit: 6 iterations. Status=0, F=  200.4024
-----------------------------------------------------------------------
Discrete choice (multinomial logit) model
Dependent variable              Choice
Log-likelihood function     -200.40241
Estimation based on N =      197, K = 13
Inf.Cr.AIC =    426.8  AIC/N =   2.167
R2=1-LogL/LogL* Log-L fncn R-sqrd R2Adj
Constants only must be computed directly
            Use NLOGIT ;...;RHS=ONE$
Chi-squared[10]          =    132.82111
Prob [ chi squared > value ] =   .00000
Response data are given as ind. choices
Number of obs.=  197, skipped     0 obs
```

CHOICE	Coefficient	Standard Error	z	Prob. $\|z\|>Z*$	95% Confidence Interval	
BS	-1.88276**	.81887	-2.30	.0215	-3.48771	-.27781
ACTPT	-.06035***	.01845	-3.27	.0011	-.09651	-.02420
INVCPT	-.08584*	.05032	-1.71	.0880	-.18447	.01279
INVTPT	-.01108	.00829	-1.34	.1817	-.02733	.00518
EGTPT	-.04119**	.02048	-2.01	.0443	-.08134	-.00104
TRPT	-1.15456***	.39991	-2.89	.0039	-1.93837	-.37074
TN	-1.67956**	.83234	-2.02	.0436	-3.31091	-.04821
BW	-1.87943**	.81967	-2.29	.0219	-3.48595	-.27290
INVCCR	-.00443	.27937	-.02	.9873	-.55199	.54312
INVTCAR	-.04955***	.01264	-3.92	.0001	-.07433	-.02477

```
    TC|    -.11006              .09195 -1.20 .2313   -.29029    .07016
    PC|    -.01791              .01799 -1.00 .3195   -.05317    .01735
EGTCAR|    -.05807*             .03310 -1.75 .0793   -.12294    .00680
-------- +--------------------------------------------------------------
```

> *As an aside*, The name used for the parameter may be whatever the analyst so desires so long as the number of characters used in naming the parameter does not exceed eight (although there are one or two reserved names, **one** being just such a name). While we might name the parameter **actpt** for the fuel design attribute we could have used **act** instead (i.e., **act*act**). While the parameter can take any name, the variable name must be that of a variable located within the data set. Thus should the analyst mistakenly type the command:
>
> ```
> ;Model:U(ba) = actpt*atc /
> ```
>
> the following error message would appear, as no such variable exists (i.e., atc) within the data set.
>
> ```
> Error:  1085: Unidentified name found in atc
> ```

It is very important to check the spelling within each of the command lines to avoid unwanted errors. Returning to Equation (11.1), the utility functions may be written as Equations (11.2a) and (11.2b), focussing on one attribute and the ASCs:

$$V_{bs} = -1.88 - 0.0604 \times actpt \tag{11.2a}$$

$$V_{tn} = -1.680 - 0.0604 \times actpt. \tag{11.2b}$$

For the present, we note that the parameter estimates for the **actpt** attribute are equal for both alternatives but the constant terms of each of the alternatives differ (i.e., −1.88 for *bs* and −1.680 for *tn*).

If the **actpt** parameter in the second utility function were given a different name than that in the first utility function (e.g., *acttn*), separate alternative-specific parameters would be estimated. For example:

```
;Model:
   u(bs) = bs + actpt*act +... /
   u(tn) = tn + acttn*act + ... /
```

would produce the following parameter estimates:

```
   BS|    -1.48273*    .83393   -1.78  .0754    -3.11720    .15174
ACTPT|     -.12439***  .03220   -3.86  .0001     -.18750   -.06128
   TN|    -2.25316***  .85647   -2.63  .0085    -3.93181   -.57452
ACTTN|     -.02117     .02176    -.97  .3305     -.06382    .02147
```

The utility functions from Equation (11.1) thus become:

$$V_{bs} = -1.88 - 0.1244 \times \text{actpt} \tag{11.3a}$$

$$V_{tn} = -2.253 - 0.0212 \times \text{acttn}. \tag{11.3b}$$

The parameter estimates for the access time attribute are allowed to vary across the alternatives. We now have two parameter estimates, one for each alternative, defined as alternative-specific parameters.

As an aside, if a parameter is given a name with nine or more characters (e.g., a parameter is given the name *parameter*), Nlogit will make use of the first eight characters only. A not uncommon mistake when specifying alternative-specific parameters is to provide two or more parameters with names which are differentiated only after the eighth character (e.g., *parameter1* and *parameter2*). As Nlogit makes use only of the first eight characters the estimated model will produce a single generic parameter titled *paramete* rather than the two or more alternative-specific parameters desired by the analyst (e.g., *parameter1* and *parameter2*).

One final note is necessary before the reader can begin estimating models. The logit model, from which the basic choice model is derived, is homogenous of degree zero in the attributes. In layman's terms, this suggests that attributes and SDCs that are invariant across alternatives, such as age, number of vehicles, etc., will fall out of the probabilities and the model will not be estimable. This is true also of the constant term. The correct way to allow for them, as shown in Chapter 3, is to include them in a maximum of $J-1$ alternatives, where J is total number of alternatives (i.e., four in the data set being used in this chapter). Importantly, J is the total that applies across the sample and not the number of alternatives that any one individual may have in their choice set.

As an aside, in the command above we have specified alternative-specific parameter estimates for the *invc* attribute for car compared to all public transport alternatives, where the latter have a generic parameter estimate.

11.3 Interpreting the MNL model output

In this section we will concentrate on interpreting the output from the basic model reported above and not concern ourselves with how to improve the model's overall performance. Subsequent sections will add to the output generated as well as to our understanding of choice analysis.

Breaking this output into two sections, the first section of the output provides the analyst with useful information regarding the data used to estimate the model, as well as the model fit. The heading informs the analyst that a discrete choice model was estimated using the method of maximum likelihood estimation (MLE).

11.3.1 Determining the sample size and weighting criteria used

Returning to the NLOGIT output, the model type and the dependent or LHS variable is named:

```
Discrete choice (multinomial logit) model
Dependent variable                Choice
```

The choice variable used was *choice*, which is consistent with the commands used for the analysis. We have not used any variable to weight the data (see Chapter 13). The number of observations refers to the number of choice sets used within the analysis and not the number of individual respondents. Since we are using the revealed preference (RP) data in the case study, there is one observation per respondent:

```
Number of obs.=   197, skipped    0 obs
```

11.3.2 Interpreting the number of iterations to model convergence

Continuing with our interpretation of the Nlogit output, the next line of output informs the analyst how many iterations were taken to locate the solution reported (i.e., to fit the model):

```
Iterations completed    5
```

We have already mentioned that MLE is an iterative process. A large number of iterations before model convergence is an indication to the analyst that something is amiss. With a few exceptions, the number of iterations taken for simple choice models will rarely exceed 25. If for MNL models more than 25 iterations are observed to have occurred, the analyst should be suspicious of the final model produced. However, more complex models may require up to 100 iterations before convergence.

As an aside, the analyst may specify the maximum number of iterations allowable by Nlogit in estimating any given model. This is achieved by adding the command **;maxit = n** (where **n** = the maximum number of iterations). That is:

```
NLOGIT
;lhs = choice, cset, altij
;choices = <names of alternatives>
; maxit = n
;Model:
U(<alternative 1 name>) = <utility function 1>/
U(<alternative 2 name>) = <utility function 2>/
...
U(<alternative i name>) = <utility function i>$
```

By specifying the maximum number of iterations, the analyst must be aware that the model produced may be sub-optimal if convergence was not achieved prior to this number of iterations being reached.

11.3.3 Determining overall model significance

The next line of output provides the log-likelihood (LL) function estimate and the LL function estimate for the choice model:

```
Log-likelihood function     -3220.150
```

Because we have used MLE and not ordinary least squares (OLS) as the estimation procedure, we cannot rely upon the use of the statistical tests of model fit commonly associated with OLS regression. We cannot use an F-statistic to determine whether the overall model is statistically significant or not.

To determine whether the overall model is statistically significant, the analyst must compare the LL function of the choice model at convergence to the LL function of some other, "base model." To explain why this is so, recall that values of LL functions closer to zero represent better model fits. For this example, the LL function at convergence is −200.402, but we invite the reader to consider just how close this is to zero if there exists no upper bound on the value that a LL function can take. Unless we have some point of comparison, there is no way to answer this question.

Traditionally, two points of comparison have been used. The first point of comparison involves comparing the LL function of the fitted model with the LL function of a model fitted independent of any information contained within the data. The second point of comparison involves comparing the LL function of the fitted model against the LL function of a model fitted using only information on the market shares as they exist within the data set. To explain the origin of these two base comparison models (note that different literature has alternatively referred to these models as "base models," "constants only models," and "null models"), an understanding of two important properties of discrete choice models is necessary.

The first property relates the dependent variable of a discrete choice model to the output of the model estimation process. The dependent variable of a discrete choice model, is binary (i.e., 0, 1), yet the outcome of the model estimation process is choice probabilities, not choices *per se*. As we show later, summing the choice probabilities for an alternative estimated from a choice model over all observations will reproduce the choice or market share for that alternative.

The second property pertains to the role that constant terms play within the model. The simplest explanation is that a constant term represents the average influence of unobserved factors influencing choice decisions. If a constant is estimated such that it is specific to an alternative (i.e., an ASC), then the constant represents the unobserved factors influencing choice decisions as they pertain to the particular alternative for which it was estimated. An interesting question then becomes: if a constant term is representative of "unobserved" influences, how is it estimated?

Consider the basic equation of a discrete choice model. Assume a binary choice model (i.e., the model has only two alternatives) in which the only parameters estimated for that model are the constant terms. Further, assume that the utilities (i.e., V_is) for the two alternatives are equal to one and zero. Why zero?

Recall that logit models are homogenous of degree zero in the attributes. As such, the analyst is only ever able to estimate the utility for $J-1$ ASCs. In estimating a model with $J-1$ ASCs with no other attributes, at least one utility function is estimated with an average utility of zero (i.e., the utility function for the $J^{th} - 1$ alternative). As the exponential of zero equals one, the utility for this alternative will be represented as one. Assuming utility values of one and zero for the two alternatives, respectively, the probability of the first alternative being chosen, all else being equal, is calculated using the choice probability below:

$$p = \frac{e^1}{e^1 + e^0} = \frac{2.72}{2.72 + 1} = 0.73. \tag{11.4}$$

An increase of one unit in the utility level associated with the first alternative produces an increase in the probability of selecting that alternative to 0.88. We show this calculation in Equation (11.5):

$$p = \frac{e^2}{e^2 + e^0} = \frac{2}{2+1} = 0.88. \tag{11.5}$$

Increasing the utility of the first alternative from one to two produced an increase in the probability of selecting that alternative of a magnitude of 0.15. Now consider a further one unit increase in the utility associated with the first alternative (i.e., the utility increases from two to three); the probability of selecting the first alternative now becomes Equation (11.6):

$$p = \frac{e^3}{e^3 + 1} = 0.95. \tag{11.6}$$

This represents an increase in the probability of choosing the first alternative of 0.07 from when the utility of the first alternative was observed to be two. An equal change in magnitude in the utility level (e.g., a one unit increase) produced a different change in the magnitude of the change in the choice probabilities. A discrete choice model is non-linear in the probabilities (NB, plotting the probabilities over changes in a utility function, holding everything else equal, will produce the familiar S-shaped or sigmoid curve; see Figure 11.1).

While the probabilities obtained from a choice model will be non-linear when plotted, the utility functions (i.e., the V_is) are estimated as per the

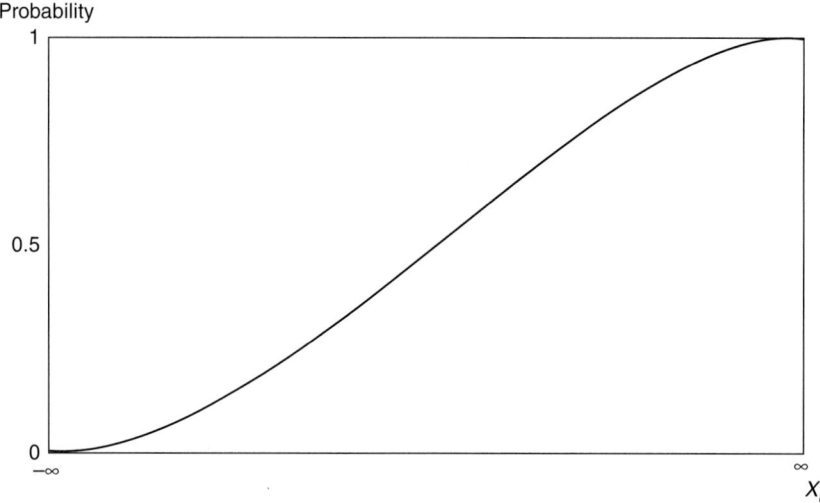

Figure 11.1   The sigmoid curve

functional form suggested in Equation (11.4). That is, the utility functions themselves are linear. Noting this point and following the same logical argument used to show that the base level of a dummy coded variable is perfectly confounded with the average utility of a given alternative (see Chapter 3), it can be shown that if the utility function for an alternative is estimated with only an ASC (i.e., no other parameters are estimated), the ASC will be equal to the average utility for that alternative.

Returning to our initial binary choice example, and assuming that the two utilities discussed are utilities estimated from a model employing ASCs only, the two utilities represent the average utilities for the two alternatives. Assuming that the original utilities are the true utilities for each alternative, the average utilities for alternatives 1 and 2 are one and zero, respectively (noting that these are relative utilities and hence the average utility for the second alternative is not strictly zero), and the probabilities of choice as calculated from Equation (11.4) for these two alternatives are 0.73 and 0.27 respectively, *ceteris paribus*.

But what of the first base comparison model? This model is estimated ignorant of any information contained within the data (hence it is sometimes referred to as the *no information model*). For this model, the true choice proportions are ignored and instead the model is estimated as if the choice or market shares are equal across the alternatives. This is equivalent to estimating a model with only a generic constant term for each of the $J - 1$ alternatives (assuming fixed choice sets).

Independent of whether one uses the first or second model as a basis of comparison, if the fitted model does not statistically improve the LL function (i.e., the LL of the model is statistically closer to zero than the comparison or base model's LL function value) then the additional attributes do not improve the overall model fit beyond the comparison or base model. That suggests that the best estimate available to the analyst is the market share assumed (i.e., either the actual market shares or equal market shares, dependent upon the comparison model employed).

The first comparison model assuming equal market shares among the alternatives has fallen out of favor. This is because an assumption of equal market shares is likely to be unrealistic, and given information in the data on choices, the analyst has available information on the actual sample market shares. So why not use the information available? For this reason, it is now more common to use the actual sample market shares available in the data as the comparison or base model to test for improvements in model fits.

A base model using the market shares within the data is equivalent to a model estimated with ASCs only. The commands necessary in Nlogit to generate this base model involve providing unique names for the constant terms for each alternative. The Nlogit outputs for this model have to be obtained using either the simple **;rhs=one** command syntax, since the LL is not reported in the model output associated with the **;model:** command syntax, or simply add **;asc** to the full model. An example is given below. By including **;choices = bs,tn,bw,cr**, the parameter estimates will be named after each alternative; otherwise, they will (as shown in the second output) be given a name associated with the order of the alternatives such as **A_Alt.1**:

```
reject;SPRP=0$
Nlogit
    ;lhs = choice, cset, altij
    ;choices = bs,tn,bw,cr
    ;rhs=one$
Normal exit:   4 iterations. Status=0, F=    250.9728
------------------------------------------------------------------------
Discrete choice (multinomial logit) model
Dependent variable                Choice
Log-likelihood function       -250.97275
Estimation based on N =      197, K =   3
Inf.Cr.AIC   =      507.9 AIC/N =     2.578
R2=1-LogL/LogL* Log-L   fncn R-sqrd R2Adj
Constants only must be computed directly
             Use NLOGIT ;...;RHS=ONE$
Response data are given as ind. choices
Number of obs.=    197, skipped     0 obs
```

CHOICE	Coefficient	Standard Error	z	Prob. |z|>Z*	95% Confidence Interval	
A_BS	-.80552***	.20473	-3.93	.0001	-1.20678	-.40425
A_TN	-.53207***	.19616	-2.71	.0067	-.91654	-.14760
A_BW	-.62947***	.20120	-3.13	.0018	-1.02381	-.23514

```
***, **, * ==>  Significance at 1%, 5%, 10% level.
Model was estimated on Aug 25, 2013 at 09:31:34 AM
------------------------------------------------------------------------
|-> Nlogit
    ;lhs = choice, cset, altij
    ;rhs=one$
Normal exit:   4 iterations. Status=0, F=    250.9728
------------------------------------------------------------------------
Discrete choice (multinomial logit) model
Dependent variable                Choice
```

```
Log-likelihood function        -250.97275
Estimation based on N =      197, K =    3
Inf.Cr.AIC  =      507.9 AIC/N =     2.578
R2=1-LogL/LogL* Log-L fncn R-sqrd R2Adj
Constants only must be computed directly
            Use NLOGIT ;...;RHS=ONE$
Response data are given as ind. choices
Number of obs.=    197, skipped     0 obs
```

CHOICE	Coefficient	Standard Error	z	Prob. |z|>Z*	95% Confidence Interval	
A_Alt.1	-.80552***	.20473	-3.93	.0001	-1.20678	-.40425
A_Alt.2	-.53207***	.19616	-2.71	.0067	-.91654	-.14760
A_Alt.3	-.62947***	.20120	-3.13	.0018	-1.02381	-.23514

To determine whether a model is statistically significant, the analyst compares the LL function of the estimated model (i.e., −200.4024) to that of the base comparison model (i.e., −250.9727). If the LL function of the estimated model can be shown to be a statistical improvement over the LL function of the base model (i.e., statistically closer to zero), then the model may be thought of as being statistically significant overall. Put another way, the base model represents the average utility for each of the alternatives and represents the market shares present within the data set. If an estimated model does not improve the LL function in comparison to the base model, then the additional parameters estimated do not add to the predictive capability of the base model. The analyst is best to use the average utility (and hence the market shares observed within the data set) as their estimate of the utility derived for each alternative for each decision maker.

To compare the LL function of an estimated model against the LL of its related base model we use the likelihood-ratio test (LRT, described in Chapter 7). The formula for the test is:

$$-2\left(\text{LL}_{\text{base model}} - \text{LL}_{\text{estimated model}}\right) \sim \chi^2_{(\text{number of new parameters estimated in the estimated model})}$$

$$(11.7)$$

Taking the difference of the LL reported for the base model in the output, (i.e., −250.97275) and the LL of the estimated model (i.e., −200.40241) and multiplying this value by minus two, the minus two log-likelihood (−2LL) statistic equals 101.14068. To determine whether an estimated model is superior to its related base model, the −2LL value obtained is compared to a Chi-square

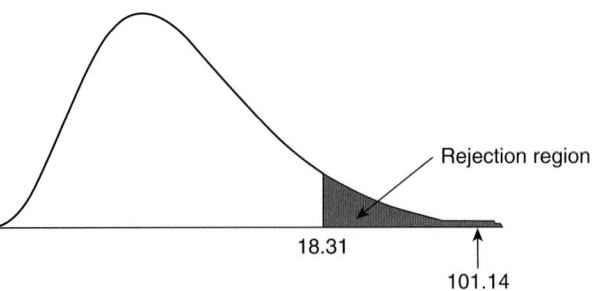

Figure 11.2 −2LL Chi-square test

statistic with degrees of freedom equal to the difference in the number of parameters estimated for the two models (assuming that the sample size remains constant). For this example, the base model requires five parameters be estimated (i.e., five ASCs) while the estimated model estimates a total of 13 parameters (i.e., three ASC and 10 attribute parameters). This suggests that the estimated model requires the estimation of 10 parameters more than the market share base comparison model. As such, the analyst is required to compare the calculated −2LL value to a χ^2 statistic with 10 degrees of freedom. From Chi-squared tables we note that $\chi^2_{10 \text{ d.f.}}$ equals 18.31 at α equals 0.05.

If the −2LL value exceeds the critical Chi-square value then the analyst rejects the null hypothesis that the specified model is no better than the base comparison model. If, on the other hand, the −2LL value is less than the Chi-square value, then the analyst cannot conclude that the specified model is better than the base model and, hence, the best estimate of utility is the average utility estimated from the base comparison model. We show this test in Figure 11.2. Clearly, here the inclusion of attribute parameters outperforms the base (market shares only) model.

In the case of all constant terms being specified within the model as ASCs, Nlogit will automatically perform the LL ratio test (however this test is performed using *the equal choice shares* for the base comparison model). This is represented by the lines of output:

```
Chi-squared[10]              =    132.82111
Prob [ chi squared > value ] =     .00000
```

From the model outputs, we can see the LRT has a value of 132.821, which is greater than the 101.14 based on a comparison with the market shares base model. We can deconstruct this value to obtain the equal shares LL, by dividing 132.82 by 2 to give 66.41, and then adding this to the LL of −200.410, to give 266.812 which, as expected, is greater than the market shares LL of −250.972.

To interpret the above output, the analyst compares the value shown in the line *Prob [chi squared > value]* (i.e., 0.00000 here) known as the *significance* or *p-value* (short for probability value) to some level of acceptance, commonly referred to as alpha, α, for that test. Usually the level of acceptance is taken as 0.05. If the p-value is less than the level of alpha, then the analyst *rejects* the null hypothesis that the estimated model is no better than the base comparison model. If, on the other hand, the p-value exceeds the level of alpha, then the analyst *cannot reject* the hypothesis and must conclude that the estimated model is no better than the base comparison model.

11.3.4 Comparing two models

Assuming that the same choice variable is used, the analyst may compare two different choice model specifications using the LRT described in Section 11.3.3. To demonstrate, consider the following model in which the cost attribute associated with the three public transport alternatives (*bs, tn, bw*) is allowed to vary across alternatives (i.e., the cost attribute is now alternative-specific):

```
Nlogit
    ;lhs = choice, cset, altij
    ;choices = bs,tn,bw,cr?/ 0.2,0.3,0.1,0.4
    ;model:
    u(bs) = bs + actpt*act + invcbs*invc + invtpt*invt2 + egtpt*egt +
trpt*trnf /
    u(tn) = tn + actpt*act + invctn*invc + invtpt*invt2 + egtpt*egt +
trpt*trnf /
    u(bw) = bw + actpt*act + invcbw*invc + invtpt*invt2 + egtpt*egt +
trpt*trnf /
    u(cr) =                    invccr*invc + invtcar*invt + TC*TC + PC*PC +
egtcar*egt $
Normal exit:   6 iterations. Status=0, F=    196.0186
---------------------------------------------------------------------------
Discrete choice (multinomial logit) model
Dependent variable               Choice
Log-likelihood function       -196.01863
Estimation based on N =      197, K =   15
Inf.Cr.AIC   =     422.0 AIC/N =    2.142
R2=1-LogL/LogL*  Log-L fncn R-sqrd R2Adj
Constants only must be computed directly
             Use NLOGIT ;...;RHS=ONE$
Chi-squared[12]             =     141.58867
```

```
Prob [ chi squared > value ] =   .00000
Response data are given as ind. choices
Number of obs.=    197, skipped     0 obs
```

CHOICE	Coefficient	Standard Error	z	Prob. |z|>Z*	95% Confidence Interval	
BS	-2.25230***	.84138	-2.68	.0074	-3.90138	-.60322
ACTPT	-.06562***	.01934	-3.39	.0007	-.10352	-.02772
INVCBS	-.02240	.05021	-.45	.6555	-.12082	.07601
INVTPT	-.01108	.00828	-1.34	.1809	-.02732	.00515
EGTPT	-.04404**	.02029	-2.17	.0299	-.08381	-.00428
TRPT	-1.19899***	.40765	-2.94	.0033	-1.99796	-.40002
TN	-.57070	.93951	-.61	.5436	-2.41210	1.27070
INVCTN	-.31378***	.09977	-3.14	.0017	-.50932	-.11823
BW	-1.50557	.97820	-1.54	.1238	-3.42281	.41167
INVCBW	-.13612	.10375	-1.31	.1895	-.33946	.06722
INVCCR	.00303	.28138	.01	.9914	-.54847	.55452
INVTCAR	-.05215***	.01263	-4.13	.0000	-.07690	-.02739
TC	-.09731	.09399	-1.04	.3006	-.28153	.08692
PC	-.01717	.01817	-.94	.3447	-.05278	.01844
EGTCAR	-.05440*	.03198	-1.70	.0889	-.11708	.00828

Using the LL ratio test we compute the -2LL ratio using the same procedure as before, only this time the LL of the base comparison model is replaced by the largest LL of the two models under comparison. If we naively use the first estimated model's LL function value first and the second estimated model's LL second, the possibility exists that the LL function for the first model will be smaller than that of the second model. In such cases, the computed Chi-square **test statistic** will be negative (i.e., the same problem when generic constants are specified). Thus the test becomes:

$$-2(LL_{Largest} - LL_{Smallest}) \sim \chi^2_{(\text{Difference in the number of parameters estimated between the two models})}.$$

$$(11.8)$$

The LL of the previous model was -200.4024, while the LL of the new model is -196.0186; hence, we replace the LL for the base model with the LL of the second model. Substituting the LL values for the old and new model into Equation (11.8), we obtain:

$$-2 \times \left(-196.018 - (-200.40) \right) \sim \chi^2_{(12-10)\text{ d.f.}}$$

$$4.382 \sim \chi^2_{(2)\text{ d.f.}}$$

The degrees of freedom for the critical Chi-square statistic is equal to the difference between the number of parameters estimated between the two models. As the first model estimated 10 parameters and the new model 12 parameters, the degrees of freedom for the test is two. From Chi-square tables, the Chi-square critical value with two degrees of freedom taken at a 95 percent confidence level is 5.99.

Comparing the test statistic of 4.382 to the Chi-square critical value of 5.99, we note that the test statistic is smaller than the critical value. Given this, the analyst is not able to reject the hypothesis that the new model does not statistically improve the LL over the previous model, and conclude that the LL of the new model is statistically no closer to zero than that of the previous model.

11.3.5 Determining model fit: the pseudo-R^2

It is often convenient to convert the LL outputs into a measure that is analogous to the overall fit or R^2 of a linear regression model. The R^2 statistic associated with choice models is not exactly analogous to the R^2 statistic of the linear regression model. This is because the linear regression model is, as the name suggests, linear, while the MNL model underlying choice analysis is non-linear. As such, an R^2 of 0.24 for a regression model is not equal to a pseudo-R^2 of 0.24 for a choice model. We show this later.

It is possible to calculate a pseudo-R^2 for a choice model. To do so we use Equation (11.9) (from Chapter 7):

$$R^2 = 1 - \frac{LL_{\text{Estimated model}}}{LL_{\text{Base model}}}. \tag{11.9}$$

Note that some analysts reportedly use the algebraically equivalent Equation (11.10) instead of Equation (11.9) to calculate the pseudo-R^2. In either case, the same R^2 value will be calculated:

$$R^2 = \frac{LL_{\text{Base model}} - LL_{\text{Estimated model}}}{LL_{\text{Base model}}}. \tag{11.10}$$

Substituting the values from estimated model output and base (known market shares only) model output into Equation (11.9) we obtain:

$$R^2 = 1 - \frac{-200.402}{250.972} = 0.2015.$$

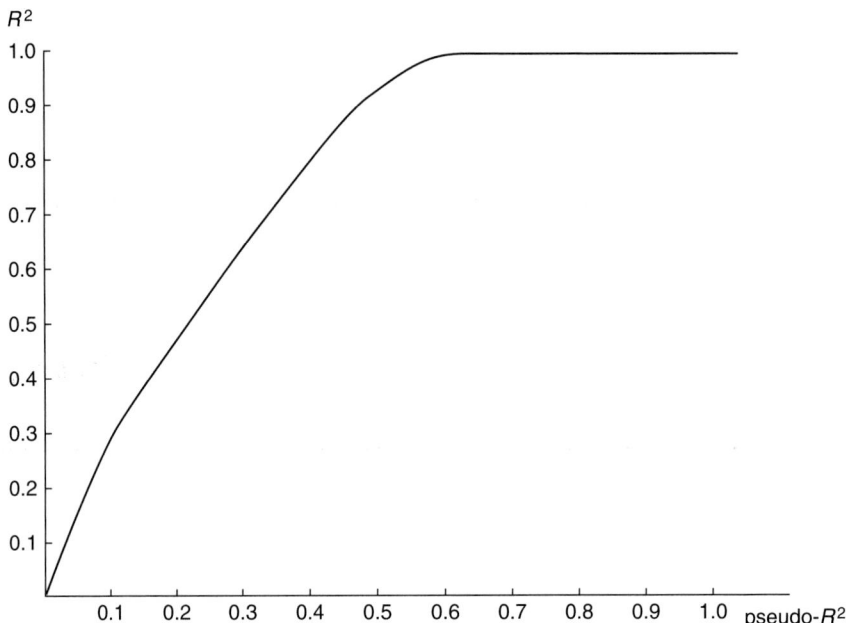

Figure 11.3   Mapping the pseudo-R^2 to the linear R^2

For this example, we use the pseudo-R^2 value of 0.2015. As noted previously, the pseudo-R^2 of a choice model is not exactly the same as the R^2 of a linear regression model. Fortunately, there exists a direct empirical relationship between the two (Domencich and McFadden 1975). Figure 11.3 shows the mapping of the relationship between the two indices.

Figure 11.3 suggests that a pseudo-R^2 value of 0.2015 still represents a bad model fit. This is not a surprising result given that the model fitted included a single attribute parameter.

> *As an aside*, in our experience, a pseudo-R^2 of 0.3 represents a decent model fit for a discrete choice model. Indeed from Figure 11.3 it can be seen that a pseudo-R^2 of 0.3 represents an R^2 of approximately 0.6 for the equivalent R^2 of a linear regression model. In fact, pseudo-R^2 values between the range of 0.3 and 0.4 can be translated as an R^2 of between 0.6 and 0.8 for the linear model equivalent.

11.3.6 Type of response and bad data

The last remaining output of the first section of output reports the type of response data used and the number of observations used for modeling:

```
Response data are given as ind. choices
Number of obs.=   197, skipped    0 obs
```

Nlogit allows modeling of a number of different types of choice data. For this book we concentrate solely on individual level data; however, it is also possible to model choices based on proportions data, frequency data, and ranked data. It is more likely that the beginner will be exposed to individual level choice data. For those wishing to explore these other data formats, the Nlogit reference manuals provide an excellent discussion on how to use them.

The number of observations used for modeling is reported a second time in the output; however, this time it is accompanied with a record of how many *bad* observations were skipped in model estimation. For simple MNL models, this record of bad observations becomes relevant when conducting the test of the Independence of Irrelevant Alternatives (IIA) (discussed in Chapter 7).

11.3.7 Obtaining estimates of the indirect utility functions

The second section of output for the simple MNL discrete choice model is that of the parameter estimates of the choice model. Those familiar with regression output from most other statistical packages will note a parallel with the output provided by Nlogit for discrete choice models and those of regression analysis. Any similarity is deceptive.

CHOICE	Coefficient	Standard Error	z	Prob. $|z|>Z*$	95% Confidence Interval	
BS	-1.88276**	.81887	-2.30	.0215	-3.48771	-.27781
ACTPT	-.06035***	.01845	-3.27	.0011	-.09651	-.02420
INVCPT	-.08584*	.05032	-1.71	.0880	-.18447	.01279
INVTPT	-.01108	.00829	-1.34	.1817	-.02733	.00518
EGTPT	-.04119**	.02048	-2.01	.0443	-.08134	-.00104
TRPT	-1.15456***	.39991	-2.89	.0039	-1.93837	-.37074
TN	-1.67956**	.83234	-2.02	.0436	-3.31091	-.04821
BW	-1.87943**	.81967	-2.29	.0219	-3.48595	-.27290
INVCCR	-.00443	.27937	-.02	.9873	-.55199	.54312
INVTCAR	-.04955***	.01264	-3.92	.0001	-.07433	-.02477
TC	-.11006	.09195	-1.20	.2313	-.29029	.07016
PC	-.01791	.01799	-1.00	.3195	-.05317	.01735
EGTCAR	-.05807*	.03310	-1.75	.0793	-.12294	.00680

The first column of output provides the variable names supplied by the analyst. The second column provides the parameter estimates for the variables mentioned in the first column of output. Ignoring the statistical significance of each of the parameters (or the lack thereof) for the present, we can use the information gleaned from the above output to write out the utility functions for each of the alternatives. Doing so requires knowledge of how the utility functions were specified earlier. For the above example, writing out the utility functions to conform to the earlier model specification yields Equations (11.11a) through (11.11d):

$$u(bs) = -1.8828 - 0.06035^{*}act - 0.08584^{*}invc - 0.01108^{*}invt2$$
$$- 0.04119^{*}egt - 1.15456^{*}trnf.$$

(11.11a)

$$u(tn) = -1.6796 - 0.06035^{*}act - 0.08584^{*}invc - 0.01108^{*}invt2$$
$$- 0.04119^{*}egt - 1.15456^{*}trnf.$$

(11.11b)

$$u(bw) = -1.8794 - 0.06035^{*}act - 0.08584^{*}invc - 0.01108^{*}invt$$
$$- 0.04119egt - 1.15456^{*}trnf.$$

(11.11c)

$$u(cr) = -0.00443^{*}invc - 0.4955^{*}invt2 - 0.05807^{*}egt.$$ (11.11d)

To demonstrate, consider the utility an individual derives when faced with a bus fare of $1 (per trip). If we ignore all attributes except invc, and considering only the impact upon the utility of travelling by bus, Equation (11.11a) becomes:

$$V_{cart} = -1.8828 - 0.08584^{*}invc \times 1 = -1.968.$$

The utility derived from a choice model as shown above is meaningful only when considered relative to that of the utility for a second alternative. Thus, a utility of −1.968 is meaningful only when compared with the utility calculated for that of each of the other alternatives. Assuming that the utility for the *tn* alternative was estimated as being −1.765, the utility of the *bs* alternative relative to that of the *tn* alternative is given as the difference of the two. That is:

$$V_{bs} - V_{tn} = -1.968 - (-1.765) = -0.203.$$

Clearly, the *tn* alternative is preferred to that of the *bs* alternative, *ceteris paribus*. The negative sign suggests disutility in contrast to utility.

Each of the utility functions shown in Equations (11.11a) through (11.11d) represent the constituent components of the MNL equation (Chapter 4) reproduced as Equation (11.12):

$$\text{Prob}(i \mid j) = \frac{\exp V_i}{\displaystyle\sum_{j=1}^{J} \exp V_j} \; ; \, j = 1, \ldots, i, \ldots, J \; i \neq j. \tag{11.12}$$

To calculate the probability that an alternative will be selected over all other available alternatives, the utility function for that alternative is treated as the numerator in Equation (11.12) (i.e.,V_i). As such, to calculate the selection probabilities of each of the alternatives will require as many equations as there exist alternatives.[1]

Using a specific example, assuming that the analyst wishes to determine the probability of selection of the *bs* alternative, expanding Equation (11.12) for the mode case study we obtain:

$$\text{Prob}(bs \mid j) = \frac{e^{V_{bs}}}{e^{V_{bs}} + e^{V_{tn}} + e^{V_{bw}} + e^{V_{ce}}} \tag{11.13}$$

and substituting Equations (11.11a) through (11.11d) we arrive at:

$$\text{Prob}(bs \mid j) = \frac{e^{(-1.8828 \, -0.06035^*act \, -0.08584^*invc \, -0.01108^*invt2 \, -0.04119^*egt \, -1.15456^*trnf)}}{\begin{array}{l}(e^{(-1.8828 \, -0.06035^*act \, -0.08584^*invc \, -0.01108^*invt2 \, -0.04119^*egt \, -1.15456^*trnf)} \\ + e^{(-1.6796 \, -0.06035^*act \, -0.08584^*invc \, -0.01108^*invt2 \, -0.04119^*egt \, -1.15456^*trnf)} \\ + e^{(-1.8794 \, -0.06035^*act \, -0.08584^*invc \, -0.01108^*invt2 \, -0.04119^*egt \, -1.15456^*trnf)} \\ + e^{(-0.00443^*invc \, -0.4955^*invt2 \, -0.05807^*egt)})\end{array}}.$$

$$\tag{11.14}$$

As noted previously, while the utility functions derived from a discrete choice model are linear, the probability estimates are not. It is possible to provide a direct behavioral interpretation of the parameter estimates when discussing

---

[1] This is not strictly true, as the probabilities must sum to one and hence one can calculate the probability of the last alternative given knowledge of the probabilities of all the other alternatives.

utilities (although only in a relative sense) but not when discussing probabilities. This is a result of the use of exponentials in Equation (11.14). In Chapter
12, we discuss the concepts of marginal effects and elasticities which provide a
direct and meaningful behavioral interpretation of the parameter estimates
when dealing with probabilities. The next column of output lists the standard
errors for the parameter estimates.

The parameter estimates obtained are subject to error. The amount of
error is given by the standard error of the coefficient. A common question
asked by analysts is whether a variable contributes to explaining the choice
response. What we are attempting to accomplish through modeling is an
explanation of the variation in the dependent variable (i.e., choice) observed
within the population of sampled individuals. Why do some individuals
choose alternative A over alternative B, while others ignore these alternatives
completely and choose alternative C? By adding variables to a model, the
analyst is attempting to explain this variation in the choice of alternative. If
an explanatory variable does not add to the analyst's understanding of
choice, statistically the weight attached to that variable will equal zero.
That is:

$$\beta_i = 0. \tag{11.15}$$

In linear regression analysis, this test is usually performed via a t- or F-test. For
choice analysis based upon MNL models, neither the t- or F-statistic is
available. Fortunately, the asymptotically equivalent test is available. Known
as the *Wald statistic*, the test statistic is both calculated and interpreted in the
same manner as the t-test associated with linear regression models. The Wald
statistic (see also Chapter 7) for each parameter, given in the fourth column of
the output is:

$$Wald = \frac{\beta_i}{\text{standard error}_i}. \tag{11.16}$$

To determine whether an explanatory variable is statistically significant
(i.e., $\beta_i \neq 0$) or not (i.e., $\beta_i = 0$), the analyst compares the Wald statistic
given in the output to a critical Wald value. In the limit, this critical Wald
value is equivalent to the t-statistic and hence the value used for comparison
is that of the t-statistic taken at various levels of confidence. Assuming a
95 percent confidence level (i.e., alpha = 0.05) the critical Wald value is 1.96
(many round this to 2.0). If the absolute value of the Wald test statistic
given in the output is greater than the critical Wald value, the analyst may

reject the hypothesis that the parameter equals zero and conclude that the explanatory variable is statistically significant. If, on the other hand, the absolute value of the Wald test statistic given in the output is less than the critical Wald value, the analyst cannot reject the hypothesis that the parameter equals zero and therefore must conclude that the explanatory variable is not statistically significant.

The final column of output provides the *probability value* (known as a *p*-value) for the Wald test of the previous column.

As with the log ratio Chi-square test, the analyst compares the *p*-value to some pre-determined confidence level as given by alpha. Assuming a 95 percent confidence level, alpha equals 0.05. *p*-values less than the determined level of alpha suggest that that parameter is not statistically equal to zero (i.e., the explanatory variable is statistically significant), while *p*-values that exceed the level of alpha as assigned by the analyst indicate that a parameter is statistically equal to zero (and hence the explanatory variable is not statistically significant). At the same level of confidence, both the Wald test and the *p*-value will draw the same conclusion for the analyst.

> *As an aside*, the output produced by Nlogit is best saved to a Word file in courier font with point size 8. When you copy and paste the output as is, it will look very messy in other default fonts and sizes (e.g., 12 point Times Roman).

11.4 Handling interactions in choice models

The examples we have used to this point have assumed that there are no significant interaction effects present within the data. However, attributes and SDCs are not necessarily independent (and hence additive). For example, the marginal utility (the estimate parameters) associated with invehicle cost may vary according to an individual's personal income. We can test this by integrating (or conditioning) *invc* on **personal; income** (pinc). The following Nlogit command syntax may be used to generate just such an interaction variable:

```
create; cst_pinc=invc*pinc$
```

The Nlogit model with this interaction term associated with the *cr* alternative is given below. We have included **;asc** so that we can obtain all of the LL results of interest:

```
Nlogit
    ;lhs = choice, cset, altij
    ;choices = bs,tn,bw,cr?/ 0.2,0.3,0.1,0.4
    ;asc
    ;model:
    u(bs) = bs + actpt*act + invcpt*invc + invtpt*invt2 + egtpt*egt +
trpt*trnf +cpinc*cst_pinc/
    u(tn) = tn + actpt*act + invcpt*invc + invtpt*invt2 + egtpt*egt +
trpt*trnf /
    u(bw) = bw + actpt*act + invcpt*invc + invtpt*invt2 + egtpt*egt +
trpt*trnf /
    u(cr) =                    invccr*invc + cpinc*cst_pinc+invtcar*invt +
TC*TC + PC*PC + egtcar*egt $
Normal exit:   4 iterations. Status=0, F=    250.9728
---------------------------------------------------------------------
Discrete choice (multinomial logit) model
Dependent variable              Choice
Log-likelihood function        -250.97275
Estimation based on N =    197, K =   3
Inf.Cr.AIC  =    507.9 AIC/N =    2.578
R2=1-LogL/LogL*  Log-L fncn R-sqrd R2Adj
Constants only   -266.8130  .0594 .0542
Response data are given as ind. choices
Number of obs.=   197, skipped    0 obs
```

CHOICE	Coefficient	Standard Error	z	Prob. |z|>Z*	95% Confidence Interval	
A_BS	-.80552***	.20473	-3.93	.0001	-1.20678	-.40425
A_TN	-.53207***	.19616	-2.71	.0067	-.91654	-.14760
A_BW	-.62947***	.20120	-3.13	.0018	-1.02381	-.23514

```
***, **, * ==>  Significance at 1%, 5%, 10% level.
Model was estimated on Aug 26, 2013 at 08:57:38 AM
---------------------------------------------------------------------
Normal exit:   6 iterations. Status=0, F=    198.2643
---------------------------------------------------------------------
Discrete choice (multinomial logit) model
Dependent variable              Choice
Log-likelihood function        -198.26430
Estimation based on N =    197, K =   14
Inf.Cr.AIC  =    424.5 AIC/N =    2.155
R2=1-LogL/LogL*  Log-L fncn R-sqrd R2Adj
Constants only   -250.9728  .2100 .1894
Chi-squared[11]              =    105.41691
Prob [ chi squared > value ] =    .00000
Response data are given as ind. choices
Number of obs.=   197, skipped    0 obs
```

CHOICE	Coefficient	Standard Error	z	Prob. |z|>Z*	95% Confidence Interval	
BS	-2.05677**	.82596	-2.49	.0128	-3.67561	-.43792
ACTPT	-.06192***	.01863	-3.32	.0009	-.09844	-.02540
INVCPT	-.13789**	.05430	-2.54	.0111	-.24430	-.03147
INVTPT	-.01216	.00834	-1.46	.1448	-.02851	.00419
EGTPT	-.04135**	.02074	-1.99	.0462	-.08200	-.00071
TRPT	-1.12894***	.40268	-2.80	.0051	-1.91818	-.33970
CPINC	.00121**	.00058	2.09	.0363	.00008	.00235
TN	-1.42844*	.84540	-1.69	.0911	-3.08540	.22852
BW	-1.53740*	.83780	-1.84	.0665	-3.17947	.10466
INVCCR	-.09990	.28535	-.35	.7263	-.65918	.45938
INVTCAR	-.04997***	.01258	-3.97	.0001	-.07463	-.02530
TC	-.10533	.09264	-1.14	.2555	-.28690	.07624
PC	-.01824	.01813	-1.01	.3145	-.05377	.01730
EGTCAR	-.05702*	.03284	-1.74	.0825	-.12139	.00734

Marginal utility of *cr* cost = −0.09990 + 0.00121*cst_pinc. The inclusion of the interaction of cost with income has resulted in the *invc* parameter estimater becoming statistically insignificant (*t*-value of −0.35). The influence of personal income is to scale the role of *invc* for *cr* up or down as income changes. If the *invc* parameter were significant then we would find that increasing personal income reduces the marginal disutility of *invc* associated with the *cr* alternative. Since *invc* is not significant, we might question the behavioral (as distinct from the statistical) gain in this functional form.

11.5 Measures of willingness to pay

A common objective in the use of discrete choice models is the derivation of measures designed to determine the amount of money individuals are willing to forfeit in order to obtain some benefit from the undertaking of some specific action or task. Such measures are referred to as measures of willingness to pay (WTP). In simple linear models,[2] WTP measures are calculated as the ratio of two parameter estimates, *holding all else constant*. Provided that at least one attribute is measured in monetary units, the ratio of the two parameters will provide a financial indicator of WTP.

---

[2] As models of discrete choice are linear in the utility functions, the choice modeler is able to take advantage of this fact.

One such important WTP measure in transportation studies (related to the case study data in this chapter) is the value of travel time savings (VTTS) defined as the amount of money an individual is willing to outlay in order to save a unit of time spent travelling, *ceteris paribus*. Specifically, such measures are used in determining road and public transportation pricing. WTP measures are also important to environmental economic studies in which a not uncommon objective is the valuation of non-monetary attributes such as air or water quality.

> *As an aside*, if VTTS are to be estimated for two or more alternatives and all attributes to be used in the calculation of the WTP measure are specified generic, the resulting VTTS will be generic to all alternatives.

In calculating a measure of WTP, it is important that both attributes to be used in the calculation are found to be statistically significant, otherwise no meaningful WTP measure can be established. For the above example, the VTTS is to be calculated from the cost and time parameters, which are both statistically significant. If, as is the case with VTTS, one attribute is measured in monetary terms, it is important that that attribute be treated as the denominator in the ratio of the two parameters to be used. As such, the VTTS from the above model may be calculated as follows:

$$\text{VTTS} = \left(\frac{\beta_{invt2}}{\beta_{invc}}\right) \times 60$$
$$= \left(\frac{-0.01108}{-0.08584}\right) \times 60 = 7.745 \ \$/\text{per hour}$$

We have multiplied the VTTS measure by 60 to give a measure of WTP measured in dollars per hour rather than dollars per minute.

> *As an aside*, WTP measures are calculated as the ratios of two parameters, and as such are sensitive to the attribute level ranges used in the estimation of both parameters. Some researchers have recently observed differences in WTP measures derived from SP and RP data sources, and have claimed that these differences may be the result of the hypothetical nature of SP data in which respondents are not bound by real life constraints in the choices made. As such, many prefer WTP measures derived from RP data where such constraints are binding. What is only now being acknowledged is that such differences may in part be the result of different attribute level ranges being employed across different studies. Even for WTP measures derived from different data sets of similar type (e.g., SP and SP or RP and RP), differences in the attribute levels ranges may account for some if not all of

any differences observed in the WTP measures derived. It is important, therefore, that researchers report the attribute level ranges used in deriving WTP measures if any objective comparison is to be made across studies.

More complex WTP measures can be obtained for non-linear models in which the valuation of an attribute is itself a function of the level of an attribute and other interacted influences. We discuss this in Chapter 12 on MNL and Chapter 15 on mixed logit (ML) models.

11.6 Obtaining utility and choice probabilities for the sample

Two underlying outputs of estimation of choice models are the overall utility associated with an alternative and the associated choice probability, obtained using the form of Equation (11.13).

The output for the first four respondents is summarized below. This data is obtained as a cut and paste into Excel from the data variable list in Nlogit. This is seen by clicking on the project file NW_SPRP.lpj, and then the variable list where the probabilities and utilities are stored under the names chosen in the command syntax:

```
Nlogit
;lhs = choice, cset, altij
;choices = bs,tn,bw,cr
;utility=util
;prob=prob
;model:
u(bs) = bs + actpt*act + invcpt*invc + invtpt*invt2 + egtpt*egt
+ trpt*trnf /
u(tn) = tn + actpt*act + invcpt*invc + invtpt*invt2 + egtpt*egt
+ trpt*trnf /
u(bw) = bw + actpt*act + invcpt*invc + invtpt*invt2 + egtpt*egt
+ trpt*trnf /
u(cr) =                  invccr*invc + invtcar*invt + TC*TC +
PC*PC + egtcar*egt $
```

Id	Set	Altij	cset	choice	prob	util
1	0	1	3	1	0.075	−5.500
1	0	2	3	0	0.819	−3.117
1	0	3	3	0	0.106	−5.163
2	0	1	4	1	0.157	−4.461
2	0	2	4	0	0.155	−4.472

Id	Set	Altij	cset	choice	prob	util
2	0	3	4	0	0.015	−6.785
2	0	4	4	0	0.673	−3.004
3	0	1	4	0	0.018	−7.562
3	0	2	4	0	0.242	−4.968
3	0	3	4	1	0.287	−4.796
3	0	4	4	0	0.453	−4.342
4	0	1	4	0	0.054	−5.492
4	0	2	4	0	0.337	−3.651
4	0	3	4	1	0.426	−3.417
4	0	4	4	0	0.183	−4.262

In the spreadsheet above, we can see that respondent 1 has 3 alternatives in their choice set and the other three respondents have all 4 alternatives in their choice set. The choice probabilities sum to 1.0 across the 3 or 4 alternatives in a respondent's choice set. Looking at respondent 1, we see that the (relative) marginal disutility associated with the train (tn) alternative (altij = 2) is the lowest (−3.117), and hence the choice probability is the highest. Analysts can create a spreadsheet for the entire sample and then present the findings in a way that may suit them. Alternatively, as is common, the utility and choice probability data is not reported in this detail, with the focus on aggregate shares and other behaviorally useful outputs such as elasticities, partial (or marginal) effects and predictions based on scenario analysis of before and after attribute levels.

The commands to undertake these behaviorally interesting applications are presented in Chapter 12, using the same data as above. It is now time to move to Chapter 12 and to introduce the extended set of outputs available in Nlogit.

Appendix 11A: The labeled choice data set used in the chapter

In 2003, the Institute of Transport Studies (ITS) (University of Sydney), on behalf of the New South Wales state government, undertook a patronage demand study as part of an evaluation of possible investment options in public transport infrastructure in the north-west sector of metropolitan Sydney.[3]

---

[3] The north-west sector is approximately 25 kilometres from the Sydney central business district (CBD). It is the fastest-growing sector of Sydney in terms of residential population and traffic build up. It is also one of the wealthiest areas with high car ownership and usage and a very poor public transport service with the exception of a busway system along the M2 tollroad into the CBD.

The principal aim of the study was to establish the preferences of residents within the study area for private and public transport modes for commuting and non-commuting trip purposes. Once known, the study called for the preferences to be used to forecast patronage levels for various currently non-existing transport modes, specifically possible new heavy rail, light rail, or busway modes.

To capture information on the preferences of residents, an SC experiment was generated and administered using CAPI technology. Sampled residents were invited to review a number of alternative main and access modes (both consisting of public and private transport options) in terms of levels of service and costs within the context of a recent trip, and to choose the main mode and access mode that they would use if faced with the same trip circumstance in the future. Each sampled respondent completed 10 choice tasks under alternative scenarios of attribute levels and, in each instance, choosing the preferred main and access modes. The experiment was complicated by the fact that alternatives available to any individual respondent undertaking a hypothetical trip depended not only on the alternatives that that respondent had available at the time of the "reference" trip, but also upon the destination of the trip. If the trip undertaken was intra-regional, then the existing busway (M2) and heavy rail modes could not be considered viable alternatives, as neither mode travels within the bounds of the study area. If, on the other hand, the reference trip was inter-regional (e.g., to the CBD), then respondents could feasibly travel to the nearest busway or heavy rail train station (outside of the origin region) and continue their trip using these modes. Further, not all respondents have access to a private vehicle for the reference trip, due either to a lack of ownership or that the vehicle was not available at the time when the trip was made. Given that the objective of the study was to derive an estimate of the patronage demand, the lack of availability of privately owned vehicles (through either random circumstance or non-ownership) should be accounted for in the SC experiment. Failure to account for the non-availability of the private vehicle alternative would likely result in biased patronage demand forecasts, in terms of both the main mode chosen and the mode chosen to access the main mode.

The master experimental design for the mode SC study required a total of 47 attributes (46 in four levels and 1 in six levels for the blocks) and had 60 runs; that is, there are 6 blocks of 10 choice sets each. The design was constructed using a procedure that simultaneously optimized the minimization of the D-error of the design as well as the correlations (for a discussion of D-error see for example, Huber and Zwerina, 1996). The final design had correlations no greater than ± 0.06. The design generated allowed for the estimation of all main mode and access mode alternative-specific main effects. Within each block, the order of the choice sets has been randomized to control for order effect biases. The experiment consisted of different task configurations designed to reflect the alternatives realistically available to a respondent given the reference trip circumstance reported by the respondent earlier in the CAPI interview: the configurations consisted of (i) with/without car, (ii) inter-/intra-regional trips, (iii) new light rail versus new heavy rail, new light rail versus new busway, and new heavy rail versus new busway. These configurations were included to provide more realism in the scenarios shown to individual respondents. In order to maintain efficiency and minimize correlations within the data set, a maximum number of complete designs have to be filled within each configuration. Using the CAPI program, if the first respondent has a car available for an intra-regional trip with new light rail and heavy rail alternatives present, she is assigned to block 1 for that configuration. If the second respondent is in the exact same configuration, she is assigned to the second block otherwise she is assigned to block 1 of the appropriate design configuration. Once a configuration has all blocks completed, the process starts at block 1 again.

The trip attributes associated with each mode are summarized in Table 11A.1.

For currently existing modes, the attribute levels were pivoted off the attribute levels captured from respondents for the reference trip (Figure 11A.1). Respondents were asked to complete information regarding the reference trip not only for the mode used for the reference trip, but also for the other modes

Table 11A.1 Trip attributes in stated choice design

For existing public transport modes		For new public transport modes	For the existing car mode
Fare (one-way)		Fare (one-way)	Running cost
In-vehicle travel time		In-vehicle travel time	In-vehicle travel time
Waiting time		Walk time	Toll cost (one-way)
Access mode:	Waiting time	Transfer waiting time	Daily parking cost
	Car time	Access mode: walk time	Egress time
	Bus time	Car time	
	Bus fare	Bus time	
Egress time		Access mode fare (one-way)	
		Bus fare	
		Egress time	

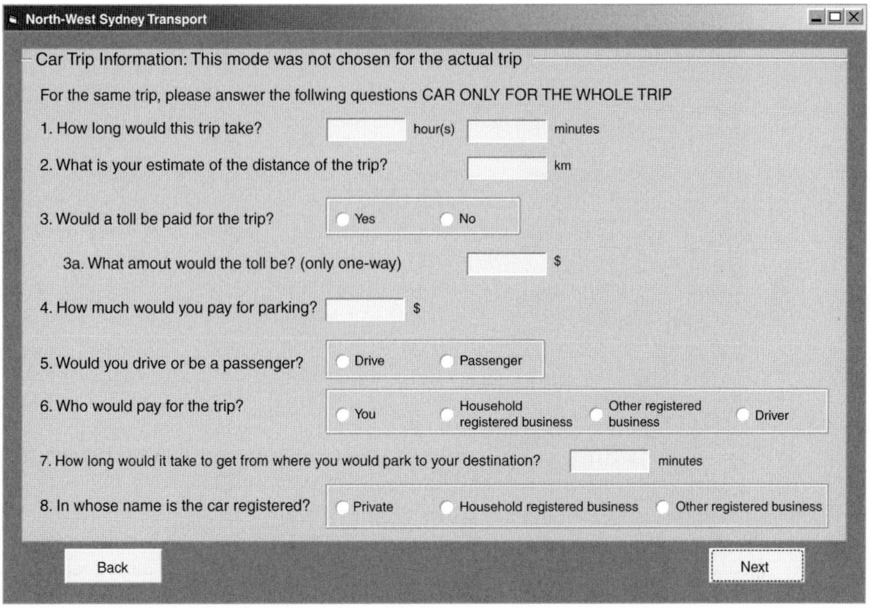

Figure 11A.1 Example screen to establish current car mode trip profile

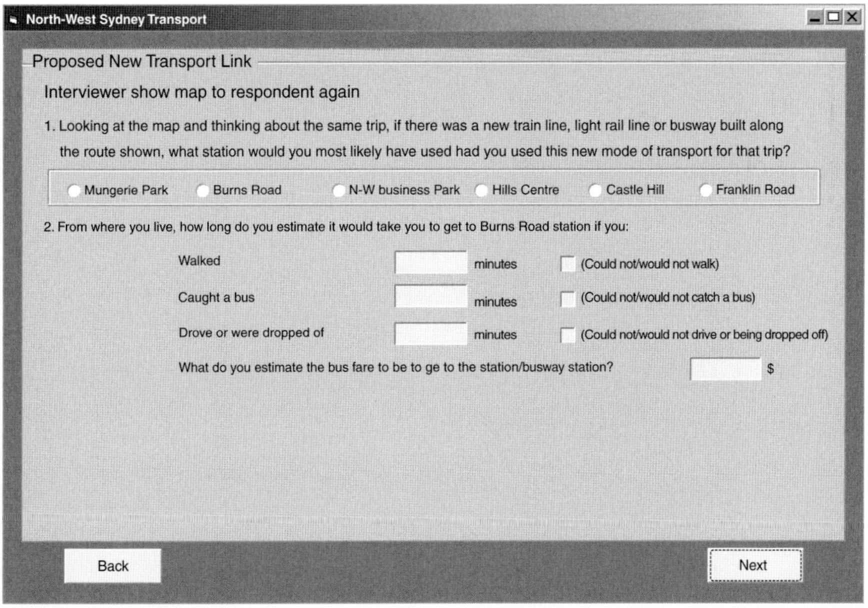

Figure 11A.2 Example screen to establish new public mode station and access profile

North-West Sydney Transport

Practice Game

		Light Rail connecting to Existing Rail Line	New Heavy Rail	Bus	Existing M2 Busway	Existing Train line	Car
Main Mode of Tansport	Fare (one-way) / running cost (for car)	$7.50	$4.50	$6.00	$5.50	$7.50	$5.60
	Toll cost (one-way)	N/A	N/A	N/A	N/A	N/A	$2.20
	Parking cost (one day)	N/A	N/A	N/A	N/A	N/A	$8.00
	In-vehicle travel time	124 mins	113 mins	103 mins	45 mins	45 mins	90 mins
	Service frequency (per hour)	10	3	3	6	3	N/A
	Time spent transfering at a rail station	4 mins	6 mins	N/A	N/A	N/A	N/A
Getting to Main Mode	Walk time OR	4 mins	3 mins	15 mins	60 mins	15 mins	N/A
	Car time OR	1 mins	1 mins	4 mins	13 mins	5 mins	N/A
	Bus time	2 mins	2 mins	N/A	15 mins	8 mins	N/A
	Bus fare	$2.00	$2.00	N/A	$2.25	$3.10	N/A
	Time Getting from Main Mode to Destination	15 mins	8 mins	15 mins	30 mins	8 mins	5 mins

Thinking about each transport mode separately, assuming you had taken that mode for the journey described, how would you get to each mode?

- Walk / Drive / Catch a bus (Light Rail)
- Walk / Drive / Catch a bus (New Heavy Rail)
- Walk / Drive (Bus)
- Walk / Drive / Catch a bus (Existing M2 Busway)
- Walk / Drive / Catch a bus (Existing Train line)

Which main mode would you choose?
- Light Rail
- New Heavy Rail
- Bus
- Existing Busway
- Existing Train
- Car

Back   Next

Figure 11A.3 Example inter-regional stated choice screen

North-West Sydney Transport

Practice Game

		Light Rail connecting to Existing Rail Line	New Heavy Rail	Bus	Car
Main Mode of Tansport	Fare (one-way) / running cost (for car)	$2.20	$3.30	$3.75	$1.35
	Toll cost (one-way)	N/A	N/A	N/A	$4.00
	Parking cost (one day)	N/A	N/A	N/A	$5.00
	In-vehicle travel time	10 mins	14 mins	23 mins	30 mins
	Service frequency (per hour)	13	4	2	N/A
	Time spent transferring at a rail station	8 mins	0 mins	N/A	N/A
Getting to Main Mode	Walk time OR	8 mins	10 mins	1 mins	N/A
	Car time OR	1 mins	1 mins	0 mins	N/A
	Bus time	5 mins	2 mins	N/A	N/A
	Bus fare	$2.00	$3.00	N/A	N/A
	Time Getting from Main Mode to Destination	8 mins	6 mins	2 mins	2 mins

Thinking about each transport mode separately, assuming you had taken that mode for the journey described, how would you get to each mode?

- Walk / Drive / Catch a bus (Light Rail)
- Walk / Drive / Catch a bus (New Heavy Rail)
- Walk / Drive (Bus)

Which main mode would you choose?
- Light Rail
- New Heavy Rail
- Bus
- Car

Back   Next

Figure 11A.4 Example intra-regional stated choice screen

they had available for that trip. While asking respondents to provide information for non-chosen alternatives may potentially provide widely incorrect attribute levels, choices made by individuals are made based on their perceptions of the attribute levels of the available alternatives and not the reality of the attribute levels of those same alternatives. As such, it was felt that asking respondents what they thought the levels were for the non-chosen alternatives was preferable than imposing those levels on the experiment based on some heuristic given knowledge of the attribute levels for the actual chosen alternative. A series of questions was asked to identify the candidate station for the new public transport mode (see Figures 11A.2 and 11A.3). An illustrative choice scenario screen is shown in Figure 11A.4.

12 Handling unlabeled discrete choice data

12.1 Introduction

Before we continue to look at some of the richer sets of behavioral outputs from the basic MNL model, we want to make an important diversion. Discrete choice data may come in one of many forms. Aside from revealed preference (RP) and stated preference (SP) data (see Chapter 6), discrete choice data may be further categorized as being either labeled or unlabeled in nature. In labeled choice data, the names of alternatives have substantive meaning to the respondent beyond their relative order of appearance in a survey (e.g., the alternatives might be labeled Dr House, Dr Cameron, Dr Foreman, Dr Chase). In unlabeled choice data, the names of the alternatives convey only the relative order of their appearance within each survey task, (e.g., drug A, drug B, drug C). Aside from affecting what outputs can appropriately be derived for the study (e.g., elasticities have no substantive meaning in unlabeled experiments), from the perspective of the overall study this decision is important, as it might directly impact upon the type and number of parameters that can or will be estimated as part of the study. As we show below, typically, unlabeled experiments will involve the estimation of generic parameters only, whereas labeled experiments may involve the estimation of alternative-specific and/or generic parameter estimates, hence potentially resulting in more parameter estimates than with an identical, though unlabeled, experiment

12.2 Introducing unlabeled data

In this chapter, we discuss the intricacies of modeling unlabeled discrete choice data. To do so, we make use of a case study involving a route choice unlabeled choice experiment. As part of a larger study investigating route

Table 12.1 Attributes and priors used in the case 1 experimental design

Attribute	Levels	Prior
Free-flow (free road)	8, 12, 16, 20	N(−0.04, 0.015)
Slowed-down time (free road)	6, 9, 12, 15	N(−0.05, 0.015)
Free-flow (toll road)	3.6, 5.2, 7	N(−0.06, 0.02)
Slowed-down time (toll road)	3.6, 5.2, 7	N(−0.08, 0.02)
Number of traffic lights	5,7,9	N(−0.08, 0.02)
Petrol costs	3.3, 3.4, 3.8, 4.2	N(−0.6, 0.2)
Toll costs	1.5, 1.7, 1.9, 2.1	N(−0.4, 0.15)

choice preferences in November 2011, data were collected from 109 respondents who were presented with a choice experiment involving the choice between two unlabeled routes. Unlike previous route choice toll road studies, the 2011 study presented respondents with alternative routes describing the amount of time spent in congested and uncongested traffic conditions broken down into time spent on free roads and time spent on toll roads (i.e., time spent on free public roads that is in free-flow and slowed-down traffic conditions, and time spent on toll roads in free-flow and slowed-down traffic conditions). Respondents were asked to trade-off these four time components with the number of traffic lights along the entire route, and the car running costs (petrol, etc.), and a toll payment. The attribute levels used in designing the choice experiment are given in Table 12.1 and an illustrative choice screen in Figure 12.1.

12.3 The basics of modeling unlabeled choice data

The modeling of unlabeled choice experiments is somewhat unique in terms of how such data should be handled relative to labeled choice data (which includes most RP data, as well as labeled stated choice experiments). The first question often asked is whether to include alternative-specific constants (ASCs) when modeling unlabeled choice data. Despite previous reservations, there exist no theoretical reasons as to why ASCs should not be estimated when dealing with unlabeled choice data, and several behavioral reasons why they should. For example, research has demonstrated the potential for rating scales to exhibit left to right survey response biases (e.g., Lindzey 1954; Payne 1976; Carp 1974; Holmes 1974), and there exists no reason to suspect that such effects do not extend to stated preference type surveys. Should such

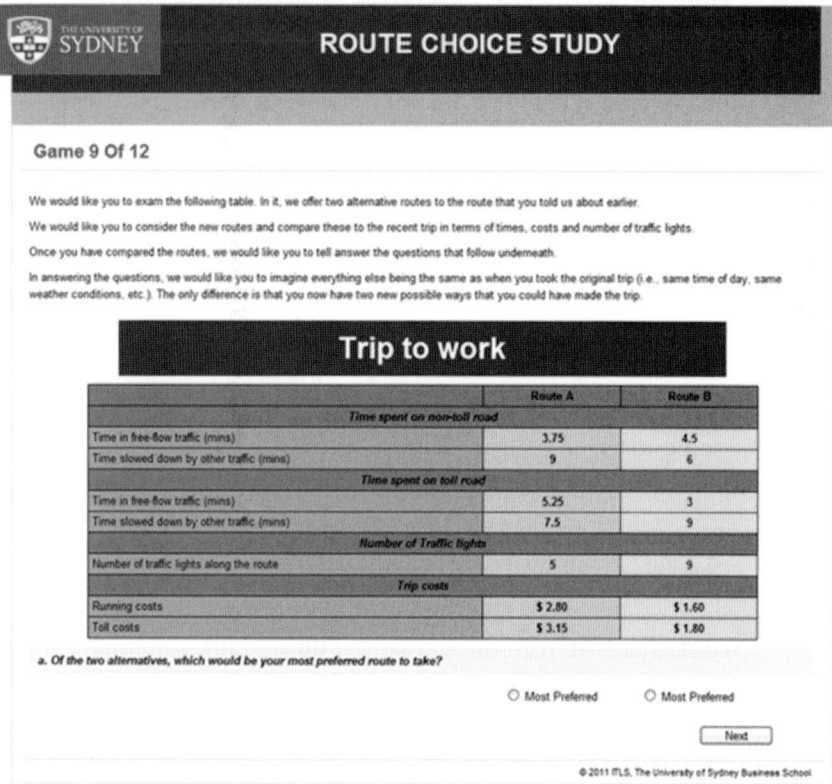

Figure 12.1: Example of unlabeled choice task screen

effects exist, then, *all else being equal,* the choice shares for alternatives presented first in a choice task (typically on the LHS or top of the survey) should be greater than those shown later in the same choice task (typically those presented on the RHS or bottom of the survey), and failure to account for such data patterns will likely bias the remaining parameter estimates (of course, the bias related to positioning is language specific, with English being read top to bottom, left to right). Such effects may be present independent of any possible experimental design biases that may exist, where one alternative may be consistently more attractive than others throughout the design. Independent of the cause, it is recommended that analysts include ASCs in *J*–1 alternatives when dealing with unlabeled choice data, which can be later removed if found to be statistically insignificant.

The second difference between how one should handle the estimation of unlabeled choice data and labeled choice data is in how one should treat the non-constant parameter estimates. Unlike ASCs, which may have some behavioral relevance, the estimation of alternative-specific parameter estimates for unlabeled choice data has no behavioral relevance whatsoever. Despite the possibility that one or more parameters may be found to be statistically different between unlabeled choice alternatives, there exists no behavioral reason why this might be the case. For example, there exists no behavioral reason why the cost parameter for one unlabeled alternative would differ from that of a second unlabeled alternative, as neither alternative should by definition be perceptually different beyond the attribute level combinations shown in the multitude of choice tasks. Further, the presence of such information is unlikely to be useful to the analyst, as each alternative is by definition unbranded, and it would be impossible to determine which estimate to apply to a branded alternative if the model where to be applied post-estimation in some form of predictive exercise. As such, the non-constant estimates for unlabeled choice experiments should always be treated as generic estimates.

To demonstrate the possible influences of estimating (or not) an ASC, consider Models 1 and 2 as reported in Table 12.2 estimated on a route choice unlabeled experiment (the Nlogit syntax for all models reported herein are reported in Appendix 12A). Model 1 is estimated with no ASC while Model 2 has an ASC associated with the first alternative, despite the data being derived from an unlabeled choice experiment (see Figure 12.1). Log-likelihood ratio (LRT) tests suggest that both models provide statistically better model fits than a model with a single ASC ($-2LL = 38.892, \chi^2_6 = 12.592$ for Model 1 and $-2LL = 143.094, \chi^2_7 = 14.061$ for model 2), while an LRT comparing Models 1 and 2 suggest that Model 2 statistically fits the data better than Model 1 ($-2LL = 104.202; \chi^2_1 = 3.841$). Examination of the ASC in Model 2 reveals it to be statistically significant and positive indicating that, *all else being equal*, respondents tended to select the first unlabeled alternative more often than the second (the actual choice shares are 0.692 for the first alternative and 0.308 for the second). An examination of the experimental design reveals, however, that on average the second alternative has slightly better values for three of the attributes, the same values for two of the attributes, and marginally worse values for two of the attributes (see Table 12.3). Further, a visual inspection of the design itself reveals nothing untoward that would induce respondents to have a greater propensity for selecting the first alternative over the second.

Aside from producing a statistically better model fit for the data, the results of Model 2 are more behaviorally plausible. One would expect, *all else being equal*, that the marginal disutility for travelling in congested traffic conditions (represented by slowed-down time) would be greater than the marginal disutility for travel time during uncongested traffic conditions (free-flow

Table 12.2 Model results from unlabeled choice experiment

| | Model 1 | | Model 2 | | Model 3 | | | |
| | | | | | Alternative 1 | | Alternative 2 | |
	Par.	(t-rat.)	Par.	(t-rat.)	Par.	(t-rat.)	Par.	(t-rat.)
Constant (alternative 1)	–	–	0.614	(9.89)	–	–	–	–
Free-flow (free road)	−0.066	(−7.27)	−0.076	(−7.91)	−0.014	(−0.39)	−0.136	(−3.61)
Slowed-down time (free road)	−0.079	(−7.54)	−0.087	(−7.90)	−0.052	(−2.18)	−0.128	(−5.28)
Free-flow (toll road)	−0.069	(−2.24)	−0.067	(−2.07)	−0.190	(−2.62)	0.038	(0.57)
Slowed-down time (toll road)	−0.059	(−1.47)	−0.078	(−1.85)	0.003	(0.05)	−0.130	(−2.19)
Number of traffic lights	−0.042	(−1.69)	−0.038	(−1.48)	0.102	(0.70)	−0.188	(−1.27)
Petrol costs	−0.510	(−5.65)	−0.540	(−5.74)	−0.432	(−1.88)	−0.623	(−2.48)
Toll costs	−0.531	(−2.51)	−0.635	(−2.89)	−1.737	(−1.80)	0.538	(0.56)
Model fit statistics								
LL(β)	−843.020		−790.919		−787.162			
LL(0)	−906.637		−906.637		−906.637			
$\rho^2(0)$	0.070		0.128		0.132			
Adj. $\rho^2(0)$	0.065		0.122		0.122			
LL(ASC only)	−862.466		−862.466		−862.466			
ρ^2(ASC only)	0.023		0.083		0.087			
Adj. ρ^2(ASC only)	0.065		0.122		0.132			
norm. AIC	1.300		1.222		1.225			
norm. BIC	1.327		1.253		1.280			
Sample								
Number of respondents	109		109		109			
Number of observations	1308		1308		1308			

Table 12.3 Descriptive statistics by alternative for unlabeled choice experiment

| | Alternative A | | Alternative B | |
	Mean	Std Dev.	Mean	Std Dev.
Free-flow (free road)	14.15	4.48	13.85	4.46
Slowed-down time (free road)	10.56	3.33	10.44	3.38
Free-flow (toll road)	5.26	1.38	5.28	1.40
Slowed-down time (toll road)	5.29	1.38	5.25	1.40
Number of traffic lights	7.00	1.63	7.00	1.64
Petrol costs	3.58	0.45	3.62	0.45
Toll costs	1.80	0.22	1.80	0.22

time). For Model 1, however, the opposite is true for time spent travelling on a toll road (i.e., −0.069 for free-flow time relative to −0.059 for slowed-down time). This anomaly is corrected in Model 2, where the marginal disutility for slowed-down time is observed to be greater than that of time spent in free-flow conditions (i.e., −0.067 for free-flow time and −0.078 for slowed-down time, respectively).

The inclusion of ASCs in discrete choice models estimated on data collected from unlabeled choice experiments, therefore, has behavioral meaning (such as left to right survey response bias); however, the issue remains as to what to do with any ASCs post-estimation. If one is interested only in calculating effects such as the marginal willingness to pay (WTP) for certain attributes, then the inclusion of the ASCs does not matter, as they are ignored in any such calculation. If, on the other hand, one wishes to use the utility functions for some form of predictive exercise, then the presence of an ASC may be problematic. That is, presuming that unlabeled choice experiments should be used in just such an exercise, which is highly doubtful as most exercises of this nature will be most likely to be between branded alternatives or product classes. Even if the results of an unlabeled choice experiment are used for something akin to prediction, the ASCs could either be simply ignored (as they represent the average of the unobserved effects for the survey task (often repeated over multiple hypothetical questions, with various combinations of attribute levels)). These would be expected to differ to the average of the unobserved effects for a real market (which often represents a single choice which will have a specific attribute level combination that cannot possibly be the same as all the combinations shown in a stated choice experiment, although the levels may overlap), or will be recalibrated so that the base market shares for the model match those of the real observed market. In either case, the ASCs from the modeling exercise are effectively ignored.

As well as estimating ASCs for unlabeled choice experiments, it is also possible to estimate alternative-specific parameter estimates. Model 3 in Table 12.2 allows for alternative-specific parameter estimates (however, we have removed the ASC in this model; as this model is behaviorally meaningless, the removal of the ASC matters not). As can be seen from the model results, the parameters for the free-flow time spent on non-tolled roads and slowed-down time on toll roads are statistically significant at the 95 percent level for the second alternative but not for the first alternative, as is the petrol cost parameter, while the free-flow time for the first alternative is statistically significant at the 95 percent level but not statistically significant for the second alternative. The slowed-down time on free roads parameter is significant at the 95 percent level for both alternatives, although it is almost 2.5 times greater in magnitude for alternative 2 than for alternative 1.

It is worth noting that Model 3 produces a better model fit for the data relative to Model 1 ($-2LL = 111.715$; $\chi^2_7 = 14.067$), although not relative to Model 2 ($-2LL = 7.513$; $\chi^2_6 = 12.592$). As such, if the choice was solely between Model 1 and Model 3 on the grounds of model fit alone, Model 3 would be the preferred model. Nevertheless, as discussed previously, Model 3 is behaviorally meaningless and impossible to use in practice. For example, assuming one were to use Model 3 to work out the relative utilities for travelling along two well known roads, Elm Street and Wall Street, the analyst would need to first figure out which estimates belong to which street (i.e., is Elm Street represented by the estimates for Alternative A or B?), before working out the attribute levels to apply. Note that this is not like the issue of ASCs, where one can simply ignore them. In working out the relative utilities for two routes, one has to assign a specific marginal (dis)utility for the travel time and cost components of the trip.

12.4 Moving beyond design attributes when using unlabeled choice data

The models reported in Section 12.3 allowed only the attributes of the design to enter into the various **indirect utility functions**. In this section, we extend the discussion to explore how additional covariate information, such as socio-demographic variables, may be used to enhance the performance of models estimated on unlabeled choice data. There currently exist two main ways that covariates may enter into the indirect utility functions of discrete choice models, irrespective of whether the data is labeled or unlabeled in nature. Discrete choice models require variables to differ across alternatives in order to be able to estimate the model parameters (overlap between values is possible in some choice observations, however, so long as each variable displays some degree of variation between the alternatives over the entire data set). If a variable remains constant across all alternatives, then it becomes impossible to isolate the specific influence that variable had in terms of the utility derived from any one alternative. As such, variables such as socio-demographics, which remain constant across all alternatives (a respondent hopefully does not change gender because they are considering alternative A instead of Alternative B), cannot directly enter into the indirect utility functions of all J alternatives of the model (as the respondent presumably remains female when considering both alternatives, it is impossible to determine whether their gender played any role in their observed choices; this differs from an attribute such as price, which will likely differ across alternatives where if a respondent (whether male or female) is observed to select the lowest price alternative in the majority of cases, then price is likely to have influenced their choice). The first way to introduce covariates into discrete choice models is therefore to enter them into up to $J-1$ indirect utility functions. In this way, the covariate is treated in effect as being zero for the indirect utility function(s) that it is left out of, which artificially creates differences for the variable between the alternatives. This then allows for estimation of the effect for the indirect utility functions that it enters into. In such an instance, the parameter is interpreted as representing the marginal utility that that covariate produces for the up to $J-1$ indirect utility functions that it is associated with, relative to the ones that it does not belong to.

When dealing with unlabeled choice experiments, it is often assumed that one should enter covariates into the indirect utility functions of the model only as interaction terms with the design attributes, or as some other transformation involving the design attributes rather than directly as main effects. The reasoning behind such thinking is that the inclusion of covariates in up to $J-1$ indirect utility functions is behaviorally meaningless when dealing with unlabeled choice data, and that the model results cannot be applied meaningfully at a later stage. Thus, the second way covariates may enter into the indirect utility functions of discrete choice models is via interaction terms, or some other transformation involving the variable and one or more other variables that vary across the alternatives in the data. An interaction term represents the multiplication of two or more variables, although one could also include effects for the summation (or some other transformation, including division) of two or more variables, provided at least one of them varies within the data. By relating a variable that is constant within each choice observation with one or more variables that vary, the resulting new variable will also vary across the alternatives. As the new variable is no longer constant across the alternatives, it may enter into the indirect utility functions of all J alternatives, although the analyst may also enter it into less than J alternatives if so desired (although this should be avoided when dealing with unlabeled choice experiments). When allocated to all J indirect utility functions, interaction terms can be used not only for behavioral interpretation, but also for other calculations such as marginal WTP, as well as for predictive exercises, much like main effects. The more accepted approach to including covariates into the indirect utility functions of models estimated on unlabeled choice data is, therefore, via interaction terms with one or more of the design attributes.

Table 12.4 Model results from unlabeled choice experiment with socio-demographic characteristics

	Model 4		Model 5	
	Par.	*(t-rat.)*	*Par.*	*(t-rat.)*
Constant (alternative 1)	0.166	(0.73)	0.623	(9.97)
Free-flow (free road)	−0.076	(−7.93)	−0.096	(−7.42)
Slowed-down time (free road)	−0.087	(−7.91)	−0.107	(−7.66)
Free-flow (toll road)	−0.065	(−2.01)	−0.136	(−3.11)
Slowed-down time (toll road)	−0.082	(−1.96)	−0.148	(−2.89)
Number of traffic lights	−0.037	(−1.45)	−0.038	(−1.49)
Petrol costs	−0.545	(−5.78)	−0.546	(−5.78)
Toll costs	−0.649	(−2.95)	−0.644	(−2.92)
Age (alternative 1)	0.009	(2.02)	–	–
Income × free road travel time	–	–	−0.066	(−7.27)
Income × toll road travel time	–	–	0.001	(2.36)
Model fit statistics				
LL(β)	−788.867		−785.867	
LL(0)	−906.637		−906.637	
$\rho^2(0)$	0.130		0.133	
Adj. $\rho^2(0)$	0.124		0.127	
LL(ASC only)	−862.466		−862.466	
ρ^2 (ASC only)	0.085		0.089	
Adj. ρ^2(ASC only)	0.124		0.127	
norm. AIC	1.220		1.217	
norm. BIC	1.256		1.256	
Sample				
Number of respondents	109		109	
Number of observations	1308		1308	

Using the same data as before, Models 4 and 5 reported in Table 12.4 allow for socio-demographic variables to enter into the indirect utility functions in the two ways just mentioned. In Model 4, age enters into the indirect utility function of the first alternative only as a main effect. Model 4 represents an extension of Model 2 by allowing age to enter into the indirect utility function of the first alternative only, in direct contravention to conventional thinking. As can be seen, the parameter for age is statistically significant at the 95 percent level, and the model provides a statistically significant improvement in terms of model fit relative to Model 2 ($-2LL = 4.104$; $\chi_7^2 = 3.841$). Far from having no behavioral interpretation, the positive age parameter suggests that older respondents are more likely to select the first alternative relative to the second, *all else being equal*, and hence be more subject to left to right response bias when answering the survey tasks. The fact that the ASC is now found to be statistically insignificant at the 95 percent level suggests that what previously appeared to be differences in the average of the unobserved effects for the two unlabeled hypothetical alternatives is largely explained by the age of the respondents.

The concern that one cannot use such a model at a later stage is also erroneous. As with ASCs, any covariates estimated as main effects in choice models dealing with unlabeled choice data may be simply ignored. That is, if the objective of the study is to obtain marginal WTP values for the different design attributes, then any covariates will be irrelevant in any case. If, on the other hand, one wishes to take the estimated indirect utility functions and use them in some form of predictive exercise then, similar to the ASCs, any estimated covariates should simply be ignored. This is because such covariates will likely be acting as explanatory variables describing potential biases in the preference patterns of the alternatives observed in unlabeled choice data which, if accounted for, should lead to less bias in the parameters for the remaining design attribute estimates.

In Model 5, we interact the respondents' reported income level with the total time spent on free roads, and the total time spent on toll routes. Both interaction terms are entered into the model and both are statistically significant at the 95 percent level of confidence. The interaction term between income and total time spent on free roads is negative, suggesting that, holding time constant, respondents with higher income levels have a greater disutility for spending time on free roads than lower income earners. The interaction term for income and time spent on toll roads, however, is positive, suggesting that higher income earners are less sensitive than lower income earners to spending time on toll roads, *all else being equal*. While the inclusion of such interactions is widely accepted within the literature dealing with unlabeled choice experiments they can, and often do, produce counterintuitive results. For example, consider a trip made by a person earning $90,000 per year involving 20 minutes spent in free-flow conditions and 15 minutes in congested conditions on a toll road. Based on the above results, the model would predict the total utility associated with time spent on the toll road to be positive (i.e., $-0.136 \times 20 + -0.148 \times 15 + 0.001 \times (20 + 15) \times 90$; noting that income is entered into the data in 000s of units). In this way, the model would predict that such a person prefers to travel more (has a higher marginal utility) for travelling on toll roads!

Of course, one is not limited to estimating interaction effects (or other similar data transformations) between the design attributes and covariates. It is also possible to include interaction terms between one or more of the design

Table 12.5 Model results from unlabeled choice experiment with interaction terms

	Model 6		Model 7	
	Par.	(t-rat.)	Par.	(t-rat.)
Constant	0.612	(9.86)	0.621	(9.94)
Free-flow (free road)	−0.071	(−7.24)	−0.092	(−6.96)
Slowed-down time (free road)	−0.273	(−2.54)	−0.293	(−2.70)
Free-flow (toll road)	−0.174	(−2.50)	−0.243	(−3.20)
Slowed-down time (toll road)	−0.145	(−2.54)	−0.215	(−3.34)
Number of traffic lights	−0.279	(−1.98)	−0.279	(−1.97)
Petrol costs	−0.644	(−5.74)	−0.649	(−5.77)
Toll costs	−0.570	(−2.56)	−0.578	(−2.58)
Free-road travel time × toll road travel time × Number of traffic lights	0.001	(1.74)	0.001	(1.73)
Income × free road travel time	–	–	0.0003	(2.37)
Income × toll road travel time	–	–	0.001	(2.35)
Model fit statistics				
LL(β)	−789.404		−784.369	
LL(0)	−906.637		−906.637	
$\rho^2(0)$	0.129		0.135	
Adj. $\rho^2(0)$	0.123		0.128	
LL(ASC only)	−862.466		−862.466	
ρ^2(ASC only)	0.085		0.091	
Adj. ρ^2(ASC only)	0.123		0.128	
norm. AIC	1.221		1.216	
norm. BIC	1.256		1.260	
Sample				
Number of respondents	109		109	
Number of observations	1308		1308	

attributes (Model 6), or combinations of various types of interaction terms (Model 7) within a single model. In Model 6, a three-way interaction term between the total time spent on free roads, the total time spent on toll roads, and the number of traffic lights, is included in the model. The resulting interaction term is not statistically significant at the 95 percent level of confidence (although it is at the 90 percent level). Ignoring the statistical significance of the interaction term, this model would suggest that, holding travel time constant, respondents prefer more traffic lights to fewer or, inversely, holding the number of traffic lights constant, respondents prefer longer travel times (fortunately, as stated above, the parameter is statistically insignificant, however, and in any case the model is inferior to Model 5 based on the LRT test $((-2LL = 6.000; \chi_1^2 = 3.841))$. Model 7 includes both types of interaction terms in a single model. In this model, the three-way interaction term between the total time spent on free roads, the total time spent on toll roads, and the number of traffic lights, remains statistically insignificant at the 95 percent level of confidence; however, the interaction term between income and total time spent on free roads switches sign and becomes positive. This finding hints at the possible existence of an interaction between income, total time spent on free roads, and the number of traffic lights, given that time spent on free roads is common across the two estimated interaction terms (such a model is reported in Appendix 12A as Model 7A, where this interaction is found to be statistically significant).

Appendix 12A: Unlabeled discrete choice data Nlogit syntax and output

```
RESET
IMPORT;FILE="N:\ITLS\Fittler\Johnr\Studies\DCM2\Data\Route.csv"$
Last observation read from data file was    2616
dstats;rhs=*$
Descriptive Statistics for 31 variables
```

Variable	Mean	Std.Dev.	Minimum	Maximum	Cases	Missing
ID	55.0	31.47028	1.0	109.0	2616	0
SET	6.500000	3.452713	1.0	12.0	2616	0
CSET	2.0	0.0	2.0	2.0	2616	0
ALTIJ	1.500000	.500096	1.0	2.0	2616	0
CHOICE	.500000	.500096	0.0	1.0	2616	0
FFNT	14.0	4.472991	8.0	20.0	2616	0
SDTNT	10.50000	3.354743	6.0	15.0	2616	0
FFT	5.266667	1.389110	3.600000	7.0	2616	0
SDTT	5.266667	1.389110	3.600000	7.0	2616	0
LGHTS	7.0	1.633305	5.0	9.0	2616	0
PC	3.600000	.447299	3.0	4.200000	2616	0
TC	1.800000	.223650	1.500000	2.100000	2616	0
GEN	.192661	.981453	-1.000000	1.0	2616	0
AGE	48.73394	13.36184	24.0	70.0	2616	0
INC	58.99083	42.11309	10.0	200.0	2616	0
LGHT5E	0.0	.816653	-1.000000	1.0	2616	0
LGHT7E	0.0	.816653	-1.000000	1.0	2616	0
LGHT5D	.333333	.471495	0.0	1.0	2616	0
LGHT7D	.333333	.471495	0.0	1.0	2616	0
FFNT20E	0.0	.707242	-1.000000	1.0	2616	0
FFNT16E	0.0	.707242	-1.000000	1.0	2616	0

```
FFNT12E|        0.0      .707242    -1.000000        1.0    2616    0
FFNT20D|     .250000     .433095         0.0         1.0    2616    0
FFNT16D|     .250000     .433095         0.0         1.0    2616    0
FFNT12D|     .250000     .433095         0.0         1.0    2616    0
--------+------------------------------------------------------------------
```

Model 0: ASC only model (MNL)
```
nlogit
;lhs=choice,cset,Altij
;choices=A,B
;model:
U(A) = SP1   $
Normal exit:   1 iterations. Status=0, F=     862.4658
```

```
Discrete choice (multinomial logit) model
Dependent variable                Choice
Log likelihood function      -862.46576
Estimation based on N =    1308, K =   1
Inf.Cr.AIC  =    1726.9 AIC/N =     1.320
Model estimated: Jul 22, 2013, 16:40:56
R2=1-LogL/LogL* Log-L fncn R-sqrd R2Adj
Constants only must be computed directly
              Use NLOGIT ;...;RHS=ONE$
Response data are given as ind. choices
Number of obs.= 1308, skipped     0 obs
-----------+----------------------------------------------------------
```
CHOICE	Coefficient	Standard Error	z	Prob. |z|>Z*	95% Confidence Interval	
SP1	.52881***	.05724	9.24	.0000	.41661	.64100

```
-----------+----------------------------------------------------------
Note: ***, **, * ==>  Significance at 1%, 5%, 10% level.
```

Model 1: No ASCs model (MNL)
```
nlogit
;lhs=choice,cset,Altij
;choices=A,B
;model:
U(A) = FFNT*FFNT + SDTNT*SDTNT + FFT*FFT + SDTT*SDTT + LGHTS*LGHTS +
PC*PC + TC*TC /
U(B) = FFNT*FFNT + SDTNT*SDTNT + FFT*FFT + SDTT*SDTT + LGHTS*LGHTS +
PC*PC + TC*TC $
Normal exit:   5 iterations. Status=0, F=     843.0197
```

```
Discrete choice (multinomial logit) model
Dependent variable                Choice
Log likelihood function      -843.01971
Estimation based on N =    1308, K =   7
Inf.Cr.AIC  =    1700.0 AIC/N =     1.300
Model estimated: Jul 22, 2013, 16:41:08
```

R2=1-LogL/LogL* Log-L fncn R-sqrd R2Adj
Constants only must be computed directly
                Use NLOGIT ;...;RHS=ONE$
Response data are given as ind. choices
Number of obs.= 1308, skipped   0 obs

```
-----------+---------------------------------------------------------------------
           |                 Standard              Prob.        95% Confidence
    CHOICE | Coefficient     Error        z       |z|>Z*          Interval
-----------+---------------------------------------------------------------------
      FFNT |  -.06635***     .00913     -7.27     .0000       -.08424    -.04845
     SDTNT |  -.07891***     .01046     -7.54     .0000       -.09942    -.05840
       FFT |  -.06902**      .03080     -2.24     .0250       -.12939    -.00866
      SDTT |  -.05925        .04022     -1.47     .1407       -.13807     .01957
     LGHTS |  -.04155*       .02455     -1.69     .0906       -.08968     .00657
        PC |  -.50961***     .09016     -5.65     .0000       -.68632    -.33289
        TC |  -.53125**      .21181     -2.51     .0121       -.94639    -.11611
-----------+---------------------------------------------------------------------
```

Note: ***, **, * ==> Significance at 1%, 5%, 10% level.

Model 2: Model with ASCs (MNL)
nlogit
;lhs=choice,cset,Altij
;choices=A,B
;model:
U(A) = SP1 + FFNT*FFNT + SDTNT*SDTNT + FFT*FFT + SDTT*SDTT + LGHTS*LGHTS +
PC*PC + TC*TC /
U(B) =   FFNT*FFNT + SDTNT*SDTNT + FFT*FFT + SDTT*SDTT + LGHTS*LGHTS +
PC*PC + TC*TC $
Normal exit: 5 iterations. Status=0, F=   790.9189

Discrete choice (multinomial logit) model
Dependent variable   Choice
Log likelihood function   -790.91889
Estimation based on N =   1308, K =   8
Inf.Cr.AIC =   1597.8 AIC/N =   1.222
Model estimated: Jul 22, 2013, 16:53:20
R2=1-LogL/LogL* Log-L fncn R-sqrd R2Adj
Constants only must be computed directly
                Use NLOGIT ;...;RHS=ONE$
Chi-squared[7]   =   143.09375
Prob [chi squared > value] =   .00000
Response data are given as ind. choices
Number of obs.= 1308, skipped   0 obs

```
-----------+---------------------------------------------------------------------
           |                 Standard              Prob.        95% Confidence
    CHOICE | Coefficient     Error        z       |z|>Z*          Interval
-----------+---------------------------------------------------------------------
       SP1 |   .61373***     .06205      9.89     .0000        .49211     .73535
      FFNT |  -.07570***     .00957     -7.91     .0000       -.09446    -.05695
```

SDTNT|	-.08702***	.01102	-7.90	.0000	-.10862	-.06542
FFT|	-.06657**	.03219	-2.07	.0386	-.12965	-.00348
SDTT|	-.07768*	.04191	-1.85	.0638	-.15981	.00446
LGHTS|	-.03774	.02555	-1.48	.1397	-.08782	.01234
PC|	-.54011***	.09408	-5.74	.0000	-.72450	-.35573
TC|	-.63533***	.21946	-2.89	.0038	-1.06546	-.20519

Note: ***, **, * ==> Significance at 1%, 5%, 10% level.

Model 3: Model with ASCs and alternative specific parameter estimates (MNL)
```
nlogit
;lhs=choice,cset,Altij
;choices=A,B
;model:
U(A) = FFNT1*FFNT + SDTNT1*SDTNT + FFT1*FFT + SDTT1*SDTT + LGHTS1*LGHTS +
PC1*PC + TC1*TC /
U(B) = FFNT2*FFNT + SDTNT2*SDTNT + FFT2*FFT + SDTT2*SDTT + LGHTS2*LGHTS +
PC2*PC + TC2*TC $
```
Normal exit: 6 iterations. Status=0, F=   787.1623

```
Discrete choice (multinomial logit) model
Dependent variable                Choice
Log likelihood function       -787.16235
Estimation based on N =   1308, K =  14
Inf.Cr.AIC  =   1602.3 AIC/N =    1.225
Model estimated: Jul 22, 2013, 16:41:09
R2=1-LogL/LogL* Log-L fncn R-sqrd R2Adj
Constants only must be computed directly
            Use NLOGIT ;...;RHS=ONE$
Response data are given as ind. choices
Number of obs.= 1308, skipped   0 obs
```

CHOICE|	Coefficient	Standard Error	z	Prob. |z|>Z*	95% Confidence Interval	
FFNT1|	-.01434	.03705	-.39	.6987	-.08695	.05827
SDTNT1|	-.05159**	.02369	-2.18	.0294	-.09802	-.00517
FFT1|	-.19045***	.07280	-2.62	.0089	-.33314	-.04776
SDTT1|	.00306	.06659	.05	.9634	-.12746	.13358
LGHTS1|	.10187	.14639	.70	.4865	-.18506	.38879
PC1|	-.43176*	.22998	-1.88	.0605	-.88250	.01899
TC1|	-1.73703*	.96762	-1.80	.0726	-3.63354	.15948
FFNT2|	-.13612***	.03775	-3.61	.0003	-.21011	-.06214
SDTNT2|	-.12767***	.02418	-5.28	.0000	-.17506	-.08027
FFT2|	.03843	.06780	.57	.5709	-.09446	.17132
SDTT2|	-.12972**	.05911	-2.19	.0282	-.24558	-.01387
LGHTS2|	-.18825	.14848	-1.27	.2049	-.47925	.10276
PC2|	-.62250**	.25125	-2.48	.0132	-1.11493	-.13007
TC2|	.53755	.95324	.56	.5728	-1.33076	2.40586

```
------------+------------------------------------------------------------------
```
Note: ***, **, * ==> Significance at 1%, 5%, 10% level.
```
------------------------------------------------------------------------------
```
Model 4: Model with age (MNL)
nlogit
;lhs=choice,cset,Altij
;choices=A,B
;model:
U(A) = SP1 + FFNT*FFNT + SDTNT*SDTNT + FFT*FFT + SDTT*SDTT + LGHTS*LGHTS +
PC*PC + TC*TC + AGE*AGE /
U(B) =   FFNT*FFNT + SDTNT*SDTNT + FFT*FFT + SDTT*SDTT + LGHTS*LGHTS +
PC*PC + TC*TC $
Normal exit: 5 iterations. Status=0, F=   788.8667
```
------------------------------------------------------------------------------
```
Discrete choice (multinomial logit) model
Dependent variable   Choice
Log likelihood function   -788.86673
Estimation based on N =   1308, K =   9
Inf.Cr.AIC =   1595.7 AIC/N =   1.220
Model estimated: Jul 22, 2013, 16:41:09
R2=1-LogL/LogL* Log-L fncn R-sqrd R2Adj
Constants only must be computed directly
            Use NLOGIT ;...;RHS=ONE$
Chi-squared[8]   =   147.19806
Prob [chi squared > value] =   .00000
Response data are given as ind. choices
Number of obs.= 1308, skipped   0 obs
```
----------+-------------------------------------------------------------------
```

CHOICE	Coefficient	Standard Error	z	Prob. |z|>Z*	95% Confidence Interval	
SP1	.16611	.22903	.73	.4683	-.28278	.61500
FFNT	-.07604***	.00959	-7.93	.0000	-.09483	-.05725
SDTNT	-.08732***	.01104	-7.91	.0000	-.10896	-.06567
FFT	-.06489**	.03224	-2.01	.0441	-.12807	-.00170
SDTT	-.08234*	.04206	-1.96	.0503	-.16478	.00009
LGHTS	-.03715	.02560	-1.45	.1466	-.08732	.01302
PC	-.54493***	.09427	-5.78	.0000	-.72970	-.36015
TC	-.64909***	.22016	-2.95	.0032	-1.08060	-.21758
AGE	.00923**	.00457	2.02	.0432	.00028	.01818

```
----------+-------------------------------------------------------------------
```
Note: ***, **, * ==> Significance at 1%, 5%, 10% level.
```
------------------------------------------------------------------------------
```
Model 5: Model with income and travel time interaction effects (MNL)
CREATE;TFRINC=(FFNT+SDTNT)*INC$
CREATE;TTRINC=(FFT+SDTT)*INC$
nlogit
;lhs=choice,cset,Altij
;choices=A,B

```
;model:
U(A) = SP1 + FFNT*FFNT + SDTNT*SDTNT + FFT*FFT + SDTT*SDTT + LGHTS*LGHTS +
PC*PC + TC*TC + TFRINC*TFRINC + TTRINC*TTRINC /
U(B) =       FFNT*FFNT + SDTNT*SDTNT + FFT*FFT + SDTT*SDTT + LGHTS*LGHTS +
PC*PC + TC*TC + TFRINC*TFRINC + TTRINC*TTRINC $
Normal exit:   5 iterations. Status=0, F=    785.8665
```

```
Discrete choice (multinomial logit) model
Dependent variable                Choice
Log likelihood function      -785.86650
Estimation based on N =   1308, K =  10
Inf.Cr.AIC  =   1591.7 AIC/N =    1.217
Model estimated: Jul 22, 2013, 16:55:23
R2=1-LogL/LogL* Log-L fncn R-sqrd R2Adj
Constants only must be computed directly
            Use NLOGIT ;...;RHS=ONE$
Chi-squared[ 9]          =    153.19852
Prob [ chi squared > value ] =    .00000
Response data are given as ind. choices
Number of obs.= 1308, skipped    0 obs
```
-----------+--

CHOICE	Coefficient	Standard Error	z	Prob. |z|>Z*	95% Confidence Interval	
SP1	.62278***	.06246	9.97	.0000	.50037	.74520
FFNT	-.09609***	.01296	-7.42	.0000	-.12148	-.07070
SDTNT	-.10713***	.01398	-7.66	.0000	-.13453	-.07974
FFT	-.13630***	.04384	-3.11	.0019	-.22223	-.05038
SDTT	-.14823***	.05134	-2.89	.0039	-.24886	-.04760
LGHTS	-.03828	.02571	-1.49	.1366	-.08868	.01212
PC	-.54577***	.09447	-5.78	.0000	-.73092	-.36062
TC	-.64372***	.22030	-2.92	.0035	-1.07551	-.21194
TFRINC	.00033**	.00014	2.38	.0173	.00006	.00061
TTRINC	.00117**	.00050	2.36	.0183	.00020	.00215

-----------+--
```
Note: ***, **, * ==> Significance at 1%, 5%, 10% level.
```

Model 6: Model with travel time interaction and traffic lights (MNL)
```
Create;INT*INT= (SDTT+SDTT)*(SDTNT+FFT)*LGHTS$
Nlogit
;lhs=choice,cset,Altij
;choices=A,B
;model:
U(A) = SP1 + FFNT*FFNT + SDTNT*SDTNT + FFT*FFT + SDTT*SDTT + LGHTS*LGHTS +
PC*PC + TC*TC + INT*INT /
U(B) =       FFNT*FFNT + SDTNT*SDTNT + FFT*FFT + SDTT*SDTT + LGHTS*LGHTS +
PC*PC + TC*TC + INT*INT $
Normal exit:   5 iterations. Status=0, F=    789.4044
```

```
Discrete choice (multinomial logit) model
Dependent variable                Choice
Log likelihood function     -789.40436
Estimation based on N =    1308, K =   9
Inf.Cr.AIC  =    1596.8 AIC/N =    1.221
Model estimated: Jul 23, 2013, 10:56:41
R2=1-LogL/LogL* Log-L fncn R-sqrd R2Adj
Constants only must be computed directly
            Use NLOGIT ;...;RHS=ONE$
Chi-squared[ 8]          =     146.12280
Prob [ chi squared > value ] =    .00000
Response data are given as ind. choices
Number of obs.= 1308, skipped     0 obs
```

CHOICE	Coefficient	Standard Error	z	Prob. |z|>Z*	95% Confidence Interval	
SP1	.61213***	.06211	9.86	.0000	.49039	.73386
FFNT	-.07133***	.00985	-7.24	.0000	-.09063	-.05203
SDTNT	-.27262**	.10752	-2.54	.0112	-.48335	-.06188
FFT	-.17361**	.06957	-2.50	.0126	-.30996	-.03725
SDTT	-.14517**	.05717	-2.54	.0111	-.25722	-.03312
LGHTS	-.27900**	.14123	-1.98	.0482	-.55581	-.00218
PC	-.64429***	.11222	-5.74	.0000	-.86425	-.42434
TC	-.57026**	.22286	-2.56	.0105	-1.00706	-.13345
INT	.00080*	.00046	1.74	.0824	-.00010	.00170

```
Note: ***, **, * ==>  Significance at 1%, 5%, 10% level.
```

Model 7: Model with travel time and traffic lights interaction (MNL)
```
Nlogit
;lhs=choice,cset,Altij
;choices=A,B
   ;model:
U(A) = SP1 + FFNT*FFNT + SDTNT*SDTNT + FFT*FFT + SDTT*SDTT + LGHTS*LGHTS +
PC*PC + TC*TC + INT*INT + TFRINC*TFRINC + TTRINC*TTRINC /
U(B) =       FFNT*FFNT + SDTNT*SDTNT + FFT*FFT + SDTT*SDTT + LGHTS*LGHTS +
PC*PC + TC*TC + INT*INT + TFRINC*TFRINC + TTRINC*TTRINC $
Normal exit:   5 iterations. Status=0, F=    784.3687
```
```
Discrete choice (multinomial logit) model
Dependent variable                Choice
Log likelihood function     -784.36867
Estimation based on N =    1308, K =  11
Inf.Cr.AIC  =    1590.7 AIC/N =    1.216
Model estimated: Jul 23, 2013, 10:41:14
R2=1-LogL/LogL* Log-L fncn R-sqrd R2Adj
Constants only must be computed directly
            Use NLOGIT ;...;RHS=ONE$
```

```
Chi-squared[10]              =      156.19418
Prob [ chi squared > value ] =     .00000
Response data are given as ind. choices
Number of obs.=  1308, skipped      0 obs
-----------+------------------------------------------------------------------------
           |                   Standard              Prob.          95% Confidence
   CHOICE|  Coefficient        Error        z      |z|>Z*             Interval
-----------+------------------------------------------------------------------------
      SP1|    .62133***         .06253      9.94    .0000          .49878      .74388
     FFNT|   -.09164***         .01316     -6.96    .0000         -.11743     -.06584
    SDTNT|   -.29250***         .10834     -2.70    .0069         -.50483     -.08016
      FFT|   -.24314***         .07597     -3.20    .0014         -.39204     -.09423
     SDTT|   -.21521***         .06443     -3.34    .0008         -.34150     -.08893
    LGHTS|   -.27948**          .14199     -1.97    .0490         -.55778     -.00119
       PC|   -.64940***         .11256     -5.77    .0000         -.87001     -.42878
       TC|   -.57785***         .22378     -2.58    .0098        -1.01646     -.13925
      INT|    .00080*           .00046      1.73    .0841         -.00011      .00171
   TFRINC|    .00033**          .00014      2.37    .0177          .00006      .00061
   TTRINC|    .00117**          .00050      2.35    .0187          .00019      .00214
-----------+------------------------------------------------------------------------
```
Note: ***, **, * ==> Significance at 1%, 5%, 10% level.

Model 7A: Model with income, travel time and traffic lights (MNL)
nlogit
;lhs=choice,cset,Altij
;choices=A,B
;model:
U(A) = SP1 + FFNT*FFNT + SDTNT*SDTNT + FFT*FFT + SDTT*SDTT + LGHTS*LGHTS +
PC*PC + TC*TC + TFRINC*TFRINC + TFRINCL*TFRINCL + TTRINC*TTRINC /
U(B) =   FFNT*FFNT + SDTNT*SDTNT + FFT*FFT + SDTT*SDTT + LGHTS*LGHTS +
PC*PC + TC*TC + TFRINC*TFRINC + TFRINCL*TFRINCL + TTRINC*TTRINC $
Normal exit: 5 iterations. Status=0, F=   784.7284

```
Discrete choice (multinomial logit) model
Dependent variable                 Choice
Log likelihood function       -784.72837
Estimation based on N =   1308, K =   11
Inf.Cr.AIC   =   1591.5 AIC/N =    1.217
Model estimated: Jul 23, 2013, 11:15:55
R2=1-LogL/LogL* Log-L fncn R-sqrd R2Adj
Constants only must be computed directly
            Use NLOGIT ;...;RHS=ONE$
Chi-squared[10]              =      155.47478
Prob [ chi squared > value ] =     .00000
Response data are given as ind. choices
Number of obs.=  1308, skipped      0 obs
```

CHOICE	Coefficient	Standard Error	z	Prob. |z|>Z*	95% Confidence Interval	
SP1	.61946***	.06254	9.91	.0000	.49689	.74202
FFNT	-.09649***	.01302	-7.41	.0000	-.12201	-.07096
SDTNT	-.10790***	.01399	-7.71	.0000	-.13531	-.08048
FFT	-.14047***	.04400	-3.19	.0014	-.22670	-.05423
SDTT	-.15297***	.05153	-2.97	.0030	-.25398	-.05197
LGHTS	-.07981**	.03784	-2.11	.0350	-.15398	-.00563
PC	-.54678***	.09442	-5.79	.0000	-.73185	-.36172
TC	-.64716***	.22059	-2.93	.0033	-1.07951	-.21481
TFRINC	.00014	.00019	.74	.4564	-.00023	.00052
TFRINCL	.27610D-04	.1835D-04	1.50	.1325	-.83593D-05	.63580D-04
TTRINC	.00125**	.00050	2.50	.0125	.00027	.00224

Note: nnnnn.D-xx or D+xx => multiply by 10 to -xx or +xx.
Note: ***, **, * ==> Significance at 1%, 5%, 10% level.

13 Getting more from your model

Where facts are few, experts are many.

(Donald R. Gannon)

13.1 Introduction

In Chapter 11 we presented the standard output generated by Nlogit for the multinomial logit (MNL) choice model. By the addition of supplementary commands to the basic command syntax, the analyst is able to generate further output to aid in an understanding of choice. We present some of these additional commands now. As before, we demonstrate how the command syntax should appear and detail line by line how to interpret the output. The revealed preference (RP) data in the North West travel choice data set is used to illustrate the set of commands and outputs.

The entire command set up and model output is given up front to make it easy for the reader to see at a glance the commands that are used in this chapter. The command set up has two choice models; the first is the MNL model estimated to obtain the standard set of parameter estimates as well as useful additional outputs such as elasticities, partial (or marginal effects) and prediction success; the second MNL model uses the parameter estimates from the first model to undertake "what if" analysis using **;simulation** and **;scenario**, that involves selecting the relevant alternatives and attributes you want to change to predict the absolute and relative change in the choice shares. Arc elasticities can be inferred from the scenario analysis, since it provides before and after choice shares associated with before and after attribute levels.

> *As an aside*, note that some rows begin with a question mark (**?**) or a question mark is inserted after a command. The question mark informs Nlogit to ignore everything that follows to the right within that line of the command. In this way, the analyst may use the

> question mark to make comments to the right of **?** that may aid in understanding what it is that the command is supposed to do, or allow the analyst to return to a previous command without having to retype it, simply by deleting the question mark.

Reading in the data using the export command

```
Reset
IMPORT;FILE="C:\Books\DCMPrimer\Second Edition 2010\Latest Version\Data
and nlogit set ups\SPRPLabelled\NW_SPRP.csv"$
```

Transforming variables

```
Create;if(altij<4)invt2=wt+invt$
```

Saving the data including transformation as an .lpj file for future use

```
Save;FILE="C:\Books\DCMPrimer\Second Edition 2010\Latest Version\Data
and nlogit set ups\SPRPLabelled\NW_SPRP.lpj"$
```

Selecting the subset of the data of interest

```
? ****** Revealed Preference Data only ******
sample;all$
reject;SPRP=0$ Eliminating the stated preference data
```

Descriptive statistics and correlation matrix

```
dstats;rhs=*$
dstats;rhs=choice,act,invc,invt2,invt,egt,trnf,pinc,gender;output=2$
```

Initial MNL model (preceding simulation and scenario application)

```
?To open a file to store elasticity outputs:
OPEN;export="C:\Books\DCMPrimer\Second Edition 2010\Latest Version\Data and nlo-
git set ups\SPRPLabelled\NWelas.csv"$
Timer$ Always useful to include this command to see how long it takes to run a
model

|-> Nlogit
    ;lhs = choice, cset, altij
    ;choices = bs,tn,bw,cr
    ;show
    ;descriptives;crosstabs
    ;effects:invc(*)/invt2(bs,tn,bw)/invt(cr)/act[bs,tn,bw]
    ;export=matrix
    ;pwt
    ;model:
u(bs) = bs + actpt*act + invcpt*invc + invtpt*invt2 + egtpt*egt + trpt*trnf /
u(tn) = tn + actpt*act + invcpt*invc + invtpt*invt2 + egtpt*egt + trpt*trnf /
```

```
u(bw) = bw + actpt*act + invcpt*invc + invtpt*invt2 + egtpt*egt + trpt*trnf /
u(cr) =                              invtcar*invt + TC*TC + PC*PC + egtcar*egt $
```

Simulation and scenario analysis

```
Timer$
Nlogit
;lhs = choice, cset, altij
;choices = bs,tn,bw,cr
;model:
u(bs) = bs + actpt*act + invcpt*invc + invtpt*invt2 + egtpt*egt + trpt*trnf /
u(tn) = tn + actpt*act + invcpt*invc + invtpt*invt2 + egtpt*egt + trpt*trnf /
u(bw) = bw + actpt*act + invcpt*invc + invtpt*invt2 + egtpt*egt + trpt*trnf /
u(cr) =                              invtcar*invt + TC*TC + PC*PC + egtcar*egt $
;Simulation
?Two applications, reducing invt2 by 0.8 and 0.9;Scenario: invt2(bs,tn,bw) = 0.9
& invt2(bs,tn,bw) = 0.8 $
```

> *As an aside*, be careful when selecting names for parameters. For example, suppose we accidentally used the same parameter name for transfer time and the train constant (i.e., *tn*). This model has an error in it. You are then using the symbol *tn* in the first three utility functions as the parameter that multiplies attribute *trnf*. You are also using symbol *tr* as the parameter that is the constant term in the utility function for *tn*. So, you are forcing *tr* to do three things. The constant is unlikely to show up in the show table for train. The reason it does not look like the train equation in **;show** as a constant term is because Nlogit is using an internal code to impose the constraint that the *tn* that is the constant term in the second equation also multiplies the attribute *trnf* in that same equation. Unfortunately, the routine that is trying to display the utility functions is getting confused by the extra (hidden) notation.

13.2 Adding to our understanding of the data

13.2.1 Descriptive output (Dstats)

Good modeling practices require that the analyst check their data before embarking on formal model estimation. The most useful command in Nlogit to do this is **Dstats**. In addition to obtaining the mean, standard deviation, and range (minimum, maximum) of each variable, **Dstats** indicates whether there are missing data on each variable (coded in the data as −999). The range is especially useful since it enables you to check whether there are values that may be outliers. A correlation matrix may be obtained by adding **;output=2**. The command allows for 223 variables. In this version of

Nlogit (August 2013 onwards) there is a new command **CORR ; Rhs = <list of variables> $**. It is the same as **Dstats** but it skips the descriptives and goes right to the correlation matrix. There is no need for **;Output=2**.

As an aside, Missing data are handled by listwise deletion. In order to compute the correlations, the program goes through the observations. If any of the variables have missing data, the observation is dropped.

As an aside, If you want to mean centre a variable, it can easily be done by using **CREATE ; CenteredX = Dev(x) $**

```
|-> dstats;rhs=*;output=2$
Descriptive Statistics for  21 variables
```

Variable	Mean	Std.Dev.	Minimum	Maximum	Cases	Missing
ID	99.44980	56.56125	1.0	197.0	747	0
SET	0.0	0.0	0.0	0.0	747	0
ALTIJ	2.456493	1.116136	1.0	4.0	747	0
ALTN	2.456493	1.116136	1.0	4.0	747	0
CSET	3.859438	.411368	2.0	4.0	747	0
CHOICE	.263722	.440945	0.0	1.0	747	0
ACT	10.80245	12.18600	0.0	210.0	572	175
INVC	5.559839	3.418899	0.0	42.0	747	0
INVT	52.68407	27.28067	2.0	501.0	747	0
TC	3.765714	2.705246	0.0	7.0	175	572
PC	11.60571	13.55063	0.0	60.0	175	572
EGT	8.551539	8.468263	0.0	100.0	747	0
TRNF	.316434	.465491	0.0	1.0	572	175
WT	4.402098	7.893725	0.0	35.0	572	175
SPRP	1.0	0.0	1.0	1.0	747	0
AGE	42.98260	12.59956	24.0	70.0	747	0
PINC	63.19277	41.61792	0.0	140.0	747	0
HSIZE	3.755020	2.280048	1.0	30.0	747	0
KIDS	1.005355	1.110502	0.0	4.0	747	0
GENDER	.500669	.500335	0.0	1.0	747	0
INVT2	43.07497	36.47828	0.0	511.0	747	0

```
dstats;rhs=choice,act,invc,invt2,invt,egt,trnf,pinc,gender;output=2$
```

Note: if you only want the correlation matrix you can use, for example, **corr; rhs=choice,act,invc,invt2,invt,egt,trnf,pinc,gender$**

```
|-> corr;rhs=choice,act,invc,invt2,invt,egt,trnf,pinc,gender$
Covariances and/or Correlations Using Listwise Deletion
Correlations computed for   9 variables.
Used    747 observations. Sum of weights =      572.0000
-----------+-----------------------------------------------------------------------
Cor.Mat.|  CHOICE     ACT     INVC     INVT2    INVT      EGT      TRNF     PINC
-----------+-----------------------------------------------------------------------
  CHOICE| 1.00000  -.08354  -.08363  -.10836  -.05707  -.06937  -.22558  -.01405
     ACT| -.08354  1.00000  -.04605  -.15266  -.13956   .11016  -.10042  -.05123
    INVC| -.08363  -.04605  1.00000   .21607   .15946   .12703   .23386   .06777
   INVT2| -.10836  -.15266   .21607  1.00000   .97151  -.02915   .46712  -.01704
    INVT| -.05707  -.13956   .15946   .97151  1.00000  -.02880   .29381  -.00967
     EGT| -.06937   .11016   .12703  -.02915  -.02880  1.00000  -.04104  -.09068
    TRNF| -.22558  -.10042   .23386   .46712   .29381  -.04104  1.00000   .01164
    PINC| -.01405  -.05123   .06777  -.01704  -.00967  -.09068   .01164  1.00000
-----------+-----------------------------------------------------------------------
Cor.Mat.|  CHOICE     ACT     INVC     INVT2    INVT      EGT      TRNF     PINC
-----------+-----------------------------------------------------------------------
  GENDER|  .04319   .04920   .04548  -.00660  -.00409   .02912   .00176   .22643
-----------+------------
Cor.Mat.|  GENDER
-----------+------------
  GENDER| 1.00000
```

Note that for this data set there is at least one missing variable for each observation and so the command **;corr;rhs=*$** does not allow a matrix, and reports the following:

```
|-> corr;rhs=*$
Covariances and/or Correlations Using Listwise Deletion
See DSTAT for (dropped) variables with no valid observations.
Correlations computed for  21 variables.
Used    747 observations. Sum of weights =         .0000
*****************************************************************
After listwise deletion, your sample has no observations.
Use DSTAT;Rhs=<your list>$ to see counts of missing data.
Note:This can occur even if all variables have some data.
*****************************************************************
```

13.2.2 ;Show

The **;show** command may be used to generate output informative of both the market shares and utility structures. The estimated model is set out below and is followed by the **;show** command output in two sections. The first section of the **;show** command output can be further divided into two segments. The first segment details information on the nested structure of the model. For the basic MNL model, there is no output as no nesting structure exists (this is relevant to the Nested logit model described in Chapter 14). Part of the second segment of the **;show** command output is relevant to the basic MNL choice model. The output in Nlogit details the choice proportions or market shares as they appear within the data.

From this output it can be seen that the *bus (BS)* was chosen 19.29 percent of the time while the *train (TR)* alternative was chosen 23.35 percent of the time. The other choice proportions are also shown. This information is important; indeed, the base comparison model used to determine overall model significance is a simple replication of these choice proportions.

The next two columns of output are not relevant to the basic MNL choice model as described to this point. The first of the two columns discloses any endogenous weighting that may have been utilized. We discuss this in a later section of the chapter. The last column discloses information with regard to a test of IID (behaviorally equivalent to the IIA assumption; see Chapter 4).

The second section of the **;show** command output reconstructs the shapes of the utility functions. The columns detail the names given to the parameters estimated within the system of utility functions of the choice model. The rows of the output represent the alternatives. The cells within the matrix formed by the parameter names and alternatives available indicate which alternative an estimated parameter is associated with, and to which variable that parameter belongs. It can be seen that constants are estimated for all but the *car (CR)* alternative, while a parameter named *invt* is estimated for all of the alternatives except *car*.

```
|-> LOAD;file="C:\Books\DCMPrimer\Second Edition 2010\Latest Version\Data and nlo-
git set ups\SPRPLabelled\NW_SPRP.sav.lpj"$
Project file contained   12167 observations.
|-> reject;SPRP=0$
|-> Nlogit
    ;lhs = choice, cset, altij
    ;choices = bs,tn,bw,cr /0.2,0.3,0.1,0.4
    ;show
    ;descriptives;crosstabs
    ;model:
    u(bo)   bo | actpt*act | invcpt*invc + invtpt'invt2 + egtpt*egt + trpt*trnf /
    u(tn) = tn + actpt*act + invcpt*invc + invtpt*invt2 + egtpt*egt + trpt*trnf /
    u(bw) = bw + actpt*act + invcpt*invc + invtpt*invt2 + egtpt*egt + trpt*trnf /
    u(cr) =                           invtcar*invt + TC*TC + PC*PC + egtcar*egt $
```

Sample proportions are marginal, not conditional.
Choices marked with * are excluded for the IIA test.

```
+--------------------+---------+-----
|Choice   (prop.)|Weight|IIA
+--------------------+---------+-----
|BS        .19289| 1.037|
|TN        .23350| 1.285|
|BW        .21320|  .469|
|CR        .36041| 1.110|
+--------------------+---------+-----
```

```
+-----------------------------------------------------------------------------+
| Model Specification:  Table entry is the attribute that                     |
| multiplies the indicated parameter.                                         |
+-----------+---------+-------------------------------------------------------+
| Choice  |******| Parameter                                                 |
|         |Row  1| BS        ACTPT    INVCPT    INVTPT    EGTPT               |
|         |Row  2| TRPT      TN       BW        INVTCAR   TC                  |
|         |Row  3| PC        EGTCAR                                          |
+-----------+---------+-------------------------------------------------------+
|BS       |      1| Constant ACT      INVC      INVT2     EGT                 |
|         |      2| TRNF     none     none      none      none                |
|         |      3| none     none                                            |
|TN       |      1| none     ACT      INVC      INVT2     EGT                 |
|         |      2| TRNF     Constant none      none      none                |
|         |      3| none     none                                            |
|BW       |      1| none     ACT      INVC      INVT2     EGT                 |
|         |      2| TRNF     none     Constant  none      none                |
|         |      3| none     none                                            |
|CR       |      1| none     none     none      none      none                |
|         |      2| none     none     none      INVT      TC                  |
|         |      3| PC       EGT                                             |
+-----------------------------------------------------------------------------+
```

Normal exit: 6 iterations. Status=0, F=   190.4789

```
------------------------------------------------------------------------------
```

Discrete choice (multinomial logit) model
Dependent variable   Choice
Log likelihood function   -190.47891
Estimation based on N =   197, K = 12
Inf.Cr.AIC =   405.0 AIC/N =   2.056
R2=1-LogL/LogL* Log-L fncn R-sqrd R2Adj
Constants only must be computed directly
            Use NLOGIT ;...;RHS=ONE$
Chi-squared[9]   =   152.66810
Prob [chi squared > value] =   .00000
Vars. corrected for choice based sampling
Response data are given as ind. choices
Number of obs.=   197, skipped   0 obs

CHOICE	Coefficient	Standard Error	z	Prob. |z|>Z*	95% Confidence Interval	
BS	-1.68661**	.74953	-2.25	.0244	-3.15566	-.21756
ACTPT	-.04533***	.01667	-2.72	.0065	-.07800	-.01265
INVCPT	-.08405	.07151	-1.18	.2399	-.22421	.05611
INVTPT	-.01368	.00840	-1.63	.1033	-.03013	.00278
EGTPT	-.04892*	.02934	-1.67	.0954	-.10642	.00858
TRPT	-1.07979***	.41033	-2.63	.0085	-1.88403	-.27555
TN	-1.39443*	.72606	-1.92	.0548	-2.81748	.02862
BW	-2.48469***	.74273	-3.35	.0008	-3.94041	-1.02897
INVTCAR	-.04847***	.01032	-4.70	.0000	-.06870	-.02825
TC	-.09183	.08020	-1.14	.2522	-.24902	.06537
PC	-.01899	.01635	-1.16	.2457	-.05104	.01307
EGTCAR	-.05489*	.03198	-1.72	.0861	-.11756	.00779

***, **, * ==> Significance at 1%, 5%, 10% level.
Model was estimated on Aug 16, 2013 at 08:43:34 AM

13.2.3 ;Descriptives

The next output is generated by the command **;descriptives**. As with all other commands such as the **;show** command, the ;**descriptives** command usually precedes the utility function specification within the command syntax. To avoid repetition, we discuss this series of output for the *bus (BS)* alternative only. The remaining output generated is interpreted in exactly the same manner. The heading informs the analyst which alternative the output is associated with. After the heading, the **;descriptives** the command output is broken into three segments. The first segment of this output gives the parameter estimates for the variables assigned to that alternative via the utility function specification.

The second segment of the **;descriptives** command output indicates the mean and standard deviation for each of the variables as specified within the utility function for that alternative for the entire sample used for the estimation of the model. For the *BS* alternative, the mean and standard deviation for the entire sample for invehicle time (*invt*) is 71.79 and 43.55 minutes, respectively.

The last segment of this output details the mean and standard deviation for the variables assigned to that alternative for those *who chose that alternative* only. In this instance, there exist 197 respondents, of whom 38 chose *BS*. For the invehicle time attribute, the mean and standard deviation for those individuals who chose BS is 52.0 and 17.75 minutes, respectively.

```
+--------------------------------------------------------------------------------+
|                  Descriptive Statistics for Alternative BS                     |
|      Utility Function           |                    |      38.0 observs.       |
|      Coefficient                | All      197.0 obs.|that chose BS             |
|  Name          Value  Variable  | Mean     Std. Dev. |Mean       Std. Dev.      |
|  --------------------  --------- | -------------------+----------------------    |
|  BS            -1.6866  ONE      |  1.000       .000  |  1.000        .000       |
|  ACTPT          -.0453  ACT      |  5.944      4.662  |  5.053       4.312       |
|  INVCPT         -.0840  INVC     |  7.071      3.872  |  7.237       6.015       |
|  INVTPT         -.0137  INVT2    | 71.797     43.551  | 52.000      17.747       |
|  EGTPT          -.0489  EGT      |  8.680      7.331  |  9.105      10.467       |
|  TRPT          -1.0798  TRNF     |   .442       .498  |   .079        .273       |
+--------------------------------------------------------------------------------+

+--------------------------------------------------------------------------------+
|                  Descriptive Statistics for Alternative TN                     |
|      Utility Function           |                    |      46.0 observs.       |
|      Coefficient                | All      187.0 obs.|that chose TN             |
|  Name          Value  Variable  | Mean     Std. Dev. |Mean       Std. Dev.      |
|  --------------------  --------- | -------------------+----------------------    |
|  ACTPT          -.0453  ACT      | 16.016      8.401  | 15.239       6.651       |
|  INVCPT         -.0840  INVC     |  4.947      2.451  |  4.065       2.435       |
|  INVTPT         -.0137  INVT2    | 45.257     15.421  | 43.630       9.903       |
|  EGTPT          -.0489  EGT      |  8.882      6.788  |  7.196       5.714       |
|  TRPT          -1.0798  TRNF     |   .230       .422  |   .174        .383       |
|  TN            -1.3944  ONE      |  1.000       .000  |  1.000        .000       |
+--------------------------------------------------------------------------------+

+--------------------------------------------------------------------------------+
|                  Descriptive Statistics for Alternative BW                     |
|      Utility Function           |                    |      42.0 observs.       |
|      Coefficient                | All      188.0 obs.|that chose BW             |
|  Name          Value  Variable  | Mean     Std. Dev. |Mean       Std. Dev.      |
|  --------------------  --------- | -------------------+----------------------    |
|  ACTPT          -.0453  ACT      | 10.707     17.561  |  5.405       4.854       |
|  INVCPT         -.0840  INVC     |  7.000      3.599  |  6.405       1.345       |
|  INVTPT         -.0137  INVT2    | 50.904     20.300  | 54.643      15.036       |
|  EGTPT          -.0489  EGT      | 10.027      9.811  |  8.286       5.932       |
|  TRPT          -1.0798  TRNF     |   .271       .446  |   .095        .297       |
|  BW            -2.4847  ONE      |  1.000       .000  |  1.000        .000       |
+--------------------------------------------------------------------------------+

+--------------------------------------------------------------------------------+
|                  Descriptive Statistics for Alternative CR                     |
|      Utility Function           |                    |      71.0 observs.       |
|      Coefficient                | All      175.0 obs.|that chose CR             |
|  Name          Value  Variable  | Mean     Std. Dev. |Mean       Std. Dev.      |
|  --------------------  --------- | -------------------+----------------------    |
|  INVTCAR        -.0485  INVT     | 55.406     24.166  | 43.324      15.839       |
|  TC             -.0918  TC       |  3.766      2.705  |  2.592       2.708       |
|  PC             -.0190  PC       | 11.606     13.551  |  5.859      10.184       |
|  EGTCAR         -.0549  EGT      |  6.469      9.348  |  3.958       4.634       |
+--------------------------------------------------------------------------------+
```

13.2.4 ;Crosstab

The pseudo-R^2 we discussed in Chapter 12 is but one method of determining how well a choice model is performing. An often more useful method of determining model performance is to examine a **contingency table** of the predicted choice outcomes for the sample, based on the model produced versus the actual choice outcomes as they exist within the data. To generate such a contingency table, Nlogit uses the command **;crosstab**. If the contingency table generated by Nlogit is too large (which is not the case in our application), it does not appear within the output file as with other output generated by Nlogit. To access the contingency table, the analyst must then use the *Matrix: Crosstab* button similar to the *LstOutp* button described in Chapter 10.

```
+---------------------------------------------------------------------+
| Cross tabulation of actual choice vs. predicted P(j)                |
| Row indicator is actual, column is predicted.                       |
| Predicted total is F(k,j,i)=Sum(i=1,...,N) P(k,j,i).                |
| Column totals may be subject to rounding error.                     |
+---------------------------------------------------------------------+
```

```
----------+----------------------------------------------------------------
NLOGIT Cross Tabulation for 4 outcome Multinomial Choice Model
XTab_Prb|         BS           TN           BW           CR        Total
----------+----------------------------------------------------------------
      BS|     12.0000      12.0000      4.00000      10.0000      38.0000
      TN|     10.0000      19.0000      5.00000      12.0000      46.0000
      BW|     9.00000      18.0000      8.00000      7.00000      42.0000
      CR|     8.00000      13.0000      5.00000      45.0000      71.0000
   Total|     40.0000      61.0000      22.0000      74.0000      197.000
```

```
+---------------------------------------------------------------------+
| Cross tabulation of actual y(ij) vs. predicted y(ij)                |
| Row indicator is actual, column is predicted.                       |
| Predicted total is N(k,j,i)=Sum(i=1,...,N) Y(k,j,i).               |
| Predicted y(ij)=1 is the j with largest probability.                |
+---------------------------------------------------------------------+
```

```
----------+----------------------------------------------------------------
NLOGIT Cross Tabulation for 4 outcome Multinomial Choice Model
XTab_Frq|         BS           TN           BW           CR        Total
----------+----------------------------------------------------------------
      BS|     13.0000      13.0000      .000000      12.0000      38.0000
      TN|     8.00000      22.0000      2.00000      14.0000      46.0000
      BW|     8.00000      24.0000      2.00000      8.00000      42.0000
      CR|     5.00000      10.0000      .000000      56.0000      71.0000
   Total|     34.0000      69.0000      4.00000      90.0000      197.000
```

Within the contingency table produced by Nlogit, the rows represent the number of choices made by those sampled for each alternative, while the columns represent the number of times an alternative was predicted to be selected, as based on the choice model specified by the analyst. This prediction is based on two aggregation rules, as shown in the two cross-tabulations above. The first **crosstab** sums the probabilities associated with each alternative across the sample; the second **crosstab** sums the choice probabilities, with the predicted choice corresponding to the alternative for which the highest probability is observed. We prefer the first approach, but we recognize that some disciplines such as marketing typically adopt the second approach, and assign a probability of 1.0 to the highest probability and zero otherwise. This strictly violates the whole idea of a probabilistic choice model associated with random utility maximization (RUM). Analysts should be aware of this point, and always check what set of rules is being used when others present evidence on prediction success.

The diagonal elements of the contingency table represent the number of times the choice model correctly predicted the choice of alternative as observed in the data. The off-diagonal elements represent, in the aggregate, the number of times the choice model incorrectly predicted which alternative a decision maker would select given the levels of the attributes of the alternatives and socio-economic characteristics (SECs) for that decision maker, as they exist within the data set.

It is possible to derive a measure of the aggregate proportion of correct predictions. This is done by summing across the number of correct predictions and dividing by the total number of choices made. Our choice model correctly predicted the mode chosen 93 (i.e., 13 + 22 + 2 + 56) times out of the total of 197 choices made. Thus the overall proportion of correct predictions equals 0.472. Thus for the data, this particular choice model correctly predicted the actual choice outcome for 47.2 percent of the total number of observations.

13.3 Adding to our understanding of the model parameters

A result of the non-linear logit transformation is that there exists no straightforward behavioral interpretation of a parameter estimate of a choice model beyond the sign of the parameter, which indicates whether the associated variable of interest has either a positive or negative effect upon the choice probabilities. Indeed for ordered logit models (see Chapter 18) (in contrast to the unordered choices herein), even the sign has no behavioral meaning. To arrive at a behaviorally meaningful interpretation, it is possible for the analyst to calculate either the elasticities or marginal effects of the choice probabilities with respect to some particular attribute or SEC. We now discuss both elasticities and partial or marginal effects.

13.3.1 Starting values

Nlogit allows the analyst to specify the starting point for a search, although we strongly recommend that the beginner refrain from changing Nlogit from its default start value. Assuming the analyst wishes to change the default starting point, this must be done for each variable in the model specification for which the starting point is to be changed. That is, there is no global way in Nlogit to change the starting point for all parameters to be estimated. The command to change the starting value for a parameter involves placing to the right of the parameter the starting value that the analyst wishes the search algorithm to begin with, in brackets (( )). This can also be done for constant terms. That is

```
;Model: U(<alternative 1 name>) = <constant(value_i) > + <parameter(value_j) > *
<variable> /
```

will commence the search for the constant coefficient at value$_i$ and the search for the variable parameter at value$_j$ (NB: that i can equal j). For example,

```
NLOGIT
;lhs = choice, cset, altij
;choices = cart, carnt, bus, train, busway, LR
;model:
U(cart)    = asccart(-0.5) + ptcst(-1)*fuel /
U(carnt)   = asccarnt       + pntcst*fuel /
U(bus)     = ascbus         + cst(-0.8)*fare /
U(train)   = asctn          + cst*fare/
U(busway)  = ascbusw        + cst*fare /
U(LR)      =                  cst*fare $
```

Note that the starting point for the search for the *CART* alternative ASC will be −0.5 and −1 for the *CART* fuel attribute. The command also specifies that the search start point for the fare attribute of the *BUS* alternative will be −0.8. The astute reader will note that in the above command the fare attribute has been specified as generic across all of the public transport alternatives. In the case of generic parameter estimates, it is only necessary to specify the start point for one alternative. Thus, the start point for the fare attributes of the train, busway, and light rail alternatives will also be −0.8. The start values for the fuel parameter of the *CARNT* alternative will be zero, as will the constant terms (save for the *CART* alternative) as no starting point was given for these. We omit the results from this exercise for this example as the results generated are no different to the results if no start point is given.

> *As an aside*, it will often be necessary to constrain certain parameters of choice models so that they equal some value. One form of constraint already discussed occurs when the analyst specifies generic parameter estimates across the utility functions of two or more alternatives. The estimated value will not be known in advance by the analyst. Often, however, the analyst will be required to fix one or more parameters so that they equal some known fixed value.

To constrain a parameter (or a constant) to some pre-determined fixed value we place to the right of the parameter to be fixed square brackets ([ ]) and write in the specific parameter value. We do not use round brackets, which indicate a starting value for a parameter to be estimated – see above. The command syntax is

```
;Model:
U(<alternative 1 name>) = <constant[value_i]> + <parameter[value_j]>*<variable>
```

13.3.2 ;effect: elasticities

The theory underlying the concept of elasticity (or elasticity of choice) was set out in Chapter 8. From Louviere *et al.* (2000, 58), direct and cross-elasticities may be defined as:

A direct elasticity measures the percentage change in the probability of choosing a particular alternative in the choice set with respect to a given percentage change in an attribute of that same alternative. A cross-elasticity measures the percentage change in the probability of choosing a particular alternative in the choice set with respect to a given percentage change in a competing alternative.

The two main methods of calculation are the arc elasticity method and the point elasticity method. The default Nlogit output is a point elasticity (except where a dummy variable is used, in which case an arc elasticity is provided, based on the average of the before and after probabilities and attribute levels). We discuss arc elasticities in Section 13.3.3 and how they can be derived for any measurement unit (e.g., ratio or ordinal) using Nlogit's simulation capability.

> *As an aside*, while it is possible to calculate point elasticities for categorically coded variables, the results will be meaningless. Consider a gender variable where male is coded zero and female coded one. In such a case the elasticity would be interpreted as the percentage change in the probability of choice given a 1 percent change in gender (we

will not offer a guess as to what this 1 percent change in gender is). Thus while Nlogit will provide elasticity estimates for dummy and effects coded variables, the output generated cannot be meaningfully interpreted. Large changes in a variable such as a 100 percent change do, however, make sense when discussing categorically coded variables (e.g., from dummy code 1 to 0). Thus, such variables have to be handled using the arc elasticity formula discussed later if the analyst requires elasticities. We therefore calculate and interpret the point elasticities for continuous level data.

To calculate elasticities using Nlogit, the analyst uses the command **;effects**. For this command, the analyst must specify which variable the elasticity is to be calculated for (i.e., which X_{ik}) and for which alternative (i.e., which alternative is i). The command looks thus:

```
;effects: <variableₖ(alternativeᵢ)>
```

For this command, the analyst types the variable name and not the parameter name for which the elasticity is to be calculated, followed by the desired alternative(s) which is placed in round (( )) brackets. It is possible using Nlogit to calculate the elasticity for a single variable over several alternatives if that variable relates to more than one alternative. Thus one could calculate the point elasticities for the invehicle time attribute for both the *BS* and *TN* alternatives. This is done by typing the name of the alternatives within the round brackets separated by a comma, as shown below:

```
;effects: <variableₖ(alternativeᵢ, alternativeⱼ)>
```

It is also possible in Nlogit to calculate the point elasticities for more than one variable at a time. For example, the analyst may calculate both the elasticity for the *invehicle attribute* for the *BS* alternative and the elasticity for the *invehicle cost* attribute for the *TN* alternative. In such cases, the commands indicating the point elasticities to be estimated are divided by a slash (/) thus:

```
;effects: <variableₖ(alternativeᵢ) / variableₕ(alternativeᵢ)>
```

The default aggregation method employed by Nlogit is that of *naive pooling*, a method that the authors advise against. To use the probability weighted sample enumeration (PWSE) method, the command **;pwt** must also be added to the command syntax. If this command is not added, the analyst will notice the telltale sign that the cross-point elasticities will all be equal. Note that the analyst may also have Nlogit compute the point elasticities using the sample means of the data by replacing the **;pwt** command with **;means**. As stated previously, we advise against this approach as well.

In general form, the command syntax for point elasticities within the Nlogit command for the data used in this chapter is:

```
?( ) is for elasticities, [  ] is for partial or marginal effects:
;effects:invc(*)/invt2(bs,tr,bw)/invt(cr)/act[bs,tr,bw]
;pwt
```

The elasticity output is presented below. We have used the asterisk symbol (*) to denote all alternatives. As such, the command syntax above will produce elasticities for all alternatives associated with a specific attribute. This applies even if a specific attribute is not associated with every alternative. Another way of defining the relevant alternatives is to list their names in the command such as **invt2(bs,tr,bw)**. The diagonal estimates are direct elasticities and the off-diagonal estimates are cross-elasticities. For example, −0.3792 is the direct elasticity associated with invehicle cost and bus, and indicates that a 1 percent increase in the invehicle cost of bus will, *all other influences held constant*, lead to a 0.3792 reduction in the probability of choosing the bus. 0.1033 tells us that a 1 percent increase in the invehicle cost of bus will, *all other influences held constant*, result in a 0.1033 percent increase in the probability of choosing the train (however, be warned about the value of cross-elasticities in a model such as MNL where IID applies, as discussed above, where differences in all cross-elasticities in a row are due to the **;pwt** command, which uses the sample enumeration instead of averaging over observations using naive pooling).

We show below the empirical implications of examples when **;pwt** is excluded and included. Note that the cross-elasticities are the same under naive pooling and differ when **;pwt** is used. Although this difference may be of concern, at the individual respondent level they are the same. The probability weighting causes differences in the results, which are substantial.

```
No ;pwt:
Timer$
Nlogit
;lhs = choice, cset, altij
;choices = bs,tn,bw,cr
;show
;descriptives;crosstabs
?( ) is for elasticities, [ ] is for partial or marginal effects:
;effects:invc(*)/invt2(bs,tn,bw)/invt(cr)/act[bs,tn,bw];export=matrix
? ;export=tables
;export=both
?;pwt
?;wts=gender
;model:
```

```
u(bs) = bs + actpt*act + invcpt*invc + invtpt*invt2 + egtpt*egt + trpt*trnf /
u(tn) = tn + actpt*act + invcpt*invc + invtpt*invt2 + egtpt*egt + trpt*trnf /
u(bw) = bw + actpt*act + invcpt*invc + invtpt*invt2 + egtpt*egt + trpt*trnf /
u(cr) =                             invtcar*invt + TC*TC + PC*PC + egtcar*egt $
```

Elasticity wrt change of X in row choice on Prob[column choice]

```
-----------+-------------------------------------------------
INVC       |      BS        TN        BW        CR
-----------+-------------------------------------------------
        BS|   -.4866     .1077     .1077     .1077
        TN|    .1230    -.2716     .1230     .1230
        BW|    .0600     .0600    -.5014     .0600
```

```
;pwt included
Timer$
Nlogit
;lhs = choice, cset, altij
;choices = bs,tn,bw,cr
;show
;descriptives;crosstabs
?( ) is for elasticities, [ ] is for partial or marginal effects:
;effects:invc(*)/invt2(bs,tn,bw)/invt(cr)/act[bs,tn,bw];export=matrix
? ;export=tables
;export=both
;pwt
?;wts=gender
;model:
```

```
u(bs) = bs + actpt*act + invcpt*invc + invtpt*invt2 + egtpt*egt + trpt*trnf /
u(tn) = tn + actpt*act + invcpt*invc + invtpt*invt2 + egtpt*egt + trpt*trnf /
u(bw) = bw + actpt*act + invcpt*invc + invtpt*invt2 + egtpt*egt + trpt*trnf /
u(cr) =                             invtcar*invt + TC*TC + PC*PC + egtcar*egt $
```

Elasticity wrt change of X in row choice on Prob[column choice]

```
-----------+-------------------------------------------------
INVC       |      BS        TN        BW        CR
-----------+-------------------------------------------------
        BS|   -.3624     .1068     .1245     .0697
        TN|    .1100    -.2186     .1470     .0786
        BW|    .0662     .0719    -.4419     .0351
```

13.3.3 Elasticities: direct and cross – extended format

It is often the case that the analyst would like to transfer the elasticities to a table in Excel, especially when there is a lot of elasticity output. This is possible using the **Export** command. Various options are available to select the outputs of interest.

The default **;Effects:** ... **specification** gets you the compact matrix form. If you add **;Full** to the command, you get the full output, which produces a set of

tables with standard errors. These are the same regardless of what you export.
The output associated with **;Full** is given below.

```
;effects:invc(*)/invt2(bs,tn,bw)/invt(cr);full;pwt
+------------------------------------------------------------------+
| Elasticity              averaged over observations.|
| Effects on probabilities of all choices in model: |
| * = Direct Elasticity effect of the attribute.    |
+------------------------------------------------------------------+
```

Average elasticity   of prob(alt) wrt INVC   in BS

Choice	Coefficient	Standard Error	z	Prob. |z|>Z*	95% Confidence Interval	
BS	-.36240***	.01748	-20.73	.0000	-.39666	-.32813
TN	.10679***	.00573	18.64	.0000	.09556	.11801
BW	.12445***	.00619	20.11	.0000	.11232	.13658
CR	.06967***	.00548	12.72	.0000	.05894	.08041

***, **, * ==> Significance at 1%, 5%, 10% level.
Model was estimated on Aug 16, 2013 at 08:59:06 AM

Average elasticity   of prob(alt) wrt INVC   in TN

Choice	Coefficient	Standard Error	z	Prob. |z|>Z*	95% Confidence Interval	
BS	.10998***	.00549	20.04	.0000	.09923	.12073
TN	-.21858***	.01046	-20.90	.0000	-.23908	-.19809
BW	.14703***	.00647	22.71	.0000	.13434	.15972
CR	.07856***	.00575	13.67	.0000	.06730	.08982

***, **, * ==> Significance at 1%, 5%, 10% level.
Model was estimated on Aug 16, 2013 at 08:59:07 AM

Average elasticity   of prob(alt) wrt INVC   in BW

Choice	Coefficient	Standard Error	z	Prob. |z|>Z*	95% Confidence Interval	
BS	.06621***	.00336	19.73	.0000	.05963	.07279
TN	.07187***	.00356	20.19	.0000	.06490	.07885
BW	-.44186***	.01090	-40.53	.0000	-.46323	-.42050
CR	.03508***	.00256	13.69	.0000	.03005	.04010

```
***, **, * ==>  Significance at 1%, 5%, 10% level.
Model was estimated on Aug 16, 2013 at 08:59:07 AM
---------------------------------------------------------------------------------

---------------------------------------------------------------------------------
Average elasticity      of prob(alt) wrt INVT2      in BS
-----------+---------------------------------------------------------------------
           |                  Standard              Prob.       95% Confidence
    Choice |  Coefficient      Error        z      |z|>Z*         Interval
-----------+---------------------------------------------------------------------
       BS |   -.53699***      .02234     -24.03    .0000     -.58078    -.49320
       TN |    .16167***      .00725      22.29    .0000      .14746     .17588
       BW |    .18748***      .00803      23.35    .0000      .17174     .20322
       CR |    .09949***      .00562      17.69    .0000      .08846     .11051
-----------+---------------------------------------------------------------------
***, **, * ==>  Significance at 1%, 5%, 10% level.
Model was estimated on Aug 16, 2013 at 08:59:07 AM
---------------------------------------------------------------------------------

---------------------------------------------------------------------------------
Average elasticity      of prob(alt) wrt INVT2      in TN
-----------+---------------------------------------------------------------------
           |                  Standard              Prob.       95% Confidence
    Choice |  Coefficient      Error        z      |z|>Z*         Interval
-----------+---------------------------------------------------------------------
       BS |    .17929***      .00722      24.83    .0000      .16514     .19345
       TN |   -.32857***      .01242     -26.46    .0000     -.35292    -.30423
       BW |    .22322***      .00848      26.34    .0000      .20661     .23983
       CR |    .10993***      .00684      16.07    .0000      .09652     .12334
-----------+---------------------------------------------------------------------
***, **, * ==>  Significance at 1%, 5%, 10% level.
Model was estimated on Aug 16, 2013 at 08:59:07 AM
---------------------------------------------------------------------------------

---------------------------------------------------------------------------------
Average elasticity      of prob(alt) wrt INVT2      in BW
-----------+---------------------------------------------------------------------
           |                  Standard              Prob.       95% Confidence
    Choice |  Coefficient      Error        z      |z|>Z*         Interval
-----------+---------------------------------------------------------------------
       BS |    .08354***      .00430      19.41    .0000      .07510     .09198
       TN |    .09170***      .00461      19.87    .0000      .08265     .10074
       BW |   -.55150***      .01554     -35.48    .0000     -.58197    -.52104
       CR |    .04165***      .00308      13.54    .0000      .03562     .04768
-----------+---------------------------------------------------------------------
***, **, * ==>  Significance at 1%, 5%, 10% level.
Model was estimated on Aug 16, 2013 at 08:59:07 AM
---------------------------------------------------------------------------------
```

```
--------------------------------------------------------------------------------
Average elasticity       of prob(alt) wrt INVT      in CR
----------- +-------------------------------------------------------------------
           |                 Standard              Prob.        95% Confidence
  Choice|  Coefficient        Error        z      |z|>Z*           Interval
----------- +-------------------------------------------------------------------
       BS|    .55295***        .03454    16.01    .0000        .48525     .62064
       TN|    .55344***        .03597    15.39    .0000        .48295     .62394
       BW|    .53235***        .03500    15.21    .0000        .46376     .60094
       CR|   -.91217***        .06191   -14.73    .0000      -1.03351    -.79084
----------- +-------------------------------------------------------------------
***, **, * ==>   Significance at 1%, 5%, 10% level.
```

The elasticity output above is presented in the Nlogit output on the screen. In addition, you can also save the output in various levels of detail as an Excel comma delimited (CSV) file. To do this, you have to open a file prior to running the Nlogit model commands. An example used here is:

```
OPEN;export="C:\Books\DCMPrimer\Second Edition 2010\Latest Version\Data
and nlogit set ups\SPRPLabelled\NWelall.csv"$
```

We suggest you use a file name that has meaning in terms of the elasticities you want to export, and that each time you run the model you rename the file to keep a set of separate files on the various model run outputs.

To be able to export findings to the spreadsheet, you have to add extra commands within the model set up. There are three options available. In the model (such as Nlogit or later other forms such as RPlogit or LClogit), in addition to the effects command you control the export of results by selecting **;Export = matrix** to get the compact matrices, **;Export = table**s to get the **;Full** output, but no matrices, and **;Export = both** to get all available outputs. **;Export=both** mimics in the CSV file what you get with **;Full** on your screen. These features handle all model forms, and any number of choices. (The CSV file is limited to 254 choices if you are exporting to Excel 2003. Excel 2007 allows 65,536 columns.) We illustrate the output by running Nlogit with **;Export=both**.

```
OPEN;export="C:\Books\DCMPrimer\Second Edition 2010\Latest Version\Data
and nlogit set ups\SPRPLabelled\NWelall.csv"$
Nlogit
...
;effects:invc(*)
;full
?;export=matrix
?  ;export=tables
;export=both
;pwt
...$
```

What you see in the **NWelall.csv** file is given below:

Average elasticity of prob(alt) wrt INVC in BS
Average elasticity of prob(alt) wrt INVC in TN
Average elasticity of prob(alt) wrt INVC in BW
Average elasticity of prob(alt) wrt INVT2 in BS
Average elasticity of prob(alt) wrt INVT2 in TN
Average elasticity of prob(alt) wrt INVT2 in BW
Average elasticity of prob(alt) wrt INVT in CR
Partial Effects for Multinomial Choice Model
Table 1: Attribute is INVC in choice BS
Elasticity: * = own

	Choice	Mean	Standard Deviation
*	BS	−0.3624	0.01748
	TN	0.10679	0.00573
	BW	0.12445	0.00619
	CR	0.06967	0.00548

Table 2: Attribute is INVC in choice TN
Elasticity: * = own

	Choice	Mean	Standard Deviation
	BS	0.10998	0.00549
*	TN	−0.21858	0.01046
	BW	0.14703	0.00647
	CR	0.07856	0.00575

Table 3: Attribute is INVC in choice BW
Elasticity: * = own

	Choice	Mean	Standard Deviation
	BS	0.06621	0.00336
	TN	0.07187	0.00356
*	BW	−0.44186	0.0109
	CR	0.03508	0.00256

Partial effects with respect to attribute INVC
Entry = dlogPr(Col_alt) / dlog(×|Row_alt)

INVC	BS	TN	BW	CR
BS	−0.3624	0.10679	0.12445	0.06967
TN	0.10998	−0.21858	0.14703	0.07856
BW	0.06621	0.07187	−0.44186	0.03508

Partial effects with respect to attribute INVC
Entry = dlogPr(Col_alt) / dlog(x|Row_alt) (z ratio)
(******) => a std. dev. of zero when the effect is always zero.

INVC	BS	TN	BW	CR
BS	−.36240(−20.73)	.10679(18.64)	.12445(20.11)	.06967(12.72)
TN	.10998(20.04)	−.21858(−20.90)	.14703(22.71)	.07856(13.67)
BW	.06621(19.73)	.07187(20.19)	−.44186(−40.53)	.03508(13.69)

13.3.4 Calculating arc elasticities

Consider the direct point elasticity for a decision maker given a unit increase in price from \$1 to \$2 and a decrease in the probability of choice from 0.6 to 0.55. Estimation using Equation (13.1) yields the following elasticity:

$$E^{P_{iq}}_{X_{ikq}} = \frac{0.6 - 0.55}{1 - 2} \cdot \frac{2}{0.55} = -0.182.$$

We interpret this result as being indicative of a 0.182 percent decrease in the probability of selecting the alternative to which the price change occurred given a 1 percent change in the price variable, *ceteris paribus*.

The above appears straightforward; however, note that we chose to use the after change price and after change probability to calculate the point elasticity. That is, X_{ikq} of Equation (13.1) equals 2 and P_{iq} equals 0.55. What if we chose to use the before change price and before change probability to estimate the direct point elasticity for our decision maker? The elasticity then becomes:

$$E^{P_{iq}}_{X_{ikq}} = \frac{0.6 - 0.55}{1 - 2} \cdot \frac{1}{0.6} = -0.08.$$

Using the before change values for X_{ikq} and P_{iq} suggests that a 1 percent change in price will yield an 0.08 percent decrease in the probability of selecting the alternative for which the price change occurred, *ceteris paribus*. There thus exists a discrepancy of some 0.1 percent between using the before change values and the after change values to calculate the point elasticity for the above example.

Which is the correct elasticity to use? For multi-million dollar projects, the answer to this question may prove critical. Rather than answer the above question, economists prefer to answer a different question. That is, is the magnitude of difference in an elasticity calculated using the before and after change values sufficiently large enough to warrant concern? If the difference is marginal, then it matters not whether the before or after change values are used. If the magnitude of difference is non-marginal, however, then the analyst may calculate the elasticity using another method, known as the *arc elasticity method*. What constitutes a marginal or non-marginal difference is up to the individual analyst.

The calculation of arc elasticity involves using an average of the before or after change values. Thus Equation (8.20) in Chapter 8 becomes:

$$E^{P_{iq}}_{X_{ikq}} = \frac{\partial P_{iq}}{\partial x_{ikq}} \cdot \frac{\bar{x}_{ikq}}{\bar{P}_{iq}}. \tag{13.1}$$

For the previous example, using Equation (13.1), the calculated elasticity now becomes:

$$E^{P_{iq}}_{x_{ikq}} = \frac{0.6 - 0.55}{1 - 2} \cdot \frac{1.5}{0.575} = -0.13.$$

Note that the arc elasticity will lie somewhere, but not necessarily halfway, between the direct elasticities calculated using the before and after change values. If you need to obtain an arc elasticity, then Nlogit can provide the *before* and *after* outputs necessary to apply Equation (13.1) via the **;simulation** and **;scenario** commands, which we discuss in Section 13.4. Before doing so, we discuss marginal or partial effects, which are an alternative output to the elasticity outputs (indeed, elasticities are calculated using the information from the partial effects).

13.3.5 Partial or marginal effects

The theory associated with this topic is presented in Section 8.4.3 of Chapter 8. A partial or marginal effect reflects the rate of change in one variable relative to the rate of change in a second variable. Unlike elasticities, marginal effects are not expressed as percentage changes. Rather marginal effects are expressed as *unit changes*. More specifically, we interpret the marginal effect for a choice model as the change in probability given a unit change in a variable, *ceteris paribus*.

The command to generate marginal effects is similar to the command to generate point elasticities, the sole difference being that the round brackets used within the elasticity command (( )) are replaced with *square* brackets ([ ]). All else remains as for the elasticity command. Hence, in general the marginal effects command will look thus:

```
;effects: <variableₖ[alternativeᵢ]>
```

As with elasticities, it is also possible to obtain marginal effects for a single variable on several alternatives through a single command. To do so, the command will take the following form:

```
;effects: <variableₖ[alternativeᵢ, alternativeⱼ]>
```

It is also possible to generate the marginal effects of several variables within a single command line by separating the individual marginal effects with a slash (/), as shown below:

```
;effects: <variableₖ[alternativeᵢ] / variableₕ[alternativeᵢ]>
```

An example using the model estimated in this chapter is given below:

```
[  ] is for partial or marginal effects:
;effects:invc(*)/invt2(bs,tr,bw)/invt(cr)/act[bs,tr,bw]

;effects:act[bs,tn,bw];full;pwt
```

Average partial effect on prob(alt) wrt ACT   in BS

Choice	Coefficient	Standard Error	z	Prob. |z|>Z*	95% Confidence Interval	
BS	-.00857***	.00020	-43.20	.0000	-.00896	-.00818
TN	.00350***	.00017	20.71	.0000	.00317	.00383
BW	.00184***	.00011	16.76	.0000	.00162	.00205
CR	.00277***	.00014	19.80	.0000	.00249	.00304

***, **, * ==> Significance at 1%, 5%, 10% level.
Model was estimated on Aug 16, 2013 at 09:03:03 AM

Average partial effect on prob(alt) wrt ACT   in TN

Choice	Coefficient	Standard Error	z	Prob. |z|>Z*	95% Confidence Interval	
BS	.00416***	.00018	23.04	.0000	.00381	.00451
TN	-.00939***	.00014	-66.97	.0000	-.00966	-.00911
BW	.00316***	.00017	18.66	.0000	.00282	.00349
CR	.00385***	.00017	22.06	.0000	.00351	.00419

***, **, * ==> Significance at 1%, 5%, 10% level.
Model was estimated on Aug 16, 2013 at 09:03:03 AM

Average partial effect on prob(alt) wrt ACT   in BW

Choice	Coefficient	Standard Error	z	Prob. |z|>Z*	95% Confidence Interval	
BS	.00195***	.00011	17.31	.0000	.00173	.00217
TN	.00276***	.00015	18.60	.0000	.00247	.00305
BW	-.00620***	.00018	-35.10	.0000	-.00654	-.00585
CR	.00131***	.7888D-04	16.58	.0000	.00115	.00146

nnnnn.D-xx or D+xx => multiply by 10 to -xx or +xx.
***, **, * ==> Significance at 1%, 5%, 10% level.
Model was estimated on Aug 16, 2013 at 09:03:03 AM

> *As an aside*, as the choice probabilities must sum to one, the marginal effects which represent the change in the choice probabilities are mathematically constrained to sum to zero, thus representing a net zero change over all alternatives. This is not true of elasticities.

The **PARTIALS** command and most model commands with **;Marginals** will use finite differences for partial effects. This is not feasible for the partial effects in the multinomial logit model. If the analyst does want these results, they will have to calculate the marginal effects manually (for categorically coded variables), or even better use the **;simulation** command (see Section 13.3.6) to obtain the change in choice shares resulting from a pre-specified change in the dummy variable, such as setting gender = 1 and then = 0, and compare the results. Looking ahead, the scenario command would be **;Scenario: gender(bs,tn,bw) = 1.0 & gender(bs,tn,bw) = 0.0 $**

Be careful in interpreting the standard errors and confidence intervals here. The elasticities are computed by computing the average across the sample observations. The standard error shown is computed as the standard deviation of this sample of elasticities. Thus, it is not a "sampling standard error," as would normally be computed for a parameter estimator. The "confidence interval" shown displays for you the range that contains roughly 95 percent of the sample observations on the elasticities, not a 95 percent confidence interval for a parameter estimator. As noted, the choice invariant cross-effect that you see in the table above is a feature of the multinomial logit model. Other models such as the nested logit (see Chapter 14) will not display this result.

13.3.6 Partial or marginal effects for binary choice

We can use the data set above in a binary choice format to also illustrate partial effects for binary choices. Fundamentally, the model describes the process of choosing one among a set of alternatives and, in response to changes in the attributes such as an increase in cost or travel time, the substitution of one alternative for another. Suppose that we simplify the model to describe only the choice of whether to drive or not. The choice model above implies the marginal probability:

$$\text{Prob}(cr = 1 | \mathbf{x}_{cr}) = \frac{\exp(\alpha_{cr} + invtcar \times invt + tc \times tc + pc \times pc + egtcar \times egt)}{1 + \exp(\alpha_{cr} + invtcar \times invt + tc \times tc + pc \times pc + egtcar \times egt)}$$
$$= \Lambda(\alpha_{cr} + \beta'_{cr}\mathbf{x}_{cr}).$$

$$(13.2)$$

This is a binary logit model. We can fit this model by restricting focus to the rows of data that apply to *cr*, and modeling the choice variable, *choice*, which equals one for those who chose *cr*, and zero for those who did not. Thus:

```
logit ; if[altij = 4] ; lhs = choice ; rhs = one,invt,tc,pc,egt $
```

The estimated model is shown below. Before examining the binary logit model, it is interesting to compare the estimates with those that were obtained as part of the earlier MNL model. They are shown in the table below. They are strikingly similar, though this is to be expected. The differences can be explained by two sources: sampling variability – 175 observations is not a very large sample – and the violation of the IIA assumption that we explored in Chapter 7. In a larger sample, and under the assumption of IIA, we would expect to get the same estimated model whether based on the full MNL or a marginal model for just one of the choices.

```
-------------------------------------------------------------------------------
Binary Logit Model for Binary Choice
Dependent variable                   CHOICE
Log likelihood function           -88.60449
Restricted log likelihood        -118.17062
Chi squared [  4](P= .000)         59.13226
Significance level                   .00000
McFadden Pseudo R-squared          .2501987
Estimation based on N =     175, K =    5
Inf.Cr.AIC   =     187.2 AIC/N =     1.070
-----------+-------------------------------------------------------------------
           |                Standard              Prob.        95% Confidence
    CHOICE | Coefficient     Error      z       |z|>Z*           Interval
-----------+-------------------------------------------------------------------
  Constant|    3.01108***     .61209    4.92    .0000     1.81141   4.21075
      INVT|    -.04110***     .01042   -3.94    .0001     -.06152   -.02068
        TC|    -.14627*       .07817   -1.87    .0613     -.29948    .00694
        PC|    -.02721        .01721   -1.58    .1139     -.06093    .00652
       EGT|    -.07195**      .03287   -2.19    .0286     -.13638   -.00753
-----------+-------------------------------------------------------------------
***, **, * ==>  Significance at 1%, 5%, 10% level.
These are the estimates from the MNL shown earlier
    INVTCAR|    -.04847***    .01032   -4.70 .0000     -.06870 -.02825
        TC|    -.09183        .08020   -1.14 .2522     -.24902  .06537
        PC|    -.01899        .01635   -1.16 .2457     -.05104  .01307
    EGTCAR|    -.05489*       .03198   -1.72 .0861     -.11756  .00779
```

How do the attributes in the model impact upon the probability of the choice? The partial effects are:

$$\frac{\partial \text{Prob}(cr = 1|\mathbf{x})}{\partial \mathbf{x}} = \Lambda(\alpha_{cr} + \boldsymbol{\beta}'_{cr}\mathbf{x}_{cr}) \times [1 - \Lambda(\alpha_{cr} + \boldsymbol{\beta}'_{cr}\mathbf{x}_{cr})]\boldsymbol{\beta}_{cr}. \tag{13.3}$$

That is, they are a multiple of the coefficient vector. The general result is that, in the choice model, the parameters are related to, but are not equal to, the partial effects that we are interested in. Nlogit will include partial effects with the model results if **;Partials** is added to the model command. For this choice model:

```
------------------------------------------------------------------------------
Partial derivatives of E[y] = F[*]  with
respect to the vector of characteristics
Average partial effects for sample obs.
-----------+------------------------------------------------------------------
           |   Partial      Standard                Prob.     95% Confidence
  CHOICE|    Effect          Error      z       |z|>Z*          Interval
-----------+------------------------------------------------------------------
      INVT|   -.00691***    .00177    -3.91     .0001     -.01038    -.00345
        TC|   -.02461*      .01311    -1.88     .0606     -.05031     .00109
        PC|   -.00458       .00291    -1.57     .1154     -.01027     .00112
       EGT|   -.01210**     .00554    -2.18     .0290     -.02297    -.00124
-----------+------------------------------------------------------------------
***, **, * ==>  Significance at 1%, 5%, 10% level.
------------------------------------------------------------------------------
```

Note that the results reported are "average partial effects"; they are computed by averaging the partial effects over the sample observations. The standard errors are computed using the delta method (see Chapter 7). The necessary Jacobian is given as in Equation (13.4):

$$\Gamma = \frac{\partial^2 \text{Prob}(cr = 1|\mathbf{x})}{\partial \mathbf{x} \partial(\alpha_{cr}, \boldsymbol{\beta}')}$$
$$= \Lambda(\alpha_{cr} + \boldsymbol{\beta}'_{cr}\mathbf{x}_{cr}) \times [1 - \Lambda(\alpha_{cr} + \boldsymbol{\beta}'_{cr}\mathbf{x}_{cr})][1 - 2\Lambda(\alpha_{cr} + \boldsymbol{\beta}'_{cr}\mathbf{x}_{cr})]\boldsymbol{\beta}_{cr}(1, \mathbf{x}'_{cr})$$
$$\tag{13.4}$$

For example, a partial effect or the change in the probability per unit change in the toll cost is estimated to be −0.02461. We need now to determine what is a reasonable change in the toll cost. Earlier, when we fit the MNL, we learned about the attributes for each alternative (with **;Describe**). For *car*, we found:

```
+------------------------------------------------------------------------+
|                Descriptive Statistics for Alternative CR               |
|      Utility Function          |              |      71.0 observs.     |
|        Coefficient             |   All    175.0 obs.|that  chose CR     |
|  Name        Value   Variable  |   Mean   Std. Dev.|Mean      Std. Dev. |
|  -------------------  --------- | ------------------+------------------- |
|  INVTCAR   -.0485   INVT        |  55.406   24.166 |  43.324    15.839  |
|  TC        -.0918   TC          |   3.766    2.705 |   2.592     2.708  |
|  PC        -.0190   PC          |  11.606   13.551 |   5.859    10.184  |
|  EGTCAR    -.0549   EGT         |   6.469    9.348 |   3.958     4.634  |
+------------------------------------------------------------------------+
```

Thus, the toll cost has a mean of about 3.766 and varies from zero to about 9. So, a one unit change in the toll cost, TC actually is a reasonable experiment. We thus infer from our results that if the toll cost rises by 1, the probability of choosing to drive will fall by 1×0.02461. To complete this experiment, we note that in the sample of 175 individuals, 71 (or 41 percent) chose *cr*. So, the average probability is about 0.41, and increasing the toll by 1 would likely decrease the probability to 0.385, or roughly 67 individuals. So, this is a fairly substantial impact, though it is difficult to see that based on just the model coefficients, or even just the partial effects. A visualization is much more informative, which can be provided using the **Simulate** command in Nlogit, which we present in Section 13.4.

13.4 Simulation and "what if" scenarios

The simulation capability of Nlogit allows the analyst to use an existing model to test how changes in attributes and SDCs impact upon the choice probabilities for each of the alternatives. This requires a two-step process:

1. Estimate the model as previously described (automatically saving outputs in memory);
2. Apply the **Simulation** command (using the stored parameter estimates) to test how changes in the attribute and SDC levels impact upon the choice probabilities.

Step 1 involves the analyst specifying a choice model that will be used as a basis of comparison for subsequent simulations. The Step 2 involves performing the simulation to test how changes in an attribute or SDC impact upon the choice probabilities for the model estimated in step 1.

The **Simulation** command in Nlogit is as follows:

```
;Simulation = <list of alternatives>
;Scenario: <variable(alternative)> = <[action]magnitude of action>$
```

The **;simulation** command may be used in one of two ways. Firstly, the analyst may restrict the set of alternatives used in the simulation by specifying which alternatives are to be included. For example, the command:

```
;Simulation = bs,tn
```

will restrict the simulation to changes in the *bs* (bus) and *tn* (train) alternatives. All other alternatives will be ignored.

The analyst may include all alternatives by not specifically specifying any alternatives. Thus:

```
;Simulation
```

will have Nlogit perform the simulation on all alternatives specified within the = **<list of alternatives>** command.

The remainder of the command syntax instructs Nlogit on what changes to simulate. A number of points are required to be made. Firstly, the command begins with a semi colon (;) but the command **;scenario** is followed with a colon (:). Next the variable specified must be included within at least one of the utility functions and must belong to the alternative specified in the round brackets. It is possible to simulate a change in an attribute belonging to more than one alternative by specifying each alternative within the round brackets separated by a comma. Thus:

```
;Scenario: invt2(bs,tn)
```

will simulate a change in the invehicle time attribute of both the *bs* and *tn* alternatives.

The actions specifications are as follows:

= will be the specific value which the variable indicated is to take for each decision maker (e.g., **invt2(bs) = 20** will simulate invehicle time equal to 20 minutes for the *bus* alternative for all individuals); or

= [+] will add the value following to the observed value within the data for each decision maker (e.g., **invt2(bs = [+]20** will add 20 minutes to the observed value of the invehicle time attribute for the *bus* alternative for each individual); or

= [−] will subtract the value following from the observed value within the data for each decision maker (e.g., **invt2(bs) = [-]20** will subtract 20 minutes from the observed value of the invehicle time attribute for the *bus* alternative for each individual); or

= [*] will multiply the observed value within the data by the value following for each individual (e.g., **invt2 (bs)** = [*]**2.0** will double the observed value of the invehicle time attribute for the *bus* alternative for each decision maker); or

= [/] will divide the observed value within the data by the value following for each individual (e.g., **invt2 (bs)** = [/]**2.0** will halve the observed value of the invehicle time attribute for the *bus* alternative for each individual).

The **Simulation** command may specify that more than one attribute is to change, and changes may be different across alternatives. To specify more than one change, the command syntax is as above, however new scenarios are separated with a slash (/). We show this below:

```
;Simulation = <list of alternatives>
;Scenario: <variable1(alternativei)> = <[action]magnitude of action> /
<variablek(alternativej)> = <[action]magnitude of action> $
```

We use the following model specification to demonstrate Nlogit's simulation capability:

```
The initial Nlogit model is first estimated, and then the following model is estimated:
|-> Nlogit
    ;lhs = choice, cset, altij
    ;choices = bs,tn,bw,cr
    ;model:
    u(bs) = bs + actpt*act + invcpt*invc + invtpt*invt2 + egtpt*egt + trpt*trnf /
    u(tn) = tn + actpt*act + invcpt*invc + invtpt*invt2 + egtpt*egt + trpt*trnf /
    u(bw) = bw + actpt*act + invcpt*invc + invtpt*invt2 + egtpt*egt + trpt*trnf /
    u(cr) =                              invtcar*invt + TC*TC + PC*PC + egtcar*egt
    ;Simulation?;arc
    ;Scenario: invt2(bs,tn,bw) = 0.9 & invt2(bs,tn,bw) = 0.8 $
+----------------------------------------------------------------+
| Discrete Choice (One Level) Model                              |
| Model Simulation Using Previous Estimates                      |
| Number of observations                  197                    |
+----------------------------------------------------------------+

+-------------------------------------------------------------------- +
|Simulations of Probability Model                                    |
|Model: Discrete Choice (One Level) Model                            |
|Simulated choice set may be a subset of the choices.                |
|Number of individuals is the probability times the                  |
|number of observations in the simulated sample.                      |
|Column totals may be affected by rounding error.                     |
|The model used was simulated with   197 observations.|
+-------------------------------------------------------------------- +
```

```
Specification of scenario 1 is:
Attribute  Alternatives affected              Change type              Value
---------- ------------------------------------  ------------------------  ----------
INVT2      BS        TN        BW               Fix at new value          .900
---------------------------------------------------------------------------------

The simulator located    197 observations for this scenario.
Simulated Probabilities (shares) for this scenario:
+-------------- +-------------------+-------------------+------------------------ +
|Choice        |      Base         |     Scenario      | Scenario - Base        |
|              |%Share Number      |%Share Number      |ChgShare ChgNumber      |
+-------------- +-------------------+-------------------+------------------------ +
|BS            | 20.203      40 | 26.718      53 |  6.515%         13 |
|TN            | 31.126      61 | 32.596      64 |  1.470%          3 |
|BW            | 11.075      22 | 12.479      25 |  1.404%          3 |
|CR            | 37.596      74 | 28.207      56 | -9.389%        -18 |
|Total         |100.000     197 |100.000     198 |  .000%           1 |
+-------------- +-------------------+-------------------+------------------------ +
```

We leave it to the reader to interpret the output above, but note that we use this model as the basis for demonstrating the simulation capability that follows. The output generated is as follows. Note that even though the model is specified as before, Nlogit does not reproduce the standard results shown above. Only the simulation results shown below are produced.

The first output indicates the total number of observations available for use for the simulation. This should equate to the number of observations used in the base choice model. The next output box informs the analyst that the simulation may be performed on a subset of the available alternatives as specified with the **;simulation = <list of alternatives>** command. The remainder of the information provided by this output box informs the reader as to how to interpret the remainder of the simulation output.

The third output box instructs the analyst what simulation change(s) were modeled and which attributes and which alternatives those changes apply to. We leave it to the reader to discover which heading applies to which action.

The last Nlogit simulation output indicates how the actions specified in the simulation impact upon the choice shares for each of the alternatives. The first section of this output provides the base shares for the base or constants-only model (not to be confused with the base choice calibration model estimated at step 1 of the simulation). The third column of the output demonstrates how the changes specified by the analyst impact upon these base choice shares.

In the example, a reduction of invehicle time for bus, train, and busway to 90 percent of the *before* value will produce an estimated market share for the *bus* alternative of 26.718, up from 20.203, *ceteris paribus*. The same change will produce market shares of 32.596, 12.479, and 28.207 for the *train, busway,* and *car* alternatives, respectively, *ceteris paribus*.

The final column provides the change in choice shares for each of the alternatives both as a percent and in raw numbers for the sample. Thus, a reduction of invehicle time for bus, train, and busway to 90 percent of the *before* value, *ceteris paribus*, decreases the *car* share as a percent by 9.39, that translates to 18 of the original 71 choices for that alternative now switching to another alternative. Of these 13, 3, and 3 of those choices are predicted to switch to the bus, train, and busway alternatives, respectively. We ignore any rounding errors.

> *As an aside*, it is possible to conduct more than one simulation concurrently and compare the results of each simulation using Nlogit. To do so, the analyst separates the simulations within the scenario command by use of the **&** character, as we have done in the example. We show this below for two simulations, although it is possible to perform more than two. The comparisons generated are pairwise comparisons, and as such Nlogit will generate output comparing each possible combination of simulation scenario specified by the analyst.

13.4.1 The binary choice application

Using the model on binary choice in Section 13.3.5, we can get a more detailed picture of the impact of the toll cost on the choice of car versus non-car by computing the probabilities at different values of TC and examining the predicted probabilities. The command syntax is:

```
simulate ; if[altij=4];  scenario: & tc = 0(.5)10 ; plot(ci)$
```

This will simulate the choice probability for values of TC ranging from 0 to 10 in steps of 0.5, tabulate the results, and plot the average predicted probability with a confidence interval. These are the results:

```
-------------------------------------------------------------------
Model Simulation Analysis for Logit Probability Function
-------------------------------------------------------------------
Simulations are computed by average over sample observations
-------------------------------------------------------------------
User Function     Function   Standard
(Delta method)     Value      Error    |t|   95% Confidence Interval
-------------------------------------------------------------------
Avrg. Function    .40571     .03101   13.09    .34495     .46648
TC    =   .00     .50437     .06555    7.69    .37589     .63286
TC    =   .50     .49078     .05928    8.28    .37459     .60698
```

TC	=	1.00	.47717	.05326	8.96	.37279	.58155
TC	=	1.50	.46354	.04762	9.73	.37020	.55688
TC	=	2.00	.44993	.04259	10.56	.36644	.53341
TC	=	2.50	.43634	.03844	11.35	.36100	.51167
TC	=	3.00	.42279	.03547	11.92	.35328	.49231
TC	=	3.50	.40931	.03399	12.04	.34270	.47592
TC	=	4.00	.39591	.03414	11.60	.32900	.46281
TC	=	4.50	.38260	.03583	10.68	.31237	.45283
TC	=	5.00	.36941	.03879	9.52	.29337	.44544
TC	=	5.50	.35634	.04266	8.35	.27274	.43995
TC	=	6.00	.34343	.04711	7.29	.25110	.43575
TC	=	6.50	.33067	.05189	6.37	.22897	.43238
TC	=	7.00	.31810	.05682	5.60	.20673	.42947
TC	=	7.50	.30572	.06177	4.95	.18465	.42678
TC	=	8.00	.29354	.06663	4.41	.16295	.42414
TC	=	8.50	.28159	.07134	3.95	.14177	.42142
TC	=	9.00	.26988	.07584	3.56	.12123	.41852
TC	=	9.50	.25840	.08008	3.23	.10145	.41536
TC	= 10.00		.24719	.08404	2.94	.08247	.41190
TC	= 10.50		.23624	.08769	2.69	.06438	.40811

Figure 13.1 expands on our earlier results. We can see that at the average toll of about 3.8, the average predicted probability is about 0.4; we found 0.41 earlier. As the toll changes from 0 to 10, we can see the predicted probability falling from a bit over 0.5 down to about 0.25. We can see clearly, with these tools, the implication of the estimated model for the relationship between toll cost and the choice to drive versus not drive.

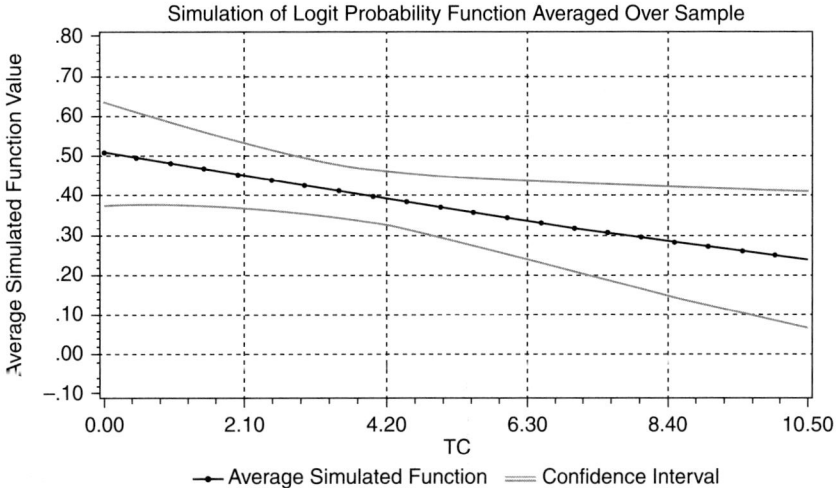

Figure 13.1 Experiment I: simulated scenario with confidence intervals

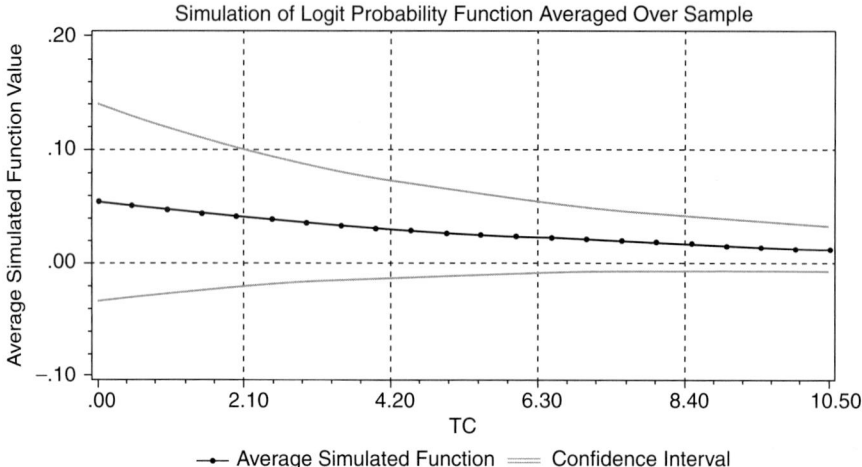

Figure 13.2 Experiment II: simulated scenario with confidence intervals

Consider another experiment (Figure 13.2). The (means, standard deviations) for invehicle time, parking cost, and egress time are (55,24), (12,14), and (6,9), respectively. The results above correspond roughly to the scenario at the means of these variables. We will try an experiment to see the impact of making driving extremely expensive in all dimensions by fixing these three attributes at the extreme values in the sample for everyone:

```
simulate ; if[altij=4]; scenario: & tc = 0(.5)10; plot(ci); set:invt=80,
pc=30,egt=25$
```

The scenario makes driving extremely unattractive.

13.4.2 Arc elasticities obtained using ;simulation

Since the simulated scenarios produce discrete changes in the probabilities from discrete changes in attributes, it is convenient to compute arc elasticities using the results. You can request estimates of arc elasticities in **;Simulation** by adding **;Arc** to the command. Like point elasticities, these be computed either unweighted or probability weighted by adding **;Pwt** to the command. If you include more than one scenario you will get additional output that compares the scenarios. The following results are produced by adding **;Arc** and running two scenarios:

```
|-> Nlogit
   ;lhs = choice, cset, altij
   ;choices = bs,tn,bw,cr
   ;model:
   u(bs) = bs + actpt*act + invcpt*invc + invtpt*invt2 + egtpt*egt + trpt*trnf /
   u(tn) = tn + actpt*act + invcpt*invc + invtpt*invt2 + egtpt*egt + trpt*trnf /
   u(bw) = bw + actpt*act + invcpt*invc + invtpt*invt2 + egtpt*egt + trpt*trnf /
   u(cr) =                            invtcar*invt + TC*TC + PC*PC + egtcar*egt
   ;Simulation;arc
   ;Scenario: invt2(bs,tn,bw) = 0.9 & invt2(bs,tn,bw) = 0.8 $
+------------------------------------------------------------+
| Discrete Choice (One Level) Model                          |
| Model Simulation Using Previous Estimates                  |
| Number of observations                    197              |
+------------------------------------------------------------+

+----------------------------------------------------------------------+
|Simulations of Probability Model                                      |
|Model: Discrete Choice (One Level) Model                              |
|Simulated choice set may be a subset of the choices.                  |
|Number of individuals is the probability times the                    |
|number of observations in the simulated sample.                       |
|Column totals may be affected by rounding error.                      |
|The model used was simulated with    197 observations.|
+----------------------------------------------------------------------+


------------------------------------------------------------------------------
Estimated Arc Elasticities Based on the Specified Scenario. Rows in the table
report 0.00 if the indicated attribute did not change in the scenario
or if the average probability or average attribute was zero in the sample.
Estimated values are averaged over all individuals used in the simulation.
Rows of the table in which no changes took place are not shown.
------------------------------------------------------------------------------
Attr Changed in | Change in Probability of Alternative
------------------------------------------------------------------------------
Choice BS       | BS        TN        BW        CR
   x = INVTPT   |   -.236    -.064     -.102      .192
Choice TN       | BS        TN        BW        CR
   x = INVTPT   |   -.218    -.065     -.104      .187
Choice BW       | BS        TN        BW        CR
   x = INVTPT   |   -.217    -.065     -.102      .186
Note, results above aggregate more than one change. They are not elasticities.
------------------------------------------------------------------------------


------------------------------------------------------------------------------
Specification of scenario 1 is:
Attribute   Alternatives affected          Change type            Value
-----------   ---------------------------------   -----------------------------   -----------
INVT2       BS       TN       BW          Fix at new value          .900
------------------------------------------------------------------------------
```

The simulator located   197 observations for this scenario.
Simulated Probabilities (shares) for this scenario:

Choice	Base		Scenario		Scenario - Base	
	%Share	Number	%Share	Number	ChgShare	ChgNumber
BS	20.203	40	26.718	53	6.515%	13
TN	31.126	61	32.596	64	1.470%	3
BW	11.075	22	12.479	25	1.404%	3
CR	37.596	74	28.207	56	-9.389%	-18
Total	100.000	197	100.000	198	.000%	1

Specification of scenario 2 is:

Attribute	Alternatives affected			Change type	Value
INVT2	BS	TN	BW	Fix at new value	.800

The simulator located   197 observations for this scenario.
Simulated Probabilities (shares) for this scenario:

Choice	Base		Scenario		Scenario - Base	
	%Share	Number	%Share	Number	ChgShare	ChgNumber
BS	20.203	40	26.725	53	6.522%	13
TN	31.126	61	32.604	64	1.478%	3
BW	11.075	22	12.482	25	1.407%	3
CR	37.596	74	28.189	56	-9.407%	-18
Total	100.000	197	100.000	198	.000%	1

The simulator located   197 observations for this scenario.
Pairwise Comparisons of Specified Scenarios
Base   for this comparison is scenario 1.
Scenario for this comparison is scenario 2.

Choice	Base		Scenario		Scenario - Base	
	%Share	Number	%Share	Number	ChgShare	ChgNumber
BS	26.718	53	26.725	53	.007%	0
TN	32.596	64	32.604	64	.008%	0
BW	12.479	25	12.482	25	.003%	0
CR	28.207	56	28.189	56	-.018%	0
Total	100.000	198	100.000	198	.000%	0

13.5 Weighting

It is not an uncommon practice for an analyst to weight data so that the data conforms to some prior view of the world. Consider an example where an analyst has sample data from a population for which census data (i.e., data on the entire population) is also available. While the research objective studied by the analyst may mean that the sample data collected will contain data on variables not included in the census data, any commonality in terms of variables collected between the two data sets may be used to re-weight the sample data to correspond with the distributions of the total population as observed in the census data.

The information held by the analyst may be used in one of two ways to weight the data. Firstly, if the information pertains to the true market shares of the alternatives, the weighting criteria to be applied is said to be *endogenous*, endogenous meaning internal to the choice response. The market shares for the alternatives are represented by the choice variable within the data set. If the information held by the analyst relates to any variable other than the choice variable, the weighting criteria to be applied is said to be *exogenous*, exogenous meaning external to the system. The distinction between **endogenous weighting** and **exogenous weighting** is important, as they are handled differently by Nlogit. We will now discuss both forms of weighting.

13.5.1 Endogenous weighting

In the case of discrete choice models, endogenous weighting of data occurs on the dependent choice variable and occurs when the analyst has information from other sources regarding the true market shares for each of the alternatives included within the model. This is of particular use when the analyst has employed choice-based weighting as the sampling technique.

The above should offer a clue as to the type of data in which the use of endogenous weighting should be employed. For stated preference (SP) data, the choice of alternative is made within the context of a choice set, and since different decision makers may observe different choice sets with alternatives assigned different attribute levels dependent upon the experimental design, the concept of true market shares is meaningless. Thus both endogenous weighting and choice-based sampling is meaningful solely within the context of RP data collection.

To apply endogenous weighting to a sample, a supplementary command syntax indicating the true market shares is attached to the **;choices = names of alternatives** command line. The additional command syntax is separated from the **;choices = names of alternatives** command by a slash (/), and the population market shares as proportions (summing exactly to 1.00) are assigned in the order of the alternatives as given in the **;choices = names of alternatives** syntax. The true shares are separated by a comma. We show this below:

NLOGIT
;lhs = choice, cset, altij
;choices = <names of alternatives> / <weight assigned to alt₁,> <weight assigned to alt₂,> ... , <weight assigned to altⱼ>
;Model:
U(<alternative 1 name>) = <utility function 1>
U(<alternative 2 name>) = <utility function 2>
...
U(<alternative i name>) = <utility function i$>

To demonstrate endogenous weighting, consider the following choice model where the population shares are given as 0.2, 0.3, 0.1, 0.4, respectively for bus, train, busway, and car:

```
|-> Nlogit
    ;lhs = choice, cset, altij
    ;choices = bs,tn,bw,cr /0.2,0.3,0.1,0.4
    ;show
    ;descriptives;crosstabs
    ;effects:invc(*)/invt2(bs,tn,bw)/invt(cr)/act[bs,tn,bw]
    ;full
    ;export=both
    ;pwt
    ;model:
    u(bs) = bs + actpt*act + invcpt*invc + invtpt*invt2 + egtpt*egt + trpt*trnf /
    u(tn) = tn + actpt*act + invcpt*invc + invtpt*invt2 + egtpt*egt + trpt*trnf /
    u(bw) = bw + actpt*act + invcpt*invc + invtpt*invt2 + egtpt*egt + trpt*trnf /
    u(cr) =                             invtcar*invt + TC*TC + PC*PC + egtcar*egt $
```

```
Sample proportions are marginal, not conditional.
Choices marked with * are excluded for the IIA test.
+---------------------+--------+------+
|Choice    (prop.) |Weight|IIA
+---------------------+--------+------+
|BS           .19289| 1.037|
|TN           .23350| 1.285|
|BW           .21320|  .469|
|CR           .36041| 1.110|
+---------------------+--------+------+
```

```
+-------------------------------------------------------------------------+
| Model Specification:  Table entry is the attribute that                 |
| multiplies the indicated parameter.                                     |
+-----------+--------+----------------------------------------------------+
| Choice    |******| Parameter                                            |
|           |Row  1| BS        ACTPT     INVCPT    INVTPT    EGTPT          |
|           |Row  2| TRPT      TN        BW        INVTCAR   TC             |
|           |Row  3| PC        EGTCAR                                      |
+-----------+--------+----------------------------------------------------+
|BS         |     1| Constant  ACT       INVC      INVT2     EGT            |
|           |     2| TRNF      none      none      none      none           |
|           |     3| none      none                                        |
|TN         |     1| none      ACT       INVC      INVT2     EGT            |
|           |     2| TRNF      Constant  none      none      none           |
|           |     3| none      none                                        |
|BW         |     1| none      ACT       INVC      INVT2     EGT            |
|           |     2| TRNF      none      Constant  none      none           |
|           |     3| none      none                                        |
|CR         |     1| none      none      none      none      none           |
|           |     2| none      none      none      INVT      TC             |
|           |     3| PC        EGT                                         |
+-------------------------------------------------------------------------+

Normal exit:  6 iterations. Status=0, F=    190.4789


-------------------------------------------------------------------------

Discrete choice (multinomial logit) model
Dependent variable            Choice
Log likelihood function      -190.47891
Estimation based on N =    197, K =  12
Inf.Cr.AIC  =    405.0 AIC/N =    2.056
R2=1-LogL/LogL* Log-L fncn R-sqrd R2Adj
Constants only must be computed directly
          Use NLOGIT ;...;RHS=ONE$
Chi-squared[ 9]          =    152.66810
Prob [ chi squared > value ] =   .00000
Vars. corrected for choice based sampling
Response data are given as ind. choices
Number of obs.=   197, skipped    0 obs
```

CHOICE	Coefficient	Standard Error	z	Prob. $\|z\|>Z^*$	95% Confidence Interval	
BS	-1.68661**	.74953	-2.25	.0244	-3.15566	-.21756
ACTPT	.04653***	.01667	0.79	.0065	.07000	.01253
INVCPT	-.08405	.07151	-1.18	.2399	-.22421	.05611
INVTPT	-.01368	.00840	-1.63	.1033	-.03013	.00278
EGTPT	-.04892*	.02934	-1.67	.0954	-.10642	.00858
TRPT	-1.07979***	.41033	-2.63	.0085	-1.88403	-.27555
TN	-1.39443*	.72606	-1.92	.0548	-2.81748	.02862

```
      BW|    -2.48469***      .74273     -3.35     .0008    -3.94041    -1.02897
 INVTCAR|     -.04847***      .01032     -4.70     .0000     -.06870     -.02825
      TC|     -.09183         .08020     -1.14     .2522     -.24902      .06537
      PC|     -.01899         .01635     -1.16     .2457     -.05104      .01307
  EGTCAR|     -.05489*        .03198     -1.72     .0861     -.11756      .00779
-----------+------------------------------------------------------------------------

***, **, * ==> Significance at 1%, 5%, 10% level.
Model was estimated on Aug 16, 2013 at 09:42:26 AM
------------------------------------------------------------------------------------
```

```
+--------------------------------------------------------------------------+
|              Descriptive Statistics for Alternative BS                    |
|    Utility Function          |                 |    38.0 observs.         |
|      Coefficient             | All     197.0 obs.|that chose BS           |
|   Name        Value  Variable | Mean    Std. Dev.|Mean       Std. Dev.    |
|  ------------------- ---------- |--------------------+------------------   |
|  BS         -1.6866  ONE       |   1.000     .000|   1.000      .000      |
|  ACTPT       -.0453  ACT       |   5.944    4.662|   5.053     4.312      |
|  INVCPT      -.0840  INVC      |   7.071    3.872|   7.237     6.015      |
|  INVTPT      -.0137  INVT2     |  71.797   43.551|  52.000    17.747      |
|  EGTPT       -.0489  EGT       |   8.680    7.331|   9.105    10.467      |
|  TRPT       -1.0798  TRNF      |    .442     .498|    .079      .273      |
+--------------------------------------------------------------------------+
```

```
+--------------------------------------------------------------------------+
|              Descriptive Statistics for Alternative TN                    |
|    Utility Function          |                 |    46.0 observs.         |
|      Coefficient             | All     187.0 obs.|that chose TN           |
|   Name        Value  Variable | Mean    Std. Dev.|Mean       Std. Dev.    |
|  ------------------- ---------- |--------------------+------------------   |
|  ACTPT       -.0453  ACT       |  16.016    8.401|  15.239     6.651      |
|  INVCPT      -.0840  INVC      |   4.947    2.451|   4.065     2.435      |
|  INVTPT      -.0137  INVT2     |  45.257   15.421|  43.630     9.903      |
|  EGTPT       -.0489  EGT       |   8.882    6.788|   7.196     5.714      |
|  TRPT       -1.0798  TRNF      |    .230     .422|    .174      .383      |
|  TN         -1.3944  ONE       |   1.000     .000|   1.000      .000      |
+--------------------------------------------------------------------------+
```

```
+--------------------------------------------------------------------------+
|              Descriptive Statistics for Alternative BW                    |
|    Utility Function          |                 |    42.0 observs.         |
|      Coefficient             | All     188.0 obs.|that chose BW           |
|   Name        Value  Variable | Mean    Std. Dev.|Mean       Std. Dev.    |
|  ------------------- ---------- |--------------------+------------------   |
|  ACTPT       -.0453  ACT       |  10.707   17.561|   5.405     4.854      |
|  INVCPT      -.0840  INVC      |   7.000    3.599|   6.405     1.345      |
|  INVTPT      -.0137  INVT2     |  50.904   20.300|  54.643    15.036      |
|  EGTPT       -.0489  EGT       |  10.027    9.811|   8.286     5.932      |
|  TRPT       -1.0798  TRNF      |    .271     .446|    .095      .297      |
|  BW         -2.4847  ONE       |   1.000     .000|   1.000      .000      |
+--------------------------------------------------------------------------+
```

```
+-------------------------------------------------------------------+
|          Descriptive Statistics for Alternative CR                |
|    Utility Function      |             |        71.0 observs.      |
|     Coefficient          | All    175.0 obs.|that chose CR         |
|  Name      Value  Variable| Mean     Std. Dev.|Mean     Std. Dev.  |
|  ---------------- ---------- | ------------------ +------------------ |
|  INVTCAR  -.0485  INVT    |  55.406    24.166| 43.324   15.839    |
|  TC       -.0918  TC      |   3.766     2.705|  2.592    2.708    |
|  PC       -.0190  PC      |  11.606    13.551|  5.859   10.184    |
|  EGTCAR   -.0549  EGT     |   6.469     9.348|  3.958    4.634    |
+-------------------------------------------------------------------+
```

```
+------------------------------------------------------------+
| Cross tabulation of actual choice vs. predicted P(j)       |
| Row indicator is actual, column is predicted.              |
| Predicted total is F(k,j,i)=Sum(i=1,...,N) P(k,j,i).       |
| Column totals may be subject to rounding error.            |
+------------------------------------------------------------+
```

```
-----------+-------------------------------------------------------
NLOGIT Cross Tabulation for 4 outcome Multinomial Choice Model
XTab_Prb|       BS         TN         BW         CR        Total
-----------+-------------------------------------------------------
     BS|   12.0000    12.0000    4.00000    10.0000    38.0000
     TN|   10.0000    19.0000    5.00000    12.0000    46.0000
     BW|   9.00000    18.0000    8.00000    7.00000    42.0000
     CR|   8.00000    13.0000    5.00000    45.0000    71.0000
  Total|   40.0000    61.0000    22.0000    74.0000    197.000
```

```
+-------------------------------------------------------------+
| Cross tabulation of actual y(ij) vs. predicted y(ij)        |
| Row indicator is actual, column is predicted.               |
| Predicted total is N(k,j,i)=Sum(i=1,...,N) Y(k,j,i).        |
| Predicted y(ij)=1 is the j with largest probability.        |
+-------------------------------------------------------------+
```

```
-----------+-------------------------------------------------------
NLOGIT Cross Tabulation for 4 outcome Multinomial Choice Model
XTab_Frq|       BS         TN         BW         CR        Total
-----------+-------------------------------------------------------
     BS|   13.0000    13.0000    .000000    12.0000    38.0000
     TN|   8.00000    22.0000    2.00000    14.0000    46.0000
     BW|   8.00000    24.0000    2.00000    8.00000    42.0000
     CR|   5.00000    10.0000    .000000    56.0000    71.0000
  Total|   34.0000    69.0000    4.00000    90.0000    197.000
```

```
+------------------------------------------------------------+
| Derivative           averaged over observations.           |
| Effects on probabilities of all choices in model:          |
| * = Direct Derivative effect of the attribute.             |
+------------------------------------------------------------+
```

```
-----------------------------------------------------------------------------------------
Average elasticity      of prob(alt) wrt INVC      in BS
----------+------------------------------------------------------------------------------
          |                    Standard               Prob.        95% Confidence
   Choice | Coefficient        Error        z        |z|>Z*          Interval
----------+------------------------------------------------------------------------------
      BS  |   -.36240***        .01748    -20.73      .0000        -.39666     -.32813
      TN  |    .10679***        .00573     18.64      .0000         .09556      .11801
      BW  |    .12445***        .00619     20.11      .0000         .11232      .13658
      CR  |    .06967***        .00548     12.72      .0000         .05894      .08041
----------+------------------------------------------------------------------------------
***, **, * ==>  Significance at 1%, 5%, 10% level.
Model was estimated on Aug 16, 2013 at 09:42:27 AM
-----------------------------------------------------------------------------------------

-----------------------------------------------------------------------------------------
Average elasticity      of prob(alt) wrt INVC      in TN
----------+------------------------------------------------------------------------------
          |                    Standard               Prob.        95% Confidence
   Choice | Coefficient        Error        z        |z|>Z*          Interval
----------+------------------------------------------------------------------------------
      BS  |    .10998***        .00549     20.04      .0000         .09923      .12073
      TN  |   -.21858***        .01046    -20.90      .0000        -.23908     -.19809
      BW  |    .14703***        .00647     22.71      .0000         .13434      .15972
      CR  |    .07856***        .00575     13.67      .0000         .06730      .08982
----------+------------------------------------------------------------------------------
***, **, * ==>  Significance at 1%, 5%, 10% level.
Model was estimated on Aug 16, 2013 at 09:42:27 AM
-----------------------------------------------------------------------------------------

-----------------------------------------------------------------------------------------
Average elasticity      of prob(alt) wrt INVC      in BW
----------+------------------------------------------------------------------------------
          |                    Standard               Prob.        95% Confidence
   Choice | Coefficient        Error        z        |z|>Z*          Interval
----------+------------------------------------------------------------------------------
      BS  |    .06621***        .00336     19.73      .0000         .05963      .07279
      TN  |    .07187***        .00356     20.19      .0000         .06490      .07885
      BW  |   -.44186***        .01090    -40.53      .0000        -.46323     -.42050
      CR  |    .03508***        .00256     13.69      .0000         .03005      .04010
----------+------------------------------------------------------------------------------
***, **, * ==>  Significance at 1%, 5%, 10% level.
Model was estimated on Aug 16, 2013 at 09:42:27 AM
-----------------------------------------------------------------------------------------

-----------------------------------------------------------------------------------------
Average elasticity      of prob(alt) wrt INVT2     in BS
----------+------------------------------------------------------------------------------
          |                    Standard               Prob.        95% Confidence
   Choice | Coefficient        Error        z        |z|>Z*          Interval
----------+------------------------------------------------------------------------------
      BS  |   -.53699***        .02234    -24.03      .0000        -.58078     -.49320
```

```
    TN|    .16167***    .00725    22.29    .0000    .14746    .17588
    BW|    .18748***    .00803    23.35    .0000    .17174    .20322
    CR|    .09949***    .00562    17.69    .0000    .08846    .11051
-----------+------------------------------------------------------------------
```

***, **, * ==> Significance at 1%, 5%, 10% level.
Model was estimated on Aug 16, 2013 at 09:42:28 AM

Average elasticity   of prob(alt) wrt INVT2   in TN
-----------+--

| | | Standard | | Prob. | 95% Confidence |
Choice	Coefficient	Error	z	|z|>Z*	Interval
BS	.17929***	.00722	24.83	.0000	.16514	.19345
TN	-.32857***	.01242	-26.46	.0000	-.35292	-.30423
BW	.22322***	.00848	26.34	.0000	.20661	.23983
CR	.10993***	.00684	16.07	.0000	.09652	.12334

***, **, * ==> Significance at 1%, 5%, 10% level.
Model was estimated on Aug 16, 2013 at 09:42:28 AM

Average elasticity   of prob(alt) wrt INVT2   in BW
-----------+--

| | | Standard | | Prob. | 95% Confidence |
Choice	Coefficient	Error	z	|z|>Z*	Interval
BS	.08354***	.00430	19.41	.0000	.07510	.09198
TN	.09170***	.00461	19.87	.0000	.08265	.10074
BW	-.55150***	.01554	-35.48	.0000	-.58197	-.52104
CR	.04165***	.00308	13.54	.0000	.03562	.04768

***, **, * ==> Significance at 1%, 5%, 10% level.
Model was estimated on Aug 16, 2013 at 09:42:28 AM

Average elasticity   of prob(alt) wrt INVT   in CR
-----------+--

| | | Standard | | Prob. | 95% Confidence |
Choice	Coefficient	Error	z	|z|>Z*	Interval
BS	.55295***	.03454	16.01	.0000	.48525	.62064
TN	.55344***	.03597	15.39	.0000	.48295	.62394
DW	.53235***	.03500	15.21	.0000	.46376	.60094
CR	-.91217***	.06191	-14.73	.0000	-1.03351	-.79084

***, **, * ==> Significance at 1%, 5%, 10% level.
Model was estimated on Aug 16, 2013 at 09:42:28 AM

```
------------------------------------------------------------------------------
Average partial effect  on prob(alt) wrt ACT      in BS
----------- +-----------------------------------------------------------------
           |                 Standard            Prob.       95% Confidence
  Choice| Coefficient      Error       z      |z|>Z*         Interval
----------- +-----------------------------------------------------------------
      BS|   -.00857***      .00020    -43.20   .0000    -.00896    -.00818
      TN|    .00350***      .00017     20.71   .0000     .00317     .00383
      BW|    .00184***      .00011     16.76   .0000     .00162     .00205
      CR|    .00277***      .00014     19.80   .0000     .00249     .00304
----------- +-----------------------------------------------------------------
***, **, * ==>  Significance at 1%, 5%, 10% level.
Model was estimated on Aug 16, 2013 at 09:42:28 AM
------------------------------------------------------------------------------
```

```
------------------------------------------------------------------------------
Average partial effect  on prob(alt) wrt ACT      in TN
----------- +-----------------------------------------------------------------
           |                 Standard            Prob.       95% Confidence
  Choice| Coefficient      Error       z      |z|>Z*         Interval
----------- +-----------------------------------------------------------------
      BS|    .00416***      .00018     23.04   .0000     .00381     .00451
      TN|   -.00939***      .00014    -66.97   .0000    -.00966    -.00911
      BW|    .00316***      .00017     18.66   .0000     .00282     .00349
      CR|    .00385***      .00017     22.06   .0000     .00351     .00419
----------- +-----------------------------------------------------------------
***, **, * ==>  Significance at 1%, 5%, 10% level.
Model was estimated on Aug 16, 2013 at 09:42:28 AM
------------------------------------------------------------------------------
```

```
------------------------------------------------------------------------------
Average partial effect  on prob(alt) wrt ACT      in BW
----------- +-----------------------------------------------------------------
           |                 Standard            Prob.       95% Confidence
  Choice| Coefficient      Error       z      |z|>Z*         Interval
----------- +-----------------------------------------------------------------
      BS|    .00195***      .00011     17.31   .0000     .00173     .00217
      TN|    .00276***      .00015     18.60   .0000     .00247     .00305
      BW|   -.00620***      .00018    -35.10   .0000    -.00654    -.00585
      CR|    .00131***    .7888D-04    16.58   .0000     .00115     .00146
----------- +-----------------------------------------------------------------
nnnnn.D-xx or D+xx => multiply by 10 to -xx or +xx.
***, **, * ==>  Significance at 1%, 5%, 10% level.
Model was estimated on Aug 16, 2013 at 09:42:28 AM
------------------------------------------------------------------------------
Elasticity wrt change of X in row choice on Prob[column choice]
----------- +-------------------------------------------------
INVC   |      BS        TN       BW        CR
----------- +-------------------------------------------------
      BS|   -.3624     .1068     .1245     .0697
      TN|    .1100    -.2186     .1470     .0786
      BW|    .0662     .0719    -.4419     .0351
```

```
Elasticity wrt change of X in row choice on Prob[column choice]
-----------+-----------------------------------------------------
INVT2   |       BS        TN        BW        CR
-----------+-----------------------------------------------------
     BS|   -.5370     .1617     .1875     .0995
     TN|    .1793    -.3286     .2232     .1099
     BW|    .0835     .0917    -.5515     .0417


Elasticity wrt change of X in row choice on Prob[column choice]
-----------+-----------------------------------------------------
INVT    |       BS        TN        BW        CR
-----------+-----------------------------------------------------
     CR|    .5529     .5534     .5323    -.9122


Derivative wrt change of X in row choice on Prob[column choice]
-----------+-----------------------------------------------------
ACT     |       BS        TN        BW        CR
-----------+-----------------------------------------------------
     BS|   -.0086     .0035     .0018     .0028
     TN|    .0042    -.0094     .0032     .0039
     BW|    .0019     .0028    -.0062     .0013
```

The findings can be compared to those presented earlier throughout the chapter where we have not used endogenous weighting. There are some notable differences in the key behavioral outputs. We leave it to the reader to explore the differences, but note that endogenous weighting can often make a significant difference to findings such as elasticities and market share changes resulting from a scenario application.

However, we want to draw the reader's attention to the choice proportions given in the ;**show** command output. Given that this model is estimated with RP data, assuming some form of random sampling, the choice proportions should equal the actual market shares for each of the alternatives.

13.5.2 Weighting on an exogenous variable

The above discourse relates to the weighting of data for choice analysis based on the choice variable of that data. Weighting data on any variable other than the choice variable requires a different approach. The Nlogit command for exogenous weighting is:

```
;wts = <name of weighting variable>
```

We have chosen to weight the data by gender. The exogenous weighting command is included in the model and the full set of results is again presented. You can compare the findings with the initial model outputs and the ones where endogenous weighting was used above:

```
|-> Nlogit
    ;lhs = choice, cset, altij
    ;choices = bs,tn,bw,cr? /0.2,0.3,0.1,0.4
    ;show
    ;descriptives;crosstabs
    ;effects:invc(*)/invt2(bs,tn,bw)/invt(cr)/act[bs,tn,bw]
    ;full
    ;export=both
    ;pwt
    ;wts=gender
    ;model:
    u(bs) = bs + actpt*act + invcpt*invc + invtpt*invt2 + egtpt*egt + trpt*trnf /
    u(tn) = tn + actpt*act + invcpt*invc + invtpt*invt2 + egtpt*egt + trpt*trnf /
    u(bw) = bw + actpt*act + invcpt*invc + invtpt*invt2 + egtpt*egt + trpt*trnf /
    u(cr) =                                invtcar*invt + TC*TC + PC*PC + egtcar*egt $
```

Sample proportions are marginal, not conditional.
Choices marked with * are excluded for the IIA test.

```
+---------------------+---------+------
|Choice    (prop.)|Weight|IIA
+---------------------+---------+------
|BS         .21429| 1.000|
|TN         .24490| 1.000|
|BW         .24490| 1.000|
|CR         .29592| 1.000|
+---------------------+---------+------
```

```
+----------------------------------------------------------------------------------- +
| Model Specification:  Table entry is the attribute that        |
| multiplies the indicated parameter.                            |
+-----------+--------+-----------------------------------------------------------+
| Choice  |******| Parameter                                                 |
|         |Row  1| BS        ACTPT     INVCPT    INVTPT    EGTPT     |
|         |Row  2| TRPT      TN        BW        INVTCAR   TC        |
|         |Row  3| PC        EGTCAR                                 |
+-----------+--------+-----------------------------------------------------------+
|BS       |      1| Constant ACT       INVC      INVT2     EGT       |
|         |      2| TRNF      none      none      none      none      |
|         |      3| none      none                                    |
|TN       |      1| none      ACT       INVC      INVT2     EGT       |
|         |      2| TRNF      Constant none      none      none      |
|         |      3| none      none                                    |
|BW       |      1| none      ACT       INVC      INVT2     EGT       |
|         |      2| TRNF      none      Constant none      none      |
|         |      3| none      none                                    |
|CR       |      1| none      none      none      none      none      |
|         |      2| none      none      none      INVT      TC        |
|         |      3| PC        EGT                                    |
+----------------------------------------------------------------------------------- +
```

Normal exit: 6 iterations. Status=0, F=   100.0337

```
-------------------------------------------------------------------------------
Discrete choice (multinomial logit) model
Dependent variable              Choice
Weighting variable              GENDER
Log likelihood function     -100.03373
Estimation based on N =      197, K =   12
Inf.Cr.AIC  =     224.1 AIC/N =     1.137
R2=1-LogL/LogL* Log-L fncn R-sqrd R2Adj
Constants only must be computed directly
              Use NLOGIT ;...;RHS=ONE$
Chi-squared[ 9]         =      70.31989
Prob [ chi squared > value ] =   .00000
Response data are given as ind. choices
Number of obs.=   197, skipped     0 obs
```

```
----------+---------------------------------------------------------------------
          |              Standard            Prob.      95% Confidence
   CHOICE | Coefficient    Error      z     |z|>Z*        Interval
----------+---------------------------------------------------------------------
       BS |  -2.83181**    1.33516   -2.12   .0339    -5.44867    -.21495
    ACTPT |   -.06195**     .02505   -2.47   .0134     -.11105    -.01284
   INVCPT |   -.07101       .05536   -1.28   .1996     -.17952     .03750
   INVTPT |   -.00740       .01222    -.60   .5452     -.03136     .01657
    EGTPT |   -.04317       .02651   -1.63   .1035     -.09513     .00879
     TRPT |  -1.45832**     .57124   -2.55   .0107    -2.57794    -.33870
       TN |  -2.60598**    1.30510   -2.00   .0459    -5.16394    -.04802
       BW |  -2.72118**    1.31273   -2.07   .0382    -5.29409    -.14828
   INVTCAR|   -.06989***    .02210   -3.16   .0016     -.11320    -.02659
       TC |   -.11222       .13550    -.83   .4075     -.37780     .15335
       PC |   -.00487       .02631    -.18   .8533     -.05643     .04670
    EGTCAR|   -.11837*      .06617   -1.79   .0736     -.24805     .01132
----------+---------------------------------------------------------------------
```

```
***, **, * ==>  Significance at 1%, 5%, 10% level.
Model was estimated on Aug 16, 2013 at 09:44:20 AM
-------------------------------------------------------------------------------
```

```
+---------------------------------------------------------------------------- +
|          Descriptive Statistics for Alternative BS                          |
|    Utility Function          |                  |    38.0 observs.          |
|    Coefficient               | All      197.0 obs.|that chose BS            |
| Name       Value  Variable   | Mean     Std. Dev.|Mean       Std. Dev.     |
| -----------------------      | ---------------------+----------------------- |
| BS         -2.8318  ONE      | 1.000      .000|  1.000        .000        |
| ACTPT       -.0619  ACT      | 5.944     4.662|  5.053       4.312        |
| INVCPT      -.0710  INVC     | 7.071     3.872|  7.237       6.015        |
| INVTPT      -.0074  INVT2    | 71.797   43.551| 52.000      17.747        |
| EGTPT       -.0432  EGT      | 8.680     7.331|  9.105      10.467        |
| TRPT       -1.4583  TRNF     |  .442      .498|   .079        .273        |
+---------------------------------------------------------------------------- +
```

```
+-------------------------------------------------------------------------+
|              Descriptive Statistics for Alternative TN                  |
|      Utility Function        |                   |   46.0 observs.      |
|        Coefficient           | All      187.0 obs.|that chose TN         |
|  Name        Value  Variable | Mean     Std. Dev.|Mean        Std. Dev. |
|  ----------------   -------- | ----------------- +--------------------- |
|  ACTPT      -.0619  ACT      | 16.016      8.401| 15.239        6.651   |
|  INVCPT     -.0710  INVC     |  4.947      2.451|  4.065        2.435   |
|  INVTPT     -.0074  INVT2    | 45.257     15.421| 43.630        9.903   |
|  EGTPT      -.0432  EGT      |  8.882      6.788|  7.196        5.714   |
|  TRPT      -1.4583  TRNF     |   .230       .422|   .174         .383   |
|  TN        -2.6060  ONE      | 1.000       .000| 1.000          .000   |
+-------------------------------------------------------------------------+


+-------------------------------------------------------------------------+
|              Descriptive Statistics for Alternative BW                  |
|      Utility Function        |                   |   42.0 observs.      |
|        Coefficient           | All      188.0 obs.|that chose BW         |
|  Name        Value  Variable | Mean     Std. Dev.|Mean        Std. Dev. |
|  ----------------   -------- | ----------------- +--------------------- |
|  ACTPT      -.0619  ACT      | 10.707     17.561|  5.405        4.854   |
|  INVCPT     -.0710  INVC     |  7.000      3.599|  6.405        1.345   |
|  INVTPT     -.0074  INVT2    | 50.904     20.300| 54.643       15.036   |
|  EGTPT      -.0432  EGT      | 10.027      9.811|  8.286        5.932   |
|  TRPT      -1.4583  TRNF     |   .271       .446|   .095         .297   |
|  BW        -2.7212  ONE      | 1.000       .000| 1.000          .000   |
+-------------------------------------------------------------------------+


+-------------------------------------------------------------------------+
|              Descriptive Statistics for Alternative CR                  |
|      Utility Function        |                   |   71.0 observs.      |
|        Coefficient           | All      175.0 obs.|that chose CR         |
|  Name        Value  Variable | Mean     Std. Dev.|Mean        Std. Dev. |
|  ----------------   -------- | ----------------- +--------------------- |
|  INVTCAR    -.0699  INVT     | 55.406     24.166| 43.324       15.839   |
|  TC         -.1122  TC       |  3.766      2.705|  2.592        2.708   |
|  PC         -.0049  PC       | 11.606     13.551|  5.859       10.184   |
|  EGTCAR     -.1184  EGT      |  6.469      9.348|  3.958        4.634   |
+-------------------------------------------------------------------------+


+-------------------------------------------------------------+
| Cross tabulation of actual choice vs. predicted P(j)        |
| Row indicator is actual, column is predicted.               |
| Predicted total is F(k,j,i)=Sum(i=1,...,N) P(k,j,i).        |
| Column totals may be subject to rounding error.             |
+-------------------------------------------------------------+
```

```
----------+----------------------------------------------------------------
NLOGIT Cross Tabulation for 4 outcome Multinomial Choice Model
XTab_Prb|        BS           TN           BW           CR          Total
----------+----------------------------------------------------------------
      BS|    12.0000      9.00000      9.00000      8.00000      38.0000
      TN|    11.0000     15.0000      11.0000      8.00000      46.0000
      BW|    8.00000     12.0000      17.0000      4.00000      42.0000
      CR|    9.00000     10.0000      11.0000      41.0000      71.0000
   Total|    40.0000     47.0000      49.0000      61.0000      197.000
```

```
+-----------------------------------------------------------------+
| Cross tabulation of actual y(ij) vs. predicted y(ij) |
| Row indicator is actual, column is predicted.        |
| Predicted total is N(k,j,i)=Sum(i=1,...,N) Y(k,j,i). |
| Predicted y(ij)=1 is the j with largest probability. |
+-----------------------------------------------------------------+
```

```
----------+----------------------------------------------------------------
NLOGIT Cross Tabulation for 4 outcome Multinomial Choice Model
XTab_Frq|        BS           TN           BW           CR          Total
----------+----------------------------------------------------------------
      BS|    12.0000      9.00000      7.00000      10.0000      38.0000
      TN|    9.00000     15.0000      11.0000      11.0000      46.0000
      BW|    1.00000     9.00000      29.0000      3.00000      42.0000
      CR|    2.00000     5.00000      11.0000      53.0000      71.0000
   Total|    24.0000     38.0000      58.0000      77.0000      197.000
```

```
+---------------------------------------------------------------+
| Derivative           averaged over observations.|
| Effects on probabilities of all choices in model: |
| * = Direct Derivative effect of the attribute.    |
+---------------------------------------------------------------+
```

```
------------------------------------------------------------------------------
Average elasticity      of prob(alt) wrt INVC      in BS
----------+------------------------------------------------------------------
          |              Standard           Prob.     95% Confidence
   Choice| Coefficient    Error       z    |z|>Z*       Interval
----------+------------------------------------------------------------------
      BS|   -.31580***    .01558   -20.27   .0000    -.34634    -.28526
      TN|    .09303***    .00644    14.44   .0000     .08041     .10566
      BW|    .09952***    .00505    19.71   .0000     .08963     .10942
      CR|    .05877***    .00684     8.59   .0000     .04537     .07218
----------+------------------------------------------------------------------
*** , ** , * ==> Significance at 1%, 5%, 10% level.
Model was estimated on Aug 16, 2013 at 09:44:21 AM
------------------------------------------------------------------------------
```

```
--------------------------------------------------------------------------------
Average elasticity      of prob(alt) wrt INVC      in TN
----------+---------------------------------------------------------------------
          |               Standard             Prob.        95% Confidence
  Choice|  Coefficient    Error       z      |z|>Z*          Interval
----------+---------------------------------------------------------------------
    BS|    .06945***      .00431    16.10    .0000      .06100     .07791
    TN|   -.21258***      .00930   -22.86    .0000     -.23080    -.19436
    BW|    .08800***      .00475    18.51    .0000      .07868     .09731
    CR|    .04771***      .00386    12.36    .0000      .04014     .05527
----------+---------------------------------------------------------------------
***, **, * ==>  Significance at 1%, 5%, 10% level.
Model was estimated on Aug 16, 2013 at 09:44:21 AM
--------------------------------------------------------------------------------


--------------------------------------------------------------------------------
Average elasticity      of prob(alt) wrt INVC      in BW
----------+---------------------------------------------------------------------
          |               Standard             Prob.        95% Confidence
  Choice|  Coefficient    Error       z      |z|>Z*          Interval
----------+---------------------------------------------------------------------
    BS|    .11703***      .00566    20.68    .0000      .10593     .12812
    TN|    .12681***      .00560    22.65    .0000      .11584     .13779
    BW|   -.29347***      .00942   -31.14    .0000     -.31194    -.27500
    CR|    .05798***      .00473    12.24    .0000      .04870     .06726
----------+---------------------------------------------------------------------
***, **, * ==>  Significance at 1%, 5%, 10% level.
Model was estimated on Aug 16, 2013 at 09:44:21 AM
--------------------------------------------------------------------------------
--------------------------------------------------------------------------------
Average elasticity      of prob(alt) wrt INVT2      in BS
----------+---------------------------------------------------------------------
          |               Standard             Prob.        95% Confidence
  Choice|  Coefficient    Error       z      |z|>Z*          Interval
----------+---------------------------------------------------------------------
    BS|   -.29476***      .01229   -23.97    .0000     -.31886    -.27066
    TN|    .08683***      .00398    21.84    .0000      .07904     .09463
    BW|    .09679***      .00430    22.51    .0000      .08836     .10521
    CR|    .05176***      .00316    16.39    .0000      .04557     .05795
----------+---------------------------------------------------------------------
***, **, * ==>  Significance at 1%, 5%, 10% level.
Model was estimated on Aug 16, 2013 at 09:44:21 AM
--------------------------------------------------------------------------------


--------------------------------------------------------------------------------
Average elasticity      of prob(alt) wrt INVT2      in TN
----------+---------------------------------------------------------------------
          |               Standard             Prob.        95% Confidence
  Choice|  Coefficient    Error       z      |z|>Z*          Interval
----------+---------------------------------------------------------------------
    BS|    .07183***      .00339    21.17    .0000      .06519     .07848
```

```
TN|    -.20345***     .00667    -30.52    .0000    -.21652    -.19039
BW|     .08449***     .00382     22.15    .0000     .07701     .09197
CR|     .04188***     .00301     13.92    .0000     .03598     .04778
----------+----------------------------------------------------------------
```
***, **, * ==> Significance at 1%, 5%, 10% level.
Model was estimated on Aug 16, 2013 at 09:44:21 AM

Average elasticity   of prob(alt) wrt INVT2   in BW

Choice	Coefficient	Standard Error	z	Prob. |z|>Z*	95% Confidence Interval	
BS	.09563***	.00483	19.82	.0000	.08618	.10509
TN	.10477***	.00524	19.98	.0000	.09449	.11505
BW	-.23755***	.00775	-30.64	.0000	-.25275	-.22235
CR	.04470***	.00385	11.59	.0000	.03714	.05225

***, **, * ==> Significance at 1%, 5%, 10% level.
Model was estimated on Aug 16, 2013 at 09:44:21 AM

Average elasticity   of prob(alt) wrt INVT   in CR

Choice	Coefficient	Standard Error	z	Prob. |z|>Z*	95% Confidence Interval	
BS	.57281***	.04751	12.06	.0000	.47968	.66594
TN	.55769***	.04869	11.45	.0000	.46226	.65312
BW	.50559***	.04303	11.75	.0000	.42125	.58994
CR	-1.21166***	.08014	-15.12	.0000	-1.36873	-1.05459

***, **, * ==> Significance at 1%, 5%, 10% level.
Model was estimated on Aug 16, 2013 at 09:44:22 AM

Average partial effect on prob(alt) wrt ACT   in BS

Choice	Coefficient	Standard Error	z	Prob. |z|>Z*	95% Confidence Interval	
BS	-.01172***	.00028	-42.57	.0000	-.01226	-.01118
TN	.00385***	.00020	19.21	.0000	.00346	.00424
BW	.00463***	.00025	18.83	.0000	.00415	.00511
CR	.00347***	.00019	18.21	.0000	.00309	.00384

***, **, * ==> Significance at 1%, 5%, 10% level.
Model was estimated on Aug 16, 2013 at 09:44:22 AM

```
-----------------------------------------------------------------------------
Average partial effect  on prob(alt) wrt ACT       in TN
-----------+-----------------------------------------------------------------
           |                Standard              Prob.      95% Confidence
    Choice | Coefficient     Error        z      |z|>Z*         Interval
-----------+-----------------------------------------------------------------
       BS|   .00413***      .00020     20.41    .0000      .00373    .00453
       TN|  -.01225***      .00023    -53.37    .0000     -.01269   -.01180
       BW|   .00576***      .00028     20.80    .0000      .00522    .00630
       CR|   .00370***      .00021     17.76    .0000      .00329    .00410
-----------+-----------------------------------------------------------------
***, **, * ==>  Significance at 1%, 5%, 10% level.
Model was estimated on Aug 16, 2013 at 09:44:22 AM
-----------------------------------------------------------------------------

-----------------------------------------------------------------------------
Average partial effect  on prob(alt) wrt ACT       in BW
-----------+-----------------------------------------------------------------
           |                Standard              Prob.      95% Confidence
    Choice | Coefficient     Error        z      |z|>Z*         Interval
-----------+-----------------------------------------------------------------
       BS|   .00513***      .00025     20.13    .0000      .00463    .00563
       TN|   .00594***      .00029     20.59    .0000      .00537    .00650
       BW|  -.01279***      .00021    -60.05    .0000     -.01321   -.01237
       CR|   .00311***      .00020     15.83    .0000      .00272    .00349
-----------+-----------------------------------------------------------------
***, **, * ==>  Significance at 1%, 5%, 10% level.
Model was estimated on Aug 16, 2013 at 09:44:22 AM
-----------------------------------------------------------------------------


Elasticity wrt change of X in row choice on Prob[column choice]
-----------+-------------------------------------------------
INVC     |      BS        TN        BW        CR
-----------+-------------------------------------------------
       BS|   -.3158     .0930     .0995     .0588
       TN|    .0695    -.2126     .0880     .0477
       BW|    .1170     .1268    -.2935     .0580

Elasticity wrt change of X in row choice on Prob[column choice]
-----------+-------------------------------------------------
INVT2    |      BS        TN        BW        CR
-----------+-------------------------------------------------
       BS|   -.2948     .0868     .0968     .0518
       TN|    .0718    -.2035     .0845     .0419
       BW|    .0956     .1048    -.2376     .0447

Elasticity wrt change of X in row choice on Prob[column choice]
-----------+-------------------------------------------------
INVT     |      BS        TN        BW        CR
-----------+-------------------------------------------------
       CR|    .5728     .5577     .5056   -1.2117
```

```
Derivative wrt change of X in row choice on Prob[column choice]
-----------+-----------------------------------------------------
ACT        |      BS        TN        BW        CR
-----------+-----------------------------------------------------
        BS|  -.0117     .0039     .0046     .0035
        TN|   .0041    -.0122     .0058     .0037
        BW|   .0051     .0059    -.0128     .0031
```

The only indication provided by Nlogit to suggest that exogenous weighting has occurred is shown in the following line of output, in which Nlogit names the variable used for weighting. No other indication is provided:

```
Weighting variable                    GENDER
```

Comparing the model weighted on an exogenous variable to that without such a weight, the reader will note a change in the LL function as well as changes in the parameters estimated, as well as behavioral outputs such as elasticities and scenario application.

The application of endogenous and exogenous weighting provides a timely reminder about the role that sampling (and effective sample responses) plays in its influence on key behavioral outputs.

13.6 Willingness to pay

An important output from choice models is the *marginal rate of substitution* (MRS) between specific attributes of interest, with a financial variable typically being in the trade-off so that the MRS can be expressed in dollar terms. The MRS is more commonly referred to as a willingness to pay (WTP) estimate. The underlying theory is presented in Section 8.4.3 of Chapter 8. A simple linear calculation of the WTP is given in Section 12.6 of Chapter 12. In this section we focus on a non-linear form and employ the Wald procedure to obtain (as discussed in Section 7.2.1.2 of Chapter 7) the mean estimate, the standard error, and confidence levels for the VTTS.

The command syntax below is used to obtain the WTP estimate for the value of travel time savings for the non-linear model in which the VTTS is itself a function of the levels of relevant attributes *invt* and *invc* in the VTTS function expressed as $/minute:

```
fn1 = -(invtz+invtcz*invc) / (invtcz*invt + 2*invcqz*invc)
```

The mean VTTS is $1.67/minute:

```
|-> reject;SPRP=0$
|-> create
   ;invtc=invc*invt
   ;invcq=invc*invc$
|-> Nlogit
   ;lhs = choice, cset, altij
   ;choices = bs,tn,bw,cr
   ;model:
   u(bs) = bs + invtz*invt2 +invtcz*invtc+invcqz*invcq/
   u(tn) = tn + invtz*invt2 +invtcz*invtc+invcqz*invcq/
   u(bw) = bw + invtz*invt2 +invtcz*invtc+invcqz*invcq/
   u(cr) =      invtz*invt + invtcz*invtc+invcqz*invcq$
Normal exit:   6 iterations. Status=0, F=    230.4580
```

```
-----------------------------------------------------------------------
Discrete choice (multinomial logit) model
Dependent variable                  Choice
Log likelihood function       -230.45797
Estimation based on N =     197, K =    6
Inf.Cr.AIC  =     472.9 AIC/N =    2.401
R2=1-LogL/LogL* Log-L fncn R-sqrd R2Adj
Constants only must be computed directly
            Use NLOGIT ;...;RHS=ONE$
Chi-squared[ 3]            =      72.70997
Prob [ chi squared > value ] =    .00000
Response data are given as ind. choices
Number of obs.=    197, skipped    0 obs
```

CHOICE	Coefficient	Standard Error	z	Prob. $|z|>Z^*$	95% Confidence Interval	
BS	-.52833**	.26519	-1.99	.0463	-1.04809	-.00857
INVTZ	-.03639***	.00805	-4.52	.0000	-.05216	-.02061
INVTCZ	.00049	.00095	.51	.6098	-.00138	.00235
INVCQZ	-.00048	.00141	-.34	.7326	-.00325	.00229
TN	-.94074***	.22709	-4.14	.0000	-1.38582	-.49566
BW	-.87783***	.25289	-3.47	.0005	-1.37348	-.38218

```
***, **, * ==>  Significance at 1%, 5%, 10% level.
Model was estimated on Aug 23, 2013 at 10:44:19 AM
-----------------------------------------------------------------------
```

```
Elapsed time:    0 hours,  0 minutes,   .172 seconds.
|-> Wald; Parameters = b ; Covariance = varb
   ; Labels = bs,invtz,invtcz,invcqz,tn,bw
   ; fn1 = -(invtz+invtcz*invc) / (invtcz*invt + 2*invcqz*invc)
   ; Means $
```

```
--------------------------------------------------------------------------
WALD procedure. Estimates and standard errors
for nonlinear functions and joint test of
nonlinear restrictions.
Wald Statistic             =         .22617
Prob. from Chi-squared[ 1] =         .63438
Functions are computed at means of variables
-----------+--------------------------------------------------------------
           |               Standard           Prob.      95% Confidence
WaldFcns|     Function       Error      z     |z|>Z*        Interval
-----------+--------------------------------------------------------------
  Fncn(1)|     1.66632      3.50379    .48    .6344     -5.20097   8.53361
-----------+--------------------------------------------------------------
***, **, * ==>  Significance at 1%, 5%, 10% level.
--------------------------------------------------------------------------
```

The preceding syntax computes the function and the asymptotic standard error for the function shown in Equation 8.27 of Chapter 8 from Rose *et al.* (2012). It reports the function value, standard error, and confidence interval. This function can also be used to compute the results over a range of values of a variable. For example, if one wanted to do this exercise for values of *invc* ranging from 5 to 50, and plot the results, you might use:

```
; Scenario: & invc = 5(5)50; Plot(ci)
```

which will get the result for xc = 5,10,...,50, and plot the function value against the values of xc, with confidence limits. Note that the description there calls this the "mean WTP." This is not the mean WTP. It is the WTP at the means. To compute the mean WTP, the function would be computed for each observation in the sample and the functions would be averaged. This calculation can be obtained by removing **;Means** from the command above. An alternative to the delta method is the Krinsky–Robb (K&R) method. The preceding can be changed to the K&R method (see Chapter 7) by adding:

```
;K&R ; Draws = number
```

to the preceding. Some researchers suggest that the number of draws must be greater than 5,000. Perhaps 1,000 will be sufficient, so test both if unsure. It is also possible to use K&R for the average WTP. This is a huge amount of computation, though if the sample size is not too large, it should be tolerable.

13.6.1 Calculating change in consumer surplus associated with an attribute change

Analysts often wish to identify the overall consumer surplus before and after a policy change (as defined by a change in one or more of the levels of the explanatory variables). There are a number of ways of estimating the *before* and *after* consumer surplus, which in the absence of an income effect is also the compensating variation. The process in Nlogit involves the same sequence of estimation as set out in Section 13.4. First, we estimate a choice model; in the case below it is multinomial logit, but we add in the syntax **;ivb=CSmode** which keeps in memory the *before* index of consumer surplus for each sampled respondent. We need to keep the relevant parameter estimates, which is the cost parameter b(1), which is used to convert the *ivb* output from utility units to cost units. The *before* output of interest is **csB**. We then repeat the model syntax without re-estimating the model by including the simulation/scenario commands that specify the change in the attribute of interest (e.g., **invc** for the air alternative), which is increased by 50 percent, as indicated by =[*]**1.5**. Using the same parameter estimate that is stored in memory for cost, we then calculate the after level of consumer surplus, namely **csA**, and the change in consumer surplus (or net benefit) denoted below as **DeltaCS**:

```
nlogit;lhs=mode
;choices=air,train,bus,car
;ivb=CSmode
;model:
U(air)=invc*invc+invt*invt/
U(train)=invc*invc+invt*invt/
U(bus)=invc*invc+invt*invt/
U(car)=invc*invc+invt*invt$
calc;list;beta=b(1)$
matr;be=b(1:2)$
create
;csB=csmode/b(1)$
dstats;rhs= csB$

nlogit;lhs=mode
;choices=air,train,bus,car
;ivb=CSmode
;model:
U(air)=invc*invc+invt*invt/
U(train)=invc*invc+invt*invt/
U(bus)=invc*invc+invt*invt/
U(car)=invc*invc+invt*invt
;SIMULATION
```

```
;Scenario:invc(air)=[*]1.5$
calc;list;beta=b(1)$
matr;be=b(1:2)$
create
;csA=csmode/b(1)$
dstats;rhs= csA$
create;DeltaCS=csB-csa$
dtstats;rhs=DEltaCS$
```

13.7 Empirical distributions: removing one observation at a time

Analysts often want to explore the implications of each observation's contribution to estimates of parameters. A way of automating this is shown below, where an observation is removed and the model estimated; then it is reinstated and another observation removed and the model estimated:

```
MATRIX ; BETAI = INIT(2,40,0.0) $
CALC   ; I = 0 $
Calc;i1=1$
Procedure
Calc;i2=i1+287$
Sample;i1-i2$
nlogit;lhs=choice,cset,alt
;choices=curr,alta,altb
;model:u(curr,alta,altb)=totime*totime+tcost*tcost$
CALC ; I = I + 1 $
MATRIX ; BETAI(*,I) = B $  (CREATES 2 BY 40 MATRIX)
CALC;i1=i1+288$
EndProc
Execute;n=40$
```

13.8 Application of random regret model versus random utility model

The random regret model (RRM) is set out in Section 8.2 of Chapter 8, and is growing in interest and as an alternative to the RUM. The data used to investigate differences between RUM and RRM is drawn from a larger study undertaken in Sydney on the demand for alternative-fueled automobiles. Full details, including the properties of the design experiment, are given in Beck *et al.* (2012, 2013) and Hensher *et al.* (2012). The data was collected over a four-month period in 2009. The final sample used in model estimation here comprises 3,172 observations related to households who had purchased a vehicle in the previous two years.

The universal finite choice set comprises three alternatives based on fuel type: petrol, diesel, or hybrid. The hybrid alternative reflects a vehicle option that is cleaner with respect to emission levels. The vehicle type, broken down into six variants: Small, Luxury Small, Medium, Luxury Medium, Large, and Luxury Large, was done so that the experiment would have adequate attribute variance over the alternatives, particularly with respect to price, while still having a manageable number of alternatives for the design.

Nine attributes were included in the choice experiment. The typical monetary costs involved in purchasing and operating a car are included in the design. These are purchase price of the vehicle, the fuel price, and the cost of registration (including compulsory third-party insurance). The fuel efficiency of a vehicle is an important attribute, given that this is the link to which level of emissions' surcharge will be set. The remaining attributes – seating capacity, engine size, and country of manufacture – were selected to give respondents a realistic and varied set of alternatives such that cars of differing types could be evaluated and traded against within the choice experiment. Table 13.1 displays the levels that have been selected for each attribute. The purchase price for the hybrid alternative is $3,000 higher at each level in order to recognize that hybrid technology is more expensive than conventional engine technology.

The RRM and RUM are estimated as multinomial logit. The findings are summarized in Table 13.2[1]. We undertook extensive investigation into the possible influence of SECs and found statistically significant interactions of respondent age, full time employment dummy, and personal and household income with vehicle price, but not with other attributes of the alternatives.

RUM and RRM are nonnested models, and are generally assessed by means of a selection criterion, such as Akaike's (1974) Information Criterion (AIC), based on the Kullback–Leibler Information criterion (KLIC). Under KLIC, when two models are compared, minimization of the criterion only depends on the maximum likelihood of the two competing models. The AIC penalizes

---

[1] We have been asked whether "the RRM model has a higher requirement on the reliability of the SP data (depending on whether respondents seriously consider all alternatives in the SP game) because it uses the unchosen alternatives as well in estimation." We believe that although the information on attributes of alternatives is used in a different way in RRM compared to RUM, the very same issues in relation to how information on attributes is processed is present under RUM. Indeed, there are a number of studies under RUM that investigate deviations from a reference or status quo alternative that involve using data in a differencing manner (see, for example, Hess *et al.* 2008).

Table 13.1 Attribute levels for stated choice experiment

Purchase price	Small	$15,000	$18,750	$22,500	$26,250	$30,000
	Small Luxury	$30,000	$33,750	$37,500	$41,250	$45,000
	Medium	$30,000	$35,000	$40,000	$45,000	$50,000
	Medium Luxury	$70,000	$77,500	$85,000	$92,500	$100,000
	Large	$40,000	$47,500	$55,000	$62,500	$70,000
	Large Luxury	$90,000	$100,000	$110,000	$120,000	$130,000
Fuel price	Pivot off daily price	−25%	−10%	0%	10%	25%
Registration	Pivot off actual purchase	−25%	−10%	0%	10%	25%
Fuel efficiency (L/10km)	Small	6	7	8	9	10
	Medium	7	9	11	13	15
	Large	7	9	11	13	15
Engine capacity (cylinders)	Small	4	6			
	Medium	4	6			
	Large	6	8			
Seating capacity	Small	2	4			
	Medium	4	5			
	Large	5	6			
Country of manufacture	Random Allocation	Japan	Europe	South Korea	Australia	USA

the log-likelihood (LL) of each model by a quantity equal to the number of its parameters. The AIC for model selection simply consists in comparing the AIC values for the two models. If the value is positive the first model is chosen, otherwise the second will be deemed best. On the AIC test, the RRM is marginally superior on statistical fit to the RUM. All parameters have the expected sign and are statistically significant at the 95 percent confidence level, except for registration fee. The fuel-specific constants show a preference for petrol vehicles, after controlling for the observed attributes.

Figures 13.3 to 13.6 depict the RUM (ProbRUM) and RRM (ProbRRM) probability distributions across the sample overall, and for each of the alternative fuel types, as well as the differences (ProbDif) between RUM and RRM. The most notable evidence is the narrower range and more peaked distribution for RRM compared to the RUM, suggesting greater heterogeneity in predicted probabilistic choice under RUM. The incidence of greater

Table 13.2 Summary of model results (*t*-values in brackets)

Attribute	Alternatives	RUM	RRM
Vehicle price ($)	All	−0.01583 (−5.50)	−0.0096 (−5.47)
Fuel price ($/litre)	All	−0.4504 (−7.23)	−0.2970 (−7.36)
Annual emissions' surcharge ($)	All	−0.00067 (−8.61)	−0.00044 (−8.79)
Variable emissions' surcharge ($/km)	All	−0.3716 (−3.57)	−0.2344 (−3.53)
Petrol-specific constant	Petrol	0.0753 (2.00)	0.0494 (2.03)
Registration fee ($ per annum)	All	−0.00013 (−1.63)	−0.000088 (−1.68)
Fuel efficiency (litres per 100km)	All	−0.0174 (−3.15)	−0.0123 (−3.46)
Engine capacity (# cylinders)	All	−0.0274 (−2.47)	−0.0179 (−2.54)
Seating capacity	All	0.2554 (18.5)	−0.1712 (20.4)
Vehicle price interacted with:			
Age of respondent	All	−0.0002 (−3.53)	−0.00015 (−4.21)
Full time employed (1,0)	All	−0.0069 (−4.07)	−0.0052 (−5.07)
Personal income (000s)	All	0.0000445 (2.02)	0.000035 (3.34)
Household income (000s)	All	0.000029 (3.49)	0.000021 (4.17)
Korean manufactured (1,0)	All	−0.1354 (−4.11)	−0.0880 (−4.19)
Diesel-specific constant	Diesel	−0.3235 (−8.65)	−0.2137 (−9.22)
Gender (male = 1)	Hybrid	−0.1546 (−3.33)	−0.1014 (−3.45)
Model fit:			
LL at zero		−10636.764	
LL at convergence		−9,484.028	−9,472.694
Info. Criterion: AIC		1.9624	1.9602
Sample size		9,682	

observation frequency around the mean and median is most stark under RRM compared to RUM, despite overall model fits being relatively similar. There are clear differences in the choice probabilities associated with each respondent, as highlighted in the ProbDif graphs. This suggests that the implied elasticities associated with one or more attributes are likely to differ given their dependence on the choice probabilities (see below).

All the mean[2] elasticities obtained from the RUM and RRM are summarized in Table 13.3. Although the absolute magnitudes appear at first glance to be relatively similar with some exceptions, such as vehicle price, many of the elasticities are quite different in percentage terms (varying between 1.21 and 18.95 percent). The vehicle price elasticities for RRM are greater than for

[2] Mean elasticities are obtained from probability weighting the respondent-specific elasticities, where the probability weight relates to the probability of choosing a particular alternative in a choice set setting.

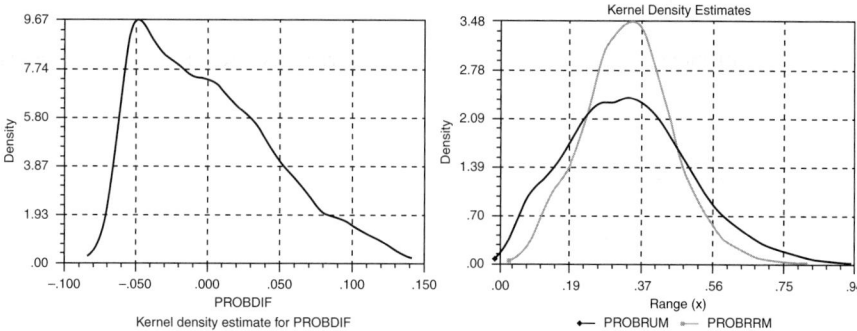

Figure 13.3   Profile of choice probabilities for RUM and RRM

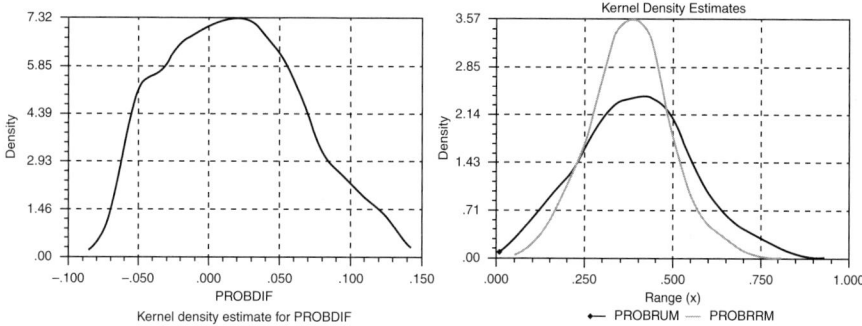

Figure 13.4   Profile of petrol choice probabilities for RUM and RRM

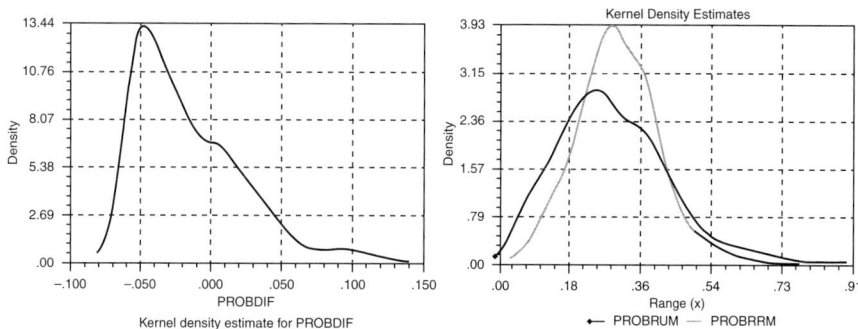

Figure 13.5   Profile of diesel choice probabilities for RUM and RRM

RUM by between 4.22 and 12.39 percent, for fuel price they are greater by between 1.21 and 9.5 percent, for fuel efficiency they are higher by between 5.31 and 18.95 percent, and for annual emissions surcharge they are higher by between 1.90 and 10.2 percent. These differences are substantial, and they

Table 13.3 Direct elasticity contrasts

Attribute	RUM			RRM		
	Petrol	Diesel	Hybrid	Petrol	Diesel	Hybrid
Vehicle price ($)	−0.931	−1.089	−1.227	−0.987	−1.135	−1.379
Fuel price ($/litre)	−0.303	−0.358	−0.331	−0.319	−0.392	−0.327
Annual emissions' surcharge ($)	−0.105	−0.102	−0.049	−0.107	−0.104	−0.054
Variable emissions' surcharge ($/km)	−0.041	−0.04	−0.019	−0.043	−0.039	−0.021
Registration fee ($ p a)	−0.062	−0.074	−0.069	−0.068	−0.075	−0.072
Fuel efficiency (litres per 100km)	−0.095	−0.113	−0.104	−0.113	−0.119	−0.118

Attribute	Absolute difference (RUM – Random regret)			Percent difference		
	Petrol	Diesel	Hybrid	Petrol	Diesel	Hybrid
Vehicle price ($)	0.056	0.046	0.152	−6.02%	−4.22%	−12.39%
Fuel price ($/litre)	0.016	0.034	−0.004	−5.28%	−9.50%	1.21%
Annual emissions' surcharge ($)	0.002	0.002	0.005	−1.90%	−1.96%	−10.20%
Variable emissions' surcharge($/km)	0.002	−0.001	0.001	−4.88%	2.50%	−5.26%
Registration fee ($ p a)	0.006	0.001	0.003	−9.68%	−1.35%	−4.35%
Fuel efficiency (litres per 100km)	0.018	0.006	0.014	−18.95%	−5.31%	−13.46%

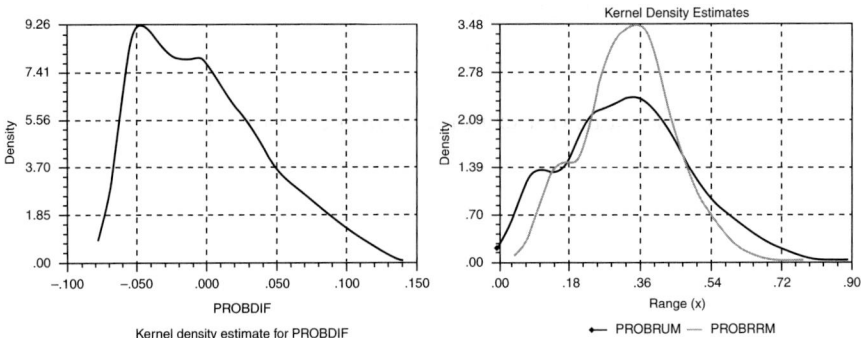

Figure 13.6 Profile of hybrid choice probabilities for RUM and RRM

suggest varying behavioral responses to a given change in a specific policy instrument across the three fuel types. All attributes are relatively inelastic, with the exception of vehicle price for diesel and hybrid fuels, with the direct elasticity associated with vehicle price being the most (in)elastic, and the vehicle emissions surcharge per kilometre being the least inelastic (the latter expected, given it relates to a kilometre of travel).

To illustrate the way that the evidence is interpreted, in the RUM a 10 percent increase in the price of a petrol vehicle results, on average, in a 9.31 percent reduction in the probability of choosing a petrol vehicle, given the choice among petrol, diesel, and hybrid, holding all other influences constant. However, this 10 percent increase in the price of a petrol vehicle in the context of the RRM takes into account the level of the vehicle price associated with the diesel or hybrid alternative. More specifically, the 9.87 percent reduction in the probability of choosing the petrol vehicle in the RRM explicitly accounts for the levels of vehicle price in the set of available alternatives, in recognition of regret that one may have chosen the wrong alternative. It is 6.02 percent higher than the RUM behavioral response, suggesting that accounting for the possibility that the wrong choice may have been made amplifies the behavioral response that one would normally attribute to a RUM-based elasticity.

The absolute mean elasticities associated with annual and variable emissions' surcharges and annual registration fee are much more similar for RUM and RRM (except for a hybrid vehicle for annual emissions' surcharge) than are the other attribute elasticities (with the exception of registration fees for diesel fueled vehicles).[3]

Overall, the mean differences are such that the RUM is not a good approximation to the RRM if random regret is a preferred representation of behavioral response, as is the case in this empirical study. This raises the important question of which elasticity estimates policy advisers should use. This bears some close thought; however, regret estimates may be more appropriate for actual potential loss (for example, being involved in an accident) or significant potential gains (for example, winning a lottery)?

13.8.1 Nlogit syntax for random regret model

```
-> rrlogit
    ;choices=Pet,Die,Hyb
    ;lhs=choice,cset,alt
    ;effects:fuel(*)/aes(*)/price(*)/ves(*)/rego(*)/fe(*);pwt
    ;model:
```

[3] It is important to note that an elasticity calculation has a number of estimates embedded in it of parameters and probabilities (see Equation (8.16) in Chapter 8), and hence it is extremely complex (if not practically impossible) to derive standard errors that are required in testing a hypothesis about the elasticity. The delta method or Krinsky-Robb tests could be implemented to do that, but for elasticities, even from a simple multinomial choice model, it is extremely complex to program, if it could be done at all. On the other hand, we would not trust an hypothesis test for an elasticity even if the standard errors were computed by the delta method.

```
U(Pet) = Petasc + price*price + fuel*fuel + rego*rego + AES*AES + VES*VES + FE*FE + EC*EC + SC*SC +
pricpage*pricpage+pricft*pricft+pricpinc*pricpinc+prichinc*prichinc+Kor*Kor /
U(Die) = Dieasc + price*price + fuel*fuel + rego*rego + AES*AES + VES*VES+ FE*FE + EC*EC + SC*SC
+pricpage*pricpage+pricft*pricft+pricpinc*pricpinc+prichinc*prichinc+Kor*Kor /
U(Hyb)                       =price*price+fuel*fuel+rego*rego+AES*AES+VES*VES+FE*FE+EC*EC+SC*SC
+pricpage*pricpage+pricft*pricft+pricpinc*pricpinc+prichinc*prichinc+Kor*Kor +male*pgend$
```

13.9 The Maximize command

Although Nlogit has numerous pre-packaged (or "hardwired") routines defined by well structured syntax, it is always possible to write out a series of functions that define the relationship between the parameters and attributes associated with each alternative. In this way, you can take advantage of the general nature of the utility expression. Although the MNL models limit the model to be linear in the parameters, although non-linear in attributes is permissible (in contrast to more complex models such as non-linear random parameter logit – see Chapter 21), it is useful to show how **Maximize** can be used to construct the MNL model.

> *As an aside*, **Maximize** gives different standard errors from the Nlogit command because **Maximize** uses only first derivatives and Nlogit uses the Hessian. There will be small differences in the standard error estimates. The example below estimates a non-linear MNL.

```
Sample ; All $
Nlogit ; Lhs = Mode ; Choices = Air,Train,Bus,Car
       ; Rhs = ttme,invc,invt,gc ; rh2=one,hinc$
? Air,Train,Bus,Car
create ; da=mode ; dt=mode[+1] ; db=mode[+2] ; dc=mode[+3] $
create ; ttmea=ttme ; ttmet=ttme[+1] ; ttmeb = ttme[+2] ; ttmec=ttme[+3] $
create ; invca=invc ; invct=invc[+1] ; invcb = invc[+2] ; invcc=invc[+3] $
create ; invta=invt ; invtt=invt[+1] ; invtb = invt[+2] ; invtc=invt[+3] $
create ; gca =gc   ; gct  =  gc[+1] ; gcb  =   gc[+2] ; gcc  =  gc[+3] $
Create ; J = Trn(-4,0) $
Reject ; J > 1 $
Maximize
; Labels = aa,at,ab,bttme,binvc,binvt,bgc, bha,bht,bhb
; Start  = 4.375,5.914,4.463,-.10289,-.08044,-.01299,.07578,.00428,-.05907,-.02295
; Fcn    = ua = aa + bttme*ttmea + binvc*invca + binvt*invta + bgc*gca + bha*hinc |
             va = exp(ua) |
          ut = at + bttme*ttmet + binvc*invct + binvt*invtt + bgc*gct + bht*hinc |
             vt = exp(ut) |
          ub = ab + bttme*ttmeb + binvc*invcb + binvt*invtb + bgc*gcb + bhb*hinc |
             vb = exp(ub) |
```

```
      uc =      bttme*ttmec + binvc*invcc + binvt*invtc + bgc*gcc        |
         vc = exp(uc) |
      IV = va+vt+vb+vc |
      P  = (da*va + dt*vt + db*vb + dc*vc)/IV |
      log(P) $
MAXIMIZE
```

| Log likelihood function   172.9437 |

Variable	Coefficient	Standard Error	b/St.Er.	P[|Z|>z]
AA	4.37035***	1.00097557	4.366	.0000
AT	5.91407***	.72338081	8.176	.0000
AB	4.46269***	.84811310	5.262	.0000
BTTME	-.10289***	.00921583	-11.164	.0000
BINVC	-.08044***	.02122791	-3.789	.0002
BINVT	-.01399***	.00288910	-4.844	.0000
BGC	.07578***	.01948463	3.889	.0001
BHA	.00428	.01507319	.284	.7767
BHT	-.05907***	.01386534	-4.260	.0000
BHB	-.02295	.02058177	-1.115	.2648

| Note: ***, **, * = Significance at 1%, 5%, 10% level. |

```
NLOGIT
```

| Log likelihood function   -172.9437 |

Variable	Coefficient	Standard Error	b/St.Er.	P[|Z|>z]
TTME	-.10289***	.01108716	-9.280	.0000
INVC	-.08044***	.01995071	-4.032	.0001
INVT	-.01399***	.00267092	-5.240	.0000
GC	.07578***	.01833199	4.134	.0000
A_AIR	4.37035***	1.05733525	4.133	.0000
AIR_HIN1	.00428	.01306169	.327	.7434
A_TRAIN	5.91407***	.68992964	8.572	.0000
TRA_HIN2	-.05907***	.01470918	-4.016	.0001
A_BUS	4.46269***	.72332545	6.170	.0000
BUS_HIN3	-.02295	.01591735	-1.442	.1493

| Note: ***, **, * = Significance at 1%, 5%, 10% level. |

13.10 Calibrating a model

When the data consists of two subsets, for example an RP data set and a counterpart SP data set, it is sometimes useful to fit the model with one of the data sets, then refit the second one while retaining the original coefficients, and just adjusting the constants. One is often interested in using the parameter estimates from one data set but re-estimating (or calibrating) on another data set only the ASCs. The example below shows the command syntax, where we have conveniently divided the data set into two "separate samples." One would normally use different data sets unless the analyst wishes to use part of a single data set as a hold out sample:

```
|-> LOAD;file="C:\Projects\NWTptStudy_03\NWTModels\ACA Ch 15 ML_RPL models\nw15jul03-
3limdep.SAV.lpj"$
Project file contained   27180 observations.


create
    ;if(employ=1)ftime=1
    ;if(whopay=1)youpay=1$
sample;all$
reject;dremove=1$  Bad data
reject;altij=-999$
reject;ttype#1$  work =1
Timer
sample;1-12060$
Nlogit
    ;lhs=resp1,cset,Altij
    ;choices=NLRail,NHRail,NBway,Bus,Bway,Train,Car
    ; Alg = BFGS
;model
    U(NLRail)= NLRAsc + cost*tcost + invt*InvTime + acwt*wait+ acwt*acctim
    + accbusf*accbusf+eggT*egresst + ptinc*pinc + ptgend*gender + NLRinsde*inside /
    U(NHRail)= TNAsc + cost*Tcost + invt*InvTime + acwt*WaitT + acwt*acctim
    + eggT*egresst + accbusf*accbusf + ptinc*pinc + ptgend*gender + NHRinsde*inside /
    U(NBway)=  NBWAsc + cost*Tcost + invt*InvTime + waitTb*WaitT
    + accTb*acctim + eggT*egresst + accbusf*accbusf+ ptinc*pinc + ptgend*gender /
    U(Bus)=    BSAsc + cost*frunCost + invt*InvTime + waitTb*WaitT
    + accTb*acctim + eggT*egresst+ ptinc*pinc + ptgend*gender/
    U(Bway)=   BWAsc + cost*Tcost + invt*InvTime + waitTb*WaitT
    + accTb*acctim + eggT*egresst + accbusf*accbusf+ ptinc*pinc + ptgend*gender /
    U(Train)=  TNAsc + cost*tcost + invt*InvTime + acwt*WaitT + acwt*acctim
    + eggT*egresst + accbusf*accbusf+ ptinc*pinc + ptgend*gender /
    U(Car)=    CRcost*costs + CRinvt*InvTime + CRpark*parkcost+ CReggT*egresst$


+-------------------------------------------------------------------------+
|WARNING:   Bad observations were found in the sample. |
|Found 565 bad observations among   2201 individuals. |
|You can use ;CheckData to get a list of these points. |
+-------------------------------------------------------------------------+

Normal exit: 32 iterations. Status=0, F=    2315.029
```

```
----------------------------------------------------------------------------------------------------
Discrete choice (multinomial logit) model
Dependent variable              Choice
Log likelihood function      -2315.02908
Estimation based on N =    1636, K =  20
Inf.Cr.AIC  =    4670.1 AIC/N =    2.855
R2=1-LogL/LogL* Log-L fncn R-sqrd R2Adj
Constants only must be computed directly
              Use NLOGIT ;...;RHS=ONE$
Response data are given as ind. choices
Number of obs.=  2201, skipped  565 obs
```

RESP1	Coefficient	Standard Error	z	Prob. |z|>Z*	95% Confidence Interval	
NLRASC	3.09077***	.35051	8.82	.0000	2.40379	3.77776
COST	-.21192***	.01316	-16.10	.0000	-.23772	-.18612
INVT	-.03428***	.00193	-17.80	.0000	-.03806	-.03051
ACWT	-.02434***	.00511	-4.76	.0000	-.03436	-.01432
ACCBUSF	-.19927***	.03169	-6.29	.0000	-.26139	-.13716
EGGT	-.02650***	.00501	-5.28	.0000	-.03633	-.01667
PTINC	-.00954***	.00247	-3.86	.0001	-.01439	-.00470
PTGEND	.50243***	.16943	2.97	.0030	.17034	.83451
NLRINSDE	-1.87282***	.45534	-4.11	.0000	-2.76528	-.98037
TNASC	2.70760***	.33840	8.00	.0000	2.04434	3.37086
NHRINSDE	-2.24667***	.55770	-4.03	.0001	-3.33974	-1.15361
NBWASC	1.97710***	.39319	5.03	.0000	1.20645	2.74774
WAITTB	-.02656	.01950	-1.36	.1731	-.06478	.01165
ACCTB	-.04328***	.01003	-4.32	.0000	-.06294	-.02363
BSASC	2.23452***	.33764	6.62	.0000	1.57275	2.89628
BWASC	2.59449***	.34292	7.57	.0000	1.92238	3.26661
CRCOST	-.12599***	.02512	-5.02	.0000	-.17523	-.07676
CRINVT	-.01732***	.00323	-5.36	.0000	-.02366	-.01099
CRPARK	-.01335*	.00707	-1.89	.0588	-.02720	.00049
CREGGT	-.02835**	.01136	-2.50	.0125	-.05061	-.00609

```
|-> sample;12061-27180$
|-> Nlogit
   ;lhs=resp1,cset,Altij
   ;choices=NLRail,NHRail,NBway,Bus,Bway,Train,Car
   ; Alg = BFGS
   ;model:
   U(NLRail)= NLRAsc + cost[]*tcost + invt[]*InvTime + acwt[]*waitt+
   acwt[]*acctim + accbusf[]*accbusf+eggT[]*egresst
                        + ptinc[]*pinc + ptgend[]*gender + NLRinsde[]*inside /
   U(NHRail)= TNAsc + cost[]*Tcost + invt[]*InvTime + acwt[]*WaitT + acwt[]*acctim
   + eggT[]*egresst + accbusf[]*accbusf
           + ptinc[]*pinc + ptgend[]*gender + NHRinsde[]*inside /
```

U(NBway)= NBWAsc + cost[]*Tcost + invt[]*InvTime + waitTb[]*WaitT + accTb[]*acctim
+ eggT[]*egresst + accbusf[]*accbusf+ ptinc[]*pinc + ptgend[]*gender /
U(Bus)= BSAsc + cost[]*frunCost + invt[]*InvTime + waitTb[]*WaitT + accTb[]*acctim
+ eggT[]*egresst+ ptinc[]*pinc + ptgend[]*gender/
U(Bway)= BWAsc + cost[]*Tcost + invt[]*InvTime + waitTb[]*WaitT + accTb[]*acctim
+ eggT[]*egresst + accbusf[]*accbusf+ ptinc[]*pinc + ptgend[]*gender /
U(Train)= TNAsc + cost[]*tcost + invt[]*InvTime + acwt[]*WaitT + acwt[]*acctim
+ eggT[]*egresst + accbusf[]*accbusf+ ptinc[]*pinc + ptgend[]*gender /
U(Car)= CRcost[]*costs + Rinvt[]*InvTime + CRpark[]*parkcost +
CReggT[]*egresst;**calibrate**$

```
+-------------------------------------------------------------------- +
|WARNING:   Bad observations were found in the sample. |
|Found 500 bad observations among   2672 individuals. |
|You can use ;CheckData to get a list of these points. |
+-------------------------------------------------------------------- +
```

Normal exit: 11 iterations. Status=0, F=   3078.057

Discrete choice (multinomial logit) model
Dependent variable   Choice
Log likelihood function   -3078.05706
Estimation based on N =   2172, K =   5
Inf.Cr.AIC =   6166.1 AIC/N =   2.839
R2=1-LogL/LogL* Log-L fncn R-sqrd R2Adj
Constants only must be computed directly
            Use NLOGIT ;...; RHS=ONE$
Response data are given as ind. choices
Number of obs.= 2672, skipped 500 obs

RESP1	Coefficient	Standard Error	z	Prob. |z|>Z*	95% Confidence Interval	
NLRASC	3.06884***	.09111	33.68	.0000	2.89027	3.24742
COST	-.21192	.....(Fixed Parameter).....				
INVT	-.03428	.....(Fixed Parameter).....				
ACWT	-.02434	.....(Fixed Parameter).....				
ACCBUSF	-.19927	.....(Fixed Parameter).....				
EGGT	-.02650	.....(Fixed Parameter).....				
PTINC	-.00954	.....(Fixed Parameter).....				
PTGEND	.50243	.....(Fixed Parameter).....				
NLRINSDE	-1.87282	.....(Fixed Parameter).....				
TNASC	2.90336***	.07806	37.19	.0000	2.75035	3.05636
NHRINSDE	-2.24667	.....(Fixed Parameter).....				
NBWASC	2.05517***	.15088	13.62	.0000	1.75946	2.35089
WAITTB	-.02656	.....(Fixed Parameter).....				
ACCTB	-.04328	.....(Fixed Parameter).....				
BSASC	2.22981***	.09925	22.47	.0000	2.03528	2.42433
BWASC	2.56348***	.09390	27.30	.0000	2.37944	2.74751

```
CRCOST|      -.12599     .....(Fixed Parameter).....
CRINVT|      -.01732     .....(Fixed Parameter).....
CRPARK|      -.01335     .....(Fixed Parameter).....
CREGGT|      -.02835     .....(Fixed Parameter).....
```

The model is first fit with the first half of the data set (**sample;1–12060**). Then, for the second estimation, we want to refit the model, but only recompute the constant terms and keep the previously estimate slope parameters. The device to use for the second model is the "[ ]" specification, which indicates that you wish to use the previously estimated parameters. The commands above will, in principle, produce the desired result, with one consideration. Newton's method is very sensitive to the starting values for this model, and with the constraints imposed in the second model will generally fail to converge. The practical solution is to change the algorithm to BFGS, which will then produce the desired result. You can do this just by adding **; Alg = BFGS** to the second command. An additional detail is that the second model will now replace the first as the "previous" model. So, if you want to do a second calibration, you have to refit the first model. To pre-empt this, you can use **;Calibrate** in the second command. This specification changes the algorithm and also instructs Nlogit not to replace the previous estimates with the current ones.

> *As an aside*, You may use this device with any discrete choice model that you fit with Nlogit. The second sample must have the same configuration as the first, and the device can only be used to fix the utility function parameters. The latter point implies that if you do this with a random parameters model, the random parameters will become fixed; that is, the variances will be fixed at zero.

14 Nested logit estimation

In mathematics you don't understand things. You just get used to them.

(John von Neumann, 1903–57)

14.1 Introduction

The majority of practical choice study applications do not progress beyond the simple multinomial logit (MNL) model discussed in previous chapters. The ease of computation, and the wide availability of software packages capable of estimating the MNL model, suggest that this trend will continue. The ease with which the MNL model may be estimated, however, comes at a price in the form of the assumption of Independence of Identically Distributed (IID) error components. While the IID assumption and the behaviorally comparable assumption of Independence of Irrelevant Alternatives (IIA) allow for ease of computation (as well as providing a closed form solution[1]), as with any assumption violations both can and do occur. When violations do occur, the cross-substitution effects (or correlation) observed between pairs of alternatives are no longer equal given the presence or absence of other alternatives within the complete list of available alternatives in the model (Louviere *et al.* 2000).

The nested logit (NL) model represents a partial relaxation of the IID and IIA assumptions of the MNL model. As discussed in Chapter 4, this relaxation occurs in the variance components of the model, together with some correlation within sub-sets of alternatives, and while more advanced models such as mixed multinomial logit (see Chapter 15) relax the IID assumption more fully,

---

[1] An equation is said to be a closed-form solution if it may be solved using mathematical operations and does not require complex, analytical calculations such as integration each time a change occurs somewhere within the system.

the NL model represents an excellent advancement for the analyst in terms of studies of choice. As with the MNL model, the NL model is relatively straightforward to estimate and offers the added benefit of being a closed-form solution. More advanced models relax the IID assumption in terms of the covariances; however, all are of open-form solution and as such require complex analytical calculations to identify changes in the choice probabilities through varying levels of attributes (see Louviere *et al.* (2000) and Train (2003, 2009), as well as the following chapters in this book). In this chapter, we show how to use NLOGIT to estimate NL models and to interpret the output, especially the output that is additional to what is obtained when estimating an MNL model. As with previous chapters, we have been very specific in terms of our explanation of the command syntax as well as the output generated.

14.2 The nested logit model commands

As with Chapters 11 and 13, we use the labeled mode choice case study as our point of reference in estimating these models. In contrast to Chapter 13, where we used the revealed preference (RP) data, we use the stated preference (SP) data in this chapter (chosen so as to show users the SP part of the data which will, in later chapters, be combined with the RP data in jointly estimating RP–SP models. We begin by examining how NL tree structures are specified in NLOGIT.

The majority of NL models estimated as part of choice studies typically have only two levels. Very few NL models are estimated with three levels, and even fewer with four levels. Nlogit has the capability to simultaneously estimate NL models with up to four levels, with sequential estimation required for additional levels. Within the literature (see also Chapter 4), the three highest levels of NL trees are named, from the highest level (level four) to the lowest level (level two), as Trunks, Limbs, and Branches. At the lowest level of NL trees (level one) resides the elemental alternatives (hereafter referred to simply as alternatives), which are sometimes referred to in the literature as *Twigs*.

NL models estimated by Nlogit may have up to a maximum of five trunks, 10 limbs, 25 branches, and 500 alternatives. Any tree structure, provided that it does not exceed the maximum number of trunks, limbs, branches, or alternatives allowed, may be estimated. Thus, provided that the total number of alternatives within the tree does not exceed 500, some branches may have only one alternative (known as a *degenerate branch*; this is discussed in more detail later), while other branches may have two or more alternatives.

Similarly, provided that the total number of limbs does not exceed 25, some trunks may have only a single branch, while others may have two or more branches. Trunks may also have any number of limbs, provided that the total number of limbs does not exceed 10 within the overall tree structure. Tree structures in which there is only a single trunk, but two or more limbs, are known as three-level NL models (we often omit the trunk level when we draw such trees; however, the level is still there). Models with only one trunk and one limb but multiple branches are, by implication, called two-level NL models (once more, it is customary when drawing such tree structures to do so without showing the single trunk and limb). Single level models, where there is only a single trunk, limb, and branch, but multiple alternatives, are also possible.

The command syntax structure for the NL model is similar to the command syntax for the MNL model discussed in Chapter 12. The addition of the following command to the MNL command syntax will estimate a NL model using Nlogit:

```
;tree =<tree structure>
```

Placing the tree specification command within the MNL command syntax, the base NL model command will look as follows:

```
NLOGIT
;lhs = choice, cset, altij
;choices =<names of alternatives>
;tree = <tree structure>
;Model:
U(alternative 1 name) = <utility function 1>/
U(alternative 2 name) = <utility function 2>/
...
U(alternative i name) = <utility function i>$
```

In defining the tree structure, the following NLOGIT conventions apply:

{} specifies a trunk (level 4);
[] specifies a limb within a trunk (level 3);
() specifies a branch within a limb within a trunk (level 2).

Entries at the same level of a tree are separated by a comma (,). The analyst may name each of the trunks, limbs, and branches; however, if no name is provided, Nlogit will provide generic names such as Trunk{l}, Lmb[$i|l$], and B($j|i,l$), where l is the lth trunk, i is the ith limb and j is the jth branch. For example, B(1|1,1) represents the first branch in limb one within the first trunk; B(1|2,1) represents the second branch in limb one within trunk one; and

B(2|2,1) represents the second branch in limb two within trunk one; Lmb[1:1] represents limb one, trunk one; and Trunk[2] represents trunk two. The naming of a trunk, limb, or branch is done by providing a name (eight characters or less) outside the relevant brackets. The alternatives are specified at the lowest level of the tree structure (i.e., at level one) and are entered within the appropriate brackets as they exist within the tree structure. Alternatives within the same trunk, limb, or branch are separated by a comma (,).

To demonstrate the above, consider the following example (not based on the SP data we use in estimation):

```
;tree = car(card,carp), PT(bus,train,busway,LR)
```

The above tree specification will estimate a NL model with the tree structure in Figure 14.1.

This structure has two branches and six alternatives, two belonging to the Car branch, and four to the public transport (PT) branch, and hence is a two-level NL model. This tree structure represents one of many possible tree structures that may be explored by the analyst. For example, the analyst may also specify the NL tree structure (using the same alternatives) as follows:

```
;tree = car(card,carnp), PTEX(bus,train), PTNW(busway,LR)
```

Graphically, the above NL tree structure would look as shown in Figure 14.2.

The tree structure in Figure 14.2 differs from that in Figure 14.1 in that there now exist three branches, each with two alternatives. For the NL model

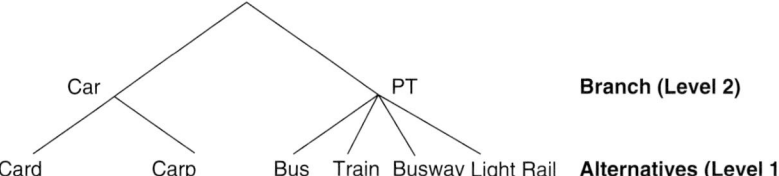

Figure 14.1   Example of an NL tree structure

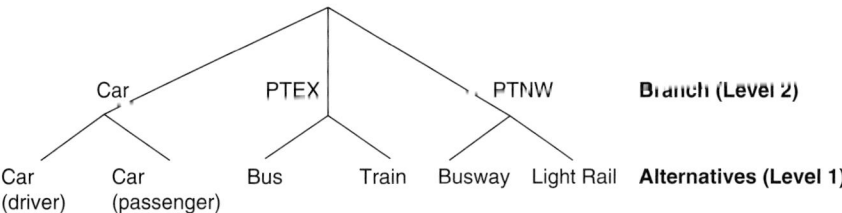

Figure 14.2   Example tree structure

represented by Figure 14.2, we have placed the bus and train alternatives within the same branch named PTEX (for existing modes) and the busway and light rail modes in the same branch named PTNW (for new modes).

> *As an aside*, although, as we have shown, it is possible to omit higher levels from NL models if the higher levels have a single limb or trunk (which we have omitted from our tree diagrams), it is also possible to acknowledge that a higher level exists by providing a name for it. For example:
>
> ```
> ;tree = Limb[car(card,carp), PTEX(bus,train), PTNW(busway,LR)]
> ```
>
> will produce exactly the same NL model as that shown in Figure 14.2. In such cases, the *inclusive value* (IV) parameter of the highest level (called Limb above) is fixed at 1.0 (see below).

Once again, the tree structure of Figure 14.2 represents but one of many possible tree structures that may be of interest. In the following tree specification, we demonstrate a third possible tree structure. In this particular structure, we have added an additional level (i.e., a limb) to the tree, thus making this a three-level NL model:

```
;tree= CAR[card,carpt], PT[PTRail(bus,train), PTRoad(busway,LR)]
```

Graphically, the above tree specification is shown in Figure 14.3.

In specifying the tree structure to be adopted, many analysts confuse NL trees with decision trees. Perhaps this is the fault of authors who tend to use, as examples, NL tree structures that have behaviorally intuitive undertones; the tree structures of Figures 14.1, 14.2, and 14.3 are examples of this. Nevertheless, any similarity of NL tree structures to decision trees is largely misleading. As discussed in Chapter 4, NL tree structures are determined so as to accommodate correlation between two or more alternatives that has a correspondence with the covariance matrix that is associated with the unobserved components of the utility expressions (i.e., on econometric and not behavioral grounds).

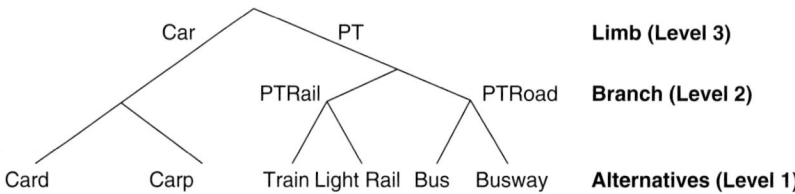

Figure 14.3 Example of a 3-level tree structure

14.2.1 Normalizing and constraining IV parameters

As discussed in Chapter 4, for all NL models, there will exist a unique IV parameter for each trunk, limb, and branch specified as part of the tree structure. As with other parameters, the analyst may constrain several of these IV parameters to be equal to some particular value (usually, but not always, 1.0). When one intends to constrain an IV parameter, the following command syntax is used:

```
;ivset: (<specification>)
```

In the form of NL we recommend (see Chapter 4), it is not necessary to use **;ivset**, and looking forward where a branch is degenerate, the IV is automatically constrained to 1.0 in line with the theoretical case. For the **;ivset** command specification, we use a colon (:) after the **;ivset** command. Whatever the specific specification adopted (discussed below), the specification is placed within round brackets (( )). That is, the convention related to the use of brackets for the tree specification command does not apply to the **;ivset** command, no matter at what level of the tree the IV parameter is to be constrained.

To constrain two or more IV parameters, the **;ivset** specification takes the following form. In this specification, each IV parameter that is to be constrained is placed within brackets, separated by a comma (,):

```
;ivset: (<IV parameter name₁>, <IV parameter name₂>, ..., <IV parameter nameₙ>)
```

For example, assuming the tree structure from Figure 14.3, the following command will constrain the inclusive value parameter of the two public transport branches to be equal:

```
;ivset: (PTrail, PTroad)
```

It is possible to constrain several IV parameters simultaneously such that various combinations of IV parameters will be equal to one another. Each new simultaneous constraint imposed is separated by a slash, as shown below:

```
;ivset: (<IV parameter name₁>, <IV parameter name₂>, ..., <IV parameter
nameᵢ>) / (<IV parameter nameⱼ>, <IV parameter nameₖ>, ..., <IV parameter
nameₙ>) / ... / (<IV parameter nameₘ>, <IV parameter nameₙ>, ..., <IV para
meter nameₚ>)
```

For example, assuming a new branch existed (called D) for the tree structure, with two new alternatives, pushbike and motorbike, the following command would constrain the IV parameters for branches A and C and B and D:

```
;ivset: (A, C) / (B, D)
```

As well as constraining the IV parameters of NL models, it is also possible for the analyst to treat them as fixed parameters. The command syntax for this is similar to that shown above for the constraining of the IV parameters, with the parameters to be fixed placed once more within the round brackets of the **;ivset** command. The value that the IV parameter is to be fixed at is specified as follows:

```
;ivset: (<specification>) = [<value>]
```

As with the constraining of several IV parameters, it is possible to constrain several IV parameters to some fixed value, simultaneously. Generically, the command syntax to do so is shown below:

```
;ivset: (<IV parameter name₁>, <IV parameter name₂>, ..., <IV parameter
name_n>) = [<value>]
```

For example, assuming the tree structure shown in Figure 14.3, the following **;ivset** command would constrain the two public transport IV parameters to equal 0.75:

```
;ivset: (PTRail, PTRoad) = [0.75]
```

It is also possible to constrain several sets of IV parameters to equal different fixed values simultaneously. We show this below with each set of IV parameters to be fixed, separated by a slash (/) in the command syntax:

```
;ivset: (<IV parameter name₁>, <IV parameter name₂>, ..., <IV parameter
name_i>) = [<value₁>] / (<IV parameter name_j>, <IV parameter name_k>, ...,
<IV parameter name_j>) = [<value₂>] / ... / / (<IV parameter name_m>, <IV
parameter name_n>, ..., <IV parameter name_p>) = [<value_w>]
```

For example, the following will constrain the PTRail branch of Figure 14.3 to 0.75 while simultaneously fixing the PTRoad IV parameter to 0.5:

```
;ivset: (PTRail) = [0.75] / ;ivset: (PTRoad) = [0.5]
```

A popular treatment is to constrain one IV parameter to 1.0, unless the analyst desires to test some hypothesis with regard to the correlation structure of the model. We reiterate, however, that this is not necessary and indeed the model may not estimate when a parameter is forced to a specific value. The remaining IV parameters, which are free to be estimated, can then be assessed relative to that which was fixed.

14.2.2 Specifying IV start values for the NL model

As with the parameter estimates of the MNL model, it is also possible for the analyst to specify the start values for the IV parameters within the NL model at which Nlogit will commence the estimation search. This is accomplished by the following command format, whereby the start value is not placed within any brackets:

```
;ivset: (<IV parameter name₁>) = value₁
```

It is possible to specify start values for several IV parameters simultaneously. For example, the following command would instruct Nlogit to start the search for the IV parameter estimates where for the Car branch, the start value is 0.8, and for the PTEX and PTNW branches, the start values are 0.75:

```
;ivset: (Car) = 0.8 / (PTEX,PTNW) = 0.75
```

> *As an aside*, by default, the Nlogit starting value for all IV parameter estimates is 1.0. The specification of starting values is not limited to the IV parameters of NL models. The analyst may also specify starting values for the remaining parameter estimates contained within the model, although the default is the MNL estimates. This may be done in a similar manner to the MNL model, where the analyst places the requested start value in round brackets (**( )**) after the parameter name. The command syntax **;start=logit** used in earlier version of Nlogit (pre Nlogit4) is redundant since the MNL estimates are always the default.
>
> *As a further aside*, when utility functions are not specified at levels 2 to 4 of the NL model (discussed later), the MNL model first estimated will be equivalent to the equivalently specified MNL model.

14.3 Estimating a NL model and interpreting the output

In setting up the command syntax, we initially estimate models in which each branch has two alternatives, leaving tree structures with a branch of one alternative (a degenerate branch) for a later section of this chapter. Given the discussion in Chapter 4, this chapter now focusses only on what was previously called the RU2 nested logit specification, which is the form that has all the accepted properties compliant with global utility maximization.

RU2 does not require any constraining of the IV parameters, although this can be chosen, as discussed in Section 14.2. The normalization for identification is an upper normalization (as shown in Chapter 4). The Nlogit command syntax for the models to be estimated in the chapter is given below:

```
LOAD;file="C:\Books\DCMPrimer\Second    Edition    2010\Latest    Version\Data  and  nlogit  set
ups\SPRPLabeled\NW_SPRP.sav.lpj"$
Project file contained   12167 observations. Note - This is all RP and SP data
reject;SPRP=1$ We are removing the RP data

Nlogit
    ;lhs = choice, cset, altij
    ;choices = NLR,NHR,NBW,bs,tn,bw,cr
    ;tree=ptnew(NLR,NHR,NBW),Allold(bs,tn,bw,cr)
    ;show
    ;RU2
    ;prob = margprob
    ;cprob = altprob
    ;ivb = ivbranch
    ;utility=mutilz
    ;model:
    u(nlr) = nlr + actpt*act + invcpt*invc + invtpt*invt2 + egtpt*egt + trpt*trnf /
    u(nhr) = nhr + actpt*act + invcpt*invc + invtpt*invt2 + egtpt*egt + trpt*trnf /
    u(nbw) = nbw + actpt*act + invcpt*invc + invtpt*invt2 + egtpt*egt + trpt*trnf /
    u(bs) = bs + actpt*act + invcpt*invc + invtpt*invt2 + egtpt*egt + trpt*trnf /
    u(tn) = tn + actpt*act + invcpt*invc + invtpt*invt2 + egtpt*egt + trpt*trnf /
    u(bw) = bw + actpt*act + invcpt*invc + invtpt*invt2 + egtpt*egt + trpt*trnf /
    u(cr) =                          invccar*invc+invtcar*invt + TC*TC + PC*PC + egtcr*egt $/
+----------------------------------------------------------------------+
|WARNING:   Bad observations were found in the sample. |
|Found 104 bad observations among   1970 individuals. |
|You can use ;CheckData to get a list of these points. |
+----------------------------------------------------------------------+
Tree Structure Specified for the Nested Logit Model
Sample proportions are marginal, not conditional.
Choices marked with * are excluded for the IIA test.
----------------------+--------------------+--------------------+--------------------+--------+-----
Trunk    (prop.)|Limb     (prop.)|Branch   (prop.)|Choice    (prop.)|Weight|IIA
----------------------+--------------------+--------------------+--------------------+--------+-----
Trunk{1} 1.00000 |Lmb[1|1] 1.00000|PTNEW     .40997|NLR      .17471| 1.000|
            |              |        |NHR      .18060| 1.000|
            |              |        |NBW      .05466| 1.000|
            |              |ALLOLD   .59003|BS       .11790| 1.000|
            |              |        |TN       .14094| 1.000|
            |              |        |BW       .20096| 1.000|
            |              |        |CR       .13023| 1.000|
----------------------+--------------------+--------------------+--------------------+--------+-----
Normal exit:   7 iterations. Status=0, F=   2730.693
----------------------------------------------------------------------------------------
Discrete choice (multinomial logit) model
Dependent variable           Choice
Log likelihood function    -2730.69253
Estimation based on N =   1866, K =  16
Inf.Cr.AIC  =   5493.4 AIC/N =    2.944
```

```
R2=1-LogL/LogL* Log-L fncn R-sqrd R2Adj
Constants only must be computed directly
              Use NLOGIT ;...;RHS=ONE$
Chi-squared[10]          =   1588.10946
Prob [ chi squared > value ] =   .00000
Response data are given as ind. choices
Number of obs.= 1970, skipped  104 obs
```

-----------+--

CHOICE	Coefficient	Standard Error	z	Prob. |z|>Z*	95% Confidence Interval	
NLR	1.84937***	.30793	6.01	.0000	1.24584	2.45291
ACTPT	-.04248***	.00467	-9.10	.0000	-.05163	-.03334
INVCPT	-.24053***	.01369	-17.57	.0000	-.26737	-.21370
INVTPT	-.03160***	.00234	-13.52	.0000	-.03618	-.02702
EGTPT	-.00414	.00400	-1.04	.3002	-.01198	.00369
TRPT	.28841**	.12646	2.28	.0226	.04055	.53626
NHR	1.95132***	.29157	6.69	.0000	1.37987	2.52278
NBW	.85378***	.28549	2.99	.0028	.29423	1.41333
BS	-.64770**	.25958	-2.50	.0126	-1.15647	-.13893
TN	-.32632	.26261	-1.24	.2140	-.84102	.18838
BW	-.03503	.26455	-.13	.8946	-.55353	.48347
INVCCAR	-.05669	.06937	-.82	.4138	-.19266	.07928
INVTCAR	-.01635***	.00319	-5.12	.0000	-.02261	-.01009
TC	-.07601**	.03093	-2.46	.0140	-.13664	-.01538
PC	-.04837***	.00882	-5.49	.0000	-.06565	-.03109
EGTCR	-.11525***	.02133	-5.40	.0000	-.15707	-.07344

-----------+--

```
***, **, * ==>  Significance at 1%, 5%, 10% level.
```

```
FIML Nested Multinomial Logit Model
Dependent variable              CHOICE
Log likelihood function     -2711.94824
Restricted log likelihood   -3660.16113
Chi squared [ 18](P= .000)   1896.42578
Significance level                .00000
McFadden Pseudo R-squared      .2590632
Estimation based on N =   1866, K =  18
Inf.Cr.AIC  =   5459.9 AIC/N =    2.926
Constants only must be computed directly
              Use NLOGIT ;...;RHS=ONE$
At start values -2730.6925  .0069******
Response data are given as ind. choices
BHHH estimator used for asymp. variance
The model has 2 levels.
Random Utility Form 2:IVparms = Mb|l,Gl
Number of obs.= 1970, skipped  104 obs
```

CHOICE	Coefficient	Standard Error	z	Prob. $\|z\|>Z*$	95% Confidence Interval	
	Attributes in the Utility Functions (beta)					
NLR	1.76991***	.28924	6.12	.0000	1.20300	2.33681
ACTPT	-.03635***	.00498	-7.29	.0000	-.04612	-.02658
INVCPT	-.21341***	.01648	-12.95	.0000	-.24572	-.18110
INVTPT	-.02617***	.00232	-11.29	.0000	-.03072	-.02163
EGTPT	-.00542	.00372	-1.46	.1454	-.01272	.00188
TRPT	.23064**	.09036	2.55	.0107	.05355	.40774
NHR	1.72411***	.28103	6.13	.0000	1.17329	2.27492
NBW	1.19653***	.25980	4.61	.0000	.68734	1.70571
BS	-.59018**	.24843	-2.38	.0175	-1.07710	-.10327
TN	-.28961	.24381	-1.19	.2349	-.76747	.18825
BW	-.02930	.23930	-.12	.9025	-.49831	.43971
INVCCAR	-.03454	.07066	-.49	.6250	-.17303	.10396
INVTCAR	-.01473***	.00325	-4.53	.0000	-.02110	-.00835
TC	-.07077**	.03124	-2.26	.0235	-.13200	-.00953
PC	-.04475***	.00886	-5.05	.0000	-.06212	-.02738
EGTCR	-.10768***	.02641	-4.08	.0000	-.15943	-.05592
	IV parameters, RU2 form = mu(b|1),gamma(1)					
PTNEW	.51010***	.05571	9.16	.0000	.40091	.61928
ALLOLD	.95074***	.08846	10.75	.0000	.77737	1.12411

Estimating the above model, Nlogit first provides the MNL output used to locate the start values for the NL and ML estimation search. The interpretation of the majority of the NL output is the same as that provided for the MNL model. We limit our discussion to new output that is either not presented with the MNL model output or where the interpretation between that provided for the MNL and NL models differs. The first difference of note is in the first line of the output box, which we reproduce below:

FIML: Nested Multinomial Logit Model

The first line of output informs the analyst that a NL model was obtained using an estimation technique known as full information maximum likelihood (FIML), which we discussed in Chapter 5. NL models may be estimated either sequentially or simultaneously. *Sequential estimation* (known as limited information maximum likelihood estimators, or LIML) involves the estimation of separate levels of the NL tree in sequential order from the lowest level to the highest level of the tree. Beginning at the branch level, LIML will estimate the utility specifications of the alternatives present within each branch, including the IV parameters, as well as the IV parameters for each branch of the tree. Once the IV parameters are estimated, the IV parameters at the branch level may be calculated. These IV parameters are then used as explanatory variables for the next level of the tree. This process is repeated until the entire tree structure of the NL Model is estimated. Hensher (1986) has shown that using LIML to estimate NL models is statistically inefficient, as the parameter estimates of levels three and higher are not minimum variance parameter estimates resulting from the use of estimates to estimate yet more estimates. For NL models with between two and four levels, it is therefore more common to use simultaneous estimation procedures that provide statistically efficient parameter estimates. The simultaneous estimation of the branches, limbs, and trunks of a NL model is achieved using FIML. The sequential estimation of each partition of the NL tree offers no advantages over the simultaneous estimation of the entire NL model other than the possibility to estimate models with greater than four levels (which will rarely be required); hence, we advise against this for the beginner. Those interested in learning more about the differences between the sequential and simultaneous estimation of NL models are referred to Louviere *et al.* (2000, 149–52), while those interested in estimating such models are referred to the reference manuals that accompany the Nlogit software.

Nlogit next reports the restricted and unrestricted LL functions for the model. The LL functions of the NL model may be interpreted in exactly the same manner as the LL functions of the MNL model. Indeed, if the two models are estimated on the same sample, the LL functions for both are directly comparable. The LL function reported is that for the model fitted as specified through the utility functions, while the unrestricted LL function is the LL function for a model estimated assuming equal choice shares (i.e., there is no knowledge of sample shares). As with the MNL model, the test of model significance for the NL model is the LL ratio test (see Chapter 7) using the reported LL values discussed above. NL performs this test automatically. The LL ratio test is chi square distributed with degrees of freedom equal to the number of parameters estimated within the model. The number of parameters is inclusive of the IV parameters estimated, but not those that were fixed (and hence not estimated). As with the MNL model, the Chi-square test statistic for this test is:

$$-2(LL_{\text{Restricted}} - LL_{\text{Unrestricted}}) \sim \chi^2_{(\text{Difference in the number of parameters estimated between the two models})}.$$

$$(14.1)$$

For the model output above, the test is shown below. The test has 18 degrees of freedom (i.e., 16 parameter estimates and 2 IV parameters):

$$-2(-3660.161 - (-2711.948)) = 1896.43 \sim \chi^2_{(18)}.$$

1896.43 is equal to the value we observe in the Nlogit output. To determine the overall model fit, the analyst may compare the test statistic to the critical chi square with 18 degrees of freedom, or use the p-value provided by Nlogit which, for this example, is zero. As the p-value is less than alpha equal to 0.05 (i.e., 95 percent confidence level), we conclude that the estimated NL model represents an improvement in the LL function of a model estimated with equal market shares. As such, we conclude that the parameters estimated for the attributes included in the utility functions improve the overall model fit.

Nlogit next estimates the pseudo-R^2. As with the MNL model, the pseudo-R^2 for the NL model is estimated using the ratio of the LL function of the model estimated here (i.e., −2711.95) over the LL function of a base model estimated assuming equal choice shares across the alternatives (i.e. −3660.16). The pseudo-R^2 becomes 0.260, as reported in the output as McFadden Pseudo R-squared:

$$R^2 = 1 - \frac{LL_{\text{Estimated model}}}{LL_{\text{Base model}}} = 1 - \frac{2711.95}{-3660.16} = 0.259.$$

When the choice set varies across individuals, as it does in the SP data we are using (where each choice set has four of the seven alternatives), it is not possible to compute the constants-only results from the market shares, and the no coefficients model does not have probabilities equal to 1/J. If you want those things calculated, you have to use **;RHS=one**, as in the model below. The LL of −3165.836 is based on the known sample choice shares, and no other information:

```
|-> Nlogit
    ;lhs = choice, cset, altij
    ;choices = NLR,NHR,NBW,bs,tn,bw,cr
    ;rhs=one$
-----------------------------------------------------------------------
Discrete choice (multinomial logit) model
Dependent variable                      Choice
Log likelihood function       -3165.83600
Estimation based on N =     1866, K =    6
Inf.Cr.AIC   =   6343.7 AIC/N =    3.400
```

```
R2=1-LogL/LogL* Log-L fncn R-sqrd R2Adj
Constants only must be computed directly
              Use NLOGIT ;...;RHS=ONE$
Response data are given as ind. choices
Number of obs.=  1970, skipped  104 obs
```

CHOICE	Coefficient	Standard Error	z	Prob. |z|>Z*	95% Confidence Interval	
A_NLR	.44365***	.08617	5.15	.0000	.27476	.61253
A_NHR	.82161***	.08696	9.45	.0000	.65116	.99205
A_NBW	-.50935***	.11979	-4.25	.0000	-.74414	-.27455
A_BS	-.18067*	.09337	-1.93	.0530	-.36368	.00234
A_TN	.08723	.08990	.97	.3319	-.08897	.26343
A_BW	.44200***	.08334	5.30	.0000	.27865	.60536

We leave it to the reader to discuss the parameters associated with each attribute. Our primary focus will be on the inclusive value (or scale) parameters. The inclusion of the IV parameters in the utility functions of NL models has important ramifications on how we present the utility functions, and how we interpret them. We may write out the utility functions for each of the alternatives directly from the output without having to be concerned with the scale parameters of the model (they all equal one). We do this in Equations (14.2a) through (14.2g):

```
u(nlr) = 1.769  -0.036*act -0.213*invc -0.026*invt2 -0.005*egt +0.231*trnf / . (14.2a)
u(nhr) = 1.724  -0.036*act -0.213*invc -0.026*invt2 -0.005*egt +0.231*trnf / . (14.2b)
u(nbw) = 1.197  -0.036*act -0.213*invc -0.026*invt2 -0.005*egt +0.231*trnf / . (14.2c)
u(bs)  = -0.591 -0.036*act -0.213*invc -0.026*invt2 -0.005*egt +0.231*trnf / . (14.2d)
u(tn)  = -0.289 -0.036*act -0.213*invc -0.026*invt2 -0.005*egt +0.231*trnf / . (14.2e)
u(bw)  = 0.029  -0.036*act -0.213*invc -0.026*invt2 -0.005*egt +0.231*trnf / . (14.2f)
u(cr)  =             -0.035*invc-0.0708*TC -0.0445*PC -0.0147*invt -0.0108*egt$ . (14.2g)
```

> *As an aside*, as with all other choice models, the utilities derived from the above utility specifications are relative. Hence, to determine the utility for any one alternative, the analyst must take the difference between the utility for that alternative and that of a second alternative.

The final results produced are the estimates of the IV parameters for each of the trunks, limbs, and branches of the model. As with the parameter estimates for the attributes specified within the utility functions, Nlogit reports for each IV parameter a standard error, a Wald statistic and a *p*-value. An interesting question arises as to what an insignificant IV parameter means. The test statistic, the Wald statistic, is calculated by dividing the IV parameter estimate by its associated standard error and comparing the resulting value to some critical value (usually ±1.96, representing a 95 percent confidence level). This test is exactly the same as the one-sample *t*-test and is used in this case to determine whether the IV parameter is statistically equal to zero. If the parameter is found to be statistically equal to zero (i.e., the parameter is not significant), the parameter remains within the 0–1 bound (it equals zero). This is important; as mentioned in Chapter 4 we have two totally independent choice models for the upper and lower levels and hence there exists evidence for a partition of the tree structure at this section of the model.

> *As an aside*, an insignificant IV parameter (i.e., one that is statistically equal to zero) suggests that the two scale parameters taken from the different levels to form the IV parameter are statistically very different (e.g., 0.1 divided by 0.8 equals 0.125 which is closer to zero than 0.1 divided by 0.2 which equals 0.5; of course, the standard errors must also be accounted for). This does not mean that the variance is not statistically significant, or there is no correlation between alternatives within a branch.

The alternative finding of a significant IV parameter estimate suggests that the parameter is not equal to zero, but does not indicate whether the parameter lies outside the upper bound of the 0–1 range (recall that an IV parameter cannot be less than zero). Thus, for significant IV parameters, a second test is required to determine whether the upper bound has been exceeded. This test may be undertaken with a simple modification to the test conducted to determine whether the parameter is statistically equal to zero. We show this modification below:

$$\text{Wald Test} = \frac{IV_{parameter} - 1}{\text{std error}}. \tag{14.3}$$

For the above example, the IV parameter for the PTNEW branch is statistically different from zero. As such, it is necessary to undertake the test described in Equation (14.4) to determine whether the variable is statistically different to one. We perform this test below:

$$\text{Wald Test} = \frac{0.5101 - 1}{0.0557} = -8.79.$$

Comparing the test statistic of −8.79 to the critical value of ±1.96 (i.e., at alpha equal to 0.05), we can reject the hypothesis that the PTNEW parameter is statistically equal to one. This finding suggests that the nested structure is indeed a statistically significant improvement over MNL, as well as being consistent with global utility maximization in that it satisfies the 0–1 bounds for the IV parameter. The same finding applies to the other branch.

If the IV parameter were not statistically equal to either zero or one, or lie within the 0–1 bound, but was statistically greater than one, the global utility maximization assumption is no longer strictly valid, and cross-elasticities with the wrong sign will be observed. The analyst will be required to (1) explore new tree structures, (2) constrain a different IV parameter using the same tree structure and re-estimate the model, or (3) move to more advanced models (see Chapter 15) in order to proceed.

As an aside, The IV parameters are related to the correlation among alternatives in the same branch (see Chapter 4):

$1 - \left(\frac{\lambda_{(i|j,l)}}{\mu_{(i|j,l)}}\right)^2$ equals the correlation of the utility functions for any pair of alternatives present within the same nest or partition of a NL model. For the above example, the correlations between the bus and train and busway and LR alternatives may be calculated as follows:

$Corr(\text{bs,tn,bw,cr}) = 1-(0.95074)^2 = 0.00964$ $Corr(\text{NLR,NHR,NBW}) = 1-(0.5101)^2 = 0.739.$

Thus, IV parameters closer to 1.0 not only indicate a smaller difference in the variance between adjoining levels, but also smaller correlation structures between the utility functions of the alternatives present within the lower level of the nest.

14.3.1 Estimating the probabilities of a two-level NL model

The estimation of the probabilities for each alternative of a NL model is more complex than the calculations for a MNL model. This is because the probability of choosing an alternative (at level 1) is conditional upon the branch to which that alternative belongs. For models with more than two levels, the probability of the branch being chosen is in turn conditional on the limb to which the branch belongs, which for four-level NL models is also conditional on the trunk to which the limb belongs. Thus, the probability that a lower level of a NL model is chosen is said to be conditional on all higher levels connected with that lower level first being chosen. For example, for the estimated model above, the probability of the bus mode being selected is conditional upon the ALLOLD branch first being chosen. Similarly, the probability of the New Light Rail (NLR) being chosen is conditional on the PTNEW branch being selected first.

Equations (14.2a) through (14.2g) represent the utility functions at level one of the NL model. Higher levels of NL models also have utility, and these utility functions at higher levels of the NL model are connected to the lower levels of the model via two means. Firstly, the utility functions of higher levels of NL models are connected to the level directly below via the inclusion of the lower level's IV parameter within the upper level's utility function. The second connection occurs through the inclusion of the IV variable (i.e., the index of expected maximum utility or EMU), which relates the utility expressions of the level directly below to that of the upper level, as detailed in Chapter 4.

That is, the utility for the jth branch belonging to limb i of trunk l is equal to the IV parameter multiplied by the IV variable (or EMU).

The unconditional probabilities for each outcome are calculated for the preceding example as the product of the conditional and marginal probabilities:

$$P(cr,AllOld) = P(cr|AllOld) \times P(AllOld)$$
$$P(bs,AllOld) = P(bs|AllOld) \times P(AllOld)$$
$$P(tn,AllOld) = P(tn|AllOld) \times P(AllOld)$$
$$P(bw,AllOld) = P(bw|AllOld) \times P(AllOld)$$
$$P(nlr, PtNew) = P(nlr|PtNew) \times P(PtNew)$$
$$P(nhr,PtNew) = P(nhr|PtNew) \times P(PtNew)$$
$$P(nbw,PtNew) = P(nbw|PtNew) \times P(PtNew)$$

These probabilities are automatically calculated by Nlogit using the formulae in Chapter 4, and can be seen and saved by adding in the syntax **;prob=<name of the variable to define the calculated probabilities>**. The predicted probabilities (the multiplication of all relevant conditional probabilities) in NL models may be retained as a new variable in the data set with the addition of the command **;prob = <name>**. This is the same command used for the MNL model to save the probabilities. Conditional probabilities for elemental alternatives (level 1 probabilities) are retained using the command syntax **;Cprob = <name>**. The IV variables (not parameters) otherwise known as EMUs may also be saved as new variables in the data set. The commands to save the IV parameters at each level are: Branch level: **IVB = <name>**, Limb level: **IVL = <name>**, and Trunk level: **IVT = <name>**.

For example, we have added in **;prob=margprob** to obtain the marginal probabilities for each of the alternatives above. Note, however, that since each respondent in the SP data set being used considered four of the seven alternatives, the marginal probabilities for each respondent are limited to the four alternatives in their choice set. For the first respondent (listed below), they had alternatives (altij) 1,3,4, and 7 in their choice set, namely NLR, NBW, bs, and cr. The marginal probabilities associated with the elemental alternatives sum to 1.0 across the entire tree. In contrast, the conditional probabilities (defined by **AltProb** in Table 14.1) sum to 1.0 within each branch. The analyst can also capture the associated utility by using a command such as **;utility=mutilz**. The results can be cut and pasted into an Excel file and then presented in various ways as tables in a report.

In addition to the various probability outputs, the IV variable is also calculated and reported (as **IvBranch** in Table 14.1). As shown in Chapter 4, the IV variable is based on the utility expressions at the level below the IV; each utility expression associated with an alternative is calculated by multiplying each parameter estimate by the relevant attribute level, adding them up plus the constant, and then taking the exponential. These are summed across all relevant alternatives (such as the four in Table 14.1 for the first respondent), and then the natural logarithm is taken of the summed exponentials. The findings are given in Table 14.1.

14.4 Specifying utility functions at higher levels of the NL tree

In Section 14.3, we assumed that all attributes were associated with the utility expressions that defined each elemental alternative. It is possible that some influence on choice may directly influence the utility at higher levels in the tree. This can be accomplished using the following command syntax, where the name provided for the utility expression is a name provided in the **;tree** specification:

```
U(<branch, limb or trunk name>) = <utility function 1>/
```

While the *attributes of elemental alternatives* may be assigned to utility expressions of higher levels of NL models, a great level of care is required by the analyst in doing so. Attribute levels distinguish between alternatives which by design are placed at level 1 of the model. Unless it can be shown that a common set of attributes is used by respondents to distinguish between higher choices (i.e., higher level partitions of the model), attributes should be assigned only at level 1 of the model. Thus, while we do not rule out the possibility that attribute levels be used in the utility expressions at higher levels of a NL model, we advise the beginner to limit themselves to the use of variables that are not attributes of alternatives, such as the socio-economic characteristics (SECs) of a respondent, or contextual variables. Intuitively, we might expect SECs to have an influence on groupings of alternatives (e.g., public transport modes versus car) that might be different to their influence, for example, between each public transport mode. In the following NL model specification, we assign personal income and gender to the upper branch **ptnew**:

Table 14.1 Useful outputs stored under the project file (data, variables)

Id	Altij	IvBranch	MargProb	AltProb	Mutilz
1	1	0.840	0.395	0.556	0.125
1	3	0.840	0.316	0.444	0.014
1	4	−0.523	0.050	0.173	−2.096
1	7	−0.523	0.239	0.827	−0.657
1	1	1.163	0.276	0.344	0.048
1	3	1.163	0.527	0.656	0.368
1	4	−0.899	0.026	0.134	−2.679
1	7	−0.899	0.171	0.866	−0.960
1	1	1.515	0.484	0.591	0.491
1	3	1.515	0.335	0.409	0.309
1	4	−0.824	0.031	0.174	−2.369
1	7	−0.824	0.149	0.826	−0.935
1	1	1.966	0.202	0.248	0.283
1	3	1.966	0.613	0.752	0.835
1	4	−0.551	0.040	0.215	−1.924
1	7	−0.551	0.145	0.785	−0.730
1	1	1.408	0.420	0.561	0.412
1	3	1.408	0.328	0.439	0.290
1	4	−0.421	0.025	0.098	−2.522
1	7	−0.421	0.227	0.902	−0.483
1	1	0.641	0.639	0.853	0.239
1	3	0.641	0.110	0.147	−0.632
1	4	−0.842	0.042	0.167	−2.420
1	7	−0.842	0.209	0.833	−0.944
1	1	1.406	0.204	0.254	0.017
1	3	1.406	0.600	0.746	0.553
1	4	−0.778	0.021	0.108	−2.769
1	7	−0.778	0.174	0.892	−0.821
1	1	0.623	0.411	0.570	0.030
1	3	0.623	0.310	0.430	−0.110
1	4	−0.696	0.074	0.265	−1.863
1	7	−0.696	0.205	0.735	−0.925
1	1	1.759	0.532	0.599	0.619
1	3	1.759	0.356	0.401	0.420
1	4	−1.303	0.017	0.156	−2.912
1	7	−1.303	0.094	0.844	−1.355
1	1	1.813	0.548	0.672	0.703
1	3	1.813	0.267	0.328	0.346
1	4	−0.633	0.016	0.086	−2.846
1	7	−0.633	0.169	0.914	−0.665

```
|-> Nlogit     ;lhs = choice, cset, altij
    ;choices = NLR,NHR,NBW,bs,tn,bw,cr
    ;tree=ptnew(NLR,NHR,NBW),Allold(bs,tn,bw,cr)
    ;show
    ;RU2
    ;prob = margprob
    ;cprob = altprob
    ;ivb = ivbranch
    ;utility=mutilz
    ;model:
    u(nlr) = nlr + actpt*act + invcpt*invc + invtpt*invt2 + egtpt*egt + trpt*trnf /
    u(nhr) = nhr + actpt*act + invcpt*invc + invtpt*invt2 + egtpt*egt + trpt*trnf /
    u(nbw) = nbw + actpt*act + invcpt*invc + invtpt*invt2 + egtpt*egt + trpt*trnf /
    u(bs)  = bs + actpt*act + invcpt*invc + invtpt*invt2 + egtpt*egt + trpt*trnf /
    u(tn)  = tn + actpt*act + invcpt*invc + invtpt*invt2 + egtpt*egt + trpt*trnf /
    u(bw)  = bw + actpt*act + invcpt*invc + invtpt*invt2 + egtpt*egt + trpt*trnf /
    u(cr)  =                       invccar*invc+invtcar*invt + TC*TC + PC*PC + egtcr*egt /
    u(ptnew)=pincz*pinc+gend*gender$
```
```
+------------------------------------------------------------------+
|WARNING:   Bad observations were found in the sample. |
|Found 104 bad observations among    1970 individuals. |
|You can use ;CheckData to get a list of these points. |
+------------------------------------------------------------------+
Tree Structure Specified for the Nested Logit Model
Sample proportions are marginal, not conditional.
Choices marked with * are excluded for the IIA test.
----------------------+---------------------+---------------------+--------------------+--------+-----
Trunk    (prop.)|Limb    (prop.)|Branch    (prop.)|Choice    (prop.)|Weight|IIA
----------------------+---------------------+---------------------+--------------------+--------+-----
Trunk{1} 1.00000|Lmb[1|1] 1.00000|PTNEW    .40997|NLR    .17471| 1.000|
         |                |           |NHR    .18060| 1.000|
         |                |           |NBW    .05466| 1.000|
         |                |ALLOLD  .59003|BS    .11790| 1.000|
         |                |           |TN    .14094| 1.000|
         |                |           |BW    .20096| 1.000|
         |                |           |CR    .13023| 1.000|
----------------------+---------------------+---------------------+--------------------+--------+-----
Normal exit:   7 iterations. Status=0, F=    2730.693
----------------------------------------------------------------------------------------------
Start values obtained using MNL model
Dependent variable          Choice
Log likelihood function    -3981.90300
Estimation based on N =   1866, K =   18
Inf.Cr.AIC  =    7999.8 AIC/N =    4.287
Log-L for Choice   model =   -2730.6925
R2=1-LogL/LogL* Log-L fncn R-sqrd R2Adj
Constants only must be computed directly
            Use NLOGIT ;...;RHS=ONE$
Chi-squared[10]        =    1588.10946
```

```
Prob [ chi squared > value ] =   .00000
Log-L for Branch   model =   -1251.2105
Response data are given as ind. choices
Number of obs.= 1970, skipped  104 obs
```

CHOICE	Coefficient	Standard Error	z	Prob. |z|>Z*	95% Confidence Interval	
	Model for Choice Among Alternatives					
NLR	1.84937***	.30793	6.01	.0000	1.24584	2.45291
ACTPT	-.04248***	.00467	-9.10	.0000	-.05163	-.03334
INVCPT	-.24053***	.01369	-17.57	.0000	-.26737	-.21370
INVTPT	-.03160***	.00234	-13.52	.0000	-.03618	-.02702
EGTPT	-.00414	.00400	-1.04	.3002	-.01198	.00369
TRPT	.28841**	.12646	2.28	.0226	.04055	.53626
NHR	1.95132***	.29157	6.69	.0000	1.37987	2.52278
NBW	.85378***	.28549	2.99	.0028	.29423	1.41333
BS	-.64770**	.25958	-2.50	.0126	-1.15647	-.13893
TN	-.32632	.26261	-1.24	.2140	-.84102	.18838
BW	-.03503	.26455	-.13	.8946	-.55353	.48347
INVCCAR	-.05669	.06937	-.82	.4138	-.19266	.07928
INVTCAR	-.01635***	.00319	-5.12	.0000	-.02261	-.01009
TC	-.07601**	.03093	-2.46	.0140	-.13664	-.01538
PC	-.04837***	.00882	-5.49	.0000	-.06565	-.03109
EGTCR	-.11525***	.02133	-5.40	.0000	-.15707	-.07344
	Model for Choice Among Branches					
PINCZ	-.00363***	.00104	-3.50	.0005	-.00566	-.00159
GEND	-.35741***	.10315	-3.47	.0005	-.55957	-.15525

```
***, **, * ==>  Significance at 1%, 5%, 10% level.

Normal exit: 32 iterations. Status=0, F=   2703.735

FIML Nested Multinomial Logit Model
Dependent variable              CHOICE
Log likelihood function     -2703.73474
Restricted log likelihood   -3660.16113
Chi squared [ 20](P= .000)   1912.85279
Significance level               .00000
McFadden Pseudo R-squared       .2613072
Estimation based on N =   1866, K =  20
Inf.Cr.AIC  =   5447.5 AIC/N =    2.919
Constants only must be computed directly
          Use NLOGIT ;...;RHS=ONE$
At start values -2742.5189   .0141******
Response data are given as ind. choices
BHHH estimator used for asymp. variance
The model has 2 levels.
Random Utility Form 2:IVparms = Mb|l,Gl
```

```
Coefs. for branch level begin with PINCZ
Number of obs.=  1970, skipped  104 obs
-----------+------------------------------------------------------------------------------
           |              Standard              Prob.        95% Confidence
   CHOICE| Coefficient     Error       z      |z|>Z*            Interval
-----------+------------------------------------------------------------------------------
           |Attributes in the Utility Functions (beta)
     NLR|    2.02074***   .29347     6.89     .0000      1.44554    2.59594
   ACTPT|    -.03467***   .00492    -7.05     .0000      -.04431    -.02503
  INVCPT|    -.20791***   .01656   -12.56     .0000      -.24036    -.17547
  INVTPT|    -.02598***   .00233   -11.15     .0000      -.03055    -.02142
   EGTPT|    -.00557      .00366    -1.52     .1287      -.01275     .00161
    TRPT|     .23514***   .08938     2.63     .0085       .05996     .41032
     NHR|    1.94280***   .28290     6.87     .0000      1.38834    2.49727
     NBW|    1.43519***   .26211     5.48     .0000       .92147    1.94891
      BS|    -.53165**    .24177    -2.20     .0279     -1.00551    -.05779
      TN|    -.23853      .23713    -1.01     .3145      -.70330     .22625
      BW|     .00840      .23337      .04     .9713      -.44899     .46580
 INVCCAR|    -.02858      .06904     -.41     .6789      -.16389     .10673
 INVTCAR|    -.01442***   .00321    -4.50     .0000      -.02070    -.00814
      TC|    -.06620**    .03052    -2.17     .0301      -.12603    -.00638
      PC|    -.04315***   .00866    -4.98     .0000      -.06013    -.02617
   EGTCR|    -.10209***   .02596    -3.93     .0001      -.15297    -.05121
           |Attributes of Branch Choice Equations (alpha)
   PINCZ|    -.00266**    .00129    -2.06     .0398      -.00519    -.00012
    GEND|    -.25315**    .11993    -2.11     .0348      -.48821    -.01809
           |IV parameters, RU2 form = mu(b|1),gamma(1)
   PTNEW|     .50367***   .05604     8.99     .0000       .39383     .61350
  ALLOLD|     .92064***   .08792    10.47     .0000       .74831    1.09296
-----------+------------------------------------------------------------------------------
```

The only difference between the base NL model and this model is the addition of the following output (as well as the influence that this has on the other parameter estimates):

```
           |Attributes of Branch Choice Equations (alpha)
   PINCZ|     -.00266**        .00129   -2.06   .0398      -.00519    -.00012
    GEND|     -.25315**        .11993   -2.11   .0348      -.48821    -.01809
```

Personal income and the gender dummy variable (**male = 1**) are statistically significant, and given the negative sign this suggests that individuals on higher incomes and males tend to have a lower utility associated with the **ptnew** branch than other respondents, *ceteris paribus*. This finding will condition the overall probability of choosing a branch and hence an alternative in the **ptnew** branch, which flows through to the allocation of probabilities throughout the entire tree. Table 14.2 reports the change in the marginal and conditional probabilities, as well as utility, for the first

Table 14.2 Comparison of findings in Table 14.1 with the NL model with upper level variables

Altij	IvBranch	MargProb	AltProb	Mutilz	Diff_MProb	Diff_AltProb	Diff_Multiz
1	1.091	0.468	0.358	0.684	0.073	−0.197	0.559
3	1.091	0.216	−0.031	0.316	−0.100	−0.475	0.302
4	−0.517	0.054	−2.098	0.172	0.004	−2.271	2.268
7	−0.517	0.262	−0.649	0.828	0.022	−1.476	1.485
1	1.301	0.366	0.281	0.475	0.089	−0.063	0.428
3	1.301	0.404	0.331	0.525	−0.123	−0.325	0.157
4	−0.871	0.030	−2.689	0.129	0.003	−2.823	2.807
7	−0.871	0.201	−0.929	0.871	0.030	−1.795	1.832
1	1.773	0.569	0.722	0.712	0.085	0.131	0.221
3	1.773	0.230	0.266	0.288	−0.105	−0.143	−0.021
4	−0.808	0.034	−2.378	0.169	0.003	−2.552	2.539
7	−0.808	0.166	−0.915	0.831	0.017	−1.741	1.766
1	2.024	0.285	0.513	0.366	0.083	0.265	0.083
3	2.024	0.494	0.790	0.634	−0.120	0.037	−0.201
4	−0.533	0.046	−1.931	0.209	0.007	−2.145	2.133
7	−0.533	0.175	−0.707	0.791	0.030	−1.493	1.521
1	1.654	0.496	0.643	0.685	0.076	0.081	0.273
3	1.654	0.228	0.251	0.315	−0.100	−0.187	0.025
4	−0.414	0.027	−2.538	0.096	0.002	−2.636	2.618
7	−0.414	0.250	−0.474	0.904	0.023	−1.376	1.387
1	1.103	0.614	0.459	0.827	−0.025	−0.393	0.588
3	1.103	0.129	−0.327	0.173	0.018	−0.474	0.805
4	−0.823	0.042	−2.425	0.163	0.000	−2.593	2.583
7	−0.823	0.215	−0.921	0.837	0.006	−1.754	1.780
1	1.478	0.290	0.252	0.377	0.086	−0.001	0.360
3	1.478	0.480	0.506	0.623	−0.120	−0.240	0.071
4	−0.781	0.024	−2.780	0.107	0.003	−2.888	2.876
7	−0.781	0.205	−0.823	0.893	0.031	−1.715	1.715
1	1.139	0.385	0.257	0.533	−0.026	−0.313	0.503
3	1.139	0.338	0.191	0.467	0.028	−0.239	0.577
4	−0.693	0.073	−1.872	0.262	−0.001	−2.137	2.125
7	−0.693	0.205	−0.918	0.738	0.000	−1.653	1.663
1	2.011	0.631	0.849	0.722	0.099	0.250	0.103
3	2.011	0.242	0.368	0.278	−0.114	−0.033	−0.142
4	−1.274	0.019	−2.928	0.149	0.001	−3.083	3.061
7	−1.274	0.108	−1.321	0.851	0.013	−2.165	2.207
1	2.098	0.623	0.930	0.778	0.075	0.258	0.075
3	2.098	0.178	0.300	0.222	−0.089	−0.028	−0.124
4	−0.638	0.017	−2.864	0.084	0.001	−2.950	2.931
7	−0.638	0.182	−0.669	0.916	0.013	−1.583	1.580

respondent for each of the 10 choice sets when we add in the upper level influences on **ptnew** compared to Table 14.1. While the differences might appear to be small, when summed across the entire data set this could amount to a noticeable change in the predicted modal shares. Interested readers could cut and paste into a spreadsheet the entire output for all respondents, and calculate the overall modal shares.

14.5 Handling degenerate branches in NL models

It is common in many applications to have partitions with only one alternative present. Such partitions are called *degenerate partitions*. For example, consider the NL tree structure shown in Figure 14.4 in which the Light Rail (LR) alternative resides within a branch by itself.

Degenerate partitions in NL models require careful consideration on how they are to be operationalized by the analyst. Given that the LR alternative is the sole alternative within branch C, it follows (see Chapter 4) that the conditional choice probability at level 1 for the LR must be equal to one. We show this below:

$$P(LR) = \frac{e^{V_{LR}}}{e^{V_{LR}}} = 1. \tag{14.4}$$

The utility function at level 2 for branch C is given as:

$$V_C = \lambda_C \left[\frac{1}{\mu_c} \times IV_{(LR)} \right] = \lambda_C \left[\frac{1}{1} \times \ln(e^{V_{LR}}) \right] = \lambda_C \times V_{LR}. \tag{14.5}$$

As the utility for a degenerate alternative can only reside at one level of the NL model (it does not matter whether we specify it at level 1 or 2), the variance must be the same at each level of a degenerate nest. That is, V_{LR} may be specified at levels 1 or 2 in the above example: however, if specified at level 1,

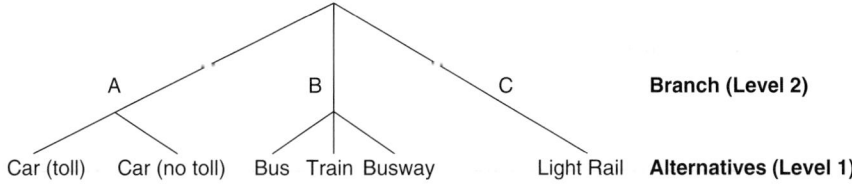

Figure 14.4 An NL tree structure with a degenerate alternative

the scale parameter, μ_C, is normalized to 1.0 while if specified at level 2, the scale parameter, λ_C, is free to vary. This is counterintuitive, since the variance (and hence scale parameters) for a degenerate alternative should be equal no matter at what level one specifies the utility function. That is, the variance structure of the NL model is such that higher level partitions incorporate the variance of lower adjoining partitions as well as that partition's own variance. With a degenerate alternative, higher level partitions should theoretically not have their own variance, as nothing is being explained at that level. As such, the only level at which the variance should be explained is at the level at which the utility function for that alternative is placed.

Normalization of the NL model using RU2 yields the following LR utility function:

$$\mu_C \times V_{1r} = \mu_C \times \beta_{11r} f\left(X_{11r}\right) + \mu_C \times \beta_{21r} f\left(X_{21r}\right) + \ldots + \mu_C \times \beta_{K1r} f\left(X_{K1r}\right). \qquad (14.6)$$

The utility function at level two of the model may be represented as follows:

$$V_C = 1\left[\frac{1}{\mu_C} \times IV_{(LR)}\right] = \frac{1}{\mu_C} \times \ln\left(e^{\mu_C V_{LR}}\right) = \frac{1}{\mu_C} \times \mu_C V_{LR} = V_{LR}. \qquad (14.7)$$

Under RU2, the scale parameters cancel each other. That is, the IV parameter is no longer identifiable! Nlogit recognizes this.

An important aspect of the above discussion, not recognized in the literature (at least that we know of), is that if a NL model has two degenerate alternatives (such as Figure 14.5), scale parameters for both must be normalized to one, which is equivalent to treating these alternatives as a single nest (with MNL properties).

Taking the above into account, the following Nlogit command syntax will estimate a NL model of the form suggested by Figure 14.4. The reader can interpret the broader output; however, we note that the IV parameters all are within the 0–1 range and are statistically significant, with the automatically constrained IV parameter for the degenerate branch:

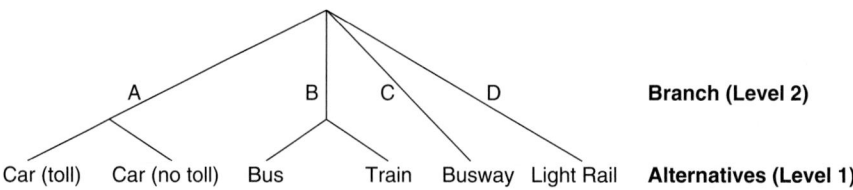

Figure 14.5 An NL tree structure with two degenerate alternatives

```
|-> Nlogit
;lhs = choice, cset, altij
    ;choices = NLR,NHR,NBW,bs,tn,bw,cr
    ;tree=ptnew(NLR,NHR,NBW),PTold(bs,tn,bw),car(cr)
    ;show
    ;RU2
    ;model:
    u(nlr) = nlr + actpt*act + invcpt*invc + invtpt*invt2 + egtpt*egt + trpt*trnf /
    u(nhr) = nhr + actpt*act + invcpt*invc + invtpt*invt2 + egtpt*egt + trpt*trnf /
    u(nbw) = nbw + actpt*act + invcpt*invc + invtpt*invt2 + egtpt*egt + trpt*trnf /
    u(bs) = bs + actpt*act + invcpt*invc + invtpt*invt2 + egtpt*egt + trpt*trnf /
    u(tn) = tn + actpt*act + invcpt*invc + invtpt*invt2 + egtpt*egt + trpt*trnf /
    u(bw) = bw + actpt*act + invcpt*invc + invtpt*invt2 + egtpt*egt + trpt*trnf /
    u(cr) =                   invccar*invc+invtcar*invt + TC*TC + PC*PC + egtcr*egt$ /
+------------------------------------------------------------------------+
|WARNING:   Bad observations were found in the sample. |
|Found 104 bad observations among   1970 individuals. |
|You can use ;CheckData to get a list of these points. |
+------------------------------------------------------------------------+
Tree Structure Specified for the Nested Logit Model
Sample proportions are marginal, not conditional.
Choices marked with * are excluded for the IIA test.
----------------------+---------------------+----------------------+--------------------+--------+------
Trunk    (prop.)|Limb    (prop.)|Branch   (prop.)|Choice    (prop.)|Weight|IIA
----------------------+---------------------+----------------------+--------------------+--------+------
Trunk{1} 1.00000|Lmb[1|1] 1.00000|PTNEW   .40997|NLR      .17471| 1.000|
                |                |                |NHR      .18060| 1.000|
                |                |                |NBW      .05466| 1.000|
                |                |PTOLD   .45981|BS       .11790| 1.000|
                |                |                |TN       .14094| 1.000|
                |                |                |BW       .20096| 1.000|
                |                |CAR     .13023|CR       .13023| 1.000|
----------------------+---------------------+----------------------+--------------------+--------+------
Normal exit:   7 iterations. Status=0, F=   2730.693
-----------------------------------------------------------------------------------------------
Discrete choice (multinomial logit) model
Dependent variable          Choice
Log likelihood function    -2730.69253
Estimation based on N =    1866, K =   16
Inf.Cr.AIC  =   5493.4 AIC/N =    2.944
R2=1-LogL/LogL*  Log-L fncn R-sqrd R2Adj
Constants only must be computed directly
            Use NLOGIT ;...;RHS=ONE$
Chi-squared[10]          -   1588.10946
Prob [ chi squared > value ] =   .00000
Response data are given as ind. choices
```

Number of obs.= 1970, skipped 104 obs

```
----------+------------------------------------------------------------------------------
          |                  Standard              Prob.        95% Confidence
   CHOICE|  Coefficient     Error        z     |z|>Z*           Interval
----------+------------------------------------------------------------------------------
      NLR|    1.84937***    .30793      6.01    .0000       1.24584    2.45291
     ACTPT|    -.04248***    .00467     -9.10    .0000       -.05163    -.03334
    INVCPT|    -.24053***    .01369    -17.57    .0000       -.26737    -.21370
    INVTPT|    -.03160***    .00234    -13.52    .0000       -.03618    -.02702
     EGTPT|    -.00414        .00400     -1.04    .3002       -.01198     .00369
      TRPT|     .28841**     .12646      2.28    .0226        .04055     .53626
       NHR|    1.95132***    .29157      6.69    .0000       1.37987    2.52278
       NBW|     .85378***    .28549      2.99    .0028        .29423    1.41333
        BS|    -.64770**     .25958     -2.50    .0126      -1.15647    -.13893
        TN|    -.32632        .26261     -1.24    .2140       -.84102     .18838
        BW|    -.03503        .26455     -.13    .8946       -.55353     .48347
   INVCCAR|    -.05669        .06937     -.82    .4138       -.19266     .07928
   INVTCAR|    -.01635***    .00319     -5.12    .0000       -.02261    -.01009
        TC|    -.07601**     .03093     -2.46    .0140       -.13664    -.01538
        PC|    -.04837***    .00882     -5.49    .0000       -.06565    -.03109
     EGTCR|    -.11525***    .02133     -5.40    .0000       -.15707    -.07344
----------+------------------------------------------------------------------------------
```

***, **, * ==> Significance at 1%, 5%, 10% level.

Normal exit: 28 iterations. Status=0, F=   2707.240

FIML Nested Multinomial Logit Model
Dependent variable   CHOICE
Log likelihood function   -2707.23966
Restricted log likelihood   -3833.05828
Chi squared [18](P= .000)   2251.63723
Significance level   .00000
McFadden Pseudo R-squared   .2937129
Estimation based on N =   1866, K = 18
Inf.Cr.AIC =   5450.5 AIC/N =   2.921
Constants only must be computed directly
          Use NLOGIT ;...;RHS=ONE$
At start values -2730.6925   .0086******
Response data are given as ind. choices
BHHH estimator used for asymp. variance
The model has 2 levels.
Random Utility Form 2:IVparms = Mb|l,Gl
Number of obs.= 1970, skipped 104 obs

```
----------+------------------------------------------------------------------------------
          |                  Standard              Prob.        95% Confidence
   CHOICE|  Coefficient     Error        z     |z|>Z*           Interval
----------+------------------------------------------------------------------------------
          |Attributes in the Utility Functions (beta)
      NLR|    1.57746***    .28668      5.50    .0000       1.01558    2.13935
```

ACTPT	-.03193***	.00427	-7.48	.0000	-.04030	-.02356
INVCPT	-.18975***	.01425	-13.32	.0000	-.21768	-.16182
INVTPT	-.02533***	.00222	-11.39	.0000	-.02968	-.02097
EGTPT	-.00345	.00323	-1.07	.2861	-.00979	.00289
TRPT	.23704***	.08485	2.79	.0052	.07073	.40335
NHR	1.52419***	.27893	5.46	.0000	.97750	2.07088
NBW	1.03683***	.26253	3.95	.0001	.52228	1.55138
BS	-.48815**	.24507	-1.99	.0464	-.96847	-.00783
TN	-.23949	.24429	-.98	.3269	-.71830	.23932
BW	-.04981	.24420	-.20	.8384	-.52842	.42881
INVCCAR	-.02154	.07367	-.29	.7700	-.16594	.12286
INVTCAR	-.01456***	.00314	-4.63	.0000	-.02072	-.00839
TC	-.07597**	.03200	-2.37	.0176	-.13870	-.01325
PC	-.04621***	.00855	-5.40	.0000	-.06297	-.02944
EGTCR	-.10939***	.02669	-4.10	.0000	-.16171	-.05707
	|IV parameters, RU2 form = mu(b|1),gamma(1)					
PTNEW	.47559***	.05019	9.48	.0000	.37722	.57395
PTOLD	.72892***	.06898	10.57	.0000	.59371	.86412
CAR	1.0	.....(Fixed Parameter).....				

The above example demonstrates the case whereby the degenerate nest is at the elemental alternative level of the model. It is possible that, for 3 level or 4 level NL models, a degenerate partition may occur at higher levels of the model. This represents a partial degeneration. Consider the 3 level NL model in Figure 14.6.

The NL model shown in Figure 14.6 places the CARNT and LR in branch A2; however, the upper nest of this partition, A1, is degenerate in the sense that A1 is the sole limb in the partition. Following the same reasoning as before, the scale parameters (and hence variances) for A1 and A2 must be equal. We show how to handle such cases in Section 14.6.

14.6 Three-level NL models

All the NL models we have estimated to date have been two-level NL models. We now estimate a three-level NL model. The Nlogit command

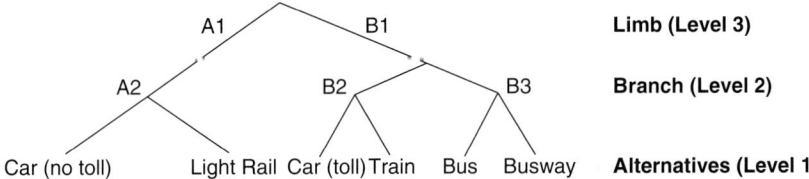

Figure 14.6 A 3-level NL tree structure with degenerate branches

to estimate a three-level NL model is given below. We were unable to find a tree structure that gave IV parameter estimates that satisfied the 0–1 condition, including adding explanatory variables at the middle and upper levels of the tree. This is often the case for three-level models. We leave it to the reader to explore the evidence, and in particular to undertake a test of differences between the various models in this chapter using the nested hypotheses tests that are presented in Chapter 7:

```
|-> Nlogit
;lhs = choice, cset, altij
    ;choices = NLR,NHR,NBW,bs,tn,bw,cr
    ;tree= ModeAU[RailN(nlr,nhr),busw(nbw,bw)], ModeBU[carbus(cr,bs,tn)]
    ;show
    ;RU2
    ;prob = margprob
    ;cprob = altprob
    ;ivb = ivbranch
    ;utility=mutilz
    ;model:
    u(nlr) = nlr + actpt*act + invcpt*invc + invtpt*invt2 + egtpt*egt + trpt*trnf /
    u(nhr) = nhr + actpt*act + invcpt*invc + invtpt*invt2 + egtpt*egt + trpt*trnf /
    u(nbw) = nbw + actpt*act + invcpt*invc + invtpt*invt2 + egtpt*egt + trpt*trnf /
    u(bs)  = bs + actpt*act + invcpt*invc + invtpt*invt2 + egtpt*egt + trpt*trnf /
    u(tn)  = tn + actpt*act + invcpt*invc + invtpt*invt2 + egtpt*egt + trpt*trnf /
    u(bw)  = bw + actpt*act + invcpt*invc + invtpt*invt2 + egtpt*egt + trpt*trnf /
    u(cr)  =                        invccar*invc+invtcar*invt + TC*TC + PC*PC + egtcr*egt$ /
+---------------------------------------------------------------------------+
|WARNING:   Bad observations were found in the sample. |
|Found 104 bad observations among    1970 individuals. |
|You can use ;CheckData to get a list of these points. |
+---------------------------------------------------------------------------+
Tree Structure Specified for the Nested Logit Model
Sample proportions are marginal, not conditional.
Choices marked with * are excluded for the IIA test.
```

Trunk	(prop.)	Limb	(prop.)	Branch	(prop.)	Choice	(prop.)	Weight	IIA
Trunk{1}	1.00000	MODEAU	.61093	RAILN	.35531	NLR	.17471	1.000	
						NHR	.18060	1.000	
				BUSW	.25563	NBW	.05466	1.000	
						BW	.20096	1.000	
		MODEBU	.38907	CARBUS	.38907	CR	.13023	1.000	
						BS	.11790	1.000	
						TN	.14094	1.000	

```
----------------------------------------------------------------------------------------
FIML Nested Multinomial Logit Model
Dependent variable                CHOICE
Log likelihood function      -2715.97371
Restricted log likelihood    -3671.38073
Chi squared [ 21](P= .000)    1910.81404
Significance level                .00000
McFadden Pseudo R-squared      .2602310
Estimation based on N =    1866, K =   21
Inf.Cr.AIC  =    5473.9 AIC/N =     2.934
Constants only must be computed directly
            Use NLOGIT ;...;RHS=ONE$
At start values -3285.7820  .1734******
Response data are given as ind. choices
BHHH estimator used for asymp. variance
The model has 3 levels.
Random Utility Form 2:IVparms = Mb|l,Gl
Number of obs.= 1970, skipped  104 obs
```

CHOICE	Coefficient	Standard Error	z	Prob. |z|>Z*	95% Confidence Interval	
	Attributes in the Utility Functions (beta)					
NLR	1.61975***	.29299	5.53	.0000	1.04549	2.19401
ACTPT	-.03474***	.00436	-7.97	.0000	-.04328	-.02620
INVCPT	-.20829***	.01592	-13.08	.0000	-.23949	-.17708
INVTPT	-.02570***	.00248	-10.36	.0000	-.03056	-.02084
EGTPT	-.00456	.00366	-1.25	.2128	-.01172	.00261
TRPT	.23276**	.09890	2.35	.0186	.03892	.42661
NHR	1.68603***	.28310	5.96	.0000	1.13118	2.24089
NBW	1.01965***	.26181	3.89	.0001	.50652	1.53279
BS	-.67008**	.26696	-2.51	.0121	-1.19332	-.14684
TN	-.38195	.26071	-1.47	.1429	-.89294	.12904
BW	.09666	.24843	.39	.6972	-.39026	.58358
INVCCAR	-.03602	.07145	-.50	.6142	-.17607	.10402
INVTCAR	-.01446***	.00339	-4.27	.0000	-.02110	-.00782
TC	-.07219**	.03172	-2.28	.0229	-.13436	-.01002
PC	-.04537***	.00906	-5.01	.0000	-.06313	-.02762
EGTCR	-.10956***	.02665	-4.11	.0000	-.16178	-.05733
	IV parameters, RU2 form = mu(b|l),gamma(l)					
RAILN	1.32941***	.17559	7.57	.0000	.98526	1.67357
BUSW	2.13830***	.29297	7.30	.0000	1.56409	2.71251
CARBUS	1.05539***	.11462	9.21	.0000	.83075	1.28003
MODEAU	1.26311***	.12687	9.96	.0000	1.01145	1.51176
MODEBU	1.05061	2.18548	.48	.6307	-3.23287	5.33408

14.7 Elasticities and partial effects

The choice invariant cross-effect associated with the MNL model is relaxed (in part at least) in the NL model that provides an additional interesting aspect of substitution, switching within as well as between branches. To provide an example, the following NL model is requested by adding:

```
; Tree = (bs,tn),(bw,cr) ; RU2 ; Effects: act (*) ; Full
```

to the model command. The following are the model results: the partial effects are accompanied by a detailed legend that describes the computations, then tables that contain more information about the elasticities (Nlogit notices that act does not appear in the utility function for *cr*, and does not produce a table for it):

```
-------------------------------------------------------------------------
FIML Nested Multinomial Logit Model
Dependent variable                 CHOICE
Log likelihood function        -197.95029
Restricted log likelihood      -273.09999
Chi squared [ 14](P= .000)      150.29941
Significance level                .00000
McFadden Pseudo R-squared         .2751729
The model has 2 levels.
Random Utility Form 2:IVparms = Mb|1,G1
Number of obs.=   197, skipped    0 obs
```

CHOICE	Coefficient	Standard Error	z	Prob. |z|>Z*	95% Confidence Interval	
Attributes in the Utility Functions (beta)					
BS	-2.02841**	.83930	-2.42	.0157	-3.67340	-.38341
ACTPT	-.09771***	.03141	-3.11	.0019	-.15927	-.03614
INVCPT	-.07608	.04673	-1.63	.1035	-.16767	.01551
INVTPT	-.01555	.01107	-1.40	.1601	-.03724	.00615
EGTPT	-.03873	.02550	-1.52	.1288	-.08871	.01125
TRPT	-1.56494***	.58604	-2.67	.0076	-2.71357	-.41632
TN	-1.69240*	.88414	-1.91	.0556	-3.42529	.04048
BW	-1.31136	.86139	-1.52	.1279	-2.99966	.37694
INVTCAR	-.05155***	.01529	-3.37	.0007	-.08152	-.02159
TC	-.09316	.08919	-1.04	.2962	-.26797	.08164
PC	-.01371	.02132	-.64	.5202	-.05550	.02808
EGTCAR	-.04927	.03045	-1.62	.1057	-.10896	.01041
IV parameters, RU2 form = mu(b|1),gamma(1)					
B(1|1,1)	.44168***	.15821	2.79	.0052	.13159	.75177
B(2|1,1)	1.07293***	.32171	3.34	.0009	.44239	1.70348

```
+-----------------------------------------------------------------------+
| Partial effects = average over observations                           |
|                                                                       |
| dlnP[alt=j,br=b,lmb=l,tr=r]                                           |
| ---------------------------    = D(k:J,B,L,R) = delta(k)*F            |
| dx(k):alt=J,br=B,lmb=L,tr=R]                                          |
|                                                                       |
| delta(k) = coefficient on x(k) in U(J|B,L,R)                         |
| F = (r=R)  (l=L)  (b=B) [(j=J)-P(J|BLR)]                              |
|   + (r=R)  (l=L) [(b=B) -P(B|LR)]P(J|BLR)t(B|LR)                      |
|   + (r=R) [(l=L)-P(L|R)] P(B|LR) P(J|BLR)t(B|LR)s(L|R)                |
|   + [(r=R) -P(R)] P(L|R)  P(B|IR) P(J|BIR)t(B|LR)s(L|R)f(R)           |
|                                                                       |
| P(J|BLR)=Prob[choice=J |branch=B,limb=L,trunk=R]                      |
| P(B|LR), P(L|R), P(R) defined likewise.                              |
| (n=N) = 1 if n=N, 0 else, for n=j,b,l,r and N=J,B,L,R.               |
| Elasticity = x(k) * D(j|B,L,R)                                       |
| Marginal effect = P(JBLR)*D = P(J|BLR)P(B|LR)P(L|R)P(R)D             |
| F is decomposed into the 4 parts in the tables.                      |
+-----------------------------------------------------------------------+

+-------------------------------------------------------------------------+
| Elasticity              averaged over observations.                     |
| Effects on probabilities of all choices in the model:                   |
| * indicates direct Elasticity effect of the attribute.                  |
+-------------------------------------------------------------------------+

+-------------------------------------------------------------------------+
| Attribute is ACT      in choice BS                                      |
|                       Decomposition of Effect if Nest    Total Effect|
|                       Trunk   Limb   Branch   Choice    Mean  St.Dev|
| Trunk=Trunk{1}                                                          |
| Limb=Lmb[1|1]                                                           |
|    Branch=B(1|1,1)                                                      |
| *     Choice=BS       .000    .000   -.173   -.131     -.304   .021 |
|       Choice=TN       .000    .000   -.173    .125     -.048   .010 |
|    Branch=B(2|1,1)                                                      |
|       Choice=BW       .000    .000    .110    .000      .110   .008 |
|       Choice=CR       .000    .000    .110    .000      .110   .008 |
+-------------------------------------------------------------------------+
| Attribute is ACT      in choice TN                                      |
|                       Decomposition of Effect if Nest    Total Effect|
|                       Trunk   Limb   Branch   Choice    Mean  St.Dev|
| Trunk=Trunk{1}                                                          |
| Limb=Lmb[1|1]                                                           |
|    Branch=B(1|1,1)                                                      |
|       Choice=BS       .000    .000   -.412    .311     -.101   .015 |
| *     Choice=TN       .000    .000   -.412   -.345     -.757   .035 |
|    Branch=B(2|1,1)                                                      |
|       Choice=BW       .000    .000    .292    .000      .292   .014 |
|       Choice=CR       .000    .000    .292    .000      .292   .014 |
+-------------------------------------------------------------------------+
```

```
| Attribute is ACT        in choice BW                                        |
|                    Decomposition of Effect if Nest      Total Effect|
|                    Trunk    Limb    Branch    Choice     Mean   St.Dev|
| Trunk=Trunk{1}                                                              |
| Limb=Lmb[1|1]                                                               |
|    Branch=B(1|1,1)                                                          |
|        Choice=BS           .000    .000     .128     .000      .128    .009 |
|        Choice=TN           .000    .000     .128     .000      .128    .009 |
|    Branch=B(2|1,1)                                                          |
| *      Choice=BW           .000    .000    -.219    -.699     -.918    .129 |
|        Choice=CR           .000    .000    -.219     .372      .153    .010 |
+----------------------------------------------------------------------------+
```

Elasticity wrt change of X in row choice on Prob[column choice]

```
-----------+-------------------------------------------------
ACT        |      BS        TN        BW        CR
-----------+-------------------------------------------------
        BS|   -.3044    -.0479     .1103     .1103
        TN|   -.1009    -.7569     .2920     .2920
        BW|    .1277     .1277    -.9183     .1530
(These are the elasticities from the MNL model)
        BS|   -.2953     .0635     .0635     .0635
        TN|    .1888    -.7289     .1888     .1888
        BW|    .0909     .0909    -.5259     .0909
```

As an example, consider the attribute access time (*act*) for bus (*bs*) travel. A change in *act* for bus can cause bus riders within the first branch to switch to train. The elasticity effect shown in the first table is −0.131. The change can also induce bus users to switch to one of the modes in the other branch (*bw* and *cr*); this effect is −0.173. The total effect of the change in access time for bus is the sum of these two values, namely −0.304. Note that −0.304 is the value shown in the summary table at the end of the displayed results. Note the cross-effects. Within the first branch, the branch effect is the same, namely −0.173. The within branch effect on *Prob(cr)* is +0.125, so the total effect is negative, −0.048. Looking at the other branch, we see that the effect of the change in access time for bus on the "alien" modes, *bw* and *cr* is the same, 0.110. There is no within branch effect in the second branch. The change in the access time for bus does not cause travellers to substitute back and forth between *bw* and *cr*. Altogether, something important has changed in this model. In the MNL model, the cross-effects are equal, so of course they all have the same sign. Here, we find that the cross-effect of *act(bus)* on the choice of train is actually negative, while it is positive for the other two modes. The implication is that when *act(bus)* increases, it induces some bus riders and some train riders to switch to either *bw* or *cr*. The MNL cannot accommodate a complicated substitution pattern such as this.

14.8 Covariance nested logit

The NL model can be extended to allow for conditioning of the IV parameters by candidate systematic sources of influence across a sample. This model is referred to as the *Covariance Heterogeneity* (CovHet) model. It is equivalent to estimating a model in which a single scale parameter (across the alternatives) is a function of alternative-specific variables: attributes associated with an alternative and each sampled individual can be included as sources of scale decomposition, adding useful behavioral information of sample heterogeneity. This extension is the source of heterogeneity introduced through covariates. For example, given the relative similarity of two alternatives, NLR and NBW, we might assume that the variance of ε_{nlr} and ε_{nbw} are given by the same function of $\mathbf{z}$; and that ε_{nlr} and ε_{nbw} are a different function of the covariates $\mathbf{z}$. That is:

$$\text{Var}[\varepsilon_{nlr}] = \sigma_1^2 \exp(\gamma' z1). \tag{14.8}$$

$$\text{Var}[\varepsilon_{nbw}] = \sigma_1^2 \exp(\gamma' z1). \tag{14.9}$$

The analyst can specify a particular functional form for the covariate expression. This model can be formulated as a NL model with IV parameters multiplied by the exponential functions. For choice k given branch j:

$$P(k|j) = \frac{exp(\beta' x_{k|j})}{\sum_j exp(\beta' x_{s|j})}. \tag{14.10}$$

For branch j:

$$P(j) = \frac{exp(\alpha' y_j + \sigma_j I_j)}{\sum_j exp(\alpha' y_j + \sigma_j I_j)}, \tag{14.11}$$

where

$$\sigma_j = \tau_j exp(\gamma' z_j). \tag{14.12}$$

A two-level model generalizes the NL model through specifying the IV utility parameter (i.e., σ_j) to be an exponential function of covariates. Analysts may be able to formulate a theory to explain the heteroskedasticity structure present in preference data of the type described by Equation (14.12).

Equation (14.12) can be transformed in terms of the scale parameter as Equation (14.13):

$$\lambda_{iq} = \exp(\psi Z_{iq}), \tag{14.13}$$

where $\boldsymbol{\psi}$ is a parameter row-vector and $\mathbf{Z_{iq}}$ are covariates. CovHet choice probabilities are given by Equation (14.14):

$$P_{iq} = \frac{\exp(\lambda_{iq}\beta X_{iq})}{\sum_{j \in C_q} \exp(\lambda_{iq}\beta X_{jq})}. \tag{14.14}$$

CovHet allows complex cross-substitution patterns among the alternatives. The derivation of CovHet when the scale factor does not vary by alternative is different than when it does. If the scale factor is *not* alternative-specific, the model can be derived using a heteroskedasticity argument (see Swait and Adamowicz 1996); when the scale factor is alternative-specific, the model can be derived as a special case of the NL model (Daly 1987; McFadden 1981; Hensher 1994; Swait and Stacey 1996). In either case, the final expression for the choice probability is given by Equation (14.14).

CovHet as a nested logit form is an appealing way of investigating the influence of contextual biases in SP studies. Swait and Adamowicz (1996), for example, hypothesize that task complexity (for SP data) and choice environment (e.g., market structure for RP data) influence the levels of variability found in preference data. They propose a specific measure to characterize complexity and/or environment, and find evidence of its impact in a number of SP data sets, as well as in an RP data source. Their measure of complexity *does not vary across alternatives*; consequently scale parameters in their model vary across individuals and SP replications, but not across alternatives. They also found that different degrees of complexity between preference data sources can impact upon the propriety of combining RP/SP data. Swait and Stacey (1996) apply CovHet to scanner panel choice data, allowing the variance (i.e., scale) to vary by person, alternative, and time period as a function of brand, socio-demographic characteristics, inter-purchase time, and state dependence. They show that accounting for non-stationarity of the variance in terms of the explanatory variables Z_{iq} enhances insight about panel behavior and greatly improves model fit with respect to standard choice models such as the MNL, NL, and even MNP models with fixed covariance matrices.

An example of a CovHet Nested logit using our SP mode choice data is given below. We have introduced one linear term *gender* to illustrate. We could have included ASCs, but did not in the example. The covariates have a positive utility parameter that suggests that when a respondent is male, *ceteris paribus*, the scale parameter increases in value. Another way of saying this is that the standard deviation of the random component is greater for males compared to females.

```
|-> Nlogit
;lhs = choice, cset, altij
    ;choices = NLR,NHR,NBW,bs,tn,bw,cr
    ;tree=ptnew(NLR,NHR,NBW),Allold(bs,tn,bw,cr)
    ;show
    ;RU2
    ;prob = margprob
    ;cprob = altprob
    ;ivb = ivbranch
    ;utility=mutilz
    ;hfn=gender
    ;model:
    u(nlr) = nlr + actpt*act + invcpt*invc + invtpt*invt2 + egtpt*egt + trpt*trnf /
    u(nhr) = nhr + actpt*act + invcpt*invc + invtpt*invt2 + egtpt*egt + trpt*trnf /
    u(nbw) = nbw + actpt*act + invcpt*invc + invtpt*invt2 + egtpt*egt + trpt*trnf /
    u(bs)  = bs + actpt*act + invcpt*invc + invtpt*invt2 + egtpt*egt + trpt*trnf /
    u(tn)  = tn + actpt*act + invcpt*invc + invtpt*invt2 + egtpt*egt + trpt*trnf /
    u(bw)  = bw + actpt*act + invcpt*invc + invtpt*invt2 + egtpt*egt + trpt*trnf /
    u(cr)  =                          invccar*invc+invtcar*invt + TC*TC + PC*PC + egtcr*egt$/
+-----------------------------------------------------------------------+
|WARNING:   Bad observations were found in the sample. |
|Found 104 bad observations among    1970 individuals. |
|You can use ;CheckData to get a list of these points. |
+-----------------------------------------------------------------------+
Tree Structure Specified for the Nested Logit Model
Sample proportions are marginal, not conditional.
Choices marked with * are excluded for the IIA test.
```

Trunk	(prop.)	Limb	(prop.)	Branch	(prop.)	Choice	(prop.)	Weight	IIA
Trunk{1}	1.00000	Lmb[1|1]	1.00000	PTNEW	.40997	NLR	.17471	1.000	
						NHR	.18060	1.000	
						NBW	.05466	1.000	
				ALLOLD	.59003	BS	.11790	1.000	
						TN	.14094	1.000	
						DW	.20096	1.000	
						CR	.13023	1.000	

```
Line search at iteration    50 does not improve fn. Exiting optimization.
-----------------------------------------------------------------------
Covariance Heterogeneity Model
Dependent variable              CHOICE
```

```
Log likelihood function      -2789.64630
Restricted log likelihood    -3660.16113
Chi squared [ 19](P= .000)   1741.02967
Significance level                .00000
McFadden Pseudo R-squared        .2378351
Estimation based on N =    1866, K =  19
Inf.Cr.AIC  =   5617.3 AIC/N =    3.010
Constants only must be computed directly
            Use NLOGIT ;...;RHS=ONE$
At start values -3285.7820  .1510******
Response data are given as ind. choices
BHHH estimator used for asymp. variance
The model has 2 levels.
Random Utility Form 2:IVparms = Mb|1,Gl
Variable IV parameters are denoted s_...
Number of obs.= 1970, skipped  104 obs
```

CHOICE	Coefficient	Standard Error	z	Prob. |z|>Z*	95% Confidence Interval	
	Attributes in the Utility Functions (beta)					
NLR	.39072	.28746	1.36	.1741	-.17270	.95414
ACTPT	-.03865***	.00459	-8.42	.0000	-.04765	-.02965
INVCPT	-.22006***	.01191	-18.47	.0000	-.24341	-.19671
INVTPT	-.01827***	.00259	-7.05	.0000	-.02335	-.01319
EGTPT	-.00234	.00413	-.57	.5704	-.01044	.00575
TRPT	.67829***	.12876	5.27	.0000	.42593	.93065
NHR	.77608***	.26665	2.91	.0036	.25346	1.29871
NBW	-.18635	.26155	-.71	.4762	-.69898	.32629
BS	-.53014**	.23336	-2.27	.0231	-.98752	-.07276
TN	-.37674	.23382	-1.61	.1071	-.83502	.08153
BW	-.02405	.23220	-.10	.9175	-.47915	.43106
INVCCAR	-.02782	.06710	-.41	.6785	-.15934	.10370
INVTCAR	-.01460***	.00281	-5.20	.0000	-.02010	-.00909
TC	-.08483***	.02915	-2.91	.0036	-.14196	-.02771
PC	-.04526***	.00763	-5.93	.0000	-.06020	-.03031
EGTCR	-.10415***	.02426	-4.29	.0000	-.15171	-.05660
	Inclusive Value Parameters					
PTNEW	.81691***	.11651	7.01	.0000	.58856	1.04527
ALLOLD	.85231***	.12494	6.82	.0000	.60743	1.09719
Lmb[1|1]	1.0	.....(Fixed Parameter).....				
Trunk{1}	1.0	.....(Fixed Parameter).....				
	Covariates in Inclusive Value Parameters					
s_GENDER	.35011***	.10854	3.23	.0013	.13737	.56284

```
***, **, * ==>  Significance at 1%, 5%, 10% level.
Fixed parameter ... is constrained to equal the value or
had a nonpositive st.error because of an earlier problem.
```

14.9 Generalized nested logit

The previous versions of Nlogit allow for one alternative to be placed in one location in a tree structure. It may be behaviorally meaningful to allow an alternative to appear in more than one branch or limb as a way of recognizing that such an alternative is related to other alternatives in different ways. That is, the correlation between specific alternatives may indeed exist in more than one part of a tree. Such a specification is known as a *generalized nested logit model*. If an alternative appears in more than one location, then it will have to be assigned through estimation and allocation parameter to recognize its contribution to specific sources of utility throughout the tree structure. In the example below, we have placed the *bw* alternative in two branches. We tested for many candidate allocations, and found that this one gave the best overall fit. In other words, we found that only the *bw* alternative resulted in model improvements with an allocation (probability) of 0.8180 and 0.1820 between PTA and PTB branches:

```
|-> Nlogit
   ;lhs = choice, cset, altij
   ;choices = NLR,NHR,NBW,bs,tn,bw,cr
   ;show
   ;RU2
   ;prob = marqprob
   ;cprob = altprob
   ;ivb = ivbranch
   ;utility=mutilz
   ;gnl
   ;tree=PTA(NLR,NHR,NBW,bw),PTB(bs,tn,bw,cr)
   ;model:
   u(nlr) = nlr + actpt*act + invcpt*invc + invtpt*invt2 + egtpt*egt + trpt*trnf /
   u(nhr) = nhr + actpt*act + invcpt*invc + invtpt*invt2 + egtpt*egt + trpt*trnf /
   u(nbw) = nbw + actpt*act + invcpt*invc + invtpt*invt2 + egtpt*egt + trpt*trnf /
   u(bs)  = bs  + actpt*act + invcpt*invc + invtpt*invt2 + egtpt*egt + trpt*trnf /
   u(tn)  = tn  + actpt*act + invcpt*invc + invtpt*invt2 + egtpt*egt + trpt*trnf /
   u(bw)  = bw  + actpt*act + invcpt*invc + invtpt*invt2 + egtpt*egt + trpt*trnf /
   u(cr)  =                   invccar*invc+invtcar*invt + TC*TC + PC*PC + egtcr*egt$/
+------------------------------------------------------------------------+
|WARNING:   Bad observations were found in the sample. |
|Found 104 bad observations among    1970 individuals. |
|You can use ;CheckData to get a list of these points. |
+------------------------------------------------------------------------+
Tree Structure Specified for the Nested Logit Model
In GNL model, choices are equally allocated to branches
Choices marked with * are excluded for the IIA test.
```

```
----------------------+----------------------+----------------------+----------------------+--------+-----
Trunk    (prop.)|Limb    (prop.)|Branch   (prop.)|Choice    (prop.)|Weight|IIA
----------------------+----------------------+----------------------+----------------------+--------+-----
Trunk{1} 1.00000|Lmb[1|1] 1.00000|PTA    .51045|NLR    .17471| 1.000|
                |                |                |NHR    .18060| 1.000|
                |                |                |NBW    .05466| 1.000|
                |                |                |BW     .10048| 1.000|
                |                |PTB    .48955|BS     .11790| 1.000|
                |                |                |TN     .14094| 1.000|
                |                |                |BW     .10048| 1.000|
                |                |                |CR     .13023| 1.000|
----------------------+----------------------+----------------------+----------------------+--------+-----
Normal exit:   7 iterations. Status=0, F=   2730.693
```

Discrete choice (multinomial logit) model
Dependent variable   Choice
Log likelihood function   -2730.69253
Estimation based on N =   1866, K = 16
Inf.Cr.AIC =   5493.4 AIC/N =   2.944
R2=1-LogL/LogL* Log-L fncn R-sqrd R2Adj
Constants only must be computed directly
          Use NLOGIT ;...;RHS=ONE$
Chi-squared[10]   =   1588.10946
Prob [chi squared > value] =   .00000
Response data are given as ind. choices
Number of obs.= 1970, skipped 104 obs

CHOICE	Coefficient	Standard Error	z	Prob. |z|>Z*	95% Confidence Interval	
NLR	1.84937***	.30793	6.01	.0000	1.24584	2.45291
ACTPT	-.04248***	.00467	-9.10	.0000	-.05163	-.03334
INVCPT	-.24053***	.01369	-17.57	.0000	-.26737	-.21370
INVTPT	-.03160***	.00234	-13.52	.0000	-.03618	-.02702
EGTPT	-.00414	.00400	-1.04	.3002	-.01198	.00369
TRPT	.28841**	.12646	2.28	.0226	.04055	.53626
NHR	1.95132***	.29157	6.69	.0000	1.37987	2.52278
NBW	.85378***	.28549	2.99	.0028	.29423	1.41333
BS	-.64770**	.25958	-2.50	.0126	-1.15647	-.13893
TN	-.32632	.26261	-1.24	.2140	-.84102	.18838
BW	-.03503	.26455	-.13	.8946	-.55353	.48347
INVCCAR	-.05669	.06937	-.82	.4138	-.19266	.07928
INVTCAR	-.01635***	.00319	-5.12	.0000	-.02261	-.01009
TC	-.07601**	.03093	-2.46	.0140	-.13664	-.01538
PC	-.04837***	.00882	-5.49	.0000	-.06565	-.03109
EGTCR	-.11525***	.02133	-5.40	.0000	-.15707	-.07344

***, **, * ==> Significance at 1%, 5%, 10% level.

```
Line search at iteration   47 does not improve fn. Exiting optimization.
------------------------------------------------------------------------
Generalized Nested Logit Model
Dependent variable               CHOICE
Log likelihood function      -2826.74184
Restricted log likelihood    -3631.06834
Chi squared [ 19](P= .000)   1608.65299
Significance level               .00000
McFadden Pseudo R-squared        .2215124
Estimation based on N =    1866, K =  19
Inf.Cr.AIC  =    5691.5 AIC/N =    3.050
Constants only must be computed directly
            Use NLOGIT ;...;RHS=ONE$
At start values -4673.8507  .3952******
Response data are given as ind. choices
The model has 2 levels.
GNL: Model uses random utility form RU1
Number of obs.= 1970, skipped  104 obs
```

CHOICE	Coefficient	Standard Error	z	Prob. |z|>Z*	95% Confidence Interval	
	Attributes in the Utility Functions (beta)					
NLR	4.13141***	.50459	8.19	.0000	3.14243	5.12040
ACTPT	-.02506***	.00448	-5.60	.0000	-.03383	-.01629
INVCPT	-.15545***	.01864	-8.34	.0000	-.19199	-.11891
INVTPT	-.01577***	.00215	-7.35	.0000	-.01998	-.01157
EGTPT	-.00717**	.00351	-2.04	.0413	-.01406	-.00028
TRPT	.14568**	.06503	2.24	.0251	.01822	.27313
NHR	4.15729***	.50362	8.25	.0000	3.17021	5.14437
NBW	3.75812***	.46082	8.16	.0000	2.85493	4.66131
BS	1.77389***	.29575	6.00	.0000	1.19423	2.35354
TN	2.12419***	.30918	6.87	.0000	1.51821	2.73017
BW	3.13939***	.35663	8.80	.0000	2.44041	3.83837
INVCCAR	.40044***	.08178	4.90	.0000	.24016	.56073
INVTCAR	-.00187	.00333	-.56	.5741	-.00839	.00465
TC	.05459	.03541	1.54	.1232	-.01482	.12400
PC	-.06278***	.01243	-5.05	.0000	-.08714	-.03842
EGTCR	-.08724***	.03266	-2.67	.0076	-.15124	-.02323
	Dissimilarity parameters. These are mu(branch).					
PTA	.37899	.36952	1.03	.3051	-.34525	1.10323
PTB	1.27466***	.11768	10.83	.0000	1.04401	1.50532
	Structural MLOGIT Allocation Model: Constants					
tNLR_PTA	0.0	(Fixed Parameter).....				
tNHR_PTA	0.0	.....(Fixed Parameter).....				
tNBW_PTA	0.0	.....(Fixed Parameter).....				
tBS_PTB	0.0	.....(Fixed Parameter).....				
tTN_PTB	0.0	.....(Fixed Parameter).....				
tBW_PTA	1.50274***	.53059	2.83	.0046	.46280	2.54269

```
  tBW_PTB|      0.0    ..... (Fixed Parameter).....
  tCR_PTB|      0.0    ..... (Fixed Parameter).....
---------- +----------------------------------------------------------------------------------
***, **, * ==> Significance at 1%, 5%, 10% level.
Fixed parameter ... is constrained to equal the value or
had a nonpositive st.error because of an earlier problem.
----------------------------------------------------------------------------------------------
Generalized Nested Logit
Estimated Allocations of Choices to Branches
Estimated standard errors in parentheses for
allocation values not fixed at 1.0 or 0.0.
         |Branch
---------- +----------------------
CHOICE   |PTA       PTB
---------- +---------- +-----------
NLR       1.0000    .0000
NHR       1.0000    .0000
NBW       1.0000    .0000
BS         .0000   1.0000
TN         .0000   1.0000
BW         .8180    .1820
         ( .0239) ( .2021)
CR         .0000   1.0000
```

Note: Allocations are multinomial logit probabilities. Underlying parameters are not shown in the output:

14.10 Additional commands

The NL model in Nlogit supports all of the additional commands described for the MNL model in Chapter 13. Thus, the *show, descriptives, crosstab, effects* (both elasticities and marginal effects; although there are some differences in their calculation), and *weight* (both exogenous and endogenous) commands may be equally applied to the NL model as to the MNL model. Similarly, the *simulation* and *scenario* capability may also be used for NL model applications. Given the similarity between the output generated using these commands for NL models and MNL models, we do not demonstrate any of these commands here.

15   Mixed logit estimation

The secret of greatness is simple: do better work than any other man in your field –
and keep on doing it.

(Wilfred A. Peterson)

15.1 Introduction

The choice modeler has available a number of econometric models. Traditionally,
the more common models applied to choice data are the multinomial logit
(MNL) and nested logit (NL) models. Increasingly, however, choice modelers
are estimating the mixed logit (ML) or random parameters logit model.[1] In
Chapter 4, we outlined the theory behind this class of models. In this chapter
we estimate a range of ML models using Nlogit, including recent developments in
scaled mixed logit (or generalized mixed logit). As with Chapters 11 and 13 (MNL
model) and Chapter 14 (NL model), we explain in detail the commands necessary
to estimate ML models as well as the interpretation of the output generated by
Nlogit. An understanding of the theory behind the ML model is presented in
Chapter 4; however we anticipate that in reading this chapter you will have a
better understanding of the model, at least from an empirical standpoint.

15.2 The mixed logit model basic commands

The ML model syntax commands build on the commands of the MNL model
discussed in Chapter 11. We begin with the *basic* ML syntax command,

[1] Other models exist such as the multinomial probit model (which assumes a normally distributed error
structure), ordered logit and probit models (used when the order of the dependent choice variable has
some meaning), latent class models (used to uncover possible different preference patterns among
assumed respondent segments), and generalized nested logit (GNL). We have deferred discussion of these
models to other chapters.

building upon this in later sections as we add to the complexity of the ML model.

The minimum set of commands necessary for the estimation of ML models in Nlogit are as follows:

```
NLOGIT
;lhs = choice, cset, altij
;choices =<names of alternatives>
;rpl
;fcn = <parameter name>(<distribution label>)
;Model:
U(alternative 1 name) = <utility function 1>/
U(alternative 2 name) = <utility function 2>/
...
```

  U(alternative i name) = <utility function i>$

You can replace **Nlogit** with **RPlogit** and drop **;rpl**.

The **;rpl** command, which stands for random parameter logit (an alternative name for the ML model), is the base command responsible for the estimation of the most general ML model form. It is this command in conjunction with the **;fcn** ('fcn' stands for 'function') command which distinguishes the ML command syntax from the basic MNL syntax. The **fcn** command is used to specify which parameters are to be treated as random parameters within the ML model framework. The utility specifications are written in the exact same format as the MNL and NL model command syntax. Within the ML model framework, parameters named in at least one utility specification as well as in the **fcn** command will be estimated as random parameter estimates. Parameters that are named solely within the utility specifications will be estimated as non-random or fixed parameters.

> *As an aside*, the term "fixed parameter" with reference to a **non-random parameter** within the ML literature can at times be confusing. In the MNL and NL model frameworks, fixed parameters are parameter estimates which are fixed at some specific value (such as zero) by the analyst. That is, they are not estimates at all but rather some analyst-specified value (although in some cases we may think of these as an analyst-inspired estimate of the true parameter value). It is also possible to fix parameter estimates within the ML model framework in a similar manner. Thus, in the ML model framework, fixed parameters may refer to either a parameter set to some pre-determined value by an analyst or a non-random parameter. For this reason, we use the phrase, "non-random" parameter rather than fixed parameter.

Within the **fcn** command, the command (**<distribution label type>**) is used to specify the distribution that the analyst wishes to impose upon each of the random parameters. The popular distributions are:

n the parameter will be normally distributed;

l the parameter will be lognormally distributed;

u the parameter will be uniformly distributed;

t the parameter will have a triangular distribution;

c the parameter is non-stochastic (i.e., the variance equals zero).

The full set of parameter distributions supported by Nlogit is summarized below. Note that one, "C," is "constant" i.e., a non-random parameter.

```
; Fcn = parameter name (type), ...
```

c nonstochastic	$\beta i = \beta$
n normal	$\beta i = \beta + \sigma vi, vi \sim N[0,1]$
s skew normal	$\beta i = \beta + \sigma vi + \lambda |wi|, \; vi, wi \sim N[0,1]$
l lognormal	$\beta i = \exp(\beta + \sigma vi), \; vi \sim N[0.1]$
z truncated normal	$\beta i = \beta + \sigma vi, \; vi \sim$ truncated normal $(-1.96 \text{ to } 1.96)$
u uniform	$\beta i = \beta + \sigma vi, \; vi \sim U[-1,1]$
f one sided uniform	$\beta i = \beta + \beta vi, \; vi \sim$ uniform$[-1,1]$
t triangular	$\beta i = \beta + \sigma vi, \; vi \sim$ triangle$[-1,1]$
o one sided triangular	$\beta i = \beta + \beta vi, \; vi \sim$ triangle$[-1,1]$
d beta, dome	$\beta i = \beta + \sigma vi, \; vi \sim 2 \times$ beta$(2,2) - 1$
b beta, scaled	$\beta i = \beta vi, \; vi \sim$ beta$(3,3)$
e Erlang	$\beta i = \beta + \sigma vi, \; vi \sim$ gamma$(1,4) - 4$
g gamma	$\beta i = \exp(\beta + \sigma vi), \; vi = \log(-\log(u1^{*}u2^{*}u3^{*}u4))$
w Weibull	$\beta i = \beta + \sigma vi, \; vi = 2(-\log ui)\sqrt{.5}, \; ui \sim U[0,1]$
r Rayleigh	$\beta i = \exp(\beta i \text{ (Weibull)})$
p exponential	$\beta i = \beta + \sigma vi, \; vi \sim$ exponential $- 1$
q exponential, scaled	$\beta i = \beta vi, \; vi \sim$ exponential
x censored (left)	$\beta i = \max(0, \beta i \text{ (normal)})$
m censored (right)	$\beta i = \min(0, \beta i \text{ (normal)})$
v exp(triangle)	$\beta i = \exp(\beta i \text{ (triangular)})$
i type I extreme value	$\beta i = \beta + \sigma vi, \; vi \sim$ standard Gumbel

> *As an aside*, For versions of Nlogit after 17 September 2012, if you have a lognormal or Johnson Sb distributed parameter, sometimes you have to flip the sign of the variable if the parameter being estimated is naturally negative, as on a cost variable. You can now build this into the model command, and leave the data alone. Use ; **FCN = –name(L)** for a lognormal coefficient, or **-name(J)** for **Sb**. Note the minus sign before the variable name. In RPlogit, if you want Sb, use (J) in the specification.

The basic format of random parameters in Nlogit's ML model (neglecting all the extra options such as mean heterogeneity, heteroskedasticity, etc.) is:

$$\beta_{k,i} = \beta_k + \sigma_k v_{k,i} \tag{15.1}$$

for parameters that vary around a fixed mean. A few deviate from this format. For example, the lognormal model is of the form:

$$\beta_{k,i} = \exp(\beta_k + \sigma_k v_{k,i}). \tag{15.2}$$

One *asymmetric distribution* is included which the authors have found to be an especially appealing distribution, called the skew normal:

$$\beta_{k,i} = \beta_k + \sigma_k V_{k,i} + \theta_k |W_{k,i}|, \tag{15.3}$$

where both $V_{k,i}$ and $W_{k,i}$ are distributed as standard normal and the latter term is the absolute value. θ_k may be positive or negative, so the skewness can go in either direction. The range of this parameter is infinite in both directions, but the distribution is skewed and therefore asymmetric.

Any of the above distributions may be assigned to any random parameter named in the **fcn** command syntax. For example, the command:

```
;fcn = invt(n)
```

will specify that a parameter named *invt* will be a random parameter drawn from a normal distribution. Note that this command refers to the parameter name and not the attribute name for an attribute entering a utility expression.

In estimating ML models, more than one parameter may be treated as a random parameter. Indeed, it is possible that all parameter estimates be treated as random. When more than one parameter is estimated as random, there is no requirement that the distributions be the same. Multiple random parameters are separated in the **fcn** command by commas (,). In the following example, the *invt* parameter will be estimated as a random parameter estimated from a normal distribution, while the *cost* parameter will be treated as a random parameter distributed with a triangular distribution:

```
;fcn=invt(n),cost(t)
```

> *As an aside*, Nlogit makes use of the first four characters of parameters named within the **fcn** specification only. This may cause problems if the first four characters of two or more random parameters are exactly the same.

The random parameters assigned over the sampled population are obtained from repeated simulated draws (see Chapter 5). The number of replications of simulated draws, R, from which the random parameters are derived, may be specified by the analyst using the following command:

```
;pts= <number of replications>
```

The default number of replications and method of simulation in Nlogit is 100 *random* draws. Train (2000) recommends that several hundred random draws be employed in estimation while Bhat (2001) recommends 1,000 random draws. Whatever number is selected, ML models are time intensive in estimation. Depending on the speed of the computer used in the estimation, as well as the number of alternatives, number of random parameters, etc. of the model, a ML model with a large number of random draws (e.g., 5,000) may take several hours before converging – like any model, it is possible that a ML model may fail to converge even after several hours of estimation. For this reason, we recommend that R be set to as low as 50 for exploratory purposes but set at much higher values once a final model specification is identified.

Historically, the approach used in the estimation of random parameter models has been to use R *random* draws from some derived empirical distribution (imposed upon each of the random parameters by the analyst). Random draws require a large number of replications if one is to be satisfied with the accuracy of the model results obtained. When combined with a sizeable sample size and a significant number of parameters to estimate, a large number of random draws is computationally time consuming. A number of intelligent draw methods are available which have been shown to provide dramatic gains in limiting the time taken for model convergence, while producing no discernible degradation in model results. Bhat (2001) reports that when using Halton intelligent draws, comparable model results to models estimated using random draws may be obtained with only one-tenth the total number of draws.

Unlike random draws that may over-sample (in assigning parameters over the sampled population) from areas of a distribution while leaving other areas of the distribution under-sampled, intelligent draw methods are designed to sample the entire parameter space in accordance with the empirical distribution imposed. For example, with a random draw, it is possible, although statistically unlikely, that one may draw observations solely from one tail of the distribution; it is for this very reason that we rely on multiple replications in estimating random parameters, as opposed to using just a single draw. Nevertheless, as suggested within the literature, fewer numerous intelligent draws appear to give empirically similar results to numerically larger numbers of random draws. Hence, intelligent draw methods are designed to reduce the possibility of drawing parameters from limited sections of a distribution and thus creating what would be considered anomalous results.

Nlogit offers two intelligent draw methods: standard Halton sequence (SHS) and shuffled uniform vectors (see Hess et al. 2004). The former method has become very popular; however, recognition that SHS may induce correlation across the space of the draws has motivated shuffling in order to reduce this correlation. The most common form of intelligent draw used in model estimation to date has been SHS.

In Nlogit, the default method of drawing from a distribution is random draws. If no command is provided by the analyst within the ML command syntax (other than the **rpl** and **fcn** commands), Nlogit will automatically employ random draws to draw off of the distribution provided in the **fcn** command for each random parameter (note that non-random parameters are estimated in the same manner as in the MNL and NL models). To make use of SHS intelligent draws, the analyst is required to add the following command syntax to the base ML command:

```
;halton
```

Rather than use random or SHS draws, *shuffled uniform vectors* may be used instead. The necessary command used to request shuffled uniform vectors is as follows (note that it is possible to use only one draw method in the estimation process; i.e., random, or SHS, or shuffled uniform vectors):

```
;shuffle
```

As an aside, In versions of Nlogit after 17 September 2012, we have added Modified Latin Hypercube sampling (MLHS) to Halton and pseudo-random draws as an option. Use **;MLHS** in the RPLogit command. In developing this option, we found that (i) MLHS gives the same answer as Halton; although not identical to the digit, but close enough; and (ii) in perfectly controlled experiments, we found that it is much faster to generate the Halton or pseudo-random draws in the data loop, that is, over and over again, than it is to generate them once before estimation and fetch them from a reservoir as needed. That is, the operation of "compute each time" is much faster than "compute once then move each time." This was surprising. The comparison was not close. Note, however, that it is not possible to compute the MLHS samples on the fly because the full set of R draws must all be drawn at the same time. The upshot is that although we expected MLHS to be faster than Halton, it appears not to be the case.

The very nature of using simulated methods to draw parameters off of a distribution means that even with the exact same model specification, each estimation task should produce a different set of model results. To avoid this possibility, it is necessary to reset the seed of the random number generator to the same value each time a ML model is estimated. The resetting of the random seed generator is by no means compulsory; the ML model will run without resetting the random seed generator; however, the results may differ with each estimation. The command to reset the seed of the random number generator is:

```
Calc; ran(<seed value>)$
```

The analyst can specify any number in the above command as the actual value adopted is of no consequence. For consistency, it is suggested that the analyst select one value and always use this (much as one would use the same PIN number for a bank account). Whatever value is used, the **calc** command must be given before the ML model syntax because the resetting of the random number generator is a separate command to that of the ML command (hence the $ at the end).

Throughout this chapter, we will use the following **calc** command to reset the random number generator but, as suggested above, any number could be used (noting that there is no replicability problem if Halton or Shuffled draws are used and the **calc** command below is not required):

```
calc;ran(12345)$
```

> *As an aside*, the order of random parameters will matter because it affects the draws (be they random or intelligent draws such as Halton) that are applied to the different parameters. Setting the seed only starts the entire chain at a specific point. It does not set the chain for each parameter. For example, think of three random parameters a,b,c, and 100 draws. The chain of draws is v1 ... v300. If ordered a,b,c, "a" gets v1-v100, "b" gets v101-v200, and "c" gets v201-v300. If ordered c,b,a, then "c" gets v1-v100, etc. Setting the seed only establishes that v1 ... v300 are the same every time. This becomes a source of any observed small differences. To ensure that the difference is not important, the analyst needs to choose a large enough number of draws. Although it would be possible to let the user supply specific seeds for each parameter, it is not worth the effort.

In the following sections we will estimate a ML model using the above commands and discuss the output generated by Nlogit for this model. In later sections, we will add to the above set of commands to estimate more complex forms of the ML model capable of detecting a wider range of effects than those discussed immediately below. We also discuss how to derive individual-specific parameter estimates and issues surrounding willingness to pay (WTP) measures derived from random parameter estimates. The final sections of the chapter show you how to estimate a generalized mixed logit model as well as the special case of scaled MNL and estimation in WTP space.

15.3 Nlogit output: interpreting the ML model

In this section we interpret the output from a ML model. As with Chapter 13, we will concentrate on interpreting the output from this model and not concern ourselves with how to improve the model's overall performance (this we leave to the reader). Subsequent sections will add to the output generated through the estimation of more complex ML models.

The ML model shown in the following example is estimated using a commuter mode choice case study presented in Appendix 11A to Chapter 11. Through the command **;halton**, we have requested that standard Halton sequences draws be used to estimate each of the random parameters. The **;fcn** command specification is used to stipulate that the *11 attributes* (drawn from a normal distribution) be treated as random parameters. Other attributes in the utility functions will be treated as non-random parameters. To reduce the amount of time necessary for model convergence (which will be useful in the classroom to reproduce the results), we have restricted the number of replications to 100:

```
sample;all$
reject;dremove=1$ Removing data with errors
reject;ttype#1$  Selecting Commuter sample
reject;altij=-999$

Nlogit
    ;lhs=resp1,cset,Altij
    ;choices=NLRail,NHRail,NBway,Bus,Bway,Train,Car
    ;par
    ;rpl
    ;fcn=invt(n),cost(n),acwt(n)  ,eggt(n),  crpark(n),accbusf(n),
        waittb(n),acctb(n),crcost(n),  crinvt(n),creggt(n)
    ;halton;pts= 100
    ;model:
    U(NLRail)= NLRAsc + cost*tcost + invt*InvTime + acwt*wait+ acwt*acctim
    + accbusf*accbusf+eggT*egresst + ptinc*pinc + ptgend*gender +
NLRinsde*inside /
    U(NHRail)= TNAsc + cost*Tcost + invt*InvTime + acwt*WaitT + acwt*acctim
    + eggT*egresst + accbusf*accbusf + ptinc*pinc + ptgend*gender +
NHRinsde*inside /
    U(NBway)=  NBWAsc + cost*Tcost + invt*InvTime + waitTb*WaitT
    + accTb*acctim + eggT*egresst + accbusf*accbusf+ ptinc*pinc + ptgend*-
gender /
    U(Bus)=     BSAsc + cost*frunCost + invt*InvTime + waitTb*WaitT
    + accTb*acctim + eggT*egresst+ ptinc*pinc + ptgend*gender/
    U(Bway)=    BWAsc + cost*Tcost + invt*InvTime + waitTb*WaitT
```

```
     + accTb*acctim + eggT*egresst + accbusf*accbusf+ ptinc*pinc + ptgend*-
gender /
    U(Train)=  TNAsc + cost*tcost + invt*InvTime + acwt*WaitT + acwt*acctim
    + eggT*egresst + accbusf*accbusf+ ptinc*pinc + ptgend*gender /
    U(Car)=    CRcost*costs + CRinvt*InvTime + CRpark*parkcost+
CReggT*egresst$
Normal exit:   6 iterations. Status=0, F=    2487.362
```

As with the NL models, Nlogit will first estimate a MNL model to derive the initial start values for each of the parameters in the ML model. In the case of the ML model, the estimation of the MNL model to obtain starting values for the parameter estimates is not optional and as such does not require the addition of commands such as **start=logit** (see Chapter 13):

```
Start values obtained using MNL model
Dependent variable              Choice
Log likelihood function    -2487.36242
Estimation based on N =  1840, K =  20
Inf.Cr.AIC  =   5014.7 AIC/N =    2.725
R2=1-LogL/LogL* Log-L fncn R-sqrd R2Adj
Constants only must be computed directly
           Use NLOGIT ;...;RHS=ONE$
Response data are given as ind. choices
Number of obs.=  1840, skipped    0 obs
```

RESP1	Coefficient	Standard Error	z	Prob. |z|>Z*	95% Confidence Interval	
INVT	-.04940***	.00207	-23.87	.0000	-.05346	-.04535
COST	-.18921***	.01386	-13.66	.0000	-.21637	-.16205
ACWT	-.05489***	.00527	-10.42	.0000	-.06521	-.04456
EGGT	-.01157**	.00471	-2.46	.0140	-.02080	-.00235
CRPARK	-.01513**	.00733	-2.07	.0389	-.02950	-.00077
ACCBUSF	-.09962***	.03220	-3.09	.0020	-.16274	-.03650
WAITTB	-.07612***	.02414	-3.15	.0016	-.12343	-.02880
ACCTB	-.06162***	.00841	-7.33	.0000	-.07810	-.04514
CRCOST	-.11424***	.02840	-4.02	.0001	-.16990	-.05857
CRINVT	-.03298***	.00392	-8.42	.0000	-.04065	-.02531
CREGGT	-.05190***	.01379	-3.76	.0002	-.07894	-.02486
NLRASC	2.69464***	.33959	7.93	.0000	2.02905	3.36022
PTINC	-.00757***	.00194	-3.90	.0001	-.01138	-.00377
PTGEND	1.34212***	.17801	7.54	.0000	.99323	1.69101
NLRINSDE	-.94667***	.31857	-2.97	.0030	1.57106	-.32227
TNASC	2.10793***	.32772	6.43	.0000	1.46562	2.75024
NHRINSDE	-.94474***	.36449	-2.59	.0095	-1.65913	-.23036
NBWASC	1.41575***	.36237	3.91	.0001	.70551	2.12599
BSASC	1.86891***	.32011	5.84	.0000	1.24151	2.49630
BWASC	1.76517***	.33367	5.29	.0000	1.11120	2.41914

This MNL model has 5 ASCs, 11 attributes (in **bold**) associated with the set of available modes, two SECs (PTINC, PTGEND), and two variables describing where the commuter's trip destination for the new rail modes (NLRINSIDE, NHRINSIDE) is inside (1) or outside (0) of the study area.

> *As an aside*, It is unusual to have an ASC that is the same in more than one utility expression; namely TNASC. However, this is appropriate in this model since NHRAIL is an extension of the TRAIN system in Sydney, and we found that this is the best representation of what is essentially the same alternative, even though the choice experiment separated this new infrastructure out from the existing (i.e., TRAIN) network.

The preceding output is interpreted in exactly the same manner as described in Chapters 11 and 13. The only discernible difference between this model and those of earlier chapters is the order in which the parameter estimates are given. Those parameter estimates that are specified as random parameters are shown first, irrespective of their order within the utility specification. All the parameters in the MNL model have the correct sign and are statistically significant at the 95 percent level of confidence.

The output provides information similar to that provided within the first output box of both the MNL and NL models. Provided in this series of output is information on the number of observations (as with the NL model, the value given is the number of alternatives considered over the sample and not the number of choice sets viewed), the number of iterations to convergence, and the LL function at convergence. Given a focus on mixed logit, the main objective of the MNL model is to obtain starting values; however, it is not uncommon for researchers to report the LL at convergence as a way of showing the gains (hopefully, they are significant) on ML over MNL. If the analyst wishes to contrast the overall LL with the fit in the absence of the set of significant attributes, adding to the command **;asc** will produce a model with only the J–1 ASCs (see below), which indicates the LL at convergence when only choice shares are known. The latter is shown below as – 3130.826 which, when compared to −2487.362, provides the necessary information to calculate the gain in model performance in the presence of the set of significant explanatory variables. The resulting pseudo-R^2 is 0.206 (manually calculated). If we were to establish the improved **fgit** relative to equal choice shares (i.e., no ASCs), then we would compare −2487.362 with −3580.475 (as reported in the ML results below), giving a pseudo-R^2 of 0.305.

```
ASCs only:
|-> Nlogit
    ;lhs=resp1,cset,Altij
    ;choices=NLRail,NHRail,NBway,Bus,Bway,Train,Car
    ;maxit=100
    ;model:
    U(NLRail)= NLRAsc/
    U(NHRail)= NHRAsc/
    U(NBway)=  NBWAsc/
    U(Bus)=    BusAsc/
    U(Train)=  TnAsc/
    U(Bway)=   BwyAsc$
Normal exit:   5 iterations. Status=0, F=    3130.826
```

```
Discrete choice (multinomial logit) model
Dependent variable              Choice
Log likelihood function      -3130.82617
Estimation based on N =   1840, K =   6
Inf.Cr.AIC  =   6273.7 AIC/N =    3.410
R2=1-LogL/LogL*  Log-L fncn R-sqrd R2Adj
Constants only must be computed directly
             Use NLOGIT ;...;RHS=ONE$
Response data are given as ind. choices
Number of obs.= 1840, skipped    0 obs
```
-----------+--

RESP1	Coefficient	Standard Error	z	Prob. |z|>Z*	95% Confidence Interval	
NLRASC	.34098***	.08886	3.84	.0001	.16683	.51514
NHRASC	.64197***	.08600	7.46	.0000	.47342	.81053
NBWASC	-.95132***	.14913	-6.38	.0000	-1.24362	-.65903
BUSASC	.00090	.08913	.01	.9920	-.17378	.17558
TNASC	.30541***	.08478	3.60	.0003	.13924	.47158
BWYASC	.02057	.09015	.23	.8195	-.15611	.19726

-----------+--

15.3.1 Model 2: mixed logit with unconstrained distributions

The first ML model presented involves 11 random parameters that have an unconstrained normal distribution. It is always recommended that analysts start with the well known normal distribution without constraints on range and sign, since this provides a good reference point from which to consider alternative distributions and a behaviorally appealing set of restrictions on the distribution. The overall fit of the ML models is −2438.811, which is an improvement over the MNL model fit of −2487.362. There is, however, an extra number of degrees of freedom (increasing from 20 in MNL to 31 in ML). The adjusted pseudo-R^2 (which accounts for the differing degrees of freedom) is 0.316 when compared with equal choice shares, but only 0.016 when contrasted with the MNL model performance (the start values). It is not unusual for ML to be marginally better on overall goodness of fit from the MNL model; however, one must be careful in relying on this single measure of performance in selecting the preferred mode since there are many behaviorally appealing outputs on ML that are not available in MNL. Specifically, as discussed later in this chapter, we often find that the WTP estimates do vary across the sample and using a single estimate (from MNL) is a behaviorally limiting condition, even if the model fit is very similar.

Also provided is a Chi-square statistic for the log-likelihood ratio test (LRT) (using as the base comparison model, a model with equal choice shares only) and information on the pseudo-R^2. In the above example, the model is statistically significant (Chi-square equal to 2283.33 with 31 degrees of freedom and a p-value equal to zero):

```
|-> Nlogit
   ;lhs=resp1,cset,Altij
   ;choices=NLRail,NHRail,NBway,Bus,Bway,Train,Car
   ;par
   ;rpl
   ;fcn=invt(n),cost(n),acwt(n)  ,eggt(n),  crpark(n),accbusf(n),
       waittb(n),acctb(n),crcost(n),  crinvt(n),creggt(n)
   ;halton;pts= 100
   ;model:
   U(NLRail)= NLRAsc + cost*tcost + invt*InvTime + acwt*wait+ acwt*acctim
   + accbusf*accbusf+eggT*egresst + ptinc*pinc + ptgend*gender +
NLRinsde*inside /
   U(NHRail)= TNAsc + cost*Tcost + invt*InvTime + acwt*WaitT + acwt*acctim
   + eggT*egresst + accbusf*accbusf + ptinc*pinc + ptgend*gender +
NHRinsde*inside /
   U(NBway)=  NBWAsc + cost*Tcost + invt*InvTime + waitTb*WaitT
   + accTb*acctim + eggT*egresst + accbusf*accbusf+ ptinc*pinc +
ptgend*gender /
   U(Bus)=    BSAsc + cost*frunCost + invt*InvTime + waitTb*WaitT
   + accTb*acctim + eggT*egresst+ ptinc*pinc + ptgend*gender/
   U(Bway)=   BWAsc + cost*Tcost + invt*InvTime + waitTb*WaitT
   + accTb*acctim + eggT*egresst + accbusf*accbusf+ ptinc*pinc +
ptgend*gender /
   U(Train)= TNAsc + cost*tcost + invt*InvTime + acwt*WaitT + acwt*acctim
   + eggT*egresst + accbusf*accbusf+ ptinc*pinc + ptgend*gender /
   U(Car)=    CRcost*costs + CRinvt*InvTime + CRpark*parkcost+
CReggT*egresst$
Normal exit:  6 iterations. Status=0, F=    2487.362
------------------------------------------------------------------------
Random Parameters Logit Model
Dependent variable                    RESP1
```

```
Log likelihood function      -2438.81169
Restricted log likelihood    -3580.47467
Chi squared [ 31](P= .000)   2283.32597
Significance level                .00000
McFadden Pseudo R-squared        .3188580
Estimation based on N =   1840, K =   31
Inf.Cr.AIC  =   4939.6 AIC/N =    2.685
R2=1-LogL/LogL*  Log-L fncn R-sqrd R2Adj
No coefficients -3580.4747 .3189  .3165
Constants only can be computed directly
             Use NLOGIT ;...;RHS=ONE$
At start values -2487.3624  .0195 .0161
Response data are given as ind. choices
Replications for simulated probs. = 100
Used Halton sequences in simulations.
Number of obs.= 1840, skipped     0 obs
```

Normal exit: 61 iterations. Status=0, F=   2438.812

RESP1	Coefficient	Standard Error	z	Prob. |z|>Z*	95% Confidence Interval	
	Random parameters in utility functions					
INVT	-.07845***	.00541	-14.50	.0000	-.08906	-.06784
COST	-.36258***	.03498	-10.36	.0000	-.43114	-.29401
ACWT	-.08227***	.00964	-8.54	.0000	-.10116	-.06337
EGGT	-.02832***	.00965	-2.93	.0033	-.04723	-.00941
CRPARK	-.08806**	.03527	-2.50	.0125	-.15719	-.01893
ACCBUSF	-.12941***	.04364	-2.97	.0030	-.21494	-.04389
WAITTB	-.10341***	.03483	-2.97	.0030	-.17167	-.03515
ACCTB	-.08388***	.01132	-7.41	.0000	-.10607	-.06169
CRCOST	-.31892***	.09142	-3.49	.0005	-.49809	-.13974
CRINVT	-.10051***	.01574	-6.39	.0000	-.13135	-.06966
CREGGT	-.12685***	.03573	-3.55	.0004	-.19687	-.05682
	Nonrandom parameters in utility functions					
NLRASC	2.89124***	.66856	4.32	.0000	1.58088	4.20160
PTINC	-.02150***	.00535	-4.02	.0001	-.03198	-.01101
PTGEND	2.95546***	.50220	5.88	.0000	1.97116	3.93976
NLRINSDE	-1.35718***	.40930	-3.32	.0009	-2.15940	-.55496
TNASC	2.08897***	.65014	3.21	.0013	.81471	3.36323
NHRINSDE	-1.44618***	.47234	-3.06	.0022	-2.37195	-.52040
NBWASC	1.33874**	.66636	2.01	.0445	.03270	2.64477
BSASC	1.59186**	.62985	2.53	.0115	.35737	2.82634
BWASC	1.54923**	.64682	2.40	.0166	.28148	2.81698
	Distns. of RPs. Std.Devs or limits of triangular					
NsINVT	.04206***	.00559	7.52	.0000	.03110	.05301
NsCOST	.31629***	.04533	6.98	.0000	.22743	.40514
NsACWT	.02742**	.01215	2.26	.0240	.00360	.05123
NsEGGT	.05633***	.01959	2.88	.0040	.01793	.09473

NsCRPARK|	.08274**	.03779	2.19	.0286	.00868	.15680
NsACCBUS|	.08363	.12494	.67	.5033	-.16125	.32850
NsWAITTB|	.06519	.06438	1.01	.3113	-.06101	.19138
NsACCTB|	.00453	.02348	.19	.8469	-.04149	.05056
NsCRCOST|	.26923***	.07536	3.57	.0004	.12153	.41693
NsCRINVT|	.04926***	.01104	4.46	.0000	.02763	.07090
NsCREGGT|	.00363	.04594	.08	.9369	-.08640	.09367

The output provides the analyst with information on the number of replications used in the simulated draws, as well as the type of draw used. In this example, the output indicates that SHS draws were used in the estimation process with 100 replications. No *bad* observations were removed during model estimation.

The last section of the output provides information on the parameter estimates of the ML model. The first and last output generated in this section relates to the random parameters estimated as part of the ML model. The first series of parameter estimate output relates to the random parameters and is used to determine whether the mean of the sample population random parameters obtained from the 100 SHS draws is statistically different to zero.

Random parameters estimated within the most basic ML framework are estimated over the sampled population from a number of draws (either random draws or intelligent draws; SHS or shuffled uniform vectors). The parameter estimates thus obtained are derived at the sample population level only. This is not the same as estimating individual-specific parameter estimates. Parameter estimates estimated at the sample population level are called *unconditional* parameter estimates, as the parameters are not conditioned on any particular individual's choice pattern but rather on the sample population as a whole. The process of estimating *unconditional* random parameters is similar to the estimation process of non-random parameters in the MNL and ML models; that is, maximization of the LL function over the data for the sample population. In a later section, we demonstrate how to estimate individual-specific or *conditional* parameter estimates. We leave it until then to discuss the differences between the two types of estimates but note that the two often produce widely varying results.

Each draw taken from some specified distribution will produce a unique sample population parameter estimate for each random parameter estimated. To avoid spurious results (for example, drawing a single observation from the tail of the distribution), R replications of draws are used. It is from these R replicated draws that the mean random parameter is derived. Simply put, the mean of each random parameter is the average of the parameters drawn over the R replications from the appropriate distribution. It is this value that is given in the above output. For the *invtime* attribute treated as generic across all public transport alternatives, the parameter estimate of −0.0784 represents the mean of the R draws over the 100 SHS draws requested within the command syntax.

The interpretation of the output associated with the mean of a random parameter estimate is much the same as with the non-random parameters discussed in Chapter 11. The *p*-value for the *invtime* attribute random parameter is 0.00, which is less than alpha equal to 0.05 (i.e., 95 percent confidence interval). As the *p*-value is less than the analyst determined critical value, we reject the null hypothesis at the 95 percent level of confidence and conclude that the mean of the random parameter is statistically different to zero. The *p*-value for the cost parameter associated with all public transport alternatives is similarly less than alpha equal to 0.05, suggesting that the mean parameter estimate of −0.3626 for this random parameter is also statistically different to zero. Both random parameters have means that are, at the sample population level, statistically different to zero.

While the first set of output relates to the means of each of the random parameters, the second series of output relates to the amount of dispersion that exists around the sample population. The parameter estimates given in the output are the derived standard deviations calculated over each of the R draws. Insignificant parameter estimates for derived standard deviations indicate that the dispersion around the mean is statistically equal to zero, suggesting that all information in the distribution is captured within the mean. Statistically significant parameter estimates for derived standard deviations for a random parameter suggest the existence of heterogeneity in the parameter estimates over the sampled population around the mean parameter estimate (i.e., different individuals possess individual-specific parameter estimates that may be different from the sample population mean parameter estimate).

As an aside, the reader will note that the names of the parameters in the above output are preceded by two letters. These letters are used to identify the analytical distribution imposed on the random parameter estimate. Random parameters drawn from normal distributions will have the letters Ns, lognormal Ls, uniform Us, triangular distributions Ts, and non-stochastic distributions Cs (we discuss the special case of using a non-stochastic distribution in a later section).

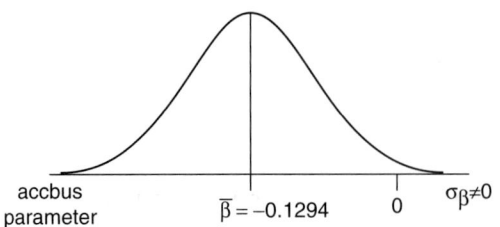

Figure 15.1   Testing dispersion of the *accbusf* random parameter

For the above example, the dispersion of the *invehicle* time random parameter represented by a derived standard deviation of 0.042 is statistically significant given a Wald statistic of 7.52 (within the ±1.96 range) and a *p*-value of 0.00 (which is less than our critical value of alpha equal to 0.05). In this case, all individuals within the sample cannot be (statistically) represented by a *invtime* parameter of −0.0784. The case for a distribution of parameter values to represent the entire sampled population is justified.

Dispersion of the access bus fare parameter (*Nsaccbus*) is statistically insignificant, as suggested by a Wald statistic of 0.67 (outside the ±1.96 critical value range) and a *p*-value of 0.5033. Unlike the *invt* parameter, the model suggests that the *accbusf* parameter should collapse to a single point representative of the entire sampled population. For the analyst, this suggests that the presence of heterogeneity over the sampled population with regard to individual level *accbusf* parameter estimates does not exist. As such, a single parameter estimate of −0.1294 is sufficient to represent all sampled individuals. We show this in Figure 15.1.

At this point, the analyst may wish to respecify the *accbusf* parameter as a non-random parameter or re-estimate the model maintaining the *accbusf* parameter as a random parameter, but assign to it some other distribution from which it may be derived. Despite supporting evidence that the *invt* parameter should be treated as a normally distributed random parameter, the analyst may also wish to assign different distributional forms to test for better model fits. Also, other parameters formally treated as non-random may be estimated as random parameters in further exploratory work. Once the analyst is content with the model results, the model should be re-estimated with a greater number of draws to confirm stability in the results.

As an aside, the statistical significance of attributes does vary as the number of draws changes, so one must exercise some judgment in the initial determination of statistically significant effects. Practical experience suggests that an attribute with a z-value over 1.5 for a small number of draws may indeed become statistically significant (i.e., over 1.96) with a larger number of draws. This has been observed more for the standard deviation parameters (i.e., those derived from normal and log-normal distributions).

In order to write out the utility functions for the above model, we need to consider Equation (15.1), that accounts for the normal distribution assumption placed upon the random parameters of the model. In the above example, we have no associated heterogeneity in the mean parameter estimate (we explore this option in a later section). As such, we may rewrite Equation (15.1) as Equation (15.4):

$$Normal : \beta_{\text{attribute mean}} + \sigma_{\text{attribute standard deviation}} \times N, \qquad (15.4)$$

where N has a standard normal distribution. For the *invtime* random parameter, we observe a mean of −0.07845 and a standard deviation of 0.04206. By way of Equation (15.1) we may write this as such, known as the marginal (dis-utility associated with the *invtime* attribute:

$$Invtd = -0.07845 + 0.04206 \times N. \qquad (15.5)$$

The commands used to obtain the estimate of *invtd* and to plot it (Figure 15.2) are as follows:

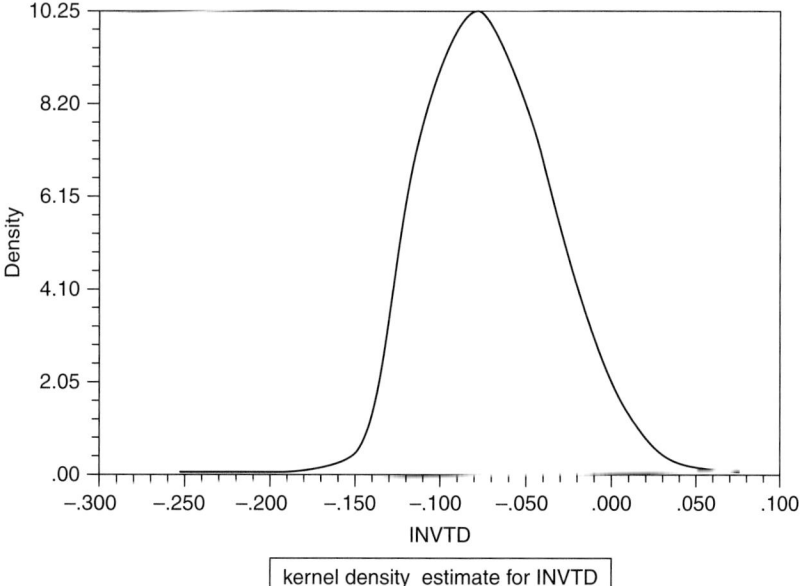

Figure 15.2   Unconstrained distribution of invehicle time for public transport modes

```
create;rna=rnn(0,1);Invtd = -0.07845 + 0.04206*rna $
?To eliminate the car alternative since this expression only
applies to public transport:
reject;altij=7$
dstats;rhs=invtd$
kernel;rhs=invtd$
                         |-> kernel;rhs=invtd$
               Kernel Density Estimator for INVTD
               Kernel Function      =       Logistic
               Observations         =           9060
               Points plotted       =           1008
               Bandwidth            =        .006106
               Statistics for abscissa values-----
               Mean                 =       -.078880
               Standard Deviation = .041972
               Skewness             =       -.019572
               Kurtosis-3 (excess)=          -.040885
               Chi2 normality test=           .014032
               Minimum              =       -.246552
               Maximum              =        .070210
               Results matrix       =         KERNEL
```

This estimated distribution is useful in many subsequent uses, such as deriving the WTP distribution. For example: to obtain an estimate of the value of invehicle time savings (VTTS), we would obtain the estimated distribution *invtd* as the numerator and then divide it by an equivalent estimated distribution to *tcostd* (i.e., $(-0.36258 + 0.31629 \times N)$), to give a VTTS in \$/min.

As an aside, the assignment of the numerator and denominator estimate to each sampled respondent is random, given the absence of any systematic influences interacting with this parameterization. The ratio of two randomized allocations produces a VTTS for each respondent which may be problematic if the numerator happens to be a high (low) estimate from the distribution and the denominator a low (high) value. This has been avoided in many studies by using a fixed parameter in the denominator. While it resolves this issue, it comes at the price of ignoring preference heterogeneity where it can be shown, as in the current model, to exist. One way to minimize the risk of this occurring is to introduce heterogeneity in the mean and/or variance of the random parameter, as shown in a later section of this chapter.

The remaining output relates to those attributes estimated as non-random parameters. Non-random parameters are interpreted in exactly the same manner as parameters estimated with the MNL or NL model forms. All parameter estimates are of the correct sign and are statistically significant. We may write out the utility functions for the above model as below:

V_{nlrail} = 2.8912+(−0.07845+0.04206×N)*invtime+(−0.36258+0.31629xN)
*tcost+(−0.08227+0.02742xN)*wait+(−0.08227+0.02742xN)*acctim
+(−0.02832+0.05633xN)*egress

+(−0.12941+0.08363xN)*accbusf−0.0215*pinc+2.95546*gender
−1.35718*nlrinside

V_{nhrail} = 2.08897+(−0.07845+0.04206×N)*invtime+(−0.36258
+0.31629xN)*tcost+(−0.08227+0.02742xN)*wait+(−0.08227
+0.02742xN)*acctim+(−0.02832+0.05633xN)*egresst
+(−0.12941+0.08363xN)*accbusf−0.0215*pinc+2.95546*gender
−1.35718*nlrinside

V_{nbway} = 1.33874+(−0.07845+0.04206×N)*invtime+(−0.36258
+0.31629xN)*tcost+(−1.0341+0.06519xN)*wait+(−0.08388
+0.00453xN)*acctim+(−0.02832+0.05633xN)*egresst
+(−0.12941+0.08363xN)*accbusf−0.0215*pinc+2.95546*gender

V_{bus} = 1.59186+(−0.07845+0.04206×N)*invtime+(−0.36258+0.31629xN)
*tcost+(−1.0341+0.06519xN)*wait+(−0.08388+0.00453xN)*acctim
+(−0.02832+0.05633xN)*egresst
+(−0.12941+0.08363xN)*accbusf−0.0215*pinc+2.95546*gender

V_{bway} = 1.54923+(−0.07845+0.04206×N)*invtime+(−0.36258+0.31629xN)
*tcost+(−1.0341+0.06519xN)*wait+(−0.08388+0.00453xN)*acctim
+(−0.02832+0.05633xN)*egresst
+(−0.12941+0.08363xN)*accbusf−0.0215*pinc+2.95546*gender

V_{train} = 2.08897+(−0.07845+0.04206×N)*invtime+(−0.36258+0.31629xN)
*tcost+(−0.08227+0.02742xN)*wait+(−0.08227+0.02742xN)*acctim
+(−0.02832+0.05633xN)*egresst
+(−0.12941+0.08363xN)*accbusf−0.0215*pinc+2.95546*gender

V_{car} = (−0.10051+0.04926×N)*invtime+(−0.31892+0.26923xN)*tcost
+(−0.08806+0.08274xN)*parkcost+(−0.12685+0.00363xN)*egresst

15.3.1.1 Graphing the distributions: the kernel density estimator

The *kernel density estimator* is a useful device for graphically presenting many of the outputs of ML models as used in the example above, especially the distributions of parameter estimates and WTP values derived from parameter distributions. It is for this reason that we introduce it in this chapter (although it is useful in the presentation of results for all model forms). The **kernel density** is a modification of the familiar histogram used to describe the distribution of a sample of observations graphically. The disadvantages of the histogram that are overcome with kernel estimators are, firstly, that histograms are discontinuous whereas (our models assume) the underlying distributions are continuous and, second, the shape of the histogram is crucially dependent on the assumed widths and placements of the bins. Intuition suggests that the first of these problems is mitigated by taking narrower bins, but the cost of doing so is that the number of observations that land in each bin falls so that the larger picture painted by the histogram becomes increasingly variable and imprecise. The kernel density estimator is a "smoothed" plot that shows, for each selected point, the proportion of the sample that is "near" it (hence the name "density"). "Nearness" is defined by a weighting function called the *kernel function*, which will have the characteristic that the farther a sample observation is from the selected point, the smaller will be the weight that it receives.

The kernel density function for a single attribute is computed using Equation (15.6):

$$f(z_j) = \frac{1}{n} \sum_{i=1}^{n} \frac{K[(z_j - x_i)/h]}{h}, \, j = 1, \ldots, M. \tag{15.6}$$

The function is computed for a specified set of values of interest, z_j, $j = 1, \ldots, M$ where z_j is a partition of the range of the attribute. Each value requires a sum over the full sample of n values, x_i, $i = 1.,,,.n$. The primary component of the computation is the kernel, or weighting function, $K[.]$, which take a number of forms. For example, the normal kernel is $K[z] = \varphi(z)$ (normal density). Thus, for the normal kernel, the weights range from $\varphi(0) = 0.399$ when $x_i = z_j$ to values approaching zero when x_i is far from z_j. Thus, again, what the kernel density function is measuring is the proportion of the sample of values that is close to the chosen z_j.

The other essential part of the computation is the smoothing (bandwidth) parameter, h, to ensure a good plot resolution. The bandwidth parameter is exactly analogous to the bin width in a common histogram. Thus, as noted earlier, narrower bins (smaller bandwidths) produce unstable histograms (kernel density estimators) because not many points are "in the neighborhood" of the value of interest. Large values of h stabilize the function, but tend to flatten it and reduce the resolution – imagine a histogram with only two or three bins, for example. Small values of h produce greater detail, but also cause the estimator to become less stable. An example of a bandwidth is given in Equation (15.7), which is a standard form used in several contemporary computer programs:

$$h = 0.9Q/n^{0.2}, \tag{15.7}$$

where $Q = \min(\text{standard deviation, range}/1.5)$.

A number of points have to be specified. The set of points z_j is (for any number of points) defined by Equation (15.8):

$$z_j = z_{LOWER} + j * [(z_{UPPER} - z_{LOWER})/M], j = 1, \ldots, M \, z_{LOWER}$$
$$= \min(x) - h \text{ to } z_{UPPER} = \max(x) + h. \tag{15.8}$$

The procedure produces an $M \times 2$ matrix in which the first column contains z_j and the second column contains the values of $f(z_j)$ and the plot of the second column against the first – this is the estimated density function.

The Nlogit command used to obtain plots of the kernel densities is:

```
;kernel;rhs=<name of parameter/variable>;Limits=<lower, upper
values>;<model form>$
```

For example, kernel;rhs=invtd;limits=0,1.5;logit$. The default is kernel; rhs=invtd$, which assumes a logistic function.

15.3.2 Model 3: restricting the sign and range of a random parameter

There are many applications in which it is believed *a priori* that the sign of a parameter must always be positive (or negative). Several of the available distributions allow you to force the sign of a parameter to be positive. These include the following types:

o one sided triangular	$\beta i = \beta + \beta vi$, $vi \sim$ triangular $(-1,1)$ $(\sigma = \beta)$
l log-normal	$\beta i = \exp(\beta + \sigma vi)$, $vi \sim N[0.1]$
x maximum	$\beta i = \text{Max}(0, \beta + \sigma \, vi)$ $vi \sim N[0.1]$
r Rayleigh	$\beta i = \exp(\beta + \sigma vi)$, $vi = 2(-\log ui) \sqrt{.5}$, $ui \sim U[0,1]$
b beta, scaled	$\beta i = \beta vi$, $vi \sim \text{beta}(3,3)$
q exponential, scaled	$\beta i = \beta vi$, $vi \sim \text{exponential}(1)$
v exp(triangle)	$\beta i = \exp(\beta i \text{ (triangular)})$

If you need to force a parameter to be negative, rather than positive, you can use these distributions anyway – just multiply the variable by −1 before estimation. (Note, in Nlogit, what we have labeled the "Rayleigh" variable is not actually a Rayleigh variable, though it does resemble one. It has a shape similar to the log-normal; however, its tail is thinner, so it may be a more plausible model.) If you specify these distributions for a parameter that would be negative if unrestricted, the estimator will fail to converge, and issue a diagnostic that it could not locate an optimum of the function (log-likelihood, LL). In addition, the maximum and minimum specifications are not continuous in the parameters, and will often not be estimable.

> *As an aside,* The constraining of a random parameter distribution is an econometric consideration based upon the underlying empirical distribution of that parameter. The reader is cautioned against confusing such a constraint on the empirical distribution with a constraint upon the behavioral distributions in the population.

A common device used to fix the sign of a parameter is to specify that it have a log-normal distribution. However, the log-normal distribution has a long, thick tail, which can imply an implausible empirical distribution of parameter values. An alternative is to use a random parameter with a finite range of variation. You may do this with the triangular, uniform or beta distribution, using:

```
; Fcn = name(o) for triangular, or ; Fcn = name(f) for uniform,
or (h) for beta
```

> *As an aside,* the constrained triangular that uses **name(o)** can also be defined by **name(t,1)**, which indicates that the mean and standard deviation are set equal.

Using the normal distribution as an example, **; Fcn = invt(n,1)** says the $\sigma_{invt} = 1 * |\beta_{invt}|$. The parameter that enters the absolute value function is the constant term in the parameter mean. This specifies that the mean of the distribution is a free parameter, β, but the two end-points of the distribution are fixed at zero and 2β, so there is no free variance (scaling) parameter. The parameter can be positive or negative.

We now re-estimate the model above, but with constrained distributions imposed on all random parameters. We have chosen a constrained triangular distribution. The triangular distribution ensures that the sign of the parameter estimate is behaviorally plausible throughout the entire distribution. The triangular distribution was promoted in Train (2003). Hensher and Greene (2003) also used it and it is increasingly being used in empirical studies. Let c be the centre and s the spread. The density starts at c – s, rises linearly to c, and then drops linearly to c + s. It is zero below c – s and above c + s. The mean and mode are c. The standard deviation is the spread divided by $\sqrt{6}$; hence the spread is the standard deviation times $\sqrt{6}$. The height of the tent at c is 1/s

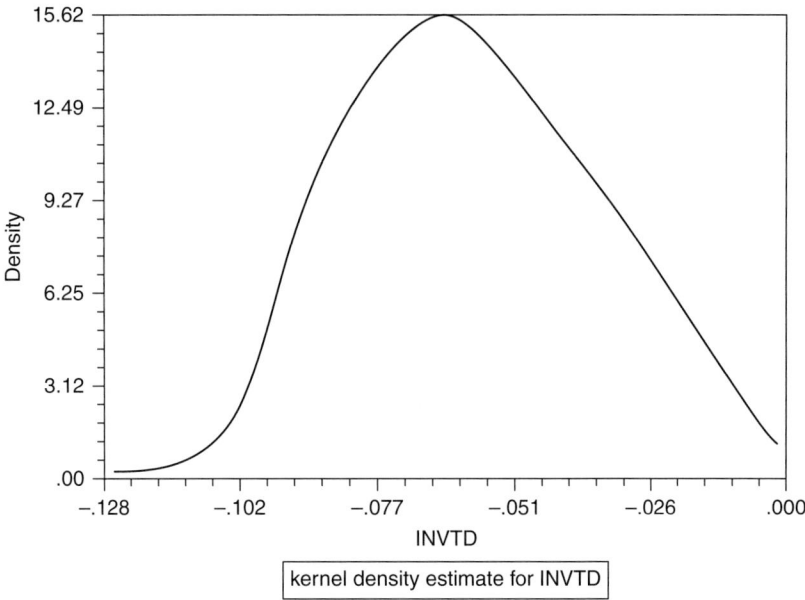

Figure 15.3 Constrained distribution of invehicle time for public transport modes

(such that each side of the tent has area $s \times (1/s) \times (1/2) = 1/2$, and both sides have area $1/2 + 1/2 = 1$, as required for a density). The slope is $1/s^2$.

The results below differ from the previous model only in the distributional assumption of the random parameters. You will see that the standard deviation parameter estimate for each random parameter is exactly equal to the mean estimate of the random parameter. This constraint ensures that the full distribution satisfies the one (negative) sign. We can show this with the following commands and the graph in Figure 15.3:

```
      create
    ;rna=rnn(0,1)
    ;V1=rnu(0,1)
    ;if(v1<=0.5)T=sqr(2*V1)-1;(ELSE) T=1-sqr(2*(1-V1))
    ;Invtd = -0.06368 + 0.06368*T $
        reject;altij=7$
        kernel;rhs=invtd;limits=-0.128,0$
    Kernel Density Estimator for INVTD
    Kernel Function      =      Logistic
    Observations         =        9060
    Points plotted       =        1008
    Bandwidth            =      .003821
    Statistics for abscissa values-----
    Mean                 =      -.063446
```

```
            Standard Deviation =      .026261
            Skewness           =      .021480
            Kurtosis-3 (excess)=     -.650728
            Chi2 normality test=     2.022592
            Minimum            =     -.128000
            Maximum            =      .000000
            Results matrix     =       KERNEL


    Nlogit
    ;lhs=resp1,cset,Altij
    ;choices=NLRail,NHRail,NBway,Bus,Bway,Train,Car
    ;par
    ;rpl
    ;fcn=invt(o),cost(o),acwt(o) ,eggt(o), crpark(o),
    accbusf(o),waittb(o),acctb(o),crcost(o),crinvt(o),creggt(o)
    ;maxit=200
    ;halton;pts= 100
    ;model:
    U(NLRail)= NLRAsc + cost*tcost + invt*InvTime + acwt*wait+ acwt*acctim
    + accbusf*accbusf+eggT*egresst + ptinc*pinc + ptgend*gender +
NLRinsde*inside /
    U(NHRail)= TNAsc + cost*Tcost + invt*InvTime + acwt*WaitT + acwt*acctim
    + eggT*egresst + accbusf*accbusf + ptinc*pinc + ptgend*gender +
NHRinsde*inside /
    U(NBway)=  NBWAsc + cost*Tcost + invt*InvTime + waitTb*WaitT
    + accTb*acctim + eggT*egresst + accbusf*accbusf+ ptinc*pinc +
ptgend*gender /
    U(Bus)=    BSAsc + cost*frunCost + invt*InvTime + waitTb*WaitT
    + accTb*acctim + eggT*egresst+ ptinc*pinc + ptgend*gender/
    U(Bway)=   BWAsc + cost*Tcost + invt*InvTime + waitTb*WaitT
    + accTb*acctim + eggT*egresst + accbusf*accbusf+ ptinc*pinc +
ptgend*gender /
    U(Train)= TNAsc + cost*tcost + invt*InvTime + acwt*WaitT + acwt*acctim
    + eggT*egresst + accbusf*accbusf+ ptinc*pinc + ptgend*gender /
    U(Car)=    CRcost*costs + CRinvt*InvTime + CRpark*parkcost+
CReggT*egresst$
Normal exit:  27 iterations. Status=0, F=    2465.753
-----------------------------------------------------------------------------

Random Parameters Logit Model
Dependent variable                  RESP1
Log likelihood function       -2465.75251
Restricted log likelihood     -3580.47467
Chi squared [ 20](P= .000)    2229.44432
Significance level                 .00000
McFadden Pseudo R-squared         .3113336
Estimation based on N =   1840, K =  20
Inf.Cr.AIC  =   4971.5 AIC/N =    2.702
```

```
R2=1-LogL/LogL* Log-L fncn R-sqrd R2Adj
No coefficients -3580.4747  .3113 .3098
Constants only can be computed directly
              Use NLOGIT ;...;RHS=ONE$
At start values -2497.0892  .0125 .0103
Response data are given as ind. choices
Replications for simulated probs. = 100
Used Halton sequences in simulations.
Number of obs.= 1840, skipped    0 obs
```

RESP1	Coefficient	Standard Error	z	Prob. |z|>Z*	95% Confidence Interval	
	Random parameters in utility functions					
INVT	-.06368***	.00329	-19.37	.0000	-.07012	-.05723
COST	-.24872***	.01958	-12.70	.0000	-.28710	-.21033
ACWT	-.06976***	.00731	-9.55	.0000	-.08407	-.05544
EGGT	-.01435**	.00565	-2.54	.0111	-.02543	-.00327
CRPARK	-.03559***	.01341	-2.65	.0079	-.06187	-.00931
ACCBUSF	-.10601***	.03622	-2.93	.0034	-.17701	-.03501
WAITTB	-.08739***	.02870	-3.04	.0023	-.14365	-.03113
ACCTB	-.07517***	.01089	-6.91	.0000	-.09651	-.05384
CRCOST	-.14957***	.04942	-3.03	.0025	-.24644	-.05271
CRINVT	-.07024***	.01107	-6.35	.0000	-.09193	-.04854
CREGGT	-.08194***	.02318	-3.53	.0004	-.12737	-.03650
	Nonrandom parameters in utility functions					
NLRASC	2.53832***	.46944	5.41	.0000	1.61824	3.45840
PTINC	-.01212***	.00290	-4.18	.0000	-.01781	-.00643
PTGEND	1.87986***	.26115	7.20	.0000	1.36801	2.39171
NLRINSDE	-1.10737***	.35603	-3.11	.0019	-1.80518	-.40956
TNASC	1.84015***	.45881	4.01	.0001	.94090	2.73940
NHRINSDE	-1.12297***	.40112	-2.80	.0051	-1.90915	-.33680
NBWASC	1.14015**	.48364	2.36	.0184	.19223	2.08807
BSASC	1.51964***	.44718	3.40	.0007	.64318	2.39611
BWASC	1.39054***	.46212	3.01	.0026	.48480	2.29629
	Distns. of RPs. Std.Devs or limits of triangular					
TsINVT	.06368***	.00329	19.37	.0000	.05723	.07012
TsCOST	.24872***	.01958	12.70	.0000	.21033	.28710
TsACWT	.06976***	.00731	9.55	.0000	.05544	.08407
TsEGGT	.01435**	.00565	2.54	.0111	.00327	.02543
TsCRPARK	.03559***	.01341	2.65	.0079	.00931	.06187
TsACCBUS	.10601***	.03622	2.93	.0034	.03501	.17701
TsWAITTB	.08739***	.02870	3.04	.0023	.03113	.14365
TsACCTB	.07517***	.01089	6.91	.0000	.05384	.09651
TsCRCOST	.14957***	.04942	3.03	.0025	.05271	.24644
TsCRINVT	.07024***	.01107	6.35	.0000	.04854	.09193
TsCREGGT	.08194***	.02318	3.53	.0004	.03650	.12737

The overall goodness of fit of the ML model with constrained distributions is −2465.75, that is not as good as the fit for the unconstrained distributions of −2438.81. This, however, is a comparison between an unconstrained normal distribution and a constrained triangular distribution. If we estimate a model with an unconstrained triangular distribution (not reported here), we find a LL at convergence of −2439.093, which is almost identical to the unconstrained normal distribution result.

15.3.3 Model 4: heterogeneity in the mean of random parameters

The distributions derived from the estimated random parameters are defined in terms of the full sample, and each respondent is randomly assigned an estimate drawn from the full distribution. While this avoids the need to be concerned about where a particular respondent might best be located on the distribution, it runs the real risk of missing out on an opportunity to establish whether a specific sampled respondent might be at the upper or lower part of the distribution as a consequence of some additional systematic source of influence. The opportunity to assess whether such systematic sources exist is referred to as adding an additional layer of heterogeneity, which may be associated with the mean of the distribution and/or the variance (or standard deviation) of the distribution. In this section, we introduce heterogeneity in the mean of a random parameter.

To introduce heterogeneity around the mean we have to include the **;rpl** command and add to it "=<**name of heterogeneity influence**>." In the application below we have added in the socio-economic effects **;rpl=pinc**. If that is all that is included as an extra command, then every random parameter will be conditioned on the personal income of a respondent, which is essentially an interaction term such that the new expression for the marginal utility of an attribute such as *invtime* is $\beta_{i,invt} = \beta + \delta_{pinc} + \sigma_{invt,i} *$ *invt*, $\sigma_{invt} = 1 \times |\beta|$.

Note that when you have a heterogenous mean, this construction becomes somewhat ambiguous. For the specification above, for example, if the uniform distribution were specified, the range of variation of the parameter, for a given value of income, is from δ_{pinc} to $\delta_{pinc} + 2\beta$. The uniform and triangular distributions with *value* = 1 are special cases, as this device allows you to anchor the distribution at zero for this case. Importantly, however, when you impose a constrained distribution on a random parameter, the inclusion of an additional term to allow for systematic heterogeneity no longer guarantees that the sign or range condition holds.

The model below is an extension of the previous model, with the addition of the 11 parameters associated with heterogeneity in the mean of the random parameters. The LL at convergence is −2444.458, compared to −2465.752 for exactly the same model without these additional parameters. With 11 degrees of freedom difference, the LRT gives −2*(21.294) = 42.588. This is greater than the critical Chi-square value with 11 degrees of freedom of 19.68, and hence we can reject the null hypothesis of no difference:

```
Nlogit
;lhs=resp1,cset,Altij
;choices=NLRail,NHRail,NBway,Bus,Bway,Train,Car
;par
;rpl=pinc
;fcn=invt(t,1),cost(t,1),acwt(t,1) ,eggt(t,1), crpark(t,1),
   accbusf(t,1),waittb(t,1],acctb(t,1),crcost(t,1),crinvt(t,1),creggt
(t,1)
;maxit=200
;halton;pts= 100
;model:
U(NLRail)= NLRAsc + cost*tcost + invt*InvTime + acwt*wait+ acwt*acctim
   + accbusf*accbusf+eggT*egresst + ptinc*pinc + ptgend*gender +
NLRinsde*inside /
U(NHRail)= TNAsc + cost*Tcost + invt*InvTime + acwt*WaitT + acwt*acctim
   + eggT*egresst + accbusf*accbusf + ptinc*pinc + ptgend*gender +
NHRinsde*inside /
U(NBway)=  NBWAsc + cost*Tcost + invt*InvTime + waitTb*WaitT
   + accTb*acctim + eggT*egresst + accbusf*accbusf+ ptinc*pinc +
ptgend*gender /
U(Bus)=    BSAsc + cost*frunCost + invt*InvTime + waitTb*WaitT
   + accTb*acctim + eggT*egresst+ ptinc*pinc + ptgend*gender/
U(Bway)=   BWAsc + cost*Tcost + invt*InvTime + waitTb*WaitT
   + accTb*acctim + eggT*egresst + accbusf*accbusf+ ptinc*pinc +
ptgend*gender /
U(Train)= TNAsc + cost*tcost + invt*InvTime + acwt*WaitT + acwt*acctim
   + eggT*egresst + accbusf*accbusf+ ptinc*pinc + ptgend*gender /
U(Car)=    CRcost*costs + CRinvt*InvTime + CRpark*parkcost+
CReggT*egresst$
Line search at iteration   47 does not improve fn. Exiting optimization.
------------------------------------------------------------------------
Random Parameters Logit Model
Dependent variable                 RESP1
Log likelihood function      -2444.45824
Restricted log likelihood    -3580.47467
Chi squared [ 31](P= .000)   2272.03287
Significance level                .00000
McFadden Pseudo R-squared        .3172810
Estimation based on N =   1840, K =   31
Inf.Cr.AIC  =   4950.9 AIC/N =    2.691
```

R2=1-LogL/LogL* Log-L fncn R-sqrd R2Adj
No coefficients -3580.4747 .3173 .3149
Constants only can be computed directly
               Use NLOGIT ;...;RHS=ONE$
At start values -2497.0892 .0211 .0176
Response data are given as ind. choices
Replications for simulated probs. = 100
Used Halton sequences in simulations.
Number of obs.= 1840, skipped 0 obs

RESP1	Coefficient	Standard Error	z	Prob. |z|>Z*	95% Confidence Interval	
Random parameters in utility functions						
INVT	-.07373***	.00579	-12.73	.0000	-.08508	-.06239
COST	-.36011***	.04029	-8.94	.0000	-.43907	-.28114
ACWT	-.07362***	.01125	-6.54	.0000	-.09567	-.05157
EGGT	-.00501	.00950	-.53	.5975	-.02363	.01360
CRPARK	-.02487	.03614	-.69	.4914	-.09570	.04596
ACCBUSF	-.25039***	.06210	-4.03	.0001	-.37210	-.12869
WAITTB	-.16222***	.04886	-3.32	.0009	-.25798	-.06646
ACCTB	-.04120***	.01453	-2.84	.0046	-.06967	-.01273
CRCOST	-.08496	.09655	-.88	.3789	-.27420	.10429
CRINVT	-.10554***	.02334	-4.52	.0000	-.15129	-.05980
CREGGT	-.10515**	.05283	-1.99	.0466	-.20870	-.00161
Nonrandom parameters in utility functions						
NLRASC	3.14865***	.75152	4.19	.0000	1.67571	4.62160
PTINC	-.02571***	.00918	-2.80	.0051	-.04371	-.00771
PTGEND	2.02553***	.32134	6.30	.0000	1.39571	2.65536
NLRINSDE	-1.10191***	.37356	-2.95	.0032	-1.83407	-.36974
TNASC	2.44911***	.74302	3.30	.0010	.99283	3.90539
NHRINSDE	-1.16338***	.42361	-2.75	.0060	-1.99365	-.33312
NBWASC	1.85999**	.76058	2.45	.0145	.36927	3.35071
BSASC	2.11085***	.73404	2.88	.0040	.67216	3.54953
BWASC	2.04147***	.74476	2.74	.0061	.58177	3.50117
Heterogeneity in mean, Parameter:Variable						
INVT:PIN	.00010**	.5127D-04	1.97	.0488	.00000	.00020
COST:PIN	.00135***	.00041	3.31	.0009	.00055	.00215
ACWT:PIN	.64733D-05	.00011	.06	.9538	-.21246D-03	.22540D-03
EGGT:PIN	-.00016	.00013	-1.20	.2287	-.00043	.00010
CRPA:PIN	-.00020	.00040	-.51	.6130	-.00098	.00058
ACCB:PIN	.00220***	.00071	3.09	.0020	.00080	.00359
WAIT:PIN	.00118**	.00051	2.30	.0215	.00017	.00219
ACCT:PIN	-.00080***	.00022	-3.72	.0002	-.00122	-.00038
CRCO:PIN	-.00098	.00120	-.82	.4127	-.00332	.00136
CRIN:PIN	.00023	.00015	1.53	.1266	-.00006	.00052
CREG:PIN	.96050D-04	.00046	.21	.8336	-.80009D-03	.99219D-03
Distns. of RPs. Std.Devs or limits of triangular						
TsINVT	.07373***	.00579	12.73	.0000	.06239	.08508

TsCOST|	.36011***	.04029	8.94	.0000	.28114	.43907
TsACWT|	.07362***	.01125	6.54	.0000	.05157	.09567
TsEGGT|	.00501	.00950	.53	.5975	-.01360	.02363
TsCRPARK|	.02487	.03614	.69	.4914	-.04596	.09570
TsACCBUS|	.25039***	.06210	4.03	.0001	.12869	.37210
TsWAITTB|	.16222***	.04886	3.32	.0009	.06646	.25798
TsACCTB|	.04120***	.01453	2.84	.0046	.01273	.06967
TsCRCOST|	.08496	.09655	.88	.3789	-.10429	.27420
TsCRINVT|	.10554***	.02334	4.52	.0000	.05980	.15129
TsCREGGT|	.10515**	.05283	1.99	.0466	.00161	.20870

```
-----------+------------------------------------------------------------------------
Parameter Matrix for Heterogeneity in Means.
Delta_RP|                 1
-----------+------------------------------------------------------------------------
         1|     .101029E-03
         2|       .00134997
         3|     .647325E-05
         4|    -.161748E-03
         5|    -.200680E-03
         6|       .00219708
         7|       .00118133
         8|    -.801656E-03
         9|    -.979918E-03
        10|     .229133E-03
        11|     .960503E-04
```

The marginal utility associated with a specific variable now includes the additional "interaction" term. For example, the marginal utility expression for *invt* is:

$MU_{invt} = -0.07373 + 0.0001*pinc + 0.07373*o$, where o is the one-sided triangular distribution. This additional term indicates that as personal income increases, the marginal utility of *invt* will increase or the marginal disutility (given the negative sign for the mean estimate) will decrease. Readers can check this out by implementing the following command:

```
create
;rna=rnn(0,1)
;V1=rnu(0,1)
;if(v1<=0.5)T=sqr(2*V1)-1;(ELSE) T=1-sqr(2*(1-V1))
          ;Invtd = =-0.07373+0.0001*pinc+0.07373*T$
          Liot;invtd$
```

15.3.4 Model 5: heterogeneity in the mean of selective random parameters

Model 4 allows for heterogeneity in the mean to be identified for all random parameters. It is often the situation that the analyst wants to limit the heterogeneity to a subset of random parameters, either for some behaviorally interesting reason or because the heterogeneity was found to be not statistically significant for specific random parameters. ML permits a specification that controls for selective use of heterogeneity in the mean.

We begin with a general variation in the form for name (type) such as *invt(n)* used in earlier models, which is **name (type|#)** or **invt (n|#)**. This simply says that all random parameters will not have an interaction term to allow for heterogeneity in the mean, where the heterogeneity is defined by one or more variables associated with the command **;rpl=het$_{var1}$, het$_{var2}$·.·...** That is, where we have name (type), heterogeneity will apply; where we have name (type|#), it will not apply.

If we want to limit the heterogeneity in the mean to a subset of attributes then we would define a pattern of 0s and 1s, where 1 includes the heterogeneity and 0 does not for the set of **het$_{var}$s** associated with **;rpl**. For example, if we specify (as below) **;rpl=pinc,gender**, and we want to include pinc but not gender, then we would specify **name (type#10)** – for example, **acwt(t|#10)**. It should be clear that **acwt(t|#00)** excludes both sources of heterogeneity, and **acwt(t|#11)** includes both sources of heterogeneity; thus **acwt(t|#11)** is equivalent to **acwt(t|#)**.

The model below specifies the various ways in which these commands can be used. Readers will see that some attributes such as access waiting time (*acwt*) are conditioned on only one of the sources of heterogeneity in the mean:

```
ACWT:PIN|     -.00011        .00011    -1.04  .2992    -.00033     .00010
ACWT:GEN|       0.0      .....(Fixed Parameter).....
```

All output is interpreted in the same way as previous model outputs:

```
    Nlogit
    ;lhs=resp1,cset,Altij
    ;choices=NLRail,NHRail,NBway,Bus,Bway,Train,Car
    ;par
    ;rpl=pinc,gender
    ;fcn=invt(t,1),cost(t,1),acwt(t|#10) ,eggt(t|#11), crpark(t|#11),
    accbusf(t,1),waittb(t|#00),acctb(t|#10),crcost(t|#00),crinvt(t,1),
creggt(t|#01)
    ;maxit=200
    ;halton;pts= 100
    ;model:
    U(NLRail)= NLRAsc + cost*tcost + invt*InvTime + acwt*wait+ acwt*acctim
    + accbusf*accbusf+eggT*egresst + ptinc*pinc + ptgend*gender +
NLRinsde*inside /
    U(NHRail)= TNAsc + cost*Tcost + invt*InvTime + acwt*WaitT + acwt*acc-
tim
```

```
       + eggT*egresst + accbusf*accbusf + ptinc*pinc + ptgend*gender +
NHRinsde*inside /
    U(NBway)=  NBWAsc + cost*Tcost + invt*InvTime + waitTb*WaitT
    + accTb*acctim + eggT*egresst + accbusf*accbusf+ ptinc*pinc +
ptgend*gender /
    U(Bus)=    BSAsc + cost*frunCost + invt*InvTime + waitTb*WaitT
    + accTb*acctim + eggT*egresst+ ptinc*pinc + ptgend*gender/
    U(Bway)=   BWAsc + cost*Tcost + invt*InvTime + waitTb*WaitT
    + accTb*acctim + eggT*egresst + accbusf*accbusf+ ptinc*pinc +
ptgend*gender /
    U(Train)=  TNAsc + cost*tcost + invt*InvTime + acwt*WaitT + acwt*acctim
    + eggT*egresst + accbusf*accbusf+ ptinc*pinc + ptgend*gender /
    U(Car)=    CRcost*costs + CRinvt*InvTime + CRpark*parkcost+
CReggT*egresst$
Normal exit:  61 iterations. Status=0, F=    2419.958
```

```
Random Parameters Logit Model
Dependent variable               RESP1
Log likelihood function       -2419.95791
Restricted log likelihood     -3580.47467
Chi squared [ 42](P= .000)     2321.03352
Significance level                .00000
McFadden Pseudo R-squared         .3241237
Estimation based on N =    1840, K =    42
Inf.Cr.AIC  =   4923.9 AIC/N =     2.676
R2=1-LogL/LogL*  Log-L fncn R-sqrd R2Adj
No coefficients -3580.4747  .3241  .3209
Constants only can be computed directly
             Use NLOGIT ;...;RHS=ONE$
At start values -2490.9804  .0285 .0239
Response data are given as ind. choices
Replications for simulated probs. = 100
Used Halton sequences in simulations.
Number of obs.= 1840, skipped    0 obs
```
-----------+---

RESP1	Coefficient	Standard Error	z	Prob. |z|>Z*	95% Confidence Interval	
	Random parameters in utility functions					
INVT	-.08356***	.00682	-12.24	.0000	-.09693	-.07018
COST	-.41734***	.04539	-9.19	.0000	-.50630	-.32838
ACWT	-.06704***	.01130	-5.93	.0000	-.08919	-.04490
EGGT	-.01839	.01237	-1.49	.1373	-.04264	.00587
CRPARK	-.03063	.03390	.90	.3662	-.09708	.03582
ACCBUSF	-.17678***	.06456	-2.74	.0062	-.30331	-.05025
WAITTB	-.09751**	.04275	-2.28	.0226	-.18131	-.01371
ACCTB	-.04498***	.01458	-3.08	.0020	-.07356	-.01640
CRCOST	-.22566***	.08519	-2.65	.0081	-.39263	-.05868

```
   CRINVT|    -.11779***      .02352    -5.01   .0000    -.16389   -.07169
   CREGGT|    -.07548*        .04090    -1.85   .0650    -.15565    .00468
         |Nonrandom parameters in utility functions
   NLRASC|    2.62184***      .75443     3.48   .0005    1.14318   4.10050
    PTINC|    -.01227         .00938    -1.31   .1908    -.03064    .00611
   PTGEND|     .75293         .86374      .87   .3834    -.93997   2.44582
 NLRINSDE|   -1.33761***      .39576    -3.38   .0007   -2.11329   -.56193
    TNASC|    1.90019**       .74336     2.56   .0106     .44324   3.35714
 NHRINSDE|   -1.43502***      .45409    -3.16   .0016   -2.32502   -.54501
   NBWASC|    1.27681*        .76510     1.67   .0952    -.22276   2.77638
    BSASC|    1.54519**       .73869     2.09   .0365     .09739   2.99299
    BWASC|    1.52209**       .74893     2.03   .0421     .05422   2.98997
         |Heterogeneity in mean, Parameter:Variable
 INVT:PIN| .97689D-05    .5756D-04      .17   .8652 -.10305D-03  .12259D-03
 INVT:GEN|     .02130***      .00558     3.82   .0001     .01037    .03223
 COST:PIN|     .00103**       .00044     2.35   .0187     .00017    .00189
 COST:GEN|     .10639***      .03678     2.89   .0038     .03430    .17848
 ACWT:PIN|    -.00011         .00011    -1.04   .2992    -.00033    .00010
 ACWT:GEN|       0.0     .....(Fixed Parameter).....
 EGGT:PIN|    -.00026*        .00015    -1.69   .0914    -.00056    .00004
 EGGT:GEN|     .01905         .01350     1.41   .1581    -.00740    .04551
 CRPA:PIN|    -.00067         .00043    -1.55   .1208    -.00152    .00018
 CRPA:GEN|     .07438**       .03317     2.24   .0249     .00937    .13940
 ACCB:PIN|     .00251***      .00075     3.33   .0009     .00103    .00399
 ACCB:GEN|    -.17458***      .05675    -3.08   .0021    -.28580   -.06335
 WAIT:PIN|       0.0     .....(Fixed Parameter).....
 WAIT:GEN|       0.0     .....(Fixed Parameter).....
 ACCT:PIN|    -.00071***      .00022    -3.18   .0015    -.00115   -.00027
 ACCT:GEN|       0.0     .....(Fixed Parameter).....
 CRCO:PIN|       0.0     .....(Fixed Parameter).....
 CRCO:GEN|       0.0     .....(Fixed Parameter).....
 CRIN:PIN|     .00031         .00020     1.55   .1211    -.00008    .00071
 CRIN:GEN|    -.01275         .01733     -.74   .4619    -.04673    .02122
 CREG:PIN|       0.0     .....(Fixed Parameter).....
 CREG:GEN|    -.07955         .06678    -1.19   .2336    -.21045    .05134
         |Distns. of RPs. Std.Devs or limits of triangular
   TsINVT|     .08356***      .00682    12.24   .0000     .07018    .09693
   TsCOST|     .41734***      .04539     9.19   .0000     .32838    .50630
   TsACWT|     .06403**       .02871     2.23   .0257     .00776    .12030
   TsEGGT|     .07389         .05149     1.44   .1513    -.02702    .17481
 TsCRPARK|     .04744         .08679      .55   .5847    -.12266    .21753
 TsACCBUS|     .17678***      .06456     2.74   .0062     .05025    .30331
 TsWAITTB|     .21195         .21625      .98   .3270    -.21190    .63580
  TsACCTB|     .01224         .06744      .18   .8559    -.11993    .14442
 TsCRCOST|     .39483         .25169     1.57   .1167    -.09848    .88814
 TsCRINVT|     .11779***      .02352     5.01   .0000     .07169    .16389
 TsCREGGT|     .05770         .10664      .54   .5885    -.15130    .26670
-----------+-------------------------------------------------------------------------
```

Parameter matrix for heterogeneity in means.

```
Delta_RP|                 1                   2
--------- +-------------------------------------
        1|     .976890E-05          .0212974
        2|      .00103315           .106390
        3|    -.114482E-03          .000000
        4|    -.260407E-03          .0190531
        5|   - .671542E-03          .0743838
        6|      .00251144          -.174575
        7|      .000000             .000000
        8|    -.709463E-03          .000000
        9|      .000000             .000000
       10|     .313569E-03         -.0127531
       11|      .000000            -.0795534
```

15.3.5 Model 6: heteroskedasticity and heterogeneity in the variances

So far, we have focussed on heterogeneity in the mean of a random parameter; however, additional sources of systematic heterogeneity (often referred to as heteroskedasticity) can be associated with the variance (or standard deviation) of the distribution.

When the model is expanded so that the random parameters model allows heterogeneity in the variances as well as in the means in the distributions of the random parameters, the additional modification is $\sigma_{ik} = \sigma_k \exp[\omega_k'\mathbf{hr}_i]$. If ω equals **0**, this returns the homoskedastic model. The implied form of the RPL model is:

$$\beta_{ik} = \beta + \delta_k{'}\mathbf{z}_i + \sigma_{ik}v_{ik} = \beta + \delta_k{'}\mathbf{z}_i + \sigma_k\exp(\omega_k{'}\mathbf{hr}_i)v_{ik}. \tag{15.9}$$

To request the heteroskedasticity model in Nlogit, you simply include:

```
; Hfr = list of variables in hri
```

The variables in $\mathbf{hr}_i$ may be any variables, but they must be choice invariant. This specification will produce the same form of heteroskedasticity in each parameter distribution – note that each parameter has its own parameter vector, ω_k.

In Section 15.3.4 we described the method of modifying the specification of the heterogenous means of the parameters so that some RPL variables in $\mathbf{z}_i$ may appear in the means of some parameters and not others. A similar construction may be used for the variances. For any parameter specification of the forms set out above, the specification may end with an exclamation point, "!" to indicate that the particular parameter is to be homoskedastic even if others are heteroskedastic. For example, the following produces a model with heterogenous means (associated with age and pinc), and one heteroskedastic variance (associated with gender):

```
; RPL= age,pinc
; Hfr = gender
; Fcn = invt(n),acwt(n|# 01 !)
```

The parameter on *invtime* has both a heterogenous mean and a heteroskedastic variance. The parameter on *waitt* has a heterogenous mean, but *age* is excluded, and a homogenous variance. Note that there are no commas before or after the !. As in the case of the means, when there is more than one Hfr variable, you may add a pattern to the specification to include and exclude them from the model. To continue the previous example, consider:

```
; RPL= age,pinc
; Hfr = gender,family,urban
; Fcn = invt(n),acwt(n|# 01 ! 101)
```

The variance for *invt* includes all three variables, but the variance for *acwt* excludes *family*.

We present a model below with three random parameters in which we specify:

```
;rpl=pinc
;fcn=invt(n),cost(n),acwt(n!01)
;hfr=gender,pinc
```

This model allows for heterogeneity in the mean (pinc) for all three random parameters and heteroskedasticity in variance for *acwt* only, but for only the second systematic source of influence listed in **;hfr=gender,pinc**. Any combination of heterogeneity in the mean and heteroskedasticity in the variance of one or more random parameters is permissible, making this a very general ML form. None of the five heteroskedasticity effects is statistically significant at the 95 percent confidence level; however, the model is sufficient to show the additional information obtained:

```
Nlogit
;lhs=resp1,cset,Altij
;choices=NLRail,NHRail,NBway,Bus,Bway,Train,Car
;par
;rpl=pinc
;fcn=invt(n),cost(n),acwt(n!01)
;hfr=gender,pinc
;maxit=100
;halton;pts= 100
```

```
;model:
U(NLRail)= NLRAsc + cost*tcost + invt*InvTime + acwt*wait+ acwt*acctim
  + accbusf*accbusf+eggT*egresst + ptinc*pinc + ptgend*gender +
NLRinsde*inside /
U(NHRail)= TNAsc + cost*Tcost + invt*InvTime + acwt*WaitT + acwt*acctim
  + eggT*egresst + accbusf*accbusf + ptinc*pinc + ptgend*gender +
NHRinsde*inside /
U(NBway)= , NBWAsc + cost*Tcost + invt*InvTime + waitTb*WaitT
  + accTb*acctim + eggT*egresst + accbusf*accbusf+ ptinc*pinc +
ptgend*gender /
U(Bus)=    BSAsc + cost*frunCost + invt*InvTime + waitTb*WaitT
  + accTb*acctim + eggT*egresst+ ptinc*pinc + ptgend*gender/
U(Bway)=   BWAsc + cost*Tcost + invt*InvTime + waitTb*WaitT
  + accTb*acctim + eggT*egresst + accbusf*accbusf+ ptinc*pinc +
ptgend*gender /
U(Train)= TNAsc + cost*tcost + invt*InvTime + acwt*WaitT + acwt*acctim
  + eggT*egresst + accbusf*accbusf+ ptinc*pinc + ptgend*gender /
U(Car)=    CRcost*costs + CRinvt*InvTime + CRpark*parkcost+
CReggT*egresst$
Line search at iteration   61 does not improve fn. Exiting optimization.
```

```
Random Parameters Logit Model
Dependent variable              RESP1
Log likelihood function    -5015.34107
Restricted log likelihood  -7376.94538
Chi squared [ 31](P= .000)   4723.20862
Significance level               .00000
McFadden Pseudo R-squared        .3201331
Estimation based on N =   3791, K =   31
Inf.Cr.AIC  =  10092.7 AIC/N =    2.662
R2=1-LogL/LogL*  Log-L fncn R-sqrd R2Adj
No coefficients  -7376.9454  .3201 .3189
Constants only can be computed directly
            Use NLOGIT ;...;RHS=ONE$
At start values -5079.7499  .0127 .0110
Response data are given as ind. choices
Replications for simulated probs. = 100
Used Halton sequences in simulations.
Heteroskedastic random parameters
BHHH estimator used for asymp. variance
Number of obs.= 3791, skipped    0 obs
```
-----------+--

RESP1	Coefficient	Standard Error	z	Prob. $\|7\|>Z^*$	95% Confidence Interval	
	Random parameters in utility functions					
INVT	-.04983***	.00294	-16.92	.0000	-.05560	-.04405
COST	-.39194***	.02686	-14.59	.0000	-.44459	-.33929
ACWT	-.06842***	.00631	-10.85	.0000	-.08078	-.05606

```
            |Nonrandom parameters in utility functions
    NLRASC|     2.85074***        .30246      9.43   .0000     2.25792    3.44355
    ACCBUSF|     -.15339***        .02562     -5.99   .0000     -.20361    -.10316
      EGGT|      -.03045***        .00347     -8.78   .0000     -.03725    -.02365
     PTINC|      -.00977**         .00400     -2.44   .0146     -.01762    -.00193
    PTGEND|       .91144***        .19264      4.73   .0000      .53387    1.28900
   NLRINSDE|      -.17376          .17724      -.98   .3269     -.52115     .17363
     TNASC|      2.39277***        .29373      8.15   .0000     1.81708    2.96846
   NHRINSDE|      -.44997**        .18872     -2.38   .0171     -.81984    -.08009
    NBWASC|      1.31471***        .32052      4.10   .0000      .68650    1.94292
    WAITTB|      -.04372**         .01867     -2.34   .0192     -.08032    -.00713
      ACCTB|     -.05003***        .00705     -7.10   .0000     -.06385    -.03622
     BSASC|      1.54373***        .28435      5.43   .0000      .98642    2.10104
     BWASC|      1.60870***        .29632      5.43   .0000     1.02793    2.18948
    CRCOST|      -.20195***        .02987     -6.76   .0000     -.26049    -.14341
    CRINVT|      -.04938***        .00452    -10.93   .0000     -.05823    -.04052
    CRPARK|      -.05814***        .00930     -6.26   .0000     -.07636    -.03992
    CREGGT|      -.09253***        .01518     -6.09   .0000     -.12229    -.06278
            |Heterogeneity in mean, Parameter:Variable
  INVT:PIN|-.72740D-04       .4752D-04      -1.53   .1258 -.16587D-03   .20390D-04
  COST:PIN|     .00090**          .00042      2.14   .0324      .00008     .00173
  ACWT:PIN|     .00017***     .6108D-04       2.77   .0056      .00005     .00029
            |Distns. of RPs. Std.Devs or limits of triangular
    NsINVT|      .01954***        .00389      5.02   .0000      .01191     .02717
    NsCOST|      .22298***        .03340      6.68   .0000      .15752     .28845
    NsACWT|      .04155***        .01443      2.88   .0040      .01328     .06983
            |Heteroskedasticity in random parameters
 sINVT|GE|      -.00086          .00371      -.23   .8159     -.00814     .00641
 sINVT|PI|       .00010      .6498D-04       1.60   .1087     -.00002     .00023
 sCOST|GE|       .03969          .03291      1.21   .2278     -.02482     .10420
 sCOST|PI|       .00107          .00204       .52   .6007     -.00293     .00506
 sACWT|GE|        0.0      .....(Fixed Parameter).....
 sACWT|PI|      -.01547          .01093     -1.41   .1572     -.03689     .00596
```

```
Parameter Matrix for Heterogeneity in Means.
Delta_RP|              1
-----------+-------------------
         1|   -.727403E-04
         2|    .900460E-03
         3|    .169300E-03
```

15.3.6 Model 7: allowing for correlated random parameters

The previous models assume that the random parameters are uncorrelated. As discussed in Chapter 4, all data sets, regardless of the number of choice situations per sampled individual (i.e., choice sets), may have unobserved effects that are correlated among alternatives in a given choice situation. ML models enable the model to be specified in such a way that the error components in different choice situations from a given individual are correlated. In Nlogit, this is achieved with the following command syntax:

```
;Correlated   (or Corr for short)
```

> *As an aside*, for current versions of Nlogit, the correlation command syntax will not work in conjunction with constraints imposed on any random parameter distributions.
> *As an aside*, The model with both correlated parameters (**;Correlated**) and heteroskedastic random parameters is not estimable. If your model command contains both **;Correlated** and **;Hfr = list**, the heteroskedasticity takes precedence, and **;Correlated** is ignored.

The following ML model is estimated allowing for correlation among the random parameters of the model:

> *As an aside*, The Nlogit version post-24 October 2014 has replaced the report of the "Lower triangle of the Cholesky Matrix" with covariances of the random parameters in the standard output of the RPL model with correlated parameters.

```
Nlogit
;lhs=resp1,cset,Altij
;choices=NLRail,NHRail,NBway,Bus,Bway,Train,Car
;par
;rpl
;corr
;fcn=invt(n),crinvt(n),cost(n)
;maxit=100
;halton;pts= 100
;model:
U(NLRail)= NLRAsc + cost*tcost + invt*InvTime + acwt*wait+ acwt*acctim
    + accbusf*accbusf+eggT*egresst + ptinc*pinc + ptgend*gender +
NLRinsde*inside /
U(NHRail)= TNAsc + cost*Tcost + invt*InvTime + acwt*WaitT + acwt*acctim
    + eggT*egresst + accbusf*accbusf + ptinc*pinc + ptgend*gender +
NHRinsde*inside /
U(NBway)=  NBWAsc + cost*Tcost + invt*InvTime + waitTb*WaitT
    + accTb*acctim + eggT*egresst + accbusf*accbusf+ ptinc*pinc +
ptgend*gender /
U(Bus)=    BSAsc + cost*frunCost + invt*InvTime + waitTb*WaitT
    + accTb*acctim + eggT*egresst+ ptinc*pinc + ptgend*gender/
U(Bway)=   BWAsc + cost*Tcost + invt*InvTime + waitTb*WaitT
    + accTb*acctim + eggT*egresst + accbusf*accbusf+ ptinc*pinc +
ptgend*gender /
U(Train)=  TNAsc + cost*tcost + invt*InvTime + acwt*WaitT + acwt*acctim
    + eggT*egresst + accbusf*accbusf+ ptinc*pinc + ptgend*gender /
U(Car)=    CRcost*costs + CRinvt*InvTime + CRpark*parkcost+
CReggT*egresst$
```

```
Normal exit:  58 iterations. Status=0, F=    2439.458

Random Parameters Logit Model
Dependent variable                    RESP1
Log likelihood function      -2439.45842
Restricted log likelihood    -3580.47467
Chi squared [ 26](P= .000)    2282.03251
Significance level                 .00000
McFadden Pseudo R-squared          .3186774
Estimation based on N =    1840, K =   26
Inf.Cr.AIC   =    4930.9 AIC/N =     2.680
R2=1-LogL/LogL* Log-L fncn R-sqrd R2Adj
No coefficients -3580.4747  .3187  .3167
Constants only can be computed directly
            Use NLOGIT ;...;RHS=ONE$
At start values -2487.3624  .0193 .0164
Response data are given as ind. choices
Replications for simulated probs. = 100
Used Halton sequences in simulations.
Number of obs.= 1840, skipped    0 obs
```

RESP1	Coefficient	Standard Error	z	Prob. $\|z\|>Z^*$	95% Confidence Interval	
Random parameters in utility functions						
INVT	-.07146***	.00436	-16.39	.0000	-.08000	-.06291
CRINVT	-.12154***	.02055	-5.91	.0000	-.16183	-.08126
COST	-.35631***	.03470	-10.27	.0000	-.42432	-.28831
Nonrandom parameters in utility functions						
NLRASC	2.37955***	.61069	3.90	.0001	1.18262	3.57649
ACWT	-.07182***	.00663	-10.84	.0000	-.08481	-.05883
ACCBUSF	-.12022***	.03781	-3.18	.0015	-.19433	-.04611
EGGT	-.01490**	.00579	-2.57	.0101	-.02626	-.00355
PTINC	-.01847***	.00529	-3.49	.0005	-.02883	-.00810
PTGEND	2.52370***	.49026	5.15	.0000	1.56280	3.48459
NLRINSDE	-1.49096***	.39110	-3.81	.0001	-2.25750	-.72443
TNASC	1.62983***	.60207	2.71	.0068	.44979	2.80987
NHRINSDE	-1.61769***	.45616	-3.55	.0004	-2.51175	-.72362
NBWASC	.98027	.62777	1.56	.1184	-.25014	2.21068
WAITTB	-.09219***	.02861	-3.22	.0013	-.14826	-.03611
ACCTB	-.08363***	.01045	-8.00	.0000	-.10410	-.06315
BSASC	1.29057**	.59560	2.17	.0302	.12322	2.45793
BWASC	1.25607**	.60974	2.06	.0394	.06100	2.45114
CRCOST	-.18887***	.06585	-2.87	.0041	-.31794	-.05979
CRPARK	-.04198**	.01830	-2.29	.0218	-.07786	-.00611
CREGGT	-.12235***	.03471	-3.52	.0004	-.19037	-.05432
Diagonal values in Cholesky matrix, L.						
NsINVT	.04154***	.00505	8.22	.0000	.03164	.05145
NsCRINVT	.05049***	.01529	3.30	.0010	.02052	.08046

```
  NsCOST|      .17326             .11511      1.51   .1323     -.05235     .39886
        |Covariances of Random Parameters
CRIN:INV|      .00253***          .00074      3.43   .0006      .00108     .00397
COST:INV|      .00158             .00197       .80   .4228     -.00228     .00544
COST:CRI|      .01348**           .00650      2.07   .0381      .00074     .02622
        |Standard deviations of parameter distributions
  sdINVT|      .04154***          .00505      8.22   .0000      .03164     .05145
sdCRINVT|      .07906***          .01510      5.24   .0000      .04946     .10866
  sdCOST|      .28348**           .13321      2.13   .0333      .02238     .54457

Cor.Mat.|    INVT    CRINVT      COST
----------+-------------------------------------------------------------------------
    INVT| 1.00000     .76952     .13421
  CRINVT|  .76952   1.00000      .60142
    COST|  .13421     .60142   1.00000
```

The above model is statistically significant with a Chi-square value of 2282.03 with 26 degrees of freedom and a pseudo-R^2 value of 0.3167. The mean of the three random parameters is statistically significant as are the standard deviation parameters; hence an examination of the spreads of each of the random parameters around their respective means reveals that all attributes exhibit preference heterogeneity. All of the non-random or fixed parameter estimates are of the expected sign and are statistically significant.

The addition of the correlation command in Nlogit produces a great deal of new output, and this is why we have limited the estimation to three random parameters. In addition to the parameter estimates in the main body of the output, there is also a correlation matrix. The correlation matrix suggests several numerically large correlations. For example, the *invt* random parameter has correlations of 0.769 and 0.134 with the *crinvt* and *cost* random parameters.

The parameters reported are, first, β from the random parameter distributions, then the non-stochastic β from the distributions of the non-random ASCs. The next results display the elements of the 3×3 lower triangular matrix, Γ. The diagonal elements appear first ("Diagonal values in Cholesky matrix L"), then the below-diagonal element(s) ("Covariances of random parameters"). The "Standard deviations of parameter distributions" are derived from Γ. The first (i.e., *sdINVT*) is $(0.04154^2)^{1/2} = 0.04154$. The second (i.e., *sdCRINVT*) is $(0.00253^2 + 0.05049^2)^{1/2} = 0.00128$. Readers can use this logic to calculate *sdCOST*. The standard errors for these estimators are computed using the delta method (discussed in Section 7.4.1).

The variance (values on the diagonal of the variance-covariance matrix) of each random parameter is calculated as the square of the reported standard deviations given in the main series of output. The calculations for this are shown below:

$$\text{Var}(invt) = 0.04154^2 = 0.00173$$
$$\text{Var}(crinvt) = 0.07906^2 = 0.00625$$
$$\text{Var}(cost) = 0.28348^2 = 0.08036$$

The covariances, reported as the off-diagonal elements of the above matrix, are calculated directly from the data (each covariance is the average of the products of deviations for each data point pair). It is therefore impossible to show this calculation, although Equation (15.10) shows the formula used in the calculation process:

$$\text{cov}(x, y) = \frac{1}{n} \sum_{i=1}^{N} (X_i - U_i)(Y_i - U_i). \tag{15.10}$$

Positive covariances suggest that larger parameter estimates for individuals along the distribution on one attribute are generally associated with larger parameter estimates for that same individual in the parameter space for the second attribute. For example, the covariance of 0.01348 between the *cost* and *crinvt* random parameters suggests that individuals with larger (i.e., more negative – the marginal utilities for this attribute are expected to be negative) sensitivities to car invehicle time are likely to have higher (negative) marginal utilities for car invehicle time. The larger the covariance, the greater the relationship between the two random parameters. Hence, 0.00158 suggests a weaker (positive) relationship between the *invt* and *cost* random parameters than between the *crinvt* and *cost* random parameters with a covariance statistic of 0.01348 (also a positive relationship; larger values of *crinvt* result in larger values of *cost*).

There exists a direct relationship between the variances and covariances and the correlations observed. The correlation coefficient used to produce the correlations is:

$$\rho = \frac{\text{cov}(X1, X2)}{\sigma_{X1} \times \sigma_{X2}}. \tag{15.11}$$

To demonstrate this relationship, consider the correlation exhibited between the *crinvt* and *cost* random parameters:

$$\rho = \frac{\text{cov}(crinvt, cost)}{\sigma_{crinvt} \times \sigma_{cost}} = \frac{0.01348}{0.07906 \times 0.28348} = 0.6014, \tag{15.12}$$

that is the correlation reported between the *crnvt* and *cost* random parameters by Nlogit (note that it is the standard deviations and not variances that make up the denominator of the correlation coefficient).

We need to discuss the Cholesky matrix in more detail so that the calculations reported in the model output can be better understood. The Cholesky decomposition matrix is a lower triangular matrix (meaning that the upper off-diagonal elements of the matrix are all zero). The above output illustrates the presence of correlated alternatives due to correlated random parameters, all normally distributed. When we have more than one random parameter and we permit correlated random parameters, then the standard deviations are no longer independent. To assess this, we have to decompose the standard deviation parameters into their attribute-specific (e.g., *invt* and *cost*) and attribute-interaction (e.g., *invt* × *cost*) standard deviations. Cholesky decomposition is the method used to do this, and has been set out in some detail in Chapter 5 where the Cholesky matrix is obtained from the variance-covariance matrix. The ML model is extended to accommodate this case by allowing the set of random parameters to have an unrestricted covariance matrix. The non-zero off-diagonal element of this matrix carries the cross-parameter correlations.

As noted, the standard deviations of random parameter estimates under conditions of correlated parameters may not be independent. To establish the independent contribution of each random parameter estimate, the Cholesky decomposition matrix separates the contribution to each standard deviation parameter made through correlation with other random parameter estimates and the actual contribution made solely through heterogeneity around the mean of each random parameter estimate, thus unconfounding the correlation structure over random parameter estimates with their associated standard deviation parameters. This allows the parameters to be freely correlated and have an unrestricted scale, as well, while ensuring that the covariance matrix that we estimate is positive definite at all times.

The first element of the Cholesky decomposition matrix will always be equal to the standard deviation parameter of the first specified random coefficient.[2] Subsequent diagonal elements of the Cholesky decomposition

---

[2] Random parameters in Nlogit are created independent of the generation of other random parameter estimates. Correlation between two random parameters is created by running the random parameter estimates through a Cholesky matrix. The distribution of the resulting vector will differ depending on the order that was specified for the coefficients in the **fcn** command. This means that different orderings of random parameters can result in different parameterizations when non-normal distributions are used. Using an example offered by Ken Train (in private correspondence with the authors), assume two random parameters X_1 and X_2 specified with normal and uniform distributions with correlation. Nlogit creates a standard normal and standard uniform that are uncorrelated, N_1 and U_2, and multiplies these by use of a Cholesky matrix. For matrix C = a 0 b c the resulting coefficients are $X_1 = a \times N_1$, which is normal, and $X_2 = b \times e_1 + c \times U_2$, which is the sum of a uniform and a normal. X_2 is not uniform but has the

matrix represent the amount of variance attributable to that random parameter when the covariances (correlations) with subsequently named random parameters have been removed. In the above example, the amount of variance directly attributable for the *crinvt* random parameter is 0.05049 and not 0.07906. Off-diagonal elements of the matrix represent the amount of cross-parameter correlations previously confounded with the standard deviation parameters of the model. For the standard deviation parameter associated with the *crinvt* random parameter, 0.07906 is attributable to a cross-product correlation with the *invt* random parameter estimate.

In writing out the marginal utility estimates of the random parameters, the analyst may either use the standard deviation parameter estimates or utilize the decomposed values obtained from the model output. The standard deviation parameter estimates reported (in Nlogit 5 but not previous versions of Nlogit) have already taken into account the additional information obtained in decomposing the sources of variation through the Cholesky decomposition method. Using the elements of the Cholesky decomposition matrix, Nlogit locates the position of all simulated individuals on each of the elements of the matrix (i.e., on the diagonal and off-diagonals of the matrix) and reconstructs the empirical distribution of the standard deviation parameter estimates. The formula for the decomposed standard deviation parameter is given in Equation (15.13):

$$\text{Standard deviation parameter} = \beta_{\text{diagonal element}} \times f(X_0) + \beta_{\text{off-diagonal element 1}} \times f(X_1) + \ldots + \beta_{\text{off-diagonal element k}} \times f(X_k), \tag{15.13}$$

where $f(X_k)$ is a location parameter used to locate individual i on some distribution for each element of the matrix. The location parameter, $f(X_k)$, may take on any distribution; however, it is most common to use the normal distribution. The marginal utilities may therefore be written as Equation (15.14):

$$\textit{Marginal Utility (attribute)} = \beta_{\text{attribute mean}} + \beta_{\text{covariate}} \times x_{\text{covariate}}$$
$$+ (\beta_{\text{diagonal element}} + \beta_{\text{off-diagonal element 1}} \times \varepsilon + \ldots + \beta_{\text{off-diagonal element k}}$$
$$\times N) \times f(N, T \text{ or } U), \tag{15.14}$$

where $f(N, T \text{ or } U)$ is the mixing distribution.

Constraints can be imposed on the Cholesky matrix as a way of allowing for some control over correlations. The command to do this is **;COR = <a pattern**

distribution defined by the sum of a uniform and normal. If the order is reversed, such that N_1 is uniform and U_2 is normal, X_1 will be uniform and X_2 will be the sum of a uniform and normal. By ordering the random parameters differently, the user is implicitly changing the distribution of the resulting coefficients.

of list of ones and zeros>. The analyst must specify the entire Cholesky matrix. For example:

;corr =

1,

1,1,

0,0,1,

0,0,0,1,

0,0,0,1,1$

This is written out in the model command as:

```
;corr=1,1,1,0,0,1,0,0,0,1,0,0,0,1,1$
```

The matrix is block diagonal. Parameter 3 is uncorrelated with all others. Parameters 1 and 2 are correlated with each other, but not correlated with 3,4,5. Parameters 4 and 5 are correlated with each other but not with 1,2,3.

> *As an aside*, the "1" on the diagonals is mandatory, and will mean a 1.0 in the Cholesky matrix. The "1" below the diagonal signals a free non-zero parameter, not necessarily 1.0. The "0" below the diagonal means that that element of the Cholesky matrix will equal zero. Specifying the Cholesky matrix is not the same as specifying the correlation matrix. That is not possible, except for the case exemplified above. You can make a whole row of the correlation matrix zero, but not a specific element.

To obtain the full distribution, now that the standard deviation parameter estimates have accounted for correlation between the random parameters, we use the same formula as before; namely (for the normal distribution):

```
create
;rna=rnn(0,1)
;Invtd =-0.07146+0.04154*rna
;Crinvtd=-0.12154+0.07906*rna
;Costd=-0.35631+0.28348*rna$
```

We can plot these distributions in Figure 15.4 using the command:

```
kernel;rhs=invtd,crinvtd,costd$
```

15.4 How can we use random parameter estimates?

The inclusion of the distributional form (i.e., *n*, *t*, *u*) within the utility formula for each random parameter estimate requires special treatment in establishing the marginal utility possessed by any individual towards the alternative for

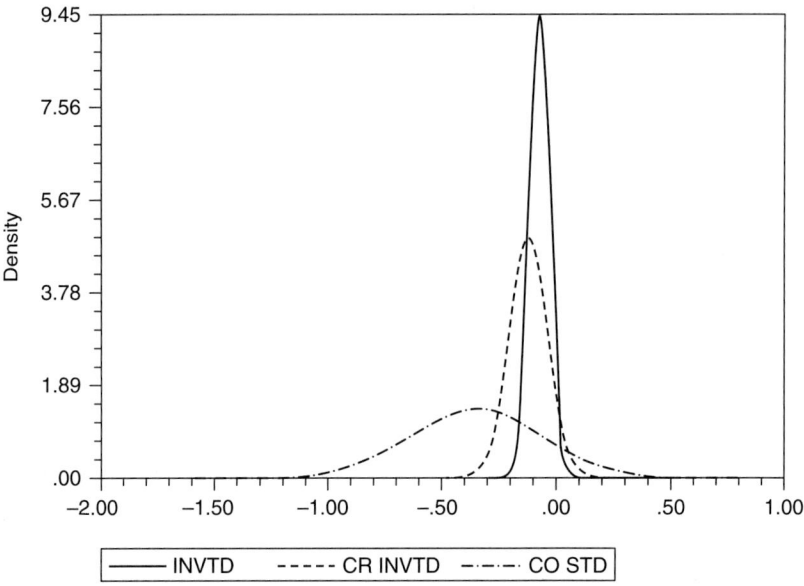

Figure 15.4 Random parameter distributions allowing for correlated random parameters

which the random parameter estimate belongs. In Section 15.5, we show you how to estimate the conditional parameter estimates (i.e., individual specific parameter estimates conditioned on the choices observed within the data) that may be used to decide where on the distribution (of marginal utility) an individual resides. These individual parameter estimates may then be used to derive individual level outputs, such as WTP measures (which can themselves be directly calculated as a distribution), elasticities, etc., or be exported to other systems such as a larger network model. The difference between conditional and unconditional estimates is presented in Section 8.1 of Chapter 8.

The ML output generated by Nlogit (as reported and discussed in previous sections of this chapter), however, is that of the unconditional parameter estimates. The output shown is representative of the entire sampled population. The output provides the mean and standard deviation of each of the random parameter distributions. As such, in using the unconditional parameter estimates, the specific location on the distribution for any given individual is unknown. If one is interested in the population profile and not that of specific individuals, this does not represent a problem. If, however, one is also interested in determining the presence of heterogeneity in the sampled population and the possible sources of heterogeneity, as shown in previous sections, then the ML model is ideal. However, once we add in heterogeneity in the mean and heteroskedasticity in the variance random parameters through inclusion of observation-specific data, we are actually influencing the specific location of an observation on the distribution.

> *As an aside*, the conditional individual level parameter estimates (discussed in Section 15.4.1) are estimated for each sampled individual (or each choice set in the case of stated choice data). The use of these individual parameter estimates, while scientifically rigorous (they are obtained Bayesian like, conditioned on the choice data), means that any output generated is limited to within the sample drawn as part of the study. Prediction outside of the sample is not possible unless one has a very robust set of mapping variables to assign a hold out sample observation to an observation used in the model estimation. Thus, if the analyst wishes to predict outside of the sample, the unconditional parameter estimates are usually preferred (see Jones and Hensher 2004).

The Nlogit commands, **utilities** and **prob** work within the ML model framework in the same manner as for the MNL and NL models. The **Simulation** command (see Chapter 13) may be used to test the policy implications resulting from changes in attribute levels; however, the results cannot be easily transferred to other domains without a robust mapping capability at the individual-observation level. That is, the analyst requires some method to map the probabilities and/or utilities obtained for sampled individuals and to a domain outside of the sample, a difficult task given the presence of the random parameter estimates. In the absence of such mapping capability, it remains possible to use the information captured in the unconditional parameter estimates to construct hypothetical samples with the same distributional information (i.e., mean, standard deviation, or spread), which in turn may be easily exported to other systems.

In summary, the unconditional parameter estimates capture information on (1) the distributional form of the marginal utilities of each random parameter (specified by the analyst), (2) the means of the distributions, and (3) the dispersion of the distributions provided in the output as the standard deviation or spread parameters. With this knowledge, it is possible to reconstruct the random parameter distribution out of sample such that the same distribution is randomly assigned over a hypothetical sample of individuals. The process to do this will depend on the distributional form of the random parameter.

15.4.1 Starting values for random parameter estimation

Nlogit 5 (post-6 September 2012) has a new facility to fully specify a *complete set of starting values for an RP model* (and, actually any other model). The syntax is **;PR0** = **<list of values>**, noting that it is PR zero. The list of values is the full set of parameters, given in the following order: β(**means of random parameters**); β(**non-random parameters**); Δ heterogeneity in mean, by rows, one for each random β; γ lower triangular Cholesky matrix; and σ = vector of diagonal elements (sigmas) for the variance matrix. All values must be provided. If there is no heterogeneity, there are no values for Δ; if there is no **;CORR**, then there are no values for γ. σ must be present if this is an RP model.

> *As an aside*, This feature is potentially dangerous. There is no way of knowing if the values you input are in the right order, or are valid at all. Nlogit has to trust the user.

15.5 Individual-specific parameter estimates: conditional parameters

The output provided by Nlogit details the population moments of the random parameter estimates for ML models. As we have shown, these population moments may be used to simulate out of sample populations and construct what are known as *unconditional parameter estimates*. Rather than rely on randomly allocating each sampled individual within a distribution as a way of allocating preference information, it is possible to utilize the additional information about the choices each individual was observed to have made as a way of increasing the accuracy of the preference allocation. One can also add in heterogeneity in the means and heteroskedasticity in the variances of random parameters, which will all be taken into account in obtaining the conditional estimates for the mean and standard deviation. In this way, it is possible to derive individual-specific parameter estimates that are *conditioned* on the choices observed to have been made (and other context effects if selected as influences on the mean and variance). The relationship between conditional and unconditional distributions is presented in Section 8.1 of Chapter 8.

Nlogit will estimate the conditional parameter estimates with the following command syntax:

```
;parameters (or ;par for short)
```

The parameters saved by **;par** are generated during estimation, not after. They are saved in memory every time the functions are computed. The last one computed is saved for the analyst to use.

> *As an aside*, If the analyst runs a subsequent model, without saving the **par** output, it will be overwritten by the **par** output of the next model run. Thus if that output is required, it is best to cut and paste it to a spreadsheet.

To demonstrate the estimation of the conditional parameter estimates, we add in **;par** to the initial random parameter model, but define all parameters as triangular rather than normal in their distribution. We omit the Nlogit output for the above model, instead choosing to concentrate on the conditional parameter estimates. The conditional parameter estimates may be found under the Matrices folder in the Untitled Project 1 box. Alternatively, if you are running a project file then you will initially click on that in order to go to the Matrices folder.

The conditional parameter estimates will be made available to the analyst by double clicking on the BETA_I option in the Matrices folder of the Untitled Project 1 box. Double clicking on this option will open up a new matrix data sheet with the saved mean conditional parameter estimates. Table 15.1 shows the stored conditional parameters for the above model for the first 20 observations (which is 2 individuals each having 10 choice sets). The column headings of the matrix are numbered, with the parameters appearing in the same order provided in the Nlogit output for the model. This means that the random parameter estimates will appear in the first few columns of the matrix, with the remaining columns devoted to the non-random parameter estimates of the model. For the above example, 11 random parameters were estimated, with the random parameters appearing in the order they were specified in the **;fcn**. Hence, the first column of the BETA_I matrix will correspond to the individual-specific conditional parameter estimates for the *invtime* parameter for all public transport alternatives and the second column of the matrix to the individual-specific conditional parameter estimates for the *invtime* attribute for the car alternative etc. (Table 15.1).

Each row of the matrix will correspond to a choice set within the data if the choice sets are assumed independent (i.e., we do not add **;pds = < number of choice sets>**). For the example data set from which these conditional parameter estimates were derived, each respondent was shown 10 choice sets each. As such, the first 10 rows of the matrix correspond to the 10 choice sets shown to the first respondent, the next 10 rows to the 10 choice sets shown to the second respondent, and so forth. The total number of rows (i.e., 3791) will therefore equal the total number of choice sets in the data.

A similar matrix is obtained for the standard deviation parameters (called SDBETA_I) (Table 15.2).

Table 15.1 A matrix (BETA_I) with the stored conditional individual-specific mean random parameter estimates for the first 20 observations

	1	2	3	4	5	6	7	8	9	10	11
1	-0.06525	-0.32382	-0.07104	0.019373	-0.18	-0.16461	-0.04422	-0.05362	-0.23926	-0.0919	-0.14548
2	-0.04744	-0.33883	-0.07225	0.021192	-0.19861	-0.16635	-0.04447	-0.05366	-0.24224	-0.11017	-0.15154
3	-0.06329	-0.10396	-0.07425	0.00044	-0.18121	-0.1671	-0.04294	-0.05438	-0.23042	-0.09626	-0.1433
4	-0.06473	-0.19812	-0.06952	0.022764	-0.17036	-0.16293	-0.04626	-0.05355	-0.23817	-0.1075	-0.13473
5	-0.05189	-0.28959	-0.07624	-0.01201	-0.18029	-0.16828	-0.04284	-0.05366	-0.23736	-0.10197	-0.13976
6	-0.04524	-0.10672	-0.0743	0.024378	-0.18661	-0.16202	-0.04282	-0.05485	-0.23612	-0.0991	-0.16997
7	-0.04847	-0.15896	-0.07727	-0.00558	-0.21356	-0.16462	-0.04536	-0.05384	-0.2442	-0.0949	-0.14407
8	-0.06662	-0.38811	-0.07153	0.005146	-0.18851	-0.16564	-0.04539	-0.05342	-0.24755	-0.09474	-0.14776
9	-0.06504	-0.40615	-0.07324	-0.01069	-0.17937	-0.16531	-0.04462	-0.05395	-0.24068	-0.1086	-0.14847
10	-0.0397	0.018877	-0.07135	-0.00669	-0.14756	-0.16768	-0.04616	-0.05319	-0.23374	-0.08921	-0.15658
11	-0.0492	-0.21267	-0.06753	-0.0448	-0.19797	-0.16468	-0.04341	-0.05343	-0.24613	-0.11663	-0.15166
12	-0.05327	-0.3638	-0.06743	-0.04518	-0.19022	-0.16632	-0.0442	-0.05361	-0.24344	-0.1107	-0.15172
13	-0.05213	-0.25684	-0.06836	-0.04347	-0.184	-0.16566	-0.04385	-0.05396	-0.23878	-0.11419	-0.14293
14	-0.05764	-0.33634	-0.0675	-0.0453	-0.21104	-0.16553	-0.04357	-0.05365	-0.24491	-0.1076	-0.13961
15	-0.05052	-0.32122	-0.06892	-0.04737	-0.211	-0.16661	-0.04484	-0.05372	-0.2419	-0.10422	-0.15075
16	-0.0545	-0.28329	-0.06769	-0.04617	-0.20192	-0.16576	-0.04483	-0.05348	-0.23865	-0.11591	-0.15911
17	-0.05237	-0.32554	-0.06852	-0.04462	-0.20299	-0.16582	-0.04399	-0.05391	-0.25099	-0.09826	-0.14926
18	-0.04894	-0.29964	-0.06789	-0.04388	-0.20783	-0.16479	-0.04407	-0.05377	-0.24728	-0.11476	-0.14587
19	-0.04699	-0.24266	-0.06695	-0.04402	-0.18382	-0.16641	-0.04499	-0.0533	-0.24253	-0.11608	-0.15123
20	-0.05252	-0.32377	-0.06861	-0.04607	-0.22832	-0.16563	-0.04269	-0.05388	-0.24311	-0.11891	-0.15281

Table 15.2 A matrix (SDBETA_I) with the stored conditional individual-specific standard deviation random parameter estimates for the first 20 observations

	1	2	3	4	5	6	7	8	9	10	11
1	0.031199	0.29129	0.026459	0.032456	0.134795	0.011739	0.01228	0.00297	0.040093	0.050788	0.052108
2	0.031523	0.292775	0.022403	0.033743	0.146696	0.013283	0.011045	0.003158	0.041787	0.054324	0.051224
3	0.029507	0.238784	0.023505	0.040933	0.141564	0.011793	0.011718	0.003033	0.047856	0.047964	0.05878
4	0.03775	0.27758	0.024759	0.033894	0.140849	0.01237	0.012009	0.003412	0.038915	0.058443	0.054172
5	0.029791	0.286637	0.023594	0.049085	0.144547	0.012586	0.011659	0.003034	0.047303	0.051284	0.051805
6	0.030241	0.232267	0.021983	0.031668	0.115001	0.012237	0.013177	0.003444	0.036469	0.047533	0.058314
7	0.031804	0.233324	0.025085	0.04306	0.143234	0.01175	0.01205	0.003089	0.041015	0.053519	0.052101
8	0.033574	0.30703	0.025877	0.036702	0.142464	0.012636	0.011948	0.003224	0.045622	0.048812	0.058346
9	0.031483	0.301836	0.023955	0.042724	0.143112	0.012086	0.011937	0.003092	0.041313	0.056293	0.051834
10	0.030159	0.193701	0.020182	0.044783	0.159352	0.010272	0.011399	0.003135	0.045978	0.041521	0.044197
11	0.031925	0.274947	0.024472	0.050083	0.138463	0.01243	0.011975	0.003316	0.04827	0.053544	0.054153
12	0.032504	0.29965	0.024447	0.051149	0.144726	0.012121	0.012543	0.003031	0.041162	0.048821	0.055704
13	0.032653	0.283942	0.025301	0.050404	0.142918	0.011713	0.011456	0.003143	0.044205	0.054323	0.049717
14	0.034164	0.284894	0.024795	0.051315	0.140456	0.012674	0.011776	0.003101	0.044222	0.049731	0.053195
15	0.031874	0.289749	0.024964	0.050456	0.144128	0.012146	0.011795	0.003188	0.040099	0.0547	0.055036
16	0.033546	0.283511	0.024346	0.053076	0.14551	0.011902	0.011687	0.003164	0.045454	0.046459	0.054099
17	0.031721	0.299869	0.024215	0.050438	0.141713	0.01238	0.011844	0.00314	0.043902	0.053115	0.05605
18	0.031277	0.280814	0.025486	0.051678	0.136842	0.012195	0.012504	0.003266	0.040964	0.053192	0.05116
19	0.031531	0.274191	0.024205	0.050843	0.141069	0.012805	0.011439	0.002944	0.045576	0.05212	0.059923
20	0.032663	0.292846	0.023786	0.05288	0.138129	0.011757	0.012222	0.003054	0.042283	0.051859	0.058133

As mentioned previously, the conditional parameter estimates are estimated for those individuals within the sample. While the conditional parameter estimates may be exported to other application settings and randomly assigned to observations in a hold out or application sample, unless the sample of respondents was drawn so as to be representative of the population from which it was derived, the conditional parameter estimates may be poor predictors of population behavioral reactions to policy changes in the scenarios tested (this may be particularly true if a non-random sample such as choice based sampling was employed). Nevertheless, while certainly true of the conditional parameter estimates, the same problem will likely be witnessed in using unconditional parameter estimates obtained from models estimated using non-representative samples.

> *As an aside*, the reason for this concern is that the choice distribution can be quite different in the application sample, and imposing the choice distribution from the estimation sample is a source of information that is a burden if the known sample choice distribution is so different. Additional information is only useful if it is portable across data settings. The use of the population moments associated with the unconditional estimates of parameters seems to be more appealing when applying a model using another sample of individuals.

Despite our earlier warning of using the conditional parameter estimates to predict out of sample, the conditional parameter estimates can often prove particularly useful. Given the non-random assignment of each individual to a specific location on the random parameter distribution (placement was conditional on the choices observed to be made), the conditional parameter estimates may be used to derive individual-specific behavioral outputs (unconditional parameter estimates are simulated randomly, hence individual behavioral outputs are less meaningful within sample; see Hensher, Greene and Rose (2005) and Section 8.1 of Chapter 8 for a detailed analysis of the differences between the two). For example, it is possible to derive individual-specific elasticities and marginal effects (see Chapter 13 for clues as to how you might do this). It is also possible to begin to build consumer segments based on the utilities held by individuals for given attributes (often called benefit segments in marketing) rather than on the traditional marketing segmentation methods of grouping consumers based on socio-demographic or psychographic information. Further, having individual-specific marginal utilities allows for the mapping between the utilities held for product bundles and other (consumer) characteristics (such as socio-demographic or psychographic information) using other statistical modeling techniques such as multiple linear regression. All this is not possible with the unconditional parameter estimates in which it is only possible to look at the simulated population in the aggregate.

15.6 Conditional confidence limits for random parameters

The stored matrices of mean and standard deviation conditional parameter estimates provide important data to use in obtaining the distributions of random parameters that are conditioned on each respondent's choice. There are many ways in which such evidence can be presented, but the most appealing method is one that can graphically show the distribution as well as indicate the confidence interval.

We show the centipede approach to examining the distribution of parameters across individuals. We have, for each individual, an estimate of the mean of the conditional distribution of parameters from which their specific vector is drawn. This is the estimate of $E[\beta_i|i]$ that is in row i of *beta_i*. We also have an estimate of the standard deviation of this conditional distribution given in row i of *sdbeta_i*. As a general result, an interval in a distribution for a continuous random variable defined by the mean plus and minus two standard deviations will encompass 95 percent or more of the mass of the distribution. This enables us to form a sort of confidence interval for β_i itself, conditioned on all the information known about the individual. To obtain this level of confidence, the interval:

$E[\beta_{ik}|$all information on individual $i] \pm 2 \times SD[\beta_{ik}|$all information on individual $i]$

will contain the actual draw for individual i. (The probability is somewhat reduced because we are using estimates of the structural parameters, not the true values.) The centipede plot feature of **PLOT** allows us to produce Figure 15.5, as follows:

```
SAMPLE ; 1-200 $
create;binvt=0;bcrinvt=0;bcost=0$
create;sinvt=0;scrinvt=0;scost=0$
name;rpi=binvt,bcrinvt,bcost$
name;rpis=sinvt,scrinvt,scost$
create;rpi=beta_i$
create;rpis=sdbeta_i$
CREATE ; lower = binvt - 2*sinvt
; upper = binvt + 2*sinvt $
CREATE ; person = Trn(1,1) $
PLOT ; Lhs = person
; Rhs = lower,upper ; Centipede
```

```
; Title = 95% Probability Intervals for invt
; Yaxis = Range
; Endpoints = 0,200 ; Bars = 0 $
```

Figure 15.5 graphs the conditional mean for each sampled person. In the figure, each vertical "leg" of the centipede plot shows the conditional confidence interval for β_{invt} for that person. The dot is the mid point of the interval, which is the point estimate. The centre horizontal bar shows the mean of the conditional means, which estimates the population mean. This was reported earlier as –0.06073. The upper and lower horizontal bars show the overall mean plus and minus twice the estimated population standard deviation – this was reported earlier as 0.08235. Thus, the unconditional population range of variation is estimated to be about 0.01375 to –0.175. In this example, we have used a constrained triangular distribution (with no heterogeneity in the mean or heteroskedasticity in the variance), and hence we have fully satisfied the negative sign across the entire distribution.

15.7 Willingness to pay issues

The WTP for an attribute is the ratio of that attribute's parameter estimate to the parameter estimate of the cost parameter. For value of travel time savings (VTTS), we multiply the resulting WTP measure by 60 if the time attribute was measured in minutes. This converts the VTTS to a measure of WTP for time per hour. We discussed in Chapters 11 and 13 how to derive measures of WTP from the MNL model. If in the ML model, the two parameters used in deriving measures of WTP are estimated as non-random parameters, the methodology of calculating WTP remains unchanged. If, however, one or the other of the parameters is estimated as a random parameter, then the WTP calculations must take this into account.

VTTS and WTP measures may be constructed using either conditional parameter estimates or the unconditional parameter estimates (population moments).

15.7.1 WTP based on conditional estimates

We have included **;par** in the model in order to obtain the matrices of conditional estimates, defined as *beta_i* and *sdbeta_i*. If we want to obtain the WTP estimates then we have to include in the model command the

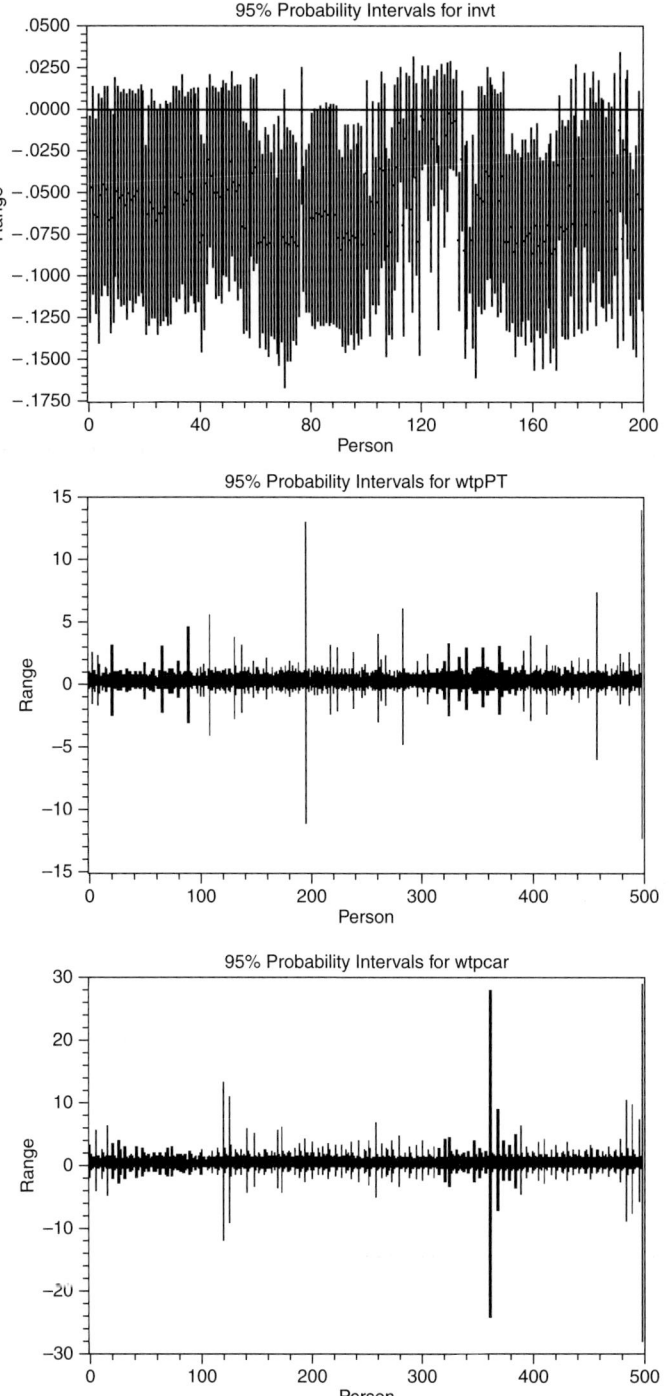

Figure 15.5 Estimates of the marginal utility of invehicle time together with confidence intervals

following (the example used herein), **;wtp=invt/cost,crinvt/crcost**, where we request two WTP estimates. This obtains two additional matrices called *wtp_i* and *sdwtp_i*:

```
;lhs=resp1,cset,Altij
;choices=NLRail,NHRail,NBway,Bus,Bway,Train,Car
;par
;rpl
;wtp=invt/cost,crinvt/crcost
;fcn=invt(t,1),cost(t,1),acwt(t,1) ,eggt(t,1), crpark(t,1),
accbusf(t,1),waittb(t,1),acctb(t,1),crcost(t,1),crinvt(t,1),creggt
(t,1)
;maxit=200
;par
;halton;pts= 100
;model:
U(NLRail)= NLRAsc + cost*tcost + invt*InvTime + acwt*waitt+
acwt*acctim + accbusf*accbusf+eggT*egresst
     + ptinc*pinc + ptgend*gender + NLRinsde*inside /
U(NHRail)= TNAsc + cost*Tcost + invt*InvTime + acwt*WaitT +
acwt*acctim
   + eggT*egresst + accbusf*accbusf
        + ptinc*pinc + ptgend*gender + NHRinsde*inside /
U(NBway)=  NBWAsc + cost*Tcost + invt*InvTime + waitTb*WaitT
   + accTb*acctim
   + eggT*egresst + accbusf*accbusf+ ptinc*pinc + ptgend*gender /
U(Bus)=    BSAsc + cost*frunCost + invt*InvTime + waitTb*WaitT
   + accTb*acctim
   + eggT*egresst+ ptinc*pinc + ptgend*gender/
U(Bway)=   BWAsc + cost*Tcost + invt*InvTime + waitTb*WaitT
   + accTb*acctim
   + eggT*egresst + accbusf*accbusf+ ptinc*pinc + ptgend*gender /
U(Train)=  TNAsc + cost*tcost + invt*InvTime + acwt*WaitT +
acwt*acctim
   + eggT*egresst + accbusf*accbusf+ ptinc*pinc + ptgend*gender /
U(Car)=    CRcost*costs + CRinvt*InvTime + CRpark*parkcost
   + CReggT*egresst$
```

The following Nlogit output is produced for the above model with the first 20 results for *wtp_i* and *sdwtp_i* given in Table 15.3 (copied into Excel with extra columns used to convert $/min. results from Nlogit to $/hour. The standard deviation estimates suggest a noticeable amount of heterogeneity in the WTP estimates within the sample. The overall mean estimate for the value of invehicle travel time savings for public transport is $21.64/hr., and for car it is $38.07/hr. The equivalent standard deviation estimates are $4.97/hr. and $8.16/hr.:

Table 15.3 A matrix with the stored conditional individual-specific WTP estimates for the first 20 observations (noting that an observation is a respondent and not a choice set in the absence of recognizing the number of choice sets using :pds = <number>)

$/min:	MvttsinvtPT	MvttsinvtCar	$/hr:	MvttsinvtPT	MvttsinvtCar	$/min:	SDvttsinvtPT	SDvttsinvtCar	$/hr:	SDvttsinvtPT	SDvttsinvtCar
1	0.396356	0.803935	23.81	48.24	1	0.400964	1.40066	24.06	84.04
2	0.304082	0.664194	18.24	39.85	2	0.301427	0.718413	18.09	43.10
3	0.573686	0.579338	34.42	34.76	3	1.09271	0.500268	65.56	30.02
4	0.399767	0.574241	23.99	34.45	4	0.380977	0.471707	22.86	28.30
5	0.33947	0.566419	20.37	33.99	5	0.372549	0.413323	22.35	24.80
6	0.371618	0.889706	22.30	53.38	6	0.459777	2.47663	27.59	148.60
7	0.325086	0.609426	19.51	36.57	7	0.247903	0.557653	14.87	33.46
8	0.461253	0.69409	27.68	41.65	8	1.03882	0.614009	62.33	36.84
9	0.359532	0.55523	21.57	33.31	9	0.360497	0.471967	21.63	28.32
10	0.488648	0.544446	29.32	32.67	10	0.634546	0.343338	38.07	20.60
11	0.338656	0.337583	20.32	20.25	11	0.199759	1.22742	11.99	73.65
12	0.322525	0.715185	19.35	42.91	12	0.261096	0.880407	15.67	52.82
13	0.318614	0.643775	19.12	38.63	13	0.399257	0.574741	23.96	34.48
14	0.339067	0.61757	20.34	37.05	14	0.302422	0.458117	18.15	27.49
15	0.378765	0.591914	22.73	35.51	15	0.511601	0.49084	30.70	29.45
16	0.341687	0.909806	20.50	54.59	16	0.380664	2.82968	22.84	169.78
17	0.378308	0.77481	22.70	46.49	17	0.515011	0.892397	30.90	53.54
18	0.310975	0.58567	18.66	35.14	18	0.28095	0.538031	16.86	32.28
19	0.326208	0.616503	19.57	36.99	19	0.308979	0.493978	18.54	29.64
20	0.345022	0.564326	20.70	33.86	20	0.304861	0.383368	18.29	23.00

```
|-> Nlogit
Random Parameters Logit Model
Dependent variable                 RESP1
Log likelihood function      -2465.75251
Restricted log likelihood    -3580.47467
Chi squared [ 20](P= .000)    2229.44432
Significance level                 .00000
McFadden Pseudo R-squared         .3113336
Estimation based on N =    1840, K =   20
Inf.Cr.AIC  =   4971.5 AIC/N =     2.702
R2=1-LogL/LogL* Log-L fncn R-sqrd R2Adj
No coefficients -3580.4747  .3113  .3098
Constants only can be computed directly
            Use NLOGIT ;...;RHS=ONE$
At start values -2497.0892  .0125 .0103
Response data are given as ind. choices
Replications for simulated probs. = 100
Used Halton sequences in simulations.
Number of obs.=  1840, skipped     0 obs
```

RESP1	Coefficient	Standard Error	z	Prob. |z|>Z*	95% Confidence Interval	
Random parameters in utility functions						
INVT	-.06368***	.00329	-19.37	.0000	-.07012	-.05723
COST	-.24872***	.01958	-12.70	.0000	-.28710	-.21033
ACWT	-.06976***	.00731	-9.55	.0000	-.08407	-.05544
EGGT	-.01435**	.00565	-2.54	.0111	-.02543	-.00327
CRPARK	-.03559***	.01341	-2.65	.0079	-.06187	-.00931
ACCBUSF	-.10601***	.03622	-2.93	.0034	-.17701	-.03501
WAITTB	-.08739***	.02870	-3.04	.0023	-.14365	-.03113
ACCTB	-.07517***	.01089	-6.91	.0000	-.09651	-.05384
CRCOST	-.14957***	.04942	-3.03	.0025	-.24644	-.05271
CRINVT	-.07024***	.01107	-6.35	.0000	-.09193	-.04854
CREGGT	-.08194***	.02318	-3.53	.0004	-.12737	-.03650
Nonrandom parameters in utility functions						
NLRASC	2.53832***	.46944	5.41	.0000	1.61824	3.45840
PTINC	-.01212***	.00290	-4.18	.0000	-.01781	-.00643
PTGEND	1.87986***	.26115	7.20	.0000	1.36801	2.39171
NLRINSDE	-1.10737***	.35603	-3.11	.0019	-1.80518	-.40956
TNASC	1.84015***	.45881	4.01	.0001	.94090	2.73940
NHRINSDE	-1.12297***	.40112	-2.80	.0051	-1.90915	-.33680
NBWASC	1.14015**	.48364	2.36	.0184	.19223	2.08807
BSASC	1.51964***	.44718	3.40	.0007	.64318	2.39611
BWASC	1.39054***	.46212	3.01	.0026	.48480	2.29629
Distns. of RPs. Std.Devs or limits of triangular						
TsINVT	.06368***	.00329	19.37	.0000	.05723	.07012
TsCOST	.24872***	.01958	12.70	.0000	.21033	.28710
TsACWT	.06976***	.00731	9.55	.0000	.05544	.08407

TsEGGT|	.01435**	.00565	2.54	.0111	.00327	.02543
TsCRPARK|	.03559***	.01341	2.65	.0079	.00931	.06187
TsACCBUS|	.10601***	.03622	2.93	.0034	.03501	.17701
TsWAITTB|	.08739***	.02870	3.04	.0023	.03113	.14365
TsACCTB|	.07517***	.01089	6.91	.0000	.05384	.09651
TsCRCOST|	.14957***	.04942	3.03	.0025	.05271	.24644
TsCRINVT|	.07024***	.01107	6.35	.0000	.04854	.09193
TsCREGGT|	.08194***	.02318	3.53	.0004	.03650	.12737

The centipede commands to plot the two distributions for the first 500 observations, together with their upper and lower confidence intervals for 95 percent probability intervals, are given as follows (noting that the matrices of interest are *wtp_i* and *sdwtp_i*, not *beta_i* and *sdbeta_i*):

```
SAMPLE ; 1-500 $
create;bwtpPT=0;bwtpcar=0$
create;swtpPT=0;swtpcar=0$
name;rpi=bwtpPT,bwtpcar$
name;rpis=swtpPT,swtpcar$
create;rpi=wtp_i$
create;rpis=sdwtp_i$
CREATE ; lower = bwtppt - 2*swtppt
   ; upper = bwtppt + 2*swtppt $

CREATE ; person = Trn(1,1) $
PLOT ; Lhs = person
   ; Rhs = lower,upper ; Centipede
   ; Title = 95% Probability Intervals for wtpPT
   ; Yaxis = Range
   ; Endpoints = 0,200 ; Bars = 0 $

CREATE ; lower = bwtpcar - 2*swtpcar
   ; upper = bwtpcar + 2*swtpcar $
CREATE ; person = Trn(1,1) $
PLOT ; Lhs = person
   ; Rhs = lower,upper ; Centipede
   ; Title = 95% Probability Intervals for wtpcar
   ; Yaxis = Range
   ; Endpoints = 0,200 ; Bars = 0 $

create
;vttsptm=60*bwtppt
;vttscrm=60*bwtpcar$
dstats;rhs=bwtppt,bwtpcar,swtpPT,swtpcar,lower,upper,vttsptm,vttscrm$
```

```
Descriptive Statistics for    8 variables
Variable|    Mean      Std.Dev.    Minimum     Maximum    Cases Missing
--------- +--------------------------------------------------------------
   BWTPPT|   .360784    .082885     .089107     .966350      500       0
```

BWTPCAR	.634560	.136013	.259644	2.074384	500	0
SWTPPT	.430219	.399642	.121706	6.034534	500	0
SWTPCAR	.759684	.822044	.267581	13.14293	500	0
LOWER	-.884808	1.540095	-24.21147	.040068	500	0
UPPER	2.153929	1.752473	.818010	28.36024	500	0
VTTSPTM	21.64706	4.973076	5.346425	57.98103	500	0
VTTSCRM	38.07363	8.160788	15.57864	124.4631	500	0

The evidence in Figure 15.5 is based on a constrained triangular distribution and results in a positive sign across the distribution for the mean estimates, which is behaviorally plausible. When we plot the 95 percent probability interval, we obtain estimates that move into the negative region, with a mean for the lower estimate of −0.8848 and a range of -$24.2/min. to $0.04/min. The upper bound has a mean of $2.15/min. with a range from $0.818/min. to $28.36/min. Although there is the hint of possible outliers, it is virtually impossible to identify them when the distribution is fully random. The only way to possibly track this down is to introduce some systematic sources of heterogeneity in the means and/or heteroskedasticity in the variances; however, this comes at the cost of losing the assurance under a constrained distribution of the mean estimates all satisfying the positive sign. Hence, the mean estimates are, in practical terms, likely to remain the best estimates we can obtain given the behavioral desire to preserve a single sign across the entire WTP distribution.

> *As an aside*, We have found that a model estimated in WTP space (see below) in contrast to utility space often improves on the sign preservation, even under unconstrained distributions, and seems to reduce the long tail common in many unconstrained distributions in utility space such as the log-normal. Furthermore, we have also found that the allowance for attribute processing rules (such as attribute non-attendance – see Chapter 21), also contributes to reducing the incidence of negative estimates of WTP where a positive estimate is behaviorally plausible.

15.7.2 WTP based on unconditional estimates

In order to obtain a WTP or VTTS measure using the unconditional parameter estimates, the population must be simulated. The following command syntax may be used to simulate a population for the above example. VTTS will be saved in the data set under the names *vttsPT* and *vttsCar*. We have multiplied the VTTS by 60 to convert from $/min. to $/hr. The mean estimates are, respectively, $19.30/hr and $38.09/hr. These are very similar to the mean estimates for the conditional distributions (namely $21.64/hr. and

$38.07/hr.), with the car value almost identical and the public transport estimate slightly lower, due essentially to sampling error. This supports the proof of equivalence in Section 8.1 of Chapter 8:

> *As an aside*, As shown below in the command syntax, when deriving estimates for each respondent on the distribution, it is important to use different names for the random normal and the triangular, otherwise you will obtain identical estimates for the numerator and denominator.

```
sample;all$
reject;dremove=1$
reject;ttype#1$  work =1
reject;altij=-999$
sample;1-500$
create
;rna=rnn(0,1)
;V1=rnu(0,1)
;V1d=rnu(0,1)
;if(v1<=0.5)T=sqr(2*V1)-1;(ELSE) T=1-sqr(2*(1-V1))
;if(v1d<=0.5)Td=sqr(2*V1d)-1;(ELSE) Td=1-sqr(2*(1-V1d))
;MUPTt=-0.06368+0.06368*T
;MUPTc=-0.24872+0.24872*Td
;VTTSPT = 60*(MUptt/muptc)$ ?60*((-0.06368+0.06368*T)/(-0.24872
+0.24872*Td))
reject;altij=7$
dstats;rhs=t,muptt,muptc,vttspt$
```

Descriptive Statistics for 4 variables
```
-----------+----------------------------------------------------------------------------
Variable|    Mean      Std.Dev.    Minimum      Maximum     Cases Missing
-----------+----------------------------------------------------------------------------
       T|   .008948     .406391    -.938382     .980076      437         0
  MUPTT|   -.063110     .025879    -.123436    -.001269      437         0
  MUPTC|   -.253697     .103243    -.478103    -.015196      437         0
 VTTSPT|   19.30139    18.36737     .167562    254.7921      437         0
-----------+----------------------------------------------------------------------------
```
```
sample;all$
reject;dremove=1$
reject;ttype#1$  work =1
reject;altij=-999$
create
;rna=rnn(0,1)
;V1=rnu(0,1)
;V1d=rnu(0,1)
;if(v1<=0.5)T=sqr(2*V1)-1;(ELSE) T=1-sqr(2*(1-V1))
```

```
;if(v1d<=0.5)Td=sqr(2*V1d)-1;(ELSE) Td=1-sqr(2*(1-V1d))
;VTTSCAR = 60*(-0.07024+0.07024*T)/(-0.14957+0.14957*Td)$
reject;altij#7$
dstats;rhs=vttscar$
```

```
Descriptive Statistics for    1 variables
-----------+----------------------------------------------------------------------------
Variable|    Mean      Std.Dev.     Minimum      Maximum      Cases Missing
-----------+----------------------------------------------------------------------------
VTTSCAR|   38.08901   40.69076     .897360     510.7445      1620        0
-----------+----------------------------------------------------------------------------
```

15.8 Error components in mixed logit models

The "kernel logit" model suggested by Ben-Akiva et al. (2002), based on an idea first proposed by Brownstone and Train (1999),[3] incorporates additional unobserved heterogeneity through effects that are associated with the individual's preferences within the choices. These appear as $M \leq J$ additional random effects:

$$U_{q,j,t} = \beta_q'\mathbf{x}_{q,j,t} + \varepsilon_{q,j,t} + c_{j1}W_{q,1} + c_{j2}W_{q,2} + \ldots + c_{jM}W_{q,M}, \qquad (15.15)$$

where the $W_{q,m}$ are normally distributed effects with zero mean, $m = 1,\ldots,$ $M \leq J$ and $C_{j,m} = 1$ if m appears in utility function j.[4] This specification can produce a simple "random effects" model if all J utilities share a single error component:

$$U_{q,j,t} = \beta_q'\mathbf{x}_{q,j,t} + \varepsilon_{q,j,t} + W_q, j = 1,\ldots,J, \qquad (15.16)$$

or an error components sort of model if one and only one alternative-specific parameter appears in each utility function, as in Equation (15.17):

$$U_{q,j,t} = \beta_q'\mathbf{x}_{q,j,t} + \varepsilon_{q,j,t} + W_{q,j}, j = 1,\ldots,J. \qquad (15.17)$$

If groups of utility functions each contain a common subset of the error components across specific nests of alternatives, then we can specify the "nested" system in Equation (15.18):

[3] The Ben-Akiva et al. (2002) paper was a reaction to the suggestion in Brownstone and Train, pointing out that identification can be difficult to assess in mixed models with these kinds of error components for alternatives and nests.
[4] Issues of specification and identification are discussed in Ben-Akiva et al. (2002).

$$U_{q,1,t} = \boldsymbol{\beta}_q'\mathbf{x}_{q,1,t} + \varepsilon_{q,1,t} + W_{q,1}$$
$$U_{q,2,t} = \boldsymbol{\beta}_q'\mathbf{x}_{q,2,t} + \varepsilon_{q,2,t} + W_{q,1}$$
$$U_{q,3,t} = \boldsymbol{\beta}_q'\mathbf{x}_{q,3,t} + \varepsilon_{q,3,t} + W_{q,2}$$
$$U_{q,4,t} = \boldsymbol{\beta}_q'\mathbf{x}_{q,4,t} + \varepsilon_{q,4,t} + W_{q,2}$$

(15.18)

and even a cross-nested model if the groups of error components overlap, as in the following example (Equation (15.19)):

$$U_{q,1,t} = \boldsymbol{\beta}_q'\mathbf{x}_{q,1,t} + \varepsilon_{q,1,t} + W_{q,1} + W_{q,2},$$
$$U_{q,2,t} = \boldsymbol{\beta}_q'\mathbf{x}_{q,2,t} + \varepsilon_{q,2,t} + W_{q,1} + W_{q,2},$$
$$U_{q,3,t} = \boldsymbol{\beta}_q'\mathbf{x}_{q,3,t} + \varepsilon_{q,3,t} + W_{q,2} + W_{q,3} + W_{q,4},$$
$$U_{q,4,t} = \boldsymbol{\beta}_q'\mathbf{x}_{q,4,t} + \varepsilon_{q,4,t} + W_{q,3} + W_{q,4}.$$

(15.19)

This extension of the ML model entails capturing an additional unobserved variance that is alternative-specific through a mixture formulation that imposes a normal distribution on such information across the sampled population. The standard deviation of these normals can be parameterized for each alternative with special cases in which there are cross-alternative equality constraints on the estimated standard deviations. Through cross-alternative constraints we can permit an alternative to appear in more than one subset of alternatives, giving it the appearance of a nested structure.

This generalization extends the Brownstone and Train (1999) model in two respects. Firstly, we allow the same kind of variance heterogeneity in the error components for alternatives and nests of alternatives as in the random parameters part:

$$\mathrm{Var}[W_{m,q}] = [\theta_m \exp(\tau_m'\mathbf{h}_q)]^2.$$

(15.20)

Second, we combine this specification with the full random parameters model laid out earlier.[5] Collecting all results, the full ML model is given by Equations (15.21–15.26):

[5] Ben-Akiva *et al.* (2002) extend the basic model somewhat by imposing a factor analytic structure on the set of kernels. This achieves a small amount of generality in allowing the variables that appear in the utility functions to be correlated. With respect to the behavioral model, little is actually obtained by this, since the assumed independent kernels above may be mixed in any fashion in the utility functions.

$$U_{q,j,t} = \boldsymbol{\beta}_q{}'\mathbf{x}_{q,j,t} + \varepsilon_{q,j,t} + \sum\nolimits_{m=1}^{M} c_{j,m} W_{q,m}. \tag{15.21}$$

$$\boldsymbol{\beta}_q = \bar{\boldsymbol{\beta}} + \Delta\mathbf{z}_q + \Gamma_q\mathbf{v}_q. \tag{15.22}$$

$$\mathbf{v}_q = \mathbf{R}\mathbf{v}_q*. \tag{15.23}$$

$$v_{q,k,t}* = \rho_k v_{q,k,t-1}* + w_{q,k,t}*. \tag{15.24}$$

$$\mathrm{Var}[v_{q,k}*] = [\sigma_k{'}\exp(\eta_k{'}\mathbf{h}_q)]^2. \tag{15.25}$$

$$\mathrm{Var}[W_{m,q}] = [\theta_m\exp(\tau_m{'}\mathbf{h}_q)]^2. \tag{15.26}$$

The conditional choice probability is now:

$$L_{q,j,t} = \mathrm{Prob}_{q,t}[j|\cdot\mathbf{X}_{q,t}, \Omega, \cdot\mathbf{z}_q, \mathbf{h}_q, \mathbf{v}_q, \mathbf{W}_q]$$
$$= \frac{\exp(\boldsymbol{\beta}'_q\mathbf{x}_{q,j,t} + \Sigma_{m=1}^{M} c_{jm} W_{mq})}{\sum_{j=1}^{J} \exp(\boldsymbol{\beta}'_q\mathbf{x}_{q,j,t} + \Sigma_{m=1}^{M} c_{jm} W_{mq})}. \tag{15.27}$$

The *unconditional* choice probability is the expected value of this logit probability over all the possible values of $\boldsymbol{\beta}_q$ and $\mathbf{W}_q$ – that is, integrated over these values, weighted by the joint density of $\boldsymbol{\beta}_q$ and $\mathbf{W}_q$. We assume that $\mathbf{v}_q$ and $\mathbf{W}_q$ are independent, so this is just the product. Thus, the unconditional choice probability is:

$$P_{jtq}(\mathbf{X}_{t,q}, \mathbf{z}_q, \mathbf{h}_q, \Omega) = \mathrm{Prob}_{q,t}[j|\mathbf{X}_{t,q}, \Omega, \mathbf{z}_q, \mathbf{h}_q]$$
$$= \int_{\mathbf{W}_q}\int_{\boldsymbol{\beta}_q} L_{q,j,t}(\boldsymbol{\beta}_q|\mathbf{X}_{q,t}, \Omega, \mathbf{z}_q, \mathbf{h}_q, \mathbf{v}_q, \mathbf{W}_q)f(\boldsymbol{\beta}_q|\Omega, \mathbf{z}_q, \mathbf{h}_q)f(\mathbf{W}_q|\Omega, \mathbf{h}_q)d\boldsymbol{\beta}_q d\mathbf{W}_q.$$
$$\tag{15.28}$$

Thus, the *unconditional* probability that individual q will choose alternative j, given the specific characteristics of their choice set and the underlying model parameters, is equal to the expected value of the conditional probability as it ranges over the possible values of $\boldsymbol{\beta}_q$ and $\mathbf{W}_q$. Finally, the contribution of individual q to the likelihood for the full sample is the product of the T conditionally (on $\mathbf{v}_q$ and $\mathbf{W}_q$) independent choice probabilities. The LL is then formed as usual. The contribution of individual q is:

$$P_q(\mathbf{X}_q, \Omega, \mathbf{z}_q, \mathbf{h}_q) =$$
$$\int_{\mathbf{W}_q} \int_{\beta_q} \prod_{t=1}^{T} L_{q,j,t}(\beta_q | \mathbf{X}_{q,t}, \Omega, \mathbf{z}_q, \mathbf{h}_q, \mathbf{v}_q, \mathbf{W}_q) f(\mathbf{v}_q | \Omega, \mathbf{z}_q, \mathbf{h}_q) f(\mathbf{W}_q | \Omega, \mathbf{h}_q) d\mathbf{v}_q d\mathbf{W}_q$$

$$(15.29)$$

and the full log likelihood is:

$$\log L(\Omega)$$
$$= \sum_{q=1}^{Q} \log \int_{\mathbf{W}_q} \int_{\beta_q} \prod_{t=1}^{T} L_{q,j,t}(\beta_q | \mathbf{X}_{tq}, \Omega, \mathbf{z}_q, \mathbf{h}_q, \mathbf{v}_q, \mathbf{W}_q) \times f(\mathbf{v}_q | \Omega, \mathbf{z}_q, \mathbf{h}_q) f(\mathbf{W}_q | \Omega, \mathbf{h}_q) d\mathbf{v}_q d\mathbf{W}_q.$$

$$(15.31)$$

Like the standard ML model, the integrals in Equation (15.31) cannot be computed analytically because there are no closed-forms solutions. However, the full expression is in the form of an expectation, which suggests that it can be approximated satisfactorily with Monte Carlo integration. Let $\mathbf{v}_{qr}$ denote the rth of R random draws from the population of $\mathbf{v}_q$ and $\mathbf{W}_{qr}$ be an accompanying random draw from the M-variate standard normal population. Using these draws, the logit probability is calculated. This process is repeated for many draws, and the mean of the resulting simulated likelihood values is taken as the approximate choice probability giving the simulated LL:

$$\log \mathrm{LS}\,(\Omega) = \frac{1}{R}\sum_{r=1}^{R} \prod_{t=1}^{T} L_{q,j,t}(\beta_q | \mathbf{X}_{q,t}, \Omega, \mathbf{z}_q, \mathbf{h}_q, \mathbf{v}_{qr}, \mathbf{W}_{qr},)$$
$$= \sum_{q=1}^{Q} \log \frac{1}{R}\sum_{r=1}^{R} \frac{\prod_{t=1}^{T} \exp[(\bar{\beta} + \Delta\mathbf{z}_q + \Gamma_q \mathbf{v}_{q,r})' \mathbf{x}_{q,j,t} + \Sigma_{m=1}^{M} c_{j,m} W_{q,m,r}]}{\sum_{m=1}^{J} \exp[(\bar{\beta} + \Delta\mathbf{z}_q + \Gamma_q \mathbf{v}_{q,r})' \mathbf{x}_{q,m,t} + \Sigma_{m=1}^{M} c_{j,m} W_{q,m,r}]} \cdot$$

$$(15.32)$$

This function is smooth and continuous in the elements of Ω and can be maximized by conventional methods. Train (2003, 2009) provides a discussion of this form of maximum simulated likelihood estimation. With sufficiently large R (number of draws), the simulated function provides an adequate approximation to the actual function for likelihood-based estimation and inference.[6]

The additional command for error components is, by example: **;ecm= (NLRail,NHRail,Train), (NBway,Bus,Bway),(Car)**. The error components

---

[6] In our application, we use Halton sequences rather than random draws to speed up and smooth the simulations. See Bhat (2001), Train (2003), or Greene (2003) for a discussion.

model may be layered on top of the random parameters (mixed) logit model by adding the ECM specification, with **; ECM = the specification of the error components**.

The full set of options and features for the ML model and the random parameters model are used in this setting as well. That includes fitted probabilities, inclusive values, all display options described, and the simulator described in Chapter 13. Do note, however, that although this model is closely related to the RP model, there is but one parameter vector and, hence, **; Par** has no effect here. The specification **; SDE = list of symbols or values** can be used in the same fashion as **; Rst = list** to constrain the standard deviations of the error components to equal each other or fixed values. For example, with four components, the specification **; SDE = 1,1,ss,ss** forces the first two to equal one and the third and fourth to equal each other. Two other specifications are available. **; SDE = a single value** forces all error components to be equal to that value. Finally, in any specification, if the value is enclosed in parentheses (()), then the value is merely used to provide the starting value for the estimator, it does not impose any constraints on the final estimates.

To allow for heteroskedasticity in variance of error components, $Var[Eim]$ = $\exp(\gamma_{mhi})$, we include the syntax **;hfe=<list of variables>**. An example of the error component commands that will be used most often is:

```
;ecm= (NLRail,NHRail,Train),(NBway,Bus,Bway),(Car)
; Hfe = pinc,gender
```

Suppose we wish to specify that only *pinc* appears in the first function, only *gender* in the second, and both in the third. The **; ECM** specification would be modified to:

```
;ecm= (NLRail,NHRail,Train!10),(NBway,Bus,Bway!01),(Car!11)
```

An exclamation point inside the parentheses after the last name signals that a specification of the heteroskedastic function is to follow. The succeeding specification is a set of zeros and ones, where a one indicates that the variable appears in the variance and a zero indicates that it does not. The number of zeros and ones provided is exactly the number of variables that appear in the **Hfe** list (already defined earlier).

As an aside, It is permissible to allow for an alternative to appear on more than one error component, as a nested structure. For example:

```
;ecm= (NLRail,NHRail,Train!10),(NBway,Bus,Bway,NLRail!01),
(Bus,Train!11)(Car!11)
```

To illustrate the application of error components and to contrast with the standard ML model, five ML models were estimated, beginning with the base model and building up to the most general model. The models are identified as follows and the results summarized in Table 15.4:

ML1: Base model with random parameters only;

ML2: ML1 plus observed heterogeneity around the mean of random parameters;

ML3: ML2 plus heteroskedasticity around the standard deviations of random parameters;

ML4: ML3 plus standard deviation of error components for alternatives and nests of alternatives;

ML5: ML4 plus heteroskedasticity in variance of error components for alternatives and nests of alternatives.

The access mode travel time relates to the chosen access mode associated with the public transport main mode.

Table 15.5 summarizes the mean and standard deviation of the parameter estimates associated with each of the specifications for each attribute and its associated decomposition.

All random parameters have a triangular distribution. We investigated model specifications with unconstrained and constrained[7] triangular distributions, and found that the specification that constrained the standard deviation to equal the mean gave the better overall model fit, as well as ensuring a behaviorally meaningful sign for estimated parameters across the entire distribution.[8] The entire set of modal attributes are specified with random parameters and all are statistically significant and of the expected sign. The models progressively improve in overall goodness of fit from a pseudo-R^2 of 0.3101 for the base model through to 0.3195 for the fully generalized model ML5. We find that personal income is a statistically significant source of influence on preference heterogeneity for the main mode public transport fares and across all models (ML2–ML5), and for bus fares on the access mode (which is available to all public modes except current bus), reducing the marginal disutility of fares for all public transport modes as personal income increases. Although personal income has an influence on public transport invehicle time in ML2, it is statistically non-significant when we move to incorporate heterogeneity around the standard deviation of the random parameter and the error components for alternatives and nests of alternatives.

---

[7] The constrained triangular has only one parameter, that is its mean and spread.
[8] The mean weighted average elasticities were also statistically equivalent.

Table 15.4 Summary of empirical results[9]: commuter trips

Note: All public transport = (new heavy rail, new light rail, new busway, bus, train, busway); time is in min.; fares and cost is in dollars ($2003). *T*-values in brackets 2230 observations, 200 Halton draws.

Attribute	Alternatives	ML1	ML2	ML3	ML4	ML5
New light rail constant	New light rail	2.411 (5.0)	3.313 (6.1)	2.978 (5.7)	4.442 (4.68)	5.011 (5.3)
New busway constant	New busway	1.019 (2.1)	1.933 (3.5)	1.561 (2.8)	2.939 (3.1)	3.487 (3.7)
Existing bus constant	Bus	1.393 (3.0)	2.273 (4.4)	1.852 (3.6)	3.255 (3.5)	3.808 (4.1)
Train constant	Existing and new train	1.709 (3.6)	2.609 (4.9)	2.246 (4.4)	3.657 (3.9)	4.213 (4.5)
Existing busway constant	Busway	1.266 (2.7)	2.183 (4.1)	1.801 (3.4)	3.178 (3.4)	3.714 (4.0)
	Random parameters –constrained triangular:					
Main mode fares	All public transport	−0.2505 (−12.1)	−0.3536 (−10.1)	−0.3512 (−10.4)	−0.3723 (−9.3)	−0.3853 (−9.4)
Car mode running and toll cost	Car	−0.1653 (−3.3)	−0.1764 (−3.3)	−0.1876 (−3.4)	−0.2152 (−2.8)	−0.2182 (−2.9)
Car parking cost	Car	−0.0340 (−2.7)	−0.0377 (−2.7)	−0.0443 (−3.0)	−0.0571 (−2.7)	−0.0558 (−2.8)
Main mode invehicle time	All public transport	−0.0640 (−19.3)	−0.0744 (−14.4)	−0.0713 (−18.5)	−0.0773 (−15.3)	−0.0785 (−15.1)
Access and wait time	All train and light rail	−0.0699 (−9.5)	−0.0716 (−9.5)	−0.0762 (−9.8)	−0.0811 (−9.1)	−0.0828 (−9.2)
Access time	All bus and busway	−.0756 (−6.9)	−0.0808 (−7.1)	−0.0839 (−6.5)	−0.0929 (−6.4)	−0.0942 (−6.3)
Wait time	All bus and busway	−0.0882 (−3.1)	−0.0907 (−3.06)	−0.1026 (−3.2)	−0.1034 (−3.0)	−0.1048 (−3.0)
Main mode invehicle time	Car	−0.0728 (−6.2)	−0.0791 (−6.2)	−0.0859 (−7.0)	−0.0796 (−5.2)	−0.0732 (−4.8)

[9] Multiple mixture runs must be conducted and a measure of variation in parameter coefficients must be reported (e.g. std. deviation in parameter estimates). Theoretically, we cannot make statistical inference from a distribution using a single point. Unfortunately, this does not address a relevant issue in our estimations. We used Halton draws to perform our integrations, so there is no simulation variance. If we repeated the estimation, we would get exactly the same estimates. In fact, there is no simulation variance because the estimates are not based on simulations. We have used the Halton technique to evaluate certain integrals. There will be an approximation error, of course. Our only control over that is to use many Halton draws, which we have done. The interpretation of the estimates as a sample of one is not correct, however. There are many other settings in which researchers must resort to approximations to evaluate integrals, such as random effects probit models which use Hermite quadrature to approximate integrals, and even the most mundane univariate probit model which uses a ratio of polynomials to approximate the standard normal cdf. The MLEs obtained in these settings are not samples of one; they are maximizers of an approximation to the LL function that cannot be evaluated exactly.

Egress travel time	All public transport	−0.0145 (−2.6)	−0.0142 (−2.5)	−0.0151 (−2.7)	−0.0169 (−2.8)	−0.0181 (−3.0)
Egress travel time	Car	−0.0814 (−3.5)	−0.0876 (−3.5)	−0.0892 (−2.8)	−0.1193 (−2.5)	−0.1084 (−2.5)
Access bus mode fare	Where is access mode	−0.1067 (−2.9)	−0.1916 (−3.65)	−0.1981 (−3.8)	−0.2118 (−3.8)	−0.2167 (−3.8)
Non-random parameters:						
Inside study area	New heavy rail	−1.119 (−2.8)	−1.207 (−2.9)	−1.300 (−3.3)	−1.497 (−3.4)	−1.419 (−3.2)
Inside study area	New light rail	−1.104 (−3.1)	−1.164 (−3.2)	−1.249 (−3.6)	−1.443 (−3.7)	−1.383 (−3.5)
Personal income	All public transport	−0.0122 (−4.1)	−0.0278 (−6.2)	−0.0211 (−4.9)	−0.0266 (−4.2)	−0.0326 (−5.0)
Gender (male = 1)	All public transport	1.905 (7.1)	1.969 (6.9)	2.662 (7.6)	3.437 (6.2)	3.493 (6.7)
Heterogeneity around mean:						
Invehicle time * personal income	All public transport		0.000124 (2.6)			
Main mode fares * personal income	All public transport	0.00135 (3.8)	0.00078 (1.90)	0.00079 (1.8)		0.00090 (2.0)
Access bus fare * personal income	All public transport except existing bus		0.00143 (2.4)	0.00146 (2.3)	0.00160 (2.3)	0.00164 (2.4)
Heterogeneity around standard deviation:						
Invehicle time *gender	All public transport			0.4007 (4.3)	0.4195 (4.5)	0.4270 (4.6)
Main mode fares * gender	All public transport			0.6384 (4.4)	0.7049 (4.4)	0.6727 (4.2)
Error components for alternatives and nests of alternatives parameters:						
Standard deviation	New light rail, new heavy rail, new busway, existing busway				0.8659 (2.2)	1.010 (2.9)
Standard deviation	Existing bus and heavy rail				0.2068 (0.32)	0.0814 (0.13)
Standard deviation	Car				3.021 (4.0)	11.158 (2.3)
Heterogeneity around standard deviation of error components effect:						
Age of commuter	Car					−0.0366 (−2.3)
LL at convergence		−2464.3	−2451.7	−2442.1	−2435.9	−2428.7
Pseudo-R²		0.3101	0.3135	0.3161	0.3176	0.3195

Table 15.5 Mean and standard deviation of random parameter estimates for entire representation of each attribute from relatively simple to more complex models
Note: Except for ML1 which has a single parameter, the other models are complex representations of multiple parameters from Table 15.4.

Mean	invtpt	costpt	acwt	eggt	crpark	accbusf	waittb	acctb	crcost	crinvt	creggt
Ave ML1	-0.0640	-0.2505	-0.0699	-0.0145	-0.0340	-0.1067	-0.0882	-0.0756	-0.1653	-0.0727	-0.0814
Std Dev ML1	0.0245	0.1003	0.0278	0.0059	0.0139	0.0435	0.0359	0.0306	0.0670	0.0283	0.0329
Ave ML2	-0.0680	-0.2744	-0.0733	-0.0148	-0.0407	-0.1125	-0.0916	-0.0831	-0.1821	-0.0869	-0.0907
Std Dev ML2	0.0287	0.1385	0.0291	0.0060	0.0166	0.1014	0.0373	0.0336	0.0738	0.0367	0.0366
Ave ML3	-0.0788	-0.3581	-0.0819	-0.0258	-0.0558	-0.1241	-0.1071	-0.0859	-0.2789	-0.1146	-0.1297
Std Dev ML3	0.0391	0.2771	0.0269	0.0465	0.0075	0.1112	0.0664	0.0002	0.1868	0.0556	0.0034
Ave ML4	-0.0923	-0.4232	-0.0942	-0.0286	-0.0763	-0.1366	-0.1231	-0.1006	-0.3866	-0.0864	-0.1735
Std Dev ML4	0.0476	0.3374	0.0299	0.0489	0.0373	0.1157	0.0979	0.0007	0.3003	0.0016	0.0161
Ave ML5	-0.0923	-0.4152	-0.0941	-0.0348	-0.1151	-0.1340	-0.1137	-0.1001	-0.2678	-0.1140	-0.1524
Std Dev ML5	0.0473	0.3236	0.0317	0.0620	0.1165	0.1051	0.0837	0.0006	0.1445	0.0602	0.0061

Notes: invtpt = invehicle time for public transport (PT); costpt = public transport fares; acwt = access and wait time for light and heavy rail; eggt = egress time for PT; crpark = car parking cost; accbusf = access bus mode fare; waittb = wait time for bus and busway; acctb = access time for bus and busway; crcost = car running cost; crinvt = car invehicle time; creggt = egress time from car.

When we add in observed heterogeneity around the standard deviations of random parameters, we find that gender has a statistically significant influence on invehicle travel time and fare for all public transport modes. The positive sign on both travel time and fares suggests that male commuters are much more heterogenous in terms of the marginal disutility associated with public mode travel time and fares compared to females.

Adding in the error components for alternatives and nests of alternatives in model ML4 is a way of allowing for additional sources of preference heterogeneity that is not accounted for by the random parameterization and its associated decomposition.[10] Importantly, however, whereas the random parameters can account for differences across individuals and alternatives, the error components for alternatives and nests of alternatives focus is on the heterogeneity profile of additional unobserved effects associated with each alternative. The standard deviation parameters associated with each alternative capture this. Although each alternative can in theory have its own unique standard deviation parameter, grouping of the modes into car, existing bus and heavy rail, and the "remaining modes" produced the best model fit (the latter being the new modes and existing busway).[11] However only two of the standard deviation effects are statistically significant, with the car having the largest standard deviation parameter.

What this suggests is that there is a noticeable amount of preference heterogeneity associated with the car alternative that is not accounted for by the random parameters of car-specific attributes, compared to the public modes. The local environment in the North West of Sydney has a high incidence of car usage compared to public transport use, and so the heterogeneity across the population might be expected to be greater for the car segment. We have explored the possible reasons for the strong error components for alternatives and nests of alternatives for the car mode and its decomposition, to reveal sources of observed heterogeneity. We find that the age of the commuter has a statistically significant influence on preference heterogeneity. We could not find any significant effects for the public transport modes. All other effects being equal, the age effect suggests that as the age of the commuter increases, the standard deviation of the error components

---

[10] Ben Akiva *et al.* (2002) show that a variance term can be estimated for each of the alternatives due to the fact that in the kernel logit model "a perfect trade-off does not exist because of the slight difference between the Gumbel and Normal distributions." By contrast probit, probit kernel and extreme value logit require that one of the variances is constrained.

[11] Existing busway is in one sense a relatively new mode and it is interesting how its variance effect aligns closer to modes under consideration, all of which have their own infrastructure, with new busway being no more than a geographical extension of the existing busway.

Table 15.6 Direct elasticities (probability weighted)
Main mode invehicle time
Direct elasticities

Elasticity of invehicle time for	With respect to	ML1	ML2	ML3	ML4	ML5
New light rail	New light rail	−1.800	−1.778	−1.763	−1.781	−2.182
New heavy rail	New heavy rail	−1.759	−1.764	−1.764	−1.720	−1.909
New busway	New busway	−2.323	−2.311	−2.282	−1.366	−2.092
Existing bus	Existing bus	−1.829	−1.798	−1.771	−2.316	−3.079
Existing busway	Existing busway	−1.673	−1.676	−1.686	−2.379	−3.010
Existing heavy rail	Existing heavy rail	−1.486	−1.495	−1.500	−2.000	−2.639
Car	Car	−1.204	−1.214	−1.202	−1.129	−1.036

for alternatives and nests of alternatives decreases, leading to a reduction in preference heterogeneity from these unobserved effects.

To gain a richer understanding of the behavioral implications of increasingly more complex models as we progress from ML1 to ML5, we present the matrix of direct elasticities (Table 15.6).[12] The direct elasticities take into account every element of Equations (15.21)–(15.26) that contribute to the percentage change in the attribute and the percentage change in the choice probability. We have selected main mode invehicle time to illustrate the differences in behavioral response across the five models.[13] The absolute values for the direct elasticities should be treated with caution since they are derived from an uncalibrated[14] stated choice model. Their purpose is simply to establish the behavioral response implications of alternative ML specifications.

The mean estimates of the direct elasticities vary marginally as we move from the base model (ML1) through to accounting for heterogeneity in the mean and standard deviations of random parameters (ML3). However, when we introduce the error components for alternatives and nests of alternatives (ML4), the elasticities change substantially for four public modes, with three increasing (existing bus, busway, and heavy rail) and one decreasing (new busway). When we account for the commuter age effect (ML5), all public mode direct elasticities further increase. Although this empirical application is

---

[12] Model fit on its own is not the best indicator of the advantages of a more complex structure. Indeed, the improvements in fit may be quite small, but the findings in terms of elasticities can be quite different.
[13] Evidence for other attributes is similar and available on request.
[14] Elasticities are strictly meaningful, in a behavioral sense, after a model has been calibrated to reproduce the known population shares. SC models whose ASCs have not been calibrated after estimation to reproduce population (in contrast to sample) shares are related to sample shares only.

Table 15.7 Value of travel time savings ($/person hr.)

		ML1	ML2	ML3	ML4	ML5
Public transport invehicle time	Mean	18.63	18.52	18.29	18.53	18.47
	Standard deviation	4.47	4.34	4.32	4.51	4.46
	Minimum	−3.13	−0.94	−5.77	−6.50	−6.31
	Maximum	29.82	29.73	31.86	34.42	34.86
	Percent Negative	0.2174	0.1630	0.3804	0.4891	0.4348
Access walk time	Mean	18.18	18.05	17.96	18.10	18.23
	Standard deviation	0.69	0.63	0.67	0.62	0.72
	Minimum	14.01	14.20	13.92	14.14	13.74
	Maximum	20.28	19.99	20.02	19.95	20.63
	Percent Negative	0	0	0	0	0
Egress time	Mean	6.61	6.61	6.65	6.32	6.46
	Standard deviation	2.26	2.30	2.29	1.97	2.06
	Minimum	−8.71	−9.04	−9.04	−7.42	−7.78
	Maximum	15.15	15.38	15.53	13.83	14.21
	Percent Negative	1.739	1.739	1.739	1.630	1.684

a single assessment of the extended ML model, it does suggest that the introduction of the error components for alternatives and nests of alternatives and its decomposition has a (potentially) significant influence on the behavioral responsiveness of the model, in contrast to the refinements centered around the random parameters alone. The cross-elasticity evidence (available on request) tells a similar story, with some elasticities increasing and others decreasing as we include the error components for alternatives and nests of alternatives.

In addition to elasticities, we derived WTP distributions for each random parameter. We have selected three WTP estimates (Table 15.7) to illustrate the influence of model specification on the mean, standard deviation, range, and incidence of negative WTP for values of travel time savings (VTTS) for public transport invehicle time, access wait time, and egress time. The VTTS are based on the ratio of the parameter estimates associated with each individual observation as drawn from the distributions for the numerator attribute and the denominator attribute (the latter being the public transport main mode fare). The numerator varies in complexity in terms of deep parameterization as we move from ML1 through to ML5.

The evidence shows a very flat profile of values across the models, suggesting little if any behavioral enhancement when progressing from the relatively simple ("parsimonious") ML1 to the more complex ML5. We might not expect any significant difference between ML4 and ML5, since the heterogeneity around the standard deviation of the error components for alternatives and nest of alternatives is car-specific. There are, however, statistically significant effects attributed to the enhancements across ML1–4, which appear to "rearrange" the contributing effects without changing the overall absolute VTTS. What this suggests is that we might expect a different valuation for specific segments of the sample (associated with the personal income and gender), which averages out to a similar overall estimate for the entire sample across all models. This is an important finding, since it supports a position that there are systematic variations in tastes attributable to person-specific effects that, while not overly important when applying the findings to a sampled population as a whole, are important when evaluating the influence of policy on specific socio-economic segments.

15.9 Generalized mixed logit: accounting for scale and taste heterogeneity

There is growing interest in establishing a mechanism to account for scale heterogeneity across individuals (essentially, the variance of a variance term or the standard deviation of utility over different choice situations), in addition to the more commonly identified taste heterogeneity in ML models. A number of authors have proposed a model that recognizes the relationship between scale and taste heterogeneity, and investigated the behavioral implications of accounting for scale heterogeneity in contrast to a term in the utility function, itself.

In this chapter, we set out a general model that extends the ML model to explicitly account for scale heterogeneity in the presence of preference heterogeneity, and compare it with models that assume only scale heterogeneity (referred to as the scale heterogenous MNL model) and only preference heterogeneity.

Scale heterogeneity is a relatively old problem (see Louviere and Eagle 2006; Louviere and Swait 1994; Hensher *et al.* 1999 for the historical context), but it is only in recent years that we have seen a concerted effort to develop estimation capability within the family of logit models to account for it at the respondent level. Fiebig *et al.* (2010) formalized the "campaign" led by Louviere and his colleagues to recognize this claimed important source of variability that has been neglected by a focus on revealing preference heterogeneity (now aligned with the ML model). Papers by Breffle and Morey (2000), Hess and Rose (2012), and Hensher and Greene (2010) are other contributions.

The generalized ML model employed here builds on the specifications of the mixed logit developed in Train (2003), Hensher and Greene (2003), and Greene (2007), among others, and the "generalized multinomial logit model" proposed in Fiebig *et al.* (2010). Full details are given in Chapter 4, but we briefly summarize the main elements here as a prelude to the estimation of models.

Briefly, the mixed multinomial logit model (MMNL) is given in Equation (15.33):

$$\text{Prob}(choice_{it} = j | \mathbf{x}_{it,j}, \mathbf{z}_i, \mathbf{v}_i) = \frac{\exp(V_{it,j})}{\sum_{j=1}^{J_{it}} \exp(V_{it,j})}, \tag{15.33}$$

where

$$V_{it,j} = \boldsymbol{\beta}_i' \mathbf{x}_{it,j} \tag{15.34a}$$

$$\boldsymbol{\beta}_i = \boldsymbol{\beta} + \Delta \mathbf{z}_i + \Gamma \mathbf{v}_i, \tag{15.34b}$$

$\mathbf{x}_{it,j}$ = the K attributes of alternative j in choice situation t faced by individual i;
$\mathbf{z}_i$ = a set of M characteristics of individual i that influence the mean of the taste parameters; and
$\mathbf{v}_i$ = a vector of K random variables with zero means and known (usually unit) variances and zero covariances.

The multinomial choice model thus far embodies both observed and unobserved heterogeneity in the preference parameters of individual i. Observed heterogeneity is reflected in the term $\Delta \mathbf{z}_i$ while the unobserved heterogeneity is embodied in $\Gamma \mathbf{v}_i$. The structural parameters to be estimated are the constant vector, $\boldsymbol{\beta}$, the $K \times M$ matrix of parameters Δ, and the non-zero elements of the lower triangular Cholesky matrix, Γ.

A number of interesting special cases are straightforward modifications of the model. Specific non-random parameters are specified by rows of zeros in Γ. A pure random parameters MNL model results if $\Delta = \mathbf{0}$ and Γ is diagonal. The basic MNL model results[15] if $\Delta = \mathbf{0}$ and $\Gamma = \mathbf{0}$.

---

[15] One can, however, allow for deterministic taste heterogeneity via interaction terms with respondent-specific characteristics.

Scale heterogeneity across choices is easily accommodated in the model already considered by random alternative-specific constants. We accommodate both observed and unobserved heterogeneity in the model. Specification (15.35) is modified accordingly as Equation (15.35):

$$\beta_i = \sigma_i[\beta + \Delta z_i] + [\gamma + \sigma_i(1 - \gamma)] \, \Gamma v_i, \tag{15.35}$$

where $\sigma_i = \exp[\overline{\sigma} + \delta' h_i + \tau w_i]$, the individual-specific standard deviation
of the idiosyncratic error term;

h_i = a set of L characteristics of individual i that may overlap with z_i;

δ = parameters in the observed heterogeneity in the scale term;

w_i = the unobserved heterogeneity, standard normally distributed;

$\overline{\sigma}$ = a mean parameter in the variance;

τ = the coefficient on the unobserved scale heterogeneity;

γ = a weighting parameter that indicates how variance in residual preference heterogeneity varies with scale, with $0 \le \gamma \le 1$.

The weighting parameter, γ, is central to the generalized model. It controls the relative importance of the overall scaling of the utility function, σ_i, versus the scaling of the individual preference weights contained in the diagonal elements of Γ. Note that if σ_i equals one (i.e., $\tau = 0$), then γ falls out of the model and Equation (15.35) reverts back to the base case random parameters model. A non-zero γ cannot be estimated apart from Γ when σ_i equals one. When σ_i is not equal to one, then γ will spread the influence of the random components between overall scaling and the scaling of the preference weights. In addition to the useful special cases of the original mixed model, some useful special cases arise in this model. If $\gamma = 0$, then a scaled mixed logit model emerges, given in Equation (15.36):

$$\beta_i = \sigma_i[\beta + \Delta z_i + \Gamma v_i]. \tag{15.36a}$$

If, further, $\Gamma = 0$ and $\Delta = 0$, a "scaled multinomial logit model (SMNL)" model is implied:

$$\beta_i = \sigma_i \beta. \tag{15.36b}$$

This generalized mixed model also provides a straightforward method of reparameterizing the model to estimate the taste parameters in WTP space, which has become a behaviorally appealing alternative way of directly obtaining an estimate of WTP (see Train and Weeks 2005; Fosgerau 2007; Scarpa, Thiene, and Hensher 2008; Scarpa, Thiene, and Train 2008; Sonnier *et al.* 2007; Hensher and Greene 2011). If $\gamma = 0$, $\Delta = 0$ and the element of β

corresponding to the price or cost variable is normalized to 1.0 while a non-zero constant is moved outside the brackets, the following reparameterized model emerges:

$$\boldsymbol{\beta}_i = \sigma_i \beta_c \left[\left(\frac{1}{\beta_c} \right) (\boldsymbol{\beta} + \boldsymbol{\Gamma} \mathbf{v}_i) \right] = \sigma_i \beta_c \left[\begin{array}{c} 1 \\ \theta_c + \boldsymbol{\Gamma}_c \mathbf{v}_i \end{array} \right]. \tag{15.37}$$

In the simple MNL case ($\sigma_i = 1$, $\boldsymbol{\Gamma} = \mathbf{0}$), this is a one to one transformation of the parameters of the original model. Where the parameters are random, however, the transformation is no longer that simple. We, as well as Train and Week (2005), have found, in application, that this form of the transformed model produces generally much more reasonable estimates of WTP for individuals in the sample than the model in the original form, in which WTP is computed using ratios of parameters (Hensher and Greene 2011).[16]

The full model, in the unrestricted form or in any of the modifications, is estimated by maximum simulated likelihood (see Chapter 5). Fiebig *et al.* (2010) note two minor complications in estimation. First, the parameter $\overline{\sigma}$ in σ_i is not separately identified from the other parameters of the model. We will assume that the variance heterogeneity is normally distributed. Neglecting the observed heterogeneity (i.e., $\boldsymbol{\delta}'\mathbf{h}_i$) for the moment, it will follow from the general result for the expected value of a log-normal variable that $E[\sigma_i] = \exp(\overline{\sigma} + \tau^2/2)$. That is, $\sigma_i = \exp(\overline{\sigma})\exp(\tau w_i)$, where $w_i \sim N(0,1)$, so $E[\sigma_i] = \exp(\overline{\sigma})E[\exp(\tau w_i)] = \exp(\overline{\sigma})\exp(E[\tau w_i] + \frac{1}{2} \operatorname{Var}[\tau w_i]) = \exp(\overline{\sigma} + \tau^2/2)$. It follows that $\overline{\sigma}$ is not identified separately from τ, which appears nowhere else in the model. Some normalization is required. A natural normalization would be to set $\overline{\sigma} = 0$. However, it is more convenient to normalize σ_i so that $E[\sigma_i^2] = 1$, by setting $\overline{\sigma} = -\tau^2/2$ instead of 0.

A second complication concerns the variation in σ_i during the simulations. The log-normal distribution implied by $\exp(-\tau^2/2 + \tau w_i)$ can produce extremely large draws and lead to overflows and instability of the estimator. To accommodate this concern, one might truncate the standard normal distribution of w_i at -1.96 and $+1.96$. In contrast to Fiebig *et al.*, who propose an acceptance/rejection method for the random draws, Nlogit uses a one-draw method, $w_{ir} = \Phi^{-1}[.025 + .95 U_{ir}]$, where $\Phi^{-1}(t)$ is the inverse of the standard normal *cdf* and U_{ir}

---

[16] The paper by Hensher and Greene (2011), like Train and Weeks (2005), supports the WTP space framework for estimating WTP distributions given that the evidence on the range is behaviorally more plausible, despite the overall goodness of fit being inferior to the utility space specifications.

is a random draw from the standard uniform population.[17] This will maintain the smoothness of the estimator in the random draws. The acceptance/rejection approach requires, on average, 1/.95 draws to obtain an acceptable draw, while the inverse probability approach always requires exactly 1.

Finally, in order to impose the limits on γ (Equation (15.35)), γ is reparameterized in terms of α, where $\gamma = \exp(\alpha)/[1 + \exp(\alpha)]$ and α is unrestricted. Likewise, to ensure $\tau \geq 0$, the model is fit in terms of λ, where $\tau = \exp(\lambda)$ and λ is unrestricted. Restricted versions in which it is desired to restrict $\gamma = 1$ or 0 and/or $\tau = 0$ are imposed directly during the estimation, rather than using extreme values of the underlying parameters, as in previous studies. Thus, in estimation, the restriction $\gamma = 0$ is imposed directly, rather than using, for example, $\alpha = -10.0$ or some other large value.

Combining all terms, the simulated LL function for the sample of data is shown in Equation (15.38):

$$\log L = \sum_{i=1}^{N} \log \left\{ \frac{1}{R} \sum_{r=1}^{R} \prod_{t=1}^{T_i} \prod_{j=1}^{J_{it}} P(j, \mathbf{X}_{it}, \boldsymbol{\beta}_{ir})^{d_{it,j}} \right\}, \tag{15.38}$$

where

$\boldsymbol{\beta}_{ir} = \sigma_{ir}[\boldsymbol{\beta} + \Delta \mathbf{z}_i] + [\gamma + \sigma_{ir}(1 - \gamma)]\, \boldsymbol{\Gamma} \mathbf{v}_{ir};$

$\sigma_{ir} = \exp[-\tau^2/2 + \boldsymbol{\delta}'\mathbf{h}_i + \tau w_{ir}];$

v_{ir} and w_{ir} = the R simulated draws on v_i and w_i;

$d_{itj} = 1$ if individual i makes choice j in choice situation t and 0 otherwise, and

$$P(j, \mathbf{X}_{it}, \boldsymbol{\beta}_{ir}) = \frac{\exp(\mathbf{x}'_{it,j}\boldsymbol{\beta}_{ir})}{\sum_{j=1}^{J_{it}}\exp(\mathbf{x}'_{it,j}\boldsymbol{\beta}_{ir})}. \tag{15.39}$$

15.10 GMX model in utility and WTP space

Given the popular interest in establishing estimates of WTP, we assume that the utility expression is separable in price, p_{ijt}, and other non-price attributes, $\mathbf{x}_{ijt}$, so that utility can be written:

---

[17] The default in Nlogit is to use $-\tau^2/2$ to center the draws on σ_i. However, in Nlogit version 5, we have removed the truncation device (forcing e(i) to lie in [−2,+2]) and instead use the normal draws without truncation. To use the new device, add ;**CENTER** to the GMXLogit command. To get a good comparison, we recommend using Halton draws for the simulation. Then, the two approaches use the same set of draws.

$$U_{ijt} = \alpha_j + \lambda_i p_{ijt} + \beta_i' \mathbf{x}_{itj} + \delta' \mathbf{z}_{ijt} + \varepsilon_{ijt}. \qquad (15.40)$$

With assumptions about the distributions of the random parameters, (λ_i, β_i), Equation (15.40) is a ML model or a generalized mixed logit model, defined "in preference space." See, e.g., Thiene and Scarpa (2009); Train and Weeks (2005); Sonnier *et al.* (2007).

It is possible to specify Equation (15.40) as utility in WTP space so that a particular set of parameters can be obtained that are direct estimates of the marginal rates of substitution between pairs of observed attributes. We rewrite Equation (15.40) as:

$$\begin{aligned} U_{ijt} &= \alpha_j + \lambda_i [p_{ijt} + (1/\lambda_i)\beta_i' \mathbf{x}_{ijt}] + \delta' \mathbf{z}_{ijt} + \varepsilon_{ijt} \\ &= \alpha_j + \lambda_i [p_{ijt} + \theta_i' \mathbf{x}_{ijt}] + \delta' \mathbf{z}_{ijt} + \varepsilon_{ijt} \end{aligned} \qquad (15.41)$$

The resulting parameter, λ_i, becomes the normalizing constant in the WTP space representation. Thus, Equation (15.41) is the WTP space form of the model in Equation (15.40).

To show the results associated with estimating various versions of the generalized MMNL in utility and WTP space, we continue to use the same data set as above. We model the parameters in preference space as $\lambda_i = (\lambda_p + \sigma_p w_i)$ and the K elements of β_i as $\beta_{ik} = (\beta_k + \sigma_k v_{ik})$, where the $K + 1$ random parameters are freely correlated. In the preference space representation, as suggested, e.g., in Thiene and Scarpa (2009), we have constrained λ_i to have one sign by writing $\lambda_i = \lambda_p \exp(\lambda_0 + \tau w_i)$. The sign of the full expression is not imposed *a priori*, but the estimate of λ is negative as expected. As before, $(w_i, \mathbf{v}_i)$ are $K + 1$ freely correlated random variables. Since the scale of λ_i is provided by λ_p, a separate λ_0 is not estimable. Note that we may write λ_i as $\exp(\log \lambda_p + \lambda_0 + \tau w_i)$, so that different combinations of λ_p and λ_0 produce the same λ_i. To remove the indeterminacy, we follow Fiebig *et al.*'s suggestion, and (with a standard normality assumption for w_i) set $\lambda_0 = -\tau^2/2$, so that $\lambda_i = \lambda_p \exp(-\tau^2/2 + \tau w_i)$ and, consequently, $E[\lambda_i] = \lambda_p$.

Equations (15.40) and (15.41) are both special cases of the Greene and Hensher (2011) implementation of Fiebig *et al.*'s (2010) model. The model in WTP space in Equation (15.41) is obtained by setting $\gamma = 0$, the row in Γ corresponding to λ_p to zero, the coefficient λ_p on p_{ijt} in β equal to 1, and relaxing the restriction $\lambda_0 = -\tau^2/2$. Thus, the model in WTP space is estimated by using a form of the generalized mixed logit model.

The models of interest are summarized in Table 15.8 (p. 691). Model 1 (M1) is the base random parameter model in preference space. Model 2 (M2) is the equivalent model in WTP space,[18] Model 3 (M3) is the generalized random parameter or ML model in preference space that accounts for taste and scale heterogeneity, and Model M1con is Model 1 with a constrained triangular distribution for the random parameters. All random parameters in Models 1 to 3 are specified with unconstrained triangular distributions and correlation among the set of random parameters.

The Nlogit command streams are given below and we summarize the results in Table 15.8 for ease of comparative assessment. We have used the command **;userp**, which is a request to use the standard ML model parameter estimates as starting values in contrast to the default MNL starting values. We find that this not only speeds up estimation, but that it helps in securing a global maximum. We have added **;pds** to recognize that there are 16 choice sets per respondent and hence the panel nature of the data is accounted for.

Model 1: utility space: RPL unconstrained distributions and correlated attributes

```
sample;all$
reject;dremove=1$
reject;ttype#1$
reject;altij=-999$
nlogit
    ;lhs=resp1,cset,Altij
    ;choices=NLRail,NHRail,NBway,Bus,Bway,Train,Car
    ;pwt
    ;rpl
    ;pds=16;halton;pts=500
    ;fcn=invt(t),waitt(t), acct(t),eggt(t),cost(t)
    ;corr;par
    ;model:
    U(NLRail)= NLRAsc+cost*tcost+invt*InvTime+waitt*waitt2+accT*acctim
+accbusf*accbusf
        + ptinc*pinc + ptgend*gender + NLRinsde*inside /
    U(NHRail)= TNAsc+cost*Tcost+invt*InvTime+waitT*WaitT+accT*acctim
+eggT*egresst
            +accbusf*accbusf+ ptinc*pinc + ptgend*gender +
NHRinsde*inside /
    U(NBway)= NBWAsc +cost*Tcost+invt*InvTime+waitT*WaitT+accT*acctim
+eggT*egress
            +accbusf*accbusf+ ptinc*pinc + ptgend*gender /
    U(Bus)=   BSAsc+cost*frunCost+invt*InvTime+waitT*WaitT+accT*acctim
+eggT*egresst
        + ptinc*pinc + ptgend*gender/
```

---

[18] The parameter on cost in Model 2 is implicitly $-0.2956 \cdot \exp(-0.4896^2 + 0.4896 \cdot w(i))$. This is also equal to $-\exp(\log(0.2956) - 0.4896^2 + 0.4896w(i)) = -\exp(-1.4585 + 0.4896 \cdot w(i))$.

```
    U(Bway)=    BWAsc+cost*Tcost+invt*InvTime+waitT*WaitT+accT*acctim
+eggT*egresst
            + accbusf*accbusf+ ptinc*pinc + ptgend*gender /
    U(Train)=  TNAsc+cost*tcost+invt*InvTime+waitT*WaitT+accT*acctim +
eggT*egresst
            + accbusf*accbusf+ ptinc*pinc + ptgend*gender /
    U(Car)=    cost*costs+invt*InvTime+CRpark*parkcost+CReggT*egresst $
Normal exit: 53 iterations. Status=0. F=    2043.845
+------------------------------------------------------------+
| Random Parameters Logit Model                              |
| Dependent variable                     RESP1               |
| Log likelihood function        -2043.845                   |
| Restricted log likelihood      -3580.475                   |
| Chi squared [  32 d.f.]         3073.26014                 |
| Significance level                .0000000                 |
| McFadden Pseudo R-squared          .4291694                |
| Estimation based on N =    1840, K =   32                  |
| AIC =      2.2564  Bayes IC =      2.3523                  |
| AICf.s. =      2.2570  HQIC =      2.2917                  |
| Model estimated: Jun 14, 2009, 11:01:27                    |
| Constants only.  Must be computed directly.                |
|               Use NLOGIT ;...;  RHS=ONE $                  |
| At start values  -2480.8579   .17615 *******               |
| Response data are given as ind. choice.                    |
+------------------------------------------------------------+
+------------------------------------------------------------+
| Notes No coefficients=> P(i,j)=1/J(i).                     |
|       Constants only => P(i,j) uses ASCs                   |
|         only. N(j)/N if fixed choice set.                  |
|         N(j) = total sample frequency for j                |
|         N    = total sample frequency.                     |
|       These 2 models are simple MNL models.                |
|       R-sqrd = 1 - LogL(model)/logL(other)                 |
|       RsqAdj=1-[nJ/(nJ-nparm)]*(1-R-sqrd)                  |
|         nJ   = sum over i, choice set sizes                |
+------------------------------------------------------------+
+------------------------------------------------------------+
| Random Parameters Logit Model                              |
| Replications for simulated probs. = 500                    |
| Halton sequences used for simulations                      |
| ---------------------------------------------              |
| RPL model with panel has  115 groups.                      |
| Fixed number of obsrvs./group=       16                    |
| Random parameters model was specified                      |
| ---------------------------------------------              |
| RPL model has correlated parameters                        |
| Number of obs.= 1840, skipped   0 bad obs.                 |
+------------------------------------------------------------+
```

Variable	Coefficient	Standard Error	b/St.Er.	P[|Z|>z]
+---------+Random parameters in utility functions				
INVT	-.07728***	.00550	-14.059	.0000
WAITT	-.03579	.02230	-1.605	.1085
ACCT	-.10950***	.01344	-8.145	.0000
EGGT	-.06294***	.01714	-3.673	.0002
COST	-.34306***	.03570	-9.609	.0000
+---------+Nonrandom parameters in utility functions				
NLRASC	1.14253***	.42031	2.718	.0066
ACCBUSF	-.06420	.04065	-1.579	.1143
PTINC	-.00812**	.00359	-2.258	.0239
PTGEND	1.50531***	.28253	5.328	.0000
NLRINSDE	-1.45966**	.60315	-2.420	.0155
TNASC	1.31882***	.33094	3.985	.0001
NHRINSDE	-3.08258***	.82333	-3.744	.0002
NBWASC	.66456*	.35718	1.861	.0628
BSASC	.78874**	.31056	2.540	.0111
BWASC	.77814**	.32520	2.393	.0167
CRPARK	-.04282***	.01191	-3.595	.0003
CREGGT	-.09378***	.02168	-4.326	.0000
+---------+Diagonal values in Cholesky matrix, L.				
TsINVT	.11099***	.00890	12.471	.0000
TsWAITT	.26302***	.03238	8.123	.0000
TsACCT	.20772***	.03179	6.535	.0000
TsEGGT	.27187***	.03497	7.774	.0000
TsCOST	.51315***	.07388	6.945	.0000
+---------+Below diagonal values in L matrix. V = L*Lt				
WAIT:INV	-.21696***	.03767	-5.759	.0000
ACCT:INV	-.04982	.03142	-1.585	.1129
ACCT:WAI	-.09559***	.02858	-3.345	.0008
EGGT:INV	-.12696***	.03412	-3.721	.0002
EGGT:WAI	-.16096***	.02775	-5.800	.0000
EGGT:ACC	-.06111**	.02515	-2.430	.0151
COST:INV	.44032***	.09948	4.426	.0000
COST:WAI	.23525***	.06574	3.579	.0003
COST:ACC	-.14034*	.07950	-1.765	.0775
COST:EGG	.23593***	.08671	2.721	.0065
+---------+Standard deviations of parameter distributions				
sdINVT	.11099***	.00890	12.471	.0000
sdWAITT	.34095***	.04140	8.236	.0000
sdACCT	.23403***	.03314	7.061	.0000
sdEGGT	.34594***	.02574	13.440	.0000
sdCOST	.76675***	.07299	10.505	.0000

Correlation Matrix for Random Parameters

Matrix COR.MAT. has 5 rows and 5 columns.

INVT	WAITT	ACCT	EGGT	COST
INVT	1.00000	-.63633	-.21287	-.36699	.57427
WAITT	-.63633	1.00000	-.17965	-.12540	-.12874
ACCT	-.21287	-.17965	1.00000	.11139	-.41003
EGGT	-.36699	-.12540	.11139	1.00000	-.07935
COST	.57427	-.12874	-.41003	-.07935	1.00000

Covariance Matrix for Random Parameters

Matrix COV.MAT. has 5 rows and 5 columns.

INVT	WAITT	ACCT	EGGT	COST
INVT	.01232	-.02408	-.00553	-.01409	.04887
WAITT	-.02408	.11625	-.01433	-.01479	-.03366
ACCT	-.00553	-.01433	.05477	.00902	-.07358
EGGT	-.01409	-.01479	.00902	.11968	-.02105
COST	.04887	-.03366	-.07358	-.02105	.58791

Cholesky Matrix for Random Parameters

Matrix Cholesky has 5 rows and 5 columns.

INVT	WAITT	ACCT	EGGT	COST
INVT	.11099	.0000000D+00	.0000000D+00	.0000000D+00	.0000000D+00
WAITT	-.21696	.26302	.0000000D+00	.0000000D+00	.0000000D+00
ACCT	-.04982	-.09559	.20772	.0000000D+00	.0000000D+00
EGGT	-.12696	-.16096	-.06111	.27187	.0000000D+00
COST	.44032	.23525	-.14034	.23593	.51315

Model 2: WTP space: unconstrained distributions and correlated attributes

(S-MNL specification)
Note: in wtp space the issue of sign is not an issue any more

```
GMXlogit;userp
;lhs=resp1,cset,Altij
;choices=NLRail,NHRail,NBway,Bus,Bway,Train,Car
;pwt
;pds=16;halton;pts=500
;fcn=invt(t),waitt(t), acct(t),eggt(t),cost(*c)
```

```
    ;corr;par
    ;gamma=[0]
    ;tau=0.3
    ;model:
    U(NLRail)= NLRAsc+cost*tcost+invt*InvTime+waitt*waitt2+accT*acctim
+accbusf*accbusf
        + ptinc*pinc + ptgend*gender + NLRinsde*inside /
    U(NHRail)= TNAsc+cost*Tcost+invt*InvTime+waitT*WaitT+accT*acctim
+eggT*egresst
            +accbusf*accbusf+ ptinc*pinc + ptgend*gender +
NHRinsde*inside /
    U(NBway)=  NBWAsc +cost*Tcost+invt*InvTime+waitT*WaitT+accT*acctim
+eggT*egress
            +accbusf*accbusf+ ptinc*pinc + ptgend*gender /
    U(Bus)=    BSAsc+cost*frunCost+invt*InvTime+waitT*WaitT+accT*acctim
+eggT*egresst
        + ptinc*pinc + ptgend*gender/
    U(Bway)=   BWAsc+cost*Tcost+invt*InvTime+waitT*WaitT+accT*acctim
+eggT*egresst
            + accbusf*accbusf+ ptinc*pinc + ptgend*gender /
    U(Train)= TNAsc+cost*tcost+invt*InvTime+waitT*WaitT+accT*acctim +
eggT*egresst
            + accbusf*accbusf+ ptinc*pinc + ptgend*gender /
    U(Car)=    cost*costs+invt*InvTime+CRpark*parkcost+CReggT*egresst $
+-------------------------------------------------------------+
| Generalized Mixed (RP) Logit Model                          |
| Dependent variable                   RESP1                  |
| Log likelihood function         -2108.366                   |
| Restricted log likelihood       -3580.475                   |
| Chi squared [  28 d.f.]         2944.21786                  |
| Significance level                 .0000000                 |
| McFadden Pseudo R-squared          .4111491                 |
| Estimation based on N =    1840, K =  28                    |
| AIC =      2.3221  Bayes IC =     2.4061                     |
| AICf.s. =     2.3226  HQIC =      2.3531                     |
| Model estimated: Jun 13, 2009, 15:05:03                     |
| Constants only.  Must be computed directly.                 |
|                Use NLOGIT ;...;  RHS=ONE $                   |
| At start values -3237.9705   .34886 *******                 |
| Response data are given as ind. choice.                     |
+-------------------------------------------------------------+
+-------------------------------------------------------------+
| Notes No coefficients=> P(i,j)=1/J(i).                      |
|       Constants only => P(i,j) uses ASCs                    |
|          only. N(j)/N if fixed choice set.                  |
|          N(j) = total sample frequency for j                |
|          N    = total sample frequency.                     |
|       These 2 models are simple MNL models.                 |
|       R-sqrd = 1 - LogL(model)/logL(other)                  |
```

```
|          RsqAdj=1-[nJ/(nJ-nparm)]*(1-R-sqrd)       |
|             nJ    = sum over i, choice set sizes   |
+----------------------------------------------------------+
+----------------------------------------------------------+
| Generalized Mixed (RP) Logit Model                 |
| Replications for simulated probs. = 500            |
| Halton sequences used for simulations              |
| -------------------------------------------------- |
| RPL model with panel has  115 groups.              |
| Fixed number of obsrvs./group=        16           |
| Random parameters model was specified              |
| -------------------------------------------------- |
| RPL model has correlated parameters                |
| Hessian was not PD. Using BHHH estimator.          |
| Number of obs.= 1840, skipped   0 bad obs.         |
+----------------------------------------------------------+
```

Variable	Coefficient	Standard Error	b/St.Er.	P[|Z|>z]
Random parameters in utility functions					
INVT	.25713***	.02822	9.111	.0000
WAITT	.17083**	.08294	2.060	.0394
ACCT	.45530***	.05277	8.628	.0000
EGGT	.29543***	.06887	4.290	.0000
COST	1.00000	......(Fixed Parameter).......		
Nonrandom parameters in utility functions					
NLRASC	1.14276***	.29200	3.914	.0001
ACCBUSF	-.06004*	.03448	-1.741	.0817
PTINC	-.01312***	.00329	-3.989	.0001
PTGEND	1.56461***	.20692	7.562	.0000
NLRINSDE	-1.28832*	.72162	-1.785	.0742
TNASC	1.55597***	.21769	7.148	.0000
NHRINSDE	-2.72308***	.77589	-3.510	.0004
NBWASC	.81411***	.24155	3.370	.0008
BSASC	1.10003***	.20211	5.443	.0000
BWASC	.97897***	.21523	4.548	.0000
CRPARK	-.04267***	.01220	-3.496	.0005
CREGGT	-.12115***	.01835	-6.601	.0000
Diagonal values in Cholesky matrix, L.					
TsINVT	.42316***	.05053	8.375	.0000
TsWAITT	1.01342***	.17256	5.873	.0000
TsACCT	.77892***	.09478	8.218	.0000
TsEGGT	.68827***	.14192	4.850	.0000
CsCOST	.000	......(Fixed Parameter).......		
Below diagonal values in L matrix. V = L*Lt					
WAIT:INV	.67315***	.16945	3.973	.0001
ACCT:INV	.30035**	.14761	2.035	.0419
ACCT:WAI	.54367***	.16706	3.254	.0011
EGGT:INV	.65431***	.15691	4.170	.0000

```
|EGGT:WAI|      .62696***           .19440          3.225    .0013 |
|EGGT:ACC|      .68610***           .14763          4.647    .0000 |
|COST:INV|        .000           .....(Fixed Parameter)....... |
|COST:WAI|        .000           .....(Fixed Parameter)....... |
|COST:ACC|        .000           .....(Fixed Parameter)....... |
|COST:EGG|        .000           .....(Fixed Parameter)....... |
+----------+Variance parameter tau in GMX scale parameter     |
|TauScale|      .48963***           .06938          7.058    .0000 |
+----------+Weighting parameter gamma in GMX model             |
|GammaMXL|        .000           .....(Fixed Parameter)....... |
+----------+Coefficient on COST    in WTP space form           |
|Beta0WTP|      -.29564***          .02380        -12.420    .0000 |
+----------+ Sample Mean     Sample Std.Dev.                   |
|Sigma(i)|      .96627**            .41441          2.332    .0197 |
+----------+Standard deviations of parameter distributions     |
|sdINVT  |      .42316***           .05053          8.375    .0000 |
|sdWAITT |     1.21661***           .18074          6.731    .0000 |
|sdACCT  |      .99625***           .12831          7.764    .0000 |
|sdEGGT  |     1.32878***           .13766          9.652    .0000 |
|sdCOST  |        .000           .....(Fixed Parameter)....... |
+----------+----------------------------------------------------------+
```

Correlation Matrix for Random Parameters
Matrix COR.MAT. has   5 rows and   5 columns.

	INVT	WAITT	ACCT	EGGT	COST
INVT	1.00000	.55330	.30148	.49242	.0000000D+00
WAITT	.55330	1.00000	.62139	.66548	.0000000D+00
ACCT	.30148	.62139	1.00000	.80965	.0000000D+00
EGGT	.49242	.66548	.80965	1.00000	.0000000D+00
COST	.0000000D+00	.0000000D+00	.0000000D+00	.0000000D+00	.0000000D+00

Covariance Matrix for Random Parameters
Matrix COV.MAT. has   5 rows and   5 columns.

	INVT	WAITT	ACCT	EGGT	COST
INVT	.17906	.28485	.12710	.27688	.0000000D+00
WAITT	.28485	1.48015	.75315	1.07582	.0000000D+00
ACCT	.12710	.75315	.99251	1.07180	.0000000D+00
EGGT	.27688	1.07582	1.07180	1.76565	.0000000D+00
COST	.0000000D+00	.0000000D+00	.0000000D+00	.0000000D+00	.0000000D+00

Cholesky Matrix for Random Parameters
Matrix Cholesky has   5 rows and   5 columns.

	INVT	WAITT	ACCT	EGGT	COST
INVT	.42316	.0000000D+00	.0000000D+00	.0000000D+00	.0000000D+00
WAITT	.67315	1.01342	.0000000D+00	.0000000D+00	.0000000D+00
ACCT	.30035	.54367	.77892	.0000000D+00	.0000000D+00
EGGT	.65431	.62696	.68610	.68827	.0000000D+00
COST	.0000000D+00	.0000000D+00	.0000000D+00	.0000000D+00	.0000000D+00

Model 3 U-specification: GMX unconstrained Ts with scale and taste heterogeneity and correlated attributes

```
sample;all$
reject;dremove=1$
reject;ttype#1$
reject;altij=-999$
GMXlogit;userp
;lhs=resp1,cset,Altij
;choices=NLRail,NHRail,NBway,Bus,Bway,Train,Car
;effects:InvTime(NLRail,NHRail,NBway,Bus,Bway,Train,Car)
;pwt
;gmx
;pds=16;halton;pts=250
;fcn=invt(t),waitt(t), acct(t),eggt(t),cost(t)
;tau=0.1   ? starting values other than 0.1 (default)
;gamma=0.1 ? starting values other than 0.1 (default)
;corr;par
```

```
+---------------------------------------------------------------+
| Generalized Mixed (RP) Logit Model                            |
| Dependent variable               RESP1                        |
| Log likelihood function        -2089.330                      |
| Restricted log likelihood      -3580.475                      |
| Chi squared [  36 d.f.]        2982.28859                     |
| Significance level               .0000000                     |
| McFadden Pseudo R-squared        .4164655                     |
| Estimation based on N =   1840, K =  36                       |
| AIC =     2.3101  Bayes IC =     2.4181                       |
| AICf.s. =     2.3109  HQIC =     2.3499                        |
| Model estimated: Jun 16, 2009, 10:25:02                       |
| Constants only.  Must be computed directly.                   |
|               Use NLOGIT ;...;  RHS=ONE $                      |
| At start values  -2425.3400  .13854 *******                   |
| Response data are given as ind. choice.                       |
+---------------------------------------------------------------+
```

```
+---------------------------------------------------------------+
| Notes No coefficients=> P(i,j)=1/J(i).                        |
|       Constants only => P(i,j) uses ASCs                      |
|         only. N(j)/N if fixed choice set.                     |
|         N(j) = total sample frequency for j                   |
|         N   = total sample frequency.                         |
|       These 2 models are simple MNL models.                   |
|       R-sqrd = 1 - LogL(model)/logL(other)                    |
|       RsqAdj=1- [nJ/(nJ-nparm)]*(1-R-sqrd)                     |
|         nJ   = sum over i, choice set sizes                   |
+---------------------------------------------------------------+
```

```
+----------------------------------------------------------------+
| Generalized Mixed (RP) Logit Model                             |
| Replications for simulated probs. = 250                        |
| Halton sequences used for simulations                          |
| ------------------------------------------------------         |
| RPL model with panel has  115 groups.                          |
| Fixed number of obsrvs./group=       16                        |
| Random parameters model was specified                          |
| ------------------------------------------------------         |
| RPL model has correlated parameters                            |
| Hessian was not PD. Using BHHH estimator.                      |
| Number of obs.= 1840, skipped   0 bad obs.                     |
+----------------------------------------------------------------+
```

Variable	Coefficient	Standard Error	b/St.Er.	P[|Z|>z]
Random parameters in utility functions				
INVT	-.07039***	.00748	-9.411	.0000
WAITT	-.05786**	.02857	-2.025	.0428
ACCT	-.11308***	.01764	-6.411	.0000
EGGT	-.07669***	.02188	-3.506	.0005
COST	-.32694***	.03399	-9.620	.0000
Nonrandom parameters in utility functions				
NLRASC	3.24088***	.51691	6.270	.0000
ACCBUSF	-.03795	.03658	-1.038	.2995
PTINC	-.01704***	.00372	-4.575	.0000
PTGEND	1.39774***	.23413	5.970	.0000
NLRINSDE	-1.03616	.93304	-1.111	.2668
TNASC	3.32005***	.46723	7.106	.0000
NHRINSDE	-2.86157***	1.05769	-2.705	.0068
NBWASC	2.63730***	.47806	5.517	.0000
BSASC	2.84240***	.44565	6.378	.0000
BWASC	2.79413***	.46306	6.034	.0000
CRCOST	-.16531***	.05666	-2.918	.0035
CRINVT	-.04816***	.00699	-6.893	.0000
CRPARK	-.06677***	.01818	-3.672	.0002
CREGGT	-.11379***	.01901	-5.985	.0000
Diagonal values in Cholesky matrix, L.				
TsINVT	.09863***	.01225	8.053	.0000
TsWAITT	.35631***	.04133	8.622	.0000
TsACCT	.19250***	.04823	3.991	.0001
TsEGGT	.23144***	.03911	5.917	.0000
TsCOST	.10869	.10289	1.056	.2908
Below diagonal values in L matrix. V = L*Lt				
WAIT:INV	-.27949***	.05096	-5.485	.0000
ACCT:INV	-.11256***	.04108	-2.740	.0061
ACCT:WAI	.12671***	.04650	2.725	.0064
EGGT:INV	-.18610***	.04405	-4.224	.0000
EGGT:WAI	.18536***	.04547	4.077	.0000
EGGT:ACC	-.09697**	.03838	-2.527	.0115

```
|COST:INV|    -.06330              .13029         -.486    .6271 |
|COST:WAI|    -.48692***           .09523        -5.113    .0000 |
|COST:ACC|    -.43282***           .08140        -5.317    .0000 |
|COST:EGG|    -.06688              .08079         -.828    .4078 |
+-----------+Variance parameter tau in GMX scale parameter    |
|TauScale|     .41034***           .03846        10.668    .0000 |
+-----------+Weighting parameter gamma in GMX model            |
|GammaMXL|     .00150              .20743          .007    .9942 |
+-----------+ Sample Mean     Sample Std.Dev.                  |
|Sigma(i)|     .97728***           .34994         2.793    .0052 |
+-----------+Standard deviations of parameter distributions    |
|sdINVT  |     .09863***           .01225         8.053    .0000 |
|sdWAITT |     .45285***           .04504        10.055    .0000 |
|sdACCT  |     .25648***           .04762         5.386    .0000 |
|sdEGGT  |     .36326***           .04182         8.686    .0000 |
|sdCOST  |     .66687***           .08705         7.661    .0000 |
```

Correlation Matrix for Random Parameters

Matrix COR.MAT. has 5 rows and 5 columns.

	INVT	WAITT	ACCT	EGGT	COST
INVT	1.00000	-.61718	-.43887	-.51230	-.09493
WAITT	-.61718	1.00000	.65957	.71766	-.51591
ACCT	-.43887	.65957	1.00000	.27655	-.80619
EGGT	-.51230	.71766	.27655	1.00000	-.21458
COST	-.09493	-.51591	-.80619	-.21458	1.00000

Covariance Matrix for Random Parameters

Matrix COV.MAT. has 5 rows and 5 columns.

	INVT	WAITT	ACCT	EGGT	COST
INVT	.00973	-.02757	-.01110	-.01836	-.00624
WAITT	-.02757	.20507	.07661	.11806	-.15580
ACCT	-.01110	.07661	.06578	.02577	-.13789
EGGT	-.01836	.11806	.02577	.13196	-.05198
COST	-.00624	-.15580	-.13789	-.05198	.44472

Cholesky Matrix for Random Parameters

Matrix Cholesky has 5 rows and 5 columns.

	INVT	WAITT	ACCT	EGGT	COST
INVT	.09863	.0000000D+00	.0000000D+00	.0000000D+00	.0000000D+00
WAITT	-.27949	.35631	.0000000D+00	.0000000D+00	.0000000D+00
ACCT	-.11256	.12671	.19250	.0000000D+00	.0000000D+00
EGGT	-.18610	.18536	-.09697	.23144	.0000000D+00
COST	-.06330	-.48692	-.43282	-.06688	.10869

Model 4: RPL t,1

```
nlogit
;lhs=resp1,cset,Altij
;choices=NLRail,NHRail,NBway,Bus,Bway,Train,Car
;pwt
;rpl
;pds=16;halton;pts=500
;fcn=invt(t,1),waitt(t,1), acct(t,1),eggt(t,1),cost(t,1)
;par
;model:
U(NLRail)= NLRAsc+cost*tcost+invt*InvTime+waitt*waitt2+accT*acctim
+accbusf*accbusf
       + ptinc*pinc + ptgend*gender + NLRinsde*inside /
U(NHRail)= TNAsc+cost*Tcost+invt*InvTime+waitT*WaitT+accT*acctim
+eggT*egresst
           +accbusf*accbusf+ ptinc*pinc + ptgend*gender +
NHRinsde*inside /
U(NBway)=  NBWAsc +cost*Tcost+invt*InvTime+waitT*WaitT+accT*acctim
+eggT*egress
           +accbusf*accbusf+ ptinc*pinc + ptgend*gender /
U(Bus)=    BSAsc+cost*frunCost+invt*InvTime+waitT*WaitT+accT*acctim
+eggT*egresst
       + ptinc*pinc + ptgend*gender/
U(Bway)=   BWAsc+cost*Tcost+invt*InvTime+waitT*WaitT+accT*acctim
+eggT*egresst
           + accbusf*accbusf+ ptinc*pinc + ptgend*gender /
U(Train)=  TNAsc+cost*tcost+invt*InvTime+waitT*WaitT+accT*acctim +
eggT*egresst
           + accbusf*accbusf+ ptinc*pinc + ptgend*gender /
U(Car)=    cost*costs+invt*InvTime+CRpark*parkcost+CReggT*egresst $
```

```
+------------------------------------------------------------+
| Random Parameters Logit Model                              |
| Dependent variable                    RESP1                |
| Log likelihood function          -2257.958                 |
| Restricted log likelihood        -3580.475                 |
| Chi squared [  17 d.f.]          2645.03271                |
| Significance level                 .0000000                |
| McFadden Pseudo R-squared          .3693690                |
| Estimation based on N =    1840, K =   17                  |
| AIC =     2.4728  Bayes IC =     2.5238                     |
| AICf.s. =     2.4730  HQIC =     2.4916                     |
| Model estimated: Jun 14, 2009, 18:04:16                    |
| Constants only.  Must be computed directly.                |
|               Use NLOGIT ;...;  RHS=ONE $                   |
| At start values  -2332.5131  .03196 *******                |
| Response data are given as ind. choice.                    |
+------------------------------------------------------------+
```

```
+----------------------------------------------------------------+
| Notes No coefficients=> P(i,j)=1/J(i).                         |
|       Constants only => P(i,j) uses ASCs                      |
|          only. N(j)/N if fixed choice set.                    |
|          N(j) = total sample frequency for j |
|          N    = total sample frequency.                       |
|       These 2 models are simple MNL models.  |
|       R-sqrd = 1 - LogL(model)/logL(other)    |
|       RsqAdj=1-[nJ/(nJ-nparm)]*(1-R-sqrd)     |
|          nJ   = sum over i, choice set sizes  |
+----------------------------------------------------------------+

+----------------------------------------------------------------+
| Random Parameters Logit Model                                 |
| Replications for simulated probs. = 500                       |
| Halton sequences used for simulations                         |
| ------------------------------------------------------- |
| RPL model with panel has  115 groups.                         |
| Fixed number of obsrvs./group=         16                     |
| Random parameters model was specified                         |
| ------------------------------------------------------- |
| Number of obs.= 1840, skipped   0 bad obs. |
+----------------------------------------------------------------+
```

Variable	Coefficient	Standard Error	b/St.Er.	P[|Z|>z]
+---------+Random parameters in utility functions				
INVT	-.06852***	.00387	-17.719	.0000
WAITT	-.09419***	.01667	-5.649	.0000
ACCT	-.11947***	.01025	-11.658	.0000
EGGT	-.04954***	.01055	-4.697	.0000
COST	-.29739***	.02281	-13.035	.0000
+---------+Nonrandom parameters in utility functions				
NLRASC	2.45939***	.32302	7.614	.0000
ACCBUSF	-.06846*	.03712	-1.844	.0651
PTINC	-.00865***	.00249	-3.478	.0005
PTGEND	1.60422***	.21467	7.473	.0000
NLRINSDE	-1.22504***	.39846	-3.074	.0021
TNASC	1.76651***	.25499	6.928	.0000
NHRINSDE	-1.15571***	.44472	-2.599	.0094
NBWASC	.96813***	.28944	3.345	.0008
BSASC	1.27769***	.23769	5.375	.0000
BWASC	1.16536***	.25118	4.639	.0000
CRPARK	-.00529	.00790	-.670	.5030
CREGGT	-.05475***	.01556	-3.519	.0004
+---------+Distns. of RPs. Std.Devs or limits of triangular.				
TsINVT	.06852***	.00387	17.719	.0000
TsWAITT	.09419***	.01667	5.649	.0000
TsACCT	.11947***	.01025	11.658	.0000

```
|TsEGGT  |      .04954***       .01055       4.697   .0000 |
|TsCOST  |      .29739***       .02281      13.035   .0000 |
+----------+-------------------------------------------------------------+
| Note: ***, **, * = Significance at 1%, 5%, 10% level.    |
+--------------------------------------------------------------------+
```

The overall goodness of fit (pseudo-R^2) varies from 0.432 for M3 to 0.369 for M4. This is a substantial improvement over the ML model whose LL at convergence is −2496.577. The LL at convergence for Models 1–4 are, respectively, −2043.85, −2108.37, −2031.63, and −2257.96. The elements of the Cholesky matrix show strong evidence of correlated attributes, which makes an uncorrelated specification inappropriate. Of particular note is the statistically significant variance parameter for scale (or τ in Equation (15.35)) equal to 0.4896 in WTP space and 0.4103 in preference space. This suggests that scale heterogeneity is present even after accounting for correlated random parameters. The estimate of γ that governs how the variance of residual taste heterogeneity varies with scale is 0.0015, and is not statistically significantly different from zero.

Similar to Train and Weeks, the generalized mixed logit model (M3) estimated in preference space with one degree of freedom less than M2 in WTP space, has the best statistical fit. In contrast, Balcombe *et al.* (2009) and Scarpa *et al.* (2008) find an improvement in terms of estimate plausibility when using WTP space, and they also find a better statistical fit. However the WTP distributions summarized in Table 15.9 are behaviorally worrying for Model 3 (and Model 1) in respect of the very large range and sign change across the full unconstrained distribution.

The WTP estimates from Model M1–M3 are summarized in Table 15.9 from conditional distributions. A close inspection of the evidence suggests that Model 2 in WTP space is preferred in that the standard deviation estimates are considerably lower and behaviorally plausible compared to Models 1 and 3. Although the GMX model in preference space has similar mean estimates to Model 2, the standard deviations are three- to six-fold greater. There are also large standard deviation estimates for Model 1, although they are slightly lower than for the GMX model; however, the mean estimates of WTP are substantially lower, and on the basis of benchmark evidence, somewhat low.

Table 15.10 is informative in this assessment; it presents a cut of the entire distribution at the lower (i.e., more negative) and upper (i.e., more positive) extremes of each distribution. We have highlighted in **bold** the WTP estimates less than −$32 and greater than $32. These are arbitrary cut-offs, but they serve

Table 15.8 Summary of model results

Note: All public transport refers to new heavy rail, new light rail, new busway, bus, train, and busway; time is in min. and cost is in dollars ($2003). *T*-values are in brackets in columns (3) to (6). Models are estimated with 500 Halton draws.

Attribute (1)	Alternatives (2)	M1: Preference space, mixed logit (3)	M2: WTP Space (4)	M3: Preference space, generalized mixed logit (5)	M4: Preference space: mixed logit with constrained triangular distn (6)
		Random parameters: mean			
Main mode invehicle time	All modes	-0.0773 (-14.06)	0.2571 (9.10)	-0.0704 (-9.41)	-0.0685 (-17.7)
Wait time	All public modes	-0.0358 (-1.61)	0.1708 (2.06)	-0.0579 (-2.03)	-0.0942 (-5.65)
Access time	All public modes	-0.1095 (-8.15)	0.4553 (8.63)	-0.1131 (-6.41)	-0.1195 (-11.66)
Egress travel time	All public transport	-0.0629 (-3.67)	0.2954 (4.29)	-0.0767 (-3.51)	-0.0495 (-4.70)
Main mode invehicle cost	All modes	-0.3431 (-9.61)	1.00 (fixed)	-0.3269 (-9.62)	-0.2974 (-13.04)
		Non-random parameters:			
New light rail constant	New light rail	1.1425 (2.72)	1.1428 (3.91)	3.2409 (6.27)	2.4594 (7.61)
New busway constant	New busway	0.6646 (1.86)	0.8141 (3.37)	2.6373 (5.52)	0.9681 (3.35)
Existing bus constant	Bus	0.7887 (2.54)	1.1000 (5.44)	2.8424 (6.38)	1.2777 (5.38)
Train constant	Existing and new train	1.3188 (3.99)	1.5560 (7.15)	3.3201 (7.11)	1.7665 (6.93)
Existing busway constant	Busway	0.7781 (2.39)	0.9790 (4.55)	2.7941 (6.03)	1.1654 (4.64)
Access bus mode fare	Where bus is access mode	-0.0642 (-1.58)	-0.0600 (-1.74)	-0.0380 (-1.04)	-0.0685 (-1.84)
Car parking cost	Car	-0.0428 (-3.60)	-0.0427 (-3.50)	-0.0668 (-3.7)	-0.0053 (-0.67)
Egress travel time	Car	-0.0938 (-4.33)	-0.1212 (-6.60)	-0.1138 (-5.99)	-0.0547 (-3.52)
Personal income ($000s)	Public transport	-0.0081 (-2.26)	-0.0131 (-3.99)	-0.0170 (-4.58)	-0.0087 (-3.38)

Table 15.8 (cont.)

Attribute(1)	Alternatives(2)	M1: Preference space, mixed logit(3)	M2: WTP Space (4)	M3: Preference space, generalized mixed logit(5)	M4: Preference space: mixed logit with constrained triangular distn(6)
Gender (male = 1)	Public transport	1.5053 (5.33)	1.5646 (7.56)	1.3977 (5.97)	1.6042 (7.47)
New light rail inside trip	New light rail	−1.4597 (−2.42)	−1.2883 (−1.79)	−1.0362 (−1.11)	−1.2250 (−3.07)
New heavy rail inside trip	New heavy rail	−3.0826 (−3.74)	−2.7231 (−3.51)	−2.8616 (−2.71)	−1.1557 (−2.60)
Random parameters: standard deviation					
Main mode invehicle time	All modes	0.1109 (12.47)	0.4232 (8.38)	0.0986 (8.05)	−0.0685 (−17.7)
Wait time	All public modes	0.3409 (8.24)	1.0134 (5.87)	0.4529 (10.06)	−0.0942 (−5.65)
Access time	All public modes	0.2340 (7.06)	0.7789 (8.22)	0.2565 (5.39)	−0.1195 (−11.66)
Egress travel time	All public transport	0.3459 (13.44)	0.6883 (4.85)	0.3633 (8.69)	−0.0495 (−4.70)
Main mode invehicle cost	All modes	0.7668 (10.51)	0.00 (fixed)	0.6669 (7.66)	−0.2974 (−13.04)
Cholesky matrix: diagonal					
Main mode invehicle time	All modes	0.1109 (12.47)	0.4232 (8.38)	0.0986 (8.05)	–
Wait time	All public modes	0.2630 (8.12)	1.0134 (5.87)	0.3563)8.62	–
Access time	All public modes	0.2077 (6.54)	0.7789 (8.22)	0.1925 (3.99)	–
Egress travel time	All public transport	0.2719 (7.77)	0.6883 (4.85)	0.2314 (5.92)	–
Main mode invehicle cost	All modes	0.5132 (6.95)	0.00 (fixed)	0.1087 (1.06)	–
Cholesky matrix: below-diagonal					
Wait: invehicle time		−0.2170 (5.76)	0.6732 (3.97)	−0.2795 (5.49)	–
Access: invehicle time		−0.0498 (1.59)	0.3004 (2.04)	−0.1126 (2.74)	–

	(1)	(2)	(3)	(4)
Access: wait time	−0.0956 (−3.35)	0.5437 (3.25)	0.1267 (2.73)	—
Egress: invehicle time	−0.1270 (−3.72)	0.6543 (4.17)	−0.1861 (−4.22)	—
Egress: wait time	−0.1609 (−5.80)	0.6270 (3.23)	0.1854 (4.08)	—
Egress: access time	−0.0611 (−2.43)	0.6861 (4.65)	−0.0970 (−2.53)	—
Invehicle cost: invehicle time	0.4403 (4.43)	0.00 (fixed)	−0.0633 (−0.49)	—
Invehicle cost: wait time	0.2353 (3.58)	0.00 (fixed)	−0.4869 (−5.11)	—
Invehicle cost: access time	−0.1403 (−1.78)	0.00 (fixed)	−0.4328 (−5.32)	—
Invehicle cost: egress time	0.2359 (2.72)	0.00 (fixed)	−0.0669 (−0.83)	—
Variance parameter in scale (τ):	—	0.4896 (7.06)	0.4103 (10.67)	—
Weighting parameter gamma (γ):	—	0.00 (fixed)	0.0015 (0.007)	—
Parameter for cost (WTP space)	—	−0.2956 (−12.4)	—	—
Sigma:				
Sample mean	—	0.9663	0.9773	—
Sample standard deviation	—	0.4144	0.3499	—
Model fit:				
LL at zero		−3580.48		
LL at convergence	−2043.85	−2108.37	−2031.63	−2257.96
Information criterion AIC	4328.23	4427.22	4202.31	4643.79
Pseudo-R^2	0.429	0.411	0.433	0.369
Number of parameters	37	38	39	
Sample size	1840			

Table 15.9 Willingness to pay ($ per person hr.)
Notes: ( ) = standard deviation, [ ] = range, { } = mean after removing outliers (< −32 and > 32), ns = not statistically significant

Attribute	M1: preference space, mixed logit	M2: WTP space	M3: Preference space, general-ized mixed logit
Main mode invehicle time	**8.70** (42.78) [−313.1 to 120.6] {**12.24**}	**16.35** (8.16) [−7.3 to 31.07] {**16.35**}	**17.68** (55.25) [−222.9 to 392.6] {**12.19**}
Access time	**7.32** (89.3) [−475.9 to 393.9] {**9.52**}	**24.07** (19.51) [−12.96 to 78.94] {**13.86**}	**23.05** (121.4) [−419.8 to 869.2] {**5.96**}
Egress travel time	**11.25** (78.5) [−331.6 to 474.9] {**5.41**}	**15.71** (24.72) [−33.17 to 99.63] {**6.41**}	**18.58** (74.1) [−146.3 to 417.6] {**5.34**}

to illustrate the extent of "extreme values" under alternative model assumptions. The WTP space Model 2 has by far fewer extreme positive and negative estimates, with both Models 1 and 3 in preference space being subject to substantial extremes.

The evidence in preference space in Tables 15.9 and 15.10 reinforces the ongoing challenge for better ways of containing the heterogeneity to a behavioral realm that is deemed to be "plausible."[19] Given that we rely on analytical distributions that are in many ways arbitrary (even though some like the log-normal have a sign restriction but also a very long tail), efforts to impose constraints on distributions in order to contain the heterogeneity around a mean (e.g., a constrained triangular) have met with criticism as being unable to recognize the possibility of poor data quality. For example, Hensher and Greene (2003), among others, have promoted the triangular distribution, where the mean parameter is constrained to equal its spread (i.e., $\beta_{jk} = \beta_k + |\beta_k| \, T_j$, and T_j is a triangular distribution ranging between −1 and +1), and the density of the distribution rises linearly to the mean from zero before declining to zero again at twice the mean. Therefore, the distribution must lie between zero and some estimated value (i.e., the β_{jk}). As such, all individual-specific parameter estimates are constrained to be of the same sign.

[19] Although we have chosen the unconstrained triangular distribution, we have found very similar evidence of long tails and/or sign changes when using a number of analytical distributions such as normal, log-normal, Rayleigh, and asymmetric normal.

Table 15.10 Lower and upper WTP estimates (ML = Model 1; WTPS = Model 2, GMX = Model 3)

invtML	invtWTPS	invtGMX	waitML	waitWTPS	waitGMX	accessML	accessWTPS	accessGMX	egressML	egressWTPS	egressGMX
-313.09	-7.30	-222.93	-428.23	-45.84	-310.01	-475.92	-12.96	-419.77	-331.55	-33.17	-146.29
-162.36	-4.93	-105.74	-328.34	-39.20	-151.60	-406.29	-11.09	-316.98	-300.54	-31.37	-141.04
-149.48	-2.84	-74.72	-261.68	-31.63	-102.91	-237.82	-4.60	-284.73	-230.83	-28.64	-88.48
-81.69	-2.54	-69.59	-177.33	-21.42	-100.32	-192.72	-4.44	-207.14	-79.20	-27.77	-64.28
-40.79	0.11	-50.56	-158.86	-20.82	-97.58	-177.31	-3.93	-166.94	-77.01	-26.17	-43.76
-16.98	0.64	-36.22	-110.22	-20.40	-97.00	-129.31	-2.22	-123.99	-75.90	-23.36	-39.43
-13.24	0.55	-9.87	-81.37	-19.41	-77.11	-116.35	-1.27	-115.63	-54.61	-22.19	-37.96
-12.49	0.57	-8.37	-76.67	-19.31	-52.31	-99.36	-0.64	-111.72	-44.62	-21.84	-32.43
-5.22	0.31	-7.21	-67.64	-19.21	-30.87	-89.62	0.48	-5.38	-40.19	-15.57	-25.45
-2.94	1.38	-6.79	-44.67	-19.06	-27.87	-69.30	2.35	-4.57	-31.68	-15.32	-25.28
0.67	2.07	-1.94	-38.80	-18.55	-27.18	-45.36	2.36	-4.13	-27.36	-14.55	-22.59
...	...	...	...	...	...	...	...	...	...	...	...
17.35	21.53	19.95	10.07	14.53	12.31	23.52	33.66	34.56	17.89	23.75	16.34
17.48	21.46	20.59	10.27	15.07	13.19	24.07	34.08	34.64	18.94	25.65	16.51
17.49	22.00	20.97	10.93	15.10	13.26	24.50	35.73	34.69	19.01	26.72	18.09
18.14	22.50	21.39	11.77	16.77	15.83	27.26	35.74	35.03	19.03	28.52	19.07
18.37	22.40	22.10	12.71	18.01	16.07	27.41	36.45	35.32	19.63	29.44	19.71
18.53	22.41	22.47	15.50	18.96	19.68	29.19	37.43	35.75	20.62	30.05	20.33
19.42	22.52	23.42	16.20	20.05	21.56	30.73	38.06	36.18	20.86	30.63	22.44
19.43	23.08	23.56	16.88	20.48	22.00	32.08	39.61	37.28	21.02	32.28	22.86
19.95	23.51	23.94	18.15	20.96	22.37	33.75	39.80	38.22	21.85	32.84	25.81
20.84	23.64	25.33	20.64	22.46	22.64	34.21	39.98	39.72	28.82	33.35	27.92
21.07	23.77	27.54	20.91	22.98	27.47	34.31	40.30	40.49	29.86	33.40	29.24
21.87	23.96	27.86	20.91	23.56	27.86	34.64	40.68	41.28	30.15	33.55	30.25
22.20	24.06	28.42	23.22	24.46	28.65	37.97	41.81	41.43	30.47	33.59	31.45
22.22	24.10	29.18	27.53	27.11	29.18	38.17	42.17	43.51	32.93	35.05	31.74
22.73	24.24	30.62	27.61	27.95	30.44	38.46	42.22	45.89	34.40	35.75	32.85
24.96	24.25	30.63	29.87	30.39	34.40	40.18	42.69	47.13	36.05	37.87	33.94
25.53	24.43	30.97	31.11	31.29	37.65	41.13	43.32	50.02	37.12	37.96	33.96
25.92	24.50	31.07	32.25	31.58	38.56	44.29	44.45	53.03	37.27	38.18	34.88
26.21	24.51	31.25	34.27	31.75	41.31	46.29	45.37	53.80	37.40	39.27	36.10
27.63	24.66	32.53	34.59	32.23	45.15	46.54	47.85	58.93	53.30	44.71	36.98
27.75	25.09	35.25	35.85	34.87	47.82	52.39	48.23	61.81	57.93	45.67	41.84
29.22	25.22	39.91	36.68	36.42	48.87	56.12	48.41	63.91	60.82	46.27	42.82
29.48	25.46	42.68	38.44	37.01	49.48	56.44	51.46	78.78	63.84	47.49	44.81
30.36	26.10	43.42	39.42	39.17	61.99	58.21	51.73	84.01	64.95	49.10	48.00
31.04	26.30	50.65	51.81	44.74	68.52	69.14	52.14	86.22	65.21	50.01	56.48
34.73	26.33	58.06	52.70	46.91	80.23	73.21	54.27	95.08	71.11	50.35	59.56
35.23	26.40	59.44	53.33	47.16	83.70	78.17	54.50	101.80	75.33	54.96	59.94
37.96	26.48	61.50	54.01	50.13	103.79	90.56	56.65	162.19	78.94	55.52	66.96
38.97	26.55	64.33	140.38	59.39	137.37	111.07	61.53	177.26	97.21	63.42	78.93
42.08	27.39	93.52	157.04	59.52	176.00	116.23	66.08	192.59	130.60	64.13	103.18
56.05	28.38	101.26	157.46	63.18	244.44	136.66	69.05	211.45	148.38	77.43	233.66
61.21	29.57	116.45	160.58	64.05	374.80	151.11	75.21	298.92	162.58	79.45	381.36
107.47	30.72	276.16	184.47	68.57	406.42	224.87	75.72	437.25	275.43	83.91	411.82
120.62	31.07	392.64	394.87	77.17	460.66	393.93	78.94	869.15	474.97	99.63	417.57

Empirically the distribution is symmetrical about the mean,[20] which not only allows for ease of interpretation, but also avoids the problem of long tails often associated with drawing from a log-normal distribution.

To enable a comparison of the WTP estimates above with a popular version of a ML model with a constrained triangular distribution on all random parameters, we also estimated Model 1 with constrained triangular distributions for each of the random parameters (Table 15.8, last column: M4), and compare the mean WTP with Models 1–3 (Table 15.8). To be able to assess the differences in the mean estimates, we calculate standard errors for the parameter estimates used to obtain the WTP estimates. Given the focus on the mean, we can implement Equation (21) of Scarpa and Rose (2008), reproduced here as Equation (15.42):

$$\text{Variance of mean WTP} = \beta^{-2}\left[Var(\alpha) - 2\alpha\beta^{-1}Cov(\alpha,\beta) + \left(\frac{\alpha}{\beta}\right)^{2}Var(\beta)\right].$$

(15.42)

To obtain the standard errors around the mean, reported in Table 15.11, we take the square root of Equation (15.42), given the variance and covariance of the numerator (α) and the denominator (β) parameters. In WTP space, we

Table 15.11 Mean estimates of willingness to pay (\$/person hr.) Standard errors in brackets

	Value of time savings:		
Triangular distributions	Invehicle time	Access time	Egress time
U-space constrained MXL (M1con)	16.31 (2.047E–07)	29.31 (4.093E–06)	12.32 (2.114E–06)
U-space unconstrained MXL (M1)	8.70 (1.335E–06)	7.32 (1.055E–05)	11.25 (9.258E–09)
WTP space unconstrained GMX (M2)	16.35 (0.00079)	24.07 (0.0028)	15.71 (0.0047)
U-space unconstrained GMX (M3)	17.68 (9.787E–07)	23.05 (2.701E–05)	18.58 (0.0057)

[20] There has been a lot said about the appropriateness of the constrained triangular distribution. To place this in the correct context, there is support in the literature for the point that the sign across the distribution must make sense in terms of some acceptable hypothesis. That is the crucial initial point (regardless of the specific constraint imposed on the specific distribution) and there is a long history in economics in selecting a log-normal distribution precisely for this reason. This is a widely held position in the literature on risk. There is a literature supporting the sense of constrained distributions, where the constraint relates to an appropriate sign on the coefficient across the full distribution. The log-normal is one such example which through its functional form ensures that the sign is always the same; however, this comes at a high cost of a very long tail to the right. Some authors have investigated the triangular distribution and especially the constrained triangular distribution (referred to by them as the "Flared" Triangular Distribution), as a symmetric and an asymmetric distribution.

only have a variance term for (α/β). There are no cross-overs between model pairs when calculated at the 95 percent confidence intervals, suggesting that the means of the distributions are statistically significantly different.

We find a strong equivalence between the evidence on mean WTP for invehicle time savings when imposing a constrained distribution (e.g., constrained triangular) in preference space (M4) and that obtained in a WTP space GMX model with an unconstrained distribution (M2), and to a lesser extent for the GMX model (M3). When scale heterogeneity is not allowed for (M1) with an unconstrained distribution, we find significantly different evidence (close to 50 percent lower mean WTP). The situation is similar for the WTP for access time savings, although there is a slightly larger divergence between M4 and both of M2 and M3. The evidence for the WTP for egress time savings is less conclusive; although the GMX models in WTP and preference space are the larger estimates (respectively, \$15.71 and \$18.58), the WTP space estimate sits almost midway between the unconstrained GMX and constrained ML models in utility space.

Given a particular interest in the possibility that estimates in WTP space might be a popular alternative way in the future (there is definitely growing interest) to the currently "popular" use of ML models with constrained distributions, there is encouraging evidence, at least for two of the three attributes, to speculate that appropriate constraining of distributions in preference space might be an empirical approximation for the outcome in WTP space. While we do not claim that we have found the rationale for justifying a constrained distribution in preference space if the WTP in WTP space is a benchmark reference, we might describe the evidence as potentially encouraging, but in need of further confirmation from other data sets and other analytical distributions.

15.11 SMNL and GMX models in utility space

In this final section, we present an SMNL and GMX model and contrast them with the standard MNL and ML models. The four models of interest are summarized in Table 15.12. Model 1 (M1) is the standard MNL model, Model 2 (M2) is the base random parameter (or mixed logit) model (MXL) in utility space, Model 3 (M3) is the generalized random parameter or mixed logit model (GMXL) that accounts for taste and scale heterogeneity, and Model 4 (M4) is the scale heterogeneity model (SMNL) without taste heterogeneity.

All random parameters are specified with unconstrained triangular distributions and correlation among the set of random parameters. The correlation is accommodated by an unrestricted lower triangular matrix, $\mathbf{\Gamma}$. All random parameters are estimated using a panel specification. We ran a series of models (MXL, GMXL, SMNL) with varying numbers of intelligent draws (50 through to 1,000). The results stabilized at 500 draws.[21] The fixed and random parameter estimates associated with the trip time and cost attributes are of the expected sign and statistically significant.[22] Personal income (only significant for GMXL) appears in the utility expression for public transport, indicating that a person on a higher income has a lower probability of choosing public transport (compared to car use).

The overall goodness of fit (pseudo-R^2) varies from 0.410 for GMXL3 to 0.295 for MNL. MXL and GMXL that allow for taste heterogeneity are a substantial improvement over the MNL model, whose LL at convergence is -2522.49. In contrast scale MNL is marginally improved over MNL. The Akaike Information Criterion (AIC)[23] clearly indicates that one should choose GMXL over the other models.

The elements of the Cholesky matrix (shown in Table 15.12 as the diagonal and below-diagonal values) show strong evidence of correlated attributes, which makes an uncorrelated specification inappropriate. Of particular note is the statistically significant variance parameter for scale (or τ), equal to 0.4109 in the GMXL model and 1.418 for SMNL. This suggests that scale heterogeneity is present even after accounting for correlated random parameters. The estimate of γ in GMXL, which governs how the variance of residual taste heterogeneity varies with scale, is 0.00028, but is statistically not significantly different from zero.

A useful behavioral output to compare models is the mean estimates of direct elasticity (Table 15.13), since these provide direct evidence on the relative sensitivity of each model in respect of modal shares associated with a change in the level of a specific trip attribute. The formula for calculating the mean elasticities for models MXL and GMXL is given in Equation (15.43):

$$Est.Avg. \frac{\partial logP_j}{\partial logx_{k,l}} = \frac{1}{N}\sum_{i=1}^{N}\int_{\beta_i}[\delta_{j,l} - P_l(\beta_i, X_i)]\beta_k x_{k,l,i}d\beta_i, \qquad (15.43)$$

---

[21] We have found that using start values from ML for GMXL is preferable than using MNL start values.
[22] We did not find any statistically significant "h" effects as per Equation (15.17).
[23] AIC $= 2k - 2\text{Ln}(L)$, where k is the number of parameters in the model, and L is the maximized value of the likelihood function for the estimated model.

Table 15.12 Summary of model results

Note. All public transport is *new* heavy rail, light rail, and busway; and *existing* bus, train, and busway; time is in min. and cost is in dollars ($2003). *T*-values are in brackets.

Attribute	Alternatives	M1: multinomial logit (MNL)	M2: Mixed logit (MXL)	M3: Generalized mixed logit (GMXL)	M4: Scale MNL (SMNL)
Random parameters: mean		All non-random parameters			
Main mode invehicle time	All public modes	-0.0481 (23.67)*	-0.0537 (12.6)	-0.0735 (9.95)	-0.0576 (22.10)*
Wait time	All public modes	-0.0270 (2.11)*	-0.0747 (3.17)	-0.0660 (2.36)	-0.0306 (3.39)*
Access time	All public modes	-0.0592 (12.6)*	-0.1064 (8.25)	-0.1087 (7.97)	-0.0666 (14.53)*
Egress travel time	All public transport	-0.0150 (3.1)*	-0.1127 (6.45)	-0.0985 (4.11)	-0.0196 (6.17)*
Main mode invehicle cost	All public modes	-0.1845 (13.5)*	-0.2947 (7.70)	-0.3164 (8.48)	-0.2358 (18.66)*
		Non-random parameters:			
New light rail constant	New light rail	2.4098 (6.44)	1.9450 (4.38)	3.3733 (6.84)	2.4026 (13.70)
New busway constant	New busway	1.249 (3.56)	1.628 (4.37)	2.8672 (6.08)	1.2493 (6.92.)
Existing bus constant	Bus	1.8142 (5.87)	1.8458 (5.31)	3.1042 (7.33)	1.8140 (11.61)
Train constant	Existing and new train	2.1039 (6.63)	2.215 (5.89)	3.4937 (7.87)	2.1132 (13.85)
Existing busway constant	Busway	1.6058 (5.07)	1.8235 (4.99)	3.0240 (6.82)	1.6088 (10.7)
Access bus mode fare	Where bus is access mode	-0.07673 (2.41)	-0.0547 (1.50)	-0.0321 (1.02)	-0.0735 (3.14)
Car cost	Car	-0.1128 (4.05)	-0.2044 (4.53)	-0.1634 (3.09)	-0.1367 (5.51)
Car invehicle time	Car	-0.0340 (8.80)	-0.0480 (8.16)	-0.0482 (7.62)	-0.0307 (10.21)
Car parking cost	Car	-0.0139 (1.97)	-0.0429 (3.25)	-0.06278 (4.27)	-0.0675 (7.07)
Egress travel time	Car	-0.0561 (4.07)	-0.0957 (5.96)	-0.1206 (5.13)	-0.0902 (6.65)
Personal income ($000s)	Public transport	-0.0026 (1.4)	-0.0016 (1.56)	-0.0099 (2.72)	-0.0003 (1.71)
		Random parameters: standard deviation			
Main mode invehicle time	All public modes	–	0.0753 (8.35)	0.1030 (7.68)	–
Wait time	All public modes	–	0.2795(7.07)	0.4318 (8.52)	–
Access time	All public modes	–	0.1937 (5.97)	0.2230 (6.07)	–
Egress travel time	All public transport	–	0.3012 (8.55)	0.3974 (9,87)	–
Main mode invehicle cost	All public modes	–	0.6502 (6.45)	0.6961 (7.08)	–
Cholesky matrix: diagonal values					
Main mode invehicle time	All public modes	–	0.0753 (8.35)	0.1030 (7.68)	–
Wait time	All public modes	–	0.2243(7.65)	0.3274 (7.31)	–
Access time	All public modes	–	0.0995 (2.98)	0.1919 (5.28)	–

Table 15.12 (cont.)

Attribute	Alternatives	M1: multinomial logit (MNL)	M2: Mixed logit (MXL)	M3: Generalized mixed logit (GMXL)	M4: Scale MNL (SMNL)
Egress travel time	All public transport	–	0.2447 (7.58)	0.2741 (6.63)	–
Main mode invehicle cost	All public modes	–	0.5325 (6.91)	0.4146 (3.38)	–
Cholesky matrix: below-diagonal values					
Wait: invehicle time	All public modes	–	0.1667 (4.16)	-0.2814 (4.93)	–
Access: invehicle time	All public modes	–	0.0104 (0.36)	-0.0893 (2.08)	–
Access: wait time	All public modes	–	-0.1658 (5.44)	0.0703 (2.27)	–
Egress: invehicle time	All public transport	–	0.1381 (3.41)	-0.2505 (4.66)	–
Egress: wait time	All public modes	–	-0.1077 (2.67)	0.1240 (2.33)	–
Egress: access time	All public modes	–	-0.0129 (0.30)	0.0684 (1.09)	–
Invehicle cost: invehicle time	All public modes	–	-0.0865 (0.75)	0.0613 (0.47)	–
Invehicle cost: wait time	All public modes	–	0.2490 (2.32)	-0.4509 (3.79)	–
Invehicle cost: access time	All public transport	–	0.1192 (1.22)	0.3006 (2.88)	–
Invehicle cost: egress time	All public modes	–	0.2358 (2.48)	-0.1238 (1.02)	–
Variance parameter in scale (τ):		–		0.4109 (7.39)	1.1418 (12.11)
Weighting parameter γ:		–		0.00028 (0.007)	–
Sigma:					
Sample mean		–	–	0.9758	0.8185
Sample standard deviation		–	–	0.3504	0.8347
Model fit:					
LL at zero		-3580.48			
LL at convergence		-2522.49	-2156.88	-2111.62	-2415.54
McFadden pseudo-R^2		0.295	0.398	0.410	0.325
Info. criterion: AIC		5076.97	4375.75	4289.25	4865.07
Sample size		1840			
VTTS ($/person hr.)					
Main mode invehicle time	All public modes	15.64	10.92 (16.92)#	12.60 (6.58)	14.66
Wait time	All public modes	8.78	17.09 (33.84)	13.01 (48.9)	7.79
Access time	All public modes	19.25	18.94 (19.94)	20.94 (4.60)	16.95
Egress travel time	All public transport	4.88	18.80 (30.79)	15.55 (30.25)	4.99
Invehicle time	Car	18.08	14.09	17.60	13.48

Note:
* fixed parameters; # standard deviations in brackets for VTTS.

Table 15.13 Direct time and cost elasticities *Note*: Uncalibrated models, standard deviations in brackets.

Attribute	Alternative	M1: Multinomial logit*	M2: Mixed logit	M3: Generalized mixed logit	M4: Scale MNL*
Invehicle time	New light rail (invt-NLR)	−1.674 (1.021)	−1.421 (0.758)	−1.481 (0.796)	−1.106 (0.462)
	New heavy rail (invt-NHR)	−1.595 (0.945)	−1.399 (0.684)	−1.533 (0.752)	−1.172 (0.530)
	New busway (invt-NBWY)	−2.133 (0.976)	−1.744 (0.652)	−1.936 (0.747)	−1.415 (0.465)
	Bus (invt-Bus)	−1.773 (0.995)	−1.356 (0.581)	−1.475 (0.650)	−1.260 (0.456)
	Busway (invt-Bway)	−1.540 (0.880)	−1.317 (0.703)	−1.465 (0.809)	−1.188 (0.530)
	Train (invt-Train)	−1.344 (0.752)	−1.227 (0.609)	−1.340 (0.731)	−1.035 (0.469)
	Car (invt-Car)	−1.215 (0.709)	−0.894 (0.648)	−0.763 (0.441)	−0.847 (0.853)
Cost	New light rail (cost-NLR)	−0.699 (0.446)	−0.883 (0.512)	−0.775 (0.475)	−0.493 (0.236)
	New heavy rail (cost-NHR)	−0.704 (0.452)	−0.756 (0.391)	−0.733 (0.389)	−0.547 (0.272)
	New busway (cost-NBWY)	−1.143 (0.496)	−0.917 (0.507)	−0.943 (0.468)	−0.806 (0.319)
	Bus (cost-Bus)	−0.942 (0.486)	−0.826 (0.384)	−0.815 (0.389)	−0.770 (0.326)
	Busway (cost-Bway)	−0.646 (0.414)	−0.758 (0.396)	−0.739 (0.427)	−0.522 (0.264)
	Train (cost-Train)	−0.832 (0.483)	−0.713 (0.368)	−0.686 (0.351)	−0.626 (0.281)
	Car (cost-Car)	−0.580 (0.339)	−0.537 (0.387)	−0.363 (0.209)	−0.528 (0.530)

Note:
*The standard deviations are an artifact of different choice probabilities and not a result of preference heterogeneity.

where j and l index alternatives, x indexes the attribute, and i indicates the individual. The integrals cannot be computed directly, so they are simulated in the same fashion (and at the same time) as the LL function. Using R simulated draws from the distribution of β_i, we obtain the simulated values of the means of the elasticities (Equation 15.44):

$$Est.Avg.\frac{\partial logP_j}{\partial logx_{k,l}} = \frac{1}{N}\sum_{i=1}^{N}\frac{1}{R}\sum_{r=1}^{R}[\delta_{j,l} - P_l(\beta_{i,r}, X_i)]\beta_{k,i,r}x_{k,l,i}. \quad (15.44)$$

Although some models are capable of producing elasticity distributions, the scale heterogeneity model SMNL is of the MNL form, and hence only mean estimates for each person are meaningful. The best way to compare the evidence across the four models is to take the ML model (essentially the "reference" given the focus on contrasting GMXL and SMNL with MXL) and difference the mean estimates for each other model against this model.

Beginning with the invehicle time mean elasticities,[24] the SMNL model (M4) has the greatest consistently negative difference[25] relative to MXL (M2), remaining directionally negative for all modal alternatives, indicating that all mean elasticities are higher for ML compared to scale MNL. In contrast, ML has higher mean elasticity estimates than MNL (M1) and GMXL (M3), with the one exception of car invehicle time for GMXL.

This evidence, albeit from one study, suggests that the SMNL model, that excludes consideration of attribute preference heterogeneity, produces noticeably lower mean estimates of the elasticities for invehicle travel time. For the cost attribute, the same findings apply for ML compared to SMNL; however, the directional implication is not clear in comparisons of MXL with MNL and GMXL.

When we undertake a statistical test of differences (using the mean and standard deviation) between various model pairs (see Table 15.14), we find on the t-ratio of differences test that there is no statistically significant difference between the mean estimates, without exception.[26] Hence the extension from MNL to ML to generalized mixed logit, and the focus only on scale heterogeneity, does not impact materially on the evidence on direct elasticities, despite the actual mean estimates that are typically used in practice being different in absolute terms.

This empirical evidence suggests that although recognition of preference and scale heterogeneity through observed attributes improves on the goodness of fit of the models, and aligns the mean elasticity estimates "closer" to those of the popular ML model (which assumes scale homogeneity), the differences are not statistically significant. However, despite this evidence, practitioners tend to focus on applying the mean estimates, and hence when only scale heterogeneity is accommodated the mean elasticity estimates are, with a few exceptions, noticeably lower than both ML and generalized mixed logit.

This evidence, admittedly from a single study, raises doubts about the substantive empirical merits of allowing for scale heterogeneity in the absence

---

[24] The elasticities are based on uncalibrated models and as such the numerical magnitudes are only valid in the comparisons across models. These models cannot be used to forecast patronage without calibration using revealed preference shares on existing modes.

[25] Since all elasticities are negative, a lower value is an absolute lower value (e.g. −0.435 is lower than −0.650).

[26] We also undertook a bootstrap calculation (as per Section 7.3.3) for two of the variables to ensure that the t-ratio test was a useful approximation. The resulting standard errors confirm that the t-ratios are a good approximation.

Table 15.14 Tests of statistical significance between elasticity estimates

Attribute	Alternative	MXL versus MNL	MXL versus GMXL	MXL versus SMNL	GMXL versus SMNL
Invehicle time	New light rail (invt-NLR)	0.199	−0.055	0.355	0.407
	New heavy rail (invt-NHR)	0.168	−0.131	0.193	0.393
	New busway (invt-NBWY)	0.331	−0.194	0.411	0.592
	Bus (invt-Bus)	0.362	−0.137	0.130	0.271
	Busway (invt-Bway)	0.198	−0.138	0.147	0.286
	Train (invt-Train)	0.121	−0.119	0.250	0.351
	Car (invt-Car)	0.334	0.167	0.044	0.087
Cost	New light rail (cost-NLR)	−0.197	0.155	0.692	0.532
	New heavy rail (cost-NHR)	0.087	0.042	0.439	0.392
	New busway (cost-NBWY)	0.319	−0.038	0.185	0.242
	Bus (cost-Bus)	0.187	0.020	0.111	0.089
	Busway (cost-Bway)	−0.196	0.033	0.496	0.432
	Train (cost-Train)	0.196	0.053	0.188	0.133
	Car (cost-Car)	0.084	0.396	0.014	−0.290

of the influence of preference heterogeneity, given that Model 3 is the preferred model. When both sources of heterogeneity are captured, the statistical fit of the GMXL model is superior (with a 2 degrees of freedom difference), suggesting that accounting for both preference and scale heterogeneity is a significant improvement over the standard ML model. In terms of the behavioral implications associated with mean direct elasticities, however, this tends to result in slightly lower travel time estimates and slightly higher travel cost estimates; however, given the standard deviations, the difference is not statistically significant.

Finally, we report the mean estimates of VTTS (Table 15.9). We calculated the mean WTP (and standard deviation where appropriate) using the unconditional estimates, and we used the generic invehicle cost random parameter to obtain VTTS. There are differences in the mean estimates for all time attributes; however, the differences between ML and GMXL are not statistically significant on a test of differences, given the standard errors. What does appear notable is the presence of lower mean estimates for SMNL compared to MNL (recognizing that the value for egress time is very similar). The behavioral implications are far from clear other than that the ML and generalized mixed logit models appear to produce higher mean estimates than the models that assume preference homogeneity. This finding is known from other studies (see Hensher 2010).

In the context of WTP, Daly *et al.* (2012) have expressed concern about the properties of some common choices of distributions for the cost coefficient in models estimated in preference space. In particular, the authors present a *mathematical* proof to show that, when the domain of the distribution for the cost coefficient includes zero, none of the moments of the WTP distribution exists. If the distribution approaches zero, but does not include zero, then the existence of the moments depends on the specific shape of the distribution as it approaches zero. For the triangular distribution bounded at zero, the mean of the inverse exists, while the variance does not.[27] In experiments using a finite number of draws in simulation, this problem is masked; indeed, Daly *et al.* (2012) confirm their theoretical results using simulations with 10^7 draws.

It should be said that the proofs by Daly *et al.* are limited to the case of uncorrelated coefficients (or to correlated normal coefficients), while the present application allows for correlation between the time and cost coefficients which is essential when introducing scale heterogeneity, since it induces correlation (as stated most eloquently by Train and Weeks 2005). Nevertheless, Daly *et al.* (2012) also discuss how the same reasoning should apply in the case of correlated coefficients, and from this perspective the variances reported for the WTP indicators herein should be treated with caution. Having investigated numerous distributions over many years, we suggest that many distributions are controversial, especially when used as ratios of parameters to obtain measures of WTP, and that the growing popularity of estimating models in WTP space (in contrast to preference space) may well be the focus in the future.

15.12 Recognizing scale heterogeneity between pooled data sets

The extension of interest here is to allow τ to be a function of a series of dummy variables that identifies the presence of scale heterogeneity between different data sets, such as a revealed preference (RP) and a stated preference (SP) data set.

---

[27] Albeit that problems with it going to infinity are slightly less pronounced than, say, with the uniform bounded at zero, so that a limited simulation may produce apparently reasonable results.

This is a simple but important extension, as follows: $\tau = \tau + \eta d_s$ where η is a data set-specific scale parameter and $d_s = 1$ for data source s and zero otherwise, with $s = 1,2 \ldots, S-1$. Hence we allow for differences in the GMXL scale factor between RP and SP data sets through the inclusion of a dummy variable d_s ($s = SP = 1$, $s = RP = 0$) associated with σ_{irs}, i.e., $\sigma_{irs} = \exp(-\tau(\tau + \eta d_s)^2/2 + (\tau + \eta d_s)w_{ir})$. We discuss joint estimation of RP–SP data in Chapter 19; however, the use of the SMNL or GMX model permits a new variant which is illustrated in model estimation and interpreted in Chapter 19.

16 Latent class models

16.1 Introduction

Although the multinomial logit model (MNL) has provided the foundation for the analysis of discrete choice modeling, its basic limitations, most notably its assumption of independence from irrelevant alternatives (IIA), have motivated researchers to consider alternative specifications. The mixed logit (ML) model (see Chapter 15) is probably the most significant among a number of innovations in terms of the range of behavior it can accommodate and its overall flexibility. The latent class model (LCM) presented in this chapter is in some respects a semi-parametric variant of the MNL model that resembles the ML model. It is somewhat less flexible than the ML model in that it approximates the underlying continuous distribution with a discrete one; however, it does not require the analyst to make specific assumptions about the distributions of parameters across individuals. Thus, each model has its limitations and virtues. However, as we will show below, the most advanced version of LCM permits continuous distributions in each discrete class for the class-specific parameters.

Latent class modeling provides an alternative approach to accommodating heterogeneity in models such as MNL and ML (see Everitt 1988 and Uebersax 1999). The natural approach assumes that parameter vectors, β_i, are distributed among individuals with a discrete distribution, rather than the continuous distribution that lies behind the ML model. Thus, it is assumed that the population consists of a finite number, Q, of groups of individuals. The groups are heterogenous, with common parameters, β_q, for the members of the group, but the groups themselves are different from one another. We assume that the classes are distinguished by the different parameter vectors, though the fundamental data generating process, the probability density for the interesting variable under study, is the same.

The analyst does not know from the data which observation is in which class, hence the term *latent* classes. The model assumes that individuals are distributed heterogenously with a discrete distribution in a population. In this chapter, we will begin with the standard LCM, with fixed parameters that are usually unconstrained so that they are different between classes, but between-class restrictions can be imposed if they make sense. We then introduce a more advanced LCM in which random parameters are imposed within each class. In addition to the standard interpretation of latent classes, we also recognize the growing popularity of the LCM to investigate attribute processing rules (see Chapter 21), through the use of the restrictions imposed on particular parameters within a class. When we do this for fixed and/or random parameters, we are defining a class as having a specific behavioral meaning and, as such, we refer to each class as a probabilistic decision rule. The examples used in the chapter include both standard latent class and latent class with random parameters, as well as the treatment of attribute processing.

16.2 The standard latent class model

The LCM for the analysis of individual heterogeneity has a history in several literatures. See Heckman and Singer (1984a, 1984b) for theoretical discussion. However, a review of the literature suggests that the vast majority of the received applications have been in the area of models for counts using the Poisson or negative binomial models. Greene (2001) provides an early survey of the literature. Swait (1994) and Bhat (1997) are early examples of the application of LCM to the analysis of discrete choice among multiple alternatives.

The underlying theory of the LCM posits that individual behavior depends on observable attributes and on latent heterogeneity that varies with factors that are unobserved by the analyst. We can analyze this heterogeneity through a model of discrete parameter variation. Thus, it is assumed that individuals are implicitly sorted into a set of Q classes, but which class contains any particular individual, whether known or not to that individual, is unknown to the analyst. The central behavioral model is a logit model for discrete choice among J_i alternatives, by individual i observed in T_i choice situations, given in Equation (16.1):

Prob[choice j by individual i in choice situation t | class q]

$$= \frac{\exp(\mathbf{x}'_{it,j}\boldsymbol{\beta}_q)}{\sum_{j-1}^{J_i} \exp(\mathbf{x}'_{it,j}\boldsymbol{\beta}_q)} = F(i,t,j\,|\,q). \qquad (16.1)$$

The number of observations and the size of the choice set may vary by individual respondent. In principle, the choice set could vary by choice situation as well. The probability for the specific choice made by an individual can be formulated in several ways; for convenience, we allow y_{it} to denote the specific choice made, so that the model, given in Equation (16.2), provides:

$$P_{it\,|\,q}(j) = \text{Prob}(y_{it} = j\,|\,\text{class} = q). \qquad (16.2)$$

For convenience, we simplify this further to $P_{it|q}$. We have used a generic notation for the density of the random variable of interest to suggest that this formulation will provide a means of extending the LCM to other frameworks, though we restrict our attention here to the discrete choice model. Note that this is a "panel data" sort of application, in that we assume that the same individual is observed in several choice situations.

We assume that, given the class assignment, the T_i events are independent. This is a possibly strong assumption, especially given the nature of the sampling design used in most choice analyses – such as a stated choice (SC) experiment in which the individual answers a sequence of survey questions. In fact, there might well be correlation in the unobserved parts of the random utilities. The latent class does not readily extend to autocorrelation. Thus, for the given class assignment, the contribution of individual i to the likelihood would be the joint probability of the sequence $\mathbf{y}_i = [y_{i1}, y_{i2}, \ldots y_{iT}]$, given as Equation (16.3):

$$P_{i|q} = \prod_{t=1}^{T_i} P_{it|q}. \qquad (16.3)$$

The class assignment is, however, unknown. Let H_{iq} denote the prior probability for a class q for individual i (we consider posterior probabilities below). Various formulations have been used for this (see Greene 2001). A particularly convenient form is the MNL model shown in Equation (16.4):

$$H_{iq} = \frac{\exp(\mathbf{z}'_i\boldsymbol{\theta}_q)}{\sum_{q=1}^{Q} \exp(\mathbf{z}'_i\boldsymbol{\theta}_q)}, \ q = 1, \ldots, Q, \boldsymbol{\theta}_Q = \mathbf{0}, \qquad (16.4)$$

where z_i denotes a set of observable characteristics (or covariates) which enter the model for class membership. Roeder *et al.* (1999), using this same formulation, denote z_i the "risk factors." The Qth parameter vector is normalized to zero to secure identification of the model. In some model specifications there may be no covariates, in which case the only element in z_i would be the constant term, "1," and the latent class probabilities would be simple constants which, by construction, sum to one. The likelihood for individual i is the expectation (over classes) of the class-specific contributions, as shown in Equation (16.5):

$$P_i = \sum_{q=1}^{Q} H_{iq} P_{i|q}. \tag{16.5}$$

The log-likelihood (LL) for the sample is shown in Equation (16.6):

$$\ln L = \sum_{i=1}^{N} \ln P_i = \sum_{i=1}^{N} \ln \left[\sum_{q=1}^{Q} H_{iq} \left(\prod_{t=1}^{T_i} P_{it|q} \right) \right]. \tag{16.6}$$

Maximization of the LL with respect to the Q structural parameter vectors, β_q, and the $Q-1$ latent class parameter vectors, θ_q, is a conventional problem in maximum likelihood estimation (see Chapter 5).[1] In comparison to more familiar maximum likelihood problems, this is a relatively difficult optimization problem, though not excessively so. For a given choice of Q, the choice of good starting values seems to be crucial. The asymptotic covariance matrix for the full set of parameter estimators is obtained by inverting the analytic second derivatives matrix of the LL function.

An issue to be confronted is the choice of Q, the number of classes. This is not a parameter in the interior of a convex parameter space, so one cannot test hypotheses about Q directly. If there is a known Q^* that is greater than the "true" Q, then it is possible to "test down" to Q by using, for example, likelihood-ratio tests (LRTs). A model with $Q + 1$ classes encompasses one with Q if the parameters in any two of the $Q + 1$ classes are forced to equality. This does move the problem up one level, since the Q^* must now be assumed

[1]   The EM algorithm has become popular in LCM estimation. Implementing the expectation maximization (EM) algorithm by iterating between computing the posterior class probabilities, re-estimating the model parameters in each class by using a probability weighted LL function, has been employed for all manner of LC models, not just multinomial choice models, for many years. It is a generic algorithm, but it has little to recommend it beyond its simple elegance. It is slow and requires the analyst to go back into the computation at the end to compute the asymptotic covariance matrix for the estimators. Software such as Latent Gold, for example, has been using this method. There is a misconception on the part of some that the method is a new model, or somehow produces a different estimator from the MLE. Neither is the case. See http://en.wikipedia.org/wiki/Expectations%E2%80%93maximization_algorithm.

known, but testing down from a specified Q^* is straightforward. "Testing up" from a small Q (one) is not valid, since the estimates obtained for any model that is too small are inconsistent. Roeder *et al.* (1999) suggest using the Bayesian Information Criterion (BIC) in Equation (16.7):

$$\text{BIC(model)} = \ln L + \frac{(\text{model size})\ln N}{N}. \tag{16.7}$$

With the parameter estimates of $\boldsymbol{\theta}_q$ in hand, the prior estimates of the class probabilities are $\hat{H}_{iq}$. Using Bayes' theorem, we can obtain a posterior estimate of the latent class probabilities using Equation (16.8):

$$\hat{H}_{q|i} = \frac{\hat{P}_{i|q}\hat{H}_{iq}}{\sum_{q=1}^{Q} \hat{P}_{i|q}\hat{H}_{iq}}. \tag{16.8}$$

The notation $\hat{H}_{q|i}$ is used to indicate the respondent-specific estimate of the class probability, conditioned on their estimated choice probabilities, as distinct from the unconditional class probabilities that enter the LL function. A strictly empirical estimator of the latent class within which the individual resides would be that associated with the maximum value of $\hat{H}_{q|i}$. We may also use these results to obtain posterior estimates of the individual specific parameter vector, as shown in Equation (16.9):

$$\hat{\boldsymbol{\beta}}_i = \sum_{q=1}^{Q} \hat{H}_{q|i}\hat{\boldsymbol{\beta}}_q. \tag{16.9}$$

The same result can be used to estimate marginal effects in the logit model in Equation (16.10):

$$\sigma_{km,itj|q} = \frac{\partial \ln F(i,t,j\,|\,q)}{\partial x_{it,km}} = x_{it,km}[1(j=k) - F(i,t,k\,|\,q)]\beta_{m|q} \tag{16.10}$$

for the effect on individual i's choice probability j in choice situation t of attribute m in choice probability k. The posterior estimator of this elasticity is given as Equation (16.11):

$$\hat{\sigma}_{km,tj|i} = \sum_{q=1}^{Q} \hat{H}_{q|i}\hat{\sigma}_{km,ji|q}. \tag{16.11}$$

An estimator of the average of this quantity over data configurations and individuals would be as in Equation (16.12):

$$\hat{\bar{\sigma}}_{km,j} = \frac{1}{N} \sum_{i=1}^{N} \frac{1}{T_i} \sum_{t=1}^{T_i} \hat{\sigma}_{km,tj|i}. \tag{16.12}$$

16.3 Random parameter latent class model

In this section, we extend the LCM to allow for heterogeneity both within and across groups. That is, we allow for variation of the parameter vector within classes as well as between classes. The extended model is a straightforward combination of the ML and latent class models. To accommodate the two layers of heterogeneity, we allow for continuous variation of the parameters within classes. The latent class aspect of the model is given as Equations (16.13) and (16.14):

$$f(y_i|\mathbf{x}_i, \text{class} = q) = g(y_i|\mathbf{x}_i, \boldsymbol{\beta}_{i|q}). \tag{16.13}$$

$$\text{Prob}(\text{class} = q) = \pi_q(\boldsymbol{\theta}), q = 1, \ldots, Q. \tag{16.14}$$

The within class heterogeneity (similar to mixed logit, ML) is structured as in Equations (16.15) and (16.16):

$$\boldsymbol{\beta}_{i|q} = \boldsymbol{\beta}_q + \mathbf{w}_{i|q}. \tag{16.15}$$

$$\mathbf{w}_{i|q} \sim E[\mathbf{w}_{i|q} | \mathbf{X}] = \mathbf{0}, \ \text{Var}[\mathbf{w}_{i|q}|\mathbf{X}] = \boldsymbol{\Sigma}_q, \tag{16.16}$$

where the use of $\mathbf{X}$ indicates that $w_{i|q}$ is uncorrelated with all the exogenous data in the sample. We will assume below that the underlying distribution for the within class heterogeneity is normal with mean $\mathbf{0}$ and covariance matrix $\boldsymbol{\Sigma}$. In a given application, it may be appropriate to further assume that certain rows and corresponding columns of $\boldsymbol{\Sigma}_q$ equal zero, indicating that the variation of the corresponding parameter is entirely across classes.

The contribution of individual i to the LL for the model is obtained for each individual in the sample by integrating out the within class heterogeneity and then the class heterogeneity. We will allow for a panel data setting as is common with SC or best–worst data. The observed vector of outcomes is denoted $\mathbf{y}_i$ and the observed data on exogenous variables are collected in $\mathbf{X}_i = [\mathbf{X}_{i1},..,\mathbf{X}_{iTi}]$. The individual is assumed to engage in T_i choice situations, where $T_i \geq 1$. The generic model is given in Equation (16.17):

$$f(\mathbf{y}_i \mid \mathbf{X}_i, \boldsymbol{\beta}_1, \ldots, \boldsymbol{\beta}_Q, \boldsymbol{\theta}, \boldsymbol{\Sigma}_1, \ldots, \boldsymbol{\Sigma}_Q) = \sum\nolimits_{q=1}^{Q} \pi_q(\boldsymbol{\theta}) \int_{w_i} \prod\nolimits_{t=1}^{T_i} f[y_{it} \mid (\boldsymbol{\beta}_q + \mathbf{w}_i), \mathbf{X}_{it}] h(\mathbf{w}_i \mid \boldsymbol{\Sigma}_q) d\mathbf{w}_i.$$

(16.17)

We can now parameterize the class probabilities using a MNL formulation to impose the adding up and positivity restrictions on $\pi_q(\boldsymbol{\theta})$, as shown in Equation (16.18):

$$\pi_q(\boldsymbol{\theta}) = \frac{\exp(\boldsymbol{\theta}_q)}{\Sigma_{q=1}^{Q} \exp(\boldsymbol{\theta}_q)} \quad q = 1, \ldots, Q; \, \theta_Q = 0.$$

(16.18)

A useful refinement of the class probabilities model is to allow the probabilities to be dependent on individual data, such as demographics including age and income. The class probability model becomes the form given in Equation (16.19):

$$\pi_{iq}(\mathbf{z}_i, \boldsymbol{\theta}) = \frac{\exp(\boldsymbol{\theta}'_q \mathbf{z}_i)}{\Sigma_{q=1}^{Q} \exp(\boldsymbol{\theta}'_q \mathbf{z}_i)} \quad q = 1, \ldots, Q; \, \theta_Q = 0.$$

(16.19)

The model employed in this application is a "latent class, mixed multinomial logit" (LC_MMNL) model. Individual i chooses among J alternatives, with conditional probabilities given as Equation (16.20):

$$f[\mathbf{y}_{it} \mid (\boldsymbol{\beta}_q + \mathbf{w}_i), \mathbf{X}_{it}] = \frac{\exp[\Sigma_{j=1}^{J} y_{it,j}(\boldsymbol{\beta}_q + \mathbf{w}_i)' \mathbf{x}_{it,j}]}{\sum\nolimits_{j=1}^{J} \exp[\Sigma_{j=1}^{J} y_{it,j}(\boldsymbol{\beta}_q + \mathbf{w}_i)' \mathbf{x}_{it,j}]} \quad j = 1, \ldots, J,$$

(16.20)

where $y_{it,j} = 1$ for the j corresponding to the alternative chosen and 0 for all others, and $\mathbf{x}_{it,j}$ is the vector of attributes of alternative j for individual i in choice situation t.

Just like mixed logit, the integrals cannot be evaluated analytically. We use maximum simulated likelihood (along the same lines as mixed logit) to evaluate the terms in the LL expression. The contribution of individual i to the simulated LL is the log of Equation (16.21):

$$f^S(\mathbf{y}_i \mid \mathbf{X}_i, \boldsymbol{\beta}_1, \ldots, \boldsymbol{\beta}_Q, \boldsymbol{\theta}, \boldsymbol{\Sigma}_1, \ldots, \boldsymbol{\Sigma}_Q) = \sum\nolimits_{q=1}^{Q} \pi_q(\boldsymbol{\theta}) \frac{1}{R} \sum\nolimits_{r=1}^{R} \prod\nolimits_{t=1}^{T_i} f[\mathbf{y}_{it} \mid (\boldsymbol{\beta}_q + \mathbf{w}_{i,r}), \mathbf{X}_{it}],$$

(16.21)

where $\mathbf{w}_{i,r}$ is the rth of R random draws (Halton draws in our implementation) on the random vector $\mathbf{w}_i$. Collecting all terms, the simulated LL is given as Equation (16.22):

$$\log L^S = \sum_{i=1}^{N} \log \left[\sum_{q=1}^{Q} \pi_q(\boldsymbol{\theta}) \frac{1}{R} \sum_{r=1}^{R} \prod_{t=1}^{T_i} f[y_{it}|(\boldsymbol{\beta}_q + \mathbf{w}_{i,r}), \mathbf{X}_{it}] \right].$$

$$(16.22)$$

The functional forms for $\pi_q(\boldsymbol{\theta})$ and $f[y_{it}|(\boldsymbol{\beta}_q+\mathbf{w}_{i,r}),\mathbf{X}_{it}]$ are given in Equations (16.18) or (16.19), and (16.20), respectively.

Willingness to pay (WTP) estimates are computed using the familiar result, WTP $= -\beta_x/\beta_{\text{cost}}$. Since there is heterogeneity of the parameters within the classes as well as across classes, the WTP result has to be averaged to produce an overall estimate. The averaging is undertaken for the random parameters within each class, then again across classes using the posterior probabilities as weights. Collecting the results, the procedure is shown in Equation (16.23):

$$\widehat{WTP} = \frac{1}{N} \sum_{i=1}^{N} \sum_{qAPR=1}^{QAPR} \{\pi_{qAPR}(\hat{\boldsymbol{\theta}})|i\} \left[\frac{\frac{1}{R}\sum_{r=1}^{R} L_{ir|qAPR} \dfrac{-\hat{\beta}_{time,ir|qAPR}}{\hat{\beta}_{cost,ir|qAPR}}}{\frac{1}{R}\sum_{r=1}^{R} L_{ir|q}} \right]$$

$$= \frac{1}{N} \sum_{i=1}^{N} \sum_{qAPR=1}^{QAPR} \{\pi_{qAPR}(\hat{\boldsymbol{\theta}})|i\} \frac{1}{R}\sum_{r=1}^{R} W_{ir|qAPR} \widehat{WTP}_{time,ir|qAPR}. \qquad (16.23)$$

R is the number of draws in the simulation and r indexes the draws,

$$\hat{\beta}_{time,ir|qAPR} = \hat{\beta}_{time|qAPR} + \hat{\sigma}_{time|qAPR} w_{time,ir|qAPR}$$

and likewise for $\hat{\beta}_{cost,ir|qAPR}$, $L_{ir|qAPR}$ is the contribution of individual i to the class-specific likelihood – this is the product term that appears in Equations (16.21) and (16.22) – $\pi_{qAPR}(\hat{\boldsymbol{\theta}})|i$ is the estimated posterior class probability for individual i (Equation (16.24)), and APR refers to the attribute processing regime which could be full attendance or non-attendance to specific attributes:

$$\pi_{qAPR}(\hat{\boldsymbol{\theta}})|i = \frac{\pi_{qAPR}(\hat{\boldsymbol{\theta}}) \frac{1}{R}\sum_{r=1}^{R} \prod_{t=1}^{T_i} f[y_{it}|(\hat{\boldsymbol{\beta}}_{qAPR} + \mathbf{w}_{i,r}), \mathbf{x}_{it}]}{\sum_{qAPR=1}^{QAPR} \pi_{qAPR}(\hat{\boldsymbol{\theta}}) \frac{1}{R}\sum_{r=1}^{R} \prod_{t=1}^{T_i} f[y_{it}|(\hat{\boldsymbol{\beta}}_{qAPR} + \mathbf{w}_{i,r}), \mathbf{x}_{it}]}.$$

$$(16.24)$$

16.4 A case study

We will illustrate the set ups in Nlogit for both the standard LCM and the LC_MMNL model, using data drawn from a study undertaken in the context of toll versus free roads, which utilized a SC experiment involving two SC alternatives (i.e., route A and route B), which are pivoted around the knowledge base of travelers (i.e., the current trip). The trip attributes associated with each route are summarized in Table 16.1.

Each alternative has three travel scenarios – "arriving x minutes earlier than expected," "arriving y minutes later than expected," and "arriving at the time expected." Each is associated with a corresponding probability[2] of occurrence to indicate that travel time is not fixed but varies from trip to trip. For all attributes except the toll cost, minutes arriving early and late, and the probabilities of arriving on time, early, or late, the values for the SC alternatives are variations around the values for the current trip. Given the lack of exposure to tolls for many travelers in the study catchment area, the toll levels are fixed over a range, varying from no toll to $4.20, with the upper limit determined by the trip length of the sampled trip.

In the choice experiment, the first alternative is described by attribute levels associated with a recent trip, with the levels of each attribute for Routes A and B pivoted around the corresponding level of actual trip alternative with the probabilities of arriving early, on time, and late provided. Commuters and

Table 16.1 Trip attributes in stated choice design

Routes A and B
Free-flow travel time
Slowed-down travel time
Stop/start/crawling travel time
Minutes arriving earlier than expected
Minutes arriving later than expected
Probability of arriving earlier than expected
Probability of arriving at the time expected
Probability of arriving later than expected
Running cost
Toll cost

---

[2] The probabilities are designed and hence exogenously induced to respondents, similar to other travel time variability studies.

Game 5

Illustrative Choice Experiment Screen

Make your choice given the route features presented in this table, thank you.

	Details of your recent trip	Route A	Route B
Average travel time experienced			
Time in free flow traffic (minutes)	20	14	12
Time slowed down by other traffic (minutes)	20	18	20
Time in stop/start/crawling traffic (minutes)	20	26	20
Probability of time of arrival			
Arriving 9 minutes earlier than expected	30%	30%	10%
Arriving at the time expected	30%	50%	50%
Arriving 6 minutes later than expected	40%	20%	40%
Trip costs			
Running costs	$2.25	$3.26	$1.91
Toll costs	$2.00	$2.40	$4.20
If you make the same trip again, which route would you choose?	O Current Road	O Route A	O Route B
If you could only choose between the two new routes, which route would you choose?		O Route A	O Route B

Figure 16.1 An illustrative choice scenario

non-commuters in a Metropolitan area in Australia were sampled. A telephone call was used to establish eligible participants from households. During the telephone call, a time and location were agreed for a face-to-face Computer Assisted Personal Interview (CAPI). In total, 588 commuters and non-commuters (with less than 120 minutes' trip length) were sampled for this study, each responding to 16 choice sets (games), resulting in 9,408 observations for model estimation. The experimental design method of *D*-efficiency used here is specifically structured to increase the statistical performance of the models with smaller samples than are required for other less efficient (statistically) designs such as orthogonal designs (see Rose *et al.* 2008). An illustrative choice scenario is given in Figure 16.1.

16.4.1 Results

The findings are presented in Table 16.2 for four models. All of the Nlogit set ups are presented in section 16.5.2. Although we have not yet introduced attribute processing (see Chapter 21), LCMs have become popular in estimated choice models where analysts are interested in investigating the role of various processing heuristics such as **attribute non-attendance** (ANA) or **attribute aggregation** when they are in common metric units (ACMA). Although it is not necessary to read Chapter 21 at this juncture, given the

Table 16.2 Summary of models

Sample size N = 588 observations. For random parameter models, we used constrained t-distributions and 500 Halton draws. T-ratios are in parentheses.
Times in min. and costs in dollars (AU$2008). MNL model LL = −6729.90

Latent class, fixed parameters, no ANA, no ACMA (Model 1)

Attributes	Class 1	Class 2	Class 3	Class 4	Class 5
Free-flow time	−0.1945 (−7.81)	−0.0743 (−3.58)	−0.0398 (−4.41)	−0.0312 (−1.45)	−0.0033 (−0.26)
Slowed-down and Stop/start/crawling time	−0.2360 (−10.5)	−0.1728 (−7.53)	−0.0782 (−6.46)	−0.1521 (−6.81)	−0.0559 (−4.96)
Running cost	−0.2723 (−3.89)	−2.2544 (−7.89)	−0.4155 (−8.86)	−1.5577 (−7.66)	−0.3854 (−5.53)
Toll cost	−0.2836 (−4.81)	−2.6709 (−8.11)	−0.3309 (−8.61)	−1.2353 (−8.33)	−0.1112 (−2.49)
Reference alt (1,0)	−0.1727 (−0.76)	−0.0823 (−0.38)	0.4211 (2.75)	3.9570 (9.26)	−2.1696 (−6.92)
Commuter trip purpose (1,0)	0.2368 (0.89)	3.2134 (8.72)	−2.8170 (−12.8)	−3.9950 (−7.92)	3.5705 (9.52)
Probability of early arrival	−0.0088 (−1.24)	−0.0303 (−2.88)	−0.0105 (−2.40)	−0.0011 (−0.13)	−0.0190 (−3.17)
Probability of late arrival	−0.0222 (−2.98)	−0.0398 (−3.43)	−0.0198 (−4.17)	−0.0349 (−4.22)	−0.0250 (−3.78)
Stated choice alt 1 (1,0)	−0.1022 (−0.77)	0.2673 (1.34)	−0.0568 (−0.74)	−0.2041 (−1.11)	0.0205 (0.20)
Class membership probability	0.124 (6.39)	0.309 (12.7)	0.184 (9.27)	0.277 (11.3)	0.107 (6.41)
Log-likelihood	−4817.72				
AIC/N	1.035				
McFadden pseudo-R²	0.5339				

Latent class, fixed parameters, FAA, ANA, ACMA (Model 2)

Attributes	FAA 1	FAA 2	FAA 3	ANA 1	ANA 2	ACMA
Free-flow time	−0.0671 (−3.19)	−0.1749 (−6.92)	−0.0378 (−3.25)	fixed	−0.0572 (−3.67)	−0.0419 (−2.22)
Slowed-down and Stop/start/crawling time	−0.1657 (−8.46)	−0.2175 (−13.5)	−0.0417 (−3.69)	−0.1590 (−5.10)	fixed	−0.0419 (−2.22)
Running cost	−2.7308 (−10.3)	−0.2396 (−3.61)	−0.7456 (−10.7)	−0.1628 (−2.20)	−0.3965 (−4.39)	−0.3603 (−4.14)
Toll cost	−2.6509 (−11.2)	−0.2831 (−5.75)	−0.5218 (−11.4)	0.0483 (−0.62)	−0.2912 (−4.07)	−0.3603 (−4.14)
Reference alt (1,0)	−0.2306 (−1.35)	−0.0025 (−0.01)	−0.0280 (−0.22)	−1.4529 (−3.50)	−4.1894 (−6.82)	3.8812 (12.0)
Commuter trip purpose (1,0)	0.3193 (1.45)	0.6366 (2.84)	−0.1712 (−0.86)	−0.1023 (−0.19)	0.4522 (0.44)	0.6772 (1.78)
Probability of early arrival	−0.0063 (−0.71)	−0.0093 (−1.62)	−0.0246 (−5.16)	−0.0073 (−0.90)	−0.0024 (−0.35)	0.0054 (0.37)
Probability of late arrival	−0.0396 (−4.66)	−0.0205 (−2.99)	−0.0390 (−7.23)	−0.0008 (−0.08)	−0.0109 (−1.42)	0.0009 (0.06)
Stated choice alt 1 (1,0)	−0.2523 (−2.75)	−0.0220 (−0.18)	−0.2523 (−2.75)	−0.1743 (−1.38)	0.3169 (2.55)	0.2824 (0.86)
Class membership probability	0.243 (10.8)	0.154 (7.08)	0.174 (7.66)	0.056 (3.95)	0.051 (4.95)	0.322 (14.3)
LL	−4711.59					
AIC/N	1.013					
McFadden pseudo-R²	0.5441					

Table 16.2 (cont.)

	Latent class, random parameters, no ANA, no ACMA (Model 3)			
Attributes	Class 1	Class 2	Class 3	Class 4
Random parameters (constrained triangular distribution)				
Free-flow time	−0.0216 (−0.89)	−0.0237 (−1.59)	−0.0779 (−8.64)	−0.0366 (−6.03)
Slowed-down and Stop/start/crawling time	0.00055 (0.03)	−0.0514 (−4.80)	−0.1116 (−17.9)	−0.0641 (−10.9)
Running cost	−0.7729 (−5.22)	−0.5957 (−7.99)	−0.5065 (−10.4)	−0.2229 (−6.24)
Toll cost	−1.3314 (−12.2)	−0.4316 (−5.52)	−0.2060 (−4.57)	−0.0879 (−2.61)
Fixed parameters				
Reference alt (_,0)	1.2552 (5.95)	0.3044 (1.61)	0.2439 (1.52)	−0.4626 (−3.37)
Commuter trip purpose (1,0)	−0.2665 (−0.77)	−0.5026 (−2.67)	−0.4992 (−3.90)	−0.5344 (−4.15)
Probability of early arrival	−0.0228 (−1.55)	−0.0038 (−0.62)	−0.0261 (−6.04)	−0.0096 (−2.51)
Probability of late arrival	0.0042 (0.24)	−0.0227 (−3.59)	−0.0269 (−5.54)	−0.0052 (−1.24)
Stated choice alt 1 (1,0)	−0.2283 (0.69)	−0.0231 (−0.18)	−0.0301 (−0.35)	0.0710 (1.16)
Class membership probability	0.367 (14.57)	0.202 (7.38)	0.211 (8.11)	0.221 (8.19)
LL			−4803.2	
AIC/N			1.033	
McFadden pseudo-R^2			0.5352	

	Latent class, random parameters, FAA, ANA, ACMA (Model 4)			
Attributes	FAA 1	ANA 1	ANA 2	ACMA
Random parameters (constrained triangular distribution)				
Free-flow time	−0.0495 (−5.39)	fixed	−0.0845 (−8.58)	−0.3561 (−36.8)
Slowed-down and Stop/start/crawling time	−0.0608 (−8.82)	−0.0839 (−14.6)	fixed	−0.3561 (−36.8)
Running cost	−0.6603 (−12.9)	−0.3114 (−6.25)	−0.0799 (−1.74)	−0.4662 (−12.9)
Toll cost	−0.5858 (−29.7)	−0.3352 (−10.1)	−0.2462 (−8.15)	−0.4662 (−12.9)
Fixed parameters				
Reference alt (1,0)	1.8524 (22.6)	0.1051 (0.84)	−1.1228 (−8.76)	0.1678 (1.21)
Commuter trip purpose (1,0)	0.1945 (2.49)	0.2533 (2.45)	−0.7462 (−4.17)	0.0635 (0.56)
Probability of early arrival	−0.0019 (−0.41)	−0.0327 (−6.91)	−0.0053 (−1.11)	−0.0135 (−1.59)
Probability of late arrival	−0.0231 (−4.23)	−0.0451 (−9.33)	−0.0118 (−2.29)	−0.0103 (−1.33)
Stated choice alt 1 (1,0)	−0.0952 (−0.82)	−0.1442 (−1.32)	0.3708 (5.79)	0.7924 (5.98)
Class membership probability	0.656 (22.5)	0.167 (7.48)	0.0611 (4.41)	0.116 (5.39)
LL			−4705.2	
AIC/N			1.010	
McFadden Pseudo-R^2			0.5447	

focus on estimating LCMs the examples may benefit from a quick read of Chapter 21.

The first and third models in Table 16.2 assume full attribute attendance (FAA), which is the standard fully compensatory assumption of the majority of choice modeling applications, while the second and fourth models allow for mixtures of FAA, ANA, and ACMA. The first two models assume fixed parameters for all attributes, while the third and fourth models include random parameters for the travel time and cost attributes. The random parameters are defined by a constrained triangular distribution (see Chapter 15 for details) with scale parameter equal to the mean estimate.[3]

The development of the models follows a natural sequence of behavioral realism (or "complexity") from Model 1 through to Model 4. Under the assumption of FAA, selecting the number of classes is explained below, along lines well recognized in the latent class literature. We estimated Model 1 under alternative numbers of classes (ranging from two through to seven classes), with five classes having the best overall goodness of fit (including AIC). When we move to Model 2, which assumes fixed parameters, but introduces ANA and ACMA, we have to define the ANA and ACMA classes and investigate how many classes should remain as FAA. In a number of studies (e.g., Scarpa *et al.* 2009; Campbell *et al.* 2011; McNair *et al.* 2012), users of LCMs (including Hensher and Greene 2010) imposed only one FAA class when investigating attribute processing rules; however there are good reasons why a number of classes might be considered (just as in Model 1), given that taste heterogeneity can continue to exist between FAA classes in the presence of elements of attribute processing. The introduction of multiple FAA classes may also go some way to reducing the chance that the attribute processing classes end up capturing taste heterogeneity as well as attribute processing, which is a risk when the taste coefficients are not constrained across classes.

Model 2 is the final model under fixed parameters, varying the number of FAA classes and specific ANA and ACMA classes. Model 3 overlays Model 1 with random parameters on the four time and cost attributes of the choice experiment; however, the number of classes is reduced to four on overall goodness of fit. Estimating this model takes many hours. Finally, we introduce Model 4, which builds on all previous models and is also freely defined in

---

[3] We investigated unconstrained distributions including log-normal, but models either failed to converge or produced imprecise parameter estimates, most notably on the standard deviations of the random parameters. This is consistent with Collins *et al.* (2013), who found that constraining the sign of the random parameter distribution is necessary when ANA is handled through latent classes. Literally over 100 hours of model estimation time was undertaken in the estimation of the random parameter versions of the models.

terms of the number of FAA classes, the ANA and ACMA classes, and the distributional assumptions imposed on each random parameter.[4] Estimation of Model 4 also takes many hours with many models failing to converge (see n. 3). The number of FAA classes under random parameters is reduced to one compared to three under fixed parameters (Model 2), possibly suggesting that some amount of preference heterogeneity that was accommodated through three classes under fixed parameters in Model 2 has been captured in a single class in Model 4 through within class preference heterogeneity. The final four models reported below are the outputs of this process.

A question naturally arises: how can the analyst determine the number of classes, Q? Since Q is not a free parameter, a LRT is not appropriate though, in fact, log L will increase when Q increases. Researchers typically use an information criterion, such as AIC, to guide them toward the appropriate value. For Model 1, the AIC was the lowest for five classes, at 1.035 (LL of −4817.72); whereas for Model 3, with random parameters, we found four classes had the lowest AIC (1.033 and a LL of −4803.2, slightly better than Model 1). Heckman and Singer (1984a) also suggest a practical guidepost in selecting the number of classes; namely, that if the model is fit with too many classes, estimates will become imprecise, even varying wildly. Signature features of a model that has been overfit include exceedingly small estimates of the class probabilities, wild values of the structural parameters, and huge estimated standard errors. For the models that account for ANA and ACMA (Models 2 and 4), the number of classes is pre-defined by the number of restrictions on parameters that are imposed to distinguish the attribute processing strategies of interest; however, the number of classes with full attribute attendance is free and can be determined along the same lines as Models 1 and 3.

With respect to the ANA and ACMA conditions that might be imposed, authors have suggested that responses to supplementary questions on whether a respondent claims that they ignore specific attributes and/or added them up may be useful to signal the possibility of specific attribute processing strategies. For the sample of 588 observations, the following incidence of reported ANA was obtained: free-flow time (28 percent), slowed-down and stop start time (27 percent), running cost (17 percent), and toll cost (11 percent). The incidence of ACMA is as follows: total time (60.5 percent) and total cost (80 percent). The reliability of such data has been questioned in many papers (see, e.g., Hess and Hensher 2010); however, despite the concerns about the

---

[4] We investigated correlations among the random parameters in the unconstrained distributions; however, such models were an inferior statistical fit over Model 4 reported in Table 16.2.

believability of such evidence, there is a case to support the presence of heterogeneity in attribute processing. The above incidence rates of ANA motivate the selection of the restrictions imposed on the models that account for ANA and ACMA, although the final classes were based on extensive investigation of alternative restrictions and show that the link with the stated supplementary question responses is tenuous (in line with the general trend in the literature). The number of classes in Models 2 and 4 are determined by the number of attribute processing rules of interest plus an assessment of the number of FAA classes using AIC as a statistical guide, as well as the suggestions of Heckman and Singer.

The incorporation of the ANA and ACMA attribute processing rules (Models 2 and 4) increases the overall goodness of fit compared to the model without allowance for attribute processing. The overall LL improves from −4817.71 (Model 1) to −4711.59 (Model 2) under fixed parameters, and from −4803.2 (Model 3)[5] to −4705.2 (Model 4) under random parameters. On the AIC test, adjusted for sample size, it improves from 1.035 to 1.013, respectively, for Models 1 and Model 2 and from 1.033 to 1.010, respectively, for Models 3 and 4. Model 4 is only a marginal improvement over Model 2 on overall fit, and after extensive investigation of possible reasons (including changing the number of Halton draws from 250 up to 1,500 with 250 increments), we could not find any circumstance under which Model 4 performs considerably better than Model 2. What this suggests to us is that the added layer of behavioral complexity to allow for taste heterogeneity may indeed be adding little once attribute processing is accounted for. This finding is reinforced by the worse fit for Model 3 with random parameters in the absence of attribute processing (−4803.2) in contrast to Model 2 with attribute processing under fixed parameters (−4711.59). It is noteworthy that including three FAA classes in Model 2 is also a way of capturing (discrete) random preference heterogeneity in a probabilistic decision process model, which introduces useful behavioral information that aligns to a comparison of two alternative specifications of random preference heterogeneity. What this indicates is an expectation that Model 2 may be capturing some amount of the random

---

[5] We also ran Model 3 as a standard ML model. Three models were estimated – an unconstrained triangular distribution with and without correlated random parameters, and a constrained triangular distribution that does not permit correlated parameters. The respective LLs (and AIC) at convergence were −5512.22 (1.176), −5568.57 (1.187), and −6158.89 (1.311). In all cases, these models are inferior, statistically, to Models 1–4 in Table 16.2, although an expected improvement over MNL (−6729.90, 1.433). Given that Model 4 outperforms the standard ML model, then Model 4 is additionally an improvement over a model with preference heterogeneity accommodated with continuous random taste heterogeneity (as opposed to the Model 1 with discrete preference heterogeneity).

Table 16.3 WTP estimates Weighted average VTTS (2008 AUD$/person hr.) using weights for components of time and components of cost (standard deviations in brackets)

	Model 1	Model 2	Model 3	Model 4
Free-flow time	6.86 (2.25)	8.91 (2.01)	5.90 (3.17)	12.78 (0.79)
Slowed-down and stop/start time	12.38 (3.12)	14.78 (1.38)	8.72 (3.91)	12.30 (1.14)
Total time	10.17 (2.77)	12.42 (1.63)	7.59 (3.61)	12.49 (1.00)

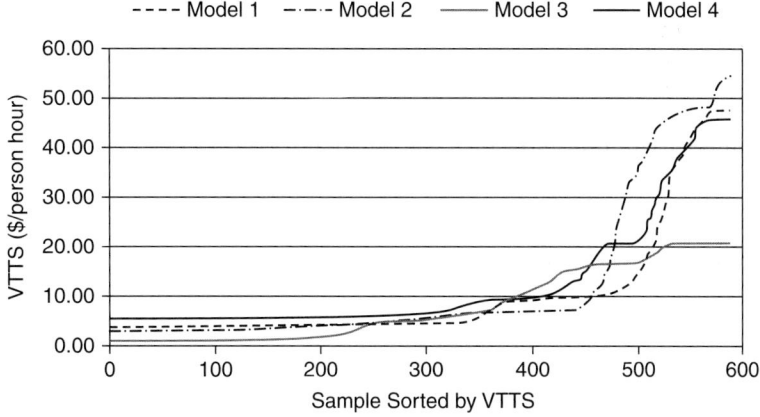

Figure 16.2 Distribution of VTTS for all models

preference heterogeneity that Model 4 is seeking to reveal, which was not obtained in Model 4 through multiple classes of FAA.

When we consider the class allocation, up to a probability, some interesting findings emerge. Class membership probabilities are statistically significant in all models, with a good spread of membership in all models. A comparison of Models 2 and 4 is especially interesting, given the difference in the treatment of the parameters (fixed or random) under a common set of attribute processing rules. Introducing random parameters to account for taste heterogeneity with a class of probabilistic decision rules reduces the probability of membership of the ACMA class from 0.322 to 0.116. A closer look at the classes representing ANA shows an increase in a move back to full attribute attendance under a random parameter specification from 0.571 (the sum of three FAA classes) to 0.656, and an increase in membership probabilities for the ANA classes. This might suggest that an amount of attribute processing (both ANA and ACMA) is being accommodated through random parameters embedded in FAA. Specifically, one implication is that a low marginal disutility associated with attributes that are otherwise assigned a zero value in

ANA are instead associated with a very low marginal disutility and appear in FAA; and small differences in marginal disutility are revealed under ACMA in contrast to equal marginal disutility. There does, however, remain a sizeable (but smaller) incidence of ANA and ACMA.

WTP estimates for the value of total travel time savings ($/hr.) based on equation (16.23), obtained for all four models, are summarized in Table 16.3 and in Figure 16.2. The averaging is undertaken for the random parameters as per Equation (16.23). We find that the mean estimates increase as we account for attribute processing. On a test of statistical differences of VTTS estimates, the z values are greater than 1.96 (ranging from 13.72 for M1 versus M3 to 31.7 for M3 versus M4), except for the comparison of Models 2 and 4 ($z = 0.85$). Thus we can conclude that adding a layer of random parameters to the model that accounts for FAA, ANA, and ACMA does not result in a statistically significant difference in the mean estimate of VTTS (M2 versus M4); however, this is not the situation for comparisons between the fixed parameter models M1 and M2, or between the random parameters models M3 and M4, where attribute processing clearly influences VTTS in an upward direction.

We also observe that the incorporation of attribute processing reduces the standard deviation of the VTTS quite considerably for both the fixed and random parameter models, as well as increasing the mean estimate of VTTS. What this suggests is that it is the allowance for attribute processing, and not the allowance for preference heterogeneity within classes through random parameters, that is the key influence on the higher mean estimate of VTTS and accompanying lower standard deviation. Model 3 is of particular interest, since it suggests that in the absence of allowance for FAA, ANA, and ACMA, the mean estimate of VTTS is significantly deflated but with an inflated standard deviation when preference heterogeneity through random parameters is accommodated.

16.4.2 Conclusions

This section has introduced a generalization of the fixed parameter LCM through a layering of random parameters within each class, and the redefinition of classes as probabilistic decision rules associated with two specific attribute processing rules. We implemented this extended model structure in the context of a toll versus free road choice setting and estimated four models as a way of seeking an understanding of the role of attribute processing in the presence of fixed or random parameters within each probabilistic decision rule class.

What we find, for the data set analyzed, is that if attribute processing is handled through discrete distributions defined in a sufficiently flexible way, adding an additional layer of taste heterogeneity through random parameters within a latent class delivers only a very small improvement in the statistical and behavioral contribution of the model. The flexibility is achieved by not equality constraining coefficients across classes and, crucially, allowing multiple FAA classes to be specified. Compared to the random parameter approach, this model is simple, fast to estimate, and in the empirical setting presented here, very close in model fit to the model that included continuously distributed random parameters.

One implication is that a random parameter treatment in this setting may be confounding with attribute processing; and that including attribute processing in the absence of continuously distributed random parameters is preferred to including continuously distributed random parameters in the absence of attribute processing. This is an important finding that might suggest the role that attribute processing rules play in accommodating attribute heterogeneity, and that random parameters within a class are essentially a potential confounding effect. We offer this finding as a potential concern, conditioned on evidence from one data set, about the possible presence of an identification problem when attribute processing and random parameters within class are simultaneously considered.

Despite the marginal influence of preference heterogeneity[6] in the overall fit of the models, we find potentially important behavioral evidence to suggest that inclusion of random parameters may be a way of accommodating small marginal disutilities (in contrast to ANA set equal to zero marginal disutility), and small differences in marginal disutilities (in contrast to equal marginal disutilities under ACMA), as observed by a "move back" to FAA when fixed parameters become random parameters under attribute processing. If this argument has merit, we may have identified one way of recognizing what the broader literature (e.g., Hess *et al.* 2011; Campbell *et al.* 2011) refers to as low sensitivity, in contrast to zero sensitivity.

The findings are specific to the data set being analyzed;[7] however, like any empirical study, there is a need to assess the findings and conclusions on a number of data sets. We encourage the research community to undertake this

---

[6] Noting that in all of the estimated models, we have preference heterogeneity of some kind, whether discrete or continuous.

[7] We are aware of only two studies that have estimated random parameter latent class models allowing for ANA (Hess *et al.* 2012, Collins *et al.* 2013). They are not directly comparable with the current evidence in this chapter because they do not allow for ACMA and multiple FAA classes, using instead a single FAA class. The main finding, however, of both of these studies is that the inclusion of random parameters and ANA does improve the model fit. There is thus a consistent message under different assumptions re the role of random parameters. Studies that introduce random parameters into LCMs without attribute processing

task, not only for the attribute processing strategies we have assessed, but for a broader set of heuristics on how attributes are processed (see Chapter 21). There is the possibility that our findings might be different for different data sets; this is, however, not a concern about our evidence, but rather a reminder that behavioral processes are often context dependent. If additional studies support the evidence here on many occasions, then there is a case for recognizing the practical value of selecting a latent class framework with fixed parameters for attribute processing, given that inclusion of random parameters adds very little in terms of predictive performance while adding significant complexity in estimation.

Other authors have used the latent class structure to compare processing heterogeneity with regard to several types of behavioral processes, with other types of heterogeneity (e.g., scale, see Thiene *et al.* 2012, and taste, see Hess *et al.* 2012). Although they deal with different decision processes and use different model specifications, they offer general findings on the confounding issue that is discussed in this chapter. They propose, like us, a latent class (or probabilistic decision process) approach with some conditions imposed on classes to reflect a decision process. They then layer additional heterogeneity on top (random taste or scale) to establish the robustness of both the specifications of heterogeneity, and the alternative model specifications that represent the different decision processes. They conclude that the latent class approach has great merit as a framework within which to represent multiple decision processes with and without a random parameter treatment.

16.5 Nlogit commands

16.5.1 Standard command structure

The command syntax is:

```
LCRPLogit
; Choices = ...
; Model: or ; Rhs/Rh2=... as usual
; RPL
; FCN = specification of the RP part, as usual
    but only allows normal, constant, triangular, uniform or (O) which is (t,1)
; Halton, etc.
```

are Greene and Hensher (2012), who found clear improvement with random parameters added to a LCM; Bujosi *et al.* (2010), who also found an improvement, albeit with the random parameters making only a small contribution (in line with only a small improvement of a RPL model over the MNL), and Vij *et al.* (2012), who does not report the LCM without random parameters, so a comparison cannot be made.

```
; Draws = number of draws
; PTS = number of classes
; LCM = variables in class probabilities (optional)
$
```

16.5.2 Command structure for the models in Table 16.2

```
load;file=C:\projects-active\Northlink\Modeling\Brisb08_30Oct.sav$
create
;time = ff+sdt+sst
;cost=rc+tc
;if(tc#0)tollasc=1
;sdst=sdt+sst
;ttime=ff+sdst
;tcost=rc+tc$
```

Model 1: latent class, fixed parameters, no ANA, no ACMA

Note: this model does not impose restrictions of parameter estimates

```
Timer$
LCLogit
    ;lhs=choice1,cset3,Alt3
    ;choices=Curr,AltA,AltB
    ;pds=16 ?stated choice data with 16 choice scenarios
    ;pts=5  ? number of classes - program allows up to 30 classes as of 22
July 2008
    ;maxit=140 ; tlg = .0001
    ;par
    ;wtp=ff/rc,ff/tc,sdst/rc,sdst/tc
    ;lcm ?=<list variables,separated by a comma>
    ;model:
    U(Curr) = FF*FF + SDST*SDT + sdst*sst+RC*rc +TC*Tc +ref
             +commref*commute+prea*prea+prla*prla/
    U(AltA) = FF*FF + SDST*SDT + sdst*sst+ RC*rc +TC*Tc+scl
             +prea*prea+prla*prla/
    U(AltB) = FF*FF + SDST*SDT + sdst*sst+ RC*rc +TC*Tc
             +prea*prea+prla*prla$
```

Model 2: latent class, fixed parameters, FAA, ANA, ACMA

Note: This model uses restrictions to define the probabilistic decision rules for each class

```
Timer$
LCLogit
    ;lhs=choice1,cset3,Alt3
    ;choices=Curr,AltA,AltB
    ;pds=16
    ;pts=6     ;maxit=140 ; tlg = .0001
    ;par
    ;wtp=ff/rc,ff/tc,sdst/rc,sdst/tc
```

```
;lcm
;model:
U(Curr) = FF*FF + SDST*SDT + sdst*sst+RC*rc +TC*Tc +ref
          +commref*commute +prea*prea+prla*prla/
U(AltA) = FF*FF + SDST*SDT + sdst*sst+ RC*rc +TC*Tc+sc1
          +prea*prea+prla*prla/
U(AltB) = FF*FF + SDST*SDT + sdst*sst+ RC*rc +TC*Tc
          +prea*prea+prla*prla
;rst=
? FAA1:
b1ff,b2sdt,b3rc,b4tc,bref,bcomr,bpea,bpla,bsc1,          ? class 1
? FAA 2:
bx1aff,bx2sdt,bx3rc,bx4tc,bxref,bxcomr,bxpea,bxpla,bxsc1, ? class 2
? FAA 3:
by1ff,by2sdt,by3rc,by4tc,byref,bycomr,bypea,bypla,bsc1,  ? class 3
? ANA 1:
0,b2asdt,b3arc,b4atc,bref2,bcomr2,bpea2,bpla2,bsc2,      ? class 4
? ANA 2:
b1bff,0,b3brc,b4btc,bref3,bcomr3,bpea3,bpla3,bsc3,       ? class 5
? ACMA:
bffsdt,bffsdt,brctc,brctc,bref4,bcomr4,bpea4,bpla4,bsc4$ ? class 6
```

```
Normal exit:  5 iterations. Status=0, F=    6729.896
-----------------------------------------------------------------------------------
Discrete choice (multinomial logit) model
Dependent variable               Choice
Log likelihood function     -6729.89591
Estimation based on N =    9408, K =    9
Inf.Cr.AIC  =  13477.8 AIC/N =    1.433
Model estimated: Aug 15, 2012, 11:39:56
R2=1-LogL/LogL* Log-L fncn R-sqrd R2Adj
Constants only must be computed directly
          Use NLOGIT ;...;RHS=ONE$
Chi-squared[ 7]          =   1346.80425
Prob [ chi squared > value ] =   .00000
Response data are given as ind. choices
Number of obs.= 9408, skipped    0 obs
```

CHOICE1	Coefficient	Standard Error	z	Prob. |z|>Z*	95% Confidence Interval	
FF|1	-.04582***	.00444	-10.33	.0000	-.05452	-.03713
SDST|1	-.07619***	.00349	-21.83	.0000	-.08303	-.06935
RC|1	-.42178***	.02512	-16.79	.0000	-.47101	-.37256
TC|1	-.35400***	.01609	-22.00	.0000	-.38553	-.32247
REF|1	.92294***	.04728	19.52	.0000	.83027	1.01561
COMMRE|1	-.14690***	.04786	-3.07	.0021	-.24069	-.05310
PREA|1	-.00973***	.00190	-5.13	.0000	-.01344	-.00601
PRLA|1	-.01483***	.00212	-7.00	.0000	-.01897	-.01068
SC1|1	-.00575	.04111	-.14	.8888	-.08631	.07482

Note: ***, **, * ==> Significance at 1%, 5%, 10% level.

Normal exit: 99 iterations. Status=0, F=   4711.589

Latent Class Logit Model
Dependent variable   CHOICE1
Log likelihood function   -4711.58936
Restricted log likelihood -10335.74441
Chi squared [54 d.f.]   11248.31011
Significance level   .00000
McFadden Pseudo R-squared   .5441461
Estimation based on N =   9408, K =   54
Inf.Cr.AIC =   9531.2 AIC/N =   1.013
Model estimated: Aug 15, 2012, 11:41:35
Constants only must be computed directly
              Use NLOGIT ;...;RHS=ONE$
At start values -6610.3727 .2872******
Response data are given as ind. choices
Number of latent classes =   6
Average Class Probabilities
      .243   .154   .174   .056   .051   .322
LCM model with panel has   588 groups
Fixed number of obsrvs./group=   16
Number of obs.= 9408, skipped   0 obs
-----------+---
           | Standard   Prob.   95% Confidence
   CHOICE1 | Coefficient   Error   z |z|>Z*   Interval
-----------+---
           |Utility parameters in latent class -->> 1
     FF|1 | -.06709***   .02103   -3.19   .0014   -.10831   -.02586
   SDST|1 | -.16573***   .01960   -8.46   .0000   -.20414   -.12733
     RC|1 | -2.73083***   .26533   -10.29   .0000   -3.25085   -2.21080
     TC|1 | -2.65091***   .23603   -11.23   .0000   -3.11352   -2.18829
    REF|1 | -.23063   .17085   -1.35   .1771   -.56550   .10424
 COMMRE|1 | .31932   .21971   1.45   .1461   -.11132   .74995
   PREA|1 | -.00633   .00888   -.71   .4754   -.02373   .01106
   PRLA|1 | -.03959***   .00849   -4.66   .0000   -.05624   -.02294
    SC1|1 | -.25230***   .09170   -2.75   .0059   -.43202   -.07258
           |Utility parameters in latent class -->> 2
     FF|2 | -.17490***   .02527   -6.92   .0000   -.22444   -.12537
   SDST|2 | -.21745***   .01608   -13.52   .0000   -.24898   -.18593
     RC|2 | -.23961***   .06638   -3.61   .0003   -.36971   -.10951
     TC|2 | -.28308***   .04927   -5.75   .0000   -.37964   -.18651
    REF|2 | -.00246   .22280   -.01   .9912   -.43915   .43423
 COMMRE|2 | .63655***   .22396   2.84   .0045   .19759   1.07550
   PREA|2 | -.00933   .00577   -1.62   .1059   -.02063   .00198
   PRLA|2 | -.02048***   .00686   -2.99   .0028   -.03392   -.00704
    SC1|2 | -.02195   .12462   -.18   .8602   -.26620   .22231
           |Utility parameters in latent class -->> 3
     FF|3 | -.03775***   .01162   -3.25   .0012   -.06052   -.01499

SDST|3|	-.04167***	.01129	-3.69	.0002	-.06380	-.01953
RC|3|	-.74556***	.06940	-10.74	.0000	-.88159	-.60954
TC|3|	-.52183***	.04589	-11.37	.0000	-.61178	-.43188
REF|3|	-.02800	.12786	-.22	.8267	-.27860	.22261
COMMRE|3|	-.17115	.19993	-.86	.3920	-.56300	.22069
PREA|3|	-.02458***	.00477	-5.16	.0000	-.03392	-.01524
PRLA|3|	-.03904***	.00540	-7.23	.0000	-.04962	-.02846
SC1|3|	-.25230***	.09170	-2.75	.0059	-.43202	-.07258

|Utility parameters in latent class -->> 4

FF|4|	0.0	.....(Fixed Parameter).....				
SDST|4|	-.15900***	.03116	-5.10	.0000	-.22008	-.09792
RC|4|	-.16277**	.07392	-2.20	.0277	-.30765	-.01788
TC|4|	-.04834	.07820	-.62	.5365	-.20161	.10494
REF|4|	-1.45290***	.41557	-3.50	.0005	-2.26740	-.63841
COMMRE|4|	-.10226	.55082	-.19	.8527	-1.18184	.97733
PREA|4|	-.00731	.00817	-.90	.3707	-.02332	.00870
PRLA|4|	-.00080	.01059	-.08	.9401	-.02156	.01997
SC1|4|	-.17428	.12632	-1.38	.1677	-.42186	.07330

|Utility parameters in latent class -->> 5

FF|5|	-.05722***	.01558	-3.67	.0002	-.08775	-.02670
SDST|5|	0.0	.....(Fixed Parameter).....				
RC|5|	-.39648***	.09028	-4.39	.0000	-.57343	-.21953
TC|5|	-.29121***	.07148	-4.07	.0000	-.43131	-.15110
REF|5|	-4.18940***	.61385	-6.82	.0000	-5.39252	-2.98628
COMMRE|5|	.45216	1.03277	.44	.6615	-1.57203	2.47636
PREA|5|	-.00244	.00706	-.35	.7294	-.01628	.01140
PRLA|5|	-.01090	.00766	-1.42	.1546	-.02592	.00411
SC1|5|	.31690**	.12431	2.55	.0108	.07325	.56054

|Utility parameters in latent class -->> 6

FF|6|	-.04186**	.01888	-2.22	.0266	-.07886	-.00485
SDST|6|	-.04186**	.01888	-2.22	.0266	-.07886	-.00485
RC|6|	-.36033***	.08714	-4.14	.0000	-.53112	-.18954
TC|6|	-.36033***	.08714	-4.14	.0000	-.53112	-.18954
REF|6|	3.88123***	.32235	12.04	.0000	3.24942	4.51303
COMMRE|6|	.67715*	.37999	1.78	.0747	-.06761	1.42191
PREA|6|	.00536	.01458	.37	.7134	-.02323	.03394
PRLA|6|	.00097	.01758	.06	.9561	-.03349	.03542
SC1|6|	.28243	.32994	.86	.3920	-.36424	.92909

|Estimated latent class probabilities

PrbCls1|	.24302***	.02258	10.76	.0000	.19876	.28727
PrbCls2|	.15408***	.02175	7.08	.0000	.11145	.19672
PrbCls3|	.17353***	.02265	7.66	.0000	.12914	.21792
PrbCls4|	.05631***	.01424	3.95	.0001	.02840	.08422
PrbCls5|	.05076***	.01025	4.95	.0000	.03067	.07084
PrbCls6|	.32231***	.02259	14.27	.0000	.27803	.36658

```
-----------+------------------------------------------------------------------
```

Note: ***, **, * ==> Significance at 1%, 5%, 10% level.
Fixed parameter ... is constrained to equal the value or
had a nonpositive st.error because of an earlier problem.

```
------------------------------------------------------------------------------
```

Elapsed time: 0 hours, 1 minutes, 43.43 seconds.

Model 3: latent class, random parameters, no ANA, no ACMA

```
Timer$
LCRPLogit  ?Command for the random parameter version of LCM
    ;lhs=choice1,cset3,Alt3
    ;choices=Curr,AltA,AltB
    ;pds=16
    ;rpl;halton
    ;draws=500
    ;fcn=ff(t,1),sdst(t,1),rc(t,1),tc(t,1)    ?constrained triangular dis-
tribution
    ;wtp=ff/rc,ff/tc,sdst/rc,sdst/tc
    ;pts=4
    ;maxit=100 ; tlg = .0001
    ;par
    ;lcm
    ;model:
    U(Curr) = FF*FF + SDST*SDsT +RC*rc +TC*Tc +ref+commref*commute
              +prea*prea+prla*prla/
    U(AltA) = FF*FF + SDST*SDsT + RC*rc +TC*Tc +sc1 +prea*prea+prla*prla/
    U(AltB) = FF*FF + SDST*SDsT + RC*rc +TC*Tc+prea*prea+prla*prla$
```

Model 4: latent class, random parameters, FAA, ANA, ACMA

```
Timer$
LCRPLogit
    ;lhs=choice1,cset3,Alt3
    ;choices=Curr,AltA,AltB
    ;pds=16
    ;rpl;halton
    ;draws=500
    ;fcn=ff(t,1),sdst(t,1),rc(t,1),tc(t,1)  ?constrained triangular dis-
tribution
    ;pts=4
    ;maxit=100 ; tlg = .0001
    ;par
    ;wtp=ff/rc,ff/tc,sdst/rc,sdst/tc
    ;lcm
    ;model:
    U(Curr) = FF*FF + SDST*SDsT +RC*rc +TC*Tc +ref +commref*commute
              +prea*prea+prla*prla/
    U(AltA) = FF*FF + SDST*SDsT + RC*rc +TC*Tc +sc1 +prea*prea+prla*prla/
    U(AltB) = FF*FF + SDST*SDsT + RC*rc +TC*Tc+prea*prea+prla*prla$
    ;rst=
    ?Both the mean and standard deviation parameters must be set to zero
if an attribute
    ?is not attended to.
    ?FAA1: full attribute attendance, Last 4 (bolded) restrictions are
the random
    ?parameter standard deviation parameters:
    b1ff,b2sdt,b3rc,b4tc,bref,bcomr,bpea,bpla,bsc1,b1ff,b2sdt,b3rc,b4tc,
    ?ANA1: Attribute non attendance for free flow time, Last 4 (bolded)
restrictions are
```

?the random parameter standard deviation parameters:
0,b2asdt,b3arc,b4atc,bref2,bcomr2,bpea2,bpla2,bsc2,**0,b2asdt,b3arc,
b4atc,**
?ANA2: Attribute non attendance for free flow time, Last 4 (bolded)
restrictions are
?the random parameter standard deviation parameters:
b1bff,0,b3brc,b4btc,bref3,bcomr3,bpea3,bpla3,bsc3,**b1bff,0,b3brc,
b4btc,**
?ACMA: Attribute non attendance for slowed down and stop/start time,
Last 4 (bolded)
?restrictions are the random parameter standard deviation parameters:
bffsdt,bffsdt,brctc,brctc,bref4 bcomr4,bpea4,bpla4,bsc4,**bffsdt,
bffsdt,brctc,brctc**$
Normal exit: 5 iterations. Status=0, F=   6729.896

Start values obtained using MNL model
Dependent variable   Choice
Log likelihood function   -6729.89591
Estimation based on N =   9408, K =   9
Inf.Cr.AIC =   13477.8 AIC/N =   1.433
Model estimated: Aug 14, 2012, 18:40:28
R2=1-LogL/LogL* Log-L fncn R-sqrd R2Adj
Constants only must be computed directly
                Use NLOGIT ;...;RHS=ONE$
Chi-squared[7]   =   1346.80425
Prob [chi squared > value] =   .00000
Response data are given as ind. choices
Number of obs.= 9408, skipped   0 obs

CHOICE1	Coefficient	Standard Error	z	Prob. |z|>Z*	95% Confidence Interval	
FF	-.04582***	.00444	-10.33	.0000	-.05452	-.03713
SDST	-.07619***	.00349	-21.83	.0000	-.08303	-.06935
RC	-.42178***	.02512	-16.79	.0000	-.47101	-.37256
TC	-.35400***	.01609	-22.00	.0000	-.38553	-.32247
REF	.92294***	.04728	19.52	.0000	.83027	1.01561
COMMREF	-.14690***	.04786	-3.07	.0021	-.24069	-.05310
PREA	-.00973***	.00190	-5.13	.0000	-.01344	-.00601
PRLA	-.01483***	.00212	-7.00	.0000	-.01897	-.01068
SC1	-.00575	.04111	-.14	.8888	-.08631	.07482

Note: ***, **, * ==> Significance at 1%, 5%, 10% level.

Line search at iteration   30 does not improve fn. Exiting optimization.

Latent Class Mixed (RP) Logit Model
Dependent variable   CHOICE1
Log likelihood function   -5079.15871
Restricted log likelihood -10335.74441

```
Chi squared [  35 d.f.]      10513.17141
Significance level                .00000
McFadden Pseudo R-squared        .5085832
Estimation based on N =    9408, K =   35
Inf.Cr.AIC  =  10228.3 AIC/N =     1.087
Model estimated: Aug 14, 2012, 20:31:49
Constants only must be computed directly
             Use NLOGIT ;...;RHS=ONE$
At start values -6683.7324  .2401******
Response data are given as ind. choices
Replications for simulated probs. = 250
Halton sequences used for simulations
Number of latent classes =          4
Average Class Probabilities
     .656   .167   .061   .116
LCM model with panel has     588 groups
Fixed number of obsrvs./group=       16
BHHH estimator used for asymp. variance
Number of obs.= 9408, skipped    0 obs
```

CHOICE1	Coefficient	Standard Error	z	Prob. |z|>Z*	95% Confidence Interval	
	Estimated latent class probabilities					
PrbCls1	.65579***	.02911	22.53	.0000	.59874	.71284
PrbCls2	.16687***	.02230	7.48	.0000	.12316	.21057
PrbCls3	.06110***	.01385	4.41	.0000	.03395	.08824
PrbCls4	.11625***	.02158	5.39	.0000	.07394	.15856

Note: ***, **, * ==> Significance at 1%, 5%, 10% level.

Random Parameters Logit Model for Class 1

CHOICE1	Coefficient	Standard Error	z	Prob. |z|>Z*	95% Confidence Interval	
	Random parameters in utility functions					
FF	-.04946***	.00917	-5.39	.0000	-.06743	-.03148
SDST	-.06084***	.00690	-8.82	.0000	-.07436	-.04731
RC	-.66031***	.05104	-12.94	.0000	-.76035	-.56027
TC	-.58579***	.01975	-29.66	.0000	-.62450	-.54708
	Nonrandom parameters in utility functions					
REF	1.85240***	.08213	22.55	.0000	1.69143	2.01337
COMMREF	.19452**	.07803	2.49	.0127	.04158	.34746
PREA	-.00190	.00466	-.41	.6839	-.01104	.00724
PRLA	-.02309***	.00545	-4.23	.0000	-.03377	-.01240
SC1	-.09518	.11576	-.82	.4109	-.32206	.13170
	Distns. of RPs. Std.Devs or limits of triangular					
TsFF	.04946***	.00917	5.39	.0000	.03148	.06743
TsSDST	.06084***	.00690	8.82	.0000	.04731	.07436

TsRC|	.66031***	.05104	12.94	.0000	.56027	.76035
TsTC|	.58579***	.01975	29.66	.0000	.54708	.62450

Note: ***, **, * ==> Significance at 1%, 5%, 10% level.

Random Parameters Logit Model for Class 2

CHOICE1		Coefficient	Standard Error	z	Prob. |z|>Z*	95% Confidence Interval
	Random parameters in utility functions						
FF|	0.0	.....(Fixed Parameter).....				
SDST|	-.08394***	.00575	-14.59	.0000	-.09522	-.07267
RC|	-.31141***	.04981	-6.25	.0000	-.40904	-.21378
TC|	-.33516***	.03321	-10.09	.0000	-.40024	-.27008
	Nonrandom parameters in utility functions						
REF|	.10510	.12448	.84	.3985	-.13888	.34909
COMMREF|	.25332**	.10329	2.45	.0142	.05087	.45577
PREA|	-.03274***	.00474	-6.91	.0000	-.04203	-.02345
PRLA|	-.04505***	.00483	-9.33	.0000	-.05452	-.03558
SC1|	-.14416	.10940	-1.32	.1876	-.35858	.07027
	Distns. of RPs. Std.Devs or limits of triangular						
TsFF|	0.0	.....(Fixed Parameter).....				
TsSDST|	.08394***	.00575	14.59	.0000	.07267	.09522
TsRC|	.31141***	.04981	6.25	.0000	.21378	.40904
TsTC|	.33516***	.03321	10.09	.0000	.27008	.40024

Note: ***, **, * ==> Significance at 1%, 5%, 10% level.
Fixed parameter ... is constrained to equal the value or
had a nonpositive st.error because of an earlier problem.

Random Parameters Logit Model for Class 3

CHOICE1		Coefficient	Standard Error	z	Prob. |z|>Z*	95% Confidence Interval
	Random parameters in utility functions						
FF|	-.08447***	.00984	-8.58	.0000	-.10376	-.06517
SDST|	0.0	.....(Fixed Parameter).....				
RC|	-.07992*	.04593	-1.74	.0818	-.16993	.01009
TC|	-.24623***	.03022	-8.15	.0000	-.30546	-.18701
	Nonrandom parameters in utility functions						
REF|	-1.12277***	.12822	-8.76	.0000	-1.37407	-.87147
COMMREF|	-.74618***	.17901	-4.17	.0000	-1.09703	-.39533
PREA|	-.00531	.00479	-1.11	.2670	-.01470	.00407
PRLA|	-.01181**	.00515	-2.29	.0217	-.02190	-.00172
SC1|	.37083***	.06399	5.79	.0000	.24541	.49626
	Distns. of RPs. Std.Devs or limits of triangular						
TsFF|	.08447***	.00984	8.58	.0000	.06517	.10376

TsSDST	0.0	.....(Fixed Parameter).....				
TsRC	.07992*	.04593	1.74	.0818	-.01009	.16993
TsTC	.24623***	.03022	8.15	.0000	.18701	.30546

Note: ***, **, * ==> Significance at 1%, 5%, 10% level.
Fixed parameter ... is constrained to equal the value or
had a nonpositive st.error because of an earlier problem.

Random Parameters Logit Model for Class 4

CHOICE1	Coefficient	Standard Error	z	Prob. |z|>Z*	95% Confidence Interval	
	Random parameters in utility functions					
FF	-.35611***	.00968	-36.80	.0000	-.37508	-.33714
SDST	-.35611***	.00968	-36.80	.0000	-.37508	-.33714
RC	-.46622***	.03600	-12.95	.0000	-.53677	-.39567
TC	-.46622***	.03600	-12.95	.0000	-.53677	-.39567
	Nonrandom parameters in utility functions					
REF	.16776	.13888	1.21	.2271	-.10444	.43996
COMMREF	.06350	.11302	.56	.5743	-.15803	.28502
PREA	-.01353	.00850	-1.59	.1114	-.03020	.00313
PRLA	-.01026	.00770	-1.33	.1827	-.02536	.00483
SC1	.79241***	.13254	5.98	.0000	.53263	1.05218
	Distns. of RPs. Std.Devs or limits of triangular					
TsFF	.35611***	.00968	36.80	.0000	.33714	.37508
TsSDST	.35611***	.00968	36.80	.0000	.33714	.37508
TsRC	.46622***	.03600	12.95	.0000	.39567	.53677
TsTC	.46622***	.03600	12.95	.0000	.39567	.53677

Note: ***, **, * ==> Significance at 1%, 5%, 10% level.

Elapsed time: 1 hours, 51 minutes, 24.38 seconds.

16.5.3 Other useful latent class model forms

16.5.3.1 LCM with scale

Scale may be of interest in LCMs, as it is in ML models. We can extend the standard LCM to accommodate the fact that the latent classes may comprise sub-sets of respondents that, while having the same preference marginal utilities, differ in their level of uncertainty and, hence, variance. We achieve this using a scale adjusted LCM. Assume that within each latent class there is a class-specific scale parameter, λ_q each associated with scale membership probabilities π_q. where, $0 \leq \pi_s \leq 1$, $\sum_{s=1}^{S} \pi_s = 1$ and λ_1 is normalized to 1 for purposes of identification. Then the probability of choice conditional on taste class q is shown in Equation (16.25):

$$Pr(j \mid q) = \frac{\exp(\lambda_q \mathbf{x}'_{it,j} \boldsymbol{\beta})}{\sum_{j=1}^{J_i} \exp(\lambda_q \mathbf{x}'_{it,j} \boldsymbol{\beta})}.$$ (16.25)

The overall probability of the sequence of t choices is given in Equation (16.26):

$$Pr(j_1, \ldots, j_{T_i}) = \sum_{q=1}^{Q} \pi_q \left[\prod_{t=1}^{T_i} \left(\frac{\exp(\lambda_q \mathbf{x}'_{it,j} \boldsymbol{\beta})}{\sum_{j=1}^{J_i} \exp(\lambda_q \mathbf{x}'_{it,j} \boldsymbol{\beta})} \right) \right].$$ (16.26)

This latent class estimator is any LCM specification, with **;SLCL**. An example is provided below. It is important to recognize that the comparison of parameter estimates between a MNL and a LCM is not possible, since each model is subject to a different scaling of the parameter estimates that is related to the scale factor of the unobserved Gumbel error component. For each model, these scale parameters are normalized in estimation (essentially to 1.0), thereby preventing any meaningful comparison of parameter estimates between the two models. The comparison of the marginal rates of substitution (i.e., WTP) between attributes in the one model does make sense, since the scale effect is neutralized.

> *As an aside*, The scaled LC model is not a simulation-based estimator. The scale factors are fixed parameters, not random parameters.

```
Lclogit   ? or Slclogit and you must remove ;slscl syntax
    ;lhs=mode
    ;rhs=one,gc,ttme
    ;choices=air,train,bus,car
    ;pts=2;pds=7
    ;rst=bg,bt,aa,at,ab,
        bg,bt,aa,at,ab
    ;maxit=100
    ;slcl$

Normal exit:   6 iterations. Status=0, F=    199.9766

-----------------------------------------------------------------------------
Discrete choice (multinomial logit) model
Dependent variable               Choice
Log likelihood function       -199.97662
Estimation based on N =     210, K =    5
Inf.Cr.AIC   =    410.0 AIC/N =    1.952
R2=1-LogL/LogL* Log-L fncn R-sqrd R2Adj
```

```
Constants only   -283.7588  .2953 .2873
Chi-squared[ 2]           =   167.56429
Prob [ chi squared > value ] =   .00000
Response data are given as ind. choices
Number of obs.=   210, skipped      0 obs
```

MODE	Coefficient	Standard Error	z	Prob. |z|>Z*	95% Confidence Interval	
GC|1	-.01578***	.00438	-3.60	.0003	-.02437	-.00719
TTME|1	-.09709***	.01044	-9.30	.0000	-.11754	-.07664
A_AIR|1	5.77636***	.65592	8.81	.0000	4.49078	7.06194
A_TRAI|1	3.92300***	.44199	8.88	.0000	3.05671	4.78929
A_BUS|1	3.21073***	.44965	7.14	.0000	2.32943	4.09204

```
***, **, * ==>  Significance at 1%, 5%, 10% level.
Model was estimated on Aug 06, 2013 at 02:03:42 PM
```

```
Maximum of   200 iterations. Exit iterations with status=1.
```

```
Scaled Latent Class MNL Model
Dependent variable                 MODE
Log likelihood function      -195.43089
Restricted log likelihood    -291.12182
Chi squared [  7](P= .000)    191.38186
Significance level               .00000
McFadden Pseudo R-squared       .3286972
Estimation based on N =    210, K =    7
Inf.Cr.AIC  =     404.9 AIC/N =     1.928
R2=1-LogL/LogL* Log-L fncn R-sqrd R2Adj
No coefficients  -291.1218  .3287 .3212
Constants only   -283.7588  .3113 .3035
At start values  -199.9788  .0227 .0118
Response data are given as ind. choices
Number of latent classes =           2
Average Class Probabilities
     .462  .538
LCM model with panel has       30 groups
Fixed number of obsrvs./group=        7
BHHH estimator used for asymp. variance
Number of obs.=   210, skipped      0 obs
```

MODE	Coefficient	Standard Error	z	Prob. |z|>Z*	95% Confidence Interval	
	Random LCM parameters in latent class -->> 1					
GC|1	-.00943**	.00382	-2.47	.0136	-.01692	-.00194
TTME|1	-.05564***	.01988	-2.80	.0051	-.09461	-.01668

```
 A_AIR|1|    3.17876***   1.15653   2.75  .0060   .91200  5.44553
A_TRAI|1|    2.09976***    .75408   2.78  .0054   .62179  3.57773
 A_BUS|1|    1.53427***    .59347   2.59  .0097   .37108  2.69745
         |Random LCM      parameters in latent class -->>  2
   GC|2|     -.00943**     .00382  -2.47  .0136  -.01692  -.00194
 TTME|2|     -.05564***    .01988  -2.80  .0051  -.09461  -.01668
A_AIR|2|     3.17876***   1.15653   2.75  .0060   .91200  5.44553
A_TRAI|2|    2.09976***    .75408   2.78  .0054   .62179  3.57773
 A_BUS|2|    1.53427***    .59347   2.59  .0097   .37108  2.69745
         |Estimated latent class probabilities
 PrbCls1|    .46193**      .21651   2.13  .0329   .03758   .88628
 PrbCls2|    .53807**      .21551   2.50  .0125   .11569   .96045
         |Scale Factors for Class Taste Parameters
Cls1_Scl|    3.18345***    .16857  18.88  .0000  2.85306  3.51385
Cls2_Scl|         1.0    .....(Fixed Parameter).....
-----------+----------------------------------------------------------------
***, **, * ==>  Significance at 1%, 5%, 10% level.
Fixed parameter ... is constrained to equal the value or
had a nonpositive st.error because of an earlier problem.
-----------------------------------------------------------------------------
```

16.5.3.2 The "2^K" model for attribute non-attendance

Hess and Rose (2007), Hensher and Greene (2010), and Campbell *et al.* (2010) use a latent class framework as a way of capturing a probabilistic decision process, in which specific restrictions are imposed on the utility expressions for each class, to represent hypotheses of pre-defined attribute processing strategies. However, while a number of the classes relate to attribute non-attendance; these papers excluded the possibility of combinations of more than one attribute non-attendance rule. Investigating all combinations, while appealing, becomes increasingly complex and infeasible as the number of attributes (K) increases, given a 2^K rule for the combination of attendance or non-attendance (see Hole 2011). With four attributes, for example, we have 16 possible combinations, and with eight attributes we have 256.

Non-attendance is accommodated by supposing that individuals sort themselves into one of 2^K (or $q=1,\ldots,Q$) classes, distinguished by which of the attributes were considered in their choice process. If the configuration chosen by the individual is not directly observed (as, for example, in a supplementary question), then in the model this sorting can only be done probabilistically. In the context of the LC model, we can model this by writing Equation (16.27):

$$\text{Prob}(i,j\,|\,q) = \frac{\exp(\boldsymbol{\beta}'_q \mathbf{x}_{i,j})}{\Sigma_{j=1}^{J}\exp(\boldsymbol{\beta}'_q \mathbf{x}_{i,j})}. \qquad (16.27)$$

β_q is one of the 2^K possible vectors β in which m of the elements are zero and $K-m$ are non-zero. Specifically, q can be thought of as a masking vector of the form $(\delta_1, \delta_2, \delta_3, \delta_4, \dots)$, where each δ takes the possible values 0,1. β_q is then the "element for element product" of this masking vector, with the standard coefficient vector β, indicating that the masking vector interacts with the coefficient vector. For example, for two attributes (classes), the parameter vectors would appear $\beta_1=(0,0)$, $\beta_2=(\beta_A,0)$, $\beta_3=(0,\beta_B)$, $\beta_4=(\beta_A,\beta_B)$.[8] However, it is an important part of the underlying theory that the class q is not defined by the attribute taking value zero within the class but by the corresponding coefficient taking the value zero. Thus the "random parameters" aspect of the model is a discrete distribution of preference structures across individuals who are distinguished by whether they pay attention to the particular attribute or not.

Since (in our case) the sorting is not observable, we cannot directly construct the likelihood function for estimation of the parameters. In keeping with the latent class approach, we need to estimate a set of probabilities (π_q) that each individual i falls into class q. While this could be conditioned on individual characteristics, in this case we have assumed that the same set applies equally to all respondents, so that the probabilities reflect the class proportions.

Hence the marginal probability that individual i will choose alternative j is found by averaging over the classes, as in Equation (16.28):

$$\text{Prob}(i,j) = \sum_{q=1}^{2^K} \pi_q \frac{\exp(\beta'_q x_{i,j})}{\sum_{j=1}^{J} \exp(\beta'_q x_{i,j})} \text{ where } \sum_{q=1}^{2^K} \pi_q = 1. \qquad (16.28)$$

As formulated, this is a type of finite mixture, or LCM. It differs from more familiar formulations in that the non-zero elements in β_q are the same across the classes and the classes have specific behavioral meaning, as opposed to merely being groupings defined on the basis of responses, as in the strict latent class formulation, hence the reference to a probabilistic decision process model. Estimation of the probabilistic decision process model is as straightforward as a latent class MNL model with linear constraints on the coefficients, as suggested above.

It should be noted that although the 2^k approach offers plenty of scope to investigate a number of attribute non-attendance profiles, we are of the view that imposing behaviorally plausible conditions through the restriction

---

[8] In this example, there is one unrestricted parameter vector in the model, shown as $\beta_4 = (\beta_A, \beta_B)$. The other parameter vectors are constructed from the same two parameters, either by setting one or both elements to zero or by equating elements to those in β_4. Thus, $\beta_3 = (0, \beta_B)$ is obtained as a linear restriction on β_4, namely that one element equal zero and a second element equal the corresponding element in β_4.

command is a preferred options. The 2^K approach can serve as a useful screening mechanism to complement the final behavioral specification of the LCM with restrictions that defines the probabilistic decision rules for each class.

The command syntax is as follows:

```
LCLOGIT ; Lhs = choice, etc.
        ; Choices = list of names
        ; LCM = list of variables in class probabilities
(optional)
        ; RHS = list of endogenous attributes
        ; RH2 = anything interacted with ASCs, such as ASCs.
(optional)
        ; Pts = 102 or 103 or 104
... any other options, such as ;PDS. $
```

The 102, 103 or 104 means that in the RHS list, the first 2, 3, or 4 attributes are endogenous, and there will be 2^2 or 2^3 or 2^4 classes. Nlogit allows up to 4 **endogenous** attributes, which produces 16 classes. Altogether it allows up to 300 parameters. It does proliferate parameters very fast. If you have pts = 104 and 3 other attributes you would have $16*(3 + 4 + 1) = 128$ parameters. This is the binding constraint, even though the parameters are repeated in the formulation of the model. The model output below, estimated with **;pts=103**, has 2^3 (or 8) classes in which various parameters are set to zero:

```
LClogit
    ;lhs=choice1,cset3,Alt3
    ;choices=Curr,AltA,AltB
    ;rhs=congt,rc,tc
    ;rh2=one
    ;lcm
    ;pts=103
    ;pds=16$
Normal exit:   5 iterations. Status=0. F=      3461.130
--------------------------------------------------------------------------------
Discrete choice (multinomial logit) model
Dependent variable                     Choice
Log likelihood function      -3461.12961
Estimation based on N =    4480, K =    5
Information Criteria: Normalization=1/N
              Normalized    Unnormalized
AIC              1.54738      6932.25923
Fin.Smpl.AIC     1.54738      6932.27264
Bayes IC         1.55453      6964.29612
Hannan Quinn     1.54990      6943.55032
Model estimated: Sep 16, 2010, 14:03:16
R2=1-LogL/LogL* Log-L fncn R-sqrd R2Adj
Constants only must be computed directly
            Use NLOGIT ;...; RHS=ONE$
```

```
Chi-squared[ 3]              =     467.23551
Prob [ chi squared > value ] =    .00000
Response data are given as ind. choices
Number of obs.= 4480, skipped      0 obs
-----------+------------------------------------------------------------------
          |                   Standard              Prob.
  CHOICE1| Coefficient        Error         z     z>|Z|
-----------+------------------------------------------------------------------
  CONGT|1|      -.07263***       .00464    -15.65   .0000
    RC|1|      -.33507***       .03749     -8.94   .0000
    TC|1|      -.27047***       .02198    -12.31   .0000
A_CURR|1|       .89824***       .05751     15.62   .0000
A_ALTA|1|      -.05025          .05603      -.90   .3698
-----------+------------------------------------------------------------------
Note: ***, **, * ==>  Significance at 1%, 5%, 10% level.
------------------------------------------------------------------------------

Normal exit:  45 iterations. Status=0. F=    2752.517
------------------------------------------------------------------------------
Endog. Attrib. Choice LC Model
Dependent variable              CHOICE1
Log likelihood function      -2752.51660
Restricted log likelihood    -4921.78305
Chi squared [  12 d.f.]       4338.53291
Significance level                .00000
McFadden Pseudo R-squared      .4407481
Estimation based on N =   4480, K =  12
Information Criteria: Normalization=1/N
            Normalized   Unnormalized
AIC              1.23416      5529.03319
Fin.Smpl.AIC     1.23417      5529.10304
Bayes IC         1.25132      5605.92173
Hannan Quinn     1.24021      5556.13183
Model estimated: Sep 16, 2010, 14:03:30
Constants only must be computed directly
              Use NLOGIT ;...;RHS=ONE$
At start values -3330.8229  .1736******
Response data are given as ind. choices
Number of latent classes =           8
LCM model with panel has     280 groups
Fixed number of obsrvs./group=       16
Hessian is not PD. Using BHHH estimator
Number of obs.= 4480, skipped      0 obs
-----------+---------------------------------------    -----------------
          |                   Standard              Prob.
  CHOICE1| Coefficient        Error         z     z>|Z|
-----------+------------------------------------------------------------------
          |Utility parameters in latent class -->> 1
  CONGT|1|      -.30457***       .01395    -21.84   .0000
    RC|1|     -1.17009***       .11770     -9.94   .0000
```

```
     TC|1|    -1.74733***      .06142    -28.45   .0000
 A_CURR|1|      .49643***      .03933     12.62   .0000
 A_ALTA|1|     -.09441*        .05202     -1.81   .0695
         |Utility parameters in latent class -->> 2
  CONGT|2|     -.30457***      .01395    -21.84   .0000
     RC|2|    -1.17009***      .11770     -9.94   .0000
     TC|2|      .000     .....(Fixed Parameter).....
 A_CURR|2|      .49643***      .03933     12.62   .0000
 A_ALTA|2|     -.09441*        .05202     -1.81   .0695
         |Utility parameters in latent class -->> 3
  CONGT|3|     -.30457***      .01395    -21.84   .0000
     RC|3|      .000     .....(Fixed Parameter).....
     TC|3|    -1.74733***      .06142    -28.45   .0000
 A_CURR|3|      .49643***      .03933     12.62   .0000
 A_ALTA|3|     -.09441*        .05202     -1.81   .0695
         |Utility parameters in latent class -->> 4
  CONGT|4|      .000     .....(Fixed Parameter).....
     RC|4|    -1.17009***      .11770     -9.94   .0000
     TC|4|    -1.74733***      .06142    -28.45   .0000
 A_CURR|4|      .49643***      .03933     12.62   .0000
 A_ALTA|4|     -.09441*        .05202     -1.81   .0695
         |Utility parameters in latent class -->> 5
  CONGT|5|     -.30457***      .01395    -21.84   .0000
     RC|5|      .000     .....(Fixed Parameter).....
     TC|5|      .000     .....(Fixed Parameter).....
 A_CURR|5|      .49643***      .03933     12.62   .0000
 A_ALTA|5|     -.09441*        .05202     -1.81   .0695
         |Utility parameters in latent class -->> 6
  CONGT|6|      .000     .....(Fixed Parameter).....
     RC|6|    -1.17009***      .11770     -9.94   .0000
     TC|6|      .000     .....(Fixed Parameter).....
 A_CURR|6|      .49643***      .03933     12.62   .0000
 A_ALTA|6|     -.09441*        .05202     -1.81   .0695
         |Utility parameters in latent class -->> 7
  CONGT|7|      .000     .....(Fixed Parameter).....
     RC|7|      .000     .....(Fixed Parameter).....
     TC|7|    -1.74733***      .06142    -28.45   .0000
 A_CURR|7|      .49643***      .03933     12.62   .0000
 A_ALTA|7|     -.09441*        .05202     -1.81   .0695
         |Utility parameters in latent class -->> 8
  CONGT|8|      .000     .....(Fixed Parameter).....
     RC|8|      .000     .....(Fixed Parameter).....
     TC|8|      .000     .....(Fixed Parameter).....
 A_CURR|8|      .49643***      .03933     12.62   .0000
 A_ALTA|8|     -.09441*        .05202     -1.81   .0695
         |Estimated latent class probabilities
PrbCls1|      .19647***      .03139      6.26   .0000
PrbCls2|      .04384         .04113      1.07   .2865
PrbCls3|      .02196         .08561       .26   .7975
```

```
PrbCls4|      .36672***      .06064      6.05   .0000
PrbCls5|      .12073***      .03316      3.64   .0003
PrbCls6|      .08326**       .03644      2.28   .0223
PrbCls7| .24037D-13         2.31182       .00  1.0000
PrbCls8|      .16702***      .03154      5.30   .0000
-----------+---------------------------------------------------------------
Note: nnnnn.D-xx or D+xx => multiply by 10 to -xx or +xx.
Note: ***, **, * ==>  Significance at 1%, 5%, 10% level.
Fixed parameter ... is constrained to equal the value or
had a nonpositive st.error because of an earlier problem.
------------------------------------------------------------------------------
```

17 Binary choice models

17.1 Introduction

This chapter introduces one of the fundamental pillars of choice modeling, the canonical model for choice between two alternatives. At the most basic level, the model describes the activity between taking an action and not taking that action – i.e., whether or not to use public transport to commute to work, whether or not to purchase a car, whether or not to accept an offered plan for delivery of a utility service such as electricity, and so on. A straightforward extension that provides a bridge to most of the choice models discussed elsewhere in this book describes the choice between two specific alternatives – i.e., whether to use public transport or drive one's own car to commute to work, whether to choose a new technology (e.g., electric) vehicle or a conventionally powered vehicle, or whether to choose a utility plan that includes time varying rates or one that does not (but includes other desirable features).

We begin with the essential binary choice between an outcome and "not." Issues of specification, estimation, and inference are detailed. We will then extend the model in several directions, concluding with multiple equation situations and analysis of panel data. Some of the econometric presentation is an interpretation of material already covered in earlier chapters; however, we believe it is useful to include the material here as a way of relating the essential elements to the popular binary choice model.

17.2 Basic binary choice

We begin with two essential assumptions that underlie the choice modeling strategy throughout this book:

- **Consumer preferences can be described by random utility**. The utility a consumer receives from a choice can be described by a function that responds to observable characteristics of the chooser and attributes of the choice as well as unobserved or unobservable aspects of the choice process. We will even be more specific and assume a particular model:

$$U_{ij} = \beta_j' \mathbf{x}_{ij} + \varepsilon_{ij}. \tag{17.1}$$

- The vector $\mathbf{x}_{ij}$ contains characteristics of the chooser, such as age, gender, income, etc. and attributes of the choice, such as price or other features. Note that the characteristics would vary across different individuals, but would be the same from one choice to the next, while the attributes would differ across choices and, presumably, across individuals as well (as different individuals might face different choices). The coefficients, or marginal utilities, β_j, are the parameters that we are interested in learning about from the observed data. Finally, the random term, ε_{ij}, represents the latent, random (i.e., unobserved) factors that drive the choice process for an individual. A crucial assumption is that ε_{ij} is not correlated with $\mathbf{x}_{ij}$ – i.e., that $\mathbf{x}_{ij}$ is **exogenous** in the random utility function. (For a helpful example in which this is not the case, consider the automobile brand choice model in Berry, Levinsohn, and Pakes (1995), in which attributes of the cars, that are not in the model, are correlated with the prices of the cars, that are in the model. Since the car attributes do drive utility, and are priced in the prices of the cars, but are not measured, they are embedded in the random term, instead. Since the price (which is in $\mathbf{x}_{ij}$) responds to these features, price is endogenous in their model.) We note, finally, that the assumption that the utility function is linear is a convenience that could be restrictive. We do consider nonlinear utility functions elsewhere in the book (see Chapter 20). Non-linearity will add considerable complexity, but no generality at this point. We can learn all we need by using linear utility functions at this point.

- **Consumers make their choices so as to maximize utility**. This assumption is not entirely uncontroversial – we consider the possibility that they minimize random regret elsewhere (see Chapter 8) – but almost so. Consider the two cases mentioned earlier. In choosing between taking an action and not taking that action, we assume that the consumer chooses so that the utility of the choice presented – we'll call that choice 1 – is greater than the universe of other alternatives:

$$U_{i1} = \beta_1' \mathbf{x}_{i1} + \varepsilon_{i1} > U_{i0} = ?. \tag{17.2}$$

- Since we have not specified the "other" alternatives, we have no device to specify that utility function. For lack of a preferable specification, we assume that the utility of the other alternative is zero:

$$U_{i0} = 0, \tag{17.3}$$

- and hence a utility-maximizing chooser will choose action 1 if:

$$U_{i1} = \boldsymbol{\beta}_1'\mathbf{x}_{i1} + \varepsilon_{i1} > 0.^1 \tag{17.4}$$

- They will choose action "0" if U_{i1} is not positive. Note, again, the use of zero as the boundary is a *normalization*. The binary choice is thus determined. If the random variable U_{i1} is positive, the individual will choose alternative 1. It is useful to note in passing the dual interpretation of this result. If the individual chooses alternative 1, they reveal to the observer that random utility 1 is positive.
- Now consider the second specification suggested above, in which there are two well defined alternatives, each providing their own utility. The utility-maximizing consumer will compare the utilities provided by the two alternatives:

$$\begin{aligned} U_{i1} &= \boldsymbol{\beta}_1'\mathbf{x}_{i1} + \varepsilon_{i1}, \\ U_{i0} &= \boldsymbol{\beta}_0'\mathbf{x}_{i0} + \varepsilon_{i0} \end{aligned} \tag{17.5}$$

- and, by our description will choose alternative 1 if:

$$U_{i1} > U_{i0}$$

or

$$U_{i1} - U_{i0} > 0.$$

- Combining terms, our utility-maximizing chooser picks alternative 1 if:

$$\begin{aligned} U_{i1} - U_{i0} &= \left(\boldsymbol{\beta}_1'\mathbf{x}_{i1} + \varepsilon_{i1}\right) - \left(\boldsymbol{\beta}_0'\mathbf{x}_{i0} + \varepsilon_{i0}\right) \\ &= \boldsymbol{\beta}_1'\mathbf{x}_{i1} - \boldsymbol{\beta}_0'\mathbf{x}_{i0} + \varepsilon_{i1} - \varepsilon_{i0} \\ &= \boldsymbol{\beta}_1'\mathbf{x}_{i1} - \boldsymbol{\beta}_0'\mathbf{x}_{i0} + \varepsilon_i \\ &= \boldsymbol{\beta}'\mathbf{x}_i + \varepsilon_i \\ &> 0 \end{aligned} \tag{17.6}$$

---

[1] A technical fine point: for this formulation to be completely consistent, we will ultimately require β_1 to contain a constant term. If not then, rather than zero, we will have to choose some arbitrary constant for U_{i0} and that will end up being the constant term in β_1.

- and they choose alternative 0 if $\boldsymbol{\beta}'\mathbf{x}_i + \varepsilon_i \leq 0$. So, in the end, the possibly subtle difference between our two cases is just a question of how we formulate the deterministic parts of the utility functions. We will return to this shortly.

17.2.1 Stochastic specification of random utility for binary choice

The next step in the model formulation is to lay out the specification of the random part of the random utility function. There are two directions in the modern literature, semi-parametric and fully parametric.[2] Semi-parametric approaches, e.g., Klein and Spady (1993), forgo the assumption of a particular distributional model for random utility. The vast majority of applications of choice modeling takes the additional step of narrowing the model specification with a particular distribution. Two models that dominate the literature are the probit model that is based on the normal distribution and the logit model that departs from the type I Extreme value distribution (or, by a narrower interpretation, the logistic distribution).[3] Assuming that ε_{i1} and ε_{i0} are normally distributed, the probability that the individual chooses alternative 1 is:

$$
\begin{aligned}
\text{Prob}(U_{i1} > 0) &= \text{Prob}(\boldsymbol{\beta}_1'\mathbf{x}_{i1} + \varepsilon_{i1}) > 0 \\
&= \text{Prob}(\varepsilon_{i1} > -\boldsymbol{\beta}_1'\mathbf{x}_{i1}) \\
&= \text{Prob}(\varepsilon_{i1} \leq \boldsymbol{\beta}_1'\mathbf{x}_{i1}) \\
&= \text{Prob}(\varepsilon_{i1} - \mu_1 \leq \boldsymbol{\beta}_1'\mathbf{x}_{i1} - \mu_1) \\
&= \Phi\left(\frac{\boldsymbol{\beta}'_1\mathbf{x}_{i1} - \mu_1}{\sigma_1}\right)
\end{aligned}
\tag{17.7}
$$

where μ_1 and σ_1 are the mean and standard deviation of ε_{i1} and $\Phi(.)$ is the standard normal CDF.

We return to the role of the constant term in the model. If $\boldsymbol{\beta}_1$ contains a constant term, say α, then $\boldsymbol{\beta}_1'\mathbf{x}_{i1} - \mu_1 = (\alpha - \mu_1) - \boldsymbol{\gamma}_1'\mathbf{x}_{i1}{}^*$, where $\boldsymbol{\gamma}_1$ is the rest of

---

[2] We are ultimately interested in rich specifications that involve complicated choice processes based on numerous attributes and that take advantage of observable data on individual heterogeneity such as income, age, gender, location, etc. The third path for model building, non-parametric analysis, for all its generality, is difficult to extend to these multi-layered settings. We will not be considering non-parametric analysis in this book. Readers are referred to more specialized sources such as Henderson and Parmeter (2014) or Li and Racine (2010) for discussions of this topic.

[3] Modern software such as NLOGIT and Stata provide menus of distributions for binary choice models that include seven or more choices. Those beyond the probit and logit are easy to program, but not particularly convincing methodologically. The availability of these exotic models (e.g., ArcTangent) is not a persuasive motivation for using them as a modeling platform. For better or worse, the probit and logit models remain the dominant choices. We will consider the choice between these two shortly.

$\boldsymbol{\beta}_1$ and $\mathbf{x}_{i1}{}^*$ is the rest of $\mathbf{x}_{i1}$ not including the constant. So, the model with a constant term equal to α and mean of ε_{i1} equal to μ is exactly the same as the model with mean of ε_{i1} equal to zero and a constant term equal to $(\alpha - \mu_1) = \alpha^*$. This means that, in our model, we must either drop α or we must drop μ_1. It turns out to be much more convenient later to normalize μ_1 to zero and let the constant term in the utility function be called α, or γ_0, etc.

Now, consider the variance. At this point, our model is:

$$\text{prob}(U_{i1}>0) = \text{Prob}(\boldsymbol{\beta}'_1\mathbf{x}_{i1} + \varepsilon_{i1}) > 0 = \Phi\left(\frac{\boldsymbol{\beta}'_1\mathbf{x}_{i1}}{\sigma_1}\right). \tag{17.8}$$

Bearing in mind that we do not observe utility, but only whether utility is positive or not (i.e., only whether the individual chooses alternative 1 or not), consider what happens if we scale the whole model by a positive constant, say C. Then:

$$
\begin{aligned}
\text{Prob(chooser chooses alternative 1)} \quad &= \text{Prob}(CU_{i1}>C \times 0)\\
&= \text{Prob}[C(\beta_1 \mathbf{x}_{i1} + \varepsilon_{i1})] >C \times 0\\
&= \text{Prob}(C\varepsilon_{i1}<C\beta_1 \mathbf{x}_{i1})\\
&= \Phi\left(\frac{C\boldsymbol{\beta}'_1\mathbf{x}_{i1}}{C\sigma_1}\right) = \Phi\left(\frac{\boldsymbol{\delta}'_1\mathbf{x}_{i1}}{\theta_1}\right) = \Phi\left(\frac{\boldsymbol{\beta}'_1\mathbf{x}_{i1}}{\sigma_1}\right)
\end{aligned}
\tag{17.9}
$$

The implication is that our model is the same regardless of what σ_1 is. To remove the indeterminacy, we set σ_1 to 1. This makes sense. It is important to note that this is not an "assumption" (at least, not one with any content or implication). This is a *normalization* based on how much information about our model will be contained in the observed data. Intuitively, the data contain no information about scaling of the utility function, only its sign as revealed by whether choice 1 is made or not. This sign does not change if σ changes. (In fact, when our model is based on the logistic distribution, the assumed standard deviation is $\pi/\sqrt{6}$, not 1. The essential point is that it is a fixed known value, not a parameter to be estimated.)

To complete this part of the specification, we return to the choice between two specific alternatives:

$$
\begin{aligned}
\text{Choose alternative 1 if } U_{i1} - U_{i0} \quad &= (\boldsymbol{\beta}_1{}'\mathbf{x}_{i1} + \varepsilon_{i1}) - (\boldsymbol{\beta}_0{}'\mathbf{x}_{i0} + \varepsilon_{i0})\\
&= \boldsymbol{\beta}_1{}'\mathbf{x}_{i1} - \boldsymbol{\beta}_0{}'\mathbf{x}_{i0} + \varepsilon_{i1} - \varepsilon_{i0} > 0. \tag{17.10}\\
&= \boldsymbol{\beta}'\mathbf{x}_i + \varepsilon_i > 0
\end{aligned}
$$

One detail left unconsidered thus far is the possibility of correlation between ε_{i1} and ε_{i0}. Denote that correlation ρ_{10}. Note, once again, the information contained in the sample. We only observe whether choice 1 or choice 0 is made. The decision turns on the difference of the two utility functions. Whether the correlation of ε_{i1} and ε_{i0} is non-zero (ρ) or not has no influence on the observed outcome. The upshot is that when modeling the utility-maximizing choice between two alternatives, we have no information on correlation across the two utility functions, as we can only observe the sign of the difference. Therefore, we normalize the correlation at zero. (Once again, it is important to note, this is not a substantive assumption. It is a normalization that is mandated by the fact that we only observe the one sign of the difference of the utility functions.[4])

17.2.2 Functional form for binary choice

The assumption of a linear function for the deterministic part of the utility function is a bit less restrictive than it might appear. The function is assumed to be linear in the parameters, but can involve any transformations of the elements of $\mathbf{x}_{it}$, such as logs, squares, products, powers, and so on. It is possible to accommodate great flexibility of the utility function while still retaining the convenience of the "linear" utility function.

We have suggested the two candidates for the distribution of the random part of the random utility function, normal and logistic. The implication of the normality assumption has been shown earlier. Starting from the case of choosing alternative 1 or not, and letting Y_{i1} denote the eventual outcome variable, we have:

$$
\begin{aligned}
U_{i1} &= \boldsymbol{\beta}_1{}'\mathbf{x}_{i1} + \varepsilon_{i1} \\
Y_{i1} &= 1[U_{i1} > 0],
\end{aligned}
\tag{17.11}
$$

where the indicator function $1[condition]$ equals one if the condition is true and zero if not. With these normalizations, our model in terms of the observed data is:

---

[4] We have left one final loose end in this derivation. In the two specific-choice cases, we have two random terms. Could they have different variances – $\sigma_1{}^2$ and $\sigma_0{}^2$? Under some additional assumptions, yes. Note, for example, with $\rho = 0$, we now require that $(\sigma_1{}^2 + \sigma_0{}^2) = 1$. Obviously, it is not possible to estimate both, or to distinguish σ_1 from σ_0. However, one might think that if σ_1 were fixed at some value, then we could estimate σ_0. Under some circumstances, it is indeed possible to estimate the ratio, σ_1/σ_0. This is a complication of the model, a type of heteroskedasticity, that we will consider later. For the present, given the simple assumptions we have made so far, the data do not provide information about this type of heteroskedasticity either.

$$
\begin{aligned}
\text{Prob}(Y_{i1} = 1|\mathbf{x}_{i1}) &= \text{Prob}(U_{i1} > 0) \\
&= \text{Prob}(\boldsymbol{\beta}_1{}'\mathbf{x}_{i1} + \varepsilon_{i1}) > 0, \\
&= \Phi(\boldsymbol{\beta}'_{1,p}x_{i1})
\end{aligned}
\tag{17.12}
$$

where $\Phi(.)$ denotes the standard normal CDF. In the statement above, we have assumed that the mean and variance of ε are zero and one, respectively. If, instead, we build our model around the logistic distribution, then Prob $(Y_{i1} = 1|\mathbf{x}_{i1}) = \Lambda(\boldsymbol{\beta}_{1,L}'\mathbf{x}_{i1})$, where $\Lambda(.)$ denotes the standard logistic distribution:

$$
\Lambda(\boldsymbol{\beta}'x_i) = \frac{\exp(\boldsymbol{\beta}'x_i)}{1 + \exp(\boldsymbol{\beta}'x_i)}.
\tag{17.13}
$$

A question to be considered is whether the two coefficient vectors will be the same. Empirically, the answer is definitely not. The widely observed empirical regularity is that, to a reasonable approximation, we will find that estimates of the logit coefficient, $\boldsymbol{\beta}_{1,L}$, will be approximately 1.6 times estimates of $\boldsymbol{\beta}_{1,P}$. This actually makes sense. We will revisit this later, but it is useful to explore the result a bit here. The probabilities are non-linear functions. As such, their derivatives, the "partial effects" of the "$\mathbf{x}$" on the probabilities, are not the coefficients in the linear utility functions, but a scaled version of them. In particular, for the two models, for a particular variable, $x_{i1,k}$:

$$
\partial\text{Prob}(Y_{i1} = 1|\mathbf{x}_{i1})/\partial x_{i1,k} = f(.)\boldsymbol{\beta}_{1,k},
\tag{17.14}
$$

where $f(.)$ is the respective density (normal or logistic) and $\boldsymbol{\beta}_{1,k}$ is the corresponding coefficient. The two models do appear to involve different coefficients, but at the same time the slopes, or partial effects implied by the two models are (as we would hope), essentially the same. If so, then for the particular variable, x_k, the partial effects:

$$
\phi(\ldots)\boldsymbol{\beta}_{1,k}(\text{Probit}) = \lambda(\ldots)\boldsymbol{\beta}_{1,k}(\text{Logit})
\tag{17.15}
$$

should be approximately equal. If these are to be the same, then:

$$
\boldsymbol{\beta}_{1,k}(\text{Logit})/\boldsymbol{\beta}_{1,k}(\text{Probit}) \approx \phi(\ldots)/\lambda(\ldots).
\tag{17.16}
$$

Over much of the range of the probabilities that one encounters in practice, say about 0.4 to about 0.6, this ratio is near 1.6 (or a bit less). This explains the empirical regularity. The estimator, to the extent that it is able, scales the coefficients so that the predicted partial effects are roughly the same.

Consider, finally, the second choice case we examined, two specific alternatives:

$$
\begin{aligned}
\text{Choose alternative 1 if } U_{i1} - U_{i0} &= (\boldsymbol{\beta}_1{}'\mathbf{x}_{i1} + \varepsilon_{i1}) - (\boldsymbol{\beta}_0{}'\mathbf{x}_{i0} + \varepsilon_{i0}) \\
&= \boldsymbol{\beta}_1{}'\mathbf{x}_{i1} - \boldsymbol{\beta}_0{}'\mathbf{x}_{i0} + \varepsilon_{i1} - \varepsilon_{i0} \\
&= \boldsymbol{\beta}'\mathbf{x}_i + \varepsilon_i \\
&> 0.
\end{aligned}
\tag{17.17}
$$

If the two random components have a type I Extreme value distribution, with cdf (see Chapter 4):

$$
F(\varepsilon_{ij}) = \exp(-\exp(-\varepsilon_{ij})) \tag{7.18}
$$

then the probability that the individual chooses alternative 1 is:

$$
\mathrm{Prob}(U_{i1} - U_{i0} > 0 | \mathbf{x}_{i1}, \mathbf{x}_{i0}) = \frac{\exp(\boldsymbol{\beta}'_1 \mathbf{x}_{i1})}{\exp(\boldsymbol{\beta}'_1 \mathbf{x}_{i1}) + \exp(\boldsymbol{\beta}'_0 \mathbf{x}_{i0})}. \tag{17.19}
$$

We should note some special cases. First, consider a variable, z_i, such as age or income, and let the coefficients of z_i be γ_1 and γ_0. The choice probability is:

$$
\mathrm{Prob}(U_{i1} - U_{i0} > 0 | \mathbf{x}_{i1}, \mathbf{x}_{i0}) = \frac{\exp(\boldsymbol{\beta}'_1 \mathbf{x}_{i1} + \gamma_1 z_i)}{\exp(\boldsymbol{\beta}'_1 \mathbf{x}_{i1} + \gamma_1 z_i) + \exp(\boldsymbol{\beta}'_0 \mathbf{x}_{i0} + \gamma_0 z_i)}. \tag{17.20}
$$

Suppose that the two coefficients for income are the same. Then the probability is:

$$
\begin{aligned}
\mathrm{Prob}(U_{i1} - U_{i0} > 0 | \mathbf{x}_{i1}, \mathbf{x}_{i0}, z_i) &= \frac{\exp(\boldsymbol{\beta}'_1 x_{i1} + \gamma_1 z_i)}{\exp(\boldsymbol{\beta}'_1 x_{i1} + \gamma z_i) + \exp(\boldsymbol{\beta}'_0 x_{i0} + \gamma z_i)} \\
&= \frac{\exp(\gamma z_i)\exp(\boldsymbol{\beta}'_1 \mathbf{x}_{i1})}{\exp(\gamma z_i)\exp(\boldsymbol{\beta}'_1 \mathbf{x}_{i1}) + \exp(\gamma z_i)\exp(\boldsymbol{\beta}'_0 \mathbf{x}_{i0})} \\
&= \frac{\exp(\boldsymbol{\beta}'_1 \mathbf{x}_{i1})}{\exp(\boldsymbol{\beta}'_1 \mathbf{x}_{i1}) + \exp(\boldsymbol{\beta}'_0 \mathbf{x}_{i0})}.
\end{aligned}
\tag{17.21}
$$

Income has disappeared from the probability. This implies a general result. When comparing the utility functions of different alternatives, the coefficients on variables that do not vary between (among) the choices must have different coefficients (also detailed in Chapter 3).

A second case to examine is that in which the coefficients on attributes of the choices are the same – that is typical when the coefficients are interpreted as marginal utilities that do not change from one choice to the next. The relevant probability is:

$$
\begin{aligned}
\text{Prob}(U_{i1} - U_{i0} > 0 | \mathbf{x}_{i1}, \mathbf{x}_{i0}) &= \frac{\exp(\boldsymbol{\beta}'\mathbf{x}_{i1})}{\exp(\boldsymbol{\beta}'\mathbf{x}_{i1}) + \exp(\boldsymbol{\beta}'\mathbf{x}_{i0})} \\
&= \frac{\exp(\boldsymbol{\beta}'\mathbf{x}_{i1})/\exp(\boldsymbol{\beta}'\mathbf{x}_{i0})}{\exp(\boldsymbol{\beta}'\mathbf{x}_{i1})/\exp(\boldsymbol{\beta}'\mathbf{x}_{i0}) + \exp(\boldsymbol{\beta}'\mathbf{x}_{i0})/\exp(\boldsymbol{\beta}'\mathbf{x}_{i0})} \\
&= \frac{\exp[\boldsymbol{\beta}'(\mathbf{x}_{i1} - \mathbf{x}_{i0})]}{\exp[\boldsymbol{\beta}'(\mathbf{x}_{i1} - \mathbf{x}_{i0})] + 1}.
\end{aligned} \tag{7.22}
$$

The natural result is that when comparing the utilities of alternatives in which the marginal utilities are the same, we base the comparison on the differences between the attributes.

The preceding shows different aspects of the functional form for binary choice models. We will use a generic format, given in Equation (17.23) to indicate the general result, and note the special cases when they arise in our applications:

$$
\text{Prob}(Y_i = 1|\mathbf{x}_i) = F(\boldsymbol{\beta}'\mathbf{x}_i); \quad \text{Prob}(Y_i = 0|\mathbf{x}_i) = 1 - F(\boldsymbol{\beta}'\mathbf{x}_i). \tag{17.23}
$$

17.2.3 Estimation of binary choice models

The log-likelihood (LL) function for the binary choice model is given as in Equation (17.24):

$$
\text{LogL} = \sum\nolimits_{y_i=0} \log[\text{Prob}(Y_i = 0|\mathbf{x}_i)] + \sum\nolimits_{y_i=1} \log[\text{Prob}(Y_i = 1|\mathbf{x}_i)]. \tag{17.24}
$$

The two distributions we are interested in are symmetric. For both probit and logit models:

$$
1 - F(\boldsymbol{\beta}'\mathbf{x}) = F(-\boldsymbol{\beta}'\mathbf{x}). \tag{17.25}
$$

So $\text{Prob}(Y_i = 0|\mathbf{x}_i) = F(-\boldsymbol{\beta}'\mathbf{x}_i)$. We can combine these results in a convenient form by using:

$$
q_i = 2y_i - 1. \tag{17.26}
$$

Thus, $q_i = 1$ if $y_i = 1$ and $q_i = -1$ when $y_i = 0$. With this device:

$$\text{Log}L = \sum_{i=1}^{n} \log[F(q_i\boldsymbol{\beta}'\mathbf{x}_i)]. \tag{17.27}$$

Estimates of the parameters are obtained by maximizing this function with respect to the vector $\boldsymbol{\beta}$. This is a conventional optimization problem. (See, e.g., Greene (2012) and Chapter 5). Estimates of the standard errors for the maximum likelihood estimates (MLEs) can be obtained by the familiar methods set out in Chapter 5.

Let F_i denote the probability that Y_i equals one, given $\mathbf{x}_i$, $F(\boldsymbol{\beta}'\mathbf{x}_i)$, let f_i denote its derivative, the PDF, and f_i' denote the second derivative of F_i. These functions are Λ_i, $\Lambda_i(1-\Lambda_i)$, and $\Lambda_i(1-\Lambda_i)(1-2\Lambda_i)$ for the logit model and Φ_i, φ_i, and $(-\boldsymbol{\beta}'\mathbf{x}_i)\varphi_i$ for the probit model. Reverting back to the explicit form of the LL in Equation (17.28):

$$\log L = \sum_{i=1}^{n}(1 - y_i)\log(1 - F_i) + y_i\log F_i \tag{17.28}$$

we obtain (after a bit of simplification) Equation (17.29):

$$\frac{\partial \log L}{\partial \boldsymbol{\beta}} = \sum_{i=1}^{n}\left[\left(\frac{y_i - F_i}{F_i(1 - F_i)}\right)f_i\right]\mathbf{x}_i = \sum_{i=1}^{n} g_i\mathbf{x}_i. \tag{17.29}$$

This derivative is equated to zero to obtain the MLE of $\boldsymbol{\beta}$. To obtain an expression for the estimator for the asymptotic covariance matrix of the MLE, we differentiate this once again, with respect to $\boldsymbol{\beta}'$, as shown in Equation (17.30):

$$\frac{\partial^2 \log L}{\partial \boldsymbol{\beta}\partial \boldsymbol{\beta}'} = \sum_{i=1}^{n}\left[\left(\frac{y_i - F_i}{F_i(1 - F_i)}\right)f_i' + \left(\frac{F(1 - F)(-f_i) - (y_i - F)(f_i - 2Ff_i)}{[F(1 - F)]^2}\right)f_i\right]\mathbf{x}_i\mathbf{x}_i'$$

$$= \sum_{i=1}^{n} H_i\mathbf{x}_i\mathbf{x}' \tag{17.30}$$

This messy expression simplifies considerably for the two models we are considering. Using the derivative results given earlier, for the probit model, it reduces to:

$$H_i = -q_i\,(\boldsymbol{\beta}'\mathbf{x}_i)\varphi_i/\Phi_i - [q_i\varphi_i/\Phi_i],^2 \tag{17.31}$$

where $\varphi(.)$ and $\Phi(.)$ are evaluated at $q_i\boldsymbol{\beta}'\mathbf{x}_i$. For the logit model the result is even simpler:

$$H_i = -\Lambda_i\,(1-\Lambda_i), \tag{17.32}$$

where Λ_i is evaluated at $\boldsymbol{\beta}'\mathbf{x}_i$. The empirical estimator of the asymptotic covariance matrix for the MLE would be as per Equation (17.33):

$$V = Est.Asy.Var[\hat{\boldsymbol{\beta}}_{MLE}] = [-\sum\nolimits_{i=1}^{n} H(\hat{\boldsymbol{\beta}}'_{MLE}\mathbf{x}_i)\mathbf{x}_i\mathbf{x}'_i]^{-1}. \tag{17.33}$$

The theoretical estimator would be based on $E[H_i]$. The same expression would apply for the logit model: $E[H_i] = H_i$. (Notice that H_i does not involve y_i for the logit model.) For the probit model:

$$E[H_i] = \frac{-[\phi(\hat{\boldsymbol{\beta}}'_{MLE}\mathbf{x}_i)]^2}{\Phi(\hat{\boldsymbol{\beta}}'_{MLE}} \mathbf{x}_i)\Phi(-\hat{\boldsymbol{\beta}}'_{MLE}\mathbf{x}_i). \tag{17.34}$$

The estimator then is:

$$V_E = \left[-\sum\nolimits_{i=1}^{n} E[H(\hat{\boldsymbol{\beta}}'_{MLE}\mathbf{x}_i)]\mathbf{x}_i\mathbf{x}'_i\right]^{-1}. \tag{17.35}$$

A third estimator is based on the information equality, $E[g_i] = 0$ and $E[-H_i] = E[g_i^2]$. Thus the so-called BHHH (Berndt, Hall, Hall, and Hausman) estimator is:

$$V_{BHHH} = \left[\sum\nolimits_{i=1}^{n} g_i^2\mathbf{x}_i\mathbf{x}'_i\right]^{-1}. \tag{17.36}$$

A "robust" estimator is often suggested in the contemporary literature:

$$V_{ROBUST} = V_E \left[\sum\nolimits_{i=1}^{n} g_i^2\mathbf{x}_i\mathbf{x}'_i\right]. \tag{17.37}$$

In order for this estimator to be robust to a failure of the assumptions of the model, it is necessary for the estimator of $\boldsymbol{\beta}$, itself, to remain a consistent estimator of the vector $\boldsymbol{\beta}$ that is of interest. No failure of the model assumptions that we have been able to devise retains this property. On the other hand, in the absence of a failure of the model assumptions, V_{ROBUST} estimates the same matrix as the other three candidates, so it is merely some redundant computation.

17.2.4 Inference-hypothesis tests

The binary choice models specified so far are conventional, though non-linear models, that are estimated using maximum likelihood. The standard menu of tools for **hypothesis testing** and inference (see Chapter 7) such as confidence intervals are available. As a "regular" estimator, the MLE is consistent and asymptotically normally distributed with estimators of the covariance matrix, as shown in Section 17.2.4. Thus, confidence intervals for coefficients are constructed using the usual critical values (1.96 for 95 percent, 2.58 for 99 percent) and estimated standard errors equal to the square roots of the diagonal elements of the estimated asymptotic covariance matrices shown earlier. For testing hypotheses, the Wald (*t*)-statistics and likelihood ratio statistics are the usual choices. Details on hypothesis testing are given in Chapter 7.

17.2.5 Fit measures

It is often of interest to assess the fit of the binary choice model to the data. There is no direct analogue to the R^2 in a linear regression context, largely because the model is non-linear, but also because, unlike in a linear regression, there is no binary choice counterpart to a sum of squared residuals or a fixed "variation" to be explained by the model. One measure often suggested that is based on the LL function is the *Pseudo-R^2*, which is defined by:

$$Pseudo\text{-}R^2 = 1 - \frac{\log L(\text{model})}{\log L(\text{base model})}. \tag{17.38}$$

The base model would be a model that contains only a constant term. It is easy to show that for any binary choice model (probit, logit, other), the base model would have:

$$\log L_0 = N_1 \log P_0 + N_1 \log P_1, \tag{17.39}$$

where N_j is the number of observations that take value $j, j = 0,1$ and $P_j = N_j/N$, the sample proportion. Since the LL for a binary choice model must be negative, and $\log L_0$ is more negative than $\log L$ for the model, the *Pseudo-R^2* must be between zero and one. Whether it is a better measure of fit than the LL function, itself, is debatable. However, it should be useful for comparing one model to another when the sample and the dependent variable are the same for the two. Other measures of fit for the binary choice model are sometimes based on the success of a prediction rule for the outcome variable, such as:

$$\hat{y}_i = 1[F(\hat{\boldsymbol{\beta}}' \mathbf{x}_i) > .5]. \tag{17.40}$$

The logic being that if the model predicts that $y = 1$ is more likely than $y = 0$, predict $y = 1$, and vice versa. Then, different tallies of success and failure of the rule, such as Cramer's measure:

$$\hat{\lambda} = \frac{\sum_{i=1}^{N} y_i \hat{F}}{N_1} - \frac{\sum_{i=1}^{N}(1 - y_i)\hat{F}}{N_0}$$

$$= (\text{Mean } \hat{F} \mid \text{ when } y = 1) - (\text{Mean } \hat{F} \mid \text{ when } y = 0). \tag{17.41}$$

17.2.6 Interpretation: partial effects and simulations

As in any non-linear model, the coefficients, β, are not the partial (or marginal) effects that are usually of interest. For any variable that appears in the random utility function:

$$\frac{\partial \text{Prob}(Y_i = 1 | \mathbf{x}_i)}{\partial \mathbf{x}_{ik}} = \frac{dF(\beta' \mathbf{x}_i)}{d(\beta' \mathbf{x}_i)} \beta_k = \delta_{ik}(\beta, \mathbf{x}_i). \tag{17.42}$$

The derivative term is the density that corresponds to the probability model, i.e., the normal density, φ_i for the probit model and $\Lambda_i(1 - \Lambda_i)$ for the logit model. In all cases, the partial effects are scaled versions of the coefficients. Two issues that arise in computing partial effects are:

- Since the partial effects involve the data, at which values of $\mathbf{x}_i$ should δ_{ik} be computed? "Partial Effects at the Means" are often obtained by replacing $\mathbf{x}_i$ in the computation with the sample means of the data. More common in the recent literature is the Average Partial Effect, which is computed by evaluating δ_{ik} at each sample point in the data set and averaging the results.
- Since the partial effects are non-linear functions of the parameter estimates (and the data), some method is needed to calculate standard errors for the estimates of $\delta_{ik}(\beta, \mathbf{x}_i)$. The delta method and the Krinsky–Robb method discussed in Chapter 7 are generally used for this purpose.

In many applications, the exogenous variables, $\mathbf{x}_i$, include demographics such as gender, marital status, age categories, and so on, that are coded as binary variables. The derivative expression above would be inappropriate for measuring the impact of a binary variable. The more common calculation is a first difference:

$$\Delta \text{Prob}(Y_i | \mathbf{x}, z) = \text{Prob}(Y_i = 1 | \mathbf{x}_i, z_i = 1) - \text{Prob}(Y_i = 1 | \mathbf{x}_i, z_i = 0)$$
$$= F(\beta' \mathbf{x}_i + \gamma) - F(\beta' \mathbf{x}_i) \tag{17.43}$$

where z_i is the dummy variable in question, and γ is the coefficient on z_i in the model.

We note again a point made elsewhere. Depending on the context, one might be interested in scaling the estimated partial effects. A partial effect of, say, 0.2 reflects a quite different outcome when the base outcome has a probability of, say, 0.3, from which a partial effect represents a 67 percent change in the probability, compared to a base probability of, say, 0.8, from which the 0.2 effect would represent only a 25 percent change in the probability. To resolve this ambiguity, researchers often use semi-elasticities or elasticities, depending on the variable changing. In the example just given, we used the semi-elasticity $(\partial P/\partial x)/P = \partial \log P/\partial x$ to resolve the scale ambiguity. In a different context, it might be more useful to use the full elasticity, $\varepsilon = \partial \log P/\partial \log x$. In the application below, the relevant "x" is income. Partial effects might be more informative in terms of proportional (percentage) changes rather than absolute (dollar or Euro) changes. We do note, however, that when the change being examined is a dummy variable, the semi-elasticity would be the only sensible measure.

When using a logit model, analysts sometimes examine "odds ratios" rather than measures of rates of change. The odds ratio for a probabiity is $\text{Prob}(Y_i{=}1|\mathbf{x}_i)/\text{Prob}(Y_i{=}0|\mathbf{x}_i)$. For the binary logit model:

$$\text{Odds ratio} = \frac{\exp(\boldsymbol{\beta}'\mathbf{x})/[1 + \exp(\boldsymbol{\beta}'\mathbf{x})]}{1/[1 + \exp(\boldsymbol{\beta}'\mathbf{x})]} = \exp(\boldsymbol{\beta}'\mathbf{x}). \qquad 17.44)$$

Consider, now, the change in the odds that results from a change in a dummy variable, z:

$$(\text{Odds ratio}|z = 1) - (\text{Odds ratio}|z = 0) = \exp(\boldsymbol{\beta}'\mathbf{x} + \gamma) - \exp(\boldsymbol{\beta}'\mathbf{x}) = \exp(\boldsymbol{\beta}'\mathbf{x})$$
$$[\exp(\gamma) - 1]. \qquad (17.45)$$

Thus, the odds ratio (or "odds") is measured to increase if $\gamma > 0$, is unchanged if $\gamma = 0$, and decrease when $\gamma < 0$. Researchers often display "odds ratios" instead of coefficients in reported results. We should note a few aspects of this computation. The "odds ratio," $\exp(\gamma)$, is actually one plus the *change* in the odds ratio, not an odds ratio itself.[5] Second, the conceptual experiment underlying the change is a full one unit change in the variable associated with the coefficient. Thus, the computation is generally not useful for continuous variables such as income or dosage level, though it might be for a measure of time such as age or trip duration. Third, using the delta method, one would compute the standard error for an estimated odds ratio, c, as

---

[5] For any variable, say z, the ratio of odds ratios when z changes by one unit is $OR(\mathbf{x},z+1)/OR(\mathbf{x},z) = \exp(\beta_z)$.

Table 17.1 Panel data sample sizes

	Full sample		Panel group sizes
Year	Number of observations	T_i	Number of observations
1984	3,874	1	1,525
1985	3,794	2	1,079
1986	3,792	3	825
1987	3,666	4	926
1988	4,483	4	1,051
1991	4,340	6	1,000
1994	3,377	7	887

$\exp(c) \times$ standard.error(c). But, the standard error should not be used to test the usual hypothesis of whether the odds ratio is zero – the odds ratio, $\exp(\gamma)$, cannot be zero. The relevant hypothesis is that it equals one. Likewise, confidence intervals, at least conceptually, should be centered at one, not zero. There is no clear advantage to reporting "odds ratios" instead of coefficients in a binary logit model – there is, however, a clear disadvantage when the coefficients are not associated with dummy variables. Nonetheless, this is fairly common in the received literature, so we note it here for completeness.

17.2.7 An application of binary choice modeling

In Riphahn, Wambach, and Million (2003), the authors were interested in the association of insurance holding with increased use of the health care system. They analyzed a panel data set extracted from the German Socioeconomic Panel Data (GSOEP). The measured activity was the number of visits to a physician in the last quarter prior to the survey year by the household head. In the German health care system that they studied, there are two types of health care insurance, the "public" type, which covers basic health care and an "add on," which augments the public health insurance and covers some additional services such as spectacles and additional hospital costs. (One must have the public insurance to purchase the add on insurance.) We will use these data to illustrate binary choice modeling.[6] The sample is an unbalanced panel of 27,326 person years, as summarized in Table 17.1.

The panel contains 7,293 groups. For the moment, we will ignore the panel data nature of the data set, and treat it as if it were a cross-section – that is, as if there were no latent correlation across the observations. (We will find below

---

[6] The data can be downloaded from the *Journal of Applied Econometrics* data archive.

Table 17.2 Insurance takeup in the GSOEP sample

```
CROSSTAB ; Lhs = public ; Rhs = addon $
Cross Tabulation ------------------+
|       |          ADDON          |
+-----------+------------------+--------+
|  PUBLIC|      0           1| Total|
+-----------+------------------+--------+
|        0|   3123          0|  3123|
|        1|  23689        514| 24203|
+-----------+------------------+--------+
|   Total|  26812        514| 27326|
+-----------+------------------+--------+
```

that this is clearly not the case. We assume it for the present for simplicity.) The sample of observations on the insurance takeup variables is shown in Table 17.2. The variables we will examine are summarized in Table 17.3.

Tables 17.4 and 17.5 display estimated probit and logit models for the add on insurance takeup variable. There is (as should be expected) little to distinguish the two models. The LLs and other diagnostic statistics are the same. Based on the chi squared value, the model as a whole is found to be statistically significant. The patterns of signs and significance of the coefficients are the same for the two models as well. The predicted scaling effect between the logit and probit coefficients is evident in the results as well, though the difference is greater than the familiar 1.6 in our results. This is to be expected. Recall, the scaling acts to (more or less) equalize the partial effects predicted at the middle of the data for the two models. In our add on insurance model, the average outcome is only 0.0188, which is far from 0.5 where the 1.6 result is most obvious. But, here the anticipated ratio would be:

$$\text{Ratio} = \frac{\phi(\Phi^{-1}(.0188))}{\Lambda(\Lambda^{-1}(.0188))[1 - \Lambda(\Lambda^{-1}(.0188))]} = \frac{.04593}{.0188(1 - .0188)} \approx 2.5. \quad (17.46)$$

Given this result, we should expect the logit coefficients in Table 17.5 to be roughly 2.5 times the probit coefficients in Table 17.4, which they are. For example, the AGE coefficient in Table 17.5, 0.01776, is about 2.6 times that in Table 17.4, 0.00678. The results suggest that older, more educated, female, and higher income individuals are more likely than others to take up the add on insurance. Marital status and presence of young children in the household matter less than the other variables. Predictably, those who perceive themselves as more healthy are less likely to take up the add on insurance. (The add on insurance enhances the coverage for hospitalization.) Table 17.5 also shows

Table 17.3 Descriptive statistics for binary choice analysis

```
DSTAT ; Rhs = public,addon,age,educ,female,married,hhkids,
income,healthy $
```

Variable	Mean	Std.Dev.	Minimum	Maximum	
PUBLIC	.885713	.318165	0.0	1.0	●
ADDON	.018810	.135856	0.0	1.0	●
AGE	43.52569	11.33025	25.0	64.0	
EDUC	11.32063	2.324885	7.0	18.0	
FEMALE	.478775	.499558	0.0	1.0	●
MARRIED	.758618	.427929	0.0	1.0	●
HHKIDS	.402730	.490456	0.0	1.0	●

(Presence of children under 16 in the household)

INCOME	.352135	.176857	.001500	3.067100

(Monthly household net income/1000)

HEALTHY	.609529	.487865	0.0	1.0	●

(Health satisfaction coded 0–10 is greater than 6)

Note: ●Indicates a binary variable.

Table 17.4 Estimated probit model for add on insurance takeup

```
NAMELIST ; X=one,age,educ,female,married,hhkids,income,healthy $
PROBIT ; Lhs = addon ; Rhs = x $
Binomial Probit Model
Dependent variable                ADDON
Log likelihood function     -2434.77285
Restricted log likelihood   -2551.44776
Chi squared [  7](P= .000)    233.34982
Significance level              .00000
McFadden Pseudo R-squared      .0457289
Estimation based on N =  27326, K =   8
Inf.Cr.AIC  =    4885.5 AIC/N =    .179
```

ADDON	Coefficient	Standard Error	z	Prob. $|z|>Z^*$	95% Confidence Interval	
Index function for probability						
Constant	-3.57370***	.13618	-26.24	.0000	-3.84061	-3.30678
AGE	.00678***	.00195	3.48	.0005	.00297	.01060
EDUC	.06906***	.00702	9.84	.0000	.05531	.08281
FEMALE	.13083***	.03774	3.47	.0005	.05685	.20480
MARRIED	.01863	.04978	.37	.7083	-.07895	.11620
HHKIDS	.04660	.04342	1.07	.2832	-.03851	.13171
INCOME	.74817***	.08360	8.95	.0000	.58432	.91203
HEALTHY	-.01372	.03918	-.35	.7261	-.09052	.06307

Table 17.5 Estimated logit model for add on insurance takeup

```
NAMELIST ; X=one,age,educ,female,married,hhkids,income,healthy $
LOGIT ; Lhs = addon ; Rhs = x $
LOGIT ; Lhs = addon ; Rhs = x ; Odds $
Binary Logit Model for Binary Choice
Log likelihood function     -2440.84843
Restricted log likelihood   -2551.44776
Chi squared [  7](P= .000)    221.19866
Significance level                .00000
McFadden Pseudo R-squared        .0433477
Estimation based on N =  27326, K =    8
Inf.Cr.AIC  =   4897.7 AIC/N =    .179
```

ADDON	Coefficient	Standard Error	z	Prob. |z|>Z*	95% Confidence Interval	
Constant	-7.52008***	.32912	-22.85	.0000	-8.16513	-6.87502
AGE	.01776***	.00479	3.71	.0002	.00837	.02715
EDUC	.16248***	.01571	10.34	.0000	.13169	.19327
FEMALE	.32623***	.09219	3.54	.0004	.14555	.50691
MARRIED	.08638	.12260	.70	.4810	-.15390	.32667
HHKIDS	.10535	.10537	1.00	.3174	-.10118	.31187
INCOME	1.50172***	.17015	8.83	.0000	1.16823	1.83521
HEALTHY	-.01242	.09585	-.13	.8969	-.20027	.17544

ADDON	Odds Ratio	Standard Error	z	Prob. |z|>Z*	95% Confidence Interval	
AGE	1.01792***	.00488	3.71	.0002	1.00836	1.02748
EDUC	1.17643***	.01848	10.34	.0000	1.14020	1.21265
FEMALE	1.38573***	.12774	3.54	.0004	1.13535	1.63610
MARRIED	1.09023	.13366	.70	.4810	.82826	1.35219
HHKIDS	1.11109	.11708	1.00	.3174	.88162	1.34056
INCOME	4.48940***	.76387	8.83	.0000	2.99225	5.98656
HEALTHY	.98766	.09466	-.13	.8969	.80212	1.17320

```
***, **, * ==>  Significance at 1%, 5%, 10% level.
Odds ratio = exp(beta); z is computed for the original beta
```

the "odds ratios" for the estimated logit model. Which of these results is more informative would be up to the analyst. We find the coefficients and associated partial effects generally more informative.

Table 17.6 displays several fit measures for the probit model (the results are essentially the same for the logit model) and illustrates the difficulty of contriving a scalar analog to the familiar R^2 used for linear regression. As

Table 17.6 Fit measures for estimated probit model

```
PROBIT ; Lhs = addon ; Rhs = x ; Summary $
+-------------------------------------------------------+
| Fit Measures for Binomial Choice Model |
| Probit   model for variable ADDON     |
+-------------------------------------------------------+
|                Y=0        Y=1      Total|
| Proportions  .98119     .01881   1.00000|
| Sample Size   26812        514     27326|
+-------------------------------------------------------+
| Log Likelihood Functions for BC Model  |
|              P=0.50     P=N1/N    P=Model|
| LogL =    -18940.94   -2551.45  -2434.77|
+-------------------------------------------------------+
| Fit Measures based on Log Likelihood   |
| McFadden = 1-(L/L0)              =  .04573|
| Estrella = 1-(L/L0)^(-2L0/n) =   .00870|
| R-squared (ML)                  =  .00850|
| Akaike Information Crit.         =  .17879|
| Schwartz Information Crit.       =  .18119|
| Veall and Zimmerman             =  .05381|
+-------------------------------------------------------+
| Fit Measures Based on Model Predictions|
| Efron                          =  .00676|
| Ben Akiva and Lerman           =  .96347|
| Cramer                         =  .01066|
+-------------------------------------------------------+

+-----------------------------------------------------------------+
|Predictions for Binary Choice Model.  Predicted value is |
|1 when probability is greater than  .500000, 0 otherwise.|
|Note, column or row total percentages may not sum to     |
|100% because of rounding. Percentages are of full sample.|
+--------+-----------------------------+----------------------------------+
|Actual|        Predicted Value       |                                  |
|Value |    0               1         | Total Actual  |
+--------+---------------+---------------+----------------------------------+
|  0    | 26811 ( 98.1%)|     1 (   .0%)| 26812 ( 98.1%)|
|  1    |   514 (  1.9%)|     0 (   .0%)|   514 (  1.9%)|
+---------+---------------+---------------+----------------------------------+
|Total | 27325 (100.0%)|     1 (   .0%)| 27326 (100.0%)|
+---------+---------------+---------------+----------------------------------+
```

Table 17.6 (cont.)

```
+------------------------------------------------------------------------+
|Crosstab for Binary Choice Model.  Predicted probability |
|vs. actual outcome. Entry = Sum[Y(i,j)*Prob(i,m)] 0,1.    |
|Note, column or row total percentages may not sum to      |
|100% because of rounding. Percentages are of full sample.|
+--------+-----------------------------+---------------------------------+
|Actual|       Predicted Probability       |                     |
|Value |    Prob(y=0)          Prob(y=1)    | Total Actual       |
+--------+----------------+----------------+---------------------------------+
| y=0  |  26312 ( 96.3%)|    499 (  1.8%)|  26812 ( 98.1%)|
| y=1  |    498 (  1.8%)|     15 (  .1%)|    514 (  1.9%)|
+--------+----------------+----------------+---------------------------------+
|Total |  26811 ( 98.1%)|    514 (  1.9%)|  27326 (100.0%)|
+---------+----------------+----------------+---------------------------------+
```

LOGIT ; Lhs = addon ; Rhs = x ; Marginal Effects $
PROBIT ; Lhs = addon ; Rhs = x ; Marginal Effects $

```
----------------------------------------------------------------------------
```

Partial derivatives of E[y] = F[*] with
respect to the vector of characteristics
Average partial effects for sample obs.

Logit|	Partial Effect	Standard Error	z	Prob. |z|>Z*	95% Confidence Interval	
AGE|	.00032***	.8707D-04	3.71	.0002	.00015 .00049	
EDUC|	.00296***	.00028	10.45	.0000	.00240 .00351	
FEMALE|	.00600***	.00172	3.49	.0005	.00263 .00937	#
MARRIED|	.00154	.00213	.72	.4709	-.00264 .00571	#
HHKIDS|	.00194	.00196	.99	.3228	-.00190 .00578	#
INCOME|	.02733***	.00309	8.86	.0000	.02128 .03338	
HEALTHY|	-.00023	.00175	-.13	.8971	-.00366 .00320	#

Probit|	Partial Effect	Standard Error	z	Prob. |z|>Z*	95% Confidence Interval	
AGE|	.00030***	.8640D-04	3.46	.0005	.00013 .00047	
EDUC|	.00304***	.00033	9.36	.0000	.00241 .00368	
FEMALE|	.00581***	.00169	3.43	.0006	.00249 .00913	#
MARRIED|	.00081	.00215	.38	.7054	-.00340 .00503	#
HHKIDS|	.00207	.00195	1.06	.2882	-.00175 .00590	#
INCOME|	.03299***	.00382	8.63	.0000	.02550 .04048	
HEALTHY|	-.00061	.00174	-.35	.7270	-.00402 .00280	#

nnnnn.D-xx or D+xx => multiply by 10 to -xx or +xx.
***, **, * ==> Significance at 1%, 5%, 10% level.
Partial effect for dummy variable is E[y|x,d=1] - E[y|x,d=0].
Standard errors computed using the delta method.

```
----------------------------------------------------------------------------
```

noted, there are two types of measures suggested for the binary choice model. The first is based on the LL, and modifies McFadden's original suggestion:

$$Pseudo\text{-}R^2 = 1 - LogL/LogL_0, \tag{17.47}$$

where $LogL$ is the LL for the estimated model and $LogL_0$ is the same for a model that contains only a constant term. It is difficult to interpret the *Pseudo-R²* for a specific model. It is definitely not a measure of variation explained. It does vary between zero and one, though it is unlikely ever to get very close to one, and it does increase when a variable is added to the model. Looking at the highly significant results in Table 17.4, the very low value of 0.04573 might seem surprising. The model could be useful for comparing models based on the same dependent variable and the same sample. Note that the change in the measure from a model A to a model B would simply be:

$$\Delta Pseudo\text{-}R^2 = (LogL_A - LogL_B)/LogL_0 \tag{17.48}$$

that is a multiple, $0.5/LogL_0$, of the likelihood-ratio statistic. Other measures are suggested that are based on $LogL$, such as the ones shown in Table 17.4 (there are others[7]), including:

$$R_{ML}{}^2 = 1 - \exp(\chi^2/n), \tag{17.49}$$

where the χ^2 is $2(LogL - LogL_0)$ is used analogously to the overall F in a regression model to test the joint hypothesis that all of the coefficients save the constant are zero. The wide variation in the measures, along with the *Information criteria*:

$$AIC = (-2LogL + 2K)/n \tag{17.50a}$$

and

$$BIC = (-2logL + logn\ logK)/n \tag{17.50b}$$

are suggestive of the difficulty of devising a coherent measure of "fit" on this basis. The same problem arises in comparing fit based on model prediction. The usual fit measures of this type are based on the prediction rule $\hat{y}_i = 1[\hat{P}_i > .5]$.

---

[7] We note the availability of a Stata program called FitStat that will produce about twenty different "fit" measures for binary choice models.

The range of values for our model based on:

$$\text{Efron} = 1 - \frac{\Sigma_i (y_i - \hat{P}_i)^2}{\Sigma_i (y_i - \frac{n1}{n})^2} \tag{17.51}$$

and

$$\text{Ben-Akiva and Lerman} = \frac{\Sigma_i y_i \hat{P}_i + (1 - y_i)(1 - \hat{P}_i)}{n} \tag{17.52}$$

renders this calculation essentially uninformative. For better or worse, a cross-tabulation such as the two shown at the bottom of Table 17.6 may be helpful. The table also helps to illustrate another vexing aspect of measuring fit for choice models. From the first cross-tabulation, we find that our model actually "fits" the data extremely well. The familiar prediction rule predicts 26,812 of 27,326, or 98.1 percent of the observations correctly. This is because the model (almost) never predicts $y_i = 1$, so it gets nearly all of the overwhelming number of zero observations correct, while failing to predict any of the one observations correctly. This will always occur with heavily unbalanced data such as these. It is not a flaw of the model. It is a flaw of the methodology of attempting to construct (contrive) a fit measure that is intended to mimic R^2 in regression.

Table 17.7 shows the estimated partial effects for the estimated probit and logit models. Several of the regressors are binary. The table indicates that those effects have been computed using the partial differences, rather than the scaled coefficients. The magnitudes of the effects in Table 17.6 illustrate a point made earlier. Consider the partial effect for female. The value is about 0.006. This seems like a trivial change in the probability until we account for the fact that the average probability of takeup in the sample is only about 0.0188. Thus, the difference between female and male, all else constant, is about 0.006/0.0188 or almost a one-third difference. This is, in fact, a very large (and statistically significant) effect. In Table 17.8, we report these effects for the logit model as semi-elasticities instead of simple derivatives. The impacts on the probabilities are much clearer in this table.

Table 17.8 illustrates another practical aspect of computing partial effects. In Table 17.7, the effects shown are computed by first obtaining the sample means of the variables in the model, then computing the effects at the means. In the lower half of the table, the partial effects are evaluated for each

Table 17.7 Estimated partial effects for logit and probit models

```
PARTIALS ; Effects : <x> ; Summary $
Semielasticities
```

```
Partial Effects for Logit:Probability(ADDON=1)
```
Partial Effects Computed at data Means. Log derivatives
```
*==> Partial Effect for a Binary Variable
```

(Delta method)	Partial Effect	Standard Error	|t|	95% Confidence Interval	
AGE	.01748	.00472	3.71	.00824	.02672
EDUC	.15989	.01550	10.31	.12950	.19027
FEMALE	.32102	.09075	3.54	.14315	.49889
MARRIED	.08501	.12064	.70	-.15145	.32146
HHKIDS	.10366	.10369	1.00	-.09957	.30690
INCOME	1.47777	.16767	8.81	1.14915	1.80639
HEALTHY	-.01222	.09432	.13	-.19708	.17264

observation in the sample separately, then averaging the effects. This usually makes relatively little difference in the results, though that is not axiomatic – the difference in a relatively small sample can be substantive. As a general rule, researchers prefer to use the latter approach, average partial effects, when possible. Table 17.8 illustrates another, practical complication. The sample means of the data do not reveal which variables are dummy variables and which are not, whereas that aspect is obvious when computing the average partial effects. One might be interested in a combination of these two ways of evaluating partial effects. In Table 17.9, we have computed the average partial effect for 40-year-old individuals with average income and 16 years of education.

The partial effect for AGE in Table 17.6 illustrates, once again, the ambiguity of the simple derivatives as measures of the impact of the variables on the outcome under study. The estimated effect of 0.0003 seems extremely small. But, again, the probability of takeup varies around 0.0188, and AGE ranges from 25 to 65 in the data set. A change in age of 10 years would be associated with a 0.003 impact on the probability, which is about 1/6 of the value. Figure 17.1 and Table 17.10 trace the estimated probability of takeup over the range of the sample data. We

Table 17.8 Estimated semi-elasticities

```
PARTIALS ; Effects : <x> ; Summary ; Means$
Partial Effects for Logit:Probability(ADDON=1)
```
Partial Effects Averaged Over Observations
```
*==> Partial Effect for a Binary Variable
```

(Delta method)	Partial Effect	Standard Error	|t|	95% Confidence Interval	
AGE	.01743	.00470	3.71	.00822	.02664
EDUC	.15942	.01542	10.34	.12921	.18964
* FEMALE	.31731	.08814	3.60	.14455	.49007
* MARRIED	.08475	.12018	.71	-.15080	.32030
* HHKIDS	.10325	.10307	1.00	-.09877	.30527
INCOME	1.47347	.16695	8.83	1.14625	1.80069
* HEALTHY	-.01218	.09403	.13	-.19649	.17212

Table 17.9 Partial effect on takeup of marital status

```
PARTIALS ; effects: married ; set: income = mean, age = 40, educ = 16 $
```
```
Simulation and partial effects are computed with fixed settings
INCOME  = sample mean    =        .3521
AGE     =                      40.0000
EDUC    =                      16.0000
```
```
Partial Effects  Analysis for Probit:Probability(ADDON=1)
```
```
Effects on function with respect to MARRIED
Results are computed by average over sample observations
Partial effects for binary var MARRIED  computed by first difference
```

df/dMARRIED (Delta method)	Partial Effect	Standard Error	|t|	95% Confidence Interval	
APE. Function	.00135	.00358	.38	-.00567	.00836

find that the average occurs at about age 40, which we can see in Table 17.3. But, over the range of the data, from 25 to 64, the estimated takeup probability ranges from 0.014 to 0.026 – i.e., it nearly doubles. This is not a trivial effect at all.

Table 17.10 Effect of change in age on takeup probability

```
SIMULATE ; Scenario: & Age = 25(3)64 ; Plot $
```

```
Model Simulation Analysis for Probit:Probability(ADDON=1)
```

```
Simulations are computed by average over sample observations
```

User Function (Delta method)	Function Value	Standard Error	$\lvert t \rvert$	95% Confidence Interval	
Avrg. Function	.01882	.00082	23.08	.01722	.02042
AGE = 25.00	.01388	.00140	9.91	.01114	.01663
AGE = 28.00	.01459	.00128	11.38	.01208	.01710
AGE = 31.00	.01533	.00116	13.24	.01306	.01759
AGE = 34.00	.01609	.00104	15.55	.01406	.01812
AGE = 37.00	.01689	.00092	18.28	.01508	.01871
AGE = 40.00	.01773	.00084	21.04	.01608	.01938
AGE = 43.00	.01860	.00081	22.83	.01700	.02020
AGE = 46.00	.01951	.00086	22.61	.01782	.02120
AGE = 49.00	.02045	.00099	20.60	.01851	.02240
AGE = 52.00	.02144	.00119	17.95	.01910	.02378
AGE = 55.00	.02246	.00145	15.46	.01961	.02531
AGE = 58.00	.02352	.00176	13.38	.02008	.02697
AGE = 61.00	.02463	.00210	11.72	.02051	.02875
AGE = 64.00	.02578	.00248	10.38	.02091	.03065

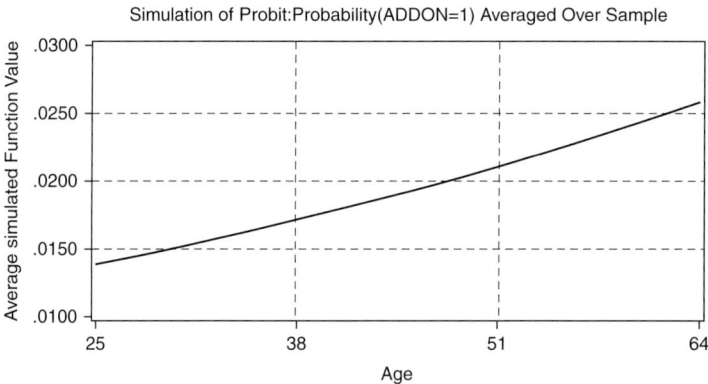

Figure 17.1 Model simulation

There are many variants of the binary choice models that we have developed here. These are treated in a variety of sources such as Greene (2012) and Cameron and Trivedi (2005). In the next two sections, we will describe two of these that appear in many studies in the literature, some panel data models, and three bivariate probit models.

17.3 Binary choice modeling with panel data

The GSOEP data we are using for our applications are an unbalanced panel, as described at the beginning of Section 17.2.8. The natural next step in the analysis would be to accommodate, or take advantage of, the panel data nature of the data set. At the start, this is occasionally a source of some confusion. What distinguishes a "panel data'"treatment from what we have already done in Section 17.2? In what follows, we will take a working framework for panel data analysis to mean some sort of treatment or specification that explicitly recognizes the correlation of unobservable or unobserved heterogeneity across the observations within a group. Consider the base case of our random utility model in Equation (17.53):

$$
\begin{aligned}
U_{it} &= \boldsymbol{\beta}'\mathbf{x}_{it} + \varepsilon_{it}, \\
Y_{it} &= 1[U_{it} > 0].
\end{aligned}
\tag{17.53}
$$

The double subscript, "it" indicates that the observation applies to individual i in period t. In particular, for our example of takeup of add on insurance, we have observed the individual in several (up to seven) years. This understanding need not apply to a time series of observations such as this, however. There are many SC experiments, some described elsewhere in this book, in which the sampled individual is offered a sequence of choice settings – for example, for different configurations of travel mode, or road formats, or utility contracts. Each of these is logically the same as the panel data case suggested.

Thus far, we have not distinguished a "panel data" approach from what we have already done. The model above is precisely what we have used in our example. But it would seem obvious that an element of the random utility specification would be characteristics of the chooser that are intrinsic and unchanging aspects of their preferences. A modification of the RUM that would accommodate this possibility would be as in Equation (17.54):

$$
\begin{aligned}
U_{it} &= \boldsymbol{\beta}'\mathbf{x}_{it} + \alpha_i + \varepsilon_{it}, \\
Y_{it} &= 1[U_{it} > 0].
\end{aligned}
\tag{17.54}
$$

The new term, α_i, would include intrinsic characteristics of the individual i that are unmeasured and unobserved by the analyst. (Observed heterogeneity, such as gender, would present no interesting challenge here – observed heterogeneity would simply be included in $\mathbf{x}_{it}$.)

As in the linear regression setting, in order to proceed with the analysis in the presence of this possibly crucial new variable, assumptions are necessary. The two standard cases that carry over from the regression case to this binary choice model are:

- Fixed effects: $E[a_i \mid x_{i1}, x_{i2}, \ldots, x_{iT}] = g(X_i)$. The heterogeneity is correlated with X_i.
- Random effects: $E[a_i \mid x_{i1}, x_{i2}, \ldots, x_{iT}] = 0$. The heterogeneity is not correlated with X_i.

For each case, we consider the implication of the condition for the conventional MLE, and then examine formal procedures that extend the familiar model to this new setting.

17.3.1 Heterogeneity and conventional estimation: the cluster correction

As a starting point, we consider the implication of the "effects" model for the MLE we computed earlier. That is, what should the analyst expect if they proceed with estimation and simply ignore the possible presence of a_i? This topic is treated in detail elsewhere, such as in Wooldridge (2010) and Greene (2012). We will only sketch the results.

The fixed effects case is a classic omitted variable problem. The impact on the conventional MLE is unpredictable. It is likely to be catastrophic. For a suggestive example, we have re-estimated our add on takeup model using the conventional MLE and a fixed effects estimator described below that is known to be consistent. The results are completely different. Note, for example, the coefficient on income, which switches sign while remaining large and significant (Table 17.11).

As a general result, in the presence of random effects, the "pooled" MLE is also likely to be inconsistent, but in a much more benign fashion. By a direct extension, we can see from the RUM that:

$$\text{Prob } (Y_{it} = 1 \mid x_{it}) = F[\beta' x_{it} / (1 + \sigma_\alpha^2)^{1/2}] = F(\delta' x_{it}). \tag{17.55}$$

That is, the effect of the random effects is to scale the estimator of β toward zero. If the objective is to estimate β, the implication is clear. In fact, δ is an interesting result. In order to compute the partial effects that are generally of interest in this model, given that there are random effects, the result of interest is:

$$E_\alpha[\partial \text{Prob } (Y_{it}=1 \mid x_{it}, \alpha_i)/\partial x_{it}] = \delta f(\delta' x_{it}). \tag{17.56}$$

This means that the familiar MLE actually does estimate something of interest. (This is called the "population averaged model.")

Table 17.11 Fixed effects and conventional estimators

```
Conventional MLE
    AGE|     .15123***    .01687    8.97   .0000     .11818    .18429
MARRIED|     .26558       .25255    1.05   .2930    -.22941    .76057
 HHKIDS|    -.25233       .16020   -1.58   .1152    -.56631    .06166
 INCOME|    -.92199***    .35569   -2.59   .0095   -1.61913   -.22485
HEALTHY|     .01249       .11790     .11   .9156    -.21858    .24357
Fixed Effects estimator
    AGE|     .00538***    .00191    2.81   .0049     .00163    .00913
MARRIED|    -.02123       .04877    -.44   .6634    -.11681    .07436
 HHKIDS|     .05539       .04279    1.29   .1955    -.02847    .13926
 INCOME|     .93684***    .07768   12.06   .0000     .78459   1.08909
HEALTHY|     .01817       .03842     .47   .6362    -.05713    .09347
```

As might be expected, because the observations within a group are correlated (through the common α_i), although the MLE is a consistent estimator of a parameter of interest, the conventional standard errors are inappropriate. A "robust" estimator of the asymptotic covariance matrix for δ, the so-called "cluster" estimator, is computed as in Equation (17.57):

$$V_{CLUSTER} = H^{-1}\left[\frac{N}{N-1}\sum_{i=1}^{N}\left(\sum_{t=1}^{T_i} g_{it}\mathbf{x}_{it}\right)\left(\sum_{t=1}^{T_i} g_{it}\mathbf{x}'_{it}\right)\right]H^{-1}, \qquad (17.57)$$

where $\mathbf{H}$ is an estimator of the expected second derivatives matrix and the inner sums are over the T_i observations in group i. The pattern of increases in the standard errors that appears in Table 17.12 is typical when there is correlation across the members of a group.

17.3.2 Fixed effects

The fixed effects model can be fitted by adding individual dummy variables to the probit or logit equation. Two problems arise. Firstly, as in linear regression, this approach does not allow time (or choice) invariant variables, such as FEMALE in our model (see Greene 2012). Second, even if the fixed effects model is the right model to be fitting, the MLE with N dummy variables in the equation is inconsistent. It is biased away from zero due to a phenomenon called the *incidental parameters problem* (see Greene 2004a).

There is an alternative approach that is based on conditioning the estimator on a sufficient statistic for α_i, that being $\Sigma_t Y_{it}$. This is the "Chamberlain estimator" (Chamberlain 1980; Rasch 1960). The compelling

Table 17.12 Cluster correction of standard erorrs

```
---------------------------------------------------------------------------------
Binomial Probit Model
Dependent variable                     ADDON
Log likelihood function       -2434.77285
Restricted log likelihood     -2551.44776
Chi squared [  7](P= .000)     233.34982
Significance level                .00000
McFadden Pseudo R-squared        .0457289
Estimation based on N =  27326, K =   8
Inf.Cr.AIC  =   4885.5 AIC/N =      .179
-----------+---------------------------------------------------------------------
```

ADDON	Coefficient	Standard Error	z	Prob. |z|>Z*	95% Confidence Interval	
	Index function for probability					
Constant	-3.57370***	.13618	-26.24	.0000	-3.84061	-3.30678
AGE	.00678***	.00195	3.48	.0005	.00297	.01060
EDUC	.06906***	.00702	9.84	.0000	.05531	.08281
FEMALE	.13083***	.03774	3.47	.0005	.05685	.20480
MARRIED	.01863	.04978	.37	.7083	-.07895	.11620
HHKIDS	.04660	.04342	1.07	.2832	-.03851	.13171
INCOME	.74817***	.08360	8.95	.0000	.58432	.91203
HEALTHY	-.01372	.03918	-.35	.7261	-.09052	.06307
	Corrected					
	Index function for probability					
Constant	-3.57370***	.18152	-19.69	.0000	-3.92947	-3.21792
AGE	.00678***	.00262	2.59	.0096	.00165	.01192
EDUC	.06906***	.00854	8.09	.0000	.05232	.08579
FEMALE	.13083**	.05359	2.44	.0146	.02579	.23587
MARRIED	.01863	.06800	.27	.7841	-.11466	.15192
HHKIDS	.04660	.05644	.83	.4090	-.06403	.15723
INCOME	.74817***	.07961	9.40	.0000	.59214	.90421
HEALTHY	-.01372	.04845	-.28	.7770	-.10868	.08123

```
***, **, * ==>  Significance at 1%, 5%, 10% level.
---------------------------------------------------------------------------------
```

disadvantage of this estimator is that because the effects (the constant terms) are conditioned out of the model and not estimated, it is not possible to compute predicted probabilities or partial effects. As such, the fixed effects approach is of limited usefulness, and only appears fairly rarely in received applications.

17.3.3 Random effects and correlated random effects

The random effects model can be consistently estimated by different methods. The tractable LL function for the observed data is obtained by integrating the unobserved heterogeneity out of the function:

$$logL = \sum_{i=1}^{n} \log \int_{\alpha_i} \prod_{t=1}^{T_i} \Phi[q_{it}(\boldsymbol{\beta}'\mathbf{x}_{it} + \sigma_\alpha v_i)]\phi(v_i). \tag{17.58}$$

Two approaches to the integration, Hermite quadrature and Monte Carlo simulation, are used in modern software. Both approaches lead to consistent estimators of $(\boldsymbol{\beta},\sigma_\alpha)$. (Note we have used a simpifying device to write α_i as $\sigma_\alpha v_i$ where $v_i \sim N[0,1]$.)[8]

The random effects model has the appeal that, under the right assumptions, it produces a feasible, consistent maximum likelihood estimator. It also does not restrict the set of variables to be time varying – our FEMALE dummy variable need not be omitted from the random effects model. The assumption that the effects are uncorrelated with the other variables in the model is rather stringent, however, and sometimes not persuasive. An intermediate approach in recent applications, called the "correlated random effects model," uses a correction attributed to Mundlak (1978). The model can be viewed as a two-level specification, given in Equation (17.59):

$$U_{it} = \boldsymbol{\beta}'\mathbf{x}_{it} + \alpha_i + \varepsilon_{it},$$
$$\alpha_i = \tau'\bar{\mathbf{x}}_i + u_i \tag{17.59}$$
$$Y_{it} = 1[U_{it} > 0].$$

Inserting the second equation into the first, then proceeding as before, we have a random effects model to which the vector of group means (for the time varying variables) is added to control for the correlation between the effects and the other variables (Tables 17.13, 17.14).

The Mundlak approach (adding the group means to the model) suggests a method of distinguishing between fixed and random effects. In Equation (17.59), if the coefficients on the group means are all zero, then what remains is a random effects model. The presence of the group means in the model is necessitated by the conditions of the fixed effects model. Thus, a joint test of the null hypothesis that the coefficients on the means are all zero is, *de facto*, a

[8] Quadrature- and simulation-based estimation are discussed at length in Greene (2012). See also Chapter 5.

Table 17.13 Estimated random effects probit model

```
Random Effects Binary Probit Model
Dependent variable                    ADDON
Log likelihood function       -2074.52056
Restricted log likelihood     -2434.77285
Chi squared [  1](P= .000)      720.50459
Significance level                .00000
(Cannot compute pseudo R2.  Use RHS=one
to obtain the required restricted logL)
Estimation based on N =   27326, K =   9
Inf.Cr.AIC  =    4167.0 AIC/N =      .152
Unbalanced panel has    7293 individuals
- ChiSqd[1] tests for random effects  -
LM    ChiSqd  119.010    P value   .00000
LR    ChiSqd  720.505    P value   .00000
Wald ChiSqd  719.973    P value   .00000
```

ADDON	Coefficient	Standard Error	z	Prob. $|z|>Z*$	95% Confidence Interval	
Constant	-6.36645***	.38660	-16.47	.0000	-7.12418	-5.60873
AGE	.01270***	.00410	3.10	.0020	.00466	.02073
EDUC	.13825***	.01883	7.34	.0000	.10134	.17516
FEMALE	.20629**	.08670	2.38	.0173	.03636	.37622
MARRIED	.07684	.09917	.77	.4384	-.11753	.27120
HHKIDS	-.00050	.07958	-.01	.9950	-.15647	.15547
INCOME	.91548***	.16357	5.60	.0000	.59490	1.23607
HEALTHY	-.01976	.06949	-.28	.7762	-.15596	.11645
Rho	.67934***	.02532	26.83	.0000	.62971	.72896

***, **, * ==> Significance at 1%, 5%, 10% level.

test of the null hypothesis of the random effects model against a broader alternative. We can use a likelihood-ratio test (LRT). The LL for the random effects model is −2074.52. That for the model that contains the means is −2028.73. Twice the difference is 91.58. The critical value for the Chi-square distribution with 6 degrees of freedom is 12.59. The null hypothesis of random effects would be rejected in favor of a fixed effects specification.

17.3.4 Parameter heterogeneity

The ML (random parameters) and latent class logit models approaches can also be extended to the binary choice model (and many other models). The

Table 17.14 Random effects probit model with Mundlak correction

```
Random Effects Binary Probit Model
Dependent variable                   ADDON
Log likelihood function     -2028.73447
Restricted log likelihood   -2399.32048
Chi squared [  1](P= .000)    741.17202
Significance level              .00000
(Cannot compute pseudo R2.  Use RHS=one
to obtain the required restricted logL)
Estimation based on N =  27326, K =  14
Inf.Cr.AIC  =   4085.5 AIC/N =    .150
Unbalanced panel has   7293 individuals
- ChiSqd[1] tests for random effects  -
LM   ChiSqd 124.805   P value  .00000
LR   ChiSqd 741.172   P value  .00000
Wald ChiSqd 768.117   P value  .00000
```

ADDON	Coefficient	Standard Error	z	Prob. $\|z\|>Z*$	95% Confidence Interval	
Constant	-6.43558***	.42036	-15.31	.0000	-7.25947	-5.61170
AGE	.09354***	.01365	6.85	.0000	.06679	.12030
EDUC	.31768***	.11955	2.66	.0079	.08336	.55199
FEMALE	.19886**	.09113	2.18	.0291	.02025	.37747
MARRIED	.10220	.18454	.55	.5797	-.25950	.46390
HHKIDS	-.22203**	.10976	-2.02	.0431	-.43714	-.00691
INCOME	-.51888*	.29725	-1.75	.0809	-1.10149	.06372
gmnAGE	-.08598***	.01524	-5.64	.0000	-.11585	-.05611
gmnEDUC	-.20215*	.12262	-1.65	.0992	-.44248	.03818
gmnMARRI	-.08657	.23608	-.37	.7138	-.54928	.37614
gmnHHKID	.42567**	.16948	2.51	.0120	.09348	.75785
gmnINCOM	2.48938***	.43306	5.75	.0000	1.64061	3.33816
gmnHEALT	-.06500	.12769	-.51	.6107	-.31526	.18527
Rho	.69858***	.02521	27.71	.0000	.64917	.74798

```
***, **, * ==>  Significance at 1%, 5%, 10% level.
```

results below illustrate how to introduce this sort of heterogeneity into the binary choice model. (We have used the PUBLIC insurance takeup for this exercise.) Table 17.15 shows a random parameters model. The fixed parameters values of the coefficients are given in parentheses with the means of the distributions. A random parameters approach suggests that one should reinterpret the meaning of statistically different from zero. The fixed parameters

Table 17.15 Estimated random parameters probit model

```
|-> probit ;lhs=public;rhs=x ;rpm
    ;fcn=one(n),age(n),educ(n),female(n),married(n),
    hhkids(n),income(n),healthy(n);draws=50 ; halton ; panel $
```

```
------------------------------------------------------------------------------------
Random Coefficients  Probit   Model
Dependent variable                PUBLIC
Log likelihood function       -4891.63913
Restricted log likelihood     -8286.28230
Chi squared [  8](P= .000)    6789.28633
Significance level                .00000
McFadden Pseudo R-squared         .4096702
Estimation based on N =  27326, K =  16
Inf.Cr.AIC  =   9815.3 AIC/N =    .359
Unbalanced panel has    7293 individuals
Simulation  based on     50 Halton draws
PROBIT (normal)  probability model
```

PUBLIC	Coefficient	Standard Error	z	Prob. |z|>Z*	95% Confidence Interval	
Means for random parameters						
Constant	7.83885***	.18319	42.79	.0000	7.47982	8.19789 (3.66772)
AGE	.07695***	.00277	27.78	.0000	.07152	.08238 (-.00032)
EDUC	-.49791***	.01142	-43.62	.0000	-.52028	-.47553 (-.16650)
FEMALE	.48625***	.04488	10.83	.0000	.39829	.57421 (0.11244)
MARRIED	-.04305	.05388	-.80	.4243	-.14865	.06256 (-.02192)
HHKIDS	-.14061***	.04905	-2.87	.0041	-.23675	-.04447 (-.06797)
INCOME	-1.48888***	.10494	-14.19	.0000	-1.69456	-1.28320 (-.98684)
HEALTHY	-.19400***	.04808	-4.03	.0001	-.28824	-.09975 (-.14718)
Scale parameters for dists. of random parameters						
Constant	.14833***	.02184	6.79	.0000	.10552	.19115
AGE	.08601***	.00171	50.27	.0000	.08265	.08936
EDUC	.07635***	.00222	34.43	.0000	.07200	.08069
FEMALE	.29918***	.03350	8.93	.0000	.23353	.36484
MARRIED	.37962***	.02566	14.79	.0000	.32932	.42992
HHKIDS	.39077***	.03360	11.63	.0000	.32491	.45662
INCOME	.15412***	.04781	3.22	.0013	.06041	.24784
HEALTHY	.07441***	.02514	2.96	.0031	.02514	.12369

```
------------------------------------------------------------------------------------
***, **, * ==>  Significance at 1%, 5%, 10% level.
------------------------------------------------------------------------------------
```

coefficient on FEMALE is 0.112, with an implied population standard deviation of zero. The estimated random parameters model suggests that the coefficient on FEMALE for group i is $0.48625 + 0.29918\nu_i$, that is, a normal distribution with a mean of 0.486 and a standard deviation of 0.299. The estimated fixed value is about 1.25 standard deviations from the estimated mean. Zero is well over two standard deviations from the estimated mean, which suggests nearly all of the mass of the distribution of the random parameter on FEMALE is above zero. The null hypothesis of the fixed (non-random) parameters model can be tested against the alternative of the random hypothesis using a LRT. The necessary values for this model are shown in Table 17.15. The Chi-square statistic of 6789.29 is far larger than the critical value for 8 degrees of freedom, so the fixed parameter model is rejected.

17.4 Bivariate probit models

There are many extensions of the binary choice models, including models for heteroskedasticity, different functional forms, non-parametric and semi-parametric approaches, Bayesian estimators, multiple equations approaches, multinomial and ordered outcomes models, and so on, that could fill a book-length examination of the topic.[9] We have insufficient space to survey the topic here. We will consider one extension, the bivariate probit model, which provides a platform for several interesting applications.

The basic form of the bivariate probit model adds a second equation to the formulation of the choice model:[10]

$$
\begin{aligned}
& y_{i1}{}^* = \boldsymbol{\beta}_1{}'\mathbf{x}_{i1} + \varepsilon_{i1}, \; y_{i1} = 1[y_{i1}{}^* > 0], \\
& y_{i2}{}^* = \boldsymbol{\beta}_2{}'\mathbf{x}_{i2} + \varepsilon_{i2}, \; y_{i2} = 1[y_{i2}{}^* > 0], \\
& (\varepsilon_{i1}, \varepsilon_{i2}) \sim \mathrm{BVN}[(0,0), (1,1,\rho)].{}^{[11]}
\end{aligned}
\tag{17.60}
$$

The model adds some complexity to the specification. However, before proceeding, we note that one could, in the context of this two-equation model, simply ignore the bivariate aspect and examine the two equations separately. The purpose of the two-equation specification is to accommodate and analyze

---

[9] See, for example, Greene and Hensher (2010), which includes nearly 100 pages specifically on binary choice modeling.

[10] The model can be extended to more than two equations in analogous fashion. When the number of equations exceeds two, the probabilities become much more difficult to compute. See Section 4.3 for a discussion.

[11] There is no natural form of the bivariate logit model, so from this point forward, we will focus on the probit model.

Table 17.16 Cross-tabulation for health care utilization

```
Cross Tabulation--------------------+
|           |       HOSPITAL        |
+-----------+--------------------+---------+
|  DOCTOR|        0          1| Total|
+-----------+--------------------+---------+
|         0|    9715        420| 10135|
|         1|   15216       1975| 17191|
+-----------+--------------------+---------+
|    Total|   24931       2395| 27326|
+-----------+--------------------+---------+
```

the correlation across the equations.[12] For an example, our health care data includes two measures of utilization of the health care system, number of doctor visits, and number of inpatient hospital visits. We have recoded these to be DOCTOR = 1(DocVisits > 0) and HOSPITAL = 1(HospVisits > 0). One would expect these to be correlated, though not perfectly so. Table 17.16 shows the mix of these two variables in our data.

Given that the two-choice responses are binary, even after accounting for the exogenous variables, ρ would not be defined as the familiar Pearson product moment correlation as used for continuous variables; the so-called "tetrachoric correlation"[13] is used as the appropriate measure of the correlation between two binary variables. Looking at the data in Table 17.1, it is unclear what to expect for the value of ρ. In view of the large off-diagonal element, one might suspect it to be large and negative. We would measure the simple, unconditional tetrachoric correlation for two binary variables as the correlation coefficient in a bivariate probit model that contained only two constant terms, and no regressors. For these data, that value is about +0.31. As exogenous variables are added to the model, the correlation will move toward zero. Some of the correlation across equations that is accounted for by omitted variables is eliminated as the variables are added to the equations.

The LL for estimation of the bivariate probit model parameters is given in Equation (17.61):

[12] A technical motivation for fitting the two equations jointly is the possible gain in efficiency (reduction in standard errors) that might attend the FIML estimator compared to the two LIML estimators. This effect is likely to be minor, however, as suggested in our application.

[13] The tetrachoric correlation is used when it is assumed that there are normally distributed latent continuous variables underlying the observed binary variables. The tetrachoric correlation estimates the correlation between the assumed underlying continuous variables. The formal definition of the tetrachoric correlation for two binary variables is exactly consistent with what we would define as the correlation of the two random terms in our bivariate probit model.

$$\log L = \sum\nolimits_{i=1}^{N} \log \Phi_2[(q_{i1}\boldsymbol{\beta}'_1\mathbf{x}_{i1}),(q_{i2}\boldsymbol{\beta}'_2\mathbf{x}_{i2}),(q_{i1}q_{i2}\rho)]. \tag{17.61}$$

Calculation of the bivariate normal probabilities is a bit complicated, but in general this model is, like its one variable counterpart, quite conventional. There are hundreds of applications to be found in the empirical literature. The various derivatives and calculations needed to obtain an asymptotic covariance matrix for the MLE and for computing the partial effects are fairly involved – they appear in detail in Greene (2012, Chapter 17).

Because there are two equations, it is now unclear what partial effects will be useful. That will depend on the context. Among the candidates are:

Joint Probability $(Y_1 = j_1,\ Y_2 = j_2) = F[q_1(\boldsymbol{\beta}_1'\mathbf{x}_1),q_2(\boldsymbol{\beta}_2'\mathbf{x}_2),(q_1q_2\rho)]$, $j_m = 0,1$, $q_m = 2j_m - 1$.

Conditional Probability $(Y_A = j_A \mid Y_B = j_B) = F[q_A(\boldsymbol{\beta}_A'\mathbf{x}_A),q_B(\boldsymbol{\beta}_B'\mathbf{x}_B),(q_Aq_B\rho)]/ \Phi[q_B(\boldsymbol{\beta}_B'\mathbf{x}_B)]$.

(Either Y_1 or Y_2 may be the conditioning variable, A or B.)

Marginal Probability: $\Phi[q_B(\boldsymbol{\beta}_B'\mathbf{x}_B)]$.

For one example, Table 17.18 (based on Table 17.17) shows the partial effects of the regressors on the conditional probability that the individual had at least one hospital visit, given that they had at least one doctor visit.

There are many variants of the bivariate (and multivariate) probit models in the received applications. We will consider two that are fairly common.

17.4.1 Simultaneous equations

In some settings, a simultaneous equations type of formulation of the model might seem natural, such as that in Equation (17.62):

$$y_{i1}^* = \boldsymbol{\beta}_1'\mathbf{x}_{i1} + \gamma_1 y_{i2} + \varepsilon_{i1},\ y_{i1} = 1[y_{i1}^* > 0],$$
$$y_{i2}^* = \boldsymbol{\beta}_2'\mathbf{x}_{i2} + \gamma_2 y_{i1} + \varepsilon_{i2},\ y_{i2} = 1[y_{i2}^* > 0], \tag{17.62}$$
$$(\varepsilon_{i1},\varepsilon_{i2}) \sim BVN[(0,0),(1,1,\rho)].[14]$$

---

[14] There is no natural form of the bivariate logit model, so from this point forward, we will focus on the probit model.

Table 17.17 Estimated bivariate probit model

```
FIML Estimates of Bivariate Probit Model
Dependent variable          DOCTOR/HOSPITAL      DOCTOR           HOSPITAL
Log likelihood function       -24482.14617   (-16743.56041)   (-7879.87240)
Estimation based on N =   27326, K =    20
Inf.Cr.AIC =   49004.3 AIC/N =    1.793
```

DOCTOR / HOSPITAL	Coefficient	Standard Error	z	Prob. |z|>Z*	95% Confidence Interval	
Index equation for DOCTOR						
Constant	.17158**	.07242	2.37	.0178	.02963	.31352 (.17055)
AGE	.00715***	.00083	8.64	.0000	.00553	.00878 (.00717)
EDUC	.00101	.00383	.26	.7928	-.00650	.00851 (.00087)
FEMALE	.34371***	.01631	21.08	.0000	.31175	.37568 (.34460)
MARRIED	.07889***	.02096	3.76	.0002	.03781	.11996 (.07918)
HHKIDS	-.14079***	.01850	-7.61	.0000	-.17706	-.10452 (-.14005)
INCOME	-.03993	.04656	-.86	.3911	-.13119	.05132 (-.03940)
HEALTHY	-.62363***	.01725	-36.16	.0000	-.65743	-.58983 (-.62273)
PUBLIC	.10403***	.02653	3.92	.0001	.05202	.15603 (.10426)
Index equation for HOSPITAL						
Constant	-1.06885***	.10255	-10.42	.0000	-1.26984	-.86786 (-1.05991)
AGE	.00073	.00110	.67	.5060	-.00142	.00288 (.00071)
EDUC	-.01399**	.00555	-2.52	.0116	-.02486	-.00312 (-.01392)
FEMALE	.09115***	.02208	4.13	.0000	.04788	.13443 (.08876)
MARRIED	-.04748*	.02814	-1.69	.0916	-.10264	.00769 (-.04750)
HHKIDS	-.00067	.02612	-.03	.9796	-.05187	.05053 (-.00218)
INCOME	.09906	.06143	1.61	.1069	-.02135	.21947 (.08852)
HEALTHY	-.43431***	.02278	-19.07	.0000	-.47896	-.38967 (-.43646)
PUBLIC	.02439	.03941	.62	.5360	-.05286	.10164 (.02092)
ADDON	.21403***	.07227	2.96	.0031	.07237	.35568 (.24306)
Disturbance correlation						
RHO(1,2)	.25357***	.01474	17.21	.0000	.22469	.28246 (0.00000)

Table 17.18 Partial effects for bivariate probit model

```
partials;effects: x ; Summary ; Means
  ; Set:public=1,addon=1 ; Prob(hospital=1|doctor=1) $
-------------------------------------------------------------------------------
Simulation and partial effects are computed with fixed settings
PUBLIC   =                      1.0000
ADDON    =                      1.0000
-------------------------------------------------------------------------------

-------------------------------------------------------------------------------
Partial Effects for Biv.Probit,Prob(HOSPITAL=1|DOCTOR=1)
Partial Effects Computed at data Means
==> Partial Effect for a Binary Variable
-------------------------------------------------------------------------------
```

| | Partial | Standard | | | |
(Delta method)	Effect	Error	|t|	95% Confidence Interval	
AGE	-.00005	.00025	.18	-.00055	.00045
EDUC	-.00329	.00133	2.48	-.00590	-.00069
FEMALE	.01084	.00517	2.10	.00071	.02097
MARRIED	-.01346	.00662	2.03	-.02645	-.00048
HHKIDS	.00411	.00609	.67	-.00783	.01605
INCOME	.02431	.01423	1.71	-.00358	.05220
HEALTHY	-.08240	.00800	10.29	-.09808	-.06671

Our doctor/hospital application might seem to fit this case. Unfortunately, this model is not estimable. (The easily misunderstood term "incoherent" is generally used for this case.) The coherency problem for this model is that there is no "reduced form." Each variable requires knowledge of the other for determination. There is no way to determine the two variables in terms of the exogenous information in the model.[15] An intermediate form of the model is more amenable. The "recursive bivariate probit model" is used as shown in Equation (17.63). See Burnett (1997) and Greene (1998):

$$y_{i1}^* = \beta_1'x_{i1} \quad\quad + \varepsilon_{i1},\ y_{i1} \quad = 1[y_{i1}^* > 0],$$
$$y_{i2}^* = \beta_2'x_{i2} + \gamma_2 y_{i1} + \varepsilon_{i2},\ y_{i2} = 1[y_{i2}^* > 0], \quad\quad (17.63)$$
$$(\varepsilon_{i1}, \varepsilon_{i2}) \sim \text{BVN}[(0,0),(1,1,\rho)].^{16}$$

[15] Early treatments of this model, e.g., in Maddala (1983), wrote the formulation on the RHS in terms of the latent index rather than the observed outcomes. This does overcome the coherency problem, but it is not a natural formulation of the behavioral aspect of the specification.

[16] There is no natural form of the bivariate logit model, so from this point forward, we will focus on the probit model.

A *recursive system* is qualitatively different from the simpler bivariate probit model in that it allows for the binary response from the first equation to appear on the right-hand side of the second equation, but in a setting where the variables are likely to be spuriously related due to observed as well as unobserved independent variables (see Arendt and Holm 2007). This additional dimension is one of three reasons why we might observe the binary variables, y_1 and y_2, to be correlated: (i) a causal relation due to the influence of y_1 on y_2 through the parameter γ, (ii) y_1 and y_2 may depend on correlated observed variables (the **x**s), and (iii) y_1 and y_2 may depend on correlated unobserved variables (the ε_is).

The first equation is in reduced form. By using the first equation in the second, it is possible to define a reduced form for the entire model in terms of the probabilities of the outcomes. Estimation of the model is carried out by treating it as a conventional bivariate probit model. The explicit form of the LL function accommodates the simultaneous equations nature of the model, as given in Equation (17.64):

$$\log L = \sum_{i=1}^{N} \log \Phi_2[q_{i1}(\boldsymbol{\beta}'_1 \mathbf{x}_{i1}), q_{i2}(\boldsymbol{\beta}'_2 \mathbf{x}_{i2} + \gamma_2 y_{i1}), (q_{i1} q_{i2} \rho)]. \tag{17.64}$$

For example, there is no Jacobian term as there is in a linear simultaneous equations model. See Maddala (1983, 124) and Greene (2012). The terms that comprise the likelihood are as follows:

$$\begin{aligned}
\text{Prob}[y_1 = 1, y_2 = 1 \,|\, \mathbf{x}_1, \mathbf{x}_2] &= \phi_2\,(\boldsymbol{\beta}_1' \mathbf{x}_1, \;\boldsymbol{\beta}_2' \mathbf{x}_2 + \gamma, \;\rho) \\
\text{Prob}[y_1 = 1, y_2 = 0 \,|\, \mathbf{x}_1, \mathbf{x}_2] &= \phi_2(\boldsymbol{\beta}_1' \mathbf{x}_1, \;-\boldsymbol{\beta}_2' \mathbf{x}_2 - \gamma, \;-\rho) \\
\text{Prob}[y_1 = 0, y_2 = 1 \,|\, \mathbf{x}_1, \mathbf{x}_2] &= \phi_2(-\boldsymbol{\beta}_1' \mathbf{x}_1, \;\boldsymbol{\beta}_2' \mathbf{x}_2, -\rho) \\
\text{Prob}[y_1 = 0, y_2 = 0 \,|\, \mathbf{x}_1, \mathbf{x}_2] &= \phi_2(-\boldsymbol{\beta}_1' \mathbf{x}_1, \;-\boldsymbol{\beta}_2' \mathbf{x}_2, \;\rho)
\end{aligned} \tag{17.65a}$$

The formulation of the recursive model produces a useful complication of the partial effects. Consider the second variable in the model. As noted, there are several candidates for the function of interest in the partial effects. For any of those functions, the model will involve a joint probability of the form in Equation (17.65):

$$F\,(y_1, y_2) = F\,(y_2|y_1)\text{Prob}\,(y_1). \tag{17.65b}$$

Now, consider an exogenous variable that appears in both equations, such as the **x** vector in our model for doctor and hospital visits. The partial effect of this **x** will consist of a "direct" effect measured by the effect on its appearance in $\mathbf{x}_2$, plus an "indirect" effect that is essentially transmitted to this function for

Table 17.19 Estimated recursive bivariate probit model

```
FIML - Recursive Bivariate Probit Model
Log likelihood function      -24482.00697
Estimation based on N =   27326, K =   21
Inf.Cr.AIC  =   49006.0 AIC/N =    1.793
```

DOCTOR / HOSPITAL	Coefficient	Standard Error	z	Prob. $\|z\|>Z*$	95% Confidence Interval	
Index equation for DOCTOR						
Constant	.17243**	.07240	2.38	.0172	.03052	.31434
AGE	.00714***	.00083	8.63	.0000	.00552	.00876
EDUC	.00105	.00383	.28	.7831	-.00645	.00855
FEMALE	.34310***	.01630	21.05	.0000	.31115	.37504
MARRIED	.07873***	.02095	3.76	.0002	.03767	.11980
HHKIDS	-.14104***	.01850	-7.62	.0000	-.17730	-.10477
INCOME	-.04037	.04649	-.87	.3851	-.13149	.05074
HEALTHY	-.62386***	.01724	-36.18	.0000	-.65765	-.59006
PUBLIC	.10386***	.02653	3.91	.0001	.05185	.15586
Index equation for HOSPITAL						
Constant	-.95119***	.24768	-3.84	.0001	-1.43664	-.46574
AGE	.00105	.00123	.86	.3906	-.00135	.00345
EDUC	-.01381**	.00550	-2.51	.0121	-.02459	-.00302
FEMALE	.10684***	.03454	3.09	.0020	.03915	.17453
MARRIED	-.04281	.02916	-1.47	.1421	-.09996	.01434
HHKIDS	-.00702	.02824	-.25	.8037	-.06237	.04833
INCOME	.09680	.06115	1.58	.1134	-.02306	.21665
HEALTHY	-.45827***	.04724	-9.70	.0000	-.55086	-.36569
PUBLIC	.02973	.04021	.74	.4597	-.04908	.10853
ADDON	.21151***	.07133	2.97	.0030	.07170	.35132
DOCTOR	-.16944	.31561	-.54	.5914	-.78803	.44915
Disturbance correlation						
RHO(1,2)	.34630**	.17038	2.03	.0421	.01237	.68023

```
***, **, * ==>  Significance at 1%, 5%, 10% level.
```

y_2 through its effect on y_1 and thence to y_2. For example, the conditional mean for y_2 given y_1 is as given in Equation (17.66):

$$F[y_2 \mid y_1 = 1, \mathbf{x}_1, \mathbf{x}_2] = \Phi_2 \left(\boldsymbol{\beta}_1' \mathbf{x}_1, \boldsymbol{\beta}_2' \mathbf{x}_2 + \gamma y_1 \, \rho \right) / \Phi \left(\boldsymbol{\beta}_1' \mathbf{x}_1 \right). \qquad (17.66)$$

This decomposition is shown in Table 17.20 for the health care model estimated in Table 17.19. Alternatively, the unconditional mean function is as shown in Equation (17.67):

Table 17.20 Decomposition of partial effects in recursive model

```
------------------------------------------------------------------
Decomposition of Partial Effects for Recursive Bivariate Probit
Model is   DOCTOR = F(x1b1), HOSPITAL = F(x2b2+c*DOCTOR  )
Conditional mean function is E[HOSPITAL|x1,x2] =
Phi2(x1b1,x2b2+gamma,rho) + Phi2(-x1b1,x2b2,-rho)
Partial effects for continuous variables are derivatives.
Partial effects for dummy variables (*) are first differences.
Direct effect is wrt x2, indirect is wrt x1, total is the sum.
There is no distinction between direct and indirect for dummy
variables.  Each of the two effects shown is the total effect.
```

Variable	Direct Effect	Indirect Effect	Total Effect
AGE	.0001652	-.0000521	.0001130
EDUC	-.0021676	-.0000077	-.0021753
FEMALE*	.0142578	.0142578	.0142578
MARRIED*	-.0074301	-.0074301	-.0074301
HHKIDS*	-.0000573	-.0000573	-.0000573
INCOME	.0151988	.0002947	.0154935
HEALTHY*	-.0707113	-.0707113	-.0707113
PUBLIC*	.0038366	.0038366	.0038366
ADDON*	.0379158	.0000000	.0379158

$$
\begin{aligned}
E[y_2|\mathbf{x}_1,\mathbf{x}_2] &= \Phi(\boldsymbol{\beta}_1'\mathbf{x}_1)E[y_2|y_1=1,\mathbf{x}_1,\mathbf{x}_2] + [1-\Phi(\boldsymbol{\beta}_1'\mathbf{x}_1)]E[y_2|y_1=0,\mathbf{x}_1,\mathbf{x}_2] \\
&= \Phi_2(\boldsymbol{\beta}_1'\mathbf{x}_1,\boldsymbol{\beta}_2'\mathbf{x}_2+\gamma,\rho) + \Phi_2(-\boldsymbol{\beta}_1'\mathbf{x}_1,\boldsymbol{\beta}_2'\mathbf{x}_2,-\rho)
\end{aligned}
$$

$$(17.67)$$

(Mathematical decomposition of this interpretation is developed in Greene 2012.)

17.4.2 Sample selection

A second variant of the bivariate probit model is a form of the sample selection model introduced in Heckman (1979). To consider a substantive example, in our model for takeup of the add on insurance, there is an observation criterion; only those who purchase the public insurance are eligible for the add on. We might then condition our analysis of add on insurance by selecting on those eligible for it.[17] The formulation of the model is given in Equation (17.68):

---

[17] A common application in the received literature studies loan default (the binary outcome of interest) for those loan applicants whose application is accepted (i.e., are selected).

$$y_{i1}* \ = \ \boldsymbol{\beta}_1'\mathbf{x}_{i\,1} + \varepsilon_{i\,1}, \ y_{i\,1} = 1[y_{i1}* \ > \ 0],$$

$$y_{i2}* \ = \ \boldsymbol{\beta}_2'\mathbf{x}_{i\,2} + \varepsilon_{i\,2}, \ y_{i\,2} = 1[y_{i2}* \ > \ 0, y_{i1} = 1], \ \text{unobserved when } y_{i\,1} = 0.$$

$$(\varepsilon_{i1}, \varepsilon_{i2}) \ \sim \ \text{BVN}[(0,0), (1,1,\rho)].^{18}$$

$$(17.68)$$

There are three types of observations in the sample. The "non-selected" observations are those for which $y_{i1} = 0$. For these observations, the contribution to the likelihood for the sample is only $\text{Prob}(y_{i1} = 0)$ – no other data are observed. For "selected" observations, the observation contributes the joint probability as it appears in the bivariate models we examined earlier. Combining terms, we get:

$$\log L = \begin{matrix} \sum_{y_{i1}=0} \log\Phi[-\boldsymbol{\beta}'_1\mathbf{x}_{i1}] + \\ \sum_{y_{i1}=1} \log\Phi_2[\boldsymbol{\beta}'_1\mathbf{x}_{i1}, q_{i2}(\boldsymbol{\beta}'_2\mathbf{x}_{i2}), q_{i2}\rho] \end{matrix}. \qquad (17.69)$$

Table 17.21 displays the estimates of the model. In specifying the model, we have defined the equation for public based on the usual demographics. The add on insurance is associated with employer provided health insurance, so our equation for add on includes several variables related to that, such as whether the individual is self-employed, is a public servant (BEAMT), and whether they have a "blue collar" or "white collar" job. The model contains a direct test of the "selection effect." If ρ equals zero in the model, then the log likelihood becomes:

$$\begin{aligned} \log L &= \begin{matrix} \sum_{y_{i1}=0} \log\Phi[-\boldsymbol{\beta}'_1\mathbf{x}_{i1}] + \\ \sum_{y_{i1}=1} \log\{\Phi[\boldsymbol{\beta}'_1\mathbf{x}_{i1}]\Phi[q_{i2}(\boldsymbol{\beta}'_2\mathbf{x}_{i2})]\} \end{matrix} . \qquad (17.70) \\ &= \sum_{i=1}^{N} \log\Phi[q_{i1}\boldsymbol{\beta}'_1\mathbf{x}_{i1}] + \sum_{y_{i1}=1} \log\Phi[q_{i2}(\boldsymbol{\beta}'_2\mathbf{x}_{i2})] \end{aligned}$$

This LL would be maximized by fitting separate probit models for y_{i1} and y_{i2}, using the observed data on y_{i2}. This would not require any consideration of a "selection" mechanism. In our results in Table 17.21, we find that the estimated correlation is significantly different from zero, which does suggest a selection effect in the data.

---

[18] There is no natural form of the bivariate logit model, so from this point forward, we will focus on the probit model.

Table 17.21 Sample selection finding

```
|-> bivar;lhs=addon,public; rh1=x
; rh2=one,income,bluec,whitec,self,beamt,working,handdum
; selection$
```

```
FIML Estimates of Bivariate Probit Model
Log likelihood function     -8444.03135
Estimation based on N =   27326, K =   17
Inf.Cr.AIC  =   16922.1 AIC/N =      .619
Selection model based on PUBLIC
Selected obs. 24203, Nonselected:   3123
```

ADDON PUBLIC	Coefficient	Standard Error	z	Prob. |z|>Z*	95% Confidence Interval	
	Index equation for ADDON					
Constant	-4.01976***	.14230	-28.25	.0000	-4.29866	-3.74086
AGE	.00815***	.00205	3.97	.0001	.00413	.01217
EDUC	.10382***	.00827	12.55	.0000	.08760	.12003
FEMALE	.14023***	.03910	3.59	.0003	.06360	.21686
MARRIED	.00773	.05268	.15	.8834	-.09553	.11099
HHKIDS	.07127	.04647	1.53	.1251	-.01981	.16235
INCOME	.73490***	.10751	6.84	.0000	.52419	.94561
HEALTHY	.00504	.03983	.13	.8993	-.07302	.08310
	Index equation for PUBLIC					
Constant	1.78225***	.03012	59.16	.0000	1.72321	1.84129
INCOME	-1.23390***	.05474	-22.54	.0000	-1.34120	-1.12661
BLUEC	1.09021***	.07627	14.29	.0000	.94071	1.23970
WHITEC	.33480***	.05926	5.65	.0000	.21864	.45095
SELF	-.70417***	.06332	-11.12	.0000	-.82827	-.58007
BEAMT	-2.04608***	.06408	-31.93	.0000	-2.17167	-1.92049
WORKING	.05679	.05733	.99	.3219	-.05558	.16916
HANDDUM	.12921***	.03241	3.99	.0001	.06569	.19273
	Disturbance correlation					
RHO(1,2)	.36012***	.08599	4.19	.0000	.19158	.52866

```
***, **, * ==>  Significance at 1%, 5%, 10% level.
```

17.4.3 Application I: model formulation of the *ex ante* link between acceptability and voting intentions for a road pricing scheme

The model examined in this application is the recursive bivariate probit model of Section 17.4.1. A road pricing scheme is proposed. Respondents indicate their acceptance ($y_1=1$) or rejection ($y_1=0$) of the proposal, and their intention to vote yes ($y_2=1|y_1$) or not ($y_1=0|y_1$) The model suggested is summarized in Equation (17.71):

$$y_{i1}* = \boldsymbol{\beta}_1'\mathbf{x}_{i1} + \varepsilon_{i1}, \, y_{i1} = 1[y_{i\,1}* > 0] \text{ (acceptance)},$$

$$y_{i2}* = \boldsymbol{\beta}_2\mathbf{x}_{i\,2} + \gamma y_{i\,1} + \varepsilon_{i\,2}, \, y_{i\,2} = 1[y_{i2}* > 0] \text{ (vote)}, \tag{17.71}$$

$$[\varepsilon_{i1}, \varepsilon_{i2}] \sim N_2[(0,0),(1,1),\rho], \, -1 < \rho < 1.$$

Observations on y_1 and y_2 are available for all individuals; y_{ij} (j=1,2) are the unobserved variables representing the latent utility or propensity of choosing to *Accept* or *Vote* for a specific RP scheme.

The endogenous nature of *Accept* is explicitly accounted for in the formulation of the LL. The LL is expressed in terms of Prob (*Vote* =1, *Accept* =1) = Prob (*Vote* =1 |*Accept* = 1)*Prob (*Accept* =1). The marginal probability for *Accept* = 1 is $\Phi(\boldsymbol{\beta}_1'\mathbf{x}_1)$ and the conditional probability for (*Vote* =1|*Accept* = 1) is $\Phi_2(\boldsymbol{\beta}_1'\mathbf{x}_1, \boldsymbol{\beta}_2'\mathbf{x}_2 + \gamma_1 Accept\, \rho)/\Phi(\boldsymbol{\beta}_1'\mathbf{x}_1)$. Collecting terms, we have:

$$\text{Prob}[Vote = 1, Accept = 1|\mathbf{x}_1, \mathbf{x}_2] = \Phi_2 (\boldsymbol{\beta}_1'\mathbf{x}_1, \boldsymbol{\beta}_2'\mathbf{x}_2 + \gamma(Accept=1)). \tag{17.72}$$

The corresponding contributions to the likelihood for the other three possible outcomes are shown in Equation (17.73):

$$\text{Prob}[Vote = 1, Accept = 0|\mathbf{x}_1, \mathbf{x}_2] = \Phi_2 (\boldsymbol{\beta}_1'\mathbf{x}_1, -(\boldsymbol{\beta}_2'\mathbf{x}_2 + \gamma(Accept = 0)), -\rho)$$
$$\text{Prob}[Vote = 0, Accept = 1|\mathbf{x}_1, \mathbf{x}_2] = \Phi_2(-\boldsymbol{\beta}_1'\mathbf{x}_1, \, \boldsymbol{\beta}_2'\mathbf{x}_2 + \gamma(Accept = 1), -\rho)$$
$$\text{Prob}[Vote = 0, Accept = 0|\mathbf{x}_1, \mathbf{x}_2] = \Phi_2(-\boldsymbol{\beta}_1'\mathbf{x}_1, -(\boldsymbol{\beta}_2'\mathbf{x}_2 + \gamma(Accept = 0))\rho).$$
$$\tag{17.73}$$

(We have included the terms $\gamma(Accept=0)$ to make explicit the form of the model. Of course, if *Accept* = 0, the whole term is zero.)

17.4.3.1 The road pricing data collection approach

The survey instrument was a Computer Assisted Personal Interview (CAPI), resident on a server, accessed via laptops used by interviewers who sat with the respondents, at locations made through appointments, to provide any advice that was required in working through the survey, while not offering answers to any of the questions.

The data used in the models are extracted from a stated choice experiment that consisted of three alternatives: two labeled alternatives representing a cordon-based charging scheme and a distance-based charging scheme, randomly assigned to road pricing schemes 1 and 2, and the status quo. Each alternative was described by separate attributes representing the average amount of tolls and fuel outlaid weekly, the annual vehicle registration charge, and the allocation of revenues raised to improve public transport, to improve and expand upon the existing road network, to reduce income tax, to contribute to general government revenue, and to be used to compensate toll road companies for loss of toll revenue. The cordon-based charging scheme and a distance-based alternative were also described by either a peak and off-peak cordon-based charging amount or a peak or off-peak per kilometre distance-based charge. Both non-status quo alternatives were also described by the year proposed when the scheme would commence.

A Bayesian D-efficient experimental design was implemented for the study (see Rose *et al.* 2008). The design was generated in such a way that the cost-related attribute levels for the status quo were first acquired from respondents during preliminary questions in the survey, while associated attributes for the cordon-based and distance-based charging schemes were pivoted off of these as minus percentage shifts representing a reduction in such costs for these schemes. Pivoted attributes included average fuel costs and annual registration fees. Fuel costs were reduced by anywhere between zero percent and 50 percent of the respondent reported values, either representing no reduction in fuel tax or up to a potential 100 percent reduction in fuel taxes. Registration fees were reduced to between zero percent and 100 percent from the respondent-reported values (see Rose *et al.* 2008 and Chapter 6 for a description of pivot type designs). Toll was only included in the status quo alternative, being set to zero for the non-status quo alternatives since it is replaced by the road pricing regime.[19]

The allocation of revenues raised was fixed for the status quo alternative, but varied in the cordon-based and distance-based charging schemes over choice tasks. The allocation of revenue was varied from zero percent to 100 percent for a given revenue stream category. Within a charging scheme, the allocation of revenue was such that the sum had to equal 100 percent across all possible revenue allocations.

The cordon-based charging alternative was described by a peak and off-peak cordon charge. The peak charge varied between $2.00 and $20.00, while the off peak charge varied between $0.00 and $15.00. Likewise, the distance-based charge was described by two distance-based charging attributes, one for trips taken during peak periods and the second for off-peak trips. The per kilometre charge for the peak period ranged from $0.05 per kilometre to $0.40 per kilometre, while the off-peak distance-based charge varied between $0.00

---

[19] The context here is one where tolls already exist, which might be replaced by a (more flexible) road pricing scheme. This context differs a lot from countries (i.e., several countries in Europe) that do not have tolls on a major scale, and where the issue is to introduce a form of road pricing that will not be replacing tolls. Getting support might then be more difficult.

and $0.30 per kilometre. The ranges selected were based on ranges that we believed would contain the most likely levels if implemented. The design was generated in such a way that the peak cordon-based, and peak per kilometre-based, charges were always equal to or greater than the associated off-peak charges. Finally, the cordon-based and distance-based charging schemes were described by the year the scheme would be implemented. In each case, this was varied between 2013 (representing one year from the time of the survey) and 2016 (representing a four-year delay from the time of the survey). An example of a choice screen is given in Figure 17.2.

17.4.3.2 Bivariate probit models

A series of probit models was estimated to establish the relationship between the probability of voting for an RP scheme in a referendum and the probability that the RP scheme would be acceptable if introduced. The initial hypothesis is that support in a referendum is dependent substantively on the RP scheme (as described by its charging regime – cordon- or distance-based, the actual charging levels, and the revenue allocation plan) being acceptable to the self-interested individual (see Hensher *et al.* 2012). Without public acceptance *ex ante*, there is a very high risk of the referendum vote in support of a scheme failing.[20]

Characteristics	Status Quo	RPScheme 1	RPScheme 2
Implementation of the scheme			
Year scheme will be introduced	---	2015	2016
Description of the scheme	Current Experience	Cordon Based ($/day)	Distance Based ($/km)
Predicted impact on you personally			
Weekly toll charges	$ 2.40	$ 0.00	$ 0.00
Weekly fuel outlay	$ 40.00	$ 28.00	$ 24.00
Annual vehicle registration fee (per annum)	$ 320.00	$ 320.00	$ 240.00
Peak period (7–9am, 4–6pm) congestion charge (total based on travel by car last week)	---	$ 11.00	$ 0.12 / km ($ 14.40 for 120 kms)
Off-peak period congestion charge (total based on travel by car last week)	---	$ 3.00	$ 0.12 / km ($ 3.60 for 30 kms)
Revenue Raised will be allocated as:			
improving public transport	---	80 %	0 %
improving existing and construct new roads	30 %	0 %	0 %
reducing personal income tax	---	0 %	80 %
general government revenue	65 %	20 %	0 %
private toll road companies (to compensate for removal of tolls)	5 %	0 %	20 %

Figure 17.2 Illustrative voting and acceptance choice screen

[20] Public acceptance can be achieved *ex ante* through a pilot scheme such as the Stockholm pilot, which is a real demonstration of the merits of RP reform (see Eliasson *et al.* 2009). Alternatively, we have to rely on identifying the extent of public acceptability of very specific RP schemes, *ex ante*, and ensure that the support is sufficient to obtain a positive outcome in a referendum.

Proposed Cordon Charge Area In Sydney CBD

Taxis, and residents living inside the cordon zone would be exempt from the cordon charge.

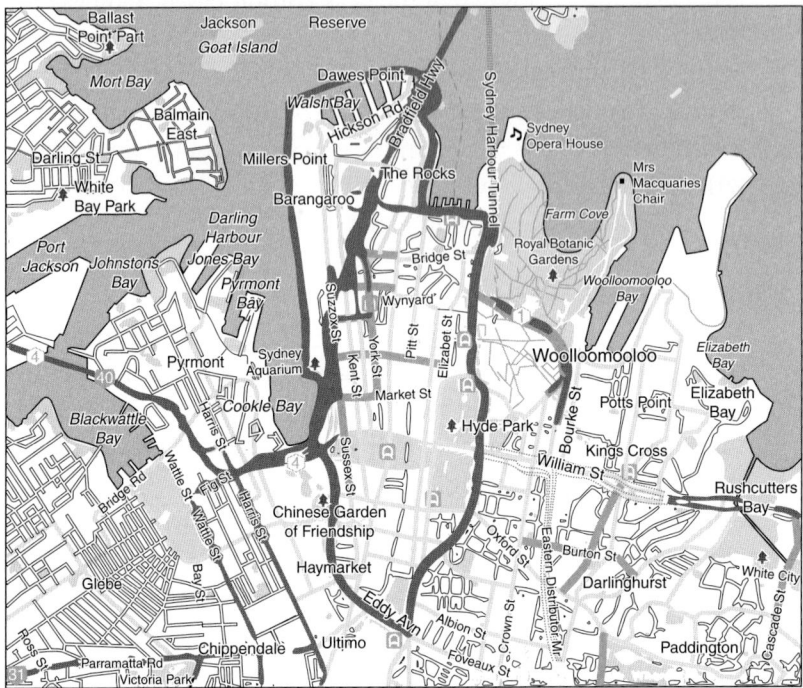

Figure 17.2 (cont.)

Separate models were initially estimated for the voting response and the acceptability response; then recursive bivariate models were estimated with non-random parameters. The final two models (3 and 4) are recursive bivariate probits with random parameters for the RP scheme costs, distinguishing the current cost components (i.e., registration and fuel costs) (Non-RP Cost) and the proposed new costs associated with a cordon and a distance-based charging regime (RP Costs). Models 3 and 4 differ by the inclusion in Model 4 of the *Accept* variable on the RHS of the *Vote* model. All models are summarized in Tables 17.22 and 17.23.[21] The set of explanatory variables was guided in part by the findings in Hensher *et al.* (2012) as well as an extensive investigation of the rich array of data items available. It is notable that the

---

[21] The alternatives defining each binary response are taken from four choice scenario screens. To account for the possibility that the response associated with a particular alternative is conditioned on the offered set of three alternatives, we included three dummy variables to represent the four choice scenarios. These variables were highly statistically non-significant and were excluded from the final models, giving us confidence in the approach we have adopted.

Table 17.22 Models of referendum voting and acceptance of road pricing schemes: 1

Sample = 2,400 observations from 200 individuals, with allowance for panel nature of data (i.e., 12 observations per individual). The covariance matrix is adjusted for data clustering in Models 1 and 2; t-values in brackets.

Choice response:	Independent probit — M1		Bivariate probit (recursive simultaneous)			
			M2: Non-random parameters		M3: Random parameters	
	Voting	Acceptance	Voting	Acceptance	Voting	Acceptance
Constant	−0.8853 (−11.6)	−0.3231 (−2.02)	−0.8988 (−12.3)	−0.3875 (−2.63)	−0.8647 (−8.75)	−0.4556 (−4.36)
Cordon scheme (1,0)	0.3807 (4.02)	0.3081 (3.49)	0.3857 (4.17)	0.3375 (3.82)	0.3747 (8.07)	0.2285 (4.31)
Non-RP costs per week	−0.0069 (−5.44)	−0.0080 (−4.94)	−0.0072 (−6.66)	−0.0080 (−5.07)	−0.0087 (−7.22)	−0.0105 (−8.88)
RP costs (per week)	−0.0122 (−7.25)	−0.0113 (−5.62)	−0.0116 (−7.88)	−0.0111 (−8.71)	−0.0200 (−10.7)	−0.0227 (−14.6)
Peak km (per week)	0.0019 (7.56)	0.0016 (2.47)	0.0020 (7.59)	0.0016 (2.83)	0.0022 (3.52)	0.0031 (7.00)
Off-peak km (per week)	0.0012 (5.78)	0.0011 (2.88)	0.0013 (7.12)	0.0011 (3.06)	0.0014 (3.78)	0.0014 (4.67)
CBD trips per week*income	0.0025 (3.43)	0.0051 (3.01)	0.0019 (2.33)	0.0053 (3.07)	0.0031 91.70)	0.0075 (5.42)
Improving public transport (0–100)	0.0108 (8.00)	0.0072 (4.99)	0.0108 (8.19)	0.0073 (5.06)	0.0119 (11.0)	0.0088 (7.41)
Improving existing and constructing new roads (0–100)	0.0074 (4.78)	0.0080 (4.87)	0.0076 (5.07)	0.0080 (5.40)	0.0076 (6.03)	0.0082 (5.94)
Reducing personal income tax (0–100)	0.0084 (5.95)	0.0051 (3.64)	0.0082 (5.83)	0.0054 (3.94)	0.0089 (7.78)	0.0067 (5.72)
Support trial of RP scheme (1,0)		0.3505 (2.14)		0.4341 (3.31)		0.4704 (6.71)
No. of privately registered cars		0.0731 (1.99)		0.0558 (1.67)		0.1165 (4.54)
Random parameter diagonal elements:						
Non-RP costs ($ per week)					0.0010 (1.68)	0.0053 (11.6)
RP costs ($ per week)					0.0227 (11.1)	0.0131 (10.3)
Random parameter off-diagonal elements:						
RP cost (V), RP cost (A)					−0.0256 (−13.9)	
NRP cost (V), NF cost (A)					−0.0044 (−5.42)	

Table 17.22 (cont.)

Choice response:	Independent probit M1		Bivariate probit (recursive simultaneous)			
			M2: Non-random parameters		M3: Random parameters	
	Voting	Acceptance	Voting	Acceptance	Voting	Acceptance
NRP cost (V), RP cost (V)					−0.0005 (−0.76)	
NRP cost (V), RP cost (A)					0.0027 (4.30)	
NRP cost (V), RP cost (V)					−0.0021 (−4.17)	
NRP cost (V), NRP cost (A)					−0.0058 (−10.9)	
Unconditional cross-equation correlation (rho)			0.8805 (37.9)		0.919 (62.8)	
Model fit:						
LL (0)	−1527.63	−1576.63	−3104.26			
LL at convergence	−1361.63	−1440.37	−2467.99		−2407.062	
AIC (sample adjusted)	1.143	1.210	2.076		2.033	

Table 17.23 Models of referendum voting and acceptance of road pricing schemes: 2

Choice response:	Bivariate probit (recursive simultaneous and endogeneity) M4:	
	Voting	Acceptance
Constant	−1.811 (−5.89)	−0.5445 (−4.40)
Acceptance (1,0)	1.0238 (3.22)	
Cordon scheme (1,0)	0.3877 (7.49)	0.2086 (3.85)
Non-RP costs (per week)	−0.0079 (−5.48)	−0.0104 (−8.49)
RP costs (per week)	−0.0177 (−7.89)	−0.0227(−13.9)
Peak km (per week)	0.0020 (2.98)	0.0034 (7.05)
Off-peak km (per week)	0.0013 (3.25)	0.0013 (4.18)
CBD trips per week*income	0.0022 (1.00)	0.0084 (5.81)
Improving public transport (0–100)	0.0121 (10.0)	0.0089 (7.27)
Improving existing and constructing new roads (0–100)	0.0071 (5.06)	0.0082 (5.94)
Reducing personal income tax (0–100)	0.0090 (6.97)	0.0065 (5.52)
Support trial of RP scheme (1,0)		0.5183 (5.68)
No. of privately registered cars		0.1467 (5.07)
Random parameter diagonal elements:		
Non-RP costs ($ per week)	0.0008 (0.88)	−0.0079 (−5.48)
RP costs ($ per week)	0.0237 (9.93)	−0.0227 (−13.9)
Random parameter off-diagonal elements:		
RP cost (V), RP cost (A)		−0.0270 (−13.4)
NRP cost (V), RP cost (A)	−0.0055 (−6.07)	
NRP cost (V), RP cost (V)	−0.0004 (−0.53)	
NRP cost (V), RP cost (A)	0.0028 (4.47)	
NRP cost (V), RP cost (V)	−0.0031 (−5.45)	
NRP cost (V), NRP cost (A)	0.0084 (13.5)	
Unconditional cross-equation correlation (rho)		0.6684 (6.67)
Model fit:		
LL (0)		−3104.26
LL at convergence		−2402.12
AIC (sample adjusted)		2.030

only socio-economic influence was personal income, through an interaction with the number of weekly trips to and from the Central Business District (CBD), the location where either a cordon- or a distance-based charge would be applicable.

For a stated choice "panel" data specification of four choice sets and three alternatives per respondent, as used here, the standard errors for all bivariate probit models are corrected for clustering in the sample. Let $\mathbf{V}$ be the estimated asymptotic covariance matrix which ignores the clustering. Let $\mathbf{g}_{ij}$ denote the first derivatives of the LL with respect to all model parameters for observation (individual) i in cluster j, and G the number of clusters. Then, the corrected asymptotic covariance matrix is given in Equation (17.74), a variant of Equation (17.57):

$$\text{Est.Asy.Var}\,[\hat{\boldsymbol{\beta}}] = \text{V}\left(\frac{G}{G-1}\right)\left[\sum_{i=1}^{G}\left(\sum_{j=1}^{n_i}\mathbf{g}_{ij}\right)\left(\sum_{j=1}^{n_i}\mathbf{g}_{ij}\right)'\right]\text{V},$$

(17.74)

where $\mathbf{V} = \mathbf{H}{-}1\ \mathbf{OPG}\ \mathbf{H}{-}1$ and $\mathbf{H}$ is the negative of the second derivatives, and **OPG** is the sum of the outer products of the gradients of the terms in the LL function.

There is a noticeable improvement in the overall goodness of fit in moving from the independent probit Model 1 (−2,802.0) to the bivariate probit Model 2 (−2,477.99) with non-random parameters. When we add in random parameters for the two cost variables, the LL for Model 3 improves even further (−2407.062), with an additional improvement in Model 4 (−2402.12) when *Accept* is introduced as a RHS endogenous variable in the *Vote* model. The endogeneity of *Accept* is statistically significant, suggesting that the acceptability of a RP scheme is a positive and important influence on the probability of voting for the scheme in a referendum, after allowing for a set of exogenous effects. The mean elasticity estimates discussed later reaffirm the strength of the influence.

The estimate of the correlated disturbances (rho) is 0.919 in Model 3 with a standard error of 0.01465, producing a very high *t*-ratio. The Wald statistic for the test of the hypothesis that rho equals zero is $(0.919/0.01465)^2 = 3{,}943.84$. For a single restriction, the critical value from the Chi-square table is 3.84; hence the hypothesis is well and truly rejected. Model 3 does not include the endogenous effect of acceptance on referendum voting. When we allow for the endogeneity of acceptance (Model 4), rho declines, as expected, but is still relatively correlated at 0.6684 with a *t*-ratio of 6.67, again rejecting the null hypothesis on the Wald test. The non-random parameters bivariate probit Model 2 has a correlated disturbance of 0.8805, statistically significant but slightly lower than the correlation in Model 3 with two random parameters, which is interesting of itself and suggests that the inclusion of preference heterogeneity appears to induce some amount of increased association between the unobserved influences. It is not clear why this is the case.

The random parameters in Models 3 and 4 have unbounded normal distributions, and have been specified such that the correlation of the random parameters (through the Cholesky decomposition) has been allowed for in the derivation of the standard deviations of the distributions. Figures 17.3 and 17.4 are presented to highlight the extent to which the distribution of the conditional means of the two price attributes are in the negative domain for the 95 percent probability intervals. They show that the conditional mean for each sampled individual is predominantly below zero, but there are some positive estimates as well. Given that the assumed distribution is unbounded, some amount of sign change can be expected.[22]

Looking at the non-random parameter variables, we find strong statistical significance. The interaction between the number of weekly CBD trips and personal income is positive, suggesting, all other influences remaining constant, that individuals who have higher personal incomes and have high travel activity to and from the CBD tend to support RP reforms to a greater extent, and would have a higher probability of voting for them, presumably because they can afford this, and see the time benefits associated with reductions in traffic congestion.[23] The number of privately registered cars has a positive and statistically significant influence on the probability of accepting a scheme; however, when we included all cars available to a household (i.e., include household business registered and employer provided cars), the number of vehicles was not statistically significant. This may be due to the fact that the non-privately registered cars are subject to generous tax concessions and/or fully compensated expenses for vehicle kilometres travelled and may be ambivalent to the reforms.

There is positive evidence that individuals who support a trial (91.8 percent of the sample) have a greater probability of accepting a scheme that converts to an increased probability of voting in favor in a referendum. Finally, the cordon-based scheme dummy variable suggests that a CBD cordon-based charging scheme is perceived to be more acceptable, and will engender a higher probability of a vote compared to a distance-based charging scheme. This is not surprising, supporting the finding in Hensher *et al.* (2013), given

---

[22] We did assess a log-normal, a constrained triangular, and a constrained normal, but the unconstrained normal gave the best fit (converged well), and identified very few non-negative values in the distribution as confirmed by Figures 17.3 and 17.4.

[23] The time benefits were not directly communicated. There are, however, clues as to how respondents perceive the benefits beyond monetary cost implications, notably potential travel time benefits. The response to how effective the scheme is in reducing congestion must have some link to a view of improved travel time. It was mentioned up front that these road pricing reforms are designed to reduce traffic congestion.

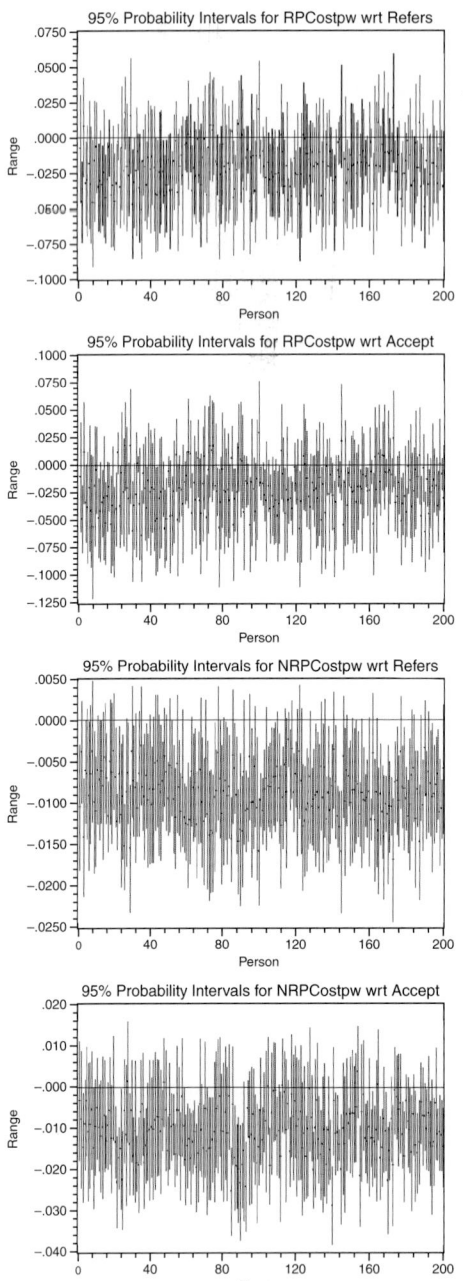

Figure 17.3   Confidence limits on conditional means of random parameters in Model 3

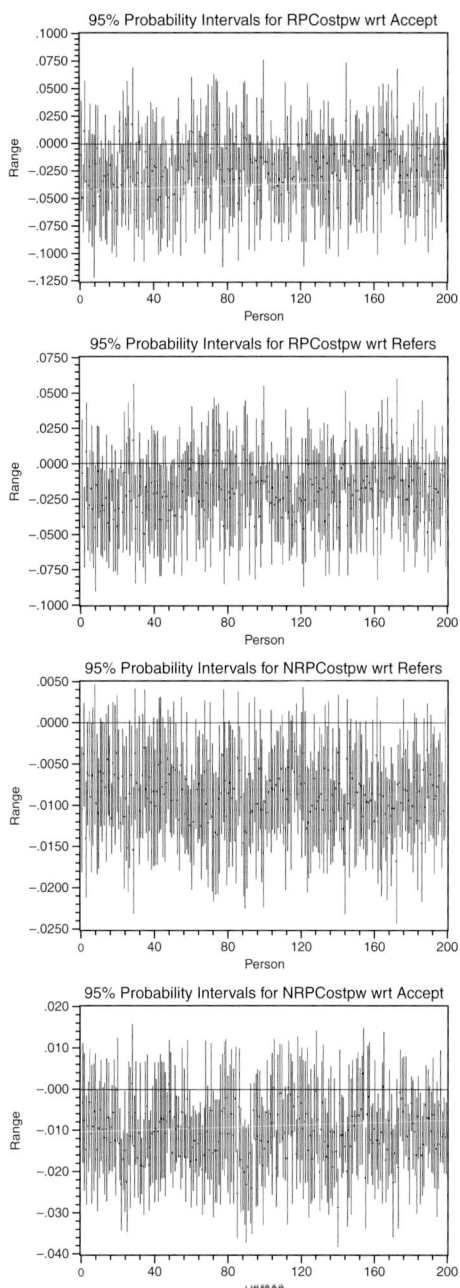

Figure 17.4   Confidence limits on conditional means of random parameters in Model 4

that it does not impact on kilometres undertaken outside of the CBD, which is the great majority of daily kilometres.

Regardless of the merits of each reform package in terms of the impact on levels of traffic congestion, there are very strong arguments opposing any reform if it discriminates between individuals on vertical equity grounds (i.e., the impact on individuals in different personal income groups). There is a large literature on the topic (e.g., Ison 1998; King *et al.* 2007; Levinson 2010; and Peters and Kramer 2012). Despite the recognition that revenue allocation[24] can be a major lever to gain community support for road pricing reform, as shown by statistically significant parameters for the three sources of funding hypothecation (i.e., public transport, roads, and reductions in personal income tax), there is also a view and evidence that revenue redistribution cannot resolve all equity and fairness concerns. Initial travel patterns also matter (Eliasson and Mattsson 2006), especially the concern that individuals undertaking most of the trips will be the ones most affected by any change, even if the impact is higher levels of time benefits. Defining trip exposure in terms of weekly peak and off-peak kilometres, we obtain positive and statistically significant parameter estimates for both *Accept* and *Vote* models. What this suggests is that car users who are more exposed to the road network through higher kilometres are more accepting of RP reform, and more likely to vote for reforms, compared to light users of the network. This has important implications for the often made claim that it is not fair to impose such charges on those who use the network more intensively than those who travel fewer kilometres. This appears, in general, not to be the situation. The strength of the level of exposure is given in the elasticity estimates below.

The key elasticity results are summarised in Table 17.24 and relate to the percentage change in the probability of an RP scheme being acceptable and that you would vote for it in a referendum (i.e., $E[y1|y2=1]$) with respect to a percentage change in the variable of interest.[25] It is very informative to compare the elasticities associated with *Vote* and *Accept* in separate probit

---

[24] Manville and King (2013) also raise the concern about credible commitment from government in using the revenue in line with community supports for reform. Hensher *et al.* (2013) found that only 22 percent of the sample had confidence that government would allocate revenue in the way they would like it allocated.

[25] We have no basis of calibrating when the reform schemes are not in existence in real markets. Furthermore, there is only one market choice observed, and hence there is no revealed preference model. The evidence in Li and Hensher (2011), which includes a review of revealed preference evidence, focuses on changes in travel. It is not possible to contrast our evidence with other studies because the focus is on voting and acceptance elasticities that, as far as we are aware, do not exist in other studies.

Table 17.24 Summary of direct elasticities (t-values in brackets)

| | Independent probit | | Bivariate probit | | |
| | M1: | | M2: Non-random parameters | M3: Random parameters | M4: Random parameters with Endogeneity |
	Voting	Acceptance	Voting (=1)	Acceptance (=1) (compared to V1A0, V0A1, V0A0)	
Non-RP costs ($ per week)	-0.432 (4.95)	-0.267 (4.54)	-0.182 (2.75)	-0.226 (2.82)	-0.327 (3.48)
RP costs ($ per week)	-0.234 (5.38)	-0.126 (4.00)	-0.097 (3.00)	-0.1301(2.10)	-0.190 (2.77)
Peak km (per week)	0.155 (7.46)	0.070 (2.74)	0.090 (4.23)	0.058(1.26)	0.089 (1.45)
Off-peak km (per week)	0.199 (5.75)	0.096 (3.07)	0.121 (3.80)	0.121 (2.22)	0.180 (2.36)
Improving public transport (0–100)	0.131 (10.7)	0.048 (6.46)	0.082 (8.98)	0.092 (8.39)	0.123 (5.97)
Improving existing and constructing new roads (0–100)	0.190 (5.11)	0.098 (5.46)	0.095 (3.12)	0.101 (3.300)	0.136 (3.17
Reducing personal income tax (0–100)	0.116 (7.42)	0.038 (4.32)	0.072 (5.91)	0.079 (5.92)	0.107 (5.07)

models with the bivariate probit models. In general, the direct price elasticities are lower (i.e., less sensitivity) under joint estimation of *Vote* and *Accept* in Models 2 and 3 compared to Model 1, where the jointness is captured through correlated disturbances but with no RHS endogeneity. When *Accept* is included as an endogenous influence on *Vote* in Model 4, the direct elasticity estimate seems to move closer to the average of the independent probit estimates of model 1, being lower than the *Vote* mean estimate but higher than the *Accept* mean estimate.

A particularly important finding is for road pricing costs per week (RPCost). We have −0.130 for Model 3 and −0.190 for Model 4, whereas the elasticities associated with *Vote* and *Accept* alone (Model 1) are, respectively, −0.234 and −0.126. This suggests in Model 1 that if one focusses only on acceptability, we obtain a much lower mean direct elasticity than if one just focusses on referendum voting. What this indicates is that a scheme has to be acceptable for it to receive a higher probability of voting for it in a referendum, given the scheme costs and other contextual influences. This reinforces the well argued views that public acceptability is crucial to obtaining increased buy in, and a resultant higher probability of a yes vote in a referendum (Goodwin 1989; Hensher *et al.* 2013; Schade *et al.* 2007; Ubbels and Verhoef 2006).

Without exception, all mean estimates of direct elasticities are inelastic and below |0.5|. The lower direct elasticities for RP Cost compared to Non-RP Cost reflect the relative cost of each source, which indicates that any additional costs, if existing costs remain, are quite a lot less than 50 percent of the total cost under a proposed scheme. The elasticities associated with current trip exposure in terms of peak and off-peak kilometres are very informative, suggesting for Model 4, our preferred model, that a 25 percent increase in weekly peak and off-peak kilometres (chosen as a reasonable change, given that average peak and off-peak kilometres per week are 70.68 and 145.9 kilometres, respectively) results, respectively, in a 2.25 and 4.5 percent increase in the joint probability of accepting and voting for a proposed RP scheme. The revenue allocation preferences are also informative; all other influences being held constant, if all the RP scheme funds raised were hypothecated to public transport (compared to none), the percentage change in the probability of accepting and voting for a specific RP scheme would increase by 12.3 percentage points; likewise, the equivalent impact if all funds were allocated to improvements in existing and new roads is 13.6 percent, with a 10.7 percent increase if all monies were hypothecated to reduced personal income taxes. Given the "closeness" of these percentage changes, any mix of revenue allocation that is hypothecated as a mixture of the three

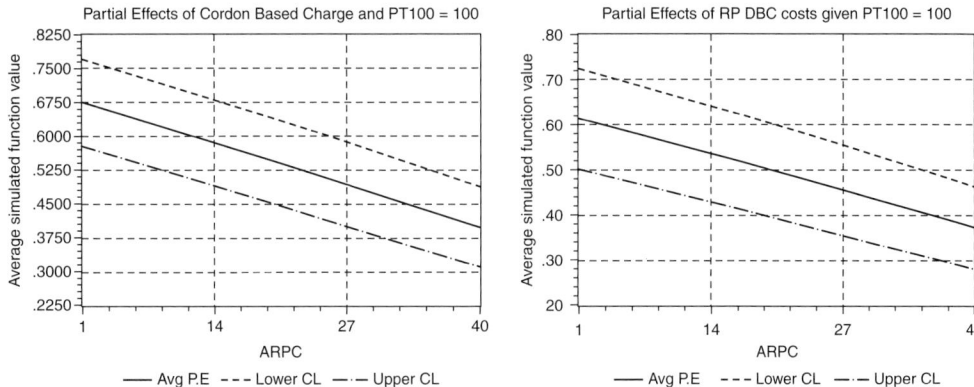

Figure 17.5 Impact of (a) cordon-based and (b) distance-based charging per week given that all revenue is hypothecated to public transport
Notes: ARPC = road pricing cost per week, Avg.P.E. – average partial effect, PT100 = all revenue is allocated to public transport.

revenue allocation categories would result in an increase in the percentage change in the probability of accepting and voting for a specific RP scheme of around 11 percent.

Although the evidence above is illuminating in identifying the potential influence of RP reform pricing, trip activity, and revenue allocation, it is even more informative to establish the extent to which a particular scheme might get over the line in a referendum. We have assessed weekly outlays varying from $1 to $40 in $1 increments, equivalent to a CBD cordon-based daily entry fee of $0.2 to $8, and equivalent to a charge of 0.5 to 20 cents per kilometre under a distance-based charging regime for an average weekly total of 200 kilometres.

The model is set up in such a way that the assessment of a CBD cordon-based charge compared to a system wide distance-based charging scheme has to account for the role of the cordon-based dummy variable in the model. What we find is that if we can contain the CBD cordon charge to a maximum of $5 for entry per day and at any time of a weekday between 7 a.m. and 6 p.m., or a distance-based charge of 10c/kilometre, then the likelihood of a scheme being voted for with an outcome greater than 50 per cent is encouraging (See Figures 17.5a and 17.5b). This is based on all of the revenue hypothecated to public transport that will, given the evidence herein and in Hensher *et al.* (2013), improve the stakes.

If we ignore the allocation of revenue, the probability of more than 50 percent of residents voting for a CBD cordon-based or a distance-based charging scheme is likely to fail; the cordon-based charge of $5 will only obtain 34 percent support and the distance-based charge of 10c/kilometre will result in 32 percent support.

17.4.4 Application II: partial effects and scenarios for bivariate probit

In this section, we use another data set to illustrate the bivariate probit model. The data was collected in 2013 from six Australian cities (Sydney, Melbourne, Canberra, Adelaide, Brisbane, and Perth). The differences in preferences between the six cities are of interest as one way of determining if there exist contextual biases (including exposure through use of specific transport investments) in the preferences of populations towards or against the voting rule and the earmarking of increased tax for transport investments.

The findings from the estimation of the bivariate probit model are summarized in Table 17.25. We investigated the potential role of each of the available socio-economic variables as well as a city-specific dummy variable and a transport-related variable, namely the recent use or otherwise of public transport.

The Nlogit syntax is given below:

```
Bivariate Probit
    ;lhs=votegood,votetp
    ;rh1=one,age,ftime,can
    ;rh2=one,usept,male,pinc,ptime,retired,brs
    ;hf2=commute
    ;partial effects$
```

Looking at the voting model (Model 1), we find that age, full time employment status, and living in Canberra are all negative and statistically significant influences. The negative sign indicates, all other things held constant, that as a person's age increases, and they are full time employed (compared to other employment status, including not in the workforce) that the probability of supporting the voting mechanism decreases. One might speculate as to whether older people are more disillusioned with the effectiveness of a referendum style vote given that the historical record in Australia is, with rare exception, one of rejection of support for a specific issue. Interestingly, residents of Australia's capital city, Canberra, have a very strong tendency (relative to residents of the other five cities), to not support a voting mechanism tied to the idea of using it for governments to decide which projects to invest in. This is reinforced by the percent support (not reported here), which is much lower than in all the other cities.

The evidence associated with earmarked taxation for transport investments (Model 2) yields six statistically significant influences, with five having

Table 17.25 Summary of bivariate probit model results

Model 1: Support for a voting approach		Model 2: Support for earmarked tax increases spent on transport investment	
Variable	Parameter estimate (*t*-ratio)	Variable	Parameter estimate (*t*-ratio)
Constant	1.0603 (8.84)	Constant	−1.0846 (−13.4)
Age (yr.)	−0.0051 (−2.12)	Use public transport (1,0)	0.3701 (5.71)
Full time employed (1,0)	−0.1482 (−2.36)	Male (1,0)	0.2470 (3.72)
Canberra (1,0)	−0.5490 (−4.20)	Personal income ($000)	0.0027 (3.38)
		Part time employed (1,0)	0.2363 (2.86)
		Retired (1,0)	0.2339 (2.48)
		Brisbane (1,0)	−0.1999 (−2.28)
Variance effect: Commute (1,0)	0.5101 (1.81)		
Disturbance correlation	0.136		
LL	−2295.13		

positive parameter estimates, and one a negative estimate. The findings suggest that males, individuals part time employed, or who are retired, and who are on higher personal incomes, tend to have a higher probability of supporting the earmarking of increased taxation to invest in transport. Furthermore, users of public transport have a higher probability of support for earmarking than non-users, possibly reflecting the parlous state of funding for public transport in Australian cities compared to investment in roads.

The only capital city dummy variable that is statistically significant is Brisbane. The negative sign suggests that Brisbane residents relative to the other cities have a lower probability of supporting the earmarking of increased taxation to transport investments. It is unclear why this might be the case, although one suggestion is that the survey was undertaken in the first year of a new (liberal) government in Queensland, and to date they have been cutting back on the transport investment commitments of the previous Labor government. However, offsetting this possible reasoning is the fact that increased taxation is likely to be imposed by a Federal government, and if this is the perspective adopted by individuals, then the explanation is somewhat ambiguous, including a mistrust of the Federal Labor party who have not committed significant funds to the Brisbane transport system; however neither have they done so for the other cities, with the possible exception of Perth.

Table 17.26 Summary of elasticities, confidence interval at 95 percent in second bracket set

Model 1: Support for a voting approach		Model 2: Support for earmarked tax increases spent on transport investment	
Variable	Elasticity (*t*-ratio)	Variable	Elasticity (*t*-ratio)
Age (yr.)	−0.0716 (2.01) (−0.141, −0.002)	Use public transport (1,0)	−0.0114 (3.22) (−0.018, −0.004)
Full time employed (1,0)	−0.0485 (2.30) (−0.089, −0.007)	Male (1,0)	−0.0076 (2.70) (0.0318, −0.0021)
Canberra (1,0)	−0.2398 (3.27) (−0.3836, −0.0961)	Personal income ($000)	−0.0048 (2.51) (-.0085, −0.0010)
		Part time employed (1,0)	−0.0072 (2.29) (−0.0133, −0.0010)
		Retired (1,0)	−0.0071 (2.16) (−0.0136, −0.0007)
		Brisbane (1,0)	−0.0062 (1.97) (0.00004, −0.0124)

Finally, the two equations are correlated, with a 0.136 correlation of the error disturbances. Although the interpretation of the mean parameter estimates is informative, what is of greater relevance are the implied elasticities associated with each explanatory variable, since they provide evidence on the extent of influence of a change in the level of an exogenous variable on the preference probability for supporting a vote and the earmarking of taxation increases. The results are summarized in Table 17.26, including the *t*-ratios and 95 percent confidence intervals.

All the mean elasticity estimates are statistically significant, and all are relatively inelastic. The elasticities associated with dummy variables (i.e., all but age and personal income) are arc elasticities based on the average of the before and after levels of an explanatory variable and the probability preference. The most significant effect is the Canberra dummy variable, which suggests, *ceteris paribus*, that when a resident lives in Canberra compared to any of the other five cities, the probability of not supporting a voting mechanism decreases by 23.98 percent. The next sizeable effect is much smaller, namely the respondent's age, if one focuses on a 1 percent change (−0.0716). Given an average age of 43 years, a 10 percent increase in age (to 47.3 years old) reduces the probability of supporting the voting mechanism by 7.16 percent. We ran a scenario on these two variables in which we predicted the joint probability of voting support given support for earmarked tax increases for transport investment. The results are shown in Table 17.27,

Table 17.27 Simulated scenario of role of Canberra and age on preference probability

```
Model Simulation Analysis for Bivariate Probit E[y1|y2=1] function
-------------------------------------------------------------------------------
Simulations are computed by average over sample observations
-------------------------------------------------------------------------------
User Function   Function   Standard
(Delta method)   Value      Error     |t|   95%  Confidence Interval
-------------------------------------------------------------------------------
Avrg. Function  .81575     .01599    51.00       .78440       .84710
-------------------------------------------------------------------------------

CAN    =   .00  -----------------------------------------------------------------
AGE    = 22.00  .85132     .01874    45.43       .81459       .88805
AGE    = 32.00  .83909     .01654    50.73       .80667       .87151
AGE    = 42.00  .82622     .01585    52.14       .79516       .85728
AGE    = 52.00  .81271     .01747    46.53       .77847       .84694
AGE    = 62.00  .79857     .02141    37.30       .75660       .84053
AGE    = 72.00  .78381     .02712    28.90       .73066       .83696
-------------------------------------------------------------------------------

CAN    =  1.00  -----------------------------------------------------------------
AGE    = 22.00  .68838     .05158    13.35       .58730       .78947
AGE    = 32.00  .66999     .05018    13.35       .57163       .76834
AGE    = 42.00  .65117     .05005    13.01       .55307       .74926
AGE    = 52.00  .63197     .05138    12.30       .53127       .73267
AGE    = 62.00  .61244     .05422    11.30       .50617       .71870
AGE    = 72.00  .59261     .05845    10.14       .47806       .70717
```

reinforcing what the implied elasticities suggest. Typically there is a 0.17 to 0.19 probability difference between Canberra and other cities for each age level.

The implied elasticity impacts are much smaller in Model 2, with all dummy variables resulting in less than a 1 percent change in the probability of supporting earmarked taxation. Sizeable percentage increases in income, for example 20 percent, can have a noticeable influence on the percentage change in the probability of supporting earmarked taxation increases.

The elasticity evidence suggests that we have identified influences on the propensity to support the voting mechanism or otherwise that are much stronger in their role than the statistically significant influences on supporting earmarked taxation or not.

18 Ordered choices

18.1 Introduction

A growing number of empirical studies involves the assessment of influences on a choice among ordered discrete alternatives. Ordered logit and probit models are well known, including extensions to accommodate random parameters (RP) and heteroskedasticity in unobserved variance (see, e.g., Bhat and Pulugurtha 1998; Greene 2007). The ordered choice model allows for non-linear effects of any variable on the probabilities associated with each ordered level (see, e.g., Eluru *et al.* 2008). However, the traditional ordered choice model is potentially limited, behaviorally, in that it holds the threshold values to be fixed. This can lead to inconsistent (i.e., incorrect) estimates of the effects of variables. Extending the ordered choice random parameter model to account for threshold random heterogeneity, as well as underlying systematic sources of explanation for unobserved heterogeneity, is a logical extension in line with the growing interest in choice analysis in establishing additional candidate sources of observed and unobserved taste heterogeneity.[1]

A substantive application here is used to illustrate the behavioral gains from generalizing the ordered choice model to accommodate random thresholds in the presence of RP. It is focussed on the influences on the role that a specific attribute processing strategy, of preserving each attribute or ignoring it, plays when choosing among unlabeled attribute packages of alternative tolled and non-tolled routes for the commuting trip in a stated choice experiment (see Hensher 2001a, 2004, 2008). The ordering represents the number of attributes attended to from the full set. Despite a growing number of studies focussing on these issues (see, e.g., Cantillo *et al.* 2006; Hensher 2006; Swait 2001;

---

[1] A number of authors have introduced random thresholds (e.g., Cameron and Heckman 1998; Cunha *et al.* 2007; Eluru *et al.* 2008) but have not integrated this into a generalized model with RP and/or decomposition of random thresholds by systematic sources.

Campbell *et al.* 2008), the entire domain of every attribute is treated as relevant to some degree, and included in the utility expressions for every individual. While acknowledging the extensive study of non-linearity in attribute specification, which permits varying marginal (dis)utility over an attribute's range, including account for asymmetric preferences under conditions of gain and loss (see Hess *et al.* 2008), this is not the same as establishing *ex ante* the extent to which a specific attribute might be totally excluded from consideration for all manner of reasons, including the influence of the design of a choice experiment when stated choice data is being used.

18.2 The traditional ordered choice model

The ordered probit model was proposed by Zavoina and McElvey (1975) for the analysis of categorical, non-quantitative choices, outcomes, and responses. Familiar applications now include bond ratings, discrete opinion surveys such as those on political questions, obesity measures (Greene *et al.* 2008), preferences in consumption, and satisfaction and health status surveys such as those analyzed by Boes and Winkelmann (2004, 2007). The model foundation is an underlying random utility or latent regression model (Equation (18.1)):

$$y_i^* = \boldsymbol{\beta}'\mathbf{x}_i + \varepsilon_i, \tag{18.1}$$

in which the continuous latent utility, y_i^*, is observed in discrete form through a censoring mechanism (Equation 18.2):

$$
\begin{aligned}
y_i \;&=\; 0 \ \text{if} \ \mu_{-1} \;<\; y_i^* \;<\; \mu_0, \\
&=\; 1 \ \text{if} \ \mu_0 \;\;\;\;<\; y_i^* \;<\; \mu_1, \\
&=\; 2 \ \text{if} \ \mu_1 \;\;\;\;<\; y_i^* \;<\; \mu_2, \\
&=\; \cdots \\
&=\; J \ \text{if} \ \mu_{J-1} \;<\; y_i^* \;<\; \mu_J.
\end{aligned}
\tag{18.2}
$$

The model contains the unknown marginal utilities, $\boldsymbol{\beta}$, as well as $J+2$ unknown threshold parameters, μ_j, all to be estimated using a sample of n observations, indexed by $i = 1,\ldots,n$. The data consist of the covariates, $\mathbf{x}_i$, and the observed discrete outcome, $y_i = 0,1,\ldots,J$. The assumption of the properties of the "disturbance," ε_i, completes the model specification. The conventional assumptions are that ε_i is a continuous disturbance with conventional CDF, $F(\varepsilon_i|\mathbf{x}_i) = F(\varepsilon_i)$, with support equal to the real line, and with density $f(\varepsilon_i) = F'(\varepsilon_i)$.

The assumption of the distribution of ε_i includes independence from (or exogeneity of) x_i. The probabilities associated with the observed outcomes are given as Equation (18.3):

$$\text{Prob}[y_i = j \mid x_i] = \text{Prob}[\varepsilon_i < \mu_j - \beta'x_i] - \text{Prob}[\mu_{j-1} - \beta'x_i], j$$
$$= 0, 1, \ldots, J. \tag{18.3}$$

Several normalizations are needed to identify the model parameters. Firstly, given the continuity assumption, in order to preserve the positive signs of the probabilities we require $\mu_j > \mu_{j-1}$. Second, if the support is to be the entire real line, then $\mu_{-1} = -\infty$ and $\mu_J = +\infty$. Finally, assuming (as we will) that x_i contains a constant term, we will require $\mu_0 = 0$. With a constant term present, if this normalization is not imposed, then adding any non-zero constant to μ_0 and the same constant to the intercept term in β will leave the probability unchanged. Given the assumption of an overall constant, only $J-1$ threshold parameters are needed to partition the real line into the $J+1$ distinct intervals.

Given that data such as ranking data defining the observed ordered choice contain no unconditional information on the scaling of the underlying unobserved variable, if y_i^* is scaled by any positive value then scaling the unknown μ_j and β by the same value preserves the observed outcomes; and, hence, a free unconditional variance parameter, $\text{Var}[\varepsilon_i] = \sigma_\varepsilon 2$, is not identified without further restriction. We thus impose the identifying restriction $\sigma_\varepsilon = $ a known constant, $\bar{\sigma}$. The usual approach to this normalization, assuming that ε is independent of x, is to assume that $\text{Var}[\varepsilon_i \mid x_i] = 1$ in the probit model and $\pi 2/3$ in the logit model – in both cases to eliminate the free structural scaling parameter. The standard treatments in the received literature complete the ordered choice model by assuming either a standard normal distribution for ε_i, producing the ordered probit model, or a standardized logistic distribution (mean zero, variance $\pi 2/3$), which produces the ordered logit model. Applications appear to be well divided between the two. A compelling case for a particular distribution remains to be put forward.

With the full set of normalizations in place, the likelihood function for estimation of the model parameters is based on the implied probabilities given in Equation (18.4):

$$\text{Prob}[y_i = j \mid x_i] = F(\mu_j - \beta'x_i) - F(\mu_{j-1} - \beta'x_i) > 0, j = 0, 1, \ldots, J. \tag{18.4}$$

Estimation of the parameters is a straightforward problem in maximum likelihood estimation (see, e.g., Greene 2008; Pratt 1981). Interpretation of the model parameters is, however, much less so (see, e.g., Daykin and Moffitt 2002). There is no natural conditional mean function, so in order to attach behavioral meaning to the parameters one typically refers to the probabilities themselves. The partial effects in the ordered choice model are as shown in Equation (18.5):

$$\frac{\partial \text{Prob}[y_i = j|\mathbf{x}_i]}{\partial \mathbf{x}_i} = [f(\mu_{j-1} - \boldsymbol{\beta}'\mathbf{x}_i) - f(\mu_j - \boldsymbol{\beta}'\mathbf{x}_i)]\boldsymbol{\beta}. \tag{18.5}$$

The result shows that neither the sign nor the magnitude of a coefficient is informative about the corresponding behavioral characteristic in the model, so the direct interpretation of the coefficients (or their "significance") is fundamentally ambiguous. A counterpart result for a dummy variable in the model would be obtained by using a difference of probabilities, rather than a derivative (Boes and Winkelmann 2007; Greene 2008, Chapter E22). One might also be interested in the cumulative values of the partial effects, such as shown in Equation (18.6) (see, e.g., Brewer *et al.* 2006). The last term in this set is zero by construction:

$$\frac{\partial \text{Prob}[y_i \leq j|\mathbf{x}_i]}{\partial \mathbf{x}_i} = \left(\sum_{m=0}^{j} [f(\mu_{m-1} - \boldsymbol{\beta}'\mathbf{x}_i) - f(\mu_m - \boldsymbol{\beta}'\mathbf{x}_i)]\right)\boldsymbol{\beta}. \tag{18.6}$$

18.3 A generalized ordered choice model

A number of authors, beginning with Terza (1985), have questioned some of the less flexible aspects of the model specification. The partial effects shown above vary with the data and the parameters. It can be shown that, for the probit and logit models, this set of partial derivatives will change sign exactly once in the sequence from 0 to J, a property that Boes and Winkelmann (2007) label the "single crossing" characteristic. Boes and Winkelmann (2007) also note that for any two continuous covariates, x_{ik} and x_{il}:

$$\frac{\partial \text{Prob}[y_i = j|\mathbf{x}_i]/\partial x_{i,k}}{\partial \text{Prob}[y_i = j|\mathbf{x}_i]/\partial x_{i,l}} = \frac{\beta_k}{\beta_l}. \tag{18.7}$$

This result in Equation 18.7 is independent of the outcomes. The ordered choice models above have the property in Equation 18.8; that is, the partial effects are each a multiple of the same $\boldsymbol{\beta}$:

$$\partial \text{Prob}[y_i \geq j | \mathbf{x}_i] / \partial \mathbf{x}_i = K_j \boldsymbol{\beta}, \tag{18.8}$$

where K_j depends on X_j. This is a feature of the model that has been labeled the "parallel regressions" assumption. Another way to view this feature of the ordered choice model is through the J binary choices implied by Equation 18.8. Let z_{ij} denote the binary variable defined by:

$$z_{ij} = 1 \text{ if } y > j, j = 0, 1, \ldots, J - 1.$$

The choice model implies:

$$\text{Prob}[z_{ij} = 1 \mid x_i] = F(\boldsymbol{\beta}' x_i - \mu_j).$$

The threshold parameter can be absorbed into the constant term. In principle, one can fit these $J-1$ binary choice models separately. That the same β appears in all of the models is implied by the ordered choice model. However, one need not impose this restriction; the binary choice models can be fitted separately and independently. Thus, the null hypothesis of the ordered choice model is that the βs in the binary choice equations are all the same (apart from the constant terms). A standard test of this null hypothesis, due to Brant (1990), is used to detect the condition that the β_j vectors are different. The Brant test frequently rejects the null hypothesis of a common slope vector in the ordered choice model. It is unclear what the alternative hypothesis should be in this context. The generalized ordered choice model that might seem to be the natural alternative is, in fact, internally inconsistent – it does not constrain the probabilities of the outcomes to be positive. It would seem that the Brant test is more about functional form or, perhaps, some other specification error. See Greene and Hensher (2010, Chapter 6).

Recent analyses, e.g., Long (1997), Long and Frees (2006), and Williams (2006), have proposed a "generalized ordered choice model." An extended form of the ordered choice model that has attracted much (perhaps most) of the recent attention, is the "generalized ordered logit" (or probit) model (e.g., by Williams 2006). This model is defined in Equation (18.9):

$$\text{Prob}[y_i = j | \mathbf{x}_i] = \text{Prob}[\varepsilon_i \leq \mu_j - \boldsymbol{\beta}_j' \mathbf{x}_i] - \text{Prob}[\mu_{j-1} - \boldsymbol{\beta}_{j-1}' \mathbf{x}_i],$$

$$j = 0, 1, \ldots, J, \tag{18.9}$$

where $\boldsymbol{\beta}_{-1} = 0$ (see, e.g., Williams 2006; Long 1997; Long and Frees 2006). The extension provides for a separate vector of marginal utilities for each jth outcome. Bhat and Zhao (2002) introduce heteroskedasticity across observational units, in a spatial ordered response analysis context, along the lines of the generalized ordered logit form.

The generalization of the model suggested above deals with both problems (single crossing and parallel regressions), but it creates new ones. The heterogeneity in the parameter vector is an artifact of the coding of the dependent variable, not a manifestation of underlying heterogeneity in the dependent variable induced by behavioral differences. It is unclear what it means for the marginal utility parameters to be structured in this way. Consider, for example, that there is no underlying structure that could be written down in such a way as to provide a means of simulating the data generating mechanism. By implication, $y_i^* = \boldsymbol{\beta}_j' \mathbf{x}_i + \varepsilon_i$ if $y_i = j$. That is, the model structure is endogenous – one could not simulate a value of y_i from the data generating mechanism without knowing in advance the value being simulated. There is no reduced form. The more difficult problem of this generalization is that the probabilities in this model need not be positive, and there is no parametric restriction (other than the restrictive model version we started with) that could achieve this. The probability model is internally inconsistent. The restrictions would have to be functions of the data. The problem is noted by Williams (2006), but dismissed as a minor issue. Boes and Winkelmann (2007) suggest that the problem could be handled through a "non-linear specification." Essentially, this generalized choice model does not treat the outcome as a single choice, even though that is what it is.

To put a more positive view, we might interpret this as a semi-parametric approach to modeling what is underlying heterogeneity. However, it is not clear why this heterogeneity should be manifest in parameter variation across the outcomes instead of across the individuals in the sample. One would assume that the failure of the Brant test to support the model with parameter homogeneity is, indeed, signaling some failure of the model. A shortcoming of the functional form as listed above (compared to a different internally consistent specification) is certainly a possibility. We hypothesize that it might also be picking up unobserved heterogeneity across individuals. The model we develop here accounts for individual heterogeneity in several possible forms.

18.3.1 Modeling observed and unobserved heterogeneity

Since Terza (1985), with the exception of Pudney and Shields (2000), most of the "generalizations" suggested for the ordered choice models have been about functional form – the single crossing feature and the parallel regressions (see, also, Greene 2008). Our interest in this chapter is, rather, in a specification that accommodates both observed and unobserved heterogeneity across individuals. We suggest that the basic model structure, when fully specified, provides for sufficient non-linearity to capture the important features of choice behavior. The generalization that interests us here will incorporate both observed and unobserved heterogeneity in the model itself.

The basic model assumes that the thresholds, μ_j, are the same for every individual in the sample. Terza (1985), Pudney and Shields (2000), Boes and Winkelmann (2007), Bhat and Pulugurta (1998), and Greene *et al.* (2008), all present cases that suggest that individual variation in the set of thresholds is a degree of heterogeneity that is likely to be present in the data, but is not accommodated in the model. Pudney and Shields discuss a clear example in the context of job promotion, in which the steps on the promotion ladder for nurses are somewhat individual-specific.

Greene (2002, 2008) argues that the fixed parameter version of the ordered choice model, and more generally, many microeconometric specifications, do not adequately account for the underlying, unobserved heterogeneity likely to be present in observed data. Further extensions of the ordered choice model presented in Greene (2008) include full RP treatments and discrete approximations under the form of latent class, or finite mixture models. These two specific extensions are also listed by Boes and Winkelmann (2004, 2007), who also describe a common effects model for panel data, and Bhat and Pulugurta (1998) as candidates for extending the model.

The model that assumes homogeneity of the preference parameters, β, across individuals, also assumes homogeneity in the scaling of the random term, ε_i. That is, the homoskedasticity assumption, $\text{Var}[\varepsilon_i|\mathbf{x}_i] = 1$, is restrictive in the same way that the homogeneity assumption is. Heteroskedasticity in terms of observables in the ordered choice model is proposed in Greene (1997), and reappears as a theme in Williams (2006).

The model proposed here generalizes the ordered choice model in the direction of accommodating heterogeneity, rather than in the direction of adding non-linearities to the underlying functional form. The earliest extensions of the ordered choice model focused on the threshold parameters. Terza's (1985) extension suggested:

$$\mu_{ij} = \mu_j + \boldsymbol{\delta}'\mathbf{z}_i. \tag{18.10}$$

where $\mathbf{z}_i$ are individual-specific exogenous variables that represent sources of systematic variation around the mean estimate of a threshold parameter. The analysis of this model continued with Pudney and Shields' (2000) "generalized ordered probit model" whose motivation, like Terza's, was to accommodate *observable* individual heterogeneity in the threshold parameters as well as in the mean of the regression. We (and Pudney and Shields) note an obvious problem of identification in this specification. Consider the generic probability with this extension:

$$\mathrm{Prob}[y_i \leq j|\mathbf{x}_i, \mathbf{z}_i] = F(\mu_j + \boldsymbol{\delta}'\mathbf{z}_i - \boldsymbol{\beta}'\mathbf{x}_i) = F[\mu_j - (\boldsymbol{\delta}^{*'}\mathbf{z}_i + -\boldsymbol{\beta}'\mathbf{x}_i)], \boldsymbol{\delta}^*$$
$$= -\boldsymbol{\delta}.$$
$$\tag{18.11}$$

It is less than obvious whether the variables, $\mathbf{z}_i$, are actually in the threshold or in the mean of the regression. Either interpretation is consistent with the model. Pudney and Shields argue that the distinction is of no substantive consequence for their analysis.

Formal modeling of heterogeneity in the parameters as representing a feature of the underlying data also appears in Greene (2002) (version 8.0) and Boes and Winkelmann (2004), both of whom suggest a RP approach to the model. In Boes and Winkelmann, it is noted that the nature of an RP specification induces heteroskedasticity, and could be modeled as such. The model would appear as follows:

$$\boldsymbol{\beta}_i = \boldsymbol{\beta} + \mathbf{u}_i, \tag{18.12}$$

where $\mathbf{u}_i \sim N[\mathbf{0}, \boldsymbol{\Omega}]$. Inserting this in the base case model and simplifying, we obtain Equation 18.13:

$$\mathrm{Prob}[y_i \leq j|\mathbf{x}_i] = \mathrm{Prob}[\varepsilon_i + \mathbf{u}_i'\mathbf{x}_i \leq \mu_j - \boldsymbol{\beta}'\mathbf{x}_i] = F\left(\frac{\mu_j - \boldsymbol{\beta}'\mathbf{x}_i}{\sqrt{1 + \mathbf{x}_i'\boldsymbol{\Omega}\mathbf{x}_i}}\right), \tag{18.13}$$

Equation 18.13 could be estimated by ordinary means, albeit with a new source of non-linearity – the elements of $\boldsymbol{\Omega}$ must now be estimated as well.[2]

---

[2] The authors' suggestion that this could be handled semi-parametrically without specifying a distribution for $\mathbf{u}_i$ is incorrect, because the resulting heteroskedastic probability written above only preserves the standard normal form assumed if $\mathbf{u}_i$ is normally distributed as well as ε_i.

Boes and Winkelmann (2004, 2007) did not pursue this approach. Greene (2002) analyzes essentially the same model, but proposes to estimate the parameters by maximum simulated likelihood.

Curiously, none of the studies listed above focus on the issue of scaling, although Williams (2006), citing Allison (1999), does mention it. A heteroskedastic ordered probit model with the functional form in Equation (18.14) appears at length in Greene (1997), and is discussed in some detail in Williams (2006):

$$\text{Var}[\varepsilon_i \mid \mathbf{h}_i] = \exp(\boldsymbol{\gamma}'\mathbf{h}_i)^2. \tag{18.14}$$

In microeconomic data, scaling of the underlying preferences is as important a source of heterogeneity as displacement of the mean, perhaps even more so. But, it has received considerably less attention than heterogeneity in location.

In what follows, we will propose a formulation of the ordered choice model that treats heterogeneity in a unified, internally consistent fashion. The model contains three points at which individual heterogeneity can substantively appear: in the random utility model (RUM) (the marginal utilities), in the threshold parameters, and in the scaling (variance) of the random components. As argued above, this form of treatment seems more likely to capture the salient features of the data generating mechanism than the received "generalized ordered logit model," which is more narrowly focused on functional form.

18.3.2 Random thresholds and heterogeneity in the ordered choice model

We depart from the base case of the usual ordered choice model:

$$\text{Prob}[y_i = j \mid \mathbf{x}_i] = F(\mu_j - \boldsymbol{\beta}'\mathbf{x}_i) - F(\mu_{j-1} - \boldsymbol{\beta}'\mathbf{x}_i) > 0, j = 0, 1, \dots, J. \tag{18.15}$$

In order to model heterogeneity in the utility functions across individuals, we construct a hierarchical model in which the coefficients vary with observable variables, z_i (typically such as demographics as age and gender), and randomly due to individual specific unobservables, v_i. The coefficients appear as:

$$\boldsymbol{\beta}_i = \boldsymbol{\beta} + \boldsymbol{\Delta}\mathbf{z}_i + \boldsymbol{\Gamma}\mathbf{v}_i, \tag{18.16}$$

where $\mathbf{\Gamma}$ is a lower triangular matrix and $\mathbf{v}_i \sim N[\mathbf{0},\mathbf{I}]$. The coefficient vector in the utility function, $\boldsymbol{\beta}_i$ is normally distributed across individuals with conditional mean:

$$E[\boldsymbol{\beta}_i | \mathbf{x}_i, \mathbf{z}_i] = \boldsymbol{\beta} + \boldsymbol{\Delta} \mathbf{z}_i \qquad (18.17)$$

and conditional variance:

$$\text{Var}[\boldsymbol{\beta}_i | \mathbf{x}_i, \mathbf{z}_i] = \mathbf{\Gamma}\mathbf{\Gamma}' = \mathbf{\Omega}. \qquad (18.18)$$

The model is formulated with $\mathbf{\Gamma} v_i$ rather than, say just v_i with covariance matrix $\mathbf{\Omega}$ purely for convenience in setting up the estimation method. This is a random parameters formulation that appears elsewhere, e.g., Greene (2002, 2005). The random effects model is a special case in which only the constant is random. The Mundlak (1978) and Chamberlain (1980) approach to modeling fixed effects is also accommodated by letting $z_i = \bar{x}_i$ in the equation for the overall constant term.

We are also interested in allowing the thresholds to vary across individuals. See, for example, King *et al.* (2004) for a striking demonstration of the payoff to this generalization. The thresholds are modeled randomly and non-linearly as:

$$\mu_{ij} = \mu_{i,j-1} + \exp(\alpha_j + \boldsymbol{\delta}'\mathbf{r}_i + \sigma_j w_{ij}), w_{ij} \sim N[0,1], \qquad (18.19)$$

with normalizations and restrictions $\mu_{-1} = -\infty$, $\mu_0 = 0$, $\mu_J = +\infty$. For the remaining thresholds, we have Equation (18.20):

$$
\begin{aligned}
\mu_1 &= \exp(\alpha_1 + \boldsymbol{\delta}'\mathbf{r}_i + \sigma_1 w_{j1}) \\
&= \exp(\boldsymbol{\delta}'\mathbf{r}_i) \exp(\alpha_1 + \sigma_1 w_{j1}) \\
\mu_2 &= \exp(\boldsymbol{\delta}'\mathbf{r}_i) [\exp(\alpha_1 + \sigma_1 w_{j1}) + \exp(\alpha_2 + \sigma_2 w_{j2})], \\
\mu_j &= \exp(\boldsymbol{\delta}'\mathbf{r}_i)\left(\Sigma_{m=1}^{j}\exp(\alpha_m + \sigma_m w_{im})\right), j = 1, \ldots, J-1 \\
\mu_J &= +\infty.
\end{aligned}
\qquad (18.20)
$$

Though it is relatively complex, this formulation is necessary for several reasons: (1) It ensures that all of the thresholds are positive, (2) it preserves the ordering of the thresholds, (3) it incorporates the necessary normalizations. Most importantly, it also allows observed variables and unobserved heterogeneity to play a role in both the utility function and in the thresholds.

The thresholds, like the regression itself, are shifted by both observable ($\mathbf{r}_i$) and unobservable (w_{ij}) heterogeneity. The model is fully consistent, in that the probabilities are all positive and sum to one by construction. If $\boldsymbol{\delta} = \mathbf{0}$ and $\sigma_j = 0$, then the original model is returned, with $\mu_1 = \exp(\alpha_1)$, $\mu_2 = \mu_1 + \exp(\alpha_2)$, and so on. Note that if the threshold parameters were specified as linear functions rather than as in Equation (18.19), then it would not be possible to identify separate parameters in the regression function and in the threshold functions.

Finally, we allow for individual heterogeneity in the variance of the utility function as well as in the mean. This is likely to be an important feature of data on individual behavior. The disturbance variance is allowed to be heteroskedastic, now specified randomly as well as deterministically. Thus:

$$\text{Var}[\varepsilon_i | \mathbf{h}_i, e_i] = \sigma_i^2 = \exp(\boldsymbol{\gamma}'\mathbf{h}_i + \tau e_i)^2, \tag{18.21}$$

where $e_i \sim N[0,1]$. Let $\mathbf{v}_i = (v_{i1}, \ldots, v_{iK})'$ and $\mathbf{w}_i = (w_{i1}, \ldots, w_{i,J-1})'$.

Combining all terms, the conditional probability of outcome j is:

$$\text{Prob}[y_i = j | \mathbf{x}_i, \mathbf{z}_i, \mathbf{h}_i, \mathbf{r}_i, \mathbf{v}_i, \mathbf{w}_i, e_i] = F\left[\frac{\mu_{ij} - \boldsymbol{\beta}'_i \mathbf{x}_i}{\exp(\boldsymbol{\gamma}'\mathbf{h}_i + \tau e_i)}\right]$$
$$- F\left[\frac{\mu_{i,j-1} - \boldsymbol{\beta}'_i \mathbf{x}_i}{\exp(\boldsymbol{\gamma}'\mathbf{h}_i + \tau e_i)}\right], \tag{18.22}$$

where it is noted, once again, that both μ_{ij} and β_i vary with observed variables and with unobserved random terms. The log-likelihood (LL) is constructed from the terms in Equation (18.22). However, the probability in Equation (18.22) contains the unobserved random terms, v_i, w_i, and e_i. The term that enters the LL function for estimation purposes must be unconditioned on the unobservables. Thus, they are integrated out, to obtain the unconditional probabilities:

$$\text{Prob}[y_i = j \,|\, \mathbf{x}_i, \mathbf{z}_i, \mathbf{h}_i, \mathbf{r}_i] =$$
$$\int_{\mathbf{v}_i, \mathbf{w}_i, e_i} \left(F\left[\frac{\mu_{ij} - \boldsymbol{\beta}'_i \mathbf{x}_i}{\exp(\boldsymbol{\gamma}'\mathbf{h}_i + \tau e_i)}\right] - F\left[\frac{\mu_{i,j-1} - \boldsymbol{\beta}'_i \mathbf{x}_i}{\exp(\boldsymbol{\gamma}'\mathbf{h}_i + \tau e_i)}\right] \right) f(\mathbf{v}_i, \mathbf{w}_i, e_i) d\mathbf{v}_i d\mathbf{w}_i de_i.$$
$$\tag{18.23}$$

The model is estimated by maximum simulated likelihood. The simulated LL function is given in Equation (18.24):

$$\log L_S(\boldsymbol{\beta}, \boldsymbol{\Delta}, \boldsymbol{\alpha}, \boldsymbol{\delta}, \boldsymbol{\gamma}, \boldsymbol{\Gamma}, \boldsymbol{\sigma}, \boldsymbol{\tau})$$

$$= \sum_{i=1}^{n} \log \frac{1}{M} \sum_{m=1}^{M} \left(F\left[\frac{\mu_{ij,m} - \boldsymbol{\beta}'_{i,m}\mathbf{x}_i}{\exp(\boldsymbol{\gamma}'\mathbf{h}_i + \tau e_{i,m})}\right] - F\left[\frac{\mu_{i,j-1,m} - \boldsymbol{\beta}'_{i,m}\mathbf{x}_i}{\exp(\boldsymbol{\gamma}'\mathbf{h}_i + \tau e_{i,m})}\right] \right).$$

$$(18.24)$$

$\mathbf{v}_{i,m}$, $\mathbf{w}_{i,m}$, $e_{i,m}$ are a set of M multivariate random draws for the simulation.[3] This is the model in its full generality. Whether a particular data set will be rich enough to support this much parameterization, particularly the elements of the covariances of the unobservables in $\boldsymbol{\Gamma}$, is an empirical question that will depend on the application.

One is typically interested in estimation of parameters such as β in Equation (18.24) to learn about the impact of the observed independent variables on the outcome of interest. This generalized ordered choice model contains four points at which changes in observed variables can induce changes in the probabilities of the outcomes – in the thresholds, μ_{ij}, in the marginal utilities, β_i, in the utility function, $\mathbf{x}_i$, and in the variance, σ_i^2. These could involve different variables or they could have variables in common. Again, demographics such as age, sex, and income, could appear anywhere in the model. In principle, then, if we are interested in all of these, we should compute all the partial effects:

$$\frac{\partial \text{Prob}(y_i = j|\mathbf{x}_i, \mathbf{z}_i, \mathbf{r}_i, \mathbf{h}_i)}{\partial \mathbf{x}_i} = \text{direct of variables in the utility function,}$$

$$\frac{\partial \text{Prob}(y_i = j|\mathbf{x}_i, \mathbf{z}_i, \mathbf{r}_i, \mathbf{h}_i)}{\partial \mathbf{z}_i} = \text{indirect of variables that affect the parameters } \beta,$$

$$\frac{\partial \text{Prob}(y_i = j|\mathbf{x}_i, \mathbf{z}_i, \mathbf{r}_i, \mathbf{h}_i)}{\partial \mathbf{h}_i} = \text{indirect of variables that affect the variance of } \varepsilon_i,$$

$$\frac{\partial \text{Prob}(y_i = j|\mathbf{x}_i, \mathbf{z}_i, \mathbf{r}_i, \mathbf{h}_i)}{\partial \mathbf{r}_i} = \text{indirect of variables that affect the thresholds.}$$

The four terms (in order) are the components of the partial effects (a) due directly to change in x_i, (b) indirectly due to change in the variables, z_i, that

---

[3] We use Halton sequences rather than pseudo-random numbers. See Train (2003, 2009) for a discussion.

influence β_i, (c) due to change in the variables, h_i, in the variance, and (d) due to changes in the variables, r_i, that appear in the threshold parameters, respectively. The probability of interest is:

$$\text{Prob}(y_i = j | \mathbf{x}_i, \mathbf{z}_i, \mathbf{h}_i, \mathbf{r}_i) = \int_{\mathbf{v}_i, \mathbf{w}_i, e_i} \left(F\left[\frac{\mu_{ij} - (\boldsymbol{\beta} + \boldsymbol{\Delta}\mathbf{z}_i + \mathbf{LDv}_i)'\mathbf{x}_i}{\exp(\boldsymbol{\gamma}'\mathbf{h}_i + \tau e_i)} \right] - F\left[\frac{\mu_{i,j-1} - (\boldsymbol{\beta} + \boldsymbol{\Delta}\mathbf{z}_i + \mathbf{LDv}_i)'\mathbf{x}_i}{\exp(\boldsymbol{\gamma}'\mathbf{h}_i + \tau e_i)} \right] \right) f(\mathbf{v}_i, \mathbf{w}_i, e_i) d\mathbf{v}_i d\mathbf{w}_i de_i,$$

$$\mu_{ij} = \exp(\boldsymbol{\delta}'\mathbf{r}_i) \left(\Sigma_{m=1}^{j} \exp(\alpha_m + \sigma_m w_{im}) \right), j = 1, \ldots, J - 1.$$

(18.25)

(LD) * (LD)' = GAMMA. L is a lower triangular matrix with ones on the diagonal, D is a diagonal matrix, and D-squared is the diagonal matrix of the Cholesky values of GAMMA. If we let Q = D-squared, then GAMMA = L*Q*L'. This is the Cholesky decomposition of GAMMA. The set of partial effects is shown in Equation set (18.26):

$$\frac{\partial \text{Prob}(y_i = j | \mathbf{x}_i, \mathbf{z}_i, \mathbf{h}_i, \mathbf{r}_i)}{\partial \mathbf{x}_i} =$$

$$\int_{\mathbf{v}_i, \mathbf{w}_i, e_i} \left(\frac{1}{\exp(\boldsymbol{\gamma}'\mathbf{h}_i + \tau e_i)} \left\{ f\left[\frac{\mu_{ij} - \boldsymbol{\beta}'_i \mathbf{x}_i}{\exp(\boldsymbol{\gamma}'\mathbf{h}_i + \tau e_i)} \right] - f\left[\frac{\mu_{i,j-1} - \boldsymbol{\beta}'_i \mathbf{x}_i}{\exp(\boldsymbol{\gamma}'\mathbf{h}_i + \tau e_i)} \right] \right\} (-\boldsymbol{\beta}_i) \right) f(\mathbf{v}_i, \mathbf{w}_i, e_i) d\mathbf{v}_i d\mathbf{w}_i de_i$$

(18.26a)

$$\frac{\partial \text{Prob}(y_i = j | \mathbf{x}_i, \mathbf{z}_i, \mathbf{h}_i, \mathbf{r}_i)}{\partial \mathbf{z}_i} =$$

$$\int_{\mathbf{v}_i, \mathbf{w}_i, e_i} \left(\frac{1}{\exp(\boldsymbol{\gamma}'\mathbf{h}_i + \tau e_i)} \left\{ f\left[\frac{\mu_{ij} - \boldsymbol{\beta}'_i \mathbf{x}_i}{\exp(\boldsymbol{\gamma}'\mathbf{h}_i + \tau e_i)} \right] - f\left[\frac{\mu_{i,j-1} - \boldsymbol{\beta}'_i \mathbf{x}_i}{\exp(\boldsymbol{\gamma}'\mathbf{h}_i + \tau e_i)} \right] \right\} (-\boldsymbol{\Delta}'\mathbf{x}_i) \right) f(\mathbf{v}_i, \mathbf{w}_i, e_i) d\mathbf{v}_i d\mathbf{w}_i de_i.$$

(18.26b)

$$\frac{\partial \text{Prob}(y_i = j | \mathbf{x}_i, \mathbf{z}_i, \mathbf{h}_i, \mathbf{r}_i)}{\partial \mathbf{h}_i} =$$

$$\int_{\mathbf{v}_i, \mathbf{w}_i, e_i} \left(\left\{ \begin{array}{l} f \left[\dfrac{\mu_{ij} - \boldsymbol{\beta}'_i \mathbf{x}_i}{\exp(\boldsymbol{\gamma}' \mathbf{h}_i + \tau e_i)} \right] \left(\dfrac{\mu_{ij} - \boldsymbol{\beta}'_i \mathbf{x}_i}{\exp(\boldsymbol{\gamma}' \mathbf{h}_i + \tau e_i)} \right) - \\[4mm] f \left[\dfrac{\mu_{i,j-1} - \boldsymbol{\beta}'_i \mathbf{x}_i}{\exp(\boldsymbol{\gamma}' \mathbf{h}_i + \tau e_i)} \right] \left(\dfrac{\mu_{i,j-1} - \boldsymbol{\beta}'_i \mathbf{x}_i}{\exp(\boldsymbol{\gamma}' \mathbf{h}_i + \tau e_i)} \right) \end{array} \right\} (-\boldsymbol{\gamma}) \right) f(\mathbf{v}_i, \mathbf{w}_i, e_i) d\mathbf{v}_i d\mathbf{w}_i de_i$$

$$(18.26c)$$

$$\frac{\partial \text{Prob}(y_i = j | \mathbf{x}_i, \mathbf{z}_i, \mathbf{h}_i, \mathbf{r}_i)}{\partial \mathbf{r}_i} =$$

$$\int_{\mathbf{v}_i, \mathbf{w}_i, e_i} \left(\left\{ \begin{array}{l} f \left[\dfrac{\mu_{ij} - \boldsymbol{\beta}'_i \mathbf{x}_i}{\exp(\boldsymbol{\gamma}' \mathbf{h}_i + \tau e_i)} \right] \left(\dfrac{\mu_{ij}}{\exp(\boldsymbol{\gamma}' \mathbf{h}_i + \tau e_i)} \right) - \\[4mm] f \left[\dfrac{\mu_{i,j-1} - \boldsymbol{\beta}'_i \mathbf{x}_i}{\exp(\boldsymbol{\gamma}' \mathbf{h}_i + \tau e_i)} \right] \left(\dfrac{\mu_{i,j-1}}{\exp(\boldsymbol{\gamma}' \mathbf{h}_i + \tau e_i)} \right) \end{array} \right\} (\boldsymbol{\delta}) \right) f(\mathbf{v}_i, \mathbf{w}_i, e_i) d\mathbf{v}_i d\mathbf{w}_i de_i .$$

$$(18.26d)$$

Effects for particular variables that appear in more than one part of the model are added from the corresponding parts. Like the LL function, the partial effects must be computed by simulation. If a variable appears only in $\mathbf{x}_i$, then this formulation retains both the "parallel regressions" and "single crossing" features of the original model. Nonetheless, the effects are highly non-linear in any event. However, if a variable appears anywhere else in the specification, then neither of these properties will necessarily remain.

18.4 Case study

The context of the application, using stated choice data from a larger study reported in Hensher (2004, 2006), is an individual's choice among unlabeled attribute packages of alternative tolled and non-tolled routes for the car commuting trip in Sydney (Australia) in 2002. In this chapter we are interested in one feature of the way in which individuals process attribute information, namely attribute inclusion or exclusion, given a maximum of five attributes per alternative. The dependent variable in the ordered choice model is the number of ignored attributes, or the number of attributes attended to from the full fixed set associated with each alternative package of route attributes. The utility function is defined over the attribute information processed by each individual, with candidate influences on each individual's decision heuristic, including the dimensions of the choice experiment (e.g., number of alternatives, range of attributes), the framing of the design attribute levels relative to a reference alternative (see below), an individual's socio-economic characteristics (SECs), and attribute accumulation where attributes are in common units (see also Hensher 2006).

The establishment of attribute inclusion/exclusion (also referred to as preservation/non-preservation)[4] in making choices in a stated choice context is often associated with design dimensionality and the so-called *complexity* of the stated choice experiment (Hensher 2006). It is typically implied that designs with more items to evaluate are more complex than those with fewer items[5] (for example, Arentze *et al.* 2003; Swait and Adamowicz 2001a, 2001b), impose a cognitive burden, and are consequently less reliable, in a behavioral sense, in revealing preference information. This is potentially misleading, since it suggests that complexity is an artefact of the *quantity* of information, in contrast to the *relevance* of information (Hensher 2006). In any setting where an individual has to process the information on offer and make a choice, psychologists interested in human judgment theory have studied numerous heuristics that are brought to bear in aiding simplification of the decision task (Gilovich *et al.* 2002). The accumulating life experiences of individuals are also often brought to bear as reference points to assist in selectively evaluating the information placed in front of them. These features of human processing and cognition are not new to the broad literature on judgment and decision making, where heuristics are offered up as deliberative analytic procedures intentionally designed to simplify choice. The presence of a large amount of information, whether requiring active search and consideration or simply assessment when placed in front of an individual (the latter being the case in choice experiments), has elements of cognitive overload (or burden) that results in the adoption of rules to make processing manageable and acceptable (presumably implying that the simplification is worth it in terms of trading off the benefits and costs of a consideration of all the information on offer or potentially available with some effort). It is not easy

---

[4] The chapter focusses on attribute preservation and non-preservation; however, it is important to recognize that one way in which the number of attributes is "reduced," without attribute elimination, is by adding up common metric attributes. Hence it is important that we consider this as well, and control for the possibility that some attributes are not eliminated but added up.

[5] Complexity also includes attributes that are lowly correlated, in contrast to highly correlated, the latter supporting greater ease of assessment in that one attribute represents other attributes.

to distinguish between simplified processing because the context is of little interest or the effort is not worth it, versus a genuine interest in the task but with some *ex ante* biases that translate into heuristics that capture how an individual desires to treat specific pieces of information. Either way, we see gains in investigating attribute processing and in time being able to separate out real behavioral processing from processing for convenience (that lacks behavioral validity in respect to the choice of interest) given the task. Importantly we suggest that the amount of information to process is less important than the relevance of the information, and indeed there are situations where so little information makes processing "complex" in the sense that the decision maker requires much more detail to define a choice of relevance.

The alternative attribute packages offered to individuals to evaluate are pivoted around the car commuting experiences of sampled respondents. The use of a respondent's experience, embodied in a reference alternative, to derive the attribute levels of the experiment, is supported by a number of theories in behavioral and cognitive psychology and economics, such as prospect theory, case-based decision theory, and minimum-regret theory (see Starmer 2000; Hensher 2006). Reference alternatives in stated choice experiments[6] act to frame the decision context of the choice task within some existing memory schema of the individual respondents, and hence make preference revelation more meaningful at the level of the individual.

Four stated choice sub-designs have been embedded in one overall design (Table 18.1). Each commuter evaluated one randomly assigned sub-design; however, across the full set of stated choice experiments, the designs differed in terms of the range and levels of attributes, the number of alternatives, and the number of choice sets. The combination of these dimensions of each design is often seen as the source of design "complexity," and it is within this setting that we have varied the dimensions of an stated choice experiment that each respondent is asked to evaluate and, through supplementary questions, established which attributes were "ignored" in the evaluation and selection of an alternative.

Previous studies were used to identify candidate design dimensions. The five design dimensions are shown in Table 18.2. Five attributes were selected for each alternative, based on previous evidence (see Hensher 2001), to characterize the options: free flow time, slowed-down time, stop/start time, variability of trip time, and total cost. Hensher (2006) explored how varying

---

[6] Hensher (2004), Train and Wilson (2008), and Rose *et al.* (2008) provide details of the design of pivot-based experiments.

the number of attributes affects information processing, aggregating attributes according to four patterns, noting that aggregated attributes are combinations of existing attributes.[7] We have selected a generic design (i.e., unlabeled alternatives) to avoid confounding the effect of the number of alternatives with the labeling (e.g., car, train). The attribute ranges are given in Table 18.1 with the sub-design dimensions shown in Table 18.2.

As a generic design, each of the alternatives, added as we move from two to three to four alternatives in a choice set (based on Table 18.1), are exactly the same. That is, for any two alternatives associated with a given design, we should not expect to find the parameter for an attribute (e.g., "free-flow travel time") to be different for the set of non-reference alternatives. Therefore we do not need the attribute "free-flow time alternative one" to be orthogonal to the attribute "free-flow time alternative two," etc. up to "free-flow time $J-1$ alternatives." The designs are computer generated. A preferred choice experiment design is one that maximizes the determinant of the covariance matrix, which is itself a function of the estimated parameters. Knowledge of the parameters, or at least some priors (such as signs) for each attribute, from past studies, provides a useful input. We found that in so doing, the search eliminates dominant alternatives. The method used finds the D-optimality plan very quickly (see Rose and Bliemer 2008; Choice Metrics 2012).

The *actual* levels of the attributes shown to respondents are calculated relative to those of the experienced reference alternative – a recent car commuter trip. The levels applied to the choice task differ depending on the range of attribute levels and the number of levels for each attribute. The design dimensions are translated into stated choice screens, illustrated in Figure 18.1. The range of the attribute levels varies *across* designs. Each sampled commuter is given a varying number of choice sets (or scenarios), but the number of alternatives remains fixed. Elicitation questions associated with attribute inclusion and exclusion are shown in Figure 18.2.

18.4.1 Empirical analysis

Computer Aided Personal Interview (CAPI) surveys were completed in the Sydney metropolitan area in 2002.[8] A stratified random sample was applied, based on the residential location of the household. Screening questions

---

[7] This is an important point because we did not want the analysis to be confounded by extra attribute dimensions.

[8] Interviews took between 20 and 35 minutes, with an interviewer present who entered an individual's responses directly into the CAPI instrument on a laptop.

Table 18.1 Attribute profiles for the design

(units = %)	Base range			Wider range			Narrower range		
Levels:	2	3	4	2	3	4	2	3	4
Free-flow time	± 20	−20, 0, +20	−20,−10,+10,+20	−20, +40	−20,+10,+40	−20, 0,+20,+40	± 5	−5, 0,+5	−5, −2.5, +2.5, +5
Slow-down time	± 40	−40, 0, +40	−40,−20,+20,+40	−30, +60	−30,+15,+60	−30, 0,+30,+60	± 20	−20, 0, +20	−20, −2.5, +2.5, +20
Stop/start time	± 40	−40, 0, +40	−40,−20,+20,+40	−30, +60	−30,+15,+60	−30, 0,+30,+60	± 20	−20, 0, +20	−20, −2.5, +2.5, +20
Uncertainty of travel time	± 40	−40, 0, +40	−40,−20,+20,+40	−30, +60	−30,+15,+60	−30, 0,+30,+60	± 20	−20, 0, +20	−20, −2.5, +2.5, +20
Total costs	± 20	−20, 0, +20	−20,−10,+10,+20	−20, +40	−20,+10,+40	−20, 0,+20,+40	± 5	−5, 0,+5	−5, −2.5, +2.5, +5

Table 18.2 Sub-designs of the overall design for five attributes

Choice set of size	Number of alternatives	Number of attributes	Number of levels of attributes	Range of attribute levels
15	2	5	2	Wider than base
9	2	5	4	Base
6	3	5	4	Narrower than base
12	4	5	3	Narrower than base

Note: Column 1 refers to the number of choice sets. The four rows represent the set of designs. The number of alternatives does not include the reference alternative.

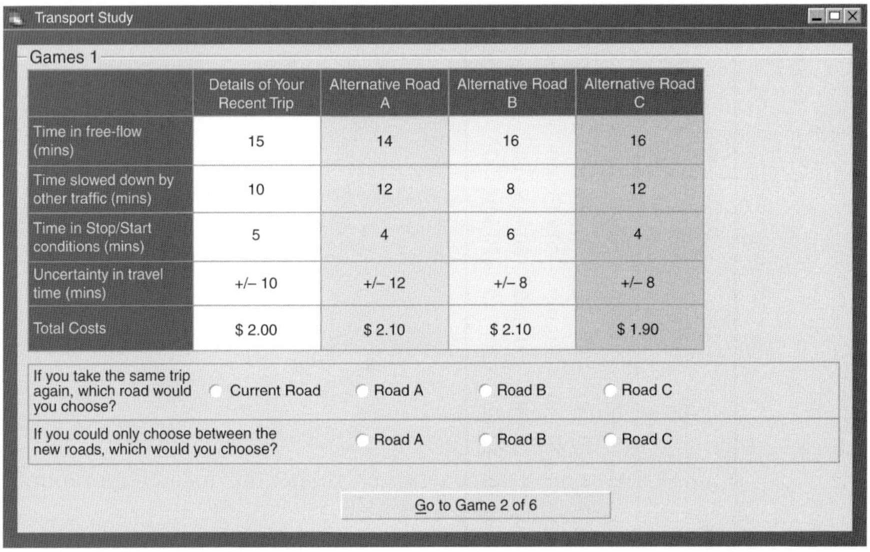

Figure 18.1   Example of a stated choice screen

established eligibility in respect of commuting by car. Further details are given in Hensher (2006). Final models are given in Table 18.3 for 2,562 observations.

The explanatory variables in the model were guided by the extant literature on heuristics and biases in choice and judgment (see Gilovich *et al.* 2002), as well as empirical evidence from previous studies on attribute processing by Hensher (2006). We selected candidate influences on the number of attributes actually processed (i.e., deemed relevant) under three broad categories: (i) design dimensions of the choice experiment, (ii) framing around the reference or base alternative, in line with the theoretical argument promoted in prospect

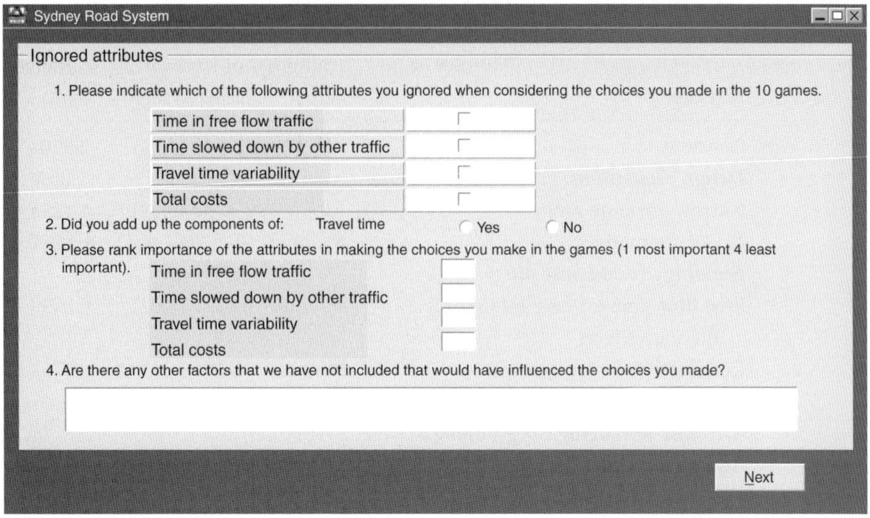
Sydney Road System

Ignored attributes

1. Please indicate which of the following attributes you ignored when considering the choices you made in the 10 games.

Time in free flow traffic	
Time slowed down by other traffic	
Travel time variability	
Total costs	

2. Did you add up the components of: Travel time Yes No

3. Please rank importance of the attributes in making the choices you make in the games (1 most important 4 least important). Time in free flow traffic

Time slowed down by other traffic

Travel time variability

Total costs

4. Are there any other factors that we have not included that would have influenced the choices you made?

Next

Figure 18.2 CAPI questions on attribute relevance

theory for reference points, and (iii) the literature on heuristics that suggests that attribute packaging or attribute accumulation[9] is a legitimate rule for some individuals in stage 1 editing under prospect theory (Gilovich *et al.* 2002).

The generalized ordered logit model has a preferred goodness of fit over the traditional ordered logit model. With four degrees of freedom difference, the likelihood ratio of 181.92 is statistically significant on any acceptable chi squared test level. The generalized model has included a random parameter form for congestion time framing and has accounted for two systematic sources of variation around the mean of the random threshold parameter (i.e., the accumulation of travel time and gender).

The evidence identifies a number of statistically significant influences on the number of attributes attended to, given the maximum number of attributes provided. The range of the attributes and the number of alternatives[10] in the choice set condition mean attribute preservation, and the number of levels of an attribute has a systematic influence on the variance of the unobserved

[9] Accumulation, grouping, and aggregation are essentially the same constructs; namely, where two or more attributes with a common metric unit are treated as a combined attribute.

[10] The difference in the number of alternatives (from two to four, excluding the reference alternative) represents a range typically found in SC studies. The actual screens, with the reference alternative in place, have between three and five alternatives. The number of alternatives is fixed per respondent but varies across the sample.

Table 18.3 Ordered logit models (2,562 observations)

Attribute	Units	Ordered logit	Generalized ordered logit
Constant		2.9682 (4.17)	2.9504 (2.79)
Design dimensions:			
Narrow attribute range	1,0	1.3738 (3.59)	1.4275 (2.35)
No. of alternatives	Number	−0.9204 (−4.1)	−1.0205 (−2.87)
Framing around base alt:			
Free-flow time for base minus SC alternative level	Minutes	0.0329 (4.02)	0.0599 (3.44)
Congested time for base minus SC alternative level	Minutes	−0.0083 (−1.80)	0.0761 (2.20)
Attribute packaging (or grouping):			
Adding travel time components	1,0	−0.7407 (−4.25)	−0.8700 (−3.33)
Variance decomposition:			
Number of levels	Number	0.1043 (2.35)	0.3357 (4.48)
Free-flow time for base minus SC alternative level	Minutes	−0.0164 (−2.75)	−0.0332 (−4.04)
Who pays (1= commuter personally)	1,0	−0.3070 (5.74)	−0.3721 (−3.89)
Threshold parameters:			
μ_1		0	0
μ_2 mean		3.0973 (5.74)	0.8753 (3.71)
Standard deviation of $\mu\mu_2$ threshold parameter			0.0767 (0.018)
Threshold parameter Decomposition:			
Adding travel time components	1,0		1.7447 (10.83)
Gender (male =1)	1,0		0.3366 (2.80)
Standard deviation of random regression parameters:			
Congested time for base minus SC alternative level	1,0		0.2652 (2.48)
Count of choice responses:		max # attributes minus #ignored	obs
0		5–0	1415
1		5–1	1080
2		5–2	66
LL		−1871.80	−1780.85

Note: SC = Stated choice.

effects (or the error term). We framed the level of each attribute relative to that of the experienced car commute as (i) free-flow time for reference (or base) minus the level associated with an alternative in the stated choice design, and (ii) the congested travel time for the base minus the level associated with each stated choice alternative's attribute level. The parameter estimates are statistically significant and negative suggesting that the more that an stated choice attribute level ("free-flow time" and "congested time" (= slowed-down plus stop/start time)) deviates from the reference alternative's level, the more likely that an individual will process an increased number of attributes. The attribute packaging effect for travel time has a negative parameter, suggesting that those individuals who add up components of travel time tend to preserve more attributes; indeed, aggregation is a way of simplifying the choice task without ignoring attributes. In the sample, 82 percent of observations undertook some attribute packaging.

The evidence here cannot establish whether an attribute reduction strategy is *strictly* linked to behavioral relevance, or to a coping strategy for handling cognitive burden, both being legitimate paradigms. It does, however, provide indications on what features of a stated choice experiment have an influence on how many attributes provided within a specific context are processed. It is likely that the evidence is application-specific, but extremely useful when analysts compare the different studies and draw inferences about the role of specific attributes.

The threshold parameter has a statistically significant mean and two sources of systematic variation across the sample around the mean threshold parameter estimate. Across the sample, there were three levels of the ordered choice observed: level 0 is where all attributes are preserved, level 1 is where 4 of the 5 attributes were preserved, and level 3 is where 3 of the 5 attributes were preserved. No respondent preserved only 1 or 2 attributes. Hence given three levels of the choice variable, there are two threshold parameters, one between levels 0 and 1 and one between levels 1 and 2 (see the explanation in paragraph following Equation 18.3). As indicated in section 2.1, a normalization is required so that a constant can be identified. We set the threshold parameter for between levels 0 and 1 equal to zero (μ_1) and estimate the parameter between levels 1 and 2 (μ_2).[11]

---

[11] Estimation of the threshold parameters is not a main object of fitting the ordered choice model *per se*. The flexibility of the threshold parameters is there to accommodate the variety of ways that individuals will translate their underlying continuous preferences into the discrete outcome. The main objective of the estimation is the prediction of and analysis of the probabilities, e.g., the partial effects. The threshold parameters do not have any interesting interpretation of their numerical values in their own right.

Table 18.4 Marginal effects for three choice levels derived from ordered logit models

Attribute	Ordered logit	Generalized ordered logit
	Average number of attributes ignored	Average number of attributes ignored
	Design dimensions:	
Narrow attribute range	−0.4148, 0.3893, 0.0255	−0.2502, 0.2242, 0.0259
Number of alternatives	0.2779, −0.2608, −0.0171	0.1789, −0.1603, −0.0256
Framing around base alt:		
Free-flow time for base minus SC alternative level	−0.0099, 0.0093, 0.0006	−01017, 0.0094, 0.0011
Congested time for base minus SC alternative level	0.0025, −0.0024, −0.0002	−0.0134, 0.0119, 0.0014
	Attribute packaging:	
Adding travel time components	0.2237, −.2099, −0.0137	0.1525, −0.1367, −0.0158
Variables in threshold		
Add travel time components	–	0.0000, 0.06510, −0.06510
Gender (male =1)	–	0.0000, 0.01785, −0.01785
	Variance decomposition:	
Number of levels	−0.1104, 0.0249, 0.0856	−0.01740, 0.0103, 0.0071
Free-flow time for base minus SC alternative level	−0.2386, 0.0537, 0.1849	0.0026, −0.0015, −0.0010
Who pays (1 = individual, 0 = a business)	0.0740, −0.0167, −0.0573	0.0502, −0.0297, −0.0071

Notes: The three marginal effects per attribute refer to the levels of the dependent variable. SC = Stated choice.

We investigated an unconstrained random parameter normal distribution; however, the standard deviation parameter estimate was not statistically significant from zero. The evidence, however, justifies the inclusion of a non-fixed threshold parameter, with a higher mean estimate across the sampled population when an individual aggregates the travel time components and when they are male. This is an important finding since it justifies the new formulation of the threshold parameters in ordered choice models as behaviorally meaningful.

A direct interpretation of the parameter estimates is not informative, given the logit transformation of the choice dependent variable (see Equations (18.5) and (18.26)). We therefore provide the marginal (or partial) effects in Table 18.4 which have substantive behavioral meaning, defined as the derivatives of the choice probabilities (Equation (18.25)). A marginal effect is the influence a one unit change in an explanatory variable has on the probability of selecting a particular outcome, *ceteris paribus*.[12] The marginal effects need not have the same sign as the model parameters. Hence, the statistical significance of an estimated parameter does not imply the same significance for the marginal effect.

We take a closer look at each model, discussing the evidence for design dimensions, framing around the base, attribute packaging, variance decomposition, and other effects. The magnitude and direction of influence is given in Table 18.4 for the marginal effects that have to be interpreted relative to each of the three levels of the *number of attributes ignored*.

In commenting on the marginal effects, it should be noted that, for the generalized ordered logit model, some attributes have more than one role; for example, the framing of free-flow time is both a main effect influence as well as a source of variance decomposition (i.e., systematic source of heterogeneity) for the unobserved variance; and the attribute accumulation for travel time is both a main effect and a systematic source of influence on the distribution of the random threshold parameter. The generalized ordered choice model (GOCM) takes all of these sources into account in identifying the marginal effects for each level of the choice variable. In contrast, where an attribute has multiple roles in the traditional ordered choice model (TOCM), the marginal effects are calculated separately. The marginal effects associated with variance decomposition in GOCM has two unique influences (i.e., the number of levels of an attribute and "who pays for the trip," together with the framing around the base alternative for free-flow time which is present elsewhere[13]).

The dummy variable for the "narrow attribute range" has the highest marginal effect, although its influence is moderated in GOCM compared to TOCM. The probability of considering more (compared to fewer) attributes from the offered set decreases as an attribute's range narrows, *ceteris paribus*. That is, respondents tend to ignore more attributes when the difference between attribute levels is small. This result is perhaps due to the fact that evaluation of small differences is more difficult or perceptually less relevant than evaluation of large differences. An important implication

---

[12] This holds for continuous variables only. For dummy (1,0) variables, the marginal effects are the derivatives of the probabilities given a change in the level of the dummy variable.

[13] For the "Free-flow time for base minus SC alternative level," we report this in variance decomposition to show its relatively small effect compared to the overall effect of this variable given in another row in the table.

is that if an analyst continues to include, in model estimation, an attribute across the entire sample that is *ignored by a respondent*, then there is a much greater likelihood of mis-specified parameter estimates in circumstances where the attribute range is narrower rather than wider.

The marginal effects for the narrow attribute range are positive when one (i.e., 5–1) or two attributes (i.e., 5–2) are ignored. Importantly the positive effect is greater when one attribute is ignored than when two are ignored. This suggests that the probability of considering four or three attributes from the offered set increases as an attribute's range goes from narrow to non-narrow, *ceteris paribus*, but to a greater extent for four attributes. What we are observing across all three levels of the dependent variable is a U- (or inverted U-) shaped response, which appears to be the case for all attributes in GOCM. Thus for the narrow attribute range we have the highest probability of preserving four attributes than of preserving three attributes, given that the probability of preserving all attributes is decreased. Given the observed profile of the sampled respondents preserving five, four, and three attributes (Table 18.2), where there are only 66 observations in the last category (compared to 1,415 and 1,080 in 5–0 and 5–1), we have greater confidence in the relative marginal effects of preserving all (i.e., five) attributes and four attributes.

As we increase the "number of alternatives" to evaluate (over the range of two to four plus the reference alternative), *ceteris paribus*, the importance of considering all attributes increases, as a way of making it easier to differentiate between the alternatives. This finding runs counter to some views – for example, that individuals will tend to ignore increasing amounts of attribute information as the number of alternatives increases. Our evidence suggests that the processing strategy is dependent on the nature of the attribute information, and not strictly on the quantity. The negative marginal effects for ignoring one and two attributes (or preserving four and three attributes) suggest that these rules are less likely to be adopted as the number of alternatives increases.

The theoretical argument promoted in prospect theory for reference points is supported by our empirical evidence. We have framed the level of each attribute relative to that of the experienced car commute trip as (i) free-flow time for current (or base) minus the level associated with an attribute and alternative in the stated choice design, and (ii) the congested travel time for the base minus the level associated with each stated choice alternative's attribute. The more that an stated choice attribute level deviates from the reference alternative's level, the more likely that an individual will process an increased number of attributes. This evidence was found for both the "free-flow time" and "congested time" framing effects. Conversely, as the stated choice design attribute level moves closer to the reference alternative's level, individuals appear to use some approximation rule, in which closeness suggests similarity, and hence ease of eliminating specific attributes, because their role is limiting in differentiation.

Reference dependency not only has a direct (mean) influence on the number of attributes ignored; it also plays a role via its contribution to explaining heteroskedasticity in the variance of the unobserved effects. This has already been accounted for in the GOCM marginal effects for free-flow time framing. It is separated out in the TOCM. The effect of widening the gap between the base and stated choice "free-flow time" reduces the heteroskedasticity of the unobserved effects across the respondents, increasing the acceptability of the constant variance condition when simpler models are specified.

In GOCM, the congested time framing effect is represented by a distribution across the sample. The random parameter has a statistically significant standard deviation parameter estimate, resulting in the distribution shown in Figure 18.3. The range is from -0.857 to 1.257; hence there is a sign change around the mean of 0.70833 and standard deviation of

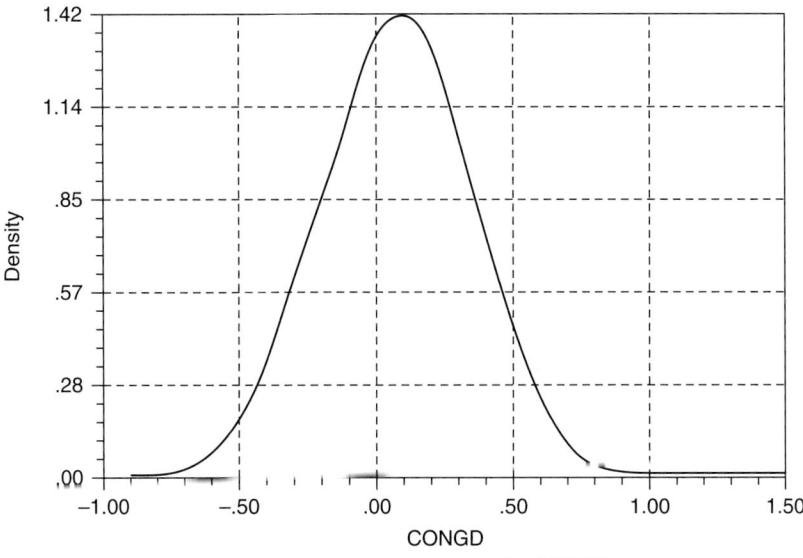

CONGD

Kernel density estimate for CONGD

Figure 18.3 Distribution of preference heterogeneity for congested time framing

0.2657. This results in the same mean marginal effect sign in GOCM as free-flow time framing; however, when we treated congested time framing as having fixed parameters (in TOCM, where the standard deviation parameter was not statistically significant), the signs are swapped for all levels of the choice variable. The evidence from the GOCM is intuitively more plausible.

The attribute accumulation rule in stage 1 editing under prospect theory is consistently strong for the aggregation of travel time components. The positive marginal effect for the dummy variable "adding three travel time components" indicates that, on average, respondents who add up the time components in assessing the alternatives tend also to ignore more attributes. There is clear evidence that a relevant simplification rule is the re-packaging of the attribute set, where possible, through addition. This is not a cancellation strategy, but a rational way of processing the information content of component attributes, and then weighting this information (in some unobserved way) in comparing alternatives.

The SECs of respondents proxy for other excluded contextual influences. A respondent's role in paying the toll was identified, through its influence on the variance decomposition of the unobserved effects, as a statistically significant socio-economic influence on the number of attributes considered. We have no priors on the likely sign of the influence on variance. The positive marginal effect for who pays suggests that those who pay themselves (in contrast to a business paying) tend to result in a higher probability of preserving more attributes, although the influence is slightly less in GOCM compared to TOCM. This might mean that males do care more about the time/cost trade-off, in contrast to a situation where only time matters if someone else pays for the travel. Gender was a systematic source of influence on the threshold parameter, increasing its mean estimate for males.

18.5 Nlogit commands

Generalized ordered choice model:

$$y^* = \beta(i)'x(i) + \varepsilon_i$$
$\beta(i) = \beta + \Gamma w(i)$, $w(i) \sim N[0,I]$, Γ = diagonal matrix of standard deviations
$\varepsilon(i) \sim N[0,\sigma(i)^2]$, $\sigma(i) = \exp[\gamma'z(i) + \tau v(i)]$ $v(i) \sim N[0,1]$

Thresholds for ordered choice:

$\mu(j) = \mu(j{-}1) + \exp[\alpha(j) + \delta'w(i) + \theta(j)u(i,j)]$ $u(i,j) \sim N[0,1]$.
$\mu(0) = 0$, model contains a constant.

Allows panel data treatment. Random draws are fixed over periods. Nothing else need be. Note that the random parameters in the model are the βs. The variance term, $\sigma(i)$, is random because of $\tau v(i)$ as well:

ORDE; Lhs = . . .
           ; Rhs = One,. . .   (β)
           ; RTM(α, θ)
           ; RPM to request random betas (Γ)
           ; RVM to request random element in $\sigma(i)$ (τ)
           ; LIMITS = list of variables for thresholds (δ)
           ; HET ; Hfn = list of variables (γ)

Allows ;RST so can specify restrictions such as some parameters random.
Allows ; PDS = definition or ;PANEL for panel data treatment.
Uses simulation, so use ;HALTON ; PTS:

```
Load;file=c:\papers\wps2005\ARC_VTTS_0103\FullDataDec02\dodMay03_05.sav$
sample;all$
reject;altz<5$ To reject base alt
reject;naig=0$
reject;naig<6$
reject;naig>8$

Ordered;lhs=naign5
    ;rhs=one,?nlvls,
    ntb,nalts1,fftd,congt1d,addtim
    ;het;hfn= fftd,nlvls,whopay ?,coycar,pinc
    ;RST=b1,b2,b3,b4,b5,b6,b7,0,b9,b10,0,0,0,0,b15,0,b17,b18,b19
    ;RTM
    ;RPM
    ;LIMITS=addtim,gender
    ;halton;pts=20
    ; maxit=31
    ; alg = bfgs ?bhhh
    ; tlg=0.001,tlb=0.001
    ;logit ;marginal effects$
Normal exit from iterations. Exit status=0
|    -----------------------------------------------------+
| Ordered Probability Model                          |
| Maximum Likelihood Estimates                       |
| Dependent variable                   NAIGN5        |
| Weighting variable                   None          |
```

```
| Number of observations            2562   |
| Iterations completed                19   |
| Log likelihood function      -1871.798   |
| Number of parameters                10   |
| Info. Criterion: AIC =         1.46901   |
|    Finite Sample: AIC =        1.46904   |
| Info. Criterion: BIC =         1.49184   |
| Info. Criterion:HQIC =         1.47728   |
| Restricted log likelihood    -2014.040   |
| McFadden Pseudo R-squared      .0706254   |
| Chi squared                   284.4847   |
| Degrees of freedom                   8   |
| Prob[ChiSqd > value] =         .0000000   |
| Model estimated: Jan 03, 2009, 10:06:39AM   |
| Underlying probabilities based on Logistic   |
+-----------------------------------------------------------+
```

```
+------------------------------------------------------------------------------- +
|      TABLE OF CELL FREQUENCIES FOR ORDERED PROBABILITY MODEL      |
+------------------------------------------------------------------------------- +
|             Frequency       Cumulative  < =   Cumulative  > =  |
|Outcome   Count   Percent   Count   Percent   Count   Percent |
|-------------- ---------  ------------ ----------  ----------- ----------  -------- |
|NAIGN5=00   1415   55.2693   1415   55.2693   2562   100.0000 |
|NAIGN5=01   1080   42.1546   2495   97.4239   1147   44.7307 |
|NAIGN5=02     66    2.5761   2561   100.0000     67    2.5761 |
+------------------------------------------------------------------------------- +
```

Variable	Coefficient	Standard Error	b/St.Er.	P[|Z|>z]	Mean of X
+-----------+Index function for probability					
Constant	2.96818***	.71141277	4.172	.0000	
NTB	1.37380***	.38246834	3.592	.0003	.4098361
NALTS1	-.92037***	.22538433	-4.084	.0000	3.7283372
FFTD	.03290***	.00819172	4.017	.0001	5.4910226
CONGT1D	-.00829*	.00472072	-1.757	.0789	-7.7076503
ADDTIM	-.74074***	.17412229	-4.254	.0000	.8243560
+-----------+Variance function					
FFTD	-.01642***	.00597604	-2.748	.0060	5.4910226
NLVLS	.10434**	.04445941	2.347	.0189	2.9086651
WHOPAY	-.30698***	.09874916	-3.109	.0019	1.3981265
+-----------+Threshold parameters for index					
Mu(1)	3.09732***	.53996121	5.736	.0000	

```
+------------------------------------------------------------------------------- +
| Note: ***, **, * = Significance at 1%, 5%, 10% level.      |
+------------------------------------------------------------------------------- +
```

```
+------------------------------------------------------------ +
| Marginal Effects for OrdLogit                               |
+------------- +------------- +------------- +------------ +
| Variable  | NAIGN5=0  | NAIGN5=1  | NAIGN5=2  |
+------------- +------------- +------------- +------------ +
| ONE       |   -.89617 |    .84119 |    .05498 |
| NTB       |   -.41479 |    .38934 |    .02545 |
| NALTS1    |    .27788 |   -.26084 |   -.01705 |
| FFTD      |   -.00993 |    .00933 |    .00061 |
| CONGT1D   |    .00250 |   -.00235 |   -.00015 |
| ADDTIM    |    .22365 |   -.20993 |   -.01372 |
| FFTD      |   -.23861 |    .05368 |    .18493 |
| NLVLS     |   -.11044 |    .02485 |    .08559 |
| WHOPAY    |    .07399 |   -.01665 |   -.05734 |
+------------- +------------- +------------- +------------ +
```

```
+-----------------------------------------------------------------------------+
| Cross tabulation of predictions. Row is actual, column is predicted.  |
| Model = Logistic  .  Prediction is number of the most probable cell.  |
+---------- +--------- +------- +------ +------ +------- +------- +------ +------ +------- +------ +-----+
| Actual|Row Sum|  0  |  1  |  2  |  3  |  4  |  5  |  6  |  7  |  8  |  9 |
+---------- +--------- +------- +------ +------ +------- +------- +------ +------ +------- +------ +-----+
|       0|   1416| 1157|   0|  259|
|       1|   1080|  707|   0|  373|
|       2|     66|    0|   0|   66|
+---------- +--------- +------- +------ +------ +------- +------- +------ +------ +------- +------ +-----+
|Col Sum|   2562| 1864|   0|  698|   0|   0|   0|   0|   0|   0|   0|
+---------- +--------- +------- +------ +------ +------- +------- +------ +------ +------- +------ +-----+
```
Maximum iterations reached. Exit iterations with status=1.

```
+------------------------------------------------------------ +
| Random Thresholds Ordered Choice Model                      |
| Maximum Likelihood Estimates                                |
| Dependent variable                    NAIGN5               |
| Weighting variable                       None               |
| Number of observations                   2562               |
| Iterations completed                       31               |
| Log likelihood function             -1786.163               |
| Number of parameters                       13               |
| Info. Criterion: AIC =                1.40450               |
|    Finite Sample: AIC =               1.40455               |
| Info. Criterion: BIC =                1.43418               |
| Info. Criterion:HQIC =                1.41526               |
| Restricted log likelihood           -1871.798               |
| McFadden Pseudo R-squared             .0457499              |
| Chi squared                          171.2693               |
| Degrees of freedom                          9               |
| Prob[ChiSqd > value] =                .0000000              |
| Model estimated: Jan 03, 2009, 10:15:43AM                   |
| Underlying probabilities based on Logistic                  |
+------------------------------------------------------------ +
```

```
+-----------+-----------------+---------------------+----------+----------+--------------+
|Variable| Coefficient | Standard Error |b/St.Er.|P[|Z|>z]| Mean of X|
+-----------+-----------------+---------------------+----------+----------+--------------+
+-----------+Latent Regression Equation                                             |
|Constant|   3.74598***      1.22345010      3.062     .0022                   |
|NTB     |   2.08729***       .70866123      2.945     .0032       .4098361|
|NALTS1  |   1.48161***       .45390074     -3.264     .0011      3.7283372|
|FFTD    |    .07748***       .02409329      3.216     .0013      5.4910226|
|CONGT1D |   -.15712***       .05886616     -2.669     .0076     -7.7076503|
|ADDTIM  |   -.51850**        .24831851     -2.088     .0368       .8243560|
+-----------+Intercept Terms in Random Thresholds                                   |
|Alpha-01|  1.03162***       .25056918      4.117     .0000                   |
+-----------+Standard Deviations of Random Thresholds                               |
|Alpha-01|     .000***    ......(Fixed Parameter).......                        |
+-----------+Variables in Random Thresholds                                         |
|ADDTIM  |   2.24714***       .14484003     15.515     .0000                   |
|GENDER  |    .61618***       .08785327      7.014     .0000                   |
+-----------+Standard Deviations of Random Regression Parameters                    |
|Constant|     .000***    ......(Fixed Parameter).......                        |
|NTB     |     .000***    ......(Fixed Parameter).......                        |
|NALTS1  |     .000***    ......(Fixed Parameter).......                        |
|FFTD    |     .000***    ......(Fixed Parameter).......                        |
|CONGT1D |    .36898***       .14216626      2.595     .0094                   |
|ADDTIM  |     .000***    ......(Fixed Parameter).......                        |
+-----------+Heteroscedasticity in Latent Regression Equation                       |
|FFTD    |   -.03170***       .00904323     -3.505     .0005                   |
|NLVLS   |    .21577***       .07512713      2.872     .0041                   |
|WHOPAY  |   -.62202***       .09368992     -6.639     .0000                   |
+-----------+------------------------------------------------------------------------+
| Note: ***, **, * = Significance at 1%, 5%, 10% level.                         |
+-------------------------------------------------------------------------------+

+-------------------------------------------------------------------------------+
|Fixed Parameter... indicates a parameter that is constrained to equal |
|a fixed value (e.g., 0) or a serious estimation problem. If you did   |
|not impose a restriction on the parameter, check for previous errors.|
+-------------------------------------------------------------------------------+

=================================================================================
||Summary of Marginal Effects for Ordered Probability Model (probit)  ||
||Effects are computed by averaging  over observs. during simulations.||
=================================================================================
||          Regression Variable ONE              Regression Variable NTB
||          ==============================      ==============================
Outcome   Effect  dPy<=nn/dX dPy>=nn/dX      Effect  dPy<=nn/dX dPy>=nn/dX
======    ==============================      ==============================
Y = 00    -.49177    -.49177      .00000     -.27402     -.27402      .00000
Y = 01     .45903    -.03274      .49177      .25577     -.01824      .27402
Y = 02     .03274     .00000      .03274      .01824      .00000      .01824
```

```
==========================================================================
||          Regression Variable NALTS1        Regression Variable FFTD
||          ==============================     ==============================
Outcome    Effect  dPy<=nn/dX dPy>=nn/dX       Effect  dPy<=nn/dX dPy>=nn/dX
=======    ==============================      ==============================
Y = 00     .19450     .19450     .00000       -.01017    -.01017     .00000
Y = 01    -.18155     .01295    -.19450        .00949    -.00068     .01017
Y = 02    -.01295     .00000    -.01295        .00068     .00000     .00068
==========================================================================
||          Regression Variable CONGT1D       Regression Variable ADDTIM
||          ==============================     ==============================
Outcome    Effect  dPy<=nn/dX dPy>=nn/dX       Effect  dPy<=nn/dX dPy>=nn/dX
=======    ==============================      ==============================
Y = 00     .02063     .02063     .00000        .06807     .06807     .00000
Y = 01    -.01925     .00137    -.02063       -.06354     .00453    -.06807
Y = 02    -.00137     .00000    -.00137       -.00453     .00000    -.00453
==========================================================================
Indirect Partial Effects for Ordered Choice Model
Variables in thresholds
Outcome   ADDTIM       GENDER
Y = 00    .000000      .000000
Y = 01    .065100      .017851
Y = 02   -.065100     -.017851
Variables in disturbance variance
Outcome   FFTD         NLVLS        WHOPAY
Y = 00    .002556     -.017397      .050153
Y = 01   -.001512      .010293     -.029673
Y = 02   -.001044      .007104     -.020479
```

19 Combining sources of data

19.1 Introduction

This chapter provides a review of the methods in practice, and advances in recent years, of ways of combining revealed preference (RP) and stated preference (SP) data in the estimation and application of choice models. The focus is on both the theory underlying the pooling of data sources as a guide to relevant practice, as well as a step by step outline of how choice models are structured and estimated. We use a mode choice example involving existing and new modes to illustrate the practicalities of application.

Choice model specification, estimation, and application has a very long history, centered originally on the use of RP data. Behavior observed in an actual market through the collection of RP data contains information about a current market equilibrium process. Figure 19.1(a) shows a simple transport example of a market with five modes (walk, bicycle, bus, train, and car) and certain cost and speed characteristics.

The technology frontier reflected in choice data collected from an existing market can be characterized by the following (Louviere *et al.* 2000):

- *Technological relationships*: By definition, RP data describes only those alternatives that exist, which implies that existing attribute levels and correlations between attributes will be in any model estimated from such data.
- *Product sets*: Products are either in or not in a particular market, so it may be difficult to separate product-related effects from attribute impacts. For example, the product "train" carries with it a series of images and associations that may not be separable from certain forms of access modes and associated levels of service, fare, and travel time.
- *Market and personal constraints*: Market and personal constraints are reflected in such data. The embodiment of constraints in real market data

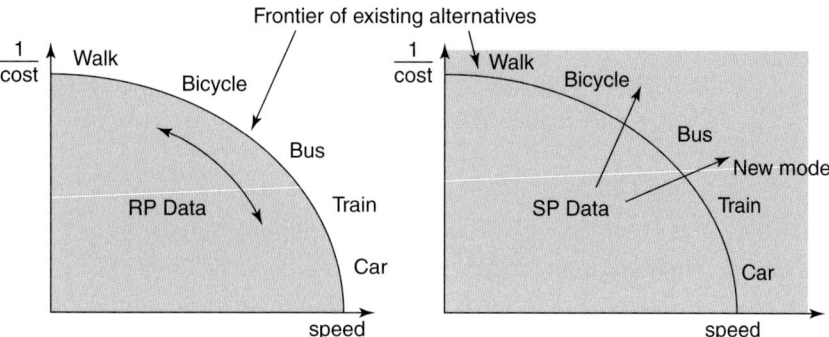

Figure 19.1 SP and RP data generation process

are generally a good thing, but some activities are directed towards such constraints, and RP data may not contain sufficient variability to permit identification of such effects.

RP data have high reliability and face validity in terms of the actual choice reported (after all, these are real choices made by individuals who committed their actual, limited resources to make the choices possible). There remains concern about the reliability of data on attributes associated with non-chosen alternatives. RP data are particularly well suited to short-term forecasting of small departures from the current state of affairs, which emphasizes the tactical nature of the support that RP-based models can give. On the other hand, these same characteristics make RP data quite inflexible, and often inappropriate, if we wish to forecast to a different market than the historical one. Shifts in the technological frontier, as opposed to movements along the frontier, call for different data. Figure 19.1(b) shows how SP data come into their own. SP choice data can be used to model existing markets (including the stretching of attribute levels of existing alternatives that are not observed in real markets), but its strengths become even more apparent if we wish to consider fundamentally different markets than existing ones. Some of the characteristics of SP data are as follows:

- *Technological relationships*: Within reason, SP data can cover a much wider range of attributes and levels than RP data. Technological relationships can be whatever the experiment designer wishes (although attribute correlations often are built into SP experiments), so that SP models tend to be more robust than RP models;

- *Product sets*: Like technology, product presence/absence can be designed into SP data. It is also possible to explore issues like line and/or brand extensions (e.g., Lufthansa Airlines' vacation packages), co-branding (e.g., Qantas and British Airways) without costly investments in actual market trials.
- *Market and personal constraints*: Market constraints often can be simulated and observed with SP data, either with attribute levels or presence/absence manipulations. In fact, even information availability issues (e.g., real market advertising and/or word-of-mouth) can be studied via SP methods, although these typically are more limited than would be the case in real markets. It is generally difficult to simulate changes in personal constraints in SP tasks and obtain meaningful results.

Thus, SP data can capture a wider and broader array of preference-driven behaviors than RP data. SP data are particularly rich in attribute trade-off information, because wider attribute ranges can be built into experiments, which in turn allows models estimated from SP data to be more robust than models estimated from RP data (see Louviere *et al.* 2000; Rose and Bliemer 2008). On the other hand, SP data are hypothetical and experience difficulty taking into account certain types of real market constraints; hence, SP-derived models may not predict well in an existing market *without* calibration of alternative-specific constants (ASCs) (as discussed in Chapters 6 and 10). As a consequence, SP-derived models may be more appropriate to predict structural changes that occur over longer time periods, although experience suggests that they also perform well in short-run prediction *if* calibrated to initial conditions.

Given that each type of data has strengths and weaknesses, there is appeal in exploiting the strengths and ameliorating the weaknesses. The process of pooling RP and SP data and estimating a model from the pooled data, called *data enrichment*, is the way to achieve this. This process, originally proposed by Morikawa (1989), was to use SP data to help identify parameters that RP data could not, and thereby improve the efficiency (i.e., obtain more precise and stable estimates) of model parameters. Early contributions to this literature are Ben-Akiva and Morikawa (1991); Ben-Akiva, Morikawa, and Shiroishi (1991); Bradley and Daly (1994); Hensher and Bradley (1993); Hensher (1998). A common theme of this paradigm is that RP data are viewed as the standard of comparison, and SP data are seen as useful only to the extent that they ameliorate certain undesirable characteristics of RP data.

The "data enrichment paradigm" view is illustrated in Figure 19.2 (from Louviere, Hensher, and Swait 2000), which suggests that the analyst's goal is to

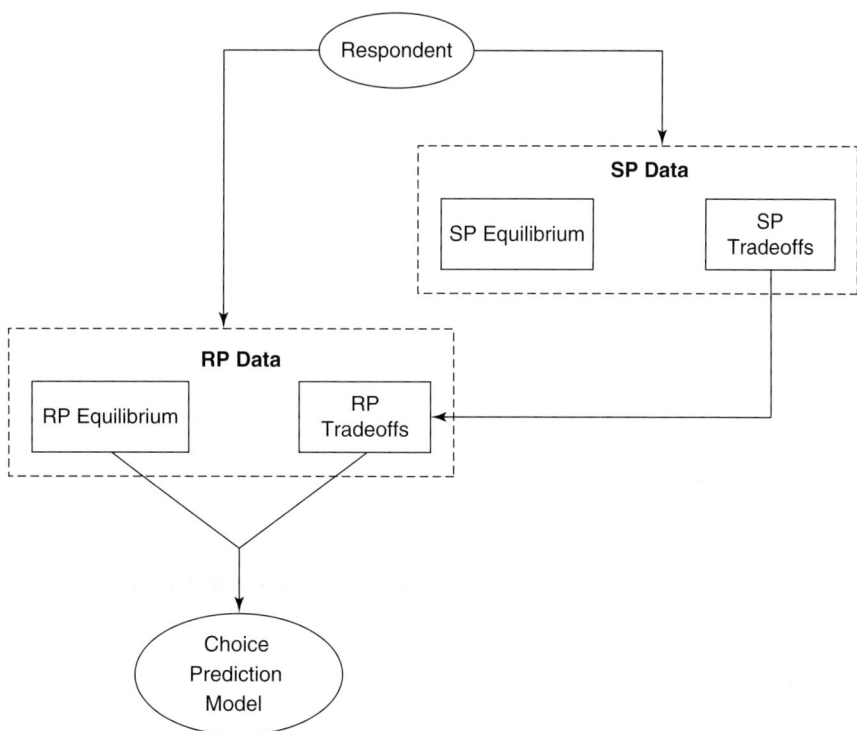

Figure 19.2 Enrichment Paradigm 1

produce a model that can forecast in real market future scenarios. RP data are collected that contain information about the equilibrium and attribute trade-offs in a particular current market. The RP information (especially the attribute trade-offs) may be deficient (i.e., identification may be problematic, or efficiency low), and hence SP data are also collected, although the RP and SP data may come from the same or different individuals. Significantly, the only SP information used involves the attribute trade-offs, which are pooled with the RP data to derive a final choice model.

The choice sets need not be the same across the two data sources (i.e., the alternatives, attributes, and/or attribute levels may differ). The combination of two data sources will allow the analyst to estimate models using information that, if they had only one of the data sources available, they might not otherwise have been able to estimate due to missing data on attributes or attribute levels. The ability to include non-existent alternatives and manipulate currently non-experienced attributes and attribute levels via an SP choice experiment is appealing. In cases where an alternative is present in

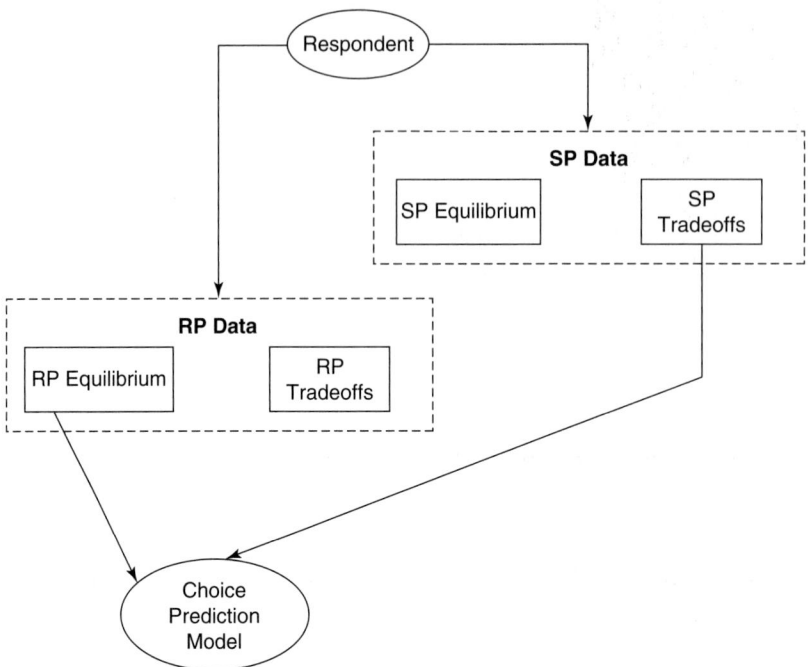

Figure 19.3 Enrichment Paradigm 2

the RP data set but not the SP data set, the analyst will have no other option but to use the RP data (ill conditioned or not) to estimate the preference function for that alternative. Similarly, where an alternative is present within the SP component of a data set but not within the RP component, the analyst will have to use the SP data to obtain the preference function for that alternative, including the SP ASCs. Indeed the only circumstance when the SP ASCs are of relevance is when there is not an RP equivalent alternative.

A different view is represented by the work of Swait, Louviere, and Williams (1994), and illustrated in Figure 19.3. Their view is that each source of data should be used to capture those aspects of the choice process for which it is superior. For example, RP data are used to obtain current market equilibria, but the trade-off information contained in RP data are ignored because of its deficiencies. SP data typically cover multiple "markets," or at least a wider range than a single RP market, hence the trade-off information in SP is used, but equilibrium information is ignored. With regard to the latter, SP data provide information about equilibria over a large range of situations not necessarily directly relevant to the final objective, namely prediction in an actual RP market.

Suppose two preference data sources are available, one RP and another SP, and both deal with the same form of behavior (say, choice of commuter mode). Each data source has a vector of attributes, and at least some of them are common to both data sets. For purposes of exposition, let the common attributes be X^{RP} and X^{SP} in the RP and SP data sets, respectively, and let there also be unique attributes Z and W, respectively, for each data set. Invoking the now familiar random utility framework (see Chapter 3), we assume that the latent utility underlying the choice process in both data sets is given by Equations (19.1) and (19.2):

$$U_i^{RP} = \alpha_i^{RP} + \beta^{RP} X_i^{RP} + \omega Z_i + \varepsilon_i^{RP}, \forall i \in C^{RP} \tag{19.1}$$

$$U_i^{SP} = \alpha_i^{SP} + \beta^{SP} X_i^{SP} + \delta W_i + \varepsilon_i^{SP}, \forall i \in C^{SP}, \tag{19.2}$$

where i is an alternative in choice sets C^{RP} or C^{SP}, αs are data source-specific ASCs, β^{RP} and β^{SP} are utility parameters for the common attributes, and ω and δ are utility parameters or parameters for the unique attributes in each data set. The choice sets need not be the same in the two data sources, and in fact the alternatives need not be the same. One attraction of SP data is its ability to manipulate and observe the effects on choice of introducing new alternatives and/or removing existing ones from consideration.

If we assume that the unobserved influences or error terms in Equations (19.1) and (19.2) are independent and identically distributed (IID) Extreme value type 1 (EV1) within both data sources that are associated, respectively, with scale factors λ^{RP} and λ^{SP} (see Chapter 3, and Ben Akiva and Lerman 1985), the corresponding multinomial logit (MNL) choice models can be expressed as follows:

$$P_i^{RP} = \frac{\exp[\lambda^{RP}(\alpha_i^{RP} + \beta^{RP} X_i^{RP} + \omega Z_i)]}{\sum\limits_{j \in C^{RP}} \exp[\lambda^{RP}(\alpha_j^{RP} + \beta^{RP} X_j^{RP} + \omega Z_j)]}, \forall i \in C^{RP}. \tag{19.3}$$

$$P_i^{SP} = \frac{\exp[\lambda^{SP}(\alpha_i^{SP} + \beta^{SP} X_i^{SP} + \delta W_i)]}{\sum\limits_{j \in C^{SP}} \exp[\lambda^{SP}(\alpha_j^{SP} + \beta^{SP} X_j^{SP} + \delta W_j)]}, \forall i \in C^{SP}. \tag{19.4}$$

The scale factor plays a crucial role in the data enrichment process. Equations (19.3) and (19.4) make it clear that any particular scale factor and the parameters of its associated choice model are inseparable and multiplicative ($\lambda \kappa$), where κ is some parameter vector. Thus, it is not possible to identify a scale factor *within* a particular data source under MNL. Nonetheless, the scale factor associated with any data source fundamentally affects the values of the estimated parameters, such that the larger (smaller) the scale, the bigger (smaller) the parameters.

There is an identification problem because scale (λ) and utility (β) parameters are confounded and cannot be separated in any one data source which, in turn, implies that *one cannot directly compare parameters from different choice models*. For example, one cannot compare the travel time coefficients from two data sources directly to determine whether one is larger than the other. In particular, one cannot determine whether the observed difference is the result of differences in scale, true parameters, or both. Even if two data sources were generated by the *same utility function* (i.e., the same β parameters), but have different scale factors λ_1 and λ_2, the estimated parameters will differ (in one case they are $\lambda_1\beta$, and in the other $\lambda_2\beta$).

Let us return to comparing two data sources that we believe reflect the same utilities, but (potentially) different scales. For example, in combining RP and SP data, the key question is whether $(\lambda_1\beta_1) = (\lambda_2\beta_2)$. We can rearrange the latter expression to obtain $\beta_1 = (\lambda_2/\lambda_1)\,\beta_2$. The scale factor in an MNL model is *inversely* related to the variance of the error term as follows for all alternatives and respondents (see Chapter 3):

$$\sigma^2 = \pi^2/6\lambda^2. \tag{19.5}$$

Thus, the higher the scale, the smaller the variance, which in turn implies that models that fit well will also display larger scales. The implication of these observations about the behavior of the scale parameter is that it plays a role in choice models that is rather unique compared to more familiar statistical models like ordinary least squares (OLS) regression (with which many researchers are acquainted). That is, the model parameters and the characteristics of the error terms are intimately (even inextricably!) related. In the case of choice models, it is necessary to think of the variance (or, equivalently, *scale*) as an integral part of the model specification instead of being a nuisance parameter. The relationship between mean and variance exhibited by the MNL model also is a property shared by many other choice model forms, such as nested logit (NL) and mixed logit (ML).

Our primary interest lies in testing the equality of the parameter vectors for SP and RP data. The process of combining the two data sources involves imposing the restriction that *the common attributes* have the same parameters in both data sources, i.e., $\beta^{RP} = \beta^{SP} = \beta$. However, because of the scale factor,

things are not so simple. Since the estimated model parameters are confounded with the scale factors for each data set (see Equations (19.3) and
(19.4)); even after imposing the restriction of common attribute parameter
equality, we still must account for the scale factors, as shown in Equations
(19.6) and (19.7) (note the absence of the superscript for β compared to
Equations (19.4) and (19.5)):

$$P_i^{RP} = \frac{\exp[\lambda^{RP}(\alpha_i^{RP} + \beta X_i^{RP} + \omega Z_i)]}{\sum\limits_{j \in C^{RP}} \exp[\lambda^{RP}(\alpha_j^{RP} + \beta X_j^{RP} + \omega Z_j)]}, \quad \forall i \in C^{RP}. \tag{19.6}$$

$$P_i^{SP} = \frac{\exp[\lambda^{SP}(\alpha_i^{SP} + \beta X_i^{SP} + \delta W_i)]}{\sum\limits_{j \in C^{SP}} \exp[\lambda^{SP}(\alpha_j^{SP} + \beta X_j^{SP} + \delta W_j)]}, \quad \forall i \in C^{SP}. \tag{19.7}$$

Equations 19.6 and 19.7 make it clear that if we wish to pool these two data
sources to obtain a better estimate of β, we cannot avoid controlling for the
scale factors. Data enrichment involves pooling the two choice data sources
under the restriction that common parameters are equal, while controlling for
the scale factors. Thus, the pooled data should enable us to estimate α^{RP}, β, ω,
λ^{RP}, α^{SP}, δ, and λ^{SP}. However, we cannot identify both scale factors, so one
must be normalized. It is conventional to assume that the scale of the RP data
set is one ($\lambda^{RP} \equiv 1$), and so the estimate of λ^{SP} represents a *relative scale* with
respect to the RP data scale. Equivalently, we can view the problem as
estimating the SP variance relative to the RP variance ($\sigma_{RP}^2 = \pi^2/6$).

The final parameter vector to be jointly estimated is $\psi = (\alpha^{RP}, \beta, \omega, \alpha^{SP}, \delta,$
$\lambda^{SP})$. Assuming that the two data sources come from independent samples, the
LL of the pooled data is simply the sum of the multinomial log likelihoods of
the RP and SP data:

$$L(\psi) = \sum_{n \in RP} \sum_{i \in C_n^{SP}} y_{in} \ln P_{in}^{RP}(X_{in}^{RP}, Z_{in}|\alpha^{RP}, \beta, \omega)$$

$$+ \sum_{n \in SP} \sum_{i \in C_n^{RP}} y_{in} \ln P_{in}^{SP}(X_{in}^{SP}, W_{in}|\alpha^{SP}, \beta, \delta, \lambda^{SP}). \tag{19.8}$$

$y_{in} - 1$ if person n chooses alternative i, and $= 0$ otherwise. This function must
be maximized with respect to ψ to determine the ML parameter estimates,
which can be accomplished in several ways, but we outline one of the easier
methods (known as the NL "trick") before introducing a more complex state
of the art method using ML and error components.

19.2 The nested logit "trick"

A full information maximum likelihood (FIML) method to estimate model parameters and relative scale factor(s) simultaneously optimize Equation (19.8) with respect to all parameters. To pool the RP and SP data, we have to assume that the data generation process for both data sources is IID EV1 with different scale factors, but location (or mean) parameters that share some components but also have other unique components. Thus, MNL choice models must underlie the choices within each data source, as in Equations (19.6) and (19.7).

Now consider Figure 19.4, which illustrates a nested logit (NL) model with two levels and two clusters (or branches) of alternatives. Cluster 1 contains alternatives in the set C_1, and Cluster 2 alternatives in the set C_2. NL models are a hierarchy of MNL models, linked via a tree structure. MNL models underlie the data within each cluster, hence the constant variance (i.e., scale) assumption must hold within clusters. However, between clusters, scale factors can differ. By explicitly accommodating different variances between clusters, NL provides a simple way to accomplish the estimation required to fuse the RP and SP data sources.

The standard MNL model for each branch is given in Equations (19.9) and (19.10):

$$P(i|C_i) = \frac{\exp[V_i/\theta_1]}{\sum\limits_{j \in C_1} \exp[V_j/\theta_1]}. \tag{19.9}$$

$$P(k|C_2) = \frac{\exp[V_k/\theta_2]}{\sum\limits_{j \in C2} \exp[V_j/\theta_2]}. \tag{19.10}$$

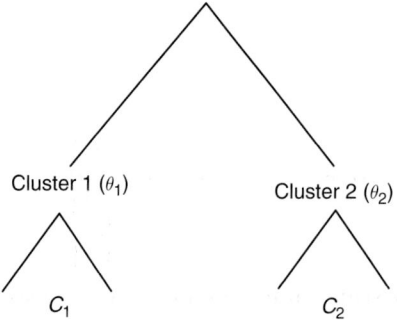

Cluster 1 (θ_1) Cluster 2 (θ_2)

C_1 C_2

Figure 19.4   Two-level, two-nest NMNL model

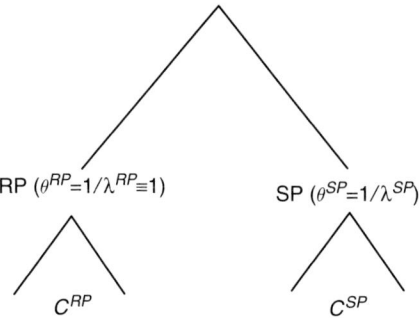

Figure 19.5   Combining SP and RP data using the NMNL model

V_i is the systematic portion of the utility of alternative i. The inclusive value parameters θ_1 and θ_2 play an interesting role in Equations (19.9) and (19.10). That is, the systematic utility of all alternatives in the respective sub-nest of the tree is multiplied by the inverse of the inclusive value. The choice model in each sub-nest is MNL, which implies that the scale of the utilities of the sub-nest is equal to the inverse of the sub-nest inclusive value. The ratio of the variances for the two clusters is given in Equation (19.11):

$$\frac{\sigma_1^2}{\sigma_2^2} = \frac{\pi^2/6\lambda_1^2}{\pi^2/6\lambda_2^2} = \frac{1/\lambda_1^2}{1/\lambda_2^2} = \left(\frac{\theta_1}{\theta_2}\right)^2. \tag{19.11}$$

Imagine that Cluster 1 in Figure 19.4 was renamed "RP" and Cluster 2 renamed "SP," as in Figure 19.5. Thus, if we estimate a NL model from the two data sources, we obtain an estimate of the scale factor of one data set relative to that of the other, and our estimation objective is accomplished. This approach was proposed by Bradley and Daly (1993) and Hensher and Bradley (1993), who called the hierarchy in Figure 19.5 an *artificial tree structure*. That is, the tree has no obvious behavioral meaning, but is a useful modeling convenience. Nlogit as a NL model (see Chapter 14) can be used to obtain FIML estimates of the inverse of the relative scale factors. One can identify only one of the relative scale factors, so Figure 19.5 normalizes the inclusive value of the RP data to unity.

The nested structure in Figure 19.5 assumes that the inclusive value parameter(s) associated with all SP alternatives are equal, and fixes the RP inclusive value parameter to unity. This assumption allows one to identify and estimate the variance, and hence scale parameter, of the SP data set relative to the RP normalization, but forces within data set homoskedasticity.

Importantly, however, the NL estimation approach to the identification and estimation of relative scale ratios can be readily generalized. For example, another tree structure can be proposed that will allow scale parameters of each SP alternative to be estimated relative to that of all RP alternatives (as shown in Hensher 1998). Further generalization is possible if one treats the entire artificial tree as a set of degenerate alternatives (i.e., each cluster is a single alternative), resulting in a unique scale parameter for each alternative. This is essentially the heteroskedastic extreme value (HEV) model, introduced initially by Bhat (1995). However, identification conditions should be carefully evaluated before undertaking either exercise.

This procedure has been used successfully in searching for an improved behavioral structure for alternatives associated with one source of preference data (i.e., SP *or* RP data) as well as for multiple sources of preference data (e.g., combined SP *and* RP data). In the RP–SP context, it was referred to by Hensher and Bradley as "a trick," in the sense that the underlying conditions to comply with utility maximization such as the 0–1 bound on the inclusive value variable linking two levels in a nest (McFadden 1981), while applicable between alternatives *within* SP and *within* RP choice sets, are not relevant *between* data sets – the scale difference between data sets (typically normalizing to unity on one data source) is the only agenda.

In the majority of NL applications, the predictability of the set of NL structures studied is driven by the revelation of differences in SP–RP scale parameters and/or the partitioning of alternatives within a given data set in what is best described as "commonsense" or intuitive partitions; for example, the marginal choice between car and public transport and then the choice between bus and train, conditional on choosing public transport. Hensher (1999) generalized the role of scale parameters through the use of the heteroskedastic HEV search engine to allow for differences in scale, as a guide to a "preferred" NL structure,[1] not only between data sets but between alternatives within and between data sets.

Common practice associated with the pooling of SP–RP data sources is to discard the RP parameter estimates and the SP constant terms and use the remaining parameters to form composite utility functions for a travel demand prediction model. For SP alternatives with no corresponding RP alternative, we have no choice but to use the SP constant terms. In discarding the

---

[1] The NL structure is an econometric formulation to account for differences in variance of the unobserved effects, or scale differences. While analysts tend to use behavioral intuition in partitioning the nest, this is not the basis of nesting. Hence it is quite feasible for mixtures of SP and RP alternatives to reside in the one branch.

parameter estimates from the RP data set and retaining the constant terms, it is necessary in creating the composite utility functions to recalibrate the RP constant terms. To demonstrate why, consider Equation (19.12), that is the equation used to calculate constant terms in discrete choice models:

$$\beta_{0i}^{RP} = \overline{V}_i^{RP} - \sum_{k=1}^{k} \beta_k^{RP} \overline{x}_k^{RP}. \tag{19.12}$$

The latter part of Equation (19.12) accounts for the RP parameter estimates that are to be discarded in constructing the composite utility functions while failing to account for the SP parameter estimates that are to be used. So why use the RP attributes in the first place? In estimating the initial SP–RP NL model, the inclusion or exclusion of an attribute in either data set will affect all other parameter estimates within the model. Hence, failure to include the RP attributes in the RP component of the NL model (i.e., simply estimate the RP model with constants only) will impact upon the SP parameter estimates obtained from the model. Thus it is necessary, despite potential problems with RP parameter estimates (given data issues), to include the RP attributes in the model, otherwise all information for these components will be accounted for solely by the unobserved effects of the RP utility functions which enter the utility functions through the $\overline{V}_i^{RP}$ (nevertheless, at the same time, the constant terms will preserve information on the choice shares within the data set).

The calibration of the RP constant terms occurs through Equation (19.13):

$$\beta_{0i}^{RP} = \overline{V}_i^{RP} - \sum_{k=1}^{k} \lambda^{SP} \beta_k^{SP} \overline{x}_k^{RP}. \tag{19.13}$$

In Equation (19.13), the RP parameter estimates are replaced by the SP parameter estimates obtained from the initial SP–RP model (taking into account scale differences that may exist between the two data sets) while the remaining components of Equation (19.12) are left as are. To operationalize Equation (19.13) requires the analyst to re-estimate the constant terms of alternatives common across the data sets, fixing the RP parameter estimates to the values observed for the SP parameters. Parameters unique to the RP data set should be allowed to be estimated freely. If population market shares are known, then the estimated model can introduce weights, known as *choice-based weights* (see a later section) to reflect the relationship between the sample shares and the known population shares. The constants associated with the RP alternatives will then approximate the relevant constants without post-calibration. A caveat: if the data used in model estimation is different to the data being used in applications (as is often the case in transport studies where network data are used in application and individual level data in estimation), then further calibration is required.

19.3 Beyond the nested logit "trick"

The NL model is a member of the family of GEV models (McFadden 1981) that cannot accommodate a number of specification requirements of data that have repeated observations from the same respondent. This occurs with SP choice sets that exhibit potential correlation due to repeated observations. In addition to potential observation correlation, joint SP–RP estimation can induce a "state dependence" effect, defined as the influence of the actual (revealed) choice on the stated choices (SCs) of the individual. State dependence can manifest itself as a positive or negative effect of the choice of an alternative on the utility associated with that alternative in the stated responses (Bhat and Castelar 2002). It is a reflection of accumulated experience and the role that reference dependency plays in choosing (Hensher 2006).

It is possible that the effect of state (reference) dependence is positive for some individuals and negative for others (see Ailawadi *et al.*, 1999), suggesting that an unconstrained analytical distribution for the random parameterization of state dependence is appropriate. A positive effect may be the result of habit persistence, inertia to explore another alternative, or learning combined with risk aversion. A negative effect could be the result of variety seeking or the result of latent frustration with the inconvenience associated with the currently used alternative (Bhat and Castelar 2002).

Most SP–RP studies disregard state dependence and adopt fixed parameters (i.e., homogeneity of attribute preference). Bhat and Castelar (2002) accommodate such unobserved heterogeneity in the state dependence effect of the RP choice on SP choices. Brownstone and Train (1999), on the other hand, accommodate observed heterogeneity in the state dependence effect by interacting the RP choice dummy variable with the socio-demographic characteristics of the individual and SP choice attributes.

This section outlines a ML model (as per Chapter 15) that can account for a between alternative error structure including correlated choice sets, SP–RP scale difference, unobserved preference heterogeneity, and state or reference dependency. It draws on contributions from Bhat and Castelar (2002). An empirical example is used to illustrate the direct elasticity differences between the traditional NL "trick" model and the more flexible ML model.

We begin with the basic form of the MNL model, with alternative specific constants, α_{ji}, and attributes, x_{ji}, for individuals i = 1,. . .,N in choice setting t and a choice set comprising a number of alternatives including the qth and the jth:

$$\text{Prob}(y_{it} = j_t) = \frac{\exp(\alpha_{ji} + \beta'_i x_{jit})}{\sum_{q=1}^{J_i} \exp(\alpha_{qi} + \beta'_i x_{qit})}. \tag{19.14}$$

The random parameter model emerges as the form of the individual-specific parameter vector, β_i. The most familiar, simplest version of the model (see Chapter 14) specifies:

$$\beta_{ki} = \beta_k + \sigma_k v_{ik},$$

and, $\qquad\qquad\qquad\qquad\qquad\qquad\qquad\qquad\qquad\qquad\qquad$ (19.15)

$$\alpha_{ji} = \alpha_j + \sigma_j v_{ji},$$

where β_k is the population mean, v_{ik} is the individual-specific heterogeneity, with mean zero and standard deviation one, and σ_k is the standard deviation of the distribution of β_{ik}s around β_k. The choice specific constants, α_{ji}, and the elements of β_i are distributed randomly across individuals with fixed means. The v_{jki}s are individual and choice-specific unobserved random disturbances – the source of the heterogeneity. For the full vector of K random coefficients in the model, we may write the full set of random parameters as:

$$\rho_i = \rho + \Gamma v_i, \tag{19.16}$$

where Γ is a diagonal matrix which contains σ_k on its diagonal. For convenience, we gather the parameters, choice-specific or not, under the subscript "k." We can allow the random parameters to be correlated by allowing Γ to be a triangular matrix with non-zero elements below the main diagonal, producing the full covariance matrix of the random coefficients as $\Sigma = \Gamma\Gamma'$. The standard case of uncorrelated coefficients has $\Gamma = \text{diag}(\sigma_1, \sigma_2, \ldots, \sigma_k)$. If the coefficients are freely correlated, Γ is a full, unrestricted, lower triangular matrix and Σ will have non-zero off-diagonal elements.

An additional layer of individual heterogeneity may be added to the model in the form of the error components that capture influences that are related to alternatives, in contrast to attributes (see also Chapter 15). We do this by constructing a set of independent individual terms, E_{im}, m = 1,..., M ~ N[0,1], that can be added to the utility functions. This device allows us to create what amounts to a random effects model and, in addition, a very general type of nesting of alternatives. Let θ_m be the scale parameter (standard deviation) associated with these effects. Then, each utility function can be constructed as:

$$U_{ijt} = \alpha_{ji} + \boldsymbol{\beta}_j' \mathbf{x}_{jit} + (\text{any of } \theta_1 E_{i1}, \theta_2 E_{i2}, \ldots, \theta_M E_{iM}). \tag{19.17}$$

Consider, for example, a four-outcome structure:

$$
\begin{aligned}
U_{i1t} &= V_{i1t} + \theta_1 E_{i1} + \theta_2 E_{i2} \\
U_{i2t} &= V_{i2t} + \qquad\qquad \theta_2 E_{i2} \\
U_{i3t} &= V_{i3t} + \theta_1 E_{i1} \qquad\quad + \theta_3 E_{i3} \\
U_{i4t} &= V_{i4t} \qquad\qquad\qquad\qquad\quad + \theta_4 E_{i4}
\end{aligned}
$$

Thus, U_{i4t} has its own uncorrelated effect, but there is a correlation between U_{i1t} and U_{i2t} and between U_{i1t} and U_{i3t}. This example is fully populated, so the covariance matrix is block diagonal with the first three freely correlated. The model might usefully be restricted in a specific application. A convenient way to allow different structures is to introduce the binary variables, $d_{jm} = 1$, if the random term E_m appears in utility function j and zero otherwise. The full model with all components is given in Equation (19.18), based on Greene and Hensher (2007):

$$\text{Prob}(y_{it} = j) = \frac{\exp\left[\alpha_{ji} + \boldsymbol{\beta}_i' \mathbf{x}_{jit} + \sum_{m=1}^{M} d_{jm} \theta_m E_m\right]}{\sum_{q=1}^{J_i} \exp\left[\alpha_{qi} + \boldsymbol{\beta}_i' \mathbf{x}_{qit} + \sum_{m=1}^{M} d_{qm} \theta_m E_{im}\right]}. \tag{19.18}$$

$(\alpha_{ji}, \boldsymbol{\beta}_i) = (\alpha_j, \boldsymbol{\beta}) + \boldsymbol{\Gamma}\boldsymbol{\Omega}_i \mathbf{v}_i$ are random ASCs and taste parameters; $\boldsymbol{\Omega}_i = \text{diag}(\omega_{i1}, \omega_{i2}, \ldots)$ and $\boldsymbol{\beta}, \alpha_{ji}$ are constant terms in the distributions of the random taste parameters. Elements ω of the variance-covariance matrix represent the full generalized matrix. Uncorrelated parameters with homogenous means and variances are defined by $\beta_{ik} = \beta_k + \sigma_k v_{ik}$ when $\boldsymbol{\Gamma} = \mathbf{I}$, $\boldsymbol{\Omega}_i = \text{diag}(\sigma_1, \ldots, \sigma_k)$, $\mathbf{x}_{jit}$ are observed choice attributes and individual characteristics, and v_i is random unobserved taste variation, with mean vector 0 and covariance matrix I. The individual specific underlying random error components are introduced through the term

E_{im}, $m = 1,\ldots,M$, $E_{im} \sim N[0,1]$, given $d_{jm} = 1$ if E_{im} appears in utility for alternative j and 0 otherwise, and θ_m is a dispersion factor for error component m.

The probabilities defined above are conditioned on the random terms, v_i, and the error components, E_i. The unconditional probabilities are obtained by integrating v_{ik} and E_{im} out of the conditional probabilities: $P_j = E_{v,E}[P(j|v_i,E_i)]$. This multiple integral, which does not exist in closed form, is approximated by sampling *nrep* draws from the assumed populations and averaging. See, for example, Bhat (2003); Revelt and Train (1998); Train (2003); Brownstone *et al.* (2000) for discussion. Parameters are estimated by maximizing the simulated log likelihood given in Equation (19.19):

$$\log L_s = \sum\nolimits_{i=1}^{N} \log \frac{1}{R} \sum\nolimits_{r=1}^{R} \prod\nolimits_{t=1}^{T_i} \frac{\exp[\alpha_{ji} + \boldsymbol{\beta}'_{ir}\mathbf{x}_{jit} + \Sigma_{m=1}^{M} d_{jm}\theta_m E_{im,r}]}{\sum\nolimits_{q=1}^{J_i} \exp[\alpha_{qi} + \boldsymbol{\beta}'_{ir}\mathbf{x}_{qit} + \Sigma_{m=1}^{M} d_{qm}\theta_m E_{im,r}]}$$

(19.19)

with respect to $(\beta, \Gamma, \Omega, \theta)$, where R = the number of replications, $\beta_{ir} = \beta + \Gamma\Omega_i v_{ir}$ is the rth draw on β_i, v_{ir} is the rth multivariate draw for individual i, and $E_{im,r}$ is the rth univariate normal draw on the underlying effect for individual i. The multivariate draw, v_{ir}, is actually K independent draws. Heteroskedasticity is induced first by multiplying by Ω_i, then the correlation is induced by multiplying $\Omega_i v_{ir}$ by Γ.

The ASCs in Equation (19.19) are linked to the Extreme value Type 1 (EV1) distribution for the random terms, after accounting for unobserved heterogeneity induced via distributions imposed on the observed attributes, and the unobserved heterogeneity that is alternative-specific and accounted for by the error components. The error components account for correlated observations across choice sets administered to individual i as well as unobserved (to the analyst) differences across decision makers in the intrinsic preference for a choice alternative (or preference heterogeneity). The parameter associated with each error component is $\delta\sigma$, neither of which appears elsewhere in the model. We induce meaning by treating this parameter pair as θ, which identifies the variance of the alternative-specific heterogeneity. What we are measuring is variation around the mean, hence the reference to a dispersion parameter.

Some specific features of the model of interest in joint estimation with multiple data sets are the possibility of "state (reference) dependence" engendered in the SP data as a derivative of an RP market context; and the differences in the scale parameters for the SP data relative to the RP data. Formally, state dependence is defined (Bhat and Castelar 2002) as:

$$\varphi_q(1 - \delta_{qt,RP}), \tag{19.20}$$

where $\delta_{qt,RP} = 1$ if an RP observation, 0 otherwise, and φ_q is the parameter estimate of state dependence which can be fixed or random. This variable enters the utility expression for each SP alternative, with the capability to select a generic specification.

The scale parameter for one data set (or set of alternatives) relative to the other set, the latter normalized to 1.0, is obtained through the introduction in one data set, the SP data,[2] of a set of ASCs that have a zero mean and free variance (Brownstone et al. 2000). The scale parameter is calculated using the formula in Equation (19.21):

$$\lambda_{qt} = [(1 - \delta_{qt,RP})\lambda] + \delta_{qt,RP}, \tag{19.21}$$

where $\delta_{qt,RP}$ is as defined as above and λ is inversely proportional to the estimated standard deviation of the ASC of an alternative, according to the EV1 distribution, where $\lambda = \pi/\sqrt{6}\text{StdDev} = 1.28255/\text{Std Dev of ASC}$.

This model with error components for each alternative is identified. Unlike other specifications (e.g., Ben-Akiva et al. 2002) that apply the results to identifying the scale factors in the disturbances in the marginal distributions of the utility functions, the logic does not apply to identifying the parameters on the attributes; and in the conditional distribution we are looking at here, the error components are acting like attributes, not disturbances. We are estimating the θ parameters as if they were weights on attributes, not scales on disturbances, and hence the way that the conditional distribution is presented. The parameters are identified in the same way that the βs on the attributes are identified. Since the error components are not observed, their scale is not identified. Hence, the parameter on the error component is $(\delta_m\sigma_m)$, where σ_m is the standard deviation. Since the scale is unidentified, we would normalize it to one for estimation purposes, with the understanding that the sign and magnitude of the weight on the component are carried by θ. The sign of δ_m is not identified, since the same set of model results will emerge if the sign of every draw on the component were reversed – the estimator of δ would simply change sign with them. As such, we normalize the sign to plus, and estimate $|\delta_m|$, with the sign and the value of σ_m normalized for identification purposes.

---

[2] We select the SP data set in the empirical application but the RP data set could have been chosen.

19.4 Case study

The data were drawn from a SC experiment that was conducted in six Australian capital cities in the mid 1990s: Sydney, Melbourne, Brisbane, Adelaide, Perth, and Canberra (Hensher *et al.* 2005). The universal choice set comprised the currently available modes plus two "new" modes, light rail and bus-based transitway (often referred to as a busway). Respondents evaluated scenarios describing ways to commute between their current residence and workplace location using different combinations of policy sensitive attributes and levels.

Four alternatives appeared in each travel choice scenario: (a) car drive alone, (b) car ride share, (c) bus or busway, and (d) train or light rail. Twelve types of showcards described scenarios involving combinations of trip length (3) and public transport pairs (4): bus versus light rail, bus versus train (heavy rail), busway versus light rail, and busway versus train. Appearance of public transport pairs in each choice set shown to respondents was based on an experimental design.

Five three-level attributes were used to describe public transport alternatives: (a) total invehicle time, (b) frequency of service, (c) closest stop to home, (d) closest stop to destination, and (e) fare. The attributes of the car alternatives were: (a) travel time, (b) fuel cost, (c) parking cost, (d) travel time variability and, for toll roads, (e) departure times and (f) toll charge.[3] The design allows orthogonal estimation of alternative-specific main effect models for each mode option.

In addition to the SC data, each respondent provided details of a current commuting trip for the chosen mode and one alternative mode. This enabled us to estimate a joint SP and RP model of choice of mode for the commuting trip. The data and detailed descriptions of the sampling process and data profile are provided in the first edition of this book – Hensher *et al.* (2005).

Final models for the NL "trick" model and the ML models have been estimated with and without accounting for the differences in the sample and population shares for the RP alternatives. The population shares for each urban area are given in Table 19.1, and have been used in the models as choice-based weights for the pooled cities' data to adjust the parameters, especially the ASCs for the RP utility expressions. This is necessary when estimating elasticities, given that the formula includes the choice probability

---

[3] In the empirical mode here, we found that the aggregation of fuel and toll costs gave the best statistical fit. The Departure time choice model based on this data is given in Louviere *et al.* (1999).

Table 19.1 Commuter mode share population weights

	Canberra	Sydney	Melbourne	Brisbane	Adelaide	Perth
Drive alone	57.58	48.99	60.12	56.25	60.67	65.02
Ride share	24.18	18.12	17.8	21.0	20.06	18.62
Bus	9.82	9.55	3.29	6.21	8.51	7.61
Train/Tram	0.0	14.74	12.12	7.78	2.53	1.89
Walk	4.14	4.78	3.57	3.63	3.31	2.53
Other	4.28	3.82	3.10	5.13	4.93	4.33
Total Number	131,955	1,557,288	1,348,859	553,697	418,507	45,5024

Source: CDATA91 Census Table: Journey to Work.

for the specific alternative. Deciding if the elasticities are sensitive to allowance for choice-based weighting is an empirical matter, considered below.

The sample modal shares are relatively similar to the population modal shares. In model estimation, we use the population shares based on the first four alternatives only. These four alternatives represent, respectively, 91.58 percent, 91.4 percent, 93.33 percent, 91.28 percent, 91.7 percent, and 93.14 percent of all modal trips to work in the six capital cities.

While choice-based weighting is straightforward in a NL model (as a weighted estimation maximum likelihood (WESML) method), where the estimator is exact and does not use simulation, this is not guaranteed to work with the simulation-based estimators because they do not compute a second derivatives matrix where the method invokes the BHHH estimator. Our software attempts to compute the WESML estimator; however, sometimes its approximation to the Hessian is not positive definite and it reverts to the adjustment of means but with no correction of standard errors. An alternative is exogenous weighting; however, this fix also omits the covariance matrix, and hence the asymptotic standard errors (and hence the *t*-ratios) are not guaranteed to be efficient. The WESML approximation worked on our data due, we suspect, to having sample modal shares that were relatively similar to the population (in brackets) modal shares; namely, 0.61 (0.63), 0.17 (0.22), 0.13 (0.08), and 0.09 (0.07), respectively for the RP alternatives drive alone, ride share, bus and train. However, we warn analysts who might unawaringly assume that choice-based weights apply without question to ML models.

The final models are summarized in Table 19.2. The ML models are a statistically significant improvement in overall goodness of fit after controlling for different numbers of parameters. The level of service variables are generic within the car and public transport modes, and travel cost is generic across all modes. Preference heterogeneity for each of these attributes is accounted for by random parameters. We investigated a large number of analytical distributions, including, normal, lognormal and triangular, and found that the constrained triangular distribution gave the best fit as well as satisfying the negative sign condition of each parameter estimate.[4] The differences in the NL and ML models with and without choice-based weights are small, and hence we focus on interpreting the choice-based weighted models, noting that the only noticeable difference is in the ride share constant, which has been reduced at the mean after the application of the choice-based weighting.

The state (or reference) dependence effect was treated as a random parameter and was also assessed as a constrained and an unconstrained normal and triangular distribution. For this data set we have not been able to establish any statistically significant influence of the actual (revealed) choice on the SCs of the individual, reporting the constrained triangular results in Table 19.2.

The scale parameters for subsets of the SP alternatives were found to be statistically significant and greater than one for the *bus and busway* (1.079) and *train and light rail* (1.20) modes; although not statistically significantly different from 1.0, the normalized value for the RP data. The *car* modes had a scale parameter of 2.367, suggesting a much lower variance on the unobserved effects associated with the EV1 random component; however, it has a *t*-ratio of 1.16. What this suggests is that there is no serious violation of scale differences between the SP and RP data. This may be due in part to the capturing of relevant unobserved heterogeneity through attributes (i.e., random parameters) and alternatives (i.e., error components).

A number of alternative groupings of alternatives in the error components found that combining the *drive alone* mode across the RP and SP data sets gave statistically significant parameter estimate of 2.758 and 1.992, respectively, in contrast to the fixed 1.0 for the full set of public modes (in SP and RP data sets). This suggests that there is substantial unobserved heterogeneity associated with the car alternatives, and especially the car drive alone alternative, that is greater than that associated with the public transport alternatives. This finding is intuitive given the large body of literature that suggests

---

[4] The triangular distribution was first used for random coefficients by Train and Revelt (2000) and Train (2001), later incorporated into Train (2003). Hensher and Greene (2003) also used it and it is increasingly being used in empirical studies. Let c be the center and s the spread. The density starts at c−s, rises linearly to c, and then drops linearly to c+s. It is zero below c−s and above c+s. The mean and mode are c. The standard deviation is the spread divided by $\sqrt{6}$; hence, the spread is the standard deviation times $\sqrt{6}$. The height of the tent at c is 1/s (such that each side of the tent has area s×(1/s)×(1/2)=1/2, and both sides have area 1/2+1/2=1, as required for a density). The slope is $1/s^2$. The mean weighted average elasticities were also statistically equivalent.

Table 19.2 Model results for "nested logit" trick versus panel mixed logit for combined SP and RP choice data

Attribute	Alternative(s)	NL	NL with choice-based weights	ML (RP – EC panel)	ML with choice-based weights
Invehicle cost	All	-0.5802 (-14.7)	-.5880 (-12.7)	R: -.8534 (-14.17)*	R: -.8551 (-14.46)*
Main mode time	SP and RP – DA, RS	-0.0368 (-6.4)	-.0365 (-3.8)	R: -0.1119 (-13.7)*	R: -0.1123 (-13.4)*
Main mode time	SP and RP – BS,TN,LR, BWY	-0.0566 (-8.2)	-.0598 (-8.2)	R: -0.0679 (-8.42)*	R: -0.0680 (-8.39)*
Access & egress mode time	SP and RP – BS,TN,LR, BWY	-0.0374 (-8.5)	-.0370 (-7.3)	R: -0.0524 (-9.72)*	R: -0.0518 (-9.84)*
Personal income	SP and RP – DA	0.0068 (2.30)	.0074 (2.4)	0.01638 (3.46)	0.01684 (3.72)
Drive alone constant	DA – RP	0.7429 (2.48)	1.1381 (3.1)	2.3445 (7.26)	2.3221 (7.31)
Ride share constant	RS – RP	-0.8444 (-3.1)	-.2802 (0.86)	-0.9227 (-2.91)	-0.8301 (-2.65)
Drive alone constant	DA – SP	0.0598 (0.36)	.0324 (0.18)		
Ride share constant	RS – SP	-0.2507 (-1.8)	-.2598 (-1.7)		
Train-specific constant	TN -SP	0.1585 (1.4)	.1655 (1.4)		
Light rail-specific constant	LR – SP	0.3055 (2.81)	.3119 (2.8)		
Busway-specific constant	BWY – SP	-0.016 (-0.14)	-.0171 (-.14)		
Bus-specific constant	BS – RP	0.0214 (0.81)	-.0716 (-.22)	0.1383 (0.51)	0.0709 (0.26)
Random parameter standard deviations:					
Invehicle cost	All			0.8534 (-14.17)*	.8551 (-14.46)*
Main mode time	SP and RP – DA, RS			0.1119 (-13.7)*	0.1123 (-13.4)*
Main mode time	SP and RP – BS,TN,LR, BWY			0.0679 (-8.42)*	0.0680 (-8.39)*
Access & egress mode time	SP and RP – BS,TN,LR, BWY			0.0524 (-9.72)*	0.0518 (-9.84)*
State dependence	DA, RS, BS, TN			0.0917 (-.81)*	0.0834 (-.75)*
SP to RP scale parameter	DA, RS			2.963 (0.89)	2.367 (1.16)
	BS, BWY			1.077 (6.48)	1.079 (6.64)
	TN, LR			1.058 (6.31)	1.200 (5.34)
	SP and RP – DA			2.877 (13.2)	2.758 (13.7)

Error component (Alternative-specific heterogeneity)			1.845 (8.5)	1.992 (9.1)
Scale parameters	SP and RP – RS			
	SP and RP – DA, RS	1.00 (fixed)	1.00 (fixed)	
	SP and RP – BS,TN,LR, BWY	0.7321 (8.85)	0.7218 (6.57)	
Sample size		2688	2688	2688	2688
LL at convergence		−2668.1	−2637.8	−2324.7	−2327.86

Notes: * = Constrained triangular random parameter, R = random parameter mean estimates, DA – drive alone, RS – ride share, BS – bus, TN – train, LR – light rail, BWY – busway. We used 500 Halton draws to perform our integrations, so there is no simulation variance. EC = Error components.

that the influencing attributes on car use are often more extensive (especially when including socio-demographic conditioning) than the set that determines public transport use. Given the generally dominant role of the car in many cities (notably 70–85 percent modal share in Australian cities), one might expect greater preference heterogeneity in the car choosers and hence an increasing likelihood of greater unobserved heterogeneity. Interestingly, the scale parameter in the NL model of 0.7218 for public transport suggests greater unobserved heterogeneity for public transport modes than for the car; however, while this may be the appropriate interpretation for this model, the absence of accounting for correlated choice sets, random preference heterogeneity in the attributes and in the alternatives makes the comparison somewhat trite.

19.4.1 Nlogit command syntax for Table 19.2 models

Nested logit – no choice-based weights

```
Timer
NLOGIT
    ;lhs=chosen,cset,altij
    ;choices=RDA,RRS,RBS,RTN,SDA,SRS,SBS,STN,SLR,SBW
    ;effects:fc(rda,rrs)/at(rda,rrs)/
pf(rbs,rtn)/mt(rbs,rtn)/ae(rbs,rtn)
    ;pwt
    ;tree= car(RDA,RRS,SDA,SRS),PT(RBS,RTN,SBS,STN,SLR,SBW)
    ;ivset: (car)=[1.0]
    ;rul
    ;model:
    U(RDA) =rdasc+ flptc*fc+tm*at +pinc*pincome/
    U(RRS) = rrsasc+ flptc*fc+tm*at/
    U(RBS) = rbsasc + flptc*pf+mt*mt+acegt*ae/
    U(RTN) =           flptc*pf+mt*mt+acegt*ae/
    U(SDA) = sdasc  + flptc*fueld+ tm*time+pinc*pincome/
    U(SRS) = srsasc + flptc*fueld+ tm*time /
    U(SBS) =          flptc*fared+ mt*time+acegt*spacegtm/
    U(STN) = stnasc + flptc*fared+ mt*time+acegt*spacegtm/
    U(SLR) = slrasc + flptc*fared+ mt*time+acegt*spacegtm/
    U(SBW) = sbwasc+  flptc*fared+ mt*time+acegt*spacegtm$
```

Nested logit – choice-based weights

```
Timer
NLOGIT
    ;lhs=chosen,cset,altij
    ;choices=RDA,RRS,RBS,RTN,SDA,SRS,SBS,STN,SLR,SBW
    /0.63,0.22,0.08,0.07,1.0,1.0,1.0,1.0,1.0,1.0
```

```
;effects:fc(rda,rrs)/at(rda,rrs)/
pf(rbs,rtn)/mt(rbs,rtn)/ae(rbs,rtn)
;pwt
;tree= car(RDA,RRS,SDA,SRS),PT(RBS,RTN,SBS,STN,SLR,SBW)
;ivset: (car)=[1.0]
;rul
;model:
U(RDA) =rdasc+ flptc*fc+tm*at +pinc*pincome/
U(RRS) = rrsasc+ flptc*fc+tm*at/
U(RBS) = rbsasc + flptc*pf+mt*mt+acegt*ae/
U(RTN) =           flptc*pf+mt*mt+acegt*ae/
U(SDA) = sdasc  + flptc*fueld+ tm*time+pinc*pincome/
U(SRS) = srsasc + flptc*fueld+ tm*time /
U(SBS) =          flptc*fared+ mt*time+acegt*spacegtm/
U(STN) = stnasc + flptc*fared+ mt*time+acegt*spacegtm/
U(SLR) = slrasc + flptc*fared+ mt*time+acegt*spacegtm/
U(SBW) = sbwasc+  flptc*fared+ mt*time+acegt*spacegtm$
```

Mixed logit – no choice-based weights

```
Timer
RPLOGIT
    ;lhs=chosen,cset,altij
    ;choices=RDA,RRS,RBS,RTN,SDA,SRS,SBS,STN,SLR,SBW
    ;descriptives;crosstab
    ;effects:fc(rda,rrs)/at(rda,rrs)/pf(rbs,rtn)/mt(rbs,rtn)/ae(rbs,rtn)
    ;pwt
    ;tlf=.001;tlb=.001;tlg=.001
    ;rpl
    ;fcn= spascc(n,*,0),spascb(n,*,0),spasct(n,*,0),
     tm(t,1),mt(t,1),acegt(t,1), rpnsd(t,1),flptc(t,1)
    ;par
    ;halton;pts= 150
    ;pds=4
    ;ecm= (RDA,SDA), (RRS,SRS)
    ;model:
U(RDA) = rdasc+ flptc*fc+tm*at+pinc*pincome/
U(RRS) = rrsasc+ flptc*fc+tm*at/
U(RBS) = rbsasc + flptc*pf+mt*mt+acegt*ae/
U(RTN) =          flptc*pf+mt*mt+acegt*ae/
U(SDA) = spascc +flptc*fueld+ tm*time+pinc*pincome+rpnSD*rpn/
U(SRS) = spascc+flptc*fueld+ tm*time +rpnSD*rpn/
U(SBS) = spascb+flptc*fared+ mt*time+acegt*spacegtm+rpnSD*rpn/
U(STN) = spasct +flptc*fared+ mt*time+acegt*spacegtm+rpnSD*rpn/
U(SLR) = spasct +flptc*fared+ mt*time+acegt*spacegtm/?+rpnSD*rpn/
U(SBW) = spascb +flptc*fared+ mt*time+acegt*spacegtm$ +rpnSD*rpn$
```

Mixed logit – choice-based weights

```
-> Timer
-> RPLOGIT
   ;lhs=chosen,cset,altij
   ;choices=RDA,RRS,RBS,RTN,SDA,SRS,SBS,STN,SLR,SBW
   /0.63,0.22,0.08,0.07,1.0,1.0,1.0,1.0,1.0,1.0
   ;descriptives;crosstab
   ;effects:fc(rda,rrs)/at(rda,rrs)/pf(rbs,rtn)/mt(rbs,rtn)/ae(rbs,rtn)
   ;pwt
   ;tlf=.001;tlb=.001;tlg=.001
   ;rpl
   ;fcn= spascc(n,*,0),spascb(n,*,0),spasct(n,*,0),
    tm(t,1),mt(t,1),acegt(t,1), rpnsd(t,1),flptc(t,1)
   ;par
   ;halton;pts= 150
   ;pds=4
   ;ecm= (RDA,SDA), (RRS,SRS)
   ;model:
   U(RDA) = rdasc+ flptc*fc+tm*at+pinc*pincome/
   U(RRS) = rrsasc+ flptc*fc+tm*at/
   U(RBS) = rbsasc + flptc*pf+mt*mt+acegt*ae/
   U(RTN) =          flptc*pf+mt*mt+acegt*ae/
   U(SDA) = spascc +flptc*fueld+ tm*time+pinc*pincome+rpnSD*rpn/
   U(SRS) = spascc+flptc*fueld+ tm*time +rpnSD*rpn/
   U(SBS) = spascb+flptc*fared+ mt*time+acegt*spacegtm+rpnSD*rpn/
   U(STN) = spasct +flptc*fared+ mt*time+acegt*spacegtm+rpnSD*rpn/
   U(SLR) = spasct +flptc*fared+ mt*time+acegt*spacegtm/?+rpnSD*rpn/
   U(SBW) = spascb +flptc*fared+ mt*time+acegt*spacegtm$ +rpnSD*rpn$
```

19.5 Even more advanced SP–RP models

As a consequence of the growing interest in incorporating both preference heterogeneity and scale heterogeneity in choice models (detailed in Chapters 4 and 15), as a way of recognizing an increasing number of ways in which sources of utility among a set of alternatives can be captured, including correlation induced by repeated observations on each sampled respondent, new model forms have been developed. Generalized mixed logit (GMXL) (set out in Chapter 15), is an extension of ML, to incorporate scale heterogeneity. The small but growing number of applications of GMXL has parameterized scale heterogeneity as a single estimate in a data set used in model estimation. However, it is often the case that analysts pool data from more than one source, such as the SP and RP sources discussed in this chapter, or multiple SP sources, inducing the potential for differences in the scale factor between the data sources. What appears absent from the literature is the capture of both scale heterogeneity for a pooled data set and data-specific scale heterogeneity effects. While this might appear to be a small extension, it is a crucial add on given the expected increase in the use of GMXL using multiple data sources.[5]

We now move beyond the NL "trick" and the extensions developed in Section 19.4 to the most generalized version of a choice model to combine multiple data sets, decomposing scale heterogeneity to identify data-specific scale effects.

The extension of interest here is to allow τ (see Chapter 15) to be a function of a series of dummy variables that identify the presence of scale heterogeneity between different data sets, such as an SP and an RP data set. The use of the SMNL or GMX model permits a new variant of SP–RP model estimation. This is a simple but important extension, as follows: $\tau = \tau + \eta d_s$ where η is a data set-specific scale parameter and $d_s = 1$ for data source s and zero otherwise, with $s = 1, 2, \ldots, S-1$. Hence we allow for differences in the GMXL scale factor between SP and RP data sets through the inclusion of a dummy variable d_s (s=SP=1, s=RP=0) associated with σ_{irs}, i.e., $\sigma_{irs} = \exp(-\tau(\tau + \eta d_s)^2/2 + (\tau + \eta d_s)w_{ir})$.

We use the same data set as in Section 19.4. The GMX command syntax in Nlogit is given at the end of this section.

The results from the estimation of the GMXL models are summarized in Table 19.3. We have estimated two models, in addition to a baseline ML model (M1). Model 2 (M2) accounts for scale heterogeneity without distinguishing data sets, and Model 3 (M3) is M2 plus an allowance for scale heterogeneity between data sets (using the command **;hft=spdum**).

The Bayes information criterion (BIC) is increasingly used as the preferred measure of comparison of overall fit of choice models. When estimating model parameters using maximum likelihood estimation, it is possible to increase the likelihood by adding parameters, which may result in over-fitting. BIC resolves this problem by introducing a penalty term for the number of parameters in the model. BIC is an increasing function of the variance of the unobserved effects and an increasing function of the number of free parameters estimated. Hence, a lower BIC implies fewer explanatory variables, better fit, or both. The model with the lower value of BIC is the one to be preferred.

From the evidence in Table 19.3, we would conclude that Model 3 is the preferred model but that Models 1 and 2 are virtually indistinguishable on overall

---

[5] We have been asked on many occasions to advise researchers how to accommodate scale differences between data sets under conditions of scale heterogeneity.

Table 19.3 Summary of model results. *t*-values are in brackets. 500 Halton draws, with panel structure accommodated and all random parameters are constrained *t*-distributions[6]

Attributes and mode-specific constants	Alternative(s)	ML. Model 1 (M1)	GMX with scale heterogeneity within pooled RP and SP data Model 2 (M2)	GMX with scale heterogeneity within and between pooled RP and SP data Model 3 (M3)	Attribute mean and standard deviation Note: *italics* is car
Invehicle cost ($)	All	−0.6223 (−13.8)	−0.7243 (−12.8)	−0.1284 (−4.57)	2.36 (*1.92*), 1.46 (*1.07*)
Main mode time (min.)	SP and RP – DA, RS	−0.1198 (−12.5)	−0.1447 (−12.7)	−0.0449 (−5.04)	23.31 (*17.55*)
Main mode time (min.)	SP and RP – BS,TN,LR, BWY	−0.0838 (−10.5)	−0.0966 (−9.1)	−0.0127 (−4.09)	15.96 (10.83)
Access & egress mode time (min.)	SP and RP – BS,TN,LR, BWY	−0.0459 (−9.26)	−0.0523 (−7.9)	−0.0060 (−4.20)	18.86 (13.52)
Personal income ($000s)	SP and RP – DA	0.0080 (2.25)	0.0081 (2.26)	0.0065 (2.61)	34,600 (*16,480*)
Drive alone constant	DA – RP	1.2438 (3.29)	1.4345 (3.53)	2.5409 (11.2)	
Ride share constant	RS – RP	−0.5641 (−1.61)	−0.3776 (−1.01)	0.9096 (4.64)	
Drive alone constant	DA – SP	0.2625 (2.59)	0.8109 (2.74)	2.7805 (11.18)	
Ride share constant	RS – SP	0.4070 (1.71)	0.5431 (2.00)	2.4598 (10.34)	
Train-specific constant	TN -SP	0.2271 (2.01)	0.2382 (2.04)	0.1648 (1.53)	
Light rail-specific constant	LR – SP	0.3995 (3.99)	0.4147 (4.00)	0.3618 (3.67)	
Bus-specific constant	BS – SP	0.0125 (0.10)	0.0127 (0.10)	0.0486 (0.34)	
Bus-specific constant	BS – RP	−0.1363 (−0.50)	−0.1484 (−0.53)	0.3347 (1.61)	

[6] See n.4.

Random parameter standard deviations:

Invehicle cost	All	-0.6223 (-13.8)	-0.7243 (-12.8)	-0.1284 (-4.57)
Main mode time	SP and RP – DA, RS	-0.1198 (-12.5)	-0.1447 (-12.7)	-0.0449 (-5.04)
Main mode time	SP and RP – BS,TN,LR, BWY	-0.0838 (-10.5)	-0.0966 (-9.1)	-0.0127 (-4.09)
Access & egress mode time	SP and RP – BS,TN,LR, BWY	-0.0459 (-9.26)	-0.0523 (-7.9)	-0.0060 (-4.20)
Variance parameter in scale (τ)		–	0.5260 (11.67)	0.8649 (14.95)
Heterogeneity in GMXL scale factor (SP)		–	–	1.6209 (7.90)
Sample size			2688	
LL at zero			-6189.45	
LL at convergence		-2549.24	-2544.68	-2518.67
Pseudo-R^2		0.5881	0.5889	0.5931
Bayes information criterion (BIC)		1.9349	1.9345	1.9241
Value of travel time savings:				AU1995$ per person hr.
Main mode time	SP and RP – DA, RS	11.55 (0.98)	12.21 (1.32)	20.99 (2.12)
Main mode time	SP and RP – BS,TN,LR, BWY	8.08 (0.54)	7.69 (0.78)	5.92 (0.45)
Access & egress mode time	SP and RP – BS,TN,LR, BWY	4.42 (0.13)	4.32 (0.62)	2.82 (0.72)

fit.[7] This latter evidence suggests that accounting for scale heterogeneity without allowing for scale differences between data sources in the GMXL scale factor does not improve the overall behavioral explanation offered by ML. This is reinforced by the similarity of the mean values of travel time savings between Models 1 and 2.

Despite this finding, however, we have a statistically significant parameter estimate for the coefficient on the overall unobserved scale heterogeneity, τ, in Model 2 (t-ratio of 11.67). What this suggests is that, although we have identified the presence of unobserved scale heterogeneity, when this is fed into the calculation of the standard deviation, σ_{ir}, or the individual-specific standard deviation of the idiosyncratic error term, equal to $\exp(-\tau^2/2 + \tau w_{ir})$, assuming an estimate for w_{ir}, the unobserved heterogeneity is standard normally distributed; the "mean of the standard deviation" and the "standard deviation of the standard deviation" are such that the overall influence is not significantly different from unity.

When we allow for differences in the GMXL scale factor between SP and RP data sets in Model 3, through the inclusion of a dummy variable d_s (s=SP=1, s=RP=0) associated with σ_{irs}, i.e., $\sigma_{irs} = \exp(-\tau(\tau + \eta d_s)^2/2 + (\tau + \eta d_s)w_{ir})$, to capture data set-specific scale differences, we find a significant difference in overall fit on BIC as well as mean estimates of value of travel time savings (VTTS).[8] The mean sigma for the SP data is 0.810 (with a standard deviation of 1.058); the mean sigma for RP data is 0.96542 (with a standard deviation of 0.9534). These distributions are plotted in Figure 19.6. We observe greater variance in unobserved heterogeneity in the SP data (i.e., lower scale)

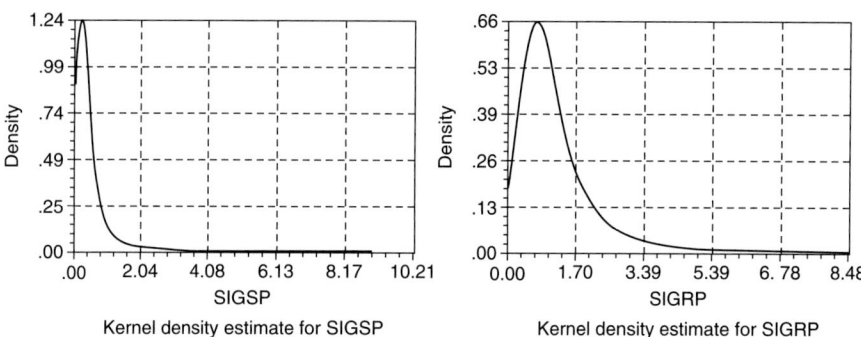

Figure 19.6 Distribution of scale standard deviation for SP and RP choices

---

[7] The similarity of Models 1 and 2 in the model fit highlights the flexibility of the ML model; even the less flexible model performs equally well when systematic scale heterogeneity is present.

[8] The standard errors associated with the VTTS are such that Models 1 and 2 are not significantly different in terms of mean estimates of VTTS, whereas Models 2 and 3 are.

compared to the RP data (noting that the numerical scale on the horizontal axis differs). This seems plausible given that the SP data induce greater variation in the levels of the observed attributes, and have the real possibility of a greater uncertainty in choice in contrast to the binary RP setting where experience has clarified the levels of attributes of at least the chosen alternative.

The evidence, albeit from one data set, suggests that data-specific scale differences play a potentially important role in accounting for scale differences between pooled data sets that matters behaviorally. Another way of interpreting this finding is that although the role of scale heterogeneity may be of intrinsic value, there is a need to include data source-specific scale conditioning through adjustments in the overall measure of scale heterogeneity in pooled data sets, reinforcing the approach adopted in earlier studies and in Section 19.4 that use closed form models (with fixed parameters) such as the NL "trick" on combining data sets to reveal scale differences. Allowing for scale heterogeneity alone across two or more data sets appears not sufficient for this one empirical application.

The Nlogit syntax is provided below, together with the model output, for GMX:

```
RESET
load;file=c:\spmaterial\sprpdemo\sprp.sav$
Project file contained    9408 observations.
sample;all$
reject;altij=1$
reject;altij=5$
reject;altij=6$
sample;all$
create;if(sprp=2)spdum=1$
gmxlogit;userp  ? userp is a command to obtain mixed logit parameter
estimates as
                ?starting values instead of MNL estimates
    ;lhs=chosen,cset,altij
    ;choices=RPDA,RPRS,RPBS,RPTN,SPDA,SPRS,SPBS,SPTN,SPLR,SPBW
    ;pwt
    ;tlf=.001;tlb=.001;tlg=.001
    ;gmx
    ;tau=0.5
    ;gamma=[0]
    ;hft=spdum
    ;maxit=50
    ;fcn=tm(t,1),mt(t,1),acegt(t,1),flptc(t,1)
    ;par
    ;halton;pts= 500;pds=4
    ;model:
    U(RPDA) = rdasc  + flptc*fcost+tm*autotime+pinc*pincome/
    U(RPRS) = rrsasc + flptc*fcost+tm*autotime/
```

```
    U(RPBS)  = rbsasc + flptc*mptrfare+mt*mptrtime+acegt*rpacegtm/
    U(RPTN)  =          flptc*mptrfare+mt*mptrtime+acegt*rpacegtm/
    U(SPDA)  = sdasc  + flptc*fueld+ tm*time+pinc*pincome/
    U(SPRS)  = srsasc + flptc*fueld+ tm*time/
    U(SPBS)  = spascb + flptc*fared+ mt*time+acegt*spacegtm/
    U(SPTN)  = stnasc + flptc*fared+ mt*time+acegt*spacegtm/
    U(SPLR)  = slrasc + flptc*fared+ mt*time+acegt*spacegtm/
    U(SPBW)  =          flptc*fared+ mt*time+acegt*spacegtm$ /
Normal exit:  32 iterations. Status=0. F=    2552.033
-----------------------------------------------------------------------------
Generalized Mixed (RP) Logit Model
Dependent variable                   CHOSEN
Log likelihood function       -2552.03320
Restricted log likelihood     -6189.34873
Chi squared [  15 d.f.]        7274.63106
Significance level                .00000
McFadden Pseudo R-squared         .5876734
Estimation based on N =   2688, K =   15
Information Criteria: Normalization=1/N
              Normalized    Unnormalized
AIC              1.90999      5134.06640
Fin.Smpl.AIC     1.91006      5134.24604
Bayes IC         1.94290      5222.51469
Hannan Quinn     1.92190      5166.05919
Model estimated: Nov 10, 2010, 11:22:59
Constants only must be computed directly
              Use NLOGIT ;...;RHS=ONE$
At start values -2639.1224   .0330******
Response data are given as ind. choices
Replications for simulated probs. = 150
Halton sequences used for simulations
RPL model with panel has      672 groups
Fixed number of obsrvs./group=         4
Heteroscedastic scale factor in GMX
Hessian is not PD. Using BHHH estimator
Number of obs.= 2688, skipped    0 obs
-----------+-----------------------------------------------------------------
           |                 Standard              Prob.
    CHOSEN| Coefficient      Error       z      z>|Z|
-----------+-----------------------------------------------------------------
           |Random parameters in utility functions
        TM|    -.04494***       .00891    -5.04  .0000
        MT|    -.01267***       .00310    -4.09  .0000
     ACEGT|    -.00603***       .00143    -4.20  .0000
     FLPTC|    -.12843***       .02809    -4.57  .0000
           |Nonrandom parameters in utility functions
     RDASC|     2.54095***      .22659    11.21  .0000
      PINC|      .00653***      .00250     2.61  .0090
     RRSASC|     .90963***      .19592     4.64  .0000
```

```
    RBSASC|     .33469           .20850     1.61   .1084
     SDASC|    2.78047***        .24859    11.18   .0000
    SRSASC|    2.45986***        .23793    10.34   .0000
    SPASCB|     .04858           .14129      .34   .7310
    STNASC|     .16475           .10802     1.53   .1272
    SLRASC|     .36175***        .09868     3.67   .0002
          |Distns. of RPs. Std.Devs or limits of triangular
      TsTM|     .04494***        .00891     5.04   .0000
      TsMT|     .01267***        .00310     4.09   .0000
   TsACEGT|     .00603***        .00143     4.20   .0000
   TsFLPTC|     .12843***        .02809     4.57   .0000
          |Heteroscedasticity in GMX scale factor
    sdSPDUM|    1.62087***        .20507     7.90   .0000
          |Variance parameter tau in GMX scale parameter
  TauScale|     .86493***        .05786    14.95   .0000
          |Weighting parameter gamma in GMX model
  GammaMXL|       .000     .....(Fixed Parameter).....
          | Sample Mean    Sample Std.Dev.
  Sigma(i)|    3.63344         3.42762     1.06   .2891
-----------+-------------------------------------------------------------------
Note: ***, **, * ==>  Significance at 1%, 5%, 10% level.
Fixed parameter ... is constrained to equal the value or
had a nonpositive st.error because of an earlier problem.
--> create
    ;if(sprp=2)spdum=1$
--> create
    ;V=rnu(0,1)     ? uniform
    ;if(v<=0.5)T=sqr(2*V)-1;(ELSE) T=1-sqr(2*(1-V))
    ;tmb=-.04494+.04494*t
    ;mtb=-.01267+.012678*t
    ;acegtb=-.00603+.00603*t
    ;costb=-.12843+.12843*t
    ;vtm=60*tmb/costb
    ;vmt=60*mtb/costb
    ;vacegt=60*acegtb/costb
    ;z=rnn(0,1)
    ;sigsp=exp((-(0.86493+1.62087)^2)/2+(0.86493+1.62087)*z)
    ;sigrp=exp((-(0.86493)^2)/2+(0.86493)*z)$

--> dstats;rhs=vtm,vmt,vacegt,sigrp,sigsp$
Descriptive Statistics
Variable|   Mean      Std.Dev.   Minimum      Maximum      Cases Missing
-----------+-------------------------------------------------------------------
      VTM| 20.99509    .139574E-11  20.9951      20.9951      9408       0
      VMT|  5.91781    .00610       5.74363      5.92104      9408       0
   VACEGT|  2.81710    .745729E-13  2.81710      2.81710      9408       0
    SIGRP|  1.01330   1.10680       .216893E-01  32.4036      9408       0
    SIGSP|  1.24960   30.89010      .220529E-05  2927.59      9408       0
```

19.6 Hypothetical bias

The extent to which individuals might behave inconsistently, when they do not have to back up their choices with real commitments, is linked to the notion of hypothetical bias, and is becoming a major question in choice research as we build up a substantial portfolio of empirical evidence on estimates of willingness to pay (WTP) for specific attributes from choice experiments (CEs).[9]

In the context of travel behavior, we have one influential paper by Brownstone and Small (2005), which concludes with the suggestion, based on a toll road context in California, that there are significant differences between RP and SC marginal WTP when the latter is obtained from choice experiments. RP studies can vary from those based on actual market evidence or revealed behavior (e.g., Brownstone and Small 2005), to RP experiments (e.g., Isacsson 2007), through to traditional discrete choice studies based on a known choice and one or more non-chosen alternatives defined on a respondent's perceptions of attribute levels; or some synthesis rule based on physical networks (as in transport studies), or averaging of attribute levels of non-chosen alternatives using information from individuals who chose a particular alternative (e.g., with a common origin and destination in a trip making context).

Efforts to study the influence of hypothetical bias on marginal WTP (MWTP)[10] and total WTP (TWTP)[11] in a choice experiment context have been confined largely, but not exclusively, to agricultural and resource applications (see Alfnes and Steine 2005; Alfnes *et al.* 2006; Lusk and Schroeder 2004; Carlsson and Martinsson 2001). The evidence is mixed in respect of the relative MWTP as one external validity test of a choice model's behavioral realism. For example, Carlsson and Martinsson (2001) and Lusk and Schroeder (2004), in comparing preferences between a hypothetical and an

---

[9] We use the phrase "choice experiment" (CE) to refer to the methods commonly adopted in transportation studies to evaluate packages of attributes, referred to as alternatives, and to then make a choice or to rank order the alternatives.

[10] We use the phrase "marginal willingness to pay" (MWTP) to refer to the valuation of a specific attribute.

[11] Total WTP is a language common in health, environmental, and resource studies to represent the change in total consumer surplus between the null alternative and the application of interest. The estimate is based on the total utility difference in dollars of a base alternative and a scenario where an attribute takes a specific value (e.g., unconstrained mouse hunting versus banning mouse hunting).

actual choice experiment, found no evidence of difference in the MWTP; in contrast, Isacsson (2007), in the context of trading time with money, found that the MWTP based on the hypothetical experiment was almost 50 percent lower at the mean than the real experiment MWTP, supporting the conclusions by Brownstone and Small (2005, 279) in a transport context that "the value of time saved on the morning commute is quite high (between $20 and $40 per hour) when based on revealed behavior, and less than half that amount when based on hypothetical behavior."

Lusk and Schroeder (2004) and Alfnes and Steine (2005) found significant differences in TWTP,[12] calculated by comparing a null alternative with an application scenario. Carlsson and Martinsson (2001) did not investigate TWTP because they did not have an opt-out or "none of these" alternative (described by some researchers as a serious design flaw[13] – see Harrison 2006), and hence they forced respondents to make a choice that included some level of payment. Although not conclusive, the literature "suggests" that the presence or absence of the opt-out or "no choice" alternative often does make a noticeable difference to the evidence. For example, Ladenburg et al. (2007), based on a review of the evidence from a number of studies and their own empirical investigations, conclude:

Assuming that the observed effect of the opt-out reminder reflects that the stated preferences are brought closer to the true preferences, adding a relatively short-scripted opt-out reminder ... will effectively reduce hypothetical bias further.

Although this specific source of potential hypothetical bias needs consideration, the evidence from many quality studies is well summarized in Murphy et al. (2005, 317):

it is likely that a number of factors affect hypothetical bias and therefore no single technique will be the magic bullet that eliminates this bias.

An assessment of the evidence, including meta analyses (e.g., List and Gallet 2001; Murphy et al. 2004) points to a number of potentially key influences on

---

[12] The literature in agricultural, resource, and environmental valuation does not calibrate the ASCs, even when the application has real market alternatives with a known market share (e.g. Lusk and Schroeder 2004). This may in part explain the significant differences in the total WTP in contrast to the non-significant differences in MWTP.

[13] The recognition of the role of the opt-out or null alternative has been described by Glenn Harrison as a potentially key insight into why conjoint choice experiments *may* allow analysts to do tight statistical calibration for hypothetical bias (personal communication, February 9, 2008).

the findings in respect of MWTP and TWTP. These include the nature of the good being studied (private or public); any connotations in terms of environmental consciousness (feel good, yeah-say); the presence or absence of an opt-out alternative; the opportunity to calibrate ASCs on all or on a subset of alternatives that are observed in actual markets; the role of supplementary data to condition the choice outcome, hypothetical or real, that can be encapsulated in the notion of information processing (e.g., identifying heuristics such as the imposition of a threshold on the way one processes attributes or ignoring certain attributes that impact on choices that may be generic to an individual or specific to the experimental circumstance, including referencing[14] around a known experience[15] – see Hensher 2006, 2008; Rose *et al.* 2008), and in items that identify "the confidence with which they would hypothetically purchase the good at the stated alternative or attribute" (Harrison 2007).

The focus of the section is on the MWTP evidence from choice experiments (CEs) in the transportation context, and the extent to which evidence on hypothetical bias from a wider literature, including the more extensive literature on contingent valuation, can offer guidance on how CEs might be structured to narrow the gap between actual market WTP and WTP derived from hypothetical choice experiments.

In Section 19.6.1, we present a number of key themes to highlight approaches used to estimate MWTP, the main focus of this section, and to identify possible sources of hypothetical bias revealed in the literature. This is followed by a limited empirical assessment, using a number of traditional RP and CE data sets, given the absence of non-experiment real choices observed in a natural environment,[16] designed to suggest directional influences of specific CE elements on the gap between RP and CE MWTP. We then consider the role of the numerator and the denominator in the empirical estimation of MWTP, which suggests that a closer look at referencing within a

---

[14] Referencing is the extent to which an application has an identifiable real observation to benchmark against (e.g., choice among existing tolled and free routes used to establish market shares and MWTP for time savings), in contrast to the valuation of specific attributes such as noise and safety where a real observation of MWTP is not usually known or able to be assessed unambiguously.

[15] The use of referencing the CE design to a real activity, as in toll road studies, is generally lacking in the literature outside of transportation. Glenn Harrison makes the valid point that this may be a two-edged frame, biasing responses. One way of establishing the presence of bias is to incorporate the reference into the design as a treatment which is present and absent across the within subject experiment. This is also a way of assessing endogeneity (see Train and Wilson 2008).

[16] Where the individuals do not know they are in an experiment (see Harrison and List 2004) or what I refer to as "at a distance."

CE, and how it is handled in model estimation, may be an important way of grounding the choice design in reality, especially where the travel activity is characterized by habitual behavior, such as commuting, and in helping to establish MWTP that are closer to the evidence from real market choice (i.e., revealed behavior). The section concludes with suggestions on where future empirical efforts should be focussed if we are to have confidence in empirical evidence from CE studies that can be used as if it were obtained "at a distance" from observing behavior in real markets. This contrasts with empirical evidence from traditional RP that models can be used as a reference benchmark where it is believed that this is close to real market WTP, enabling us to gauge the extent to which specific treatments of SC WTP might close the gap and reduce hypothetical bias.[17]

19.6.1 Key themes

This section draws together key assumptions and approaches used in the empirical identification of MWTP. To make some sense of the literature, we begin with a classification based on the nature of the data (real, experimental); followed by a discussion of the key behavioral paradigm (CV, CE); the role of specific features linked in general to uncertainty such as opt-out, cheap-talk and referencing; and efforts to introduce calibration and bias functions to reduce hypothetical bias.

19.6.1.1 Data spectrum

The terms revealed, real and actual values, are typically used interchangeably in the literature to refer to situations in which an individual makes a consequential economic commitment. In experimental studies, this typically involves payment for a good or service by the participant. Most studies of hypothetical bias assume that these cash-based estimates are unbiased. On the other hand, stated or hypothetical values refer to survey responses that lack any salient economic commitment and typically a hypothetical scenario.[18] A review of the literature suggests that we can reasonably classify evidence on MWTP in terms of three broad categories, each with a set of underlying

---

[17] One referee provided extensive comment in support of conventional RP choice models as evidence of WTP in real markets. This is controversial; however, given the extensive use of RP models as if they reproduce real market trading among attributes, we have incorporated this benchmark in the section.

[18] One way of distinguishing salient and non-salient circumstances is that a salient economic commitment would be consistent with "I prefer X and Y and I actually chose X." A non-salient economic commitment would be "I prefer X to Y but there is no guarantee I will actually choose X."

variations. The classification suggests that the term "revealed preference" (RP), common in many studies, is not strictly equivalent to "real market data." The choice response in RP studies may be a real market response, but the data typically imposed on each respondent for non-chosen alternatives are controversial (as is concern in general about lack of variance and measurement error),[19] and it is one reason, among others, that SC methods have blossomed for MWTP identification.

Real markets, where we can *observe* actual behavior, are able to identify the levels of attributes offered by each available alternative, as perceived by the decision making unit. A distinction within the category is based on the presence or absence of an experimental treatment. The *non-experimental focus* entails non-artefactual or anonymous observation of individuals "at a distance" (i.e., without having to ask any questions; in a sense, the individual does not know they are being studied), and recording their choice and attribute levels of relevant alternatives.[20] While this avoids any experimental bias, it often exhibits measurement error associated, in particular, with the non-chosen alternative(s) (e.g., choice between a tolled and free route, between modes of transport), although examples in areas such as choice of quality beef in a supermarket (see Lusk and Schroeder 2004) can avoid measurement error through unambiguous labeling of the attributes of each alternative on offer. This focus, however, is unlikely to be rich enough to observe the processing strategy adopted in respect to attributes and alternatives, which does influence the MWTP (Chapter 21), including the identification of the relevant choice set from which the observed outcome is obtained. However, as shown in a number of recent papers (e.g. Hensher and Greene 2008; Hensher and Layton 2008), it is possible to infer the probability of a processing rule being invoked without having to ask each individual.[21]

The *experimental focus* involves giving individuals money or having them earn it to undertake real choices and actions. There is typically a baseline participation fee, together with a sum of money and other attributes that vary

---

[19] As Ben-Akiva *et al.* (1994) state, "the possibilities to elicit real WTP measures are limited because they can be varied only on a small scale."

[20] For example, in a high occupancy toll lane (HOT) context in California, the analyst is able to measure the travel times using third-party methods (e.g. car following), and identifying the toll as a posted price, as was the situation reported in Brownstone and Small (2005).

[21] It is not yet clear whether the analytical methods implemented to identify the use of various process rules up to a probability are an improvement on the self-stated supplementary questions asked of respondents as to how they processed the attribute data in CEs (e.g., non-attended to specific attributes, added up common metric unit attributes). See also Chapter 21.

according to the alternative chosen (e.g., Isacsson 2007; Lusk and Schroeder 2004). A concern with this focus is that the participation fee may be driving the outcome, as distinct from revealing true behavior under circumstances where the financial means is internally derived by the individual and is a real trade, in terms of opportunity cost. Carlsson and Martinson (2001) suggest that:

our test of external validity may not be seen as a test of truthful revelation but rather as a test of external validity between hypothetical and actual experiments.

RP data, common in many studies, is based on surveying individuals and asking them to describe a recent or current actual alternative, and one or more non-chosen (possibly non-experienced) alternatives with/without any information to identify the attribute processing strategies used. Whereas the actual choice outcome is known, the levels of the attributes are either reported by the respondent or drawn from a synthetic source, such as a modal network in transportation studies (see Daly and Ortúzar 1990 for a critical assessment where they show that models estimated with network data, rather than detailed data, did not even support the preferred model structure). Either way, the information associated with the non-chosen alternatives is potentially subject to non-marginal errors in respect of what levels would be experienced if an individual were to choose that alternative in a real market.[22]

SC data can be classified into two broad classes – contingent valuation (CV)[23] and choice experiments (CE). Both are methods of estimating the

---

[22] To investigate the possibility of bias caused by systematic misperception of travel times, Ghosh (2001) used perceived time savings to help explain route, mode, and transponder choice in a tolled versus non-tolled lane choice setting. Perception error (defined as perceived minus actual time savings) was added as an explanatory variable. He found that commuters with larger positive perception errors are more likely to use the toll facility; however, the RP values of time savings are not changed by including this variable, suggesting that RP results may not be affected by perceptual problems. Ghosh was not able to identify whether or not SP results are so affected (see also Brownstone and Small 2005).

[23] The term was apparently first introduced in 1947 by S.V. Ciriacy-Wantrup, who thought that the appropriate procedures employed interviews in which subjects are "asked how much money they are willing to pay for successive additional quantities of a collective extra-market good." One implicit assumption of this definition is that contingent value is not needed for ordinary market goods. But with respect to those goods that are not bought and sold, some device as to replace the set of prices that markets happily make explicit. Toward that end the tester prepares an array of questions about some particular subject matter in order to elicit how much they would be prepared to pay – the so-called WTP – in order to secure the provision of some public good. Alternatively, they are asked how much money someone would have to pay them – the so-called WTA – to discontinue some public project that they hold dear. There is sharp disagreement as to how useful the best of these studies is in making value determinations for widespread studies on the valuation of a full set of public goods – the creation of a national park, the preservation of wildlife in an estuary, the control of epidemics, the pursuit of national security, or whatever.

non-market value of attributes or amenities, such as values of endangered species, recreational or scenic resources, air pollution, and travel time savings. These measured values are generally based on the WTP for improved attribute or amenity levels. In the CV context, there are several questions that have been used, in both a controlled experiment and in practice. Among those are dichotomous, open ended, payment card, and bidding games. *Dichotomous choice* is a bid offered to the respondent that he/she can accept or reject, while in the open ended question the respondent is asked for his or her maximum WTP for something that is of most interest, such as an improved quality environment. The payment card is a mode of question shown to the respondent with several bids printed on it. The respondent is asked if any of those bids is close to their maximum WTP. Finally, the bidding game refers to the sequence of bids offered to the respondent so that his or her maximum WTP can be elicited (Frykblom 1997).

The choice experiment approach (see Rose and Bliemer 2007 for a recent review) is based on surveying individuals using a variety of instruments (e.g., pencil and paper, CAPI, internet-based survey) and asking them to assess a set of analyst-defined alternatives, and to express their preferences through first preference rank (i.e., choosing one), full or partial ranking, and rating all alternatives, with/without analyst knowledge of the attribute processing strategy (APS). There are many variants including labelled or unlabeled choice sets (attributes and alternatives) – sometimes referred to as multiple price lists in experimental economics which, when generalized to many attributes, are referred to as multiple attribute lists (equivalent to multiple price lists – see Harrison 2007). These can also have variants such as referenced alternatives based on a pivot around a real action (which are increasingly common in transport studies – see Rose *et al.* 2008), and allowance for attribute processing, exogenously or endogenously (see Tversky and Kahneman 1981; Hensher 2008; Swait 2001) with various heuristics to define attribute boundaries (Hensher and Layton 2008 and Chapter 21).

19.6.2 Evidence from contingent valuation to guide choice experiments

Although the main focus here is on MWTP and choice experiments, in which the empirical investigation of hypothetical bias is somewhat limited, there is much to be learned from CV studies in guiding the design and application of CEs and any supplementary data that set the context and condition the choice response. There is a burgeoning literature on hypothetical bias associated with contingent valuation (see, for example, Portney 1994;

Hanemann 1994; Diamond and Hausman 1994), summarized in Harrison (2006, 2007) and Carson *et al.* (1996) under the broad heading of making CEs incentive compatible.[24] Much of the focus in CV studies is on assessing hypothetical bias in TWTP; however, there are some useful signals on what may be sources of hypothetical bias in estimation of MWTP that can be taken into account in the estimation of MWTP in CEs.

19.6.2.1 CV evidence

The method of CV has been the subject of heavy criticism, with much of this debate focusing on the validity of the results, in particular the hypothetical nature of the experiments (see Carson *et al.* 1996). The accumulating evidence suggests that individuals in such hypothetical CV studies exaggerate their TWTP and MWTP for private and public goods, in part due to the problems associated with the poor representation of other relevant attributes when the CV focus is on one attribute only. Several attempts have been made to reduce the influence of this hypothetical bias. *Cheap talk* scripts seemed to be one of the most successful attempts. Initially suggested by Cummings *et al.* (1995, 1995a), cheap talk is an attempt to bring down the hypothetical bias by describing and discussing the propensity of respondents to exaggerate stated WTP for a specific good at a specific price. Using private goods, classroom experiments, or closely controlled field settings, cheap talk proved to be potentially successful (see Cummings and Taylor 1999). While the hypothetical mean TWTP without cheap talk was significantly higher than TWTP using actual economic commitments, the hypothetical TWTP with a cheap talk script could not be shown to be statistically significantly different from the actual TWTP. In general we would conclude that the evidence is mixed and the debate is still wide open.

List and Gallet (2001)[25] used a meta analysis to explore whether there are any systematic relationships between various methodological differences and hypothetical bias. Their results indicate that the magnitude of hypothetical bias was statistically less for (a) WTP, as compared to willingness to accept (WTA) applications, (b) private as compared to public goods, and (c) one

---

[24] A process is said to be incentive compatible if all of the participants fare best when they truthfully reveal any private information the mechanism asks for. As an illustration, voting systems which create incentives to vote dishonestly *lack* the property of incentive compatibility. In the absence of dummy bidders, a second-price auction is an example of a mechanism that is incentive compatible. There are different degrees of incentive compatibility: in some games, truth-telling can be a dominant strategy. A weaker notion is that truth-telling is a Bayes–Nash equilibrium: it is best for each participant to tell the truth, provided that others are also doing so. See Harrison (2007).

[25] Their empirical analysis is an update of Foster *et al.* (1997).

elicitation method, the first-price sealed bid, as compared to the Vickrey second-price auction baseline.

Murphy *et al.* (2004) also report the results of a meta analysis of hypothetical bias in 28 CV studies that reported WTP and used the same mechanism for eliciting both hypothetical and actual values. The 28 papers generated 83 observations with a median ratio of hypothetical to actual value of 1.35, and a distribution with a severe positive skewness. They found that a choice-based elicitation mechanism, such as dichotomous and multiple choice, referendum, payment card, and conjoint, is important in reducing bias. There is some weak evidence that bias increases when public goods are being valued (reinforcing the evidence of List and Gallet 2001), and that some calibration methods (see below) may be effective at reducing bias. However, the results are quite sensitive to model specification, which will remain a problem until a comprehensive theory of hypothetical bias is developed.

There are a number of CV studies that utilize calibration techniques to control for hypothetical bias. Studies that employ *ex ante*, or instrument calibration, techniques such as budget reminders or cheap talk scripts (Cummings and Taylor 1999; List 2001), attempt to get unbiased responses from participants. *Ex post*, or statistical calibration techniques, on the other hand, recognize that responses are biased and they attempt to control for it using laboratory experiments to calibrate field data (Fox *et al.* 1998) or uncertainty adjustments (Poe *et al.* 2005).

Blackburn *et al.* (1994) define a "known bias function" as one that is an *ex post* systematic statistical function of the SECs of the sample. If this bias is not mere noise, then one can say that it is "knowable" to a decision maker. They then test if the bias function is transferable to a distinct sample valuing a distinct good, and conclude that it is. In other words, they show that one can use the bias function estimated from one instance to calibrate the hypothetical responses in another instance, and that the calibrated hypothetical responses statistically match those observed in a paired real elicitation procedure. Johannesson *et al.* (1999) extend this analysis to consider responses in which subjects report *the confidence with which they would hypothetically purchase the good at the stated price*, and find that information on that confidence is a valuable predictor of hypothetical bias.

The idea of instrument calibration (first used in Harrison 2006), in contrast to statistical calibration, has generated two important innovations in the way in which hypothetical questions have been posed: recognition of some uncertainty in the subject's understanding of what a "hypothetical yes" means (Blumenschein *et al.* 1998, 2001), and the role of cheap talk scripts directly encouraging subjects to avoid hypothetical bias (Cummings and Taylor 1998; List 2001; Aadland and Caplan 2003; Brown *et al.* 2003). The evidence for these procedures is mixed. Allowing for some uncertainty can allow one to adjust hypothetical responses to better match real responses. Although this could be estimable, it normally presumes that one knows *ex ante* what threshold of uncertainty is appropriate to apply (see Swait 2001). However, simply showing that there exists a threshold that can make the hypothetical responses match the real responses, once you look at the hypothetical and real responses, is not particularly useful unless that threshold provides some out-of-sample predictive power. Similarly, the effects of cheap talk appear to be context-specific, which simply means that one has to test its effect in each context rather than assume that it works in all contexts.[26] There is a case to build in uncertainty *ex ante* in experimental design, given that outcomes are uncertain for many reasons (see Harrison 2006a). This recognizes that a plan is not the same as an actual action of implementation. For example, in studies investigating the role of various congestion charging schemes in contexts where they currently do not exist, introducing an attribute that attaches a probability of such a scheme actually happening is one way to control for subjective assessment shrouded in various beliefs about the reality of the offer. Greater certainty (or lesser uncertainty of an outcome) is known to influence preferences.

19.6.2.2 CE evidence

CEs are typically framed in a manner that adds realism, in that they closely resemble individual purchasing or use decisions. There are surprisingly few published studies that test for hypothetical bias in CE (exceptions being Alfnes and Steine 2005; Lusk 2003; Lusk and Schroeder 2004; Cameron *et al.* 2002; Carlsson and Martinsson 2001; List *et al.* 2001; Johansson-Stenman and Svedsäter 2003; Brownstone and Small 2005; Isacsson 2007). Both Carlsson and Martinsson (2001) and Cameron *et al.* (2002) fail to reject a hypothesis of equal MWTP in both a real and a hypothetical setting, while Johansson-Stenman and Svedsäter (2003) reject the equality of MWTPs, and Lusk and Schroeder (2004) find that hypothetical TWTP for the good exceeds real TWTP, but fails to reject the equality of MWTPs for changes in the single

---

[26] The increasing role that in-depth interviews and focus groups are playing in the definition of choice experiments has been found by the author to add substantial credibility to the experiments. Recent studies in the context of determining the MWTP for music in gym classes, and at nightclubs and discos, which was subsequently used in Federal Court of Australia arbitrations on music royalties, confirms this.

attributes. Carlsson *et al.* (2005) also conclude that they cannot reject the hypothesis of a hypothetical bias for MWTP in choice experiments.

List *et al.* (2006) explore CEs that conveniently provide information on the purchase decision as well as the attribute value vector. The empirical work revolves around examining behavior in two very different field settings. In the first field study, they explored hypothetical bias in the purchase decision by eliciting contributions for a threshold public good in an actual capital campaign. To extend the analysis a level deeper, in a second field experiment they examined both the purchase decision and the marginal value vector via inspection of consumption decisions in an actual marketplace. In support of CEs, both field experiments provide some evidence that hypothetical choice experiments combined with "cheap talk," be it light or heavy, can yield credible estimates of the purchase decision. *Furthermore, they find no evidence of hypothetical bias when estimating MWTP.* Yet, they do find that the cheap talk component might induce internal inconsistency of subjects' preferences in the choice experiment.

Lusk (2003) explored the effect of cheap talk on WTP that was elicited via a mass mail survey (n = 4,900) for a novel food product, golden rice. Employing a double-bounded dichotomous choice question, he found that estimated WTP, calculated from hypothetical responses with cheap talk, was significantly less than WTP estimated from hypothetical responses without cheap talk. However, consistent with List (2001), he found that cheap talk does not reduce WTP for *experienced*, or in our case *knowledgeable*, consumers. For all consumers, average WTP for golden rice exceeds the price of traditional white rice. The evidence that cheap talk tends to attenuate hypothetical bias only for subjects less familiar with the good being valued by List (2001) and Lusk (2003) reinforces the importance of referencing, a key focus of the current discussion.

In addition, the potential effect of "realism" (Cummings and Taylor 1998) or "consequentialism" (Landry and List 2007), or the role of "limit cards" (Backhaus *et al.* 2005) further supports the appeal of referencing around an experience good or alternative. The "limit cards" approach requests the respondent to place an imaginary "limit card" behind the stimulus he considers just sufficient to generate a choice. In this manner, the limit card combines the first-preference response in CE studies with a ranking position that separates acceptable stimuli from those that are not deemed capable of leading to a choice. The underlying theoretical argument to support limit cards is that individuals evaluate "decision" alternatives at a subjective level, called the *comparison level*, which is not dissimilar to the idea of a reference alternative. In some sense, this literature is related to information processing which is now recognized as having a role to play in minimizing hypothetical bias (see Chapter 21). Backhaus *et al.* (2005) use a weekend trip to three capital cities (Paris, Rome, and Vienna) as the choice context to show that the mean WTP, based on limit conjoint analysis, is very close to the real WTP; in contrast, the CV mean estimates are substantially different.

The most relevant condition for choice analysis is *salience*, which requires that the reward be directly related to the decision the subject makes during a study. Paying a respondent a fixed amount is not salient, because there is no relationship between the respondent's performance/actions and the reward he or she receives. There is no reason to expect that the respondent's behavior during a study will be consistent with his or her behavior during a similar, real world, economic activity. Ding *et al.* (2007) suggest that traditional marketing research often relies on conjoint analysis in which participants are either paid nothing or a non-salient reward to answer questions about hypothetical purchase decisions. Such studies struggle to uncover true consumer preferences because participants have little stake in the answers they give. They developed an approach that provides participants with incentives based on actual behavior. Ding *et al.* conducted field experiments in a Chinese restaurant to test their incentive-aligned approach. Participants stated their meal preferences and eventually had to pay for and eat the preferred meal. Using the traditional hypothetical conjoint approach, they were able to predict consumer's top choice only 26 percent of the time. In contrast, using the incentive-aligned approach, they were able to predict consumer's top choice 48 percent of the time.

There are two innovative urban transport studies using CEs that investigate hypothetical bias. Using a simple dichotomous choice experiment with two attributes, Isacsson (2007) suggests that there is a bias in estimates of the value of time savings associated with public transport, based on hypothetical choices. Real values tend to be higher than values derived from hypothetical choices. This replicates the findings of Brownstone and Small (2005). Assuming an exponential distribution for the value of time savings, real choices in Isacsson produced an estimated mean value of time savings which was twice as large as the corresponding hypothetical value. This evidence in CEs in transportation applications is the inverse to the general findings in CV studies that conclude that hypothetical WTP estimated in stated preference surveys is most often found to be an overstatement of true WTP (see, e.g., Harrison and Rutstrom 2008; List and Gallet 2001; Murphy *et al.* 2005).

19.6.2.3 Summary

In summary, this section has identified a number of candidate influences on the magnitude of hypothetical bias. The key influences are the use of cheap talk to assist in attenuating bias, especially where there is a lack of experience; the ability to opt-out in contrast to a forced choice, which is linked to referencing in that the respondent's opt-out is maintenance of the status quo; and the use of processing strategies such as "limit cards" or questions to establish the threshold limits for the set of alternatives that is treated as serious decision alternatives.

What we appear to have is a strong recommendation for greater clarity of the CE (i) in terms of a translation of offerings in real markets, (ii) in the manner in which experience is embedded in the CE (through, in particular, pivoting around an experienced good), and (iii) in the way that we capture information to delineate the process heuristics that each individual uses in evaluating the attributes and alternatives.

In the remaining sections, we focus on the role that referencing (linked to opt-out) can play in reducing hypothetical bias, taking the Brownstone and Small (2005) study as one influential and current benchmark in travel behavior research of evidence on MWTP obtained from observing real behavioral decisions relative to CE evidence. We also acknowledge that many researchers regard the MWTP from traditional RP studies (with all their known deficiencies) as another "benchmark of interest," which often produces higher mean estimates than CE studies. An investigation into the role of process heuristics is provided elsewhere in Hensher and Greene (2008).

19.6.3 Some background evidence in transportation studies

The general lack of evidence from real markets observed "at a distance" in the transportation context limits the comparisons here to a range of empirical paradigms, ranging from the traditional RP choice data through to various CE specifications. Drawing on a number of (non-referenced) data sets collected by the authors over the last twenty years, we ran separate traditional RP and traditional (i.e. non-referenced) CE models as ML error component models (see Table 19.4). The VTTS was calculated for each RP and CE choice set and compared. These non-pivot (pencil and paper face to face survey) CE designs have attribute levels determined by a specific trip length segment, and are not individualized to each person's current or recent trip.[27]

---

[27] Both of these features may well be at the center of the sources of hypothetical bias.

Table 19.4 Summary of illustrative Australian empirical evidence on VTTS: traditional CE versus RP

Study title	Context	Mean VTTS ($ per person hr.)	Ratio RP/CE (using 95 percent confidence limits on a symmetrical distribution)
RP versus CE evidence			
Sydney-Melbourne 1987	Long-distance non-commuting; labeled mode choice	Error component: RP: 9.74±6.23 CE: 5.81±3.01	1.67±2.1
Six Australian capital cities 1994	Urban commuting; labeled mode choice	Error component: RP: 3.51±1.47 CE: 4.20±2,13	0.838±0.7
Sydney Pricing Tribunal 1995	Urban commuting; labeled mode and ticket type choice	MNL RP: 6.73±3.94 CE: 6.11± 3.22	1.10±1.2
		Error component: RP: 6.87±4.58 CE: 6.26±2.95	1.09±1.56

Note: All studies used a face to face pencil and paper survey.

The evidence suggests that the ratio RP/CE is not significantly different from 1.0 in any of the three studies[28] and hence we cannot reject the null hypothesis of no evidence of hypothetical bias. If the "truth" resided in the RP model, which in these three studies has the usual concerns with the identification of the relevant set of non-chosen alternatives (including the measurement error problem), then we would indeed conclude that hypothetical bias is not an issue. The influential paper by Brownstone and Small (2005), especially in the United States, however, has convinced a growing number of researchers and practitioners that MWTP from CE studies is significantly under-estimated compared to *revealed behavior* studies, and hence there is a need to seek out a possible explanation(s) for this. Brownstone and Small (2005) suggest that the traditional RP estimate is not a benchmark compared to real market observation.[29] Importantly Brownstone and Small's model looks like the usual RP model, but the data is obtained from a sample of a traveller's actually observed choosing between a variable priced tolled lane and a free lane. The attributes are measured by external procedures so that the levels of times and

---

[28] A referee described this evidence as "a good result."

[29] We acknowledge personal communication with Ken Small and David Brownstone in early 2008.

costs actually experienced for both alternatives in the choice set are not subject to the usual concerns associated with asking individuals.

Given the dominance of habit (in contrast to variety seeking) in much of modal and route trip activity for a given trip purpose, there is appeal in focussing on choice situations where preference inference (and hence MWTP) might be better identified without "forcing" non-chosen alternatives into the decision space, unless one can capture data along the lines of Brownstone and Small (see n. 28). Our preference-revelation paradigm promotes the use of a reference (or status quo) alternative in the design of CEs, which is also the opt-out under conditions of actual experience. This appears to offer great promise in the derivation of estimates of MWTP that have a closer link to the real market activity *of each individual.*

Reference alternatives have an important role to play in giving sense to the levels of the attributes offered in the CE choice scenarios. Using a CAPI and internet-based surveys, we can now automatically individualize the attribute levels in CEs relative to a reference experience (e.g., a recent travel activity). That is, the levels seen by each individual will differ according to the levels associated with a reference alternative, even where the design levels (as percentage variations around the reference point) are the same. What is not clear is whether the reference alternative should be included in the choice set used in model estimation. In Table 19.5 we investigated this issue, using a 2004 toll road study in Sydney. Respondents were asked (i) to make a choice among the reference alternative and two CE alternatives, and (ii) to choose among the CE alternatives. What we find suggests that there is a difference, albeit small, in the mean VTTS, which is smaller when the error components specification is used, in contrast to the simple MNL form. The confidence intervals[30] for the

Table 19.5 Empirical evidence on CE-based VTTS (mean $ per person hr. and statistical uncertainty) for pivot data paradigm, treating time and cost parameters generic across all alternatives

Study title	Context	Model including reference alternative	Model excluding reference alternative (a form of opt-out)
Toll Study Sydney 2004	Urban commuting, unlabeled choice	MNL: 18.6±6.3	MNL: 17.85±7.7
		Error component 18.1±7.4	Error component 17.83±8.1

[30] These are important because the estimated VTTS are ratios of random variables, so they are also random.

above values were estimated using the *t*-ratio method equation derived by Armstrong *et al.* (2001):

$$V_{S,I} = \left(\frac{\theta_t \cdot t_c}{\theta_c \cdot t_t}\right) \cdot \frac{(t_t t_c - \rho t^2)}{(t_c^2 - t^2)} \pm \left(\frac{\theta_t \cdot t_c}{\theta_c \cdot t_t}\right) \cdot \frac{\sqrt{(\rho t^2 - t_t t_c)^2 - (t_t^2 - t^2)(t_c^2 - t^2)}}{(t_c^2 - t^2)},$$

(19.22)

where t_t and t_c correspond to the *t*-ratios for parameter estimates for travel time and cost, θ_t and θ_c, respectively; t is the critical value of the statistics given the degree of confidence required; and ρ is the coefficient of correlation between both parameter estimates. This expression assures positive upper and lower bounds for the VTTS if the parameters involved are statistically different from zero.

On a test of differences, the error component model findings are not statistically different at the 95 percent confidence level. This test, however, says nothing about the added value of the reference alternative as a way of identifying the marginal disutility of time and cost associated with an alternative chosen in an actual market setting, complete with all the real world constraints that an individual takes into account in choosing that alternative.

Constraining parameters across the reference and CE design alternatives, which is common in the majority of CEs, may actually be clouding real information on the difference of the marginal disutility of time and cost of a real alternative and a hypothetical alternative that may be sources of differences in VTTS.

The WTP derived from CEs reported in Tables 19.4 and 19.5 are ratios of parameter estimates, and are typically sensitive to small changes in the numerator and/or denominator estimates, which may be differentially impacting on each alternative (although suppressed when parameters are generic across the reference and CE alternatives). In other words, deviations between RP and CE WTP estimates due to hypothetical bias might be confounded by deviations introduced by something as simple as adding another attribute to one or more alternatives.[31] In the following sections, we need to take a closer look at the richness of the information in the numerator and denominator of a WTP calculation, and the additional information offered in

---

[31] A study by Steimetz and Brownstone (2005) cited in Brownstone and Small (2005) bootstraps the distribution of WTP and takes the mean of this distribution as a point estimate in an effort to accommodate this numerator and denominator sensitivity. I thank a referee for pointing this out.

a reference-based CE, through separation of the utility expressions for the reference (i.e. current market decision outcome) and CE alternatives.

19.6.3.1 Marginal WTP: numerator and denominator effects

Wardman (2001) and Brownstone and Small (2005) suggest a range of reasons as to why CE and RP MWTP may differ (they do not investigate TWTP[32]). Wardman (2001, 120) suggests that a lower CE MWTP can be explained (in part) by (i) strategic response bias, especially on the parameter of cost which appears in the denominator of the calculation of WTP in dollars, associated with greater sensitivity to cost variation that a choice experiment generates; (ii) the ability in a CE to "adopt simplified decision rules such as ignoring attributes of lesser importance or which vary less"; and (iii), a variation on (ii), to ignore attribute variations which are not realistic, thereby reducing mean parameter estimates. He suggests that this is more likely to be an issue for the parameter estimate (such as travel time) which is the numerator of the WTP calculation.

Brownstone and Small (2005) also offer some explanations for these differences,[33] also cited in Isacsson (2007). The most appealing is that individuals display (time) inconsistency in their actual behavior, or more generally constraints associated with real actions that are not accounted for in CEs. It is suggested that these constraints tend to result in higher cost choices more frequently in real life than in hypothetical surveys.[34] They also consider the misperception of travel time. They ask individuals to report the time savings they think could be realized by using express lanes.[35] This belief elicitation was non-incentivized. Individuals typically report an estimate (based on the mean), twice the actual time savings. Brownstone and Small (2005, 288) suggest two possible explanations: (i) individuals focus on total delays on part of the trip instead of the full origin–destination trip, and (ii) impatience

---

[32] TWTP is predominantly a focus of environmental, health, marketing, and agricultural applications.

[33] Brownstone and Small (2005) suggest that the mean VTTS in a toll HOT lane versus free route context is in the range USD$20–$40 per person hr., which is about 50 percent higher than the evidence from SP studies (i.e., $USD13–$16). The high end USD$40 is a self-selected group who had already obtained a transponder that enabled them to use the express lane if they so chose, and hence they would be expected to have the highest VTTS.

[34] Higher attribute levels tend, holding unit of measurement fixed, to result in lower parameter estimates, and hence with the cost parameter in the denominator, we obtain a higher mean MWTP for RP situations compared to SP situations.

[35] David Brownstone (personal communication, February 28, 2008) advises that many of the respondents in the CE RP comparisons actually switched between the tolled and untolled alternatives regularly (at least once a week). He suggests that it would be interesting to repeat the estimation on the subset of these switchers, who are quite familiar with both alternatives.

with heavy traffic leads to exaggeration of actual delay time. These reasons are then used to suggest that the same level of an attribute in a CE will lead to the same reaction, and hence a lowering of the parameter estimate for time.

Hensher (2006, 2008) and Hensher and Greene (2008) promote the idea of attribute processing as a behaviorally meaningful way of ensuring that individuals use the heuristics that they also use in real markets (although there may be additional CE-specific effects given the amount of information being offered for processing, which may not change the heuristic set but simply invoke a specific processing rule). We do not see Wardman's point (ii) as a CE-specific issue, since this happens also in RP settings. Supplementary questions should be asked to reveal such processing rules for CE *and* RP data, or model specifications defined to test for and capture specific process heuristics, up to a probability (see Hensher and Greene 2008; Hensher and Layton 2008). Furthermore Wardman's point (iii) is linked implicitly to the promotion of pivot designs (see Rose *et al.* 2008) that can, if carefully designed, reduce this feature of many poorly designed CEs (see below).

Brownstone and Small's suggestion in the context of time savings realized by using the express lane (2005, 88), is controversial; namely, that "if people experiencing a 10-min time delay remember it as 20 min, then they probably react to a hypothetical question involving a 20-min delay in the same way that they react to a real situation involving a 10-min delay. This would cause their measured value of time savings in the hypothetical situation to be exactly half the value observed in real situations." Unlike RP data, where one is asked to indicate the level (and in some cases the difference) or, as in the case of Brownstone and Small, use some other means of measuring not related to a specific individual's actual trip, such as floating cars and loop detectors, in a CE the level is actually given to each sampled respondent. Hence an individual is processing a given level of an attribute, used in model estimation, which is not the same as asking an individual for an attribute level or obtaining it from a third-party source, for the non-chosen alternative, or the difference, and then constructing an attribute level for the non-chosen alternative. In one sense, this removes an element of uncertainty associated with a respondent having to construct a level of an attribute associated with a non-chosen alternative in an RP study.

The MWTP (e.g., VTTS) is shorthand for the ratio of two distinct quantities – the marginal (dis)utility of an attribute of interest (e.g., travel time), and the marginal (dis)utility of money (Hensher and Goodwin 2004). Both are confounded by changes in tastes, leisure activities, education, and opportunities or choice set open to sampled individuals, as well as the data collection paradigm (Hensher 2006; Harrison 2006, 2007). Given the different context of a CE in general, it must be recognized that CE studies should be annexures to RP studies that can supplement where RP data is deficient. Pivot designs, discussed below, may well be the way forward.

19.6.4 Pivot designs: elements of RP and CE

RP data is generally regarded as rich in information on the chosen alternative, but problematic on the attributes describing the non-chosen alternatives. This is due, in large measure, to a lack of experience with non-chosen alternatives, common in transportation contexts, many of which exhibit strong patterns of habitual behavior with high levels of inertia required to motivate any serious consideration of alternatives. Variety seeking is not common with many transportation choices, especially in urban settings. There will always be perceptual bias, which many would argue is not a bias but a product of the exposure and overt experience an individual has accumulated in respect of these alternatives. There is a large literature that embodies ideas of reinforced preference towards the chosen alternative (see, for example, Tversky and Kahneman 1981; Gilboa and Schmeidler 2001). The recent development in referencing or pivot designs (see Rose *et al.* 2008; Hess *et al.* 2008) is in part a response to the observation[36] that individuals are, in many situations, habitual in behavior, especially in the short to medium term in many transport "choices" such as the daily commute, in contrast to variety seeking; and it often requires a perceptually different level of offering of an alternative (defined in terms of behavioral thresholds on specific attributes and/or mixes of attributes) before an individual will *consider* switching and then *possibly* switching. Given that cross-section studies, which are the typical data source for MWTP, are seen as representing long run behavior, we have to contemplate mixtures of habitual and variety seeking behavioral responses, even where the bias towards the reference alternative is strong.[37] This is consistent with CEs offering alternatives around the reference alternative that are different labeled alternatives (e.g., public transport instead of car for the commute), in addition to the unlabeled CE alternatives where one is

---

[36] This is generally the case with the most popular transportation application of commuter mode or route choice.

[37] We acknowledge discussions with Ken Small on this point.

varying the attribute levels of the reference alternative. Conversion of consideration into action is an important threshold question.

Given the problems in identifying "reliable" (in an *ex post* choosing sense) levels of attributes of non-chosen alternatives, with systematic misperception of travel times suggested by Brownstone and Small (2005, 288) as a possible source of differences in RP and CE MWTP, there is potential merit in seeing pivot-based choice experiments as richer in reality than traditional RP with forced (and often artificially constructed) alternatives. A CE pivot experiment (CE_PV) recognizes that an individual has chosen an alternative in a real market setting and that this alternative is reasonably assumed to be the utility maximizing outcome (given all the perceptions and awareness that exist in actual markets).[38] An individual when asked to evaluate a well designed labeled or unlabeled CE_PV, is in relatively familiar territory compared to an RP context where attribute levels of non-chosen alternatives are typically unknown and "wild guesses" are not uncommon. Specifically a CE_PV experiment offers design variations around an experienced alternative, which are selected to ensure that the attributes and their mix are comprehensive and comprehensible (Hensher 2006). Pivoting is one way of promoting *relevancy* in attribute levels, in line with ideas in prospect theory (Tversky and Kahneman 1981). It also eliminates the need to input a "no choice" alternative.

Hensher (2001) demonstrates that CE-based WTP estimates depend largely on the *context* of the alternatives presented, such as "start/stop" traffic versus "free-flow" traffic (as Wardman (2001) does, but to a lesser extent). This illustrates the importance of pivoting CE alternatives off of real world experience – enabling respondents to apply some meaningful context to these hypothetical alternatives. Second, the RP-based findings of Hensher (2006a) suggest that VTTS estimates can reflect additional congestion costs (a finding confirmed by Steimetz 2008). As such, a possible explanation for the divergence between RP and CE estimates is that CE respondents cannot visualize all of the congestion costs that would, in the real world, accompany the hypothetical travel times presented to them. But pivoting off of a real world

---

[38] Hensher *et al.* (2005) have suggested that one might estimate stand alone CE models to obtain robust parameter estimates on each attribute and then calibrate the constants to reproduce the base market shares observed in real markets. This removes the need to estimate RP models. This approach is conditional on assuming that the parameter estimates obtained from RP alternatives, be they from a stand alone RP model or a joint (rescaled) RP–CE model, are statistically and behaviorally less reliable, than from CE alternatives, and especially the reference alternative.

alternative might enable respondents to visualize such costs, offering some promise of tightening the gap between RP and CE results.

To investigate the role of referencing around an experienced alternative (essentially an RP observation in an actual market), we re-estimated some models that were developed for VTTS studies in the context of tolled versus non-tolled routes in Australia and New Zealand. We focus on (habitual) commuting activity in the Sydney region in 2004 and in a regional context in New Zealand in 2007. A typical CE screen is shown in Figure 19.7 (taken from the Sydney study), extracted from a computer aided personal survey instrument.

The initial Sydney model estimation involved estimation of a choice between the reference alternative, defined in terms of a recent or current commuting trip, and two CE alternatives, the latter developed as a *D*-efficient design (see Rose *et al.* 2008 and Chapter 7), with actual attribute levels pivoted around the reference alternative's levels. The subsequent Sydney model focussed on the choice between the two CE alternatives (essentially a forced choice). The New Zealand study involved exactly the same model specification. ML models with error components (to account for scale)[39] were estimated, with the parameters for travel time for each of the reference and CE alternatives specified as random with triangular distributions.[40] Separate fixed parameters were estimated for cost (running and toll cost, as applicable).[41] We also included two constants to account for any biases in favor of the reference alternative and the first-ordered CE alternative.

The key findings are summarized in Table 19.6.[42] The models in Table 19.6 had the best overall goodness of fit (on a likelihood ratio test, or LRT). The VTTS estimates are conditional estimates based on the full distributions, and not the means. For the Sydney study, the mean of the VTTS distribution for the reference alternative is $26.99 per person hr. (standard deviation of $7.94);

---

[39] In part to recognize the greater uncertainty about the stated choice designed alternatives relative to the reference alternative for each respondent.

[40] The models used simulated MLE with 500 Halton draws and accounted for the correlation between 16 choice scenarios shown to each sampled respondent.

[41] Sillano and Ortúzar (2005) argue that: "constraining a taste coefficient to be fixed over the population, *may* make it grow in a less than average proportion (i.e. the parameters that are allowed to vary grow more than the parameters that should vary over the population, but are constrained to be fixed)." If this is the case, then it would apply to both the reference and CE alternatives. In addition, the majority of empirical RP studies using ML also impose this condition.

[42] This included unconstrained triangular and normal distributions for travel time, and random parameters specifications for travel cost. The MNL model had a significantly worse overall fit (see note to Table 19.3), and produced ratios of RP:CE mean VTTS of 1.46 and 1.05, respectively, for Sydney and New Zealand.

Table 19.6 Summary of findings for pivot-based models
Mean parameter estimates (for times and costs only)[43]

Study	Reference alternative		CE alternatives	
	Time	Cost	Time	Cost
Sydney	−0.1008 (−7.7)	−0.2239 (−12.049)	−0.0669 (−16.6)	−0.2138 (−11.3)
New Zealand	−0.2128 (−9.25)	−0.4774 (−2.1)	−0.1783 (−16.80)	−0.7634 (−32.9)

	WTP estimates:			
Study	Reference alternative	CE alternatives	Forced choice (CE only)	Ratio Ref:CE
	Mean (standard deviation)			
Sydney	26.99(7.94)	17.92 (7.82)	23.24 (7.52)	1.51
New Zealand	27.34 (7.46)	13.65 (4.31)	11.28 (5.35)	2.00

Note: LL for Sydney (912 observations) and New Zealand (1,840 observations) models are, respectively, −662.51 and −1187.96 (MNL LLs are, respectively, −837.8 and −1630.2).

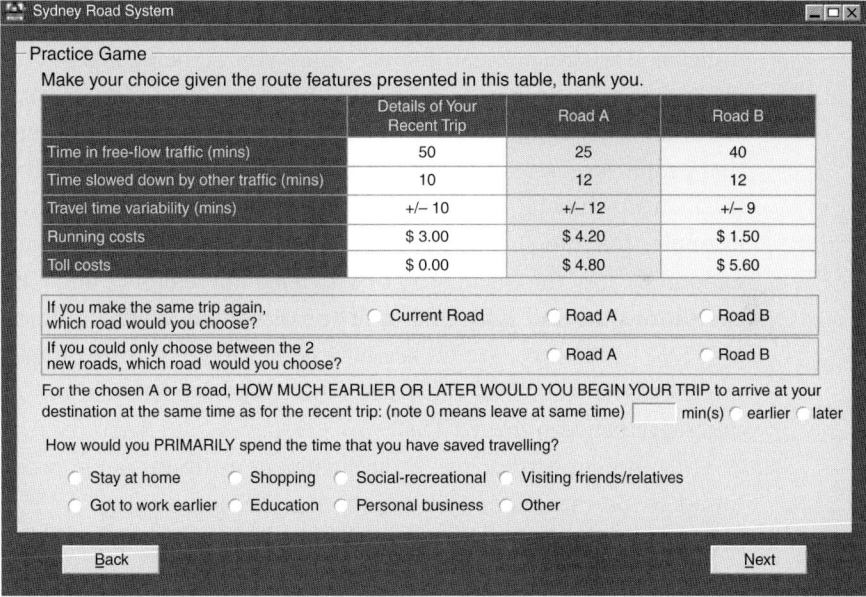

Figure 19.7   Illustrative stated choice screen from a CAPI

the mean for the CE alternatives is $17.92 (standard deviation of $7.82), derived from the model that includes the reference alternative. The forced choice

---

[43] We do not report the reference ASC and the SC dummy variable for choice scenario 1, both of which account for the mean influence of other attributes and context.

models produced a mean VTTS of $23.24 per person hr. (standard deviation of $7.52). The ratio of the Reference to CE alternatives mean VTTS is 1.51. For the New Zealand study, the mean VTTS for the reference alternative is $27.34 per person hr. (standard deviation of $7.46); the mean for the CE alternatives is $13.65 (standard deviation of $4.31), derived from the model that includes the reference alternative. The forced choice models gave a mean VTTS of $11.28 per person hr. (standard deviation of $5.35). The ratio of the Reference to CE alternatives mean VTTS is 2.00. A t-ratio test of differences shows that the WTP associated with the reference alternative and the CE alternative are statistically significant at the 95 percent confidence level.

We find that the marginal disutility associated with travel time in the reference alternative is substantially higher (especially for Sydney) than that associated with the CE design alternatives, and is either similar (i.e., Sydney) or lower (i.e. New Zealand) for cost; resulting in the higher mean VTTS for the reference (or real market) alternative. The evidence from other studies by Hensher and Louviere (see Hensher 2006; Louviere and Hensher 2001) that the attribute range has the greatest influence on MWTP than any other dimension of choice experiments,[44] with MWTP being higher with a reduced attribute range, supports the findings here; the CE design alternatives have a wider attribute range relative to the range of attributes of other alternatives that people face in real choices, and hence a lower mean VTTS than the mean VTTS from the real market alternative. If we take the Sydney sample as an example, the ratio of the range of each attribute in the numerator and denominator of the calculation of VTTS for the reference and CE alternatives is 1.42 for time and 1.48 for cost. The ratio of the reference alternative to CE VTTS is 1.51; hence, are we seeing a coincidence or something of empirical interest as a statistical calibration (*ex post*) adjustment to "explain" the difference between the VTTS?

To comment further on the influence of attribute range, which has been found to be the major dimension of a CE influencing WTP, research in marketing (e.g., Ohler *et al.* 2000) suggests that heterogeneity systematically varies with attribute range and distribution, as do model ASCs and goodness

---

[44] Hensher and Louviere have found, in many studies, that the MWTP increases as the range of attribute levels decreases, and vice versa. In CE studies it is common to have a wider range of an attribute to assess; that is essentially what CEs are all about, creating a behaviorally richer variance. However, this may come at a price, in that real markets are not so rich in variability, and hence when actual market data are used we observe after estimation higher MWTP compared to an SC experiment. This naturally begs the question: does the ratio of the range of each attribute in the numerator and denominator of the calculation of MWTP for the reference and CE observations account for part or all of the difference in the mean MWTP?

of fit measures (see also McClelland and Judd 1993), but preference model parameters remain largely unaffected. Thus, it is unclear what to make of empirical heterogeneity results because they may prove to be largely contextual; that is, they are associated with particular patterns of attribute ranges and samples of people, and cannot be generalized without taking differences in attribute ranges and people into account. The need to take into account links with characteristics of choosers and heterogeneity distributions has been recognized (see Hensher 2006), but there has been little recognition of the fact that if one changes the range and/or distribution of attributes in design matrices, this can lead to significant differences in inferences about heterogeneity. Simply put, the greater relevance in preserving the attribute content under a wider range will mean that such an attribute is relatively more important to the outcome than it is under a narrow range specification, and hence a higher mean WTP is inferred (Louviere and Hensher 2001).

The empirical evidence on VTTS from the two studies is in line with the relative magnitudes of SC and RP mean MWTP found by Brownstone and Small (2005)[45] as long as we accept that under habitual behavior the reference alternative has important information on the marginal disutility of attribute levels associated with the experienced alternative. The difference between our studies and those of Brownstone and Small is that we focussed on a known trip, and assumed that most commuters had little idea about the non-chosen alternative(s). The latter, one might argue, in an RP setting, exists to enable the estimation of a choice model, and to give variability in trip attributes. Under conditions of habitual behavior, a well designed pivot-based CE can deliver the relevant market information as well as attribute variability, while avoiding the problems in identifying meaningful data on non-chosen alternatives, especially in contexts where habit and inertia are very strong elements of real market behavior. The findings support the relative magnitudes of MWTP found by Brownstone and Small (2005) and Isacsson (2007). If one desires to use traditional RP MWTP as the benchmark, which in the non-transport literature suggests that the MWTP from CE studies is on the low side, then the findings here are consistent with closing the gap on hypothetical bias. If RP and CE studies in transport cannot establish any evidence on hypothetical bias, then one wonders why we have invested so much in CEs.[46]

---

[45] Given the 2004 exchange rate of AUD\$1=\$USD\$0.689, the Sydney evidence for the reference alternative is USD\$39.48, compared to the SC estimate of (i) USD\$19.93 for the model that includes the reference alternative, or (ii) USD\$16.08 when the forced choice among two CE alternatives is used.

[46] Except where the focus is on new alternatives and possibly very large attribute changes associated with existing alternatives that are outside the range of market experience.

The appeal of pivoting is not to imply specifying time and cost parameters as generic across all alternatives, but to recognize the role of CE data in generating variability about the real market experience (i.e., the pivot) in order to be able to estimate parameters. The argument is that this looks like offering a richer attribute preference-revelation setting than either (i) the current view on RP, with problematic identification of non-chosen alternatives, and (ii) the treatment of the CE alternatives as having "equal" status as the pivot alternative in real market identification. Crucially, however, we need the CE alternatives (without measurement error, but subject to respondent perception), to provide the necessary variation in attribute data to reveal preferences. The support for this approach is in part reinforced by the evidence from Brownstone and Small (2005) and Isacsson (2007) on the relativity of the market WTP against the CE evidence from studies where actual trade-offs are being observed and measured in real markets.

The empirical evidence here suggests that, for all the years of interest in CEs, and the debate about the role of traditional RP and CE data, we may have missed or masked an important message; namely, that CEs with referencing back to a real market activity, especially where it is chosen on repeated occasions, may provide a suitable specification, short of capturing data "at a distance," where the latter has evaded every single travel study to date.[47] If we recognize that the requirement to seek data on at least one non-chosen alternative in RP modeling is linked to the creation of the variance necessary to estimate a model, then this imposition in the context of habitual behavior may be accommodated by variance revelation through a CE pivot design, where the only information required from real markets relates to the habitually selected alternative.

We strongly recommend further research into the proposition that future CEs should consider using a real market reference alternative as a pivot in the design of the choice scenarios.[48] This not only grounds the experiment in

---

[47] Brownstone and Small measured travel times of each alternative with floating cars (on SR91) and loop detectors on I-15, which is the closest we have come to real independent observation.

[48] This should include, or at least consider, the development of models in which we can account for sign dependent preferences with respect to a reference point outcome (e.g., Hess *et al.* 2008), as suggested by cumulative prospect theory (CPT). Seror (2007), in the context of women's choices about pre-natal diagnosis of Down syndrome, concluded that CPT fitted the observed choices better than expected utility theory and rank dependent utility theory. Such a finding has been questioned by a number of researchers, claiming that many studies have been far too casual about what "the" reference point is, and allowed their priors, that loss aversion is significant to drive their specification of the reference point. See Andersen *et al.* (2007b). In general, the notion of a reference point makes good sense in typical transport applications.

reality *at an individual respondent level*, it also enables estimation of alternative-specific parameters for relevant attributes that enable the derivation of estimates of MWTP for the real market alternative and, separately, for the CE alternatives. Pivot-based CE data have the power of richness to enable respondents to express preferences involving not only the actual memory but also *related hypothetical memories constructed from it* (Hensher 2006). We do, however, emphasize that the evidence here in support of the directional and magnitude differences between WTP associated with RP and CE alternatives should not be seen as anything more than encouraging consistency and hence reducing the gap in respect of hypothetical bias. Natural field experiments are required to test this preliminary finding.

19.6.5 Conclusions

This section on hypothetical bias has brought together elements of the literature on revealed and SC studies (CV and CE) to identify the nature and extent of hypothetical bias, and what might be sensible specifications of data and models to reduce the gap between the MWTP estimates likely to exist in actual markets, when observed "at a distance," and estimates from CEs.

In suggesting that the mean MWTP for time savings is lower when trading time and cost in utility expressions associated with SC alternatives compared to RP alternatives, we recognize that there is limited (but powerful) evidence promoting this relativity from the very influential paper by Brownstone and Small (2005),[49] reinforced by Isacsson (2007). A way forward within the context of CEs, when the interest is on estimating the MWTP under conditions of habit, which is common in many transport applications, is to recognize the real market information present in a reference alternative. What we find, empirically, is that when a pivoted design is used for constructing CEs, and the model is specified to have estimated parameters of time and cost that are different for the reference alternative than the hypothetical alternatives, the estimated VTTS is higher for the reference alternative than for the hypothetical alternatives. This model specification is not the specification that researchers have generally used with data from pivoted experimental designs. Usually, time and cost are specified to have the same parameters for

---

[49] The Brownstone and Small paper is increasingly being referenced by bankers engaged in toll road project financing.

the reference and hypothetical alternatives. The proposal here for reducing hypothetical bias (given the Brownstone–Small "benchmark"), is to use a pivoted design and allow different parameters for the reference and hypothetical alternatives.

Despite the importance of good experimental design, the disproportionate amount of focus in recent years on the actual design of the CE, in terms of its statistical properties, may be at the expense of substantially placing less focus on real behavioral influences on outcomes that require a more considered assessment of process (see Chapter 7), especially referencing that is grounded in reality.

There are many suggestions from the literature, derived from mixtures of empirical evidence, carefully argued theoretical and behavioral positions, and speculative explanation. The main points to emerge, that appear to offer sensible directions for specifications of future choice studies, are:

1. The inclusion of a well scripted presentation (including cheap talk scripts), explaining the objectives of the choice experiment.
2. Inclusion of the opt-out or null alternative, avoiding a forced choice setting unless an opt-out is not sensible.
3. Pivoting the attribute levels of a CE around a reference alternative that has been experienced, and/or there is substantial awareness of, and estimating unique parameter estimates for the reference alternative, in order to calculate estimates of the MWTP for an alternative that is actually chosen in a real market.
4. The ability to calibrate the ASCs through choice-based weights on alternatives where actual shares are known. This may not be feasible in many applications, but where there is evidence of actual market shares on the same alternatives, this is essential if a valid comparison of TWTP is to be made.[50]
5. The inclusion of supplementary questions designed to identify the attribute processing strategy adopted, as well as a question to establish "*the confidence with which an individual would hypothetically purchase or use the good (or alternative) that is actually chosen in the choice experiment*"; the latter possibly being added into the CE after each choice scenario and after an additional response in the form of a rating of the alternatives, possibly

---

[50] Where the data relates to labeled alternatives (e.g., specific routes or modes), the pooling of data across individuals, who each evaluated the attribute packages around their chosen alternative, enables construction of a choice model that looks like the traditional RP model form. This can then be calibrated with choice-based weights.

along the lines of "limit cards." Fuji and Garling (2003) offer some ideas on the certainty scale question.

6. Identifying constraints that may impact on actual choices that might be ignored in CEs, which encourage responses without commitment. Once identified, these constraints should be used in revising choice responses. How this might be defined is a challenge for ongoing research.

We also support future empirical studies that can confirm or deny the growing body of evidence on hypothetical bias in CEs. Using a toll road context as an example, an empirical study might be undertaken of the following form:

1. The context is the choice among competing existing tolled and non-tolled routes including the option to consider none-of-these.
2. The attributes of interest should be, as a minimum, door-to-door travel time and cost, where the latter is running cost and toll cost for the tolled route, and running cost for the non-tolled route.
3. The sampled individuals are persons who currently use one of the two routes. This defines a reference alternative.
4. There are two groups:
   a. *Group A* participate in a SC experiment with no endowment and no randomly selected alternative for implementation, as is often the practice in CV studies.
   b. *Group B* is given an endowment (e.g., a $20 subsidy voucher) and told that the voucher is a subsidy towards the toll on any tolled route, which is valid for up to two weeks. The money is not a reward for participation. This is common practice in many CV and dichotomous choice studies in environmental and agricultural applications.

We have selected the two groups as a way to test some of the imposed conditions common in many of the studies outside of transportation, as reported here.

5. For each choice scenario, the sampled individual is asked to choose between (i) the reference alternative, two design alternatives, and an opt-out alternative, (ii) the reference alternative and two design alternatives, (iii) the two design alternatives and an opt-out alternative, and (iv) the two design alternatives.
6. Where the travel time is earlier or later than when one normally travels, we should identify the extent to which the individual is able to adjust their commitments to commence and/or finish the trip. This is a way of

attempting to identify schedule inconvenience raised by Brownstone and Small (2005) as one reason for the divergence between RP and CE VTTS.

7. A supplementary *certainty scale* question after each choice scenario, along lines suggested by Johannesson *et al.* (1999), on a scale 0 (very unsure) to 10 (very sure), to indicate how sure or certain the respondent is that they would actually choose that route (or not at all) at the indicated price and travel time.

Part IV

Advanced topics

20 Frontiers of choice analysis

20.1 Introduction

Some of the most exciting developments in discrete choice modeling involve the need to allow for non-linearity in the parameter estimates associated with attribute definitions. For example, some attributes can be measured by a mean and a standard deviation associated with an individual observation over repeated occasions in the one utility expression in a given choice set. This suggests that the attribute variability may be seen differently by a heterogenous sample of individuals, in which some are risk averse, some are risk taking, while others might be risk neutral.

To accommodate both taste (preference) heterogeneity and **risk attitude**, where the latter might be some **power function** of the attribute distribution, requires a capability to embed non-linearity in parameters in a utility expression. This chapter presents a way of doing this, and illustrates such a capability with a case study. The method is referred to as non-linear random parameter logit (NLRPL).

20.2 A mixed multinomial logit model with non-linear utility functions

The general form of NLRPL departs from a standard linear-in-parameters random utility model (RUM), with utility functions defined over J_{it} choices available to individual i in choice situation t:

$$W(i, t, m) = U(i, t, m) + \varepsilon_{itm}, \quad m = 1, \ldots, J_{it}; t = 1, \ldots, T_i;$$
$$i = 1, \ldots, N \tag{20.1}$$

with the IID, type I Extreme value distribution assumed for the random terms ε_{itm}. Conditioned on $U(i,t,m)$, the choice probabilities take the familiar multinomial logit (MNL) form:

Prob(choice j is made in choice situation t by individual i):

$$P(i,t,j) = \frac{\exp[U(i,t,j)]}{\sum_{m=1}^{J_{it}} \exp[U(i,t,m)]}. \tag{20.2}$$

The utility functions that accommodate non-linearity in the unknown parameters, even where the parameters are non-random, are built up from an extension of the mixed multinomial logit (MMNL) structure, along similar lines to Anderson *et al.* (2012), but with extensions to incorporate scale heterogeneity:

$$U(i,t,m) = \sigma_i[V_m(\mathbf{x}_{itm}, \boldsymbol{\beta}_i, \mathbf{w}_i)], \tag{20.3}$$

$$V_m(\mathbf{x}_{itm}, \boldsymbol{\beta}_i, \mathbf{w}_i) = h_m(\mathbf{x}_{itm}, \boldsymbol{\beta}_i) + \sum_{k=1}^{K} d_{km}\, \theta_k w_{ik}, \tag{20.4}$$

$$\boldsymbol{\beta}_i = \boldsymbol{\beta} + \Delta \mathbf{z}_i + \Gamma \mathbf{v}_i, \tag{20.5}$$

$$\sigma_i = \exp[\lambda + \delta' \mathbf{c}_i + \varphi u_i]. \tag{20.6}$$

The various parts allow several degrees of flexibility. In Equation (20.4), the function $h_m(..)$ is an *arbitrary non-linear function* that defines the underlying utilities (preferences) across alternatives with an error component structure (shown as the last term). The fact that the mixed logit (ML) form set out is extremely general, such that it could fit any specifications in any choice model, is the appeal of the approach. The form of the utility function itself may vary across the choices. Heterogeneity in the preference parameters of the model is shown in Equation (20.5) in line with the ML model, where $\boldsymbol{\beta}_i$ varies around the overall constant, $\boldsymbol{\beta}$, in response to observable heterogeneity through $\mathbf{z}_i$ and unobservable heterogeneity in $\mathbf{v}_i$. The parameters of the distribution of $\boldsymbol{\beta}_i$ are the overall mean (i.e., $\boldsymbol{\beta}$), the structural parameters on the observed heterogeneity, Δ, and the Cholesky square root (lower triangle) of the covariance matrix of the random components, Γ. The random components are assumed to have known, fixed (usually at zero) means, constant known variances (usually one), and to be uncorrelated. In the most common applications, multivariate standard normality would be assumed for $\mathbf{v}_i$. The covariance matrix of $\boldsymbol{\beta}_i$ would then be $\Omega = \Gamma\Gamma'$. Parameters that are not random are included in the general form of the model, by imposing rows of zeros in Γ, including the diagonal elements. A non-random parameters model would have $\Gamma = \mathbf{0}$ in its entirety.

Thus far, with $\theta_k = 0$ and $\sigma_i = 1$, the model is an extension of the MMNL model developed by McFadden and Train (2000), Train (2003), and Hensher and Greene (2003), in which the utility functions may be general non-linear functions of the attributes of the choices and characteristics of the individual contained in $\mathbf{x}_{itm}$ *and* the parameters, $\boldsymbol{\beta}_i$.

The scaling term in Equation (20.6) allows for an overall random scaling of the preference structure across individuals (as in the SMNL and GMX models). Like preference weights in the utility functions, the scaling parameter, σ_i, varies with observed and unobserved heterogeneity, c_i and u_i, respectively. In general cases, the mean parameter in σ_i, namely, λ, is not separately identified, and a normalization is required; a natural choice is zero. However, it is useful to normalize the scale parameter around unity. Assuming for the moment that $\boldsymbol{\delta} = \mathbf{0}$, if u_i is standard normally distributed with a non-zero κ, a separate variance parameter for u_i is not identified, then σ_i is log-normally distributed with expected value $E[\sigma_i] = \exp(\lambda + (\varphi)^2/2\,\sigma_u^2) = \exp(\lambda + (\varphi)^2/2)$. To center this at unity, therefore, we use the normalization $\lambda = -\varphi^2/2$. With this restriction, if $\boldsymbol{\delta} = 0$ and u_i is normally distributed, as we assume, then $E[\sigma_i] = 1$, which is a useful normalization for the cross-individual heteroskedasticity. Correlation across the utility functions is induced by the correlation of the observed attributes and characteristics, and by the common latent features of the individual u_i in σ_i and $\mathbf{v}_i$ in $\boldsymbol{\beta}_i$.

Equation set (20.1)–(20.6) is an encompassing model that has as special cases the various specifications discussed earlier (from MNL to MMNL, error components, SMNL, and GMX). Parameters of the model are estimated by maximum simulated likelihood. The log-likelihood (LL) function based on Equations (20.1)–(20.6) is:

$$\log L(\boldsymbol{\beta},\Delta,\Gamma,\boldsymbol{\theta},\boldsymbol{\delta},\varphi|\mathbf{X},\mathbf{y},\mathbf{z},\mathbf{c},\mathbf{w},\mathbf{v},\mathbf{u}) = \sum\nolimits_{i=1}^{N} \log\prod\nolimits_{t=1}^{T_i} P(i,t,j\,|\,\mathbf{w}_i,\mathbf{v}_i,u_i).$$

$$(20.7)$$

The conditioning is on the unobservables $\mathbf{w},\mathbf{v},\mathbf{u}$, and the observables, $\mathbf{X}_i, \mathbf{y}_i, \mathbf{z}_i$, $\mathbf{c}_i$ where $(\mathbf{X},\mathbf{z},\mathbf{c})_i$ is the full data set of attributes and characteristics, $\mathbf{x}_{i,t,m}$, and observed heterogeneity, $\mathbf{z}_i$ and $\mathbf{c}_i$; and $\mathbf{y}_i$ is a full set of binary indicators, y_{itm}, that marks which alternative is chosen, $y_{itj} = 1$, and which are not, $y_{itm} = 0$, in each choice situation. In full:

$$P(i, t, j) = \prod_{q=1}^{J_{it}} \left[\frac{\exp[U(i, t, j)]}{\sum_{m=1}^{J_{it}} \exp[U(i, t, m)]} \right]^{y_{itq}}. \tag{20.8}$$

In order to estimate the model parameters, it is necessary to obtain the LL unconditioned on the unobservable elements. The unconditional LL is:

$$\log L(\boldsymbol{\beta}, \boldsymbol{\Delta}, \boldsymbol{\Gamma}, \boldsymbol{\theta}, \boldsymbol{\delta}, \boldsymbol{\varphi}|X, y, z, c) = \sum_{i=1}^{N} \log \int_{\mathbf{w}_i, \mathbf{v}_i, u_i} \prod_{t=1}^{T_i} \begin{bmatrix} P(i, t, j \mid \mathbf{w}_i, \mathbf{v}_i, u_i) \times \\ f(\mathbf{w}_i, \mathbf{v}_i, u_i) \end{bmatrix} d\mathbf{w}_i d\mathbf{v}_i du_i. \tag{20.9}$$

Given the presence of $\boldsymbol{\Gamma}$, $\boldsymbol{\theta}$, and $\boldsymbol{\varphi}$, no new parameters are introduced in $f(\mathbf{w}_i, \mathbf{v}_i, u_i)$. Since the integrals do not exist in closed form, they are approximated, using simulation. The simulated LL function is:

$$\log L_S(\boldsymbol{\beta}, \boldsymbol{\Delta}, \boldsymbol{\Gamma}, \boldsymbol{\theta}, \boldsymbol{\delta}, \boldsymbol{\varphi}|X, y, z, c) = \sum_{i=1}^{N} \log \frac{1}{R} \sum_{r=1}^{R} \prod_{t=1}^{T_i} P[i, t, j \mid \mathbf{w}_i(r), \mathbf{v}_i(r), u_i(r)], \tag{20.10}$$

where $P[i,t,j|\mathbf{w}_i(r), \mathbf{v}_i(r), u_i(r)]$ is computed from Equations (20.2) and (20.3)–(20.6) using R simulated draws, $\mathbf{w}_i(r)$, $\mathbf{v}_i(r)$, and $u_i(r)$ from the assumed populations. Thus:

$$V_m[\mathbf{x}_{itm}, \boldsymbol{\beta}_i(r), \mathbf{w}_i(r)] = h_m[\mathbf{x}_{itm}, \boldsymbol{\beta}_i(r)] + \Sigma_k d_{km} \, \theta_k w_{ik}(r), \tag{20.11}$$

$$\boldsymbol{\beta}_i(r) = \boldsymbol{\beta} + \boldsymbol{\Delta} \mathbf{z}_i + \boldsymbol{\Gamma} \mathbf{v}_i(r), \tag{20.12}$$

$$\sigma_i(r) = \exp[\lambda + \boldsymbol{\delta}' \mathbf{c}_i + \boldsymbol{\varphi} u_i(r)]. \tag{20.13}$$

For optimization, the derivatives of the simulated LL function must be simulated as well. For convenience, let the joint conditional probability of the T_i choices made be:

$$P_{S,i}(r) = \prod_{t=1}^{T_i} P[i, t, j \mid \mathbf{w}_i(r), \mathbf{v}_i(r), u_i(r)] \tag{20.14}$$

and the simulated unconditional probability be denoted as in Equation (20.15):

$$P_{S,i} = \frac{1}{R} \sum_{r=1}^{R} P_{S,i}(r) = \frac{1}{R} \sum_{r=1}^{R} \prod_{t=1}^{T_i} P[i, t, j \mid \mathbf{w}_i(r), \mathbf{v}_i(r), u_i(r)] \tag{20.15}$$

so that

$$\log L_S(\boldsymbol{\beta}, \boldsymbol{\Delta}, \boldsymbol{\Gamma}, \boldsymbol{\theta}, \boldsymbol{\delta}, \boldsymbol{\varphi} | \mathbf{X}, \mathbf{y}, \mathbf{z}, \mathbf{c}) = \sum_{i=1}^{N} \log P_{S,i}. \tag{20.16}$$

Denote by $vec(\boldsymbol{\Delta})$ and $vec(\boldsymbol{\Gamma})$ the column vectors formed by stacking the rows of $\boldsymbol{\Delta}$ and $\boldsymbol{\Gamma}$, respectively. Then:

$$\frac{\partial \log L_S(\boldsymbol{\beta}, \boldsymbol{\Delta}, \boldsymbol{\Gamma}, \boldsymbol{\theta}, \boldsymbol{\delta}, \boldsymbol{\varphi} \,|\, \mathbf{X}, \mathbf{y}, \mathbf{z}, \mathbf{c})}{\partial \begin{pmatrix} \boldsymbol{\beta} \\ vec(\boldsymbol{\Delta}) \\ vec(\boldsymbol{\Gamma}) \end{pmatrix}}$$

$$= \sum_{i=1}^{N} \frac{1}{P_{S,i}} \frac{1}{R} \sum_{r=1}^{R} [P_{S,i}(r)] \sum_{t=1}^{T_i} \begin{pmatrix} \left(\mathbf{g}_j[i, t, j, (r)] - \bar{\mathbf{g}}[i, t, (r)] \right) \\ \left(\mathbf{g}_j[i, t, j, (r)] - \bar{\mathbf{g}}[i, t, (r)] \right) \otimes \mathbf{z}_i \\ \left(\mathbf{g}_j[i, t, j, (r)] - \bar{\mathbf{g}}[i, t, (r)] \right) \otimes \mathbf{v}_i \end{pmatrix}, \tag{20.17}$$

where

$$\mathbf{g}_j[i, t, j, (r)] = \frac{\partial h_j[\mathbf{x}_{itj}, \boldsymbol{\beta}_i(r)]}{\partial \boldsymbol{\beta}_i(r)} \tag{20.18}$$

and

$$\bar{\mathbf{g}}[i, t, (r)] = \sum_{m=1}^{J_{it}} P[i, t, m \,|\, \mathbf{w}_i(r), \mathbf{v}_i(r), u_i(r)] \, \mathbf{g}_m[i, t, m, (r)]. \tag{20.19}$$

For the random error components:

$$\frac{\partial \log L_S}{\partial \theta_k} = \sum_{i=1}^{N} \frac{1}{P_{S,i}} \frac{1}{R} \sum_{r=1}^{R} P_{S,i}(r) \sum_{t=1}^{T_i} \frac{[\sigma_i(r) w_{ik}(r)] \times}{\left[d_{kj} - \sum_{m=1}^{J_{it}} P[i, t, m \,|\, \mathbf{w}_i(r), \mathbf{v}_i(r), u_i(r)] \, d_{km} \right]}. \tag{20.20}$$

Finally,

$$
\frac{\partial \log L_{S,i}}{\partial \begin{pmatrix} \delta \\ \tau \end{pmatrix}} = \sum_{i=1}^{N} \frac{1}{P_{S,i}} \frac{1}{R} \sum_{r=1}^{R} P_{S,i}(r) \frac{\partial \sigma_i(r)}{\partial \begin{pmatrix} \delta \\ \varphi \end{pmatrix}} \sum_{t=1}^{T_i}
$$

$$
\times \left[\begin{array}{c} V_j[x_{itj}, \beta_i(r), w_i(r)] - \\ \left(\sum_{m=1}^{J_{it}} \dfrac{P[i, t, m | \mathbf{w}_i(r), \mathbf{v}_i(r), u_i(r)] \times}{V_m[x_{itm}, \beta_i(r), w_i(r)]} \right) \end{array} \right] \tag{20.21}
$$

and

$$
\frac{\partial \sigma_i(r)}{\partial \begin{pmatrix} \delta \\ \varphi \end{pmatrix}} = \sigma_i(r) \begin{pmatrix} c_i \\ u_i - \varphi \end{pmatrix}. \tag{20.22}
$$

Partial effects and other derivatives of the probabilities are typically associated with scaled versions of the parameters in the model. In the simple MNL model, the elasticity of the probability of the jth choice with respect to change in the lth attribute of alternative m (see Chapter 10) is:

$$
\frac{\partial \log P(i, t, j)}{\partial \log x_{l,itm}} = [\delta_{jm} - P(i, t, m)] \beta_l x_{l,itm}, \tag{20.23}
$$

where $\delta_{jm} = 1[j = m]$. In the model considered here, it is necessary to replace β_l with $\partial h_m(\mathbf{x}_{itm}, \beta_i) / \partial x_{l,itm} = D_{l,itm}$ Since the utility functions may differ across alternatives, this derivative need not be generic. In addition, the derivative would have to be simulated since the heterogeneity in β_i would have to be averaged out. The estimated average partial effect, averaged across individuals and periods, is estimated using:

$$
APE(l \mid j, m) = \frac{1}{N} \sum_{i=1}^{N} \frac{1}{T_i} \sum_{t=1}^{T_i} \frac{1}{R} \sum_{r=1}^{R} [\delta_{jm}
$$
$$
- P[i, t, m | \mathbf{w}_i(r), \mathbf{v}_i(r), u_i(r)]] \frac{\partial h_m[\mathbf{x}_{itm}, \beta_i(r)]}{\partial x_{l,itm}} x_{l,itm}. \tag{20.24}
$$

Estimates of willingness to pay (WTP) require derivatives of the utility functions with respect to certain attributes. These take the familiar forms, though using derivatives of the utility functions rather than simple coefficients. In both cases it is necessary to simulate the derivatives as suggested above. Nlogit does this simultaneously with computation of the likelihood function.

20.3 Expected utility theory and prospect theory

The NLRPL model is an appropriate form for estimating models associated with **expected utility theory** (EUT) and other non-linear behavioral frameworks such as prospect theory, including rank dependent utility theory and cumulative prospect theory. In this section we summarize the key elements of these theoretical and behavioral frameworks as a behaviorally appealing way of using the NLRPL model.

Random utility maximization (RUM) theory was proposed by Marschak (1959) for discrete choices and formally introduced to behavioral choice modeling by McFadden (1974). RUM assumes that a representative individual acts as if they are a utility maximizer and will accordingly choose the alternative that maximizes utility. Given the inability of the analyst to observe all sources of utility, the utility can only be represented in a modeling framework up to a probability. A growing number of studies have investigated other behavioral paradigms such as EUT, rank dependent utility theory, and prospect theory.

EUT, originally developed by Bernoulli in 1738, recognizes that individual decision making is made under uncertainty or risk (i.e., the outcome is not deterministic). It assumes that an individual compares the expected utility (EU) values associated with particular options. That is, individuals are assumed to compare "the weighted sums obtained by adding the utility values of outcomes multiplied by their respective probabilities" (Mongin 1997, 342). Von Neumann and Morgenstern (1947) extended EUT into game theory, with a focus on how decision makers maximize their EU by considering the potential reactions of other agents. Von Neumann and Morgenstern (1947) and Savage (1954), in the case of risk and uncertainty, respectively, are the authors of EUT. EUT has been extensively applied in a growing number of fields such as experimental economics, environmental economics, and health economics. A recent application of EUT in traveler behavior studies is in the context of measuring travel time reliability.

Unlike RUM models, which typically assume a linear-additive utility function for the observed or representative consumer component (i.e., $U = \sum_k (\beta_k \times x_k)$, where β_k are the estimated parameters and x_k are the attributes that underlie individual preferences), EUT models postulate a non-linear functional form, i.e., $U = x^r$ (see Harrison and Rutström 2009), typically with one attribute (given the focus often on lotteries). A basic EUT model is given in Equation (20.25):

$$E(U) = \sum_m (p_m \cdot x_m^r),\tag{20.25}$$

where $E(U)$ is the expected utility; $m\ (=1,\ldots,M)$ are the possible outcomes for an attribute and $m \geq 2$; p_m is the probability associated with the mth outcome; x_m is the value for the mth outcome; and r is the parameter to be estimated which explains respondents' attitudes towards risk ($r < 1$: risk averse; $r = 1$: risk neutral (which implies a linear function form); $r > 1$: risk loving).

20.3.1 Risk or uncertainty?

Knight (1921), in the first study that addressed the distinction between uncertainty and risk, argued that the economic environment is characterized by unmeasurable uncertainty rather than measurable risk. Mongin (1997) further explained that risk can be fully measured either by using historical results or by observation, suggesting that it is not feasible to measure or quantify uncertainty due to its stochastic nature. Travel time variability is an example of an event that is both random and unsystematic. For example, Noland and Polak (2002) emphasized that the difference between travel time variability and congestion is linked in that travelers have difficulty in predicting the former (e.g., congestion caused by unforeseen road accidents or service cancellations) from day to day, while they can, to some extent, predict the variation in travel time due to congestion (e.g., peak hours versus off-peak hours). Hence, travel time variability is a type of uncertainty rather than risk.

However, the distinction between uncertainty and risk has not been clearly addressed in many literatures. In traveler behavior research, for example, some studies use "risk" to describe variability in travel time. Senna (1994) used risk averse, neutral, or loving to specify individuals' risk attitudes in the face of travel time variability, in a EUT framework. Batley and Ibáñez (2009) interpreted travel time variability as "time risk." The concept of travel time variability is strictly uncertainty rather than risk, with any ambiguity leading to a crucial problem in understanding travel time reliability. Experimental economists have empirically identified the difference between attitudes towards risk and uncertainty, by using one choice task to estimate attitudes toward risk (i.e., objective), and another task for the same respondents to estimate attitudes toward uncertainty (i.e., subjective) (see Andersen et al. 2007b).

Knight (1921) used known and unknown probabilities to distinguish between risk and uncertainty, similar to the ambiguous versus unambiguous probabilities proposed by Ellsberg (1961). Based on EUT, Savage (1954) developed subjective expected utility theory (SEUT) to understand decision making under uncertainty, which uses subjective probabilities to weight utilities. Some authors (e.g., Bates *et al.* 2001) have suggested that the variability in travel time should be represented by subjective probabilities (i.e., a subject's perception of unreliability in travel times, which may differ across subjects). The majority of travel time reliability studies that have incorporated EUT have exogenously imposed probabilities in stated choice (SC) experiments. For example, Small *et al.* (1999) and Asensio and Matas (2008) provided respondents with the probabilities associated with different travel times. Although other authors have not displayed probabilities in their surveys, they have treated travel times as equi-probably distributed when calculating the expected value. This is however, also an exogenous probability weighting (see e.g., Bates *et al.* 2001; Hollander 2006; Batley and Ibáñez 2009).

This endogeneity issue might be the biggest challenge for future research. One way of accounting for this is to develop models to estimate subjective probabilities. This has been undertaken in experimental economics, by jointly estimating individuals' attitudes and subjective probabilities using structural maximum likelihood methods (see Anderson *et al.* 2007b). Theoretically, we can emulate experimental economists. However, their choice contexts are rather simple – i.e., binary choice (two alternatives only) and one attribute (e.g., the price of lottery). Hence, to estimate subjective probabilities would be a difficult task in discrete choice analysis where we commonly allow for many alternatives and many attributes. In addition to the estimation of subjective probabilities, Slovic (1987) suggested that "objective" assessment may also be used, for example, using probabilities provided by experts who have full knowledge on all possible outcomes, or by asking for respondent perceptions. However, this "objective" strategy would involve changes in the design of SC experiments. For example, instead of designing probabilities of occurrence of different levels associated with an attribute and showing the designed probabilities in a choice experiment (CE), analysts would ask a respondent for their subjective understanding of probability distributions.

However, do individuals make decisions exactly in an EU manner? Many experimental economic and psychological studies have questioned this assumption theoretically and empirically (Allais 1953; Luce and Suppes 1965). An alternative that is growing in popularity is the non-EU theory, prospect theory.

20.3.2 The appeal of prospect theory

Prospect theory, proposed by Kahneman and Tversky (1979), is often referred to as 'original PT' (OPT), which offers a number of significant differences relative to normative EUT. The five key features are (i) Kahneman and Tversky's assumption of the conceived choice behavior process in which subjects *first frame (or edit) the offered prospects*, particularly by coding them as gains and losses relative to a reference point, and successively evaluate these edited prospects and then choose the prospect of highest value; (ii) *reference dependence*, to recognize different value functions for gains and losses with respect to the reference point, often the current wealth position (Laury and Holt 2000), rather than a utility function defined over final wealth in EU models (i.e., $U = f(x + w)$ where x is the payoff of a lottery ticket, and w is the current wealth position); (iii) *diminishing sensitivity*, associated with the decreasing marginal value of both gains and losses (e.g., many psychological studies found a concave utility function over monetary gains and a convex utility function over monetary losses); (iv) *loss aversion*, defined as the disutility of a loss, is valued higher than the utility of an equivalent gain; and (v) the use of non-linear probability weighting to transform original probabilities to explain Allais' paradox, the violation of EUT (Allais 1953) mechanism in EU models, where probabilities of occurrence are directly used as weights.

Tversky and Kahneman (1992) extended the OPT version in response to an idea initially proposed by Quiggin (1982), in which the transformed probabilities are influenced by the rank of the (attribute) outcomes in terms of preference, referred to as cumulative prospect theory (CPT). The functional form for the decision weights is then specified in line with Quiggin's **rank-dependent utility theory** (RDUT). By incorporating rank dependent decision weights, CPT is capable of revealing personality characteristics (pessimism or optimism) (Diecidue and Wakker 2001). Prospect theory also introduces a framework to model risk attitudes in terms of non-linearity in weighted probabilities, which are captured though sensitivity towards outcomes (i.e., the curvature of utility) in EU models (Wakker 2008). Van de Kaa (2008) provides an extended overview of the basic assumptions of prospect theory and a comparison with those of utility theory (including EUT).

The initial classic contribution by Kahneman and Tversky (1979) posited prospect theory as a set of generic assumptions, in which functions are characterized by qualitative properties such as a convex–concave value function, and an inversely S-shaped weighted probability, rather than particular functional forms such as the approximation of the value function as the power of attribute levels and the probability weighting function that Tversky and Kahneman used in their later article (Kahneman and Tversky 1992). In the 1992 paper, they posited CPT not as a different theory but as "a new *version* of Prospect Theory," and they included even more restrictive simplifying assumptions that may be used to describe observed behavior in particular contexts (e.g., a linear approximation of the power function).

Tversky and Kahneman (1992) provided parametric formulae for the value functions under a constant relative risk aversion (CRRA) assumption, as well as a one-parameter probability weighting function. The value function in the gain domain for $x \geq 0$ is $V = x^\alpha$ and in the loss domain, where $x < 0$, it is $V = -\lambda(-x)^\beta$. α and β are the exponents of the value function over gains and losses, respectively, and λ is the coefficient of loss aversion postulating that a loss is treated as more serious than a gain of equal size.[1] The probability weighting function suggested by Tversky and Kahneman (1992) is given in Equation (20.26). There are a number of alternative weighting functions, e.g., a two-parameter weighting function proposed by Goldstein and Einhorn (1987) given in Equation (20.27), and another version of a one-parameter weighting function derived by Prelec (1998), given in Equation (20.28):

$$w(p_m) = \frac{p_m^\gamma}{[p_m^\gamma + (1 - p_m)^\gamma]^{\frac{1}{\gamma}}}. \tag{20.26}$$

$$w(p_m) = \frac{\tau p_m^\gamma}{\tau p_m^\gamma + (1 - p_m)^\gamma}. \tag{20.27}$$

$$w(p_m) = \exp(-(-\ln p_m)^\gamma). \tag{20.28}$$

$w(p)$ is the probability weight function; p_m is the probability associated with the mth outcome for an alternative with multiple possible outcomes; and γ is the probability weighting parameter to be estimated, which measures the degree of curvature of the weighting function. τ in Equation (20.27) measures the elevation of the probability weighting function ($w(p)$).

In an OPT model, the value function is directly weighted by a probability weighting function (i.e., $OP(V) = \sum_m w(p_m)V(x_m)$), where the transformed probabilities are independent of outcomes. However, in a CPT model, the transformation, $\pi(p)$, often referred to as **decision weights**, is performed over

---

[1] The corresponding values estimated by Tversky and Kahneman are 0.88 for α, 0.88 for β and 2.25 for λ.

Li and Hensher (2015) have proposed a very general framework for studying risky prospects that enables identification of the preferred form in contrast to evaluating a limited number of predefined functional forms.

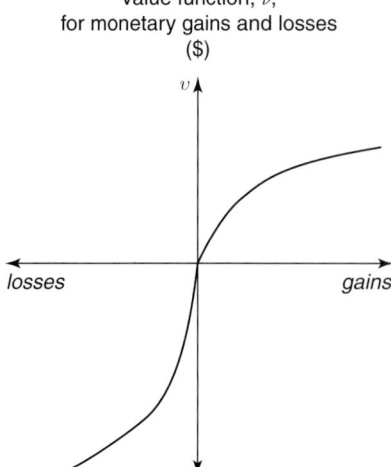

Value function, ν,
for monetary gains and losses
($)

Prospect Theory: developed on controlled
laboratory experiments (Kahneman and
Tversky 1979; Tversky and Kahneman 1992)

Figure 20.1   Typical PT value functions over monetary gains and losses

the cumulative probability distribution, where all potential outcomes are typically ranked in increasing order in terms of preference (from worst to best, see
Equation 20.4).[2] Hence, the cumulative prospect value is defined as:
$CP(V) = \sum_m \pi(p_m) V(x_m)$:

$$\pi(p_m) = w(p_m + p_{m+1} + \ldots + p_n) - w(p_{m+1} + \ldots + p_n) \text{ for}$$

$$m = 1, 2, \ldots, n - 1; \text{ and } \pi(p_n) = w(p_n). \tag{20.29}$$

Empirical estimation in Tversky and Kahneman (1992) produced the value
functions for gains and losses shown in Figure 20.1, where the increase in
monetary gains (losses) leads to more satisfaction (dissatisfaction) and
respondents tend to be risk averse over certain gains, while risk seeking over
certain losses for a very small niche sample. Tversky and Kahneman also
estimated an inverse S-shaped weighting function (see Figure 20.2). By combining the curvature of the value functions and the probability weighting
functions, a four-fold pattern of risk attitudes[3] is revealed: risk seeking for low
probability gains and high probability losses, and risk aversion for high

[2]   Outcomes can also be ranked from best to worst (see e.g., Diecidue and Wakker 2001).
[3]   Risk-averse is where a sure alternative is preferred to a risky alternative (i.e., with multiple possible
outcomes) of equal expected value; risk-seeking is where a risky alternative is preferred to a sure
alternative of equal expected value.

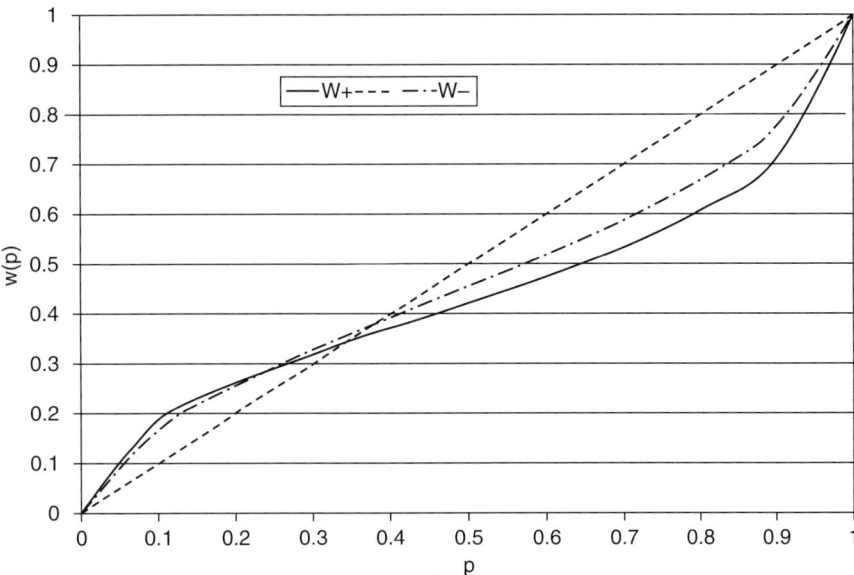

Figure 20.2 Probability weighting functions for gains (W^+) and losses (W^-) from Tversky and Kahneman (1992); smooth line is average, - - - is gains, and –·– is losses.

probability gains and low probability losses, which is a common finding of prospect theory studies based on monetary gains and losses (Fox and Poldrack 2008).

A full PT model must address the following criteria in a systematic and parametric manner: (i) *reference dependence* (i.e., separate value functions defined over gains and losses); (ii) *diminishing sensitive* (i.e., the curvatures of value functions suggesting decreasing marginal value of both gains and losses) and *loss aversion*; (iii) *non-linear probability weighting*. In an OPT model, the probability weighting function is independent of outcomes; while in a CPT model, the decision weights are *rank dependent*. In addition to the above characteristics, OPT includes the editing process. CPT also allows for different probability weight functions for probabilities of gains and probabilities of losses.

For the one-parameter probability weighting function in Equation 20.26, γ^+ and γ^- represent the probability weighting parameter in the gain and loss domains, respectively. As an example, Tversky and Kahneman estimated a probability weighting parameter in their CPT model of 0.61 for gains (γ^+) and 0.69 for losses (γ^-). However, some CPT studies assume the same weighting parameter for gains and losses, and even the same risk attitude parameter (e.g., Harrison and Rutström 2008). Although there are some variations in these prospect theory studies, a focus is to understand risk attitudes and the shape of probability weighting empirically.

The decision weighted value function, $(W(V))$, is given as in Equation (20.30):

$$W(V) = \sum_m [w(p_m) \times V]. \tag{20.30}$$

Camerer and Ho (1994) suggest that the decision weighting function should be used, rather than EUT linear probability weighting, given that the former is able to capture individual subjective beliefs and improve model fit. With regard to non-linear decision weighting, a common finding is that people tend to over-weight outcomes with lower probabilities, and to under-weight outcomes with higher probabilities (see, e.g., Tversky and Kahneman 1992; Camerer and Ho 1994; Tversky and Fox 1995). This is because probabilities are weighted by an inverse S-shaped probability weighting function (see Figure 20.2 when $\gamma = 0.56$). Roberts et al. (2006) have found opposite results (i.e., over-weighting outcomes with higher probabilities and under-weighting outcomes with lower probabilities), by applying decision weights in the context of individuals' preferences for environmental quality.

Constant absolute risk aversion (CARA) and constant relative risk aversion (CRRA) are the two main options for analyzing the attitude towards risk, where the CARA model form postulates an exponential specification for the utility function, and the CRRA form is a power specification (e.g., $U = x^{\alpha}$). For the non-linear utility specification, the CRRA form rather than CARA is used in this study, given that CARA is usually a less plausible description of the attitude towards risk than CRRA (see Blanchard and Fischer 1989). Blanchard and Fischer (1989, 44) further explain that "the CARA specification is, however, sometimes analytically more convenient than the CRRA specification, and thus also belongs to the standard tool kit." CRRA has been widely used in behavioral economics and psychology (see, e.g., Tversky and Kahneman 1992; Holt and Laury 2002; Harrison and Rutström 2009) and often delivers "a better fit than alternative families" (Wakker 2008, 1329). We estimate the constant *relative* risk aversion (CRRA) model form as a general power specification (i.e., $U = x^{1-\alpha}/(1-\alpha)$), more widely used than the simple x^{α} form (Andersen et al. 2012; Holt and Laury 2002).

20.4 Case study: travel time variability and the value of expected travel time savings

It is well accepted in travel behavior research that the decision making environment in which travel choices are made involves assessment of attributes that have risk (and uncertainty[4]) associated with them; for example, the variability associated with travel time for the same repeated trip. Although recent choice analysis research has focused on alternative treatments of attributes under the broad rubric of heuristics and attribute processing (see Hensher 2010 for an overview and Chapter 21), there has been a somewhat limited effort to formally include, in travel choice analysis, the "obvious" observation that attribute levels vary in repeated travel activity (e.g., travel times for the daily commute), and hence attribute risk and perceptual conditioning[5] is ever present which, if ignored, become yet another confounding source of unobserved utility associated with alternatives on offer (see van de Kaa 2008).

Travel time variability has become an important research focus in the transportation literature, in particular traveler behavior research. Within a linear utility framework, the scheduling model and the mean–variance model, typically developed empirically within the SC theoretic framework, are two dominant approaches to empirical measurement of the value of time variability (see e.g., Small *et al.* 1999; Bates *et al.* 2001; Li *et al.* 2010 for a review). However, with a few exceptions, the majority of the existing travel time variability studies ignored two important components of decision making under risk that are present in responses to travel time variability: non-linear probability weighing (or perceptual conditioning), and risk attitudes, although some of the studies recognized travel time variability in their SC experiments in terms of a series of travel times for a trip (e.g., 5 or 10). These traditional approaches for travel time variability are implemented under "linear probability weighting" and "risk neutrality."

Incorporating perceptual conditioning (through decision weights), borrowed from prospect theory, into a EUT specification of particular attributes, but staying within an overall RUM framework, offers a new variant on EU, which we call attribute-specific extended EUT (EEUT). A number of parametric functional forms for such decision weights have been developed in the

---

[4] Risk refers to a circumstance where the chooser knows with precision the probability distribution of possible outcomes (e.g., when the analyst indicates the chance of specific travel times occurring over repeated commuting trips). Uncertainty refers to a situation where a chooser is not offered such information, and is required to assess the probabilities of potential outcomes with some degree of vagueness and ambiguity (e.g., when an analyst indicates that a trip could take as long as x minutes and as quick as y minutes, without any notion of likely occurrence).

[5] The Allais paradox (Allais 1953) suggests that probabilities given in choice experiments are in reality transformed by decision makers in the face of risky choices. To account for the perceptual translation of agents, non-linear probability weighting was introduced by a number of authors to transform the analyst-provided probabilities into chooser perceptions.

published literature, together with alternative treatments of risk embedded in the value function. The case study here draws on the contribution of Hensher *et al.* (2011).

This EEUT functional form embedded within a RUM model allows for non-linearity in an attribute-specific value specification (α) conditioned on probability weighting ($w(p)$), with the attribute of interest entering non-linearly. The specification of the attribute has an associated chance of each level occurring over R occasions (r = 1,...,R). The overall utility function for this representation of one attribute expressed as EEUT, is given in Equations (20.31) and (20.32):

$$EEUT(U) = \beta_x\{[W(P_1)x_1^{1-\alpha} + W(P_2)x_2^{1-\alpha} + \ldots + W(P_R)x_R^{1-\alpha}]/(1-\alpha)\}. \tag{20.31}$$

$$U = EEUT(U) + \sum_{z=1}^{Z} \beta_z S_z. \tag{20.32}$$

$W(P)$ is a non-linear probability weighting function which converts raw probabilities (P) associated with attribute x_1, x_2, ... x_R with R levels over R occurrences, as shown typically in a SC experiment (see below); and α has to be estimated, where $(1-\alpha)$ indicates the attitude towards risk.[6] There are also a number of other variables (S) in the utility expression that are not specified this way, and are added in as linear in parameters. The presence of α, γ, and τ in Equations (20.27) and (20.31) results in an embedded attribute-specific treatment in the overall utility expression associated with each alternative, that is non-linear in a number of parameters. Only if $(1 - \alpha) = 1$, and γ and τ =1 does Equation (20.31) collapse to a linear utility function. Estimation of this model requires a non-linear logit form, as set out in Section 20.2.

20.4.1 Empirical application

The empirical focus here is on estimating the non-linear probability weighted travel time variability profiles using four probability weighting functional forms, and deriving measures of WTP for travel time variability-embedded values of travel time savings (VTTS). The data are drawn from a study

---

[6] The experimental design and modeling framework accommodates decisions under risk, although travel time variability is best described under uncertainty rather than risk. Research should also address choice made under uncertainty (in the face of travel time variability) in terms of both experimental design and modeling approaches.

Table 20.1 Trip attributes in stated choice design

Routes A and B (for a given Departure Time)
Recent trip time components:
Free flow travel time
Slowed down travel time
Stop/start/crawling travel time
Total trip time associated with other repeated trips:
Time associated with a quicker trip
Time associated with a slower trip
Occurrence probabilities for each trip time:
Probability of trip being quicker
Probability of trip being slower
Probability of recent trip time
Trip cost attributes:
Running cost
Toll Cost

undertaken in Australia in the context of toll versus free roads, which utilised a SC experiment involving two SC alternatives (i.e., route A and route B) pivoted around the knowledge base of travelers (i.e., the current trip). The trip attributes associated with each route are summarized in Table 20.1.

Each alternative has three travel scenarios – "a quicker travel time than recent trip time," "a slower time than recent trip time," and "the recent trip time."[7] Respondents were advised that *departure time remains unchanged*. Each is associated with a corresponding probability[8] of occurrence to indicate that travel time is not fixed but varies from time to time. For all attributes except the toll cost, minutes for quicker and shorter trips, and the probabilities associated with the three trip times, the values for the SC alternatives are variations around the values for the most recent trip. Given the lack of exposure to tolls for many travelers in the study catchment area, the toll levels are fixed over a range, varying from no toll to $4.20, with the upper limit determined by the trip length of the sampled trip. The variations used for each attribute are given in Table 20.2, based on a range that we have shown in various studies (see Li *et al.* 2010) to be meaningful to respondents, while still delivering sufficient variability to identify attribute preference.

---

[7] The data was not collected specifically to study trip time variability, and hence the limit of three travel times, in contrast to the five levels used by Small *et al.* (1999) and 10 levels used by Bates *et al.* (2001), where the latter studies focused specifically on travel time variability (or reliability).

[8] The probabilities are designed and hence exogenously induced to respondents, similar to other travel time variability studies.

Table 20.2 Profile of the attribute range in the stated choice design

Attribute	Level 1	Level 2	Level 3	Level 4	Level 5	Level 6	Level 7	Level 8
Free flow time	−40%	−30%	−20%	−10%	0%	10%	20%	30%
Slowed down time	−40%	−30%	−20%	−10%	0%	10%	20%	30%
Stop/Start time	−40%	−30%	−20%	−10%	0%	10%	20%	*30%*
Quicker trip time	−5%	−10%	−15%	−20%	–	–	–	–
Slower trip time	10%	20%	30%	40%	–	–	–	–
Prob. of quicker time	10%	20%	30%	40%	–	–	–	–
Prob. of most recent trip time	20%	30%	40%	50%	60%	70%	80%	–
Prob. of slower trip time	10%	20%	30%	40%	–	–	–	–
Running costs	−25%	−15%	−5%	5%	15%	25%	35%	45%
Toll costs	$0.00	$0.60	$1.20	$1.80	$2.40	$3.00	$3.60	$4.20

There are three versions of the experimental design, depending on the trip length (10 to 30 minutes, 31 to 45 minutes, and more than 45 minutes, the latter capped at 120 minutes), with each version having 32 choice situations (or scenarios) blocked into two sub-sets of 16 choice situations each. An example of a choice scenario is given in Figure 20.3. The first alternative is described by attribute levels associated with a recent trip, with the levels of each attribute for Routes A and B pivoted around the corresponding level of actual trip alternative.

In total, 280 commuters were sampled for this study. The experimental design method of *D*-efficiency used here is specifically structured to increase the statistical performance of the models with smaller samples than are required for other less (statistically) efficient designs, such as orthogonal designs (see Rose and Bliemer 2008 and Chapter 7).

The socio-economic profile of the data is given in Table 20.3, and the descriptive overview of choice experiment attributes is given in Table 20.4.

The descriptive statistics for the time and probability variables are given in Table 20.5.

The design assumes a fixed level for a shorter or longer trip within each choice scenario. However, across the choice scenarios, we vary the probability of a shorter, a longer, and a recent trip time, and hence recognize the stochastic nature of the travel time distribution (see Table 20.2 where, for example, the probability of travel time occurrence varies from 10 percent to 40 percent in the CE).

Game 5

Illustrative Choice Experiment Screen

Make your choice given the route features presented in this table, thank you.

	Details of your recent trip	Route A	Route B
Average travel time experienced			
Time in free flow traffic (minutes)	25	14	12
Time slowed down by other traffic (minutes)	20	18	20
Time in stop/start/crawling traffic (minutes)	35	26	20
Probability of travel time			
9 minutes quicker	30%	30%	10%
As above	30%	50%	50%
6 minutes slower	40%	20%	40%
Trip costs			
Running costs	\$2.25	\$3.26	\$1.91
Toll costs	\$2.00	\$2.40	\$4.20
If you make the same trip again, which route would you choose?	O Current Road	O Route A	O Route B
If you could only choose between the two new routes, which route would you choose?		O Route A	O Route B

Figure 20.3 Illustrative stated choice screen

20.4.2 Empirical analysis: mixed multinomial logit model with non-linear utility functions

We focus on an MMNL model. MNL estimates are given in Hensher *et al.* (2011). For the random parameters, unconstrained normal distributions are applied to the *Expected time* parameter and the *Cost* parameter. Given that the distributions for α and γ are quite likely to be asymmetrical, skewed normal distributions are used for these two parameters. The skewed normal distribution is given as $\beta_{k,i} = \beta_k + \sigma_k V_{k,i} + \theta_k |W_{k,i}|$, where both $V_{k,i}$ and $W_{k,i}$ are distributed as standard normal. This form is in line with Equation (20.5) except that we have not included the covariate term, $\mathbf{\Delta z}_i$ (observable heterogeneity through $\mathbf{z}_i$)[9] but have added in the extra term to allow for skewness or asymmetry. The second term is the absolute value. θ_k may be positive or negative, so the skewness can go in either direction. The range of this parameter is infinite in both directions, but since the distribution is skewed, it is therefore asymmetric.

We can derive the value of an expected travel time savings (VETTS) as given in Equation (20.33). The only difference across the four models is in the form of the probability weighting functions:[10]

[9] In the mixed logit specification, we did investigate the role of socioeconomic characteristics as sources of systematic heterogeneity associated with the random parameters; however we were unable to find any statistically significant influences.

[10] In the experimental design, there are three possible travel times for each alternative route within a choice set.

Table 20.3 Descriptive socio-economic statistics

Purpose	Statistic	Gender (1=female)	Income	Age
Commuter	Mean	0.575	$67,145	42.52
	Std. Deviation	0.495	$36,493	14.25

Table 20.4 Descriptive statistics for costs and time, by segment

	All times of day		Peak		Off-Peak	
	Mean	Std. Dev.	Mean	Std. Dev.	Mean	Std. Dev.
Running costs	$3.15	$2.56	$3.58	$3.01	$2.92	$2.26
Toll costs	$1.41	$1.50	$1.40	$1.50	$1.41	$1.51
Total time	39.29	16.58	36.93	16.25	40.54	16.61

Table 20.5 Travel times and probabilities of occurrence (13,440 cases)

Variable	Mean	Std. Dev.	Minimum	Maximum
P_S	0.25	0.11	0.1	0.4
P_L	0.25	0.11	0.1	0.4
P_{MR}	0.50	0.15	0.2	0.8
X(quicker)	4.80	3.14	0	18
Y(slower)	9.60	6.28	1	36
MR_T	39.29	16.58	10	119
S_T	34.48	14.98	7	115
L_T	48.89	21.09	11	150
PT_S	8.61	5.61	0.8	40.8
PT_L	12.12	7.68	1.1	56.4
PT_{MR}	19.69	10.57	2	95.2

Notes: P_S, P_L and P_{MR} are probabilities for quicker, slower, and recent trip time, MR_T is the most recent travel time (the sum of three components: free flow, slowed down and stop/start times), X(quicker) and Y(slower) are the amounts of quicker and slower times compared with most recent time; which are designed and presented in the experiment. S_T is the actual quicker (or shorter) travel time ($=MR_T -X(quicker)$); L_T is the actual slower (or longer) travel time ($=MR_T +Y(slower)$); PTE ($=P_S * E_T$), PT_L ($=P_L * L_T$) and PT_{MR} ($=P_{MR} * MR_T$) are probability weighted values for quicker, slower and most recent time respectively.

Table 20.6 Mixed multinomial logit (MMNL) within an *EEUT* framework

Variable	Coefficient	*t*-ratio
Nonrandom parameters:		
Reference constant	0.5129	2.69
Tollasc	−0.6766	−4.32
Age (years)	0.0305	7.26
Means for random parameters:		
Alpha (α)	0.4727	14.56
Gamma (γ)	0.7355	2.33
Expected Time (minutes)	−0.3708	−4.69
Cost ($)	−0.8554	−9.88
Standard deviations for random parameters:		
Alpha (α)	1.5896	18.21
Gamma (γ)	1.3276	3.12
Expected Time (minutes)	0.6911	4.82
Cost ($)	1.1720	9.53
Skew normal θ for Alpha	−1.8673	−20.01
Skew normal θ for Gamma	0.3469	0.57
No. of observations	4480	
Information Criterion : AIC	5444.59	
LL	−2709.29	
VETTS	**7.73 (0.53)**	

Simulation based on 250 Halton draws[11]

$$VETTS_{Mi} = \frac{\beta_{ti}[W(P_1)t_1^{-\alpha i} + W(P_{2i})t_2^{-\alpha i} + W(P_3)t_3^{-\alpha i}]}{\beta_{Costi}} \quad i = 1, .., 4 \text{ models.}$$

$$(20.33)$$

The modeling results of an EEUT MMNL model, using Equation 20.26 as the preferred functional form for the decisions weights, are summarized in Table 20.6. All parameter estimates are statistically significant above the 95 percent confidence interval, with the exception of the Skewed normal θ parameter component underlying γ.

Compared to MNL, the MMNL model delivers significant improvement in model fit (AIC: 5,444.59 versus 6,850.86; LL: −2,709.29 versus −3,418.43).

---

[11] We ran models with 100 draws, 250 draws and 500 draws. The model with 250 draws has a better model fit than other two models (log-likelihood: −2731.55 for 100 draws; −2709.29 for 250 draws; −2745.48 for 500 draws). Models took between 10 and 25 hours to estimate and converge. Further details of Halton draws are provided in Bhat (2001) and Halton (1970).

The mean α estimate is 0.4727, hence 1 minus α is smaller than unity, suggesting a risk seeking attitude on average. It is interesting to reveal the attitude towards risk at the disaggregate level; 65.7 percent of the sampled car commuters (280 in total) have positive α estimates while 34.3 percent of them have a negative α, suggesting that part of the sampled respondents have risk taking attitudes $(1 - \alpha > 1)$ while others tend to be risk averse $(1 - \alpha < 1)$. This finding (i.e., a higher proportion of risk taking car commuters) also explains a generic risk taking attitude from the previous MNL models (e.g., MNL Model 2: $1 - \alpha = 0.6166 < 1$). Senna (1994) assumed that his sampled commuters with flexible arrival times were risk averse when making risky time-related decisions, where the assumed risk attitude parameter was 1.4 (>1), and his sampled commuters with fixed arrival times were risk taking with the assumed parameter of 0.5 (<1). The mix of risk taking and risk averse attitudes revealed by the MMNL model may be attributed to commuters with a fixed arrival time and commuters with flexible arrival times, both sampled in our study.

With regard to γ (probability weighting) at the individual level, the γ estimate ranges from 0.9261 to 4.1734, with a mean of 1.7419 and a standard deviation of 0.5884. We have plotted (in Excel) the probability weighting function in Figure 20.4, where the dotted line represents the probability weighting function for the respondent who has the lowest γ value ($= 0.9261$) which is close to a straight line, and the dashed line represents the probability weighting function for the respondent with the highest γ value ($= 4.1734$), under which the raw probabilities are significantly under-weighted. On average ($\gamma = 1.7419$), our sampled car commuters tend to under-weight the given probabilities shown in the experiment, given that the design probabilities for the quicker and slower trips range from 0.1 to 0.4, and the probabilities for the recent trip range from 0.2 to 0.8.[12]

Under the MMNL model, the VETTS values range from \$6.30 per person hr. to \$9.56 per person hr. The mean VETTS is \$7.73 per person hr. with a standard deviation of \$0.53 per person hr. These values are impressive and encouraging, given that there are four random parameters in the MMNL model (two skewed normal distributions and two normal distributions) with both time and cost conditioned on random parameters, and yet the model is still well behaved in terms of such a meaningful estimated range

---

[12] Under the probability weighting function with $\gamma = 1.7419$, within the range of our designed probabilities, only when the raw probability is 0.8, the transformed probability is slightly higher (i.e., 0.807).

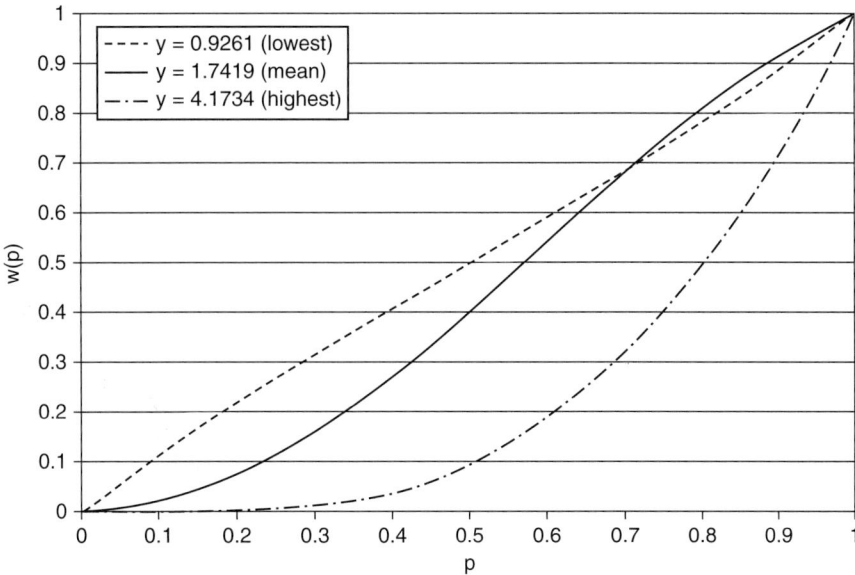

Figure 20.4 Individual probability weighting function curves (MMNL)

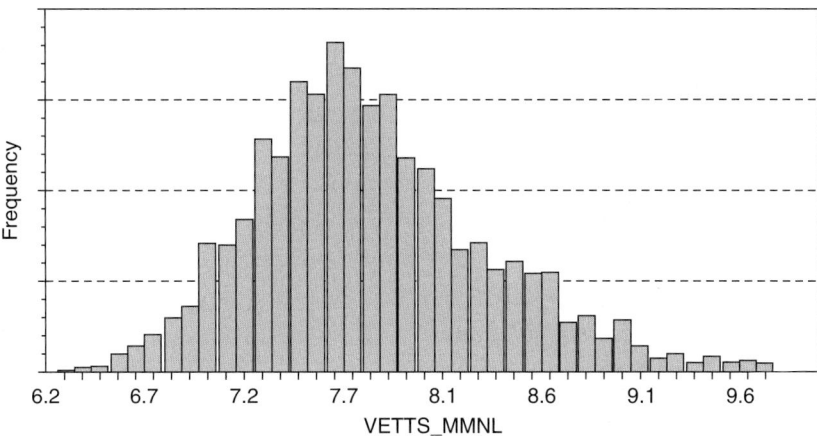

Figure 20.5 Distribution of VETTS (unit: $/person hour) in MMNL model

(see Figure 20.5), giving increased behavioral realism relative to the simple MNL model. It is common to observed extreme values and sign changes in distributions of WTP in many studies where unconstrained distributions are used (see Hensher 2006). The log-normal circumvents a sign change but typically exhibits a very long tail. Constrained distributions that assume no sign change have behavioral appeal, but have been criticized as being arbitrary in their imposed constraints, and many distributions have been treated as symmetric, which also has limitations. In this case study we have successfully accommodated unconstrained distributions and asymmetry, resulting in behaviorally plausible distributions.[13]

Despite the behavioral advantages of more complex models (such as MMNL), the challenge of using these models is in how to select an appropriate set of WTP estimates to use in practical applications (see Hensher and Goodwin 2004), which often seek a single mean estimate, and occasionally a number of mean estimates representing each part (e.g., thirds) of a distribution. This difficulty has been associated with almost all previous studies where the models are established on the linear utility specification (without risk attitude and probability weighting). However, in this case study, where preferences, attitude towards risk, and probability weighting are all accommodated in one single model, the MMNL model delivers a much lower standard deviation around the mean WTP estimate than its corresponding MNL model (MMNL: $0.53 per person hr. versus $3.21 per person hr.).[14] In a traditional linear MMNL model under risk neutrality and linear probability weighting, variations in random parameters have empirically tended to lead to a much wider range of estimates or higher standard deviations. However, in this non-linear model allowing for risk attitudes and probability weighting, and more importantly unobserved heterogeneity, extreme and/or sign changing estimates of VETTS are totally absent, and hence the model delivers a much more behaviorally "appealing" range of WTP (VETTS: $6.30 per person hr. to $9.65 per person hr.). Therefore, this non-linear EEUT MMNL model not only provides a much better model fit and improved behavioral explanation, but also offers appealing empirical inputs into practical applications.[15]

---

[13] Some applied studies often remove the extreme tails when using unconstrained distributions.

[14] The standard deviation in the MNL model is caused by different levels of probabilities and times (see Equation 20.31).

[15] This commentary does not suggest that there may be other influences at play; however attributing the findings to preferences, probability weighting, and attitude toward risks does not preclude the role of other effects. The evidence nevertheless is very encouraging and suggests that consideration of these additional behavioral dimensions has merit.

20.5 NLRPLogit commands for Table 20.6 model

> *As an aside*, NLRPlogit as a non-linear utility function cannot know in advance where the missing data are. Hence, regardless of whether a variable is included in a specific utility expression or not, if it is coded −999 and associated with any alternative that is included in the model, then it will create an error message (error number 509) and it is almost certain that the model will not estimate.

```
Timer$
? Generic for E, L, On and random parameters for risk attitude, time, cost
and Gammap
NLRPLogit
    ; Lhs = Choice1,cset3,alt3
    ; Choices = Curr,AltA,AltB
    ; checkdata
    ; maxit=10
    ; Labels = bref,betac, gammap,btolla,bage ,alphar, betatelo, ttau
    ; Start = 0.48, -0.33,0.21,-0.3,0.03 ,0.05,-0.34, 1.9
    ; Fn1 = earltr=(earlta^(1-alphar))/(1-alphar) ?equation 20.26
    ; Fn2 = latetr=(lateta^(1-alphar))/(1-alphar)
    ; Fn3 = ontr=(time^(1-alphar))/(1-alphar)
    ; Fn4 = wpo = (Ttau*pronp^gammap)/(Ttau*pronp^gammap + (1-pronp)^gammap)
    ; Fn5 = wpe = (Ttau*preap^gammap)/(Ttau*preap^gammap + (1-preap)^gammap)
    ; Fn6 = wpl = (Ttau*prlap^gammap)/(Ttau*prlap^gammap + (1-prlap)^gammap)
    ; Fn7 = Util1 = bref+wpe*(betatelo*earltr) +wpl*(betatelo*latetr) +betac*cost +
      wpo*(betatelo*ontr) +btolla*tollasc +bage*age1
    ; Fn8 = Util2 =    +wpe*(betatelo*earltr) +wpl*(betatelo*latetr) +betac*cost +
      wpo*(betatelo*ontr) +btolla*tollasc
    ; Fn9 = Util3 =    +wpe*(betatelo*earltr) +wpl*(betatelo*latetr) +betac*cost +
      wpo*(betatelo*ontr) +btolla*tollasc
    ; Model: U(Curr)=Util1/U(AltA) = util2/U(AltB) = util3
    ;RPL;halton;draws=250;pds=16;parameters;fcn=alphar(s), gammap(s),ttau (s),
        betatelo(n), betac(n)$? unconstrainted, some risk averse(alpha<0), some = 1
Nonlinear Utility Mixed Logit Model
Dependent variable              CHOICE1
Log likelihood function     -2755.94897
Restricted log likelihood   -4921.78305
Chi squared [  16 d.f.]      4331.66816
Significance level               .00000
McFadden Pseudo R-squared       .4400507
Estimation based on N =   4480, K =  16
Information Criteria: Normalization=1/N
              Normalized   Unnormalized
```

```
AIC                1.23748     5543.89794
Fin.Smpl.AIC       1.23750     5544.01983
Bayes IC           1.26036     5646.41600
Hannan Quinn       1.24554     5580.02945
Model estimated: Dec 10, 2010, 02:07:17
Constants only must be computed directly
            Use NLOGIT ;...;RHS=ONE$
At start values -4770.8696  .4223******
Response data are given as ind. choices
Replications for simulated probs. = 250
Halton sequences used for simulations
NLM model with panel has     280 groups
Fixed number of obsrvs./group=      16
Hessian is not PD. Using BHHH estimator
Number of obs.= 4480, skipped    0 obs
```

```
-----------+------------------------------------------------------------------
           |                    Standard              Prob.
  CHOICE1| Coefficient         Error       z     z>|Z|
-----------+------------------------------------------------------------------
           |Random parameters in utility functions
   ALPHAR|     .12802          .13272     .96    .3348
   GAMMAP|     .54470**        .26367    2.07    .0388
     TTAU|    1.75367         1.94962     .90    .3684
 BETATELO|    -.36685**        .15753   -2.33    .0199
    BETAC|    -.52151***       .09049   -5.76    .0000
           |Nonrandom parameters in utility functions
     BREF|     .44095***       .17019    2.59    .0096
   BTOLLA|    -.55830***       .17080   -3.27    .0011
     BAGE|     .01959***       .00353    5.55    .0000
           |Distns. of RPs. Std.Devs or limits of triangular
  SsALPHAR|    .26627***       .05738    4.64    .0000
  SsGAMMAP|    .18904          .28876     .65    .5127
    SsTTAU|    .05726          .78852     .07    .9421
  NsBETATE|    .48363**        .20742    2.33    .0197
   NsBETAC|    .13883          .16863     .82    .4103
  Theta_01|   -.59014**        .23723   -2.49    .0129
  Theta_02|   -.10310          .57432    -.18    .8575
  Theta_03|   -.10181         2.82528    -.04    .9713
-----------+------------------------------------------------------------------
Note: ***, **, * ==>  Significance at 1%, 5%, 10% level.
------------------------------------------------------------------------------
```

Elapsed time: 11 hours, 31 minutes, 51.64 seconds.

```
*************************EEUT****************************************************
```
? *earlta*, *lateta*, and *time* are three possible travel times per trip when arriving early, late and on time; and *preap*, *prlap*, and *pronp* are associated probabilities of occurrence correspondingly.

```
Nonlinear Utility Mixed Logit Model
Dependent variable                 CHOICE1
Log likelihood function      -2709.29810
Restricted log likelihood    -4921.78305
Chi squared [  13 d.f.]       4424.96991
Significance level                .00000
McFadden Pseudo R-squared        .4495292
Estimation based on N =    4480, K =  13
Information Criteria: Normalization=1/N
             Normalized    Unnormalized
AIC             1.21531      5444.59620
Fin.Smpl.AIC    1.21533      5444.67771
Bayes IC        1.23390      5527.89212
Hannan Quinn    1.22186      5473.95305
Model estimated: Dec 04, 2010, 06:55:30
Constants only must be computed directly
            Use NLOGIT ;...;RHS=ONE$
At start values -3956.6542  .3153******
Response data are given as ind. choices
Replications for simulated probs. = 250
Halton sequences used for simulations
NLM model with panel has      280 groups
Fixed number of obsrvs./group=        16
Hessian is not PD. Using BHHH estimator
Number of obs.= 4480, skipped    0 obs
```

CHOICE1	Coefficient	Standard Error	z	Prob. z>|Z|
Random parameters in utility functions				
ALPHAR	.47266***	.03246	14.56	.0000
GAMMAP	.73554**	.31511	2.33	.0196
BETATELO	-.37076***	.07905	-4.69	.0000
BETAC	-.85541***	.08658	-9.88	.0000
Nonrandom parameters in utility functions				
BREF	.51293***	.19047	2.69	.0071
BTOLLA	-.67658***	.15648	-4.32	.0000
BAGE	.03046***	.00420	7.26	.0000
Distns. of RPs. Std.Devs or limits of triangular				
SsALPHAR	1.58959***	.08727	18.21	.0000
SsGAMMAP	1.32758***	.42526	3.12	.0018
NsBETATE	.69113***	.14333	4.82	.0000
NsBETAC	1.17198***	.12297	9.53	.0000
Theta_01	-1.86732***	.09333	-20.01	.0000
Theta_02	.34601	.00859	.57	.5687

```
Note: ***, **, * ==>  Significance at 1%, 5%, 10% level.
```

```
 Elapsed time:    15 hours, 32 minutes, 29.18 seconds.
*******************************************RDUT****************************************
Ranking order in terms of preference under RDUT: Late arrival<Early arrival<On-time
arrival
NLRPLogit
     ; Lhs = Choice1,cset3,alt3
     ; Choices = Curr,AltA,AltB
     ; checkdata
     ; maxit=10
     ; Labels = bref,betac, gammap,btolla,bage ,alphar, betatleo
     ; Start =  0.9, -0.6,     1.5,  -0.6, 0.01    ,0.7,-1.2
     ; Fn1 = earltr=(earlta^(1-alphar))/(1-alphar)
     ; Fn2 = latetr=(lateta^(1-alphar))/(1-alphar)
     ; Fn3 = ontr=(time^(1-alphar))/(1-alphar)
     ; Fn4 = wpo = (pronp^gammap)/((pronp^gammap + (1-pronp)^gammap)^(1/gammap))
     ; Fn5 = wpe = (pr23^gammap)/((pr23^gammap + (1-pr23)^gammap)^(1/gammap))-
(pronp^gammap)/((pronp^gammap + (1-pronp)^gammap)^(1/gammap))
     ; Fn6 = wpl = 1-(pr23^gammap)/((pr23^gammap + (1-pr23)^gammap)^(1/gammap))
     ; Fn7 = Util1 = bref+wpe*(betatleo*earltr*D) +wpl*(betatleo*latetr*D) +betac
*cost + wpo*(betatleo*ontr*D) +btolla*tollasc +bage*age1
     ; Fn8 = Util2 = +wpe*(betatleo*earltr*D) +wpl*(betatleo*latetr*D) +betac
*cost + wpo*(betatleo*ontr*D) +btolla*tollasc
     ; Fn9 = Util3 = +wpe*(betatleo*earltr*D) +wpl*(betatleo*latetr*D) +betac
*cost + wpo*(betatleo*ontr*D) +btolla*tollasc
     ; Model: U(Curr)=Util1/U(AltA) = util2/U(AltB) = util3
     ;RPL;halton;draws=250;pds=16;parameters;fcn=alphar(n), gammap(n), betatleo(o)$
-----------------------------------------------------------------
Nonlinear Utility Mixed Logit Model
Dependent variable              CHOICE1
Log likelihood function     -2850.11800
Restricted log likelihood   -4921.78305
Chi squared [   9 d.f.]      4143.33010
Significance level               .00000
McFadden Pseudo R-squared     .4209176
Estimation based on N =    4480, K =    9
Information Criteria: Normalization=1/N
             Normalized    Unnormalized
AIC            1.27639       5718.23601
Fin.Smpl.AIC   1.27640       5718.27627
Bayes IC       1.28926       5775.90241
Hannan Quinn   1.28093       5738.55998
Model estimated: Jan 07, 2011, 00:53:05
Constants only must be computed directly
              Use NLOGIT ;...;RHS=ONE$
At start values -4440.5198  .3582******
Response data are given as ind. choices
Replications for simulated probs. = 250
Halton sequences used for simulations
NLM model with panel has     280 groups
```

```
Fixed number of obsrvs./group=        16
Hessian is not PD. Using BHHH estimator
Number of obs.= 4480, skipped      0 obs
---------- +--------------------------------------------------------------------
          |                      Standard             Prob.
CHOICE1 | Coefficient            Error      z    z>|Z|
---------- +--------------------------------------------------------------------
          |Random parameters in utility functions
  ALPHAR |     .78670***          .01365   57.62   .0000
  GAMMAP |    2.85297***         1.07067    2.66   .0077
BETATLEO |   -1.41922***          .05006  -28.35   .0000
          |Nonrandom parameters in utility functions
    BREF |    1.24792***          .16207    7.70   .0000
   BETAC |    -.35066***          .05036   -6.96   .0000
  BTOLLA |    -.76509***          .17930   -4.27   .0000
    BAGE |     .00326             .00325    1.00   .3169
          |Distns. of RPs. Std.Devs or limits of triangular
NsALPHAR |     .18777***          .02013    9.33   .0000
NsGAMMAP |    2.60405***          .68164    3.82   .0001
TsBETATL |    1.41922***          .05006   28.35   .0000
---------- +--------------------------------------------------------------------
Note: ***, **, * ==>  Significance at 1%, 5%, 10% level.
-------------------------------------------------------------------------------
Elapsed time:    17 hours, 48 minutes, 51.57 seconds.
```

20.6 Hybrid choice models

20.6.1 An overview of hybrid choice models

In recent years, there has been a growing interest in implementing model systems that encapsulate the endogeneity of "soft" variables such as attitudes and opinions. Although the literature on this topic dates back to at least 1997 (Ben Akiva *et al.* 1997, 1999; Swait 1994), it is only in the post-2007 period that we have seen an explosion of papers on the topic, which has become known in broad terms as hybrid choice models (HCM).

Daly *et al.* (2012) provide a very lucid discussion of the case for recognizing the role of soft variables in a manner that is different to simply including them as explanatory variables in a single choice model. We draw on their insights in this section. The focal point is a recognition that "decision makers differ from one another, and the treatment of differences in sensitivities (and hence choices) across individual decision makers is one of the main areas of interest in choice modeling. While these differences can often be directly linked to socio-demographic characteristics such as age and income, a case has repeatedly been made that underlying attitudes and perceptions may be equally important predictors for these differences, notwithstanding that these attitudes and perceptions may once again be explained by sociodemographic characteristics" (Daly *et al.* 2013, 37).

Although socio-demographic characteristics are directly measurable, the same does not apply to underlying perceptions and attitudes, which are unobserved in the same way that respondent-specific sensitivities are not known. Referred to as *latent variables*, these factors cannot be observed directly; rather, they can at best be inferred from other variables called *indicators* (Golob 2001). Attitudes and opinions are typically measured on a psychometric scale such as the popular Likert scale, and as responses to survey questions about attitudes, perceptions, or decision making protocols they are used as proxies of the underlying latent attitudes.

Attitudes reflect latent variables corresponding to the characteristics of the decision maker and reflect individuals' needs, values, tastes, and capabilities. Attitudes are formed over time and are affected by experience and external factors including socio-economic characteristics (SECs) (Walker and Ben Akiva 2002). Perceptions measure the individual's cognitive capacity to represent and evaluate the levels of the attributes of different alternatives. Perceptions are relevant because the choice process depends on how attribute levels are perceived by the individual beliefs of a specific consumer (Bolduc and Daziano 2010). The consequence of this recognition (which is in many ways well known through the earlier contributions of authors such as Joreskog and his software, LISREL), is that choice analysts are now jointly estimating attitudinal and choice models, focussing on the role of latent attitudes.

Historically, in the context of discrete choice modeling, we can begin with the workshop summary reports (Ben Akiva *et al.* 1997, 1999), from the Choice Symposium conference series that proposes a broad framework defined on observed variables (x), latent variables (x^*), observed indicators (I), utilities (U), choices (Y), and unobserved random terms ($\gamma,\varepsilon,\omega$). See Figure 20.6 for a graphical representation. The functional specification becomes:

$$x^* = x^*(x, \gamma), \tag{20.33a}$$

$$U = U(x, x^*, \varepsilon) \tag{20.33b}$$

$$Y = Y(U) \quad \text{(estimated as any form such as MNL, nested logit, MNP}\big) \tag{20.33c}$$

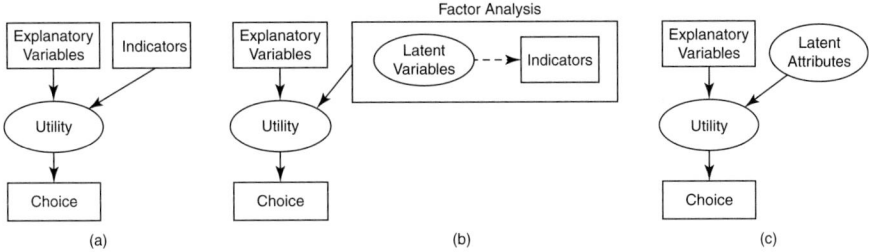

Figure 20.6   Incorporating latent variables in discrete choice models using different methods

$$I = I(x, x^*, \omega) \text{ (Binary, ordered, continuous).} \tag{20.33d}$$

The proposed reduced form is:

$$I = I(x, x^*, Y, \omega). \tag{20.34}$$

This is a relatively simple model to estimate by maximum-likelihood estimation (MLE). As long as U does not involve I, and I does not involve Y, the likelihood partitions are relatively simple to estimate. Ben Akiva *et al.* (2002) continue the development of this general model, suggesting simulation-based estimators, including Bayesian estimation. They also raise the important issue of model identification.

The use of attitudes in discrete choice models, in particular, is not new, and a number of different approaches has been used in past work. The most direct approach relies on using choice models with indicators. In this case, indicators of the underlying latent variable are treated as error-free explanatory predictors of choice (see Figure 20.6a). In other words, rather than correctly treating indicators as functions of underlying attitudes, they are treated as direct measures of the attitudes. The main disadvantages of this approach are that strong agreement with an attitudinal statement does not necessarily translate into a causal relationship with choice. Additionally, indicators are highly dependent on the phrasing of the survey and, furthermore, they are not available for forecasting. Incorporating the indicators of latent variables as explanatory variables also ignores the fact that latent variables contain measurement error, and can thus lead to inconsistent estimates (Ashok *et al.* 2002).

Finally, indicators are arguably correlated with the error of the choice model, i.e. there are unobserved effects that influence both a respondent's choice and his/her responses to indicator questions. This thus creates a risk of endogeneity bias. An alternative is a sequential estimation approach using factor analysis or structural equation modeling (SEM) for the latent variable component and discrete choice models for the choice component of the model. Factor analysis can be either confirmatory (CFA) or confirmatory with covariates – that is a multiple indicator multiple cause (MIMIC) model. The factor analysis approach involves analysis of the interrelationships between attitudinal indicators and a statistical procedure that transforms the correlated indicators into a smaller group of uncorrelated (latent) variables called *principal components* or *factors*. This procedure requires a single measurement equation. On the other hand, SEM involves two parts: a measurement model and a structural model. SEMs capture three relationships: the relationship among factors (latent variables), the relationship among observed variables, and the relationship between factors and observed variables that are not factor indicators.

As a next step, the latent variables are entered in the utility equations (see Figure 20.6b) of the choice models. The latent variables contain measurement error, and in order to obtain consistent estimates the choice probability must be integrated over the distribution of latent variables, where the distribution of the factors is obtained from the factor analysis model. This method recognizes that both the choice and the response to the indicator questions are driven by the same underlying latent variable. The key disadvantage of this approach is that the latent estimates are inefficient, i.e., they are derived from the attitudinal information only and do not take account of the actual choices that the respondent has made (see, e.g., Morikawa *et al.* (2002)). Past work has also made use of internal market analysis, in which both the latent attributes of the alternatives and consumer preferences are inferred from preference or choice data. In this restrictive approach (Figure 20.6c), the observed choices are the only indicators used, and therefore the latent attributes are alternative-specific and do not vary among individuals in a market segment (see, e.g., Elrod 1988; Elrod and Keane 1995).

With a view to improving on the above methods, recent research efforts have led to the formulation of a combined model structure offering a general treatment of the inclusion of latent variables in discrete choice models. In particular, this model framework comprises two components: a discrete choice model and a latent variable model (Figure 20.7).

Daly *et al.* (2012), Bolduc and Daziano (2012), and Prato *et al.* (2012) are all recent examples of various ways of specifying and estimating hybrid choice models. Rather than attempt to summarize each model form, we prefer to benefit by the options offered in these and other papers and set up a very

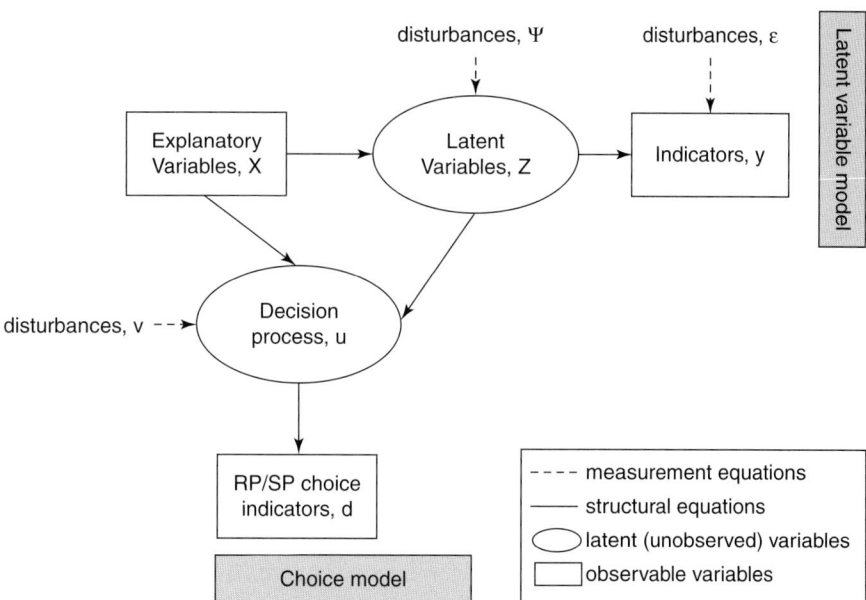

Figure 20.7   The integrated latent variable and discrete choice modeling framework
Sources: Walker and Ben-Akiva (2002), Bolduc *et al.* (2005).

general model system (which will be offered in Nlogit 6). The various elements are presented below.

20.6.2 The main elements of a hybrid choice model

Latent attitude variables (z^*): since z^*, the underlying opinions and attitudes of respondents, is unobserved, any assumption other than continuous and normally distributed is unlikely not to make sense. We start with Equation (20.35):

$$z^* = \Gamma w + \eta. \tag{20.35}$$

There are L such "latent" variables that depend on M observed variables w. η is normally distributed with zero mean and covariance matrix Σ_η. In principle, Σ_η can be any positive definite matrix. We speculate that anything other than a diagonal matrix will be identified, although the diagonal elements might not be identified either, and so in such a setting Σ_η is often likely to be defined as equal to I_L.

Observed indicators (I): there are Q observed indicators of the attitudes or opinions (the "soft" variables), written as in Equation (20.36):

$$I = I(z^*, z, u). \tag{20.36}$$

I is an observation mechanism, z is a set of observables which can be related to alternatives, SECs, and choice context (e.g., survey method), and u is the random disturbances. This differs from many of the contributions on HCM, although it is closest to Daly *et al.* (2012) in that I is not additive in the unobservable u. To take the simplest case, suppose the one indicator is a binary variable determined by a probit observation mechanism. Then:

$$I = 1[\gamma'z + \tau z^* + \mu > 0], \tag{20.37}$$

where γ and τ are parameters to be estimated. We can specify that μ is normally distributed with mean zero and covariance Σ_μ. Whether Σ_μ can differ from an identity matrix depends on the nature of the observation mechanism. If I is binary, the diagonal elements must be 1. Non-zero off-diagonal elements can be non-zero, for example, in a bivariate or multivariate probit set up. The indicators could be continuous, binary, ordered, or even "censored."

Multinomial choice utility functions: the choice set contains J alternatives. Utility functions are defined on a multinomial logit platform:

$$U^* = U^*(x, z^*, I) + \varepsilon, \tag{20.38}$$

where ε has the usual *iid* Extreme value distribution, producing a conditional MNL model. More advanced models are also permissible, such as ML.

We can now define y generically as the indicator of the choice within a maximum random utility setting, as per usual. z^* at this stage has a very general form and role in the choice model.

Likelihood function: the LL is composed, ultimately, of the joint densities of the observed outcomes, the multinomial choice, and the observed indicators. The form of the joint density is given in Equation 20.39:

$$P(y, I | w, z, x) = \int_{z^*} P_{\text{choice}}(y | z^*, w, x, z, I) P_{\text{indicators}}(I | z^*, w, x, z) f(z^* | w) dz^*. \tag{20.39}$$

This is maximized over the model parameters using maximum simulated likelihood. This differs from the formulation in other papers that we are aware of in an important way. There is a crucial insight missing in the formulation of the choice model part of the system where other papers treat the "measurement equations" of the latent variable, that is the equations of the observed indicators, as separate from the equations of the choice model. In the template above, I appears as a condition in the choice model. In papers such as Daly *et al.* (2012), Daziano and Bolduc (2012) and Prato *et al.* (2012), conditioned on z^*, the choice and measurement equations are independent; I does not appear in the choice model. This seems unnecessary, and narrows the model. This is related to an important issue – what appears in the choice model, the latent variable or the observed indicator (or both)? There is no problem having both I and z^* appear in P_{choice}. The product of the two densities as shown above is still the joint density of the observed variables. The logic of the construction is exactly the same as that which underlies, for example, the recursive bivariate probit model (see Chapter 17).

How z^* and I appear in the choice model is arbitrary. It would be natural for them to appear linearly in the utility functions. But they could play a role in the scaling (of variances) as well. Overall, there are almost guaranteed to be identification problems in the model, requiring the imposition of quite a few restrictions. On the other hand, a natural extension of the model, which will further complicate identification, is to allow the elements of β in the utility functions to be random as in a ML model.

It is useful at this stage to set out some notation and to suggest, in a little more detail, the links between various parts of an overall structural equation model system, which is essentially the nature of a HCM. The task is to combine choice responses, individual level indicators, choice task level indicators, and alternative level indicators with latent attitude indicators.

Notation: define i = individual, $i=1,\dots,N$; t = choice situation, $t = 1,\dots,T$; j = alternative, $j=1,\dots,J$ (J can vary by person, but this may become intractible if it does); z^* = latent attitude.

Since z^* is unobserved, it must exist at the individual level, so z_i may be driven by observable variables, h_i, and unobservables, u_i. If z_i is not driven by observables, then it is identified only by its presence in either the indicator or choice equations. Otherwise, there could be structural "causal" equations, $z_i^* = \Gamma m_i + u_i$. (Think "multiple causes" and "multiple indicators.") As discussed above, there are likely to be major identification issues. m_i is a set of person- and/or context-specific exogenous variables. Examples of data related to each element are given below.

I_i = indicator observed at the person level: an example at the respondent level is a response on a Likert scale (1 to 5) to the question: "how important is saving greenhouse gas emissions in travel to you personally?" Equation (20.36) might then be $I_i = I_i(z_i^*, w_i, v_i)$, where w = observed data, and v = the random disturbance. In addition, we might also be interested in information obtained at the choice task level. An example might be: "Are you interested in a task that examines how you feel about toll roads?" Let us define A_{it} = indicator observed at choice task level as $A_{it} = A_{it}(z_i^*, w_i, w_{it}, v_{it})$ (although we note that it is unlikely that there would be a separate w_{it}). We may also be interested in an indicator observed at the alternative level (Q_{ij}) such as a question: "Is this alternative acceptable to you?" This would not vary at the choice task level. The feeling about an alternative should not vary at the task level unless the analyst intends to vary the tasks in a way that can be modeled separately. In SC experiments, it is more common to vary alternatives at a choice set level because of the attribute levels. What we are assessing here is a perception of the attribute package levels. In a number of studies, authors have asked this at a choice set level. The presence of z_i^* and/or v_{ij} in Q_{ij} makes the choice set endogenous:

$$Q_{ij} = Q_{ij}(z_i^*, w_i, v_{ij}). \tag{20.40}$$

The contribution to the LL of the various elements is as follows. Conditioned on z_i^*:

$$P(i|z_i^*, \ldots) = \begin{Bmatrix} \{I_i(z_i^*, w_i, v_{it})\}\times \\ \left\{\prod_{j=1}^{J} Q_{ij}(z_i^*, w_i, v_{ij})\right\}\times \\ \left\{\prod_{t=1}^{T} \text{Choice}_{itj}(z_i^*, x_{it1}, \ldots, x_{itJ}, w_i)\times A_{it}(z_i^*, w_i, v_{it})\right\}. \end{Bmatrix} \tag{20.41}$$

To obtain the contribution to the LL, we integrate z_i^* out of $P(i|z_i^*, \ldots)$, then take logarithms.

The data arrangements are set out below as a way of assisting in understanding data requirements. We will assume that a variable number of choices and a variable number of choice tasks, while feasible, can be ignored with both fixed across a sample. Assume three alternatives in a choice set, and a SC experiment with two choice tasks. The schema below in Table 20.7 suggests one attribute in the choice model, up to three Q_j indicator, one or two A_{it} task level models, and one I_i person level indicator equation. In each case, there could be multiple models, though a model with more than one Q_j alternative specific model equation would be somewhat complex.

Table 20.7 Example of data arrangements for a hybrid choice model

Row	Choice Task	Choice variable	Attributes Variables	Q_j indicator (see note 1) Indicators	Vars	A_{it} Indicator (see note 2) Indicators	Vars	I_i Indicator (see note 3) Indicators	Vars	M_i Causes (see note 4) Vars
Rows 1–3:										
1	1	$Y_{1,1}$	$X_{1,1}$	Q_1	h_1	A_1	f_1	I	g	m
2	1	$Y_{2,1}$	$X_{2,1}$	Q_2	h_2	A_1	f_1	I	g	m
3	1	$Y_{3,1}$	$X_{3,1}$	Q_3	h_3	A_1	f_1	I	g	m
Rows 4–6:										
4	2	$Y_{1,2}$	$X_{1,2}$	Q_1	h_1	A_2	f_2	I	g	m
5	2	$Y_{2,2}$	$X_{2,2}$	Q_2	h_2	A_2	f_2	I	g	m
6	2	$Y_{3,2}$	$X_{3,2}$	Q_3	h_3	A_2	f_2	I	g	m

Note 1: Block of 3 rows is repeated with each choice task. Only the data given with the first task are actually used, since these indicator models use N observations to fit each of the J models.

Note 2: Each row is repeated within the choice task. Only the first row in each choice task block is actually used. Each of the T Choice task indicator models is fit with N observations.

Note 3: Each row is repeated for every row of the individual's data set. Only the first row is actually used. The individual model is fit with N observations in total.

Note 4: Same configuration of I_i indicators. Equation for z^* is fit at the individual level.

The preceding addresses all the data and synchronization issues the analyst is likely to want to specify in Nlogit, even if for any one application there are redundant data in the table above, as shown in the notes. Examples of model applications using the one common data set up are as follows, noting that the entire data set for this person is rows 1–6.

1. To fit an individual level, I_i model, I will use row 1 only, and ignore rows 2–6.
2. To fit a choice task level model relating to choice task 1, I will use row 1. If there is also a question about choice task 2, I would use row 4. Rows 2–3 and 5–6 would be ignored.
3. To fit a model about alternative 1, I would use row 1. To fit an equation about alternative 2, I would use row 2. To fit an equation about alternative 3, I would use row 3. Rows 4–6 would be ignored.

Rows that are not used are filled with the corresponding data mainly to "coerce" the user into always providing the correct data in the internal rows of the block. This will provide a way for the user to keep the data straight. An additional advantage of this structure is that the simulation that will be needed to integrate out the random part of the attitude variables will run at the same rate as the random parameters synchronization.

The proposed syntax for the command (in release Nlogit 6) is:

```
HybridLogit
; Lhs = choice variable
; Choices = list of choices
[; specification of utility functions using the standard arrangements]
[;RPL ; Fcn = the usual specification]   allow some random parameter spe-
cification
; Attitudes : name (choices in which it appears)  [= list of variables ]  /
             name (choices in which it appears)  [= list of variables] ...
; Indicators: name (level, type) = list / level is Individual, Choice, Task
              name (level, type) = list ...$ type is Continuous,Binary,Scale
```

21 Attribute processing, heuristics, and preference construction

This chapter was co-authored with Waiyan Leong and Andrew Collins.

21.1 Introduction

Any economic decision or judgment has an associated, often subconscious, psychological process prodding it along, in ways that makes the "neoclassical ambition of avoiding [this] necessity . . . .unrealizable" (Simon 1978, 507). The translation of this fundamental statement on human behavior has become associated with the identification of the heuristics that individuals use to simplify preference construction and hence make choices, or to make the representation of what matters relevant, regardless of the degree of complexity as perceived by the decision maker and/or the analyst. Despite this recognition in behavioral research as long ago as the 1950s (see Svenson 1998), that cognitive processes have a key role in preference revelation, and the reminders throughout the literature (see McFadden 2001b; Yoon and Simonson 2008) about rule-driven behavior, we still see relatively little of the decision processing literature incorporated into discrete choice modeling which is, increasingly, becoming the mainstream empirical context for preference measurement and willingness to pay (WTP) derivatives.

There is an extensive literature focussing on these matters that might broadly be described as heuristics and biases, and which is crystallized in the notion of *process*, in contrast to *outcome*. Choice has both elements of process and outcome, which in combination represent the endogeneity of choice in choice studies. The failure to recognize process and the maintenance of a linear additive utility expression under full attribute and parameter preservation is an admission, by default, that individuals, when faced with a choice situation, deem all attributes (and alternatives) relevant, and that a *compensatory decision rule* is used by all agents to arrive at a choice. In recent years we have started to see a growing interest in alternative processing strategies at the

937

attribute, alternative, and choice set levels, with empirical evidence suggesting that inclusion of process matters in a non-marginal way in the determination of estimates of WTP, elasticities, and choice outcomes. This chapter focuses on the role of heuristics in information processing in choice experiments (CEs), since this is the setting within which the major contributions have been made, but we remind readers that the heuristics also apply in the context of revealed preference (RP) data.

Although there should be no suggestion that fully compensatory choice rules are always invalid – indeed they may be, in aggregate, an acceptable representation of many process circumstances – there is a strong belief that process heterogeneity exists as a consequence of mixtures of genuine cognitive processing strategies that simplify decision making in real markets, for all manner of reasons, and the presence of new states that are in particular introduced through the design of CEs that are no more than new circumstances to process. Whether the processing rules adopted are natural to real choices, or are artefacts of the design of an experiment, or some other survey instrument (including RP surveys) in front of an individual, is in some senses irrelevant; what is relevant is the manner in which such choice assessments are processed in respect of the role that each design attribute and the mixture of attributes and alternatives plays in the outcome. Yoon and Simonson (2008) and Park *et al.* (2008)[1] provide some interesting perspectives from marketing research on preference revelation.

There is a substantial extant literature in the psychology domain as regards the influence of various factors on the amount of information processed in decision tasks. Evidence demonstrates the importance of such factors as time pressure (e.g., Diederich 2003), cognitive load (e.g., Drolet and Luce 2004), and task complexity (Swait and Adamowicz 2001a) in influencing the decision strategy employed during complex decision tasks. There is also a great deal of variability in the decision strategies employed in different contexts, and this variability adds to the complexity in understanding the behavioral mechanisms involved in decision making and choice. There is also a debate on what constitutes "complexity" in the eyes of the decision maker (in contrast to the assumptions of the analyst), with some authors such as Hensher (2006) suggesting that relevance is what matters and that what is complex to one agent may not be so to another. We discuss this in more detail below.

---

[1] Park *et al.* (2008) promotes the idea of starting with a basic product profile and upgrading it one attribute at a time, identifying the WTP for that additional attribute given the budgets available.

The typology of decision strategies developed by Payne *et al.* (1992) is particularly useful in providing a framework within which to understand decision strategies. They characterized decision strategies along three dimensions: basis of processing, amount of processing, and consistency of processing. Decision strategies are said to differ in regards to whether many attributes within an alternative are considered before another alternative is considered (*alternative-based* processing) or whether values across alternatives on a single attribute are processed before another attribute is processed (*attribute-based* processing). Strategies are also said to differ in terms of the amount of information processed (i.e., in terms of whether any information is ignored or not processed before a decision may be made, or added up if it is in a common metric unit). Finally, decision strategies can also be grouped in terms of whether the same amount of information for each alternative is examined (*consistent* processing) or whether the amount of processing varies depending on the alternative (*selective* processing).

On the basis of this typology, Payne *et al.* (1993) identified six specific decision strategies, three of which are attribute-based and three alternative-based approaches. The attribute-based approaches include elimination-by-aspects (EBA), lexicographic choice (LEX), and majority of confirming dimensions (MCD) strategies. The alternative-based approaches include weighted additive (WADD), satisficing (SAT), and equal-weight (EQW) strategies. These strategies are further described in Table 21.1 (see Payne *et al.* (1993) for a full description of these strategies). The main argument posited by Payne *et al.* (1993) was that individuals constructed strategies depending on the task demands and the information they were faced with.

In the random utility framework, the WADD utility assumption as the mainstay functional form of these models allows an individual q's preferences

Table 21.1 Typology of decision strategies
Source: Payne *et al.* 1993.

Strategy	Attribute or alternative-based	Amount of information	Consistency
EBA	Attribute-based	Depends on values of alternatives and cut-offs	Selective
LEX	Attribute-based	Depends on values of alternatives and cut-offs	Selective
MCD	Attribute-based	Ignores probability or weight information	Consistent
WADD	Alternative-based	All information processed	Consistent
SAT	Alternative-based	Depends on values of alternatives and cut-offs	Selective
EQW	Alternative-based	Ignores probability or weight information	Consistent

(or utility) for any alternative j comprising k attributes to be written as $U_{jq} = \sum_{k=1}^{K} \beta_{jkq} X_{jk} + \varepsilon_{jq}$. In this equation, X_{jk} are the values of attribute k in alternative j, β_{jkq} denotes the taste parameters or the weights that individual q associates with X_{jk}, and ε_{jq} represents an unobservable random term that affects utility, but is unknown to the analyst. By writing utility in this manner, the analyst assumes that the respondent systematically works through all alternatives, evaluating each alternative in the manner described in the equation above, before choosing the alternative with the highest value.

Given that rationally adaptive behavioral models are more likely to be behaviorally valid descriptions of choice behavior, one might discount the WADD strategy, since it assumes that all information is processed (this remains a **testable assumption**, however). Strictly, WADD is not a heuristic; by definition, a heuristic is a rule of thumb – a simplifying strategy – whereas WADD is seen to be the normative rule. Furthermore, where there is an interest in stochastic representations of *attribute-based* processes which may not be consistent across different decision tasks, there are two potentially useful strategies that can help to explain choice behavior. Table 21.1 suggests that the only two attribute-based strategies capable of explaining inconsistent and variable decision strategies are EBA and LEX, which satisfy the criterion of stochastic specifications of attribute processing (AP) strategies.

EBA (see Starmer 2000) involves a determination of the most important attribute (usually defined by the attribute with the highest weight/probability) and the cut-off value for that attribute (i.e., a threshold). An alternative is eliminated if the value of its most important attribute falls below this cut-off value. This process of elimination continues for the second most important attribute, and so on, until a final alternative remains. Thus, the EBA strategy is best characterized as a *"threshold"* AP strategy, although we note that attribute threshold processing does not have to confine itself to a sequential assessment along the lines of EBA (see Swait 2001; Hensher and Rose 2009).

The LEX strategy, in its strictest sense, involves a direct comparison between alternatives on the *most important* attribute. In the event of a tie, the second most important attribute is used as a comparison, and so on until an alternative is chosen. The LEX strategy is thus best characterized as a *"relative comparison"* strategy. Thus, we can clearly differentiate two classes of AP strategies: threshold and relative comparison.

A major deficit in these strategies is that although they assume selectivity in AP across different decision task contexts, they assume consistency in attribute strategy within the same decision context. In other words, once a strategy is selected for a given task (or choice), it does not change within the task.

This issue is further complicated by an influential psychological theory which identifies two main stages in the decision process. Differentiation and consolidation (Diff Con) theory, developed by Svenson and Malmsten (1996), assumes that decision making is a goal oriented task which incorporates the pre-decision process of *differentiation* and the post-decision process of *consolidation*. This theory is crucial in encouraging a disaggregation of the entire decision process.

The two issues discussed above, regarding the *adaptive* nature of strategies and the *disaggregation* of the decision process, are issues that can only be assessed realistically within a paradigm that relaxes the deterministic assumption of most rational and normative models of decision making. In other words, a stochastic specification of AP capable of accommodating the widespread consensus in the decision making literature that decision making is an active process which may require different strategies in different contexts and at different stages of the decision process (e.g., Stewart *et al.* 2003). As the relevance of attributes in a decision task changes so, too, must our approach to modeling the strategies that individuals employ when adapting to such changes.

There is widespread evidence in the psychology literature concerning the behavioral variability, unpredictability, and inconsistency regularly demonstrated in decision making and choices (e.g., Gonzáles-Vallejo 2002; Slovic 1995), reflecting an assumption that goes back at least to Thurstone's law of comparative judgment (1927). One of the particularly important advantages of using a stochastic representation of decision strategies, as promoted here, is that it enables a more behaviorally realistic analysis of variation in decision strategies.

Recent research by Hensher (2006, 2008), Greene and Hensher (2008), Layton and Hensher (2010), Hensher and Rose (2009), Hensher and Layton (2010), Hess and Hensher (2010), Puckett and Hensher (2008), Swait (2001), Cantillo *et al.* (2006), Cameron (2008), Scarpa *et al.* (2008), Beharry and Scarpa (2008), Cantillo and Ortúzar (2005), and Hensher *et al.* (2009), among others, are examples of a growing interest in the way that individuals evaluate a package of attributes associated with ordered or unordered mutually exclusive alternatives in real or hypothetical markets, and make choices.[2] The accumulating empirical evidence suggests that individuals use

---

[2] This chapter does not consider other aspects of process in CEs such as uncertainty in the choice response. See Lundhede *et al.* (2009).

a number of strategies derived from heuristics to represent the way that information embedded within attributes defining alternatives is used to process the context and arrive at a choice outcome. These include cancellation or attribute exclusion, degrees of attention paid to attributes in a package of attributes, referencing of new or hypothetical attribute packages around a recent or past experience, imposing thresholds on attribute levels to represent acceptable levels (e.g., Swait 2001; Hensher and Rose 2009), and attribute aggregation where they are in common units (see Gilovich *et al.* 2002 for a series of papers that synthesize the evidence under the theme of heuristics and biases). Importantly, the heuristics are likely to be context-specific, such that the nature of the information shown in stated choice (SC) experiments, for example, conditions in part the choice of rules adopted.

Hensher (2006b, 2008) argues that individuals appear to adopt a range of "coping" or editing strategies in hypothetical choice settings that are consistent with how they normally process information in real markets. CEs have varying amounts of information to process but, importantly, aligning "choice complexity" with the amount of information to process is potentially misleading. *Relevance* is what matters (Hensher 2006b), and the heuristics adopted by individuals to evaluate a circumstance is what needs to be captured through frameworks that can empirically identify rules adopted by individuals.

There are at least two ways in which the information on processing might be identified. One involves direct questioning of respondents after each choice scenario (what we refer to as *self-stated intentions*); the other involves probabilistic conditions imposed on the model form through specification of the utility expressions associated with each alternative, that enables inference on the way that specific attributes are processed. Both may be complementary.

The purpose of this chapter is to review some of the important findings and theoretical models that have emerged from the literature that might be used to improve the choice modeling process and show how we can incorporate these ideas into the estimation of choice models. The focus of this chapter draws on both direct questioning and functional forms to investigate the role of mixtures of processing rules to establish the behavioral implications on choice outcomes, marginal willingness to pay (MWTP) and choice elasticities. The functional forms presented here, as well as responses to self-stated intention questions, enable the analyst to infer, up to a probability, the presence of some very specific AP strategies such as common-metric attribute aggregation, common-metric parameter transfer, and attribute non-attendance in the presence or otherwise of attribute thresholds and referencing.

21.2 A review of common decision processes

There is much in the psychology literature that points to the use of quick mental processing rules known as heuristics that are relied on to manage the vast number of decisions that must be made in everyday life. It is recognized that the WADD rule, if followed strictly to the letter, is cognitively demanding and time consuming (Payne *et al.* 1993). Furthermore, it implies an assumption of stable, well articulated preferences which appears to hold only under conditions where the choice task is familiar or when the respondent has experience with the various alternatives that are presented. When these conditions fail to apply, preferences are not determined in advance of the choice situation, but are instead constructed in response to the characteristics of the choice task. As Payne *et al.* (1999, 245) put it, the construction process involves an interaction between "the properties of the human information processing system and the properties of the choice task."

Rather than static decision processes that are repeatedly applied to different choice contexts, behavioral decision research tells us that "individuals have a repertoire of decision strategies for solving decision problems" (Bettman *et al.* 1998, 194). Table 21.2 (based on Table 21.1) describes some classic decision strategies that have been identified in the decision research literature (Payne *et al.* 1993).

Bettman *et al.* (1998) propose a choice goals framework to understand how individuals come to use particular decision strategies. They argue that respondents attempt to trade-off between two conflicting goals: maximizing the accuracy of a decision and minimizing the cognitive effort required to reach that decision. The effort–accuracy trade-off is on view in the majority of decision cases, although individuals may also pursue other goals like minimizing negative emotions and maximizing the ease of justifying the decision. Bettman *et al.*'s framework resonates with Jones' (1999) thesis that people are "intendedly rational," but limits imposed by human cognitive and emotional architecture constrain decision making behavior.

To assess cognitive effort, decision strategies can be decomposed into *elementary information processes* (EIPs) – such as READ, COMPARE, ADD, MULTIPLY, ELIMINATE, and so on. An EBA strategy can be thought of as (i) *reading* the weight of each attribute; (ii) *comparing* the weight just read with the largest weight found previously until the most important attribute is found; (iii) *reading* a cut-off threshold for that attribute; (iv) *reading* the attribute value across all alternatives; (v) *comparing* each value

Table 21.2 Classic decision strategies

Decision rule	Description
Weighted additive rule (WADD)	Develops overall evaluation of an alternative by multiplying each attribute value by its importance weight and then summing up each of these products over all attributes. The alternative with the highest value is chosen.
Equal weight heuristic (EQW)	Like WADD, all alternatives and all attributes are considered, but each attribute is weighted equally. The alternative with the highest value is chosen.
Satisficing heuristic (SAT)	Alternatives are considered one at a time in the order they are presented. Each attribute is compared to a pre-defined cut-off. If any attribute fails to meet the cut-off, that alternative is rejected, and the next alternative considered. The first alternative with all attribute levels meeting the cut-off is chosen.
Lexicographic (LEX)	Determine the most important attribute and evaluate all alternatives on that attribute. The alternative with the best value on that attribute is chosen. If there is a tie, the second most important attribute is considered, and so on.
Elimination-by-aspects (EBA)	Determine the most important attribute and its cut-off value. Evaluate all alternatives on that attribute. Eliminate the alternative whose attribute level fails to meet the cut-off. Carry on with the second most important attribute, etc. until one alternative remains
Majority of confirming dimensions (MCD)	Process pairs of alternatives. Compare the values of each attribute and the alternative with the winning number of attributes is retained. The retained alternative is compared with the next alternative. Stop when all the alternatives have been evaluated.

against the cut-off; and (vi) *eliminating* alternatives whose attribute values fail to meet the cut-off. Cognitive effort for the decision strategy is then expressed as a function of the total number of EIPs and types of EIPs. The reason for varying cognitive effort with EIP type is that in empirical estimates EIPs have been found to differ in cognitive effort requirements – for example, MULTIPLY takes over 2 seconds versus under half a second for COMPARE.

To define the accuracy of a decision strategy, Payne *et al.* (1993) suggest comparing the WADD value of the choice in relation to the normative WADD rule. Such a relative accuracy measure is proposed in Equation (21.1):

$$\text{Relative Accuracy} = \frac{\text{Weighted additive value}_{\text{choice}} - \text{Weighted additive value}_{\text{worst}}}{\text{Weighted additive value}_{\text{best}} - \text{Weighted additive value}_{\text{worst}}}.$$

$$(21.1)$$

For the common heuristics described earlier, Payne *et al.* conclude that relative accuracy does not decrease very much when the number of alternatives increases, but the cognitive effort, measured in terms of the EIP workload, increases much more rapidly for the WADD strategy than for the heuristics. Thus, as the number of alternatives grows in a choice task, the heuristics appear to be more efficient from an effort–accuracy trade-off perspective. This means that with, say six or eight alternatives given to the respondent, the effort–accuracy framework predicts a shift from compensatory to non-compensatory choice strategies. Such shifts have indeed been observed in empirical settings through process tracing methods (see Section 21.5.3). Respondents have been known to use attribute-based strategies like EBA early in the process to reduce the number of alternatives before using an alternative-based strategy such as additive utility to arrive at the final outcome, in what has been called a *phased decision strategy.*

More generally, in relatively less complex choice tasks, where complexity, according to Payne *et al.*, refers to task characteristics such as the number of alternatives, number of attributes, and time pressure,[3] the effort–accuracy perspective predicts that compensatory decision strategies such as the WADD model tend to be more frequently employed. This idea of complexity can be distinguished from Hensher's (2006d) notion of relevance, which pertains to providing more complete descriptions of attributes in the choice task and allowing respondents to form their own processing rules with regards to relevance. Hence, a choice task that disaggregates, say, a time attribute in its various components such as free-flow time, slowed-down time and stop-start time may be more relevant than aggregating these components into an overall "time" attribute.

Given more attributes to process, someone using a fully compensatory strategy is required to exert greater cognitive effort. When there are more attributes, there is consistent evidence showing that respondents become more selective in their information search, by reducing the proportion of information searched (Sundstrom 1987; Olshavsky 1979; Payne 1976), but evidence is mixed as to whether this represents a fundamental change in decision strategy (Sundstrom 1987) or whether this is a case of different weights being applied (Olshavsky 1979). Compared to the WADD rule, it is also unclear how the relative efficiencies of the heuristics stack up in this situation. Unlike what happens when the number of alternatives increases, Payne *et al.* show that the relative accuracy of the heuristics like LEX and SAT

---

[3] Although in most CEs, time pressure is not experimentally manipulated.

decreases as the number of attributes increases, the exception to this being the EBA rule.[4] Neither has the question of whether too many attributes can overload respondents and lead to a degradation of choice quality been resolved. Some authors like Malhotra (1982) argue for this position, but Bettman *et al.* (1998) suggest that increases in the amount of information given to respondents need not be harmful as long as they select information that reflects their values, rather than basing their decision on surface features of the choice task such as salience or format.

So far, the discussion of Payne *et al.*'s effort–accuracy framework posits a top down approach, where the respondent weighs the costs and benefits of adopting each of the various decision strategies, and then chooses the one which best meets the effort–accuracy trade-off for the required task. A complementary view involves preference construction as "bottom up" or "data-driven" (Payne *et al.*, 1993, 171), where respondents shape or change decision strategies by exploiting previously encountered problem structures. Decision problems are subsequently restructured as an intermediate step, making them more amenable to analysis using certain heuristics. Information in choice tasks might be transformed through rounding or standardizing values in a common metric. Information might also be rearranged or further simplified by deeming certain attributes irrelevant. The restructuring serves to reduce the perceived complexity of the choice task (Payne and Bettman 1992; Jones 1999).

21.3 Embedding decision processes in choice models

21.3.1 Two-stage models

Arising from the earlier findings of individuals engaging in phased decision strategies, several authors have attempted to model a two-stage decision process whereby a subset of alternatives is selected from a larger universal set and the final choice is made from the reduced set. *Screening rules* are typically invoked in the first stage. These could be based on the history of past choices, or on the attribute levels of alternatives in the current choice situation. A general form of a two-stage model, attributed to Manski (1977), is given in Equation (21.2):

---

[4] With an increase in the number of attributes, the EBA rule requires the chosen alternative to surpass more cut-off values.

$$P_{jq} = \sum_{C \in G} P_q(j|C)P_q(C),\tag{21.2}$$

where P_{jq} is the probability of individual q choosing alternative j, $P_q(j|C)$ is the probability of individual q choosing alternative j given the reduced choice set C, and $P_q(C)$ is the probability that the reduced choice set of q is C, among all the non-empty subsets of a master choice set M.

Expanding on the Manski equation, Cantillo and Ortúzar (2005) have assumed a first-stage elimination involving the use of a rejection mechanism based on individual-specific thresholds of attribute levels. Alternatives which survive the first-stage screening are then evaluated in the usual compensatory manner within the random utility framework.

Cantillo and Ortúzar suggest that "the threshold could be taken as the most favorable value among those that the attribute can take for the set of potential alternatives; it could also be the value that the attribute takes for the chosen alternative, or simply any reference value" (Cantillo and Ortúzar 2005, 644). Hence, there is a great amount of flexibility as to how the individual-specific thresholds are modeled. In general, the vector of thresholds for individual q, $\mathbf{T}_q$, may be specified as a $m \times 1$ vector, where m is the number of attributes subject to threshold considerations, $0 \leq m \leq K$. For Cantillo and Ortúzar, $\mathbf{T}_q$ is assumed to be a random vector distributed according to a joint density function $\Omega(\boldsymbol{\delta})$ with mean $E[\mathbf{T}_q] = \overline{\mathbf{T}}_q$ and a variance-covariance matrix $\mathrm{var}[\mathbf{T}_q] = \boldsymbol{\Sigma}_q$. Because Cantillo and Ortúzar consider a transport context where alternatives are specified in terms of time, cost, and accident rate, thresholds represent the upper bound of the acceptable range of attribute levels. Hence, an alternative j is included in the second-stage consideration if $X_{jkq} \leq T_{kq}$, for all attributes which are threshold constrained. $\overline{\mathbf{T}}_q$ may also be allowed to vary as a function of socio-demographic factors.

21.3.2 Models with "fuzzy" constraints

In most two-stage models, it is assumed that the decision maker would reject any alternative whenever its attribute(s) fail to meet at least one of the constraints. While maintaining the assumption that a lower or upper bound self-imposed constraint exists for each attribute, Swait (2001; see also Hensher *et al.* 2013) relaxes the assumption of a "hard" cut-off constraint and assumes that cut-offs can be violated, but at a cost to overall utility through a penalty in the utility function. If attributes in a particular alternative violate their respective constraints, that alternative can still be chosen provided sufficient compensation in the other attributes is available to outweigh the dis-benefit of violating the cut-off in the given attributes.

The utility function of alternative j is written in Equation (21.3) as follows:

$$U_j = \sum_k \beta_{jk} X_{jk} + \sum_k (\omega_k \lambda_{jk} + v_k \kappa_{jk}) + \varepsilon_j. \tag{21.3}$$

λ_{jk} and κ_{jk} are the respective penalties of violating the lower bound and upper bound constraints. Let the lower bound cut-off and the upper bound cut-off for attribute k be denoted c_k and d_k respectively, where c_k and d_k may be allowed to vary across individuals. λ_{jk} and κ_{jk} may be defined in terms of c_k and d_k as follows in expression (21.4):

$$\lambda_{jk} = \begin{cases} 0 \ \text{if} \ c_k \ \text{does not exist} \\ \max(0, c_k - X_{jk}) \end{cases} \quad \kappa_{jk} = \begin{cases} 0 \ \text{if} \ d_k \ \text{does not exist} \\ \max(0, X_{jk} - d_k) \end{cases} \tag{21.4}$$

ω_k and v_k are the marginal disutilities of violating the lower and upper cut-offs for attribute k.

To estimate his model, Swait obtains self-reported cut-off information from respondents. However, if such information is unavailable, as might be expected in most CE data where attribute level thresholds are not explicitly accounted for in the modeling, it might still be worthwhile to consider using attribute levels of the reference alternative as "pseudo-cut-off" values for c_k and d_k. Such a representation would be consistent with both the reference dependency and loss aversion concepts established in many behavioral studies. Reference alternatives may simply be the status quo or, in the spirit of more recent work on **reference point revision**, those alternatives which were chosen in previous choice sets. Another point of observation is that because c_k and d_k are essentially thresholds the stochastic models of threshold formation mentioned in Section 21.3.1 would also be relevant to this discussion and are a possible extension of the model.

Hensher *et al.* (2013) have developed a model that incorporates the upper and lower bound attribute thresholds, in a choice model where the relevance of an alternative is also taken into account. The model form for the utility expression that encapsulates the thresholds is given in Equation (21.5), which can be estimated using the NLRPLOGIT command set out in Chapter 20:[5]

---

[5] An alternative form for the alternative acceptability conditioning is the exponential form: $\exp(\delta_j \sum_{h=1}^{H} (A_{jq} + \gamma R_{hq}))$. Empirically, the difference is negligible in terms of predictive power and elasticity outputs.

$$U_{jq} = 1 + \delta_j \sum_{h=1}^{H} (A_{jq} + \gamma R_{hq})[\alpha_j + \sum_{k=1}^{K} \beta_{kj} X_{kjq}$$

$$+ \sum_{l=K+1}^{L} \beta_l \{0 : \max(0, X_{ljq} - X_{lq}min)\}$$

$$+ \sum_{m=L+1}^{M} \beta_m \{0 : \max(0, X_{mq}max - X_{mjq})\}] + \varepsilon_j, \qquad (21.5)$$

where A_{ji} is defined as a dummy variable denoting whether an alternative is perceived to be acceptable (1) or not (0) by the qth individual, R_{hq} is a dummy variable indicating whether the hth attribute level is in the perceived attribute threshold rejection region (1) or not (0) of the qth individual, γ and δ_j are estimated parameters, α_j is an alternative-specific constant (ASC), and β_{kj} are the preference parameters associated with the kth attribute (X) and jth alternative. The inclusion of R_{hq} recognizes that the role of attributes is fundamental to the perception of alternative acceptability. The cut-off penalties are a linear function of the amount of constraint violation and are defined as *{0: max(0, X_{ljq}–X_{lmin})}*, the lower cut-off effect and deviation of the attribute level from the minimum cut-off attribute threshold where the attribute level is below the minimum cut-off (i.e., the cut-off exists), and zero otherwise (if the cut-off does not exist), and *{0:max(0, X_{min} –X_{mjq})}*, the upper cut-off effect and deviation of the attribute level from the maximum cut-off attribute threshold where the attribute level is above the maximum cut-off (i.e., the cut-off exists), and zero otherwise (if the cut-off does not exist). X_{kjq} is the kth attribute associated with the jth alternative and qth individual, with $l = K+1, \ldots, L$ attribute lower cut-offs; $m = L+1, \ldots, M$ attribute upper cut-offs; $q = 1, \ldots, Q$ respondents; and β_l and β_m estimated penalty parameters.

This has highlighted that decision process heterogeneity is likely to be an inherent component in CEs and the usual approach of assuming a single decision rule that is used by all respondents may be too much of an over-simplification. One approach used by Swait (2009) to formalize decision process heterogeneity is to consider a mixed PDF random utility model, where an alternative may be evaluated in one of several discrete states, corresponding to different decision rules or cognitive processes. One of these states pertains to the usual utility maximizing, fully compensatory condition, while other states represent a more extreme version of attractiveness or unattractiveness, which aims to capture the possible use of a non-compensatory strategy, context dependence and/or attribute independence. Equation (21.6) illustrates Swait's model for a simple two-condition scenario, where respondent q assigns alternative j to either the first event that represents the trade-off condition in the usual sense, or the alternative event representing a rejection condition, where the utility for alternative j is not defined over attribute values:

$$U_{jq} \begin{cases} = V_{jq} + \varepsilon_j \text{ with probability } q_{jq} \\ = -\infty \text{ with probability } p_{jq} \end{cases}. \tag{21.6}$$

Swait's (2009) model can be set up to embed the EBA heuristic as part of choice set formation. The EBA heuristic states that an alternative is eliminated if the attribute of that alternative fails to meet a certain threshold. This allows p_j, the probability of an alternative being in the rejection condition, to be written as a function of a disjunctive screening rule: it takes just one attribute to fail the threshold cut-off before the alternative is eliminated. Conversely, q_j, which is the probability that an alternative is in the usual random utility-maximizing, fully compensatory trade-off condition, is written in the conjunctive sense: all attributes must meet the threshold criteria before subsequent processing takes place.

Using a similar concept employed by Cantillo and Ortúzar (2005), Swait (2009) assumes that for each attribute of interest, individual-specific thresholds are randomly distributed across the population. His specific assumption for the distribution of τ is normal with mean $\bar{\tau}_k$ and variance σ_k^2. In an unlabeled experiment, τ may be assumed to be generic across alternatives. If the EBA heuristic is applied to only one aspect – for example, cost – then Equation (21.7) is obtained:

$$p_{jq} = \Pr(\tau_{qk} < X_{jk}) = \Pr\left(Z < \frac{X_{jqk} - \bar{\tau}_k}{\sigma_k}\right) = \Phi\left(\frac{X_{jqk} - \bar{\tau}_k}{\sigma_k}\right)$$

$$q_{jq} = 1 - p_{jq} = 1 - \Phi\left(\frac{X_{jqk} - \bar{\tau}_k}{\sigma_k}\right). \tag{21.7}$$

The above can be generalized to elimination by m aspects, $1 \leq m \leq K$, in which case a joint density function for the vector of thresholds, $\tau_q = (\tau_1, \tau_2, \ldots, \tau_m)'$ is required.

Like Cantillo and Ortúzar (2005), Swait (2009)'s approach is one way of formalizing Payne et al.'s (1993) phased or two-stage decision hypothesis in the sense that non-compensatory rules are used as the basis of "rejecting" an alternative. Using Payne et al.'s terms, this would be akin to reducing the complexity of the choice task. The remaining alternatives are evaluated in the usual compensatory manner. The difference, however, is that while Payne *et al.* see the elimination of alternatives as a deterministic process, Swait allows each alternative to be rejected up to a probability, thereby introducing some "fuzziness" into choice set formation.

Despite sharing some similarities to two-stage models, Swait's model departs from the strict two-stage model in the sense that there is a non-zero probability of all alternatives being in the rejection condition, in which case the alternatives are simply selected according to a random choice rule. This contrasts with the typical two-stage model, where the set of all possible choice subsets in the second stage does not include the null, thereby excluding the possibility that all alternatives are "rejected." Hence, Swait's assumption may not necessarily be valid in a CE with status quo alternatives, as a situation where all alternatives, including the status quo, are in the rejection condition is not likely to arise. Even if all the experimentally designed (hypothetical) alternatives are in the rejection condition, it seems reasonable to assume in this scenario that the status quo alternative would be chosen.

Swait's model can flexibly incorporate various decision rules through an appropriate specification of the functional form for q_j. To model the EBA heuristic, q_j can be expressed in terms of the probability of one or more attributes of the alternative fulfilling certain threshold criteria. Instead of a conjunctive rule involving thresholds, q_j can be expressed as an increasing function of the number of "best" attributes in an alternative, which would then take the interpretation of the MCD heuristic being used as a screening rule. By "best," X_{jk} could be the highest across all alternatives, if the attribute is one that generates utility, or the lowest across all alternatives, if the attribute is one that generates disutility (e.g., cost, time attributes). A variant of this approach might be to follow Hensher and Collins (2011) in embedding the MCD heuristic, proxied by the number of "best" attributes that each alternative possesses, into the trade-off condition. Swait suggests that even more complex hybrid rules that depend on alternative, person and/or choice context characteristics can be considered.

The following discussion outlines a sketch of how Swait's two-mix model can be used to test the lexicographic rule. Instead of "elimination" and "trade-off," the two evaluation conditions may be thought of as "dominance" and "trade-off," where dominance is assigned a utility of $+\infty$. If only one alternative is in the "dominant" condition, that alternative will be selected, while if two or more alternatives are in the "dominant" condition, the random choice rule applies.

The probability of an alternative being in the "dominant" condition, denoted by p_{jq}, may be assumed to have as one of its arguments the indicator function $1(X_{jk} \succ X_{ik} \forall j \neq i)$. The symbol "$\succ$" denotes a preference relationship where the LHS variable is preferred to the RHS variable. This indicator function equals 1 if the level of the kth attribute of the jth alternative is "best" among all alternatives in the choice set. Ties could be included in the definition of "best."

The indicator function needs to be weighted by the importance that the respondent attaches to that attribute. The reason is that despite an alternative scoring best on an attribute, if that attribute turns out to be relatively unimportant from the respondent's perspective, the probability of that alternative being chosen on the basis of the lexicographic rule should still turn out to be comparatively small. To weight the attributes, one could normalize by the squared part-utilities $\dfrac{(\beta_{jk} X_{jk})^2}{\sum\limits_{k} (\beta_{jk} X_{jk})^2}$, ensuring that all part-utilities are non-negative or by the logit function $\dfrac{\exp(\beta_{jk} X_{jk})}{\sum\limits_{k} \exp(\beta_{jk} X_{jk})}$. To simplify the model, prior known values of β_{jk} or some other measure of importance weights might be used.

The lexicographic rule sometimes contains the notion of a just noticeable difference rule or lexicographic semi-order (Payne *et al.*, 1993). This rule states that the kth attribute of the jth alternative must exceed the second-best level of that same attribute found in another alternative i by at least the amount τ_k, otherwise the alternatives are considered to be tied. The indicator function may be modified as follows: $1(|X_{jk} - X_{ik}^{(2)}| > \tau_k)$. Because τ_k is usually not observed nor elicited directly, distributional assumptions would be needed for τ_k, as with the EBA case. If none of the alternatives shows a noticeable difference from the others, then all the alternatives are simply assigned to the fully compensatory trade-off condition.

21.3.3 Other approaches

An alternative approach focuses on inferring decision processes from observed choice outcomes, by directly embedding certain heuristics into the systematic component of utility, for example, through latent class models (LCMs) (Hensher and Collins 2011; Hensher and Greene 2010; McNair *et al.* 2010, 2011; Scarpa *et al.* 2009; Swait and Adamowicz 2001a; Hole 2011). In transport applications, LCMs (see Chapter 16) have been used to test the heuristics of common-metric attribute aggregation, attribute non-attendance, and decision rules like MCD to explain choice in the context of a toll road/ non-toll road alternative (Hensher 2010; Hensher and Collins 2011). The overall conclusion from this line of inquiry is that accounting for (decision) process heterogeneity – that is, allowing heuristic use to vary by subgroups of respondents (up to a probability) – leads to improvements in model fits compared to the standard multinomial logit (MNL) model. In instances where supplementary questions are a part of the survey instrument, accounting for self-stated responses to questions of whether attributes were added up or certain attributes ignored has further improved the explanatory power of the models.

> *As an aside*, a simple latent class approach may be used to model the lexicographic rule.[6] As a non-compensatory rule, the lexicographic rule may be characterized by a high β for the attribute of importance and low or zero βs for the rest of the attributes. This might suggest a latent class structure that assigns respondents' probabilistically to a fully compensatory utility model or to various classes that constrain all but one of the βs to zero. This approach interprets the lexicographic rule as an extreme form of attribute non-attendance. However, this specification does not model the second stage, and any higher order considerations of the lexicographic rule, which states that in case of a tie the second most important attribute is considered, and so on.

Hierarchical Bayes modeling has also proven useful when estimating heterogeneity in cases where the decision sequence, constraints, and thresholds are latent. Gilbride and Allenby (2004) model the two-stage decision processing strategy identified in Payne *et al.* (1993) by assuming that screening rules exist to restrict a larger choice set into a smaller subset of alternatives for final evaluation. The screening rules considered include (i) a compensatory screening rule, where the deterministic portion of utility in the traditional compensatory sense must exceed a threshold; (ii) a conjunctive screening rule, where all attribute values must be acceptable; and (iii) a disjunctive rule, where at least one attribute value needs to be acceptable. These thresholds are determined endogenously and are allowed to vary by respondents, not unlike the approach taken by Swait (2009) and Cantillo and Ortúzar (2005). In conclusion, Gilbride and Allenby find that the conjunctive screening model explains the data best. Further extensions of this work include modeling the EBA processing rule and an economic screening rule which allows eliminations of alternatives if the loss of expected utility (through the elimination) falls below a certain threshold, which could be

---

[6] Some exploratory analysis would also be useful to check if a respondent is consistently choosing the alternative which is best according to a given attribute. Histograms of the frequency that such choices are made can be plotted.

interpreted as the benefits accruing from a reduction in cognitive effort (Gilbride and Allenby 2006).

A point may be noted about how complexity as defined by Payne *et al.* (1993) has been incorporated into choice models. Swait and Adamowicz (2001b) argue that complexity leads to higher variance in preferences and hence the scale factor can be expressed as a function of complexity. Entropy is used as a proxy for their complexity measure, where entropy is defined in Equation (21.8):

$$H_{qt} = -\sum_{j \in S} \pi_{jqt} \log(\pi_{jqt}),\tag{21.8}$$

where π_{jqn} is the probability of alternative j chosen by individual q in choice situation n, and this is given in Equation (21.9):

$$\pi_{jqt} = \frac{\exp(\beta X_{jqt})}{\sum\limits_{j \in S} \exp(\beta X_{jqt})}.\tag{21.9}$$

The entropy measure allows for the degree of preference similarity (the difficulty of making trade-offs) to influence complexity, as entropy reaches its maximum when each of the J alternatives are indistinguishable and has an equal probability of being chosen. The scale of choice task t for individual q is given in Equation (21.10):

$$\mu_{qt} = \exp(\theta_1 H_{qt} + \theta_2 H_{qt}^2).\tag{21.10}$$

The use of the quadratic form is to account for non-linear effects of complexity on decision processes. Specifically, at low levels of complexity, easy decisions requiring little cognitive effort lead to more preference consistency across respondents (scale is high), while moderate levels of complexity lead to more preference inconsistency (lower scale) as respondents resort to using simplifying heuristics. At extreme levels of complexity, alternatives are all approximately similar in utility terms, thus the error variance should begin to decline after a certain point. Writing the scale factor in the form above leads to a specific form of heterogeneity across respondents. Swait and Adamowicz (2001a) also use the same idea of entropy to model complexity; the difference however, is the use of entropy as an explanatory variable for respondent choice.

21.4 Relational heuristics

21.4.1 Within choice set heuristics

Individuals have also been found to use heuristics that are relational and perceptual in nature. By "relational," these heuristics emphasize the comparison of ratings of one alternative against another, allowing the value obtained from an alternative to *also* depend on the local choice context. The models proposed by Kivetz *et al.* (2004) are motivated by empirical findings of an extremeness aversion principle, the so-called **compromise effect**, which leads respondents to favor an in-between alternative when extreme alternatives which do not dominate each other are available in the choice set. Contextual models such as a loss aversion model and a context concavity model have been put forward, both of which incorporate the use of reference points and which account for loss aversion or concavity in gains in the context of the current choice set. In these models, rather than a reference alternative, reference attribute levels are used instead. In the loss aversion model, the reference point is taken to be the mid point of the attribute range of the alternatives in the local choice set, and not necessarily the existing status quo choice option. The value function is defined in Equation (21.11) as:

$$V_j = \sum_k \left[v_{jk}(X_{jk}) - v_{rk}(X_{rk}) \right] \times 1 \left(v_{jk}(X_{jk}) \geq v_{rk}(X_{rk}) \right)$$

$$+ \sum_k \lambda_k \left[v_{jk}(X_{jk}) - v_{rk}(X_{rk}) \right] \times 1 \left(v_{jk}(X_{jk}) < v_{rk}(X_{rk}) \right). \tag{21.11}$$

V_j is the value of alternative i (given a choice set S), $v_{jk}(X_{jk})$ is the utility of attribute k of alternative j, λ_k is the loss aversion parameter for attribute k, and X_{rk} indicates the value of attribute k at the reference point in choice set S.

The context concavity model takes the attribute value with the lowest part-utility as the reference point and codes the utility of other attribute values as gains against the reference. The model specification is shown in Equation (21.12):

$$V_j = \sum_k \left(v_{jk}(X_{jk}) - v_{rk}(X_{rk}) \right)^{c_k}. \tag{21.12}$$

As gains are concave relative to the reference, c_k is introduced as a concavity parameter for attribute k. X_{rk} in this case is the attribute value that gives the

Table 21.3 Worked example for the contextual concavity model

	Alt 1	Alt 2	Alt 3
Attribute 1:			
Assumed value for $v_{j1}(X_{j1})$	5.4	10.2	20.3
$v_{j1}(X_{j1}) - v_{r1}(X_{r1})$	0	4.8	14.9
$\left(v_{j1}(X_{j1}) - v_{r1}(X_{r1})\right)^{0.5}$, assuming $c_1 = 0.5$	0	2.2	3.9
Attribute 2:			
Assumed value for $v_{j2}(X_{j2})$	30.3	23.7	15.2
$v_{j2}(X_{j2}) - v_{r2}(X_{r2})$	15.1	8.5	0
$\left(v_{j2}(X_{j2}) - v_{r2}(X_{r2})\right)^{0.3}$, assuming $c_2 = 0.3$	2.3	1.9	0
$V_j = \left(v_{j1}(X_{j1}) - v_{r1}(X_{r1})\right)^{0.5} + \left(v_{j2}(X_{j2}) - v_{r2}(X_{r2})\right)^{0.3}$	2.3	**4.1**	3.9

lowest utility on attribute k across all alternatives in the choice set. Using some assumed values for the part-utilities, Table 21.3 illustrates how the contextual concavity model leads to an increased relative preference for the intermediate alternative (Alt 2). More generally, the concavity parameter implies diminishing marginal sensitivity to gains, thus benefiting the in-between alternative with its moderate gains on the attributes, compared to the extreme alternatives.

Tversky and Simonson (1993) have also proposed a componential context model, also called a **relative advantage model** (RAM) by Kivetz *et al.* (2004). This model is shown in Equation (21.13). The Nlogit commands for the RAM model are given in Appendix 21A, using data described in Section 21.7:

$$V_j = \sum_k v_k(X_{jk}) + \theta \sum_{j \in S} R(j, i). \tag{21.13}$$

$R(j,i)$ denotes the relative advantage of alternative j over alternative i, and θ is the weight given to the relative advantage component of the model. The parameter θ can be taken as an indication of the strength of the choice context in determining preferences. Using Tversky and Simonson's notation, $R(j,i)$ can be defined as follows: first, for a pair of alternatives (j, i), consider the advantage of j over i with respect to an attribute k, denoted in Equation (21.14) by

$$A_k(j, i) = \begin{cases} v_k(X_{jk}) - v_k(X_{ik}) \text{ if } v_k(X_{jk}) \geq v_k(X_{ik}), \\ 0 \text{ otherwise} \end{cases} \tag{21.14}$$

Define the disadvantage of j over i with respect to an attribute k as an increasing convex function $\delta_k(.)$, where $\delta_k(t) \geq t$, of the corresponding advantage function $A_k(i,j)$, i.e., $D_k(i,j) = \delta_k(A_k(i,j))$. The convex function $\delta_k(.)$ takes the loss aversion principle into consideration. Relative advantage of j over i is then defined in Equation (21.15):

$$R(j,i) = \frac{\sum\limits_k A_k(j,i)}{\sum\limits_k A_k(j,i) + \sum\limits_k D_k(j,i)} = \frac{A(j,i)}{A(j,i) + D(j,i)}. \tag{21.15}$$

$R(j,i) = 0$ if S contains two or fewer elements. The $R(j,i)$ term captures extremeness aversion because extreme alternatives, although enjoying large advantages on some attributes, also possess large disadvantages on at least one attribute. The loss aversion principle from prospect theory (see Chapter 20) leads to these alternatives being less favored compared to the in-between alternatives that have smaller advantages and disadvantages. It should be noted that, unlike the context dependent effect in the loss aversion and the context concavity models, the Tversky and Simonson model assumes that each alternative is compared against all other alternatives in the choice set.

Kivetz *et al.* (2004) assume, in Equation (21.16), the following functional form for $D_k(j,i)$:

$$D_k(j,i) = A_k(i,j) + L_k A_k(i,j)^{\psi_k}. \tag{21.16}$$

L_k is a loss aversion parameter (*a priori* expected to be greater than zero) and ψ_k is a power parameter (*a priori* expected to be greater than one). Rather than an actual description of the underlying behavioral processes, Kivetz *et al.* (2004) observe that these models might be used in an "as-if" manner to improve predictive validity. Their evaluation shows that embedding such intra-choice set relational heuristics, especially loss aversion and context concavity, improves predictions of choices and provides promising leads for future research.

Even as Kivetz *et al.* (2004) claim that extremeness aversion is a "robust" and "important" finding that has been neglected by choice modelers, Gourville and Soman (2007) document cases of extremeness seeking when choice sets are non-alignable. A non-alignable choice set entails alternatives "that vary along discrete, non-compensatory attributes, such that one alternative may possess one set of desirable features, while a second alternative may possess a different set of desirable features" (Gourville and Soman 2007,

10). An example of a non-alignable choice set is the choice among multiple car models, with say one alternative having a high quality car stereo with rear seat DVD entertainment (but no sun roof), and another alternative having the sun roof, but no rear seat entertainment. Hence, the trade-off across attributes is discrete, such that by choosing one alternative the desirable features of another may have to be given up completely. In cases of non-alignable choices, Gourville and Soman found that respondents displayed an increased tendency to either of the extreme alternatives (i.e., a low price, basic model or a high price, fully loaded model) when the size of the choice set is increased. Consumers are posited to increasingly rely on an all-or-nothing strategy, choosing the basic low priced alternative or the high priced, fully loaded alternative.

Gourville and Soman do not reject extremeness aversion outright, but qualify that such aversion occurs when the attributes are alignable, i.e., when attributes can be traded off incrementally. For example, a choice involving a low priced, low processing speed computer model and a medium priced, medium processing speed model is alignable and the introduction of an extreme high priced, high processing speed option causes the market share of the intermediate option to go up. Gourville and Soman suggest that more research needs to be done to investigate the impact of hybrid alignable/non-alignable attributes in the choice set, which arguably characterizes most real world decision making. Although an interesting heuristic, the context in which many CEs are designed seems to preclude the wider applicability of extremeness seeking. Rather, the value of this discussion about alignable and non-alignable attributes serves to emphasize the possibility that in most applications where the attributes that determine choice are alignable, extremeness aversion will prevail.

21.4.2 Between choice set dependence

This notion of "relational" can be extended to allow preceding choice tasks or choice outcomes to impact current choice. As noted by Simonson and Tversky, "in deciding whether or not to select a particular option, people commonly compare it to other alternatives that are currently available as well as with relevant alternatives that have been encountered in the past" (Simonson and Tversky 1992, 282). As most CEs require respondents to answer a series of sequential choice tasks, Simonson and Tversky imply that preferences over attributes are not necessarily independent across choice sets.

Indeed, the discrete choice literature has begun to amass evidence supporting the Simonson and Tversky hypothesis that the past matters. In responding to sequences of choice tasks, there are signs that indicate reference point revision (DeShazo 2002). Hensher and Collins (2011) find that if a non-reference (i.e., non-status quo) alternative is chosen in the preceding choice set $n-1$ the reference in the current choice set n is revised and its utility increases. This suggests a shift in the value function around a new reference point.

"Ordering anomalies," where choice is biased by the sequence of attribute values observed in the preceding choice set(s), are also not uncommon (Day and Prades 2010). For example, if a price attribute of one alternative is seen to increase from one choice set to another, the proportion of respondents choosing that alternative in the second choice set is smaller than if the second choice set was the first choice set, i.e., if there was no preceding choice set for comparison. A proposed explanation is a "good deal/bad deal" heuristic (Bateman *et al.* 2008) or a trade-off contrast (Simonson and Tversky 1992), whereby current preferences are revised on the basis of previous price or cost attributes. This finding may be viewed as a specific example of a more general phenomenon of preference reversal (Tversky *et al.* 1990).

Strategic misrepresentation has also been invoked as one justification for incorporating previous choices as a reference point in the current choice set. The argument from a public goods provision context is that people aim to increase the likelihood of their most preferred alternative being implemented by deliberately withholding the truth about their preferences in the current choice task if chosen alternatives in previous choice tasks have better attribute values than those in the current choice task. Strategic misrepresentation assumes that the respondents have stable and well formed preferences, but that a discrepancy exists between stated preferences (SP) and underlying true preferences. A weaker version of strategic misrepresentation allows respondents to consider the likelihood that the good would not be provided if they did not reveal their true preferences, and hence to only reject truth-telling probabilistically (McNair *et al.* 2010).

The key to modeling strategic representation is to assume that the status quo option is not only chosen when it is preferred to the other alternatives, but also chosen when a previously chosen alternative is preferred to the alternatives in the current choice task. When the latter happens, the attributes of the status quo are replaced by the attributes of this alternative, once such an alternative has been chosen in a preceding choice set.

Another explanation for considering features of previously seen choice sets in the current choice set involves a **value learning** heuristic, which assumes truth-telling, but poorly formed initial preferences. Hence, preferences can be influenced by the starting point and subsequent attribute values (McNair *et al.* 2010), with the "good-deal/bad-deal" heuristic being a specific case in point. It is possible that in a group of respondents, several heuristics are at work and no one heuristic dominates. McNair *et al.* (2010) show that responses to a sequence of binary choice tasks involving the provision of an underground electricity network are consistent with both a weak form of strategic misrepresentation and with a "good deal/bad deal" heuristic, while in an equality constrained LCM, strategic misrepresentation and value learning can be modeled as distinct classes of heuristics for subgroups of respondents (McNair *et al.* 2010).

Underpinning value learning and strategic misrepresentation is the notion of reference point revision. In a direct test of how reference points are shifted when non-status quo alternatives are chosen, Hensher and Collins (2011) found that compared to the choice of a status quo alternative, the choice of a non-reference alternative (i.e., non-status quo alternative) in a given choice set leads to a utility increase for the non-status quo alternatives in the subsequent choice set. Briesch *et al.* (1997) argue that when previously encountered attributes or alternatives are used as a reference, judgments are assumed to be memory-based because information is retrieved from memory and then compared to what is currently available in the choice set. Memory-based judgments "are likely to occur when consumers are able and are motivated to recall past prices from memory and use this information for the task at hand" (Briesch *et al.* 1997, 204). Thus, a vastly superior dominant alternative encountered in a choice set creates conditions for memory-based judgments to take place and it seems likely that such an alternative will be held in the memory as a reference point in future choice sets. Findings from Briesch *et al.* lend some support to this hypothesis. In the context of high frequency purchases of various consumer goods, they evaluated various econometric specifications of references involving past or current prices, and found that a reference specification dependent on memory-based past prices provided the best overall model fit. With a sufficient number of choice sets per respondent, it may be possible to examine various specifications of how previously encountered choice tasks enter the utility expression. For example, it would be possible to test whether all intervening choice sets matter, perhaps using a decay function that allows the more recent choice history to weight more prominently. On the other hand, the data may be adequately explained by appealing to a handful of critical decision points, for example, at the first choice set, because of anchoring and starting point biases, at the most preferred alternative or at the most recent choice set, because of the peak-end heuristic.

The idea of modeling past influences on current decisions via a decay function has been explored by Swait *et al.* (2004). In the context of time series discrete choice models, where the decisions of a panel of respondents are recorded over a period of time, it may be appropriate to account for both state dependence and habit persistence. State dependence may be defined as "current preferences being affected by previous choices," while habit persistence refers to how "current preferences are affected by previous preferences" (Swait *et al.* 2004, 96). In the model specification, the current utility (at time *t*) of alternative *j* defined through a meta-utility function (Equation (21.17)):

$$\hat{V}_{jt} = \prod_{s=0}^{t} \alpha_{js}\exp(V_{j,t-s}), \tag{21.17}$$

where meta-utility is dependent on all past (static) utilities, $V_{j,t-s}$, which is itself dependent only on the attributes in the period $t - s$. The link between current utility and historical observed utilities is achieved through a path dependence parameter, $\alpha_{js}, 0 \le \alpha_{js} \le 1, \alpha_{j0} = 1$, where α_{js} might also be interpreted as the weights associated with the previous periods. Taking logs to obtain a linear additive form and adding past and contemporaneous error terms results in Equation (21.18):

$$\ln(\hat{V}_{jt}) = \sum_{s=0}^{t} V_{j,t-s} + \sum_{s=0}^{t} \ln(\alpha_{js}) + \sum_{s=0}^{t} \varepsilon_{j,t-s}. \tag{21.18}$$

As the first RHS term of Equation (21.18) contains all past attribute levels, this equation can also be seen to link "current utility to historical observed attribute levels in a fashion that is consistent with learning about attributes or updating" (Swait *et al.* 2004, 98). Attribute levels in previous periods are combined with current attribute levels in a form of temporal averaging. State dependence can be modeled using a dummy variable that equals 1 for alternative *j* in choice set *i* if the same alternative had been chosen in choice set *t – 1*. The variance structure of the disturbance term is allowed to vary over time, providing a form of temporal heteroskedasticity. One final observation to make is that in the repeated CE context, this model provides another way of investigating the role of the value learning heuristic.

An alternative specification proposed by Cantillo *et al.* (2006) assumes a just noticeable difference heuristic in linking the attribute levels in the preceding choice set to the attributes in the current choice set. A change in the attribute level from choice task $n-1$ to choice task n is assumed to be perceptible only if $|\Delta X_{k,n}| = |X_{k,n} - X_{k,n-1}| \geq \delta_k$, for non-negative threshold values δ_k of attribute k. Like several of the threshold formulations described earlier, thresholds can be assumed to be individual-specific, randomly distributed across the population and may also depend on socio-demographic characteristics.

Cantillo *et al.* assume that respondents only perceive the part of the attribute level change that is bigger than the threshold, as in Equation (21.19):

$$X_{jkqn} = X_{jkq,n-1} + sgn(\Delta X_{jkqn})\max(|\Delta X_{jkqn}| - \delta_{kq}, 0). \tag{21.19}$$

If m of the K attributes have an associated perception threshold, utility can be written in Equation (21.20) as:

$$U_{jqn} = V_{jqn} + \varepsilon_{jqn} = \sum_{k=1}^{m} \beta_{jkq} X_{jkqn} + \sum_{k=m+1}^{K} \beta_{jkq} X_{jkqn} + \varepsilon_{jqn}$$

$$= \sum_{k=1}^{m} \beta_{jkq} \left[X_{jkq,n-1} + \Delta X_{jkqn} \left(1 - \frac{\delta_{kq}}{|\Delta X_{jkqn}|} \right) I_{jkq} \right] + \sum_{k=m+1}^{K} \beta_{jkq} X_{jkqn} + \varepsilon_{jqn}, \tag{21.20}$$

where $I_{jkq} = \begin{cases} 1 \text{ if } |\Delta X_{jkqn}| \geq \delta_{kq} \\ 0 \text{ otherwise} \end{cases}$

To complete the model, a joint density function needs to be assumed for δ_k. Cantillo *et al.* assume that all δ_k are independently distributed over a triangular distribution. The value for m is determined exogenously, by allowing the perception of each attribute to be threshold constrained at a time.

Cantillo *et al.*'s just noticeable difference heuristic provides one way of allowing respondents to "change" the attribute values presented to them in a particular choice task, thereby relaxing the assumption in most choice models that respondents take the attribute levels as given. In applications where variability matters – for example, in transport where both travel times and variability of travel times are important determinants of choice (see Hensher and Li 2012) – the travel time attribute may itself be changed or edited by the respondent, with the magnitude of the edit possibly depending on the variability attribute and any associated threshold.

The provision of an alternative may itself be a subject of uncertainty. McNair *et al.* (2011) have attempted to model this aspect of the choice data by assigning probability weights to each of the alternatives in the choice set. These weights are determined on the basis that respondents expect a higher cost alternative to be more readily provided. Moreover, a history of accepting alternatives with the higher cost in previous choice sets also improves the probability that the alternatives in the current choice set will be provided.

21.5 Process data

21.5.1 Motivation for process data collection

Given what is still unknown about human decision making, there appears to be some merit in understanding decision processes from a process viewpoint. A process is "a sequence of events, information acquisition steps, and/or decisions that eventually lead to an outcome" (Pendyala and Bricka 2006, 513). Process data is intended to:

describe the sequences, procedures, and ways in which people make decisions by focussing on how people collect, absorb, assimilate, interpret, and use information to make decisions. In short, process data intend to reveal the cognitive process underlying decision-making behavior. (Pendyala and Bricka 2006, 513)

The collection of additional process data is thought to complement existing estimation techniques by offering new covariates to help explain the variance in the data (Bradley 2006).

21.5.2 Monitoring information acquisition

One well established process tracing technique involves monitoring how respondents acquire information in a decision task. Usually, the respondent is presented with hidden values in a matrix comprising alternatives in columns and attributes in rows. Respondents are then asked to uncover, by clicking on the relevant box, as few attribute values as are necessary to make a choice. This method allows a researcher to obtain data on what information is sought by the respondent, in what order the information is retrieved, how much information is examined, and the time spent on acquiring each piece of information (Payne *et al.* 1993). Earlier versions of monitoring information acquisition allowed the respondent to either keep all previously opened boxes uncovered (Payne 1976) or to restrict the currently available information to only one box at a time, i.e., once a new piece of information is acquired, the previous information is hidden again (Olshavsky 1979). The current practice appears to favor the latter option (Riedl *et al.* 2008; Payne *et al.* 1993). Puckett and Hensher (2006, 2009) developed CEs that allowed respondents to "grey out" attributes that they ignored (i.e., did not attend to) for each alternative, allowing for the level of the attribute as well as the attribute *per se*. They also permitted common-metric attributes (e.g., running costs and toll costs) to be added.

This technique of monitoring information acquisition was used by Kaye-Blake *et al.* (2009) to assess the amount of information processed by respondents in an agricultural context involving the choice of potatoes. In choice sets with six attributes and three alternatives, they found that slightly more than 20 percent of the available information was not accessed and almost half of all alternatives had at least one attribute not attended to. Better model fit statistics were obtained when revealed attribute non-attendance (as evidenced by the attributes left uncovered in the choice set) was accounted for, compared to the base case of assumed full information processing. This is evidence supporting the case for process data. Unfortunately, they do not report the order or sequence of clicks that would allow the calculation of process tracing metrics. Using these metrics to identify the decision strategies used in their choice context would have been a relevant and timely contribution to the field.

Process tracing metrics as applied to the monitoring of information acquisition have undergone substantial refinement since they were introduced some thirty years ago. Earlier metrics included proportion of information searched, variability of information searched per alternative, and a search index (Payne 1976), but more recently Riedl *et al.* (2008) have suggested alternative metrics to improve the identification of various decision strategies. Two of these are described below.

Metric 1: ratio of alternative-wise transitions to attribute-wise and mixed transitions
Define an alternative-wise transition (AltT) as one where the two successive boxes to be opened are different attributes within the same alternative, an attribute-wise transition (AttrT) as one where the two successive boxes to be opened are the same attribute across different alternatives, and a mixed

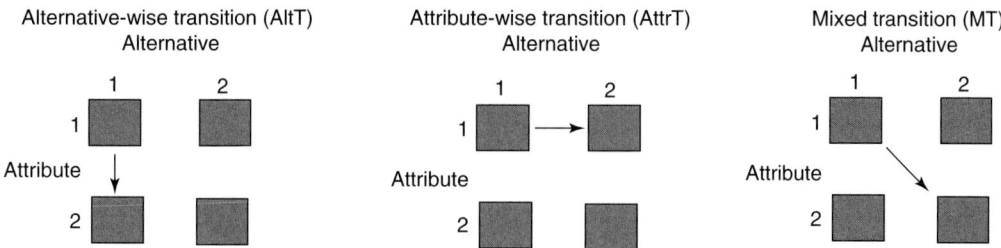

Figure 21.1 Graphical illustration of possible transitions in a choice experiment

transition (MT) as one that differs across alternatives and attributes. Figure 21.1 provides an illustration of these transition types.

The WADD utility decision rule implies consideration of all attribute values within an alternative before transitioning to the next alternative. In a matrix with k attributes and j alternatives, the WADD and EQW rules predict that the number of AltTs to be $(k-1) * j$ and the number of AttrTs + MTs to be $j-1$. The closer a respondent's measure of $\frac{AltT}{AttrT+MT}$ is to $\frac{(k-1)*j}{j-1}$, the more likely WADD or EQW has been used.

Metric 2: correlation between attribute rank (AR) and the number of boxes opened for each attribute (NBOX)

EBA and LEX strategies imply an attribute-wise search, with a selective amount of information processed for each attribute. These strategies also imply the elimination of alternatives prior to arriving at a final choice.

In this metric, define a box rank to be the nth box that is opened by the respondent, hence, the first box that is opened gets a box rank of 1 and so on. The attribute rank (AR) is defined as the mean of all box ranks for that attribute. The earlier the attribute is considered during the decision process, the lower its AR will be. NBOX is the number of boxes that were opened for each attribute.

A typical EBA simulation is illustrated in Figure 21.2. Here a "+" sign indicates that the attribute value exceeds the threshold value, while a "−" sign indicates that the attribute value falls short of the threshold and thereby eliminates that particular alternative from further consideration. In this example, the (AR, NBOX) data pairs form the following sequence: (3,5), (7,3), (9.5,2).

It will be noted that the EBA and LEX strategies imply a negative correlation between AR and NBOX. In contrast, compensatory strategies like EQW and WADD should give a zero correlation, as a consistent set of information is

	Alt1	Alt2	Alt3	Alt4	Alt5	AR	NBOX
Attr1	1+	2–	3+	4–	5+	3	5
Attr2	8+		7–		6+	7	3
Attr3	9–				10+	9.5	2
Attr4						–	0

Figure 21.2 Typical EBA simulation

processed per alternative, resulting in NBOX for each attribute being a constant factor across all attributes.

An alternative metric for the MCD heuristic

Riedl *et al.* (2008) propose to identify the MCD heuristic by tracking latencies. Essentially, when $j \geq 3$, a respondent following the MCD rule will evaluate at least one alternative more than once (assuming that the attribute values are not kept in short-term memory), and the total time taken to evaluate each alternative can then be compared against the other. Instead of using latency data, as suggested by Riedl *et al.*, it may be simpler to track the number of times an alternative is acquired. For example, when $j = 3$, one alternative will be acquired two times, and when $j = 4$, either one alternative will be acquired three times, or two alternatives acquired two times. Another metric uses the notion of *transitions* defined earlier. As the MCD heuristic implies a consistent search across all attributes, with k attributes and j alternatives in the choice set, the number of AttrTs is $k*(j-1)$.

It would be a relatively straightforward process to collect some of these metrics as part of a CE, perhaps at the end of all the choice tasks given to the respondent. This data might be used to improve the probability estimates of assigning an individual to a particular class of heuristics in a mixed PDF model (e.g., Swait 2009) or in a class assignment model. Nevertheless, even with the suggested metrics, decision strategies – or, more precisely, classes of decision strategies – are only identifiable up to a probability.

21.6 Synthesis so far

One of the main objectives of CEs and the SP technique is to find "a robust and reliable method for valuing the non-market impacts of public policies on individuals" (Sugden 2005). Research from psychology and other related disciplines has found systematic patterns of inconsistencies with the standard economic assumptions. It is generally accepted that preferences are to a large extent constructed and dependent on the choice environment and choice context. The decision that is finally observed by the analyst would most likely have been filtered through some simplifying rules or heuristics. It therefore appears that improvements in the robustness and reliability of choice models can be realized by incorporating these behavioral considerations into model specifications.

This chapter so far has shown that the existing literature has already made some headway towards embedding such patterns of human behavior into choice models. While collecting better process data to more fully comprehend the decision making process is certainly one important step for future work, it is still possible even without process data to test most of the heuristics discussed in this chapter using the information that would have been collected in the course of a typical CE.[7] A summary of the candidate heuristics and a possible model form that can be easily tested with existing data are listed in Table 21.4.

Table 21.4 Summary of candidate heuristics and example model forms testable on existing data sets

Heuristic	Example of methodology that embeds heuristic into choice model
H.1 Elimination-by-aspects	
H.1.1	See Swait (2009), for a k-mix discrete-continuous PDF model that allows each alternative to be in one of k conditions up to a probability.
H.1.2	See Cantillo and Ortúzar (2005) for a two-stage model involving a first-stage elimination through attribute thresholds.
H.1.3	See Swait (2001) and Hensher and Rose (2012) for a model that allows the attribute cut-offs to be violated.
H.2 Majority of confirming dimensions	
	See Hensher and Collins (2011) for a latent class approach; Swait (2009) can be adapted to embed MCD.
H.3 Lexicographic rules	
H.3.1	Use of a latent class approach to model the lexicographic rule.
H.3.2	Adaptation of Swait's (2009) discrete-continuous PDF model to the lexicographic rule and lexicographic semi-order rule.
H.4 Attribute non-attendance and common-metric attribute aggregation	
	See Hensher (2010) for a latent class approach. Also Scarpa et al. (2008b) and Layton and Hensher (2010).

---

[7] Assumptions will have to be made about latent constructs, for example, thresholds and reference points.

Table 21.4 (cont.)

H.5 The effect of choice complexity in choice models

    See Swait and Adamowicz (2001a) and Swait and Adamowicz (2001b).

H.6 Extremeness aversion heuristic

H.6.1   See Kivetz *et al.* (2004) for the contextual concavity formulation.

H.6.2   See Kivetz *et al.* (2004) for the loss aversion model.

H.6.3   See Kivetz *et al.* (2004) for the RAM.

H.7 Strategic misrepresentation

    See McNair *et al.* (2011).

H.8 Value learning

    See McNair *et al.* (2011).

H.9 Reference point revision

    See Hensher and Collins (2011).

H.10 Temporal and state dependence

    See Swait *et al.* (2004).

H.11 A Just-noticeable difference heuristic in attribute level updating

    See Cantillo *et al.* (2006).

A significant portion of the literature has observed that model outputs such as welfare estimates and WTP are substantially different when standard assumptions are relaxed and more behaviorally plausible assumptions put in. It may therefore be worthwhile revisiting some of our existing data sets to see how our results and conclusions would change if we were to now consider embedding heuristics into our choice models.

21.7 Case study I: incorporating attribute processing heuristics through non-linear processing

To illustrate the implications of a number of AP strategies, we use a data set drawn from a study undertaken in Sydney in 2004, in the context of car driving commuters making choices from a range of level of service packages defined in terms of travel times and costs, including a toll where applicable. The SC questionnaire presented respondents with sixteen choice situations, each giving a choice between their current (reference) route and two alternative routes with varying trip attributes. The sample of 243 effective interviews, each responding to 16 choice sets, resulted in 3,888 observations for model estimation.

To ensure that we captured a large number of travel circumstances and potential AP rules, we sampled individuals who had recently undertaken trips of various travel times, in locations where toll roads currently exist.[8] To ensure some variety in trip length, an individual was assigned to one of the three trip length segments based on a recent commuting trip: no more than 30 minutes, 31 to 60 minutes, and more than 61 minutes (capped at 2 hours). A telephone call was used to establish eligible participants from households stratified geographically, and a time and location agreed for a face-to-face Computer Assisted Personal Interview (CAPI).

A statistically efficient design (see Rose and Bliemer 2008; Sándor and Wedel 2002), that is pivoted around the knowledge base of travellers, is used to establish the attribute packages in each choice scenario, in recognition of supporting theories in behavioral and cognitive psychology and economics, such as prospect theory. A pivot design recognizes the useful information contained in an RP alternative, capturing the accumulated exposure to the studied context. Further details of the design of the CE and merits of pivot or referenced designs are provided in Hensher and Layton (2010) and Hensher (2008).

The two SC alternatives are unlabeled routes. The trip attributes associated with each route are free-flow time, slowed-down time, trip time variability, running cost, and toll cost. All attributes of the SC alternatives are based on the values of the current trip. Variability in travel time for the current alternative was calculated as the difference between the longest and shortest trip time provided in non-SC questions. The SC alternative values for this attribute are variations around the total trip time. For all other attributes, the values for the SC alternatives are variations around the values for the current trip. The variations used for each attribute are given in Table 21.5.

The experimental design has one version of 16 choice sets (games). The design has no dominance given the assumptions that less of all attributes is better.[9] The distinction between free-flow and slowed-down time is designed to promote the differences in the quality of travel time between various routes – especially a tolled route and a non-tolled route – and is separate to the influence of total time. Free-flow time is interpreted with reference to a trip at 3 a.m. in the morning when there are no delays due to traffic.[10] An example of an SC screen is shown in Figure 21.3.

---

[8] Sydney has a growing number of operating toll roads, hence drivers have had a lot of exposure to paying tolls.

[9] The survey designs are available from the author on request.

[10] This distinction does not imply that there is a specific minute of a trip that is free flow *per se*, but it does tell respondents that there is a certain amount of the total time that is slowed down due to traffic, etc. and hence a balance is not slowed down (i.e., it is free flow as one observes typically at 3 a.m. in the morning).

Table 21.5 Profile of attribute range in stated choice design

	Free-flow time	Slowed-down time	Variability	Running costs	Toll costs
Level 1	− 50%	− 50%	+ 5%	− 50%	− 100%
Level 2	− 20%	− 20%	+ 10%	− 20%	+ 20%
Level 3	+ 10%	+ 10%	+ 15%	+ 10%	+ 40%
Level 4	+ 40%	+ 40%	+ 20%	+ 40%	+ 60%

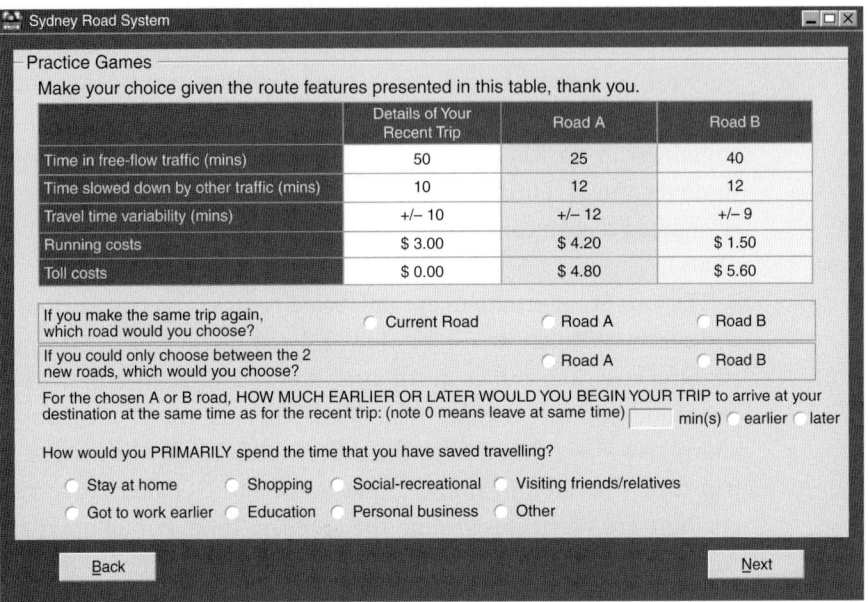

Figure 21.3   Example of a stated choice screen

21.7.1 Common-metric attribute aggregation

In this section, we explore a line of inquiry in which we consider the relationship between pairs of attributes associated with the same alternative that are defined on a common metric (e.g., minutes or dollars) in order to gain evidence on how such attributes might be processed in preference revelation. We speculate the presence of an underlying continuous probability distribution for the way that pairs of attributes are processed when the units are common. The appeal of this approach is that, unlike studies that investigate alternative behavioral processing rules such as compensatory (i.e., all attributes are treated in the same level of a hierarchy in trading among them) versus EBA, we allow for a mix of regimes across a sample. In contrast, most studies impose the same rule on the entire estimation sample, and contrast two regimes as two separate models. That is, *they assume consistency in attribute strategy within the same decision context for the entire sample.*

Consider a utility function for alternative i defined in terms of two attributes labeled x_1 and x_2 (these might be free-flow time and congestion time, both in common units) and other attributes such as running cost and toll cost x_3 and x_4:

$$U_i = f(x_{i1}, x_{i2}, x_{i3}, x_{i4}) + \varepsilon_i, \tag{21.21}$$

where

$$f(x_{i1}, x_{i2}, x_{i3}, x_{i4}) = \begin{cases} \beta_1\, x_{i1} + \beta_2\, x_{i2} + \beta_3\, x_{i3} + \beta_4\, x_{i4} & if\,(x_{i1} - x_{i2})^2 > \alpha \\ \beta_{12}(x_{i1} + x_{i2}) + \beta_{i3}\, x_{i3} + \beta_{i4}\, x_{i4} & if\,(x_{i1} - x_{i2})^2 < \alpha \end{cases}. \tag{21.22}$$

β_1, β_2, β_3, β_4, β_{12}, are parameters and α is an unknown threshold. The term $(x_{i1} - x_{i2})^2$ represents the square of the distance between x_{i1} and x_{i2}. A squared form supports efficient computation, but another form could be used. Intuitively, when the difference between the common metric attributes x_{i1} and x_{i2} is great enough, the agent's process preserves attribute partitioning, and thus treats each attribute as separate entities and evaluates their contribution to utility in the standard random utility model (RUM) manner with parameters β_1 and β_2. On the other hand, when the difference between the common metric attributes x_{i1} and x_{i2} is relatively small, the agent's process aggregates the attributes and thus treats the sum of x_{i1} and x_{i2} as a single attribute with utility weight β_{12}.

We enrich the model by allowing α_n for person n to be randomly distributed (with $\alpha_n > 0$). A useful candidate distribution is that α_n is exponential with mean $1/\lambda$ and density $g(\alpha) = \lambda e^{-\lambda \alpha}$. This density allows for some fraction of the population to behave essentially as standard utility maximizers at the level of a very specific alternative (where for repeated observations, we impose the condition of independence in respect of the way the heuristic operates). Still others behave as standard utility maximizers when attributes are dissimilar, but aggregate when attributes are similar. Importantly, this density also allows for a tail of others who more frequently are aggregating the two attributes. The probability conditions are given in Equation (21.23). In this model, we assume that there is an exponentially distributed threshold parameter, IID across alternatives and respondents, that indicates how the respondent views the attribute components.[11] This non-linear utility function permits a probabilistic preservation or aggregation of each attribute:

$$P_i\left((x_{i1} - x_{i2})^2 > \alpha\right) = 1 - \exp^{-\lambda}(x_{i1} - x_{i2})^2. \tag{21.23}$$

Integrating over the α_n we write U_i in conditional form:

$$
\begin{aligned}
U_i = f\left(x_{i1}, x_{i2} \mid \left[(x_{i1} - x_{i2})^2 > \alpha\right]\right) P_i\left(\left[(x_{i1} - x_{i2})^2 > \alpha\right]\right) \\
+ f\left(x_{i1}, x_{i2} \mid \left[(x_{i1} - x_{i2})^2 < \alpha\right]\right) P_i\left(\left[(x_{i1} - x_{i2})^2 < \alpha\right]\right) + \varepsilon
\end{aligned}
\tag{21.24}
$$

Equation (21.24), together with the equivalent treatment of x_{i3} and x_{i4}, implies that:

$$
\begin{aligned}
U_i = (\beta_1 x_{i1} + \beta_2 x_{i2})\left(1 - \exp^{-\lambda_1 (x_{i1} - x_{i2})^2}\right) + \beta_{12}(x_{i1} + x_{i2})\left(\exp^{-\lambda_1 (x_{i1} - x_{i2})^2}\right) \\
+ (\beta_3 x_{i3} + \beta_4 x_{i4})\left(1 - \exp^{-\lambda_2 (x_{i3} - x_{i4})^2}\right) + \beta_{34}(x_{i3} + x_{i4})\left(\exp^{-\lambda_2 (x_{i3} - x_{i4})^2}\right) + \varepsilon_i
\end{aligned}
\tag{21.25}
$$

Equation (21.25) is a non-linear form in $x_{i1}, x_{i2}, x_{i3}, x_{i4}$. As λ_q $q = 1,2$, tends toward ∞ the distribution becomes degenerate at zero. In this case, all individuals are always standard utility maximizers who partition the common-metric attributes, and we obtain the linear additive form (21.26):

$$U_i = \beta_1 x_{i1} + \beta_2 x_{i2} + \beta_3 x_{i3} + \beta_4 x_{i4} + \varepsilon_i. \tag{21.26}$$

If λ_q tends toward 0 then every individual becomes a common-metric aggregator, as they perceive no difference between the two attributes[12] (Equation 21.27):

---

[11] One can allow for the α_ns to be constant across alternatives for a given respondent. We discuss the formulation and report results for such a model later. At this juncture, we find it clearest to present the model in terms of uncorrelated α_ns.

[12] As an example, imagine an experimental design with x_1 and x_2 being dummy variables, and the only combinations considered are (1,0) and (0,1). In both cases $(x_1 - x_2)^2 = 1$, and so we have condition:
$$U = (\beta_1 x_1 + \beta_2 x_2)(1 - \exp^{-\lambda}) + \beta_{12}(x_1 + x_2)(\exp^{-\lambda}) + \varepsilon.$$
If $x_1 = 1$ and $x_2 = 0$, we have condition (a): $U = (\beta_1 x_1)(1 - \exp^{-\lambda}) + \beta_{12}(x_1)(\exp^{-\lambda}) + \varepsilon$
equivalent to (b): $U = (\beta_1 x_1) + (\beta_{12} - \beta_1)x_1(\exp^{-\lambda}) + \varepsilon = \{\beta_1 + (\beta_{12} - \beta_1)(\exp^{-\lambda})\} x_1 + \varepsilon.$
The same functional expression applies for x_2. In both cases we have a co-mingling of parameters. If we include the combinations of (1,1) and (0,0), then we have Equation (c): $U = \beta_{12}(x_1 + x_2) + \varepsilon.$

$$U_i = \beta_{12}\left(x_{i1} + x_{i2}\right) + \beta_{34}\left(x_{i3} + x_{i4}\right) + \varepsilon_i. \tag{21.27}$$

Equation (21.25) is the estimable utility expression for each alternative in a stated or revealed choice model, under the assumption that an independent α_{in} is drawn for each alternative i and each individual n. To estimate the model by the method of maximum likelihood, compute the probability that $U_{in} \geq U_{jn}$, $\forall\, i \neq j$, where U_{in} and U_{jn} are defined as in Equation (21.25). The model can be extended to make the parameter α_n a fixed number for each individual, so that the same threshold parameter is used in evaluating all alternatives by a given individual (but different across individuals). The model can be further extended to account for a panel of repeated choices that we utilize in our empirical application. The panel model can most succinctly be described as follows. Define a set of T choice occasions by $t = 1, \ldots, T$. Then define $f(x_{it1}, x_{it2}, x_{it3}, x_{it4}\,|\,\alpha_n)$ analogously to Equation (21.22) as the deterministic portion of the utility function for alternative i on occasion t for person n given their threshold parameter and the resulting evaluation of the common-metric attributes. Then the choice model for T choices may be written as:

$$\int \left[P\Big(f(x_{it1}, x_{it2}, x_{it3}, x_{it4}\,|\,\alpha_n) + \varepsilon_{it} \geq f(x_{jt1}, x_{jt2}, x_{jt3}, x_{jt4}\,|\,\alpha_n) + \varepsilon_{jt}, \right.$$

$$\left. \forall t = 1 : T,\, it \neq jt \Big) \right] g(\alpha_n)\, d\alpha_n. \tag{21.28}$$

To compute Equation (21.28) one must utilize the sequence of choices and integrate the resulting panel choice probability over the density of the threshold parameter, α_n.

We can derive the relevant WTP for travel time savings for free-flow and slowed-down time, and a weighted average total time, and contrast it with the results from the traditional linear models. The WTP function is now highly non-linear. The derivative of the utility expression with respect to a specific attribute is given in Equation (21.29), using free-flow time (defined as x_1) and in Equation (21.30) using slowed-down time, (x_2), as examples of the common form, suppressing the subscript for an alternative. The difference is in the specific parameters and the sign change before the number "2." Exactly the same functional form for Equations (21.29) and (21.30) applies to running cost and toll cost, respectively. The WTP for free-flow time, for example, defined in terms of running cost would be:

$(\partial U/\partial x_1)/(\partial U/\partial x_3)$:

$$\partial U/\partial x_1 = \beta_1\left(1 - \exp^{-\lambda(x_1-x_2)^2}\right) + 2(\beta_1 x_1 + \beta_2 x_2)\lambda(x_1 - x_2)\exp^{-\lambda(x_1-x_2)^2}$$
$$+ \beta_{12}\exp^{-\lambda(x_1-x_2)^2} - 2\beta_{12}(x_1 + x_2)\lambda(x_1 - x_2)\exp^{-\lambda(x_1-x_2)^2}.$$

$$(21.29)$$

$$\partial U/\partial x_2 = \beta_1\left(1 - \exp^{-\lambda(x_1-x_2)^2}\right) + 2(\beta_1 x_1 + \beta_2 x_2)\lambda(x_1 - x_2)\exp^{-\lambda(x_1-x_2)^2}$$
$$+ \beta_{12}\exp^{-\lambda(x_1-x_2)^2} - 2\beta_{12}(x_1 + x_2)\lambda(x_1 - x_2)\exp^{-\lambda(x_1-x_2)^2}.$$

$$(21.30)$$

The set up to estimate this model in Nlogit is given below:

```
load;file=C:\Projects-Active\M4East_F3_2004plus\M4Data04\m4noncom.sav$
This was not a panel data set
.LPJ save file contained   10704 observations.
This .LPJ file did not make full use of the data area.
Data set is being rearranged to increase the number of variables that you
can create.  This may take a minute
or two.  Please wait.
Sample ; All $
create
    ;if(toll>0)tollasc=1
    ;totc=cost+toll
    ;tt=ff+sdt
    ;zz=sdt/(ff+sdt)$
reject;cset3=-999$
?To begin, perfectly replicate the basic MNL.
? Putting data on one line J=1
create ; dcu=choice1 ; ds1=choice1[+1] ; ds2=choice1[+2]$   choice
create ; ffcu=ff ; ffs1=ff[+1] ; ffs2 = ff[+2]  $  free-flow time
create ; sdcu=sdt ; sds1=sdt[+1] ; sds2 = sdt[+2]  $  slowed down time
create ; rccu=cost ; rcs1=cost[+1] ; rcs2 = cost[+2]  $ running cost
create ; tccu=toll ; tcs1=toll[+1] ; tcs2 = toll[+2]  $ toll cost
create ; varcu=var ; vcs1=var[+1] ; vcs2 = var[+2]  $ reliability
Create ; J = Trn(-3,0) $
Reject ; J > 1 $
Maximise
    ; Labels = bff,bsdt,brc,btoll,bvar,nonsqasc
    ; Start  = -.068,-.083,-.306,.403,-.013,0.319
    ; Fcn    = uc = bff*ffcu + bsdt*sdcu + brc*rccu + btoll*tccu
    + bvar*varcu|
              vc = exp(uc)  |
```

```
    us1 =     nonsqasc +  bff*ffs1 + bsdt*sds1 + brc*rcs1 + btoll*tcs1
    + bvar*vcs1|
    vs1 = exp(us1) |
    us2 =     nonsqasc + bff*ffs2 + bsdt*sds2 + brc*rcs2 + btoll*tcs2
    + bvar*vcs2|
                vs2 = exp(us2) |
    IV = vc+vs1+vs2|
    P  = (dcu*vc + ds1*vs1 + ds2*vs2)/IV |
    log(P) $
Normal exit from iterations. Exit status=0.
```

```
+--------------------------------------------------------------+
| User Defined Optimization                                    |
| Maximum Likelihood Estimates                                 |
| Dependent variable              Function                     |
| Weighting variable                  None                     |
| Number of observations              3568                     |
| Iterations completed                  12                     |
| Log likelihood function         2734.620                     |
| Number of parameters                   0                     |
| Info. Criterion: AIC =          -1.53286                     |
|    Finite Sample: AIC =         -1.53286                     |
| Info. Criterion: BIC =          -1.53286                     |
| Info. Criterion:HQIC =          -1.53286                     |
| Restricted log likelihood        .0000000                    |
| Chi squared                     5469.240                     |
| Degrees of freedom                     6                     |
| Prob[ChiSqd > value] =           .0000000                    |
| Model estimated: May 12, 2008, 09:35:23AM                    |
+--------------------------------------------------------------+
```

```
+----------+------------------+--------------------+----------+-----------+
|Variable| Coefficient  | Standard Error |b/St.Er.|P[|Z|>z] |
+----------+------------------+--------------------+----------+-----------+
|BFF     |    -.06832***       .00328040   -20.827   .0000 |
|BSDT    |    -.08434***       .00372181   -22.660   .0000 |
|BRC     |    -.31202***       .02005974   -15.554   .0000 |
|BTOLL   |    -.41086***       .01251124   -32.839   .0000 |
|BVAR    |     .00875***       .00241100     3.630   .0003 |
|NONSQASC|    -.15699**        .06419372    -2.445   .0145 |
+----------+-------------------------------------------------------------+
| Note: ***, **, * = Significance at 1%, 5%, 10% level.       |
+-------------------------------------------------------------------------+
```

?Then fit the nonlinear model.
```
Create;dffsdtc=0.01*(ffcu-sdcu)^2; drctcc=0.01*(rccu-tccu)^2;sumttc=ffcu
+sdcu;sumcc=rccu+tccu$
Create;dffsdts1=0.01*(ffs1-sds1)^2;drctcs1=0.01*(rcs1-tcs1)^2;
sumtts1=ffs1+sds1;sumcs1=rcs1+tcs1$
Create;dffsdts2=0.01*(ffs2-sds2)^2;drctcs2=0.01*(rcs2-tcs2)^2;
sumtts2=ffs2+sds2;sumcs2=rcs2+tcs2$
dstats;rhs=ffcu,sdcu,ffs1,sds1,ffs2,sds2,rccu,tccu,rcs1,tcs1,rcs2,tcs2,
```

```
dffsdtc,dffsdts1,dffsdts2,drctcc,drctcs1,drctcs2$
Maximise
    ; Labels = bff,bsdt,brc,btoll,bvar,nonsqasc,?btollasc,
    betacc,betatt,acc1,att1
    ; Start = -.068,-.083,-.306,-.403,-.009,-.156,0,0,0,0
    ; maxit = 20
    ; Fcn    = uc =
    (brc*rccu + btoll*tccu)*(1-exp(-acc1*drctcc))
    + betacc*sumtcc*exp(-acc1*drctcc)
    + (bff*ffcu + bsdt*sdcu)*(1-exp(-att1*dffsdtc))
    +betatt*sumttc*exp(-att1*dffsdtc) + bvar*varcu|
               vc = exp(uc) |
    us1 =    nonsqasc +
    (brc*rcs1 + btoll*tcs1)*(1-exp(-acc1*drctcs1))
    +betacc*sumtcs1*exp(-acc1*drctcs1)
    (bff*ffs1 + bsdt*sds1)*(1-exp(-att1*dffsdts1))
    +betatt*sumtts1*exp(-att1*dffsdts1)
    + bvar*varcu|
              vs1 = exp(us1) |
    us2 =    nonsqasc +      (brc*rcs2 + btoll*tcs2)*(1-exp(-acc1*drctcs2))
    +betacc*sumtcs2*exp(-acc1*drctcs2)
    (bff*ffs2 + bsdt*sds2)*(1-exp(-att1*dffsdts2))
    +betatt*sumtts2*exp(-att1*dffsdts2)
    + bvar*varcu|
              vs2 = exp(us2) |
    IV = vc+vs1+vs2|
    P  = (dcu*vc + ds1*vs1 + ds2*vs2)/IV |
    log(P) $
Maximum iterations reached. Exit iterations with status=1.
```

```
+--------------------------------------------------------------+
| User Defined Optimization                                    |
| Maximum Likelihood Estimates                                 |
| Dependent variable                 Function                  |
| Weighting variable                     None                  |
| Number of observations                 3568                  |
| Iterations completed                     21                  |
| Log likelihood function            2969.138                  |
| Number of parameters                      0                  |
| Info. Criterion: AIC =             -1.66431                  |
|    Finite Sample: AIC =            -1.66431                  |
| Info. Criterion: BIC =             -1.66431                  |
| Info. Criterion:HQIC =             -1.66431                  |
| Restricted log likelihood          .0000000                  |
| Chi squared                        5938.276                  |
| Degrees of freedom                       10                  |
| Prob[ChiSqd > value] =             .0000000                  |
| Model estimated: May 12, 2008, 09:38:46AM                    |
+--------------------------------------------------------------+
```

Variable	Coefficient	Standard Error	b/St.Er.	P[|Z|>z]
BFF	.29530	.93089447	.317	.7511
BSDT	.27320	.83889932	.326	.7447
BRC	-.02064	.01463281	-1.411	.1583
BTOLL	-.36827***	.01514496	-24.317	.0000
BVAR	-.00900	.122518D+09	.000	1.0000
NONSQASC	-.61223***	.06787733	-9.020	.0000
BETACC	-.21771***	.02015601	-10.801	.0000
BETATT	-.06792***	.00292412	-23.227	.0000
ACC1	20.8150***	3.27880870	6.348	.0000
ATT1	.00021	.00067015	.317	.7510

21.7.2 Latent class specification: non-attendance and dual processing of common-metric attributes in choice analysis

Processing heuristics presented can be evaluated within a LCM framework (see Chapter 16). The underlying theory of the LCM posits that individual behavior depends on observable attributes and on latent heterogeneity that varies with factors that are unobserved by the analyst. It is assumed that individuals are implicitly sorted into a set of Q processing classes, but which class contains any particular individual, whether known or not to that individual, is unknown to the analyst. The behavioral model is a logit model for discrete choice among J_i alternatives, by individual i observed in T_i choice situations, given in Equation (21.31):

Prob[choice j by individual i in choice situation t | class q]

$$= \frac{\exp(x'_{it,j}\beta_q)}{\sum_{j=1}^{J_i} \exp(x'_{it,j}\beta_q)}. \tag{21.31}$$

The class assignment is unknown. Let H_{iq} denote the prior probability for class q for individual i. A convenient form is the MNL (Equation 21.32):

$$H_{iq} = \frac{\exp(z'_i\theta_q)}{\sum_{q=1}^{Q} \exp(z'_i\theta_q)}, \quad q = 1,\ldots,Q, \theta_Q = \mathbf{0}, \tag{21.32}$$

where $\mathbf{z}_i$ denotes a set of observable characteristics which enter the model for class membership. To account for possible heuristics defined in the domains of attribute non-attendance, aggregation, and common-metric parameter transfer, we impose restrictions on the parameters within each latent class, each class representing a particular process heuristic. For example, to impose the condition of non-attendance of a specific attribute we set its parameter to zero; to impose common-metric aggregation we constrain two parameters to be equal; and to allow for parameter transfer we define a single parameter based on the parameter associated with a specific attribute.

Example command set ups for attribute non-attendance and parameter transfer are given below:

```
Nlogit
    ;lhs=choice1,cset3,Alt3
    ;choices=Curr,AltA,AltB
    ;pds=16
    ;pts= 9 ? program allows up to 30 classes as of 22 July 2008
    ;maxit=200
    ;lcm ?=igcosts ?,igff?,igsd,igtoll
    ;model:
    U(Curr) = FF*FF + SDT*SDT + RC*Cost +TC*Toll
    +FFt*FF + fft*SDT + RCt*Cost +rCt*Toll+sdtt*FF + sdtt*SDT + tCt*Cost +TCt...
    U(AltA) = ?nonSQ +
    FF*FF + SDT*SDT + RC*Cost +TC*Toll+FFt*FF + SDTt*SDT + RCt*Cost +TCt*Toll
    +FFt*FF + fft*SDT + RCt*Cost +rCt*Toll+sdtt*FF + sdtt*SDT + tCt*Cost +TCt...
    U(AltB) = ?nonSQ +
    FF*FF + SDT*SDT + RC*Cost +TC*Toll+FFt*FF + SDTt*SDT + RCt*Cost +TCt*Toll
    +FFt*FF + fft*SDT + RCt*Cost +rCt*Toll+sdtt*FF + sdtt*SDT + tCt*Cost +TCt...
    ;rst=
    b1,b2,b3,b4,0,0,0,0,          ? full attendance
    b1a,b2a,0,b4a,0,0,0,0,        ? ignore running cost
    0,b2b,b3b,b4b,0,0,0,0,        ? ignore free-flow time
    b1c,b2c,b3c,0,0,0,0,0,        ? ignore toll cost
    b1d,0,b3d,b4d,0,0,0,0,        ? ignore slowed down time
    0,0,b3e,b4e,0,0,0,0,          ? ignore free flow and slowed down time
    b1f,b2f,0,0,0,0,0,0,          ? ignore running and toll costs
    0,b2g,0,b4g,0,0,0,0,          ? ignore free-flow time and running cost
    0,b2h,0,0,0,0,0,0$,           ? ignore free-flow time, running and toll cost
Nlogit
    ;lhs=choice1,cset3,Alt3
    ;choices=Curr,AltA,AltB
    ;pds=16
    ;pts= 6 ? program allows up to 30 classes as of 22 July 2008
    ;maxit=200
    ;lcm ?=igcosts ?,igff?,igsd,igtoll
    ;model:
```

```
U(Curr) = FF*FF + SDT*SDT + RC*Cost +TC*Toll
+FFt*FF + fft*SDT + RCt*Cost +rCt*Toll+sdtt*FF + sdtt*SDT + tCt*Cost +TCt...
U(AltA) = ?nonSQ +
FF*FF + SDT*SDT + RC*Cost +TC*Toll+FFt*FF + SDTt*SDT + RCt*Cost +TCt*Toll
+FFt*FF + fft*SDT + RCt*Cost +rCt*Toll+sdtt*FF + sdtt*SDT + tCt*Cost +TCt...
U(AltB) = ?nonSQ +
FF*FF + SDT*SDT + RC*Cost +TC*Toll+FFt*FF + SDTt*SDT + RCt*Cost +TCt*Toll
+FFt*FF + fft*SDT + RCt*Cost +rCt*Toll+sdtt*FF + sdtt*SDT + tCt*Cost +TCt...
;rst=
b1,b2,b3,b4,0,0,0,0,0,0,0,0,        ?full attendance
0,0,b3,b4,b5,b6,0,0,0,0,0,0,        ?transfer beta sdt to ff
b1,b2,0,0,b7,b8,0,0,0,0,0,0,        ?transfer beta toll to rc
0,0,b3,b4,0,0,0,0,b9,b10,0,0,       ?transfer beta ff to sdt
0,0,0,0,0,0,0,0,b9,b10,b11,b12,     ?transfer beta ff to sdt and beta rc to tc
b1,b2,0,0,0,0,0,0,0,0,b11,b12$      ?transfer beta rc to tc
```

21.7.3 Evidence on marginal willingness to pay: value of travel time savings

In this section, we bring together the evidence on VTTS when one or more processing strategies are accounted for in modeling choice outcomes. The estimated models are not presented here since they are given in Layton and Hensher (2010), Hensher and Layton (2010), Hensher and Rose (2009), and Hensher and Greene (2010). In all cases, we have accounted for the panel structure of the data. Our interest is on establishing the extent of under- or over-estimates of mean VTTS in contrast to full relevance and compensatory rules when account is taken of a number of process rules set out above.

To obtain a VTTS distribution for each of free-flow and slowed-down time, we have to either simulate the distribution across values for the attribute(s) of interest or apply the formula to a sample of observations. We chose the latter, using the same data used to estimate the models. Given that the denominator in the WTP expression is a weighted average of the role of running cost and toll cost, where the weights reflect the incidence of running and toll cost and the numerator includes both attributes with a common metric, the WTP for a specific trip time component (i.e., free-flow or slowed-down time) is dependent on a mix of levels of all four attributes.

We summarize the evidence in Table 21.6, including the reference source. The major finding is that all mean estimates of VTTS are higher when one or more processing rules are accounted for, in contrast to the traditional MNL model that assumes full attribute and parameter preservation. There is a clear

Table 21.6 Summary of WTP estimates (2004$/person hr.)

Process rule	VTTS: free-flow time	VTTS: slowed-down time	VTTS: Weighted average time	Reference
Full preservation of attributes and parameters	11.76	15.72	14.07	Hensher and Greene (2010)
Process I: attribute aggregation	12.87	16.78	15.10	Layton and Hensher (2010)[13]
Process II: parameter transfer	13.37	19.44	16.91	Hensher and Layton (2010)
Process III: attribute non-attendance	15.28 (1.91)	22.05 (2.74)	19.23	Hensher and Rose (2009)
Process IV: latent class mixture of all rules	–	–	19.62	Hensher and Greene (2010)

trend here that, if reinforced by other data sets, sends a warning about the under-estimation of VTTS when processing heuristics are not accounted for. The extent of under-estimation appears significant; for the overall weighted average travel time it ranges from a high of 34.7 percent for the full set of process rules in the LCM to a low of 7.3 percent for attribute aggregation for both time and cost.[14]

We take a closer look at the findings from the LCM, summarized in Table 21.7. There is a range of mean estimates of VTTS across the latent classes. The range is $1.35 to $42.19, after dividing the marginal disutility of each time component by the weighted average cost parameter, where the weights are the levels of running and toll cost. To obtain an overall sample

---

[13] In order to estimate the model as a panel, Layton and Hensher (2010) used a combination of many start values and simulated annealing (code written by E.G.Tsionas, 9 April 1995, available at the American university Gauss Archive: www.american.edu/academic.depts/cas/econ/gaussres/GAUSSIDX.HTM). Using the maximum from the simulated annealing approach, we then computed one Newton–Raphson iteration using 500 replications of the simulator, and computed the covariance from all terms except for λ_t and λ_c.

[14] It is worth noting that the attribute aggregation model (Process I) allowed for aggregation of both the time and the cost components. By contrast, the LCM (Process IV) only found time aggregation statistically significant, but did identify a significant effect from the heuristic that transferred the toll cost parameter to the running cost attribute. What this latter evidence suggests is that individuals do not tend to add up the cost components, but tend to re-weight their influence by the parameter transfer rule.

Table 21.7 Values of travel time savings (2004$/person hr.)

NAT = not attended to ParT = parameter transfer	Class member-ship probability	Free-flow time	Slowed-down time	Total time
Traditional MNL		11.76	15.72	**14.07**
LCM:				
All attributes attended to	0.2817	5.87	9.89	8.22
Free-flow NAT	0.1119		23.02	23.02
Toll cost NAT	0.0359	3.95	8.93	6.85
Slowed-down time NAT	0.0643	1.35		1.35
Running cost and slowed-down time NAT	0.0497	42.19		42.19
Free-flow and slowed-down time added	0.2978		37.57	37.57
Free-flow to slowed-down and vice versa ParT	0.0758		4.57	4.57
Free-flow to slowed-down ParT and running cost to toll cost and vice versa ParT	0.0829		9.26	9.26
Class membership weighted VTTS				**19.62**

Source: Hensher and Greene (2010).

average, we have to weight each mean estimate by the probability of class membership.

The overall sample weighted average for total time is $19.62, which contrasts with $14.07 for the traditional MNL specification (Hensher and Greene 2011, Table 3). The mean estimate of VTTS is 39.4 percent higher when process heterogeneity is accounted for across three classes of heuristics. A closer look at the contribution of each heuristic suggests that attribute addition for the two time components produces the highest mean estimate contribution to VTTS, after controlling for class membership. Ignoring free-flow time is the next contributor, followed by full attendance to all attributes. Ignoring running cost and slowed-down time is the next contribution (Table 21.7).

21.7.4 Evidence from self-stated processing response for common-metric addition

The focus of the previous sections was on exploring a way in which we are able to allow for the possibility of heterogeneity in the way that individuals process common-metric attributes in making choices, focussing on a number of potential heuristics, without having to ask supplementary (deterministic) elicitation questions. In addition to the SC experiment, in the survey we did,

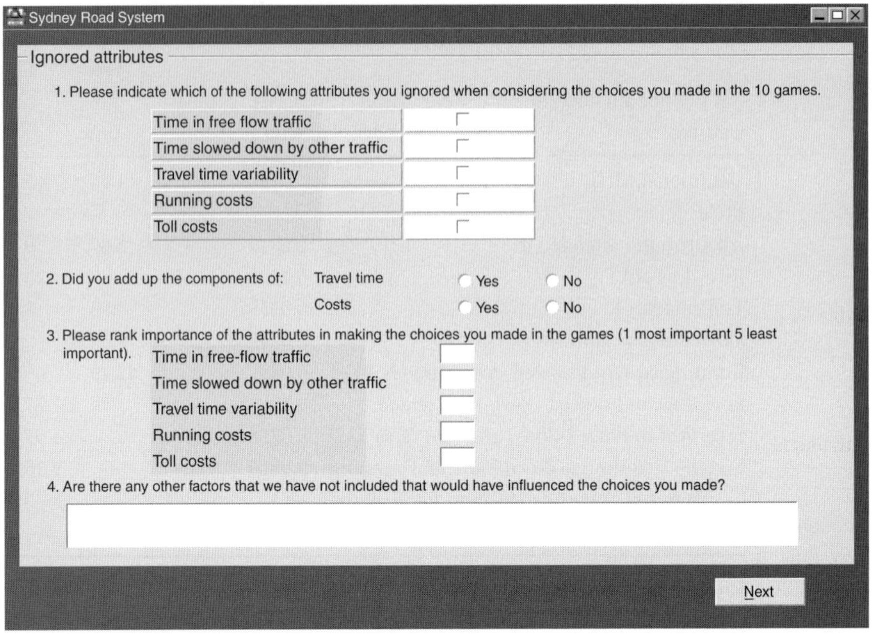

Figure 21.4   4 CAPI questions on attribute relevance

however, ask supplementary elicitation questions shown in Figure 21.4.[15] In this section, we investigate the possible implications of conditioning the preference function used to derive WTP estimates, using the response to the supplementary question of whether an attribute was not attended to. A large percentage of the respondents stated, in supplementary questions (see Hensher 2008), that they added the components: 88.06 percent and 76.5 percent, respectively for time and cost.

We estimated five panel-specification models – two mixed logit (ML) (with and without error components) and three LCMs. One ML model ignored the AP rule and the other accommodated it through the specification of separate parameters to capture the following conditions: (i) added up times but not costs, (ii) added up costs but not times, (iii) added up both times and costs,

---

[15] This question was asked after completion of all 16 choice tasks. An alternative approach is to ask these questions after each choice task, as was the case in Puckett and Hensher (2009), and Scarpa *et al.* (2010). Our preference is for choice task-specific self-stated processing questions, especially where the attribute level matters; however, this comes at the risk of cognitive burden and the possibility that the number of choice tasks might need to be reduced. We also recognize the potential limitation of such questions, and the need to investigate question structure and the believability/plausibility of the evidence.

and (iv) all four attributes preserved as separate components. One LCM defined four class memberships as per (i)–(iv) above without recourse to information from the supplementary questions, whereas another LCM conditioned class membership on conditions (i)–(iv). A base LCM assumed that all attributes were treated separately but three classes were identified with statistically significant latent class probabilities. The findings are summarized in Table 21.8. MLs and LCMs are well documented in the literature.

Table 21.8 Influence of self-stated APS on VTTS

(i) ML models (panel specification)

Attributes	ML model (constrained triangular for random parameters), *t*-ratios in brackets except for VTTS which is standard deviation	
	No allowance for self-stated APS	Allowance for self-stated APS
Random parameters:		
Free-flow time (FF)	−0.10023 (−17.33)	−0.0497 (−3.64)
Slowed-down time (SDT)	−0.1147 (−21.94)	−0.687 (−5.98)
Aggregated FF and SDT	–	−0.1236 (−22.5)
Running cost (RC)	−0.4167 (−14.58)	−0.1945 (−4.11)
Toll cost (TC)	−0.188 (−22.99)	−0.2905 (−9.70)
Aggregated RC and TC	–	−0.6103 (−21.62)
Fixed parameter:		
Non-reference alternative dummy	−0.1344 (−2.88)	−0.1669 (−3.61)
LL at convergence	−2762.80	−2711.88
LL at zero	4271.41	
Weighted average VTTS *($Aus2004 per person hr.)*	**$15.87 ($10.14)**	**$20.12 ($16.01)**

(ii) ML models (panel specification) with error component

Attributes	ML model (constrained triangular for random parameters), *t*-ratios in brackets except for VTTS which is standard deviation	
	No allowance for self-stated APS	Allowance for self-stated APS
Random parameters:		
Free-flow time (FF)	−0.11190 (−31.45)	−0.08113 (5.50)
Slowed-down time (SDT)	−0.12746 (−34.25)	−0.07514(−7.06)
Aggregated FF and SDT	–	−0.13076 (−19.37)
Running cost (RC)	−0.49740 (−19.74)	−0.23583(−3.96)
Toll cost (TC)	−0.55193(−32.95)	−0.26234(−7.489)

(ii) (cont.)

Attributes		ML model (constrained triangular for random parameters), *t*-ratios in brackets except for VTTS which is standard deviation
Aggregated RC and TC	–	−0.65814(−17.19)
Fixed parameter:		
Non-reference alternative dummy	0.18195 (1.95)	−0.27233 (−2.13)
Standard deviation of latent random effect	*2.43423 (24.5)*	*2.3357 (28.21)*
LL at convergence	−2485.03	−2447.43
LL at zero		4271.41
Weighted average VTTS ($Aus2004 per person hr.)	**$16.11($10.87)**	**$22.63 ($23.26)**

(iii) LCMs (panel specification)
Base model:

	Class 1	Class 2	Class 3
Free-flow time	−0.04006 (−4.7)	−0.2022 (−28.9)	−0.0338 (−7.5)
Slowed-down time	−0.0603 (−9.6)	−0.2009 (−31.6)	−0.0749 (−22.0)
Running cost	−0.3323 (−8.9)	−0.3399 (−10.7)	−0.4739 (−15.3)
Toll cost	−0.2883 (−10.7)	−0.3417 (−24.2)	−0.6115 (−33.6)
Non-reference alternative	2.5043 (12.3)	0.3947 (−7.2)	−1.0281 (−23.3)
Class membership probability	0.263 (6.92)	0.361 (10.45)	0.376 (11.14)
LL at convergence		−2542.74	
LL at zero		−4271.41	
Weighted average VTTS ($Aus2004 per person hr.)		**$17.89**	

Models allowing for AP:

	No allowance for self-stated APS		Allowance for self-stated APS	
Latent class attributes:	Class membership probability	Parameter estimates for FF, SDT,RC,TC, NONSQ (*t*-ratios in brackets)	Class membership probability	Parameter estimates for FF,SDT,RC,TC,NONSQ (*t*-ratios in brackets)
All attributes treated separately	0.379	−.049,−.090,−.638,−.743, −.622 (−5.5,−13.0,−11.3, −19.1,−6.9)	0.381	−.055,−.092,−.648, −.748, −.637 (−5.0,−12.1,−10.1, −16.3,−6.7)
Time components aggregated	0.050	−.057,−.057,−0.29,−0.38, −3.9 (−3.3,−3.3,−1.9, −9.2,−11.1)	0.052	−.054,−.054,−.332, −.370, −3.82 (−3.2,−3.2,−2.0, −8.4,−10.4)

Table 21.8 (*cont.*)

	No allowance for self-stated APS		Allowance for self-stated APS	
Latent class attributes:	Class membership probability	Parameter estimates for FF, SDT,RC,TC, NONSQ (*t*-ratios in brackets)	Class membership probability	Parameter estimates for FF,SDT,RC,TC,NONSQ (*t*-ratios in brackets)
Cost components aggregated	0.318	−.217,−.212,−.319,−.319, −.428 (−26.9,−29.2, −19.1,−19.1,−6.8)	0.310	−.221,−.215,−.317,−.317, −.410 (−25.1,−27.8, −17.5,−17.5,−6.3)
Time and cost components aggregated	0.253	−.052 ,−.052,−.282, −.282,2.58 (−17.4,−17.4, −25.4,−25.4,22.2)	0.257	−.050,−.050,−.277, −.277,2.49 (−16.1,−16.1, −23.2,−23.2,21.9)
Theta in class probability:				
				Constant, FF,SDT,FFSDT,RC,TC,RCTC
				Note: All covariates are in min. or dollars except the constant. ∗statistically significant: ∗= 5% , ∗∗= 10% level
All attributes treated separately				1.35∗∗,−.006,.003,−.005,−.33,−.079,−.093 (2.4,−.17,.14,−.61,−1.1,−.45,−1.4)
Time components aggregated				−1.59,.18∗,−.45,.009,.52,−.61,−.13 (−1.2,1.9,−1.4,.44,1.6,−1.1,−.7)
Cost components aggregated				1.16∗,−.02,−.03,−.009,.35∗,−.15,−.13∗ (1.9,−.7,−1.1,−.9,1.7,−.9,−1.7)
LL at convergence		−2427.57		−2399.64
LL at zero		−4271.41		
Weighted average VTTS ($Aus2004 per person hr.)		**$18.02 ($15.02)**		**$18.05 ($15.28)**

For ML, we have selected a quasi-constrained triangular distribution in which the spread[16] estimate is constrained to equal the mean estimate for the random parameters. If the scale equals 1.0, the range is 0 to 2 ß₁ (see Chapter 15). This is an appealing way of capturing the random taste heterogeneity, avoiding the search for such heterogeneity at the extremes of unconstrained distributions. The triangular distribution was first used for random coefficients by Train and Revelt (2000), later incorporated into Train (2003, 2009), and it is increasingly being used in empirical studies.

---

[16] The spread is the standard deviation times $\sqrt{6}$.

The overall goodness of fit for the models with allowance for self-stated attribute processing strategy (APS) are statistically better than when self-stated APS is not accounted for. The ML models differ in the way that the time and cost attributes are included in the utility expressions, but in both models all parameters have the expected negative signs and are statistically significant at the 1 percent level. Given the different ways that free-flow and slowed-down time are handled, the most sensible representation of VTTS is as a weighted average estimate, with weights associated with the contribution of each of the three specifications of cost and of time. The VTTS in Table 21.7 (p. 981) are based on conditional distributions (that is, conditional on the alternative chosen). The VTTS in the ML model is significantly higher when the self-stated APS is accounted for, i.e., $20.12 (22.63 with error components) per person hr. compared to $15.87 ($16.11 with error components) per person hr.

The LCM is based on four attribute addition rules (i)–(iv), and all time and cost parameters are statistically significant at the 1 percent level and of the expected sign when class membership is conditioned on the self-stated APS; however, when the self-stated APS are not included, all but one parameter is statistically significant at the 1 percent level, the exception being running cost in the second latent class, which has a 10 percent significance level. The overall log-likelihood (LL) at convergence is greatly improved over the ML model for both LCMs, suggesting that the discrete nature of heterogeneity captured through latent class is a statistical improvement over the continuous representation of heterogeneity in the ML model. The weighted average VTTS are derived first across classes for each attribute, based on conditional distributions associated with the probability of class membership of each respondent within each class, and then a further weighting is undertaken using weights that reflect the magnitudes of the components of time and cost.

The weighted average VTTS in the two LCMs that account for AP are virtually identical. What this suggests is that once we have captured the alternative processing rules, through the definition of latent classes, the inclusion of the self-stated APS rules as conditions on class membership do not contribute additional statistically useful evidence to revise the findings, in the aggregate. This is consistent with the statistical non-significance of most of the self-stated APS variables; with only three parameters having a 10 percent significance level (excluding the constants). There were no parameters with 1 or 5 percent significance levels. However, when we contrast this evidence to the base LCM that makes no allowance for AP, the mean VTTS is only slightly lower (i.e., $17.89 per person hr. compared to $18.02, and $14.07 for the MNL model). What this may suggest is that the latent class specification may have done a good job in approximating the way in which attributes are processed.

These findings support the hypothesis that allowance for AP rules tends to result, on average, in a higher mean estimate of WTP for travel time savings. This is consistent directionally with other studies undertaken by Rose *et al.* (2005) and Hensher and Layton (2010).

21.8 Case study II: the influence of choice response certainty, alternative acceptability, and attribute thresholds

Choice studies can be characterized by three key elements – attributes, alternatives, and choice responses. For over forty years, researchers have studied the relationship between these elements and developed a rich suite of modeling tools to understand the role of observed and unobserved influences on choice outcomes within a random utility theoretic framework in which uncertainty is intrinsically linked to the analysts' absence of full information on the real sources of individual choice making. In recent years, an increasing number of analysts has highlighted a concern with the assumption, in the majority of choice studies, that all attributes are traded in a fully compensatory manner, and are by implication all relevant, and that each attribute and its trade is treated by the individual decision maker as totally certain (see e.g., Hensher and Collins 2011). Three issues that might be considered to reflect how individuals make choices in survey settings are the relevance of attribute levels, especially the perceptual thresholds that individuals use to define whether an attribute is in or out of the consideration range, the overall acceptability of an alternative as described by a package of attribute levels, and the extent to which the respondent is certain of actually choosing the alternative that they indicated was their preferred alternative if it were offered in a real market.

The hypothetical bias literature, in particular, has focussed on the certainty of response associated with a CE if the alternative were offered in a real market. Johannesson *et al.* (1999) and Fuji and Gärling (2003) offer some ideas on the certainty scale. Supplementary questions are increasingly being included to establish "the confidence with which an individual would hypothetically purchase or use the good (or alternative) that is actually chosen in the choice experiment," the latter being added into the CE after each choice scenario and, in some studies, after an additional response in the form of a rating of the alternatives, possibly along the lines of "limit-cards" (see

Section 19.6.2.2). Johannesson *et al.* (1999) proposed a supplementary *certainty scale* question after each choice scenario, on a scale 0 (very unsure) to 10 (very sure), to indicate how sure or certain the respondent is that they would actually choose a particular alternative (or not at all) at the indicated attribute levels. This response metric can be used to exogenously weight the sample to represent a way of placing a higher weight on those choices that one has more confidence in actually being made.[17]

At the same time, there is also a growing literature on *attribute thresholds*, with some studies imposing analytical distributions on cut-offs (including just noticeable differences such as Cantillo *et al.* 2006), and other studies asking supplementary questions (e.g., Swait 2001) prior to the SC questions, to establish lower and upper bounds on acceptable attribute levels. Studies in transportation in the 1970s (e.g., Hensher 1975) highlighted the presence of asymmetric thresholds, but did not incorporate them into choice models.

Although there is a growing literature on the role of choice response certainty and the thresholds that decision makers impose on attributes in making choices there appears, however, to have been little research into the perceived acceptability of each alternative on preferences, which we will show below plays a significant role in linking attributes to choice. It is surprising that this feature of choice models has not been given as much treatment as the other issues, although some researchers may argue that this is the same idea as consideration sets, despite the latter being focussed on the mix of alternatives, in line with choice set formation.

Given that the respondent evaluates packages of attributes defining each alternative, there is appeal in acknowledging the influence of the consequent perceived acceptability of an alternative on choice. Observed (in the experiment) attributes and defined alternatives are related, and hence the intersection between these two features must be recognized and accounted for in any specification that evaluates the influence of attributes and alternatives. Attributes are processed in many ways (see Hensher 2010 and Leong and Hensher 2012 for reviews); of particular interest is the role of perceived attribute thresholds (or lower and upper cut-offs) that are used by respondents to condition the acceptability of an alternative.

This section investigates the influence of acceptability of each alternative, attribute thresholds, and choice response certainty, on automobile purchase

---

[17] An interesting way of including response certainty into a model is to create a relative measure around a reference alternative, where the latter has been chosen in a real market and hence its certainty value is 10 on the 1–10 scale. Deviations from 10 may be more informative than the actual certainty scale value.

preferences in Sydney in the context of choosing among petrol, diesel, and hybrid fueled vehicles (associated with specific levels of fuel efficiency and engine capacity) when faced with a mix of vehicle prices, fuel prices, fixed annual registration fees, annual emission surcharges, and vehicle kilometre emission surcharges.

21.8.1 Accounting for response certainty, acceptability of alternatives, and attribute thresholds

Beginning with the standard utility expression associated with the jth alternative contained in a choice set of $j = 1,\ldots,J$ alternatives, we assume that an index defining the acceptability of the jth alternative and qth individual, A_{jq}, conditions the utility expression. The functional form can be denoted by $U_{jq}{}^* = A_{jq}U_{jq} = A_{jq}(V_{jq} + \varepsilon_j)$, where $U_{jq}{}^*$ is the standard utility expression conditioned on the perceived acceptability of an alternative. This conditioning is a form of heteroskedasticity. A_{jq} recognizes that individual-specific perceptions, proxied by statements on relevance of attributes defining an alternative and the alternative *per se*, condition the marginal (dis)utility of each and every attribute, observed and unobserved, associated with the jth alternative in a pre-defined choice set. In the current context, we modify the definition of $U_{jq}{}^*$ as $A_{jq}V_{jq} + \varepsilon_j$, leaving the random component un-contaminated directly by the function A_j. This enables us to adopt a logit form under random-utility maximization. An example of heteroskedastic conditioning, implemented in Section 21.8.3, is $A_{jq} = \left(1 + \delta_j(AC_{jq} + \sum_{h=1}^{H} \gamma_h R_{h_q})\right)$, where AC_{jq} is a variable denoting whether an alternative is perceived to be acceptable or not by the qth individual, R_{hq} is a dummy variable indicating whether the hth attribute level is in a perceived attribute threshold rejection region or not for the qth individual, and δ_j and γ_h are estimated parameters.[18] The inclusion of R_{hq} recognizes that the role of attributes is fundamental to the perception of alternative acceptability.

We assume that individuals adopt attribute thresholding in the way they process offered attribute levels associated with each alternative, and that these thresholds are independent of the alternative, but not its acceptability. Attribute thresholds have lower and upper bounds, which may be subject to

---

[18] This is not strictly scale heterogeneity – see the following paragraphs – although it appears like deterministic scale as a function only of covariates. In contrast, scale heterogeneity as represented in SMNL is a stochastic treatment which may be partially decomposed via the deterministic addition of covariates.

measurement error, and also may be revised depending on the levels offered by other attributes. That is, there is "softness" (in the language of Swait 2001) in the binding nature of perceived threshold levels reported by the qth individual. To capture the notion of threshold, we define a lower cut-off and an upper cut-off. Accounting for attribute thresholds is equivalent to introducing functions that are incremental effects on the linear attribute effect throughout an attribute's entire range, and only get activated if the corresponding cut-off is in use. These cut-off penalties are a linear function of the amount of constraint violation and are defined as: $\{0{:}max(0, X_{ljq}-X_{lmin})\}$, the lower cut-off effect and deviation of the attribute level from the minimum cut-off attribute threshold where the attribute level is below the minimum cut-off (i.e., the cut-off exists), and zero otherwise (if the cut-off does not exist); and $\{0{:}max(0, X_{min} -X_{mjq})\}$, the upper cut-off effect and deviation of the attribute level from the maximum cut-off attribute threshold where the attribute level is above the maximum cut-off (i.e., the cut-off exists), and zero otherwise (if the cut-off does not exist). Defining X_{kjq} as the kth attribute associated with the jth alternative and qth individual, with $l = K+1,\ldots,L$ attribute lower cut-offs; $m = L+1,\ldots,M$ attribute upper cut-offs; $q=1,\ldots,Q$ respondents, and β_l and β_m estimated penalty parameters, we write the threshold penalty expression as:

$$\sum\nolimits_{l=K+1}^{L} \beta_l\{0 : \max(0, X_{ljq} - X_{lq}min)\} + \sum\nolimits_{m=L+1}^{M} \beta_m\{0 : \max(0, X_{mq}max - X_{mjq}).$$

(21.33)

In the current application, both upper and lower bounds are behaviorally meaningful. For example, some individuals might only be interested in 6 cylinder cars and would not consider 4 and 8 cylinder cars. Likewise low prices and very high prices might be rejected for different reasons, with purchasers often looking within a specific price range given their preferences.

We also define $Cert_{cs}$ to represent levels of surety. To allow for the influence of response certainty, which is choice set (cs)-specific, we assume that the entire utility function associated with each alternative must be exogenously weighted by the index of certainty, defined here on a 10-point scale, where 1 is the lowest level of certainty.

The model form for the utility expression that encapsulates the elements presented above is given in Equation (21.34)[19]:

---

[19] An alternative form for the alternative acceptability conditioning is the exponential form: $\exp(\delta_j(AC_{jq} + \sum_{h=1}^{H} \gamma R_{hq}))$. Empirically, the difference is negligible in terms of predictive power and elasticity outputs.

$$U_{jq} = (1 + \delta_j \left(AC_{jq} + \sum_{h=1}^{H} \gamma_h R_{hq} \right) \left[\alpha_j + \sum_{k=1}^{K} \beta_{kj} X_{kjq} \right.$$

$$+ \sum_{l=K+1}^{L} \beta_l \{0 : \max(0, X_{ljq} - X_{lq}\min)\}$$

$$\left. + \sum_{m=L+1}^{M} \beta_m \{0 : \max(0, X_{mq}\max - X_{mjq})\} \right] + \varepsilon_j. \qquad (21.34)$$

All terms are defined above except α_j which are ASCs.

Equation (21.34) is a non-linear utility function, which in its general form departs from a standard RUM with utility functions defined over J_{qt} choices available to individual q in choice situation t, given in Equation (21.35):

$$U_{jqt} = V_{jqt} + \varepsilon_{jqt}, j = 1, \ldots, J_{qt}; t = 1, \ldots, T_q; q = 1, \ldots, Q, \qquad (21.35)$$

with the IID, Type I EV distribution assumed for the random terms ε_{jqt}. Conditioned on V_{jqt}, the choice probabilities take the familiar MNL form in Equation (21.36):

$$Prob_{jqt} = \frac{\exp V_{jqt}}{\sum_{j=1}^{J_{qt}} \exp V_{jqt}}. \qquad (21.36)$$

When we allow for heteroskedasticity (Model 5 below), Equation (21.36) becomes Equation (21.37):

$$Prob_{jqt} = \frac{\exp[(1 + \delta_j(AC_{jq} + \sum_{h=1}^{H} \gamma_h R_{hq}))V_{jqt}]}{\sum_{j=1}^{J_{qt}} \exp[(1 + \delta_j(AC_{jq} + \sum_{h=1}^{H} \gamma_h R_{hq}))V_{jqt}]}. \qquad (21.37)$$

The utility functions that accommodate non-linearity in the unknown parameters, even where the parameters are non-random, can be built up from an extension of the ML structure, along similar lines to Anderson *et al.* (2012), but with extensions to incorporate scale heterogeneity (σ_q) (see Fiebig *et al.* 2010 and Greene and Hensher 2010 and Chapter 20). An example of this is through the following system of equations:

$$V_{jqt} = \sigma_q[V_j(X_{jqt}, \boldsymbol{\beta}_{jq})], \qquad (21.38)$$

$$V_j(\mathbf{x}_{jqt}, \boldsymbol{\beta}_{jq}) = h_j(\mathbf{x}_{jqt}, \boldsymbol{\beta}_{jq}), \qquad (21.39)$$

$$\boldsymbol{\beta}_{jq} = \boldsymbol{\beta}_j + \Delta \mathbf{z}_q + \Gamma \mathbf{v}_{jq}, \qquad (21.40)$$

$$\sigma_q = exp(\lambda + \delta' c_q + \tau u_q). \tag{21.41}$$

In Equation (21.39), the function $h_j(..)$ is an *arbitrary non-linear function* that defines the underlying preferences across alternatives. The form of the utility function, itself, may vary across the choices, and accommodates the hetero-skedastic form in Equation (21.37). Heterogeneity in the preference para-meters of the model is shown in Equation (21.40) (the ML form), where β_{qj} varies around the overall constant β_j in response to observable heterogeneity through z_q and unobservable heterogeneity in v_q. The parameters of the distribution of β_q are the overall mean (i.e., β_j), the structural parameters on the observed heterogeneity, Δ, and the Cholesky square root (lower triangle) of the covariance matrix of the random components, Γ. The random compo-nents are assumed to have known, fixed (usually at zero) means, constant known variances (usually one), and to be uncorrelated. In the most common applications, multivariate standard normality would be assumed for v_q. The covariance matrix of β_q is $\Omega = \Gamma\Gamma'$. Parameters that are not random (e.g., MNL and the model form with heteroskedastic conditioning (HMNL)) are included in the general form of the model, by imposing rows of zeros in Γ including the diagonal elements. A non-random parameters model would have $\Gamma = 0$ in its entirety.

When σ_q (the individual-specific standard deviation) equals 1, the model is an extension of the ML model developed by McFadden and Train (2000), Train (2003), and Hensher and Greene (2003), in which the utility functions may be general non-linear functions of the attributes of the choices and characteristics of the individual contained in X_{jqt} and the parameters, β_{jq}. Invoking the scaling term in Equation (21.41) allows for an overall random scaling of the preference structure across individuals. Like preference weights in the utility functions, the scaling parameter, σ_q, varies with observed and unobserved heterogeneity, c_q and u_q, respectively. In general cases, the mean parameter in σ_q, denoted as λ, is not separately identified, and a normalization is required; a natural choice is zero. However, it is useful to normalize the scale parameter around unity. Assuming for the moment that $\delta = 0$, if u_q is standard normally distributed with a non-zero τ, the coefficient on the unobserved scale heterogeneity, a separate variance parameter for u_q is not identified, then σ_q is log-normally distributed with expected value $E[\sigma_q] = \exp(\lambda + \tau^2/2 \sigma_u^2) = \exp(\lambda + \tau^2/2)$. To centre this at unity, therefore, we use the normalization $\lambda = -\tau^2/2$. With this restriction, if $\delta = 0$ and u_q is normally distributed, as we assume, then $E[\sigma_q] = 1$, which is a useful normalization for the cross-individual heteroskedasticity. This model is the most general one we will estimate and is called heteroskedastic Gumbel scale MNL (HG-SMNL). All parameters of the models are estimated by maximum simulated likelihood. This most general model is given in Equation (21.42):

$$Prob_{jqt} = \frac{\exp[\sigma_q(1 + \delta_j(AC_{jq} + \sum_{h=1}^{H} \gamma_h R_{hq}))V_{jqt}]}{\sum_{j=1}^{J_{qt}} \exp[\sigma_q(1 + \delta_j(AC_{jq} + \sum_{h=1}^{H} (AC_{jq} + \gamma_h R_{hq}))V_{jqt}]}. \quad (21.42)$$

In summary, in the section following the discussion of the CE, we present the findings for six models. The form of the utility expression that incorporates all three features is non-linear, a form known as heteroskedastic MNL (Model 5) or with scale heterogeneity allowed for (Model 6). To establish the contribution of these features, we begin with the standard MNL (Model 1) and ML models (Model 3), then move on to choice certainty weighted MNL (Model 2) and ML (Model 4), and finish with heteroskedastic MNL (HMNL) (Model 5) and the extension to heteroskedastic Gumbel scale MNL (HG-SMNL) (Model 6).

21.8.2 The choice experiment and survey process

We draw on a CE that was designed for a study whose main objective was to identify possible ways to reduce emissions from automobile ownership and use in the context of respondents who had purchased a new vehicle in 2007, 2008, or 2009, denoted their current or reference vehicle. The CE was accompanied by supplementary questions on attribute thresholds before the SC experiment, together with questions linked to each CE on the acceptability of an alternative and the certainty that the respondent would actually make that choice.

The labeled CE was defined on three fuel type alternatives – petrol, diesel, and hybrid. Within each fuel class each alternative was further defined by a vehicle class: small, luxury small, medium, luxury medium, large and luxury large, to ensure that the experiment would have adequate attribute variance as well as meaningful attribute levels over the alternatives, particularly with respect to price, while still having a manageable number of alternatives for the design. Nine attributes were included in the CE, refined via a review of the available literature on vehicle purchasing, as well as through a pilot survey (Beck *et al.* 2012, 2013) and preliminary analysis of secondary data sets. The attributes and their levels are summarized in Table 21.9.

Table 21.9 Attribute levels for choice experiment

	Levels	1	2	3	4	5
Purchase price	*Small*	$15,000	$18,750	$22,500	$26,250	$30,000
	Small luxury	$30,000	$33,750	$37,500	$41,250	$45,000
	Medium	$30,000	$35,000	$40,000	$45,000	$50,000
	Medium luxury	$70,000	$77,500	$85,000	$92,500	$100,000
	Large	$40,000	$47,500	$55,000	$62,500	$70,000
	Large luxury	$90,000	$100,000	$110,000	$120,000	$130,000
Fuel price	*Pivot off daily price*	−25%	−10%	0%	10%	25%
Registration	*Pivot off actual purchase*	−25%	−10%	0%	10%	25%
Annual emissions surcharge	*Pivot off fuel efficiency*	Random allocation of one of five levels				
Variable emissions surcharge	*Pivot off fuel efficiency*	Random allocation of one of five levels				
Fuel efficiency (L/100km)	*Small*	6	7	8	9	10
	Medium	7	9	11	13	15
	Large	7	9	11	13	15
Engine capacity (cylinders)	*Small*	4	6			
	Medium	4	6			
	Large	6	8			
Seating capacity	*Small*	2	4			
	Medium	4	5			
	Large	5	6			

Both of the surcharges are determined by the type of fuel a vehicle uses and the fuel efficiency of that vehicle. For a given vehicle, if it is fueled by petrol, owners would pay a higher surcharge than if it were fueled by diesel, which is in turn more expensive than if it were a hybrid. Once the car has been specified in terms of fuel type and efficiency, there are five levels of surcharge that could be applied.

The CE is a *D*-efficient design, where the focus is on the asymptotic properties of the standard errors of estimates, given the priors of attribute parameters. Prior parameter estimates obtained from substantive pilot surveys are used to minimize the asymptotic variance-covariance matrix which leads to lower standard errors and more reliable parameter estimates, for a given sample size (see Rose and Bliemer 2008 and Chapter 6 for details). The methodology focusses not only on the design attributes which are expanded out through treatment repetition, i.e., multiple choice sets, but also on the non-expanded socio-demographics and other contextual variables that are replicated as constants within each observation, and whose inclusion should have the greater influence on the efficient sample size.

A reference alternative is included in the experimental design to add to the relevance and comprehension for the attribute levels being assessed (see Rose *et al.* 2008). In the process of designing the CE, there were a number of conditions on the interaction of the attributes and alternatives (Beck *et al.* 2012):

1. The annual and variable surcharges that are applied to an alternative are each conditional on the type of fuel used and the fuel efficiency of the vehicle in question.
2. If the reference alternative is petrol (diesel), the petrol (diesel) fueled alternative must have the same fuel price as the reference alternative.
3. The annual and variable surcharge for the hybrid alternative cannot be higher than that of another vehicle when the alternative vehicle has the same fuel efficiency rating or is more inefficient than the hybrid.
4. To ensure that respondents faced a realistic choice set, given the vehicle size of the reference alternative, one of the remaining alternatives was restricted to be the same size as the reference, another was allowed to vary plus/minus one body size, and the third was allowed to vary freely. The condition was applied to the alternatives at random.

As the reference alternative is part of the design as a basis for comparison and to act as a pivot for the experimental design, the only attributes displayed are the known attributes of the alternative. For the petrol, diesel, and hybrid alternatives, all attributes vary, and the combinations of levels are optimized via the design process. While we always have the same four fuel type alternatives in each choice set (i.e., reference, petrol, diesel, hybrid), the size of each vehicle for each alternative will vary randomly and is endogenous to the design. The level of the annual and variable surcharge that appears in each alternative is conditional on the fuel type and efficiency of the vehicle. The values of fuel price and registration (including compulsory third-party (CTP) insurance) pivot off an actual experience as follows:

- Fuel price pivots around the daily fuel price as entered by the interviewer. There are five levels of fuel price (−25%, −10%, no change, +10%, +25%).
- Registration (including CTP) pivots around the actual cost provided by the respondent. There are five levels of registration (−25%, −10%, no change, +10%, +25%).
- The annual emissions surcharge is determined by the type of fuel used by the alternative and the fuel efficiency of that vehicle. For each fuel type and

fuel efficiency combination, there are five levels of surcharge that apply (Table 21.9).

- The variable emissions surcharge is determined by the type of fuel used by the alternative and the fuel efficiency of that vehicle. For each fuel type and fuel efficiency combination, there are five levels of surcharge that apply (Table 21.9).

An internet-based survey with face to face assistance of an interviewer was programmed. An eligible respondent had to have purchased a new vehicle in 2007, 2008, or 2009. Details of response rates and reasons for non-eligibility are summarized in Beck *et al.* (2012). The survey was completed online at a central location (varied throughout the Sydney metropolitan area to minimize travel distance for respondents). Respondents provided details of the vehicles within the household, and details of the most recent (or a potential) purchase. Eight choice sets are provided (with an example shown in Figure 21.5), with all

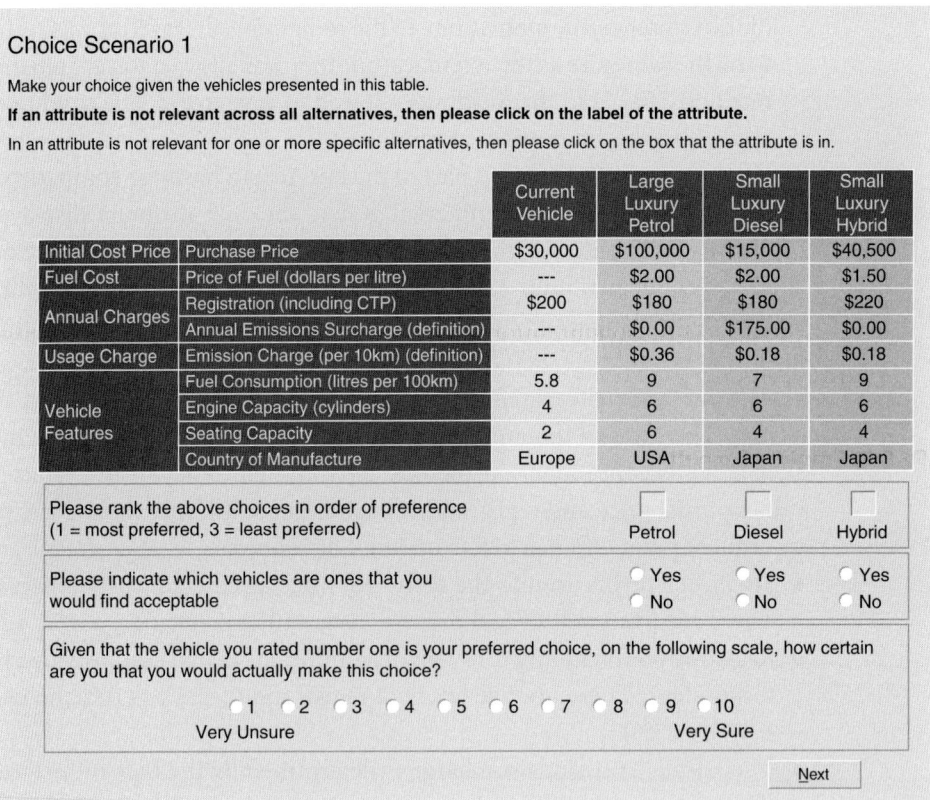

Figure 21.5   Illustrative stated choice screen

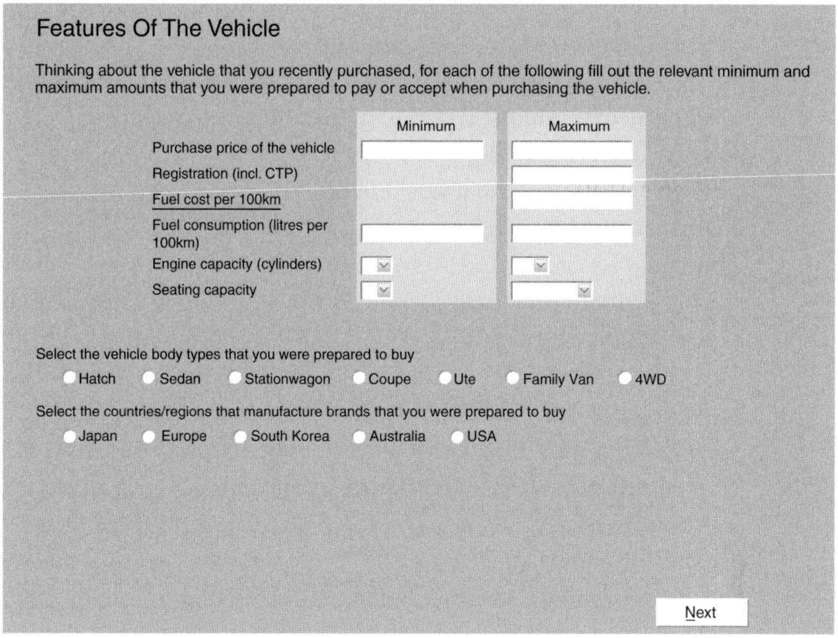

Figure 21.6   Attribute threshold questions (preceding the choice set screens)

participants asked to review the alternatives, decide which attributes are relevant,[20] and then indicate their preferred outcome, as well as an indication of which alternatives are acceptable, and what is the certainty of actually making the choice if it were available now in a real market. A prior screen (Figure 21.6) sought information on the lower and upper thresholds of attributes.

21.8.3 Empirical results

The data was collected over a four-month period in 2009. The final sample used in model estimation comprises 1,568 choice sets for 196 household observations, a subset of the full data set. Given the focus in this chapter on the role of attribute thresholds, acceptability of alternatives, and choice response certainty, we refer readers to Hensher *et al.* (2011) and Beck *et al.*

---

[20] The survey is programmed so that respondents can click on various rows, columns, and cells within a choice scenario if they find that attribute, alternative, or level to be ignored or irrelevant. This information is stored so that for each and every choice set completed by every respondent, data are collected on what information was important in making a decision and what information was discarded.

(2012) for details of the data set, confining the presentation to the data elements relevant to the modeling undertaken below. Table 21.10 summarizes the data used in the estimation of the six models.

Of particular interest is that 65 percent of the alternatives were perceived to be acceptable, suggesting that a large percentage were perceived as not acceptable given the attribute levels offered. The mean certainty scale value is 7.14 on the 1–10 scale, suggesting that certainty is greater than the mid point, although a lot of respondents are not totally sure.

The attribute threshold responses are very illuminating. Taking the attribute rejection evidence for the combined minimum and maximum cut-offs, 83.2 percent of the CE levels for vehicle price are outside of the upper and lower bounds for the price attribute that respondents indicated they are prepared to pay or accept. In contrast, the percentages for the other attributes are, respectively, 52.5 percent for the price of fuel, 45.2 percent for the annual registration charge, 49 percent for fuel consumption in litres/100km, 37.5 percent for engine capacity, and 57.9 percent for seating capacity. These are sizeable percentages, and raise some fundamental questions about empirical evidence if thresholds are ignored.

Separating out the lower and upper cut-off thresholds (defined by an attribute rejection range dummy variable), we see that the percentage that exceed the upper (i.e., maximum) cut off are greater than the lower (i.e., minimum) cut-off, except for seating capacity. The rejection percentage is as high as 71.4 percent for the upper vehicle price and 5 percent for the lower engine capacity. The actual differences between the minimum (maximum) perceived threshold levels and the levels shown in the CE are also summarized in Table 21.10. For example, the average vehicle price in the CE is $16,780 above the threshold maximum; and fuel consumption is 1.38 litres per 100km above the upper threshold, on average.

This descriptive evidence on attribute thresholds raises the interesting question as to whether future SC studies should take this information into account in designing the range of attribute levels. The modeling evidence below explicitly accounts for the influence of attribute thresholds and the acceptability of each alternative (both correlated) has on prediction success and mean direct elasticity estimates.

The results for all six choice models are summarized in Table 21.11. Models 1 and 2 are basic MNL models, distinguished by the exogenous weighting of the certainty scale, and models 3 and 4 are the equivalent ML models that have associated random parameters for all eight design attributes to account for preference heterogeneity, with an unconstrained normal distribution assumed

Table 21.10 Descriptive overview of key data items

Attribute	Units	Mean	Stand. dev.	Minimum	Maximum
Certainty scale	1–10	7.14	2.11	1 (unsure)	10 (sure)
Alternative acceptable (AC)	1,0	0.65	–	0 (unacceptable)	1 (acceptable)
Attributes:					
Price	$000s	51.82	28.45	15	133
Fuel	$/litre	1.22	0.22	0.75	1.66
Registration charge	$annual	872	501	225	4125
Annual emission surcharge	$annual	224	210	0	900
Variable emission charge	$/km	0.16	0.14	0	0.6
Fuel efficiency	Litres/100km	10.07	2.89	6	15
Engine capacity	#cylinders	5.47	1.36	4	8
Seating capacity	#seats	4.18	1.34	2	6
Threshold forms:					
Minimum price	$000s	25.30	13.37	1	95
Maximum price	$000s	35.03	16.08	14	120
Maximum registration charge	$annual	18.67	27.67	1	260
Maximum fuel price	$/litre	1.87	2.77	1	26
Minimum fuel efficiency	Litres/100km	6.75	2.45	1	12
Maximum fuel efficiency	Litres/100km	11.45	6.18	5	60
Minimum engine capacity	#cylinders	4.42	0.86	4	8
Maximum engine capacity	#cylinders	5.23	1.26	4	8
Minimum seating capacity	#seats	4.49	1.24	2	7
Maximum seating capacity	#seats	5.30	0.95	2	7
Full range, accept and reject:					
Min price – price	$000s	−26.52	28.21	−130	80
Price – max price	$000s	16.78	27.89	−90	114
Fuel – max fuel	$/litre	0.52	2.58	−19.1	1.49
Min fuel efficiency (FE) – FE	Litres/100km	−3.32	3.41	−14	5
Min fuel efficiency (FE) – max FE	Litres/100km	−1.38	6.69	−54	10
Registration –max registration	$annual	−147	789	−4177	2950
Min engine capacity (EC) – EC	#cylinders	−1.04	1.45	−4	4
Engine capacity (EC) – max EC	#cylinders	0.24	1.61	−4	4
Min seating capacity (SC) – SC	#seats	0.31	1.77	−4	5
Seating capacity – max SC	#seats	−1.11	1.49	−5	4
Outside attribute thresholds:					
Min price – price	$000s	1.104	4.75	0	80
Price – max price	$000s	19.80	24.3	0	114
Fuel – max fuel	$/litre	0.207	0.30	0	1.49
Min Fuel efficiency (FE) – FE	Litres/100km	0.203	0.62	0	5
Min fuel efficiency (FE) – max FE	Litres/100km	1.15	1.91	0	10
Registration – max registration	$annual	109	284	0	2950
Min engine capacity (EC) – EC	#cylinders	0.11	0.47	0	4

Table 21.10 (cont.)

Attribute	Units	Mean	Stand. dev.	Minimum	Maximum
Engine capacity (EC) – max EC	#cylinders	0.69	1.07	0	4
Min seating capacity (SC) – SC	#seats	0.84	1.11	0	5
Seating capacity – max SC	#seats	0.17	0.52	0	4
Attribute rejection range dummy:					
Minimum price	1,0	0.118	–	0	1
Maximum price	1,0	0.714	–	0	1
Maximum registration charge	1,0	0.452	–	0	1
Maximum fuel price	1,0	0.525	–	0	1
Minimum fuel efficiency	1,0	0.128	–	0	1
Maximum fuel efficiency	1,0	0.362	–	0	1
Minimum engine capacity	1,0	0.050	–	0	1
Maximum engine capacity	1,0	0.321	–	0	1
Minimum seating capacity	1,0	0.455	–	0	1
Maximum seating capacity	1,0	0.124	–	0	1
Attribute rejection dummy – min and max:					
Price	1,0	0.832	–	0	1
Fuel	1,0	0.525	–	0	1
Registration	1,0	0.452	–	0	1
Fuel efficiency	1,0	0.490	–	0	1
Engine capacity	1,0	0.375	–	0	1
Seating capacity	1,0	0.579	–	0	1

for all attribute parameters. The remaining two models are extensions of MNL in which we account for the acceptability of each alternative at a choice set level and the perceived attribute thresholds. Model 6 differs from Model 5 by the estimation of an additional parameter to account for scale heterogeneity. The overall goodness of fit of the models improves substantially as we move from Model 1 to Model 6; however, the evidence from comparing Models 1 and 3 with Models 2 and 4 is that the exogenous weighting by the certainty scale has a very small (almost negligible) influence on the overall model fit. Models 5 and 6 are significantly better fitting models (with exogenous weighting included), with fits improving by a factor of close to twice compared to the ML models. The allowance for scale heterogeneity is significant in overall gain in fit (given one degree of freedom difference between Models 5 and 6).

In-sample prediction success increases substantially when we allow for the acceptability of each alternative and the attribute thresholds. In Table 21.11, we report the percentage improvement in prediction of Models 5 and 6 compared to Model 4. The predictive gain is impressive, ranging from 28.3 percent to 91.6 percent. The improved performance in predicting the choice of the diesel alternative is the most spectacular.

Taking a closer look at specific parameter estimates, in Models 5 and 6, the negative parameters of −0.5684 (Model 5) and −0.7157 (Model 6), estimated in the sub-function (1−0.7157 × alternative acceptability) conditioned on the attribute rejection range dummy variable, suggests that the relative disutility of the jth alternative decreases[21] when this alternative (1) is perceived to be acceptable in contrast to not acceptable (0); and when the price attribute is in the rejection range (given the attached parameter estimate is −0.2332 for Model 5 and −0.1848 for Model 6); this disutility is further tempered and increases. The negative parameter for the lower and upper cut-off penalties recognizes that a price level outside of the lower and upper perceived thresholds of preference will add disutility, increasing the overall relative disutility. What we then have in this formulation is a way of recognizing and adjusting the marginal disutility of an attribute associated with an alternative in a particular choice set. To complete the adjustment, the full set of utility expressions associated with a choice set for the qth individual is weighted by the perceived certainty that the chosen alternative would actually be chosen.

All (main effects) design attributes except engine capacity and seating capacity have a negative sign across all models, as is expected given that they are financial or fuel consumption attributes. The number of cylinders preferred varies across the sample, and can move from having more preferred to less and vice versa. The same applies to seating capacity. Both signs can be interpreted with meaning. The sign is the same in Models 1 to 4, but changes when we move to Models 5 and 6; however, until we combine all of the other attribute-related influences, we are unable to establish if there is a continuation of the sign between the first four and last two models.

The Nlogit set up for Model 6 is given below (see Chapter 20 for more details on the non-linear model form):

```
Timer$
NLRPlogit
;lhs=choice,cset,alt
;choices=Pet,Die,Hyb
;maxit=50
;pars
```

---

[21] It should be noted that the overall utility expression is negative, and hence the heteroskedastic effect reduces the disutility when the alternative is acceptable, compared to not acceptable, as might be expected.

```
;rpl =prrejz,flrejz,rgrejz,ferejz,ecrejz,screjz
;fcn=altac(c)
;halton;draws=50
;pds=panel
;smnl;tau=0.1
;wts=cert,noscale
;output=3;crosstab;printvc
;start = -.647,-.0993,-1.8085,-.00451,-0.00245,-.6388,-.15051,.06247,-.0709,
        .18976,-.45376,-0.0893,0.02961,-1.13807,-.04491,0.12248,-0.00057,
        -0.13019,.41258,-.69951,-.02448
;labels =altac,pric,fue,reg,ae,ve,fel,ecl,scl,petasc,dasc
        ,prcld,prchd,fuehd,feld,fehd,rghd,ecld,echd,scld,schd
;prob=probvw1;utility=utilvw1
;fn1= ealtacc=(1+altac*altaccz)      ? linear
;fn2= Vaa=pric*price + fue*fuel+reg*rego +AE*AES+VE*VES +FEl*FE+ECl*EC+
SCl*SC
;fn3= vab= prcld*prcldf+prchd*prchdf+fuehd*fuelhdf+feld*feldf+fehd*fehdf
           +rghd*rghdf+ecld*ecldf+echd*echdf+scld*scldf+schd*schdf
;fn4 = Util1 = ealtacc*(Petasc + Vaa+Vab)?+Vac)
;fn5 = Util2 = ealtacc*(Dasc + Vaa+Vab)   ?+Vac)
;fn6 = Util3 = ealtacc*(Vaa+Vab)          ?+Vac)?
;?ecm=(pet),(hybrid)
;model:
U(pet)   = Util1 /U(die)   = Util2 /U(hyb)   = Util3 $
```

Table 21.11 Summary of model results (*t*-values are in brackets)

500 Halton draws, with panel structure accommodated in Models M3–M6. Random parameters are standard
  normal

	Alts	M1: MNL	M2: MNL	M3: Mixed Logit	M4: Mixed Logit	M5: H– MNL	M6: H– SMNL
Exogenous weighting on response choice certainty	–	No	Yes	No	Yes	Yes	Yes
A$_{jq}$: conditioned on acceptability of each alternative and attributes outside threshold range	–	No	No	No	No	Yes	Yes
Attribute perceived thresholds built in	–	No	No	No	No	Yes	Yes
Attributes:							
Alternative acceptable (1,0)	–	–	–	–	–	−0.5684 (−11.1)	−0.7157 (−16.2)
Vehicle price ($)	All	−0.0264 (−15.8)	−0.0262 (−41.3)	−0.0522 (−11.4)	−0.0532 (−31.4)	−0.0525 (−8.7)	−0.0765 (−4.9)

Table 21.11 (cont.)

	Alts	M1: MNL	M2: MNL	M3: Mixed Logit	M4: Mixed Logit	M5: H– MNL	M6: H– SMNL
Fuel price ($/litre)	All	−0.4785	−0.5283	−0.7790	−0.9099	−1.8049	−1.8017
		(−3.1)	(−8.9)	(−3.5)	(−10.7)	(−10.9)	(−4.6)
Annual emissions surcharge ($)	All	−0.0008	−0.0008	−0.0016	−0.0018	−0.0011	−0.0034
		(−3.9)	(−11.2)	(−4.9)	(−13.9)	(−8.5)	(−6.6)
Variable emissions surcharge ($/km)	All	−0.6509	−0.7342	−1.1852	−1.2361	−0.6358	−0.6445
		(−2.4)	(−7.2)	(−2.8)	(−7.6)	(−3.2)	(−1.2)
Registration fee ($/per annum)	All	−0.0006	−0.0006	−0.0009	−0.0010	−0.0014	−0.0050
		(−3.2)	(−7.8)	(−2.8)	(−8.2)	(−8.4)	(−7.2)
Fuel efficiency (litres/ 100km)	All	−0.0536	−0.0624	−0.0870	−0.0899	−0.0929	−0.2091
		(−3.7)	(−11.4)	(−4.0)	(−11.1)	(−5.5)	(−4.1)
Engine capacity (# cylinders)	All	−0.0367	−0.0409	−0.0661	−0.0760	0.1617	0.0632
		(−1.3)	(−3.8)	(−1.6)	(−4.9)	(4.5)	(0.6)
Seating capacity	All	0.2749	0.2645	0.4852	0.4948	−0.1715	−0.0634
		(8.0)	(20.8)	(7.4)	(19.3)	(−3.8)	(−0.6)
Petrol-specific constant	Petrol	0.0760	0.1375	0.0812	0.1332	0.1759	0.1967
		(0.96)	(4.6)	(0.8)	(3.5)	(3.7)	(1.5)
Diesel-specific constant	Diesel	−0.3456	−0.3301	−0.5232	−0.5167	−0.3111	−0.5330
		(−4.5)	(−11.2)	(−5.1)	(−13.3)	(−6.5)	(−4.0)
Random parameters: standard deviation:							
Vehicle price ($)	All	–	–	0.0430	0.0464	–	–
				(9.2)	(20.9)		
Fuel price ($/litre)	All	–	–	0.8854	0.9882	–	–
				(1.8)	(5.5)		
Annual emissions surcharge ($)	All	–	–	0.0024	0.0025	–	–
				(5.7)	(16.0)		
Variable emissions surcharge ($/km)	All	–	–	2.6288	2.5970	–	–
				(4.4)	(12.0)		
Registration fee ($/per annum)	All	–	–	0.0018	0.0019	–	–
				(4.0)	(11.9)		
Fuel efficiency (litres/ 100km)	All	–	–	0.0987	0.0996	–	–
				(3.8)	(9.8)		
Engine capacity (# cylinders)	All	–	–	0.2422	0.2391	–	–
				(4.0)	(10.5)		
Seating capacity	All	–	–	0.6375	0.6919	–	–
				(8.4)	(22.8)		
Attribute threshold cut-off effects:							
Max (0, AttPriceLower-Price)	All	–	–	–	–	−0.0625	−0.0224
						(−6.5)	(−1.0)
		–	–	–	–		

Table 21.11 (cont.)

	Alts	M1: MNL	M2: MNL	M3: Mixed Logit	M4: Mixed Logit	M5: H–MNL	M6: H–SMNL
Max (0,Price-AttPriceUpper)						0.0296 (4.8)	−0.0596 (−2.8)
Max (0,Fuel-AttFuelUpper)	All	–	–	–	–	1.1772 (4.8)	−1.1126 (−2.0)
Max(0, AttPriceLower-FuelEff)	All	–	–	–	–	0.0335 (0.6)	0.0192 (0.1)
Max (0,Price-AttFuelEffUpper)	All	–	–	–	–	−0.0651 (−2.6)	−0.1343 (−1.9)
Max (0,Regn-AttRegnUpper)	All	–	–	–	–	−0.0001 (−0.3)	−0.0008 (−0.5)
Max (0, AttECLower-EngCap)	All	–	–	–	–	−0.1093 (−1.7)	−0.1366 (−0.6)
Max (0,EngCap-AttECUpper)	All	–	–	–	–	−0.3079 (−6.9)	−0.4470 (−3.4)
Max (0, AttSCLower-StCap)	All	–	–	–	–	−0.5271 (−10.7)	−0.7387 (−5.5)
Max (0,StCap-AttSCUpper)	All	–	–	–	–	−0.0080 (−0.1)	−0.0364 (−0.2)
Acceptability of alternative conditioned on attribute thresholds:							
Price outside thresholds (1,0)	All	–	–	–	–	−0.2332 (−4.9)	−0.1848 (−4.4)
Fuel price outside thresholds (1,0)	All	–	–	–	–	−0.1236 (−6.6)	−0.0850 (−3.3)
Regn outside thresholds (1,0)	All	–	–	–	–	−0.0238 (−1.5)	−0.0275 (−1.0)
Fueleff outside thresholds (1,0)	All	–	–	–	–	−0.0539 (−3.1)	−0.1031 (−3.6)
EngCap outside thresholds (1,0)	All	–	–	–	–	−0.0053 (−0.3)	−0.0104 (−0.4)
StCap outside thresholds (1,0)	All	–	–	–	–	−0.0276 (−1.5)	−0.0806 (−2.6)
Variance parameter in scale (τ):							
Sigma:	–	–	–	–	–	–	0.1144 (23.6)
Sample mean	–	–	–	–	–	–	0.9609
Sample standard deviation	–	–	–	–	–	–	0.8896
Model fit:							
LL at zero	–	−1722.62	−12294.57	−1722.62	−12294.57	−12294.57	−12294.57
LL at convergence	–	−1532.42	−10868.78	−1392.55	−9986.23	−7706.5	−7509.94

Table 21.11 (cont.)

	Alts	M1: MNL	M2: MNL	M3: Mixed Logit	M4: Mixed Logit	M5: H– MNL	M6: H– SMNL
McFadden Pseudo-R^2	–	0.110	0.116	0.192	0.188	0.373	0.390
Info. Criterion: AIC	–	1.9674	13.8760	1.7992	12.7605	9.8642	9.6147
Sample size	–	1568					
In-Sample Prediction success:		*Summing the choice probabilities across the sample*					
Petrol (608)	–	272	278	274	276	367 (32.9%)	402 (45.7%)
Diesel (416)	–	140	138	143	142	232 (63.4%)	272 (91.6%)
Hybrid (544)	–	232	230	242	241	309 (28.3%)	327 (35.7%)

Of particular note in Model 6 is the statistically significant parameter τ that reveals the presence and extent of scale heterogeneity. There is clear evidence of scale heterogeneity in the presence of preference heterogeneity, and even the latter is not revealed through random parameters but through the role of acceptability of an alternative and the perceived attribute thresholds.

One behaviorally appealing way to compare the models is to calculate the direct elasticities for each of the attributes in the CE. The elasticity formula is given in Equation (21.43a):

$$Elas_{kjq} = (1 - Prob_{jq}) \times X_{kjq} \times \frac{\partial V_{jq}}{\partial X_{kjq}}, \tag{21.43a}$$

where $\frac{\partial V_{jq}}{\partial X_{kjq}}$ is the parameter estimate (or marginal disutility) associated with the kth attribute in the jth alternative for the qth individual in Models 1 to 6, and is the form in Equation (21.43) for Models 5 and 6. The general form given in equation (21.43b) is derived from Equation (21.34), where all terms are as defined in previous equations:

$$\frac{\partial V_{jq}}{\partial X_{kjq}} = \beta_k(1 + 2\gamma_h X_{hjq} - \delta_j AC_{jq}) + \beta_l(1 + \delta_j A_{jq} - \gamma_h X_{hl}\text{min} + 2\gamma_h X_{hjq})$$
$$+ \beta_m(-1 - \delta_j AC_{jq} + \gamma_h X_{hm}\text{max} - 2\gamma_h X_{hjq}) \tag{21.43b}$$

In Equation (21.43b), the second (third) term falls out when the lower (upper) cut off is satisfied (i.e., when the attribute level for the hth (or kth) attribute associated with the jth alternative and qth individual is outside of the perceived attribute threshold acceptance level. The marginal disutility expression (see Equation (21.44) which is an interpretation of Equation (21.43)) for price in Model 6 accounts for the mean non-penalized marginal disutility, the penalized lower and upper bound cut-offs where the price level offered is outside of the minimum and maximum threshold levels (zero otherwise), and the conditioning of the price on acceptability of an alternative when price is in the attribute rejection range:

$$
\begin{aligned}
MU_{price} = (-0.7157 \ + \ 0.1848 \times \text{price}) \times [-0.0765 \times \text{price} \\
- \ 0.0224 \times \text{lower\_cutoff\_penalty} \\
- \ 0.0596 \times \text{upper\_cutoff\_penalty}].
\end{aligned}
\tag{21.44}
$$

For the penalty functions, we expect a negative parameter estimate. To interpret the estimates associated with $\sum_{l=K+1}^{L} \beta_l \{0 : \max(0, X_{ljq} - X_{lq}\min)\} + \sum_{m=L+1}^{M} \beta_m \{0 : \max(0, X_{mq}\max - X_{mjq})\}$, we note that when the threshold is satisfied (i.e., the attribute level in the CE is greater than the lower value for the lower cut-off and/or less than the upper value for the upper cut-off), the variable is set equal to zero; however, if the attribute level is less than the lower cut-off or higher than the upper cut-off, the penalty variable is invoked. A negative parameter estimate indicates that if, say, price moves further away from (and below) the lower cut-off, the overall disutility of price increases. Likewise if the price moves further above the upper cut-off, then marginal disutility also increases. The evidence in Models 5 and 6 supports this interpretation (except for statistically non-significant estimates).

For Models 5 (and 6), the mean parameter estimates defining overall marginal disutility are −1.2823 (−0.866) (vehicle price), −2.121(−1.872) (fuel price), −0.0015 (−0.0047) (annual emissions surcharge), −0.835 (−0.899) (variable emissions surcharge), −0.019 (−0.0069) (annual registration charge), −0.196 (−0.189) (fuel efficiency), 0.277 (0.191) (engine capacity), and −0.242 (0.725) (seating capacity). It appears that engine and seating capacity retain their sign in Model 5, but seating capacity has a change of sign in Model 6 after accounting for all attribute influencing elements.

The mean direct elasticity estimates are summarized in Table 21.12. The biggest influence on the difference in the direct elasticities in Models 5 and 6 in contrast to Models 1 to 4 is the conditioning on the acceptability of each alternative, although attribute thresholds have a contribution. To our surprise

Table 21.12 Summary of mean direct elasticity results Three estimates for petrol, diesel, and hybrid; all elasticities are probability weighted

Attribute	M1: MNL	M2: MNL	M3: ML	M4: ML	M5: H-MNL	M6: H-SMNL
Vehicle price ($)	−.844,	−.830,	−.751,	−.734,	−1.59,	−1.908,
	−.991,	−.991,	−.937,	−.923,	−1.28.	−1.59,
	−1.09	−1.09	−.805	−.786	−2.09	−1.968
Fuel price ($/litre)	−.357,	−.389,	−.359,	−.404,	−.425,	−.291,
	−.429,	−.477,	−.434,	−.494,	−.333,	−.227,
	−.382	−.425	−.362	−.411	−.409	−.286
Annual emissions	−.140,	−.149,	−.144,	−.150,	−.072,	−.155,
surcharge ($)	−.152,	−.165,	−.133,	−.140,	−.047,	−.098,
	−.063	−.069	−.066	−.070	−.025	−.052
Variable emissions	−.082,	−.092,	−.072,	−.074,	−.027,	−.020,
surcharge ($/km)	−.084,	−.095,	−.071,	−.073,	−.018,	−.013,
	−.042	−.048	−.037	−.038	−.011	−.009
Registration fee	−.327,	−.301,	−.268,	−.303,	−.260,	−.651,
($/per annum)	−0394,	−.369,	−.332,	−.380,	−.208,	−.536,
	−.353	−.330	−.270	−.308	−.258	−.664
Fuel efficiency	−.338,	−.390, -	−.315,	−.315,	−.038,	−.202,
(litres/100km)	−.406,	−.477,	−.383,	−.386,	−.032,	−.128,
	−.356	−.419	−.314	−.317,	−.043	−.148
Engine capacity	−.121,	−.134, -	−.129,	−.143,	.229,	.088,
(# cylinders)	−.148,	−.167,	−.154,	−.174,	.193,	.079,
	−.134	−.151	−.129	−.146	.246	.109
Seating capacity	0.717,	.682,	.777,	.767,	−.146,	.341,
	.840,	.814,	1.01,	1.02,	−.120,	.261,
	.751	.728	.766	−.763	−.142	.271

Note: Standard deviations are available on request.

the exogenous weighting by the certainty scale had no noticeable impact on the mean elasticities, where the models with and without such weighting are compared (i.e., MNL Model 1 versus 3 and ML Model 2 versus 4). This is an interesting finding given the arguments and evidence offered by the few studies (e.g., Johannesson *et al.* 1999) that have investigated a certainty scale.

We also calculated the marginal rate of substitution between vehicle price and each of the other attributes in Models 5 and 6, the two models of most interest. These are summarized in Table 21.13. The most interesting evidence is for fuel price and variable emissions charge relative to vehicle price. A change in the variable emissions charge ($/km) and in fuel prices ($/litre) both

Table 21.13 Summary of marginal rates of substitution

Marginal rate of substitution between vehicle price ($) and:	M5: H-MNL	M6: H-SMNL
Fuel price ($/litre)	1.632 (1.14)	2.447 (1.476)
Annual emissions surcharge ($)	0.0011 (0.0008)	0.0062 (0.0026)
Variable emissions surcharge ($/km)	0.649 (0.467)	1.179 (0.596)
Registration fee ($/per annum)	0.0015 (0.001)	0.0091 (0.0038)
Fuel efficiency (litres/100km)	0.0219 (0.041)	−0.235 (0.271)
Engine capacity (# cylinders)	−0.210 (0.159)	−0.262 (0.280)
Seating capacity	0.163 (0.197)	−0.974 (1.301)

Note: The vehicle price marginal disutility is in the denominator. One can construct other ratios by taking two of the marginal rates of substitution (MRS) and dividing one into the other. For example, the MRS between fuel price and annual emission surcharge in Model 5 is 0.0011/0.649 = 0.00169. Standard deviations in brackets.

have a non-marginal impact on the vehicle price paid and vice versa in terms of substitution and purchase of vehicle decisions. The other subsitution rates are relatively low, with the possible exception of engine capacity.

21.8.4 Conclusions

This section has presented a framework within which important processing influences on choice making at the respondent and choice set level can be incorporated into a RUM. Drawing on the existing literature that suggests that choice attribute thresholds and response certainty have behaviorally significant influences on the probability of a choice, we extend the processing set to investigate the role that perceived acceptance of an alternative also has. The model specification that incorporates these three influences is referred to as a heteroskedastic MNL model and modified as heteroskedastic scale MNL when scale heterogeneity is accounted for.

A comparison of the models shows the significant improvement in predictive power as well as different mean direct elasticities for the HMNL and HG-SMNL (compared to simple MNL and ML) models, due in large measure to the "scaling" of the standard utility expression by a function that accounts for the acceptability of each alternative and perceived attribute thresholds, as well as accounting for scale heterogeneity. The evidence also suggests, in particular, that alternative acceptance appears far more influential than response certainty in improving the predictive performance of the choice model.

The approach and evidence presented suggests that we should not ignore supplementary information on how alternatives and attributes are processed prior to a choice response as well as accommodating the degrees of certainty of actually making the choice. Indeed the improvement in prediction performance and significantly different direct elasticities is sufficient enough to recognize the role that supplementary data plays, regardless of whether one believes in the credibility of such information.

An ongoing research challenge is to gain a greater understanding and reliability concerning a range of supplementary questions in aiding our understanding of how individuals view the information content of SC experiments, in contrast to assuming, through ignorance, that all information is relevant and treated as if all attributes and alternatives are subject to the same trading regime.

21.9 Case study III: interrogation of responses to stated choice experiments – is there sense in what respondents tell us?

SC experiments are used extensively to create data capable of modeling choices in order to obtain parameter estimates that describe the preferences of individuals for specific attributes of alternatives within a pre-defined choice setting (Louviere *et al.* 2000). The popularity of such CEs is in part a product of the lack of appropriate RP data in situations where choosing among a number of alternatives can be observed in real markets, but also due to the ability, within a single unified theoretical framework, to investigate the potential takeup of alternatives which do not currently exist in terms of the levels and mix of attributes and/or uniqueness beyond a set of prescribed attributes.

It is common practice for analysts to pool the data from a sample of respondents, accounting for the presence of multiple observations for each respondent, and then to estimate a discrete choice model, accounting to varying degrees for observed and unobserved preference heterogeneity, and more recently also scale heterogeneity (see Fiebig *et al.* 2010 and Greene and Hensher 2010 as examples). There is also a growing interest in investigating the role that specific AP heuristics play in conditioning the influence of each attribute associated with each alternative (see Hensher 2010 for an overview; Hess and Hensher 2010; and Cameron and DeShazo 2010), using a variety of supplementary questions on how attributes are processed and/or developing model functional forms that capture specific heuristics. Another area of growing interest, particularly in the non-market valuation literature, is research into behavioral explanations for the preference changes that appear to occur over a sequence of choice tasks, using parametric (Bateman *et al.* 2008; Day *et al.* 2009; McNair *et al.* 2010a) and non-parametric tests (Day and Prades 2010) as well as equality constrained LCMs (McNair *et al.* 2012).

What we believe is not given enough emphasis is the extent to which we can learn from an interrogation of each response at the choice set level, and set up candidate rules, or heuristics (often referred to as "rules of thumb") that align with one or more possible processing rules used by an individual, within and between sequentially administered choice sets, to reveal their choice response. Specifically, the analysis here is looking for evidence that would be consistent with respondents' use of heuristics to make choices in SC experiments. This matters because of the small, but accumulating empirical evidence, that alternative AP strategies (APS) do influence behavioral outputs such as estimates of WTP and model predictive capability (see Hensher 2010 for an overview). While we can never be certain that a specific rule is applied, we are seeking out a way to gain confidence in the evidence, given that some pundits believe that respondents are known to make choices that have no "rational" attachment.

To illustrate the focus of this chapter, we reproduce, in Table 21.14, data from one respondent in one of many CEs the authors have conducted,[22] in the context of choosing among three routes for a commuter trip, where the first route description is the reference or status quo (SQ) alternative associated with a recent trip. The design attributes are free-flow time (FF), slowed-down time (SDT), running cost (Cost), toll if applicable (Toll), and overall trip time variability (Var) (times are in min., costs in dollars, and time variability in plus or minus min.). We begin with the most commonly assumed normative processing rule that assumes (in the absence of any known AP heuristic) that all attributes (and levels) are relevant, and that a fully compensatory processing strategy is active at the choice set level. Focussing on these five attributes only, we highlight in shaded grey the most attractive attribute level (e.g., lowest FF), which varies across the attributes, and propose that if an alternative had the most attractive level on one or more attributes, and that alternative was chosen, then we can reasonably suggest that the respondent was "plausible" in their choice, assuming that the heuristic being used to process the choice set preserves (i.e., does not ignore) the attribute(s) with the "most attractive level(s)" based, of course, on only the offered attributes.

---

[22] We undertook exactly this same exercise on a number of data sets and a number of respondents in each data set, and the message was the same or very similar.

Table 21.14 Example of 16 choice scenario responses evaluated by one respondent

Choice scenario	Alternative	TotTime	TotCost	Var	FF	SDT	Cost	Toll	Choice	Plausible = Y
1	1 (SQ)	40	5.4	25	12	28	3.2	2.2	0	Y
1	2	48	5.7	8	14	34	2.6	3.1	1	Y
1	3	36	8	6	14	22	4.5	3.5	0	Y
2	1 (SQ)	40	5.4	25	12	28	3.2	2.2	1	Y
2	2	40	7.1	8	6	34	4.5	2.6	0	Y
2	3	44	4.7	6	10	34	1.6	3.1	0	Y
3	1 (SQ)	40	5.4	25	12	28	3.2	2.2	0	Y
3	2	28	7	8	14	14	3.5	3.5	1	Y
3	3	40	2.6	6	6	34	2.6	0	0	Y
4	1 (SQ)	40	5.4	25	12	28	3.2	2.2	0	Y
4	2	28	4.5	2	14	14	4.5	0	1	Y
4	3	48	4.2	8	14	34	1.6	2.6	0	Y
5	1 (SQ)	40	5.4	25	12	28	3.2	2.2	0	Y
5	2	44	8	4	10	34	4.5	3.5	0	Y
5	3	36	1.6	2	14	22	1.6	0	1	Y
6	1 (SQ)	40	5.4	25	12	28	3.2	2.2	1	Y
6	2	48	5.1	6	14	34	1.6	3.5	0	Y
6	3	48	3.5	4	14	34	3.5	0	0	Y
7	1 (SQ)	40	5.4	25	12	28	3.2	2.2	1	Y
7	2	44	6.6	2	10	34	3.5	3.1	0	Y
7	3	48	6.1	8	14	34	2.6	3.5	0	Y
8	1 (SQ)	40	5.4	25	12	28	3.2	2.2	0	Y
8	2	36	7.6	6	14	22	4.5	3.1	0	Y
8	3	20	5.1	4	6	14	1.6	3.5	1	Y
9	1 (SQ)	40	5.4	25	12	28	3.2	2.2	1	Y
9	2	48	4.2	2	14	34	1.6	2.6	0	Y
9	3	28	6.6	8	6	22	3.5	3.1	0	Y
10	1 (SQ)	40	5.4	25	12	28	3.2	2.2	0	Y
10	2	20	4.7	4	6	14	1.6	3.1	1	Y
10	3	44	7	2	10	34	3.5	3.5	0	Y
11	1 (SQ)	40	5.4	25	12	28	3.2	2.2	0	Y
11	2	32	1.6	8	10	22	1.6	0	1	Y
11	3	28	6.1	6	14	14	3.5	2.6	0	Y
12	1 (SQ)	40	5.4	25	12	28	3.2	2.2	1	Y
12	2	48	2.6	4	14	34	2.6	0	0	Y
12	3	40	7.1	2	6	34	4.5	2.6	0	Y
13	1 (SQ)	40	5.4	25	12	28	3.2	2.2	0	Y
13	2	24	5.2	6	10	14	2.6	2.6	1	Y
13	3	48	7.6	4	14	34	4.5	3.1	0	Y
14	1 (SQ)	40	5.4	25	12	28	3.2	2.2	0	Y
14	2	40	3.5	6	6	34	3.5	0	1	Y

Table 21.14 (cont.)

Choice scenario	Alternative	TotTime	TotCost	Var	FF	SDT	Cost	Toll	Choice	Plausible = Y
14	3	32	5.2	4	10	22	2.6	2.6	0	Y
15	1 (SQ)	40	5.4	25	12	28	3.2	2.2	0	Y
15	2	36	6.1	4	14	22	3.5	2.6	0	Y
15	3	28	5.7	2	14	14	2.6	3.1	1	Y
16	1 (SQ)	40	5.4	25	12	28	3.2	2.2	0	Y
16	2	28	6.1	2	6	22	2.6	3.5	1	Y
16	3	24	4.5	8	10	14	4.5	0	0	Y

Applying the same logic across all of the sixteen choices that each respondent made, we found that 51 of the 300 respondents were consistently selecting options that were best on the same attribute, where the experimental design did not allow them to consistently choose such that two or more attributes were always best.

There could be other reasons why an alternative is chosen, regardless of the attribute levels and their relative performance, such as satisfaction with the status quo or the adoption of a minimum regret calculus, in contrast to a utility maximization calculus (see Chorus 2010 and Hensher *et al.* 2013). Indeed, if a respondent focuses on only one attribute, then we might be observing a consistent EBA heuristic. However, on the face of the observed attribute evidence, the 16 choice scenarios satisfy a "plausible choice" test in 16 situations. Five of the choice scenarios show the status quo as the preferred alternative (**bolded** in the choice column in Table 21.14). It may also be that this example individual adopts one or more AP rules in evaluating the choice scenarios, which may be the basis of choice in any of the 16 choice sets, regardless of whether they have passed the "plausibility" test used above. We investigate a number of these AP rules in the following sections.

Furthermore, supplementary data associated with the respondents' perception of whether specific attributes were ignored or added up (where they have a common metric) might also be brought to bear, to add additional insights into the choice responses. No attributes were ignored by this respondent, as reported by responses to supplementary questions. Looking at the possibility that this individual may also have added up FF and SDT and/or Cost and Toll, we cannot find any evidence within the "plausible choice" test that it would have failed if attribute addition (TotTime, TotCost) had not been applied, although this may have assisted in making the choice.

The following sections undertake a more formal inquiry using another data set collected in 2007 in New Zealand, to delve more deeply into alternative "plausible choice" tests as well as the role of non-compensatory heuristics in aiding our understanding of how SC sets are processed in assisting the selection of a choice outcome. We briefly describe the data, followed by a statistical assessment of them in the search for possible rules (or heuristics) that explain specific choice responses under specific assumptions. The investigated rules and tests focus on the influence of the choice sequence on choice response, a pairwise alternative plausibility test and the presence of dominance, the influence of non-trading, dimensional versus holistic AP, the influence of relative attribute levels, and revision of the reference alternative as value learning across sequenced choice sets. We then discuss the evidence, and conclude with a proposal to include two new explanatory variables in choice models to capture the number of attributes in an alternative that are "best" as well as value learning, together with a statement of the degree of confidence one might have in the behavioral sense of the data emanating from an SC experiment.

21.9.1 The data setting

As part of a larger study to evaluate the costs and benefits of a new toll road proposal in New Zealand, we undertook field work in late 2007 to identify the preferences of a sample of 136 commuters, 116 non-commuters, and 126 individuals traveling on employer business in the catchment area around Tauranga in the North Island of New Zealand. An SC experiment was included, together with questions that sought information on a recent trip which was used to construct both the reference (i.e., status quo) alternative, and the two other alternatives, which had levels that pivoted around the status quo alternative. There were 16 choice scenarios in which the respondent compared the levels of times and costs of a current/recent trip against two alternative opportunities to complete the same trip described by other levels of times and costs. The respondent had to choose one of these alternatives. The profile of the attribute range is given in Table 21.15 with an illustrative SC scenario screen in Figure 21.7. The experimental design was composed of two blocks of 16 choice scenarios each, and can be found in full in Appendix 21B. Respondents were randomly assigned to one of the two blocks, with the order in which the 16 choice scenarios were presented also randomized. The levels

Table 21.15 Profile of attribute range in choice experiment

Attribute	Levels
Free-flow time (variation around reference level)	−30%, −15%, 0, 15%, 30%
Slowed-down time (variation around reference level)	−30%, −15%, 0, 15%, 30%
Trip time variability	±0%, ±,5%, ±10%, ±15%
Running cost (variation around reference level)	−40%, −10%, 0 ,20%, 40%
Toll cost	$0, $0.5, $1, $1.5, $2, $2.5, $3, $3.5, $4

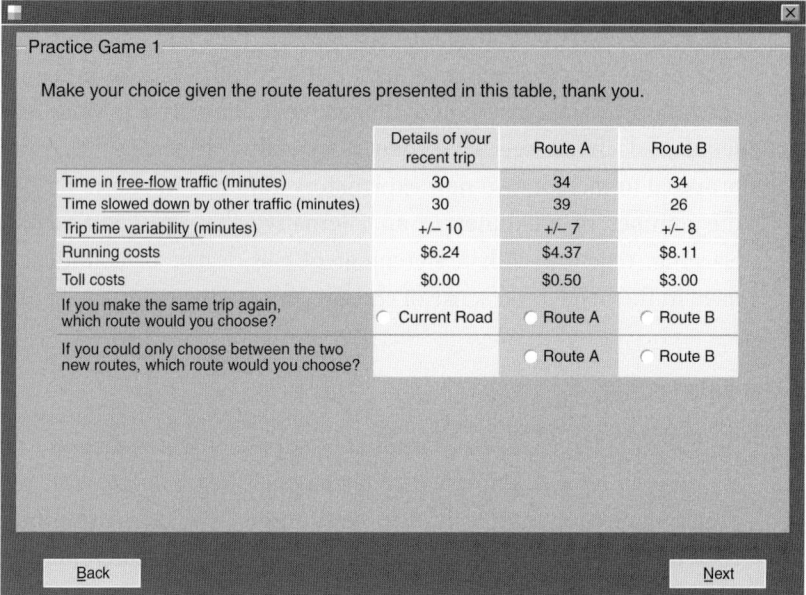

Figure 21.7   Example of a stated choice screen

of the design were optimized in accordance with efficient design theory, with a
d-error measure employed (see Rose and Bliemer 2008 and Chapter 6 for
details).

A few additional rules were imposed on the design:

(i)   Free-flow and slowed-down times[23] in the non-reference alternatives
      were set to a base of 5 min. if the respondent entered zero for their
      current trip.

---

[23] The distinction between free-flow and slowed-down time is solely to promote the differences in the
quality of travel time between various routes – especially a tolled route and a non-tolled route, and is
separate to the influence of total time.

(ii) To obtain sensible trip time variability levels in minutes, we asked respondents to suggest a range of departure times experienced to ensure they arrived at their destination at the planned arrival time. This range was used to identify the actual trip time variability given the percentages used in the design. Where the departure times were reported as the same as the recent reference trip, we set an artificial base as per the same rule in (i).

(iii) Given that tolled routes were currently not available at the time of the survey, the proposed new tolled route was assigned a range of values. Construction of the new toll road was approved in 2010, with a proposed fixed toll in the range evaluated.

In addition, supplementary questions were asked upon completion of all 16 choice scenarios on whether specific attributes were ignored. The entire survey instrument was programmed as a Computer Assisted Personal Interview (CAPI), that enabled the attribute levels to be tailored to (i.e., pivoted around) each respondent's recent trip experience. An interviewer was present and guided the respondents through the survey screens. All data is automatically captured in a data base. The software has built in checks to ensure that all data provided were logical where appropriate (e.g., the travel time, given distance, delivered a meaningful average trip speed). Given the focus of this chapter, other details of the study are not provided.

21.9.2 Investigating candidate evidential rules

As a prelude to investigating a number of candidate heuristics (or evidential rules) that might contribute to explaining choice response, we continue the theme of "plausible choice" in the contexts of full attribute relevance and omitting those attributes that the respondent claimed not to have considered. The following analyses are performed at both the choice set and respondent level, where we use the word "observation" to refer to a choice set assessment, and "respondent" to refer to the assessment over all (16) choice sets, with the latter providing evidence that those respondents who fail the various tests are exhibiting different behavioral tendencies overall, not just in response to a specific feature of the experimental design. We assess the implications of the evidence on WTP estimates, before investigating five speculative but interesting heuristics associated with (i) pairwise alternative plausibility and the presence of dominance, (ii) the influence of non-trading, (iii) the role of dimensional versus holistic AP, (iv) the influence of relative attribute levels, and (v) the revision of the reference alternative as value learning across sequenced choice sets.

The "plausible choice" test presented above for one respondent can be applied across the 6,048 observations in the New Zealand data. Appendix 21C details all 54 choice sets (or scenarios) where the test failed. An alternative that would fail the test if chosen was present in 291 choice scenarios, resulting in a failure rate of 18.6 percent. Note that the lack of a toll in some alternative (i.e., non-tolled routes) meant that the reference alternative always had at least one best attribute, and so if it was chosen, the "plausible choice" test could not fail. Table 21.16 also shows the proportion (and counts) of plausible choice sets by choice task sequence number. When all attributes are assumed to be relevant we find, across all 16 choice sets, that 99.12 percent of the observations pass the "plausible choice" test associated with one or more attributes being best on the chosen alternative (with the percentage varying across the 16 choice sets from 100 percent to 98.4 percent). When we omit those attributes which the respondent claimed not to have considered, i.e., they were ignored, 95.78 percent of the observations pass this test (with the percentage varying

Table 21.16 Influence of choice sequence on choice response

Choice set sequence	Assuming full attribute relevance		Allowing for attribute being ignored	
	Proportion plausible	Count non-plausible	Proportion plausible	Count non-plausible
1	0.9894	4	0.9471	20
2	1.0000	0	0.9497	19
3	0.9894	4	0.9392	23
4	0.9894	4	0.9603	15
5	0.9974	1	0.9524	18
6	0.9841	6	0.9603	15
7	0.9921	3	0.9841	6
8	0.9947	2	0.9550	17
9	0.9841	6	0.9444	21
10	0.9894	4	0.9656	13
11	0.9894	4	0.9603	15
12	0.9921	3	0.9550	17
13	0.9894	4	0.9550	17
14	0.9894	4	0.9524	18
15	0.9894	4	0.9709	11
16	1.0000	0	0.9735	10

across the 16 choice sets from 98.41 percent to 94.44 percent), suggesting that regardless of respondents' claims of attributes being ignored or not, there is a very high incidence of plausible choosing. The evidence also suggests that there is no noticeable deterioration in plausible choice response as the respondent works through the choice sets from set 1 to set 16. At the respondent level, we find that the 54 choice observations that failed the "plausible choice" test were spread across 49 respondents.

The structure of the design has an impact on the incidence of observations that fail the "plausible choice" test. If full attribute attendance is assumed, then the test cannot be failed if every alternative in the experimental design has at least one best attribute. In this empirical setting, only one alternative in the design did not have a best level (choice scenario 31 in Appendix 21B), which might have had some role in keeping the incidence rate low (54 observations out of a possible 291). Other choice scenarios also allowed the test to fail as a consequence of the forced variability in slowed-down and free-flow time when the recent trip values were less than 5 min. (rule (i) discussed earlier). Once ignored attributes are taken into account, the number of scenarios in which the test is failed can in no way be inferred from the experimental design. While there are a finite (albeit large) number of combinations with which the attributes can be ignored or preserved, the analyst does not know *a priori* which of these will be chosen. Looking at the entire data set, it can be determined that when accounting for the reported ignoring of attributes, 255 observations are implausible out of a possible 1,699 choice scenarios where an implausible choice could have been made, spread across 99 respondents.

We also ran two simple logit models (not reported here) to explore the possible influence of the commuter's age, income and gender on whether the choice response for each choice set was plausible (1) or not (0) under the "plausible choice" test. One model assumed full attribute relevance and the other accounted for the attributes that the respondents stated as ignored (or not preserved[24]). Income and gender had no influence, but age had a statistically significant impact when accounting for whether an attribute was ignored or not, with the probability of satisfying the "plausible choice" test increasing as the commuter ages.

---

[24] We are starting to see, in the literature, a number of ways of indicating that attributes are ignored. A popular language, especially in the environmental literature, is "attribute non-preservation" or "attribute non-attendance."

Choice task response latencies have been used by Haaijer *et al.* (2000) and Rose and Black (2006) to improve the model fit of the final choice models of interest. We took an alternative approach, investigating the relationship between the "plausible choice" test (both under full attribute relevance and allowing for attributes to be ignored) and the amount of time to complete each of the 16 choice scenarios (i.e., the response latency). Statistically significant relationships were found between the choice scenario completion time and the "plausible choice" test, both under full attribute relevance and when AP was taken into account, and are reported in Table 21.17 (i) at the choice set level, and Table 21.17 (ii) at the respondent level. We find that for respondents who satisfied the "plausible choice" test at the choice set level, the average time to complete a choice set was 27.47 seconds, with a standard deviation of 26.03 seconds; however when we account for the choice set response being implausible at the observation level, we find that the mean time decreases by 5.21 seconds under full attribute relevance and 5.58 seconds when ignoring attributes is accounted for. When we do the same comparison at the respondent

Table 21.17 Influences on choice scenario completion time

(i) Choice set level
Simple OLS regression

	Full attribute relevance	Allowing for attribute being ignored
Constant	22.2963 (17.1)	22.1163 (30.8)
Full relevance plausible choice test (1,0)	5.2159 (3.96)	
Plausible choice test under attribute non-preservation (1,0)	–	5.5856 (7.5)
Adjusted R^2	0.00035	0.0019
Sample size		6,048

(ii) Respondent level

	Full attribute relevance	Allowing for attribute being ignored
Constant	23.2659 (53.9)	24.7287 (73.63)
Full relevance plausible choice test (1,0)	4.8474 (10.1)	
Plausible choice test under attribute non-preservation (1,0)	–	3.6691 (9.01)
Adjusted R^2	0.00040	0.0037
Sample size		6,048

level, we find for respondents who have at least one choice set not satisfying the plausibility test that the average time to complete a choice screen decreases by 4.84 and 3.66 seconds for full attribute relevance and attribute non-attendance, respectively, relative to the respondents who pass the test. One possible explanation for this difference in completion time is that those who pass the "plausible choice" test are more engaged in the choice task. Alternatively, those who fail the test might be employing some other heuristic that allows them to make a more rapid choice. Clearly, no definitive causal inferences can be drawn, despite speculative opinion that such respondents might be less engaged in the task.

The Nlogit set up for Table 21.17 is given below (together with the create commands that apply to subsequent tables):

```
read;file=C:\papers\WPs2016\choicesequence\data\NZdata_rat.xls$
reject;respid=16110048$
create
    ;ratd=rat=ratig
    ;rat1d=rat1-ratig1
    ;rat2d=rat2-ratig2
    ;rat3d=rat3-ratig3
    ;if(alt3=1)refalt=1
    ;if(alt3=2)scalt2=1
    ;if(alt3=3)scalt3=1
    ;time=FF+Sdt$
create
    ;if(shownum=1)cseq1=1
    ;if(shownum=2)cseq2=1
    ;if(shownum=3)cseq3=1
    ;if(shownum=4)cseq4=1
    ;if(shownum=5)cseq5=1
    ;if(shownum=6)cseq6=1
    ;if(shownum=7)cseq7=1
    ;if(shownum=8)cseq8=1
    ;if(shownum=9)cseq9=1
    ;if(shownum=10)cseq10=1
    ;if(shownum=11)cseq11=1
    ;if(shownum=12)cseq12=1
    ;if(shownum=13)cseq13=1
    ;if(shownum=14)cseq14=1
    ;if(shownum=15)cseq15=1
    ;if(shownum=16)cseq16=1$
create
    ;alt2a=alt3-1
    ;if(refff<0)refffb=refff    ?ref alt ff better (b) than sc
    ;if(refff=0)refffe=refff    ?ref alt ff equal (e) to sc
    ;if(refff>0)refffw=refff$   ?ref alt ff worse (w) than sc
```

```
create
    ;if(refsdt<0)refsdtb=refsdt   ?ref alt sdt better (b) than sc
    ;if(refsdt=0)refsdte=refsdt   ?ref alt sdt equal (e) to sc
    ;if(refsdt>0)refsdtw=refsdt   ?ref alt sdt worse (w) than sc
    ;if(refvar<0)refvarb=refvar   ?ref alt var better (b) than sc
    ;if(refvar=0)refvare=refvar   ?ref alt var equal (e) to sc
    ;if(refvar>0)refvarw=refvar$  ?ref alt var worse (w) than sc
create
    ;if(refrc<0)refrcb=refrc   ?ref alt rc better (b) than sc
    ;if(refrc=0)refrce=refrc   ?ref alt rc equal (e) to sc
    ;if(refrc>0)refrcw=refrc   ?ref alt rc worse (w) than sc
    ;if(reftc<0)reftcb=reftc   ?ref alt tc better (b) than sc
    ;if(reftc=0)reftce=reftc   ?ref alt tc equal (e) to sc
    ;if(reftc>0)reftcw=reftc$ ?ref alt tc worse (w) than sc
create
    ;if(alt3=1&choice1=1)ref=1
    ;if(alt3=2&choice1=1)sc2=1
    ;if(alt3=2&choice1=1)sc3=1
    ;if(rat=1&choice1=1)ratref=1$
create
    ;bestt=bestff+bestsdt+bestvar+bestrc+besttc
    ;bet=beff+besdt+bevar+berc+betc
    ;if(bestffi=-888)bestffic=0;(else)bestffic=bestffi
    ;if(bestsdti=-888)bestsdic=0;(else)bestsdic=bestsdti
    ;if(bestvari=-888)bestvarc=0;(else)bestvarc=bestvari
    ;if(bestrci=-888)bestrcic=0;(else)bestrcic=bestrci
    ;if(besttci=-888)besttcic=0;(else)besttcic=besttci
    ;besttc=bestffic+bestsdic+bestvarc+bestrcic+besttcic
    ;if(beffi=-888)beffic=0;(else)beffic=beffi
    ;if(besdti=-888)besdic=0;(else)besdic=besdti
    ;if(bevari=-888)bevarc=0;(else)bevarc=bevari
    ;if(berci=-888)bercic=0;(else)bercic=berci
    ;if(betci=-888)betcic=0;(else)betcic=betci
    ;betc=beffic+besdic+bevarc+bercic+betcic$
create
    ;if(chSQ=16)allSQ=1;(else)allSQ=0
    ;if(chSQ=0)allHyp=1;(else)allHyp=0
    ;rpVar=WstLngth-BstLngth
    ;rpVarPct=rpVar/WstLngth
    ;rpCongPc=Slowed/TrpLngth$
Create
    ;if(income<0)income=-888;if(QuotaVeh=2)business=1;(else)business=0
    ;numIg=IgFFTime+IgSlowTm+IgTrpVar+IgRnCost+IgTlCost$
sample;all$
reject;respid=16110048$              ? 570 freeflow
reject;respid=2110012$               ? 270 freeflow
reject;respid=16110070$              ? 270 freeflow
reject;respid=2611008$               ? 240 freeflow
create
```

```
    ;if(alt3=1&choice1=1)ref=1
    ;if(alt3=2&choice1=1)sc2=1
    ;if(alt3=2&choice1=1)sc3=1
    ;refl=ref[-3]
    ;sc1l=sc2[-3]
    ;sc2l=sc3[-3]$
create
    ;if(refl=1)newref=1
    ;if(sc1l=1)newrefa=1
    ;if(sc2l=1)newrefa=1$
create
    ;if(shownum=1)newrefa=0
    ;if(shownum=1)refcs1=1
    ;if(shownum=1)newrefa=0$
sample;all$
reject;choice1=-999$
create
    ;if(alt3=1&choice1=1)ref=1
    ;if(alt3=2&choice1=1)sc2=1
    ;if(alt3=2&choice1=1)sc3=1
    ;if(rat=1&choice1=1)ratref=1$
crmodel;lhs=chtime;rhs=one,ratig;het$
-------------------------------------------------------------
Ordinary     least squares regression ..............
LHS=CHTIME   Mean                  =        27.46613
             Standard deviation    =        26.03400
             Number of observs.    =           18336
Model size   Parameters            =               2
             Degrees of freedom    =           18334
Residuals    Sum of squares        = 12403768.05060
             Standard error of e   =        26.01047
Fit          R-squared             =          .00186
             Adjusted R-squared    =          .00181
Model test   F[ 1, 18334] (prob) =    34.2(.0000)
White heteroskedasticity robust covariance matrix.
Br./Pagan LM Chi-sq [ 1] (prob) =  67.92 (.0000)
Model was estimated on Apr 29, 2010 at 09:37:58 AM
-----------+-------------------------------------------------------------------
           |                Standard          Prob.        Mean
   CHTIME| Coefficient      Error      z     z>|Z|       of X
-----------+-------------------------------------------------------------------
Constant|    22.1163***     .71810    30.80  .0000
   RATIG|     5.58563***    .74490     7.50  .0000      .95779
-----------+-------------------------------------------------------------------
Note: ***, **, * ==>  Significance at 1%, 5%, 10% level.
-------------------------------------------------------------
--> crmodel;lhs=chtime;rhs=one,ratigre;het$
-------------------------------------------------------------
Ordinary     least squares regression .................
```

```
LHS=CHTIME   Mean                    =        27.46613
             Standard deviation      =        26.03400
             Number of observs.      =           18336
Model size   Parameters              =               2
             Degrees of freedom      =           18334
Residuals    Sum of squares          =  12380133.52919
             Standard error of e     =        25.98568
Fit          R-squared               =          .00376
             Adjusted R-squared      =          .00371
Model test   F[  1, 18334] (prob) =      69.3(.0000)
White heteroskedasticity robust covariance matrix.
Br./Pagan LM Chi-sq [  1]  (prob) = 154.03 (.0000)
Model was estimated on Oct 05, 2010 at 02:12:30 PM
-----------+------------------------------------------------------------
           |                  Standard              Prob.          Mean
    CHTIME | Coefficient       Error        z      z>|Z|           of X
-----------+------------------------------------------------------------
  Constant |   24.7287***       .33585     73.63   .0000
   RATIGRE |   3.66907***       .40729      9.01   .0000         .74607
-----------+------------------------------------------------------------
Note: ***, **, * ==>  Significance at 1%, 5%, 10% level.
------------------------------------------------------------------------
--> crmodel;lhs=chtime;rhs=one,rat;het$
------------------------------------------------------------------------
Ordinary    least squares regression ..............
LHS=CHTIME   Mean                    =        27.46613
             Standard deviation      =        26.03400
             Number of observs.      =           18336
Model size   Parameters              =               2
             Degrees of freedom      =           18334
Residuals    Sum of squares          =  12422528.56599
             Standard error of e     =        26.03013
Fit          R-squared               =          .00035
             Adjusted R-squared      =          .00030
Model test   F[  1, 18334] (prob) =       6.4(.0111)
White heteroskedasticity robust covariance matrix.
Br./Pagan LM Chi-sq [  1]  (prob) =  28.83 (.0000)
Model was estimated on Oct 05, 2010 at 02:12:50 PM
-----------+------------------------------------------------------------
           |                  Standard              Prob.          Mean
    CHTIME | Coefficient       Error        z      z>|Z|           of X
-----------+------------------------------------------------------------
  Constant |   22.2963***      1.30304     17.11   .0000
       RAT |   5.21592***      1.31734      3.96   .0001         .99116
-----------+------------------------------------------------------------
Note: ***, **, * ==>  Significance at 1%, 5%, 10% level.
------------------------------------------------------------------------
--> crmodel;lhs=chtime;rhs=one,ratre;het$
------------------------------------------------------------------
```

```
Ordinary     least squares regression ...........
LHS=CHTIME   Mean                    =        27.46613
             Standard deviation      =        26.03400
             Number of observs.      =           18336
Model size   Parameters              =               2
             Degrees of freedom      =           18334
Residuals    Sum of squares          = 12377055.95118
             Standard error of e     =        25.98245
Fit          R-squared               =          .00401
             Adjusted R-squared      =          .00396
Model test   F[  1, 18334] (prob) =    73.8(.0000)
White heteroskedasticity robust covariance matrix.
Br./Pagan LM Chi-sq [  1]  (prob) = 150.31 (.0000)
Model was estimated on Oct 05, 2010 at 02:13:06 PM
-----------+-----------------------------------------------------------------
           |                   Standard             Prob.        Mean
    CHTIME| Coefficient        Error        z     z>|Z|         of X
-----------+-----------------------------------------------------------------
Constant|     23.2659***       .43104     53.98   .0000
   RATRE|      4.84736***      .48001     10.10   .0000        .86649
-----------+-----------------------------------------------------------------
Note: ***, **, * ==>  Significance at 1%, 5%, 10% level.
-----------------------------------------------------------------------------
```

21.9.3 Derivative willingness to pay

The next task is to estimate choice models at the choice set and respondent level that distinguish between (i) the full sample (6,048 observations or 378 respondents) assuming all attributes are relevant (Full), (ii) the full sample with choice scenarios removed when the "plausible choice" test failed (5,994 observations, 329 respondents) (Plausible), (iii) the full sample taking into account attribute ignoring as an APS (6,048 observations, 378 respondents) (Full APS), and (iv) the full APS sample with choice scenarios removed when the "plausible choice" test failed (5,793 observations, 279 respondents) (Plausible APS). The findings on VTTS are summarized in Table 21.18.[25] We have also included the percentage changes in the mean VTTS estimates as a way of identifying the behavioral implications of failing the "plausible choice" test, as defined by the observed attributes that at least one attribute is the best for the chosen alternative, regardless of whether it was the reference alternative or not.

At the choice set level (Table 21.18(i)), while the differences are marked in some cases, none of the differences in mean VTTS are statistically different,

---

[25] All parameter estimates are statistically significant in all four models.

Table 21.18 Implications of "plausible choice" test on mean VTTS

(i) Choice set level

	Running cost					
	All attributes relevant			Allowing for attribute being ignored		
$/person hour (VTTS):	Full	Plausible	Difference	Full APS	Plausible APS	Difference
Free-flow time	$13.01	$12.53	3.81%	$12.02	$11.62	3.44%
Slowed-down time	$13.93	$13.85	0.58%	$14.52	$14.53	−0.07%
Trip time variability	$2.57	$2.53	1.58%	$2.33	$2.95	−21.02%
	Toll cost					
	All attributes relevant			AP strategy applied		
$/person hour (VTTS):	Full	Plausible	Difference	Full APS	Plausible APS	Difference
Free-flow time	$10.16	$10.51	−3.33%	$9.08	$9.73	−6.68%
Slowed-down time	$10.88	$11.61	−6.29%	$10.96	$12.17	−9.94%
Trip time variability	$2.00	$2.12	−5.66%	$1.76	$2.47	−28.75%
Weighted average VTTS:	12.49	12.29	1.63%	11.84	11.83	0.09%

(ii) Respondent level

	Running cost					
	All attributes relevant			Allowing for attribute being ignored		
$/person hour (VTTS):	Full	Plausible	Difference	Full APS	Plausible APS	Difference
Free-flow time	$13.01	$13.08	−0.54%	$12.02	$13.37	−10.10%
Slowed-down time	$13.93	$15.06	−7.50%	$14.52	$16.89	−14.03%
Trip time variability	$2.57	$3.47	−25.94%	$2.33	$3.01	−22.59%
	Toll cost					
	All attributes relevant			APS applied		
$/person hour (VTTS):	Full	Plausible	Difference	Full APS	Plausible APS	Difference
Free-flow time	$10.16	$11.57	−12.19%	$9.08	$10.73	−15.38%
Slowed-down time	$10.88	$13.33	−18.38%	$10.96	$13.56	−19.17%
Trip time variability	$2.00	$3.07	−34.85%	$1.76	$2.42	−27.27%
Weighted average VTTS:	10.34	12.01	−13.91%	9.55	11.44	−16.52%

especially the weighted average VTTS (where the weights relate to the attribute levels for free-flow and slowed-down time, and running and toll cost), using the delta test to obtain standard errors. This is the case even when over 4 percent of the sample is removed due to a suspicion of implausible choice behavior. This finding suggests that the underlying model is robust, and able to cope with a small percentage of seemingly implausible decisions. However, when we compare the mean VTTS at the respondent level (in Table 21.18(ii)), we find statistically significant differences, given standard errors calculated using the delta method and 1,000 random draws. This is an important finding, suggesting that the behavioral implications in terms of VTTS are not of concern when we focus on individual choice sets, but when we remove entire respondents who fail the plausible test on at least one choice set, the differences are significant. The respondent level evidence supports the findings of Scarpa *et al.* (2007), who found that the WTP estimates were of a different magnitude when "irrational" respondents were removed, which were of a considerably higher proportion than in the current study.

21.9.4 Pairwise alternative "plausible choice" test and dominance

So far, we have not discussed the possibility of dominance and what role it might play as an embedded feature of the design, as well as a response issue. We need to introduce some definitions related to dominance in order to be clear as to what features of the CE setting we are investigating. Dominance has two possible interpretations. The first, which is more common, relates to *design issues*, where one would distinguish between (i) the choice set level, where an alternative is equal or better on all attributes to another alternative, and (ii) across all choice sets shown to a respondent, where a particular alternative is always better on all attributes (noting this never happens in our CE designs). The second relates to *response issues*, where (i) at the choice set level, the respondent chooses an alternative that is best on all attributes, and (ii) at the respondent level across all choice sets, where a particular alternative is always chosen regardless of whether it is always the best in each choice set. We focus on the second interpretation, but report the extent of dominance (as a design issue) in the design being used. It must be noted, however, that design and response issues are not independent. In particular, the presence of design dominance allows a respondent in a single choice scenario to choose an alternative that is equal or inferior on all attributes to another alternative. One reason for this might be a preference for or against an alternative, where this might lead to all choice responses being made for that alternative or class of alternatives (e.g., status quo (SQ) or not status quo). If we considered SQ to be an attribute of the alternatives, then the preference for or against SQ might break the dominance condition. However we do not know *a priori* what the sign will be for any one respondent.

A weaker plausibility test compares the pairs of alternatives, allowing a choice to be considered consistent with a number of plausible heuristics such as EBA, even when it contains no best attributes, if it has at least one better attribute than the rejected alternative on a pairwise comparison. If the pair includes the reference alternative, it may be that this contrast delivers an outcome that passes a pairwise "plausibility choice" test on more occasions.

On closer inspection, of the 54 choice sets that failed the full choice set "plausible choice" test from the 6,048 choice sets in the sample, all but one satisfied the pairwise "plausible choice" test, with 20 of the chosen alternatives having the better level on all five attributes, 17 on four attributes, 14 on three attributes, and two on two attributes. This suggests that if a three-way and/or a two-way assessment of alternatives are both candidate processing strategies, then only one respondent failed both "plausibility choice" tests on only one choice set.

Could it be that just as, as some researchers suggest, there is a bias towards the reference alternative, there might be circumstances where the bias is reversed?[26] For modeling, it may be appropriate to remove the reference alternative and treat their processing strategy as elimination-by-alternatives, allowing the reference alternative to be specified as "non-existent." This is equivalent to ignoring an alternative in contrast to an attribute. Within this data set, 23 respondents chose the reference alternative for all 16 choice tasks, while a further 17 respondents chose the alternative for 15 out of 16 choice tasks. However, with 70 respondents never choosing the reference alternative, total avoidance of the reference alternative was much more common than total avoidance of the two hypothetical alternatives.

At a choice set level, if a chosen alternative passes the pairwise comparison test, that is, it is better on at least one attribute than the alternative to which it is compared, we can state that it is not dominated by the other alternative. Expressed another way, the alternative in question is dominated by the other alternative if, for every attribute, the attribute level is equal to or worse than the other alternative. While the pairwise "plausible choice" test applied above to those who failed the three-way "plausible choice" test found only one case of response dominance at the choice set level, an examination of *all choice sets for each respondent* uncovered a wider pattern of choice of a dominated alternative for 46 (out of 6,048) observations. Of the total of 6,048 choice

---

[26] Within the environmental economics literature this is actually an often quoted criticism of eliciting preferences through stated preference (SP) methods (i.e., that people act strategically in an hypothetical setting and are more likely to choose a non-reference as it provides them with an "option" to choose it, even though they would be unlikely to do so in reality). Related to this issue of strategic decision making is yeah-saying (especially in environmental economics case studies). Within the context of the transport application here, this is far less likely to be of concern; however, it is important to recognize this matter in applications more aligned to environmental economics.

Table 21.19 Response dominance in full sample

Number of observations for which each alternative dominated the chosen alternative		Choice behavior over all 16 tasks for those choice observations that were dominated	
Reference	10	Always chose reference alternative	9
SC Alternative 2	7	Never chose reference alternative	10
SC Alternative 3	28	Mix of reference and other alternatives	27
Reference and SC Alternative 2	1	–	–
Total	**46**	**Total**	**46**

scenarios, 667 contained a dominated alternative,[27] meaning that 6.9 percent of choice tasks containing dominance led to the choice of a dominated alternative. The 46 cases of dominated alternatives being chosen are summarized in Table 21.19 (where the focus is on response and design dominance). The first two columns indicate which alternative *dominated* the chosen alternative, i.e., which alternative was equal or better on all attributes, but still not chosen (e.g., there were 10 choice observations where the reference alternative was best on all attributes but not chosen; in contrast there were 28 choice observations where SC alternative 3 was best but not chosen). Of note is this high number for alternative 3, stemming from choice scenario 20 in the experimental design (see Appendix 21B), where the reference alternative was inferior, on the presented attributes, to the third alternative. One plausible explanation is that respondents are not paying as close attention to the third alternative, and hence missing a superior alternative. This explanation is supported by the results from the base MNL model (see Table 21.22, p. 1039) where an ASC for the second alternative is positive and significant. In particular, the third alternative might have been missed because most of the two hypothetical alternatives had a toll attached, whereas the reference alternative never did.[28] Those respondents who placed greater disutility on a toll might have disengaged from the hypothetical alternatives, or considered all of them as toll road alternatives. If this is the case, then it is likely that this phenomenon is occurring in

---

[27] The 667 choice scenarios containing dominance primarily stemmed from three choice scenarios containing dominance in the experimental design (see Appendix 21C, choice scenarios 15, 20, and 25). However, the application of various rules to ensure variation in the attribute levels of the hypothetical alternatives might have led to the presentation and capture of choice scenarios containing dominance that was not present in the experimental design.

[28] The experimental design did not contain a scenario where the second alternative dominated the reference alternative. However, the application of various rules as outlined in n. 28 led to this condition in some of the choice scenarios in the data set.

other choice scenarios, when dominance is not present, to the detriment of the quality of the data set. Care should be taken to minimize the chance of this happening, via clear instructions to the respondent and, if relevant, appropriate training of the interviewers administering the survey.

To be truly effective, the dominance check requires an unlabeled experiment, such that the only points of comparison between alternatives are the attributes. In this experiment, while the two hypothetical routes are unlabeled, the reference alternative represents their current route, and thus other factors might be influencing whether they choose the reference alternative or one of the remaining two alternatives. For nine dominated observations, shown in the last column of Table 21.19, the respondent always chose the reference alternative over the 16 choice tasks. This suggests that they were not trading over the attributes, such that a new alternative with superior attributes was not preferred. Conversely, for 10 dominated observations, the respondent never chose the reference alternative, instead trading only between the two hypothetical alternatives. The respondent might have been dissuaded from the reference alternative by their actual experiences of it. Alternatively, inferences might be made about omitted attributes, leading to seemingly implausible choices being made (Lancsar and Louviere 2006). The remaining observations were by respondents who chose the reference alternative and a hypothetical alternative at least once each. We have no clear explanation for their choice of a dominated alternative. A preference for, or aversion to, the reference alternative might still have been in effect, except with some trading across these alternatives. Alternatively, the dominance might be the consequence of not paying attention, for example to the third alternative, as discussed above.

The above examination of dominance assumed that none of the attributes was ignored. Just as the number of alternatives in a data set that lead to failure in the "plausible choice" test will be impacted by the particular APS of the individual, so too will the presence of dominance in a choice task. If an alternative is already dominated by another alternative, then the omission of attributes in the comparison will either retain the dominance or lead to a tie between the two alternatives. However, a pair of alternatives that, under full attribute attendance, present trade-offs, with some attributes better and worse for each alternative, might degenerate into a condition where one alternative dominates the other. Choice of a dominated alternative in this scenario might be indicative of several things. A genuine mistake might have been made either at the time of choice or when revealing which attributes were ignored. Alternatively, the AP rules might vary across choice tasks, even though they were gathered once after the completion of the choice scenarios in this study (see Puckett *et al.* 2007 for a study where APSs were collected after every choice scenario). A consequence of this condition is that even when a design is generated that has no dominance when full attribute attendance is assumed, the choice scenarios might appear to the respondent to contain dominance when their specific APS is taken into account, and this might have implications for the effectiveness and/or efficiency of the design. A potentially very important area of future research is the design of SC experiments that are robust to a mix of APSs.

21.9.5 Influences of non-trading

It is often suggested that respondents are non-traders as a result of always selecting the same alternative, especially the reference alternative, across all choice sets. There are many reasons posited including lack of interest in the CE, regret avoidance, and inertia. We investigated design attribute levels and respondent-specific characteristics as possible sources of influence in Table 21.20 (Model 1) at the respondent level, where the binary dependent variable equals 1 for 23 observations who always choose the reference alternative across all 16 choice sets, and zero otherwise for the remaining 355 respondents. Increased trip length decreases the probability of the respondent always choosing the reference alternative, as does a business trip purpose (in contrast to commuting and non-commuting). Two attributes that we had expected to be significant were not, namely the variability in total time as a percentage of the worst time for the reference alternative, and the percentage of total trip time in slowed-down conditions.

We then ran a binary logit model (Model 2) to investigate possible systematic sources of influence on the choice of the reference alternative *at a choice set* level. This model delivered some very significant sources of influence, suggesting variety seeking behavior (i.e., moving away from always choosing the reference alternative) as income increases, trip length increases, the trip is for business, the amount of toll road experience increases, and as there is engagement in AP, leading to an increasing number of attributes being ignored by the respondent (the latter obtained from supplementary questions). This latter evidence might be due to the presence of greater engagement in evaluating the new alternatives. Also, with greater variability in travel times across the reference alternative, respondents are less likely to stay with the reference alternative, as expected. However, the sign for the percentage of time being in slowed-down conditions is positive, which is the opposite effect to total time variability. A closer look at the data confirms that there is relatively more congestion with shorter trips, which increases the probability of choosing the reference alternative.

Table 21.20 Respondent and design influences on choice of reference alternative

	Full relevance			Ignored attributes
	Model 1	Model 2	Model 3	Model 4
	Reference Alternative chosen for **all** tasks	Reference Alternative chosen for single task	Base model 2 with extra influences	Base model 2 with extra influences
Constant	−1.4881 (−1.59)	1.1683 (9.34)	–	–
Time to complete a choice set (seconds)	–	0.0095 (7.95)	–	–
Trip length (km)	−0.0293 (−2.34)	−0.0185 (−15.9)	−0.0107 (−8.70)	−0.0111 (−8.94)
Personal gross income ($000s)	0.0102 (1.24)	−0.0034 (−3.21)	−0.0044 (−4.01)	−0.0042 (−3.72)
Business trip (compared to commuting and non-commuting)	−1.670 (−2.22)	−0.4048 (−6.78)	−0.3999 (−6.47)	−0.3995 (−6.34)
Ref alt time variability as percentage of Ref alt worst time	−1.6012 (−1.02)	−0.9469 (−4.86)	−1.1422 (−5.58)	−1.0013 (−4.84)
Percentage of total trip time in slowed down conditions	0.5060 (0.46)	0.3588 (2.46)	0.6835 (4.31)	0.4521 (2.92)
Amount of recent experience on toll roads (0–6)	−0.0147 (−0.11)	−0.0342 (−2.03)	−0.0465 (−2.65)	−0.0416 (−2.33)
Number of ignored attributes	0.1862 (0.94)	−0.0747 (−2.79)	–	–
Reference constant (1,0)	–	–	1.1828 (9.61)	1.1299 (9.11)
SC1 constant (1,0)	–	–	0.0730 (1.83)	0.0677 (1.69)
Free-flow time (min.)	–	–	−0.0850 (−26.6)	−0.0904 (−26.65)
Slowed-down time (mins)	–	–	−0.0953 (−15.3)	−0.1081 (−15.6)
Trip time variability (plus/ minus min.)	–	–	−0.0067 (−1.14)	−0.0102 (−1.48)
Running cost ($)	–	–	−0.3906 (−20.7)	−0.4481 (−20.9)
Toll cost ($)	–	–	−0.5448 (−27.4)	−0.6303 (−30.7)
BIC	0.5357	1.3027	1.7817	1.7296
LL at convergence	−77.50	−3930.20	−5331.12	−5173.80
Sample size	378	6048	6048	6048

Having identified some statistically significant influences on bias in favor of, or against, the reference alternative across all choice sets, and at a choice set level, we expanded on the binary choice base Model 2 to accommodate the full set of three alternatives under full attribute relevance (Model 3) and under attribute non-preservation (Model 4). The extra reference alternative-specific characteristics were highly significant, and the reference constant became marginally significant and positive, suggesting that we have accounted for a growing number of the reasons why respondents do not choose the reference alternative. The Bayes Information Criterion (BIC), which accounts for the number of parameter estimates, judges a model by how close its fitted values tend to be to the true values, in terms of a certain expected value (Akaike 1974). The BIC value assigned to a model *ranks* competing models and indicates which is the best among the given alternatives, and is preferred over the LL criterion when the number of parameters changes (as a way of avoiding over-fitting). Model 4, with a lower BIC, is a significant improvement over Model 3.

The Nlogit set ups for Table 21.20 are given below. First, we ran a binary logit model where the dependent variable is whether the reference alternative was always chosen across the choice tasks. There is one observation per respondent, and so only 378 observations. Not much is significant (Model 1). The variables are as follows:

RPVARPCT: RP variability as a percentage of RP worst trip time ((Worst observed TT – Best observed TT)/Worst observed TT); RPCONGPC: percentage of total trip time in slowed-down conditions; CHTIME: choice task time; BUSINESS: 1 if it was a business trip; TOLLREXP: amount of recent experience on toll roads 0=none, 6=a lot; NUMIG: number of ignored attributes:

```
sample;all$
reject;choice1=-999$
reject;shownum#1$
reject;alt3#1$
logit;lhs=allSQ
;rhs=one,rpVarPct,rpCongPc,TrpLngth,income,business,TollRExp,numIg$
Normal exit:   6 iterations. Status=0. F=    77.50044
-----------------------------------------------------------------------------
Binary Logit Model for Binary Choice
Dependent variable                ALLSQ
Log likelihood function      -77.50044
Restricted log likelihood    -86.67182
Chi squared [   7 d.f.]       18.34277
Significance level              .01052
McFadden Pseudo R-squared      .1058174
Estimation based on N =    378, K =    8
Information Criteria: Normalization=1/N
```

```
                   Normalized   Unnormalized
AIC                  .45238       171.00088
Fin.Smpl.AIC         .45342       171.39112
Bayes IC             .53566       202.48003
Hannan Quinn         .48544       183.49447
Model estimated: Apr 20, 2010, 11:37:55
Hosmer-Lemeshow chi-squared =    5.50370
P-value=  .70263 with deg.fr. =        8
-----------+--------------------------------------------------------------------
Variable| Coefficient    Standard Error  b/St.Er. P[|Z|>z]   Mean of X
-----------+--------------------------------------------------------------------
         |Characteristics in numerator of Prob[Y = 1]
Constant|    -1.48841        .93467         -1.592   .1113
RPVARPCT|    -1.60119       1.56593         -1.023   .3065      .35627
RPCONGPC|      .50599       1.10958           .456   .6484      .24711
TRPLNGTH|     -.02932**      .01255         -2.337   .0194    47.2328
  INCOME|      .01021        .00827          1.235   .2168    48.7725
BUSINESS|    -1.69986**      .76525         -2.221   .0263      .33333
TOLLREXP|     -.01474        .13872          -.106   .9154     3.23810
   NUMIG|      .18624        .19859           .938   .3483     1.06878
```

Next we ran a binary logit model where the dependent variable is whether the reference alternative was chosen at the choice set level (i.e., a single task). The actual levels and the two other alternatives did not enter the specification. This is a move away from the non-traders. There is now one observation per choice task (Model 2):

```
sample;all$
reject;choice1=-999$
reject;alt3#1$
create;if(income<0)income=-888$
create;if(QuotaVeh=2)business=1;(else)business=0$
create;numIg=IgFFTime+IgSlowTm+IgTrpVar+IgRnCost+IgTlCost$
logit;lhs=choice1
        ;rhs=one,rpVarPct,rpCongPc,TrpLngth,income,chTime,business,
TollRExp,numIg$
Normal exit:   5 iterations. Status=0. F=    3930.201
--------------------------------------------------------------------------------
Binary Logit Model for Binary Choice
Dependent variable             CHOICE1
Log likelihood function     -3930.20098
Restricted log likelihood   -4173.24521
Chi squared [   8 d.f.]       486.08846
Significance level               .00000
McFadden Pseudo R-squared       .0582387
Estimation based on N =    6048, K =   9
Information Criteria: Normalization=1/N
              Normalized   Unnormalized
AIC             1.30265     7878.40197
```

```
Fin.Smpl.AIC      1.30265       7878.43178
Bayes IC          1.31263       7938.76931
Hannan Quinn      1.30611       7899.35726
Model estimated: Apr 20, 2010, 11:45:19
Hosmer-Lemeshow chi-squared =  13.49219
P-value=  .09600 with deg.fr. =        8
-----------+--------------------------------------------------------------------
Variable| Coefficient    Standard Error  b/St.Er. P[|Z|>z]    Mean of X
-----------+--------------------------------------------------------------------
        |Characteristics in numerator of Prob[Y = 1]
Constant|    1.16828***       .12511      9.338    .0000
RPVARPCT|    -.94686***       .19474     -4.862    .0000       .35627
RPCONGPC|     .35880**        .14562      2.464    .0137       .24711
TRPLNGTH|    -.01854***       .00117    -15.899    .0000      47.2328
  INCOME|    -.00338***       .00105     -3.206    .0013      48.7725
  CHTIME|     .00952***       .00120      7.954    .0000      27.5595
BUSINESS|    -.40478***       .05967     -6.783    .0000       .33333
TOLLREXP|    -.03420**        .01682     -2.033    .0420      3.23810
   NUMIG|    -.07470***       .02674     -2.794    .0052      1.06878
```

Next we added these variables into the base model (as Model 3). The LL improves from −5,428 to −5,331. The extra SQ attributes were highly significant, and the SQ ASC became marginally significant and positive, suggesting that we have accounted for many of the reasons why they do not like the SQ. Similar improvements can be found with attribute non-attendance and is reported below as well (LL from −5265 to −5173).

```
sample;all$
reject;choice1=-999$
nlogit;lhs=choice1,cset3,Alt3
;choices=Cur1,AltA1,AltB1
;checkdata
;model:
U(Cur1)  = Rp1 + ff*ff +sdt*sdt+ VR*var + RC*RC +TC*TC + rpVarPct*rpVarPct +
           rpCongPc*rpCongPc + TrpLngth*TrpLngth + income*income
           + business*business + TollRExp*TollRExp /
U(AltA1) = SP1 + ff*ff +sdt*sdt+ VR*var + RC*RC +TC*TC/
U(AltB1) =       ff*ff +sdt*sdt+ VR*var + RC*RC +TC*TC$
No bad observations were found in the sample
Normal exit:  6 iterations. Status=0. F=   5331.118
----------------------------------------------------------
Discrete choice (multinomial logit) model
Dependent variable              Choice
Log likelihood function    -5331.11780
Estimation based on N =    6048, K =  13
Information Criteria: Normalization=1/N
            Normalized   Unnormalized
AIC             1.76723    10688.23560
Fin.Smpl.AIC    1.76724    10688.29592
```

```
Bayes IC         1.78165     10775.43287
Hannan Quinn     1.77224     10718.50435
Model estimated: Apr 20, 2010, 11:54:50
R2=1-LogL/LogL* Log-L fncn R-sqrd R2Adj
Constants only must be computed directly
                Use NLOGIT ;...; RHS=ONE$
Chi-squared[11]         =   2188.40655
Prob [ chi squared > value ] =   .00000
Response data are given as ind. choices
Number of obs.= 6048, skipped    0 obs
-----------+----------------------------------------------------------
Variable| Coefficient    Standard Error  b/St.Er. P[|Z|>z]
-----------+----------------------------------------------------------
      RP1|    1.18281***        .12313       9.606   .0000
       FF|    -.08501***        .00320     -26.585   .0000
      SDT|    -.09529***        .00623     -15.297   .0000
       VR|    -.00665           .00582      -1.142   .2536
       RC|    -.39061***        .01891     -20.661   .0000
       TC|    -.53475***        .01951     -27.406   .0000
  RPVARPCT|   -1.14221***       .20469      -5.580   .0000
  RPCONGPC|    .68348***        .15862       4.309   .0000
  TRPLNGTH|    -.01073***       .00123      -8.704   .0000
    INCOME|    -.00443***       .00111      -4.005   .0001
  BUSINESS|    -.39997***       .06181      -6.471   .0000
  TOLLREXP|    -.04646***       .01750      -2.654   .0079
      SP1|     .07302*          .03992       1.829   .0674
      SP1|     .07302*          .03992       1.829   .0674
```

In the final model (Model 4) we allowed for ignored attributes (replacing, for example ff with ffi which has ignored attributes recoded as −888).

```
nlogit;lhs=choice1,cset3,Alt3
;choices=Cur1,AltA1,AltB1
;checkdata
;model:
U(Cur1)  = Rp1 + ffi*ffi +sdti*sdti+ VRi*vari + RCi*RCi +TCi*TCi
    + rpVarPct*rpVarPct + rpCongPc*rpCongPc + TrpLngth*TrpLngth + inco-
me*income
    + business*business + TollRExp*TollRExp /
U(AltA1) = SP1 + ffi*ffi +sdti*sdti+ VRi*vari + RCi*RCi +TCi*TCi/
U(AltB1) =       ffi*ffi +sdti*sdti+ VRi*vari + RCi*RCi +TCi*TCi$
No bad observations were found in the sample
+----------------------------------------------------------------------+
| Data Contain Values -888 indicating attributes that |
| were ignored by some individuals in making choices  |
| Coefficients listed multiply these attributes:      |
| Coefficient label.  Number of individuals found     |
|     FFI                       944                    |
|     SDTI                      1504                   |
|     VRI                       2240                   |
```

```
|    RCI                      1120                        |
|    TCI                       656                        |
+--------------------------------------------------------+
Normal exit:   6 iterations. Status=0. F=     5173.796
---------------------------------------------------------
Discrete choice (multinomial logit) model
Dependent variable                   Choice
Log likelihood function      -5173.79563
Estimation based on N =     6048, K =   13
Information Criteria: Normalization=1/N
                Normalized    Unnormalized
AIC                1.71521      10373.59125
Fin.Smpl.AIC       1.71522      10373.65158
Bayes IC           1.72963      10460.78853
Hannan Quinn       1.72021      10403.86000
Model estimated: Apr 20, 2010, 11:58:13
R2=1-LogL/LogL* Log-L fncn R-sqrd R2Adj
Constants only must be computed directly
              Use NLOGIT ;...; RHS=ONE$
Chi-squared[11]           =    2503.05090
Prob [ chi squared > value ] =    .00000
Response data are given as ind. choices
Number of obs.= 6048, skipped    0 obs
-----------+---------------------------------------------
Variable| Coefficient    Standard Error   b/St.Er. P[|Z|>z]
-----------+---------------------------------------------
      RP1|    1.12992***         .12399        9.113   .0000
      FFI|    -.09039***         .00339      -26.645   .0000
     SDTI|    -.10809***         .00692      -15.623   .0000
      VRI|    -.01017            .00686       -1.481   .1387
      RCI|    -.44807***         .02141      -20.930   .0000
      TCI|    -.63032***         .02054      -30.689   .0000
  RPVARPCT|  -1.00122***         .20707       -4.835   .0000
  RPCONGPC|     .46208***        .15852        2.915   .0036
  TRPLNGTH|    -.01111***        .00124       -8.940   .0000
    INCOME|    -.00419***        .00113       -3.717   .0002
  BUSINESS|    -.39950***        .06305       -6.336   .0000
  TOLLREXP|    -.04157**         .01788       -2.325   .0201
      SP1|     .06773*           .04018        1.686   .0918
```

21.9.6 Dimensional versus holistic processing strategies

Another pairwise test could be based on the MCD rule (Russo and Dosher 1983), which is concerned with the total count of superior attributes in each alternative. Under this test, pairs of attributes are compared in turn, with an

Table 21.21 Number of strictly best attributes per alternative

Number of best attributes	Full relevance				Allowing for attribute being ignored			
	All alternatives		Chosen alternative		All alternatives		Chosen alternative	
	Count	Percentage	Count	Percentage	Count	Percentage	Count	Percentage
0	2758	15.20	467	7.72	4703	25.92	871	14.40
1	8245	45.44	2563	42.38	8697	47.93	2950	48.78
2	5482	30.21	2118	35.02	3862	21.29	1707	28.22
3	1382	7.62	709	11.72	777	4.28	439	7.26
4	277	1.53	191	3.16	105	0.58	81	1.34
5	0	0.00	0	0.00	0	0.00	0	0.00
Total	18144	100	6048	100	18144	100	6048	100
Mean		1.35		1.60		1.06		1.32

alternative winning if it has a greater number of better attribute levels. The paired test continues until there is an overall winner. In our case, additionally, it might be that the reference alternative is dropped first, resulting in only a one-pair test.

To test for the MCD heuristic in this data set, a total count of best attributes was generated for each alternative, and then entered into the utility expressions for all three alternatives. To contribute to the count for an alternative, an attribute had to be *strictly better* than that attribute in all other alternatives in the choice set. That is, no ties were allowed.[29] The distribution of the number of best attributes is shown in Table 21.21, both for the full relevance sample and accounting for attributes being ignored, with separate reporting for all alternatives and the chosen alternative only. The distribution for the chosen alternative is skewed towards a higher number of best attributes in both cases, and higher means can also be observed, which is plausible. This alone does not suggest that MCD is being employed, as it would be expected that alternatives with a higher number of best attributes would also tend to have higher relative utilities.

A close inspection shows that the percentage of alternatives with zero strictly best attributes is much higher when allowing for attributes being ignored than in the "full relevance" group (compared to the other rows of evidence). This might suggest that respondents are more likely to ignore an attribute when at least one attribute is outranked. On this evidence, if found true in other data sets, it has important behavioral implications, since the

---

[29] Accounting for ties did not materially affect the findings.

analyst may wish to remove alternatives in model estimation where the number of best attributes is zero.

The model results are reported in Table 21.22, with Model 1 representing the base model, with all attributes assumed to be considered. Model 2 extends this base model, such that both the attribute levels and the number of best attributes impact on representative utility. The latter is highly significant, and positive in sign, so that as the number of best attributes increases, an alternative is more likely to be chosen, as would be expected. Additionally, an improvement in BIC, which accounts for the number of parameter estimates, can be observed.

Model 3 reports a model where only the number of best attributes and the ASCs are included, and the attribute levels are omitted. While the number of best attributes is highly significant, the model fit is considerably worse, suggesting that the number of best attributes cannot substitute for the attribute levels themselves.

The Nlogit set ups for Table 21.22 are given below:

Table 21.22 Influence of majority of confirming dimensions

	Full Relevance			Allowing for attributes being ignored		
	Model 1	Model 2 Base plus # best attributes	Model 3 # best attributes	Model 4	Model 5 Base plus # best attributes	Model 6 # best attributes
	Base			Base		
Reference constant (1,0)	0.0065	−0.0418	0.5228	−0.0417	−0.0797	0.5149
	(0.13)	(−0.84)	(15.96)	(−0.89)	(−1.67)	(15.6)
SC1 constant (1,0)	0.074	0.0862	0.1339	0.0669	0.0821	0.1422
	(1.88)	(2.16)	(3.75)	(1.67)	(2.04)	(3.95)
Free-flow time (min.)	−0.0899	−0.0853		−0.0949	−0.0884	–
	(−28.3)	(−26.0)		(−28.0)	(−24.9)	
Slowed-down time (min.)	−0.0963	−0.0826	–	−0.1146	−0.0983	–
	(−16.1)	(−12.7)		(−16.9)	(−13.4)	
Trip time variability (plus/minus min.)	−0.0177	−0.0053	–	−0.0184	−0.0041	–
	(−3.07)	(−0.85)		(−2.68)	(−0.56)	
Running cost ($)	−0.4147	−0.3871	–	−0.4735	−0.4354	–
	(−22.2)	(−20.1)		(−22.4)	(−19.7)	
Toll cost ($)	−0.5312	−0.5274	–	−0.6271	−0.6123	–
	(−27.5)	(−27.4)		(−31.0)	(−30.2)	
# of attributes in an alternative that are best	–	0.1041	0.3136	–	0.1269	0.4370
		(4.95)	(19.79)		(5.24)	(23.9)

Table 21.22 (cont.)

	Full Relevance			Allowing for attributes being ignored		
	Model 1	Model 2 Base plus # best	Model 3 # best	Model 4	Model 5 Base plus # best	Model 6 # best
	Base	attributes	attributes	Base	attributes	attributes
	VTTS ($/person hr.):					
Free-flow time (based on running cost parameter estimate)	13.01	13.22		12.03	12.18	
Free-flow time (based on toll cost parameter estimate)	10.15	9.70		9.08	8.66	
Slowed-down time (based on running cost parameter estimate)	13.93	12.80		14.52	13.55	
Slowed-down time (based on toll cost parameter estimate)	10.88	9.40		10.96	9.63	
Weighted average VTTS:	*12.48*	*12.20*		*11.85*	*11.58*	
	Number of observations with attribute ignored:					
Free-flow time	–			944		
Slowed-down time	–			1504		
Trip time variability	–			2240		
Running cost	–			1120		
Toll cost	–			656		
Model fit:						
LL at convergence	−5428.17	−5417.55	−6224.89	−5265.81	−5252.05	−6123.98
BIC	1.8051	1.8031	2.0628	1.7514	1.7483	2.0295
Sample size			6048			

```
sample;all$
reject;choice1=-999$
nlogit  ? Model 1
    ;lhs=choice1,cset3,Alt3
    ;choices=Cur1,AltA1,AltB1
    ;checkdata
    ;model:
    U(Cur1)  =  Rp1 + ff*ff +sdt*sdt+ VR*var + RC*RC +TC*TC /
    U(AltA1) = SP1 + ff*ff +sdt*sdt+ VR*var + RC*RC +TC*TC /
    U(AltB1) =       ff*ff +sdt*sdt+ VR*var + RC*RC +TC*TC $
Normal exit:  7 iterations. Status=0. F=    5428.170
```

```
---------------------------------------------------------------------------
Discrete choice (multinomial logit) model
Dependent variable                      Choice
Log likelihood function      -5428.17018
Estimation based on N =      6048, K =    7
Information Criteria: Normalization=1/N
             Normalized    Unnormalized
AIC             1.79734      10870.34036
Fin.Smpl.AIC    1.79735      10870.35890
Bayes IC        1.80511      10917.29274
Hannan Quinn    1.80004      10886.63892
Model estimated: Oct 05, 2010, 14:45:23
R2=1-LogL/LogL* Log-L fncn R-sqrd R2Adj
Constants only must be computed directly
                Use NLOGIT ;...; RHS=ONE$
Chi-squared[ 5]              =    1994.30179
Prob [ chi squared > value ] =    .00000
Response data are given as ind. choices
Number of obs.= 6048, skipped    0 obs
-----------+---------------------------------------------------------
           |                 Standard            Prob.
   CHOICE1 | Coefficient      Error       z     z>|Z|
-----------+---------------------------------------------------------
       RP1 |      .00646      .04836       .13   .8937
        FF |    -.08992***    .00317    -28.34   .0000
       SDT |    -.09629***    .00598    -16.11   .0000
        VR |    -.01774***    .00577     -3.07   .0021
        RC |    -.41466***    .01864    -22.25   .0000
        TC |    -.53116***    .01928    -27.54   .0000
       SP1 |      .07491*     .03979      1.88   .0597
-----------+---------------------------------------------------------
Note: ***, **, * ==>  Significance at 1%, 5%, 10% level.
---------------------------------------------------------------------------
nlogit ? Model 2
    ;lhs=choice1,cset3,Alt3
    ;choices=Cur1,AltA1,AltB1
    ;checkdata
    ;model:
    U(Cur1)  = Rp1 + ff*ff +sdt*sdt+ VR*var + RC*RC +TC*TC +bet*bet/
    U(AltA1) = SP1 + ff*ff +sdt*sdt+ VR*var + RC*RC +TC*TC +bet*bet/
    U(AltB1) =       ff*ff +sdt*sdt+ VR*var + RC*RC +TC*TC +bet*bet$
Normal exit:  6 iterations. Status=0, F=    5417.552
---------------------------------------------------------------------------
Discrete choice (multinomial logit) model
Dependent variable                      Choice
Log likelihood function      -5417.55217
Estimation based on N =      6048, K =    8
Inf.Cr.AIC  =  10851.1 AIC/N =    1.794
R2=1-LogL/LogL* Log-L fncn R-sqrd R2Adj
```

```
Constants only must be computed directly
            Use NLOGIT ;...;RHS=ONE$
Chi-squared[ 6]          =    2015.53780
Prob [ chi squared > value ] =   .00000
Response data are given as ind. choices
Number of obs.= 6048, skipped    0 obs
```

CHOICE1	Coefficient	Standard Error	z	Prob. |z|>Z*	95% Confidence Interval	
RP1	-.04176	.04957	-.84	.3995	-.13891	.05539
FF	-.08531***	.00328	-25.99	.0000	-.09174	-.07888
SDT	-.08263***	.00649	-12.72	.0000	-.09536	-.06990
VR	-.00533	.00627	-.85	.3956	-.01761	.00696
RC	-.38709***	.01930	-20.06	.0000	-.42492	-.34927
TC	-.52735***	.01922	-27.43	.0000	-.56503	-.48968
BET	.10405***	.02103	4.95	.0000	.06284	.14526
SP1	.08621**	.03988	2.16	.0306	.00805	.16438

```
***, **, * ==>  Significance at 1%, 5%, 10% level.
Model was estimated on Jul 18, 2013 at 04:24:12 PM
```

nlogit ? Model 3
```
    ;lhs=choice1,cset3,Alt3
    ;choices=Cur1,AltA1,AltB1
    ;checkdata
    ;model:
    U(Cur1)  = Rp1 + bet*bet/
    U(AltA1) = SP1 + bet*bet/
    U(AltB1) =       bet*bet$
Normal exit:  4 iterations. Status=0, F=    6224.889
```

```
Discrete choice (multinomial logit) model
Dependent variable              Choice
Log likelihood function    -6224.88913
Estimation based on N =   6048, K =   3
Inf.Cr.AIC  =  12455.8 AIC/N =    2.059
R2=1-LogL/LogL* Log-L fncn R-sqrd R2Adj
Constants only must be computed directly
            Use NLOGIT ;...;RHS=ONE$
Chi-squared[ 1]          =    400.86389
Prob [ chi squared > value ] =   .00000
Response data are given as ind. choices
Number of obs.= 6048, skipped    0 obs
```

CHOICE1	Coefficient	Standard Error	z	Prob. |z|>Z*	95% Confidence Interval	
RP1	.52280***	.03276	15.96	.0000	.45859	.58702
BET	.31355***	.01585	19.79	.0000	.28249	.34461

```
     SP1|      .13390***       .03567      3.75   .0002        .06399      .20380
-----------+--------------------------------------------------------------------------
*** , ** , * ==>  Significance at 1%, 5%, 10% level.
Model was estimated on Jul 18, 2013 at 04:27:17 PM
----------------------------------------------------------------------------------------
```

nlogit ? Model 4
```
    ;lhs=choice1,cset3,Alt3
    ;choices=Cur1,AltA1,AltB1
    ;model:
    U(Cur1) =  Rp1 + ff*ffi +sdt*sdti+ VR*vari + RC*RCi +TC*TCi /
    U(AltA1) = SP1 + ff*ffi +sdt*sdti+ VR*vari + RC*RCi +TC*TCi /
    U(AltB1) =        ff*ffi +sdt*sdti+ VR*vari + RC*RCi +TC*TCi $
+------------------------------------------------------------------------+
| Data Contain Values -888 indicating attributes that  |
| were ignored by some individuals in making choices   |
| Coefficients listed multiply these attributes:       |
| Coefficient label.  Number of individuals found      |
|     FF                        944                     |
|     SDT                      1504                     |
|     VR                       2240                     |
|     RC                       1120                     |
|     TC                        656                     |
+------------------------------------------------------------------------+
Normal exit:  6 iterations. Status=0. F=     5265.808
----------------------------------------------------------------
Discrete choice (multinomial logit) model
Dependent variable               Choice
Log likelihood function     -5265.80769
Estimation based on N =   6048, K =    7
Information Criteria: Normalization=1/N
            Normalized    Unnormalized
AIC             1.74365    10545.61539
Fin.Smpl.AIC    1.74366    10545.63393
Bayes IC        1.75142    10592.56777
Hannan Quinn    1.74635    10561.91395
Model estimated: Oct 05, 2010, 14:57:53
R2=1-LogL/LogL* Log-L fncn R-sqrd R2Adj
Constants only must be computed directly
            Use NLOGIT ;...; RHS=ONE$
Chi-squared[ 5]          =    2319.02676
Prob [ chi squared > value ] =    .00000
Response data are given as ind. choices
Number of obs.= 6048, skipped    0 obs
-----------+--------------------------------------------------------------
           |                 Standard            Prob.
   CHOICE1| Coefficient      Error      z     z>|Z|
-----------+--------------------------------------------------------------
      RP1|    -.04170         .04674    -.89   .3723
       FF|    -.09488***      .00338  -28.05   .0000
```

```
       SDT|    -.11458***      .00680   -16.85   .0000
        VR|    -.01841***      .00687    -2.68   .0074
        RC|    -.47348***      .02112   -22.42   .0000
        TC|    -.62708***      .02023   -30.99   .0000
       SP1|     .06694*        .04008     1.67   .0949
-----------+-------------------------------------------------------
Note: ***, **, * ==>  Significance at 1%, 5%, 10% level.
-------------------------------------------------------------------
```

Nlogit ? Model 5
```
    ;lhs=choice1,cset3,Alt3
    ;choices=Cur1,AltA1,AltB1
    ;checkdata
    ;model:
    U(Cur1)  = Rp1 + ffi*ffi +sdti*sdti+ VRi*vari + RCi*RCi +TCi*TCi
+betc*betc/
    U(AltA1) = SP1 + ffi*ffi +sdti*sdti+ VRi*vari + RCi*RCi +TCi*TCi
+betc*betc/
    U(AltB1) =       ffi*ffi +sdti*sdti+ VRi*vari + RCi*RCi +TCi*TCi
+betc*betc$
| Data Contain Values -888 indicating attributes that  |
| were ignored by some individuals in making choices   |
| Coefficients listed multiply these attributes:       |
| Coefficient label.  Number of individuals found      |
|     FFI               944                             |
|     SDTI             1504                             |
|     VRI              2240                             |
|     RCI              1120                             |
|     TCI               656                             |
+------------------------------------------------------------+
Normal exit:  6 iterations. Status=0, F=    5252.050
-------------------------------------------------------------------
Discrete choice (multinomial logit) model
Dependent variable               Choice
Log likelihood function     -5252.04953
Estimation based on N =   6048, K =    8
Inf.Cr.AIC  =  10520.1 AIC/N =    1.739
R2=1-LogL/LogL* Log-L fncn R-sqrd R2Adj
Constants only must be computed directly
            Use NLOGIT ;...;RHS=ONE$
Chi-squared[ 6]          =   2346.54309
Prob [ chi squared > value ] =   .00000
Response data are given as ind. choices
Number of obs.= 6048, skipped    0 obs
```

CHOICE1	Coefficient	Standard Error	z	Prob. |z|>Z*	95% Confidence Interval	
RP1	-.07965*	.04765	-1.67	.0946	-.17305	.01375
FFI	-.08840***	.00356	-24.87	.0000	-.09536	-.08143

```
     SDTI|     -.09825***       .00735    -13.37   .0000    -.11266    -.08384
      VRI|     -.00411          .00734      -.56   .5753    -.01850     .01028
      RCI|     -.43540***       .02205    -19.75   .0000    -.47862    -.39219
      TCI|     -.61227***       .02029    -30.18   .0000    -.65203    -.57251
     BETC|      .12694***       .02421      5.24   .0000     .07949     .17440
      SP1|      .08213**        .04020      2.04   .0410     .00334     .16092
-----------+-----------------------------------------------------------------------
***, **, * ==>  Significance at 1%, 5%, 10% level.
Model was estimated on Jul 18, 2013 at 04:33:26 PM
-----------------------------------------------------------------------------------

Nlogit ? Model 6
     ;lhs=choice1,cset3,Alt3
     ;choices=Cur1,AltA1,AltB1
     ;checkdata
     ;model:
     U(Cur1)  = Rp1 + betc*betc/
     U(AltA1) = SP1 + betc*betc/
     U(AltB1) =       betc*betc$
Normal exit:   4 iterations. Status=0, F=      6123.984
----------------------------------------------------------------------
Discrete choice (multinomial logit) model
Dependent variable              Choice
Log likelihood function     -6123.98369
Estimation based on N =     6048, K =    3
Inf.Cr.AIC  =   12254.0 AIC/N =     2.026
R2=1-LogL/LogL* Log-L fncn R-sqrd R2Adj
Constants only must be computed directly
           Use NLOGIT ;...;RHS=ONE$
Chi-squared[ 1]           =      602.67477
Prob [ chi squared > value ] =    .00000
Response data are given as ind. choices
Number of obs.=  6048, skipped     0 obs
-----------+-----------------------------------------------------------------------
           |                Standard              Prob.       95% Confidence
   CHOICE1| Coefficient      Error       z     |z|>Z*          Interval
-----------+-----------------------------------------------------------------------
      RP1|      .51486***       .03298    15.61   .0000     .45021     .57950
     BETC|      .43697***       .01827    23.91   .0000     .40116     .47279
      SP1|      .14215***       .03598     3.95   .0001     .07162     .21268
-----------+-----------------------------------------------------------------------
***, **, * ==>  Significance at 1%, 5%, 10% level.
Model was estimated on Jul 18, 2013 at 04:44:33 PM
-----------------------------------------------------------------------------------
```

The same tests were performed, after accounting for attributes stated as being ignored (Models 4–6). Any ignored attributes were not included in the count of the number of best attributes. Model 4 of Table 21.23 sets out the base model that accounts for attribute ignoring, which itself fits the data better than when all attributes are assumed to be attended to. Model 5 presents the model that accounts for both heuristics, and Model 6 represents the inclusion of the number of best attributes in the absence of explicit consideration of each attribute, after allowing for attributes that are indicated as ignored. The BIC is improved, at 1.7483 compared to 1.7514 for the base model, with the number of the best attributes parameter being statistically significant and of the expected sign.

We report the weighted average VTTS in Table 21.23 (where the weights are the levels of each attribute, namely free-flow and slowed-down time, and running and toll cost) which, at the mean estimate for the weighted average total time, appear to vary sufficiently between full relevance and allowing for attributes being ignored, but not between models within each of these AP settings when allowance is made for the number of attributes that are best. When confidence intervals are generated using a bootstrapping procedure with 1,000 random draws from normal distributions for relevant parameters, with moments set at their coefficient point estimates and standard errors (Krinsky and Robb 1986 and Chapter 8), we find, as expected, that there are no statistically significant differences between Models 1 and 2 (and between Models 4 and 5); however, the differences are statistically significant at the 95 percent confidence level between the estimates for full relevance and attribute non-attendance.

While Model 2 (Model 5) compared to Model 1 (Model 4) is an improvement on BIC, albeit relatively small, its underlying form suggests that all respondents simultaneously consider and trade between both the attribute levels in a typical compensatory fashion (both under full relevance and after ignoring some attributes if applicable), and the number of best attributes in each alternative. More plausibly, a respondent might resort solely to the MCD heuristic, or refrain from using it entirely. In recognition that there may be two classes of respondent, with heuristic application distinguishing between them, two LCMs[30] were estimated (Table 21.23). Two classes are defined,[31] where the utility expressions in each class are

---

[30] See Hensher and Greene (2010) for other examples of the identification of AP heuristics with the LCM.

[31] We investigated a three-class model in which the additional class was defined by all attributes plus the number of best attributes. The overall fit of the model did not improve and many of the attributes were not statistically significant. We also estimated a three-class model with class-specific parameter estimates for attributes included in more than one class, but many parameters were not statistically significant. A further model allowing for random parameters was investigated but did not improve on the two-class model reported in Table 21.23.

Table 21.23 Identifying role of MCD: latent class model

	Full Relevance	Allowing for attributes being ignored
Class 1		
Reference constant (1,0)	−0.4207 (−0.67)	−0.0676 (−1.06)
SC1 constant (1,0)	0.0674 (1.27)	0.0852 (1.51)
Free-flow time (min.)	−0.1234 (−16.52)	−0.1448 (−16.6)
Slowed-down time (min.)	−0.1192 (−11.37)	−0.1676 (−12.1)
Trip time variability (plus/minus min.)	−0.0145 (−1.83)	−0.0116 (−1.18)
Running cost ($)	−0.5467 (−15.04)	−0.6980 (−14.9)
Toll cost ($)	−0.7159 (−12.92)	−0.9038 (−18.0)
Class 2		
# of attributes in an alternative that are best	0.2856 (2.76)	0.2665 (3.06)
Probability of class membership:		
Class 1	0.8465 (6.25)	0.8206 (9.58)
Class 2	0.1535 (6.35)	0.1794 (8.17)
VTTS ($/person hour):		
Free-flow time (based on running cost parameter estimate)	13.54	12.45
Free-flow time (based on toll cost parameter estimate)	10.34	9.61
Slowed-down time (based on running cost parameter estimate)	13.08	14.41
Slowed-down time (based on toll cost parameter estimate)	9.99	11.13
Weighted average VTTS:	*12.60*	*12.17*
Number of observations with attribute ignored:		
Free-flow time (min.)	–	944
Slowed-down time (min.)	–	1504
Trip time variability (plus/minus min.)	–	2240
Running cost ($)	–	1120
Toll cost ($)	–	656
Model fit:		
BIC	1.7795	1.7287
LL at convergence	−5402.47	−5218.52
Sample size	6048	

constrained to represent one of the two heuristics. The first class contains the attribute levels and ASCs, as per the base model, while the second class contains only the number of best attributes. A further improvement in model fit is obtained with this model, with the BIC under full attribute relevance (and accounting for ignored attributes) improving from 1.8051 (1.7514) for the base model, to 1.8031 (1.7483) for the single class model that contains both the levels and the number of best attributes, to 1.7795 (1.7287) for the LCM. Again, the number of best attributes parameter is statistically significant and of the expected sign.

The command set up for Table 21.23 is given below:

```
nlogit  ?Full Relevance
    ;lhs=choice1,cset3,Alt3
    ;choices=Cur1,AltA1,AltB1
    ;checkdata
    ;lcm
    ;pts=2
    ;model:
    U(Cur1)  = Rp1 + ff*ff +sdt*sdt+ VR*var + RC*RC +TC*TC +bestt*bestt/
    U(AltA1) = SP1 + ff*ff +sdt*sdt+ VR*var + RC*RC +TC*TC +bestt*bestt/
    U(AltB1) =       ff*ff +sdt*sdt+ VR*var + RC*RC +TC*TC +bestt*bestt
    ;rst=
    b1,b2,b3,b4,b5,b6,0,sp1,        ? best #
    0,0,0,0,0,0,b7,0$               ? all attributes
Normal exit:  6 iterations. Status=0, F=    5429.803
---------------------------------------------------------------------
Discrete choice (multinomial logit) model
Dependent variable              Choice
Log likelihood function    -5429.80334
Estimation based on N =   6048, K =   7
Inf.Cr.AIC  =  10873.6 AIC/N =    1.798
R2=1-LogL/LogL* Log-L fncn R-sqrd R2Adj
Constants only must be computed directly
            Use NLOGIT ;...;RHS=ONE$
Chi-squared[ 6]        =   1991.03546
Prob [ chi squared > value ] =   .00000
Response data are given as ind. choices
Number of obs.= 6048, skipped    0 obs
```

CHOICE1	Coefficient	Standard Error	z	Prob. |z|>Z*	95% Confidence Interval	
RP1|1	.00638	.04836	.13	.8950	-.08840	.10117
FF|1	-.08988***	.00318	-28.30	.0000	-.09610	-.08365
SDT|1	-.09630***	.00598	-16.11	.0000	-.10802	-.08459
VR|1	-.01772***	.00578	-3.07	.0022	-.02904	-.00640
RC|1	-.41449***	.01865	-22.22	.0000	-.45105	-.37793
TC|1	-.53108***	.01929	-27.54	.0000	-.56888	-.49328
BESTT|1	0.0	.....(Fixed Parameter).....				

```
   SP1|1|      .07487*       .03979     1.88  .0598    -.00310     .15285
-----------+----------------------------------------------------------------------
***, **, * ==>  Significance at 1%, 5%, 10% level.
Fixed parameter ... is constrained to equal the value or
had a nonpositive st.error because of an earlier problem.
Model was estimated on Jul 18, 2013 at 04:29:07 PM
----------------------------------------------------------------------------------
Line search at iteration   21 does not improve fn. Exiting optimization.
----------------------------------------------------------------------------------
Latent Class Logit Model
Dependent variable               CHOICE1
Log likelihood function      -5402.47428
Restricted log likelihood    -6644.40712
Chi squared [  9](P= .000)    2483.86568
Significance level               .00000
McFadden Pseudo R-squared       .1869140
Estimation based on N =   6048, K =    9
Inf.Cr.AIC   =  10822.9 AIC/N =    1.790
Constants only must be computed directly
             Use NLOGIT ;...;RHS=ONE$
At start values -5771.1842  .0639******
Response data are given as ind. choices
Number of latent classes =            2
Average Class Probabilities
     .847   .153
Number of obs.=  6048, skipped    0 obs
-----------+----------------------------------------------------------------------
           |                  Standard          Prob.       95% Confidence
   CHOICE1| Coefficient        Error      z    |z|>Z*        Interval
-----------+----------------------------------------------------------------------
           |Random B_BESTT parameters in latent class -->>  1
   RP1|1|     -.04207         .06273    -.67   .5024    -.16503     .08088
    FF|1|     -.12341***      .00747  -16.52   .0000    -.13805    -.10877
   SDT|1|     -.11920***      .01048  -11.37   .0000    -.13974    -.09866
    VR|1|     -.01447*        .00789   -1.83   .0666    -.02993     .00099
    RC|1|     -.54671***      .03635  -15.04   .0000    -.61796    -.47546
    TC|1|     -.71594***      .04232  -16.92   .0000    -.79890    -.63299
 BESTT|1|      0.0     .....(Fixed Parameter).....
   SP1|1|      .06742         .05296    1.27   .2030    -.03639     .17123
           |Random B_BESTT parameters in latent class -->>  2
   RP1|2|      0.0     .....(Fixed Parameter).....
    FF|2|      0.0     .....(Fixed Parameter).....
   SDT|2|      0.0     .....(Fixed Parameter).....
    VR|2|      0.0     .....(Fixed Parameter).....
    RC|2|      0.0     .....(Fixed Parameter).....
    TC|2|      0.0     .....(Fixed Parameter).....
 BESTT|2|      .28569***      .10366    2.76   .0058     .08253     .48885
   SP1|2|      0.0     .....(Fixed Parameter).....
           |Estimated latent class probabilities
```

```
  PrbCls1|     .84650***      .02416     35.03   .0000      .79914    .89386
  PrbCls2|     .15350***      .02416      6.35   .0000      .10614    .20086
-----------+--------------------------------------------------------------------
***, **, * ==>  Significance at 1%, 5%, 10% level.
Fixed parameter ... is constrained to equal the value or
had a nonpositive st.error because of an earlier problem.
Model was estimated on Jul 18, 2013 at 04:29:23 PM
```
Nlogit ? Allowing for Attributes Being Ignored
```
    ;lhs=choice1,cset3,Alt3
    ;choices=Cur1,AltA1,AltB1
    ;checkdata
    ;lcm
    ;pts=2
    ;model:
    U(Cur1)   = Rp1 + ffi*ffi +sdti*sdti+ VRi*vari + RCi*RCi +TCi*TCi
+besttc*besttc/
    U(AltA1) = SP1 + ffi*ffi +sdti*sdti+ VRi*vari + RCi*RCi +TCi*TCi
+besttc*besttc/
    U(AltB1) =         ffi*ffi +sdti*sdti+ VRi*vari + RCi*RCi +TCi*TCi
+besttc*besttc
    ;rst=
    b1,b2,b3,b4,b5,b6,0,sp1,          ? best #
    0,0,0,0,0,0,b7,0$                 ? all attributes
+--------------------------------------------------------------------+
| Data Contain Values -888 indicating attributes that                |
| were ignored by some individuals in making choices                 |
| Coefficients listed multiply these attributes:                     |
| Coefficient label.  Number of individuals found                    |
|     FFI   |1                 944                                   |
|     SDTI  |1                1504                                   |
|     VRI   |1                2240                                   |
|     RCI   |1                1120                                   |
|     TCI   |1                 656                                   |
+--------------------------------------------------------------------+
Normal exit:   6 iterations. Status=0, F=    5265.808
--------------------------------------------------------------------------
Discrete choice (multinomial logit) model
Dependent variable               Choice
Log likelihood function     -5265.80769
Estimation based on N =    6048, K =    7
Inf.Cr.AIC  =  10545.6 AIC/N =    1.744
R2=1-LogL/LogL* Log-L fncn R-sqrd R2Adj
Constants only must be computed directly
            Use NLOGIT ;...;RHS=ONE$
Chi-squared[ 6]            =    2319.02676
Prob [ chi squared > value ] =    .00000
Response data are given as ind. choices
Number of obs.= 6048, skipped    0 obs
-----------+--------------------------------------------------------------------
```

CHOICE1	Coefficient	Standard Error	z	Prob. |z|>Z*	95% Confidence Interval	
RP1|1	-.04170	.04674	-.89	.3723	-.13331	.04990
FFI|1	-.09488***	.00338	-28.05	.0000	-.10151	-.08825
SDTI|1	-.11458***	.00680	-16.85	.0000	-.12791	-.10126
VRI|1	-.01841***	.00687	-2.68	.0074	-.03188	-.00494
RCI|1	-.47348***	.02112	-22.42	.0000	-.51488	-.43208
TCI|1	-.62708***	.02023	-30.99	.0000	-.66674	-.58742
BESTTC|1	0.0	.....(Fixed Parameter).....				
SP1|1	.06694*	.04008	1.67	.0949	-.01161	.14549

***, **, * ==> Significance at 1%, 5%, 10% level.
Fixed parameter ... is constrained to equal the value or
had a nonpositive st.error because of an earlier problem.
Model was estimated on Jul 18, 2013 at 04:35:50 PM

Line search at iteration   20 does not improve fn. Exiting optimization.

Latent Class Logit Model
Dependent variable   CHOICE1
Log likelihood function   -5218.51914
Restricted log likelihood   -6644.40712
Chi squared [9](P= .000)   2851.77597
Significance level   .00000
McFadden Pseudo R-squared   .2145997
Estimation based on N =   6048, K =   9
Inf.Cr.AIC = 10455.0 AIC/N =   1.729
Constants only must be computed directly
          Use NLOGIT ;...;RHS=ONE$
At start values -5652.9201 .0768******
Response data are given as ind. choices
Number of latent classes =   2
Average Class Probabilities
     .821   .179
Number of obs.= 6048, skipped   0 obs

CHOICE1	Coefficient	Standard Error	z	Prob. |z|>Z*	95% Confidence Interval	
	Random B_BESTT parameters in latent class -->> 1					
RP1|1	-.06761	.06370	-1.06	.2885	-.19245	.05724
FFI|1	-.14483***	.00873	-16.59	.0000	-.16194	-.12773
SDTI|1	-.16764***	.01387	-12.09	.0000	-.19483	-.14046
VRI|1	-.01157	.00979	-1.18	.2370	-.03076	.00761
RCI|1	-.69801***	.04691	-14.88	.0000	-.78995	-.60607
TCI|1	-.90377***	.05018	-18.01	.0000	-1.00212	-.80541
BESTTC|1	0.0	.....(Fixed Parameter).....				
SP1|1	.08521	.05658	1.51	.1321	-.02569	.19612

```
          |Random B_BESTT parameters in latent class -->>   2
    RP1|2|          0.0     .....(Fixed Parameter).....
    FFI|2|          0.0     .....(Fixed Parameter).....
   SDTI|2|          0.0     .....(Fixed Parameter).....
    VRI|2|          0.0     .....(Fixed Parameter).....
    RCI|2|          0.0     .....(Fixed Parameter).....
    TCI|2|          0.0     .....(Fixed Parameter).....
 BESTTC|2|      .26653***        .08700     3.06   .0022        .09602      .43704
    SP1|2|          0.0     .....(Fixed Parameter).....
          |Estimated latent class probabilities
 PrbCls1|       .82061***        .02197    37.36   .0000        .77755      .86366
 PrbCls2|       .17939***        .02197     8.17   .0000        .13634      .22245
-----------+--------------------------------------------------------------------------------
***, **, * ==>  Significance at 1%, 5%, 10% level.
Fixed parameter ... is constrained to equal the value or
had a nonpositive st.error because of an earlier problem.
Model was estimated on Jul 18, 2013 at 04:36:06 PM
```

These results suggest that some respondents are employing the MCD heuristic. Under the heuristic, trading is not occurring on the absolute attribute levels. What matters instead is which alternative has the *best* level for each attribute, where tallies of the number of best attributes appear to act as a supplementary step when determining the best alternative. Overall, the mean probability of class membership of each class in both models is over 80 percent for processing of the constituent attributes and between 15 and 18 percent for the number of attributes being the determining influence.

The implication is that the application of the choice model must recognize that the trading among the attributes occurs up to a probability of 85 percent (or 82 percent when accounting for ignoring) on average, with the number of best attribute levels having an influence up to a probability of 15 percent (or 18 percent) on average. This is an important finding that downplays the contribution of the marginal disutility of each attribute in the presence of the overall number of preferred attribute levels associated with an alternative. When we compare the mean estimates of VTTS for Model 2 (and Model 5) in Table 21.22 with the LCMs (Table 21.23), the mean estimates are, respectively, $12.20 and $12.60 for full relevance and $11.58 and $12.17 when attributes are ignored. The latent class mean estimates have moved closer to the mean estimates in Table 21.22 when we do not include allowance for the number of best attributes (i.e., Model 1 and 4 in Table 21.23 of $12.48 and $11.85, respectively). If the contrast is with the base models in Table 21.22, we would conclude that the VTTS estimates are not statistically significant in the presence and absence of accounting for the MCD rule; however, differences are significant when allowing for attributes to be ignored. This finding supports the evidence in studies undertaken by Hensher and his colleagues (see Hensher 2010) that allowing for attribute non-attendance has a statistically significant influence on the mean estimates of VTTS.

21.9.7 Influence of the relative attribute levels

Another test relates to the relationship between the level of an attribute associated with the reference alternative and each of the other alternatives (Ref-SC1, Ref-SC2). We distinguished between differences where a reference alternative attribute level was better, equal, and worse relative to SC1 and SC2, defined as a series of attribute specific dummy variables (e.g., free-flow time (FFT) better = 1 if reference FFT minus SC1 FFT is negative and equal to zero if reference FFT minus SC1 FFT is positive). The choice response variable refers to the alternative chosen. A simple logit model was specified in which we included the better and worse attribute forms for all five design attributes (eliminating "worse" for toll cost only because there were no observations). The model is summarized in Table 21.24. Interpreting the parameter estimates is tricky. Where an attribute refers to a better level for the reference alternative (the difference for all attributes being negative on the attribute

Table 21.24 Influence of referencing on choice response
6048 observations

Attributes defined as reference minus SC1 or minus SC2	Percent of data	Parameter estimates
Free-flow time better	37.7	0.0915 (12.1)
Free-flow time worse	62.3	0.0647 (7.45)
Slowed-down time better	47.8	0.0860 (5.25)
Slowed-down time worse	52.2	0.0770 (10.9)
Variability in time better	40.5	−0.0347 (−1.89)
Variability in time worse	59.5	0.0215 (1.84)
Running cost better	38.8	0.3090 (4.72)
Running cost worse	61.2	0.4996 (9.69)
Toll cost better	100	0.6336 (30.4)
Toll cost worse	0	–
SC alternative 2 dummy (1,2)	–	0.1186 (2.96)
LL at convergence		−3118.56

difference, as illustrated above for FFT), a positive parameter estimate suggests that when the difference narrows towards zero, making the reference alternative relatively less attractive on that attribute, the probability of choosing a non-reference alternative (SC1 or SC2) increases. The parameter estimate is positive for "better" except for trip time variability, producing the opposite behavioral response, which seems counterintuitive (although marginally significant). The opposite behavioral response is found when the reference alternative is worse; all parameter estimates are positive, suggesting that when the reference alternative becomes relatively less attractive (given it is worse), the probability of choosing SC1 or SC2 increases.

An example set up for Table 21.24 is:

```
sample;all$
reject;choice2=-999$
reject;alt3=1$
nlogit
    ;lhs=choice2,cset2,Alt2a
    ;choices=AltA1,AltB1
    ;checkdata
    ;model:
    U(AltA1) = SP2 + brefffb*refffb+brefsdtb*refsdtb+
    brefvarb*refvarb+brefrcb*refrcb +breftcb*reftcb
    + brefffw*refffw+brefsdtw*refsdtw+
    brefvarw*refvarw+brefrcw*refrcw/?+breftcw*reftcw/
    U(AltB1) =         brefffb*refffb+brefsdtw*refsdtb+
    brefvarb*refvarb+brefrcb*refrcb +breftcb*reftcb
    +brefffw*refffw+brefsdtw*refsdtw+
    brefvarw*refvarw+brefrcw*refrcw$+breftcw*reftcw$
```

21.9.8 Revision of the reference alternative as value learning

DeShazo (2002) suggested the idea of *reference point revision* in which preferences may be well formed, but respondents' value functions shift when a non-status quo option is chosen (see also McNair *et al.* 2010). The shift occurs because the selection of a non-status quo option is viewed as a transaction up to a probability, and this causes a revision of the reference point around which the asymmetric value function predicted by prospect theory is centered (Kahneman and Tversky 1979). There is an important distinction to be made between value learning, which in its broadest meaning implies that underlying preferences are changing, and reference revision, which can occur when preferences are stable but the objective is to maximize the likelihood of

Table 21.25 Identifying the role of value learning
Note: Choice set 1 is removed

	Full relevance
Revised reference (1,0) (which can be any of the three alternatives)	0.9358 (15.73)
Free-flow time (min.)	−0.01033 (−52.3)
Slowed-down time (min.)	−0.0972 (−17.4)
Trip time variability (plus/minus min.)	−0.0178 (−2.96)
Running cost ($)	−0.4810 (−36.8)
Toll cost ($)	−0.6163 (−43.2)
BIC	1.7637
LL at convergence	−5027.00
Sample size	5730

implementation of the most preferred alternative observed *over the course of the sequence of questions*. The latter is a special case of the former. We focus on value learning.

We ran a model in which we identified the chosen alternative from a previous choice set, and created a dummy variable equal to 1 associated with whatever alternative was chosen in the previous choice set, be it the initial reference alternative or one of the offered non-status quo alternatives (namely alternatives two or three). We then introduced into the utility expressions the revised reference dummy variable as a way of investigating the role of value learning. We found (see Table 21.25) a mean estimate of 0.9358 (*t*-ratio of 15.73) for this variable, which suggests that when the reference alternative is revised, in the next choice scenario it increases the utility of the new "reference" alternative. This is an important finding, supporting the hypothesis of DeShazo; it is also recognition of sequential interdependence between adjacent choice scenarios, which should be treated explicitly rather than only through a correlated error variance specification, where the latter captures many unobserved effects at the alternative level.

An example set up for Table 21.25 is:

```
sample;all$
reject;choice1=-999$
reject;shownum=1$
nlogit
    ;lhs=choice1,cset3,Alt3
    ;choices=Cur1,AltA1,AltB1
    ;checkdata
    ;model:
    U(Cur1)   =  ff*ff +sdt*sdt+ VR*var + RC*RC +TC*TC/
```

```
U(AltA1) =    newref*newrefa + ff*ff +sdt*sdt+ VR*var + RC*RC +TC*TC/
U(AltB1) =    newref*newrefa+   ff*ff +sdt*sdt+ VR*var + RC*RC +TC*TC$
```

21.9.9 A revised model for future stated choice model estimation

We present a model below as a contrast to the base model (Table 21.22, Models 2 and 5), where we include value learning, the MCD, and attribute non-attendance. This model captures a main contribution of this chapter. Accommodating value learning through reference revision involves treating the first choice set differently; to allow for this, we introduce a dummy variable for the initial reference alternative for choice set one only. We also include design and contextual variables that are correlates, to some degree, with the presence of non-trading in terms of always selecting the existing (i.e., non-revised) reference alternative across all 16 choice sets, or selection of the existing reference alternative in a specific choice set (Table 21.26).

Table 21.26 Revised full model for future applications

	Ignored attributes
Trip length (km)	−0.0098 (−7.54)
Personal gross income ($000s)	−0.0077 (−7.46)
Business trip (compared to commuting and non-commuting)	−0.3490 (−5.27)
Existing reference alternative time variability as percentage of worst time	−0.8548 (−3.91)
Percentage of total trip time in slowed-down conditions	0.5703 (3.40)
Amount of recent experience on toll roads (0–6)	−0.0304 (−1.61)
Free-flow time (min.)	−0.0909 (−23.6)
Slowed-down time (min.)	−0.0938 (−12.04)
Trip time variability (plus/minus min.)	0.0103 (1.34)
Running cost ($)	−0.4539 (−19.0)
Toll cost ($)	−0.6414 (−29.4)
# of attributes in an alternative that are best	**0.2646 (10.0)**
Value learning reference revision (1,0) which may be the original reference alternative	**0.8843 (13.8)**
Initial choice set reference dummy (1,0) for choice set 1	**1.1442 (8.99)**
BIC	1.6092
LL at convergence	−4600.45
Sample size	5793

Table 21.26 (cont.)

	Ignored attributes
Mean VTTS ($/person hr.):	
Free-flow time (based on running cost parameter estimate)	12.02
Free-flow time (based on toll cost parameter estimate)	8.50
Slowed-down time (based on running cost parameter estimate)	12.40
Slowed-down time (based on toll cost parameter estimate)	8.77
Weighted average VTTS:	11.19

The weighted mean estimate of value of travel time savings in Table 21.26 is $11.19 per person hr. This estimate can be contrasted with the findings of the "base" model (reported in Table 21.22) which only included the design attributes and constants for the existing reference alternative (without value learning), namely $12.48 under full attribute reference, or $11.85 when we allowed for attributes being ignored. At the 95 percent level of confidence, the weighted mean estimate of VTTS is significantly different and lower. The Nlogit model command for Table 21.26 (using all the create commands listed under Table 21.16) is:

```
dstata;rhs=newref,newrefa,refl,sc11,sc21$
Descriptive Statistics
All results based on nonmissing observations.
==========================================================================
Variable     Mean        Std.Dev.   Minimum    Maximum    Cases Missing
==========================================================================
All observations in current sample
--------+-----------------------------------------------------------------
 NEWREF|   .152686      .359695     .000000    1.00000    18240        0
NEWREFA|   .963268E-01  .295047     .000000    1.00000    18240        0
   REFL|   .152712      .359719     .000000    1.00000    18237        3
   SC1L|   .963426E-01  .295069     .000000    1.00000    18237        3
   SC2L|   .963426E-01  .295069     .000000    1.00000    18237        3
reject;choice1=-999$
reject;ratig=0$
nlogit
   ;lhs=choice1,cset3,Alt3
   ;choices=Cur1,AltA1,AltB1
   ;checkdata
   ;model:
   U(Cur1)  = refcs1+
   ffi*ffi +sdti*sdti+ VRi*vari + RCi*RCi +TCi*TCi
 + rpVarPct*rpVarPct + rpCongPc*rpCongPc + TrpLngth*TrpLngth + income*income
 + business*business + TollRExp*TollRExp +betc*betc/?+numig*numig/
```

```
    U(AltA1) = newref*newrefa  + ffi*ffi +sdti*sdti+ VRi*vari + RCi*RCi
    +TCi*TCi+betc*betc/
    U(AltB1) =  newref*newrefa  +  ffi*ffi +sdti*sdti+ VRi*vari + RCi*RCi
    +TCi*TCi+betc*betc$
+------------------------------------------------------------------------+
| Inspecting the data set before estimation.                             |
| These errors mark observations which will be skipped.                  |
| Row Individual = 1st row then group number of data block               |
+------------------------------------------------------------------------+
No bad observations were found in the sample
+------------------------------------------------------------------------+
| Data Contain Values -888 indicating attributes that                    |
| were ignored by some individuals in making choices                     |
| Coefficients listed multiply these attributes:                         |
| Coefficient label.  Number of individuals found                        |
|     FFI                         837                                    |
|     SDTI                       1370                                    |
|     VRI                        2113                                    |
|     RCI                         986                                    |
|     TCI                         546                                    |
|     INCOME                      648                                    |
+------------------------------------------------------------------------+
Normal exit:   6 iterations. Status=0. F=    4600.456
--------------------------------------------------------------------------
Discrete choice (multinomial logit) model
Dependent variable                   Choice
Log likelihood function      -4600.45626
Estimation based on N =    5793, K =   14
Information Criteria: Normalization=1/N
                Normalized   Unnormalized
AIC               1.59311       9228.91253
Fin.Smpl.AIC      1.59313       9228.98522
Bayes IC          1.60922       9322.21420
Hannan Quinn      1.59872       9261.37078
Model estimated: Apr 26, 2010, 07:13:05
R2=1-LogL/LogL* Log-L fncn R-sqrd R2Adj
Constants only must be computed directly
                Use NLOGIT ;...; RHS=ONE$
Response data are given as ind. choices
Number of obs.= 5793, skipped    0 obs
-----------+--------------------------------------------------------------
           |                    Standard               Prob.
    CHOICE1| Coefficient         Error        z      z>|Z|
-----------+--------------------------------------------------------------
    REFCS1|      1.14424***        .12734      8.99    .0000
      FFI|      -.09097***        .00385    -23.64    .0000
     SDTI|      -.09383***        .00779    -12.04    .0000
      VRI|       .01030           .00770      1.34    .1810
      RCI|      -.45386***        .02385    -19.03    .0000
```

TCI	-.64138***	.02183	-29.38	.0000
RPVARPCT	-.85483***	.21857	-3.91	.0001
RPCONGPC	.57034***	.16753	3.40	.0007
TRPLNGTH	-.00982***	.00130	-7.54	.0000
INCOME	-.00772***	.00104	-7.46	.0000
BUSINESS	-.34901***	.06629	-5.27	.0000
TOLLREXP	-.03038	.01887	-1.61	.1074
BETC	.26464***	.02635	10.04	.0000
NEWREF	.88427***	.06403	13.81	.0000

```
----------- +-----------------------------------------------------------
Note: ***, **, * ==>  Significance at 1%, 5%, 10% level.
-----------------------------------------------------------------------
```

21.9.10 Conclusions

What does this evidence suggest for moving forward in the use of CE data? We have identified a number of features of the choosing process that are associated with the design of the CE, and the characteristics of respondents, that influence the SC outcome. Some very specific heuristics appear to have some systematic influence on choice, in particular the number of attributes that offer the best levels for an alternative, and the revision of the reference alternative as a result of value learning, reflected in a previous choice in the choice set sequence. Building both of these features into the estimated choice model seems to be a useful step forward in recognition of process rule heterogeneity. We also believe that the simple "plausible choice" test proposed here for the entire choice set, and for pairwise alternatives, at the observation and respondent levels, is a useful tool in eliminating data, if required, that has individuals choosing an alternative that has no single attribute that is better.

Another avenue for reconciling seemingly implausible choice behavior stems from the recognition that the choice might be plausible when a decision or process rule is employed by the decision maker. We have handled several decision rules in our analysis, namely the treatment of attributes the respondent claimed not to have considered, the application of the MCD heuristic, and revision of the reference alternative as value learning. However, other processes might be employed by the respondents that are not consistent with utility maximization. For example, Gilbride and Allenby (2004) estimated a choice model that handled conjunctive and disjunctive screening rules, with choice treated as a compensatory process on the remaining alternatives. Here, a choice task that appears implausible might pass the plausibility test after some alternatives have been eliminated in the screening stage. Swait (2009) allowed the unobserved utility of the choice alternatives to be in one of several discrete states. One of the states allowed conventional utility maximization, while other states led to "alternative rejection" and "alternative dominance." Again, plausibility might prevail once the process rule is employed: in this case, once rejection and dominance has been taken into account. We propose that one way to assess these, and other new model forms, is to determine how well they can explain decisions that appear implausible when viewed through the conventional prism of utility maximization.

Of interest to the analyst are possible ways in which implausible behavior can be minimized in an SC environment. In our data, there appeared to be no link between the task order number and the rate of implausible behavior, which suggested that the number of choice tasks might not have an impact, within reasonable limits. Choice task complexity (as defined by dimensions such as number of alternatives, attributes, and attribute levels) was not varied in this analysis; however, the impact of task complexity on implausible behavior would be an interesting area of research. Also of interest is the plausibility of choice in market conditions, which may be impacted by habit, mood, time pressure, and ease with which information can be compared. We anticipate that these influences would lead to a decrease in plausibility of choice, either through an increase in errors, or an increase in use of decision rules and heuristics. If the aim of a SC task is to successfully predict market choices, encouraging plausible choice in the SC environment might not actually be the best way forward. Survey realism might instead be more important.

This section will hopefully engender an interest in further inquiry into the underlying sources of process heterogeneity that should be captured explicitly in the formulation of the utility expressions that represent the preference domain of each respondent for each alternative. Including additional attribute and AP-related explanatory variables appears to provide plausible explanations of utility maximizing behavior in choice making. Testing of the ideas presented on other data sets will enable us to establish the portability of the evidence.

21.10 The role of multiple heuristics in representing attribute processing as a way of conditioning modal choices

So far, we have introduced a large number of potentially relevant heuristics that can be embedded into a choice model. These include the MCD heuristic, which in the local choice set can be modeled as the number of "best" attributes that an alternative possesses, and a heuristic linked to reference point revision, which occurs when a non-status quo alternative is chosen in the preceding choice set.

It may make more sense to consider more than one process heuristic applying to one or more attributes. That is, an alternative approach to identifying and weighting multiple heuristics in a utility function by means of a logit-type specification for the weights of the heuristics is also appealing. We now introduce a mixed heuristics model, illustrating its merit in the context of a mode choice study.

If it is believed that there is heterogeneity in decision processes, i.e., different respondents use different heuristics (and the possibility that the same individual uses different heuristics for different attributes within and between alternatives and choice sets), one popular approach is to appeal to probabilistic decision process models (which are essentially latent class structures as discussed in Section 21.9.6) where the functional form of the heuristic under consideration is expressed through the utility expressions in each class (Hensher and Collins 2011; McNair *et al.* 2011, 2012; Hess *et al.* 2012). Typically, each class represents one heuristic, which means that each respondent is assumed to be relying only on one heuristic. However, what that heuristic (i.e., class membership) might be for each individual can only be known up to a probability.

An alternative to the LCM approach is to weight each heuristic directly in the utility function. Within the utility function, this approach allocates the proportional contribution of each heuristic to overall utility, with the possibility of linking this share outcome to the characteristics of respondents and other possible contextual influences. In a model with a total of H heuristics, the weights of each heuristic, denoted by W_h, $h=1,2,\ldots,H$ can be given by means of a logistic function shown in Equation (21.45):

$$W_h = \frac{\exp\left(\sum_l \gamma_{lh} Z_l\right)}{\sum_{h=1}^{H} \exp\left(\sum_l \gamma_{lh} Z_l\right)}. \tag{21.45}$$

Z_l denotes the value of variable l which is typically a socio-economic or context characteristic. γ_{lh} is a parameter weight that is allowed to vary according to each of the l variables and each of the m heuristics. To ensure identification of the model, it will be necessary to normalize, for every variable l, one γ_{lh}.

As an illustration of this approach, we explore a "mixture" of the linear in the parameters and linear in the attributes (LPLA) standard fully compensatory decision rule and the **non-linear worst level referencing** (NLWLR)[32] heuristic. This example is very much in the spirit of Tversky and Simonson's (1993) componental contextual model, where utility comprises a context independent effect (in this case LPLA) and a context dependent effect (in this case NLWLR). For this model, define the LPLA and NLWLR specifications (respectively as H_1 and H_2) as illustrated in Equation (21.46). For ease of illustrating this multiple heuristics approach, the utility function for each alternative is defined by only two attributes, which are the trip cost (*cost*), defined as the fare in the case of a public transport option, and the sum of running cost, toll cost, and parking cost in the case of the car option and the travel time (*TT*):

$$H_1 = -\beta_1 cost_j - \beta_2 TT_j \text{ and}$$
$$H_2 = (\beta_1 cost_{max} - \beta_1 cost_j)^{\varphi_1} + (\beta_2 TT_{max} - \beta_2 TT_j)^{\varphi_2}. \tag{21.46}$$

In the NLWLR model, respondents are assumed to make reference to the worst attribute level of each choice set. This reference may be defined as the maximum of each of the *cost* and *TT* attributes in the choice set, since higher levels of *cost* and *TT* give rise to greater disutility. Moreover, as $cost_{max}$ and TT_{max} precede the minus sign, the prior expectation is for $\hat{\beta}_k$ to be positive. If the NLWLR model is a better representation of choice behavior, then the power parameter, φ_k, is expected to satisfy the inequality $0 < \varphi_k < 1$. This arises from one of the predictions of prospect theory, which suggests that gains in utility, relative to the reference, are best represented by a concave function.

For this example, the full data set is used. A choice set in the data may comprise up to five alternatives. The utility functions for these alternatives can be written in the form of Equation (21.47):

$$U_{bus} = \beta_{0,bus} + H_2 + \varepsilon_0$$
$$U_{train} = \beta_{0,train} + W_1 H_1 + W_2 H_2 + \varepsilon_1$$
$$U_{metro} = \beta_{0,metro} + W_1 H_1 + W_2 H_2 + \varepsilon_2 \tag{21.47}$$
$$U_{other} = H_2 + \varepsilon_3$$
$$U_{taxi} = \beta_{0,taxi} + H_2 + \varepsilon_4.$$

---

[32] This model was first introduced as a contextual concavity model by Kivetz *et al.* (2004), who use it to model a specific phenomenon known as extremeness aversion. They make the prior assumption that relative to the worst performing attribute, utility is concave in the gains. This assumption is empirically testable, and we find that it does not always hold (see Leong and Hensher 2012). Hence, it may be more useful to label such a functional specification as a "non-linear worst level referencing" (NLWLR) model instead.

In a labeled experiment, there is potential for allowing some heterogeneity in decision rules across alternatives. In Equation (21.47) therefore, we have allowed the train and the metro equations to be some combination of the LPLA and NLWLR rules. The justification for this assumption might be to appeal to the observation that the train and the proposed metro share similar characteristics, hence perhaps similar decision rules might be applied for these two alternatives. At the same time, the decision rules might differ from other modes – perhaps the metro alternative might be more thoroughly evaluated since explicit attention had been drawn to the metro in the introductory screens. (See Hensher, Rose, and Collins 2011.)

We condition the heuristic weights W_1 and W_2 on two variables: the age of the respondent and the income of the respondent. In a two-heuristic model, W_1 and W_2 are given by Equation (21.48):

$$W_1 = \frac{\exp(\gamma_0^{H1} + \gamma_{age}^{H1} * age + \gamma_{inc}^{H1} * income)}{\exp(\gamma_0^{H1} + \gamma_{age}^{H1} * age + \gamma_{inc}^{H1} * income) + \exp(\gamma_0^{H2} + \gamma_{age}^{H2} * age + \gamma_{inc}^{H2} * income)}$$

$$W_2 = \frac{\exp(\gamma_0^{H2} + \gamma_{age}^{H2} * age + \gamma_{inc}^{H2} * income)}{\exp(\gamma_0^{H1} + \gamma_{age}^{H1} * age + \gamma_{inc}^{H1} * income) + \exp(\gamma_0^{H2} + \gamma_{age}^{H2} * age + \gamma_{inc}^{H2} * income)}.$$

$$(21.48)$$

The restrictions $\gamma_0^{H2} = -\gamma_0^{H1}$, $\gamma_{age}^{H2} = -\gamma_{age}^{H1}$, and $\gamma_{inc}^{H2} = -\gamma_{inc}^{H1}$ were imposed for identification.

In a model where γ_{age}^{H1} and γ_{inc}^{H1} are assumed homogenous in the sample, the heuristic weights W_1 and W_2 will still differ across respondents following the variations in the socio-economic characteristics (SECs). Table 21.27 reports the results of the estimation for a fixed parameters model. This model, which combines the LPLA and NLWLR rules, at the cost of estimating three additional parameters (φ_1, φ_2, and γ_0^{H1}) shows a substantial improvement in fit compared to the typical MNL specification with the SECs entered in the usual way. The parameters for the TT and $cost$ attributes are significant at the 1 percent level and of the correct sign.

Turning to the heuristic weights, the partial derivatives of W_m with respect to each of its l arguments are functions that take the same sign as γ_{lm}. Hence, the estimation results show that W_1, which is the weight of the LPLA heuristic is, all else equal, lower than W_2, the weight of the NLWLR heuristic. W_1 is increasing in *age* and decreasing in *income*, with the opposite effect for W_2. These are interesting findings as they demonstrate a relationship between the use of a heuristic and the SECs of a respondent. A multiple heuristics

Table 21.27 Estimation of weighted LPLA and NLWLR decision rules in utility

	$\hat{\beta}$ (z-ratio)	$\hat{\varphi}$ (z-ratio)	$\hat{\gamma}$ (z-ratio)
Travel time (TT) (min.)	0.0217 (9.40)	0.424 (6.21)	
Cost ($)	0.0418 (3.56)	0.695 (8.10)	
ASCs	−0.644 (−9.73)		
– bus	−0.447 (−9.89)		
– train	−1.405 (−8.85)		
– taxi			
Heuristic constant			−0.871 (−4.28)
Age (years)			0.0168 (4.67)
Income ($ 000)			−0.00567 (−3.51)
No. of observations	6,138		
LL	−5120.95		
LL(0)	−9878.73		
LL (MNL)	−5163.46		

approach suggested here may in fact be a preferred way of accounting for the impact of SECs on decision making.

Appendix 21A Nlogit command syntax for NLWLR and RAM heuristics

The command syntax uses the data described in Section 21.7.
Non-linear worst level referencing (NLWLR)

```
For the NLWLR heuristic, the first step is to identify the maximum or the
minimum value of an attribute in the local choice set. The following
commands identify the max/min value and replicate it for all alterna-
tives.
? Creating max variables within each choice set
create; if(alt=3)  |maxct = congtime!congtime[-1]!congtime[-2]
                   ; maxff = ff!ff[-1]!ff[-2]; maxrc = rc!rc[-1]!rc[-2]
                   ; maxtc=tc!tc[-1]!tc[-2]$
create ; if(alt=2)  |maxct=maxct[1];maxff=maxff[1];
                   maxrc=maxrc[1];maxtc=maxtc[1]$
create; if(alt=1)  |maxct=maxct[2];maxff=maxff[2];
                   maxrc=maxrc[2];maxtc=maxtc[2]$
? Creating min variables within each choice set
create; if(alt=3)  |minff = ff~ff[-1]~ff[-2]; minct = congtime~congtime[-
1]~congtime[-2]; minrc = rc~rc[-1]~rc[-2]
                   ; mintc=tc~tc[-1]~tc[-2]$
create; if(alt=2)  |minff=minff[1]; minct=minct[1];
                   minrc=minrc[1];mintc=mintc[1]$
```

```
create; if(alt=1) |minff=minff[2]; minct=minct[2];
                  minrc=minrc[2];mintc=mintc[2]$
```

? Differences can then be created, as follows.

```
create
; ffd = ff - maxff
; ctd = congtime-maxct
; rcd = rc-maxrc
; tcd = tc - maxtc$
```
? We can then implement the NLWLR heuristic using the NLRPlogit command.
The choice of starting values are crucial in this.

? NLWLR

```
NLRPlogit
;lhs=choice1,noalts,alt
;choices=Curr, AltA, AltB
;start= 0,0, -0.04, -0.06, -0.2, -0.2, 1.0, 1.0, 1.0, 1.0
;labels = ref, ASCA, ffh1, cth1, rch1, tch1, concff, concct, concrc,
conctc
;fn1 = NLWLR = (ffh1*ffd)^concff + (cth1*ctd)^concct +
                (rch1*rcd)^concrc + (tch1*tcd)^conctc
;fn2 = Util1 = ref + NLWLR
;fn3 = Util2 = ASCA + NLWLR
;model:
U(curr) = Util1/
U(altA)= Util2/
U(altB) = NLWLR$
```

Relative advantage model (RAM) model

For the RAM model, we need to create pairwise differences of each attribute across all possible pairs of alternatives. These enter into the RAM
component of the utility function
******************** Create variables for RAM
model*************************
First step is to create the pairwise attribute level differences between
the alternatives
Naming convention is d_attribute name_altj_altj', so dffsqa is the difference in ff attribute between SQ alternative and A alternative
```
create
; if(alt=1)|drcsqa = rc - rc[+1]; drcsqb = rc-rc[+2]; dtcsqa = tc - tc[+1]
; dtcsqb = tc-tc[+2];dffsqa = ff - ff[+1]; dffsqb = ff-ff[+2]
; dctsqa = congtime - congtime[+1]; dctsqb = congtime-congtime[+2]
```
? For all alt != sq, set d_attributename_altj_altj' = 0 for the moment:
```
; (else)| drcsqa = 0; drcsqb = 0; dtcsqa = 0; dtcsqb = 0
; dffsqa = 0; dffsqb = 0; dctsqa = 0; dctsqb = 0$
create
```

```
; if(alt=2)|drcasq = rc - rc[-1]; drcab =rc - rc[+1]; dtcasq = tc - tc[-1]
; dtcab =tc - tc[+1]; dffasq = ff - ff[-1]; dffab =ff - ff[+1]
; dctasq = congtime - congtime[-1]; dctab =congtime - congtime[+1]
? For all alt != A, set d_attributename_altj_altj' = 0 for the moment:
; (else)|drcasq = 0; drcab = 0; dtcasq = 0; dtcab = 0
; dffasq = 0; dffab = 0; dctasq = 0; dctab = 0$
create
; if(alt=3)|drcbsq = rc - rc[-2]; drcba =rc - rc[-1]; dtcbsq = tc - tc[-2]
; dtcba =tc - tc[-1]; dffbsq = ff - ff[-2]; dffba =ff - ff[-1]
; dctbsq = congtime - congtime[-2]; dctba =congtime - congtime[-1]
? For all alt != B, set d_attributename_altj_altj' = 0 for the moment:
; (else)| dtbsq = 0; dtba = 0; dcbsq = 0; dcba = 0; drcbsq = 0; drcba = 0;
dtcbsq = 0
; dtcba = 0; dffbsq = 0; dffba = 0; dctbsq = 0; dctba = 0$


? This is to replicate the same value of pairwise differences across all
alternatives

create
;if(alt=1)|dffasq = dffasq[+1]; dffbsq = dffbsq[+2]; dffab = dffab[+1];
dffba=dffba[+2]
          ;dctasq = dctasq[+1]; dctbsq = dctbsq[+2]; dctab = dctab[+1];
dctba=dctba[+2]
          ;drcasq = drcasq[+1]; drcbsq = drcbsq[+2]; drcab = drcab[+1];
drcba=drcba[+2]
          ;dtcasq = dtcasq[+1]; dtcbsq = dtcbsq[+2]; dtcab = dtcab[+1];
dtcba=dtcba[+2]$
create
;if(alt=2)|dffsqa = dffsqa[-1]; dffba = dffba[+1];dffsqb = dffsqb[-1];
dffbsq = dffbsq[+1]
          ;dctsqa = dctsqa[-1]; dctba = dctba[+1];dctsqb = dctsqb[-1];
dctbsq = dctbsq[+1]
          ;drcsqa = drcsqa[-1]; drcba = drcba[+1];drcsqb= drcsqb[-1];
drcbsq = drcbsq[+1]
          ;dtcsqa = dtcsqa[-1]; dtcba = dtcba[+1];dtcsqb= dtcsqb[-1];
dtcbsq = dtcbsq[+1]$
create
;if(alt=3)|dffsqb = dffsqb[-2]; dffab = dffab[-1];dffsqa = dffsqa[-2];
dffasq= dffasq[-1]
          ;dctsqb = dctsqb[-2]; dctab = dctab[-1];dctsqa = dctsqa[-2];
dctasq= dctasq[-1]
          ;drcsqb = drcsqb[-2]; drcab = drcab[-1];drcsqa = drcsqa[-2];
drcasq= drcasq[-1]
          ;dtcsqb = dtcsqb[-2]; dtcab = dtcab[-1];dtcsqa = dtcsqa[-2];
dtcasq= dtcasq[-1]$
? The following estimates the regret-RAM model
? adv_altj_altj' denotes the advantage of altj over altj'
? dadv_altj_altj' denotes the disadvantage of altj over altj'
? radv_altj_altj' denotes the relative advantage of altj over altj'
```

```
NLRPlogit  ?See Chapter 20 for Details of the NLRPLOGIT Command
;lhs=choice1,noalts,alt
;choices=Curr, AltA, AltB
;start = -0.05,-0.07, -0.25,-0.29,.08969
;labels = betaff, betact, betarc, betatc, ref
;fn1 = advsqa = log(1+exp(betaff*dffsqa)) + log(1+exp(betact*dctsqa)) +
log(1+exp(betarc*drcsqa)) + log(1+exp(betatc*dtcsqa))
;fn2 = dadvsqa = log(1+exp(-betaff*dffsqa)) + log(1+exp(-betact*dctsqa))
+ log(1+exp(-betarc*drcsqa)) + log(1+exp(-betatc*dtcsqa))
;fn3 = radvsqa = advsqa/(advsqa + dadvsqa)
;fn4 = advsqb = log(1+exp(betaff*dffsqb)) + log(1+exp(betact*dctsqb)) +
log(1+exp(betarc*drcsqb)) + log(1+exp(betatc*dtcsqb))
;fn5 = dadvsqb = log(1+exp(-betaff*dffsqb)) + log(1+exp(-betact*dctsqb))
+ log(1+exp(-betarc*drcsqb)) + log(1+exp(-betatc*dtcsqb))
;fn6 = radvsqb = advsqb/(advsqb + dadvsqb)
;fn7 = advasq = log(1+exp(betaff*dffasq)) + log(1+exp(betact*dctasq)) +
log(1+exp(betarc*drcasq)) + log(1+exp(betatc*dtcasq))
;fn8 = dadvasq = log(1+exp(-betaff*dffasq)) + log(1+exp(-betact*dctasq))
+ log(1+exp(-betarc*drcasq)) + log(1+exp(-betatc*dtcasq))
;fn9 = radvasq = advasq/(advasq + dadvasq)
;fn10 = advab = log(1+exp(betaff*dffab)) + log(1+exp(betact*dctab)) + log
(1+exp(betarc*drcab)) + log(1+exp(betatc*dtcab))
;fn11 = dadvab = log(1+exp(-betaff*dffab)) + log(1+exp(-betact*dctab)) +
log(1+exp(-betarc*drcab)) + log(1+exp(-betatc*dtcab))
;fn12 = radvab = advab/(advab + dadvab)
;fn13 = advbsq = log(1+exp(betaff*dffbsq)) + log(1+exp(betact*dctbsq)) +
log(1+exp(betarc*drcbsq)) + log(1+exp(betatc*dtcbsq))
;fn14 = dadvbsq = log(1+exp(-betaff*dffbsq)) + log(1+exp(-betact*dctbsq))
+ log(1+exp(-betarc*drcbsq)) + log(1+exp(-betatc*dtcbsq))
;fn15 = radvbsq = advbsq/(advbsq + dadvbsq)
;fn16 = advba = log(1+exp(betaff*dffba)) + log(1+exp(betact*dctba)) + log
(1+exp(betarc*drcba)) + log(1+exp(betatc*dtcba))
;fn17 = dadvba = log(1+exp(-betaff*dffba)) + log(1+exp(-betact*dctba)) +
log(1+exp(-betarc*drcba)) + log(1+exp(-betatc*dtcba))
;fn18 = radvba = advba/(advba + dadvba)
;fn19 = util1 = ref + betaff*ff + betact*congtime + betarc*rc + betatc*tc
+ (radvsqa + radvsqb)
;fn20 = util2 = betaff*ff + betact*congtime + betarc*rc + betatc*tc +
(radvasq + radvab)
;fn21 = util3 = betaff*ff + betact*congtime + betarc*rc + betatc*tc +
(radvbsq + radvba)
;model:
U(curr) = util1/
U(altA) = util2/
U(altB) = util3$
```

Appendix 21B Experimental design in Table 21.15

Columns include the alternative number (Alt.), where alternative 1 is the reference alternative, a unique choice scenario identifier (Cset), free-flow time (FF), slowed-down time (SDT), trip time variability (Var), running cost (Cost), and toll (Toll). FF, SDT, Var, and Cost are all expressed as a proportion of the recent trip values, where this proportion is added to the recent trip value. Toll is in dollars. Grey highlighting denotes the best attribute level in a choice scenario. Alternatives marked in **bold** denote a situation of dominance under full attribute attendance.

Appendix 21C Data associated with Table 21.15

		Block 1						Block 2				
Alt.	Cset	FF	SDT	Var	Cost	Toll	Cset	FF	SDT	Var	Cost	Toll
1	1	0	0	0	0	0	17	0	0	0	0	0
2		−0.15	0.3	−0.3	0.3	3.5		0.15	0.3	−0.3	−0.3	0.5
3		0.15	−0.3	−0.3	−0.3	0		0.15	−0.15	−0.15	0.3	3
1	2	0	0	0	0	0	18	0	0	0	0	0
2		−0.15	−0.3	0.3	−0.15	4		0.15	−0.15	−0.15	−0.15	2.5
3		0.3	−0.15	−0.3	0.15	1		0.15	−0.15	0.15	−0.3	1.5
1	3	0	0	0	0	0	19	0	0	0	0	0
2		0.3	−0.15	−0.15	−0.15	0		−0.3	0.15	0.15	0.3	0
3		−0.15	−0.3	−0.3	−0.3	0.5		0.3	−0.15	−0.3	0.3	0.5
1	4	0	0	0	0	0	20	**0**	**0**	**0**	**0**	**0**
2		−0.3	−0.15	0.3	−0.3	3.5		0.3	0.3	−0.3	−0.15	0.5
3		0.3	−0.3	0.3	−0.3	2.5		**−0.15**	**−0.3**	**−0.15**	**−0.15**	**0**
1	5	0	0	0	0	0	21	0	0	0	0	0
2		−0.15	−0.15	−0.3	−0.3	2.5		−0.15	0.15	0.3	−0.3	3
3		−0.3	−0.15	−0.3	−0.15	3		0.3	0.15	0.3	−0.3	2.5
1	6	0	0	0	0	0	22	0	0	0	0	0
2		0.3	0.15	−0.3	−0.3	3.5		−0.15	0.3	−0.3	0.3	1.5
3		−0.15	−0.3	−0.15	0.15	3.5		−0.15	−0.3	−0.15	−0.15	2
1	7	0	0	0	0	0	23	0	0	0	0	0
2		−0.3	0.15	0.15	−0.15	1.5		0.3	0.15	−0.15	−0.3	0
3		−0.3	0.3	−0.15	0.15	3		−0.3	0.3	0.3	−0.15	4
1	8	0	0	0	0	0	24	0	0	0	0	0
2		−0.15	−0.3	−0.3	−0.15	2.5		0.3	−0.3	0.3	0.15	0.5
3		−0.3	−0.15	0.3	0.15	2		0.15	0.3	0.15	−0.15	2.5

Alt.	Cset	Block 1					Cset	Block 2				
		FF	SDT	Var	Cost	Toll		FF	SDT	Var	Cost	Toll
1	9	0	0	0	0	0	25	0	0	0	0	0
2		-0.3	-0.3	-0.15	0.15	2		-0.3	-0.3	-0.3	0.3	0
3		0.15	-0.15	-0.3	-0.3	4		-0.3	-0.15	0.3	0.3	4
1	10	0	0	0	0	0	26	0	0	0	0	0
2		-0.15	0.3	-0.15	0.15	4		-0.3	-0.15	0.15	0.3	1
3		0.3	-0.15	0.15	-0.3	1		-0.3	0.15	0.3	-0.3	1.5
1	11	0	0	0	0	0	27	0	0	0	0	0
2		0.15	-0.3	0.15	-0.3	4		0.15	-0.15	-0.15	-0.15	3
3		-0.15	0.3	-0.3	0.15	2		-0.15	0.15	-0.15	-0.15	3.5
1	12	0	0	0	0	0	28	0	0	0	0	0
2		-0.15	0.15	0.3	-0.3	2		-0.3	-0.3	-0.15	0.15	4
3		-0.3	-0.3	0.15	-0.3	3.5		-0.15	0.15	0.15	-0.15	1.5
1	13	0	0	0	0	0	29	0	0	0	0	0
2		-0.15	-0.15	0.3	-0.15	1.5		0.15	-0.15	-0.15	0.15	0
3		-0.3	-0.15	-0.3	-0.15	4		-0.15	0.15	-0.3	0.3	0.5
1	14	0	0	0	0	0	30	0	0	0	0	0
2		0.15	-0.3	-0.15	-0.15	1		0.3	-0.15	-0.15	0.15	1
3		0.3	0.15	-0.15	-0.3	1		-0.3	-0.3	-0.15	0.3	3.5
1	15	0	0	0	0	0	31	0	0	0	0	0
2		-0.15	-0.3	0.15	-0.15	0.5		-0.3	0.3	-0.3	0.3	3
3		0.15	-0.3	0.15	0.15	3		-0.15	0.3	-0.15	0.3	0.5
1	16	0	0	0	0	0	32	0	0	0	0	0
2		-0.3	-0.3	-0.3	-0.3	2		-0.3	-0.15	0.15	-0.3	3
3		-0.15	0.3	-0.15	-0.15	0		-0.3	-0.3	-0.3	-0.15	3.5

Alt.	FF	SDT	Var	Cost	Toll	TotT	TotC	Choice
1	20	0	0	2.6	0	20	2.6	0
2	17	2	6	2.21	4	19	6.21	0
3	26	3	4	2.99	1	29	3.99	1
1	8	2	2	1.2	0	10	1.2	0
2	7	1	6	1.02	4	8	5.02	0
3	10	2	4	1.38	1	12	2.38	1
1	60	0	30	7.8	0	60	7.8	0
2	51	2	34	6.63	0.5	53	7.13	0
3	69	2	34	8.97	3	71	11.97	1
1	25	0	18	3.25	0	25	3.25	0
2	29	4	12	2.28	0.5	33	2.78	0
3	29	3	15	4.23	3	32	7.23	1

Alt.	FF	SDT	Var	Cost	Toll	TotT	TotC	Choice
1	30	0	5	3.9	0	30	3.9	0
2	39	2	6	4.49	0.5	41	4.99	1
3	34	4	6	3.32	2.5	38	5.82	0
1	22	0	2	2.86	0	22	2.86	0
2	29	2	6	3.29	0.5	31	3.79	1
3	25	4	6	2.43	2.5	29	4.93	0
1	16	0	5	2.08	0	16	2.08	0
2	21	2	6	2.39	0.5	23	2.89	1
3	18	4	6	1.77	2.5	22	4.27	0
1	20	0	5	2.6	0	20	2.6	0
2	26	2	6	2.99	0.5	28	3.49	1
3	23	4	6	2.21	2.5	27	4.71	0
1	22	0	2	2.86	0	22	2.86	0
2	29	3	4	3.29	1	32	4.29	1
3	15	2	4	3.72	3.5	17	7.22	0
1	35	10	2	5.33	0	45	5.33	0
2	46	8	4	6.13	1	54	7.13	1
3	24	7	4	6.93	3.5	31	10.43	0
1	8	2	2	1.2	0	10	1.2	0
2	10	2	4	1.38	1	12	2.38	1
3	6	1	4	1.55	3.5	7	5.05	0
1	40	5	8	5.59	0	45	5.59	0
2	28	6	5	7.27	3	34	10.27	0
3	34	6	6	7.27	0.5	40	7.77	1
1	50	10	10	7.28	0	60	7.28	0
2	35	13	7	9.46	3	48	12.46	0
3	42	13	8	9.46	0.5	55	9.96	1
1	25	5	8	3.64	0	30	3.64	0
2	18	6	5	4.73	3	24	7.73	0
3	21	6	6	4.73	0.5	27	5.23	1
1	45	45	22	9.36	0	90	9.36	0
2	32	58	16	12.17	3	90	15.17	0
3	38	58	19	12.17	0.5	96	12.67	1
1	40	40	35	8.32	0	80	8.32	0
2	28	52	24	10.82	3	80	13.82	0
3	34	52	30	10.82	0.5	86	11.32	1
1	15	0	2	1.95	0	15	1.95	0
2	10	4	4	2.54	3	14	5.54	0
3	13	4	4	2.54	0.5	17	3.04	1
1	35	40	12	7.67	0	75	7.67	0
2	24	52	9	9.97	3	76	12.97	0
3	30	52	11	9.97	0.5	82	10.47	1
1	10	25	12	3.25	0	35	3.25	0

Alt.	FF	SDT	Var	Cost	Toll	TotT	TotC	Choice
2	7	32	9	4.23	3	39	7.23	0
3	8	32	11	4.23	0.5	40	4.73	1
1	22	0	2	2.86	0	22	2.86	0
2	15	4	4	3.72	3	19	6.72	0
3	19	4	4	3.72	0.5	23	4.22	1
1	30	7	6	4.45	0	37	4.45	0
2	21	9	5	5.78	3	30	8.78	0
3	26	9	6	5.78	0.5	35	6.28	1
1	90	0	45	11.7	0	90	11.7	0
2	63	4	32	15.21	3	67	18.21	0
3	76	4	38	15.21	0.5	80	15.71	1
1	65	25	15	10.4	0	90	10.4	0
2	46	32	10	13.52	3	78	16.52	0
3	55	32	13	13.52	0.5	87	14.02	1
1	55	5	12	7.54	0	60	7.54	0
2	38	6	9	9.8	3	44	12.8	0
3	47	6	11	9.8	0.5	53	10.3	1
1	20	20	10	4.16	0	40	4.16	0
2	14	26	7	5.41	3	40	8.41	0
3	17	26	8	5.41	0.5	43	5.91	1
1	80	10	15	11.18	0	90	11.18	0
2	56	13	10	14.53	3	69	17.53	0
3	68	13	13	14.53	0.5	81	15.03	1
1	60	10	12	8.58	0	70	8.58	0
2	42	13	9	11.15	3	55	14.15	0
3	51	13	11	11.15	0.5	64	11.65	1
1	25	0	18	3.25	0	25	3.25	0
2	18	4	12	4.23	3	22	7.23	0
3	21	4	15	4.23	0.5	25	4.73	1
1	55	10	15	7.93	0	65	7.93	0
2	38	13	10	10.31	3	51	13.31	0
3	47	13	13	10.31	0.5	60	10.81	1
1	240	30	30	33.54	0	270	33.54	0
2	168	39	21	43.6	3	207	46.6	0
3	204	39	26	43.6	0.5	243	44.1	1
1	30	15	8	5.07	0	45	5.07	0
2	21	20	5	6.59	3	41	9.59	0
3	26	20	6	6.59	0.5	46	7.09	1
1	30	15	40	5.07	0	45	5.07	0
2	21	20	28	6.59	3	41	9.59	0
3	26	20	34	6.59	0.5	46	7.09	1
1	35	10	2	5.33	0	45	5.33	0
2	24	13	4	6.93	3	37	9.93	0

Alt.	FF	SDT	Var	Cost	Toll	TotT	TotC	Choice
3	30	13	4	6.93	0.5	43	7.43	1
1	15	5	6	2.34	0	20	2.34	0
2	10	6	5	3.04	3	16	6.04	0
3	13	6	6	3.04	0.5	19	3.54	1
1	15	5	2	2.34	0	20	2.34	0
2	10	6	4	3.04	3	16	6.04	0
3	13	6	4	3.04	0.5	19	3.54	1
1	25	5	18	3.64	0	30	3.64	0
2	18	6	12	4.73	3	24	7.73	0
3	21	6	15	4.73	0.5	27	5.23	1
1	40	5	8	5.59	0	45	5.59	0
2	28	6	5	7.27	3	34	10.27	0
3	34	6	6	7.27	0.5	40	7.77	1
1	20	10	8	3.38	0	30	3.38	0
2	14	13	5	4.39	3	27	7.39	0
3	17	13	6	4.39	0.5	30	4.89	1
1	25	10	10	4.03	0	35	4.03	0
2	18	13	7	5.24	3	31	8.24	0
3	21	13	8	5.24	0.5	34	5.74	1
1	25	5	8	3.64	0	30	3.64	0
2	18	6	5	4.73	3	24	7.73	0
3	21	6	6	4.73	0.5	27	5.23	1
1	17	3	4	2.44	0	20	2.44	0
2	12	4	2	3.18	3	16	6.18	0
3	14	4	3	3.18	0.5	18	3.68	1
1	45	15	15	7.02	0	60	7.02	0
2	32	20	10	9.13	3	52	12.13	0
3	38	20	13	9.13	0.5	58	9.63	1
1	30	10	10	4.68	0	40	4.68	0
2	21	13	7	6.08	3	34	9.08	0
3	26	13	8	6.08	0.5	39	6.58	1
1	35	10	8	5.33	0	45	5.33	0
2	24	13	5	6.93	3	37	9.93	0
3	30	13	6	6.93	0.5	43	7.43	1
1	8	2	2	1.2	0	10	1.2	0
2	6	3	4	1.55	3	9	4.55	0
3	7	3	4	1.55	0.5	10	2.05	1
1	17	3	8	2.44	0	20	2.44	0
2	12	4	5	3.18	3	16	6.18	0
3	14	4	6	3.18	0.5	18	3.68	1
1	20	5	12	2.99	0	25	2.99	0
2	14	6	9	3.89	3	20	6.89	0
3	17	6	11	3.89	0.5	23	4.39	1

Alt.	FF	SDT	Var	Cost	Toll	TotT	TotC	Choice
1	50	40	15	9.62	0	90	9.62	0
2	35	52	10	12.51	3	87	15.51	0
3	42	52	13	12.51	0.5	94	13.01	1
1	22	3	4	3.09	0	25	3.09	0
2	15	4	2	4.02	3	19	7.02	0
3	19	4	3	4.02	0.5	23	4.52	1
1	20	10	15	3.38	0	30	3.38	0
2	14	13	10	4.39	3	27	7.39	0
3	17	13	13	4.39	0.5	30	4.89	1
1	90	0	15	11.7	0	90	11.7	0
2	63	4	10	15.21	3	67	18.21	0
3	76	4	13	15.21	0.5	80	15.71	1
1	50	10	15	7.28	0	60	7.28	0
2	35	13	10	9.46	3	48	12.46	0
3	42	13	13	9.46	0.5	55	9.96	1
1	30	10	12	4.68	0	40	4.68	0
2	21	13	9	6.08	3	34	9.08	0
3	26	13	11	6.08	0.5	39	6.58	1
1	40	15	12	6.37	0	55	6.37	0
2	28	20	9	8.28	3	48	11.28	0
3	34	20	11	8.28	0.5	54	8.78	1

Grey highlighting denotes the best attribute level in a choice scenario.

22 Group decision making

22.1 Introduction

The literature on household economics has made substantial progress in the study of group decision making, beginning with the initial theoretical contributions (Becker 1993; Browning and Chiappori 1998; Lampietti 1999; Chiuri 2000; Vermeulen 2002), and subsequent empirical applications in various fields, such as marketing (Arora and Allenby 1999; Adamowicz *et al.* 2005), transport (Brewer and Hensher 2000; Hensher *et al.* 2007), and environmental economics (Quiggin 1998; Smith and Houtven 1998; Bateman and Munroe 2005; Dosman and Adamowicz 2006). Recent studies, for example, provide evidence of substantial differences in taste intensities between domestic partners, and make an attempt at reconciling them with observed joint choices using power functions (Dosman and Adamowicz 2006; Beharry *et al.* 2009). The evidence collected so far indicates that, for some categories of decisions, the conventional practice of selecting one member of the couple as representative of the tastes of the entire household may be biased when compared with the preference estimates underlying joint deliberation by the same couple.

Despite the existence of an extensive literature on group decision making, synthesized in Dellaert *et al.* (1998) and Vermeulen (2002), there has been a limited focus on ways in which multiple agents have been recognized in the formalization of discrete choice models. This literature can broadly be divided into two. (i) a focus on the game playing between agents in a sequential choice process that involves initial preferences (with or without knowledge of the agent's choice), followed by a process of feedback, review, and revision or maintenance of the initial preference. This approach endogenizes the preferences of other decision makers in the ultimate group decision. We call this **interactive agency choice experiments** (IACE), as developed initially by

Hensher and detailed in Brewer and Hensher (2000) and Rose and Hensher (2004). (ii) studies that develop ways of establishing the influence and power of each agent in the joint choice outcome, which may or may not use an IACE framework. Puckett and Hensher (2006) review this literature, which is primarily in marketing and household economics and has, for example, been extended and implemented in the study of freight distribution chains by Hensher *et al.* (2008), to the study of partnering between bus operators and the regulator by Hensher and Knowles (2007) and, most recently, to the household purchase of alternative fueled vehicles by Hensher *et al.* (2011) and Beck *et al.* (2012).

Schematically, the IACE structure involves a sequential engagement of two or more agents seeking to establish a consensus on their individual preferences that can, through negotiation or "give-and-take," result in an agreed or non-agreed joint choice outcome. The representation of the role of each agent is identified by an additional shadow value of the power or influence of each agent, given their own individual preferences (see Arora and Allenby 1999; Aribarg *et al.* 2002; Corfman 1991; Corfman and Lehmann 1987; Dosman and Adamowicz 2006; Hensher *et al.* 2008). We now discuss the IACE method in detail, and show how the method can be implemented in Nlogit.

22.2 Interactive agency choice experiments

Developed by Hensher and his colleagues and used to examine an employer/employee choice of telecommuting (Brewer and Hensher 2000), freight transportation (Hensher *et al.* 2007), and automobile choice (Hensher *et al.* 2008), the IACE methodology enables ongoing collaboration between respondents (termed agents), as preference shifts are tracked from initial singularly held preferences to group choices, through a process of negotiation and revision. The iterative nature of the methodology allows the analyst to track how preference structures are modified from initial preferences, which may or may not be in conflict, through to the ultimate group agreement or stalemate. The process requires agents to make initial choices independently after which, if agent choice is not in agreement, information about the choices made is fed back to each agent who would then be required to revise (or retain) their choice. The feedback and revision process extends for as many passes as the researcher desires.

Consider a scenario where two agents are independently evaluating a choice task consisting of the same set of alternatives described by the same set of attributes and attribute levels. The interactive agency process, as displayed in Table 22.1, begins with two such group members providing their initial choices independent of each other, which are then modeled. In the modeling process, utility functions are specified by the analyst which form the starting point for the analysis of the group decision:

$$V_{ai} = \alpha_{ai} + \sum_{k=1}^{K}(\beta_{ak}x_{ik}) \tag{22.1}$$

$$V_{bi} = \alpha_{bi} + \sum_{k=1}^{K}(\beta_{bk}x_{ik}), \tag{22.2}$$

where V_{ai} represents the observed utility derived by agent a for alternative i, α_{ai} represents a constant specific to alternative i (this value can also be generic across alternatives), x_{ik} is a vector of k design attributes associated with alternative i, and β_{ak} is the corresponding vector of marginal (dis)utility parameters. Note that the total utility would be a summation of this observed utility plus an error term that captures unobserved utility. Under the random utility-maximization (RUM) framework, the alternative with the highest total utility is the alternative chosen by that agent.

In the interactive agency process, the initial choices made by agents are compared. If the same alternative has been selected by both agents, then it is inferred that this would be the alternative chosen by the group. Where agreement has been reached between the parties, the choice is said to be in equilibrium. After each pass, choice tasks where no equilibrium decision was reached are sent back to each agent for re-evaluation where one or more of the agents may revise their choice. This process continues until an equilibrium choice is reached, or the analyst terminates the process.

For equilibrated choices, the same choice is observed for each member of the group (i.e., ignoring tasks where no agreement was reached). As such, the inferred utility of group g can be defined as:

$$V_{gi} = \alpha_{gi} + \sum_{k=1}^{K}(\beta_{gk}x_{ik}). \tag{22.3}$$

However, if the assumption is made that the group utility is a function of the individual preferences of each agent weighted by the level of influence of the agent (or perhaps in the case of a cooperative household, the agent's level of responsibility for the decision or the importance of the decision for one agent relative to the other), then it is possible to define the utility of group g as:

$$V_{gi} = \alpha_{gi} + \lambda_a(V_{ai}) + (1 - \lambda_a)(V_{bi}), \tag{22.4}$$

which can be reformulated as:

$$V_{gi} = \alpha_{gi} + \lambda_a\left(\sum_{k=1}^{K}(\beta_{aik}x_{ik})\right) + (1 - \lambda_a)\left(\sum_{k=1}^{K}(\beta_{bik}x_{ik})\right), \tag{22.5}$$

where λ_a is the measure of influence that agent a possesses relative to agent b. In this specification the influence measures represented by λ_a, along with any alternative-specific constant (ASC) used by the analyst, are the only parameters that vary freely within the model. In other words: parameters reflecting the tastes of group members for the different attributes are taken from the estimated individual-level models in Equations (22.1) and (22.2). Values of λ_a range from zero to one, with a zero result representing influence being held solely by agent b, and a value of one equating to the situation where the utility of agent a is wholly representative of the group. The mid point, 0.5, represents the situation where both agents contribute equally to the group's utility. To ensure that λ_a is bounded, this parameter can be defined as:

$$\lambda_a = \frac{e^{(\theta)}}{1 + e^{(\theta)}}. \tag{22.6}$$

This modeling structure lends itself to the mixed logit (ML) model.

To assist in tracking the behavioral outputs of the IACE framework we refer to each stage in which an agent reviews a choice set of alternatives and indicates their preferred alternative as a *round*. When both agents have completed a round in a sequence, we refer to the completion of a *pass*. In the example in this chapter, we have designed the IACE such that each agent can go up to three rounds before we impose a stop rule, and hence there are three passes in total. Specific agents may stop after their initial round (that is, at the completion of pass 1) if they both choose the same alternative. Agents who do not agree will continue to pass 2 (that is, rounds 3 and 4 for agents 1 and 2). In pass 2 we commence a process of feedback, review, and revision or maintenance of pass 1 preferences. In pass 2, both agents will have knowledge of the preferences of the other agent; in contrast, this is only known in pass 1 if the analyst provides this information to the subsequent agent.

If agreement occurs in pass 2 for some agents, then a subset will continue into pass 3 (rounds 5 and 6). Previous studies have found that the majority of agent pairs agree (cooperatively or non-cooperatively) by the end of round 6. One of our hypotheses is that specific attributes and their levels become the major reason for non-agreement in earlier passes, and as the negotiations unfold there appears to be some degree of give-and-take in the interests of a resolution, so that an "equilibrium" joint choice can be actioned in the market. What is of particular interest here is identifying what exogenous drivers influence agreement and non-agreement at the end of each pass, and how this knowledge can be used to identify the relative influence, and hence power, of each agent in decision making. The IACE framework, supplemented by additional contextual data, enables the analyst to investigate possible influences on agreement, and the inferred power of each agent (Table 22.1).

We propose the following model system as a way of establishing the preferences of each agent in an IACE framework and the role that each agent's individual preferences play in establishing the group preference function for choice making.

Stage 1: Each agent participates in a stated choice experiment (CE) with common choice sets. The behavioral process assumes that each agent acts *as if* they are a utility maximizer. The agent-specific models define utility expressions of the form: U(alt i, agent q) $i=1,...,J$; $q=1,...,Q$, where *alt* defines an alternative package of attribute levels. For example, with two agents and three alternatives we have U(a_1q_1), U(a_2q_1), U(a_3q_1) for agent 1 and U(a_1q_2), U(a_2q_2), U(a_3q_2) for agent 2. An unlabeled stated choice (SC) design (in our case study – see p. 1079) will be established to parameterize this independent utility maximizing choice model.

Stage 1 involves a series of rounds and passes as described above, with all agents participating in pass 1 and incrementally reducing as we move to the next pass as a result of agreement between parties. Each pass defines a set of alternatives for each agent that can be jointly modeled as ML. A by-product of the estimation of pass level models is a binary logit model for agree and non-agree. In the application setting of vehicle purchase set out in Section 22.5, there are four identical alternatives assessed by each agent, giving eight alternatives to be included in the estimation of the pass model for each agent pair.

Stage 2: This involves recognition of the final pass in which an agent pair agreed and the estimation of a single model in which the utility functions for

Table 22.1 Schematic representation of IASP evaluation

	PASS		
		$AG_1 \rightarrow AG_2$	
Alt 1	Pass 1	Alt 1 – Alt 1	Agree
Alt 2	$AG_1 \longrightarrow AG_2$	Alt 2 – Alt 2	
Alt 3		Alt 3 – Alt 3	
		Alt 1 – Alt 2	Not agree
		Alt 1 – Alt 3	
		Alt 2 – Alt 1	
		Alt 2 – Alt 3	
		Alt 3 – Alt 1	
Current		Alt 3 – Alt 2	
TC 1	Pass 2	$AG_1 \rightarrow AG_2$	Agree
TC 2	$AG_1 \longrightarrow AG_2$	Alt 1 – Alt 1	
		Alt 2 – Alt 2	Not agree
		Alt 3 – Alt 3	
		Alt 1 – Alt 2	
		Alt 1 – Alt 3	
		Alt 2 – Alt 1	
		Alt 2 – Alt 3	
		Alt 3 – Alt 1	
		Alt 3 – Alt 2	
Current	Pass 3	$AG_1 \rightarrow AG_2$	
TC 1	$AG_2 \longrightarrow AG_2$	Alt 1 – Alt 1	Agree
TC 2		Alt 2 – Alt 2	
		Alt 3 – Alt 3	
		Alt 1 – Alt 2	Not agree
		Alt 1 – Alt 3	
		Alt 2 – Alt 1	
		Alt 2 – Alt 3	
		Alt 3 – Alt 1	
		Alt 3 – Alt 2	

each agent are drawn from the pass at which the agents agreed. We refer to this phase as establishing *group equilibrium preferences*. Importantly these preferences have benefitted from the sequential process undertaken across the passes, and hence the parameterization of each attribute to reveal the preferences of each agent in joint agent choice making space is enriched by the negotiation that has been completed to establish consensus in choice, regardless of whether it was cooperative or non-cooperative. We support the proposition that the stage 1 interactive process has added important information to both parties' search for a preferred choice outcome that has to accommodate the preferences of the other party. In the application below, with four alternatives in the choice set of each agent, there will be four alternatives in the group equilibrium model, defining the pairs across the agents that are the same alternative. One of these four pairs is the chosen alternative for the two agents.

Additionally, the determination of group equilibrium preference has been influenced by the *power play* between the agents, which is something we should identify in order to gain a better appreciation of the role of each agent. If it transpires that one agent totally dominates, then there may be a case for reverting back to a single-agent modeling framework. However, it is likely that this may apply only to subsets of agent pairs, necessitating some amount of segmentation to accommodate differential power play across the population of interest.

Stage 3: All parameters estimated from stages 1 or 2 are fixed and imported[1] into a joint agent model. For example, with two agents and three alternatives, there are nine joint alternatives – $U(a_1a_1)$, $U(a_1a_2)$, $U(a_1a_3)$,...., $U(a_3a_1)$, $U(a_3a_2)$, $U(a_3a_3)$, referred to as propositions p = 1,...,P. Three of the joint propositions imply non-negotiated agreement (that is $U(a_1a_1)$, $U(a_2a_2)$, $U(a_3a_3)$). The stage 3 choice is between combinations of agent-specific propositions with one proposition the chosen pair. A model is then specified of the following form (for two agents, q, _q) (see Puckett and Hensher 2006):

$$
\begin{aligned}
U(a_1a_1) &= ASC_{a1a1} + \lambda_{qp} * (\beta_{1q}x_{1q} + \beta_{2q}x_{2q} + \ldots) \\
&\quad + (1 - \lambda_{qp}) * (\beta_{1_q}x_{1_q} + \beta_{2_q}x_{2_q} + \ldots) \quad \ldots \\
U(a_1a_3) &= ASC_{a1a3} + \lambda_{qp} * (\beta_{1q}x_{1q} + \beta_{2q}x_{2q} + \ldots) \\
&\quad + (1 - \lambda_{qp}) * (\beta_{1_q}x_{1_q} + \beta_{2_q}x_{2_q} + \ldots) \quad \ldots \\
U(a_3a_3) &= ASC_{a3a3} + \lambda_{qp} * (\beta_{1q}x_{1q} + \beta_{2q}x_{2q} + \ldots) \\
&\quad + (1 - \lambda_{qp}) * (\beta_{1-q}x_{1-q} + \beta_{2-q}x_{2-q} + \ldots) \quad .
\end{aligned}
\tag{22.7}
$$

The power measures for agents q and $\_q$ sum to one, making comparisons of agent types straightforward. If the two power measures are equal for a given attribute *mix defining a proposition* (that is, $\lambda_{qp} = (1 - \lambda_{qp}) = 0.5$), then group choice equilibrium is not governed by a dominant agent with respect to

---

[1] The ASCs may not be imported. One can also jointly estimate the attribute parameters and power weights. See Section 22.5.14.

proposition p. In other words, regardless of the power structure governing other attributes, agent types q and $\_q$ tend to reach perceptively fair compromises when bridging the gap in their preferences for each proposition. If the power measures are significantly different across agent types (for example, $\lambda_{qp} > (1 - \lambda_{qp})$ for two agents), then λ_{qp} gives a direct measure of the dominance of one agent type over the other with respect to the attribute mix in proposition p; as λ_{qp} increases, so does the relative power held by agent type q over $\_q$.

This model is straightforward to estimate, holding all βs fixed, with each λ_{qp} and the ASCs free parameters. λ_{qp} as a power indicator can be a random parameter and a function of other criteria, especially the contextual attributes, and can be specific to each attribute within and/or between propositions, or constrained as the analyst sees fit.

22.3 Case study data on automobile purchases

The data used in the implementation of the IACE framework was collected using first- and second-year marketing undergraduate students.

The focus is on choosing at automobile type assuming you are in the market today to acquire a vehicle (regardless of how many vehicles your household currently owns). The main part of the survey is an unlabeled SC experiment, administered to pairs of individuals from the same household who are asked to work through a series of CEs in an interactive way to arrive at a choice outcome.

Before commencing the SC experiment, respondents were asked a series of questions related to their currently owned vehicle. This information was then used to assign agent pairs to a vehicle type (small, medium, large, four-wheel drive, or luxury vehicle) so as to provide context for the experiment. The attributes and attribute levels of the SC experiment are shown in Table 22.2. The list is not extensive, given our primary interest in testing the capability of undertaking an IACE task using the internet. A lot of logistics effort was required to arrange to have both agents available at the same time to participate in the survey, considerably more than if one is surveying an independent agent.

209 agent pairs participated; 31 were assigned to the small vehicle condition, 66 to the medium vehicle condition, 35 to the large, 31 to four-wheel drives, and the remaining 46 to the luxury vehicle experimental condition. We have selected a sub-sample of pairs that are a male and a female.

Table 22.2 Stated choice design attributes

• Attribute	• Attribute level
• Engine size	• *Small* (1.2,1.3, 1.4, 1.5)
	• *Medium* (1.6, 1.8, 2.0, 2.2)
	• *Large* (2.3, 2.9, 3.4, 4.0)
	• *4WD* (3.2, 4.0, 4.9, 5.7)
	• *Luxury* (3.0, 4.0, 5.0, 5.7)
• Price $AUD	• *Small* ($12,000, $13,500, $15,000, $16,500)
	• *Medium* ($19,990, $21,990, $23,990, $25,990)
	• *Large* ($28,000, $30,000, $32,000, $34,000)
	• *4WD* ($52,990, $56,640, $60,300, $36,950)
	• *Luxury* ($54,950, $71,100, $87,300, $103,500)
• Air conditioning	• Yes, No
• Transmission type	• Manual, Automatic
• Fuel consumption litres/100km	• *Small* (6.2, 6.7, 7.4, 7.7)
	• *Medium* (7.6, 8.1, 8.5, 9.0)
	• *Large* (8.8, 9.8, 10.7, 11.7)
	• *4WD* (11.1, 13.1, 15.2, 17.2)
	• *Luxury* (10.9, 13, 16, 18.2)
• ABS brakes	Yes, No

The actual logistics of conducting the study involve active participation of each agent in a sequence, each evaluating alternatives set out in a series of SC screens accessed via the internet. One at a time, each agent in a pre-selected pair is asked to leave the room for a moment. The person remaining is asked, in round 1, to complete the survey and when completed they leave and the other person returns to complete the very same survey instrument. The respondents are separated to avoid discussing the answers. In Round 2, half of the returning agents are told what the other agent chose and the other half are not.

At the completion of round 1 there is an advisory that says that depending on the answers that both household members give, you may be asked to repeat the process a number of times. Instructions are provided to each agent prior to evaluating the SC screens. The instruction is as follows: "The questions we will ask each of you relate to the household purchase of hypothetical cars. We would like you to consider several hypothetical situations in which your household is interested in purchasing a new car. In each hypothetical situation, we will show you three possible cars that you may purchase. We would like you to first choose the car that you would most likely choose if it were really available. Next we would like you to choose the car that you think the other family member would most likely choose. This may be the same car, or another car."

Table 22.3 Illustrative stated choice screen

	Car A	Car B	Car C	None
Engine size	1.4	1.5	1.4	
Price	$13,500	$12,000	$16,500	
Air conditioning	No	Yes	No	
Transmission type	Manual	Automatic	Automatic	
Fuel consumption (litres/100km)	6.7	6.2	7.2	
ABS brakes	No	Yes	Yes	
I would choose	☐	☐	☐	☐
The other person would most likely choose	☐	☐	☐	☐

An example choice situation is provided and is reproduced as Table 22.3. An agent is asked to consider each car as described, choose the car that most appeals to them, and also to choose the car that they think the other household member would most likely choose. The process is repeated four times with four choice sets.

The CE uses a statistically efficient design that minimizes the elements of the asymptotic (co)variance (AVC) matrix, Ω, with the aim of producing greater *reliability* in the parameter estimates given a fixed number of choice observations. To compare the statistical efficiency of SC experimental designs, a number of alternative approaches have been proposed within the literature (see Chapter 6). The most commonly used measure is D-error (see Chapter 6):

$$\text{D-error} = (\det \Omega)^{1/k} = -\frac{1}{N} \left(\det \left(\frac{\partial LL(\beta)^2}{\partial \beta \partial \beta'} \right) \right)^{-1/k}, \qquad (22.8)$$

where k represents the number of parameters for the design, $LL(\beta)$ the log-likelihood (LL) function of the discrete choice model under consideration, N the sample size, and β the parameters to be estimated from the design. Given that we are generating designs and not estimating parameters for an already existing design, it is necessary to assume a set of priors for the parameter estimates. Given uncertainty as to the actual population parameters, it is typical to draw these priors from Bayesian distributions rather than assume fixed parameter values.

The $D_{(b)}$-error is calculated by taking the determinant, with both scaled to take into account the number of parameters to be estimated. It involves a series of multiplications and subtractions over all the elements of the matrix (see, for example, Kanninen 2002). As such, the determinant (and by implication, the $D_{(b)}$-error measure) summarizes all the elements of the matrix in a single "global" value. Thus, whilst attempts to minimize the D-error measure, on average, minimize all the elements within the matrix, it is possible that in doing so, some elements (variances and/or covariances) may in fact become larger. Despite this property, the $D_{(b)}$-error measure has become the most common measure of statistical efficiency within the literature.

22.4 Case study results

The analysis has been undertaken in a sequence that matches the IACE stages presented in Section 22.2. We start with the empirical evidence for each of the passes (Table 22.4), followed by the sources of influence on agreement versus non-agreement (Table 22.5). Table 22.6 presents the evidence on the power influence that agents play in each pass, followed by the findings for the preference model estimated on the agreement pass for each agent pair, referred to as the group equilibrium model (Table 22.7). The remaining two tables present the probability contrasts between the sequenced pass models and the pooled equilibrium passes (Table 22.8) and the sources of agreement versus disagreement in the group equilibrium model (Table 22.7).

In Table 22.4, Alternatives A–C and E–G refer to the unlabeled three vehicle alternatives, respectively, for agents 1 and 2, while Alternatives D and H are the null alternative (that is, "none" in Table 22.3) for each agent. 404 agent pairs participated in pass 1, with a progression to 164 agents pairs in pass 1, and 91 agent pairs in pass 3.

In the ML pass 1 model, the marginal disutility of the price of the vehicle for agent 1 and the fuel efficiency (litres/100km) of the vehicles for both agents were identified as random parameters with constrained triangular distributions, while vehicle price is a fixed parameter for agent 2. This supports the presence of preference heterogeneity for these two attributes for agent 1 and fuel efficiency only for agent 2. Although the alternatives are unlabeled, a "generic" constant for the three vehicle alternatives for each of the agents was positive and statistically significant (although marginally so for agent 2)[2] suggesting that there are, on average, additional unobserved influences on relative utility that contribute more than three times to the utility of the alternatives for agent 1 compared to agent 2. The implication is that agent 1

[2] The ASCs for agents 1 and 2 were estimated separately for A, B, and C, but we found that they were almost identical suggesting no order bias after controlling for the explicit attributes of alternatives. We then treated them as generic constants across A–C and E–G.

Table 22.4 Pass model results

Attribute	Alternative(s)	Pass 1 Agent 1	Pass 1 Agent 2	Pass 2 Agent 1	Pass 2 Agent 2	Pass 3 Agent 1	Pass 3 Agent 2
Random parameters:							
Vehicle price ('000s) Agent 1	A–C	−0.0842 (−3.1)					
Fuel efficiency (litres/100km)	A–C, E–G	−0.1533 (−2.5)					
Fixed parameters:							
ASC	A–C	3.496 (3.3)					
ASC	E–G		1.127 (1.7)				
Vehicle price ('000s) Agent 2	E–G		−0.033 (−1.5)				
Small vehicle (1,0)	A–C	−1.461 (−2.3)					
Small vehicle (1,0)	E–G				1.518 (1.4)		
Air conditioning (1,0)	A–C	1.130 (7.5)		0.490(2.6)		0.558 (2.1)	
Air conditioning (1,0)	E–G		1.149 (8.0)		0.88 (4.4)		0.948 (3.6)
Manual transmission (1,0)	A–C	1.321 (8.4)		0.648 (3.4)		0.419 (1.6)	
Manual transmission (1,0)	E–G		0.726 (5.1)		−.753 (3.7)		
ABS brakes (1,2)	A–C	0.5615 (3.8)		0.681 (3.5)		0.615 (2.2)	
ABS brakes (1,2)	E–G		0.5109 (3.6)				
Can drive manual (1,0)	D,H			−1.403 (−2.9)			
Married agents (1,0)	D	0.2163 (3.2)					
Agent 1 Age (years)	D					−1.719 (−1.8)	
Agent 2 Age (years)	H		−0.948 (−3.0)				
Agent 1 thought agent 2 would choose same alternative (1,0)	D			0.739 (2.2)			

Table 22.4 (cont.)

		Pass 1		Pass 2		Pass 3	
Attribute	Alternative(s)	Agent 1	Agent 2	Agent 1	Agent 2	Agent 1	Agent 2
Random parameter standard deviations							
Vehicle price (000s) Agent 1	A–C	0.0842 (3.1)					
Fuel efficiency (litres/100km)	A–C, E–G	0.1533 (2.5)					
Error component (alternative-specific heterogeneity)	D			0.0067 (1.2)			
	H				0.0925 (16.7)		
Sample size			808		328		182
LL at zero			−1680.19		−679.98		−386.75
LL at convergence			−949.07		−408.21		−237.2

Note: Alternative A–C (E–G) = automobile attribute packages for agent 1 (agent 2); Alternative D (H) = null alternative for agent 1 (agent 2) has, on average, a sizeable additional set of relevant influences on vehicle choice after controlling for the observed effects, compared to agent 2.

In pass 1, agent 1 has, on average, a bias against small vehicles, and both agents have strong preferences for air conditioning, manual transmission, and ABS brakes. In the null alternative we find that as agent 1 ages, there is an increasing probability of choosing none of the vehicles on offer, with the reverse situation for agent 2. Given the statistical significance of age, we expect it to have an important influence on whether agents agree in a pass or move to the next pass.

As we move through the passes, the number of statistically significant vehicle attributes and agent characteristics decreases. This suggests that specific attributes have an initial influence on the preferences of each agent in the pair, with a subset having a positive influence on a subset of agents agreeing. However, agents who do not agree in pass 1 and continue to review and revise in passes 2 and 3, appear to differ on a reduced set of statistically significant influences that are in the detail of vehicle specification such as air conditioning, transmission, and ABS brakes. The fact that vehicle price and fuel efficiency are statistically significant only in pass 1 is very informative, suggesting that these may well be attributes that all agents in the initial sample see as important, but that there remain a number of agent pairs who cannot agree initially without feedback and review, given knowledge of the other agents' preferences for some vehicle attributes.

In pass 2, this is revealed through the significance of a number of vehicle attributes and a statistically significant error component (or dispersion parameter) associated with the null alternative for agent 2. This suggests that there is a notable amount of heterogeneity in the unobserved variance (as distinct from the mean) associated with the null alternative that differs from that associated with the vehicle alternatives (normalized to zero).

As we move to pass 3 we note a statistically significant generic-specific constant for alternatives A–C, suggesting that there remain some unobserved effects that add to the preferences of agent 1 that are not accounted for by the observed attributes. Relative to a brother and sister agent pair, married agents in the final pass are less likely to choose the null alternative.

To gain a greater appreciation of the profile of agent pairs who agree or do not agree at each pass, we present three binary logit models in Table 22.5(a–c). The pass one "agree–non-agree" model suggests that as male agent 1 increases in age, they tend to agree, but the probability of agreeing decreases as the age of agent 2 increases. Households that have more cars tend have a reduced probability of agreeing in pass 1, maybe because the agents are more

Table 22.5 Sources of agreement

(a) Pass 1 (agree = 1)

Attribute	Binary logit	Mean of variable
Agent 1 Age (years)	0.0399 (1.1)	36.3
Agent 1 Male (1,0)	0.835 (5.4)	0.54
Agent 2 Age (years)	−0.362 (−1.0)	38.6
Agent 2 Male (1,0)	0.890 (5.9)	0.46
No. of cars in household	−0.097 (−2.5)	1.8
Agent 2 was told what other agent had chosen (1,0)	0.927 (7.7)	0.248
Agent thought other agent would choose same alt (1,0)	1.619 (13.9)	0.449
Agents are married to each other (1,0)	0.345 (1.8)	0.108
Agents live in a *de facto* relationship (1,0)	−0.586 (−3.0)	0.069
Agents are not related (1,0)	0.576 (2.4)	0.059
Sample size	3232	
LL at zero	−1502.48	
LL at convergence	−1367.06	

(b) Pass 2 (agree = 1)

Attribute	Binary logit	Mean of variable
Agent 1 Age (years)	0.447(1.0)	34.3
Agent 1 Male (1,0)	−0.374 (−1.9)	0.523
Agent 2 Age (years)	−0.148 (−3.3)	35.5
Agent 2 Male (1,0)	−.120 (−.63)	0.477
Agent 2 was told what other agent had chosen (1,0)	0.818 (5.7)	0.554
Agent thought other agent would choose same alt (1,0)	2.181 (10.4)	0.193
Agents are married to each other (1,0)	0.719 (3.4)	0.128
Agents live in a *de facto* relationship (1,0)	−0.654 (−2.6)	0.089
Agents are not related (1,0)	0.591 (2.2)	0.070
Sample size	1308	
LL at zero	−895.30	
LL at convergence	−798.12	

(c) Pass 3 (agree = 1)

Attribute	Binary logit	Mean of variable
Agent 1 Male (1,0)	−1.518 (−6.6)	0.565
Agent 2 Male (1,0)	−1.333 (−6.0)	0.434
Agent 2 Age (years)	−0.141 (−3.3)	36.8
No. of cars in household	0.226 (2.9)	1.73

Table 22.5 (cont.)

Attribute	Binary logit	Mean of variable
Agent thought other agent would choose same alt (1,0)	1.137 (4.4)	.104
Agents are married to each other (1,0)	0.786 (2.8)	0.109
Sample size		728
LL at zero		−383.39
LL at convergence		−358.56

discriminating in their own preferences for specific cars. Relative to an agent pair that is a brother and sister, agents who are married to each other are more likely to agree in all passes; compared to those in a *de facto* relationship (passes 1 and 2), who are less likely to agree; and those not related (passes 1 and 2), who are more likely to agree. Two variables of great interest relate to whether agent 2 was told what the other agent had chosen (applicable to pass 1), and a dummy variable to indicate "whether an agent thought the other agent would choose the same alternative." In pass 1, both variables are positive, suggesting a higher probability of agreement if agent 2 was told what agent 1 had chosen and where each agent had predicted that the other agent would choose the same alternative. The latter evidence is in a sense a partial logic check.

The findings presented above inform us of what attributes and socio-economic characteristics (SECs) influence the choices and hence preferences of each agent as they progress to agreement of a vehicle purchase. Another interesting product of the method is the ability to establish what role each person played in terms of influence (or power) in determining the outcome in each pass. Hensher *et al.* (2007) and Hensher and Knowles (2007) have investigated this matter in detail in the context of freight distribution chains and regulator operator cooperation in the bus sector, respectively. Equation (22.7) summarizes the econometric structure within which the role of power parameters can be parameterized.

As presented in a previous section, the free parameters in the joint utility functions are the vector of power measures, τ_{qk}, and the marginal utility estimates, carried forward from the independent choice model, are held constant across alternatives, whilst the attribute levels are the identical attribute levels present for each alternative j in mutually faced choice set p. The elements in τ_{qk} can vary across alternatives, but by definition sum to unity within each alternative. τ_{qk} as a power indicator can be a random parameter and a function of other criteria, such as SECs, and can be specific

Table 22.6 Group equilibrium model results

Attribute	Alternative(s)	ML
Random parameters:		
Vehicle price (000s)	A–C	−0.05148 (−2.1)
Fuel efficiency (litres/100km)	A–C	−0.19889 (−2.2)
Fixed parameters:		
Air conditioning (1,0)	A–C	1.4053 (8.1)
Manual transmission (1,0)	A–C	1.1743 (6.7)
ABS brakes (1,0)	A–C	0.6399 (3.8)
Agent 1 Male (1,0)	D	0.6366 (1.8)
No. of cars in household	D	0.3519 (3.2)
Null alternative constant	D	−2.4717 (−2.4)
Pass number	D	−0.8434 (−2.2)
Random parameter standard deviations		
Vehicle price (000s)	A–C	0.05148 (2.1)
Fuel efficiency (litres/100km)	A–C	0.07956 (2.2)
Error component (alternative-specific heterogeneity)	D	0.0153 (4.3)
Sample size		333
LL at zero		−679.97
LL at convergence		−358.01

Note: We only need to estimate models on A-D since both agents' agreed and attribute levels are identical per alternative. We have, however, included the SECs of each agent in the model.

to each attribute within and/or between alternatives, or constrained as the analyst sees fit.

As the power measures for agents q (λ_{qk}) and q' ($1 - \lambda_{qk}$) sum to unity for each attribute k, comparisons of influence across agent types are straightforward. If the two power measures are equal for a given attribute k (that is, $\lambda_{qk} = (1 - \lambda_{qk}) = 0.5$), then group choice equilibrium is not governed by a dominant agent with respect to attribute k. In other words, regardless of the power structure governing other attributes, agent types q and q' tend to reach perceptively fair compromises when bridging the gap in their preferences for k. If the power measures are significantly different across agent types (for example, $\lambda_{qk} > (1 - \lambda_{qk})$), then λ_{qk} gives a direct measure of the dominance of one agent type over the other with respect to attribute k; as λ_{qk} increases, so does the relative power held by agent type q over q' for k.

For example, the power measures may reveal that one agent type tends to get their way with regard to monetary concerns, whereas the other agent type tends to get their way with regard to concerns for non-financial attributes. These relationships can be examined further within subsets of agent groups (by decomposition of the random parameter specification of λ_{qk}), in order to reveal deviations from the inferred behavior at the sample level that may be present for a particular type of relationship.

It is important to note that in the case study the measure is unbounded (although it can be bounded as per Equation 22.6). That is, the only constraint on the power measures is that they sum to one across members of a group. Hence, it is possible to observe power measures either less than zero or greater than one. This is straightforward, in that a (0,1) bound is excessively restrictive for group decision making, especially for cases of trade-offs across fixed attribute bundles. The limited set of pre-specified trade-offs may make it necessary for a decision maker to offer more than requested with respect to one attribute, in order to reach agreement on an alternative. Therefore, one may observe a tendency for a given type of decision maker to offer greater concession toward the preferences of another type of decision maker for a given attribute than the initial discrepancy in preferences between the decision makers, resulting in an estimated power measure outside of the (0,1) range. The empirical evidence is given in Table 22.6.

The specific model form is a variation on the specification in Equation (22.2). We have calculated the joint probabilities of the 16 pairs of alternatives (A–D by E–H), and transformed these probabilities to log odds of joint agent probability of alternative pair for a logistics regression. The power parameters, all of which are statistically significant at the 95 percent level or better, for passes 1–3, are (0.982, 0.017), (0.960, 0.040), and (0.143, 0.867), respectively. What we observe is very informative. It suggests that, on average, agent 1 dominates the choice process in passes 1 and 2, with agent 2 coming to the fore in pass 3. The pass 3 finding suggests that, after two passes, the persistence of agent 2 in standing their ground has finally paid off and that the preferences of agent 2 in pass 3 are reflective of their real preferences, which would otherwise have been drowned by the dominance of a large subset of agents in passes 1 and 2 who dominated on average. This is crucial evidence to support the need to extract the preference data for each agent pair for the pass in which they agreed, and to estimate a model based on this data alone as an improved representation of preferences that might exist in real markets. We report the findings in Tables 22.6–22.8.

Table 22.6 establishes the influence of a random parameterization of vehicle prices and fuel efficiency; however, unlike the pass sequence, vehicle price is a random (albeit generic) parameter for both agents, now defined as a single decision maker (noting A–C = E–G and D = H). The error component dispersion parameter for the null alternative is statistically significant, suggesting the presence of significant unobserved sources of variance that impact on the choice between the three vehicle alternatives and the null. We have added in a variable to represent the number of passes leading up to agreement. The negative sign indicates that, after controlling for the influence of all other observed and unobserved effects, as the number of passes increases, the probability of choosing the null decreases. This is intuitively plausible to the extent to which each agent gathers more information on the preferences of the other party and has more opportunity to negotiate through feedback and review, resulting in an increasing probability of agreeing on a vehicle choice.

The final model provides empirical estimates of group equilibrium preferences. These enable us to establish a set of probabilities of choosing each vehicle package and the null. What is particularly interesting is the extent to which, on average, the application of the group equilibrium model results in different mean probability estimates than those obtained for each of the passes, especially pass 1, which is equivalent to the traditional one-pass SC experiment. The comparisons are summarized in Table 22.7.

If we used pass 1 as the correct preference revelation setting, essentially equivalent to what we obtain when we run an agent independent CE with no feedback and revision, relative to group choice equilibrium, alternatives AE (1,5) and BF (2,6) would have an over-estimated mean choice probability for both agents; alternative CG (3,7) has a mean estimate that is identical for agent 1 but an over-estimate in pass 1 for agent 2. The greatest difference is for the null alternative DH (4,8) where there is a significant under-estimate in pass 1. Passes 2 and 3 are not so informative since they represent the agents who do not agree in Pass 1, and which are not usually captured in the traditional non-feedback revision CE setting.

To gain some more systematic appreciation of the influences on agent agreement in the initial pass in contrast to the agreement in subsequent passes, we ran a binary logit model. The findings, given in Table 22.8, suggest that

Table 22.7 Probability contrasts

Alternative pairs	Group equilibrium	Pass 1 Agent 1	Agent 2	Pass 2 Agent 1	Agent 2	Pass 3 Agent 1	Agent 2
AE (1,5)	0.258	0.267	0.275	0.280	0.304	0.266	0.296
BF (2,6)	0.266	0.271	0.276	0.283	0.280	0.245	0.273
CG (3,7)	0.274	0.274	0.280	0.278	0.287	0.265	0.275
DH (4,8)	0.199	0.187	0.168	0.157	0.127	0.223	0.157
Total sample		404		171		35	
agree	333 comprising:	233		68		32	

Table 22.8 Sources of agreement: passes 2 and 3 versus pass 1 group equilibrium

Attribute	Binary logit	Mean of bariable
Pass 23 constant	−0.6171 (−6.7)	
Agent 1 Male (1,0)	−0.2796 (−2.3)	0.538
Age difference between agent 1 and 2	0.403 (4.5)	−11.62
Agents are married to each other (1,0)	0.6331 (3.6)	0.114
Agents live in a *de facto* relationship (1,0)	0.2700 (1.2)	0.060
Agents are not related (1,0)	1.1813 (4.6)	0.063
Sample size	1332	
LL at zero	−861.02	
LL at convergence	−829.07	

males are more likely to agree in pass 1 than females. The greater the age difference, the more likely the negotiation will continue beyond pass 1. Relative to the agent pair being a brother and sister (base), married, *de facto* and non-related couples are more likely to disagree in pass 1 and continue to a second or third pass. This reinforces the evidence for passes 1, 2, and 3 as reported in the agree–non-agree models (Table 22.5).

22.5 Nlogit commands and outputs

The Nlogit set ups are exactly the ones used to obtain the findings presented in Section 22.4. We have edited out some of the output that is not essential to guide the users in setting up the command stream. Passes 1, 2, and 3 have the same command structure except that different subsets of data are used as shown by the reject commands we have listed.

22.5.1 Estimating a model with power weights

```
Load;file =C:\Papers\WPs2011\IACECar\IACE_Car_MF.sav$
```

22.5.2 Pass 1, round 1 (agent 1) and round 2 (agent 2) ML model

```
reject;pass#1$
reject;rnd>2$
reject;alt>8$   To eliminate observations that are not applicable
create;pricez=price/1000$
```

```
rplogit
;lhs=choice1,cset,altijz
;choices=altA1,altB1,altC1,altD1,altA2,altB2,altC2,altD2?4 alternatives
for agents 1 & 2
;rpl;fcn=price1(t,1),fuelef12(t,1);halton,pts=500
;par ;utility=util1;prob=pass1p  ?storing utilities and probabilities
;model:
U(altA1)=ASC1+price1*pricez+fuelef12*fuel+smallv1*smallv+ac1*ac+trans1
*trans+abs1*abs/
U(altB1)=ASC1+price1*pricez+fuelef12*fuel+smallv1*smallv+ac1*ac+trans1
*trans+abs1*abs/
U(altC1)=ASC1+price1*pricez+fuelef12*fuel+smallv1*smallv+ac1*ac+trans1
*trans+abs1*abs/
U(altD1)=age1*ageA/
U(altA2)=asc2+price2*pricez+fuelef12*fuel+ac2*ac+trans2*trans+abs2*abs/
U(altB2)=asc2+price2*pricez+fuelef12*fuel+ac2*ac+trans2*trans+abs2*abs/
U(altC2)=Asc2+price2*pricez+fuelef12*fuel+ac2*ac+trans2*trans+abs2*abs/
U(altD2)=genderd2*genderb$
Normal exit from iterations. Exit status=0.
+-----------------------------------------------------------+
| Random Parameters Logit Model                             |
| Maximum Likelihood Estimates                              |
| Dependent variable              CHOICE1                   |
| Number of observations              808                   |
| Iterations completed                 17                   |
| Log likelihood function        -949.0695                  |
| Number of parameters                 14                   |
| Info. Criterion: AIC =          2.38384                   |
| Info. Criterion: BIC =          2.46518                   |
| Restricted log likelihood      -1680.189                  |
| McFadden Pseudo R-squared       .4351412                  |
| At start values  -950.6900   .00170 *******              |
+-----------------------------------------------------------+

+-----------------------------------------------------------+
| Random Parameters Logit Model                             |
| Replications for simulated probs. = 500                   |
| Halton sequences used for simulations                     |
+-----------------------------------------------------------+
```

Variable	Coefficient	Standard Error	b/St.Er.	P[|Z|>z]
---------+Random parameters in utility functions				
PRICE1	-.08419594	.02759731	-3.051	.0023
FUELEF12	-.15328834	.06085694	-2.519	.0118
---------+Nonrandom parameters in utility functions				
ASC1	3.49565266	1.06965972	3.268	.0011
SMALLV1	-1.46097818	.62849023	-2.325	.0201
AC1	1.13049774	.14996959	7.538	.0000

```
TRANS1    |    1.32105367     .15718658     8.404    .0000
ABS1      |     .56148756     .14904703     3.767    .0002
AGE1      |     .21633004     .06836149     3.165    .0016
ASC2      |    1.12734001     .71247313     1.582    .1136
PRICE2    |    -.03342266     .02221145    -1.505    .1324
AC2       |    1.14895147     .14369550     7.996    .0000
TRANS2    |     .72556207     .14213511     5.105    .0000
ABS2      |     .51085546     .14038488     3.639    .0003
GENDERD2  |    -.94844004     .31151874    -3.045    .0023
---------+ Derived standard deviations of parameter distributions
TsPRICE1  |     .08419594     .02759731     3.051    .0023
TsFUELEF  |     .15328834     .06085694     2.519    .0118
```

22.5.3 Pass 1, round 1 (agent 1) and round 2 (agent 2) agree model

```
create;if(relation=1)marr=1 ;if(relation=2)defacto=1 ;if(relation=3)
notrel=1$
logit
    ;lhs=agree1
    ;rhs=agea,gendera,ageb,genderb,numcars,told,choose,marr,defacto,
notrel$
Normal exit from iterations. Exit status=0.
```

```
+-------------------------------------------------------------+
| Binary Logit Model for Binary Choice                        |
| Maximum Likelihood Estimates                                |
| Dependent variable               AGREE1                     |
| Number of observations             3232                     |
| Iterations completed                 11                     |
| Log likelihood function        -1367.056                    |
| Number of parameters                 10                     |
| Info. Criterion: AIC =           .85214                     |
| Restricted log likelihood      -1502.479                    |
| McFadden Pseudo R-squared        .0901328                   |
+-------------------------------------------------------------+
```

```
+--------+--------------+--------------+---------+---------+----------+----------+----------+
|Variable| Coefficient  | Standard Error |b/St.Er.|P[|Z|>z]| Mean of X|
+--------+--------------+--------------+---------+---------+----------+----------+----------+
---------+Characteristics in numerator of Prob[Y = 1]
  AGEA    |     .03993165     .03720238    1.073    .2831    3.63366337
  GENDERA |     .83576694     .15363277    5.440    .0000     .54455446
  AGEB    |    -.03620329     .03792487    -.955    .3398    3.86138614
  GENDERB |     .89030702     .15153326    5.875    .0000     .45544554
  NUMCARS |    -.09759253     .03868549   -2.523    .0116  -18.1980198
  TOLD    |     .92658029     .12092513    7.662    .0000     .24381188
  CHOOSE  |    1.61992446     .11679118   13.870    .0000     .44925743
```

MARR	.34599887	.19231219	1.799	.0720	.10891089
DEFACTO	-.58649446	.19870484	-2.952	.0032	.06930693
NOTREL	.57650284	.23576884	2.445	.0145	.05940594

22.5.4 Sorting probabilities for two agents into a single row

```
create
    ;passA1=pass1p
    ;passB1=pass1p[+1]
    ;passC1=pass1p[+2]
    ;passD1=pass1p[+3]
    ;passA2=pass1p[+16]
    ;passB2=pass1p[+17]
    ;passC2=pass1p[+18]
    ;passD2=pass1p[+19]$
```

22.5.5 Creating cooperation and non-cooperation probabilities for the pairs

```
create
    ;coopA=passA1*passA2 ? alt A agent 1 and alt A agent 2
    ;ncoop12=passA1*passB2
    ;ncoop13=passA1*passC2
    ;ncoop14=passA1*passD2
    ;ncoop21=passB1*passA2
    ;coopB=passB1*passB2
    ;ncoop23=passB1*passC2
    ;ncoop24=passB1*passD2
    ;ncoop31=passC1*passA2
    ;ncoop32=passC1*passB2
    ;coopC=passC1*passC2
    ;ncoop34=passC1*passD2
    ;ncoop41=passD1*passA2
    ;ncoop42=passD1*passB2
    ;ncoop43=passD1*passC2
    ;coopD=passC1*passC2 $
```

22.5.6 Removing all but line 1 of the four choice sets per person in pair

```
create;lined=dmy(32,1)$
reject;lined#1$   To use only line one of the 32
namelist;cprobs=coopA,ncoop12,ncoop13,ncoop14,ncoop21,coopB,ncoop23,ncoop24,
              ncoop31,ncoop32,coopC,ncoop34,ncoop41,ncoop42,ncoop43,coopD$
namelist;passpr=passA1,passB1,passC1,passD1,passA2,passB2,passC2,passD2$
dstats;rhs=cprobs,passpr,rnd,pass,lined$
Descriptive Statistics
```

All results based on nonmissing observations.
```
=======================================================================
Variable     Mean        Std.Dev.     Minimum       Maximum         Cases
=======================================================================
```
All observations in current sample
```
-----------------------------------------------------------------
COOPA   | .763862E-01  .726007E-01  .178755E-02  .395191          101
NCOOP12 | .673697E-01  .553543E-01  .631503E-02  .344814          101
NCOOP13 | .716571E-01  .572734E-01  .383806E-02  .284068          101
NCOOP14 | .456793E-01  .452811E-01  .203701E-02  .288444          101
NCOOP21 | .728243E-01  .516858E-01  .160653E-02  .231627          101
COOPB   | .990126E-01  .112036      .155347E-02  .556135          101
NCOOP23 | .765949E-01  .641968E-01  .734792E-03  .295942          101
NCOOP24 | .508328E-01  .479378E-01  .126018E-02  .240950          101
NCOOP31 | .690486E-01  .612892E-01  .410930E-02  .326127          101
NCOOP32 | .688203E-01  .652851E-01  .287789E-02  .333120          101
COOPC   | .871799E-01  .865398E-01  .176146E-02  .411685          101
NCOOP34 | .404765E-01  .325327E-01  .178009E-02  .133559          101
NCOOP41 | .470984E-01  .420942E-01  .224879E-02  .233532          101
NCOOP42 | .440991E-01  .365063E-01  .369707E-02  .202388          101
NCOOP43 | .489374E-01  .456428E-01  .269314E-02  .211110          101
COOPD   | .871799E-01  .865398E-01  .176146E-02  .411685          101
PASSA1  | .261092      .149453      .316582E-01  .698440          101
PASSB1  | .299265      .188840      .300963E-01  .787971          101
PASSC1  | .265525      .169636      .304937E-01  .641838          101
PASSD1  | .174118      .114026      .315459E-01  .508091          101
PASSA2  | .265358      .137121      .316582E-01  .567271          101
PASSB2  | .279302      .170303      .300963E-01  .787971          101
PASSC2  | .284369      .170913      .167566E-01  .793413          101
PASSD2  | .170972      .106892      .204512E-01  .530933          101
RND     | 1.46535      .501285      1.00000      2.00000          101
PASS    | 1.00000      .000000      1.00000      1.00000          101
LINED   | 1.00000      .000000      1.00000      1.00000          101
```

22.5.7 Getting utilities on 1 line (note: focusing only on overall utilities at this stage)

```
Sample;all$
reject;pass#1$
reject;rnd>2$
reject;alt>8$   To eliminate obs that are not applicable
create
    ;utilA1=util1
    ;utilB1=util1[+1]
    ;utilC1=util1[+2]
    ;utilD1=util1[+3]
    ;utilA2=util1[+16]
    ;utilB2=util1[+17]
    ;utilC2=util1[+18]
    ;utilD2=util1[+19]$
```

22.5.8 Writing out new file for power weight application

```
write;
    pass,rnd,coopA,utilA1,utilA2,
    pass,rnd,ncoop12,utilA1,utilB2,
    pass,rnd,ncoop13,utilA1,utilC2,
    pass,rnd,ncoop14,utilA1,utilD2,
    pass,rnd,ncoop21,utilB1,utilA2,
    pass,rnd,coopB,utilB1,utilB2,
    pass,rnd,ncoop23,utilB1,utilC2,
    pass,rnd,ncoop24,utilB1,utilD2,
    pass,rnd,ncoop31,utilC1,utilA2,
    pass,rnd,ncoop32,utilC1,utilB2,
    pass,rnd,coopC,utilC1,utilC2,
    pass,rnd,ncoop34,utilC1,utilD2,
    pass,rnd,ncoop41,utilD1,utilA2,
    pass,rnd,ncoop42,utilD1,utilB2,
    pass,rnd,ncoop43,utilD1,utilC2,
    pass,rnd,coopD,utilD1,utilD2
    ;format=(15(5F12.5/)5f12.5)
    ;file=C:\Papers\WPs2011\IACECar\Pass1Power.txt$
```

22.5.9 Reading new data file

```
reset
read;file=C:\Papers\WPs2011\IACECar\Pass1Power.txt
    ;names= pass,rnd,prob,util1,util2
    ;format=(5f12.5);nobs= 1616 ;nvar=5$
dstats;rhs=*$
Descriptive Statistics
=======================================================================
Variable     Mean       Std.Dev.     Minimum     Maximum       Cases
=======================================================================
All observations in current sample
-----------------------------------------------------------------------
PASS    |   1.00000     .000000     1.00000     1.00000        1616
RND     |   1.46535     .498952     1.00000     2.00000        1616
PROB    |   .658249E-01 .655178E-01 .730000E-03 .556130        1616
UTIL1   |   .829769     1.09591    -1.73545     3.49634        1592
UTIL2   |   .849197     1.07817    -1.73545     3.49634        1336
```

22.5.10 Estimating OLS power weight model (weights sum to 1.0)

Note: Different to before, since using paired probabilities as the dependent variable.

```
create;diffut=util1-util2;lprob=log(prob/(1-prob))$
crmodel
    ;lhs=lprob
    ;rhs=one,util1,util2
    ;cls:b(2)+b(3)=1$
```

```
+-----------------------------------------------------------------------+
| Ordinary    least squares regression                                  |
| LHS=LPROB    Mean                    =  -3.124691                      |
|              Standard deviation      =   1.121428                      |
| WTS=none     Number of observs.      =       1616                      |
| Model size   Parameters             =          3                      |
|              Degrees of freedom      =       1613                      |
| Residuals    Sum of squares         =   2023.224                      |
|              Standard error of e     =   1.119966                      |
| Fit          R-squared              =   .3841372E-02                   |
|              Adjusted R-squared      =   .2606210E-02                  |
| Model test   F[  2,  1613] (prob) =    3.11 (.0449)                    |
| Diagnostic   Log likelihood         =  -2474.593                      |
|              Restricted(b=0)         =  -2477.703                      |
| Info criter. LogAmemiya Prd. Crt. =     .2284510                      |
|              Akaike Info. Criter. =     .2284510                      |
+-----------------------------------------------------------------------+
|Variable| Coefficient  | Standard Error |b/St.Er.|P[|Z|>z]| Mean of X|
+--------+--------------+----------------+--------+--------+----------+----------+
 Constant|  -3.09768641      .03061562  -101.180   .0000
 UTIL1   |    .00030301      .00023926     1.266   .2054  -14.0191879
 UTIL2   |    .00013201   .764675D-04      1.726   .0843  -172.392001
```

Resulting power weights

```
+-----------------------------------------------------------------------+
| Linearly restricted regression                                        |
| Ordinary    least squares regression                                  |
| LHS=LPROB    Mean                    =  -3.124691                      |
|              Standard deviation      =   1.121428                      |
| WTS=none     Number of observs.      =       1616                      |
| Model size   Parameters             =          2                      |
|              Degrees of freedom      =       1614                      |
| Residuals    Sum of squares         =   .2355703E+08                  |
|              Standard error of e     =   120.8116                      |
| Fit          R-squared              =  -11597.59                       |
|              Adjusted R-squared      =  -11604.78                      |
| Diagnostic   Log likelihood         =  -10039.48                      |
|              Restricted(b=0)         =  -2477.703                      |
| Info criter. LogAmemiya Prd. Crt. =    9.589701                       |
|              Akaike Info. Criter. =    9.589701                       |
| Restrictns.  F[  1,  1613] (prob) =******* (.0000)                    |
+-----------------------------------------------------------------------+
```

Variable	Coefficient	Standard Error	b/St.Er.	P[|Z|>z]	Mean of X
Constant	13.6012536	3.27626610	4.151	.0000	
UTIL1	.98290896	.00823779	119.317	.0000	-14.0191879
UTIL2	.01709104	.00823779	2.075	.0380	-172.392001

22.5.11 Pass #2 (repeating same process as for pass#1)

```
create
    ;if(pass=1)chp1=choice1
    ;if(pass=2)chp2=choice1$
reject;pass#2$
create;if(rnd=3|rnd=4)rnd34=1$
reject;rnd34#1$
reject;alt>8$  To eliminate obs that are not applicable
nlogit
    ;lhs=choice1,cset,alt
    ;choices=altA1,altB1,altC1,altD1,altA2,altB2,altC2,altD2
    ;utility=util2;prob=pass2p
    ;ecm= (altD1),(altD2)
    ;model:
    U(altA1)=ac1*ac+trans1*trans+abs1*abs+manualb1*manualb/
    U(altB1)=ac1*ac+trans1*trans+abs1*abs+manualb1*manualb/
    U(altC1)=ac1*ac+trans1*trans+abs1*abs+manualb1*manualb/
    U(altD1)= choose*choose /
    U(altA2)=smallv2*smallv+ac2*ac+trans2*trans /
    U(altB2)=smallv2*smallv
    +ac2*ac+trans2*trans /
    U(altC2)=smallv2*smallv+ac2*ac+trans2*trans /
    U(altD2)=choose*choose
```

```
Normal exit from iterations. Exit status=0.
+-------------------------------------------------------------+
| Error Components (Random Effects) model                     |
| Maximum Likelihood Estimates                                |
| Dependent variable              CHOICE1                     |
| Number of observations              327                     |
| Iterations completed                 12                     |
| Log likelihood function        -408.2055                    |
| Number of parameters                 10                     |
| Info. Criterion: AIC =          2.55783                     |
| Restricted log likelihood      -679.9774                    |
| McFadden Pseudo R-squared        .3996779                   |
| At start values   -408.2175   .00003 *******|
| Response data are given as ind. choice.                     |
+-------------------------------------------------------------+
```

```
+------------------------------------------------------------+
| Error Components (Random Effects) model                    |
| Replications for simulated probs. = 500                    |
| Number of obs.=   327, skipped   0 bad obs.                |
+------------------------------------------------------------+
+--------+--------------+---------------+---------+--------+--------+--------+
|Variable| Coefficient  | Standard Error |b/St.Er.|P[|Z|>z]|
+--------+--------------+---------------+---------+--------+--------+--------+
---------+Nonrandom parameters in utility functions
  AC1     |     .49005645      .18805095      2.606    .0092
  TRANS1  |     .64838425      .18805761      3.448    .0006
  ABS1    |     .68111715      .19230800      3.542    .0004
  MANUALB1|   -1.40274509      .48704108     -2.880    .0040
  CHOOSE  |     .73906653      .33872551      2.182    .0291
  SMALLV2 |    1.51774727     1.09623989      1.385    .1662
  AC2     |     .88020449      .20142269      4.370    .0000
  TRANS2  |     .75316259      .20134452      3.741    .0002
---------+Standard deviations of latent random effects
  SigmaE01|     .00668620      .00541920      1.234    .2173
  SigmaE02|     .09251584      .00552830     16.735    .0000
```

```
logit
    ;lhs=agree1
    ;rhs=agea,gendera,ageb,genderb,told,choose,marr,defacto,notrel$
Normal exit from iterations. Exit status=0.
```

```
+------------------------------------------------------------+
| Binary Logit Model for Binary Choice                       |
| Maximum Likelihood Estimates                               |
| Dependent variable              AGREE1                     |
| Number of observations            1308                     |
| Iterations completed                 5                     |
| Log likelihood function       -798.1246                    |
| Number of parameters                 9                     |
| Info. Criterion: AIC =         1.23414                     |
| Restricted log likelihood     -895.2948                    |
| McFadden Pseudo R-squared       .1085343                   |
+------------------------------------------------------------+
+--------+--------------+---------------+--------+---------+----------+----------+-----------+
|Variable| Coefficient  | Standard Error |b/St.Er.|P[|Z|>z]| Mean of X|
+--------+--------------+---------------+--------+---------+----------+----------+-----------+
---------+Characteristics in numerator of Prob[Y = 1]
  AGEA    |     .04472296      .04338149      1.031    .3026   3.43425076
  GENDERA |    -.37357912      .19417657     -1.924    .0544    .52293578
  AGEB    |     .11002371      .04465762      3.315    .0009   3.55351682
  GENDERB |    -.12024167      .19242782      -.625    .5321    .47706422
  TOLD    |     .81835993      .14352136      5.702    .0000    .55351682
  CHOOSE  |    2.18160246      .20911924     10.432    .0000    .19266055
  MARR    |     .71989585      .21491511      3.350    .0008    .12844037
```

```
   DEFACTO |      -.65358419        .24686418     -2.648    .0081    .08868502
   NOTREL  |       .59052518        .26551989      2.224    .0261    .07033639
create
    ;passA1=pass2p
    ;passB1=pass2p[+1]
    ;passC1=pass2p[+2]
    ;passD1=pass2p[+3]
    ;passA2=pass2p[+16]
    ;passB2=pass2p[+17]
    ;passC2=pass2p[+18]
    ;passD2=pass2p[+19]$
create
    ;coopA=passA1*passA2      ;ncoop12=passA1*passB2
    ;ncoop13=passA1*passC2
    ;ncoop14=passA1*passD2
    ;ncoop21=passB1*passA2
    ;coopB=passB1*passB2
    ;ncoop23=passB1*passC2
    ;ncoop24=passB1*passD2
    ;ncoop31=passC1*passA2
    ;ncoop32=passC1*passB2
    ;coopC=passC1*passC2
    ;ncoop34=passC1*passD2
    ;ncoop41=passD1*passA2
    ;ncoop42=passD1*passB2
    ;ncoop43=passD1*passC2
    ;coopD=passC1*passC2 $
create;lined=dmy(32,1)$
reject;lined#1$  To use only line one of the 32 (4 resp A by 4 alt and 4 ...
namelist;cprobs=coopA,ncoop12,ncoop13,ncoop14,ncoop21,coopB,ncoop23,
    ncoop24,
      ncoop31,ncoop32,coopC,ncoop34,ncoop41,ncoop42,ncoop43,coopD$
namelist;passpr=passA1,passB1,passC1,passD1,passA2,passB2,passC2,passD2$
dstats;rhs=cprobs,passpr,rnd,pass,lined$
Descriptive Statistics
=======================================================================
Variable     Mean        Std.Dev.     Minimum      Maximum       Cases
=======================================================================
-----------------------------------------------------------------------
All observations in current sample
-----------------------------------------------------------------------
COOPA    |  .849429E-01  .533277E-01  .130850E-01  .248684          46
NCOOP12  |  .890744E-01  .537367E-01  .245993E-01  .263873          46
NCOOP13  |  .920542E-01  .567748E-01  .949661E-02  .285906          46
NCOOP14  |  .425945E-01  .367116E-01  .452954E-02  .209464          46
NCOOP21  |  .739161E-01  .455627E-01  .136280E-01  .237295          46
COOPB    |  .813787E-01  .516624E-01  .155708E-01  .263873          46
NCOOP23  |  .837980E-01  .552306E-01  .111258E-01  .277152          46
NCOOP24  |  .371832E-01  .296734E-01  .341251E-02  .132585          46
```

NCOOP31	.717988E-01	.402659E-01	.100617E-01	.198032	46
NCOOP32	.792008E-01	.467621E-01	.128627E-01	.187629	46
COOPC	.845424E-01	.587186E-01	.100617E-01	.271045	46
NCOOP34	.370204E-01	.347176E-01	.387478E-02	.156443	46
NCOOP41	.390516E-01	.379878E-01	.351979E-02	.253621	46
NCOOP42	.447599E-01	.441971E-01	.165738E-02	.253621	46
NCOOP43	.400139E-01	.276343E-01	.848759E-02	.149056	46
COOPD	.845424E-01	.587186E-01	.100617E-01	.271045	46
PASSA1	.309483	.125592	.116319	.630297	47
PASSB1	.273875	.113357	.967490E-01	.575822	47
PASSC1	.274148	.121305	.816736E-01	.520661	47
PASSD1	.142494	.950604E-01	.171307E-01	.606601	47
PASSA2	.269709	.111041	.816900E-01	.498693	46
PASSB2	.294414	.124243	.609159E-01	.630508	46
PASSC2	.300409	.139099	.816431E-01	.630172	46
PASSD2	.135468	.939317E-01	.171307E-01	.518700	46
RND	3.36170	.485688	3.00000	4.00000	47
PASS	2.00000	.000000	2.00000	2.00000	47
LINED	1.00000	.000000	1.00000	1.00000	47

```
Sample;all$
reject;pass#2$
create;if(rnd=3|rnd=4)rnd34=1$
reject;rnd34#1$
reject;alt>8$  To eliminate obs that are not applicable

create
    ;utilA1=util1
    ;utilB1=util1[+1]
    ;utilC1=util1[+2]
    ;utilD1=util1[+3]
    ;utilA2=util1[+16]
    ;utilB2=util1[+17]
    ;utilC2=util1[+18]
    ;utilD2=util1[+19]$
create;lined=dmy(32,1)$
reject;lined#1$  To use only line one of the 32
write;
    pass,rnd,coopA,utilA1,utilA2,
    pass,rnd,ncoop12,utilA1,utilB2,
    pass,rnd,ncoop13,utilA1,utilC2,
    pass,rnd,ncoop14,utilA1,utilD2,
    pass,rnd,ncoop21,utilB1,utilA2,
    pass,rnd,coopB,utilB1,utilB2,
    pass,rnd,ncoop23,utilD1,utilC2,
    pass,rnd,ncoop24,utilB1,utilD2,
    pass,rnd,ncoop31,utilC1,utilA2,
    pass,rnd,ncoop32,utilC1,utilB2,
```

```
    pass,rnd,coopC,utilC1,utilC2,
    pass,rnd,ncoop34,utilC1,utilD2,
    pass,rnd,ncoop41,utilD1,utilA2,
    pass,rnd,ncoop42,utilD1,utilB2,
    pass,rnd,ncoop43,utilD1,utilC2,
    pass,rnd,coopD,utilD1,utilD2
    ;format=(15(5F12.5/)5f12.5)
    ;file=C:\Papers\WPs2011\IACECar\Pass2Power.txt$
reset
read;file=C:\Papers\WPs2011\IACECar\Pass2Power.txt
    ;names= pass,rnd,prob,util1,util2
    ;format=(5f12.5);nobs= 1616 ;nvar=5$
Last observation read from data file was      752
dstats;rhs=*$
Descriptive Statistics
=======================================================================
Variable      Mean        Std.Dev.      Minimum      Maximum        Cases
=======================================================================
All observations in current sample
-----------------------------------------------------------------------

PASS  |   2.00000      .000000       2.00000      2.00000           752
RND   |   3.36170      .480813       3.00000      4.00000           752
PROB  |   .666169E-01  .509216E-01   .166000E-02  .285910           736
UTIL1 |   1.11452      .717230      -.397410      2.55852           728
UTIL2 |   1.17962      .689951      -.274140      2.55852           472
create
    ;diffut=util1-util2
    ;lprob=log(prob/(1-prob))$
crmodel
    ;lhs=lprob
    ;rhs=one,util1,util2
    ;cls:b(2)+b(3)=1$
```

```
+-----------------------------------------------------------------+
| Ordinary     least squares regression                          |
| LHS=LPROB      Mean                 =  -24.12440                |
|                Standard deviation   =   143.8358                |
| WTS=none       Number of observs.   =       752                |
| Model size     Parameters           =         3                |
|                Degrees of freedom   =       749                |
| Residuals      Sum of squares       =   9857381.               |
|                Standard error of e  =   114.7202                |
| Fit            R-squared            =   .3655639                |
|                Adjusted R-squared   =   .3638698                |
| Model test     F[ 2,   749] (prob) = 215.79 (.0000)            |
| Diagnostic     Log likelihood       =  -4631.896                |
|                Restricted(b=0)       =  -4802.983                |
|                Chi-sq [ 2]  (prob) = 342.17 (.0000)            |
```

```
| Info criter. LogAmemiya Prd. Crt. =    9.488974    |
|              Akaike Info. Criter.  =    9.488973    |
+-----------------------------------------------------------------------+
```

Variable	Coefficient	Standard Error	b/St.Er.	P[|Z|>z]	Mean of X
Constant	-3.46215432	5.27426084	-.656	.5116	
UTIL1	.48247198	.02448741	19.703	.0000	-30.8040281
UTIL2	.01562429	.00890306	1.755	.0793	-371.227687

```
+-----------------------------------------------------------------------+
| Linearly restricted regression                                        |
| Ordinary     least squares regression                                 |
| LHS=LPROB    Mean                 =  -24.12440                         |
|              Standard deviation   =   143.8358                         |
| WTS=none     Number of observs.   =        752                         |
| Model size   Parameters           =          2                        |
|              Degrees of freedom   =        750                         |
| Residuals    Sum of squares       =   .1561210E+08                     |
|              Standard error of e  =   144.2780                         |
| Fit          R-squared            =  -.4818718E-02                     |
|              Adjusted R-squared   =  -.6158477E-02                     |
| Diagnostic   Log likelihood       =  -4804.790                        |
|              Restricted(b=0)       =  -4802.983                        |
| Info criter. LogAmemiya Prd. Crt. =   9.946140                        |
|              Akaike Info. Criter.  =   9.946140                        |
+-----------------------------------------------------------------------+
```

Variable	Coefficient	Standard Error	b/St.Er.	P[|Z|>z]	Mean of X
Constant	20.2625944	6.47789105	3.128	.0018	
UTIL1	.96009981	.01110134	86.485	.0000	-30.8040281
UTIL2	.03990019	.01110134	3.594	.0003	-371.227687

22.5.12 Pass #3 (same set up as pass#1)

```
reset
Load;file =C:\Papers\WPs2011\IACECar\IACE_Car_MF.sav$
reject;pass#3$
create;if(rnd=5|rnd=6)rnd56=1$
reject;rnd56#1$
reject;alt>8$  To eliminate obs that are not applicable
create
    ;pricez=price/1000$
create
    ;if(relation=1)marr=1
    ;if(relation=2)defacto=1
    ;if(relation=3)notrel=1$
```

```
nlogit
    ;lhs=choice1,cset,alt
    ;choices=altA1,altB1,altC1,altD1,altA2,altB2,altC2,altD2
    ;utility=util2;prob=pass2p
    ;model:
    U(altA1)=ASC1+ac1*ac+trans1*trans+abs1*abs/
    U(altB1)=ASC1+ac1*ac
    +trans1*trans+abs1*abs/
    U(altC1)=ASC1+ac1*ac+trans1*trans+abs1*abs/
    U(altD1)= marr*marr/
    U(altA2)=ac2*ac /
    U(altB2)=ac2*ac/?+trans2*trans /
    U(altC2)=ac2*ac/?+trans2*trans /
    U(altD2)=marr*marr$
```

Normal exit from iterations. Exit status=0.

```
+--------------------------------------------------------------+
| Discrete choice (multinomial logit) model                    |
| Maximum Likelihood Estimates                                 |
| Dependent variable                        Choice             |
| Number of observations                    182                |
| Iterations completed                       6                 |
| Log likelihood function        -237.1371                     |
| Number of parameters                       6                 |
| Info. Criterion: AIC =          2.67184                      |
| Info. Criterion: BIC =          2.77746                      |
| R2=1-LogL/LogL*  Log-L fncn  R-sqrd  RsqAdj                  |
| Number of obs.=   182, skipped   0 bad obs.                  |
+--------------------------------------------------------------+
```

Variable	Coefficient	Standard Error	b/St.Er.	P[|Z|>z]
ASC1	-.88925055	.38018939	-2.339	.0193
AC1	.55795018	.26762586	2.085	.0371
TRANS1	.41948069	.26803721	1.565	.1176
ABS1	.61454275	.28223996	2.177	.0295
MARR	-1.71948941	1.05072358	-1.636	.1017
AC2	.94820487	.26548810	3.572	.0004

```
logit
    ;lhs=agree1
    ;rhs=genderb,gendera,numcars,marr,choose,ageb$
```

Normal exit from iterations. Exit status=0.

```
+--------------------------------------------------------------+
| Binary Logit Model for Binary Choice                         |
| Maximum Likelihood Estimates                                 |
| Dependent variable                        AGREE1             |
| Number of observations                    728                |
| Iterations completed                       5                 |
| Log likelihood function        -358.5647                     |
```

```
| Number of parameters                    6       |
| Info. Criterion: AIC =            1.00155        |
| Restricted log likelihood       -383.3864        |
| McFadden Pseudo R-squared        .0647432        |
+-------------------------------------------------------------+
+--------+--------------+---------------+--------+--------+---------+----------+---------+
|Variable| Coefficient  | Standard Error |b/St.Er.|P[|Z|>z]| Mean of X|
+--------+--------------+---------------+--------+--------+---------+----------+---------+
---------+Characteristics in numerator of Prob[Y = 1]
 GENDERB |    -1.33326571       .22254840       -5.991    .0000      .43406593
 GENDERA |    -1.51788811       .22970120       -6.608    .0000      .56593407
 NUMCARS |      .22571487       .07816808        2.888    .0039     1.73076923
 MARR    |      .78591991       .28140716        2.793    .0052      .10989011
 CHOOSE  |     1.13743684       .26059781        4.365    .0000      .10439560
 AGEB    |     -.14127984       .04296746       -3.288    .0010     3.68681319
```

```
create
    ;passA1=pass3p
    ;passB1=pass3p[+1]
    ;passC1=pass3p[+2]
    ;passD1=pass3p[+3]
    ;passA2=pass3p[+16]
    ;passB2=pass3p[+17]
    ;passC2=pass3p[+18]
    ;passD2=pass3p[+19]$
create
    ;coopA=passA1*passA2      ;ncoop12=passA1*passB2
    ;ncoop13=passA1*passC2
    ;ncoop14=passA1*passD2
    ;ncoop21=passB1*passA2
    ;coopB=passB1*passB2
    ;ncoop23=passB1*passC2
    ;ncoop24=passB1*passD2
    ;ncoop31=passC1*passA2
    ;ncoop32=passC1*passB2
    ;coopC=passC1*passC2
    ;ncoop34=passC1*passD2
    ;ncoop41=passD1*passA2
    ;ncoop42=passD1*passB2
    ;ncoop43=passD1*passC2
    ;coopD=passC1*passC2 $
create;lined=dmy(32,1)$
reject;lined#1$  To use only line one of the 32
namelist;cprobs=coopA,ncoop12,ncoop13,ncoop14,ncoop21,coopB,ncoop23,
ncoop24,
    ncoop31,ncoop32,coopC,ncoop34,ncoop41,ncoop42,ncoop43,coopD$
namelist;passpr=passA1,passB1,passC1,passD1,passA2,passB2,passC2,passD2$
dstats;rhs=cprobs,passpr,rnd,pass,lined$
Descriptive Statistics
```

```
========================================================================
Variable    Mean        Std.Dev.     Minimum      Maximum      Cases
========================================================================
------------------------------------------------------------------------
All observations in current sample
------------------------------------------------------------------------
COOPA    | .728784E-01  .352189E-01  .254591E-01  .157090          17
NCOOP12  | .739366E-01  .357962E-01  .221670E-01  .142914          17
NCOOP13  | .976446E-01  .557435E-01  .321044E-01  .227205          17
NCOOP14  | .496361E-01  .304240E-01  .179073E-01  .130852          17
NCOOP21  | .719108E-01  .348934E-01  .166485E-01  .134326          17
COOPB    | .701286E-01  .330785E-01  .229877E-01  .134326          17
NCOOP23  | .927623E-01  .488328E-01  .290864E-01  .201830          17
NCOOP24  | .477815E-01  .255676E-01  .109036E-01  .940584E-01      17
NCOOP31  | .638935E-01  .516668E-01  .166485E-01  .250758          17
NCOOP32  | .647819E-01  .483981E-01  .189139E-01  .213877          17
COOPC    | .793098E-01  .467249E-01  .254111E-01  .213877          17
NCOOP34  | .439761E-01  .277870E-01  .693795E-02  .971526E-01      17
NCOOP41  | .408312E-01  .240431E-01  .650025E-02  .850882E-01      17
NCOOP42  | .431087E-01  .287565E-01  .498137E-02  .107663          17
NCOOP43  | .542407E-01  .319923E-01  .674357E-02  .112520          17
COOPD    | .793098E-01  .467249E-01  .254111E-01  .213877          17
PASSA1   | .294096      .106673      .105533      .462469          17
PASSB1   | .282583      .113634      .130491      .462469          17
PASSC1   | .251961      .133596      .908731E-01  .542216          17
PASSD1   | .171360      .932685E-01  .282525E-01  .317525          17
PASSA2   | .249514      .812497E-01  .127583      .462469          17
PASSB2   | .251956      .844410E-01  .112318      .462469          17
PASSC2   | .323957      .109466      .179177      .585510          17
PASSD2   | .174573      .745316E-01  .439956E-01  .310449          17
RND      | 5.35294      .492592      5.00000      6.00000          17
PASS     | 3.00000      .000000      3.00000      3.00000          17
LINED    | 1.00000      .000000      1.00000      1.00000          17
```

```
Sample;all$
reject;pass#3$
create;if(rnd=5|rnd=6)rnd56=1$
reject;rnd56#1$
reject;alt>8$   To eliminate obs that are not applicable

create
    ;utilA1=util1
    ;utilB1=util1[+1]
    ;utilC1=util1[+2]
    ;utilD1=util1[+3]
    ;utilA2=util1[+16]
    ;utilB2=util1[+17]
    ;utilC2=util1[+18]
    ;utilD2=util1[+19]$
```

```
create;lined=dmy(32,1)$
reject;lined#1$   To use only line one of the 32

write;
    pass,rnd,coopA,utilA1,utilA2,
    pass,rnd,ncoop12,utilA1,utilB2,
    pass,rnd,ncoop13,utilA1,utilC2,
    pass,rnd,ncoop14,utilA1,utilD2,
    pass,rnd,ncoop21,utilB1,utilA2,
    pass,rnd,coopB,utilB1,utilB2,
    pass,rnd,ncoop23,utilB1,utilC2,
    pass,rnd,ncoop24,utilB1,utilD2,
    pass,rnd,ncoop31,utilC1,utilA2,
    pass,rnd,ncoop32,utilC1,utilB2,
    pass,rnd,coopC,utilC1,utilC2,
    pass,rnd,ncoop34,utilC1,utilD2,
    pass,rnd,ncoop41,utilD1,utilA2,
    pass,rnd,ncoop42,utilD1,utilB2,
    pass,rnd,ncoop43,utilD1,utilC2,
    pass,rnd,coopD,utilD1,utilD2
    ;format=(15(5F12.5/)5f12.5)
    ;file=C:\Papers\WPs2011\IACECar\Pass3Power.txt$

reset
read;file=C:\Papers\WPs2011\IACECar\Pass3Power.txt
    ;names= pass,rnd,prob,util1,util2
    ;format=(5f12.5);nobs= 1616  ;nvar=5$
dstats;rhs=*$
Descriptive Statistics
=====================================================================
Variable     Mean       Std.Dev.     Minimum      Maximum       Cases
=====================================================================
---------------------------------------------------------------------
PASS    |  3.00000      .000000      3.00000      3.00000         272
RND     |  5.35294      .478766      5.00000      6.00000         272
PROB    |  .653828E-01  .416536E-01  .498000E-02  .250760         272
UTIL1   |  .196654      .475090     -.889250      .948200         248
UTIL2   |  .000000      .000000      .000000      .000000           4
create
    ;diffut=util1-util2
    ;lprob=log(prob/(1-prob))$
crmodel
    ;lhs=lprob
    ;rhs=one,util1,util2
    ;cls:b(2)+b(3)=1$
```

```
+---------------------------------------------------------------+
| Ordinary    least squares regression                          |
| Model was estimated Feb 26, 2007 at 05:13:32PM                |
|              Standard deviation   =    .7395663               |
```

```
| WTS=none     Number of observs.    =        272      |
| Model size   Parameters            =          3      |
|              Degrees of freedom    =        269      |
| Residuals    Sum of squares        =   146.2974      |
|              Standard error of e    =    .7374663     |
| Fit          R-squared             =    .1300919E-01 |
|              Adjusted R-squared     =    .5670967E-02 |
| Model test   F[  2,   269] (prob) =    1.77 (.1718)  |
| Diagnostic   Log likelihood        =  -301.6095      |
|              Restricted(b=0)       =  -303.3903      |
|              Chi-sq [  2]   (prob) =    3.56 (.1685)  |
| Info criter. LogAmemiya Prd. Crt. =   -.5981007      |
|              Akaike Info. Criter. =   -.5981016      |
+------------------------------------------------------+
```

Variable	Coefficient	Standard Error	t-ratio	P[|T|>t]	Mean of X
Constant	-3.54737221	.36873315	-9.620	.0000	
UTIL1	-.526905D-04	.00015789	-.334	.7389	-87.9677565
UTIL2	-.00068437	.00037212	-1.839	.0670	-984.308824

```
+------------------------------------------------------+
| Linearly restricted regression                       |
| Ordinary     least squares regression                |
| LHS=LPROB    Mean                  =   -2.869103      |
|              Standard deviation    =    .7395663      |
| WTS=none     Number of observs.    =        272      |
| Model size   Parameters            =          2      |
|              Degrees of freedom    =        270      |
| Residuals    Sum of squares        =   3427132.      |
|              Standard error of e    =    112.6636     |
| Fit          R-squared             =  -23120.03      |
|              Adjusted R-squared     =  -23205.67      |
| Diagnostic   Log likelihood        =  -1669.986      |
|              Restricted(b=0)       =  -303.3903      |
| Info criter. LogAmemiya Prd. Crt. =    9.456138      |
|              Akaike Info. Criter. =    9.456138      |
+------------------------------------------------------+
```

Variable	Coefficient	Standard Error	t-ratio	P[|T|>t]	Mean of X
Constant	853.392742	21.2920770	40.080	.0000	
UTIL1	.14285520	.02249866	6.349	.0000	-87.9677565
UTIL2	.85714480	.02249866	38.098	.0000	-984.308824

22.5.13 Group equilibrium

```
RESET
Load;file =C:\Papers\WPs2011\IACECar\IACE_Car_MF.sav$
```

```
-create
    ;if(agea=0)ageaa=21
    ;if(agea=1)ageaa=27
    ;if(agea=2)ageaa=32
    ;if(agea=3)ageaa=37
    ;if(agea=4)ageaa=43
    ;if(agea=5)ageaa=48
    ;if(agea=6)ageaa=53
    ;if(agea=7)ageaa=58
    ;if(agea=8)ageaa=65
    ;if(agea=9)ageaa=75$
create
    ;if(ageb=0)agebb=21
    ;if(ageb=1)agebb=27
    ;if(ageb=2)agebb=32
    ;if(ageb=3)agebb=37
    ;if(ageb=4)agebb=43
    ;if(ageb=5)agebb=48
    ;if(ageb=6)agebb=53
    ;if(ageb=7)agebb=58
    ;if(ageb=8)agebb=65
    ;if(ageb=9)agebb=75$
create
    ;if(rnd=2 & rndagree=2)requi=1
    ;if(rnd=3 & rndagree=3)requi=2
    ;if(rnd=4 & rndagree=4)requi=3
    ;if(rnd=5 & rndagree=5)requi=4
    ;if(rnd=6 & rndagree=6)requi=5$
reject;requi=0$
reject;requi>5$
create
    ;if(requi=1)equiR2=1
    ;if(requi=2)equiR3=1
    ;if(requi=3)equiR4=1
    ;if(requi=4)equiR5=1
    ;if(requi=5)equiR6=1
    ;gendB=genderb[-4]
            ?to get gender of second agent  (note one is M and one is F only)
    ;agB=agebb[-4]
            ?to get age of second agent
    ;agediff=ageaa-agebb$
reject;altij>4$
            Done because for equilibrium Agent 1 and 2 have same attributes
Not socios)
create
    ;pricez=price/1000
    ;pass23=pass2+pass3$
rplogit
    ;lhs=choice1,cset,altij
    ;choices=altA,altB,altC,altD
```

```
;rpl
;fcn=price (t,1),fuel(t,0.4)
;halton;pts=600 ?0
;par
;utility=utileq;prob=passeq
;ecm=(altd)
;model:
U(altA)=price*pricez+fuel*fuel+ac*ac+trans*trans+abs*abs/
U(altB)=price*pricez+fuel*fuel
+ac*ac+trans*trans+abs*abs/
U(altC)=price*pricez+fuel*fuel+ac*ac+trans*trans+abs*abs/
U(altD)=ASCD+gendera*gendera +pass23*pass3+pass23*pass2 +ncars
*numcars$
```
Normal exit from iterations. Exit status=0.

```
+------------------------------------------------------------+
| Random Parms/Error Comps. Logit Model                      |
| Maximum Likelihood Estimates                               |
| Dependent variable              CHOICE1                    |
| Number of observations              325                    |
| Iterations completed                 12                    |
| Log likelihood function        -358.0119                   |
| Number of parameters                 10                    |
| Info. Criterion: AIC =           2.26469                   |
| Restricted log likelihood      -450.5457                   |
| McFadden Pseudo R-squared        .2053816                  |
| Degrees of freedom                   10                    |
| At start values   -358.3682   .00099 *******|
+------------------------------------------------------------+

+------------------------------------------------------------+
| Random Parms/Error Comps. Logit Model                      |
| Replications for simulated probs. = 600                    |
| Halton sequences used for simulations                      |
| Number of obs.=   333, skipped   8 bad obs.                |
+------------------------------------------------------------+
```

Variable	Coefficient	Standard Error	b/St.Er.	P[|Z|>z]
---------+Random parameters in utility functions				
PRICE	-.05148758	.02452672	-2.099	.0358
FUEL	-.19889737	.09055701	-2.196	.0281
---------+Nonrandom parameters in utility functions				
AC	1.40531487	.17382527	8.085	.0000
TRANS	1.17429432	.17521797	6.702	.0000
ABS	.63998532	.16686204	3.835	.0001
ASCD	-2.47166656	1.04154490	-2.373	.0176
GENDERA	.63657641	.34604309	1.840	.0658
PASS23	-.84341903	.38167430	-2.210	.0271
NCARS	.35196772	.11157544	3.155	.0016
---------+Derived standard deviations of parameter distributions				
TsPRICE	.05148758	.02452672	2.099	.0358

```
 TsFUEL   |     .07955895       .03622280    2.196   .0281
---------+Standard deviations of latent random effects
 SigmaE01|     .01530389       .00358228    4.272   .0000
```

```
RESET
Load;file =C:\Papers\WPs2011\IACECar\IACE_Car_MFZ.sav$
create
    ;if(relation=1)marr=1
    ;if(relation=2)defacto=1
    ;if(relation=3)notrel=1$
dstats;rhs=*$
Descriptive Statistics
=========================================================================
Variable     Mean       Std.Dev.    Minimum     Maximum      Cases
=========================================================================
All observations in current sample
-------------------------------------------------------------------------
PASS23   |  .348348     .476626     .000000    1.00000        1332
PASSEQ   |  .250000     .188431     .103374E-01 .852799       1300
UTILEQ   | -1.50674    1.04679     -3.98054    1.19307        1300
MARR     |  .114114     .318069     .000000    1.00000        1332
DEFACTO  |  .600601E-01 .237687     .000000    1.00000        1332
NOTREL   |  .630631E-01 .243168     .000000    1.00000        1332
```

```
mlogit;lhs=pass23;rhs=one,gendera,agediff,marr,defacto,notrel$
Normal exit from iterations. Exit status=0.
+-----------------------------------------------------------+
| Binary Logit Model for Binary Choice          |
| Maximum Likelihood Estimates                  |
| Dependent variable                 PASS23     |
| Number of observations             1332       |
| Iterations completed               4          |
| Log likelihood function         -829.0678     |
| Number of parameters               6          |
| Info. Criterion: AIC =          1.25386       |
| Restricted log likelihood       -861.0290     |
| McFadden Pseudo R-squared        .0371198     |
+-----------------------------------------------------------+
```

```
+--------+--------------+---------------+--------+--------+----------+----------+-----------+
|Variable| Coefficient  | Standard Error |b/St.Er.|P[|Z|>z]| Mean of X|
+--------+--------------+---------------+--------+--------+----------+----------+-----------+
---------+Characteristics in numerator of Prob[Y = 1]
 Constant|   -.61707294    .09209337   -6.701   .0000
 GENDERA |   -.27962040    .12301604   -2.273   .0230    .53753754
 AGEDIFF |    .04027671    .00888108    4.535   .0000  -1.16216216
 MARR    |    .63308687    .17752829    3.566   .0004    .11411411
 DEFACTO |    .27004987    .24010498    1.125   .2607    .06006006
 NOTREL  |   1.18134367    .25671565    4.602   .0000    .06306306
```

```
sample;all$
reject;altij#1$
dstats;rhs=altij,passeq,utileq,pass,choice1$
Descriptive Statistics
===================================================================
Variable     Mean        Std.Dev.     Minimum       Maximum       Cases
===================================================================
All observations in current sample
-------------------------------------------------------------------
ALTIJ   |   1.00000     .000000      1.00000       1.00000        1317
PASSEQ  |   .258778     .187604      .186015E-01   .851210         325
UTILEQ  |  -1.23537    1.09126      -3.79724       1.35483         325
PASS    |   1.52468     .725380      1.00000       3.00000        1317
CHOICE1 |   .282460     .450367      .000000       1.00000        1317
sample;all$
reject;altij#2$
dstats;rhs=altij,passeq,utileq,pass,choice1$
Descriptive Statistics
===================================================================
Variable     Mean        Std.Dev.     Minimum       Maximum       Cases
===================================================================
All observations in current sample
-------------------------------------------------------------------
ALTIJ   |   2.00000     .000000      2.00000       2.00000        1317
PASSEQ  |   .266494     .200153      .192713E-01   .821879         325
UTILEQ  |  -1.20870    1.11740      -3.79555       1.35419         325
PASS    |   1.52468     .725380      1.00000       3.00000        1317
CHOICE1 |   .291572     .454659      .000000       1.00000        1317
sample;all$
reject;altij#3$
dstats;rhs=altij,passeq,utileq,pass,choice1$
Descriptive Statistics
===================================================================
Variable     Mean        Std.Dev.     Minimum       Maximum       Cases
===================================================================
All observations in current sample
-------------------------------------------------------------------
ALTIJ   |   3.00000     .000000      3.00000       3.00000        1317
PASSEQ  |   .274737     .201526      .171286E-01   .754001         325
UTILEQ  |  -1.21273    1.13896      -3.58578       1.35740         325
PASS    |   1.52468     .725380      1.00000       3.00000        1317
CHOICE1 |   .261200     .439455      .000000       1.00000        1317
sample;all$
reject;altij#4$
dstats;rhs=altij,passeq,utileq,pass,choice1$
Descriptive Statistics
All results based on nonmissing observations.
```

```
=======================================================================
Variable      Mean        Std.Dev.      Minimum       Maximum      Cases
=======================================================================
All observations in current sample
-----------------------------------------------------------------------
ALTIJ   |    4.00000      .000000       4.00000       4.00000       1317
PASSEQ  |     .199990     .148926       .102940E-01   .836078        325
UTILEQ  |   -1.90069      .687080      -3.36625       .997002        325
PASS    |    1.52468      .725380       1.00000       3.00000       1317
CHOICE1 |     .164768     .371112       .000000       1.00000       1317
```

22.5.14 Joint estimation of power weights and preference parameters

Power weight: w *beta1+ (1-w) *beta2 = w(beta1-beta2)+beta2
   "w" can take any value but w + (1 – w) = 1

Note: This is another data set, and used only to show the set up in Nlogit.

```
load;file=c:\papers\wps2015\waterqualityitaly\water_italyz.sav$
create
    ;altijz=trn(-12,0)
    ;cset=4$  To create a 1,2,...,12 code for the alternatives
NLRPLogit
    ;LHS=choice,cset,altijz
    ;choices=F1,F2,F3,F4,M1,M2,M3,M4,G1,G2,G3,G4
    ;checkdata
    ;maxit=5
    ;tlg=0.001
    ;labels=bcst1,bowk1,bomth1,bonev1,bswk1,bsmth1,bsnev1,bmdtur1,
           bmetur1,bextur1,bstn1,
    ,bsq1,
    bcst2,bowk2,bomth2,bonev2,bswk2,bsmth2,bsnev2,bmdtur2,bmetur2,
           bextur2,bstn2,
    ,bsq2,
    ,bvinz1,bvinz2,bpw
    ;start=-.04,.88,.86,1.6,1.4,1.0,2.3,-1.1,-2.4,-2.1,-1.6,
    ,2.0,
    -.04,.88,.86,1.6,1.4,1.0,2.3,-1.1,-2.4,-2.1,-1.6,
    ,2.0,
    0.3,0.3,-1?, -1
    ;Fn1=VN1= bcst1*Cost+bowk1*O_WEEK+bomth1*O_MONTH+bonev1*O_NEVER
          +bswk1*S_WEEK+bsmth1*S_MONTH+bsnev1*S_NEVER
          +bmdtur1*MILD_TUR+bmetur1*MED_TURB+bextur1*EXTR_TUR
          +bstn1*STAIN
    ;Fn2=VN1null=bvinz1*vicenza +bsq1*sq
    ;Fn3=VN2= bcst2*Cost+bowk2*O_WEEK+bomth2*O_MONTH+bonev2*O_NEVER
          +bswk2*S_WEEK+bsmth2*S_MONTH+bsnev2*S_NEVER
          +bmdtur2*MILD_TUR+bmetur2*MED_TURB+bextur2*EXTR_TUR
          +bstn2*STAIN
    ;Fn4=VN2null=bvinz2*vicenza +bsq2*sq
```

```
;Fn5=VGP=bpw*(bcst1-bcst2)*cost+bcst2*cost
+bpw*(bowk1-bowk2)*O_WEEK+bowk2*O_WEEK
+bpw*(bomth1-bomth2)*O_MONTH+bomth2*O_MONTH
+bpw*(bonev1-bonev2)*O_NEVER+bonev2*O_NEVER
+bpw*(bswk1-bswk2)*S_WEEK+bswk2*S_WEEK
+bpw*(bsmth1-bsmth2)*S_MONTH+bsmth2*S_MONTH
+bpw*(bsnev1-bsnev2)*S_NEVER+bsnev2*S_NEVER
+bpw*(bmdtur1-bmdtur2)*MILD_TUR+bmdtur2*MILD_TUR
+bpw*(bmetur1-bmetur2)*MED_TURB+bmetur2*MED_TURB
+bpw*(bextur1-bextur2)*EXTR_TUR+bextur2*EXTR_TUR
+bpw*(bstn1-bstn2)*STAIN+bstn2*STAIN
;Fn6=VGPN=bpw* (bvinz1-bvinz2)*vicenza +bvinz2*vicenza +(bsq1-bsq2)
     *SQ+bsq2*SQ
;Model:U(F1,F2,F3)=VN1/U(F4)=VN1null/
U(M1,M2,M3)=VN2/U(M4)=VN2null/
U(G1,G2,G3)=VGP/U(G4)=VGPN
;RPL;fcn=bpw(n)  bsq1(c) ?bcst1(c) ?,bcst2(t,1)
;HALTON;PAR;PDS=8,DRAWS=50
;actualy=actual
;fittedy=newfit
;prob=avgpi2
;utility=virt
;list$
+---------------------------------------------------------------------+
| Inspecting the data set before estimation.                          |
| These errors mark observations which will be skipped.               |
| Row Individual = 1st row then group number of data block            |
+---------------------------------------------------------------------+
No bad observations were found in the sample
-----------------------------------------------------------------------
Nonlinear Utility Mixed Logit Model
Dependent variable               CHOICE
Log likelihood function         -1272.258
Restricted log likelihood       -4771.021
Chi squared [  28 d.f.]          6997.52513
Significance level               .0000000
McFadden Pseudo R-squared        .7333363
Estimation based on N =   1920, K =  28
Information Criteria: Normalization=1/N
             Normalized   Unnormalized
AIC           1.35444      2600.51641
Model estimated: Sep 10, 2009, 07:04:27
Constants only must be computed directly
             Use NLOGIT ;...;RHS=ONE$
At start values -1317.8376   .0346-.6020
Replications for simulated probs. = 250
Halton sequences used for simulations
NLM model with panel has     240 groups
Fixed number of obsrvs./group=         8
```

```
Hessian is not PD. Using BHHH estimator
Number of obs.=  1920, skipped     0 obs
-----------+----------------------------------------------------------------
Variable|  Coefficient    Standard Error   b/St.Er. P[|Z|>z]
-----------+----------------------------------------------------------------
        |Random parameters in utility functions
    BPW|   -1.00883           .93154          -1.083    .2788
        |Nonrandom parameters in utility functions
  BCST1|    -.04092***        .01551          -2.638    .0083
  BOWK1|     .91477**         .43192           2.118    .0342
 BOMTH1|     .98043**         .43155           2.272    .0231
 BONEV1|    1.73792***        .40191           4.324    .0000
  BSWK1|    1.57580***        .45838           3.438    .0006
 BSMTH1|    1.06018**         .46346           2.288    .0222
 BSNEV1|    2.39058***        .51849           4.611    .0000
BMDTUR1|    -.93278***        .29028          -3.213    .0013
BMETUR1|   -2.25166***        .35153          -6.405    .0000
BEXTUR1|   -2.05929***        .45622          -4.514    .0000
  BSTN1|   -1.51921***        .23457          -6.477    .0000
   BSQ1|    2.21148***        .28336           7.804    .0000
  BCST2|    -.06447***        .01311          -4.916    .0000
  BOWK2|     .75492**         .29610           2.550    .0108
 BOMTH2|     .77723***        .28883           2.691    .0071
 BONEV2|    1.51524***        .27322           5.546    .0000
  BSWK2|    1.12851***        .39052           2.890    .0039
 BSMTH2|    1.06391***        .31058           3.426    .0006
 BSNEV2|    2.20885***        .33656           6.563    .0000
BMDTUR2|   -1.19401***        .16078          -7.426    .0000
BMETUR2|   -2.48662***        .15878         -15.661    .0000
BEXTUR2|   -2.22786***        .31499          -7.073    .0000
  BSTN2|   -1.86532***        .17592         -10.603    .0000
   BSQ2|    1.86152***        .33692           5.525    .0000
 BVINZ1|     .05225           .23155            .226    .8215
 BVINZ2|    -.33471**         .16489          -2.030    .0424
        |Distns. of RPs. Std.Devs or limits of triangular
  NsBPW|     .00015         45.92795            .000   1.0000
-----------+----------------------------------------------------------------
Note: ***, **, * = Significance at 1%, 5%, 10% level.
```

Select glossary

Terms marked * appear in the model output rather than the main text.

A-error Rule used in designing choice experiments. The design with the lowest *A*-error is called *A-optimal*. Instead of taking the determinant, the *A*-error takes the trace of the AVC matrix.

a priori Before the fact.

alternative hypothesis Outcome of the hypothesis test for which one wishes to find supporting evidence.

alternatives Options containing specified levels of attributes.

alternative-specific constant (ASC) Parameter for a particular alternative that is used to represent the role of unobserved sources of utility.

arc elasticity Elasticity calculated over a range of values for the reference variable.

attribute Specific variable that is included in an estimated model as an explanatory variable.

attribute invariance Limited variation in the levels of attributes observed in the market.

attribute level label Narrative description corresponding to an attribute.

attribute levels Specific value taken by an attribute. Experimental designs require that each attribute takes on two or more levels, which may be quantitative or qualitative.

attribute non-attendance (ANA) Rule of not attending to (or ignoring) an attribute in choosing an alternative.

attribute processing Set of rules used by respondents to assess attributes and make choices.

attributes Characteristics of an alternative.

balanced design Design in which the levels of any given attribute appear the same number of times as all other levels for that particular attribute.

best–worst Way to use choice data where the focus is on identifying the best and worst attribute or the best and worst alternative and modeling the choice with this information using various methods.

bias Force that leads to incorrect inferences regarding behavior.

blocking Use of an additional design column to assign sub-sets of treatment combinations to decision makers.

bootstrapping It is often uncertain what formula should be used to compute the asymptotic covariance matrix of an estimator. A reliable and common strategy is to use a parametric bootstrap procedure.

branch Third division of alternatives in a nested model.

calibrate To adjust the constant terms in a model in order to replicate actual market shares through model estimation.

calibration constant Constant used to allow the model to correspond to actual choice shares.

cardinal Numerical value that is directly comparable to all other such values (i.e., a value of ten is twice as good as a value of five).

ceteris paribus All other things held constant (Latin).

choice-based sampling Sampling method involving the deliberate over- and under-sampling of groups that make particular choices.

choice outcome Observed choice behavior of an individual.

choice set generation Process of identifying the choices that are relevant to a particular problem.

choice set Set of alternatives over which an agent makes a choice.

choice setting Scenario in which an agent's choice takes place.

choice shares Proportion of the population that chooses a particular alternative.

Cholesky matrix A lower off-diagonal matrix L which is used in the factorization of a matrix A, such that $A = LL'$.

closed-form Mathematically tractable, involving only mathematical operations.

coding Use of numbers to designate a particular state of an attribute (e.g., zero denotes male and one denotes female).

coefficient Scalar value by which a particular element in a model is multiplied in the estimation process.

cognitive burden Level of difficulty faced by a respondent in considering a set of choice menus.

column vector Matrix containing only one column.

compromise effect Leads respondents to favor an in-between alternative when extreme alternatives which do not dominate each other are available in the choice set.

Computer Assisted Personal Interview (CAPI) Use of a computer in face-to-face data collection.

conditional choice Choice that is predicated on a prior condition (e.g., the choice of commuting mode is conditional on the decision whether to work).

confoundment State of being unable to break apart the effects of multiple forces.

conjoint analysis Analysis of experiments in which individuals rank or rate each treatment combination.

constraints Obstacles to selecting an alternative that would yield the highest possible level of utility or satisfaction (e.g., income, time, scarcity, technology).

contingency table Cross-tabulation or actual versus predicted choices.

continuous Variable that can take an infinite level of values.

correlation Measure of the strength of the relationship that may exist between two random variables.

covariance Statistical measure representative of the degree to which two random variables vary together.

cross-section Data relating to multiple members of a population.

cumulative density function (CDF) Function yielding a value equal to the probability that a random variable is observed to take on a value less than or equal to some known value.

data cleaning Inspection of the data for inaccuracies.

decision strategies *See* **process heuristics**.

decision weights Used in prospect theoretic models to represent the role of attribute occurrence when more than one level is being considered in choice making.

degrees of freedom Number of observations in a sample minus the number of independent (linear) constraints imposed during the modeling process. These constraints are the estimated parameters.

delay choice alternative Alternative to delay a choice of alternatives.

delta method Method to obtain standard errors to test of statistical significance of parameters by computing variances of functions such as WTP.

design degrees of freedom Number of treatment combinations required to obtain the necessary degrees of freedom.

design efficiency Designing choice experiments that use information on priors and the asymptotic variance-covariance matrix (AVC) to obtain a determinant of the AVC called the *D*-error; the lowest value is the *D*-efficient design.

discrete choice Selection of one alternative among a set of mutually exclusive alternatives.

discrete Variable that can only take a finite level of values.

distribution Range over which the value of a variable may be, and the frequency with which each of those values is, observed to occur.

dummy coding Denotes the existence of a particular attribute with a one and its absence with a zero.

effect Impact of a particular treatment upon a response variable.

effects coding *See* **orthogonal coding**.

efficient design *See* **design efficiency**.

elasticity Percentage change in one variable with respect to a percentage change in another.

elemental alternatives Alternatives that are not composites of other alternatives (e.g., choosing to drive a car, choosing to take a train).

elimination-by-aspects (EBA) The EBA heuristic states that an alternative is eliminated if the attribute of that alternative fails to meet a certain threshold.

endogenous Within the control of the decision maker (e.g., which alternative to choose).

endogenous weighting Weighting of choice data based on information regarding true market shares.

error components Random components associated with each alternative which may be defined with common or different variances for one or more of the alternatives.

exogenous Outside of the control of the decision maker (e.g., gender or age).

exogenous weighting Weighting of any data besides choice.

expected utility theory (*EUT*) Recognizes that individual decision making is made under uncertainty or risk (i.e., the outcome is not deterministic).

expected value Average value of a set of values observed for a particular variable.

experiment Manipulation of one variable with the purpose of observing the effect of that manipulation upon a second variable.

experimental design Specification of attributes and attribute levels for use in an experiment.

factor level Specific value taken by a factor. Experimental designs require that each factor takes on two or more levels, which may be quantitative or qualitative.

fixed parameter Parameter with a constant value. Also refers to a non-random parameter.

foldover Reproduction of a design in which the factor levels of the design are reversed (e.g., replace 0 with 1 and replace 1 with 0).

full factorial design Design in which all possible treatment combinations are enumerated.

generalized cost Measure of cost that allows for the direct comparison of the costs of all alternatives. This involves the conversion of attribute levels into a common measure, generally a monetary value (e.g., converting travel time into a value of travel time, VTTS).

generalized mixed logit Extension of random parameter (mixed) logit to allow for heterogeneity in scale. *See* **scale heterogeneity**.

Hausman test Test for the existence of the independence of irrelevant alternatives.

heterogeneity Variation in behavior that can be attributed to differences in the tastes and decision making processes of individuals in the population.

hypothesis testing Process by which one determines the worth of an estimate of a population parameter.

hypothetical bias Extent to which individuals might behave inconsistently, when they do not have to back up their choices with real commitments.

IID condition Assumption that the unobserved components of utility of all alternatives are uncorrelated with the unobserved components of utility for all other alternatives, combined with the assumption that each of these error terms has the exact same distribution.

importance weight Relative contribution of an attribute to utility.

inclusive value (IV) Parameter estimate used to establish the extent of dependence or independence between linked choices. Also referred to as logsum and expected maximum utility.

income effect Change in quantity demanded that can be attributed to a change in an individual's income.

independence of irrelevant alternatives (IIA) Restrictive assumption, which is part of the multinomial logit (MNL) model. The IIA property states that the ratio of the choice probabilities is independent of the presence or absence of any other alternative in a choice set.

indifference curves All combinations of two attributes that yield the same level of utility.

indirect utility function Function used to estimate the utility derived from a particular set of observed attributes.

insignificant Having no systematic influence.

intelligent draws Draws that are not random draws that have characteristics that can improve the efficiency of estimates for a given sample. Examples are Halton sequences, Random and Shuffles Halton sequences, Modified Latin Hypercube Sampling.

interaction effect Effect upon the response variable obtained by combining two or more attributes which would not have been observed had each of the attributes been estimated separately.

inter-attribute correlation Subjective interrelation between two attributes (e.g., a higher price may signal higher quality).

interactive agency choice experiments (IACE) Method to jointly model the choices of more than one agent.

kernel density Smoothed plot used to describe the distribution of a sample of observations.

***Krinsky–Robb (KR) method** Non-symmetric confidence intervals can be obtained using the Krinsky–Robb method.

Krinsky–Robb (KR) test Method to obtain the standard errors associated with parameter estimates and especially when the interest is in the standard errors associated with ratios of parameters, as in WTP estimates.

labeled experiment Contains a description of the alternative (e.g., naming a particular item model).

Lagrange multiplier (LM) test Statistical test of a simple null hypothesis that a parameter of interest θ is equal to some particular value θ_0.

latent class Modeling method that recognises that the analyst does not know from the data which observation is in which class, hence the term *latent* classes. Latent class models (LCMs) can have fixed and/or random parameters as well as restriction of parameters in each class.

limb Second division of alternatives in a nested model.

lower off-diagonal matrix Matrix in which all values above and to the right of the diagonal are equal to zero.

main effect (ME) Direct independent effect of each factor upon a response variable. For experimental designs, the main effect is the difference in the means of each level of an attribute and the overall or grand mean.

majority of confirming dimensions (MCD) This processes pairs of alternatives. It compares the values of each attribute, and the alternative with the winning number of attributes is retained. The retained alternative is compared with the next alternative. We stop when all alternatives have been evaluated.

marginal effects Change in the probability of selecting an alternative with respect to a one-unit change in an attribute.

marginal rate of substitution (MRS) Amount of a particular item that must be given to an agent in order to exactly compensate that agent for the loss of one unit of another item.

marginal utility Increase in utility due to an incremental increase of an attribute.

maximum likelihood estimation (MLE) Method used to find parameter estimates that best explain the data.

moment Property of a distribution, such as its mean (first population moment of a distribution) or variance (second population moment of a distribution).

multicollinearity State of two variables being so closely correlated that the effects of one cannot be isolated from the effects of the other.

multivariate Involving more than one variable.

naive pooling Calculation of marginal effects for each decision maker without weighting by the decision maker's associated choice probability.

nested Hierarchical, or belonging to a mutually exclusive sub-set of a group of outcomes.

no choice alternative Alternative not to choose any of the alternatives in the choice set.

nominal qualitative attribute Labeled attribute for which no natural order exists.

non-linear worst level referencing (NLWLR) Process heuristic that makes the prior assumption that relative to the worst performing attribute, utility is concave in the gains.

non-random parameter Parameter that takes on only one value.

normalize To fix to a particular value in order to enable comparison.

null hypothesis Statement that outlines the possible outcome of the hypothesis test that one does not want to observe.

observation Choice made by an individual in a choice setting.

ordered choice Choice among alternatives that are ranked in a meaningful order (e.g., 0 = best, 1 = second best, 2 = worst; 0 = 0 cars, 1 = 1 car, 2 = 2 cars). *See* **ordinal scaled data**.

ordinal Numerical value that is indirectly comparable to all other such values (i.e., a value of ten is better than a value of five).

ordinal scaled data Data in which the values assigned to levels observed for an object are both unique and provide an indication of order (i.e., a ranking).

orthogonal Independent of all other factors.

orthogonal coding Coding in which all values for a given attribute sum to zero. In the case of even numbers of code levels, each positive code level is matched by its negative value. In the case of odd numbers of code levels, the median level is assigned the value zero. For example, in the two-level case, the levels assigned are − 1 and 1; in the three-level case, the levels assigned are −1, 0, and 1.

orthogonal main effects only design Orthogonal design in which only the main effects are estimated. All other interactions are assumed to be insignificant.

orthogonality Term that represents a situation of zero correlation between pairs of attributes in a choice experiment.

overidentified Having too many variables to be estimated by the available information.

panel data Data incorporating multiple observations per sampled individual.

parameter Unique weight used to describe the systematic contribution of a particular element in a model.

part-worth Proportion of utility that can be attributed to a specific attribute.

pivot design In a pivot design the attribute levels shown to the respondents are pivoted from the reference alternatives of each respondent.

point elasticity Elasticity calculated at a particular point.

power functions Way of weighting the influence of each agent in a two or more person group choice model in respect of establishing the overall role their preferences play in defining the role of either an attribute or an alternative in choice making.

preference heterogeneity Differing preferences across the population.

preferences Forces leading an individual to select one alternative over another.

probability density function (PDF) Probability distribution over the various values that a variable might take (bounded by zero and one, inclusively).

probability-weighted sample enumeration Calculation of marginal effects for each decision maker, weighted by the decision maker's associated choice probability.

probit Choice model that assumes a normal distribution for the random errors (in contrast to EV1 for logit).

process heuristics Rules used by individuals to evaluate alternatives and make choices such as attribute non-attendance, majority of confirming dimensions (MCD), and elimination-by-aspects (EBA).

profiles Combinations of attributes, each with unique levels.

prospect theory (i) Choice behavior process, in which individuals *frame (or edit) the offered prospects* as gains and losses relative to a reference point, and successively evaluate these edited prospects and then choose the prospect of highest value; (ii) *reference dependence*, to recognize different value functions for gains and losses with respect to the reference point, (iii) *diminishing sensitivity*, associated with decreasing marginal value of both gains and losses; (iv) *loss aversion*, defined as the disutility of a loss being valued higher than the utility of an equivalent gain; and (v) use of non-linear probability weighting to transform original probabilities.

*****pseudo R-squared** Measure of model fit for discrete choice models, giving the proportion of variation in the data that is explained by the model.

quantitative Involving numbers.

qualitative Involving description.

random parameter Parameter with a mean value and an associated standard deviation, yielding a distribution of estimated values.

random regret Behavioral choosing process that indicates that when choosing between alternatives, decision makers aim to minimize anticipated regret (in contrast to maximizing utility).

random utility maximization (RUM) Analysis of the maximization of utility, taking into account the unobserved sources of utility for all alternatives.

randomization Changing the order of elements.

rank-dependent utility theory (RDUT) *See* **cumulative prospect theory (CPT)**.

ratio scale Level of satisfaction or utility of an alternative relative to that of another alternative.

ratio scaled data Data in which the values assigned to levels of an object are unique, provide an indication of order, have an equal distance between scale points, and the zero point on the scale of measure used represents an absence of the object being observed (e.g., expenditure, or temperature measured in Kelvin or Rankin).

rationality Taking into account all matters that are relevant, regardless of the amount of information at one's disposal to assist one's deliberations.

reference point revision Occurs where preferences may be well formed and the reference changes.

relational heuristics Individuals have been found to use heuristics that are relational and perceptual in nature. By "relational," these heuristics emphasize the comparison of ratings of one alternative against another, allowing the value obtained from an alternative to *also* depend on the local choice context. Examples are the extremeness aversion principle, the "compromise effect."

relative advantage model (RAM) Componential context model, also called a relative advantage model (RAM). The model focuses on the relative advantage of alternative *j* over alternative *i*, and a weight is given to the relative advantage component of the model. This weight parameter can be taken as an indication of the strength of the choice context in determining preferences.

reliability Concept that results similar to those from a given sample would be obtained through repeated samples.

research question Chief question the research is intended to address.

responses Observed outcomes in a choice setting.

restricted Involving parameters that are constrained to a particular value.

revealed preference (RP) Responses observed in a market setting.

risk attitude Recognition in modeling of the presence of risk taking, risk averse, and risk neutral choosers.

satisfaction Amount or level of happiness that an alternative yields to an individual. *See* **utility**.

scale heterogeneity Recognition that the scale factor can vary across a sample.

scale parameter Parameter used to normalize utility expressions across alternatives and a reference measure used to allow for the comparison of utility for different alternatives.

scaled multinomial logit Multinomial logit (MNL) that accounts for scale heterogeneity in the presence of fixed attribute parameters

significance Probability that a given parameter estimate is equal to a particular value, generally given in reference to zero.

socio-economic characteristics (SECs) Information regarding individuals that serves as a proxy for their tastes. Examples include income, age, gender, and occupation.

standard deviation Square root of the variance.

stated choice (SC) data Data associated with a choice experiment (CE) in which respondents are offered various combinations of attributes associated with a number of alternatives and asked to choose the most preferred or to rank the alternatives. In contrast to revealed preference (RP) data, the attribute levels are predetermined by a designed experiment and the choice response is stated or hypothetical.

stated preference (SP) Responses observed in an experimental setting.

stated preference experiment Experiment involving hypothetical choice scenarios and researcher-specified attributes and attribute levels.

statistical efficiency Used in experimental design to focus on the standard errors likely to be obtained from the experiment (and to a lesser effect the covariances). Referred to as efficient designs.

stimulus refinement Brainstorming and then narrowing the range of alternatives to consider in the experiment.

stochastic Random.

substitution effect Change in quantity demanded that can be attributed to a change in the relative prices of two goods.

substitution patterns Manner in which it is inferred that people move away from one alternative toward another in response to changes in attribute levels.

tastes Component of an individual's personal preferences which are specific to that individual, rather than being tied to the relevant attributes in the choice set.

test statistic Result of a statistical test that relates some sample statistic to that of a population statistic.

testable assumption Assumption that can be refuted or confirmed.

treatment Specific factor level for a particular attribute.

treatment combination Combinations of attributes, each with unique levels.

trunk First division of alternatives in a nested model.

t-test Test statistic relating to the sample standard deviation through a normal distribution.

unbalanced design Design in which the levels of any given attribute do not appear the same number of times as all other levels for that particular attribute.

unconditional choice Choice that is independent of all previous choices.

unlabeled experiment Containing no description of the alternative (e.g., listed as "Product A").

univariate Involving one variable.

utility Level of happiness that an alternative yields to an individual.

utility maximization Act of seeking the alternative that yields the highest level of utility.

validity Significant relationship between the results inferred through estimation and real world behavior.

value learning Respondents' value functions shift when a non-status quo option is chosen.

variance Second population moment of a distribution. It provides the analyst with an understanding of how dispersed or spread observations are around the mean of a distribution.

variance estimation Statistical inference, such as some hypothesis tests, confidence intervals, and estimation generally, relies on the computation of variances of estimators.

vector Matrix containing either only one row or one column.

Wald statistic Ratio of an importance weight to its standard error. Useful for computing variances of functions.

Wald test Test of whether a Wald statistic is significantly different to zero.

willingness to pay (WTP) Amount that someone is willing to pay for an attribute; it is usually expressed in monetary terms, derived from the ratio of the parameter (or marginal utility) of the attribute of interest and the marginal utility of a monetary variable.

References

Aadland, D. and Caplan, A. J. (2003) Willingness to pay for curbside recycling with detection and mitigation of hypothetical bias, *American Journal of Agricultural Economics*, 85 (3), 492–502.

Accent Marketing and Research and Centre for Research in Environmental Appraisal & Management (CREAM) (2002) *Yorkshire Water Services*, Final Report, Prepared for Yorkshire Water, November.

ACT Gover (2003a) Community Summit, Workbook, 27 August, Canberra.

(2003b) Community Water Summit, Workshop Groups' Summary Reports, 27 August, Canberra. Available at: www.thinkwater.act.gov.au/strategy/summit_transcripts.shtml.

ACTEW Corporation (2004) Community assistance makes water restrictions a success, Media Release, 8 June.

Adamowicz, W., Hanemann, M., Swait, J., Johnson, R., Layton, D., Regenwetter, M., Reimer, T. and Sorkin, R. (2005) Decision strategy and structure in households: a groups perspective, *Marketing Letters*, 16, 387–399.

Ailawadi, K. L., Gedenk, K. and Neslin, S. A. (1999) Heterogeneity and purchase event feedback in choice models: an empirical analysis with implications for model buildings, *International Journal of Research in Marketing*, 16, 177–198.

Akaike, H. (1974) A new look at the statistical model identification, *IEEE Transactions on Automatic Control* 19 (6), 716–723.

Alfnes, F. and Steine, G. (2005) None-of-these bias in hypothetical choice experiments, Discussion Paper DP-06/05, Department of Economics and Resources Management, Norwegian University of Life Sciences, Aas.

Alfnes, F., Guttormsen, A., Steine, G. and Kolstad, K. (2006) Consumers' willingness to pay for the color of salmon: a choice experiment with real economic incentives, *American Journal of Agricultural Economics*, 88 (4), 1050–1061.

Allais, M. (1953) Le comportement de l'homme rationnel devant le risque, *Econometrica*, 21 (4), 503–546.

Allenby, G. M., Shively, T. S., Yang, S. and Garratt, M. J. (2004) A choice model for packaged goods: dealing with discrete quantities and quantity discounts, *Marketing Science*, 23 (1), 95–108.

Allison, P. (1999) Comparing logit and probit coefficients across groups, *Sociological Methods and Research*, 28, 186–208.

Anderson, D. A. and Wiley, J. B. (1992) Efficient choice set designs for estimating cross effect models, *Marketing Letters*, 3, 357–370.

Anderson, S., Harrison, G. W., Hole, A. R., Lau, M. and Rutström, E. E. (2012) Non-linear mixed logit, *Journal of Theory and Decision*, 73, 7–96.

Anderson, S., Harrison, G. W., Lau, M. and Rutström, E. (2007a) Valuation using multiple price list formats, *Applied Economics*, 39 (4), 675–682.

(2007b) Dual criteria decisions, Working Paper 06–11, Department of Economics, College of Business Administration, University of Central Florida.

Antonov, I. A. and Saleev, V. M. (1979) An economic method of computing LP_{tau} sequences, *Zh, vychisl. Mat. mat. Fiz.*, 19, 243–245, English translation, *USSR Comput. Maths. Math. Phys.*, 19, 252–256.

Arendt, J. and Holm, A. (2007) Probit models with binary endogenous regressors, 6th International Health Economics Association World Congress, Copenhagen, 8–11 July.

Arentze, T., Borgers, A., Timmermans, H. and DelMistro, R. (2003) Transport stated choice responses: effects of task complexity, presentation format and literacy, *Transportation Research Part E*, 39, 229–244.

Aribarg, A., Arora, N. and Bodur, H. O. (2002) Understanding the role of preference revision and concession in group decisions, *Journal of Marketing Research*, 39, 336–349.

Armstrong, P. M., Garrido, R. A. and Ortúzar, J. de D. (2001) Confidence intervals to bound the value of time, *Transportation Research Part E*, 7 (1), 143–161.

Arora, N. and Allenby, G. M. (1999) Measuring the influence of individual preference structures in group decision making, *Journal of Marketing Research*, 37, 476–487.

Asensio, J. and Matas, A. (2008) Commuters' valuation of travel time variability, *Transportation Research Part E*, 44 (6), 1074–1085.

Ashok, K., Dillon, W. R. and Yuan, S. (2002) Extending discrete choice models to incorporate attitudinal and other latent variables, *Journal of Marketing Research*, 39 (1), 31–46.

Ashton, W. D. (1972) *The logit transformation*, Griffin, London. Available at: www.bepress. com/bejeap/advances/vol6/iss2/art2.

Asmussen, S. and Glynn, P. W. (2007) *Stochastic Simulation: Algorithms and Analysis*, Springer, New York.

Auger, P., Devinney, T. M. and Louviere, J. J. (2007) Best–worst scaling methodology to investigate consumer ethical beliefs across countries, *Journal of Business Ethics*, 70, 299–326.

Backhaus, K., Wilken, R., Voeth, M. and Sichtmann, C. (2005) An empirical comparison of methods to measure willingness to pay by examining the hypothetical bias, *International Journal of Market Research* 47 (5), 543–562.

Balcombe, K., Fraser, I. and Chalak, A. (2009) Model selection in the Bayesian mixed logit: misreporting or heterogeneous preferences?, *Journal of Environmental Economics and Management*, 57 (2), 219–225.

Bateman, I. J., Carson, R. T., Day, B., Dupont, D., Louviere, J. J., Morimoto, S., Scarpa R. *et al.* (2008) Choice set awareness and ordering effects in discrete choice experiments, CSERGE Working Paper EDM 08-01.

Bateman, I. J., Carson, R. T., Day, B., Dupont, D., Louviere, J. J., Morimoto, S., Scarpa, R. and Wang, P. (2008) Choice set awareness and ordering effects in discrete choice experiments, CSERGE Working Paper EDM 08–01

Bateman, I. J. and Munro, A. (2005) An experiment on risky choice amongst households, *Economic Journal*, 115, 176–189.

Bates, J., Polak, J., Jones, P. and Cook, A. (2001) The valuation of reliability for personal travel, *Transportation Research Part E*, 37 (2–3), 191–229.

Batley, R. and Ibáñez, N. (2009) Randomness in preferences, outcomes and tastes: an application to journey time risk, International Choice Modelling Conference, Harrogate.

Beck, M., Rose, J. M. and Hensher, D. A. (2012) Comparison of group decision making models: a vehicle purchasing case study, Paper presented at the International Association of Traveller Behaviour Research (IATBR) Conference, Toronto, July 13–15.

(2013) Consistently inconsistent: the role of certainty, acceptability and scale in automobile choice, *Transportation Research Part E*, 56 (3), 81–93.

Becker, G. (1991) *A Treatise on the Family*, Harvard University Press, Cambridge, MA.

(1993) A theory of marriage: Part 1, *Journal of Political Economy*, 81 (4), 813–846.

Beharry, N., Hensher, D. and Scarpa, R. (2009) An analytical framework for joint vs. separate decisions by couples in choice experiments: the case of coastal water quality in Tobago, *Environmental and Resource Economics*, 43, 95–117.

Beharry, N. and Scarpa, R. (2008) Who should select the attributes in choice-experiments for non-market valuation? An application to coastal water quality in Tobago, Sustainability Research Institute, University of Leeds.

Ben-Akiva, M. E. and Bolduc, D. (1996) Multinomial probit with a logit kernel and a general parametric specification of the covariance structure, Unpublished Working Paper, Department of Civil Engineering, MIT, Cambridge, MA.

Ben-Akiva, M. E., Bolduc, D. and Bradley, M. (1993) Estimation of travel choice models with randomly distributed values of time, *Transportation Research Record*, 1413, 88–97.

Ben-Akiva, M. E., Bradley, M., Morikawa, T., Benjamin, J., Novak, T. P., Oppewal, H. and Rao, V. (1994) Combining revealed and stated preferences data, *Marketing Letters*, 5 (4), 336–350.

Ben Akiva, M. E. and Lerman, S. R. (1979) Disaggregate travel and mobility choice models and measures of accessibility, in Hensher, D. A. and Stopher, P. R. (eds.), *Behavioural Travel Modelling*, Croom Helm, London.

(1985) *Discrete Choice Analysis: Theory and Application to Travel Demand*, MIT Press, Cambridge, MA.

Ben-Akiva, M., McFadden, D., Abe, M., Boèckenholt, U., Bolduc, D., Gopinath, D., Morikawa, T., Ramaswamy,V., Rao, V., Revelt, D. and Steinberg, D. (1997). Modelling methods for discrete choice analysis, *Marketing Letters* 8 (3), 273–286.

Ben-Akiva, M., McFadden, D., Garling, T., Gopinath, D., Walker, J., Bolduc, D., Boersch-Supan, A., Delquié, P., Larichev, O., Morikawa, T., Polydoropoulou, A. and Rao, V. (1999). Extended framework for modelling choice behavior, *Marketing Letters*, 10 (3), 187–203.

Ben-Akiva, M., McFadden, D., Train, K., Walker, J., Bhat, C., Bierlaire, M., Bolduc, D., Boersch-Supan, A., Brownstone, D., Bunch, D., Daly, A., de Palma, A., Gopinath, D., Karlstrom, A. and Munizaga, M. A. (2002) Hybrid choice models: progress and challenges, *Marketing Letters*, 13 (3), 163–175.

Ben-Akiva, M. E. and Morikawa, T. (1991) Estimation of travel demand models from multiple data sources, in Koshi, M. (ed.), *Transportation and Traffic Theory*, Proceedings of the 11th ISTTT, Elsevier, Amsterdam, 461–476.

Ben-Akiva, M. E., Morikawa, T. and Shiroishi, F. (1991) Analysis of the reliability of preference ranking data, *Journal of Business Research*, 23, 253–268.

Ben-Akiva, M. E., and Swait J. (1986) The Akaike likelihood ratio index, *Transportation Science*, 20 (2), 133–136.

Bentham, J. (1789) *An Introduction to the Principles of Morals and Legislation*, Clarendon Press, Oxford.

Berkson, J. (1944) Application of the logistics function to bioassay, *Journal of the American Statistical Association,* 39, 357–65.

Bernouli, D. (1738) Specimen Theoriae Novae de Mensura Sortis, Commentarii Academiae Scientiarum Imperialis Petropolitanae, *Tomus V (Papers of the Imperial Academy of Sciences in Petersburg)*, V, 175–192.

Berry, S., Levinsohn, J. and Pakes, A. (1995) Automobile prices in market equilibrium, *Econometrica*, 63 (4), 841–890.

Bertrand, M. and Mullainathan, S. (2001) Do people mean what they say? Implications for subjective survey data, *American Economic Review Papers and Proceedings*, 91(2), 67–72.

Bettman, J. R., Luce, M. F. and Payne, J. W. (1998). Constructive consumer choice processes, *Journal of Consumer Research*, 25, 187–217.

Bhat, C. R. (1994) Imputing a continuous income variable from grouped and missing income observations, *Economics Letters*, 46 (4), 311–320.

(1995) A heteroscedastic extreme value model of intercity travel mode choice, *Transportation Research Part B*, 29 (6), 471–483.

(1997) An endogenous segmentation mode choice model with an application to intercity travel, *Transportation Science*, 31, 34–48.

(2001) Quasi-random maximum simulated likelihood estimation of the mixed multinomial logit model, *Transportation Research Part B*, 35 (7), 677–693.

(2003) Simulation estimation of mixed discrete choice models using randomized and scrambled Halton sequences, *Transportation Research Part B*, 37 (9), 837–855.

(2008) The multiple discrete-continuous extreme value (MDCEV) model: role of utility function parameters, identification considerations, and model extensions, *Transportation Research Part B*, 42 (3), 274–303.

Bhat, C. R. and Castelar, S. (2002) A unified mixed logit framework for modeling revealed and stated preferences: formulation and application to congestion pricing analysis in the San Francisco Bay area, *Transportation Research Part B*, 36, 577–669.

Bhat, C. R. and Pulugurta, V. (1998) A comparison of two alternative behavioral mechanisms for car ownership decisions, *Transportation Research Part B*, 32 (1), 61–75.

Bhat, C. R. and Zhao, H. (2002) The spatial analysis of activity stop generation, *Transportation Research Part B*, 36 (6), 557–575.

Bickel, P. J. and Doksum, K. A. (1981) An analysis of transformations revisited, *Journal of the American Statistical Association*, 76, 296–311.

Blackburn, M., Harrison, G. W. and Rutström, E. E. (1994) Statistical bias functions and informative hypothetical surveys, *American Journal of Agricultural Economics*, 76 (5), 1084–1088.

Blanchard, O. and Fischer, S. (1989) *Lectures on Macroeconomics*, MIT Press, Cambridge, MA.

Bliemer, M. C. J. and Rose, J. M. (2005a) Efficiency and sample size requirements for stated choice studies, Working Paper ITLS-WP-05-08, Institute of Transport and Logistics Studies, The University of Sydney.

(2005b) Efficient designs for alternative specific choice experiments, Working Paper ITLS-WP-05-04, Institute of Transport and Logistics Studies, the University of Sydney.

(2009) Designing stated choice experiments: the state of the art, in Kitamura, R., Yoshi, T. and Yamamoto, T. (eds.), *The Expanding Sphere of Travel Behaviour Research, Selected Papers from the 11th International Conference on Travel Behaviour Research*, Chapter 25, 495–538.

(2010a) Construction of experimental designs for mixed logit models allowing for correlation across choice observations, *Transportation Research Part B: Methodological*, 44 (6) 720–34.

(2010b) Construction of experimental designs for mixed logit models allowing for correlation across choice observations, *Transportation Research Part B: Methodological*, 44 (6) 720–34.

(2010c) Serial choice conjoint analysis for estimating discrete choice models, in Hess, S. and Daly, A. (eds.), *Choice Modelling: The State of the Art and the State of the Practice*, Emerald Group, Bingley, 139–161.

(2011) Experimental design influences on stated choice outputs: an empirical study in air travel choice, *Transportation Research Part A*, 45 (1), 63–79.

(2013) Confidence intervals of willingness-to-pay for random coefficient logit models, *Transportation Research Part B*, 58 (2), 199–214.

(2014) A unified theory of experimental design for stated choice studies, Paper presented at the 10th International Conference on Transport Survey Methods, Leura.

Bliemer, M. C. J., Rose, J. M. and Hensher, D. A. (2009) Efficient stated choice experiments for estimating nested logit models, *Transportation Research Part B*, 43 (1), 19–35.

Bliemer, M. C. J., Rose, J. M. and Hess, S. (2008) Approximation of Bayesian efficiency in experimental choice designs, *Journal of Choice Modelling*, 1 (1), 98–127.

Blumenschein, K., Johanneson, M., Yokoyama, K. K. and Freeman, P. R. (2001) Hypothetical versus real willingness to pay in the health care sector: results from a field experiment, *Journal of Health Economics*, 20 (3), 441–457.

Blumenschein, K., Johannesson, M., Blomquist, G. C., Liljas, B. and O'Coner, R. M. (1998) Experimental results on expressed certainty and hypothetical bias in contingent valuation, *Southern Economic Journal*, 65 (1), 169–177.

Bock, R. D. and Jones, L. V. (1968) *The Measurement and Prediction of Judgment and Choice*, Holden-Day, San Francisco, CA.

(2004) Income and happiness: new results from generalized threshold and sequential models, IZA Discussion Paper 1175, SOI Working Paper 0407.

Boes, S. and Winkelman, R. (2007) Ordered response models, *Allgemeines Statistiches Archiv Physica Verlag*, 90 (1), 165–180.

Bolduc, D. and Alvarez Daziano, R. (2010) On estimation of hybrid choice models, in Hess, S. and Daly, A. (eds.), *Choice Modelling: The State of the Art and the State of Practice*, Emerald Group, Bingley.

Bolduc, D., Ben-Akiva, M., Walker, J. and Michaud, A. (2005) Hybrid choice models with logit kernel: applicability to large scale models, in Lee-Gosselin, M. and Doherty, S. (eds), *Integrated Land-Use and Transportation Models: Behavioural Foundations*, Elsevier, Oxford, 275–302.

Bonini, N., Tentori, K. and Rumiati, R. (2004) Contingent application of the cancellation editing operation: the role of semantic relatedness between risky outcomes, *Journal of Behavioral Decision Making*, 17, 139–152.

Bordley, R. (2013) Discrete choice with large choice sets, *Economics Letters*, 118, 13–15.

Borsh-Supan, A. and Hajivassiliou, V. (1993) Smooth unbiased multivariate probability simulation for maximum likelihood estimation of limited dependent variable models, *Journal of Econometrics*, 58 (3), 347–368.

Box, G. E. P. and Cox, D. R. (1964) An analysis of transformations, *Journal of the Royal Statistical Society, Series B*, 26, 211–252.

Box, G. E. P. and Draper, N. R. (1987) *Empirical Model-Building and Response Surfaces*, Wiley, New York.

Bradley, M. A. (2006) Process data for understanding and modelling travel behaviour, in Stopher, P. and Stecher, C. (eds.), *Travel Survey Methods: Quality and Future Directions*, Elsevier, Oxford.

Bradley, M. A., and Daly, A. J. (1997) Estimation of logit choice models using mixed stated preference and revealed preference information, in Stopher, P. R. and Lee-Gosselin, M. (eds.), *Understanding Travel Behaviour in an Era of Change*, Pergamon, Oxford, 209–232.

Bradley, R. A. and Terry, M. E. (1952) Rank analysis of incomplete block designs. I: the method of paired comparison, *Biometrika*, 39, 324–345.

Brant, R. (1990) Assessing proportionality in the proportional odds model for ordinal logistic regression, *Biometrics*, 46, 1171–1178.

Bratley, P., Fox, B. L. and Niederreiter, H. (1992) Implementing Sobol's quasi-random sequence generator, *ACM Transactions on Computer Software*, 2 (3), 195–213.

Breffle, W. S. and Morey, E. R. (2000) Investigating preference heterogeneity in a repeated discrete-choice recreation demand model of Atlantic salmon fishing, *Marine Resource Economics*, 15, 1–20.

Brewer, A. and Hensher, D. A. (2000) Distributed work and travel behaviour: the dynamics of interactive agency choices between employers and employees, *Transportation*, 27, 117–148.

Brewer, C., Kovner, C. T., Wu, Y., Greene, W., Liu, Y. and Reimers, C. (2006) Factors influencing female registered nurses' work behavior, *Health Services Research*, 43 (1), 860–866.

Briesch, R. A., Chintagunta, P. K. and Matzkin, R. L. (2010) Nonparametric discrete choice models with unobserved heterogeneity, *Journal of Business and Economic Statistics*, 28 (2), 291–307.

Briesch, R. A., Krishnamurthi, L., Mazumdar, T. and Raj, S. P. (1997) A comparative analysis of reference price models, *Journal of Consumer Research*, 24, 202–214.

Brown, T. C., Ajzen, I. and Hrubes, D. (2003) Further tests of entreaties to avoid hypothetical bias in referendum contingent valuation, *Journal of Environmental Economics and Management*, 46 (2), 353–361.

Browning, M. and Chiappori, P. A. (1998) Efficient intra-household allocations: a general characterization and empirical tests, *Econometrica*, 66 (6), 1241–78.

Brownstone, D. and Small, K. A. (2005) Valuing time and reliability: assessing the evidence from road pricing demonstrations, *Transportation Research Part A*, 39 (4), 279–293.

Brownstone, D. and Train, K. (1999) Forecasting new product penetration with flexible substitution patterns, *Journal of Econometrics*, 89 (1–2), 109–129.

Bunch, D. S., Louviere, J. J. and Anderson, D. A. (1996) A comparison of experimental design strategies for multinomial logit models: the case of generic attributes, Working Paper, Graduate School of Management, University of California at Davis.

Burgess, G., Burgess, H., Burton, L., Howe, C. W., Johnson, L., MacDonnell, L. J. and Reitsma, R. F. (1992) Improving the environmental problem-solving process: lessons from the 1980s California drought, Working Paper, University of Colorado.

Burgess, L. and Street, D. (2003) Optimal designs for 2k choice experiments, *Communications in Statistics – Theory and Methods*, 32 (11), 2185–2206.

(2005) Optimal designs for choice experiments with asymmetric attributes, *Journal of Statistical Planning and Inference*, 134 (1), 288–301.

Burnett, N. (1997) Gender economics courses in Liberal Arts Colleges, *Journal of Economic Education*, 28 (4), 369–377.

Cai, Y., Deilami, I. and Train, K. (1998) Customer retention in a competitive power market: analysis of a 'double-bounded plus follow-ups' questionnaire, *Energy Journal*, 19 (2), 191–215.

Caflisch, R. E. (1998) Monte Carlo and quasi-Monte Carlo methods, *Acta Numerica*, 7, 1–49.

Camerer, C. and Ho, T. (1994) Violations of the betweenness axiom and non-linearity in probability, *Journal of Risk and Uncertainty*, 8 (2), 167–196.

Cameron, A. and Trivedi, P. (2005) *Microeconometrics: Methods and Applications*, Cambridge University Press.

Cameron, S. V. and Heckman, J. J. (1998) Life cycle schooling and dynamic selection bias: models and evidence for five cohorts of American males, *Journal of Political Economy*, 106 (2), 262–333.

Cameron, T. A. and DeShazo, J. R. (2010) Differential attention to attributes in utility-theoretic choice models, *Journal of Choice Modelling*, 3 (3), 73–115.

Cameron, T. A., Poe, G. L., Ethier, R. G. and Schulze, W. D. (2002) Alternative non-market value-elicitation methods: are the underlying preferences the same?, *Journal of Environmental Economics and Management*, 44 (3), 391–425.

Campbell, D., Hensher, D. A. and Scarpa, R. (2011) Non-attendance to attributes in environmental choice analysis: a latent class specification, *Journal of Environmental Planning and Management*, 54 (8), 1061–1076.

(2012) Cost thresholds, cut-offs and sensitivities in stated choice analysis: identification and implications, *Resource and Energy Economics*, 34, 396–411.

Campbell, D., Hutchinson, W. and Scarpa, R. (2008) Incorporating discontinuous preferences into the analysis of discrete choice experiments, *Environment and Resource Economics*, 43 (1), 403–417.

Cantillo, V., Heydecker, B. and Ortúzar, J. de D. (2006) A discrete choice model incorporating thresholds for perception in attribute values, *Transportation Research Part B*, 40 (9), 807–825.

Cantillo, V. and Ortúzar, J. de D. (2005) A semi-compensatory discrete choice model with explicit attribute thresholds of perception, *Transportation Research Part B*, 39 (7), 641–657.

Carlsson, F and Martinsson, P. (2001) Do hypothetical and actual marginal willingness to pay differ in choice experiments?, *Journal of Environmental Economics and Management*, 41 (2), 179–192.

(2002) Design techniques for stated preference methods in health economics, *Health Economics*, 12, 281–294.

Carlsson, F., Frykblom, P. and Lagerkvist, C-J. (2005) Using cheap-talk as a test of validity of choice experiments, *Economics Letters*, 89 (5), 147–152.

Carlsson, F., Kataria, M. and Lampi, E. (2008) Ignoring attributes in choice experiments, Proceedings of the EAERE Conference, 25–28 June, Gothenburg.

Carp, F. M. (1974) Position effects on interview responses, *Journal of Gerontology*, 29 (5), 581–587.

Carrasco, J. A. and Ortúzar, J. de D. (2002) A review and assessment of the nested logit model, *Transport Reviews*, 22, 197–218.

Carroll, J. S. and Johnson, E. J. (1990). *Decision Research: A Field Guide*, Sage, Newbury Park, CA.

Carson, R., Flores, E., Martin, K. and Wright, J. (1996) Contingent valuation and revealed preference methodologies: comparing the estimates for quasi-public goods, *Land Economics*, 72 (1), 80–99.

Carson, R., Groves, T., List, J. and Machina, M. (2004) Probabilistic influence and supplemental benefits: a field test of the two key assumptions underlying stated preferences, Paper presented at the European Association of Environmental and Resource Economists, Budapest, June.

Carson, R., Groves, T. and Machina, M. (2007) Incentive and informational properties of preference questions, *Environment and Resource Economics*, 37, 181–210.

Carson, R., Louviere, J. J., Anderson, D., Arabie, P., Bunch, D., Hensher, D. A., Johnson, R., Kuhfeld, W., Steinberg, D., Swait, J., Timmermans, H. and Wiley, J. (1994) Experimental analysis of choice, *Marketing Letters*, 5, 351–367.

Cassel, E. and Mendelsohn, R. (1985) The choice of functional forms for hedonic price equations: comment, *Journal of Urban Economics*, 18 (2), 135–142.

Caussade, S., Ortúzar, J. de D., Rizzi, L. and Hensher, D. A. (2005) Assessing the influence of design dimensions on stated choice experiment estimates, *Transportation Research Part B*, 39 (7), 621–640.

Chamberlain, G. (1980) Analysis of covariance with qualitative data, *Review of Economic Studies*, 47, 225–238.

Cherchi, E., Meloni, I. and Ortúzar, J. de D. (2002) Policy forecasts involving new train services: application of mixed rp/sp models with interaction effects, Paper presented at the XII Panamerican Conference on Transport and Traffic Engineering, Quito.

Chiuri, M. C. (2000) Individual decisions and household demand for consumption and leisure, *Research in Economics*, 54, 277–324.

Choice Metrics (2012) *NGene 1.1.1 User Manual and Reference Guide*, Choice Metrics, Sydney.

Chorus, C. G. (2010) A new model of random regret minimization, *European Journal of Transport and Infrastructure Research*, 10, 181–196.

Chorus, C. G., Arentze, T. A. and Timmermans, H. J. P. (2008a) A random regret-minimization model of travel choice, *Transportation Research Part B*, 42 (1), 1–18.

(2008b) A comparison of regret minimization and utility-maximization in the context of travel mode-choices, Proceedings of the 87th Annual Meeting of the Transportation Research Board, Washington, DC.

Cirillo, C., Lindveld, K. and Daly, A. (2000) Eliminating bias due to the repeated measurements problem in SP data, in Ortúzar, J. de D. (ed.), *Stated Preference Modelling Techniques: PTRC Perspectives 4*, PTRC Education and Research Services Ltd, London.

Cohen, E. (2009) Applying best–worst scaling to wine marketing, *International Journal of Wine Business Research*, 21 (1), 8–23.

Collins, A. T. and Rose, J. M. (2011) Estimation of stochastic scale with best–worst data, Manuscript, Institute of Transport and Logistics Studies, University of Sydney Business School, 2nd International Choice Modelling Conference ICMC 2011, University of Leeds, 6 July.

Collins, A. T., Rose, J. M. and Hensher D. A. (2013) Specification issues in a generalised random parameters attribute nonattendance model, *Transportation Research Part B: Methodological*, 56, 234–53.

Connolly, T. and Zeelenberg, M. (2002) Regret in decision making, *Current Directions in Psychological Science*, 11, 212–216.

Cook, R. D. and Nachtsheim, C. J. (1980) A comparison of algorithms for constructing exact D-optimal designs, *Techometrics*, 22, 315–324.

Cooper, B., Rose, J. M. and Crase, L. (2012) Does anybody like water restrictions? Some observations in Australian urban communities, *Australian Journal of Agricultural and Resource Economics*, 56 (1), 61–51.

Corfman, K. P. (1991) Perceptions of relative influence: formation and measurement, *Journal of Marketing Research*, 28, 125–136.

Corfman, K. P. and Lehmann, D. R. (1987) Models of cooperative group decision-making and relative influence, *Journal of Consumer Research*, 14, 1–13.

Coricelli, G., Critchley, H. D., Joffily, M., O'Doherty, J. P., Sirigu, A. and Dolan, R. J. (2005) Regret and its avoidance: a neuroimaging study of choice behaviour, *Nature Neuroscience*, 8 (9), 1255–1262.

Creel, M. D. and Loomis, J. B. (1991) Confidence intervals for welfare measures with an application to a problem of truncated counts, *Review of Economics and Statistics*, 73, 370–373.

Cummings, R. G., Harrison, G. W. and Osborne, L. L. (1995) Can the bias of contingent valuation be reduced? Evidence from the laboratory, Economics Working Paper B-95-03, Division of Research, College of Business Administration, University of South Carolina. Available at: www.bus.ucf.edu/gharrison/wp/.

Cummings, R. G., Harrison, G. W. and Rutström, E. E. (1995) Homegrown values and hypothetical surveys: is the dichotomous choice approach incentive compatible?, *American Economic Review*, 85 (1), 260–266.

Cummings, R. G. and Taylor, L. O. (1998) Does realism matter in contingent valuation surveys?, *Land Economics*, 74 (2), 203–215.

(1999) Unbiased value estimates for environmental goods: a cheap talk design for the contingent valuation method, *American Economic Review*, 89 (3), 649–665.

Cunha, F., Heckman, J. J. and Navarro, S. (2007) The identification and economic content of ordered choice models with stochastic cutoffs, *International Economic Review*, 48 (4), 1273–1309.

Daly, A. J. (1987) Estimating 'tree' logit models, *Transportation Research Part B*, 21, 251–67.

Daly, A. J., Hess, S. and Train, K. (2012) Assuring finite moments for willingness to pay in random coefficient models, *Transportation*, 39 (1), 19–31.

Daly, A. J., Hess, S., Patruni, B., Potoglou, D. *et al.* (2013) Using ordered attitudinal indicators in a latent variable choice model: a study of the impact of security on rail travel behaviour, *Transportation*, 39 (2), 267–297.

Daly, A. J. and Ortúzar, J. de D. (1990) Forecasting and data aggregation: theory and practice, *Traffic Engineering & Control*, 31, 632–643.

Daly, A. J. and Zachary, S. (1978) Improved multiple choice models, in Hensher, D. A. and Dalvi, M. Q. (eds.), *Determinants of Travel Choice*, Saxon House, Farnborough.

Day, B., Bateman, I. J., Carson, R. T., Dupont, D., Louviere, J. J., Morimoto, S., Scarpa, R. *et al.* (2009) Task independence in stated preference studies: a test of order effect explanations, CSERGE Working Paper EDM 09–14.

Day, B. and Prades, J. P. (2010) Ordering anomalies in choice experiments, *Journal of Environmental Economics and Management*, 59, 271–285.

Daykin, A. and Moffitt, P. (2002) Analyzing ordered responses: a review of the ordered probit model, *Understanding Statistics*, 3, 157–166.

Daziano, R. and Bolduc, D. (2012) Covariance, identification, and finite sample performance of the MSL and Bayes estimators of a logit model with latent attributes, *Transportation*, 40 (3), 647–670.

Debreu, G. (1960) Review of R. D. Luce, Individual Choice Behavior, *American Economic Review*, 50, 186–188.

Dellaert, B. G. C., Prodigalidad, M. and Louviere, J. J. (1998) Family members' projections of each other's preference and influence: a two-stage conjoint approach, *Marketing Letters*, 9, 135–145.

Dempster, A. P. (1967) Upper and lower probabilities induced by a multiple-valued mapping, *Ann Math. Stat.*, 38, 325–339.

DeShazo, J. R. (2002) Designing transactions without framing effects in iterative question formats, *Journal of Environmental Economics and Management*, 43, 360–385.

DeShazo, J. R. and Fermo, G. (2002) Designing choice sets for stated preference methods: the effects of complexity on choice consistency, *Journal of Environmental Economics and Management*, 44, 123–143.

Diamond, P. and Hausman, J. (1994) Contingent valuation: is some number better than no number?, *Journal of Economic Perspectives*, 8(4), 45–64.

Diecidue, E. and Wakker, P. P. (2001) On the intuition of rank-dependent utility, *Journal of Risk and Uncertainty*, 23 (3), 281–298.

Diederich, A. (2003) MDFT account of decision making under time pressure, *Psychonomic Bulletin & Review*, 10 (1), 156–166.

Ding, M., Grewal, R. and Liechty, J. (2007) An incentive-aligned mechanism for conjoint analysis, *Journal of Marketing Research*, 44 (2), 214–223, doi:10.1109/TAC.1974.1100705.

Domencich, T. and McFadden, D. (1975) *Urban Travel Demand*, North-Holland, Amsterdam.

Dosman, D. and Adamowicz, W (2006) Combining stated and revealed preference data to construct an empirical examination of intrahousehold bargaining, *Review of Economics of the Household*, 4, 15–34.

Drolet, A. and Luce, M. F. (2004) The rationalizing effects of cognitive load on emotion-based trade-off avoidance, *Journal of Consumer Research*, 31 (1), 63–77.

Dubois, D. and Prade, H. (1987) Representation and combination of uncertainty with belief functions and possibility measures, *Computational Intelligence*, 170 (11), 909–924.

(1988) Modelling uncertainty and inductive inference: a survey of recent non-additive probability systems, *Acta Psychologica*, 68, 53–78.

Dworkin, J. (1973) Global trends in natural disasters 1947–1973, Natural Hazards Research Working Paper 26, Institute of Behavioral Science, University of Colorado.

Einstein, A. (1921) Geometry and experience, Lecture at the Prussian Academy of Science, Berlin, 27 January.

El Helbawy, A. T. and Bradley, R. A. (1978) Treatment contrasts in paired comparisons: large-sample results, applications and some optimal designs, *Journal of the American Statistical Association*, 73, 831–839.

Eliasson, J., Hultzkranz, L., Nerhagen, L. and Smidfelt Rosqvist, L. (2009) The Stockholm congestion charging trial 2006: overview of effects, *Transportation Research Part A*, 43 (3), 240–250.

Eliasson, J. and Mattsson, L. G. (2006) Equity effects of congestion pricing: quantitative methodology and a case study for Stockholm, *Transportation Research Part A*, 40 (7), 602–620.

Ellsberg, D. (1961) Risk, ambiguity, and the savage axioms, *Quarterly Journal of Economics*, 75 (4), 643–669.

Elrod, T. (1988) Choice map: inferring a product-market map from panel data, *Marketing Science*, 7 (1), 21–40.

Elrod, T. and Keane, M. P. (1995) A factor-analytic probit model for representing the market structure in panel data, *Journal of Marketing Research*, 32 (1), 1–16.

Eluru, N., Bhat, C. R. and Hensher, D. A. (2008) A mixed generalized ordered response model for examining pedestrian and bicyclist injury severity level in traffic crashes, *Accident Analysis and Prevention*, 40 (3), 1033–1054.

Ericsson, K. A. and Simon, H. A. (1993) *Protocol Analysis: Verbal Reports as Data*, MIT Press, Cambridge, MA.

Eto, J., Koomey, J., Lehman, B., Martin, N., Mills, E., Webber, C. and Worrell, E. (2001) Scoping study on trends in the economic value of electricity reliability to the US economy, Technical Report, Energy Analysis Department, Lawrence Berkeley Laboratory, Berkeley, CA.

Everitt, B. (1988) A finite mixture model for the clustering of mixed-mode data, *Statistics and Probability Letters*, 6, 305–309.

Fader, P.S., Lattin, J. M. and Little, J. D. C. (1992) Estimating nonlinear parameters in the multinomial logit model, *Marketing Science*, 11 (4), 372–385.

Fang, K.-T. and Wang, Y. (1994) *Number-Theoretic Methods in Statistics*, Chapman & Hall, London.

Ferrini, S. and Scarpa, R. (2007) Designs with a-priori information for nonmarket valuation with choice-experiments: a Monte Carlo study, *Journal of Environmental Economics and Management*, 53 (3), 342–363.

Fiebig, D. G., Keane, M., Louviere, J. J. and Wasi, N. (2010) The generalized multinomial logit: accounting for scale and coefficient heterogeneity, *Marketing Science*, 29 (3), 393–421.

Fisher, R. A. (1935) *The Design of Experiments*, Hafner Press, New York.

Flynn, T. N., Louviere, J. J., Peters, T. J. and Coast, J. (2007) Best–worst scaling: what it can do for health care research and how to do it, *Journal of Health Economics*, 26, 171–189.

  (2008) Estimating preferences for a dermatology consultation using best–worst scaling: comparison of various methods of analysis, *BMC Medical Research Methodology*, 8 (76), 1–12.

Fosgerau, M. (2006) Investigating the distribution of the value of travel time savings, *Transportation Research Part B*, 40 (8), 688–707.

(2007) Using nonparametrics to specify a model to measure the value of travel time, *Transportation Research Part A*, 41 (9), 842–856.

Fosgerau, M. and Bierlaire, M. (2009) Discrete choice models with multiplicative error terms, *Transportation Research, Part B: Methodological*, 43 (5), 494–505.

Foster, V., Bateman, I. and Harley, D. (1997) Real and hypothetical willingness to pay for environmental preservation: a non-experimental comparison, *Journal of Agricultural Economics*, 48 (1), 123–138.

Fowkes, A. S. and Wardman, M. R. (1988) The design of stated preference travel choice experiments with particular regard to inter-personal taste variations, *Journal of Transport Economics and Policy*, 22, 27–44.

Fowkes, A. S., Wardman, M. and Holden, D. G. P. (1993) *Non-orthogonal stated preference design*, Proceedings of the PTRC Summer Annual Meeting, 91–97.

Fox, C. R. and Poldrack, R. A. (2008) Prospect theory and the brain, in Glimcher, P., Fehr, E., Camerer, C. and Poldrack, R. (eds.) *Handbook of Neuroeconomics*, Academic Press, San Diego, CA, 145–170.

Fox, C. R. and Tversky, A. (1998) A belief-based account of decision under uncertainty, *Management Science*, 44 (7), 870–895.

Fox, J. A., Shogren, J. F., Hayes, D. J. and Kliebenstein, J. B. (1998) CVM-X: calibrating contingent values with experimental auction markets, *American Journal of Agricultural Economics*, 80, 455–465.

Frykblom, P. (1997) Hypothetical question modes and real willingness to pay, *Journal of Environmental Economics and Management*, 34 (2), 274–287.

Fujii, S. and Gärling, T. (2003) Application of attitude theory for improved predictive accuracy of stated preference methods in travel demand analysis, *Transportation Research Part A*, 37 (4), 389–402.

Galanti, S. and Jung, A. (1997) Low-discrepancy sequences: Monte Carlo simulation of option prices, *Journal of Derivatives*, 5 (1), 63–83.

Garrod, G. D., Scarpa, R. and Willis, K. G. (2002) Estimating the benefits of traffic calming on through routes: a choice experiment approach, *Journal of Transport Economics and Policy*, 36 (2), 211–232.

Georgescu-Roegen, N. (1954) Choice, expectations, and measurability, *Quarterly Journal of Economics*, 68, 503–534.

Geweke, J. (1989) Bayesian inference in econometric models using Monte Carlo integration, *Econometrica*, 57 (6), 1317–1339.

(1991) Efficient simulation from multivariate normal and Student-t distributions subject to linear constraints, in Keramidas, M. E. (ed.), *Computer Science and Statistics: Proceedings of the Twenty-Third Symposium on the Inference*, Interface Foundation of North America, Inc., Fairfax, VA, 571–578.

Ghosh, A. (2001) Valuing time and reliability: commuters' mode choice from a real time congestion pricing experiment, PhD dissertation, Department of Economics, University of California at Irvine.

Gilboa, I. and Schmeidler, D. (2001) *A Theory of Case-Based Decisions*, Cambridge University Press.

Gilbride, T. J. and Allenby, G. M. (2004) A choice model with conjunctive, disjunctive, and compensatory screening rules, *Marketing Science*, 23 (3), 391–406.

(2006). Estimating heterogeneous EBA and economic screening rule choice models, *Marketing Science*, 25 (5), 494–509.

Gilovich, T., Griffin, D. and Kahneman, D. (eds.) (2002) *Heuristics and Biases – The Psychology of Intuitive Judgment*, Cambridge University Press.

Goett, A., Hudson, K. and Train, K. (2000) Customers' choice among retail energy suppliers: the willingness-to-pay for service attributes, *Energy Journal*, 21 (4), 1–28.

Goldstein, W. M. and Einhorn, H. J. (1987) Expression theory and the preference reversal phenomena, *Psychological Review*, 94 (2), 236–254.

Golob, T. (2001) Joint models of attitudes and behaviour in evaluation of the San Diego I-15 congestion pricing project, *Transportation Research Part A*, 35 (6), 495–514.

González, R. and Wu, G. (1999) On the shape of the probability weighting function, *Cognitive Psychology*, 38 (1), 129–166.

González-Vellejo, C. (2002) Making trade-offs: a probabilistic and context-sensitive model of choice behavior, *Psychological Review*, 109, 137–155.

Goodwin, P. (1989) The rule of three: a possible solution to the political problem of competing objectives for road pricing, *Traffic Engineering and Control*, 30, 495–497.

(1997) Solving congestion, Inaugural Lecture of the Professorship of Transport Policy, University College London. Available at: www.cts.ucl.ac.uk/tsu/pbginau.htm, retrieved 19 May 2012.

Gordon, J., Chapman, R. and Blamey, R. (2001) Assessing the options for the Canberra water supply: an application of choice modelling, in Bennett, J. and Blamey, R. (eds.), *The Choice Modelling Approach to Environmental Evaluation*, Edward Elgar, Cheltenham.

Gotwalt, C. M., Jones, B. A. and Steinberg, D. M. (2009) Fast computation of designs robust to parameter uncertainty for nonlinear settings, *Technometrics*, 51, 88–95.

Gourieroux, C., and Monfort, A. (1996) *Simulation-Based Methods Econometric Methods*, Oxford University Press.

Gourville, J. T. and Soman, D. (2007). Extremeness seeking: when and why consumers prefer the extreme. Harvard Business School Working Paper 07–092.

Greene, W. H. (1997) LIMDEP version 7.0 Reference Manual, Econometric Software, New York.

(1998a) *Econometric Analysis*, Prentice Hall, Upper Saddle River, NJ, 4th edn.

(1998b) Gender economics courses in Liberal Arts Colleges: further results, *Journal of Economic Education*, 29 (4), 291–300.

(2001) Fixed and random effects in nonlinear models, Working Paper EC-01–01, Stern School of Business, Department of Economics, New York University.

(2002) LIMDEP version 8.0 Reference Manual, Econometric Software, New York.

(2004a) The behavior of the fixed effects estimator in nonlinear models, *Econometrics Journal*, 7 (1), 98–119.

(2004b) Fixed effects and bias due to the incidental parameters problem in the Tobit model, *Econometric Reviews*, 23 (2), 125–147.

(2007) Nlogit 4, Econometric Software, New York and Sydney.

(2008) *Econometric Analysis*, Prentice Hall, Upper Saddle River, NJ, 6th edn.

(2012) *Econometric Analysis*, Prentice Hall, Upper Saddle River, NJ, 7th edn.

Greene, W. H., Harris, M., Hollingsworth, B. and Maitra, P. (2008) A bivariate latent class correlated generalized ordered probit model with an application to modelling observed obesity levels, Working Paper 08–18, Stern School of Business, New York University.

Greene, W. H. and Hensher, D. A. (2007) Heteroscedastic control for random coefficients and error components in mixed logit, *Transportation Research Part E*, 43 (5), 610–623.

(2010a) *Modelling Ordered Choices*, Cambridge University Press.

(2010b) Ordered choice, heterogeneity, and attribute processing, *Journal of Transport Economics and Policy*, 44 (3), 331–264.

(2010c) Does scale heterogeneity across individuals matter? An empirical assessment of alternative logit models, *Transportation*, 37 (3), 413–428.

(2013) Revealing additional dimensions of preference heterogeneity in a latent class mixed multinomial logit model, *Applied Economics*, 45 (14), 1897–1902.

Greene, W., Hensher, D. A. and Rose, J. (2005) Using classical simulation based estimators to estimate individual willingness to pay values: a mixed logit case study of commuters, in Scarpa, R. and Alberini, A. (eds.), *Applications of Simulation Methods in Environmental and Resource Economics*, Springer, Dordrecht, 17–34.

Griffin, R. C. and Mjelde, J. W. (2000) Valuing water supply reliability, *American Journal of Agricultural Economics*, 82, 414–426.

Gunn, H. F. (1988) Value of travel time estimation, Working Paper 157, Institute of Transport Studies, University of Leeds.

Haab, T. C. and McConnell, K. E. (2002) *Valuing Environmental Natural Resources: The Econometrics of Non-Market Valuation*, Edward Elgar, Northampton, MA.

Haaijer, R., Wagner, K. and Wedel, M. (2000) Response latencies in the analysis of conjoint choice experiments, *Journal of Marketing Research*, 37, 376–382.

Hahn, G. J., and Shapiro, S. S. (1966) *A Catalog and Computer Program for the Design and Analysis of Orthogonal Symmetric and Asymmetric Fractional Factorial Experiments*, General Electric Research and Development Center, Schenectady, NY.

Hajivassiliou, V. and McFadden, D. (1998) The method of simulated scores for the estimation of LDV models, *Econometrica*, 66 (4), 863–896.

Hajivassiliou, V. and Ruud, P. (1994) Classical estimation methods for LDV models using simulation, in Engle, R. and McFadden, D. (eds.), *Handbook of Econometrics*, North-Holland, Amsterdam.

Hall, J., Kenny, P., King., M., Louviere, J. J., Viney, R. and Yeoh, A. (2002) Using stated preference discrete choice modelling to evaluate the introduction of varicella vaccination, *Health Economics*, 11(10), 457–465.

Hallahan, K. (1999) Seven models of framing: implications for public relations, *Journal of Public Relations Research*, 11 (3), 205–242.

Halton, J. (1960) On the efficiency of certain quasi-random sequences of points in evaluating multi-dimensional integrals, *Numerische Mathematik*, 2, 84–90.

(1970) A retrospective and prospective survey of the Monte Carlo method, *SIAM Review*, 12 (1), 1–63.

Hammersley, J. M. and Morton, K. W. (1956) A new Monte Carlo technique: antithetic variates, *Proceedings of the Cambridge Philosophical Society*, 52, Part 3, 449 175.

Hanemann, W. (1994) Valuing the environment through contingent valuation, *Journal of Economic Perspectives*, 8 (4), 19–43.

Harrison, G. W. (2006a) Experimental evidence of alternative environmental valuation methods, *Environmental and Resource Economics*, 34 (1), 125–162.

(2006b) Hypothetical bias over uncertain outcomes, in List, J. A. (ed.), *Using Experimental Methods in Environmental and Resource Economics*, Edward Elgar, Northampton, MA, 41–69.

(2007) Making choice studies incentive compatible, in Kanninen, B. (ed.), *Valuing Environmental Amenities Using Stated Choice Studies*, Springer, Dordrecht, 67–110.

Harrison, G. W., Humphrey, S. and Verschoor, A. (2010) Choice under uncertainty: Evidence from Ethiopia, India and Uganda, *Economic Journal*, 120 (543), 80–104.

Harrison, G. W. and List, J. A. (2004) Field experiments, *Journal of Economic Literature*, 42 (4), 1013–1059.

Harrison, G. W. and Rutström, E. E. (2008) Experimental evidence on the existence of hypothetical bias in value elicitation methods, in Plott, C. R. and Smith, V. L. (eds.), *Handbook of Experimental Economics Results*, North-Holland, Amsterdam.

(2009) Expected utility theory and prospect theory: one wedding and a decent funeral, *Journal of Experimental Economics*, 12 (2), 133–158.

Hausman, J. (1978) Specification tests in econometrics, *Econometrica*, 46, 1251–1271.

Hausman, J. and McFadden, D. (1984) Specification tests for the multinomial logit model, *Econometrica*, 52, 1219–1240.

Heckman, J. (1979) Sample selection bias as a specification error, *Econometrica*, 47, 153–161.

Heckman, J. and Singer, B. (1984a) A method for minimizing the impact of distributional assumptions in econometric models, *Econometrica*, 52, 271–320.

(1984b) Econometric duration analysis, *Journal of Econometrics*, 24, 63–132.

Henderson, D. and Parmeter, C. (2014) *Applied Nonparametric Econometrics*, Cambridge University Press.

Hensher, D. A. (1974) A Probabilistic disaggregate model of binary mode choice, in Hensher, D. A. (ed.), Urban travel choice and demand modelling, Special Report 12, Australian Road Research Board, Melbourne, August, 61–99.

(1975) The value of commuter travel time savings: empirical estimation using an alternative valuation model, *Journal of Transport Economics and Policy*, 10 (2), 167–176.

(1986) Sequential and full information maximum likelihood estimation of a nested-logit model, *Review of Economics and Statistics*, 58(4), 657–667.

(1994) Stated preference analysis of travel choices: the state of practice, Special Issue of *Transportation* on The Practice of Stated Preference Analysis, 21 (2), 106–134.

(1998) Establishing a fare elasticity regime for urban passenger transport, *Journal of Transport Economics and Policy*, 32 (2), 221–246.

(1999) HEV choice models as a search engine for specification of nested logit tree structures, *Marketing Letters*, 10 (4), 333–343.

(2001) Measurement of the valuation of travel time savings, *Journal of Transport Economics and Policy*, 35 (1), 71–98.

(2001a) The valuation of commuter travel time savings for car drivers in New Zealand: evaluating alternative model specifications, *Transportation*, 28, 110–118.

(2002) A systematic assessment of the environmental impacts of transport policy: an end use perspective, *Environmental and Resource Economics*, 22 (1–2), 185–217.

(2004) Accounting for stated choice design dimensionality in willingness to pay for travel time savings, *Journal of Transport Economics and Policy*, 38 (2), 425–446.

(2006a) The signs of the times: imposing a globally signed condition on willingness to pay distributions, *Transportation*, 33(3), 205–222.

(2006b) Integrating accident and travel delay externalities in an urban context, *Transport Reviews*, 26 (4), 521–534.

(2006c) Revealing differences in behavioral response due to the dimensionality of stated choice designs: an initial assessment, *Environmental and Resource Economics*, 34 (1), 7–44.

(2006d) How do respondents handle stated choice experiments? – Attribute processing strategies under varying information load, *Journal of Applied Econometrics*, 21 (5), 861–878.

(2008) Joint estimation of process and outcome in choice experiments and implications for willingness to pay, *Journal of Transport Economics and Policy*, 42 (2), 297–322.

(2010a) Attribute processing, heuristics and preference construction in choice analysis, in Hess, S. and Daly, A. (eds.), *Choice Modelling: The State of Art and the State of Practice*, Emerald Group, Bingley, 35–70.

(2010b) Hypothetical bias, choice experiments and willingness to pay, *Transportation Research Part B*, 44 (6), 735–752.

Hensher, D. A., Beck, M. J. and Rose, J. M. (2011) Accounting for preference and scale heterogeneity in establishing whether it matters who is interviewed to reveal household automobile purchase preferences, *Environment and Resource Economics*, 49, 1–22.

Hensher, D. A. and Bradley, M. (1993) Using stated response data to enrich revealed preference discrete choice models, *Marketing Letters*, 4 (2), 139–152.

Hensher, D. A. and Brewer, A. M. (2000) *Transport and Economics Management*, Oxford University Press.

Hensher, D. A. and Collins, A. (2011) Interrogation of responses to stated choice experiments: is there sense in what respondents tell us? A closer look at what respondents choose in stated choice experiments, *Journal of Choice Modelling*, 4 (1), 62–89.

Hensher, D. A. and Goodwin, P. B. (2004) Implementation of values of time savings: the extended set of considerations in a tollroad context, *Transport Policy*, 11 (2), 171–181.

Hensher, D. A. and Greene, W. H. (2002) Specification and estimation of the nested logit model: alternative normalisations, *Transportation Research Part B*, 36 (1), 1–17.

(2003) Mixed logit models: state of practice, *Transportation*, 30 (2), 133–176.

(2010) Non-attendance and dual processing of common-metric attributes in choice analysis: a latent class specification, *Empirical Economics*, 39 (2), 413–426.

(2011) Valuation of travel time savings in WTP and preference space in the presence of taste and scale heterogeneity, *Journal of Transport Economics and Policy*, 45 (3), 505–525.

Hensher, D. A., Greene, W. H. and Chorus, C. (2013) Random regret minimisation or random utility maximisation: an exploratory analysis in the context of automobile fuel choice, *Journal of Advanced Transportation*, 47, 667–678.

Hensher, D. A., Greene, W. H. and Li, Z. (2011) Embedding risk attitude and decision weights in non-linear logit to accommodate time variability in the value of expected travel time savings, *Transportation Research Part B*, 45 (7), 954–972.

Hensher, D. A. and Johnson, L. W. (1981) *Applied Discrete-Choice Modelling*, Croom Helm, London/John Wiley, New York.

Hensher, D. A. and King, J. (2001) Parking demand and responsiveness to supply, pricing and location in the Sydney Central Business District, *Transportation Research Part A*, 5 (3), 177–196.

Hensher, D. A. and Knowles, L. (2007) Spatial alliances of public transit operators: establishing operator preferences for area management contracts with government, in Macario, R., Viega, J. and Hensher, D. A. (eds.), *Competition and Ownership of Land Passenger Transport*, Elsevier, Oxford, 517–546.

Hensher, D. A. and Layton, D. (2010) Common-metric attribute parameter transfer and cognitive rationalisation: implications for willingness to pay, *Transportation*, 37 (3), 473–490.

Hensher, D. A. and Li, Z. (2012) Valuing travel time variability within a rank-dependent utility framework and an investigation of unobserved taste heterogeneity, *Journal of Transport Economics and Policy*, 46 (2), 293–312.

(2013) Referendum voting in road pricing reform: a review of the evidence, *Transport Policy*, 25 (1), 186–97.

Hensher, D. A., Li, Z. and Rose, J. M. (2013) Accommodating risk in the valuation of expected travel time savings, *Journal of Advanced Transportation*, 47 (2), 206–224.

Hensher, D. A., Louviere, J. J. and Swait, J. (1999) Combining sources of preference data, *Journal of Econometrics*, 89, 197–221.

Hensher, D. A. and Mulley, C. (2014) Complementing distance based charges with discounted registration fees in the reform of road user charges: the impact for motorists and government revenue, *Transportation*, doi: 10.1007/s11116-013-9473-6.

Hensher, D. A., Mulley, C. and Rose, J. M. (2014, in press) Understanding the relationship between voting preferences for public transport and perceptions and preferences for bus rapid transit versus light rail, *Journal of Transport Economics and Policy*.

Hensher, D. A. and Prioni, P. (2002) A service quality index for area-wide contract performance assessment, *Journal of Transport Economics and Policy*, 36, 93–113.

Hensher, D. A. and Puckett, S. M. (2007) Congestion charging as an effective travel demand management instrument, *Transportation Research Part A*, 41 (5), 615–626.

Hensher, D. A., Puckett S. M. and Rose, J. M. (2007a) Extending stated choice analysis to recognise agent-specific attribute endogeneity in bilateral group negotiation and choice: a think piece, *Transportation*, 34 (6), 667–679.

Hensher, D. A., Puckett, S. and Rose, J. (2007b) Agency decision making in freight distribution chains: revealing a parsimonious empirical strategy from alternative behavioural structures, *Transportation Research Part B*, 41 (9), 924–949.

Hensher, D. A. and Rose, J.M (2007) Development of commuter and non-commuter mode choice models for the assessment of new public transport infrastructure projects: a case study, *Transportation Research Part A*, 41 (5), 428–433.

(2009) Simplifying choice through attribute preservation or non-attendance: implications for willingness to pay, *Transportation Research Part E*, 45 (4), 583–590.

(2012) The influence of alternative acceptability, attribute thresholds and choice response certainty on automobile purchase preferences, *Journal of Transport Economics and Policy*, 46 (3), 451–468.

Hensher, D. A., Rose, J. M. and Beck, M. J. (2012) Are there specific design elements of choice experiments and types of people that influence choice response certainty?, *Journal of Choice Modelling*, 5 (1), 77–97.

Hensher, D. A., Rose, J. M. and Collins, A. T. (2011) Identifying commuter preferences for existing modes and a proposed Metro, *Public Transport – Planning and Operation*, online, DOI: 10.1007/512469-010-0035-4, 3:109–147.

Hensher, D. A., Rose, J. M. and Black, I. (2008) Interactive agency choice in automobile purchase decisions: the role of negotiation in determining equilibrium choice outcomes, *Journal of Transport Economics and Policy*, 42 (2), 269–296.

Hensher, D. A., Rose, J. M. and Collins, A. (2013) Understanding buy in for risky prospects: incorporating degree of belief into the ex ante assessment of support for alternative road pricing schemes, *Journal of Transport Economics and Policy*, 47 (3), 453–73.

Hensher, D. A., Rose, J. and Greene, W. (2005a) The implications on willingness to pay of respondents ignoring specific attributes, *Transportation*, 32 (3), 203–220.

(2005b) *Applied Choice Analysis: A Primer*, Cambridge University Press.

(2012) Inferring attribute non-attendance from stated choice data: implications for willingness to pay estimates and a warning for stated choice experiment design, *Transportation*, 39 (2), 235–245.

Hensher, D. A., Shore, N. and Train, K. N. (2005) Households' willingness to pay for water service attributes, *Environmental and Resource Economics*, 32, 509–531.

Hess, S. and Hensher, D. A. (2010) Using conditioning on observed choices to retrieve individual-specific attribute processing strategies, *Transportation Research Part B*, 44 (6), 781–790.

Hess, S., Hensher, D. A. and Daly, A. J. (2012) Not bored yet – revisiting respondent fatigue in stated choice experiments, *Transportation Research Part A*, 46 (3), 626–644.

Hess, S. and Rose, J. M. (2007) A latent class approach to modelling heterogeneous information processing strategies in SP studies, Paper presented at the Oslo Workshop on Valuation Methods in Transport Planning, Oslo.

(2012) Can scale and coefficient heterogeneity be separated in random coefficients models?, *Transportation*, 39 (6), 1225–1239.

Hess, S., Rose, J. M. and Bain, S. (2010) Random scale heterogeneity in discrete choice models, Paper presented at the 89th Annual Meeting of the Transportation Research Board, Washington, DC.

Hess, S., Rose, J. M. and Hensher, D. A. (2008) Asymmetrical preference formation in willingness to pay estimates in discrete choice models, *Transportation Research Part E*, 44 (5), 847–863.

Hess, S., Stathopoulos, A. and Daly, A. (2012) Allowing for heterogeneous decision rules in discrete choice models: an approach and four case studies, *Transportation*, 39 (3), 565–591.

Hess, S., Train, K. E. and Polak, J. W. (2004) On the use of randomly shifted and shuffled uniform vectors in the estimation of the mixed logit model for vehicle choice, Paper presented at the 83rd Annual Meeting of the Transportation Research Board, Washington, DC.

(2006) On the use of a Modified Latin Hypercube Sampling (MLHS) approach in the estimation of a mixed logit model for vehicle choice, *Transportation Research Part B*, 40 (2), 147–163.

Hole, A. R. (2011) A discrete choice model with endogenous attribute attendance, *Economics Letters*, 110 (3), 203–205.

Hollander, Y. (2006) Direct versus indirect models for the effects of unreliability, *Transportation Research Part A*, 40 (9), 699–711.

Holmes, C. (1974) A statistical evaluation of rating scales, *Journal of the Market Research Society*, 16, 87–107.

Holt, C. A. and Laury, S. K. (2002) Risk aversion and incentive effects, *American Economic Review*, 92 (5), 1644–1655.

Houston, D. A. and Sherman, S. J. (1995) Cancellation and focus: the role of shared and unique features in the choice process, *Journal of Experimental Social Psychology*, 31, 357–378.

Houston, D. A., Sherman, S. J. and Baker, S. M. (1989) The influence of unique features and direction of comparison on preferences, *Journal of Experimental Social Psychology*, 25, 121–141.

Howe, C. W. and Smith, M. G. (1994) The value of water supply reliability in urban water systems, *Journal of Environmental Economics and Management*, 26, 19–30. Available at: www.sawtoothsoftware.com/technicaldownloads.shtml#ssize.

Huber, J. and Zwerina, K. (1996) The importance of utility balance in efficient choice designs, *Journal of Marketing Research*, 33, 307–317.

Hudson, D., Gallardo, K. and Hanson, T. (2006) Hypothetical (non)bias in choice experiments: evidence from freshwater prawns, Working Paper. Department of Agricultural Economics, Mississippi State University.

Hull, C. L. (1943) *Principles of Behavior*, Appleton-Century, New York.

Idson, L. C., Krantz, D. H., Osherson, D. and Bonini, N. (2001) The relation between probability and evidence judgment: an extension of support theory, *Journal of Risk and Uncertainty*, 22 (3), 227–249.

Isacsson, G. (2007) The trade off between time and money: is there a difference between real and hypothetical choices?, Swedish National Road and Transport Research Institute, Borlange.

Ison, S. (1998) The saleability of urban road pricing, *Economic Affairs*, 18 (4), 21–25.

Johannesson, M., Blomquist, G., Blumenschien, K., Johansson, P., Liljas, B. and O'Connor, R. (1999) Calibrating hypothetical willingness to pay responses, *Journal of Risk and Uncertainty*, 8 (1), 21–32.

Johansson-Stenman, O. and Svedsäter, H. (2003) Self image and choice experiments: hypothetical and actual willingness to pay, Working Papers in Economics 94, Department of Economics, Gothenburg University.

John, J. A. and Draper, N. R. (1980) An alternative family of transformations, *Applied Statistics*, 29, 190–197.

Johnson, F. R., Kanninen, B. J. and Bingham, M. (2006) Experimental design for stated choice studies, in Kanninen, B. J. (ed.) *Valuing Environmental Amenities Using Stated Choice Studies: A Common Sense Approach to Theory and Practice*, Springer, Dordrecht, 159–202.

Johnson, R. and Orme, B. (2003) Getting the most from CBC, Sawtooth Conference Paper, Sawtooth ART Conference, Beaver Creek.

Jones, B. D. (1999) Bounded rationality, *Annual Review of Political Science*, 2, 297–321.

Jones, P. M. (1998) Urban road pricing: public acceptability and barriers to implementation, in Button, K. J. and Verhoef, E. T. (eds.), *Road Pricing, Traffic Congestion and the Environment: Issues of Efficiency and Social Feasibility*, Edward Elgar, Cheltenham, 263–284.

Jones, S. and Hensher, D. A. (2004) Predicting financial distress: a mixed logit model, *Accounting Review*, 79 (4), 1011–1038.

Joreskog, K. G. and Goldberger, A. S. (1975) Estimation of a model with multiple indicators and multiple causes of a single latent variable, *Journal of the American Statistical Association*, 70 (351), 631–639.

Jou, R. (2001) Modelling the impact of pre-trip information on commuter departure time and route choice, *Transportation Research Part B*, 35 (10), 887–902.

Jovicic G. and Hansen, C. O. (2003) A passenger travel demand model for Copenhagen, *Transportation Research Part A*, 37 (4), 333–349.

Kahneman, D. and Tversky, A. (1979) Prospect theory: an analysis of decision under risk, *Econometrica*, 47 (2), 263–292.

Kanninen, B. J. (2002) Optimal design for multinomial choice experiments, *Journal of Marketing Research*, 39, 214–217.

(2005) Optimal design for binary choice experiments with quadratic or interactive terms, Paper presented at the 2005 International Health Economics Association conference, Barcelona.

Karmarkar, U. S. (1978) Weighted subjective utility: a descriptive extension of the expected utility model, *Organizational Behavior and Human Performance*, 21 (1), 61–72.

Kates, R. W. (1979) The Australian experience: summary and prospect, in Heathcote, R. L. and Thom, B. G. (eds.), *Natural Hazards in Australia*, Australian Academy of Science, Canberra, 511–520.

Kaye-Blake, W. H., Abell, W. L. and Zellman, E. (2009) Respondents' ignoring of attribute information in a choice modelling survey, *Australian Journal of Agricultural and Resource Economics*, 53, 547–564.

Keane, M. (1990) Four essays in empirical macro and labor economics, PhD thesis, Brown University.

(1994) A computationally practical simulation estimator for panel data, *Econometrica*, 62 (1), 95–116.

(2006) The generalized logit model: preliminary ideas on a research program, Presentation at Motorola–CenSoC Hong Kong Meeting, 22 October.

Keppel, G. and Wickens, D. W. (2004) *Design and Analysis: A Researcher's Handbook*, Pearson Prentice Hall, Upper Saddle River, NJ, 4th edn.

Kessels, R., Bradley, B., Goos, P. and Vandebroek, M. (2009) An efficient algorithm for constructing Bayesian optimal choice designs, *Journal of Business and Economic Statistics*, 27 (2), 279–291.

Kessels, R., Goos, P. and Vandebroek, M. (2006) A comparison of criteria to design efficient choice experiments, *Journal of Marketing Research*, 43, 409–419.

King, D., Manville, M. and Shoup, D. (2007) The political calculus of congestion pricing, *Transport Policy*, 14 (2), 111–123.

King, G., Murray, C., Salomon, J. and Tandon, A. (2004) Enhancing the validity and cross-cultural comparability of measurement in survey research, *American Political Science Review*, 98, 191–207.

King, G. and Wand, J. (2007) Comparing incomparable survey responses: new tools for anchoring vignettes, *Political Analysis*, 15, 46–66.

Kivetz, R., Netzer, O. and Srinivasan, V. (2004) Alternative models for capturing the compromise effect, *Journal of Marketing Research*, 41 (3), 237–257.

Klein, R. and Spady, R. (1993) An efficient semiparametric estimator for discrete choice models, *Econometrica*, 61, 387–421.

Knight, F. H. (1921) *Risk, Uncertainty and Profit*, University of Chicago Press.

Koss, P. and Sami Khawaja, M. (2001) The value of water supply reliability in California: a contingent valuation study, *Water Policy*, 3, 165–174.

Krantz, D. H. (1991) From indices to mappings: the representational approach to measurement, in Brown, D. and Smith, E. (eds.), *Frontiers of Mathematical Psychology: Essays in Honour of Clyde Coombs*, Springer, New York, 1–52.

Krinsky, I. and Robb, A. L. (1986) On approximating the statistical properties of elasticities, *Review of Economics and Statistics*, 68, 715–719.

Krosnick, J. A. and Schuman, H. (1988) Attitude intensity importance, and certainty and susceptibility to response effects, *Journal of Personality and Social Psychology*, 54 (6), 940–952.

Kuehl, R. O. (1994) *Statistical Principles of Research Design and Analysis*, Duxbury Press, Belmont, CA.

  (2000) *Statistical Principles of Research Design and Analysis*, Duxbury Press, Pacific Grove, CA, 2nd edn.

Kuhfeld, W. F., Tobias, R. D. and Garratt, M. (1994) Efficient experimental design with marketing research applications, *Journal of Marketing Research*, 21, 545–557.

Ladenburg, J., Olsen, S. and Nielsen, R. (2007) Reducing hypothetical bias in choice experiments, Powerpoint presentation, Institute of Food and Resource Economics, University of Copenhagen.

Lam, S. H. and Xie, F. (2002) Transit path models that use revealed preference and stated preference data, *Transportation Research Record*, 1779, 58–65.

Lampietti, J. (1999) Do husbands and wives make the same choices? Evidence from Northern Ethiopia, *Economics Letters*, 62, 253–260.

Lancaster, K. J. (1966) A new approach to consumer theory, *Journal of Political Economy*, 74 (2), 132–157.

Lancsar, E. and Louviere, J. J. (2006) Deleting 'irrational' responses from discrete choice experiments: a case of investigating or imposing preferences?, *Health Economics*, 15, 797–811.

Landry, C. E. and List, J. A. (2007) Using ex ante approaches to obtain credible signals for value in contingent markets: evidence from the field, *American Journal of Agricultural Economics*, 89 (2), 420–429.

Lattimore, P., Baker, J. and Witte, A. (1992) The influence of probability on risky choice – a parametric examination, *Journal of Economic Behavior & Organization*, 17 (3), 377–400.

Laury, S. K. and Holt, C. A. (2000) Further reflections on prospect theory, Working Paper, Department of Economics, University of Virginia, Charlottesville, VA.

Lave, C. (1970) The demand for urban mass transit, *Review of Economics and Statistics*, 52, 320–323.

Layton, D. and Hensher, D. A. (2010) Aggregation of common-metric attributes in preference revelation in choice experiments and implications for willingness to pay, *Transportation Research Part D*, 15 (7), 394–404.

Lazari, A. G. and Anderson, D. A. (1994) Designs of discrete choice experiments for estimating both attribute and availability cross effects, *Journal of Marketing Research*, 31(3), 375–383.

Lee, L. (1995) Asymptotic bias in simulated maximum likelihood estimation of discrete choice models, *Econometric Theory*, 11, 437–483.

Leong, W. and Hensher, D. A. (2012) Embedding decision heuristics in discrete choice models: a review, *Transport Reviews*, 32 (3), 313–331.

Levinson, D. (2010) Equity effects of road pricing: a review, *Transport Reviews*, 30 (1), 33–57.

Li, Q. and Racine, J. (2007) *Nonparametric Econometrics*, Princeton University Press.

(2010) Smooth varying-coefficient estimation and inference for qualitative and quantitative data, *Econometric Theory*, 26, 1607–1637.

Li, Z. and Hensher, D. A. (2010) Toll roads in Australia: an overview of characteristics and accuracy of demand forecasts, *Transport Reviews*, 30 (5), 541–569.

(2011) Prospect theoretic contributions in understanding traveller behaviour: a review and some comments, *Transport Reviews*, 31 (1), 97–117.

(2012) Congestion charging and car use: a review of stated preference and opinion studies and market monitoring evidence, *Transport Policy*, 20, 47–61.

Li, B. and Hensher, D. A. (2015) Choice analysis for risky prospects, submitted to *Journal of Econometrics*, 3 February.

Li, Z., Hensher, D. A. and Rose, J. M. (2010) Willingness to pay for travel time reliability in passenger transport: a review and some new empirical evidence, *Transportation Research Part E*, 46 (3), 384–403.

Lindzey, G. (1954) *The Handbook of Social Psychology*, Vol. II, Addison-Wesley, Reading, MA.

Lisco, T. (1967) The value of commuters' travel time: a study in urban transportation, PhD dissertation, University of Chicago.

List, J. A. (2001) Do explicit warnings eliminate the hypothetical bias in elicitation procedures?: evidence from field auctions for sportscards, *American Economic Review,* 91(5), 1498–1507.

List, J. A. and Gallet, G. (2001) What experimental protocol influence disparities between actual and hypothetical stated values?, *Environmental and Resource Economics*, 20 (2), 241–254.

List, J., Sinha, P. and Taylor, M. (2006) Using choice experiments to value non-market goods and services: evidence from field experiments, *Advances in Economic Analysis and Policy*, 6 (2), 1132–1132.

Liu, Y.-H. and Mahmassani, H. S. (2000) Global maximum likelihood estimation procedure for multinomial probit model parameters, *Transportation Research Part B, Special Issue: Methodological Development in Travel Behaviour Research*, 34B (5), 419–449.

Long, J. S. (1997), *Regression Models for Categorical and Limited Dependent Variables*, Sage, New York.

Long, J. S. and Frees, J. (2006) *Regression Models for Categorical and Limited Dependent Variables Using Stata*, Stata Press, College Station, TX.

Louviere, J. J. (2003) Random utility theory-based stated preference elicitation methods: applications in health economics with special reference to combining sources of preference data, keynote address, Australian Health Economics Society Conference, Canberra.

Louviere, J. J., Carson, R. T., Ainslie, A., Cameron, T. A., DeShazo, J. R., Hensher, D. A., Kohn, R., Marley, T. and Street, D. J. (2002) Dissecting the random component of utility, *Marketing Letters*, 13, 177–193.

Louviere, J. J. and Eagle, T. (2006) Confound it! That pesky little scale constant messes up our convenient assumptions, Proceedings of the 2006 Sawtooth Software Conference, Sawtooth Software, Sequem, Washington, DC, 211–218.

Louviere, J. J. and Hensher, D. A. (1982) On the design and analysis of simulated choice or allocation experiments in travel choice modelling, *Transportation Research Record*, 890, 11–17.

(1983) Using discrete choice models with experimental design data to forecast consumer demand for a unique cultural event, *Journal of Consumer Research*, 10 (3), 348–361.

(2001) Combining preference data, in Hensher, D. A. (ed.), *The Leading Edge of Travel Behaviour Research*, Pergamon Press, Oxford, 125–144.

Louviere, J., Hensher, D. A. and Swait, J. (2000) *Stated Choice Methods: Analysis and Applications*, Cambridge University Press.

Louviere, J. J. and Islam, T. (2008) A comparison of importance weights and willingness-to-pay measures derived from choice-based conjoint, constant sum scales and best–worst scaling, *Journal of Business Research*, 61, 903–911.

Louviere, J. J., Islam, T., Wasi, N., Street, D. and Burgess, L. (2008) Designing discrete choice experiments: do optimal designs come at a price?, *Journal of Consumer Research*, 35 (2), 360–375.

Louviere, J. J. and Lanscar, E. (2009) Choice experiments in health: the good, the bad, and the ugly and toward a brighter future, *Health Economics, Policy and Law*, 4 (4), 527–546.

Louviere, J. J., Lings, I., Islam, T., Gudergan, S. and Flynn, T. (2013) An introduction to the application of (case 1) best–worst scaling in marketing research, *International Journal of Marketing Research*, 30, 292–303.

Louviere, J. J., Meyer, R. J., Bunch, D. S., Carson, R., Dellaert, B., Hanemann, W. A., Hensher, D. A. and Irwin, J. (1999) Combining sources of preference data for modelling complex decision processes, *Marketing Letters*, 10 (3), 205–217.

Louviere, J., Oppewal, H., Timmermans, H. and Thomas, T. (2003) Handling large numbers of attributes in conjoint applications, Working Paper 3.

Louviere, J. J., Street, D., Burgess, L., Wasi, N., Islam, T. and Marley, A. A. J. (2008) Modelling the choices of individual decision makers by combining efficient choice experiment designs with extra preference information, *Journal of Choice Modelling*, 1(1), 128–163.

Louviere, J. J. and Woodworth, G. (1983) Design and analysis of simulated consumer choice or allocation experiments: an approach based on aggregate data, *Journal of Marketing Research*, 20, 350–367.

Luce, R. D. (1959) *Individual Choice Behavior*, Wiley, New York.

Luce, R. D. and Suppes, P. (1965) Preference, utility and subjective probability, in Luce, R. D., Bush, R. R. and Galanter, E. (eds.), *Handbook of Mathematical Psychology*, Vol. III, Wiley, New York.

Lui, Y. and Mahmassani, H. (2000) Global maximum likelihood estimation procedures for multinomial probit (MNP) model parameters, *Transportation Research Part B*, 34 (5), 419–444.

Lundhede, T. H., Olsen, S. B., Jacobsen, J. B. and Thorsen, B. J. (2009) Handling respondent uncertainty in choice experiments: evaluating recoding approaches against explicit modelling of uncertainty, Faculty of Life Sciences, University of Copenhagen.

Lusk, J. L. (2003) Willingness to pay for golden rice, *American Journal of Agricultural Economics*, 85 (4), 840–856.

Lusk, J. L. and Norwood, F. B. (2005) Effect of experimental design on choice-based conjoint valuation estimates, *American Journal of Agricultural Economics*, 87 (3), 771–785.

Lusk, J. and Schroeder, T. (2004) Are choice experiments incentive compatible? A test with quality differentiated beef steaks, *American Journal of Agricultural Economics*, 86 (2), 467–482.

Maddala, G. S. (1983) *Limited-Dependent and Qualitative Variables in Econometrics*, Cambridge University Press.

Maddala, T., Phillip, K. A. and Johnson, F. R. (2003) An experiment on simplifying conjoint analysis designs for measuring preferences, *Health Economics*, 12, 1035–1047.

Malhotra, N. K. (1982) Information load and consumer decision making, *Journal of Consumer Research*, 8(4), 419–430.

Manheim, C. F. (1973) Practical implications of some fundamental properties of travel demand models, *Highway Research Record*, 244, 21–38.

Manly, B. F. (1976) Exponential data transformation, *The Statistician*, 25, 37–42.

Manski, C. F. (1977) The structure of random utility models, *Theory and Decisions*, 8, 229–254.

Manski, C. F. and Lerman, S. R. (1977) The estimation of choice probabilities from choice-based samples, *Econometrica*, 45 (8), 1977–1988.

Manski, C. F. and McFadden, D. (1981) Alternative estimators and sample designs for discrete choice analysis, in Manski, C. F. and McFadden, D. (eds.), *Structural Analysis of Discrete Data with Econometric Applications*, MIT Press, Cambridge, MA, 2–50.

Manville, M. and King, D. (2013) Credible commitment and congestion pricing, *Transportation*, 40, 229–250.

Marcucci, E., Marini, M. and Ticchi, D. (2005) Road pricing as a citizen-candidate game, *European Transport*, 31, 28–45.

Marcucci, E., Stathopoulos, A., Rotaris, L. and Danielis, R. (2011) Comparing single and joint preferences: a choice experiment on residential location in three-member households, *Environment and Planning Part A*, 43 (5), 1209–1225.

Marley, A. A. J. and Louviere, J. J. (2005) Some probabilistic models of best, worst, and best–worst choices, *Journal of Mathematical Psychology*, 49, 464–480.

Marley, A. A. J. and Pihlens, D. (2012) Models of best–worst choice and ranking among multi-attribute options (profiles), *Journal of Mathematical Psychology*, 56, 24–34.

Marschak, J. (1959) Binary choice constraints and random utility indicators, in Arrow, K. J. (ed.), *Mathematical Methods in the Social Sciences*, Stanford University Press.

McClelland, G. H. and Judd, C. M. (1993) The statistical difficulties of detecting interactions and moderator effects, *Psychological Bulletin*, 144 (2), 376–390.

McFadden, D. (1968) The revealed preferences of a public bureaucracy, Department of Economics, University of California.

(1974) Conditional logit analysis of qualitative choice behavior, in Zarembka, P. (ed.), *Frontiers in Econometrics*, Academic Press: New York, 105–142.

(1981) Econometric models of probabilistic choice, in Manski, C. and McFadden, D. (eds.), *Structural Analysis of Discrete Data with Econometric Applications*, MIT Press, Cambridge, MA, 198–272.

(1984) Econometric analysis of qualitative response models, in Griliches, Z. and Intrilligator, M. (eds.), *Handbook of Econometrics*, Vol. II, Elsevier, Amsterdam.

(1989) A method of simulated moments for estimation of discrete response models without numerical integration, *Econometrica*, 57 (5), 995–1026.

(1998) Measuring willingness-to-pay for transportation improvements, in Garling, T., Laitila, T. and Westin, K. (eds.), *Theoretical Foundations of Travel Choice Modelling*, Elsevier, Oxford, 339–364.

(2001a) Disaggregate behavioural travel demand RUM side – a 30 years retrospective, in Hensher, D. A. (ed.), *Travel Behaviour Research: The Leading Edge*, Pergamon, Oxford, 17–64.

(2001b) Economic choices, Nobel Lecture, December 2000, *American Economic Review*, 91 (3), 351–378.

McFadden, D. and Train, K. (2000) Mixed MNL models for discrete response, *Journal of Applied Econometrics*, 15 (5), 447–470.

McNair, B. J., Bennett, J. and Hensher, D. A. (2010) Strategic response to a sequence of discrete choice questions, 54th Annual Conference of the Australian Agricultural and Resource Economics Society. Adelaide.

(2011) A comparison of responses to single and repeated discrete choice questions, *Resource and Energy Economics*, 33, 544–571.

McNair, B., Hensher, D. A. and Bennett, J. (2012) Modelling heterogeneity in response behaviour towards a sequence of discrete choice questions: a probabilistic decision process model, *Environment and Resource Economics*, 51, 599–616.

Meral, G. H. (1979) Local drought-induced conservation: California experiences, Proceedings of the Conference on Water Conservation: Needs and Implementing Strategies, American Society of Civil Engineers, New York.

Meyer, R. K. and Nachtsheim, C. J. (1995) The coordinate-exchange algorithm for constructing exact optimal experimental designs, *Technometrics*, 37 (1), 60–69.

Mongin, P. (1997) Expected utility theory, in Davis, J., Hands, W. and Mäki, U. (eds.) *Handbook of Economic Methodology*, Edward Elgar, London, 342–350.

Morikawa, T. (1989) Incorporating stated preference data in travel demand analysis, PhD dissertation, Department of Civil Engineering, MIT.

Morikawa, T., Ben-Akiva, M. and McFadden, D. (2002) Discrete choice models incorporating revealed preferences and psychometric data, in Franses, P. H. and Montgomery, A. L. (eds.), *Econometric Models in Marketing*, Vol. 16, Elsevier, Amsterdam, 29–55.

Morokoff, W. J. and Caflisch, R. E. (1995) Quasi-Monte Carlo integration, *Journal of Computational Physics*, 122 (2), 218–230.

Mundlak, Y. (1978) On the pooling of time series and cross sectional data, *Econometrica*, 56, 69–86.

Murphy, J., Allen, P., Stevens, T. and Weatherhead, D. (2004) A meta-analysis of hypothetical bias in stated preference valuation, Department of Resource Economics, University of Massachusetts, Amherst, MA, January.

(2005) Is cheap talk effective at eliminating hypothetical bias in a provision point mechanism?, *Environmental and Resource Economics,* 30 (3), 313–325.

Nelson, J. O. (1979) Northern California rationing lessons, Proceedings of the Conference on Water Conservation: Needs and Implementing Strategies, American Society of Civil Engineers, New York.

Niederreiter, H. (1992) Random number generation and quasi-Monte Carlo methods, CBMS-NFS Regional Conference Series in Applied Mathematics, 63, SIAM, Philadelphia, PA.

Noland, R. B. and Polak, J. W. (2002) Travel time variability: a review of theoretical and empirical issues, *Transport Reviews*, 22 (1), 39–93.

Ohler, T., Li, A., Louviere, J. J. and Swait, J. (2000) Attribute range effects in binary response tasks, *Marketing Letters*, 11 (3), 249–260.

Olshavsky, R. W. (1979) Task complexity and contingent processing in decision making: a replication and extension, *Organizational Behavior and Human Performance*, 24, 300–316.

Orme, B. (1998) Sample size issues for conjoint analysis studies, Sawtooth Software Technical Paper.

Ortúzar, J. de D., Iacobelli, A. and Valeze, C. (2000) Estimating demand for a cycle-way network, *Transportation Research Part A*, 34 (5), 353–373.

Ortúzar, J. de D. and Willumsen, P. (2011) *Transport Modelling*, Wiley, New York, 4th edn.

Pareto, V. (1906) Manuale di economia politica, con una introduzione alla scienza sociale, *Societa Editrice Libraria*, Milan.

Park, Y.-H., Ding, M. and Rao, V. (2008) Eliciting preference for complex products: a web-based upgrading method, *Journal of Marketing Research*, 45, 562–574.

Paterson, R. W., Boyle, K. J., Parmeter, C. F., Beumann, J. E. and De Civita, P. (2008) Heterogeneity in preferences for smoking cessation, *Health Economics*, 17 (12), 1363–1377.

Paulhus, D. L. (1991) Measurement and control of response bias, in Robinson, P. J., Shaver, P. R. and Wrightsman, L. S. (eds.), *Measures of Personality and Social Psychological Attitudes*, Academic Press, San Diego, CA, 17–59.

Payne, J. D. (1972) The effects of reversing the order of verbal rating scales in a postal survey, *Journal of the Market Research Society*, 14, 30–44.

Payne, J. W. (1976) Task complexity and contingent processing in decision making: an information search and protocol analysis, *Organizational Behavior and Human Performance*, 16, 366–387.

Payne, J. W. and Bettman, J. R. (1992) Behavioural decision research: a constructive processing perspective, *Annual Review of Psychology*, 43, 87–131.

Payne, J. W., Bettman, J. R. and Johnson, E. J. (1993) *The Adaptive Decision Maker*, Cambridge University Press.

Payne, J. W., Bettman, J. R. and Schkade, D. A. (1999) Measuring constructed preferences: towards a building code, *Journal of Risk and Uncertainty*, 19, 243–270.

Peeta, S., Ramos, J. L. and Pasupathy, R. (2000) Content of variable message signs and on-line driver behavior, *Transportation Research Record*, 1725, 102–103.

Peirce, C. S. (1876) Note on the Theory of the Economy of Research, *Coast Survey Report*, 197–201.

Pendyala, R. and Bricka, S. (2006). Collection and analysis of behavioural process data: challenges and opportunities, in Stopher, P. and Stecher, C. (eds.), *Travel Survey Methods: Quality and Future Directions*, Elsevier, Oxford.

Peters, R.P. and Kramer, J. (2012) Just who should pay for what? Vertical equity, transit subsidy and broad pricing: the case of New York City, *Journal of Public Transportation*, 15 (2), 117–136.

Poe, G., Giraud, K. and Loomis, J. (2005) Simple computational methods for measuring the difference of empirical distributions: application to internal and external scope tests in contingent valuation, *American Journal of Agricultural Economics*, 87 (2), 353–365.

Polak, J. (1987) A more general model of individual departure time choice transportation planning methods, Proceedings of Seminar C held at the PTRC Summer Annual Meeting, P290, 247–258.

Polak, J., Hess, S. and Liu, X. (2008) Characterising heterogeneity in attitudes to risk in expected utility models of mode and departure time choice, Paper presented at the Transportation Research Board (TRB) 87th Annual Meeting, Washington, DC.

Portney, P. R. (1994) The contingent valuation debate: why economists should care, *Journal of Economic Perspectives*, 8 (4), 3–17.

Powers, D. A. and Xie, Y. (2000) *Statistical Methods for Categorical Data Analysis*, Academic Press, New York.

Powers, E. A., Morrow, P., Goudy, W. J. and Keith, P. (1977) Serial order preference in survey research, *Public Opinion Quarterly*, 41 (1), 80–85.

Prato, C. G., Bekhor, S. and Pronello, C. (2012) Latent variables and route choice behaviour, *Transportation*, 39 (3), 299–319.

Pratt, J. (1981) Concavity of the log likelihood, *Journal of the American Statistical Association*, 76, 103–106.

Prelec, D. (1998) The probability weighting function, *Econometrica*, 66 (3), 497–527.

Puckett, S. M. and Hensher, D. A. (2009) Revealing the extent of process heterogeneity in choice analysis: an empirical assessment, *Transportation Research Part A*, 43 (2), 117–126.

(2006) Modelling interdependent behaviour utilising a sequentially-administered stated choice experiment: analysis of urban road freight stakeholders, Conference for the International Association of Transport Behaviour Research, Kyoto.

(2008) The role of attribute processing strategies in estimating the preferences of road freight stakeholders under variable road user charges, *Transportation Research Part E*, 44, 379–395.

Puckett, S. M., Hensher, D. A., Rose, J. M. and Collins, A., (2007) Design and development of a stated choice experiment for interdependent agents: accounting for interactions between buyers and sellers of urban freight services, *Transportation*, 34 (4), 429–451.

Pudney, S. and Shields, M. (2000) Gender, race, pay and promotion in the British nursing profession: estimation of a generalized ordered probit model, *Journal of Applied Econometrics*, 15 (4), 367–399.

Pullman, M. E., Dodson, K. J. and Moore, W. L. (1999) A comparison of conjoint methods when are many attributes, *Marketing Letters*, 10, 1–14.

Quan, W., Rose, J. M., Collins, A. T. and Bliemer, M. C. J. (2011) A comparison of algorithms for generating efficient choice experiments, Working Paper ITLS-WP-11-19, Institute of Transport and Logistics Studies, University of Sydney.

Quandt, R. E. (1970) *The Demand for Travel: Theory and Measurement*, D.C. Heath, Lexington, MA.

Quiggin, J. (1982) A theory of anticipated utility, *Journal of Economic Behavior and Organization*, 3 (4), 323–343.

(1994) Regret theory with general choice sets, *Journal of Risk and Uncertainty*, 8 (2), 153–165.

(1995) Regret theory with general choice sets, *Risk and Uncertainty*, 8 (2), 153–165.

(1998) Individual and household willingness to pay for public goods, *American Journal of Agricultural Economics*, 80, 58–63.

Racevskis, L. and Lupi, F. (2008) Incentive compatibility in an attribute-based referendum model, Paper presented at the American Agricultural Economics Association Annual Meeting, Orlando, FL, 27–29 July.

Rasch, G. (1960) *Probabilistic Models for Some Intelligence and Attainment Tests*, Denmark Paedogiska, Copenhagen.

Rasouli, S. and Timmermans, H. (2014) Specification of regret-based models of choice behavior: formal analyses and experimental design based evidence, Eindhoven University of Technology.

Restle, F. (1961) *Psychology of Judgment and Choice*, Wiley, New York.

Revelt, D. and Train, K. (1998) Mixed logit with repeated choices: households' choices of appliance efficiency level, *Review of Economics and Statistics*, 80 (4), 647–657.

Riedl, R., Brandstatter, E. and Roithmayr, F. (2008). Identifying decision strategies: a process- and outcome-based classification method, *Behavior Research Methods*, 40 (3): 795–807.

Riphahn, R., Wambach, A. and Million, A. (2003) Incentive effects in the demand for health care: a bivariate panel count estimation, *Journal of Applied Econometrics*, 18 (4), 387–405.

Roberts, J. A., Hann, L.-H. and Slaughter, S. A. (2006) Understanding the motivations, participation, and performance of open source software development: a longitudinal study of the Apache Projects, *Management Science,* 52 (7), 984–999.

Roeder, K., Lynch, K. and Nagin, D. (1999) Modeling uncertainty in latent class membership: a case study in criminology, *Journal of the American Statistical Association*, 94, 766–776.

Rose, J. M. (2014) Interpreting discrete choice models based on best–worst data: a matter of framing, 93rd Annual Meeting of the Transportation Research Board TRB 2014, Washington DC, 16 January.

Rose, J. M., Bain, S. and Bliemer, M. C. J. (2011) Experimental design strategies for stated preference studies dealing with non market goods, in Bennett, J. (ed.), *International Handbook on Non-Marketed Environmental Valuation*, Edward Elgar, Cheltenham, 273–299.

Rose, J. M., Bekker de-Grob, E. and Bliemer, E. (2012) If theoretical framework matters, then why are we ignoring their tenants? An (re)examination of random utility theory and beyond, Working Paper, Institute of Transport and Logistics Studies, The University of Sydney, November.

Rose, J. M. and Black, I. (2006) Means matter, but variances matter too: decomposing response latency influences on variance heterogeneity in stated preference experiments, *Marketing Letters*, 17 (4), 295–310.

Rose, J. M. and Bliemer, M. C. J. (2004) The design of stated choice experiments: the state of practice and future challenges, Working Paper ITS-WP-04-09, Institute of Transport and Logistics Studies, University of Sydney.

(2005) Sample optimality in the design of stated choice experiments, Report ITLS-WP-05-13, Institute of Transport and Logistics Studies, University of Sydney.

(2006) Designing efficient data for stated choice experiments, Proceedings of the 11th International Conference on Travel Behaviour Research, Kyoto.

(2008) Stated preference experimental design strategies, in Hensher, D. A. and Button, K. J. (eds), *Handbook of Transport Modelling*, Elsevier, Oxford, 151–179.

(2009) Constructing efficient stated choice experimental designs, *Transport Reviews*, 29 (5), 587–617.

(2011) Stated preference experimental design strategies, in Hensher, D. A. (ed.), *Transport Economics: Critical Concepts in Economics*, Vol. 1, Routledge, Oxford, 304–332.

(2012) Sample optimality in the design of stated choice experiments, in Pendyala, R. and Bhat, C. (eds), *Travel Behaviour Research in the Evolving World*, IATBR, Jaipur, 119–145.

(2013) Sample size requirements for stated choice experiments, *Transportation*, 40 (5), 1021–1041.

(2014) Stated choice experimental design theory: the who, the what and the why, in Hess, S. and Daly, A. (eds.), *Handbook of Choice Modelling*, Edward Elgar, Cheltenham.

Rose, J., Bliemer, M., Hensher, D. A. and Collins, A. (2008) Designing efficient stated choice experiments in the presence of reference alternatives, *Transportation Research Part B*, 42 (4), 395–406.

Rose, J. and Hensher, D. A. (2004) Modelling agent interdependency in group decision making: methodological approaches to interactive agent choice experiments, *Transportation Research Part E*, 40 (1), 63–79.

(2014) Tollroads are only part of the overall trip: the error of our ways in past willingness to pay studies, *Transportation*, 41 (4), 819–837.

Rose, J., Hensher, D. A. and Greene, W. (2005) Recovering costs through price and service differentiation: accounting for exogenous information on attribute processing strategies in airline choice, *Journal of Air Transport Management*, 11, 400–407.

Rose, J. M., Scarpa, R. and Bliemer, M. C. J. (2009) Incorporating model uncertainty into the generation of efficient stated choice experiments: a model averaging approach, International Choice Modelling Conference, March 30-April 1, Harrogate.

Rumelhart, D. L. and Greeno, J. G. (1968) Choice between similar and dissimilar objects: an experimental test of the Luce and Restle choice models, presented at the Midwestern Psychological Association meeting, Chicago, May.

Russell, C. S., Arey, D. G. and Kates, R. W. (1970) *Drought and Water Supply: Implications of the Massachusetts Experience for Municipal Planning*, Johns Hopkins University Press for Resources for the Future, Inc., Baltimore, MD.

Russo, J. E. and Dosher, B. A. (1983) Strategies for multiattribute binary choice, *Journal of Experimental Psychology: Learning, Memory, & Cognition*, 9 (4), 676–696.

Sakia, R. M. (1992) The Box–Cox transformation technique: a review, *The Statistician*, 41 (2), 169–178.

Sándor, Z. and Train, K. (2004), Quasi-random simulation of discrete choice models, *Transportation Research Part B*, 38 (4), 313–327.

Sándor, Z. and Wedel, M. (2002) Profile construction in experimental choice designs for mixed logit models, *Marketing Science*, 21 (4), 455–475.

(2005) Heterogeneous conjoint choice designs, *Journal of Marketing Research*, 42, 210–218.

(2001) Designing conjoint choice experiments using managers' prior beliefs, *Journal of Marketing Research*, 36, 430–444.

Savage, L. J. (1954) *The Foundations of Statistics*, Wiley, London.

Scarpa, R., Campbell, D. and Hutchinson, G. (2005) Individual benefit estimates for rural landscape improvements: the role of sequential Bayesian design and response rationality in a choice study, Paper presented at the 14th Annual Conference of the European Association of Environmental and Resource Economics, Bremen.

(2007) Benefit estimates for landscape improvements: sequential Bayesian design and respondents' rationality in a choice experiment study, *Land Economics*, 83 (4), 617–634.

Scarpa, R., Ferrini, S. and Willis, K. G. (2005) Performance of error component models for status-quo effects in choice experiments, in Scarpa, R., Ferrini, S. and Willis, K. G. (eds.), *Applications of Simulation Methods in Environmental and Resource Economics*, Springer, Dordrecht, 247–274.

Scarpa, R., Gilbride, T. J., Campbell, D. and Hensher, D. A. (2009) Modelling attribute non-attendance in choice experiments for rural landscape valuation, *European Review of Agricultural Economics*, 36 (2), 151–174.

Scarpa, R. and Rose, J. M. (2008) Designs efficiency for non-market valuation with choice modelling: how to measure it, what to report and why, *Australian Journal of Agricultural and Resource Economics*, 52 (3), 253–282.

Scarpa, R., Thiene, M. and Hensher, D. A. (2010) Monitoring choice task attribute attendance in non-market valuation of multiple park management services: does it matter?, *Land Economics*, 86 (4), 817–839, Waikato Management School, The University of Waikato.

(2012) Preferences for tap water attributes within couples: an exploration of alternative mixed logit parameterizations, *Water Resources Research Journal*, 48 (1), 1–11, doi:10.1029/2010WR010148.

Scarpa, R., Thiene, M. and Marangon, F. (2008) Using flexible taste distributions to value collective reputation for environmentally-friendly production methods, *Canadian Journal of Agricultural Economics*, 56, 145–162.

Scarpa, R., Thiene, M. and Train, K. (2008) Utility in willingness to pay space: a tool to address confounding random scale effects in destination choice to the Alps, *American Journal of Agricultural Economics*, 90 (4), 994–1010. (See also Appendix: Utility in WTP space: a tool to address confounding random scale effects in destination choice to the Alps. Available at: http://agecon.lib.umn.edu/.).

Scarpa, R., Willis, K. G. and Acutt, M. (2004) Individual-specific welfare measures for public goods: a latent class approach to residential customers of Yorkshire Water, in Koundouri, P. (ed.), *Econometrics Informing Natural Resource Management*, Edward Elgar, Cheltenham.

Schade, J. and Baum, M. (2007) Reactance or acceptance? Reactions towards the introduction of road pricing, *Transportation Research Part A*, 41 (1), 41–48.

Schade, J. and Schlag, B. (eds.) (2003) *Acceptability of Transport Pricing Strategies*, Elsevier, Oxford.

Schwanen, T. and Ettema, D. (2009) Coping with unreliable transportation when collecting children: examining parents' behavior with cumulative prospect theory, *Transportation Research Part A*, 43 (5), 511–525.

Senna, L. A. D. S. (1994) The influence of travel time variability on the value of time, *Transportation*, 21 (2), 203–228.

Seror, V. (2007) Fitting observed and theoretical choices – women's choices about prenatal diagnosis of Down syndrome, *Health Economics*, 14 (2), 161–167.

Shafer, G. (1976) *A Mathematical Theory of Evidence*, Princeton University Press.

Sillano, M. and Ortúzar, J. de D. (2005) Willingness-to-pay estimation with mixed logit models: some new evidence, *Environment and Planning A*, 37 (5), 525–550.

Simon, H. (1978) Rational decision making in organisations, *American Economic Review*, 69 (4), 493–513.

Simonson, I. and Tversky, A. (1992) Choice in context: tradeoff contrast and extremeness aversion, *Journal of Marketing Research*, 29 (3): 281–295.

Slovic, P. (1987) Perception of risk, *Science, New Series*, 236 (4799), 280–285.

(1995) The construction of preference, *American Psychologist*, 50, 364–371.

Small, K. A. (1992) Using the revenues from congestion pricing, *Transportation*, 19 (3), 359–381.

Small, K. A., Noland, R. B., Chu, X. and Lewis, D. (1999) Valuation of travel-time savings and predictability in congested conditions for highway user-cost estimation, NCHRP Report 431, Transportation Research Board, National Research Council.

Smith, V. K. and Van Houtven, G. (1998) Non-market valuation and the household, Resources for the Future, Discussion Paper 98–31, Washington, DC.

Sobol, I. M. (1967) Distribution of points in a cube and approximate evaluation of integrals, *USSR Computational Mathematics and Mathematical Physics*, 7 (4), 784–802.

Sonnier, G., Ainslie, A. and Otter, T. (2003) The influence of brand image and product style on consumer brand valuations, Working Paper, Anderson Graduate School of Management, University of California, Los Angeles, CA.

(2007) Heterogeneity distributions of willingness-to-pay in choice models, *Quantitative Marketing Economics*, 5 (3), 313–331.

Starmer, C. (2000) Developments in non-expected utility theory: the hunt for a descriptive theory of choice under risk, *Journal of Economic Literature*, 38, 332–382.

Starmer, C. and Sugden, R. (1993) Testing for juxtaposition and event splitting effects, *Journal of Risk and Uncertainty*, 6, 235–254.

Steimetz (2008) Defensive driving and the external costs of accidents and travel delays, *Transportation Research Part B*, 42 (9), 703–724.

Steimetz, S. and Brownstone. D. (2005) Estimating commuters' 'value of time' with noisy data: a multiple imputation approach, *Transportation Research Part B*, 39 (7), 565–591.

Stewart, M. B. (2004) A comparison of semiparametric estimators for the ordered response model, *Computational Statistics and Data Analysis*, 49, 555–573.

Stewart, N., Chater, N., Stott, H. P. and Reimers, S. (2003) Prospect relativity: how choice options influence decision under risk, *Journal of Experimental Psychology: General*, 132, 23–46.

Stopher, P. R. and Lisco, T. (1970) Modelling travel demand: a disaggregate behavioral approach, issues and applications, *Transportation Research Forum Proceedings*, 195–214.

Stott, H. P. (2006) Cumulative prospect theory's functional menagerie, *Journal of Risk and Uncertainty*, 32 (2), 101–130.

Street, D., Bunch, D. and Moore, B. (2001) Optimal designs for 2k paired comparison experiments, *Communications in Statistics – Theory and Method*, 30, 2149–2171.

Street, D. J. and Burgess, L. (2004) Optimal and near-optimal pairs for the estimation of effects in 2-level choice experiments, *Journal of Statistical Planning and Inference*, 118, 185–199.

Street, D. J., Burgess, L. and Louviere, J. J. (2005) Quick and easy choice sets: contructing optimal and nearly optimal stated choice experiments, *International Journal of Research in Marketing*, 22, 459–470.

Sugden, R. (2005) Anomalies and stated preference techniques: a framework for a discussion of coping strategies, *Environmental and Resource Economics*, 32, 1–12.

Sundstrom, G. A. (1987) Information search and decision making: the effects of information displays, *Acta Psychologica*, 65, 165–179.

Svenson, O. (1998) The perspective from behavioral decision theory on modelling travel choice, in Garling, T., Laitila, T. and Westin, K. (eds.), *Theoretical Foundations of Travel Choice Modelling*, Elsevier, Oxford, 141–172.

Svenson, O. and Malmsten, N. (1996) Post-decision consolidation over time as a function of gain or loss of an alternative, *Scandinavian Journal of Psychology*, 37 (3), 302–311.

Swait, J. (1994) A structural equation model of latent segmentation and product choice for cross-sectional revealed preference choice data, *Journal of Retail and Consumer Services*, 1 (2), 77–89.

(2001) A non-compensatory choice model incorporating attribute cut-offs, *Transportation Research Part B*, 35 (10), 903–928.

(2009) Choice models based on mixed discrete/continuous PDFs, *Transportation Research Part B*, 43 (7), 766–783.

Swait J. and Adamowicz, W. (1996) The effect of choice environment and task demands on consumer behaviour: discriminating between contribution and confusion, Working Paper, Department of Rural Economy, University of Alberta.

(2001a) The influence of task complexity on consumer choice: a latent class model of decision strategy switching, *Journal of Consumer Research*, 28, 135–148.

(2001b) Choice environment, market complexity, and consumer behavior: a theoretical and empirical approach for incorporating decision complexity into models of consumer choice, *Organizational Behavior and Human Decision Processes*, 49, 1–27.

Swait, J., Adamowicz, W. and van Buren, M. (2004) Choice and temporal welfare impacts: incorporating history into discrete choice models, *Journal of Environmental Economics and Management*, 47, 94–116.

Swait, J. and Louviere, J. J. (1993) The role of the scale parameter in the estimation and use of multinomial logit models, *Journal of Marketing Research*, 30, 305–314.

Swait, J., Louviere, J. J. and Williams, M. (1994) A sequential approach to exploiting the combined strengths of SP and RP data: application to freight shipper choice, *Transportation*, 21, 135–152.

Swait, J. and Stacey, E. C. (1996) Consumer brand assessment and assessment confidence in models of longitudinal choice behavior, Paper presented at the 1996 INFORMS Marketing Science Conference, March 7–10, Gainesville, FL.

Temme, D., Paulssen, M. and Dannewald, T. (2008) Incorporating latent variables into discrete choice models: a simultaneous estimation approach using SEM software, *Business Research*, 1, 220–237.

Terza, J. (1985) Ordinal probit: generalisation, *Communications in Statistics – Theory and Methods*, 14 (1), 1–11.

Thaler, R. (1999) Mental accounting matters, *Journal of Behavioral Decision Making*, 12, 183–206.

Thiene, M. and Scarpa, R. (2009) Deriving and testing efficient estimates of WTP distributions in destination choice models, *Environmental and Resource Economics*, 44, 379–395.

Thurstone, L. L. (1927) A law of comparative judgment, *Psychological Review*, 34, 278–286.

(1945) The prediction of choice, *Psychometrika*, 10, 237–253.

Toner, J. P., Clark, S. D., Grant-Muller, S. M. and Fowkes, A. S. (1998) Anything you can do, we can do better: a provocative introduction to a new approach to stated preference design, WCTR Proceedings, 107–120, Antwerp.

Toner, J. P., Wardman, M. and Whelan, G. (1999) Testing recent advances in stated preference design, Proceedings of the European Transport Conference, Cambridge.

Train, K. (1978) A validation test for a disaggregate mode choice model, *Transportation Research*, 12, 167–173.

(1997) Mixed logit models for recreation demand, in Kling, C. and Herriges, J. (eds.), *Valuing the Environment Using Recreation Demand Models*, Edward Elgar, New York.

(2000) Halton sequences for mixed logit, Working Paper, Department of Economics, University of California, Berkeley, CA.

(2003, 2009) *Discrete Choice Methods with Simulation*, Cambridge University Press.

Train, K. and Revelt, D. (2000) Customer-specific taste parameters and mixed logit, Working Paper, Department of Economics, University of California, Berkeley. Available at: http://elsa.berkeley.edu/wp/train0999.pdf.

Train, K. and Weeks, M. (2005) Discrete choice models in preference space and willing to-pay space, in Scarpa, R. and Alberini, A. (eds.), *Applications of Simulation Methods in Environmental and Resource Economics*, Springer, Dordrecht, 1–16.

Train, K. and Wilson, W. (2008) Estimation on stated-preference experiments constructed from revealed-preference choice, *Transportation Research Part B*, 40 (2), 191–203.

Truong, T. P. and Hensher, D. A. (2012) Linking discrete choice to continuous demand models within a computable general equilibrium framework, *Transportation Research Part B*, 46 (9), 1177–1201.

Tuffin, B. (1996) On the use of low-discrepancy sequences in Monte Carlo methods, *Monte Carlo Methods and Applications*, 2 (4), 295–320.

Tukey, J. W. (1957) The comparative anatomy of transformations, *Annals of Mathematical Statistics*, 28, 602–632.

(1962) The future of data analysis, *Annals of Mathematical Statistics*, 33 (1), 13.

Tversky, A. and Fox, C. (1995) Weighing risk and uncertainty, *Psychological Reviews*, 102 (2), 269–283.

Tversky, A. and Kahneman, D. (1981) The framing of decisions and the psychology of choice, *Science*, 211 (4), 453–458.

(1992) Advances in prospect theory: cumulative representations of uncertainty, *Journal of Risk and Uncertainty*, 5 (4), 297–323.

Tversky, A. and Koehler, D. (1994) Support theory: a nonextensional representation of subjective probability, *Psychological Review*, 1010, 547–567.

Tversky, A. and Simonson, I. (1993) Context-dependent preferences, *Management Science*, 39 (10), 1179–89.

Tversky, A., Slovic, P. and Kahneman, D. (1990) The causes of preference reversal, *American Economic Review*, 80 (1), 204–217.

Ubbels, B. and Verhoef, E. (2006) Acceptability of road pricing and revenue use in the Netherlands, *European Transport/Trasporti Europei*, 32, 69–94.

Uebersax, J. (1999) Probit latent class analysis with dichotomous or ordered category measures: conditional independence/dependence models, *Applied Psychological Measurement*, 23, 283–297.

Van Amelsfort, D. H. and Bliemer, M. C. J. (2005) Uncertainty in travel conditions related travel time and arrival time: some findings from a choice experiment, Proceedings of the European Transport Conference (ETC), Strassbourg.

van de Kaa, E. J. (2008) Extended prospect theory, TRAIL Research School, Delft.

Verlegh, P. W., Schifferstein, H. N. and Wittink, D. R. (2002) Range and number-of-levels effects in derived and stated measures of attribute importance, *Marketing Letters*, 13, 41–52.

Vermeulen, B., Goos, P. and Vandeboek, M. (2008) Models and optimal designs for conjoint choice experiments including a no-choice option, *International Journal of Research in Marketing*, 25 (2), 94–103.

Vermuelen, F. (2002) Collective household models: principles and main results, *Journal of Economic Surveys*, 16, 533–564.

Viney, R., Savage, E. and Louviere, J. J. (2005) Empirical investigation of experimental design properties of discrete choice experiments, *Health Economics*, 14 (4), 349–362.

von Neumann, J. and Morgenstern, O. (1947) *Theory of Games and Economic Behavior*, Princeton University Press, 2nd edn.

Vuong, Q. H. (1989) Likelihood ratio tests for model selection and non-nested hypotheses, *Econometrica*, 57 (1989), 307–333.

Wakker, P. P. (2008) Explaining the characteristics of the power (CRRA) utility family, *Health Economics*, 17 (12), 1329–1344.

Walker, J. L. and Ben-Akiva, M. E. (2002) Generalized random utility model, *Math Soc. Sc.*, 43 (3), 303–343.

Walker, J. L., Ben-Akiva, M. and Bolduc, D. (2007) Identification of parameters in normal error component logit-mixture (NECLM) models, *Journal of Applied Econometrics*, 22 (6), 1095–1125.

Wang, X. and Hickernell, F. J. (2000) Randomized Halton sequences, *Mathematical and Computer Modelling*, 32 (7–8), 887–899.

Wardman, M. (2001) A review of British evidence on time and service quality valuations, *Transportation Research Part E*, 37 (2–3), 107–128.

Watson, S. M., Toner, J. P., Fowkes, A. S. and Wardman, M. R. (2000) Efficiency properties of orthogonal stated preference designs, in Ortúzar, J. de D. (ed.), *Stated Preference Modelling Techniques*, PTRC Education and Research Services Ltd, 91–101.

Williams, H. C. W. L. (1977) On the formation of travel demand models and economic evaluation measures of user benefit, *Environment and Planning Part A*, 9 (3), 285–344.

Williams, R. (2006) Generalized ordered logit/partial proportional odds models for ordinal dependent variables, *Stata Journal*, 6 (1), 58–82.

Wilson, A. G., Hawkins, A. F., Hill, G. J. and Wagon, D. J. (1969) Calibrating and testing of the SELNEC transport model, *Regional Studies*, 3(3), 340–345.

Winiarski, M. (2003) Quasi-Monte Carlo derivative valuation and reduction of simulation bias, MSc Thesis, Royal Institute of Technology (KTH), Stockholm.

Wong, S. K. M., and Wang, Z. W. (1993) Qualitative measures of ambiguity, in Hackerman, D. and Mamdani, A. (eds.), *Proceedings of The Ninth Conference on Uncertainty in Artificial Intelligence*, Morgan Kaufmann, San Mateo, CA, 443–450.

Wooldridge, J. (2010) *Econometric Analysis of Cross Section and Panel Data*, MIT Press, Cambridge, MA.

Yanez, M. F., Raveau, S., Rojas, M. and Ortúzar, J. de D. (2009) Modelling and forecasting with latent variables in discrete choice panel models, Proceedings of the European Transport Conference, Noordwijk Conference Centre, Leeuwenhorst.

Yanez, M. F., Bahamonde-Birke, F., Raveau, S. and Ortúzar, J. de D. (2010) The role of tangible attributes in hybrid discrete choice models, Proceedings of the European Transport Conference, Glasgow.

Yanez, M. F., Raveau, S. and Ortúzar, J. de D. (2010). Inclusion of latent variables in mixed logit models: modelling and forecasting, *Transportation Research Part A: Policy and Practice*, 44 (9), 744–753.

Yoon, S.-O. and Simonson, I. (2008) Choice set configuration as a determinant of preference attribution and strength, *Journal of Consumer Research*, 35, 324–336.

Yu, J., Goos, P. and Vandeboek, M. (2006) The importance of attribute interactions in conjoint choice design and modeling, Department of Decision Sciences and Information Management Working Paper 0601.

(2008) A comparison of different Bayesian design criteria to compute efficient conjoint choice experiments, Department of Decision Sciences and Information Management Working Paper 0817.

(2009) Efficient conjoint choice designs in the presence of respondent heterogeneity, *Marketing Science*, 28 (1), 122–135.

Zavoina, R. and McElvey, W. (1975) A statistical model for the analysis of ordinal level dependent variables, *Journal of Mathematical Sociology*, Summer, 103–120.

Zeelenberg, M. (1999) The use of crying over spilled milk: a note on the rationality and functionality of regret, *Philosophical Psychology*, 12 (3), 325–340.

Zeelenberg, M. and Pieters, R. (2007) A theory of regret regulation 1.0, *Journal of Consumer Psychology*, 17 (1), 3–18.

Index